D1085572

LET'S GO:

IRELAND

is the best book for anyone traveling on a budget. Here's why:

▨ No other guidebook has as many budget listings.

In Ireland we list over 4,500 budget travel bargains. We tell you the cheapest way to get around, and where to get an inexpensive and satisfying meal once you've arrived. We give hundreds of money-saving tips that anyone can use, plus invaluable advice on discounts and deals for students, children, families, and senior travelers.

▨ Let's Go researchers have to make it on their own.

Our Harvard-Radcliffe researcher-writers travel on budgets as tight as your own—no expense accounts, no free hotel rooms.

▨ Let's Go is completely revised each year.

We don't just update the prices, we go back to the place. If a charming café has become an overpriced tourist trap, we'll replace the listing with a new and better one.

▨ No other guidebook includes all this:

Honest, engaging coverage of both the cities and the countryside; up-to-the-minute prices, directions, addresses, phone numbers, and opening hours; in-depth essays on local culture, history, and politics; comprehensive listings on transportation between and within regions and cities; straight advice on work and study, budget accommodations, sights, nightlife, and food; detailed city and regional maps; and much more.

▨ Let's Go is for anyone who wants to see Ireland on a budget.

LET'S GO PUBLICATIONS

Let's Go: Alaska & The Pacific Northwest
Let's Go: Britain & Ireland
Let's Go: California
Let's Go: Central America
Let's Go: Eastern Europe
Let's Go: Europe
Let's Go: France
Let's Go: Germany
Let's Go: Greece & Turkey
Let's Go: Ireland
Let's Go: Israel & Egypt
Let's Go: Italy
Let's Go: London
Let's Go: Mexico
Let's Go: New York City
Let's Go: Paris
Let's Go: Rome
Let's Go: Southeast Asia
Let's Go: Spain & Portugal
Let's Go: Switzerland & Austria
Let's Go: USA
Let's Go: Washington, D.C.

Map Guides (coming March 1996)

Let's Go: Boston
Let's Go: London
Let's Go: New York City
Let's Go: Paris
Let's Go: San Francisco
Let's Go: Washington, D.C.

LET'S GO

The Budget Guide to

IRELAND

Maia K. Linask
Editor

Allison Crapo
Associate Editor

St. Martin's Press ⚘ New York

HELPING LET'S GO

If you want to share your discoveries, suggestions, or corrections, please drop us a line. We read every piece of correspondence, whether a postcard, a 10-page e-mail, or a coconut. All suggestions are passed along to our researcher-writers. Please note that mail received after May 1996 may be too late for the 1997 book, but will be retained for the following edition. Address mail to:

Let's Go: Ireland
One Story Street
Cambridge, MA 02138
USA

Visit Let's Go in the travel section of **http://www.americanexpress.com/student/,** or send e-mail to:

LetsGo@delphi.com
Subject: "Let's Go: Ireland"

In addition to the invaluable travel advice our readers share with us, many are kind enough to offer their services as researchers or editors. Unfortunately, the charter of Let's Go, Inc. enables us to employ only currently enrolled Harvard-Radcliffe students.

Maps by David Lindroth copyright © 1996, 1995, 1994 by St. Martin's Press, Inc.

Map revisions pp. 3, 91, 366-7, 384-5 by Let's Go, Inc.

Distributed outside the USA and Canada by Macmillan.

ISBN: 0-312-13546-7

First edition
10 9 8 7 6 5 4 3 2 1

Let's Go: Ireland is written by Let's Go Publications, One Story Street, Cambridge, MA 02138, USA.

Contents

Maps

About Let's Go

THIRTY-SIX YEARS OF WISDOM

Back in 1960, a few students at Harvard University banded together to produce a 20-page pamphlet offering a collection of tips on budget travel in Europe. This modest, mimeographed packet was offered to passengers as an extra on their student charter flights to Europe. The following year, students traveling to Europe researched the first full-fledged edition of *Let's Go: Europe*, a pocket-sized book featuring irreverent write-ups of sights and a decidedly youthful slant. Throughout the '60s, our guides reflected the times; one section of the 1968 *Let's Go: Europe* discussed "Street Singing in Europe on No Dollars a Day," which we said "has very little to do with music." The 1969 guide to America led off with sound advice on San Francisco's Haight-Ashbury ("dig the scene"). During the '70s and '80s, we gradually added regional and city guides, and expanded coverage into the Middle East, Central America, and Asia.

We've seen a lot in 36 years. *Let's Go: Europe* is now the world's best-selling international guide, translated into seven languages. And our guides are still researched, written, and produced entirely by students who know first-hand how to see the world on the cheap. As the budget travel world expands, so does Let's Go. The first editions of *Let's Go: Central America* and *Let's Go: Southeast Asia* hit the shelves this year, and *Let's Go: India & Nepal* is right on their heels. Our useful new series of map guides combine concise city coverage with vivid foldout maps. Our new guides bring our total number of titles, with their spirit of adventure and their honesty, accuracy, and editorial integrity, to 28.

HOW WE DO IT

Each guide is completely revised and updated every year by a well-traveled set of 200 students, who work on all aspects of each guide's development. Every winter, we recruit over 110 researchers and 50 editors to write our books anew. After several months of training, Researcher-Writers hit the road for seven weeks of exploration, from Anchorage to Ankara, Estonia to El Salvador, Iceland to Indonesia. Those hired possess a rare combination of budget travel sense, writing ability, stamina, and courage. Train strikes, stolen luggage, food poisoning, and irate tourist officials are all part of a day's work. Editors work from spring to fall, massaging copy written on Himalayan bus rides into witty yet informative prose. A student staff of typesetters, cartographers, publicists, and managers keeps our lively and sophisticated team together. In September, the collected efforts of the summer are delivered to our printer, who turns them into books in record time. And even as you read this, work on next year's editions is well underway.

WHY WE DO IT

At Let's Go, our goal is to give you a great vacation. We don't think of budget travel as the last recourse of the destitute; we believe that it's the only way to travel. Living cheaply and simply brings you closer to the real people and places you've been saving up to visit. Our book will ease your anxieties and answer your questions about the basics—to help you get off the beaten track and explore. Once you learn the ropes, we encourage you to put Let's Go away now and then to strike out on your own. As any seasoned traveler will tell you, the best discoveries are often those you make yourself. When you find something worth sharing, drop us a line. We're Let's Go Publications, One Story Street, Cambridge, MA 02138, USA (e-mail: LetsGo@delphi.com).

HAPPY TRAVELS!

Researcher-Writers

Nicole Carkeek   *Clare, Galway, Sligo, Leitrim,*
                              Cavan & Monaghan, Fermanagh & Tyrone
We asked her and she told us! Nicole, a native Australian, saved and economized in true budget travel style. No one could know *Let's Go* readers any better. Always careful and comprehensive, nothing from Kilrush to Clones escaped her thorough researching. She befriended hostel owners in Galway, B&B proprietors in Westport, and restauranteurs in Omagh. Though the winds on the Aran Islands sent her chasing after copy (literally), it always arrived in Cambridge, meticulous and precise. Nicole considered staying on Hare Krishna Island, but opted to relax, after seven hectic weeks, in charming Galway.

Ryan Hackney   *Meath & Louth, Dublin, Wicklow,*
                              Kildare, Carlow, Wexford & Waterford
Ryan traversed Eastern Ireland and Dublin, forcing his way into the hearts and dining rooms of tea-and-scone-laden women everywhere. He had no difficulty finding 21 free pints in Irish pubs. Ryan, an expert beer taster, truly believes that Guinness is good for you. His dog Chaka didn't get any, though. Infallible, Ryan was daunted only by spiders in the phone booths of Kildare. Ryan hit the ground running and never stopped. He single-handedly reinvented Dublin, even while eating pints of strawberries. We nominate him as ambassador to Dublin and wish him a lifetime supply of floating, flaming whiskey!!! (see page 150).

Alice Lin   *Donegal, Antrim & Derry,*
                              Down & Armagh, Belfast, Isle of Man
Alice sends her thanks to the many people who helped her in Donegal when Bus Éireann couldn't: Pat, Leo, Leo, Shaun, Brendan, Eamon, Martin, and the Cahalan family. Hostel owners have never been so friendly as they were in Donegal. Her cooking was a pleasure to many of them. Alice, who never flinched or groaned, is a legend in her own time. Undaunted by riots or Bailey's-hating bartenders, she went the extra kilometer in the Sperrin Mountains (without being asked) and trekked through bogs on the Inishowen (she didn't even mind the mud and smells). Alice pointed us to the best that the island has to offer. Thanks for the inspiring green hackey sacks.

Heather Sullivan   *Cork, Kerry, Limerick, Tipperary*
We knew we had a real Researcher-Writer when we found someone who had been to Wyoming *and* Idaho. Her discriminating eye saw every hostel in the southwest while her discerning palate went on a search for the best brown bread in all of Ireland. Heather biked, walked, and drove around every peninsula, without regard for all the tour buses, to research islands, parks, and pubs. Heather was always full of cheer but never kissed the Blarney Stone. Having finished her stint as a travel guide writer in Ireland, she plans to return for more laid-back fun.

Daniel Silverberg   *London*
Amara Balthrop-Lewis   *London*

Acknowledgments

The ready and rapid help of Bord Fáilte and the Northern Ireland Tourist Board was invaluable. The generosity of IHH made our researchers feel at home. Thanks to Joy Somberg, Timur, Julianna, Dan W., Sean F., Jake, Mike O., and Tina. Our eternal love and gratitude to Glenn Davis, Adam Fleisher, Nathan Lump, and Tim Perlstein, who did, after all, save our GI. You gave advice, laughter, and support whenever we needed it. Our greatest thanks goes to Sean D. We couldn't have asked for a better colleague and friend. **MKL and APC**

To Melissa, Sonia, and Jennifer, who kept me sane from afar. To Sean D., who stayed calm and stayed late. To Mom and Dad, without whom I couldn't have done any of this. To Allison (frogs!), who was a friend and an editor, who made me laugh and made me grateful. And to Rob, who was so supportive, patient, helpful, and so much fun (not to mention a good cook) that I still can't believe it. Thanks. **MKL**

Thanks to my dear Maia for making my summer wonderful (oh, really?). To Liz and Tina for the multitude breaks. To Jake, Rebecca, Connie, and Adam for philosophy, love, and care. To Jen, from whom I never get far. To MDG who is always with me. I send hugs to MPO for Understanding. To my beautiful Sean, for being evil and cool (but not necessarily in that order) and rescuing me from my desk. The words are gone. And my love and thanks to my family: I never leave the farm in Idaho. May you always find me there. **APC**

Editor	Maia K. Linask
Associate Editor	Allison Crapo
Managing Editor	Sean K. Desmond
Publishing Director	Sean Fitzpatrick
Production Manager	Michael L. Cisneros
Associate Production Manager	Eunice C. Park
Cartography Manager	Samuel P. Trumbull
Associate Cartography Manager	Amanda K. Bean
Editorial Manager	Timothy S. Perlstein
Editorial Manager	Haneen M. Rabie
Financial Manager	Katarzyna Drozd
Personnel Manager	Sean K. Desmond
Publicity Manager	Timur Okay Harry Hiçyılmaz
Associate Publicity Manager	Eleni N. Gage
General Manager	Richard Olken
Assistant General Manager	Anne E. Chisholm
Office Coordinator	Jennifer L. Schuberth
Director of Advertising and Sales	Jean C. Anderson
Sales Assistant Manager	Sammy Lai
Sales Representatives	Matthew S. Abramson
	Delphine Gabbay, Godffrey Williams

How To Use This Book

The more you know about Ireland, the happier you'll be when you get there. Our **Essentials** chapter is designed expressly to help maximize your happiness. The dry-as-dust **Planning Your Trip** section has necessary information on everything you did and didn't think of asking, from customs to packing to health. It also contains a section on the specific concerns of women, minorities, bisexuals, gays, lesbians, people with disabilities, families, and older travelers. There's little we don't prepare you for. A **Getting There** section is particularly helpful for those with little experience in planning travel. It also helps seasoned travelers navigate a path trough (and along) the maze of planes, ferries, rails, and buses, which can be confusing for anyone. **Traveling in Ireland** will tell you what you may expect once you get there.

An **Introduction** explains the basics of Irish history, literature, language, and food. These essays are designed to help travelers understand what they see and thereby get the most out of their trip. They are also meant to provide some entertainment. The **Northern Ireland** introduction contains similar cultural information. More importantly, it tells you ways to stay out of trouble. Most of the book is dedicated to coverage of the regions, towns, and cities that constitute Ireland. The counties and towns in the Republic of Ireland section are organized clockwise around the coast, beginning with Dublin. Northern Ireland does just the opposite: its towns are represented in *Let's Go* from south and east to north and west. Each listing is divided up into a number of paragraphs. Practical information makes known where the tourist office, bank, and laundry (and more) are. Other sections suggest places to stay, places to eat, and places to see.

The **Isle of Man** and **London** make both great stopovers and novelties of their own. A glossary at the back of the book will help you decode both British slang and Irish language. And please use the index in the back; we're quite proud of it.

It's important, when using our books, to realize that our choices for listings are based on what we believe represents good value, not just low price. Travelers who become concerned solely with saving money are bound to have less fond memories of their travels. It's also important to know that, while Let's Go researchers try to leave no stone unturned, there are far too many such stones to include all of them in the book. Readers shouldn't let Let's Go become a bible of budget travel. It is, in essence, an enabling device. The best way to see Ireland is to meet Irish people and ask them questions about where to stay, what to see, and who they are. As a final few words of warning, there are some things which we felt it unnecessary to include in every town. Every large town or city in Ireland makes a good base for exploring the surrounding countryside, and every mountain and tower, when you get to the top, will give you a new view.

A NOTE TO OUR READERS

The information for this book is gathered by Let's Go researchers during the summer months. Each listing is derived from the assigned researcher's opinion based upon his or her visit at a particular time. The opinions are expressed in a candid and forthright manner. Other travelers might disagree. Those traveling at a different time may have different experiences since prices, dates, hours, and conditions are always subject to change. You are urged to check beforehand to avoid inconvenience and surprises. Travel always involves a certain degree of risk, especially in low-cost areas. When traveling, especially on a budget, you should always take particular care to ensure your safety.

ESSENTIALS

PLANNING YOUR TRIP

Traveling is like comedy—timing is everything. Traveling during the low or off-season (mid-Sept. to May) will reduce the damage to your bank account. Airfares are considerably lower, and you won't have to compete with squadrons of fellow tourists. However, many attractions, hostels, and tourist offices close in the off-season, and in some rural areas in west Ireland, local transportation shuts down altogether. If traveling during the off-season, the infamous Irish climate is a force to be reckoned with (see Weather, p. 21).

■ ■ ■ RESOURCES AT HOME

TOURIST BUREAUS

Irish Tourist Board (Bord Fáilte): In **U.S.:** 345 Park Ave., New York, NY 10154 (tel. (800) 223-6470 or (212) 418-0800; fax (212) 371-9052). In **Canada:** 160 Bloor St. E., Suite 1150, Toronto, Ont. M4W 1B9 (tel. (416) 929-2777; fax (416) 929-6783). In **U.K.:** 150 New Bond St., London W1Y 0AQ (tel. (0171) 493 3201; fax (0171) 493 9065). In **Australia:** Level 5, 36 Carrington St., Sydney NSW 2000 (tel. (02) 299 6177; fax 299 6323). Ask for the *Caravan and Camping Guide*, which lists Bord Fáilte-approved B&Bs and campgrounds and prices.

Northern Ireland Tourist Board: In **U.S.:** 551 Fifth Ave., New York, NY 10176 (tel. (212) 922-0101 or (800) 326-0036; fax (212) 922-0099). **Head Office:** 59 North St., Belfast, BT1 1NB, Northern Ireland (tel. (01232) 246609; fax (01232) 240960). In **U.K.:** 11 Berkeley St., London W1X 5AD (tel. (0171) 409 0487; fax (0171) 499 3731). In **Dublin:** 16 Nassau St., Dublin 2 (tel. (01) 679 1977; fax (01) 679 1863; open Mon.-Fri. 9am-5:30pm, Sat. 10am-5pm). In **Canada:** 111 Avenue Rd., Suite 450, Toronto, Ont. M5R 3J8 (tel. (416) 925-6368; fax (416) 961-2175). You can also contact any British Tourist Office for Northern Ireland info. Ask any tourist board for free brochures. *Where to Stay in Northern Ireland 1995,* a list of all B&Bs and campgrounds and their prices, is available for US$9.95 (UK£4) and *Where to Eat in Northern Ireland 1995* is available for US$6.95 (UK£2.50).

Isle of Man Tourist Information: Sea Terminal Building, Douglas IM1 2RG, Isle of Man (tel. (01624) 686766; fax 627443).

All Ireland Tourist Board: In **London:** British Travel Centre, 4 Lower Regent St., London SW1 4PQ (tel. (0171) 839 8416; fax (0171) 839 6179; Mon.-Fri. 9am-6:30pm, Sat.-Sun. 10am-4pm). In **Australia:** All Ireland Board, 25 Meredith Place, French's Forest NSW 2046, Australia (tel. (02) 975 6087; fax 975 7851).

TRAVEL SERVICES

Worldwide:

Council Travel: the travel division of Council (see below), is a full-service travel agency specializing in student, youth, and budget travel. With over 50 offices worldwide, they offer exclusively negotiated discount airfares on scheduled airlines, railpasses, hosteling cards, low-cost accommodations, guidebooks (including *Let's Go*), budget tours, travel gear, and international student (ISIC), youth (GO 25), and teacher (ITIC) identification cards. Some of the 41 offices in the U.S. include: 729 Boylston St. #201, **Boston,** MA 02116 (tel. (617) 266-1926); 1153 N. Dearborn St., **Chicago,** IL 60610 (tel. (312) 951-0585); 10904 Lindbrook Dr., **Los Angeles,** CA 90024 (tel. (310) 208-3551); 205 East 42nd St., **New York,** NY 10017 (tel. (212) 661-1450); 530 Bush St., Ground Floor, **San Francisco,** CA 94108 (tel. (415) 421-3473); 1314 NE 43rd St., Suite 210, **Seattle,** WA 98105 (tel.

(206) 632-2448). For U.S. cities not listed, call 1-800-2-COUNCIL (800-226-8624). Overseas offices include: 28A Poland St. (Oxford Circus), **London** W1V 3DB (tel. (0171) 437 7767).

International Student Travel Confederation: Store Kongensgade 40H, 1264 Copenhagen K, Denmark (tel. (33) 93 93 03, fax 33 (93) 73 77). A nonprofit confederation. Sponsors the International Student Identity Card (ISIC). Member organizations include International Student Rail Association (ISRA), Student Air Travel Association (SATA), ISIS Travel Insurance, and the International Association for Educational and Work Exchange Programs (IAEWEP).

STA Travel: 6560 North Scottsdale Rd. #F100, Scottsdale, AZ 85253 (tel. (800) 777-0112). A student and youth travel organization with over 100 offices around the world and 14 U.S. locations. Offers discount airfares (for travelers under 26 and full-time students under 32), railpasses, accommodations, tours, insurance, and ISICs. Offices include: 297 Newbury St., **Boston,** MA 02116 (tel. (617) 266 6014); 48 E. 11th St., **New York,** NY 10003 (tel. (212) 477 7166); and 51 Grant Ave., **San Francisco,** CA 94108 (tel. (415) 391 8407). In the U.K.: Priory House, 6 Wrights Lane, **London** W8 6TA (tel. (0171) 938 4711). In **New Zealand:** 10 High St., Auckland (tel. (09) 309 9723). In **Australia:** 224 Faraday St., Melbourne VIC 3050 (tel. (03) 347 6911).

In the U.S. & Canada:

Council on International Educational Exchange (Council): 205 East 42nd St., New York, NY 10017 (tel. (212) 661-1414). A private, not-for-profit organization, Council administers work, volunteer, academic, and professional programs around the world. They also offer identity cards (including the ISIC and the GO25) and a range of publications; among them the useful magazine *Student Travels* (free) and *The High-School Student's Guide to Study, Travel, and Adventure Abroad* ($13.95, postage $1.50).

Let's Go Travel: Harvard Student Agencies, 53A Church St., Cambridge, MA 02138 (tel. (800) 5-LETS GO/553-8746) or (617) 495-9649). Let's Go Travel offers railpasses, HI-AYH memberships, ISICs, International Teacher Identification cards, GO25 cards, FIYTO cards, guidebooks (including every *Let's Go*), maps, bargain flights, and a complete line of budget travel gear. All items available by mail—call or write for a catalog.

Educational Travel Center (ETC): 438 North Frances St., Madison, WI 53703 (tel. (800) 747-5551; fax (608) 256-2042). Flight information, HI-AYH memberships, Eurail and regional rail passes. Call or write for free pamphlet *Taking Off.*

International Student Exchange Flights (ISE): 5010 East Shea Blvd., #A104, Scottsdale, AZ 85254 (tel. (602) 951-1177). Budget student flights, HI-AYH memberships, BritRail and Eurail passes, International Student Exchange Identity Card (US$18), and travel guides, including the *Let's Go* series. Free catalog!

Unitravel: 1177 North Warson Rd., St. Louis, MO 63132 (tel. (800) 325-2222; fax (314) 569-2503). Offers discounted airfares on major scheduled airlines from the U.S. to Europe, Africa, and Asia.

Travel CUTS (Canadian University Travel Services, Ltd.): 187 College St., Toronto, Ont. M5T 1P7 (tel. (416) 798-CUTS/2887; fax (416) 979-8167). Canada's national student travel bureau and equivalent of Council, with 40 offices across Canada. Also in the **London:** 295-A Regent St., London W1R 7YA (tel. (0171) 637 3161). Discounted airfares, and special student fares to all destinations with valid ISIC. Issuing authority for ISIC, FIYTO and HI cards. Offers free *Student Traveler* magazine, as well as info on the Student Work Abroad Program (SWAP).

In Ireland & Britain:

Campus Travel: 52 Grosvenor Gardens, London SW1W 0AG (tel. (0171) 730 8832; fax (0171) 730 5739). 37 branches in the U.K. Student and youth fares on plane, train, boat, and bus travel. Flexible airline tickets. Discount and ID cards for students, travel insurance for students and those under 35, maps, and travel guides. Publishes travel guides. Telephone booking service: in **Europe** call (0171) 730 3402; in **North America** call (071) 730 2101; **worldwide** call (071) 730 8111; in Manchester call (0161) 273 1721; in Scotland call (0131) 668 3303.

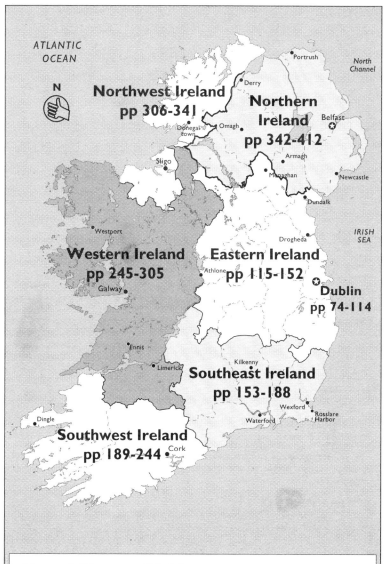

ATLANTIC OCEAN

Portrush

North Channel

N

Northwest Ireland
pp 306-341

Derry

Northern Ireland
pp 342-412

Belfast

Donegal town

Omagh

Armagh

Sligo

Monaghan

Newcastle

Dundalk

Westport

IRISH SEA

Western Ireland
pp 245-305

Drogheda

Eastern Ireland
pp 115-152

Athlone

Galway

Dublin
pp 74-114

Ennis

Limerick

Kilkenny

Southeast Ireland
pp 153-188

Dingle

Wexford

Rosslare Harbor

Waterford

Southwest Ireland
pp 189-244

Cork

Map of Chapter Divisions

Eastern Ireland
Counties: Monaghan, Cavan, Louth, Meath, Longford, Westmeath, Offaly, Laois, Kildare, and Wicklow.

Southeast Ireland
Counties: Tipperary, Kilkenny, Carlow, Wexford, and Waterford.

Southwest Ireland
Counties: Cork and Kerry.

Western Ireland
Counties: Limerick, Clare, Galway, Roscommon, Leitrim, and Mayo.

Northwest Ireland
Counties: Sligo and Donegal.

Northern Ireland
Counties: Derry, Antrim, Tyrone, Fermanagh, Armagh, and Down.

USIT: 19-21 Aston Quay, O'Connell Bridge, Dublin 2 (tel. (01) 679 88 33; fax (01) 677 88 43). In the **USA:** New York Student Center, 895 Amsterdam Ave., New York, NY 10025 (tel. (212) 663-5435). Additional offices in Cork, Galway, Limerick, Waterford, Maynooth, Coleraine, Derry, and Belfast. Sells ISIC, HI hostel cards, and *Let's Go* guidebooks. In addition to selling discounted student fares on scheduled flights, USIT books its own charter flights in the summer for some of the best flight deals.

WST Charters: 65 Wigmore St., London W1H 0JU (tel. (0171) 224 0504; fax (0171) 224 6142). ISICs and bargain flights worldwide.

READING UP

The College Connection, Inc.: 1295 Prospect St., La Jolla, CA 92037 (tel. (619) 551-9770). Publishes *The Passport*, a booklet listing hints about every aspect of traveling and studying abroad. The College Rail Connection, a division of the College Connection, sells railpasses with students discounts.

Forsyth Travel Library: P.O. Box 2975, Shawnee Mission, KS 66201 (tel. (800) 367-7984; fax (913) 384-3553). Call or write for their catalog of maps, guidebooks, railpasses, timetables, and HI memberships. They also have a separate catalog of travel gear; including soft luggage, converters and adapters, security items, and accessories.

Hippocrene Books, Inc.: 171 Madison Ave., New York, NY 10016 (tel. (212) 685-4371). Offers a free catalog of travel reference books, travel guides, maps, foreign language dictionaries, and 100 language learning guides.

Hunter Publishing: 300 Raritan Center Parkway, Edison, NJ 08818 (tel. (908) 225-1900). Publishes an extensive catalog of travel books, guides, language learning tapes, and quality maps; including *Charming Small Hotel Guides* to Italy, France, England, and Germany (each US$12.95).

Specialty Travel Index: 305 San Anselmo Avenue, Suite 313, San Anselmo, CA 94960 (tel. (415) 459-4900; fax (415) 459-4974). An extensive listing of "off the beaten track" and specialty travel opportunities, including a variety of adventures in the Irish outdoors. For copies or subscriptions, write to the address above. Single issues US$6, a 1-year subscription US$10 in the U.S., US$13 in Canada, US$12 surface mail/US$20 air mail to all other foreign addresses.

Superintendent of Documents: U.S. Government Printing Office, P.O. Box 371954, Pittsburgh, PA 15250-7954 (tel. (202) 512-1800; fax (202) 512-2250. Publishes *Your Trip Abroad* (US$1.25), *Health Information for International Travel* (US$7), and "Background Notes" on all countries ($1). Postage included.

Transitions Abroad: 18 Hulst Rd., P.O. Box 1300, Amherst, MA 01004-1300 (tel. (413) 245-3414; fax 256-0373). Publishes an invaluable magazine listing publications and resources for overseas study, work, and volunteering. They also publish *The Alternative Travel Directory*, a comprehensive guide to living, learning, and working overseas (US$19.95; postage $3).

GETTING IT ON-LINE

There is a vast amount of information available through the international computer network known as the **Internet.** Some commercial providers (such as America Online, CompuServe, and Prodigy) offer sophisticated services like **on-line reservations.** Even the most basic mode of access can provide an over-abundance of information. Most universities and many businesses offer students and employees Internet access. Commercial gateways provide Internet access to the general public for a monthly fee (usually US$20-30).

One primary means of transmission and discussion of information across the Internet are forums known collectively as Usenet, and individually as **newsgroups.** There are thousands of newsgroups accessible by users all over the world; sometimes, they're your best source for up-to-the-minute information. New groups are always sprouting up; unfortunately, not all groups are available from all systems, although your system administrator can usually add new groups on request. A basic news-reading program can be accessed on most UNIX systems by typing "rn" for "read news." A caveat: most newsgroups are unmoderated, so the quality of conversation and the reliability of information posted within them is not always certain. Before posting messages yourself, you should familiarize yourself with the standards of "netiquette" that (in theory) keep discussion polite and coordinated.

There are several "hierarchies" of newsgroups. One, the "soc" groups, primarily addresses social issues and socializing; subscribe to **soc.culture.jordan,** or the country of your choice. The "alt" groups are a less formalized collection of newsgroups; good examples are **alt.politics.france** and **alt.current-events.balkans.** "Rec" groups (such as **rec.travel.air** and **rec.travel.europe)** are oriented toward hobbies, recreation, and the arts. Some systems also provide access to the "ClariNet" newsgroups; read-only (copyrighted) groups which compile the latest wire service news. Examples of such groups are **clari.world.europe.italy** and **clari.news.asia.**

Three of the other services available on the Internet are **FTP** (file transfer protocol), **gopher,** and **World Wide Web.** Each can be used to obtain files and other information stored in areas of other computer systems accessible to the public. Thousands of such archives exist, including many with information on travel. A particularly useful archive is **rec-travel** at "ftp.cc.umanitoba.ca"; it includes travelogues, U.S. State Department Advisories, and more. Use your WWW browser to check out the handy CIA World Factbook; point to "http://www.odci.gov94fact/ fb94toc/fb94toc.html". You can also find a **guide to hosteling** at "http://www.hostels.com/hostels" (or e-mail them at "info@hostels.com").

The "Student and Budget Travel Resource Guide" lists a wide variety of online travel information. It is available through the WWW at "http:// asa.ugl.lib.umich.edu/chdocs/travel/travel-guide.html"; or e-mail to "travel-guide@umich.edu". **Northern Ireland Tourist Board** announces that they "have now joined the cyber age—on **Internet."** Including information on the Giant's Causeway, the Glens of Antrim, or the 13 U.S. Presidents who originated in Northern Ireland, information from the Northern Ireland Tourist Board is accessible on the Internet at "http://www.interknowledge.com/northern-ireland".

■■■ DOCUMENTS & FORMALITIES

When you travel, always carry on your person two or more forms of identification, including at least one photo ID. A passport and a driver's license or birth certificate usually serve as adequate proof of your identity and citizenship. Many establishments, especially banks, require several IDs before cashing traveler's checks. Never carry all your identification in the same place. If you plan to be in Ireland or Northern Ireland for a long time, register your passport with an embassy or consulate. Students should consult Youth & Student Identification (see p. 9).

File all applications several weeks (or even months) in advance of your departure date. Most offices suggest that you apply in the winter off-season (between Aug. and Dec.) for speedier service. If you are a U.S. citizen and need general information about prudent travel abroad, see the booklet *Your Trip Abroad* (US$1.25) from the Superintendent of Documents, U.S. Government Printing Office, Washington, DC 20402 (tel. (202) 783-3238). Your city's passport agency may also have copies.

CONSULATES & HIGH COMMISSIONS

Ireland: In the **U.S.:** Irish Embassy, 2234 Massachusetts Ave. NW, Washington, DC 20008 (tel. (202) 462-3939); consulates at: 345 Park Ave., 17th floor, New York, NY 10154 (tel. (212) 319-2555); Wrigley Building, rm. 911, 400 N. Michigan Ave., Chicago, IL 60611 (tel. (312) 337-1868); 655 Montgomery St., #930, San Francisco, CA 94111 (tel. (415) 392-4214); 535 Boylston St., Boston, MA 02116 (tel. (617) 267-9330). In **Canada:** 170 Metcalfe St., Ottawa, Ont. K2P 1P3 (tel. (613) 233-6281). In **Australia** and **New Zealand:** 20 Arkana St., Yarralumla ACT 2600, Australia (tel. (06) 273 3022; fax 273 3741).

Britain: In the **U.S.:** British Embassy, 3100 Massachusetts Ave. NW, Washington, DC 20008 (tel. (202) 462-1340); consulates at 845 Third Ave., New York, NY 10022 (tel. (212) 745-0200); Suite 2700, Marquis One Tower, 245 Peachtree Center Ave., Atlanta, GA 30303 (tel. (404) 524-5856); 33 North Dearborn St., Chicago, IL 60602 (tel. (312) 346-1810); First Interstate Bank Plaza, Suite 1990, 1000 Louisiana, Houston, TX 77002 (tel. (713) 659-6270); and 11766 Wilshire Blvd., Ste. 400, Los Angeles, CA 90025-6536 (tel. (310) 477-3322). Call the Embassy for additional consulates. In **Canada:** British Tourist Authority, 111 Avenue Rd. Suite 450, Toronto, Ontario M5R 3J8 (tel. (416) 925-6326; fax (416) 961-2175). In **Australia:** British High Commission, Commonwealth Ave., Yarralumla, Canberra, ACT 2600 (tel. (06) 270 6666). In **New Zealand:** British High Commission, 44 Hill St., Wellington 1 (tel. (04) 472 6049).

GETTING IN: PASSPORT REQUIREMENTS

You must have a valid **passport** to enter Ireland or Northern Ireland and to reenter your own country. Citizens of the U.S., Canada, Australia, and New Zealand may enter both the Republic of Ireland and Northern Ireland without a visa. When entering the country, dress neatly and carry proof of your financial independence (such as an air ticket to depart, enough money to cover your living expenses, etc.).

The standard period of admission is three months to Ireland, six months to Northern Ireland. To stay longer, you must show evidence that you can support yourself for an extended period of time and a medical examination is often required. Admission as a visitor from a non-EU nation does not include the right to work, which is authorized only by the possession of a work permit (see Alternatives To Tourism, p. 24). Entering either Ireland or Northern Ireland to study does not require a special visa, but immigration officers will want to see proof of acceptance by an Irish or Northern Irish school.

Passports

Before you leave, photocopy the page of your passport that contains your photograph and identifying information, especially your passport number. Carry it apart from the passport itself and leave another copy at home. If you lose your passport while traveling, immediately notify the local police and the nearest consulate of your home government. In an emergency, ask for temporary traveling papers that will permit you to return to your home country.

U.S. citizens may apply for a passport, valid for ten years (five years if under 18), at any clerk of court or post office authorized to accept passport applications, or at a U.S. Passport Agency, located in Boston, Chicago, Honolulu, Houston, Los Angeles, Miami, New Orleans, New York, Philadelphia, San Francisco, Seattle, Stamford, or Washington, DC. Refer to the "U.S. Government, State Department" section of the telephone directory's Blue Pages or call your local post office for addresses. If this is your first passport, if you are under age 18, if your current passport is more than 12 years old, or if it was issued before your 18th birthday, you must apply in person. For your first passport, you must submit the following along with a completed application form: (1) proof of U.S. Citizenship (a certified birth certificate, naturalization papers, or a previous passport); (2) ID bearing your signature and either your photo or a personal description (e.g., an unexpired driver's license or passport, student ID card, or government ID card); and (3) two identical, passport-size (2 in. by 2 in.) photographs with a white or off-white background taken within the past six months. Bring these items and $65 (under 18 $40) in check or money order. Passport Agencies accept cash only in the exact amount. Write your date of birth on the check and photocopy the data page for your records. You can renew your passport by mail (or in person) for $55. Your old passport can fulfill both requirements (1) and (2) above. Processing usually takes four weeks.

In 1986, more Americans filed for passports than ever before, meaning that in 1996, the number applying for renewals will be enormous. The U.S. Passport Agency encourages everyone to apply early, especially considering the number of people who will be filing for renewals in 1996. Passports are processed according to the departure date indicated on the application form. In March through August, processing may take longer. If you fail to indicate a departure date, the agency will assume you are not planning any immediate travel. Your passport will be mailed to you. You may pay for express mail return of your passport. Passport agencies offer rush service. If you have proof that you are departing within five working days (e.g. an airplane ticket), a Passport Agency will issue a passport while you wait. Arrive well before the office opens so you can lead the line, but expect to remain there a good part of the day. You will also be forced to pay a $30 rush fee.

Abroad, a U.S. embassy or consulate can usually issue new passports, given proof of citizenship. For more information, call the U.S. Passport Information's helpful 24-hr. recorded message (tel. (202) 647-0518), which offers general information, agency locations, opening hours, etc. Or call the recorded message of the passport agency nearest you. If your passport is lost or stolen in the U.S., report it in writing to Passport Services, 1111 19th St. NW, Department of State, Washington, DC 20522-1705, or to the nearest passport agency.

Canadian passport applications forms are available at all passport offices, post offices, and at most travel agencies. You can also apply in person at any of 28 regional offices. Application must include proof of Canadian citizenship and two identical signed photographs, which must have been taken within the last 12 months, and must also indicate the photographer, studio address, and the date the photos were taken. The application must be signed by a guarantor—someone who has known the applicant for two years and whose profession falls into one of the categories listed in the application form. The fee is CDN$35, and processing requires about three weeks if you mail your application, five working days if you make a personal appearance. Applicants over 16 should file form A, while applicants under 16 who travel with a parent should use Form B and may be included on the parent's passport. Passports are valid for five years. For further information and a list of Canadian embassies and consulates abroad, write to Info-Export (BPTE) at the External Affairs office, Ottawa, Ont. K1A OG3, or call the 24-hr. number (from Canada only; (800) 567-6868).

Australian citizens must apply for a passport in person at a local post office, a passport office, or an Australian diplomatic mission overseas. An appointment may be necessary. Passport offices are in Adelaide, Brisbane, Canberra, Darwin, Hobart, Melbourne, Newcastle, Perth, and Sydney. A parent may file an application for a child who is under 18 and unmarried. Along with your application, you must submit: (1) proof of citizenship (such as an expired passport, a birth certificate, or a citizen's certificate from the Immigration Service); (2) proof of your present name; (3) two identical, signed photos less than six months old; (4) other forms of ID (driver's license, credit card, etc.). Application fees are adjusted every three months.

Applicants for **New Zealand passports** must contact their local Link Centre, travel agent, or New Zealand Representative for an application form which they must mail to the New Zealand Passport Office, Documents of National Identity Division, Department of Internal Affairs, Box 10-526, Wellington (tel. (04) 474 8100). With a completed application, you must submit: (1) proof of citizenship; (2) proof of identity; and (3) two certified photos. The standard processing time is 10 working days from receipt of application. The application fee is NZ$80 for an application submitted in New Zealand and varies for those submitted abroad. Citizens applying from overseas should send the passport application to the nearest embassy, high commission, or consulate authorized to issue passports.

Visas

For more information, send for *Foreign Visa Requirements* (US $0.50) from Consumer Information Center, Pueblo, CO 81009 (tel. (719) 948-3334), or contact Center for International Business and Travel (CIBT), 25 West 43rd St. #1420, New York, NY 10036 (tel. (800) 925-2428 or (212) 575-2811 from NYC). This organization secures visas for travel to and from all countries. The service charge varies, but the average cost for a U.S. citizen is US$50 per visa.

Customs

Visitors to the **Republic of Ireland** must declare everything in excess of the following allowances for goods obtained outside the EU or duty and tax free in the EU: (1) 200 cigarettes, or 100 cigarillos, or 50 cigars, or 250g tobacco; (2) 1 liter of alcoholic drinks exceeding 22% vol. or 2 liters of alcoholic drinks not exceeding 22% vol.; (3) two liters of still wine; (4) 50g of perfume; (5) toilet water (1/4 liter); (6) IR£142 of other goods per adult traveler (under 15, IR£73). A maximum of 25 liters of beer may be imported as a part of, but not in addition to, the adult allowance. Goods obtained in another EU country duty-free or tax paid (up to IR£73 per person) will not be subject to additional customs duty. Travelers under 17 are not entitled to any tobacco or alcohol allowance. For more information, contact The Revenue Commissioners, Dublin Castle, Dublin 1 (tel. (01) 679 2777; fax (01) 679 27035).

British citizens or visitors arriving in Northern Ireland from outside the EU must declare any goods in excess of the following allowances: (1) 200 cigarettes, 100 cigarillos, 50 cigars, or 250 g tobacco; (2) still table wine (2 liters); (3) strong liqueurs over 22% volume (1 liter) or fortified or sparkling wine (2 liters); (4) perfume (60 cc/ml); (5) toilet water (250 cc/ml); and (6) £136 worth of all other goods including gifts and souvenirs. You must be over 17 to import liquor or tobacco. These allowances also apply to Duty Free purchases within the EU, except for the last category ("other goods"), which has an allowance of £71. Goods obtained duty- and tax-paid for personal use (regulated according to set guide levels) within the EU do not require any further customs duty. For more information about U.K. customs, contact Her Majesty's Customs and Excise, Custom House, Nettleton Road, Heathrow Airport, Hounslow, Middlesex, TW6 2LA (tel. (0181) 910-3744; fax 910-3765).

It's illegal to bring into the **U.K.** or **Ireland** any controlled drugs, horror comics, fireworks, meat, or plant or vegetable material (including fruit and bark). All animals brought into the country are subject to a six-month quarantine at the owner's expense. Neither country limits the amount of currency you may bring in, though Ireland places restrictions on the amount taken out—no more than £150 in Irish currency, plus no more than the value of IR£1200 in foreign currency. The U.K. has no such limits.

Upon returning home, you must declare all articles acquired abroad. Make a list (including serial numbers) of any valuables that you take with you from home. If you register this list with customs at the airport before departing, you'll avoid being charged import duties upon your return. Like Ireland and Northern Ireland, the U.S., Canada, Australia, and New Zealand all prohibit or restrict the import of firearms, explosives, ammunition, fireworks, plants, animals, lottery tickets, obscene literature and film, and controlled drugs. To avoid problems when carrying prescription drugs, make sure bottles are clearly marked, and have a copy of the prescription ready to show the customs officer.

U.S. citizens returning from abroad must declare all merchandise acquired abroad; including gifts, articles bought in duty-free shops, and purchases for others. Remember to have sales slips ready, since customs officials may ask for them. The first US$400 worth of merchandise may be entered duty-free; the next US$1000 worth is subject to a 10% tax. Goods are considered duty-free if they are for personal or household use (this includes gifts) and cannot include more than 100 cigars, 200 cigarettes, and one liter of alcoholic beverages. You must be over 21 to bring liquor into the U.S. To be eligible for the duty-free allowance, you must have remained abroad for at least 48 hours and cannot have used this exemption or any part of it within the preceding 30 days. You can mail unsolicited gifts duty-free if they are worth less than US$100, though you may not mail alcohol, tobacco, or perfume. Officials occasionally spot-check parcels, so mark the price and nature of the gift and the words "Unsolicited Gift" on the package. If you send back a non-gift parcel or a gift worth more than $100, the Postal Service will collect a duty for its value plus a handling charge to deliver it. If you mail home personal goods of U.S. origin, avoid duty charges by marking the package "American goods returned." For more information, consult the brochure *Know Before You Go*, available from the U.S.

Customs Service, P.O. Box 7407, Washington DC 20044 (tel. 202) 927-6724). Foreign nationals living in the U.S. are subject to different regulations and should ask for the leaflet *Customs Hints for Visitors (Nonresidents)*. Both publications are free.

Canadian citizens who remain abroad for at least one week may bring back up to CDN$300 worth of goods duty-free once every calendar year (this amount cannot be combined from various trips). Canadian citizens or residents who travel for a period between 48 hours and six days can bring back up to CDN $100 with the exception of tobacco and alcohol. You are permitted to ship goods except tobacco and alcohol home under this exemption as long as you declare them when you arrive. Citizens over the legal age (which varies by province) may import in-person (not through the mail) up to 200 cigarettes, 50 cigars, 400g loose tobacco, 1.14 liters wine or alcohol, and 24 355ml cans/bottles beer (the value of these products is included in the CDN$300 allowance). For more information, write to Canadian Customs, 2265 St. Laurent Blvd., Ottawa, Ontario, K1G 4K3 (tel. (613) 993-0534; within Canada, call (800) 461-9999).

Australian citizens over 18 may bring in up to AUS$400 worth of duty-free goods, including 1.124 liters alcohol and 250 cigarettes or 250g tobacco. For those under 18, the limit is AUS$200. There is no limit to the amount of Australian or foreign cash that may be brought into or taken out of the country. However, amounts of AUS$5000 or more (or the equivalent in foreign currency) must be reported. For information, contact the Customs Service, 5 Constitution Ave., Canberra, ACT 2601 (tel. (06) 275 6255; fax 275 6989). Australians have no limit to the amount of Australian and/or foreign cash that may be brought into or taken out of Australia.

New Zealand citizens may bring home up to NZ$700 worth of goods duty-free if they are intended for personal use or are unsolicited gifts. The *New Zealand Customs Guide for Travelers* is available at any customs office, or contact New Zealand Customs, PO Box 29, Auckland (tel. (09) 773 520; fax 309 2978).

Each **South African citizen** may import duty-free: 400 cigarettes, 50 cigars, 250g tobacco, 2 liters of wine, 1 liter of spirits, 250ml toilet water, 50ml perfume, and other items up to a value of R500. Amounts exceeding this limit but not R10,000 are dutiable at 20%. Goods acquired abroad and sent to the Republic as unaccompanied baggage do not qualify for any allowances. You may not export or import South African bank notes in excess of R500.

YOUTH & STUDENT IDENTIFICATION

Student and youth IDs can get you a lot of discounts on airfares to Ireland, trains and buses within Ireland, and admission to sights. The **International Student Identity Card (ISIC)** is the most widely recognized form of student ID; more than one million students have one. The ISIC also provides accident insurance of up to US$3000 per accident, US$25,000 for emergency medical evacuation, and US$100 per day of in-hospital care for up to 60 days, among other benefits. In addition, cardholders have access to a toll-free Traveler's Assistance hotline whose multilingual staff can provide help in medical, legal, and financial emergencies overseas.

Many student travel offices issue ISICs, including Council Travel, Let's Go Travel, and STA in the U.S.; USIT in Ireland; and any of the organizations under the auspices of the International Student Travel Confederation (ISTC) around the world (see Travel Services, p. 1). The *International Student Identity Card Handbook*, available when you purchase the card, lists by country some of the available discounts.

To apply, provide in person or by mail: (1) current, dated proof of full-time student status (e.g., a letter on school stationery signed and sealed by the registrar, or a photocopied transcript, grade report, or bursar's receipt with your name printed); (2) a 1½-inch by 2-inch photo with your name printed on the back; (3) proof of age; (4) proof of nationality; (5) name and address of beneficiary (for insurance purposes). The fee is US$18, and the card is valid from September 1 of one year to the end of the following year. Because of the proliferation of phony ISICs, many airlines and some other services now require double proof of student identity.

The US$19 **International Teacher Identity Card (ITIC)** offers identical discounts in theory, but because it's relatively new, some merchants don't know it exists and don't honor it. The application process is the same as for an ISIC; make sure to include a letter on school stationery from a department chair, principal, or other school official declaring you a full-time faculty member.

Federation of International Youth Travel Organisations (FIYTO) issues its own discount card to travelers who are not students but are under 26. Known as the **GO25 Card,** this one-year card offers many of the same benefits as the ISIC, and most organizations that sell the ISIC also sell the GO25 Card. To apply, bring: (1) proof of birthdate (copy of birth certificate, passport, or a valid driver's license); (2) a passport-sized photo (with your name printed on the back). The fee is US$16 (UK£5), which includes travel insurance (prices subject to change). For more information, contact Council on International and Educational Exchange, the official U.S. sponsor of the card (see Travel Services above).

HOSTEL MEMBERSHIP

A one-year **Hostelling International (HI)** membership permits you to stay at one of the 42 HI hostels run by **An Óige** ("ann OY-ga") in Ireland and **YHANI** ("YA-nee") in the North. It's cheaper to join HI in Ireland than in the United States: visitors from countries other than the Republic of Ireland staying at an An Óige hostel without a membership card may get full HI membership by purchasing 6 stamps (IR£1.25 each) and affixing them to an International Guest Card. The stamps may be purchased one at a time, so if you wind up staying in fewer than six HI hostels you don't waste as much money as you would on a full membership. YHANI hostels tend to be flexible about the HI membership requirement. HI cards are available from some travel agencies, including Council Travel, Let's Go Travel, and STA Travel (see Travel Services, p. 1), and from the following organizations:

An Óige (Irish Youth Hostel Association): 61 Mountjoy Street, Dublin 7, Ireland (tel. (01) 830 4555; fax (01) 830 5808). One-year membership is IR£7.50, under 18 £4, and family £7.50 for each adult with children under 16 free.

Youth Hostel Association of Northern Ireland (YHANI): 22-32 Donegal Rd., Belfast BT12 5JN, Northern Ireland (tel. (0232) 315435; fax (0232) 439699). Annual membership UK £7, under 18 UK£3, family UK£14 for up to 6 children.

Hostelling International-American Youth Hostels (HI-AYH): 733 15th St. NW, Suite 840, Washington, DC, 20005 (tel. (202) 783 6161; fax 783 6171). The American branch of HI. HI-AYH is comprised of 38 local councils. Membership cards cost US$25, renewals US$20, under 18 US$10, over 54 US$15, family cards US$35. Membership valid for 12 months from date of issue.

Canadian Hostelling Association (HI-Canada): 400-205 Catherine Street, Ottawa, Ont. K2P 1C3 (tel. (613) 237-7884; fax 237-7868). One-year membership fee CDN$26.75, under 18 CDN$12.84; 2-year CDN$37.45.

Youth Hostels Association of England and Wales (YHA): Trevelyan House, 8 St. Stephen's Hill, St. Albans, Herts AL1 2DY (tel. (01727) 855215); or 14 Southampton St., Covent Garden, London WC2E 7HY (tel. (0171) 836 1036). Enrollment fees are UK£9, under 18 UK£3. Children aged 5-18 enrolled free when a parent joins.

Australian Youth Hostels Association (AYHA): Level 3, 10 Mallett St., Camperdown NSW 2050 Australia (tel. (02) 565 1699). Fee AUS$40, renewal AUS$24, under 18 fee and renewal AUS$12.

Youth Hostels Association of New Zealand (YHANZ): P.O. Box 436, 173 Gloucester St., Christchurch 1, New Zealand (tel. (03) 379 9970; fax (03) 365 4476). Annual memberships: Senior (adult) NZ$34, Youth (15-17) NZ$12, under 15 free. Rates are lower for 2- and 3-year memberships. Life membership NZ$240. New Zealand memberships not renewable overseas.

TOP 5 Ways to Save Money While Traveling

5. Ship yourself in a crate marked "Livestock." Remember to poke holes in the crate.

4. Board a train dressed as Elvis and sneer and say "The King rides for free."

3. Ask if you can walk through the Channel Tunnel.

2. Board the plane dressed as an airline pilot, nod to the flight attendants, and hide in the rest room until the plane lands.

1. Bring a balloon to the airline ticket counter, kneel, breathe in the helium, and ask for the kiddie fare.

But if you're serious about saving money while you're traveling abroad, just get an ISIC—the International Student Identity Card. Discounts for students on international airfares, hotels and motels, car rentals, international phone calls, financial services, and more.

The International Student Identity Card

For more information call:

1-800-GET-AN-ID

Available at Council Travel offices (see ad in this book) and universities nationwide.

CIEE: Council on International Educational Exchange
205 East 42nd Street, New York, NY 10017-5706

The HI guides (*Vol. 1: Europe and the Mediterranean* and *Vol. 2: Africa, America, Asia, Australia, and New Zealand*) list up-to-date information. Get them at bookstores or directly from HI (each US$11, UK£7, $3 postage and handling).

■■■ MONEY

CURRENCY & EXCHANGE

US$1 = IR£0.63	IR£1 = US$1.59
CDN$1 = IR£0.46	IR£1 = CDN$2.15
UK£1 = IR£0.98	IR£1 = UK£1.02
AUS$1 = IR£0.46	IR£1 = AUS$2.17
NZ$1 = IR£0.41	IR£1 = NZ$2.43
SAR 1 = IR£0.17	IR£1 = SAR 5.85
US$1 = UK£0.60	UK£1 = US$1.54
CDN$1 = UK£0.49	UK£1 = CDN$2.09
AUS$1 = UK£0.48	UK£1 = A$2.10
NZ$1 = UK£0.42	UK£1 = NZ$2.36
SAR 1 = UK£0.18	UK£1 = SAR 5.67

The information in this book was researched during the summer of 1995. Inflation and the Invisible Hand may raise the prices we list by 10%.

Legal tender in the Republic of Ireland is the Irish pound (or "punt"), denoted £. It comes in the same denominations as the British pound (called "sterling" in Ireland) but is usually worth a bit less. British small change is no longer widely accepted in the Republic of Ireland. The Irish punt is difficult to convert abroad. If you're worried about exchanging your dirhams, bring some British pounds.

Legal tender in Northern Ireland and the Isle of Man is the British pound. Northern Ireland has its own bank notes, which are identical in value to English, Scottish, or Manx notes of the same denominations. Although all these notes are accepted in Northern Ireland, Northern Ireland bank notes are not accepted across the water. Remember to swap your Northern Ireland pounds for Bank of England notes before you leave. UK coins now come in logical denominations of 1p, 2p, 5p, 10p, 20p, 50p, and £1. An old "shilling" coin is worth 5p, a "florin" 10p. "Quid" is another common term for pounds sterling, and those darn crazy Irish call the plural "quid," not "quids."

Most banks are closed on Saturday, Sunday, and all public holidays. Ireland and Northern Ireland enjoy "bank holidays" several times a year. Banks in Ireland are usually open Monday to Friday 10am-4pm, closing later on Thursday. Usual weekday bank hours in Northern Ireland are Monday to Friday 9:30am-3:30pm. Some close for lunch; some close early or late one day per week.

Follow the fluctuation of rates for several weeks before you trip. If the trend is toward a stronger pound, exchange a significant amount of money at the beginning of your trip. It's more expensive to buy foreign currency than domestic. Pounds will be less costly in Ireland than at home. It is essential, however, that you exchange a small amount of money before you get on the plane. Airport exchange rates are generally not as favorable, and you won't want to be stuck in a long line to change money after your long flight. Generally, you should bring enough Irish currency (depending on when you arrive) to last the first 24-72 hours of a trip (exchanging currency will be difficult over a weekend).

Observe commission rates closely when abroad; check newspapers to get the standard rate. Bank rates are generally preferable to those of travel agencies, tourist offices, restaurants, hotels, and the dubious bureaux de change. Avoid changing money at a post office (their rates are worst of all). Since you lose money with every

Believe it or not, you can run out of green in Ireland.

If you run out of money in Ireland, you don't have to run around looking for the pot of gold. With Western Union you can receive money from the States within minutes, in case the situation arises. Plus, it's already converted into pounds.

Just call either our number in Britain, 0 800 833 833*. Ireland, 1 800 395 395*, or the United States, 1 800 325 6000*. Then pick up your money at any Western Union location in these countries.

After all, you can't always rely on the luck of the Irish.

WESTERN UNION | MONEY TRANSFER
The fastest way to send money worldwide.[SM]

* Toll free within country.

transaction, convert in large sums (provided the exchange rate is either staying constant or deteriorating), but not more than you will need. Planning a travel budget with a daily allowance is a good idea.

Traveler's Checks

Traveler's checks are generally the safest way to carry large sums of money. The major brands can be exchanged at virtually every bank in Ireland and Northern Ireland, sometimes without a commission. Traveler's checks are also accepted at the great majority of B&Bs, shops, and restaurants, though many smaller establishments only take cash. Furthermore, if lost or stolen, they can be replaced, often within a matter of hours, and many issuing agencies offer additional services, such as refund hotlines, message relaying, travel insurance, and emergency assistance.

Sign your checks immediately when you purchase them; copy the serial numbers down and keep them in a safe place (*not* in your wallet or with the checks). Also, make a photocopy and leave it with someone at home. Countersign checks *only* when you are ready to use them and when the store cashier is watching. Carry your passport when you plan to use checks. To accelerate the refund process for lost or stolen checks, keep check receipts and a record of which checks you've cashed separate from the checks themselves. Leave a photocopy of check serial numbers with someone at home as a back-up. Always keep a few extra pounds handy in case of theft or loss. Buying checks in small denominations (US$20 checks rather than US$50 ones or higher) is usually safer and more convenient—otherwise, after a small purchase, you'll still be carrying around a large amount of cash.

American Express Travelers Cheques are perhaps the most widely accepted worldwide and the easiest to replace. In Northern Ireland, though, Thomas Cook checks are just as widely recognized. If you will be visiting other countries in addition to Ireland and Northern Ireland, you should buy your checks in U.S. dollars. Few currencies are as easily exchanged worldwide, and you will save yourself the cost of repeatedly converting currency. If you are staying exclusively in Northern Ireland, you might wish to buy your checks in British pounds. In Northern Ireland, most branches of the Bank of Ireland and of Ulster Bank and some branches of other banks will not charge a commission when changing traveler's checks if you show a student ID. The following companies offer checks in U.S. dollars or British pounds—often in both:

American Express: For general information or to report stolen cheques, call tel. (1800) 626 000 in Ireland; (0800) 521313 in the U.K.; (800) CASH NOW (227-4669) in the U.S. and Canada; (008) 251902 in Australia; and (0800) 441068 in New Zealand. Dublin office: tel. (01) 677 2874 or (01) 373 6892.

Interpayment: In the U.S. and Canada: (800) 221-2426. In U.K.: (1733) 318949. In Ireland: (1800) 558876. Sells Visa traveler's checks, cashable at any **TSB** bank or Barclay's branch. Commission charge of 1% (minimum charge of £1, maximum charge of £5).

Citicorp: Sells Visa traveler's checks (currencies include US dollars and British pounds). For Citicorp information and to report lost checks, call (800) 645-6556 in the U.S. and Canada, (0171) 982 4040 in Britain, or from elsewhere call collect (813) 623 1709. Commission varies by bank (1-2%). Check holders automatically enrolled for 45 days in Citicorp's **Travel Assist Hotline** (tel. (800) 523 1199), which provides English-speaking doctor, lawyer, and interpreter referrals along with traveler's check refund assistance. Citicorp's World Courier Service guarantees hand-delivery of traveler's checks anywhere in the world.

Mastercard International: offers traveler's checks in 11 currencies. For lost or stolen checks, in North America call (800) 223-9920 or collect (609) 987-7300; elsewhere call the U.K. at (1733) 502 995 collect. Participating banks (look for the Mastercard logo) will charge a 1-2% commission; try buying the checks at a Thomas Cook office (see below) for potentially lower commissions.

Thomas Cook: also sells Mastercard Traveler's Checks. Call (800) 223-9920 in the U.S. and Canada; elsewhere call U.S. collect (609) 987-7300; from the U.K. call (0800) 622101 free or (1733) 502995 collect. Offers checks in British and Irish pounds, at a commission from 1-2%. Try buying the checks from a Thomas Cook office for potentially lower commissions.

Visa: Call (800) 227-6811 in the U.S.; in the U.K. (0171) 937 8091; from anywhere else call U.S. collect at (212) 858-8500. Sells traveler's checks by mail; call (800) 235-7366 to order them in the U.S. Any kind of Visa traveler's checks can be reported lost at the Visa number.

Electronic Banking

Most banks in Ireland and Northern Ireland have ATMs; the catch is that few of them are hooked up to international networks. In the Republic, **Visa** and **Mastercard/Access** are accepted at some Bank of Ireland ATMs and at all Allied Irish Bank (AIB) ATMs. Both banks, and Trustee Savings Bank (TSB), accept Visa and Mastercard at their foreign exchange desks during opening hours.

In Northern Ireland, First Trust, Northern, Bank of Ireland, and Ulster Bank accept Visa cards at their ATMs. **Halifax Bank** has ATMs that are on the **Plus** network; the bank has branches only in a few major cities in Northern Ireland. If your bank uses Plus, you will be able to access your own bank account through Halifax ATMs when you're in need of funds. Because ATM machines get the wholesale exchange rate, which is roughly 5% better than the retail rate most banks use, you'll generally save money by using them.

Isle of Man Bank and **Barclays** have branches in most towns on the Isle of Man. Isle of Man Banks' ATMs accept Visa, Mastercard, Plus, and Cirrus system cards; Barclays' ATMs accept Visa, Plus, and Cirrus. TSB ATMs on the Isle of Man accept Visa and Mastercard.

American Express card holders can sign up for AmEx's free Express Cash service through which you can access cash from your account at any ATM with the AmEx trademark, but each transaction costs a minimum of US$2.50 (maximum US$10), plus conversion fees and interest. For a list of ATMs where you can use your card, call AmEx in the U.S. at (800) 543-4080 (in Canada tel. (800) 933-3278). ATM machines with a "Link" logo accept AmEx.

VAT (Value-Added Tax)

Both Ireland and Northern Ireland charge value-added tax (VAT), a national sales tax on most goods and some services. In Ireland, the VAT ranges from 0% on most food and clothing to 12% in restaurants to 21% on other items, such as jewelry, cameras, and appliances. The British rate (applicable to Northern Ireland and the Isle of Man) is 17.5% on many services (such as hairdressers, hotels, restaurants, and car rental agencies) and on all goods (except books, medicine, and food). Prices stated in *Let's Go* include VAT unless otherwise specified. Visitors to Northern Ireland and the Isle of Man can get a **VAT refund** through the Retail Export Scheme. Ask the shopkeeper from whom you buy your goods for the appropriate form, which customs officials will sign and stamp when you take your purchases through customs in your carry-on baggage. Once home, send the form and a self-addressed, Northern Irish-stamped envelope to the shopkeeper, who will then send your refund. In order to use this scheme, you must export the goods within three months of purchase. The process in the Republic is equally cumbersome.

DISCOUNT CARDS

The Irish government offers a **National Heritage Card,** which allows free access to the 31 national parks, monuments, and gardens maintained by the Office of Public Works (OPW) (IR£15, students IR£6). Purchase the card in the Republic at any site overseen by the OPW. You can also purchase the OPW card at any site, and it can quickly pay for itself (especially since most sites have risen in cost). If you see more than five sites, it is definitely worthwhile.

All U.S. travelers to Northern Ireland or other British countries should seriously consider joining the **Royal Oak Foundation,** the U.S. membership affiliate of the **National Trust.** The National Trust is a British charity dedicated to preserving "places of historic interest or natural beauty" in the U.K. Royal Oak membership or membership in one of their fellow Trusts in Commonwealth countries will allow you free entry to over 240 trust sites and properties open to the public. Royal Oak membership is annually renewable at a cost of US$40 for an individual and US$65 for a family. A handbook with brief descriptions of National Trust properties in England, Wales, and Northern Ireland is included with membership. For more, U.S. and Canadian residents should contact the Royal Oak Foundation, 285 W. Broadway #400, New York, NY 10013 (tel. (800) 913-6565 or (212) 966-6565). All others should contact the National Trust's Membership Department, P.O. 39, Bromley, Kent, BR1 1NH, England (tel. (0181) 464 1111). Annual membership fees: individual UK£25; family UK£46.

GETTING MONEY FROM HOME

Do your best to avoid having money sent to you on the road; instead, carry a bank card, credit card, or a separate stash of emergency traveler's checks. If someone feeds money into your bank or credit card account back home, you'll be set. In an emergency, **wire money** through **Western Union** (tel. (800) 325-6000 in North America, (0800) 833833 in Europe) or **American Express** (tel. (800) 543-4080 in the U.S., (800) 933-3278 in Canada). Fees correspond to the amount being sent and, for AmEx, the speed (10 minutes, overnight, 3-5 days). Western Union is generally cheaper but may take longer: US$29 to send $250, $40 for $500, $50 for $1000. U.S. Citizens can also have money sent to them abroad in dire emergencies by the **State Department's Citizens' Emergency Center** (tel. (202) 647-5225, after hours (202) 647-4000). The State Department will cable a modest amount of money to consular offices for dispersal. To send money through the State Department, a person can drop it off there or cable money to the department through Western Union.

■■■ HEALTH

In the event of sudden illness or an accident, dial **999,** the general **emergency** number for the Republic of Ireland, Northern Ireland, and the Isle of Man. It's a free call from any pay phone.

GENERAL ADVICE

"Late-night pharmacy" is an oxymoron, even in larger Irish cities. In the case of an accident, your **passport** should list any information needed—the names, phone numbers, and addresses of anyone you would want to be contacted, all allergies and pre-existing medical conditions you would want doctors to be aware of (diabetes, asthma, corrective lenses, etc.), and insurance information. If you wear **glasses or contact lenses,** be sure to take an extra pair and to know your prescription. If you wear contacts, be sure that you have glasses in case you lose or tear a lens. Take extra solution with you, as it can be even pricier than usual abroad. Always go prepared with any **medication** you regularly take and may need while traveling, as well as a copy of the prescription from your doctor and a statement of any pre-existing medical conditions you may have, especially if you will be bringing insulin, syringes, or any narcotics into a foreign country. It is always a good idea to see a doctor before traveling, especially if you will be abroad for more than a month or two, if you will be hiking or camping a good deal, or if you have any serious pre-existing medical conditions.

Let's Go should not be your only information source on common health problems while traveling, hiking, or camping. Check with the publications and organizations listed at the end of this section for more information, or send for the **American Red Cross'** *First-Aid and Safety Handbook* (US$14.95) by calling or writing to the American Red Cross, 61 Medford St., Somerville, MA 02143 (tel. (800) 564-1234). In the United States, the American Red Cross also offers many first-aid and CPR courses; these have a reputation for high quality and low cost. You may want to take one before you go (contact your local American Red Cross office). A new booklet is also available from the U.S. Government Printing Office, Washington, DC 20402 (tel. (202) 783-3238) entitled *Health Information for International Travelers* ($7), which is an annual global rundown of disease, immunization, and general health advice, including risks in particular countries. **Global Emergency Medical Services** (GEMS) provides international medical assistance to travelers. Subscribers have immediate access 24 hours, 7 days a week, to an emergency room registered nurse who has on-line access to medical information that you provide your primary physician. They have a worldwide network of 6,000 English speaking medical providers in 1,800 locations in 180 countries. Subscribers also receive a pocket-sized personal portable medical record that contains important medical information. For more information, call in the U.S. (800) 860-1111 or write them at 2001 Westside Dr., Suite 120, Alpharetta, GA 30201.

For minor health problems, a compact **first-aid kit** should suffice. The following items are advisable: bandages of several sizes, a painkiller (aspirin, acetaminophen, or ibuprofen), antiseptic soap or antibiotic cream, a thermometer in a sturdy case, a Swiss Army knife with tweezers, moleskin (for blisters), insect repellent, and elastic bandages. These are less necessary: burn ointment, a decongestant, motion sickness remedy, medicine for diarrhea or stomach problems, and sunscreen.

The cold, wet climate is a far greater danger than heat in Ireland, especially if you will be hiking. Overexposure to cold brings risks of hypothermia and frostbite. **Hypothermia** is a result of exposure to cold and can occur even in the middle of the summer, especially in rainy or windy conditions or at night. The signs are easy to detect: body temperature drops rapidly, resulting in the failure to produce body heat; you may shiver, have poor coordination, feel exhausted, or have slurred speech, sleepiness, hallucinations, or amnesia. Do not let hypothermia victims fall asleep if they are in the advanced stages—their body temperature will drop further and if they lose consciousness they may die. Seek medical help as soon as possible. To avoid hypothermia, keep as dry as possible and stay out of the wind. Wind carries heat away from the body. Wear wool, especially in wet weather—it retains insulating properties even when soggy. Polypropylene also dries quickly when wet, allowing you to stay warm; however, nearly all other fabrics make you colder when wet. If you have hypothermia, remove all wet, non-wool clothing (especially all cotton). Make warm and protective clothing a priority. Dress in layers, and remember that most loss of body heat is through your head, so carry a wool hat with you and your body will thank you.

SEXUAL CONCERNS

Contraception has been legal in the Republic of Ireland for over a decade, and condoms are now widely available through prescriptions in the larger towns in both the Republic and the North. Women on the pill should bring enough to allow for possible loss or extended stays, and should remember to take time zone changes into account and to make the necessary adjustments in their medication schedules.

Abortion is illegal in Northern Ireland and the Republic, though women can now travel from Ireland to Britain expressly to obtain an abortion (see Abortion: A Slow Separation of Church and State, p. 59). The **U.K. Family Planning Association** can provide you with information on contraception and abortion in Britain; write to 27 Mortimer St., London W1N 7RJ (tel. (0171) 636 7866, fax (0171) 436 3288). You can also call the **National Abortion Federation hotline** (tel. (800) 772 9100; Mon.-Fri. 9:30am-5:30pm). Alternatively, you can contact your embassy to receive a list of doctors who perform abortions. For worldwide information on contraception, condoms, and abortion, contact the **International Planned Parenthood Federation,** Regent's College Inner Circle, Regent's Park, London NW1 4NS (tel. (0171) 486 0741). Women's centers, listed in major cities, can provide advice; remember that some are funded by the Catholic Church.

All travelers should be concerned about **Acquired Immune Deficiency Syndrome (AIDS),** transmitted through the exchange of body fluids with an infected individual (HIV-positive). Do not have sex without using a condom lubricated with **spermicide (nonoxynol-9),** or share intravenous needles with anyone. If you have any questions about HIV and AIDS, you can call the U.S. **Centers for Disease Control** (CDC)'s main **AIDS hotline** number (tel. (800) 342 2437, 24-hrs.; TTD (800) 243-7889; international hotline (404) 639-3311; Mon.-Fri. 10am-10pm). Council (see p. 1) distributes free *AIDS and International Travel*, which contains information on safe sex, HIV testing, hotline numbers, and blood transfusions while overseas.

■■■ SAFETY & SECURITY

Ireland and Northern Ireland are safer for the traveler than most other European countries. That doesn't mean nothing gets stolen. Keep your money to yourself, preferably stowed away in a money belt or necklace pouch. Be wary at busy bus and train stations, money-changing establishments, and other tourist-infested areas. Also, be alert in public telephone booths. Wherever you stow your belongings, try to keep your valuables on your person: consider this an iron-clad rule in the dorm-style rooms of some hostels. Even a trip to the shower can cost you a wallet or a camera. At night, sleep with your worldly goods under your pillow or in another safe place, and put the straps of your bag around the leg of your bed. Lockers at bus and train stations are safe. Label all your belongings with your name, address, and home phone number. For an official **Department of State travel advisory** on Ireland or the U.K., call the 24-hr. hotline at (202) 647-5225. They offer travel warnings on crime statistics, security recommendations, and miscellaneous tips on health precautions and obtaining a U.S. passport. American citizens traveling abroad can also call this number in an emergency.

DRUGS

If you are caught with any quantity of illegal or controlled drugs in Ireland or Northern Ireland, you will be arrested and tried under Irish or British law or be immediately expelled from the country. Your home government is powerless to shield you from the judicial system of a foreign country. If you are imprisoned, consular officers can visit you, provide you with a list of local attorneys, and inform your family and friends, but that's all. The London-based organization **Release** (tel. (0171) 729 9904) advises people who have been arrested on drug charges; that's about all they can do. For more information on the subject of drugs overseas, send for the free brochure *Travel Warning on Drugs Abroad* (Publication 9558) from the Bureau of Consular Affairs, U.S. Department of State, Washington, DC 20520 (tel. (202) 647-1488).

Drugs and traveling are not a good combination in any case. If you carry prescription drugs while you travel, it is vital to have a copy of the prescriptions themselves readily accessible at country borders. As far as **illegal drugs** are concerned, laws all over the world are different, but the safest bet is to avoid them. Little can ruin a vacation more quickly than a drug charge.

CONCERNS FOR WOMEN

Women travelers may be vulnerable to **urinary tract and bladder infections,** common and uncomfortable bacterial diseases which cause a burning sensation and painful, sometimes frequent, urination. Drink lots of vitamin-C-rich juice, plenty of water, and urinate often—especially right after intercourse. If untreated, these problems can lead to kidney infections, which can lead to sterility and death. If symptoms persist, see a doctor. If you often develop **vaginal yeast infections,** take medicine along with you—treatments may be not readily available.

EVEN MORE RESOURCES

Travelers with conditions that cannot be easily recognized (diabetes, epilepsy, heart conditions, allergies to antibiotics, etc.) may want to join the **Medic Alert Foundation,** P.O. Box 1009, Turlock, CA 95381-1009. Call the 24-hour hotline at (800) 432 5378. Membership provides the Medic Alert Identification Tag, an annually updated wallet card, and hotline access. The cost of membership begins at US $35 for the tag's stainless steel model. The **American Diabetes Association,** 1660 Duke St., Alexandria, VA 22314 (tel. (800) 232-3472) provides copies of the article *Travel and Diabetes* and diabetic ID cards, which carry messages in 18 languages explaining the carrier's status. In the U.S., contact your local ADA office for details.

■■■ INSURANCE

Beware of unnecessary coverage—your current policies might well extend to many travel-related accidents. Medical insurance policies, especially those from universities, often cover costs incurred abroad, though Medicare's coverage is not valid most places. Canadians are protected by their home province's health insurance plan up to 90 days after leaving the country. Australians are covered by Medicare in Britain; consult Medicare's *Health Care for Australians Travelling Overseas* or write to the Commonwealth Dept. of Health, Housing and Community Services, GPO Box 9848, Canberra.

The International Student Identity Card (ISIC) and International Teacher Identity Card (ITIC) provide US$3000 worth of accident and illness insurance, $100 per day up to 60 days of hospitalization, and up to $25,000 coverage for emergency medical evaluation; they also give you access to a toll-free Traveler's Assistance hotline whose staff can provide help in medical, legal, and financial emergencies overseas. In the United States, call (800) 626-2427; from abroad call collect (713) 267-2525. **Council** offers an inexpensive Trip-Safe plan, with options covering medical treatment and hospitalization, accidents, baggage loss, and even charter flights missed due to illness. If you are ineligible for the ISIC or ITIC, Trip-Safe extends coverage of the insurance you have. **STA** offers a more expensive and comprehensive plan; **American Express** cardholders receive car-rental and flight insurance on card purchases; see Travel Services (p. 1) or Money (p. 13). Other perks in travel insurance packages are often not worth the expense. Referral to physicians and lawyers can be obtained through a consulate; a major credit card will get you cash in case of theft. **Council Travel** (see Travel Services, p. 1) offers short-term insurance coverage specifically designed for the budget traveler. A choice of coverage levels includes sickness and accident, emergency evacuation, baggage and personal effects, trip cancellation, and a 24-hour emergency telephone assistance service.

Insurance companies usually require a copy of the police report for thefts or evidence of having paid medical expenses (doctor's statements, receipts), and may have time limits on filing. Homeowners should list the goods they take on their policy before they leave; otherwise coverage for theft or damage may be denied. Always carry your policy numbers and proof of insurance. Note that some of the plans listed below offer cash advances or guaranteed bills. If your coverage does not include on-the-spot payments or cash transferals, leave space in your budget for emergencies. If you have less than perfect faith in your travel plans, consider **trip cancellation or interruption insurance,** which protects you in case your airline or tour operator leaves you stranded at the final hour. Check the yellow pages and newspapers, and consult your travel agent. Expect to pay US$2-5 per US$100 coverage for cancellation and interruption insurance.

The following firms offer insurance against theft, loss of luggage, injury, or other emergency in the U.S.: **Access America** (tel. (800) 294 8300); **ARM Coverage, Inc./ Carefree Travel Insurance** (tel. (800) 323 3149); **GlobalCare Travel Insurance** (tel. (800) 821 2488); **Travel Guard International** (tel. (800) 826 1300). If you have no medical insurance, or if your policy does not extend overseas, the following organizations provide travel service:

Travel Assistance International: by Worldwide Assistance Services, Inc., 1133 15th St. NW, Suite 400, Washington, DC 20005-2710 (tel. (800) 821-2828), provides on-the-spot medical coverage (US$15,000-US$90,000) and unlimited medical evacuation insurance, 24-hr. emergency multilingual assistance hotline, and

worldwide local presence. Trip cancellation/interruption, baggage, and acciden-
tal death and dismemberment insurance are also offered.

Travel Insured International, Inc.: 52-S Oakland Ave., P.O. Box 280568, East
Hartford, CT 06128-0568 (tel. (800) 243-3174; fax (203) 528-8005). Insurance
against accident, baggage loss, sickness, trip cancellation/interruption, travel
delay, and default. Covers emergency medical evacuation and automatic flight
insurance.

■■■ PACK LIGHT

If you don't pack light, you will pay for your folly either in back pain or in postage
back home. The convenience of having less to carry far outweighs the inconvenience of having a limited wardrobe. That backpack or suitcase may be light as a
feather when you buy it or take it out of the closet, even manageable all the way to
the airport, but overseas it will turn into an itchy, monstrous beast. Before you leave,
pack your bag (one only!) and take it for a half-hour walk. If the walk feels like a
trudge, unpack several things. A good rule is to pack only what you absolutely need,
then get rid of half the clothes and bring more money. Remember that you can find
virtually all the supplies you might need in Ireland and U.K.

A **backpack** is ideal if you plan to cover a lot of ground, hike, or camp; get one
with several external compartments. **Frame backpacks** (US$125-300) are far more
spacious than others. **Internal frame** packs mold to your back, keep a low center of
gravity, and have enough flexibility to follow you through your contortions. They
are also more manageable and less easily mangled. **Conversion packs** are internal-
frame backpacks which transform into suitcases. **External-frame** packs don't travel
as well; bring an empty duffel to protect yours in baggage compartments. Make sure
your belt has a strong, padded hip belt, which transfers weight to your legs. Buy a
pack with one large pocket and use stuff sacks to separate your gear. **Suitcases** and
duffels are best suited for people who plan to stay only in cities and large towns.
They're the worst for schlepping from city to city. Packing a smaller **daypack** inside
your pack or in addition to your suitcase allows you to leave your big bag in the hostel while you see town. Get one with secure zippers and closures.

Choose your **clothing** with the infamous Irish weather in mind. If you plan to do
any camping, pay a little more for a lightweight poncho that unbuttons to form a
groundcloth. Make sure the poncho will cover both you and your pack. Cyclists
should devote money and energy towards finding a *truly* waterproof jacket or poncho. Ordinary "rainproof" materials will not suffice in the eternal drizzle of the
Emerald Isle. Gore-Tex or another specialized material will make your life infinitely
more comfortable. Buy a raincoat or poncho that breathes—Dunnes Stores in Ireland can sell you an inexpensive but airtight poncho, and you'll be soaked in your
own sweat within an hour if you wear it. A good rain poncho runs US$20-40. Sum-
mertime is hardly warm—packing more than one pair of shorts is needlessly optimistic, and a wool sweater comes in handy even in mid-June. Waterlogged travelers
report that sweatshirts and jeans soak up rain like a sponge.

When packing, keep in mind that laundry services are quite accessible; take fewer
clothes and wash them more often. **Footwear** is perhaps the most crucial item on
any packing list. Walking shoes are preferable to running shoes or sandals. A number of hiking shoes that cost less than US$75 will dry overnight. In any case, sturdy
rubber-soled shoes, like Rockports, are recommended. A double pair of socks—
light absorbent cotton inside and thick wool outside—will cushion feet, keep them
dry, and help prevent blisters. Bring a pair of light flip-flops for protection against
the fungal floors of some station and hostel showers.

In most European countries, including Ireland, **electricity** is 220 volts AC, enough
to fry a 110V North American appliance. Visit a hardware store for an **adapter**
(which changes the shape of the plug) and a **converter** (changes the voltage). Don't
make the mistake of using only an adapter—you'll melt your radio.

PLANNING YOUR TRIP

The following is a **checklist** of items you may need: pocketknife, tweezers, small flashlight, needle and thread, string, safety pins, rubber bands (to roll clothes), waterproof matches, a sturdy plastic water bottle, a travel alarm clock, earplugs, a cold-water soap, clothespins and line, towel or chamois (super-absorbent tiny towel), moleskin (for blisters), bags that seal shut (for damp clothing, soaps, or messy foods), a squash ball (to use as a sink plug), and a padlock.

■■■ WEATHER

The weather in Ireland and Northern Ireland is subject to frequent changes but few extremes, with an average temperature in the low to mid-60s (°F) in the summer and in the low 40s (°F) in the winter. A bright and cloudless morning sky is often followed by intermittent drizzle and mist throughout the afternoon. Count on feeling chilly and wet at least once a day.

April is the driest month in Ireland, especially on the east coast near Dublin. May and June are the sunniest months, particularly in the south and southeast, and July and August are the warmest. December and January have the worst weather of the year—wet, cold, and cloudy. It also gets dark early in winter months—kiss the sun good night at 3pm or so. The average annual max. and min. temperatures for Dublin are 8°C (47°F) and 1°C (35°F) for January, 20°C (67°F) and 11°C (51°F) for July.

■■■ SPECIFIC CONCERNS

WOMEN AND TRAVEL

Women exploring any area on their own inevitably face additional safety concerns. It's always best to trust your instincts: if you'd feel better somewhere else, don't hesitate to move on. You may want to consider staying in hostels which offer single rooms with locks on the inside or religious organizations that offer rooms for women only. Stick to centrally located accommodations and avoid late-night treks or tube rides. Hitching is *never* safe for lone women, or even for two women traveling together.

Your best answer to verbal harassment is no answer at all (a reaction is what the harasser wants). Wearing a conspicuous wedding band may help ward off over-friendly individuals. Don't hesitate to seek out a police officer or a passerby if you are being harassed. Memorize the emergency number in Ireland—it's 999 and free—and carry change for the phone and enough extra money for a bus or taxi. Carry a whistle or an airhorn on your keychain, and use it in an emergency. These warnings and suggestions are not meant to discourage women from traveling alone. Don't take unnecessary risks, but don't lose your spirit of adventure either.

The **sexism** in Ireland translates into an annoying, and sometimes comical, display of concern for women travelers: in its mildest form, it's the problematic idea that women are fragile and need protection from men. Irish men are often surprised at the independence displayed by women traveling solo. Women who have hitched report that the same men who offered them lifts have cautioned them against hitch-hiking. Irish sexism also expresses itself through assaults upon single women by drivers or hostel owners. For some women's organizations, see listings under Dublin (see p. 82). The following resources and books are useful:

Handbook For Women Travelers: by Maggie and Gemma Moss. Encyclopedic and well-written. UK£9 from Piaktus Books, 5 Windmill St., London W1P 1HF (0171) 631 0710.

Women Going Places: a women's travel and resource guide emphasizing women-owned enterprises. Geared towards lesbians, but offers advice appropriate for all women. US$14 from Inland Book Company, PO Box 12061, East Haven, CT 06512, (203) 467-4257 or order from a local bookstore.

A Journey of One's Own: by Thalia Zepatos, Eighth Mountain Press US$14.95. Interesting and full of good advice, plus a specific and manageable bibliography of books and resources.

OLDER TRAVELERS AND SENIOR CITIZENS

Seniors are eligible for a wide array of discounts on transportation, museums, movies, theater, concerts, restaurants, and accommodations. In *Let's Go: Ireland*, the discounts on admission fees listed for students are generally also valid for seniors. The term "concessions" and "OAPs" (old-age pensioners) indicate discounts for seniors. In the Republic, citizens on social welfare are entitled to free rail and bus travels. Unscrupulous foreigners who look old and Irish often try to slip by. Generally, proof of senior citizen status is required for many discounts listed, so prepare to get carded. The following organizations and publishers may be useful:

AARP (American Association of Retired Persons): 601 E St., NW, Washington, DC 20049, (202) 434-2277. Members 50 and over receive benefits and services including the AARP Motoring Plan from Amoco. (800) 334-3300 as well as discounts on lodging, car rental, and sight-seeing. Annual fee: US$8/couple; US$75/lifetime membership.

Elderhostel: 75 Federal St., 3rd floor, Boston, MA 02110-1941, tel. (617) 426-7788, fax 426-8351. You must be 55 or over and may bring a spouse of any age. Programs at colleges and universities in over 50 countries focus on varied subjects and generally last one to four weeks.

BISEXUAL, GAY, & LESBIAN TRAVELERS

Attitudes in Ireland and Northern Ireland range from tolerant to aggressively hostile. As is true elsewhere, people in rural areas may not be as accepting as those in big cities. Public displays of affection (PDA) in Ireland and most of U.K. will bring you certain verbal harassment.

You may end up double-checking the address to be sure you've entered a gay pub. Visitors will be delighted, however, by the age mix in pubs. There is less ageism in Ireland, and much less attitude. Women are sometimes welcome, sometimes not; there are almost no women-only clubs. *Gay Community News* covers mostly Irish gay-related news. Its listings page covers most gay locales in all of Ireland. *Let's Go: Ireland* has comprehensive gay pub and nightlife listings, as well as phone numbers for gay information. Check out our coverage of Belfast, Dublin, Cork, Galway, and Belmullet, Co. Mayo. In Ireland, the age of consent between anyone is 18 (see p. 59). Below are several resources intended specifically for the BGL traveler:

Are You Two...Together? A Gay and Lesbian Travel Guide to Europe: Random House, available at bookstores (US$18). A funny, well-written travel guide filled with entertaining anecdotes and handy tips; covers London, Brighton, Wales, and other European gay centers (not Ireland).

Ferrari Publications, Inc.: PO Box 37887, Phoenix, AZ 85069, tel. (602) 863 2408. Publishers of *Ferrari's Places of Interest* (US$16), *Ferrari's Places for Men* (US$15), *Ferrari's Places for Women* (US$13), and *Inn Places: US and Worldwide Gay Accommodations* (US$15). Available in bookstores, or by mail order (postage US$4.50 for the first item, US$1 for each additional item).

Gay's the Word: 66 Marchmont St., London WC1N 1AB, England (tel. (0171) 278 7654). The largest gay and lesbian bookstore in the U.K. Mail order service available. No catalogue of listings, but they will provide you with a list of titles on a given subject. Open Mon.-Wed. and Fri. 10am-6pm, Thurs. 10am-7pm, Sat. 10am-6pm, Sun. 2-6pm.

Spartacus International Gay Guides: published by Bruno Gmunder, Postfach 110729, D-1000 Berlin 30, Germany (tel. 49 (30) 615 0030). Lists hotlines, bars, restaurants, hotels, and bookstores around the world catering to gay men. Available in the U.S. from bookstores (US$30).

TRAVELERS WITH DISABILITIES

Ireland is not wheelchair-accessible. Ramps, wide doors, accessible bathrooms are less common than in the U.S., even in cities such as Dublin. Advance booking is strongly recommended; if you notify a bus company of your plans ahead of time, they will have staff ready to assist you. Not all train stations are wheelchair-accessible. Guide dogs are always conveyed free, but both the U.K. and Ireland impose a six-month quarantine on all animals entering the country and require that the owner obtain an import license (consult a British or Irish Consulate). Write to the British Tourist Authority or the Bord Fáilte for free handbooks and access guides. For **travel by Underground**, pick up the free booklet *Access to the Underground* from Tourist Information Centres and London Transport Information Centres, or by post from the Unit for Disabled Passengers (London Regional Transport, 55 Broadway, London SW1H 0BD; tel. 918 3312). London Transport's 24-hour travel information hotline is also useful (tel. 222 1234). Other helpful sources of information are:

Access Project (PHSP): 39 Bradley Gardens, West Ealing, London W13 8HE, England. Distributes access guides to London and Paris for a donation of £5. Researched by persons with disabilities. They cover traveling, accommodation, access to sights and entertainment. Includes a "Loo Guide" with a list of wheelchair-accessible toilets.

American Foundation for the Blind: 11 Penn Plaza, New York, NY 10011, tel. (212) 502-7600, open Mon.-Fri. 8:30am-4:30pm. Provides information and services for the visually impaired. For a catalogue of products, contact **Lighthouse Low-Vision Products** at (800) 829-0500.

Facts on File: 460 Park Ave. S., New York, NY 10016, (212) 683-2244. Publishes *Access to the World* (US$17), a guide to handicap-accessible accommodations and sights. Available in bookstores or by mail order.

Mobility International, USA (MIUSA): PO Box 10767, Eugene, OR 97440, tel. (503) 343-1284 voice and TDD, fax (503) 343-6812. International headquarters in Britain, 228 Borough High St., London SE1 1JX, tel. (071) 403 5688. Contacts in 30 countries. Information on travel programs, international work camps, accommodations, access guides, and organized tours for those with physical disabilities. Membership costs US$20/year, newsletter US$10. Call for a list of publications.

MossRehab Hospital Travel Information Service: 1200 W. Tabor Rd., Philadelphia, PA 19141, tel. (215) 456-9603. A telephone information resource center on international travel accessibility and other travel-related concerns for those with disabilities.

Society for the Advancement of Travel for the Handicapped: 347 Fifth Ave., Suite 610, New York, NY 10016, tel. (212) 447-7284, fax 725-8253. Publishes quarterly travel newsletter, booklets, and information sheets (free for members, US$3 each for nonmembers), which contain advice on trip planning. Annual membership is US$45, students and seniors US$25, agents and corporations US$100.

TRAVELERS WITH CHILDREN

Children enjoy Ireland; they should, considering how they get fussed over by enraptured strangers. Children will especially enjoy Ireland's many folk parks: there are excellent ones in Omagh and near Belfast. Dublin has much for kids to do and Tramore will be a prepubescent dream vacation. Children under 16 are generally charged half the adult price on trains and buses, and one-fourth the adult price for admission to sights. Children under two will generally fly (though not necessarily with a seat of their own) for 10% of the adult fare. Children from 2 to 12 are not so cheap: they only get a 25-33% discount off the adult fare and this not always. It seems to be up to the airline and pure random chance. You may want to refer to *Sharing Nature with Children* and *Backpacking with Babies and Small Children* (US$10) by **Wilderness Press**, 2440 Bancroft Way, Berkeley, CA 94704 (tel. (800) 443-7227, fax (510) 548-1355). **John Muir Publications,** P.O. Box 613, Santa Fe, NM 87504 (tel. (800) 285 4078) produces *Kidding Around: London* an educational but still distracting illustrated book (US$10-13; postage US$4). **Mason-Grant Publications,** P.O. Box 6547, Portsmouth, NH 03802 (tel. (603) 436 1608, fax (603) 427 0015) publishes *Take Your Kids to Europe* by Cynthia W. Harriman (US$14), a cartoon-filled budget family guide.

DIETARY CONCERNS

There are lots of veggie options in the land of the potato. *Let's Go* lists vegetarian restaurants wherever we find them, and lists vegetarian entrees in carnivorous restaurants. Many Irish will be mystified by requests for kosher food. National tourist offices often publish lists of kosher and vegetarian restaurants. The following organizations can offer advice on how to meet your specific dietary needs while traveling.

Bridgestone Press: 237 Lammack, Blackburn, England (tel. (01254) 245377). Publishes a number of dining guides to Ireland, including the *Vegetarian's Guide to Ireland* (IR£7).

Ballantine-Mitchell Publishers: Newbury House 890-900, Eastern Ave., Newbury Park, Ilford, Essex IG2 7HH, tel. (0181) 599 8866, fax 599 0984. Publishes *The Jewish Travel Guide*, with lists of synagogues, kosher restaurants, and Jewish institutions in over 80 countries. Available in the UK from Ballantine-Mitchell.

Vegetarian Society of the UK: Parkdale, Dunham Rd., Altringham, Cheshire WA14 4QG, tel. (0161) 928 0793. Their *International Vegetarian Travel Guide* was last published in 1991, but copies are still available for US£2. They also publish the *European Vegetarian Guide to Hotels and Restaurants,* which covers most of Western Europe. Call or send a self-addressed stamped envelope for more information.

Vegetarian Times: tel. (201) 783-1129. In addition to the *Times,* they publish *European Vegetarian Guide to Restaurants and Hotels.*

■■■ ALTERNATIVES TO TOURISM

WORK

If you are not a citizen of an EU or British Commonwealth nation, you will have difficulty finding a paying job that you are legally allowed to take. Visitors between the ages of 17 and 27 who are citizens of British Commonwealth nations (including Canada, Australia, and New Zealand) may work in Northern Ireland during their visit without work permits if the employment they take is "incidental to their holiday." Other Commonwealth citizens with a parent or grandparent born in the United Kingdom may apply for a patriality certificate, which entitles them to live and work in the U.K. without any other formalities. If you do not fit into any of these categories, you must apply for a work permit to be considered for paid employment in Northern Ireland or the Isle of Man. Contact your British Consulate or High Commission for details before you go, and the Department of Employment when you arrive. Regulations in Ireland are even stricter (and unemployment even higher).

Permits

Officially, you can hold a job in European countries only with a work permit, applied for by your prospective employer (or by you, with supporting papers from the employer). Many countries are tight-fisted with work permits due to large numbers of working-age immigrants. Often, an employer must demonstrate that a potential employee has skills that locals lack. The real Catch-22 is that normally you must physically enter the country in order to have immigration officials validate your work permit papers and note your status in your passport. This means that if you can't set up a job from afar (which requires contacts and time) and have the work permit sent to you, you must enter the country to look for a job, find an employer, and have them start the permit process, then leave the country until the permit is sent to you (up to six weeks), and finally re-enter the country to start work.

In practice, it's rarely so complicated. Friends in Europe can help expedite work permits or arrange work-for-accommodations swaps. Many permit-less agricultural workers go untroubled by local authorities, who recognize the need for seasonal help. EU citizens can work in any other EU country, and if your parents or grandparents were born in an EU country, you may be able to claim dual citizenship or at least the right to a work permit. Students can check with their universities' foreign language departments, which may have official or unofficial connections to job openings abroad.

Finding A Job

If you are a full-time student at a U.S. University, the simplest way to get a job is through work permit programs run by **Council** (see Travel Services, p. 1) and its member organizations. Council, under the **Work Abroad Program,** can issue American students a work permit (a "Blue Card") valid for six months in Northern Ireland. To qualify, you must be a full-time student or pursuing a course of eight hours or more while working towards a degree at an accredited U.S. college or university. Students may participate in the program a second time provided that their total aggregate stay (not just work time) in Northern Ireland does not exceed six months. Council's similar program for Ireland (student permit valid for only four months; permanent residents of the U.S. are also eligible), administered in conjunction with USIT, the Irish student travel association, allows you to work tax-free. The charge for participating in the Work Abroad Program is US$160. Appropriate for neophytes, the program run by Council will help find accommodations, openings, and connections.

Au pair jobs, temporary volunteer positions, and jobs at work camps and farm camps do not require a work permit, although you will need an entrance card or letter of invitation from the organization concerned. This letter does not permit you to undertake any other kind of paid employment during your stay.

Council on International Educational Exchange (Council): (see Travel Services, p. 1) helps students secure work visas through its work-exchange programs in Ireland and Britain. Also provides general information on academic, work, volunteer, and professional opportunities abroad. The free brochures *Basic Facts on Study Abroad, International Workcamps,* and *Work Abroad* are useful and available at Council locations. Also available are *Work, Study, Travel Abroad: The Whole World Handbook* (US$14, postage US$1.50); *The High-School Student's Guide to Study, Travel, and Adventure Abroad* (US$14, postage US$1.50); and *Smart Vacations: The Traveler's Guide to Learning Adventures Abroad* (US$15, postage US$1.50).

Vacation Work: 9 Park End St., Oxford OX1 1HJ, England (tel. (01865) 241978; fax 79 08 85). Produces excellent publications on work-abroad opportunities.

VFP: 43 Tiffany Rd., Belmont VT 05730 (tel. (802) 259-2759). Their *International Work Camp Directory* lists work camps in Europe, Asia, and the U.S.

Office of Overseas Schools: A/OS Room 245, SA-29, Dept. of State, Washington DC 20522-2902 (tel. (703) 875-7800). Teaching jobs abroad.

Transitions Abroad Publishing, Inc.: 18 Hulst Rd., P.O. Box 1300, Amherst, MA 01004 (tel./fax (800) 293-0373). Publishes a bimonthly magazine listing all kinds of opportunities and printed resources for those seeking to study, work, or travel abroad. They also publish an *Alternative Travel Planner,* a truly exhaustive listing of information for the "active international traveler." For subscriptions (in USA, US$1995 for 6 issues; in Canada US$26; other countries US$38). Contact them at *Transitions Abroad,* Dept. TRA, Box 3000, Danville, NJ 07834.

VOLUNTEERING

Volunteering is often the most viable (and realistic) option for those wishing to spend time in Ireland without being a tourist. Given rates of employment, visitors will have a difficult time finding a paying job that will compensate for travel and living expenses. The following organizations can provide more information.

Council on International Educational Exchange (Council): (see Travel Services, p. 1) publishes *Volunteer! The Comprehensive Guide to Voluntary Service in the U.S. and Abroad* (US$13 plus $1.50 postage). Available from Council Travel offices and Council. Council's **Voluntary Services Department,** 205 E. 42nd St., New York, NY 10017 (tel. (212) 661-1414, ex. 1139) arranges placement in workcamps for two to four weeks on environmental or community service projects worldwide, including Ireland. Registration fee for the placement service is US$165.

Volunteer for Peace: 43 Tiffany Rd., Belmont VT 05730 (tel. (802) 259-2759; fax 259-2922). A non-profit organization that arranges for speedy placement in over 800 10- to 15-person workcamps in over 15 countries, primarily in Europe and including Ireland and U.K. Gives the most complete and up-to-date listings in the annual *International Workcamp Directory* (US$12). Registration fee US$150. Some workcamps are open to 16- and 17-year-olds for US$175. Free newsletter.

Willing Workers on Organic Farms (WWOOF): c/o Annie Sampson, Crowhill, Newgrove, Tulla, Co. Clare. distributes a list of names of organic farmers in Ireland who offer room and board in exchange for help on their farms. Be sure to include an international postal reply coupon with your request.

The Archaeological Institute of America: 656 Beacon St., Boston, MA 02215-2010 (tel. (617) 353-9361; fax 353-6550), puts out the *Archaeological Fieldwork Opportunities Bulletin* (US$11 for non-members) which lists over 250 field sites throughout the world. The guide can be purchased from Kendall/Hunt Publishing, 4500 Westmark Drive, Dubuque, Iowa 52002 (tel. (800) 228-0810).

Service Civil Internation (SCI-VS): 5474 Walnut Level Rd., Crozet, VA 22932 (tel. (804) 823-1826). Arranges placements in workcamps in Europe (ages 18 and over). Registration fees US$50-250, depending on camp location.

STUDY

It's not difficult to spend a summer, a term, or a year studying in Ireland or Northern Ireland. Enrolling as a full-time student is more difficult. The requirements for admission can be hard to meet unless you attended an Irish or British secondary school. For initial information on studying in Northern Ireland, contact the British Council office in your home country. You could also turn to Council's publications *Work, Study, Travel Abroad: The Whole World Handbook* or *The High-School Student's Guide to Study, Travel, And Adventure* (see Finding a Job, above). The following organizations and programs can also deluge you with information:

Coláiste Lurgan: Indreabhán, Co. na Gaillimhe, Ireland (tel. (091) 83480). Three-week intensive Irish-language summer courses in the Connemara *gaeltacht,* 15 mi. west of Galway City (IR£260). Homestays with Irish-speaking families and kayaking included.

Oideas Gael: Gleann Cholm Cille, Co. Donegal, Ireland (tel. (073) 30248; E-mail "oidsgael@101.ie"). Offers week-long courses from June until Sept. Irish language and cultural activity courses. The program offers courses at various levels, including the option of being in a bi-lingual activity such as hillwalking, setdancing, painting, archaeology, spinning, and weaving.

Trinity College Dublin: offers a 1-year program of high-quality undergraduate courses for visiting students. Write to International Student Affairs, Arts Building, Trinity College, University of Dublin, Dublin 2, Ireland (tel. (01) 702 2011).

University College Dublin: Newman House, 86 St. Stephen's Green, Dublin 2, Ireland. Offers the **Semester in Irish Studies** (tel. (01) 706 7398) every fall semester for college juniors and seniors of all majors with solid academic records. Courses in Irish history, literature, politics, and folk culture. Its **International Summer School** (tel. (01) 706 7420) offers a 2½-week course in July on Irish tradition and contemporary culture for students over 17.

Institute of Irish Studies: 6 Holyrood Park, Dublin 4, Ireland (tel. (01) 269 2491; fax 269 5459). On the campus of Trinity College Dublin; offers 2-week courses in Irish civilization in June, July, and Aug. which cover Irish history, literature, culture, and politics (£790). Monastic Odyssey tour is offered three times a year, in which students survey the massive monastic heritage of Ireland (£990).

University College Cork: Overseas Students Information Office, University College, Cork, Ireland (tel. (021) 276871; fax 902543). 10,000 students are living large in Ireland's college town. Call or write for application and information.

University College Galway: Galway, Ireland (tel. (091) 24411; fax 25051). Offers 1-yr. and 1-semester opportunities for junior and senior year students who meet the college's entry requirements. **Summer school** courses offered July-Aug. include Irish Archaeology, Literature, Culture, Gaelic, and Creative Writing.

Universities Central Council on Admission: Jessop Ave., Cheltenham, Glos. U.K. GL50 3SH (tel. (01242) 222444). Provides information and handles applications for admission to all full-time undergraduate courses in universities and their affiliated colleges in the United Kingdom. Write to them for an application and the extremely informative and quite hefty *How to Apply for Admission to a University* handbook (£5 shipping fee overseas).

Association of Commonwealth Universities (ACU): John Foster House, 36 Gordon Sq., London U.K. WC1H 0PF (tel. (071) 387 8572). Administers scholarship programs such as the British Marshalls and publishes information about Commonwealth universities.

British Information Services: 845 Third Ave., 9th Floor, New York, NY 10022 (tel. (212) 752-5747). Gives information on study in Britain. Write for their imaginatively-named free pamphlet, *Study in Britain,* which is updated annually.

Beaver College Center for Education Abroad: 450 S. Easton Rd., Glenside, PA 19038 (tel. (800) 755-5607; fax (215) 573-2174). Operates semester- or year-long programs at 7 universities in Ireland and 37 institutions in Britain; applicants must have completed three full semesters at an accredited university. Call for brochure.

Inter-Study Programs: 42 Milsom St., Bath U.K. BA1 1DN (tel. (01225) 464769; in the U.S. call their Boston office at (617) 391-0991). Offers semester- and year-long programs in Britain and Ireland. Handles all details between program institution and your home institution, including housing and credit transfer.

Universities and Colleges Admissions Services: P.O. Box 28, Cheltenham, Glos. U.K. GL50 3SA (tel. (0242) 227788). Provides information and handles application forms for admission to full-time undergraduate courses in universities and their affiliated colleges in the U.K. Write for an application form and the informative UCAS handbook on how to apply for admission to a university.

GETTING THERE

Airfares are complex and sometimes deliberately confusing. Call every toll-free number and ask about discounts. Travel agents might not want to do the legwork to find the cheapest fares (for which they receive the lowest commissions). Have a knowledgeable budget travel agent guide you through the options; better yet, use several. Students and people under 26 should never need to pay full price. Seniors can also get deals; many airlines offer senior traveler club deals or airline passes and discounts for companions. Travel sections in Sunday newspapers often list bargain fares from the local airport. Outfox airline reps with the phone-book-sized *Official Airline Guide* (at large libraries); this monthly guide lists every scheduled flight in the world with prices. George Brown's *The Airline Passenger's Guerilla Handbook* (1990) is a more renegade resource.

Most airlines' fare structures peak between mid-June and early September. Midweek (Mon.-Thurs.) flights are 10-20% cheaper than weekend ones. Leaving from a travel hub such as New York, Boston, Atlanta, Dallas, Chicago, Los Angeles, San Francisco, Vancouver, Toronto, Sydney, or Melbourne will win you a more competitive fare, though the gains are not as great when departing from travel hubs monopolized by one airline.

Return-date flexibility is usually not an option for the budget traveler; except on youth fares purchased through the airlines, traveling with an "open return" ticket can be pricier than fixing a return date and paying to change it. Avoid one-way tickets: the flight to Europe may be economical, but the return fares can be outrageous. The commercial airlines' lowest regular offer is the **APEX** (Advance Purchase Excursion Fare); specials advertised in newspapers may be cheaper, but have correspondingly more restrictions and fewer available seats. APEX fares provide you with confirmed reservations and allow "open-jaw" tickets (landing in and returning from different cities). Reservations must usually be made at least 21 days in advance, with 7- to 14-day minimum and 60- to 90-day maximum stays and hefty cancellation and change-of-reservation penalties. For summer travel, book APEX fares early; by May you will have difficulty getting the departure date you want. Whenever flying internationally, pick up your ticket in advance of the departure date and arrive at the airport two to three hours before your flight.

■■■ FROM NORTH AMERICA

COMMERCIAL AIRLINES

Flying to London is usually the cheapest way across the Atlantic. If you plan to travel through Europe, flying through Amsterdam, Luxembourg, or Brussels can be your cheapest option. In 1995, the high-season, round-trip fares to London rarely topped US$650, and off-season rates were much lower, often hovering around US$400.

Most airlines no longer offer standby fares, once a staple of budget travel. Standby has given way to the **three-day-advance-purchase youth fare,** a cousin of the one-day variety in Europe. It's available only to those under 25 (sometimes 24) and only within three days of departure—a gamble that often pays off but could backfire if the airline's all booked up. Return dates are open, but you must come back within a year, and once again can book your return seat no more than three days ahead. Youth fares in summer aren't really cheaper than APEX, but off-season prices drop deliciously. **Icelandair** (tel. (800) 223-5500 from the U.S.) is one of the few airlines which offer this 3-day fare. Check with a travel agent for details.

A few airlines offer other discounts. Look into flights to relatively less popular destinations or smaller carriers. Icelandair also offers a "get-up-and-go" fare from New York to Luxembourg (April-June 15 and Sept.-Oct. US$398; June 15-Aug. US$598). Reservations can be made no more than three days before departure. After arrival, Icelandair offers discounts on trains and buses running from Luxembourg to other parts of Europe. Major British and Irish destinations are Belfast, Dublin, Edinburgh, and London.

CHARTER FLIGHTS AND TICKET CONSOLIDATORS

Ticket consolidators resell, at heavy discounts, commercial and charter airlines' unsold tickets. Look for tiny ads in weekend papers (in the U.S., the Sunday *New York Times* travel section is best) and start calling. Unlike tickets bought through an airline, you won't be able to use these tickets on another flight if you miss yours, and you will have to go back to the consolidator—not the airline—to get a refund. Phone around and pay with a credit card; you can't stop a cash payment if you never receive tickets. Find out everything you can about an agency and insist on a **receipt** with full details about the tickets, refunds, and restrictions; if they don't want to give you a clear summary or seem clueless, use a different company.

It's best to buy from a major organization that has experience in placing individuals on charter flights. One of the most reputable is **Council Travel** (see Travel Services, p. 1), the travel division of Council. A full-service agency specializing in student, youth, and budget travel. Council Travel has over 50 offices worldwide and offers exclusively negotiated discount airfares on scheduled airlines. Another good organization is **Unitravel,** 1177 N. Warson Rd., St. Louis, MO 63132 (tel. (800) 325 2222); they will hold all payments in a bank escrow until completion of your trip. Also try **Interworld Travel,** Douglas Entrance, 800 Douglas Rd. Suite 140, Coral Gables, FL 33134-3138 (tel. (305) 443 4929); **Rebel,** 25050 Avenue Kearney Suite

215, Valencia, CA 91355 (tel. (800) 227 3235); The **Air Travel Advisory Bureau,** Columbus House, 28 Charles Sq., London N1 6HT, England (tel. (0171) 636 5000), puts travelers in touch with the cheapest carriers out of London.

The theory behind **charter flights** is that a tour operator contracts with an airline (usually a fairly obscure one) to use their planes to fly passengers to peak-season destinations. Charter flights thus fly infrequently, have more restrictions, and may be changed or canceled at the last minute. Shoot for a scheduled air ticket if you can and pay with a credit card. You might also consider traveler's insurance. It's best to buy from a major organization that has experience in placing individuals on charter flights. One of the most reputable is **Council Travel** (tel. (800) 800-8222).

Last minute **discount clubs** and **fare brokers** offer members savings, including charter flights and tour packages. Research carefully. **Last Minute Travel Club,** 1249 Boylston St., Boston, MA 02215 (tel. (800) 527 8646 or (617) 267 9800) is one of the few travel clubs that does not require a membership fee. Other clubs are **Discount Travel International, Moment's Notice** (tel. (212) 486 0500; US$25 annual fee), and **Traveler's Advantage** (tel. (800) 835 8747; US$49 annual fee). For US$25, **Travel Avenue** will search for the lowest international airfare and provides rebates on fares over US$300 (tel. (800) 333 3335.) The often labyrinthine contracts for all these organizations bear close study; you may prefer not to stop over in Luxembourg for 11 hours.

COURIER FLIGHTS

Those who travel light should consider flying to Europe as a courier. The company hiring you will use your checked luggage space for freight; you're left with the carry-on allowance. Watch for restrictions: most flights are round-trip only with fixed-length stays (usually short), you may not be able to travel with a companion, and most flights are from New York or Boston. Round-trip fares to Western Europe from the U.S. range from US$199-349 (during the off-season) to US$399-549 (during the summer). **NOW Voyager,** 74 Varick St. 307, New York, NY 10013 (tel. (212) 431-1616), acts as an agent for many courier flights worldwide from New York, although some flights are available from Houston. They also offer special last-minute deals to such cities as London, Paris, Rome and Frankfurt which go for as little as US$200 round-trip. Also try **Halbart Express,** 147-05 176th St., Jamaica, NY 11434 (tel. (718) 656-5000), or **Courier Travel Service** (tel. (516) 763-6898). If you have travel time to spare, **Ford's Travel Guides,** 19448 Londelius St., Northridge, CA 91324 (tel. (818) 701-7414), lists **freighter companies** that take passengers for trans-Atlantic crossings. Ask for their *Freighter Travel Guide and Waterways of the World* (US$15, $2.50 postage if mailed outside U.S.). Check your bookstore or library for The *Courier Air Travel Handbook* (US$10), which explains courier travel and contains names, telephone numbers, and contact points of courier companies; order it from **Bookmasters, Inc.,** (tel. (800) 507-2665), PO Box 2039, Mansfield, OH 44905.

■■■ FROM DOWN UNDER

Travelers from Australia or New Zealand are best advised to visit a local branch of one of the specialty organizations listed for North America. **STA Travel** is probably the largest international agency you will find: they have offices in **Melbourne,** 222 Faraday St., VIC 3053 (tel. (03) 349 2411) and **Sydney,** 1st floor, 734 Harris St., Altima 20007 (tel. (02) 212 1255). Flying direct is but one (very expensive) way of getting to the British Isles. **British Airways** (tel. (0181) 897 4000) and **Qantas** both fly direct from Australia to Britain. The Irish airline **Aer Lingus** has great deals for travelers from Australia and New Zealand who fly directly to England, providing free shuttle service from London to Dublin. Any national airline between Australia and Britain can offer somewhat cheaper connecting flights on one part of the route; most travelers reportedly take **Singapore Air** or other Far East-based carriers during the initial leg of their trip.

■■■ FROM CONTINENTAL EUROPE

Air travel between Ireland and continental Europe is expensive and generally unnecessary. Most budget travelers take ferries. USIT does offer some good deals on student flights, particularly to Paris and to wherever the Irish national soccer team is playing a tournament.

BUS & FERRY

Bus Éireann, the Irish national bus company, recently inaugurated a coach service to Paris connecting from any city in Ireland. The big advantage of the new service is that it sails to Paris, France via Cork or Rosslare, thereby circumventing the dreaded "land bridge" approach of driving to the Continent via Britain. Fares are IR£74 one-way, IR£119 round-trip. Contact the Bus Éireann travel center in Cork (tel. (021) 508188) or a travel agent. **Supabus,** another bus/ferry scheme cooked up by Bus Éireann, is cheaper than the Paris service, but less elegant: rates start at IR£50 return to London from Dublin, IR£35 for single. However, inconvenient arrival and departure times mean that you won't be sleeping very well. Supabus connects in London to the immense Eurolines network, which in turn connects with many European destinations. Contact Bus Éireann for info.

FERRIES

France to Ireland

There are bumpy, crowded crossings from Cork to Le Havre (22hr.), Cherbourg (18hr.), Roscoff (14hr.), and St. Malo (18hr.); and from Rosslare to Le Havre (21hr.) and Cherbourg (17hr.).

Irish Ferries are at 2-4 Merrion Row, Dublin 2 (tel. (01) 661 0511); 9 Bridge St., Cork (tel. (021) 504333); and at Rosslare Harbour (tel. (053) 33158). Reservations can be made through Lynott Tours (800) 221-2474. They sail from Cork and Rosslare Harbour to Le Havre and Cherbourg, France. (Rosslare-Le Havre 1-3/week, 22hr.; Rosslare-Cherbourg 1-2/week, 16hr.; Cork-Le Havre June-Aug. 1/week, 20hr.; Cork-Cherbourg June-Aug. 1/week, 18hr.) Prices are the same for all sailings: single fares range from IR£166 (students £83) in mid-July down to IR£95 (students IR£48) in Oct.-April. **Eurail Passes** grant passage (not a seat, not a berth, just the right to sit on the floor of the ferry) on ferry services between Rosslare and Cherbourg/Le Havre.

Brittany Ferries, Tourist House, 42 Grand Parade, Cork (tel. (021) 277 801), sail to Roscoff and St. Malo from Cork. (Cork-Roscoff: March-Oct. 1-2/week, 14hr.; Cork-St. Malo: May-Sept. 1/week, 18hr.) One-way tickets range from IR£72 in mid-July to IR£50 in March and Oct. 11-day return fares cost IR£10 more than the one-way fare; open returns cost 40% more. (Office open Mon.-Fri. 9am-5:30pm, Sat. 9am-noon. Call for free brochure listing schedule.)

The Continent to England

Stena Sealink Line (U.K. tel. (01233) 647047) ferries across the channel between France (Calais, Diappe, and Cherbourg) and England (Dover, Newhaven, and Southampton). Sealink ferries are the most frequent and take 1½ hours (1/hr. from Dover to Calais; fares vary, floating around UK£26 one way, high season). Other routes between the Continent and England include Bergen, Norway to Newcastle (on **Scandinavian Seaways** tel. (01255) 240240); Esbjerg, Denmark to Harwich or Newcastle (Scandinavian); Gothenburg, Sweden to Harwich or Newcastle (Scandinavian); Hamburg, Germany to Harwich (Scandinavian); Hook of Holland, Belgium to Harwich (Sealink); Oostende, Belgium to Dover (Scandinavian); Rotterdam, the Netherlands to Hull; Zeebrugge, Belgium to Dover, Hull, or Felixstowe. (See below for office information.)

In May 1994, the **Channel Tunnel (Chunnel)** was completed, connecting England and France. **Eurotunnel** is the name of bi-national Franco-British company that built and owns the Chunnel. Eurotunnel's **Le Shuttle** service carries passengers

WITH OUR RAIL PASSES YOU'LL HAVE UP TO 70% MORE MONEY TO WASTE.

With savings of up to 70% off the price of point to point tickets, you'll be laughing all the way to the souvenir stand. Rail passes are available for travel throughout Europe or the country of your choice and we'll even help you fly there. So all you'll have to do is leave some extra room in your suitcase. To learn more call **1-800-4-EURAIL** (1-800-438-7245). *Rail Europe*

Rail Europe, P.O. Box 10383, Stamford, CT 06904.

with cars, buses, or campers. Car passenger service opened in 1994, coach service in March 1995. Starting in the spring of 1995, **Eurostar** hit the scene, barreling passengers from the Continent to the Isles and vice versa. Service runs from Paris' Nord Station to London's Waterloo Station (10/day; 3hr.; adult £77.50 single, £155 return, ages 11-26 £42 single, £84 return). Discounts are available with various international rail passes; call the Eurostar office in London at (0345) 881881 for more information on rates, fares, and discounts.

■■■ FROM BRITAIN

FLIGHTS

Airplanes fly between Gatwick, Stansted, Heathrow, Luton, Manchester, Birmingham, Liverpool, and Glasgow airports (in Britain) and Dublin, Shannon, Cork, Kerry, Galway, Knock, Sligo, and Waterford (in Ireland); Belfast and Derry in Northern Ireland; and Ronaldsway on the Isle of Man. British Airways, Aer Lingus, British Midlands, Manx Air, and Ryan Air are some of the companies offering service on these routes. Students can fly one-way from London to Dublin for UK£52 or less if they book through USIT. **British Midland Airways** (Belfast office: Suite 2, Fountain Centre, College St. Belfast BT1 6ET; tel. (01232) 241 188); Dublin Office: Nutley Hall, Merrion Rd., Dublin 4; tel. (01) 283 0700; reservations (01) 283 8833) flies about eight flights per day to Belfast International Airport. **British Airways** (Belfast office: 9 Fountain Centre, College St., Belfast 1; tel. (01345) 222 111) flies about nine flights per weekday, six per day on weekends. Prices range from UK£70-97 return, but can drop from time to time. Call and inquire about specials. Flights from London to Belfast generally take 1¼hr. **Manx Airlines** (tel. (01) 260 1588) flies from London to Dublin (UK£75-86 return) and from London to Belfast (UK£70-97 return). Book as early as you can to get the cheapest fare.

FERRIES

Ferries are popular and usually more economical than flights. Boats run from Fishguard Harbour and Pembroke Dock in South Wales to Rosslare in southeast Ireland; from Holyhead in north Wales to Dún Laoghaire ("dun-LEER-ee") and nearby Dublin; from Stranraer, Scotland to Larne, Northern Ireland. Some people ask car drivers to let them travel as one of four free passengers that a set of wheels gets. Ferry passengers from the Republic are taxed an additional IR£5; from England to Éire, there's a tax of UK£5. **HI members** receive a 25% discount on fares from Irish Ferries. **ISIC cardholders** receive a 25% discount from Irish Ferries and a discount on Stena-Sealink ferries. ISIC cardholders with **Travelsave stamps** save 50% on Irish Ferries. Almost all sailings in June, July, and August are "controlled sailings," which means that you must book the crossing ahead of time (a day in advance is sufficient). Low season on ferry prices runs May and October to December; midseason is June to July and September, while high season is late July to August.

To Dublin

Irish Ferries sails from Holyhead to Dublin. Single fares go for IR£19-27; from Dublin to Holyhead in summer '95, they charged IR£25 (students with ISIC IR£22-24, inquire about Travelsave stamp discounts; HI members also get a discount; bikes travel free; prices excluding IR£5 government travel tax). Call the Irish Ferries office in Dublin at 16 Westmoreland St. (tel. (01) 661 0511; fax (01) 661 0743); in Holyhead (tel. (01407) 760222 or 760223); in Pembroke (tel. (01646) 684161); in Rosslare Harbour (tel. (053) 33158); or in Cork at St. Patrick's Bridge (tel. (021) 504333; fax (021) 504651). Their after-hours information line in England is tel. (0161) 236 3936, in Ireland tel. (01) 661 0715.

Stena-Sealink Line ferries go from Holyhead, North Wales, to Dún Laoghaire, a Dublin suburb. They can be reached at 15 Westmoreland St., Dublin 2 (tel. (01) 280 8844), in Dún Laoghaire (tel. (01) 280 0205; recorded info 280 0338), in Rosslare

Harbour (tel. (053) 33115; recorded info tel. 33330), in Cork at the Tourist House, Grand Parade (tel. (021) 272965), or in Limerick at the Tourist Office, Arthurs Quay (tel. (061) 316259). Their head office is at Charter House, Park St., Ashford, Kent, England TN24 8EX (tel. (01233) 647047 or 240280). In summer '95, they charged IR£20-28 (students IR£18-24 return) for ferries from Dublin to Holyhead.

Assorted bus tickets that include ferry connections between Britain and Ireland are also available as package deals through ferry companies, travel agents, and USIT offices. **Supabus** (run by Bus Éireann) connects Dublin with London for UK£29-36, (the higher fares apply July to Aug.). Tickets can be booked through USIT, any Bus Éireann office, or any National Express office in Britain (tel. (099) 808080).

To Rosslare Harbour

Irish Ferries has an office in Rosslare; in summer '95, their ferries to Pembroke, Wales left Rosslare Harbour twice daily (4½hr.; IR£19-27, students and seniors IR£17-24, bikes free). **Stena-Sealink** ferries left Rosslare Harbour for Fishguard, South Wales twice daily. (IR£20-28, students IR£18-24, bikes free); book through any Stena-Sealink office (see above).

To Cork

Cork-Swansea Ferries, 52 South Mall, Cork (tel. (021) 271 166), run to Swansea, Wales (1/week at 9pm; IR£20, students and seniors IR£16, bikes IR£7). **Slattery's** travel agency, based in Tralee at 1 Russell St. (tel. (066) 21611) runs a combined bus/ferry deal which amounts to very cheap transport to London (IR£35 single, IR£53 return). Ferries to Cork from France and England dock at **Ringaskiddy Terminal,** nine miles south of the city. The 20-minute city bus from the ferry terminal to the Cork bus station, or vice versa, costs about IR£3.

To Belfast & Larne

The **Hoverspeed Seacat** leaves Stranraer and arrives in Belfast (July-Aug. Thurs.-Sun. 5/day, Tues.-Wed. 4/day; June and Sept. daily 4/day; 1½hr.; UK£19-21, seniors and students UK£12-14, ages 4-15 UK£10-12, bikes and tykes under 4 free; for bookings, tel. (0345) 523523). A Flexibus shuttle runs into Belfast. For pedestrians, the hovercraft is faster than ferries, comparable in price, and actually gets you to Belfast rather than dumping you in industrial Larne; drivers with autos, however, may save as much as UK£40 by taking the ferry rather than the Seacat. **Stena-Sealink** ferries (Larne tel. (01574) 273616, Stranraer tel. (01776) 2262) run from Stranraer, Scotland to Larne, Northern Ireland. (2½hr.; UK£42 return, bikes free.) Direct **train** service from London's Euston Station to Belfast's York St. Station via Sealink takes about 12hr. and costs UK£47. **P&O Ferries** (central office (01304) 212121) run between Carnryan, Scotland and Larne. (Mon.-Fri. 6/day, Sat.-Sun. 4/day; UK£18, seniors and children £9.)

To Ireland via the Isle of Man

You can easily combine a ferry across the Irish Sea with a stopover on the Isle of Man. An advantage of this routing is that you can ferry into Dublin and ferry out of Belfast at no extra charge. The Isle of Man Steam Packet Co. (Belfast tel. (01232) 351009; Douglas tel. (01232) 351009; fax (01624) 661065) charges UK£21-31 one way, students UK£15-31, bikes free; the principal ports are Heysham and Liverpool.

TRAVELING IN IRELAND

■■■ GETTING AROUND

Fares on all modes of transportation are either "single" (one way) or "return" (round-trip). "Period returns" require you to return within a specific number of days; "day return" means you must return on the same day. Always keep your ticket with you. Unless stated otherwise, *Let's Go* always lists single (one way) fares. Round-trip fares on trains and buses are rarely more than 30% above the one-way fare, and are sometimes identical.

Roads between Irish cities and towns have official letters and numbers ("N" and "R" in the Republic, "M," "A," and "B" in the North), but most locals refer to them by destination ("Kerry road," "Tralee road"). Signs and printed directions sometimes give only the numbered and lettered designations, sometimes only the destination. Most signs are in English and Irish; some destination signs are only in Irish. White roadsigns give distances in miles; on green signs, they're in kilometers.

BY TRAIN

Iarnród Éireann (Irish Rail) branches out from Dublin to larger cities, but there is limited service. For schedule information, pick up an *InterCity Rail Travellers Guide* (50p), available at most train stations. By far the most useful travel pass for students on trains and buses in Ireland is the **TravelSave stamp,** available at any USIT with an ISIC card and IR£8. Affixed to your ISIC card, this stamp decreases single fares by 50% on national rail and allows you to break your journey to visit at any stop on the way to your final destination (valid for one month). It also provides 15% discounts on bus fares (except on fares less than IR£1). A **Faircard** can get anyone under 26 up to 50% the price of any InterCity trip. Those over 26 can get the less potent **Weekender card** (up to a third off, Fri.-Tues. only). Information is available from Irish Rail information office, 35 Lower Abbey St., Dublin 1 (tel. (01) 836 6222).

While the **Eurailpass** is not accepted in Britain, it *is* accepted on trains in Ireland. (It is no longer accepted on Irish buses.) Fares for 1995 were as follows: regular Eurailpass US$498 (15 days), US$648 (21 days), or US$798 (1 month); Youthpass (for those under 26) US$398 (15 days), US$578 (1 month) or US$768 (2 months). You can also buy a Flexipass for 5, 10, or 15 days of travel within two months or a Saverpass for group discounts. It's not worth buying a Eurailpass unless you plan to travel on the Continent as well. With the pass, you can travel on Irish Ferries from Rosslare to Cherbourg or Le Havre.

Northern Ireland Railways (Belfast tel. (01232) 899411, Britrail enquiries tel. (01232) 230671) service is not extensive but covers the Northeastern coastal region well. The major line connects Dublin to Belfast (6/day; 2½hr.; UK£14, UK£21 return) and runs north through Antrim. When it reaches Belfast, this line splits, with one branch ending at Bangor and one at Larne. There is also rail service from Belfast and Lisburn west to Derry and Portrush, stopping at three towns between Antrim and the coast. British Rail passes are not valid here, but Northern Ireland Railways offers its own discounts. A valid **Northern Ireland Travelsave** stamp (UK£5, bought at the Student Travel Office, 13b The Fountain Centre, College St., Belfast, and affixed to back of ISIC) will get you 50% off all trains and 15% discounts on bus fares over UK£1 within Northern Ireland. The **Rail Runabout** ticket allows seven consecutive days of travel between April and Oct. (UK£25, children UK£12.50).

BY BUS

Buses in the Republic of Ireland reach many more destinations than trains, but are less frequent, less comfortable, and slower. The national bus company, **Bus Éireann** operates both long-distance **Expressway** buses, which link larger cities, and **Provincial** buses, which serve the countryside and smaller towns. The bus timetable book (50p) is available at Busáras in Dublin and at many tourist offices. A mélange of **private bus services** are faster and cheaper than Bus Éireann. Most of these services link Dublin to one or two towns in the west. In Donegal, private bus providers take the place of Bus Éireann's nearly nonexistent local service.

Bus Éireann's discount **Rambler** tickets mostly aren't worth buying; individual tickets often provide better value. The **Road Rambler** ticket offers unlimited bus travel within Ireland three days (IR£28), eight days (IR£68), or 15 days (IR£98). A combined **Rail and Road Rambler** ticket good for unlimited travel on rail and bus lines is also available. Purchase these from Bus Éireann at the main tourist office in Dublin, 14 Upper O'Connell St., Dublin 1 (tel. (01) 830 2222; in Cork tel. (021) 506055; in Limerick tel. (061) 313333; in Waterford tel. (051) 79000; in Galway tel. (091) 62000). You can also contact the Irish Rail information office, 35 Lower Abbey St., Dublin 1 (tel. (01) 836 6222).

Ulsterbus, Oxford St., Belfast (tel. (01232) 320 011), runs throughout the North, where there are no private bus services; coverage expands in summer, when open-top buses cover a northeastern coastal route, and full- and half-day tours leave for key tourist spots from Belfast. Pick up a regional timetable (25p) at any station. Again, the bus discount passes won't save you much money: a **Freedom of Northern Ireland** bus pass costs UK£9 for one day, UK£28 for seven consecutive days; under 16 UK£4.50, UK£14. The **Emerald Card** offers travel for eight out of 15 consecutive days (UK£105, children UK£53) or 15 out of 30 consecutive days (UK£185, children UK£93). The Emerald card allows unlimited travel on Ulsterbus, Citybus, Northern Ireland Railways, Bus Éireann, Dublin Bus, and Irish Rails. Hostelers might take advantage of the **Go as You Please pass** which offers seven days unlimited bus travel and six nights in YHANI hostels (from UK£55), available only through YHANI (see Hostel Membership, p. 11).

BY CAR

The advantages of car travel speak for themselves. Disadvantages include high gasoline prices, the unfamiliar laws and habits associated with driving in foreign lands, and the fact that in Ireland, as in Britain, **they drive on the left.** Be particularly cautious at roundabouts (rotary interchanges)—give way to traffic from the right. In both countries, the law requires drivers and front-seat passengers to wear seat belts. In Northern Ireland, rear-seat passengers are also required to buckle up—these laws are enforced. In Ireland, children under 12 are not allowed to sit in the front seat of a car. In the Republic of Ireland, roads numbered below N50 are "primary routes," which connect all the major towns; roads numbered N50 and above are "secondary routes," not as well-trafficked but still well-signposted. Regional "R-roads" are rarely referred to by number. Instead, the road takes the name of its destination. The general speed limit is 55mph (90km/h) on the open road and either 30mph (50km/h) or 40mph (65km/h) in town. There are no major highways.

Northern Ireland possesses exactly two major highways (M-roads or motorways) connecting Belfast with the rest of the province. The M-roads are supplemented by a web of "A-roads" and "B-roads." Speed limits are 60mph (97km/h) on single carriageways (non-divided highways), 70mph (113km/h) on motorways (highways) and dual carriageways (divided highways), and usually 30mph (48km/h) in urban areas. (Speed limits are always marked at the beginning of town areas. Upon leaving, you'll see a circular sign with a slash through it, signalling the end of the speed restriction.) Speed limits aren't rabidly enforced; remember though, that many of these roads are sinuous and single-track—use common sense.

Hiring (renting) an automobile is the least expensive option if you plan to drive for a month or less. Major rental companies include **Avis, Budget Rent-A-Car, Murrays Europcar, Hertz, Kenning, McCausland,** and **Swan National.** Prices range from IR£100 to IR£300 per week with insurance, unlimited mileage, plus VAT. For insurance reasons, renters are required to be over 21 and under 70. However, **Europe by Car** will rent to younger people if the paperwork is done in advance, in the U.S. All plans require sizable deposits unless you're paying by credit card. Make sure you understand the insurance agreement before you rent. Some agreements require you to pay for damages that you may not have caused. Automatics are generally more expensive to rent than manuals (stick shifts). The initial cost of renting a car and the price of petrol will astound you in Ireland. People under 21 cannot rent, and those under 25 often encounter difficulties. Try **Budget Rent-A-Car,** 151 Lower Drumcondra Rd, Dublin 9 (tel. (01) 837 9611; £45/day).

You may use an American or Canadian driver's license for six months in the U.K. and Ireland, provided you've had it for one year. If you plan on staying for a longer duration, you will need an **International Driver's Permit.** Your IDP must be issued in your own country before you depart. U.S. license holders can obtain an IDP, valid for one year, at any **American Automobile Association (AAA)** office or by writing to its main office, AAA Florida, Travel Agency Services Department, 1000 AAA Drive (mail stop 28), Heathrow, FL 32746-5080 (tel. (407) 444-4000; fax 444-4140). For further information, contact a local AAA office. The **Irish Automobile Association** is on 23 Suffolk Rd., Rockhill, Blackrock, Co. Dublin (tel. (01) 677 9481), off Grafton St. They honor most foreign automobile memberships; their 24-hr. breakdown and road service number (toll-free within Ireland) is (1800) 667788.

BY BICYCLE

Much of Ireland's and Northern Ireland's countrysides are well suited for cycling; many roads are not heavily traveled. (Single-digit N roads in the Republic, and M roads in the North, are more busily trafficked; try to avoid them.) Even well traveled routes will often cover highly uneven terrain. Begin your trip in the south or west to take advantage of prevailing winds. It's a pain to bring a bike on an airplane, and each airline has different rules. *Let's Go* lists bike shops and bike rental establishments wherever we can find them.

Rent-A-Bike, 58 Lower Gardiner St., Dublin (tel. (01) 872 5399), rents 18-speed cross-country and mountain bikes for IR£7/day, IR£30 week, plus deposit IR£30. The shops will equip you with locks, patch kits, pumps, pannier bags, handlebar bags, and helmets for IR£5 extra. You can return your bike at a different depot for about IR£5. You can also buy a used bike at the Dublin shop and sell it back four months later for half price. Rent-A-Bike depots are located in Dublin; Isaac's Hostel, Cork; An Óige Hostel, Limerick; Shannon Airport; Great Western Hostel, Galway; Scotts Garden, Killarney. All bookings should be made through the head office in Dublin (open Mon.-Sat. 9am-6pm, plus Sun. 9am-6pm in summer).

Irish Cycle Hire, Mayoralty Rd., Drogheda, Co. Louth (tel. (041) 41067 or 42338; fax 35369, has offices in Dublin, Cork, Killarney, Dingle, Donegal. They also own **Viking Rent-a-Bike** and **Railbike,** so they have many depots. The Drogheda office, which is the office to contact with any question, is open 9am-6pm. Other offices are open daily 9am-6pm. All have rates of IR£6/day, IR£30/week, with deposit IR£30. Helmets and pannier bags are available for rent at IR£5/week each. Bikes come with lock pump and repair kit. One-way rental (renting in one location and dropping off in another) is possible for IR£5. ISIC card holders get a 10% discount (also inquire about a 10% discount for *Let's Go* users, especially in Drogheda).

Raleigh Rent-A-Bike rents for IR£7 per day, IR£30 per week, plus deposit IR£40. The shops will equip you with locks, patch kits, and pumps, and for longer journeys, pannier bags (IR£5 per week). Their **One-Way Rental** plan allows you to rent a bike at one shop and drop it off at any of eight others for a flat charge of IR£12. The bike shops that participate in this scheme are in Ennis, Castletownbere, Cork, Ardara, Dublin, Galway, Limerick, and Castlebar. A list of Raleigh dealers is available at most tourist offices and bike shops. You might also contact **Raleigh Ireland Limited,** 10 Raleigh House, Kylemore Rd., Dublin 10 (tel. (01) 626 1333).

Many small local dealers and hostels also rent bikes; rates are usually IR£6-9/day and IR£25-35/week. Tourist offices sell *Cycling Ireland* (with map, IR£1.50); you should also check a travel bookstore for other Irish cycling guides if you plan to do much long-distance riding. Mountaineers Books (tel. (800) 553-4453) sells *Ireland by Bike: 21 Tours* for US$15 (plus US$3 shipping). If you are nervous about striking out on your own, **CBT Bicycle Tours** (tel. (312) 404-1710 or (800) 736-2453; fax (312) 404-1833) in the U.S. and Canada offer bicycle tours through the U.K. and Ireland that are geared toward the college-aged. They also arrange discounted airfares for their participants. You can take your bike on the **train** for IR£6, and on the **bus** for a variable charge. However, bus transport is entirely at the driver's discretion. You'll have better luck getting your bike on a bus if you depart from a terminal, not a wayside stop, if the bus is full, however, you may be out of luck completely. Adequate **maps** are a necessity; Ordnance Survey maps (1" to 1 mi.) or Bartholomew maps (½" to 1 mi.) are available in most bookstores in Ireland and the U.K., and in good ones in the U.S. A waterproof cape or poncho is an absolute must. The **Northern Ireland Tourist Board** (see Resources at Home, p. 1) distributes leaflets on various on-road biking routes in Northern Ireland and provides addresses of bike rental establishments, many of which rent mountain bikes.

ON FOOT

Ireland has lots of hiking paths and national parks at your disposal. The **Wicklow Way,** a popular trail through mountainous Co. Wicklow, has hostels designed for hikers within a day's walk of each other. The best hillwalking maps are the Ordnance Survey ½"-to-1-mi. series; IR£3.70 each. Consult *Dublin and the Wicklow Mountains—Access Routes for the Hillwalker* (IR£2.80), and the tourist office's pamphlet *Walking in Ireland* (IR£1.50).

The **Ulster Way** encircles Northern Ireland with 560 miles of marked trails. Less industrious trekkers are accommodated by frequent subdivisions. Plentiful information is available on the numerous paths that lace Northern Ireland. For the booklet *The Ulster Way* (£2), contact the **Sports Council for Northern Ireland,** House of Sport, Upper Malone Rd., Belfast BT9 5LA (tel. (01232) 381 222). If you're planning a hike through the Mourne Mountains, contact **Heart of Down Accommodations Association,** Down District Council, 24 Storangford Rd. Downpatrick, Co. Down BT30 6SR (tel. (01396) 610800).

If you're not feeling too adventurous, you can try **Tír na nÓg Tours,** 22 Store St., Fairview, Dublin 3 (tel. (01) 836 4684), which offers guided backpacking tours of Ireland. The six-day tours zip along the south and west coasts, and the tour price includes hostel accommodations along the way. Tours leave weekly throughout the year, although prices vary according to the season (ranging from £129-149).

BY THUMB

Let's Go urges you to seriously consider the risks before you decide to hitchhike. We do not recommend hitchhiking as a means of transport, and the information given below and the routes listed in the book are not intended to do so. Do not even consider hitching to or through South Armagh—it's completely unsafe.

No one should hitch without careful consideration of the risks involved. Not everyone can be an airplane pilot, but almost anyone can pretend to drive a car. Hitching means entrusting your life to a randomly selected person who happens to stop beside you on the road. You risk theft, assault, sexual harassment, and unsafe driving. Hitching in Ireland has a glowing reputation, but it does have sobering risks: two German tourists were recently murdered while hitching in Western Ireland, and a woman hitcher was raped outside Carrickfergus, Northern Ireland.

In spite of these risks, the gains are many. Favorable hitching experiences allow you to meet local people and get where you're going, especially in rural areas where public transportation is particularly sketchy. The choice, however, remains yours. Consider this section as akin to handing out condoms to high school students: we don't endorse it, but if you're going to do it anyway, we'll tell you some ways to make it safer and how to do it right.

The **decision to pick up** a hitcher can be a difficult one for a driver, so a smart hitcher will do everything possible to make it a comfortable decision. Your success as a hitcher will depend partly on **what you look like.** Look neat, smile, and don't dawdle. **Where you stand** is vital. Stand in a spot where it's easy to see you well before they have to stop, then they don't need to make a quick decision about stopping. (A quick decision will be more likely "no".) If you walk while sticking out your thumb, you'll be less likely to be picked up. Experienced hitchers pick a spot outside of built-up areas where drivers can stop and return to the road without causing an accident. Hitching on hills or curves is hazardous and unsuccessful. Successful points for hitchers include traffic circles and access roads to highways. In the Practical Information section of many cities, we list the bus lines that travelers take to strategic points for hitching out.

You can get a sense of the amount of traffic a road sees by its letter and number: in the Republic, single-digit N-roads (A-roads in the North) are as close as Ireland gets to highways, double-digit N-roads see some intercity traffic, R-roads (B-roads in the North) generally only carry local traffic but are easy hitches, and non-lettered roads are a hitcher's **purgatory.** In Northern Ireland, hitching (or even standing) on motorways (M-roads) is illegal: you may only thumb at the entrance ramps—*in front* of the nifty blue and white superhighway pictograph (a bridge over a road).

Safety issues are always imperative, even when you're traveling with another person. Avoid getting in the back of a two-door car, and never let go of your backpack. Hitchhiking at night can be particularly dangerous. Stand in a well-lit place and expect drivers to be leery of nocturnal thumbers. When you get into a car, make sure you know how to get out again in a hurry. Couples may avoid hassles with male drivers if the woman sits in the back or next to the door. If you ever feel threatened, insist on being let off, regardless of where you are. If the driver refuses to stop, act as though you're going to open the car door or vomit on the upholstery.

If you are hitching a **long distance** or to a remote spot with an intervening town between your present and desired location, you would do well to make your sign for the intervening town rather than your final destination. Shorter lifts are easier to pick up because it's easier for the driver and because more cars will be going to the nearby spot than to the distant one. Once you're picked up, if the driver is actually going to your final destination, then the driver will almost certainly take you the entire way (unless you make terrible jokes about Idaho or potatoes). If the driver is not going the entire way, then you've at least covered some of the distance and probably put yourself in a better location for hitching the rest of the way.

■■■ ACCOMMODATIONS

Bord Fáilte ("bored FAHL-tshah"; meaning "welcome board") is the Republic of Ireland's tourism authority. Actually a government department (and a fairly important one), its system for approving accommodations involves a more or less frequent inspection and a fee. Approved accommodations get to use Bord Fáilte's national bookings system and display its icon, a green shamrock on a white field. Bord Fáilte's standards are very specific and, in some cases, far higher than what hostelers and other budget travelers expect or require. Many unapproved accommodations are better and cheaper than their approved neighbors, though, of course, *some* unapproved places are real dumps. Most official tourist offices in Ireland will refer *only* to approved accommodations; some offices won't even tell you how to get to an unapproved hostel, B&B, or campground. Most tourist offices will book a room for IR£3 fee, plus a 10% deposit. **Credit card reservations** can be made through Bord Fáilte by Freefone within Ireland (tel. (01) 284 1765), or outside Ireland (tel. (01) 284 1765; fax (01) 284 1751).

HOSTELS

> ### A Hosteler's Bill of Rights
> There are certain standard features that we do not include in our hostel listings. Unless we state otherwise, you can expect that every hostel has: no lockout, no curfew, a kitchen, free hot showers, secure luggage storage, and no key deposit.

For those eager to meet fellow travelers of all ages and nationalities, ease the burden on their budgets, or recreate fond memories of summer camp, hostels are the way to go. Though curfews, lockouts, communal showers, and single-sex, dorm-style rooms might dissuade the less-seasoned traveler, hostels are generally clean, well-managed, and exceptionally reasonable in price. As the undisputed hubs of the budget-travel subculture, hostels are also great places to swap stories and tips or just meet people. And hey, these so-called youth hostels and their many tricks aren't just for kids; in Ireland more than anywhere else, senior travelers and families are invariably welcome. Some hostels are strikingly beautiful (a few are even housed in castles), while others are little more than run-down barracks. You can expect every Irish hostel to provide blankets, while you have to provide a sheet or sleepsack.

The worldwide network of hostels is **Hostelling International (HI).** A membership in any national HI affiliate allows you to stay in HI hostels in any country. Nonmembers may ask at hostels for an "International Guest Card." When they visit a hostel, an overnight fee plus one-sixth of the annual membership charge buys one stamp; a card with six stamps is proof of full HI membership. In Ireland, the HI affiliate is **An Óige,** which operates 44 hostels countrywide. Many An Óige hostels are in remote areas or small villages and seem designed mostly to serve hikers, long-distance bicyclists, anglers, and others who want to see nature rather than meet people. The North's HI affiliate is **YHANI** (Youth Hostel Association of Northern Ireland). It operates only nine hostels, all comfortable. Many HI hostels have curfews and lockouts (midday hours when everyone has to leave the building), though they're not always strict about them; almost all have laundry facilities and kitchens. Some HI hostels exist only from March to November, April to October, or May to September. The annually-updated *An Óige Handbook* (IR£1.50) lists, locates, and describes all the An Óige and YHANI hostels in both countries; its standard pricing system isn't always followed by all the hostels it lists. An Óige, YHANI and other HI addresses are under Useful Addresses (see Hostel Membership, p. 11).

In Ireland, the two significant non-HI, non-governmental hostel organizations recently merged to form **IHH.** IHH hostels have no lockout or curfew, accept all ages, require no membership card, and have a mellow atmosphere; all are Bord Fáilte-approved. Pick up a free booklet with complete descriptions of each at any IHH hostel. Get in touch with IHH by writing via the IHH Office, U.C.D. Village, Belfield, Dublin 4 (tel. (01) 260 1634).

BED & BREAKFASTS

"Bed-and-breakfast" generally means what it says: a bed in a private room in a small place, often a private home with extra rooms, whose price includes a breakfast of some sort. Irish B&Bs are most savory. Singles run about IR£12-20; doubles IR£20-34. "Full Irish breakfasts"—eggs, bacon, sausage, bread, cereal, orange juice, and coffee or tea—are often filling enough to get you through until dinner. Remember that attitudes in rural Ireland can be quite conservative. An unmarried couple traveling together may encounter some raised eyebrows, but usually no real problems. B&Bs displaying a shamrock are officially approved by the Irish Tourist Board, Bord Fáilte. They charge the prices quoted in the 1996 edition of the *Ireland Accommodation Guide,* published by Bord Fáilte and available at all tourist offices (IR£4). For all manner of accommodations in Northern Ireland, check the Northern Ireland Tourist Board's annual *Where to Stay in Northern Ireland* (UK£4), available at most tourist offices.

■ ■ ■ HIKING & CAMPING

Camping brings you closest to the land, the water, the insects, and continued financial solvency. Ireland is gratifyingly well endowed with sites. Most campsites are open from April through October, though some stay open year-round. While a few youth hostels have camping facilities (the charge is usually half the hostel charge), most campsites are privately owned and designed for people with caravans rather than tent-dwellers. You can legally set up camp only in specifically marked areas unless you get permission from the owner on whose land you plan to squat. It is legal to cross private land by **public rights of way;** any other use of private land without permission is considered trespassing. Remember, **bogs are flammable**—do not tempt fate. The *Ireland Accommodation Guide,* published by Bord Fáilte and available at all tourist offices (IR£4), hits all approved campgrounds in the Republic.

Camping in State Forests and National Parks is not allowed in Ireland, nor is camping on public land if there is an official campsite in the area. It is also illegal to light fires within 2km of these forests and parks. Designated caravan and camping parks provide all the accoutrements of bourgeois civilization: toilets, running water, showers, garbage cans, and sometimes shops, kitchen and laundry facilities, restaurants, and game rooms. In addition, many have several caravans for hire at the site. Northern Ireland treats its campers royally; there are well-equipped campsites throughout, and spectacular parks often house equally mouthwatering sites.

SAFETY

The first thing to preserve in the wilderness is you—**health, safety, and food** should be your primary concerns when you camp. A guide to outdoor survival is *How to Stay Alive in the Woods,* by Bradford Angier (Macmillan, $8). Regardless of the weather when you set out, be prepared for the worst—warm, sunny days in this area of the world can turn to sleeting rain faster than you can say "aaagghhh!"; Goretex or waterproof nylon and wool are musts. Always bring a compass (and know how to use it), sturdy shoes, a first-aid kit, a flashlight, and, for long-distance hikers, a whistle. *Never go camping or hiking for any significant time or distance by yourself.* If you're going into an area that is not well-traveled or well-marked, let a ranger or hostel warden know where and how long you're hiking in case you fail to return on schedule or need to be reached. The distress signal is six blasts on a whistle (or anything loud) repeated at regular intervals (reply is three long blasts).

Be careful about the water you drink outdoors: **do not drink directly or brush your teeth with water from a stream, lake, or river.** Parasites (notably **giardia**) and pollutants can make water unsafe. Many backpackers and campers not scrupulous about their water get infections that can stay with them for years. Symptoms of parasitic infections include swollen glands or lymph nodes, fever, rashes or itchiness, digestive problems, eye problems, and anemia. The most reliable source of water on the trail is water you boil (it does no good to simply heat it) for at least five minutes. You can make it taste better by adding a little salt or pouring it into another container. Second most reliable, and less tasty, is water that you treat with **iodine** or other chemicals such as Potable-Aqua. Water purifiers can also be useful, but are expensive and not guaranteed against all bacteria and parasites.

Bring **sunscreen** from home (it's often more expensive abroad) and apply it liberally and often, especially in sunny weather or when hiking. **Extreme cold** is a far greater danger than heat in Britain and Ireland, especially for hikers. **Hypothermia** can occur even in July, especially in rainy or windy conditions or at night (see Health, p. 16). In freezing temperatures, **frostbite** may occur. The affected skin will turn white, then waxy and cold. The victim should drink warm beverages, stay or get dry, and gently and slowly warm the frostbitten area in dry fabric or with steady body contact. *Never* rub frostbite or run hot water over it. Take serious cases to a doctor ASAP.

CAMPING

The second thing to protect while you are outdoors is the **wilderness itself.** The thousands of outdoor enthusiasts that pour into parks every year threaten to trample the land to death. Because firewood is scarce in popular parks, campers are asked to make small fires using only dead branches or brush; using a **campstove** is the more cautious way to cook. Check to see if the park prohibits campfires. To avoid digging a rain trench for your tent, pitch it on high, dry ground. Don't cut vegetation or clear campsites. If there are no toilet facilities, bury human waste at least four inches deep and 100 feet or more from any water supplies and campsites. Never bury tampons or pads; instead, seal them in plastic bags and carry them out. *Biosafe* soap or detergents may be used in streams or lakes. Otherwise, don't use soaps in or near bodies of water. Always pack up your trash in a plastic bag and carry it with you until you reach the next trash can; burning and burying pollute the environment. Remember, if you **carry it in, carry it out.**

PUBLICATIONS

Automobile Association: Norfolk House, Basingstoke, Hampshire RG24 9NY ENGLAND (tel. (01256) 20123, fax (01256) 22575) publishes *Camping and Caravanning in Europe* (£7.99).

The Mountaineers Books: 1011 Klickitat Way, Suite 107, Seattle, WA 98134 (tel. (800) 553-4453 or (202) 223-6303, fax 223-6306). Bountiful information on hiking (the *100 Hikes* series), backpacking, climbing, biking, natural history, and environmental conservation all over the world.

Sierra Club Bookstore: 730 Polk St., San Francisco, CA 94109, (tel. (415) 923-5500, fax 923-5500). Books include *Wild Britain* ($16). Ask for their *Annual Outing Catalog* (US$2). Shipping is $4 for orders up to $20, $6 for orders up to $40, $8 for orders up to $40, and $10 for any order over $80.

Wilderness Press: 2440 Bancroft Way, Berkeley, CA 94704-1676 (tel. (800) 443-7227 or (510) 843-8080, fax (510) 548 1355), publishes *Backpacking Basics* ($11), *Backpacker's Sourcebook*, and *Backpacking with Babies and Small Children* ($11), among other guides.

EQUIPMENT

Prospective campers will need to invest money in good camping equipment. Spend time skimming catalogues and questioning salespeople before buying anything. Use mail-order firms to gauge prices; order from them if you can't do as well locally. In the fall, the previous year's merchandise may be reduced as much as 50%. Purchase your equipment before you leave (see Pack Light, p. 20 for a detailed assessment of backpack options). Most of the better **sleeping bags**—down (lightweight and warm) or synthetic (cheaper, heavier, more durable, lower maintenance, and warmer when wet)—have ratings for specific minimum temperatures. Sleeping bags are rated according to the lowest outdoor temperature at which they'll keep you warm. The lowest prices for good sleeping bags are $65-80 for a summer synthetic, $135-180 for a three-season synthetic, $170-225 for a three-season down bag, and $270-550 for a down sleeping bag you can use in the winter. **Sleeping bag pads** range from US$15-30, while **air mattresses** go for about US$25-50. The best pad is the Thermarest (US$50-80), which is light, comfy, and self-inflating. Watch out for big, bulky air mattresses—a pain if you're planning to do much hiking.

When you select a **tent,** your major considerations should be shape and size. The best tents are free-standing with their own frames and suspension systems. They set up quickly and require no staking (though staking will keep your tent from blowing away). Low profile dome tents are the best all-around. When they are pitched, their internal space is almost entirely usable; this means little unnecessary bulk. Be sure your tent has a rain fly. Good two-person tents start at about $135; $200 fetches a four-person. You can, however, often find last year's version for half the price. Backpackers and cyclists prefer especially small, lightweight models (US$145 and up).

Other camping basics include a battery-operated **lantern** (*never* gas) and a simple plastic **groundcloth** to protect the tent floor. When camping in autumn, winter, or spring, bring along a "space blanket," a technological wonder that helps you retain your body heat (US$3.50-13; doubles as a groundcloth). Large, collapsible **water sacks** will significantly improve your lot in primitive campgrounds and weigh practically nothing when empty, though they can get bulky. **Campstoves** come in all sizes, weights, and fuel types, but none are truly cheap (US$30-85). Consider GAZ-powered stoves (a brand name), which come with bottled propane gas that is easy to use and widely available in Europe. Beware: stove gas can be heavy and bulky if you bring too much. A water bottle (canteens don't pack well), Ace bandage, Swiss army knife, insect repellent, and waterproof matches are other essential items.

Recreational Equipment, Inc. (REI): 6750 S. 228th St., Kent WA 98032 (tel. (800) 426-4840). Stores all over the U.S. (headquarters in Seattle). Stocks a wide range of the latest in camping gear and holds great seasonal sales. An absolutely huge selection; many things are guaranteed for life (not including normal wear and tear). Very knowledgeable staff, all of whom have outdoors experience.

Campmor, Inc.: P.O. Box 700, Saddle River, NJ 075458-0700 (tel. (800) 526-4784). Monstrous selection of equipment at low prices for a variety of backpacking and travel needs. One-year guarantee for unused or defective goods.

Eastern Mountain Sports: One Vose Farm Rd., Peterborough, NH 03458 (tel. (603) 924-7231) has stores from Colorado to Virginia to Maine. Though somewhat pricey, they provide excellent service and guaranteed customer satisfaction (a full refund if you're unhappy) on all items sold.

L.L. Bean: Casco St., Freeport, ME 04033-0001 (tel. (800) 341-4341). Supplies its own equipment and national-brand merchandise. Freeport store is open every minute of the year. Complete mail order service; 100% guarantee.

Sierra Design: 1255 Powell St., Emeryville, CA 94608 (tel. (510) 450-9555), sells excellent tents, including the 2-person "Clip Flashlight" model (US$170) that weighs less than 4 lbs. You can often find last year's version for half the price.

■■■ KEEPING IN TOUCH

MAIL

Mail can be sent internationally through **Poste Restante** (the international phrase for General Delivery) to any city or town. Mark the envelope "HOLD" and address it, for example, "Sean DESMOND, Poste Restante, Dublin, Ireland." The last name should be capitalized and underlined. The mail will go to a special desk in the central post office, unless you specify a post office by street address or postal code. When picking up your mail, bring your passport or other ID. If the clerk insists that there is nothing for you, try checking under your first name as well.

In the Republic, there are no postal codes, except in Dublin, where there are 24 widely-ignored ones. Northern Ireland uses the British system of six-character codes. *Let's Go* lists post offices in the Practical Information section for each city and most towns. Generally, letters specifically marked "air mail" are faster than postcards and provide more writing room than aerograms. Air mail letters between the Republic and American cities average 10-14 days, between Northern Ireland or the Isle of Man and America 6-10 days.

Sending mail c/o **American Express** offices is quite reliable. They will hold your mail for free if you have AmEx traveler's cheques or a card. To have mail held for longer than 30 days, write "Hold for x days" on the envelope, where x is a number. Again the sender should capitalize and underline your last name (e.g. Sean DESMOND), marking the envelope "Client Letter Service." We list AmEx office locations for most cities. A complete list is available for free from AmEx (tel. (800) 528-4800) in the booklet *Traveler's Companion*.

■■■ TELEPHONES

CALLING THERE

When calling overseas, remember time differences so as not to wake B&B proprietors in the wee hours. Dial your country's international access code (011 for the USA and Canada, 0011 for Australia, 00 for New Zealand); then the country code (44 for Britain, Northern Ireland, and the Isle of Man; 353 for the Republic of Ireland); then the regional telephone code, *dropping the initial zero*, and, finally, the local number. The phone code for the Isle of Man is 01624. *Let's Go* lists telephone codes in Practical Information sections, except when covering rural areas where more than one telephone code may apply (in those cases we list the telephone code, in parentheses, together with the number, out of parentheses). For example, when calling from the U.S. to order books from Fred Hanna's in Dublin (telephone code 01), dial 011-353-1-677-1255. Regional telephone codes range from two to six digits, and local telephone numbers range from three to seven digits.

CALLING FROM THERE

Emergency

Dial **999** anywhere in Ireland, Northern Ireland, the Isle of Man, or London for police, fire, or ambulance; no coins are required. Police in the Republic of Ireland are called *garda* ("GAR-da"), plural *gardaí* ("gar-DEE").

Republic of Ireland

Operator (not available from card phones): 190.
Directory inquiries (for the Republic and the North): 1190.
Directory inquiries for Britain: 1197.
Telecom Éireann information number: (1800) 330 330.
International operator: 114.
International access code: 00.

Using Irish pay phones can be tricky. Public phones come in two varieties: coin phones and card phones. Public coin phones will sometimes make change (it depends on which order you insert coins) but private pay phones ("one-armed bandits") in hotels and restaurants do not—once you plunk in your change, you can kiss it goodbye. In any pay phone, do not insert money until you are asked to, or until your call goes through. The frightening pip, pip noise that the phone makes as you wait for it to start ringing is normal, and can last up to 10 seconds.

Local calls cost 20p on standard pay phones; "one-armed bandits" can charge 30p or whatever they please. Local calls are not unlimited—one unit pays for four minutes. Newsagents sell **callcards** in denominations of £3.50, £7.50, or £15; they're essential for international calls. For calls direct-dialed to the U.S. during the cheapest hours, one card unit lasts 8 seconds, so a 100-unit (£15) card lasts for 13.3 minutes. Talk fast. Card phones have a digital display that ticks off the perilous plunge your units are taking. When the unit number starts flashing, you may push the eject button on the card phone; you can then pull out your expired calling card and replace it with a fresh one. If you try to wait until your card's units fall to zero, you'll be disconnected, which is a bummer. Eject your card early, and use that last remaining unit or two for a local call.

To make **international calls** from the Republic of Ireland, dial the international access code (00); then the country code (see below); area code (dropping the initial zero); and local number. Alternatively, you can access an Irish international operator at 114. Note that to call the North from the Republic, you dial (08) plus the regional phone code (*without* dropping the initial zero) plus the number. International calls from the Republic are cheapest during **economy periods.** The low-rate period to North America is Mon.-Fri. 10pm-8am and Sat.-Sun. all day; to EU countries it's Mon.-Fri. 6pm-8am and Sat.-Sun. all day; to Australia and New Zealand call Mon.-Fri. 2-8pm and midnight-8am and Sat.-Sun. all day. There are no economy rates to the rest of the world. Long distance calls within the Republic are also cheapest Mon.-Fri. 6pm-8am and Sat.-Sun. all day.

Northern Ireland, Isle of Man, London

Operator: 100.
Directory inquiries: 192. **Other enquiries:** 191.
International operator: 155.
International directory assistance: 153.
International access code: 00.

The pay phones in Northern Ireland and the Isle of Man charge 10p for local calls. A series of harsh beeps warns you to insert more money when your time is up. The digital display ticks off your credit in 1p increments so you can watch your pence in suspense. Only unused coins are returned. You may use all remaining credit on a second call by pressing the "follow on call" button (often marked "FC"). Phones don't accept 1p, 2p, or 5p coins. The dial tone is a continuous purring sound; a repeated double-purr means the line is ringing. Northern **Phonecards,** in denominations of £2, £5, £10, and £20, are sold at post offices, newsagents, or John Menzies stationery shops. The £5 and higher denominations provide extra credit. Phone booths that take cards are labeled in green; coin booths are labeled in red. Many phone booths take cards in Belfast, Derry, and other developed areas; in the rural North, they're rare. In Belfast, card phones labelled in green and blue take phonecards, credit cards (Visa or Mastercard/Access), or change. Bright blue **Mercury** phones are scattered about the Belfast city center. They take cash or credit cards (Visa or Mastercard/Access). International calls are cheaper on these phones. Card phones are common on the **Isle of Man,** where Manx Telecom **Smart Cards** come in £2, £3, £5, and £10 denominations, with 10% extra credit free. These cards are available at post offices and newsagents (look for the Three Legs of Mann sticker in the window).

To make **international calls** from Northern Ireland or the Isle of Man, dial the **international access code (00);** the country code for where you're calling (see below); the area/city code (dropping the initial zero); then the local number. **Reduced rates** for most international calls from Northern Ireland and the Isle of Man apply Monday to Friday 8pm-8am, and weekends all day. Rates are highest Monday to Friday 3-5pm. The low-rate period to Australia and New Zealand is daily midnight-7am and 2:30pm-7:30pm. Rates to the Irish Republic go down Monday to Friday 6pm-8am and weekends.

Calling Card Calls

Another dialing option is to access an operator in the country you're calling—rates are often cheaper than those for direct calls, and service a bit speedier. Long-distance companies in your home country may have economical arrangements for their clients calling home from overseas. For example, AT&T provides "USA Direct" service from Britain and Ireland; by calling a toll-free number in Ireland or the UK you can access a U.S. operator who will help you place a collect call (US$5.75 surcharge) or charge it to your AT&T calling card (US$2.50 surcharge). Rates run about US$1.75-1.85 for the first minute plus about US$1 per additional minute. The people you are calling need not subscribe to AT&T service. If you are in the North, if no one else can help, and if you can find one, use a Mercury phone; it is generally cheaper to make a connection by Mercury than by British Telecom. To reach the long-distance companies listed below when calling from a Mercury phone, dial (0500) instead of (0800). The following services will allow you to place collect calls (expensive) or charge them to a calling card (less so):

	Republic of Ireland	Northern Ireland, Isle of Man, London
Australia Direct	1800 550 061	0800 890 061
British Telecom	1800 550 144	
Canada Direct	1800 555 001	0800 890 016
Ireland Direct		0800 890 353
New Zealand Direct	1800 799 964	0800 799 964
Telekom South Africa	1800 990 353	0800 990 044
AT&T USA Direct	1800 550 000	0800 890 011
MCI WorldPhone	1800 551 001	0800 890 222

COUNTRY CODES

Republic of Ireland: 353.
Northern Ireland: from the Republic 08; from other countries 44.
London & Isle of Man: 44.
USA and Canada: 1.
Australia: 61.
New Zealand: 64.

Ireland:
Republic of Ireland
and Northern Ireland

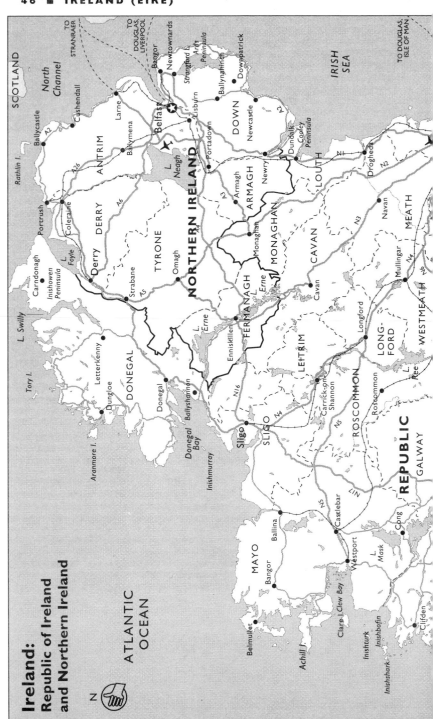

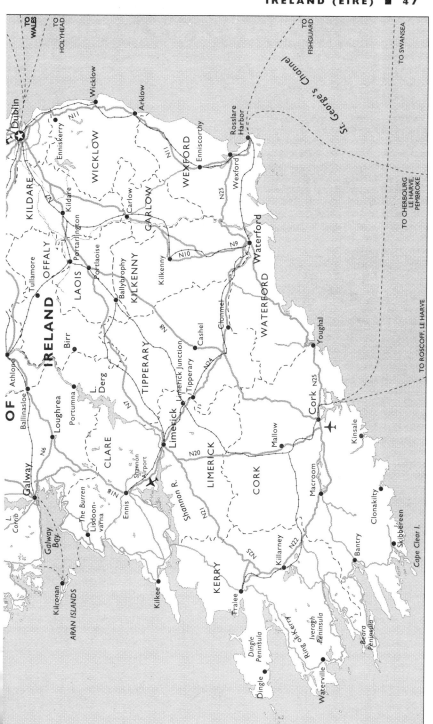

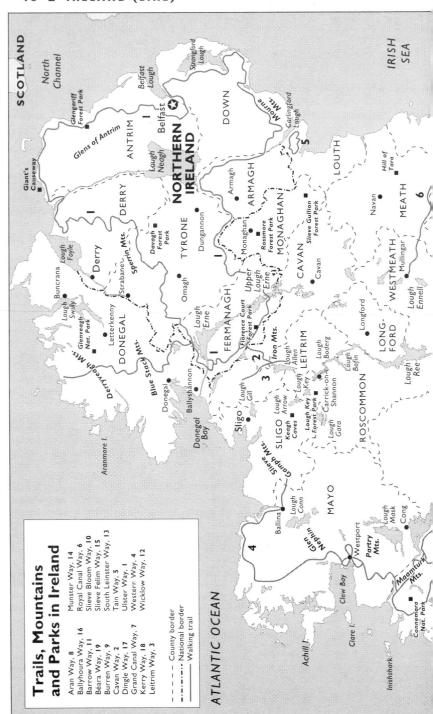

Trails, Mountains and Parks in Ireland

Aran Way, 8
Ballyhoura Way, 16
Barrow Way, 11
Béara Way, 19
Burren Way, 9
Cavan Way, 2
Dingle Way, 17
Grand Canal Way, 7
Kerry Way, 18
Leitrim Way, 3

Munster Way, 14
Royal Canal Way, 6
Slieve Bloom Way, 10
Slieve Felim Way, 15
South Leinster Way, 13
Tain Way, 5
Ulster Way, 1
Western Way, 4
Wicklow Way, 12

– – – County border
·–··–·· National border
·–··–·· Walking trail

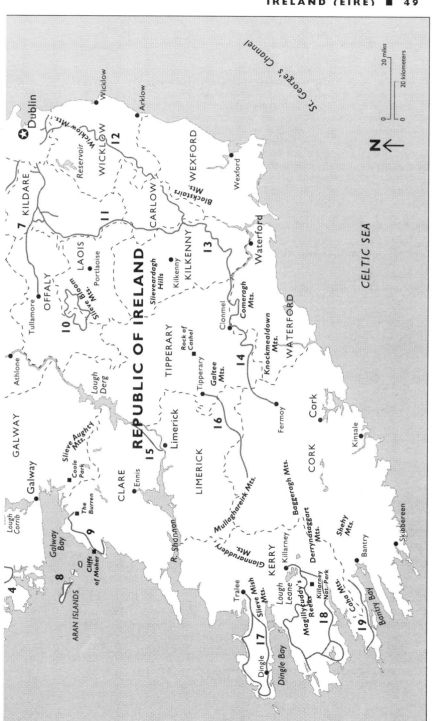

■ IRELAND (ÉIRE)

It can be hard to see Ireland through the mist of stereotypes that surrounds the island even on the clearest of days. Though much of the country is still rural and religious, there is also a developing urban culture with links to the Continent as well as to Great Britain. Traditional musicians roam Western pubs, while rockers try hard in Dublin, Cork, and Galway. The Irish language lives both in coastal villages and in national magazines, while literature in English—especially poetry—is in some ways healthier on this highly-educated island than it is elsewhere. Long hiking trails, roads, and cliff walks make a chain of windy, watery, spectacular scenery around the coast from Wexford all the way up to Inishowen, while Dublin diffuses its uniquely Irish modernity and sophistication to everything within its orbit.

■ ■ ■ HISTORY

Travel in this small nation will be more rewarding for those who take time to learn its history. *Let's Go* can provide only a very compressed account. Mark Tierney's *Modern Ireland* is a clear, brisk and comprehensive narrative covering the period from 1850 to 1968; *The Oxford History of Ireland* is a good source on earlier periods; and R.F. Foster's hefty tome *Modern Ireland: 1600-1972* is authoritative and interesting if you know a little already.

PRE-CHRISTIAN IRELAND (TO 350 AD)

The first major civilization in Ireland culminated in the **Neolithic** mound builders (4500-2500 BC). These mysterious, agrarian, and industrious people left Ireland dotted with cairns, dolmens, and passage-tombs. Beakers (perhaps for drinking mead) and stone circles (henges) of a religious/astronomical bent also arrived around 2500 BC with advances in copper working.

Bronze arrived in Ireland around 2000 BC, perhaps accompanied by Celtic invaders. The island's culture radically changed over the next 700 years. The megaliths and henges disappeared, more weapons and fortifications emerged, and a new warrior aristocracy took control and began furiously hurling weapons at each other and into rivers and bogs as part of a new weapons and water cult. The last two centuries of the Bronze Age (900-700 BC) saw an unprecedented flowering of Irish culture. Ireland in the **Irish Golden Age,** dominated by hierarchical warrior-nobles, held a central position on Atlantic trade routes stretching from Gibraltar to Sweden. Few artifacts remain from the **Irish Dark Age** (700-300 BC) which was followed by the **Celtic Iron Age.** The continental La Tène culture brought complex artwork (familiar from later, Christian texts such as the *Book of Kells*). The heroic attitudes so prominent in the *Táin* (see Legends & Folktales, p. 61) and other Irish epics, were based on events in this period.

The Roman armies who conquered England didn't think Ireland worth invading. The society they chose to leave alone was ethnically Celtic, spoke Old Irish, lived in small farming settlements, and organized itself under a loose hierarchy of regional chieftains and provincial kings. The most famous of these were the Ulaid of Ulster, chariot warriors who dominated the La Tène culture from their capital near Armagh. A complex, ultra-hierarchical legal code called the **Brehon Law** was administered by wandering judges. Bards either roamed the countryside or sought protection at a chieftain's court. Everyone else stayed in their home *túath* (tribe)— only the aristocracy and intelligentsia could travel freely.

EARLY CHRISTIANS AND VIKINGS (350-1200)

A series of hopeful missionaries Christianized Ireland in a patchwork way. The foremost of these missionaries, **St. Patrick,** was taken here as a boy slave. He escaped to England and returned (without church permission) to do God's work, landing probably in southeast Co. Down in the early 5th century. St. Patrick's exploits are legendary; not only are they retold, but many were invented later by churchmen in Armagh, who claimed that their local saint had gone on to convert the rest of the island to justify their claims to authority over the entire Irish Church.

As barbarians overran the Continent, monks fled to island safety. The enormous and hierarchical **monastic cities** of the 6th-8th centuries later earned Ireland the name, the "island of saints and scholars." From their bases in Armagh, Durrow, Derry, Kells, Clonmacnoise, Iona (in Scotland), and elsewhere, the monastics recorded the old epics, wrote long religious and legal poems in Old Irish and Latin, and illuminated gospels, of which the *Book of Durrow* and the *Book of Kells* now sit in exhibits at Trinity College. Monastic cities allied themselves with up-and-coming chieftains: Armagh owed its prominence in part to the Uí Néill (O'Neill) clan, which gradually spread from Meath into central Ulster.

Vikings raided every coastline in Northern Europe, making no exception for Ireland. Those who tired of pillaging founded larger towns in the South, such as Limerick, Waterford, and Dublin. Settled Vikings allied themselves with local chieftains, injected Scandinavian words into Irish, and left the southeast littered with Viking-derived place names, like Wexford *(Wæsfjord)*.

The first decade of the new millennium saw the rise of High King **Brian Ború** of the warlike Dál Cais clan of Clare, who challenged the Uí Néill clan for control of Ireland, and finally took Armagh in 1005. The Battle of Clontarf (1014) set Leinstermen and Vikings against Brian Ború's clan. The Dál Cais won, but Brian died in battle, leaving Ireland divided. Brian's successors continued to skirmish over who had the right to call himself "High King," while a church reorganization got rid of perceived corruption by getting rid of the monastic cities, creating a stricter hierarchy along Continental lines. Two High King claimants were new-style rulers **Rory O'Connor** and **Dermot MacMurrough.** Dermot made the mistake of requesting permission from King Henry II of England to ask English Norman nobles to help him reconquer Leinster. Henry assented, and **Richard Fitzgilbert de Clare (Strongbow)** was too willing to help. Strongbow and his Anglo-Normans arrived in 1169 and cut a bloody swath through south Leinster. Dermot died in 1171. Strongbow married Dermot's daughter, Aoife, and seemed about to proclaim an independent Norman kingdom in Ireland. Henry sent English troops to Waterford, which proved unneeded. By the time they arrived, Strongbow had sent a message to Henry, in which he affirmed his loyalty and offered to govern Leinster on England's behalf.

FEUDALISM (1200-1607)

Thus—in a flurry of miscommunications—began the English hold over Ireland. The next 200 years saw the carving up of Ireland into feudal counties and baronies, some held by the Norman-descended "Old English," some held by surviving Gaelic lords. The Old English areas had more towns and more trade: they were concentrated in Leinster, while Connacht and Ulster remained mostly Gaelic. The English parliament controlled **the Pale,** a fortified domain around Dublin. Old English and Irish fiefdoms used similar castles, ate similar foods, appreciated the same poets, and hired the same mercenaries. This cultural cross-pollination worried the Pale and the English crown, who sponsored the notorious 1366 **Statutes of Kilkenny.** These decrees banned English colonists (called "more Irish than the Irish themselves") from speaking Irish, wearing Irish styles of dress, or marrying the native Irish, and forbade the Irish from entering walled cities (like Derry). The statutes were harsh, but had little effect. Gaelic lords kept taking land from English ones. Feudal skirmishes and economic decline lasted until the rise of the "Geraldine Earls," two branches of the FitzGerald family who fought for control of south Leinster. The victors, the **Earls of Kildare,** were virtual rulers of Ireland from 1470 to 1534.

When Henry VIII broke with the Catholic Church, the Old English and the Gaelic lords stayed Catholic. The Old English wished to remain loyal both to Catholicism and to the Crown. **Thomas FitzGerald** of Kildare, Lord Offaly, sent a missive to

Henry VIII stating this position. Henry responded as if to an armed rebellion, and destroyed the power of Kildare. A newly-convened Dublin Parliament declared Henry head of the new **Church of Ireland,** whose membership remained minuscule. Feudal warfare continued for decades. A FitzGerald uprising in Munster in 1579 was harshly suppressed, planting the idea in English heads that Irish land had to be directly controlled by Protestants if it were to be considered safe and loyal. **Hugh O'Neill,** an Ulster earl, raised an army of thousands in open rebellion in the late 1590s. Gaelic lords supported him, the Old English lords were divided, and the King of Spain promised naval assistance, which arrived in Kinsale Harbour in 1601, then sat there with Spanish soldiers still on their boats as armies from England demolished O'Neill's forces. His power broken, O'Neill and his allies, the rest of the major Gaelic lords, fled Ireland in 1607 (the **Flight of the Earls).** The English used their military advantage to take control of the land and to parcel it out to Protestants.

PLANTATION & CROMWELL (1607-1688)

The English project of "planting" Ireland with Protestants and dispossessing Catholics of their land had most success in Ulster, where Scottish Presbyterians joined the expected mix of adventurers and ex-soldiers. But King Charles's representative in Ireland, Lord Wentworth, pursued a policy with few supporters outside England, closing off the South to the Scots and confiscating more land than there were Protestant takers. The dispossessed people revolted in Ulster of 1641, under a loose group of Gaelic-Irish leaders who were soon joined by **Owen Roe O'Neill,** who had returned from the Continent to lead the insurrection. The Catholic Church backed the rebels, who advanced south and in 1642 formed the **Confederation of Kilkenny,** an uneasy alliance of Church, Irish, and Old English lords. Some members of the last group considered themselves loyal to the King while rebelling against his treasonous viceroy. The arrival of the English Civil War complicated the tangle of interests: the English in Ireland were split between Parliamentarians and King's men, the Church envoy and Owen Roe O'Neill had different goals, and the Old English were still divided. Long negotiations between the Confederates and the King's envoy, Ormond, ended with **Oliver Cromwell's** victory in England and his arrival in Ireland at the head of a Puritan army.

Cromwell's tactics were unconventional: anything his army did not occupy it destroyed. Catholics were massacred; whole towns were razed. The Confederate army and Ormond's Royalists melted away. Entire tracts of land were confiscated and given to soldiers and other Protestant adventurers. The native Irish landowners could go "to hell or Connacht"—native Irish could own land only in remote and soil-poor provinces. In practice, the richest landowners found ways to stay, while the smaller farmers were uniformly displaced. The net result was that by 1660, the vast majority of land was owned, maintained, and policed by imported Protestants.

THE PROTESTANT ASCENDANCY (1688-1801)

Again, 30 years later, English political change meant Irish bloodshed. The closet-Catholic **James II,** driven from England by the "Glorious Revolution" of 1688, came to Ireland with his army, intending to conquer first this island, and then the other one. Jacobites (James's supporters) and Williamites (supporters of new, Protestant King William III) fought each other all over Ireland, with a siege in Derry ending in Williamite victory. The **Battle of the Boyne,** another Williamite win which drove James into exile again, led to the disastrous **Battle of Aughrim** and to the war's end in the **Treaty of Limerick,** which ambiguously promised Catholics civil rights that were never delivered. The unenforceable **Penal Laws** (enacted 1695-1704) limited Catholics economically and banned the public practice of their religion.

The newly-secure Anglo-Irish elite built their own culture in Dublin and the Pale with political parties, garden parties, talk, and architecture second only to London. The term "Ascendancy" was coined to describe a social elite whose distinction depended upon Anglicanism. Within this exclusive social structure, thinkers such as **Bishop George Berkeley** and **Edmund Burke** rose to prominence. **Jonathan Swift,**

Dean of St. Patrick's Cathedral, campaigned against dependency upon England by criticizing reliance upon imported manufacturing and tirelessly pamphleteering on behalf of both the Protestant Church and the rights of the Irish people. Swift was an early proponent of the limited nationalism developed by Irish Parliamentary "patriots" like **Henry Grattan** and Henry Flood, who wanted their Anglo-Irish state (under the King, and excluding Catholics) out from under the authority of the English Parliament. **James Gandon** built Dublin's best-known monuments, and Trinity College flourished as the quintessential institution of the Ascendancy. Meanwhile, displaced peasants filled Dublin's poorer quarters, creating horrific slums.

The Penal Laws made life difficult for priests, but did not prevent the growth of a Catholic, Gaelic-descended merchant class in places like Galway and Tralee. Early in the 18th century, Catholics exercised their religion furtively, using hidden, big, flat rocks (**Mass Rocks**) when altars were unavailable. Denied official education, Gaelic-Irish teens learned literature and religion in **hedge schools,** hidden assemblies whose teachers were often fugitive priests. The hedge schools later became a powerful symbol of the non-English, poor Irish 18th century. Typically, landlords were Anglo-Irish Protestants and their tenants Gaelic-Irish Catholics. The cultural divide made brutal rents and eviction policies easier for some landlords to adopt, and secret agrarian societies, like the **Defenders,** formed to punish the upper classes and defend peasant holdings.

The American and French Revolutions inspired others to ideas of independence. The **United Irishmen** began as a radical Ulster debating society. When war between England and Napoleon's France seemed likely, the United Irishmen were outlawed and reorganized themselves as a secret society, linking up with Defender cells. Their Protestant leader, **Theobald Wolfe Tone,** had hoped for a general uprising to create an independent, non-sectarian Ireland. His followers had less abstract ideals, and what erupted in May of 1798 was a bloody rising of peasants and priests, bloodiest in Co. Wexford, where **Vinegar Hill** near Enniscorthy saw the rebels' celebrated last stand. A month later, French troops under General Humbert arrived in Co. Mayo and managed to hold territory there for about a month. (French soldiers were held as prisoners of war and shipped home; Irish soldiers were executed.) By relaxing anti-Catholic laws, England had hoped to make Irish society less volatile. Wexford's rebels spooked the British into abolishing Irish "self-government" altogether. The 1801 **Act of Union** abolished the Dublin Parliament, creating "The United Kingdom of Great Britain and Ireland." Wolfe Tone committed suicide in captivity, while other United Irishmen escaped to France, building a secret network that would eventually link up with the Fenians.

O'CONNELL (1801–1841)

The gay mad whirl of Dublin vanished. The new government peppered the coastline with **Martello towers:** simple, defensible lookout towers designed to defend against another French invasion. The dispirited Anglo-Irish gentry collapsed into an accretion of landlords as agrarian violence continued. English and Continental travelers to Ireland were struck by its rural poverty.

Union meant Ireland could now send representatives to the British parliament, and the electoral reforms of the 1810s and 20s lowered the property qualifications to the point where many Irish Catholic small farmers had the vote. They voted for **Daniel O'Connell,** whose election to Parliament in 1829 essentially forced Westminster into repealing the remaining anti-Catholic laws, one of which would have barred him from taking his seat. O'Connell acquired the nickname "The Liberator." At first, his efforts within the Parliament unlocked more money to improve Irish trade, living conditions and health care, but when the unsympathetic Tories took power, O'Connell began to convene huge rallies in Ireland, showing popular support for his goal of Repealing the Act of Union. Romantic Nationalism, imported from Germany and Italy, pervaded the intellectual air, and some felt O'Connell had not gone far enough. "Young Ireland" poets and journalists, like **John Mitchel** (whom Yeats quoted: "Send war in our time, O Lord"), wanted independence, not repeal, and would work for it through violence. They tried a revolt in 1848. No one noticed or cared, since much of Ireland was starving.

FAMINE (1841-1870)

The only crop capable of providing enough nutrients per acre to support 19th century Ireland's population was the potato. From 1845-7 a new fungal disease made increasing amounts of the crops blackened and inedible. Famine ensued, exacerbated by English economic theorists, who advised the government not to tamper with free markets (that is, divert crops meant for export) even to feed the starving poor. Some individual landlords were known for their efforts on behalf of the displaced famine victims; others became known for their cruelty. Famine lasted roughly from 1847 to 1851; when the corpses were buried, rural Ireland had been decimated. Of the 1841 population of eight million, one million people had died. Another million had emigrated to Liverpool, London, Australia, and especially America, where a big Irish-American community would reward the most anti-British politicians or revolutionaries they could find. Depopulation in Connacht was even worse than those numbers implied, while the numbers of Dublin poor swelled.

What remained of the Irish peasantry was completely reorganized. The bottom layer of truly penniless farmers had been eliminated. Men married late, eldest sons inherited whole farms, and younger sons without special skills were as likely as not to leave Ireland. The Encumbered Estates Act began the fifty-year process of removing the landlord class. This was continued by a series of Land Acts and by the **Congested Districts Board**, converting Ireland by 1900 into a nation of conservative, religious, culturally uniform, Catholic smallholders (except for Dublin and northeast Ulster). The widening net of railroads—more extensive than those in use now—improved rural standards of living.

Young Ireland leftover **James Stephens** (not the poet) founded the **Irish Republican Brotherhood** or **IRB (the Fenians)** in 1858. The IRB, and its counterpart American organization, were secret societies aimed at the violent removal of the British. Fenian violence in 1867 made William Gladstone, among others, notice the Irish discontent. He became Britain's Prime Minister a year later under the slogan "Justice for Ireland." Justice consisted in disestablishing the minority Protestant Church of Ireland and battling over land reform. Combining agrarian thinkers, Fenians, and the Home Rule Party's new leader, **Charles Stewart Parnell**, the **Land League** of the 1870s pushed for reforms with O'Connell-style mass meetings.

Potatoes! The Story Behind the Starch

In the 19th century, potatoes literally sustained life for peasants on small and land-poor farms of west and southwest Ireland. A dietary staple, potatoes are the only single cheap food that can support life as a sole diet. Bulky and expensive to ship, with difficult storage requirements, potato crops were increasingly difficult to export or market. The rural peasants relied almost exclusively upon them for nourishment. On an average, an adult ate about 13 pounds of potatoes a day. Despite a dozen of smaller blights and crop failures in the earlier 19th century, the Great Famine of 1845 hit with harsh proportions. Called a "Malthusian apocalypse," the Famine dealt a devastating blow to rural communities dependent upon the crop, wiping out rural population and prompting waves of emigration. Plighted by an invisible fungus, *Phytophthora Infestans*, infected potatoes blackened and decayed, forming an inedible soft mass of potato ooze. One rural newspaper suggested: "Cut off diseased parts and steam or boil into a mash with bran and salt. When warm it is nourishing for pigs and cattle, but tainted potatoes cold are apt to disagree." Baking also purportedly made the potatoes edible. Baking them in primitive Irish cabins for 18-22 minutes at 180°F, once the foul smell oozed out and the potatoes turned white.

PARNELL & CULTURAL NATIONALISM (1870-1914)

Isaac Butt founded the Irish Home Rule Party in 1870. Its several dozen members defied him by adopting "obstructionist" tactics—making long dull speeches, introducing endless amendments, and generally trying to keep the rest of Parliament angry, bored, and ineffective until they saw fit to grant Ireland control of its own affairs. Parnell was a charismatic, Protestant aristocrat with an American mother and a hatred for everything English. Backed by Parnell's invigorated Irish party, Gladstone introduced a Home Rule Bill, which was defeated. Parnell, however, gained more esteem than ever when letters linking him to an infamous Fenian crime (the **Phoenix Park Murders**) turned out to be forgeries. In 1890 Captain O'Shea sued for divorce from his wife Katherine on the grounds that she was having an affair with Parnell. The allegations were proven true: the scandal split the Home Rulers, and all of Ireland, into Parnellites and anti-Parnellites in the same deep, acrimonious way as the Dreyfus affair split France.

While the parliamentary movement split, civil society grew. Many groups, and many journals, tried to revive or preserve what they took to be essential "Gaelic" culture—some were blatantly racist. The **Gaelic Athletic Association** tried to replace English sports with hurling, camogie, and Gaelic football and the **Gaelic League** spread the use of the Irish language. The IRB infiltrated these organizations, seeing them as means to a future mobilization. The quarrelsome **Arthur Griffith,** who advocated Irish abstention from British politics, called his tiny movement and little-read newspaper by the catchy name **Sinn Féin** ("shin fayn," which means "Ourselves Alone"). **James Connolly** led strikes in Belfast, while **James Larkin** spearheaded the enormous Dublin general strike of 1913, a short-term defeat which nevertheless established the existence of large trade unions in Ireland. From 1910-13 Northern Protestants, moved by anti-Catholic bigotry as well as by loyalty to Great Britain, had joined mass rallies, signed a Covenant, and organized themselves into the quasi-military **Ulster Volunteer Force (UVF)** to resist Home Rule. Nationalists led by Eoin MacNeill followed their example in 1913 by creating the **Irish Volunteers,** which the IRB correctly saw as a potential revolutionary force.

THE EASTER RISING (1914-1918)

In summer 1914, Irish Home Rule seemed imminent—the House of Commons had already passed a Home Rule Bill—and Ulster seemed ready to go up in flames. Neither happened. Instead, World War I intervened. Home Rule party leader **John Redmond,** also an Irish Volunteer leader, urged the Volunteers to enlist in the Army— 600,000 Irish people and 170,000 Volunteers did. An 11,000-member guard remained in Ireland, led officially by MacNéill, who knew nothing of the revolt the Volunteers' other leaders (all IRB members) were planning. If there was one architect of what followed, it was poet and schoolteacher **Padraig Pearse,** who won his co-conspirators over to an ideology of "blood sacrifice." If, Pearse believed, a small cabal of committed men might die violently and in public as martyrs for Ireland, then the entire nation would mobilize and win its independence.

Pearse was right. The rump Volunteers conducted a series of unarmed maneuvers and parades throughout 1915-6, leaving Dublin Castle convinced of their harmlessness, while the Volunteers' secret IRB leaders planned a shipment of German arms to be used in a nationwide revolt on Easter Sunday 1916. The arms arrived a day too early and were never picked up, and the British captured the man who was to meet the shipment, **Sir Roger Casement,** and hanged him. The week before Easter Sunday, those in the IRB faction who had planned the Rising showed MacNeill a forgery which purported to be a Dublin Castle order for the suppression of the Volunteers. At the same time, they told him about the arms shipments. Realizing he had been fooled for two years, but thinking that inaction risked the destruction of the Volunteers, MacNeill gave orders for the Easter Sunday mobilization. On Saturday he learned that the Castle order had been forged and that the arms had been captured, and inserted in the Sunday papers a plea ordering all Volunteers *not* to mobilize.

MacNeill and most IRB leaders had been thinking in terms of military success, which at this point was clearly impossible, but the Pearse cabal wanted blood sacrifice. On Sunday the Pearse group met and decided to have the uprising anyway on the following Monday, though it could only be organized in Dublin. Pearse, James Connolly, and others seized the General Post Office on O'Connell St. and a few other public buildings, read aloud a "Proclamation of the Republic of Ireland," and held out for only five days of firefights across downtown Dublin. Dubliners initially saw the Easter rebels as criminal annoyances, since their only tangible accomplishment was massive property damage.

The British martial-law administration in Dublin transformed popular opinion by turning **Kilmainham Gaol** into a center of martyrdom: over 10 days in May, 15 "ringleaders" received the death sentence, among them Pearse, Pearse's brother (executed basically for that reason), and James Connolly, who was shot while tied to a chair, since his wounds prevented him from standing. **Eamon de Valera** was spared because the British wrongly thought him an American citizen. By June the public mood was sympathetic to the martyrs—and increasingly anti-British. In 1917 the Volunteers were re-formed under master spy and IRB bigwig **Michael Collins** and Cathal Brugha. Under de Valera and Collins, the **Sinn Féin party,** which everyone thought had had some link to the Rising (which it hadn't), became the political voice of military Nationalism. When in 1918 the British tried to introduce a military draft in Ireland, the public turned overwhelmingly to Sinn Féin, repudiating the nonviolent plans of the Home Rule party.

INDEPENDENCE & CIVIL WAR (1919-1922)

Extremist Volunteers became known as the **Irish Republican Army (IRA),** which at first functioned as the military arm of the new Sinn Féin government. The **War of Independence** was fought between the new government and the British, who reinforced their inadequate police with the **Black and Tans,** demobilized soldiers whose nicknames came from their patched-together uniforms. The IRA's guerrillas were notorious for the atrocities they committed, but the Blacks and Tans were even more notorious. The British, under Prime Minister Lloyd George, understood that they had to get out of Ireland. Secret and hurried negotiations produced the **Anglo-Irish Treaty,** which recognized a 26-county state, since the North had by this time set up its own Protestant and Unionist government. The Treaty also imposed on Irish officials a tortuous oath of allegiance to the King of England, but not to the British government.

The Sinn Féin, the IRA, and the population split on whether to accept the Treaty. Collins said yes, de Valera said no. The representative parliament voted yes, and the capable Collins government began the business of setting up a nation, with treasury, tax collection, a foreign ministry, and an unarmed police force (the *Garda Siochana*). The part of the IRA that had opposed the treaty included **General Rory O'Connor,** who occupied the Four Courts in Dublin and took a pro-Treaty Army general hostage. Collins' government attacked the Four Courts. Two years of **civil war** followed, tearing up the countryside and dividing the population. The pro-Treaty government "won." A dwindling minority of anti-Treaty IRA officers fled deeper into Munster, but Collins was assassinated before the end of 1922.

THE DE VALERA ERA (1922-1960)

W.T. Cosgrave and his party Cumann na nGaedheal (which evolved into today's **Fine Gael** party) headed the first stable Free State administration until 1932. His government restored civil order, more or less, and brought **electrical power** to much of the West by damming the Shannon River. The anti-Treaty voters at first supported abstentionist Sinn Féin. Eamon de Valera broke with Sinn Féin and with the IRA in 1927, founding his own political party, **Fianna Fáil,** to participate in government and oppose the Treaty nonviolently. Fianna Fáil won the 1932 election, and de Valera held power for much of the next twenty years. His ideal Ireland was a nation of deeply Catholic small farmers. Fianna Fáil's economic program, accordingly, broke up the remaining large landholdings and imposed high tariffs. The tariffs produced a trade war with Britain, which battered the Irish economy until 1938. IRA hard-liners trickled out of jails in the early '30s and resumed violence, heckling Cumann na nGaedheal meetings. The **Blueshirts** formed around Eoin O'Duffy to oppose the IRA, and swiftly became a pseudo-Fascist organization with mass rallies and military-style discipline. By 1936 the Blueshirts had been suppressed and the IRA outlawed. The episode strengthened support for de Valera but tarnished the new state's public image.

In 1937 de Valera and the voters approved what is still the **Irish Constitution.** It begins "In the name of the most Holy Trinity," declares the state's name to be Éire, and establishes the legislative structure. The legislature consists of two chambers, a powerful lower house (the **Dáil**) and a less important upper house (the **Seanad** or Senate). **Taoiseach** (Prime Minister) and **Tánaiste** (Deputy Prime Minister) lead a Cabinet, while the **President** (Douglas Hyde was the first) is the ceremonial head of state. Article 2 says the state's authority extends over "the whole island of Ireland," but article 3 admits that it doesn't, "pending the reintegration of the national territory." The original Constitution referred to the special role of the **Catholic Church** in Ireland. Though Ireland remains overwhelmingly Catholic, the "special position" clause was deleted by a constitutional amendment in 1972.

Ireland was neutral during World War II. Some Irish (especially Northern Nationalists) supported the Nazis on the grounds that they, too, were fighting England, though far more Irish citizens (around 50,000) served in the British army. **"The Emergency,"** as the war was known, meant strict rationing of basic foodstuffs and severe censorship of newspapers and letters. Éire expressed its neutrality in such a way as to effectively assist the Allies; for example, downed American or British airmen were shipped north to Belfast, while downed German pilots were detained in P.O.W. camps. After the firebombing of Belfast in 1941, Northerners cheered the arrival of Dublin's fire brigade. De Valera demonstrated what he thought neutrality meant by delivering official condolences to the German ambassador on the death of Hitler—the only head of government in the world to do so.

A Fine Gael government under John Costello had the honor of officially proclaiming "the Republic of Ireland," but was plagued with problems. The balance, however, between the Church and its political role needed to be defined in almost uniformly Catholic Ireland. The Republic's Nationalism proved to be unabashedly Catholic. This position created many controversies between the new coalition government and the Church, one of which was the proposed reforms of the health care plan. **Dr. Noel Browne,** appointed as Minister of Health to the Dáil, proposed a "Mother and Child Scheme" to improve a health bill passed by the Fianna Fáil in 1947 and before Browne took office. Emphasizing a need to clarify the position of women in the health scheme—with obvious implications for women's place in other aspects of Irish society—Browne suggested three additions to the health bill, making it a state maternal plan operating without a means test: free maternity care to all mothers, child care up to the age of 16, and an education plan. Browne's plan was innovative, but was criticized for containing controversial aspects of a socialized medical care system, too reminiscent of the British National Health Service. Yet Browne did defend the program politically; it was indicted by the Catholic Church for running counter to Church teachings "in direct opposition to the rights of the family and of the individual and...liable to very great abuse."

The last de Valera government, in the late '50s, and its successor under **Sean Lemass** finally boosted the Irish economy by ditching protectionism in favor of attempts to attract foreign investment. In place of the skirmishes—verbal and military—over Constitutional issues that had dominated the '20s, Irish politics had become a contest between two ideologically similar parties who vied with each other to provide local benefits and constituent services.

RECENT HISTORY (1960-1993)

The 1960s brought Ireland into unprecedented contact with the outside world, which meant economic growth and a slowdown in emigration. Government concerned itself with developing the economy, improving education, and bolstering tourism. In 1967, the government introduced free secondary education; in 1968, it introduced free university education for those below a certain income level. Tourism became a major industry: Shannon Airport (a major employer) and Bord Fáilte, learning to market Ireland with finesse, grew big and professional. Ireland's entry into the **European Union** in 1972 was an occasion for rejoicing. In 1969, the Troubles in the North disturbed everyone but didn't alter the Republic's political or economic trends: while politicians sitll expressed nationalist sentiments, few Irish citizens cast votes based on Northern events (see History & Politics, p. 342).

Entering a European community and welcoming international visitors inevitably produced a more secular Ireland. **Garret FitzGerald** revamped Fine Gael partly under that banner. During the late '70s and early '80s, he and **Charlie Haughey**, Fianna Fáil's leader, alternated as Taoiseach, producing a bewildering set of economic programs and initiatives periodically interrupted by scandal and events in the North. The **Fianna Fáil** seemed to be caught up always in a more rhetorical Ireland than a pragmatic one. The party emphasized its conception of a United Ireland, but actually made little concrete progress to realistic improvements. Recession in the mid-'80s inspired a new wave of emigration as well as produced more complex economic problems for the party. FitzGerald had the honor of signing the 1985 **Anglo-Irish agreement,** which gave Éire an official (but not legal) role in Northern negotiations. EU membership and EU funds are as crucial as ever to Ireland's economy, and greater involvement in the Continent's culture and economy saves the Irish from having to choose between isolation and Great Britain. The Republic approved the Maastricht treaty by a 2:1 vote in June 1992.

CURRENT EVENTS

In September of 1993, Ireland elected a coalition between Fianna Fáil and the newer, smaller, leftist Labor Party. The latter's enormous success in the November '92 election surprised even the party leaders, who had not yet fielded a full slate of candidates. Newly-elected Taoiseach **Albert Reynolds** declared that stopping violence in Northern Ireland was his highest priority. Almost miraculously, Reynolds announced the August 1994 cease-fire agreement with Gerry Adams and the IRA. When faced with appointment for President of the High Court of Ireland arose, Reynolds ignored the party's coalition with the Labour Party, Tánaiste and Foreign Minister **Dick Spring** of the Labour Party, and their requests for a liberal appointee. When Reynolds appointed conservative Attorney General **Harry Whelehan** as President of the High Court on November 11, 1994, the Labour ministers walked out of the Cabinet Room. Whelehan had been heavily criticized for his lack of action in a case involving a pedophiliac priest, Father Brendan Smyth. Other scandals in the Church implicated the conservative government for protecting priests from legal charges of sexual misconduct and abuse. During the week following the appointment, Fine Gael, led by **John Bruton,** introduced a no-confidence motion against the government in Parliament. Reynolds attempted to defend his appointment of Whelehan, but was secretly pressuring him to resign. When this failed, Reynolds claimed he had been purposely misled by Whelehan. Dick Spring announced that he had discovered that Reynolds himself had withheld information regarding the Father Smyth case. Reynolds was forced to resign. The Labour Party formed a new coalition with Fine Gael, and John Bruton became Taoiseach in mid-December.

Social reform under the Labour Party and its coalition government continues to gather momentum. Although the **women's movement** has been historically tied to political activism, it has become a bona fide movement of its own. The surprise election in 1991 of President **Mary Robinson** marked a public turning point in the Republic's progressive liberalism by electing a forward-looking activist to a typically figurehead position. That liberalism seemed threatened when Ireland's High Court horrified many people in February, 1992 by ruling temporarily that a 14-year-old girl (called **X** in court papers) who said she had been raped could not leave the country to obtain an abortion. In 1983 voters had approved, by almost 2:1, a constitutional amendment endorsing "the right to life of the unborn." Since then, referendums have been passed to allow for "right to information" in Ireland (see Abortion: A Slow Separation of Church and State, p. 59). A 1986 referendum on **divorce** kept it illegal by a narrower margin, although it will soon be voted upon in another progressive referendum. Contraception has been legal for over a decade, although it is only available at licensed pharmacies.

The gay rights movement is slowly gaining legal ground. In 1980, the first legal challenge to existing laws against **homosexuality** was brought before the High Court. Lawyer Mary Robinson (who would be President) represented David Norris, a gay lecturer of Trinity College who challenged the essentially tacit laws against homosexuality. Losing in both the High Court and the Supreme Court, Robinson and Norris appealed to the European Court of Human Rights in Strasbourg. Ireland's government essentially claimed that since the laws were not enforced, there was really no need to change them. However, in 1988, the European court ordered Ireland to change its laws. Since then, the Irish government has stammered and done little, while promising to re-examine its laws. In June of 1993, the age of consent between gay men was lowered to 18 from that set in 1967 of 21 years old.

As more Irish young people spend time abroad and as more international travelers spend time here, the culture's conservatism slowly cracks. The short-term result is an enormous generation gap. Ireland continues to cringe under stress between a historically sectarian religious fervor and an increasingly secular (and European) human rights movement. Recent scandals in the Catholic Church betray public confidence, and after the Whelehan appointment and the Father Smyth case, the new government is particularly cautious. However, the hopes for solidarity of a politically and religiously unified Ireland seem to be forsaken.

Abortion: A Slow Separation of Church and State

In his latest encyclical, the *Evangelium Vitae*, Pope John Paul II made his strongest pronouncement against abortion. In November 1992, voters said no to legalizing abortion, but did approve a measure to provide "information." In March, Parliament voted to affirm the bill, but in May 1995, the abortion information law won final approval from the High Court making it legal for centers to give advice on where to go abroad for a safe clinic. Counselors can now arrange for counseling before and after the procedure, and for medical records of women to be forwarded to the medical physicians involved. In Ireland itself, terminating a pregnancy is still illegal, although over 5000 Irish women a year travel abroad to seek abortions. Many viewed the new law as anti-Catholic in sentiment, although this opinion has been modified in response to a rise in secular humanism and the improvement of human rights.

■■■ ARCHAEOLOGY

Since the Romans never tore up the countryside, more Stone, Bronze, and Iron Age remains are visible in Ireland than in most European countries. Ireland's real prehistoric past is as complicated as its legendary one, with many waves of invaders and settlers, distinguished by their styles of pottery, weaponry and burial.

Dolmens are T-shaped or table-shaped groups of three or more enormous stones, with one big flat one as the roof or tabletop. They might have been used for a number of things, but the best recent guess is that they're a kind of shrine. **Passage graves,** stone-roofed, ornamented underground hallways, lead past a series of rooms containing corpses or cinerary urns. **Stone circles** look like rings of pint-sized gravestones. They mark spots of religious importance, show up on top of passage graves, and sometimes track heavenly paths.

The late Bronze and Iron Age inhabitants built **ring forts** around their villages, made of stone or of earth. **Souterrains,** under-ground chambers, were used for storage or for hiding from marauders and were built both inside and outside the ring forts. A **clochán** is a mortarless beehive-shaped stone hut. Mysterious and smaller freestanding monuments are the **ogham** stones, property-marking obelisks which record, usually, a man's name and that of his father, in a non-Latin script made up of dots and slashes. These stones date from the early Christian period. The highest concentration of remains is probably in the Burren, Co. Clare, whose limestone moonscape kept later settlers out. The most famous, best-studied sites are the Hill of Tara and the passage graves of Brú na Bóinne, in Co. Meath.

Missionaries and monks brought new kinds of simple structures: the short *oratories* gave way to viking inspired **round towers,** dozens of which survive—a few now charge admission, but most are just sitting out there in fields and forests, in various states of disrepair. **High crosses** or **Celtic crosses,** stone crucifixes as tall as or taller than a human being, have elaborate carving on their sides which sometimes illustrates Bible stories or legends of saints.

■■■ THE IRISH LANGUAGE

Irish is a Celtic language closely related to Scottish Gaelic and Manx and more distantly to Breton and Welsh. Irish is spoken exclusively in only a few isolated parts of Ireland, called **gaeltachta.** Some prominent areas are on the Dingle Peninsula, on Cape Clear Island, in the Aran Islands, around the Ring in Co. Waterford, in Connemara in Co. Galway, and in patches of Co. Donegal. Even in the *gaeltacht,* all but a few elderly people *can* speak English—they'd just rather not. Ulster, Munster and Connacht each have dialects of Irish. Ulster and Donegal Irish, like Donegal's traditional music, has been altered by contact with Scotland and Scottish Gaelic. (Only foreigners call the Irish language "Gaelic.")

In 1600 there were as many Irish speakers worldwide as English ones: the English-speakers had more money and better armies; over the next two-and-a-half centuries more and more Irish speakers had to learn English to conduct their business. Their children and grandchildren grew up speaking English only. Mid-19th-century British efforts to introduce modern systematic schooling in rural areas resulted in teaching English. The Famine hit Irish-speaking areas hardest, and the number of Irish speakers continued to decline.

Founded by Douglas Hyde in 1893, the **Gaelic League** was created to inspire enthusiasm for Irish among people who didn't grow up speaking it or with an appreciation for it. The League aimed to spread the everyday use of Irish as part of a project to de-Anglicize the island, just as the Gaelic Athletic Association aimed to overpower English sports. Placing political import in cultural nationalism, Hyde believed that political revolution could wait and cultural change was the most important thing, though many Gaelic Leaguers disagreed. Gaboodles of adults whose first language was English took to the study of Irish: the League ballooned, becoming almost trendy. Writers who were bilingual from birth, like Flann O'Brien, enjoyed Douglas Hyde's famous mispronunciations. O'Brien's *An Béal Bocht* ("the poor mouth") satirized these new language enthusiasts.

The revolutionaries of 1916 and the new political leaders of the '20s were almost without exception excited about reinvigorating the Irish language, and tried to use government to strengthen the Irish language: the civil service exam included an Irish test, and there were some attempts to require all elementary schools to teach in it. The new policies were resented, and eventually the policies were overlooked. Preoccupied with economic development, the people and governments of the post-war Republic ignored Irish for years. The *gaeltachts* shrank, though an entire government department had the job of maintaining them.

The last fifteen years have seen more controversy over the fate of Irish. A book called **The Death of the Irish Language** used statistics and demographics to prove that there would soon be no Irish-speakers left. Its author and his methods were immediately attacked by people from other disciplines. While long-term trends in most *gaeltachts* still point to de-population and dispersal, the movement for more Irish-language media and educational requirements should help. There's already a Connemara-based Irish radio station, and agitation for Irish-language TV continues. Schoolchildren of all ages in the Republic are required to take extensive Irish courses, and all Irish universities require a knowledge of the language for admission. Voluntary elementary schools that teach all subjects in Irish are gaining some adherence in urban areas, both in the Republic and among Northern Catholics. A growing movement of **Irish-language summer camps** offer a heavy dose of culture and patriotism (see Study, p. 26). Among teens and twentysomethings, the language has gone from despised to trendy. You may hear younger English-speakers break into Irish briefly for privacy's sake. The Irish books everyone reads in Irish schools can be a relentlessly wistful, antiquated series of autobiographies, inconsistent with ideas about the modern Irish-literature community, which produces dozens of novels, poetry collections, and critical essays every year.

In Éire, all government documents must contain both Irish and English. Street signs, **bathrooms** ("Fir" means "men," "Mná" means "women"), and other public messages might show up in Irish alone (see Glossary).

■■■ LEGENDS & FOLKTALES

Scholars have been arguing for decades over which of Ireland's legends, folktales, and epics record actual events, and which ones are just good yarns. The vast repertoire includes fairy tales, war stories, revenge tales, and many, many tales of cattle raids. (Cattle was the ancient Celts' most valuable commodity—slaves and women were valued in cows.) Each story had many "authors" and passed orally down through many generations before someone (most likely a medieval monk) wrote it down. The books we have now often compile surviving bits and pieces of different versions. The Christian monks sometimes altered especially pagan details as they recorded the tales, or created tales of historical saints by appropriating stories of pre-Christian heroes or gods. The legends aren't incredibly accurate as a record of historical events, but they do give an exciting picture of ancient Irish culture: defensive about property (especially cows), warlike, sport-loving, and heavy-drinking.

The stories of the **Túatha de Danann** may well have developed to explain the burial mounds left behind by the pre-Celtic Stone Age culture. The Túatha de Danann are a race of beings somewhere between gods and men who live underground, emerging occasionally to aid their descendents, fight with the mortals, and seduce (or when all else fails, abduct) mortal beauties.

The long, famous **Book of Invasions** (*Leabhar Gabhála Éireann*) claims to be a historical record of the cultures and armies that have invaded Ireland, from Noah's daughter, Cesair, up to the Celts. The tales locate the Irish peoples' ancestry in the Greek islands. Nemed, a Scythian, became lost at sea after pursuing a mysterious tower of gold which rose out of the waves. After a year and a half of wandering, he and his ships landed in Ireland, until the next wave of settlers arrived...and the next, and the next, in wave upon wave of invasions (hence the name). Three clans of Nemed's descendants survived: one settled in the northern Greek islands, studied druidic arts, and became the Túatha de Danann. Another group was enslaved in Greece but eventually escaped, returned to Ireland as the **Fir Bolg,** and fought the Túatha de Danann. Each of the early waves of invaders had to deal with the fierce and mysterious indigenous people: the Formorians. These stories aren't the oldest Irish legends. They do, however, claim to have taken place first.

The earliest tales of the Túatha de Danann describe their lives as ordinary warriors and chieftains—only when fighting other races do their supernatural powers arise. Poets living in the chieftains' households invented the art of verse satire. These poets, and sometimes ordinary people, have the power to curse and lay a *geis,* a magic compulsion or prohibition. When the Túatha de Danann retreat to the Other

World, leaving Ireland to the Celts, the Celtic heroes acquire some of the old gods' customs and skills.

Several "cycles" or collections of tales narrate the entire life story of a hero. One of the largest is the **Ulster Cycle,** the adventures of King Conchobar of Ulster and his clan: the **Ulaid.** His archenemies are Queen Medbh of Connacht and her husband Ailill. Ulster and Connacht are continually raiding each other and exacting revenge. (In reality, the Laigin of Leinster were the arch-enemies of the Ulaid.) Ulster's champion is **Cú Chulainn** ("COO-hullin"), the king's nephew, whose adventures began at the age of five. Cú Chulainn falls in love with Emer, whose father disapproves. He sends Cú Chulainn to train with the Amazonian warrior Scathach, hoping that the Amazon will kill his potential son-in-law. Instead, she teaches him the arts of war and shows him how to wield the Gae Bolga, the sun-god's destructive spear.

The central tale of the Ulster Cycle is the **Táin bo Cuailnge** (Cattle Raid of Cooley). The definitive of the translation into English was done by Thomas Kinsella. In the tale, Medbh and Ailill's bedtime banter turns to comparing their possessions (as it often does), and Queen Medbh is alarmed to discover that her husband is richer than she is—by one bull. Determined to surpass him, she decides first to borrow, and then to steal, the most famous bull in the country: the Donn of Cooley. She assembles an army to capture the bull and invades Ulster when all the Ulster warriors are disabled. Only the 17-year-old Cú Chulainn is immune. He strikes a deal with the Queen, and fights her warriors in single combat one by one for an entire season. He beats them all, but the Connacht soldiers invade anyway and capture the Donn. The Ulstermen recover, invade Connacht, and recapture their bull. In the process the Donn escapes and kills Aillil's bull. On its triumphant return, however, the Ulster animal's heart bursts, and it dies.

Other cycles include **Tales of the Traditional Kings,** and the **Cycle of Finn, Ossian, and their Companions**. Finn McCool, or Fionn MacCumaill, leads a group of heroes that includes his son, Ossian, and his grandson, Oscar. In some stories, he is more or less a mercenary. In others, he is a king or a giant with supernatural powers and saves Ireland from monsters. In the **Pursuit of Diarmuid and Gráinne,** Finn has grown old and unattractive, but is betrothed to the young Gráinne. She meets him, has no wish to marry him, and decides to elope with Diarmuid, one of Finn's younger companions. Diarmuid refuses, but Gráinne lays a *geis* on him to flee with her. Whenever Finn catches up to the couple, Diarmuid deliberately kisses her, driving her betrothed into a jealous frenzy. After 16 years of pursuit, Finn seems willing to be reconciled: he invites Diarmuid to help hunt a famous wild boar. Having left his trusty spear at home, Diarmuid finds the creature impervious to all his weapons. The boar gores him. Diarmuid dies, and Gráinne marries Finn. Various forests

---

Irish Wakes: In the midst of life we are in death.

The purpose of a wake was to pray for the dead and to sympathize with the relatives of the dead person the night before the actual funeral. Besides mourning, the wake gave the family time to make sure the person was actually dead. For centuries in Europe, a wake was also a "waking" of the dead where the deceased would be given a final party in their honor. With the rise of Christianity, the wild wake died out on the continent but persisted in Ireland until the end of the last century. A typical Irish wake began solemnly enough as women would say prayers over the body and even keen in sorrow. But a wake was also a huge social occasion with games, storytelling, drinking, eating, and more drinking. Throughout the night, the deceased would be treated as if alive—a drink would be placed by their casket and card games were invented so the dead could be dealt a hand. As the evening wore on and the guests got drunker and rowdier, the corpse might be taken from the casket and danced with in turn. Wild wakes were not intended to show disrespect for the dead or the clergy (who strongly forbade them). Rather an Irish wake was a deeply-rooted custom of celebrating life in the house and keep death waiting at the doorstep.

and caves throughout Ireland claim to have been places at which Diarmuid and Gráinne rested during the pursuit.

Literati (including W.B. Yeats) have periodically compiled Ireland's **folktales.** Some stories involve the *sí* (sometimes spelled *sidhe*), who are residents of the Other World underground or undersea. Leprechauns are a late, degenerate version of the *sí*, who themselves are supposedly the disempowered remnants of the Túatha de Danann. Other stories are simply about ordinary folks and their pranks and troubles. For more myths and tales, try *Folktales of Ireland*, edited by Sean O'Sullivan; Yeats's *Fairy and Folk Tales of Ireland, Ancient Irish Tales,* edited by Cross and Slover, or The Irish Literary Tradition, by J.E.C. Williams and P.K.Ford.

■■■ LITERATURE

BEFORE 1600

In early Irish society, language was equal to action. What the bard (directly from the Irish *baird*) sang about battles, valor, and lineage was the only record a chieftain had by which to make decisions. Descending from druidic tradition, poetry and politics were so intertwined that the *fili*, trained poets, and *breatheamh,* judges of the Brehon Laws, were often the same people. The poet/patron relationship was fairly simple and symbiotic—the poet sang long praise poems about his lord and in return received his three meals and a roof above his head.

Aside from court reporting, the bard was a visionary and poet of nature. As with Caedom in the English tradition, the legends of Ireland's first poets were stories of inspiration and creation that bordered on shamanism. An example comes from the *Book of Invasions* when the mythical poet Ahairgain first sets foot in Ireland: "I am a plant of beauty, / I am a boar of valour, / I am a salmon in a pool, / I am a lake in a plain, / I am the strength of art." Out of this early nature poetry Ireland, with all its placenames, flora, and fauna, became a charged literary landscape.

Toward the end of the first millennium, the oral tradition of the bards gave some ground to the monastic pension for writing it all down. The monastic settlements of pre-Norman Ireland compiled enormous annals of myth, legend, and history. Divorced from the courts and their poetic economy, the monks created lasting monuments to old Irish prose. An established pagan tradition and the introduction of Christianity created a beautiful tension in Irish literature between recalling old bardic forms and incorporating a new worldview. This tension, it could be argued, exists in Irish literature to this day and is expressed fully by *Sweeney Astray*, the story of a pagan king who turns into a bird after being cursed by a monk. After the Norman incursions and the decline of the monasteries, feudal courts run by the Old English competed with Gaelic ones in hiring and maintaining traditional poets.

1600-1800

After the Battle of Kinsale, in 1601, a group of Irish writers, of whom **Geoffrey Keating** was the most famous, predicted an imminent collapse of Irish language and culture. Keating wrote simple and elegant prose as well as a comprehensive history of Ireland. Similar histories became a literary trend in the early 17th century. In this period poets drew heavily on the traditional trope of Ireland as a captive woman. **Daíbhí Ó Bruadhair's** "The Shipwreck" lamented the Treaty of Limerick. **Aogan Ó Rathaille** and **Eoghan Rua Ó Sulleabhain** were two more of the period's increasingly despairing, and impoverished, poets. Ireland in the early 1700s had enough bilingual readers to support "macaronic" works like **Seán Ó Neachtain's** *The Story of Eamon Cleary,* whose unusual, often punning effects depended on a mixture of English and Irish. Joyce would later copy such techniques. A majority of the works written in Irish at this time were dreary laments about the state of Ireland and its language and culture.

Jonathan Swift (1667-1745), for decades the Dean of St. Patrick's Cathedral in Dublin, towered above his Anglo-Irish contemporaries with his mix of moral indignation, bitterness, and wit. Besides his masterpiece, *Gulliver's Travels,* Swift wrote political pamphlets and essays decrying English exploitation (and defending the established, Protestant Church of Ireland). "A Modest Proposal" satirically suggested that the overpopulated and hungry native Irish sell their children as food. Even after his death, Swift's works dominated the Irish literary scene for the second half of the 18th century.

1800-1880

The Act of Union (1801) was a death knell for Irish writing, since the Anglo-Irish gentry could no longer afford to support the arts. Still, **Maria Edgeworth** *(Castle Rackrent)* and then **William Carleton** wrote realistic, still-read novels about the gentry and peasantry. Their books, along with those of **Gerald Griffin** and **John Banim,** made attempts at defining the nature of rural Irish society. The novels also tried to find a reason for the confusion of the present in the island's past. Many of these books depicted peasants plotting against their selfish and rich Irish masters up in the mansion. Almost as soon as these novelists died, however, their works were rejected by the **Young Ireland** movement, who decided that these earlier writers had given in, both in language and in form, to the demands of English writers and critics. The books were, essentially, too middle-class and perpetuated a false stereotype of Irish peasants.

Poets also found it difficult to sustain themselves through writing. While there was a proliferation of both poets and the literary journals for which they wrote, few could eke out a living in this line of work. (**William Allingham,** for example, wrote poetry and acted as a customs agent.) Even fewer poets became famous by writing. Indeed, there was something of a necessary dichotomy in the poetic life of Ireland at this time. Many poets, in order to survive, joined groups which espoused certain ideologies. They were thereby able to publish their work in journals, but had to conform their own views and objectives to fit those of the group. Others remained distinct from any grouping but thereby gave up any chances of fame.

Much of the poetry of the first half of the century wanted to discover an organic relationship between politics, culture, and language. A reconciliation between the English and the Irish was also attempted. Through original writings and especially through frequent translations, three main attitudes toward poetry and language evolved in Ireland. The first was that which tried to soften nationalist sentiment with a Victorian respectability—**Thomas Moore** wrote popular lyrics along these lines. Another vein of poetry adopted a militant attitude, propounding outright rebellion against English language, culture, and politics in order to maintain the Irish versions of the same. Poets of this type often wrote for *The Nation,* a Dublin-based periodical. One of the main contributors to the journal was **James Clarence Mangan,** a poet and prolific translator. Unfortunately, his knowledge of Irish was far from perfect. As a result, his translations were often rendered quite creatively. He was, in this respect, stuck between two languages, unable to find a compromise and a common meaning between the two. A third group of poets tried to find a middle way by merging English words and an Irish spirit or essence. **Samuel Ferguson,** a Belfast unionist, wrote with exactly this idea in mind. His poetry and especially his translations, both full of energy, attempted to link together Irish and Catholic with English and Protestant into a single, shared identity.

The poets of this pre-Famine period tried to portray, largely through translation, an Ireland of the old poems that no longer really existed. The matter was complicated by the fact that they were writing for two audiences with two sets of demands, one aesthetic and one political. The old image of Ireland (found in many translations), was one of fairies and myths which satisfied the former. A vision of Ireland as a rebellious colony gratified the latter audience. The lasting accomplishment of this group of mostly obscure poets was to reconcile the conflicting demands of two languages and two sets of images. By the end of the Famine, these writers were able to combine the mythical and revolutionary images of Ireland into a heroic image (which combined political and cultural aspects into one vision), pitted against the modern, urban, industrial world of England. In the end, an opposition to England was the main theme.

The Famine, a demoralizing event which left people feeling totally abandoned, greatly affected approaches to literature in Ireland. Two Irish economists, in analyzing the tragedy, made major advances in political economy. **Isaac Butt** convinced others of the falsity of a Union which claimed political unity but refused unified economic aid. **John Elliot Cairnes** exploded the idea of *laissez faire,* which he claimed was only applicable to those countries whose economic organization and division of land imitated those in England.

The "Young Ireland" group, which originally coalesced around **Thomas Davis,** drifted farther towards the left after the Famine. Davis, something of an idealist, wanted to reform a unified Irish cultural identity, one which would substantially rely on the Irish language. But he naively failed to realize that Irish culture was intimately related to both politics and economy. His theories, in their economic ignorance, seemed to ignore the centrality of the Famine. This blindness tended to alienate both readers and authors.

Following Davis's death in 1842, **Lalor** transformed the Young Ireland movement, making land the central question to which linguistic concerns were subsidiary. **Mitchel** reacted even more strongly and advocated violent activity. The Famine induced Irish authors to put economic questions ahead of political affairs, and political affairs ahead of cultural concerns. But the poems they wrote, so blatantly political, were rather shallow and obvious, suitable for the outrage which immediately followed the Famine. It was this trend in the artistic quality of writing which the future Irish Revival had to reverse.

The late-19th century also saw the removal of a number of talented authors to England. Among other reasons, many emigrated because it was easier to make a living by writing in London than in Ireland. Dublin-born **Oscar Wilde** moved to London and set up as a cultivated aesthete to write one novel and several sparklingly witty plays, including *The Importance of Being Earnest.* Prolific playwright **George**

Maria Edgeworth (1768-1849)

Maria Edgeworth (1768-1849) was the major figure in the Irish literary world after Swift and before Shaw and Yeats. A contemporary of Jane Austen, Edgeworth is, sadly, read and discussed less often than any of her peers. Edgeworth's early didactic works were greatly influenced by her father's rational and utilitarian way of thinking. Her later works, which depicted regional life, were largely determined by his decision to relocate to the family land in Ireland. This move revealed the life of provincial, Irish peasants to Maria. Her most famous and lasting work, published anonymously in 1800, was titled *Castle Rackrent, An Hibernian Tale: Taken from the Fact, and from the Manners of the Irish Squires, Before the Year 1782.* The central concern was the responsibility of landowners toward their tenants. The inspiration, clearly, came from living in rural Edgeworthstown, Co. Longford.

Much of Edgeworth's extensive body of mostly historical fiction was typical of its age. She began her career with ideas about the connection between moral worth and social position. Some of her stories reveal a subtle romantic preoccupation with the achievement of personal integrity through solitude. But her innovations and the anomalies in her writing add a twist to the writings of an author otherwise representative of her era. Edgeworth was a woman in the midst of men. She, with her family, moved to Ireland when most people went the other way (even her literature posits a westward flight). She also realized, as few at this time did, that there existed a British social reality, not entirely separable into England and Ireland. Finally, Maria Edgeworth paved the way for future literary journals by raising the question of a compromise between the modern and the antiquarian. This legacy, more than any other, substantially determined the concerns of later writers, including those of the Revival.

Bernard Shaw (1856-1950) was also born in Dublin but moved to London in 1876 where he became an active socialist. Never forgetting his Irish heritage, Shaw even used it in the service of socialist ideals, as in *John Bull's Other Island*, which depicts the increasing hardships of the Irish peasant laborer, the result of harsh Land Acts. Shaw himself identified much of his writing as Irish, in form if not always in content: "When I say I am an Irishman I mean that my language is the English of Swift and not the unspeakable drivel of the mid-19th century newspapers." Shaw won the Nobel Prize for Literature in 1925 for a body of work which includes *Arms and the Man, Candida, Man and Superman,* and *Pygmalion*.

1880-1939

Following on the heels of these literary movements and counter-movements, a vigorous and enduring effort, known today as the **Irish Literary Revival,** took over the scene. The Irish poetic and dramatic traditions were reconceived. For almost an entire century, Irish writers' central concern had been a reaction, either cultural or political, against England. Only now did Irish literature, as art and as expression, become the real work of Irish authors. And only now did an affirmation of Ireland, rather than a negation of England, become a matter of concern. The new literary theory stated that the essential spiritual life of a country existed in its culture. It therefore became the task of literature to discover the real Ireland in itself (not always in reference to England), whether Gaelic or Anglicized (or both) in form.

Interest in the Irish language suddenly revived. After the Famine, many Irish men and women reacted negatively to any attempts to preserve the Irish language. The original members of the Young Ireland group had also supported a revival of the Irish language, but their economic ignorance forced people to equate the Irish language with economic failure and Famine. At the turn of the century, Irish literature, after declining for almost a century, began to recover ground. **Peig Sayers'** *Peig*, a mournful book about growing up on the Blaskets, was written during the revival and is still read in high schools today. This memoir, like others written by Blasket Islanders, mourns the decline of Gaelic culture and language.

The Irish Literary Revival began with attempts to record peasant stories. By means of the old tales and traditions, a new elite would create a distinctively Irish literature in English. The writers of the Revival considered their own works to be chapters in a book of Irish identity—it was just such "Irishness" that literature was supposed to reveal. Affected by the revivalists, and by the Sligo of his boyhood, **William Butler Yeats's** (1865-1939) early poems create a dreamily rural Ireland of loss, longing, and legend. His early work from *Crossways* (1889) to *In the Seven Woods* (1904), won Yeats worldwide fame and the Nobel Prize.

Yeats's lifelong friend and colleague, **Lady Augusta Gregory** (1852-1932), wrote forty plays as well as a number of translations, poems, and essays. She began her career by collecting the folktales and legends of Galway. Soon, the Abbey Theatre Movement became her main concern. While helping other playwrights revise, Gregory discovered her own skill as a writer of dialogue. Her comedies, including *Spreading the News* and *The Rising of the Moon*, were most successful. A distinctive combination of reality and myth-making (of personal dreams and community pressure) clearly marks Gregory's work. By the end of the 19th century, Gregory was a staunch nationalist and spent many of her last years defending the codicil in her son's will which left his collection of art to Ireland.

The **Abbey Theatre Movement** was spearheaded by Yeats and Lady Gregory. The main purpose was "to build up a Celtic and Irish school of dramatic literature," as the prospectus stated. But conflict almost immediately arose between various contributors. Was this new body of drama to be written in verse or prose and in the realistic or the fantastic and heroic mode? Another difficulty arose in the choice of language. Ideally, the plays would be written in Irish, but practically they needed to be written in English. A sort of compromise was found in the work of John Millington Synge, who wrote English plays that were perfectly Irish in essence. Padraic

Colum wrote in plainer language about more timely issues and emotions. Finally, Sean O'Casey achieved a synthesis of urban realism and heroic poetry.

Playwrights in general, many of whose plays were put on at the Abbey Theatre, resonated with their audiences by writing with an ear for English as it is spoken by people who grew up hearing Irish. **John Millington Synge** (1871-1909) spent much of his early years traveling and living in Paris. He was a multi-faceted man who, before embarking on a literary career, "wished to be at once Shakespeare, Beethoven, and Darwin." During one of his many stays in Ireland, Synge met Yeats, who advised that he look for inspiration on the Aran Islands. This advice, which Synge followed in 1898, led him to write *The Aran Islands*, a documentary of life on the islands. His experiences also gave him the subject matter for writing his black comedy *The Playboy of the Western World*, which destroyed the pastoralist myth about Irish peasantry and humorously portrayed a rural society divided into classes. The play's first production instigated riots. **Sean O'Casey,** (1880-1964) a later playwright who also knew how to use Irish-English, created a similar uproar with *The Plough and Stars*. The play depicted the Easter Rebellion, and nationalism, in an unflattering light and sentimentalized the urban poor. This and two former plays were produced at the Abbey Theatre. O'Casey eventually emigrated to England.

The myth of the timeless, classless country peasant came under attack from these playwrights who tried to record the reality of rural life and, by a different tactic, from **James Joyce** (1882-1941). This most famous of Irish authors was born and educated in Dublin, but spent much of his time after 1904 on the continent. One of his earlier works, *A Portrait of the Artist as a Young Man,* comes nearest to autobiography. *Dubliners,* a collection of linked short stories which results in a novelesque work, is his most accessible writing. Most of the stories describe movement out of the city as being liberating, in contrast to most urban literature. Finding the short story to be an oppressive form, Joyce abandoned it for the novel. *Ulysses,* Joyce's revolutionary novel, appeared in 1922. It minutely chronicles one day in the life of the antihero, Leopold Bloom, a middle class man living his life in a stagnating Dublin. Its structure follows that of Homer's *Odyssey*—hence the title. Joyce's last book, *Finnegans Wake,* is so dependent on allusions and puns that some people find it unreadable: those who can make sense of it often see it as his masterpiece.

The turbulence of 1914, 1916, and after enabled Yeats to recreate himself as a poet of difficulty, power, and violence. "Easter 1916" described the sudden transformation the Easter rebels brought to the Irish national self-image: "All changed, changed utterly/ A terrible beauty is born." With his friends and his longtime unrequited love Maud Gonne caught up in rebel activity, Yeats was finally forced into marriage with George Hyde-Lees. Yeats then bought and renovated a stone tower, Thoor Ballylee. The tower became a symbol in an idiosyncratic and mystical system which appears in his last two decades of poems. From *The Tower* (1928) to the posthumous *Last Poems* (1939) Yeats was at his of peak of verbal invention.

Yeats ignored everyday life and suffering in Ireland in pursuit of a deeper vision. The Northern Protestant poet **Louis MacNeice** (1907-1963) compensated with a lyric persona both humane and skeptical. He took no part in the sectarian politics. His "Valediction" is the best attack ever on an idealized version of Ireland. Patrick Kavanaugh also debunked a mythical Ireland in poems such as "The Great Hunger." Other poets of the early 20th century wrote works in which the technical elegance was the redeeming feature. They made attempts to combine the popular ballad with aesthetics (the archaic and the modern), an effort which failed largely because there was no appropriate language. Poets like **Patrick Pearse, Padraic Colum, Seamus O'Sullivan,** and **Thomas MacDonagh** tried their hand at various language and forms, but none seemed totally suitable for the uniquely Irish dilemma between past and present, Gaelic and English.

The year 1929 brought the **Censorship of Publications Act,** which severely restricted the development of Irish literature. This Act was part of an Irish Ireland movement, provincial and Catholic in its beliefs. After the heroism of the Civil War and Republicanism—one which was reflected in Yeats's poetry—Ireland had suddenly become conservative. The poet **AE** fought against such repression and limitation. In the journal which he edited, AE made efforts to retain the pre-Civil War heroism and idealism. He saw the prevailing conservative and Catholic social climate as one of reaction to the romanticism that had run rampant before the Civil War. But rather than giving in to such provincialism, he envisioned (and propounded) a broad cultural synthesis which would include various cultures and religions, not just those which Ireland's new government accepted.

1939-THE PRESENT

Samuel Beckett, a Trinity graduate who fled Ireland for Paris and never came back, is generally thought of as the last product of Irish modernism. His three novels *(Molloy, Malone Dies,* and *The Unnameable),* world-famous plays *(Waiting for Godot, Endgame),* and bleak prose poems certainly look like the end of something. They distinctly convey a deathly pessimism about language, society, and life. Unsurprisingly, Beckett's influence has been felt more outside Ireland than in it. Hugh Kenner's confrontational, insightful, anecdote-packed *A Colder Eye* covers Irish modernism from early Yeats to O'Brien and Beckett.

Reviving the notion, first developed by AE, of the writer as social critic, **Seán O'Faoláin** founded *The Bell* in 1940. O'Faoláin insisted that his journal would espouse no restrictive ideology. In the artistic vein of the time, which AE has predicted, the *Bell*'s editor pleaded for "honesty" and "realism." These principles of writing were supposed to open up Ireland to her complete and complex identity. O'Faoláin wanted to search for Ireland wherever he could, not just in a Catholic and Gaelic nationalism. According to his own principles, though O'Faoláin accepted the predominant provincialism which existed and argued against it.

At the same time that O'Faoláin was, as he felt, wasting his energies on journalistic writing, the short story was becoming a popular, successful, and sophisticated art form in Ireland. More palatable and often more comprehensible than the contemporary works of Beckett, these stories frequently took the common lives of Irish men and women as their theme. But rather than buying into a narrow nationalism, these stories depicted individual liberty and energy as victims of oppressive provincialism. In so many of these stories, strict morality governs and destroys creativity. And while some kind of epiphany usually defines the climax, action does not necessarily follow such a revelation of suppressed emotions or oppressive environment and atmosphere. **Frank O'Connor, Bernard McLaverty, Sean O'Faolain,** and **Edna O'Brien** (one of few female Irish writers, she wrote a bit after the others) all achieved some overseas recognition for their short stories. Refusing to imitate the realism and lyricism typical of most short stories, **Flann O'Brien** gained an international reputation that has lasted to this day. Instead of resorting to realism, O'Brien lets loose an unrestricted literary inventiveness. Unlike other writers of the time, he set almost all his work in Dublin. O'Brien also tried to provide a comic answer to Joyce and to set himself in opposition to a cultural and linguistic lethargy: *At Swim-Two-Birds* is a book-length prank in which an author's characters conspire to keep the author asleep so that the characters can do what they please.

Poets at this time found it impossible to gain any recognition. Most became introverts and happily succumbed to provincialism. One of the rare exceptions, **Padraic Fallon** (1905-1974), continued to combine political and religious topics in his poetry but avoided the plague of nationalism. **Charles Donnelly** also resisted the regionalism of this time. He conceived of the existence of a common humanity, an idea which became the inspiration in his poetry. But while many poets, like Louis MacNiece, condemned Ireland's neutralism in World War II as cowardice, others remained entirely nationalist and unconcerned with anything but Ireland itself.

Stimulated by O'Brien, the Irish novel developed. **Brian Moore's** *The Emperor of Ice Cream* is an appealing coming-of-age story set in wartime Belfast, and **Roddy Doyle** wrote the trilogy which led to the films *The Commitments* and *The Snapper.*

After 1950, however, Irish poetry suddenly began to free itself from a stifling provincialism. This movement involved an increased contact with the continent: playwright **Brendan Behan** and poet **John Montague** both went to Paris. On the other hand, Irish writing was still unsure of its place in the world, a situation which was signaled by the increased obsession with the father-son relationship (which questioned the relationship of past to present and future). Living in the backwash of the heroic times of the Revival and the Civil War, these new Irish poets had to question their inheritance. And the answer that seemed to present itself was a new version of Ireland that was a parody of the old one.

But the same old problems persisted. Authors were still trying to bridge the gap between Gaelic and Anglo-Irish themes and languages. As an affirmation of the former, Irish language poetry revived. **Michael Hartnett** began to write solely in Irish. **Nuala ní Dhomhnaill** is a first-rate living poet whose public readings are generally bilingual. In contrast to the pessimism non-speakers associate with the Irish language, her work brings refrigerators, feminism, and smart bombs into proximity with the *Sí*. Ní Dhomhnaill is published outside Ireland in English translations (look for Paul Muldoon's). By contrast, the younger poet **Biddy Jenkinson** refuses to authorize any translation of her work into English, though it has been rendered into French. The preeminent Irish-language novel is **Maírtín Ó Cadhain's** *Cré na Cille* (Churchyard Clay), which is composed of dialogue between corpses in a graveyard.

In contrast, others, like **Maírtín Ó Direáin** (a modernist writer) and **Seán Ó Riordain,** tried to incorporate the English modes into the Irish tradition. **Derek Mahon** saw the poet as an anthropologist (rather than a student of Gaelic inheritance or of Republicanism). He was interested in the common elements that humans of all cultures shared. Most contemporary poetry is intensely private. Though some poets (**Padraid Fiacc** and **Tom Paulin**) are directly political and almost propagandistic, most treat the issue from a distance, from a mundane, every-day perspective. **Frank Ornsby,** for example, writes poetry that celebrates the rituals of domestic life. Political conflict plays no part in these pieces.

Born in rural Co. Derry, **Seamus Heaney** is the most prominent living Irish poet. His fourth book, *North* (1975), tackled the Troubles head-on. Concentrating on bogs and earth, Heaney wrote in an anti-pastoral mode. He was part of the **Field Day movement,** led by Derry poet and critic **Seamus Deane,** which produced what was billed as the definitive anthology of Irish writing (though it's since come under heavy fire for its relative lack of women writers). Heaney's contemporary, who also writes in a non-political vein, is **Paul Muldoon,** whose tools are a corrosive self-skepticism, supple couplets, and the world's best ear for weird rhymes. Influenced by MacNeice and Auden, Muldoon reflects the cosmopolitan consciousness Ireland's new wave of high cultural aspirations. Nonetheless, his rhymes and forms show the influence of the Irish language. **Ciaran Carson** uses Muldoon-like ironies in long-lined poems that tell stories about the working-class culture of Belfast and the rural North. Women's issues receive the same neglect that political conflict does. **Eavan Boland** is one of the few modern Irish poets who has even attempted to capture the experience of middle-class, suburban women. **Medbh McGuckian** is another modern and successful female Irish author, one of few.

The Field Day Movement also gave its name to a successful theater company. Native playwrights include politically-conscious **Frank McGuinness,** and **Brian Friel,** whose *Dancing at Lughnasa* was a Broadway hit. Important critics and essayists are **Conor Cruise O'Brien,** a former diplomat who writes about history, literature, politics—hell, everything. **Denis Donoghue,** whose *We Irish* is a vigorous, skeptical lit-crit grab-bag; and the provocative **Declan Kiberd,** for whom Ireland is a "postcolonial" society more like India than like England.

■■■ MUSIC & FILM

Irish traditional music is alive and well. So is Irish folk music—the two can mean different things: "folk music" often means singing with acoustic guitar accompaniment, whether it's Irish (the Clancy Brothers, Christy Moore, Luka Bloom) or not (Joni Mitchell). "Traditional music" or "trad," on the other hand, means the centu-

MUSIC & FILM

ries-old array of dance rhythms, cyclic melodics, and embellishments which has passed down from generation to generation of traditional musicians. It can be written down, but that's not its primary means of transmission. Indeed, a traditional musician's training consists largely of listening and imitating others. The tunes and forms (hornpipe, reel, etc.) are the skeletons around which the players in a trad session build the music: the same tune will produce a different result every session.

TRADITIONAL MUSIC

Irish traditional music is encountered in mainly two forms. It is often heard as impromptu sessions in pubs in the evenings or, on the other hand, can be found in recordings, which are becoming more numerous. Well-known recording artist include Altan, De Danann, and the Chieftains. Trad music is also, though rarely, performed at concerts. *Let's Go* lists many pubs with regular trad sessions, but you'll have to follow your own ears to find superior playing. Pubs in Co. Clare, Kerry, Galway, and Sligo should be especially strong. The town of Doolin, Co. Clare is over-hyped. If you want a guarantee that you'll hear OK traditional music, find a *fleadh*. These are big gatherings of trad musicians whose officially scheduled sessions often spill over into nearby pubs. **Comhaltas Ceoltóirí Éireann**, the national traditional music association, organizes *fleadhs*. Write or call them at 32 Belgrave Sq., Monkstown, Co. Dublin (tel. (01) 280 0295).

For centuries the most common way to "listen" to trad music was to dance to it. This isn't true anymore. Spontaneous traditional dancing is fading fast, replaced by formal, rigid competitions where traditional dancers are graded, like gymnasts. *Céilís*, where attendants participate in traditional Irish set-dancing, do still take place occasionally in many Irish towns, but are planned in advance: bands are hired, a venue is found, dates are set.

The instruments with which Irish trad music is most frequently played are the fiddle, the simple flute, the concertina or hand-held accordion, the tin whistle, and the *uilleann* pipes ("elbow pipes"). These pipes are similar to bagpipes, but pumped with a bellows held under the arm and more melodic than the Scottish instrument. To play traditional music well requires tremendous practice and skill, though the techniques have little in common with those of European classical music: it's often said that training in one is an impediment to playing the other. The harp, Ireland's national symbol, is rarely encountered in live trad music now, since it's big and hard to lug around. It is, however, still frequently heard in recordings.

The *bodhrán*, a hand-held Goldstein drum, wasn't seen as a legitimate instrument until the '60s, when the influential Sean Ó Riada of the Chieftains introduced it in an effort to drive rock and jazz drumming out. Today, the *bodhrán* has skillful specialists. The *Bodharán* is played either with both ends of a stick or with the bare hand. To observers, it looks easy, but playing it well takes practice and patience.

Purists get in heated arguments about what constitutes "traditional" singing: a style of unaccompanied vocals called *sean-nós* ("old-time") is more talked about than heard, though everyone says it sounds great. This style of nasal singing descends from the ancient practice of keening. It requires the vocalist to sing each verse of a song differently, either by using embellishments or varied techniques or different sounds, like clicks. Sessions in pubs will sometimes alternate fast-paced traditional instrumental music with guitar- or mandolin-accompanied folk songs.

FOLK & ROCK MUSIC

In Ireland there is surprisingly little distinction between music types—above all a fine musician is a fine musician and uses material from a variety of sources. This cross-pollination produces fabulous live musics and also a number of successful folk musicians who draw on traditional elements. Chief among this group, the inspiring and hugely popular **Christy Moore** has been called the Bob Dylan of Ireland. The ballads and anthems that Moore (among others) made popular now form something of a pub-singalong canon here—hardly a late-night session goes by without someone's moving rendition of "Ride On," "City of Chicago," or the lament "Irish Ways and Irish Laws." Other popular groups include Christy's old bands, **Moving Hearts** and **Planxty.**

This lack of distinction between different genre has had mixed results. **Van Morrison's** inspirations included American soul and blues. Submerging them into Celtic "soul," he managed to make them his own. **Horslips** became hugely popular in the '70s by trying to merge trad and rock forms, but wound up shuffling uneasily between the two. **Thin Lizzy** tried to Gaelicize early heavy metal, while a succession of groups, like Clannad, started out trad and slowly became bad rockers. The **Saw Doctors** and **Lir** live life on the edge of the rock/trad duality. Maybe the best hybridizers were the **Pogues,** London-based Irishmen whose famously drunken, punk-damaged folk songs won a wide international audience. New York-based Irish emigres **The Black 47** recently tried for Poguish success by fusing trad with rap.

The worldwide punk rock explosion, which began in the late 1970's, had brilliant effects in Belfast, where **Stiff Little Fingers** spit forth three years of excellent anthems (followed by ten years of bad hard rock). Most Northern punks rebelled against their overserious parents by emphasizing the fun part of rock and roll. They tried to create, through their songs, the de-politicized youth culture that had existed in England and America since the '50s: Starjets, Rudi, Protex, Big Self, and the very silly Radio Stars emphasized this approach in Belfast, but its most successful advocates were Derry's **Undertones.**

Punk was slower to happen in Dublin, though the **Boomtown Rats** (fronted by future Live Aid guy Bob Geldof) tried. A bit later, so did **U2:** from the adrenaline-soaked promise of 1980's *Boy,* the band slowly ascended into the rock-star stratosphere. Now, abandoned by their older, loyal fans who fell in love with their early rock style, U2 plays to media- and techno-inspired TV screens as in *Zooropa.* The smartest Irish popsters of the '80s, bands like the **Slowest Clock** and the folky **Stars of Heaven,** went almost nowhere commercially, while plenty of U2-derived bands have raced up and down British and American charts on the basis of their perceived Celtic aura. Distortion-masters **My Bloody Valentine** started in Ireland, though like the Pogues, or John Lydon, or U2, they moved to London before becoming significant. **Sinéad O'Connor** used Gaelic themes and reeling fiddles in at least one of her hits, "I Am Stretched on Your Grave." **The Golden Horde** are a talented, unpretentious punk band who still perform. Lately, the lowercase **cranberries** (from Limerick) have hit big in the U.S. New risers in the U.S. folk/rock scene are **Mary Black, the Chieftains,** and **Sharon Shannon.** Meanwhile, the rock press has christened Cork a hot spot: its flagship bands, the **Frank and Walters** and the **Sultans of Ping F.C.,** are not exactly revolutionary, but a hubbub of new zines and clubs in Cork, Dublin, and the Southeast may herald a more inventive, post-U2 era in Irish rock.

FILM

Hollywood has known about Ireland's untouched expanses of green, appealing small towns and comparatively low labor costs since the early '70s, when movies set elsewhere were sometimes made here. In the last five-odd years, however, the Irish government has begun to encourage a truly Irish film industry. An excellent art cinema has opened in Dublin, and there's an office two blocks away to encourage budding moviemakers. Based on novels by Roddy Doyle, *The Commitments* (directed by an American, Alan Parker) and *The Snapper* made audiences snap their fingers and weep with stories of kids from the depressed North Side of Dublin who form a band to play American soul music. *The Crying Game's* tight plot, tortured hero, IRA theme and ballyhooed surprise-middle won it huge audiences as well as critical praise. Some claim that it would have won an Oscar had it been released by a major American studio rather than by a private distributor. The film took place entirely in England and Northern Ireland. Its director, Neil Jordan, resides near Dublin. More recently, Irish writers and studios have produced *Widow's Peak* and *In the Name of the Father,* in which Daniel Day-Lewis expressed the Troubles in Northern Ireland.

Circle of Friends chronicles a typical love story, circa 1950, while trying simultaneously to comment on Irish rural and political life.

■■■ PUBS & FOOD

The pub is in some sense the living room of the Irish household. Locals of all ages, from every social milieu, head to the public house for conversation, food, singing and dancing, and lively *craic* ("crack"), an Irish word meaning simply "a good time." Though the clientele of the average public house is predominantly male, female travelers can feel comfortable here. People aren't normally looking for much other than communal talk and drink. You might have your ears talked off, however, especially by amateur *seanachaí* ("SHAN-ukh-ee"), traveling storytellers. In the evening, some pubs host traditional music. Local and traveling musicians, toting fiddles, guitars, *bodhráns* (a shallow, one-sided drum), and whistles, drop in around 9:30pm to start impromptu trad sessions.

Pubs in the Republic are generally open Monday to Saturday from 10:30am to 11:30pm (11pm in winter), and Sunday from 12:30 to 2pm and 4 to 11pm. (Pubs are closed from 2-4pm due to Holy hours.) Pubs in the North tend to be open Monday to Saturday from 11:30am to 11pm, and Sunday from 12:30 to 2:30pm and 7 to 10pm. Some pubs close for a few hours on weekday afternoons as well, particularly in rural areas. Pub lunches are usually served from Monday to Saturday, 12:30 to 2:30pm, while soup, soda bread, and sandwiches are served all day. Children are often not allowed in pubs after 7pm.

Beer is the default drink in Irish pubs. Cocktails are an oddity found mainly in American-style bars and discos, and most pubs stock only a few token bottles of wine. Beer comes in three varieties: **lagers** (blond, fizzy brews served cold, a bit weaker than ales or stouts—almost all American beers are lagers), **ales** (slightly darker, more bitter, and sometimes served a bit warmer than lagers), and **stouts** (thick, tar-black, and made from roasted barley to impart an almost chocolaty flavor). **Guinness** stout inspires a reverence otherwise reserved for the Holy Trinity. Known variously as "the dark stuff," "the blonde in the black skirt," or simply "I'll have a pint, please," it's a rich, dark brew with a head thick enough to stand a match in. It's also far better here than the Guinness you've had anywhere else. For a sweeter taste, try it with blackcurrant or cider. Stout takes a while to pour (usually, three to four minutes), so quit drumming the bar and be patient. **Murphy's** is a similar, although slightly sweeter, stout brewed in Cork, as is **Beamish,** a tasty "economy" stout. **Smithwicks** ale (a hoppy, English-style bitter, pronounced "Smiddicks") and **Harp** lager (made by Guinness) are both popular domestic brews. You might be surprised by the many pubs serving Budweiser or Heineken here, and the number of young people quaffing such imported lagers. In general, however, the indigenous brews are far worthier. Beer is served in imperial **pint glasses** (about 20 oz.) or half-pints (called a "glass"). If you ask for a beer you'll get a full pint, so be loud and clear if you can only stay (or stand) for a half. Or just take the pint and drink faster. A pint of Guinness costs anywhere from £1.70-2.10.

Irish whiskey (which Queen Elizabeth once declared her only true Irish friend) is sweeter and more stinging than its Scotch counterpart. It's also served in larger measures than you might be used to. Dubliners are partial to **Powers,** drinkers in Cork enjoy **Paddy,** and **Bushmills** is the favorite in the North. **Jameson** is popular everywhere. **Irish coffee** is sweetened with brown sugar and whipped cream and laced with whiskey—allegedly invented at Shannon Airport by a desperate bartender looking to appease cranky travelers on a layover, though others place the drink's origin in San Francisco. **Hot whiskey** (spiced up with lemon, cloves, and brown sugar) can provide a cozy buzz, as will the Irish version of **eggnog** (brandy, beaten egg, milk, and lemonade). In the west, you may hear some locals praise "mountain dew," a euphemism for **poitín** ("po-CHEEN"), a lethal (and illegal) distillation sometimes given to cows in labor that ranges in strength from 115 to 140 proof. Bad *poitín* can be very dangerous indeed.

Food in Ireland can be fairly expensive, especially in restaurants. The basics—and that's what you'll get—are simple and filling. "Takeaway" (take-out) fish and chips shops ("chippers") are quick, greasy, and very popular. For variation, try chips with gravy, potato cakes (flat pancakes made of potato flakes), or the infamous spiceburger (a breaded, spiced patty of fried breadcrumbs and spices). Many **pubs** serve food as well as drink, and **pub grub** is a good option for a quick and inexpensive meal. Typical pub grub includes Irish stew (meat, potatoes, carrots, and onions), burgers, soup, and sandwiches.

Another alternative is to do your own **shopping.** Soda bread will keep for about a week and is delicious. Irish dairy products are addictive. Seafood can be a bargain in some small towns. Smoked mackerel is splendid year-round. Atlantic salmon is freshest around July. Regional specialties include *crubeen* (tasty pigs' feet) in Cork, and *coddle* (boiled sausages and bacon with potatoes) in Dublin. *Colcannon,* "ploughman's lunch," and Irish stew, usually £4, are probably the essential Irish dishes. Wexford berries in the Southeast are luscious May through July.

In **Northern Ireland,** you'll find similar culinary offerings, along with a few regional specialties. Meal portions tend to be large, fried, and inevitably canopied with potatoes. A hearty Ulster Fry (fried eggs, fried bacon, fried sausage, fried potato bread, and fried tomatoes) at breakfast will tide you over until the main midday meal, and tea is often substituted for dinner around 6pm. Every town has a few tempting bakeries selling pasties (pronounced "PASS-tees", meat or vegetable wrapped in a pastry) and traditional soda bread. For a listing of Northern restaurants and pubs that serve food, check *Where to Eat in Northern Ireland,* available at most tourist offices.

TIPPING

Many restaurants in Ireland figure a service charge into the bill (some even calculate it into the cost of the dishes themselves). The menu almost always indicates whether or not service is included. For those restaurants that do not include a tip in the bill, customers should leave 10-15%. The exact amount should truly depend upon the quality of the service (as isn't usually the case in America). The one hard and fast rule is that no tip should be less than 50p.

Tipping is less common for other services, especially in rural areas, but always very welcome. Porters, parking-lot attendants, and hairdressers are usually tipped, cab drivers less so. Hotel housekeepers will welcome a show of appreciation, but B&B owners may actually be insulted at a tip. And above all, never tip the **man behind the bar.**

County Dublin

Dublin and its coastal suburbs form one economic and commercial unit, all of which can be reached by DART (Dublin Area Rapid Transit) and suburban rail. All these towns, except Bray, are in County Dublin—the administrative unit that encircles the capital. The residents from the city hop out to the suburbs on weekends, and vice versa. Fast and modern Dublin dispels many preconceptions about "backward" Ireland, but the country's greener and more traditional side hides itself just a DART ride away. Dublin's suburbs are no less distinctive than Ireland's romanticized rural villages (though they are more crowded), and some towns—notably Howth—boast patches of unsurpassed beauty.

GETTING AROUND COUNTY DUBLIN

By Bus

The distressingly lime-green **Dublin Buses,** *Bus Átha Cliath* in Irish, sport "db" logos and run around town from 6am to 11:30pm. The buses comprehensively cover the city of Dublin and its suburbs north to Balbriggan, Rush, Malahide, and Donabate, west to Maynooth and Celbridge, and south to Blessington, Dún Laoghaire, and Bray. A **NiteLink** service runs express routes to the suburbs (Thurs.-Sat. midnight, 1, 2, and 3am; £2, no passes valid). Tickets for the NiteLink are sold from a van parked on the corner of Westmoreland and College St., next to the entrance to Trinity College. Dublin has a new **wheelchair accessible** bus service around the downtown area called **OmniLink** (Mon.-Sat. 8am-11pm; 30p).

Buses are cheap (55p to £1.25) and extensive, but many don't run frequently enough. A majority of bus routes end or begin at city center, or *An Lár,* defined by the streets around O'Connell Bridge. The yellow bus timetables along the quays have insets of the city center which indicate route termini by printing the route number inside a box. It's easiest to figure out bus routes by using the *Map of Greater Dublin* (£4.10) in conjunction with the accurate **Dublin Bus Timetable** (£1.20; also good for finding termini in City Centre). Both are available from newsagents the **Dublin Bus office,** 59 O'Connell St. (tel. 873 4222 or 872 0000; open Mon.-Fri. 9am-5:30pm, Sat. 9am-1pm), which also has pamphlets detailing each individual route (free).

Among passes, choose between the **One Day Travel Wide** (£3.30, Dublin buses only), the **One Day Bus/Rail** (£4.50, valid on buses, DART, and rail service anywhere between Kilcoole, Balbriggan, and Maynooth), and the **Four-Day Explorer** (£10, 4 days of everything you get with the One Day Bus/Rail). Passes should be inserted into the scanner on the right side of the bus entrance. With a **CIE card** from the Dublin bus office (£2; a Dublin address is required, but the street address of a hostel will work), tourists can also buy a **weekly adult bus pass** (valid Sun.-Sat.; £10.50) or a **weekly adult bus/rail pass** (valid Sun.-Sat.; £14.50). With a CIE card *and* a TravelSave stamp on their ISIC cards, **students** can buy weekly bus passes for £8.50. Newsagents with the Dublin Bus "db" logo in the window sell these passes but only the Dublin bus office sells the CIE card. Individuals or groups may want to consider the transferable (anybody can use the same book) **10 Journey ticket books,** which allow ten trips of the same price (55p, 80p, £1, £1.10, or £1.25) and produce savings of 50p to £2.

By Train

The electric **DART** trains run frequently up and down the coast to serve the suburbs. From Connolly, Pearse, and Tara St. Stations in the city center, the DART shoots all the way south to Bray and north to Howth. DART trains are inevitably faster and more predictable than comparable bus rides. The DART runs every 15 minutes from 6:30am-midnight (75p to £1.60). Tickets are sold in the station and must be presented at the end of the trip. The unmistakably orange trains of the **suburban rail** network continue north to Malahide, Donabate, and Drogheda, south to Wicklow and Arklow, and west to Maynooth. These trains leave from Connolly Station, though the southern line also stops at Tara St. and Pearse Stations. Trains to Kildare leave from Heuston Station. Trains are frequent on weekdays, less so on Sunday.

■■■ DUBLIN

Dublin has a different feel than the rest of Ireland. In a country known for its relaxed pace of life and rural quietude, Dublin is fast, urban, and thumps with energy. The Irish who live outside of Dublin worry that it has taken on the characteristics of big cities everywhere: crime and a weakness for short-lived international trends. Perhaps they also fear the rapid social change in the city. The truth is that Ireland is changing, and that Dublin, holding close to one-third of the country's population in the city and its environs, is at the forefront of those changes. These circumstances make Dublin a seminal site for music and an active gay and lesbian population. The old Ireland is certainly present—castle, cathedrals, and fine old pubs saturate the city. The friendliness of the Irish people, the love of good *craic*, and the willingness to befriend a stranger, although sometimes hidden beneath a veneer or urban bustle, is always ready to burst out, whether while waiting for a bus or over a round of Guinness. While not cosmopolitan in the same sense as London or Paris, Dublin does have a degree of urban sophistication, manifested in its vibrant theater, music, and literary productions, that shows it to be taking its place among the great cities of modern Europe.

Dublin has been a port since the winter of 840-841, when Vikings built this longship port downstream from the older Celtic settlement of Áth Cliath. After a few years of regular visits, the Vikings set up a permanent town, Dubh Linn ("Black Pool"), around the modern College Green. The Viking Thingmote, or hill of assembly, stood there as administrative center for both Viking powers and the Norman Pale until William III's victory at the Battle of the Boyne in 1690. During the Protestant Ascendancy which followed (see The Protestant Ascendancy (1688-1801), p. 52), the Irish Parliament House (now the Bank of Ireland) sprang up near the old Viking center along with a Protestant English culture still evident in the architectural details of Dublin's tidy Georgian squares.

As the capital of Ireland (and thus a center of international commerce and diplomacy) since the end of the 17th century, Dublin has seen a blending of cultures which has produced an extraordinary intellectual and literary life. From Swift and Burke to Joyce and Beckett, Dublin has produced so many great writers that virtually every street contains a literary landmark. The city's public life, which takes place on the streets, in open markets, and behind inviting pub doors, is vibrant with both Irish and English energies. There's a pub to suit every mood, and the music scene inside them is world-renowned. Dublin may not embody the "Emerald Isle" that the tourist brochures promote, but it is a thriving and exciting urban center.

TO & FROM THE TRANSPORTATION HUBLIN

Rail lines, bus lines (both official and private), and the national highway system radiate from Ireland's capital. Of Ireland's major national roads, six terminate in Dublin. N5 and N6 lead to N4, and N8, N9, and N10 to N7. Because inter-city transport is so Dublin-centric, you may find it more convenient in the long run to arrange your travel in other parts of the Republic while you're in the capital. To get the best deals, check in with USIT (see p. 4) for a Travelsave stamp if you intend to take buses or trains and ask around for private bus lines. For sea and air travel into the capital, refer to the Essentials section (see To Dublin, p. 33).

Central Dublin

A B C

1

Old Cabra Rd.

Blackhorse Ave.

Glenbeigh Rd.

PHOENIX
PARK

North Circular Rd.

GrangegormanUpper

Annamoe Ter.

Prussia St.

*Zoological
Gardens*

2

North Circular Rd.

O'Devaney Gardens

Aughrim St.

Halliday Rd.

Manor St.

Kirwan St.

Infirmary Rd.

Montpelier Gds.

Manor Pl.

Main Rd.

Wellington
Monument

Montpelier Hill

Arbour Hill

Brunswick St.

King St. North

Blackhall Pl.

Queen St.

Smithfield St.

Bow St.

3

Conygham Rd.

Benburb St.

Wolfe Tone Quay

Heuston Station

Victoria Quay

Arran Quay

Usher's Quay

Island St.

St. Johns Rd. West

Steevens La.

Watling St.

Oliver Bond

4

Royal Hospital
Kilmainham

St. James's St.

Thomas St. West

Rainsford St.

Lane Bow Bridge

Guinness
Brewery

Bellevue St.

Earl St.

Old Kilmainham Rd.

Meath St.

Basin St. Upper

Summer St.

The Coombe

Ardee St.

South

Grand   Canal   Bank

Marrowbone La.

Cork St.

Brickfield
Lane

5

New Ireland Rd.

Circular
Rd.

St. Anthony's Rd.

Reuben St.

Cork St.

Donore Avenue

St. Theresa
Gds.

O'Donovan
Rd.

Dolphin Rd.

Fatima Mansions

Barn

Dufferin Ave.

S. Circular Rd.

6

Keeper Rd.

Dolphin's

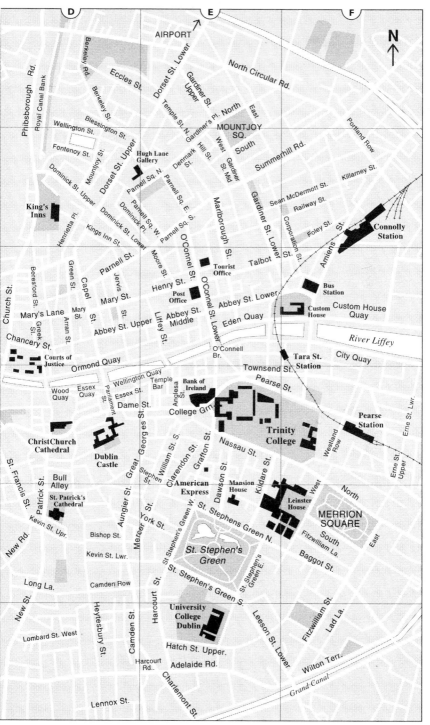

By Train

Most inter-city trains arrive at **Heuston Station** (tel. 703 2132), just south of Victoria Quay, well west of the city center and a long walk from anywhere. Any Dublin bus heading east—and several pass by every minute—will take you into the city. Buses #26, 51, and 79 go specifically to the city center. To facilitate **train and bus connections,** bus #90 makes the circuit of Dublin's three train stations and its bus station.

The other major rail terminus is **Connolly Station,** Amiens St. (tel. 836 3333), centrally located just north of the Liffey and close to Busáras (the bus station) and half-a-dozen hostels and B&Bs. Buses #20, 20A, and 90 will take weary souls south of the river, but it's faster to walk. **Pearse Station,** just east of Trinity College on Pearse St. and Westland Row, receives southbound trains from Connolly Station. Both Connolly and Pearse are also DART stations serving the north and south coasts (see Getting Around County Dublin, p. 74). **Luggage storage** is available at Heuston and Connolly Stations (items £1/day; open at Heuston Mon.-Sat. 7:15am-8:35pm, Sun. 8am-3pm and 5-9pm; at Connolly Mon.-Sat. 7:40am-9:30pm, Sun. 9:15am-1pm and 5-10pm).

Irish Rail, Iarnród Éireann in Irish, 35 Lower Abbey St. (tel. 836 6222), spews data on its own InterCity services as well as on DART, suburban trains, international train tickets, and ferries. (Open Mon.-Fri. 9am-5pm, Sat. 9am-1pm; phones open Mon.-Sat. 9am-6pm, Sun. 10am-6pm.) Trains run **from Connolly** to: Belfast (Mon.-Sat. 8/day, Sun. 3/day; 2-2½hr.; £15), Sligo (Mon.-Sat. 4/day, Sun. 3/day; 3hr. 20 min.; £27.50), and Wexford/Rosslare (Mon.-Sat. 3/day, Sun 2/day; 3hr.; £10, students £7). Trains **from Heuston** make tracks for: Cork (Mon.-Sat. 4/day, Sun. 3/day; 3¼hr.; £32), Galway (Mon.-Sat. 4/day, Sun. 2/day; 3hr.; £13), Limerick (Mon.-Sat. 9/day, Sun. 6/day; 2¾hr.; £26), Tralee (Mon.-Sat. 3/day, Sun. 2/day; 4hr.; £33.50, students £10.50), and Waterford (Mon.-Sat. 4/day, Sun. 3/day; 2¾hr.; £11).

All fares in *Let's Go* listings are for single (one-way) tickets, unless otherwise noted. Student fares (with ISIC and TravelSave stamp) are generally 50% of the adult fare. All lines, except those to Cork and Limerick, boast cheaper return (round-trip) promotion fares, for which the restrictions, often on days of travel, vary from line to line. Unlike bus tickets, train tickets sometimes allow travelers to break a journey into stages yet still pay the price of a single-phase trip. 24-hr. "talking timetables" recite info on trains to: Belfast (tel. 873 4444); Cork (tel. 872 4222); Galway/Westport (tel. 872 4777); Killarney/Tralee (tel. 873 3333); Limerick (tel. 872 4666); Sligo (tel. 873 1111); Waterford (tel. 873 0000); and Wexford/Rosslare (tel. 873 5555).

By Bus

Bus Éireann, the national bus company, covers the entire island. Its inter-city buses to Dublin arrive at **Busáras Central Bus Station,** Store St. (tel. 836 6111), directly behind the Customs House and next door to Connolly Station. **Luggage storage** is open Mon.-Sat. 8am-7:45pm, Sun. 10am-5:45pm (£1.50/item, £2/rucksack per day). Buses run from Busáras to: Belfast (4/day, Sun. 3/day; 3hr.; £9.50); Cork (4/day, Sun. 3/day; 4½hr.; £12, students £8.50); Derry (4/day, Sun. 2/day; 4½hr.; £10, students £8.80); Dingle (2/day, Sun. 1/day; 7hr.; £16, students £9.50); Donegal Town (4/day, Sun. 3/day; 4¼hr.; £10, students £8); Galway (8/day, Sun. 7/day; 4hr.; £9, students £6.50); Killarney (2-5/day, Sun. 3/day; 6hr.; £14, students £9); Limerick (8/day, Sun. 7/day; 3¼hr.; £10, students £7.50); Rosslare Harbour (5-7/day, Sun. 5-6/day; 3hr.; £9, students £6.50); Shannon Airport (6/day, Sun. 4/day; 4½hr.; £10, students £8); Sligo (3/day; 4hr.; £8, students £7); Tralee (5/day, Sun. 4/day; 6hr.; £14, students £9); Waterford (6/day; 2¾hr.; £7, students £6); Westport (3/day, Sun. 1/day; 5½hr.; £11, students £8.50); and Wexford (5-7/day, Sun. 5-6/day; 2¾hr.; £7, students £6). **Private bus companies** typically run one or two buses a day between Dublin and some other destination. Their buses are generally cheaper and slightly faster than Bus Éireann, but it's maddeningly hard to find info on them. **PAMBO** (Private Association of Motor Bus Owners), 32 Lower Abbey St. (tel. 878 8422) may be able to help (open Mon.-Fri. 10am-5pm). Private bus lines from Dublin to other cities are listed in *Let's Go* under Getting There for those cities.

By Thumb

Hitchers into Dublin generally ask drivers to drop them off at one of the myriad bus and DART stops outside the city. Hitchers out of Dublin ride a bus to the city outskirts where the motorways begin. Buses #25, 25A, 66, 66A, 67, and 67A from Middle Abbey St. travel to Lucan Rd., which turns into N4 (for Galway and the West). To find a ride to Cork, Waterford, and Limerick (N7), hitchers usually take bus #51, 51B, or 69 from Fleet St. to Naas ("nace") Rd. Wicklow, Wexford, and Rosslare are along N11, for which hitchers take bus #46 or 84 from Eden Quay or #46A from Fleet St. to Stillorgan Rd. N3 heads to Donegal and Sligo, and can be reached on bus #38 from Lower Abbey St. or #39 from Middle Abbey St. to Navan Rd. Buses #33, 41, and 41A from Eden Quay to Swords send hitchers on their way to the North, Belfast, and Dundalk (on N1).

From the Airport or Ferry Port

From **Dublin Airport** (tel. 844 4900), Dublin bus #41, 41A, or 41C (every 20min.; £1.10) takes travelers to Eden Quay in the city center. Alternatively, **Airport Express** Buses (Mon.-Sat. 6:40am-11:00pm, Sun. 7:10am-11:00pm; every 15-30 min.; £2.50) will bring you to Busáras Central Bus Station and sometimes continue to Heuston Station. A cab from the airport to the city center costs £12-14. Several cab companies offer wheelchair-accessible cabs for no extra charge (call in advance).

B&I ferries dock at the mouth of the River Liffey, just outside central Dublin. Buses #53 and 53A run from there past Alexandra Rd. and arrive near the Custom House (80p). **Stena-Sealink** ferries arrive in Dún Laoghaire (see Dún Laoghaire, p. 111), from which the DART shuttles weary passengers to Connolly Station, Pearse Station, or Tara St. Station in the city center (£1.10). Buses #7, 7A, and 8 go from Georges St. in Dún Laoghaire to Eden Quay (£1.10).

ORIENTATION

The **River Liffey** cuts central Dublin in half from west to east. The better food and more famous sights reside on the South Side (of the river), though plenty of hostels and the bus station sprout up on the grittier North Side. Almost all streets in Dublin changes their names every few blocks. Tourists should ask directions frequently and buy a map with a street index. The streets running alongside the Liffey are called quays ("keys"); their names change every block. Each bridge over the Liffey also has its own name, and all streets change names as they cross the river. If a street is split into "Upper" and "Lower," then the "Lower" part of the street is always closer to the mouth of the Liffey.

Grafton St. is basically the spine of the city. As it runs north, it changes to College Green, sandwiched by Trinity College and the former House of Lords. Farther north, the same street becomes Westmoreland and then turns into O'Connell St. as it crosses the River Liffey over O'Connell Bridge. O'Connell St. marks the northern boundary of the city center. Following Grafton St. south to St. Stephen's Green, the street name soon changes to Harcourt St.

Important north-south arteries on the south side of the Liffey are **South Great Georges St.** (west of Grafton St.) and **Wexford St.** East of Grafton St., Kildare St. connects Trinity College and St. Stephen's Green. The most important east-west streets are the many sections of Abbey St. (on the North side) and Dame St. on the South Side, which is the main channel to the Temple Bar neighborhood.

Trinity College Dublin (TCD) draws legions of bookshops and student-oriented pubs into its orbit. The more expensive and tourist-oriented shops and restaurants gravitate towards Grafton St. and St. Stephen's Green. To the west of TCD, **Temple Bar** is home to excellent pubs and trendy clubs, as well as an eclectic array of funky restaurants and, after renovations are completed in 1996, a set of art museums and workshops (this region is Dublin's version of Soho). The **North Side** has a bad reputation. Home to Dublin's working class, the regions north of the river are not as dangerous or run-down as many would have you believe. If you walk north far enough, though, the sets from *The Commitments* will look familiar. The core of

Dublin is circumscribed by North and South Circular Rd. Almost all the sights are located within this area, and you can walk from one end to the other in a half-hour.

PRACTICAL INFORMATION

Dublin Tourist Information: Main Office, 14 Upper O'Connell St. (tel. 284 4768). From Connolly Train Station, Talbot St. runs east until it becomes a pedestrian zone and hits O'Connell St., a wide road with an island down the middle. Taking O'Connell St. north (to the right), the tourist office is on the right. From Busáras Central Bus Station, Corporation St. crosses Talbot St. one block north of the bus station. The route is then the same as the route from Connolly Station. Accommodation service with £1 booking fee and 10% deposit; £2 charge to book outside Dublin. The king among billions of pamphlets is the *Map of Greater Dublin* (£4.10). American Express maintains a branch office with currency exchange here (tel. 878 6892). Bus Éireann tickets and info are available. Argus Rent-a-Car has a desk here and a free list of car rental agencies is also available. Open June Mon.-Sat. 8:30am-6pm; July-Aug. Mon.-Sat. 8:30am-8pm, Sun. 10:30am-2pm; Sept.-Feb. Mon.-Fri. 9am-5pm, Sat. 9am-3:30pm; March-May Mon.-Sat. 9am-5pm.

Branch Offices: Dublin Airport (tel. 284 4768; open daily 8am-10:30pm; mid-Sept. to mid-June 8am-10:30pm, Mon.-Sat. 8am-6pm; May to June 8am-8pm), **Dún Laoghaire Harbour,** St. Michael's Wharf (tel. 284 4768; open June-Sept. daily 8:30am-10pm; Sept.-May Mon.-Fri. 9am-5pm, Sat. 9am-1pm), and **Dublin Port,** B&I Terminal (open June-Aug.at ferry arrivals). All less busy than the main branch.

Bord Fáilte Éireann (Irish Tourist Board) Headquarters: Baggot St. Bridge (tel. 602 4000). This is the nerve center of Bord Fáilte. They dish out maps and more on the entire Republic of Ireland. (Open Mon.-Sat. 9am-5pm.)

Northern Ireland Tourist Board: 16 Nassau St. (tel. 679 1977 or (1800) 230230). Plan ahead with their help. Open Mon.-Fri. 9am-5:30, Sat. 10am-5pm.

Temple Bar Information Centre: 18 Eustace St. (tel. 671 5717). Heading away from Trinity College, make a right off Dame St. where it intersects both Eustace and Great George's St. They have info on the artsy Temple Bar, better arts information than the Dublin Tourist Office can offer, and more time to answer questions. The center publishes the useful, bimonthly *Temple Bar Guide* (free) and will give you a copy of *Gay Community News* (free). Open Mon.-Fri. 9am-7pm, Sat. 11am-7pm, Sun. noon-6pm; Oct.-May Mon.-Fri. 9:30am-6pm, Sat. noon-6pm.

Community and Youth Information Centre: Sackville Pl. (tel. 878 6844), corner of Marlborough St. A library with a wealth of resources on careers, culture, outings, travel and tourist information, accommodations (no bookings), camping, sporting events, counseling, and referrals. Bulletin boards advertise youth and special-needs groups. Open Mon.-Wed. 9:30am-6pm, Thurs.-Sat. 9:30am-5pm.

Budget Travel: USIT (Irish Student Travel Agency), 19-21 Aston Quay (tel. 679 8833), near O'Connell Bridge. The place to seek Irish travel discounts. ISIC, HI, and EYC cards; Travelsave stamps £7. Big discounts, especially for people under 26. They even book hostels. Open Mon.-Fri. 9am-6pm, Sat. 11am-4pm.

An Óige Head Office (Irish Youth Hostel Association/HI): 61 Mountjoy St. (tel. 830 4555), corner of Wellington St. Follow O'Connell St. north, continuing through all its name changes. Mountjoy St. is on the left. Book and pay for HI hostels here. Package bike and rail tours. The *An Óige Handbook* (£1.50) lists all HI hostels in Ireland and Northern Ireland. Membership £7.50, under 18 £4. Open Mon.-Fri. 9:30am-5:30pm; April-Sept. also Sat. 10am-12:30pm.

Embassies: Australia, Fitzwilton House, Wilton Terrace (tel. 676 1517). Open Mon.-Fri. 10am-noon and 2-4pm. **Britain,** 31 Merrion Rd. (tel. 269 5211). Open Mon.-Fri. 10am-noon and 2-4pm. **Canada,** 65 St. Stephen's Green South (tel. 478 1988; emergencies, call 285 1246). Open Mon.-Fri. 10am-noon and 2-4pm. **France,** 36 Ailesbury Rd. (tel. 269 4777). **Germany,** 31 Trimleston Ave. (tel. 269 3011 or 269 3123). Open Mon.-Fri. 9am-noon. **Italy,** 63 Northumberland Rd. (tel. 660 1744). **Japan,** 22 Ailesbury Rd. (tel. 269 4244). **Netherlands,** 160 Merrion Rd. (tel. 269 3444; after hours, call 298 1787). Open Mon.-Fri. 9am-12:30pm and 2-4pm. **New Zealanders** should contact their embassy in London: New Zealand House, Haymarket, London SW1Y 4QT. From Ireland, dial 00 44 (171) 930 8422. **Spain,** 17A Merlyn Pk. (tel. 269 1640; after hours, call 269 2131). Open Mon.-Fri.

9:30am-3pm. **United States,** 42 Elgin Rd., Ballsbridge (tel. 668 8777). Open Mon.-Fri. 8:30am-4pm.

Banks: Best exchange rates are in banks. **Bank of Ireland,** 6 Lower O'Connell St. (tel. 872 9799); **ATM. AIB (Allied Irish Bank),** 10 Lower O'Connell St. (tel. 873 0555); **ATM.** Both open Mon.-Wed. and Fri. 10am-4pm, Thurs. 10am-5pm.**TSB (Trustees' Savings Bank),** 12 Lower Abbey St. (tel. 878 6266). Open Mon.-Wed. and Fri. 9:30am-5pm, Thurs. 9:30am-7pm. Bureaux de change also in the General Post Office and in the tourist office main branch.

American Express: 116 Grafton St., Dublin 2 (tel. 677 2874), up the street from Trinity College gates. Travelers cheque refunds (tel. (1800) 626000). Client mail held; currency exchange (no commission for AmEx Travelers Cheques). Open Mon.-Sat. 9am-5pm, also June-Sept. Sun. 11am-4pm. Also in the tourist office on O'Connell St. (tel. 878 6892).

Post Office: General Post Office (G.P.O.), O'Connell St. (tel. 705 7000), near the tourist office. Big. Dublin is the only city in Ireland with postal codes (24 of them). Even-numbered postal codes are for areas south of the Liffey, odd-numbered are for the north. The numbers increase with distance from city center. Poste Restante pick-up at the bureau de change window closes 15 min. early. Open Mon.-Sat. 8am-8pm, Sun. 10am-6:30pm. **G.P.O. Postal Code:** Dublin 1.

Phones: Telecom Éireann (inquiries and phonecard refunds, tel. 671 4444). A fleet of **public pay telephones** docks in the General Post Office (phones open Mon.-Sat. 8am-8pm, Sun. and holidays 10:30am-6:30pm). Another anchors at the Gaiety Centre, on South King St. across from St. Stephen's Green (open Mon.-Fri. 9:30am-5pm). Both locations have a cargo of phone books covering all of Ireland. **Phone Code:** 01.

Directory Inquiries: tel. 1190, no charge.

Buses: Inter-city buses (see By Bus, p. 78) and intra-city buses (see Getting Around County Dublin, p. 74) are covered above.

Trains: (see By Train, p. 78).

Ferries: Bookings in Irish Rail office (below). Ferries to Dublin from England, Wales, and the Isle of Man are covered in Essentials (see Ferries, p. 33). Ferry port to Dublin transport is covered above (see From the Airport or Ferry Port, p. 79).

Iarnród Éireann (Irish Rail): 35 Lower Abbey St. (tel. 836 6222). Info and bookings on trains and ferries. Open Mon.-Fri. 9:15am-5pm, Sat. 9:15am-12:45pm; phones open Mon.-Sat. 9am-6pm, Sun. 10am-6pm.

Taxi: National Radio Cabs, 40 James St. (tel. 677 2222). **Co-op Taxi** (tel. 677 7777 or 676 6666). **Central Cabs** (tel. 836 5555) and **City Group Taxi** (tel. 872 7272) have wheelchair-accessible taxis (call in advance). All are 24-hr. services. Fares start at £1.80; 80p/mi.; £1.20 call-in charge.

Car Rental: Argus, 59 Terenure Rd. East, Dublin 6 (tel. 490 4444; fax 490 6328). Offices also in the tourist office on O'Connell St. and in the airport. From £38/day, £225/week for ages 26-64. Special arrangements for drivers 23-26 or 64-70.

Bike Rental: (see By Bicycle, p. 37). **Rent-A-Bike,** 58 Lower Gardiner St. (tel. 872 5931 or 872 5399; fax 836 4763). Cross-country and mountain bikes £6/day, £30/week; deposit £30. Panniers, helmets, and child seats £5/week. Bike repair. Sells bikes for about £100, buys them back for ½-price within 6 months. For £5 extra, you can return the bike to other locations. Cycling holidays for £82/week staying in An Óige hostels, £135/week staying in B&Bs. Open Mon.-Sat. 9am-6pm. **Rail-Bike,** Heuston Station, affiliated with **Irish Cycle Hire** (tel. (041) 41062). £6/day, £30/week, helmets £5/week, pannier bags £5/week; deposit £30. Return the bike you rent here to RailBike depots in the main rail stations. **Raleigh Rent-A-Bike,** Kylemore Rd., Dublin 10 (tel. 626 1333). Limited one-way rental system (£12 surcharge; deposit credit card) includes C. Harding (below). Bikes £7/day, £30/week; deposit £40. In Dublin, Raleigh dealers include: **C. Harding for Bikes,** 30 Bachelor's Walk (tel. 873 3622; fax 873 3622); **McDonald's Cycles,** 38 Wexford St. (tel. 475 2586); **Little Sport,** 3 Merville Ave., off Fairview Rd. (tel. 833 2405).

Bike Repair and Storage: Square Wheel Cycleworks, Temple Lane South (tel. 679 0838), off Dame St., below the Well-Fed Café. Excellent advice on bicycle touring, expert repair, and supervised bicycle park (20p/hr., 60p/day, £2.50/week). Open Mon.-Fri. 8:30am-6:30pm. **C. Harding,** 30 Bachelor's Walk (tel. 873

2455), has bike storage north of the Liffey and a repair service (50p/4hr., £1/day, £3.50/6 days for students; overnight parking £1.50). Open Mon.-Sat. 8:30am-6pm. Turn right off O'Connell St. before the bridge.

Luggage Storage: In the central bus and train stations (see To & From the Transportation Hublin, p. 75).

Newsagent: Read Newsagent, 24 Nassau St. (tel. 679 6011; fax 671 1684). Photocopying 2p/page. Go ahead, xerox the phone book. Cheap stationery. Foreign newspapers and periodicals. Open Mon.-Fri. 8:30am-6:30pm, Sat. 9am-6:30pm.

Library: New Central Library, ILAC Centre, Moore St. (tel. 873 4333). Video and listening facilities and a children's library. Telephone directories on shelves for EU countries and on microfilm for U.S. and Canada. Open Mon.-Thurs. 10am-8pm, Fri.-Sat. 10am-5pm.

Laundry: The Laundry Shop, 191 Parnell St. (tel. 872 3541). Closest to Busáras and North Side hostels. Wash £1.90, dry £1, soap 50p. Open Mon.-Sat. 8:30am-6pm, Thurs. 8:30am-8pm. **Laundry Room,** 8 Kevin St. Lower (tel. 478 1774), west down St. Stephen's Green South. Closest to Trinity College, Temple Bar, and South Side hostels. Wash £2, dry £1.50, soap 30p. Open Mon.-Sat. 8am-9pm, last wash 7:30pm.

Bisexual, Gay, and Lesbian Information: Gay Switchboard Dublin, Carmichael House, North Brunswick St., Dublin 7 (tel. 872 1055). Info on meetings, outdoor groups, and nightlife. Open Sun.-Fri. 8-10pm, Sat. 3:30-6pm. **Lesbian Line** (tel. 661 3777) open Thurs. 7-9pm. **National Gay and Lesbian Federation (NLGF),** the Hirschfeld Centre, 10 Fownes St. (tel. 671 0939), behind the Central Bank. Deals mostly with legal disputes and publishes *Gay Community News,* a free monthly publication covering all of Ireland. Get it here or at the Temple Bar Information Centre (see above).

AIDS Resource Centre: 14 Haddington Rd. (tel. 660 2149), off Baggot St. Advice, counseling, and HIV testing. Also operates the **Gay Men's Health Project,** Tues.7:30-9:30pm (no appointment necessary). **Dublin AIDS Alliance,** 53 Parnell Sq. (tel. 873 3799) offers counseling and info on HIV.

Hotlines: Samaritans, 112 Marlborough St. (tel. (1850) 609 090 or 872 7700), for the depressed, lonely, or suicidal. 24 hrs.**Rape Crisis Centre,** 70 Lower Leeson St. (tel. 661 4911; weekends after 5:30pm tel. 661 4564). **Women's Aid** (tel. (1800) 341 900 or 860 0033). Open Mon.-Fri. 10am-10pm, Sat. 10am-6pm. **Dublin Well Woman Centre,** 73 Lower Leeson St. (tel. 661 0083 or 661 0086), a professional health center for women. **Cura,** 30 South Anne St. (tel. 671 0598), Catholic-funded support for women with unplanned pregnancies. **Alcoholics Anonymous,** 109 South Circular Rd., Dublin 8 (tel. 679 5967). **Narcotics Anonymous** (tel. 830 0944), 24-hr. phone service for those fighting drug addiction.

Pharmacy: O'Connell's, 55 Lower O'Connell St. (tel. 873 0427). Open Mon.-Sat. 8:30am-10pm, Sun. 10am-10pm. Convenient to city bus routes. **Temple Bar Pharmacy,** 21 Essex St. East (tel. 670 9751) offers the usual plus a range of homeopathic treatments. Open Mon.-Sat. 9am-7pm.

Hospital: Meath Hospital, Heytesbury St. (24-hr. tel. 453 6555, 453 6000, or 453 6694). Buses # 16, 16a, 19, 19a, 22, 22a, and 55 run here. **Mater Misericordiae Hospital,** Eccles Street, off Dorset St. Lower (tel. 830 1122). Served by buses #10, 22, 38, and 120. **Beaumont Hospital,** Beaumont Rd. D9 (tel. 837 7755). Served by buses #27a, 51a, 101, and 103. **St. James Hospital,** James St., Dublin 8 (tel. 453 7941). Quick and professional STD treatment. Buses #17, 19, 19a, 21a, 78a, and 123 stop here.

Emergency: Dial 999; no coins required. **Garda:** Dublin Metro Headquarters, Harcourt Sq. (tel. 732 222). Store St. office (tel. 873 2222 or 478 1822), Fitzgibbon St. office (tel. 836 3113). **Garda Confidential Report Line:** tel. (1800) 666 111.

ACCOMMODATIONS

Dublin has a host of marvelous accommodations, but the ever-flowing glut of visitors ensures that real dumps stay open as well. Reserve well ahead to be sure that you've got a bed, particularly during Easter weekend, British school holidays, and the months of July and August. Private hostel rooms and B&B singles are especially hard to come by. The tourist offices will book you local accommodations for £1, but they only deal in Bord Fáilte-approved B&Bs, which aren't always cheapest. Dublin hostels that pay the fee to be plugged into Bord Fáilte's system are Avalon House, An Óige, Isaac's, Kinlay House, the Marlborough Hostel, Morehampton House, The Young Traveler, and Goin' My Way/Cardijn House. Tourist officials may turn strangely mum if you mention any of the others.

Phoenix Park may tempt the desperate, but impromptu camping there is a bad idea. If the garda or park rangers don't get you to leave, the hooligans might. **Focus Point,** 14a Eustace St. (tel. 671 2555), provides info and tries to find housing for those with "no fixed abode." The truly down-and-out can try **Simon Community,** P.O. Box 581, Lower Sheriff St. (tel. 872 0188), where volunteers run shelters and soup kitchens for the homeless.

Hostels

Hostels abound north of the River Liffey and east of O'Connell St. The hostels south of the river fill up fastest. Most are independent (unconnected to An Óige/HI). Prices range from £6 to £10 per night. Reserve ahead in the summer, especially for private rooms. **The Old School House Hostel** in Dún Laoghaire (see Accommodations, p. 112) is a hosteler's alternative to busy city life.

Avalon House (IHH), 55 Aungier St. (tel. 475 0001; fax 475 0303). South Great Georges St., off Dame St., becomes Aungier St. One of the better hostels in Dublin. The rooms are a joy to return to: groovy comforters and terracotta decor, though beds are a trifle short. Unbeatable location between Trinity and Temple Bar. Co-ed showers, toilets, and dorms (all non-smoking). 4-bed dorms are split-level: the 2 beds on each level are connected by a circular stairway. The result is B&B-level privacy at dorm prices. Late-night coffee bar (open until 1am; entrees about £2); smallish kitchen with microwave open 7:30-10am and 5-10:30pm. Bike rack; safety deposit boxes with £5 deposit; laundry £4.50/bag (but Kevin St. laundromat is cheaper). No reservations taken for 24-bed dorm. Continental breakfast and sheets included. 24-bed dorm £7.50, July-Aug. £10.50. 4-bed dorm £11/person, July-Aug. £11.50. Double £13/person, July-Aug. £13.50. Add 50p for rooms w/bath. **Disabled-access room** (2 single beds) £13.50/person.

Kinlay House (IHH), 2-12 Lord Edward St. (tel. 679 6644; fax 679 7437), the continuation of Dame St. Protestant country boys who came to work in the city once slid down the beautifully carved oak banisters in the lofty entrance hall. Today, tired backpackers trudge upstairs to collapse on comfortable beds or on soft couches in the TV room. Located in hip 'n' happening Temple Bar, featuring neat key-card system to keep the happenings outside. Lockers; laundry (£4); bike hire; 24-hr. access to luggage storage. Breakfast, towel, linen, and soap included. Single £18, Oct.-May £17.50; twin £13.50, Oct.-May £12.50, 50p more w/bath; 4- to 6-bed dorm £12, Oct.-May £11, £1 more w/bath; dorm £9.50, Oct.-May £8.50.

Isaac's (IHH), 2-4 Frenchman's Lane (tel. 874 9321), first right off Lower Gardiner St. walking up from the Custom House. Floor upon floor of rooms attractively decorated with framed prints and floral comforters. Youthful staff and guests mingle in the bustling, inexpensive café on the ground floor. Reception open 24 hrs. Bed lockout 11am-5pm. Lockers (in rooms) 50p deposit; free sheets. Fills up a week in advance for Fri. and Sat. nights. 12- to 14-bed dorm £6.25, 6- to 8-bed dorm £8, twin room £14.50/person, single or triple room £17.75/person. Continental breakfast £1.25, Irish breakfast £1.95.

Marlborough Hostel (IHH), 81-81 Marlborough St. (tel. 874 7629 or 874 7812; fax 874 5172), directly behind the O'Connell St. tourist office. Large and light rooms with super-comfy beds. Barbecues in the backyard garden in summer. Bike shed; laundry 50p; sheets 50p; kitchen with microwave; common room with peat fire. Price includes continental breakfast. Check-out 10:30am. Single £14; double £22; 4- to 10-bed dorm £7.50.

Strollers, 58 Dame St. (tel. 677 5614 or 677 5422; fax 839 0474). In the middle of Temple Bar action, about halfway between Trinity College and Dublin Castle. Strollers wins the award for best-located hostel in Dublin. It's also close to the top for luxury. Truly restful beds in bright, spotless, non-smoking rooms induce visions of sugar plums. Two minor drawbacks: loud traffic and smallish rooms. Includes sheets and continental breakfast. 8-bed dorm £10.50, quads £12.50/person, double £14.50/person. Wheelchair access.

Globetrotter's Tourist Hostel (IHH), 46 Gardiner St. Lower (tel. 873 5893). Comfortable beds top each other in high bunks. Most excellent bathrooms. Groove to Percy Sledge in the funky dining room. Open 24 hrs.; free sheets; safety deposit boxes £1.50. Includes continental breakfast. July to mid-Sept. £12/person, mid-Sept. to June £10/person or £20 for 3 nights.

Dublin International Youth Hostel (An Óige/HI), 61 Mountjoy St. (tel. 830 1766 or 830 1396). O'Connell St. changes names three times before reaching the turn left onto Mountjoy St. A convent with stained-glass windows and confessional boxes converted into a pleasing if institutional 420-bed hostel. Large rooms, squeaky wooden bunks. Secure parking. Sheets 80p; luggage storage 50p; self-service laundry £4; currency exchange. Continental breakfast included. Max. 3-night stay. Dorm £9, non-members £9.50; 4- to 6-bed dorm £10/person; twin £12/person. Oct.-May £2 less.

Abraham House, 82 Gardiner St. Lower (tel. 855 0600; fax 855 0598). Tired travelers fall into the low, soft bunks (extra-long beds optional) and heave a sigh of relief in large, open rooms. Gallons of hot water. Kitchen with microwave; 24-hr. reception. Includes sheets, towels, and light breakfast. Dorm July-Sept. £10, Oct.-June £7; twin July-Sept. £13.50, Oct.-June £11.

M.E.C., 42 North Great Georges St. (tel. 872 6301 or 872 5707), off Parnell St. This grand Georgian building was first built as the home of the Archbishop of Dublin, then served as a convent until 1987. The M.E.C. stands for Montessori Education Centre, a pre-school next door. The beautiful stairway and the lovely, high ceilings reveal the building's potential, but the interior also belies the building's age. The beds are long and a little soft, but the neighborhood is refreshingly quiet. Sheet and pillow £1; locker deposit £1.8- to 16-bed dorm £8.50/person, double £10.50/person, single £13.50. Weekly rates £35 (in high season) or £25.

Harcourt St. Hostel (An Óige/HI), 70 Harcourt St. (tel. 475 0430), one of the many names for Grafton St. More personal and better located than the An Óige monster-truck hostel. Book through the An Óige head office (61 Mountjoy St., tel. 830 4555). 10-bed dorms £9; breakfast included; sheets 85p. Open July-Aug.

Goin' My Way/Cardijn House (IHH), 15 Talbot St. (tel. 878 8484; after 6pm tel. 874 1720). A hide-away hostel with cramped rooms off 5 winding flights of stairs. Blankets and sleeping bags are available to pad the thin mattresses. Lockout noon-5pm; midnight curfew; kitchen open after 5pm. Coffee bar open all day. No secure luggage storage, but small valuables can be left in the office. Showers 50p; continental breakfast included. 6- to 8-bed dorm £7/person, 4-bed dorm £9/person, double £10/person.

The Young Traveller, St. Mary's Pl. (tel. 830 5000), Granby Rd. runs north from Parnell St. and into St. Mary's Pl. Everything's soft: weak showers and cozy beds. Free luggage storage (available for longer periods, too); car park; laundry £1.50. Continental breakfast and sheets included. 4-bed dorm £9/person, Oct.-May £7.50-8; double £10/person, Oct.-May £8.50-9.

University Housing

When Dublin's university students vamoose every summer, much of the city's spark and pluck disappears with them. But the students do leave behind their empty dorm rooms. Some student accommodations are astonishingly modern and luxurious.

Dublin City University, Glasnevin (tel. 704 5736). Bus #11, 13, or 19A from city center stops here. A short taxi ride from the airport (the tourist info booth there will book a room here). Single in 2-room suite w/kitchenette and bathroom: £17/night, £90/week; £60/week for 2-4 weeks. Twin room £24/night, £100/week. Rooms available June 18-Sept. 22.

USIT, operates University College Dublin dorms in Belfield, near Dún Laoghaire (tel. 269 7111). Access from city center on bus #10 or 46A to UCD housing. Apartment-style dorms pile up suites that each include 3 or 4 singles and a shared bathroom, kitchen, and dining room. Sports facilities; launderette; car park. £18/ person per day, £96 per week. Available June 22-Sept. 21.

The University of Dublin, Trinity Hall, Dartry Rd., Rathmines (tel. 497 1772), 3 mi. south of city center (via bus #14 or 14A). Standard dorm rooms with washbasins and desks. Single £15-20/person, double £14-18/person; 10% discount with ISIC. Includes continental breakfast. Available late June to Sept.

Bed & Breakfasts

A blanket of quality B&Bs covers Dublin and the surrounding suburbs. Those with a green shamrock sign out front are registered, occasionally checked, and approved by Bord Fáilte. B&Bs without the shamrock haven't been inspected but may very well be better-located and cheaper. B&B prices stretch from £12 to £25 per person. Near the city center, inexpensive B&Bs cluster along Upper and Lower Gardiner St., on Sheriff St., and near the Parnell Sq. area. These B&Bs are rarely warm, welcoming places, exceptions are listed below.

Neighborhood B&Bs are often spare rooms in a house that has emptied of children. They tend to be close to the city: Clonliffe Rd., Sandymount, and Clontarf are no more than a 10- or 15-minute bus ride from Eden Quay. Suburbs offer more calm and an even greater chance of finding decent B&Bs, especially for those without a reservation: B&Bs in Howth (p. 108) and Dún Laoghaire (p. 112) are just as accessible (by DART) to Dublin as many of the B&Bs listed below. Maynooth (p. 125) and Malahide (p. 110), reached by suburban rail, are also good places to seek accommodation. Aside from the regions covered below, B&Bs within the city limits are also to be found in large numbers in Raheny (Dublin 5), Drumcondra (Dublin 9), and Templeogue (Dublin 6W). Bord Fáilte's annually updated *Ireland Accommodation Guide* (£5) lists all approved B&Bs and their rates.

Sandymount

The most convenient of places to stay is this middle-class seaside neighborhood near Dublin Port, south of city center. Take bus #3 from O'Connell St., or, better still, the DART to Landsdowne Rd. or Sandymount stops.

Mrs. Bermingham, 8 Dromard Terrace (tel. 668 3861). Bus #3 from O'Connell St. or DART to Sandymount stop. Old-fashioned rooms, one with a bay window overlooking the garden, and a (new-fangled) TV in the sitting room. Soft beds with great, fluffy comforters. Owner is lots of fun. Single £15, double £26.

Mrs. R. Casey, Villa Jude, 2 Church Ave. (tel. 668 4982), off Beach Rd. Bus #3 or DART (Lansdowne Rd. stop). Mrs. Casey has nourished 7 children and countless others with her homemade bread and strapping Irish breakfasts. The parlor overflows with family photos, fresh flowers, and lace doilies. Every room is immaculate and TV-equipped. £13/person.

Mrs. Dolores Abbot-Murphy, 14 Castle Park (tel. 269 8413). Friendly owner is as sweet as candy. Each cheerful room has a TV. The dining room adds elegance to every meal. £14/person, w/bath £16. Open May-Oct.

Clontarf and Malahide Rd.

Clontarf Rd. runs along Dublin Bay across from the Dublin Port facility north of the city center. Behind it rise the startlingly pretty hills of Howth. Houses with addresses in the 200s face directly onto the Irish Sea; those with addresses in the 90s face it through a maze of smokestacks. Sea breezes and a waterfront park almost make up for the lively sight of car ferries chugging into dock. Take bus #30 from Lower Abbey St. to Clontarf Rd.

Mrs. Carmel Drain, Bayview, 265 Clontarf Rd. (tel. 833 9870). Palm tree in the front yard. Mrs. Drain herself made the sheepskin rugs, scattered throughout the house, with sheep from her brother's farm. Bayview, indeed, with mountains too. Orthopedic beds and tea and biscuits in each room. £15/person, w/bath £16.50.

Ferryview Guest House, 96 Clontarf Rd. (tel. 833 5893). Trouser press in the hall-way may well be your only chance for pressed clothes. Nautical objects abound in the cheerful, non-smoking rooms. Single £16; £15/person, w/bath £16.50.

Mrs. M. Dunwoody, 19 Copeland Ave. (tel. 833 9091), between Malahide Rd. and Howth Rd. Easy access to buses and a location 10 min. closer to the city than other B&Bs in the area. A doll collection resides in the elegant dining room. Non-smoking rooms. Single £17.50; double £28, w/bath £33.

Mrs. Patricia Barry, Bayview, 98 Clontarf Rd. (tel. 833 3950). Recently refur-bished, fresh rooms have little to do with the bay. But the beds have pink bows on them. Piano in sitting room. Super showers. £15/person, w/bath £16.50.

Mrs. Eileen Kelly, 18 Copeland Rd. (tel. 833 3760). A pretty rose garden prefaces a lovely sitting room. The beds are firm, and all rooms have TV. £14.50/person, w/bath £16.50.

Clonliffe Road

This respectable lower-middle class neighborhood seems to have a grandmotherly figure behind every door. Take bus #51A from Lower Abbey St. or take a 20-minute walk from the city center: up O'Connell St., right on Dorset St., across the Royal Canal, and finally right onto Clonliffe Rd.

Mrs. M. Ryan, 10 Distillery Rd. (tel. 837 4147), off Clonliffe Rd., on the left if you're coming from city center. Yellow paint trims this gingerbread-like house, attached to #11. Pink-haired in '93, blonde in '94, platinum in '95, the grandmoth-erly proprietor welcomes all with firm beds and warm comforters. £12/person, single £14.

Mrs. Brid Creagh, St. Aiden's B&B, 150 Clonliffe Rd. (tel. 837 6750). A small green fountain glows and gurgles in the foyer. The non-smoking rooms are bound to remind you of home. £15/person. Open April-Sept.

Mrs. Kathleen Greville, Mona B&B, 148 Clonliffe Rd. (tel. 837 6723). Firm beds and clean rooms kept tidy by a warm proprietor. And homemade bread. Single £16, double £28. Open May-Oct.

Gardiner Street

The B&Bs in this area can be a budget-traveler's purgatory. Many travelers arrive late at night and, knowing no better, are plundered here. Choose wisely, or choose a suburban B&B. Lower Gardiner St. and Upper Gardiner St. are within walking dis-tance, but buses #41, 41A, 41B, and 41C from Eden Quay are convenient for the far-ther parts of the road. Those who are walking should start up O'Connell St. and take a right onto Parnell St. to reach Gardiner St.

Leitrim House, 34 Blessington St. (tel. 830 8728), on the final stretch of what was O'Connell St. Leitrim House is 1 block past the false teeth repair shop. Bus #10 drops you off nearby, at the top of Mountjoy St. Lilac walls and flowers on the windowsill result in flowery and pleasant-smelling rooms. Reliquaries in the par-lor strike a contrast. Pampering proprietor really makes the place. £12/person.

Parkway Guest House, 5 Gardiner Place (tel. 874 0469). The rooms are plain but comfortable, and the location, just off Gardiner St. but without the noisy traffic, is excellent. Guests should feel free to play the piano in the sitting room. Single £15; double £28, w/bath £30.

Stella Maris Guest House, 13 Upper Gardiner St. (tel. 874 0835). Red deer antlers in the dining room, a stuffed pheasant in the parlor, and antique furniture every-where—it could almost be a hunting lodge. Everything here comes in large sizes: solid, dark wood beds with firm mattresses suit big rooms with tall ceilings and wide windows. Teamaker in each room. Single £20; double £34, w/bath £240.

Marian Guest House, 21 Upper Gardiner St. (tel. 874 4129). Guests have enjoyed the antique marble fireplaces in this old building for decades and also revel in the delightful rooms (all w/TV). Call ahead. June-Oct. £15/person, Nov.-May £12.

Camping

Most campsites are far from the city center, but camping equipment is available in the heart of the city. **The Great Outdoors,** Chatham St. (tel. 679 4293), off the top of Grafton St., has an excellent selection of tents, backpacks, and cookware (10% discount for An Óige/HI members; open Mon.-Wed. and Fri.-Sat. 9:30am-5:30pm, Thurs. 9:30am-8pm). **O'Meara's,** 26 Ossory Rd. (tel. 836 3233), off North Strand Rd., sells camping equipment and rents tents by the week. (Buy a 2-person tent for £30 during a sale, or rent one for £25/week. Open Mon.-Thurs. and Sat. 10am-1pm and 2-6pm, Fri. 10am-9pm, Sun. 2:30-5:30pm.) **Mavy St.,** off of O'Connell St., has several shops with packs and other equipment in an affordable price range.

Backpackers EuroHostel, 80/81 Lower Gardiner St. (tel. 836 4900). Not really a campsite, but a big room behind the hostel has mattresses where diehard budget travelers can camp out (£4) and still use all of the hostel facilities.

Shankill Caravan and Camping Park, (tel. 282 0011). Buses #45, 45A, 46, and 84, from Eden Quay, and the DART all run to Shankill. Middle-aged travelers in campers alternate with shrubs and tents. Not the ideal accommodation for seeing Dublin. The views of the hills and the 20-minute walk to the beach are much more convenient. £4.50-5.50/tent plus 50p/person. 8-min. shower 50p.

North Beach Caravan and Camping Park, Rush (tel. 843 7131 or 843 7602). Bus #33 from Eden Quay (runs every 45 min.) and the suburban train rush here. Peaceful, beach-side location in a quiet town just outside of Dublin's sphere of influence. Kitchen; indoor beds for emergencies. £3/night.

Longer Term Stays

Solo travelers expecting to spend several weeks in Dublin may want to consider a bedsit, or sublet. Long stays are often most economical when sharing the cost of renting a house or apartment with others. Rooms in outer-city locations like Marino and Rathmines fetch about £32/week (ask whether electricity, phone, and water are included). Dublin's countless university students are often looking for room-mates, usually for the summer but also on a weekly basis. The two main **notice boards** for accommodation are at USIT, 19-21 Aston Quay, and at Trinity College, near the guard's desk and the entrance to the Dublin Experience. Also check in the Student Union and the main entrance to TCD (Trinity College).

A group looking to rent a house or apartment for a few months can happily turn to **Tathony House,** Bow Lane West (tel. 679 0443) near Kilmainham Gaol. Most of their apartments contain 4 double bedrooms, kitchen, sitting area, and bathroom (1 month min. stay; bed in double £30-35/week; single £50/week). If you want some-one else to do the legwork, **Relocators,** 38 Dame St. (tel. 679 3511), opposite the Central Bank, arranges accommodation in Dublin and the suburbs. The company has set deals with landlords to get reduced rates on flats, apartments, B&Bs, and Irish cottages. Bedsits may be as little as £20/week, but a service charge of £30 is required. (Open Mon.-Fri. 9am-7:30pm, Sat. 10am-4:0pm, Sun. 11am-3:30pm.) Classified ads in the two main daily newspapers, the *Irish Times* and the *Irish Independent,* can also help in finding cheap housing, often at weekly rates.

FOOD

Dublin's **open-air markets** sell fresh and cheap fixings for those on a tight budget, and the colors and smells also make for interesting browsing. Vendors with thick east-coast accents hawk fruit, fresh Irish strawberries, flowers, and the occasional chocolate bar from their pushcarts. The frenzied **Moore St. Market,** lined with butcher shops, is the city's main trading center (open Mon.-Sat. 9am-5pm). Moore St. is two blocks west of O'Connell St. The **Thomas St. Market,** along the continuation of Dame St., is a calmer alternative for fruit and vegetable shopping (open Fri.-Sat. 9am-5pm). The **Festival Market,** at the corner of Nicholas St. and Back Lane off High St., is better known for inexpensive clothing and jewelry than for produce (open Fri.-Sun. 9am-5pm).

The cheapest **supermarkets** around Dublin are the many **Dunnes Stores,** which are at St. Stephen's Green Shopping Centre, ILAC Centre, off Henry St., and on North Earl St., off O'Connell St. (All open Mon.-Wed. and Fri.-Sat. 9am-6pm, Thurs. 9am-8pm.) **Quinnsworth** supermarkets are also widespread. In reality, there are so many grocery stores around that it's quite easy to find basic supplies. The **Runner Bean,** 4 Nassau St. (tel. 679 4833), vends wholefoods, homemade breads, and veggies, fruits, and nuts for the squirrel in you (open Mon.-Fri. 8am-6pm, Sat. 9am-6pm). **Down to Earth,** 73 South Great Georges St. (tel. 671 9702) stocks health foods, herbal medicines, and a dozen varieties of granola (open Mon.-Sat. 10am-6pm).

Temple Bar

This neighborhood is ready to implode from its masses of inexpensive and creative eateries. The Temple Bar has more ethnic diversity in its restaurants than the combined counties of Louth, Meath, Wicklow, and Longford (and probably Offaly, too).

The Well Fed Café, 6 Crow St. (tel. 677 2234), off Dame St. Inventive vegetarian dishes served by a worker's cooperative in a stripped-down, bohemian atmosphere. Peace and protest posters on the walls; idealists and disenchanteds at the tables. Adverts for indie band gigs and leaflets for liberal causes in lobby. Popular with the gay community. Brown bread and soup £1, main courses £2-2.50, apple pie with cream 80p. Open Mon.-Sat. noon-8pm. Wheelchair accessible.

Bad Ass Café, Crown Alley, off Temple Bar (tel. 671 2596). Burned down in 1994 but, like phoenixes, Bad Asses rise from the ashes. Colorful, exuberant atmosphere. The food fits right in. Besides, Sinéad O'Connor once worked here, so you can't go wrong. Lunch £3-5. Medium pizza £5, large £7. Student menu (with ISIC): coleslaw, scone and butter, "magic mushrooms," medium pizza, beverage (£5.50). Open daily 9am until "late" (past midnight).

La Mezza Luna, 1 Temple Lane (tel. 671 2840), corner of Dame St. Stars and half-moons twinkle from a midnight-blue ceiling. The food is celestial, too. You can't upstage *paglia*—smoked ham with a mushroom, cream, and wine sauce (£5), or spicy *fettucini putanesca,* with sausage, anchovies, and olives (£5). A spicy pasta pomodor (£4) fills diners to the brim. For dessert, *tiramisù:* mascapone cheese, chocolate, brandy, and cream. Open Mon.-Sat. 12:30-11pm, Sun. 4-10:30pm.

Old New Orleans, 3 Cork Hill (tel. 670 9785), across from Dublin Castle. The least expensive Cajun restaurant in town, it's spicy enough to satisfy even expatriated Louisianians. Small menu, but what they do, they do well. Vegetarian jambalaya £4.50. Open Mon.-Fri. noon-3pm, Thurs.-Sat. 6pm-midnight. No credit cards.

Poco Loco, 32 Parliament St. (tel. 679 1950), between Grattan Bridge and City Hall. Proprietor Neasa O'Riordan asks country music stars using *Let's Go* to please visit her if they happen to be in Dublin. Excellent Tex-Mex in Ireland—who knew? Enchiladas £5, vegetarian chimichangas £4. Open Mon.-Fri. noon-midnight, Sat. 5pm-midnight, Sun. 5-10pm.

Elephant and Castle, 18 Temple Bar (tel. 679 3121). Bustling service and creative menu. Yuppies galore. Burgers £3.50-8, Caesar salad £6.50, Mexican salad £8. Great dinner omelettes: pesto (£6), apple (£5), fresh air (£3). Open Mon.-Fri. 8am-11:30pm, Sat. 10:30am-11:30pm, Sun. noon-11:30pm.

Irish Film Centre, 6 Eustace St. (tel. 677 8788), off Dame St. Perfect for pre- or post-performance pleasures, this bar/restaurant serves snacks all day long and gets particularly creative at dinner. Good vegetarian selection (£5-7). Dinner reservations recommended. Open Sun.-Tues. 12:30-8:30pm, Wed.-Sat. 12:30-11pm.

Trinity College, Grafton Street, Christ Church

Leo Burdock's, 2 Werburgh St. (tel. 454 0306), uphill from Christ Church Cathedral. Luckily the steps of the Cathedral are nearby—Burdock's is take-out only, and eating Burdock's fish and chips are a religious experience from which walking shouldn't distract. Dubliners' pick for best fish and chips in the universe. Haddock or cod £2, large chips 95p. Open Mon.-Fri. 12:30-11pm, Sat. 2-11pm.

La Cave, 28 South Anne St. (tel. 679 4409), off Grafton St. An underground wine-bar replete with Frenchness. Elegant, romantic, soothing. Wines served by every measure. On Sunday nights, poets, musicians, and aesthetes gather for readings and repartee. Cheese plate £4.50 (enough for a meal), vegetarian couscous £5.50, beef braised with Dijon mustard £5.50, *table d'hôte* (complete meal; say "TAH-bluh DOTE" to fit in) £12.50. Open daily 12:30-3pm and 6pm-2am or later.

Cornucopia, 19 Wicklow St. (tel. 677 7583). This vegetarian horn of plenty overflows with huge portions. Sit down for a serious meal (vegetable and bean curry w/rice and salad £4.45) or just a snack (large lentil soup £1.50) and people-watch. Open Mon.-Wed. and Fri. 9am-8pm, Thurs. 9am-9pm, Sat. 9am-6pm.

Bewley's Cafés, (tel. 677 6761), 4 locations. A Dublin institution frequented by a delightful crowd of Dublin characters. Dark wood paneling, marble table tops, and mirrored walls complete the look. Wildly complex pastries (£1); outstanding coffee. Meals are plain but inexpensive. Branches at: 78 Grafton St., the largest (open Sun.-Thurs. 7:30am-1am, Fri.-Sat. 7:30am-2am); 12 Westmoreland St., frequented by James Joyce (open Mon.-Sat. 7:30am-9pm, Sun. 9:30am-8pm); 13 South Great Georges St. (open Mon.-Sat. 7:45am-6pm); and Mary St., past Henry St. (open Mon.-Wed. 7am-9pm, Thurs.-Sat. 7am-2am, Sun. 10am-10pm).

Trinity College, The Buttery, 20 strides inside the college gates, down the handicap ramp in the basement of the dining hall. Food for studious Irish youth. Cheap salads (£1.70). Also a stop on the *Let's Go Dublin Pub Crawl.* (Cafeteria open all year Mon.-Fri. 9:30am-6pm; restaurant open all year Mon.-Fri. noon-2pm and 4-7pm.) **The J.C.R.,** a student café to the right just inside Trinity gates, has cheap snacks when the college is in session (Oct.-May Mon.-Fri. 10am-6:30pm).

Marks Bros., 7 South Great Georges St. (tel. 667 1085), off Dame St. Thick sandwiches (£1.30-1.70) and high salads for starving artists and punks among turgid posters. 3 levels allow for solitary contemplation of James Joyce or of the causes of social stratification. Very popular among gays. Just for fun, tally up the total number of pierced body parts among the waitstaff. Legendary cinnamon buns 40p; sandwiches £1.30-1.70. Open Mon.-Sat. 10am-5pm.

The Stag's Head, 1 Dame Court (tel. 679 3701), via an alleyway off Dame St. at Stanley Racing #28. Marked by a Stag's Head logo in tile on the sidewalk. A great pub with even better grub. Boiled cabbage and potatoes £4, chicken and mushroom pie with chips and vegetables £4.50, sandwiches £1.20. Food served Mon.-Fri. 12:30-3:30pm and 5:30-7:30pm, Sat. 12:30-2:30pm.

Wed Wose Café, Exchequer St. off South Great Georges St., near the block-long wed-bwick mawket. Eclectic decor, cramped seating, and good cheap food. "Mega-bweakfast" (double bacon, egg, sausage, toast, tomato, white pudding, beans, and fwied bwead) £3; steak sandwich, fishburgers £3. Open Mon.-Sat. 7am-7pm.

Blazing Salads II, top floor of Powerscourt Townhouse Centre (tel. 671 9552), along the pedestrian route connecting South Great Georges St. with Grafton St. Far exceeds typical vegetarians' expectations, and perhaps their daring. Entrees £4.25: carrot and fennel bake, or pinto bean and vegetable casserole with organic brown rice. For dessert, brave the Arame Strudle, a Japanese sea vegetable sautéed and rolled into pastry. Open Mon.-Sat. 9am-6pm.

Brew Baker, 22 South Frederick St. (tel. 677 8288). A coffeeshop where the sandwiches, snacks, and pastries are clearly secondary accompaniments to the fundamental product: rich, dark brew (no, not Guinness). Seating outside for people-watching and seating downstairs for intimate chats. Cappuccino 85p. Open Mon.-Fri. 7:30am-6pm, Sat. 10am-5pm.

North of the Liffey

Eating here is undoubtedly less interesting than it is south of the river. O'Connell St. sports blocks of neon fast-food chains, and side streets are filled with fish-and-chips shops and newsagents stocking overpriced groceries. Your options are limited.

The Winding Stair Bookshop and Café, 40 Lower Ormond Quay (tel. 873 3292), near Bachelor's Walk. Café overlooking the river shares 2 floors with bookshelves. Contemporary Irish writing, periodicals, and soothing music decrease the pace even more. Big Greek salad £2.60, sandwiches £1.50, soup and bread £1.60. Open Mon.-Sat. 10:30am-5:30pm.

101 Talbot, 100-102 Talbot St. (tel. 874 5011), off O'Connell St., next to the "Hairy Legs" store. Non-exorbitant gourmet dishes use food in new settings. Menu changes daily: Brazil nut *ressoles* with red pepper sauce (£7), pork with avocado and strawberry dressing (£8). Lunches £5, dinner £7-8. Open Tues.-Sat. 10am-11pm, Mon. 10am-3:30pm.

Flanagan's, 61 O'Connell St. (tel. 873 1388). Normal Irish food is served in the street-level restaurant, but the pizzeria upstairs serves generous pizzas (12" 2-topping pizza £4; weekend evening special of garlic bread, salad, 12" pizza and tea £5.75). Windows look out over teeming O'Connell St. Open daily 8am-midnight.

PUBS

"Good puzzle would be cross Dublin without passing a pub," wrote James Joyce. A local radio station once offered £100 to the first person to solve the puzzle. The winner explained that you could take any route—you'd just have to visit them all on the way! While smaller (and more typical) Irish towns will pack everyone into a few gloriously generic pubs, Dublin's size allows for shapes, styles, subcultures, and specialties. Dublin is the place to hear Irish rock-and-roll. It is not, however, the best place for traditional music. The *bodhrán* is present somewhere in Dublin, but it's much easier to find in the west. Beware of pubs that advertise "traditional" music but mean traditional American country or folk. Check *In Dublin, Hot Press,* or the *Event Guide* for pub music listings, or ask around.

Many heated debates begin from the postulation that Guinness tastes slightly different from every tap. In-depth *Let's Go* research suggests that the Guinness Hop Store, attached to the Guinness Brewery (see Guinness Brewery & Kilmainham, p. 99), serves the city's best, while Mulligan's, the former world champ, currently keeps its hold on #2. Visitors should certainly do their part to contribute to this growing field of research. The **Dublin Literary Pub Crawl** (tel. 454 0228) traces Dublin's liquid history in constant reference to the literary history. The tour spews snatches of info and entrancing monologues. (Meet at The Duke, 2 Duke St. June-Aug. Mon.-Sun. 7:30pm, Mon.-Sat. 3pm, and Sun. noon; May and Sept. Mon.-Sun. 7:30pm; Oct.-April Fri.-Sat. 7:30pm, Sun. noon. £6, students £5.) The enclosed **Let's Go Dublin Pub Crawl Map** should help you stumble around town. The number following each pub listing is the key to its location on the map itself.

North of the Liffey

Fibber MaGee's, 80 Parnell St. (tel. 874 5253). A big pub full of a young crowd dancing to indie rock. You can rest your pint on tree-stump tables outside, where it's quieter. The antithesis of a "classy" pub, Fibber's has pints for only £1.65 from 10:30am-5pm every day and pints for only £1.80 every Wednesday evening as well. Local rock bands play on Sat. afternoons (cover £3). Open until 2am every night, so you can avoid the dreaded 11:30pm bar call.

Slattery's [3], 129 Capel St. (tel. 872 7971). The pub best known for traditional Irish music and set dancing. Rock and blues, too. Music nightly 9pm: trad downstairs (free), rock and blues upstairs (£2-4).

The Grattan [4], 165 Capel St. (tel. 873 3049), on the corner of Little Strand St. Cushy blue velvet seats envelop international ears attuned mostly to jazz, but also blues, folk, rock, and "Australian mad convict rock." Separate rock venue upstairs (cover £2) often features French rock bands whose mettle draws a Euro-slick, urbane crowd. Music starts 9pm.

Hughes' [2], 19 Chancery St. near Chancery Row (tel. 872 6540), behind Four Courts. A delightful venue for traditional music (nightly, no cover charge) and set dancing (Mon. and Wed. 9pm).

The Flowing Tide, 8 Abbey St. Lower (tel. 874 0842). Eclectic mix of regulars, students, and patrons and actors of the Abbey Theatre. Ground floor attracts an older, artsy crowd while the **Neptune Bar** downstairs fills with Dublin students. Pints of Guinness 10p less than the area norm.

PUBS

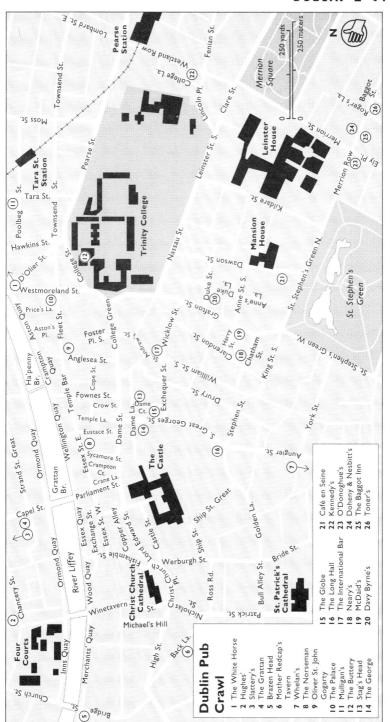

Dublin Pub Crawl

1 The White Horse
2 Hughes'
3 Slattery's
4 The Grattan
5 Brazen Head
6 Mother Redcap's Tavern
7 Whelan's
8 The Norseman
9 Oliver St. John Gogarty
10 The Palace
11 Mulligan's
12 The Buttery
13 Stag's Head
14 The George
15 The Globe
16 The Long Hall
17 The International Bar
18 McDaid's
19 Neary's
20 Davy Byrne's
21 Café en Seine
22 Kennedy's
23 O'Donoghue's
24 Doheny & Nesbitt's
25 The Baggot Inn
26 Toner's

Pearse Station

Tara St. Station

Four Courts

Trinity College

Leinster House

Mansion House

St. Stephen's Green

Christ Church Cathedral

St. Patrick's Cathedral

The Castle

Merrion Square

Temple Bar

River Liffey

0   250 yards
0   250 meters

Grafton Street & Vicinity

Davy Byrne's [20], 21 Duke St. (tel. 671 1298), off Grafton St. "Nice quiet bar. Nice piece of wood in that counter. Nicely planned. Like the way it curves there." Come see what Joyce meant in *Ulysses*. The many comfortable seats may not bring epiphany about why Joyce considered this a "moral pub," but they do enhance the enjoyment of pints.

McDaid's [19], 3 Harry St. (tel. 679 4395), off Grafton St., across from Anne St. Writer Brendan Behan frequented this cheery place. Old books adorn the walls, inspiring conversations of love and honor among the young Dubliners in the crowded downstairs and more spacious upstairs areas; occasional rock gigs.

The International Bar [17], 23 Wicklow St. (tel. 677 9250), off Grafton St. on the corner of South William St. Excellent improv comedy on Mon. nights and stand-up comedy on Wed. nights. All other nights blues (performances 9pm; cover charge £2-5). Sun. 12:30pm, ballads and traditional Irish music (no cover).

Neary's [18], 1 Chatham St. (tel. 677 8596), off Grafton St. across from the Gaiety Theatre stage door. The door also has a sign reading "The Chatham Cocktail Lounge." Actors and their entourages pop from dressing room to the pub. Cast-iron arms at the entrance hold lanterns to show you the way.

Baggot Street & Vicinity

O'Donoghue's [23], 15 Merrion Row (tel. 676 2807), between St. Stephen's Green North and Baggot St. Original home of The Dubliners, a renowned Irish band. Every night new hopefuls attempt to break through into the traditional Irish music scene (9pm winter, 9:30pm summer; no cover charge).

Café en Seine [21], 40 Dawson St. (tel. 677 4151) is built to impress. A café with dainty pastries occupies the front of the shop. A very long bar stretches through a high-ceilinged hall hung with tapestries and zany paintings. A large crowd of mixed ages packs in, unconcerned that the Seine is not at all nearby.

The White Horse [1], 1 Georges Quay (tel. 679 3068). For those early mornings when you just *need* a pint with your muesli, the White Horse opens at 7:30am every day. It's a small, simple bar, frequented by regulars who come for the trad and rock (starts around 9:30pm; no cover).

Doheny and Nesbitt's [24], 5 Lower Baggot St. (tel. 676 2945), near St. Stephen's Green. Glorious snugs and Irish stew (£2.50; served Sat.). Home to the best hot roast beef sandwich in Dublin (lunch only). Executive male bonding sessions on weekday evenings—very corporate.

Toner's [26], 139 Lower Baggot St. (tel. 676 3090). The only pub in which Yeats ever set foot. He stayed long enough to drink one sherry before insisting on going home. Dark wood snugs enable you to feel wonderfully secluded, even though it is a small and tight pub.

The Baggot Inn [25], 143 Lower Baggot St. (tel. 676 1430). According to some quirky numbering system, it's across the street from Doheny's. Frequented by U2 in the early 80s, nightly rock still attracts a jumping and bumping group. Either the calm ambience or the big-screen TV draw an older crowd in the afternoons.

Kennedy's [22], 31 Westland Row (tel. 676 2998), on the southeast corner of Trinity College campus. Boisterous TCD hangout. Jolly musicians gather to play informal sessions (Oct.-May Tues., Thurs., and Sat. June-Sept. Thurs. and Sat.).

The Buttery [12], Trinity College. Dark, smoky, and crammed with students, even at 3pm. This pub offers no extras. People come here to talk and drink, and they do both expertly. Open Mon.-Fri. noon-11pm.

Temple Bar & Vicinity

The Brazen Head [5], 20 Lower Bridge St. (tel. 679 5186), off Merchant's Quay. Dublin's oldest pub, established in 1198 as the first stop after the bridge on the way into the city. The courtyard is quite the pickup scene on summer nights.

The Stag's Head [13], 1 Dame Court (tel. 679 3701). From Dame St., the entrance to a short cut is next to #28, Stanley Racing and is marked by "Stag's Head" written in tile on the sidewalk. Beautiful Victorian pub with stained glass, mirrors, and brasswork. Shiny. Huge whisky kegs on the walls. Truly excellent grub.

The George [14], 89 South Great Georges St. (tel. 478 2983). Currently Dublin's only gay pub. Ground-floor bar is crowded with gay men and lesbians. Upstairs, **The Block** is a bar and nightclub for gay men (Fri.-Sat.).

Oliver St. John Gogarty [9], corner of Fleet St. and Anglesea St. (tel. 671 1822). Lively and convivial atmosphere in a traditionally decorated pub. Named for Joyce's nemesis and onetime roommate, who appears in *Ulysses* as Buck Mulligan. Trad sessions nightly 7:30pm (no cover) and good food. This is what pubs are all about.

The Long Hall [16], 51 South Great Georges St. (tel. 475 1590). A beautiful, long old pub with a carved polished wood bar, ornate mirrors, and endless *craic*.

Mulligan's [11], 8 Poolbeg St. (tel. 677 5582), behind Burgh Quay off Tara St. Big rep as the best pint of Guinness in Dublin, outside the brewery itself. This is a sit, smoke, and talk sort of pub. The crowd consists mainly of middle-aged man.

Whelan's [7], 25 Wexford St. (tel. 478 0766), continue down South St. Georges St. A bit of a walk away from everything. Nightly music makes it one of the hot spots for live rock in Dublin. They know it, and have a "21 and over" policy. Nightly Irish indie rock or blues (cover £2-3).

Mother Redcaps Tavern [6], Back Lane (tel. 453 8306), near Christ Church. In a spacious former shoe factory, convenient to Burdock's (see Food o' Dublin, p. 87). Traditional music Tues. and Thurs., Bluegrass on Wed. and Fri. (9pm), Sun. morning trad and ballads, Sun. night folk—and no cover charge. No wonder everyone's so happy-go-lucky and friendly. At the separate bar upstairs, Fri. and Sat. nights bring big names in trad music (and a cover, £5-6).

The Norseman [8], 29 East Essex St. (tel. 671 5135), corner of Sycamore St. behind Wellington Quay. No Vikings, no Ivar. More trendy types frequent this pub: musicians, actors, entourage. Ballads Sun. 9-11am.

The Palace [10], 21 Fleet St. (tel. 677 9290), behind Aston Quay. A classic neighborly Dublin pub has old-fashioned wood panelling and cramped quarters that encourage *craic*. Many Dubliners choose this as their favorite pub.

The Globe [15], 11 South Great Georges St. (tel. 671 1220). Music issues forth from the Roman busts on the walls. Frothy cappuccino and Guinness fuel the hip, young clientele of this café/pub. It is indeed pretentious, and yet so relaxed that you can appreciate the modernist paintings next to the bust of Julius Caesar.

TOURS

Self-Guided Walking Tours

Dublin is definitely a walking city. Most major sights lie less than a mile from O'Connell Bridge. The tourist office sells *Visitor Attractions in Dublin,* which lists the main attractions (£1.95), and many info-stuffed brochures that describe self-guided walking tours (£1 each). The **Old City Trail** begins on College Green and weaves its way through the Liberties, the markets, and Temple Bar. It's mostly a gathering of "here-once-stoods," which seldom have any relation to each other. The **Georgian Heritage Trail** is more tangibly gratifying. This theme-walk connects some of the better preserved Georgian streets, terraces, and public buildings south of the Liffey. **The Cultural Trail,** starring James Joyce and Sean O'Casey, zips among the Four Courts, the Custom House and King's Inn, the Municipal Gallery, and the Dublin Writers' Museum. It touches on most of the important historical and political sights. Lastly, the disturbingly worshipful **Rock'n'Stroll Trail** brochure makes a circuit of significant sights in Dublin's recent musical history, labelling each with a plaque. Sinéad O'Connor's waitressing job at the Bad Ass Café and U2's Windmill Lane Studios are its highlights. For Joyce fans, the tourist office provides a **Ulysses map of Dublin** (50p) that details some of Leopold Bloom's haunts. Tourists can retrace Bloom's literary actions, beginning with kidneys for breakfast. The entire walk will inevitably take 18 hours (including drinking and debauching).

Guided Walking

Among an abundance of guided walking tours, Trinity students give two good ones. The **Historical Walking Tour** (tel. 845 0241) takes two hours to instruct tourists in a crash course in Dublin's history from the Celts to the present. Great emphasis is laid on the "gritty" lives of ordinary Dubliners. (June-Sept. Mon.-Sat. at 11am, noon, and 3pm, Sun. also at 2pm. Meet at Trinity's front gate. £4, students £3.) The witty and irreverent **Trinity College Walking Tour** also touches on Dublin's history, but it concentrates on University lore. (June-Sept. 10am-4pm, leaves every 15 min. from the Info Booth inside the front gate; ½ hr.; £5, students £4, including admission to the Old Library and the Book of Kells.) For a unique perspective on Irish history, **Sli Na Ban**, or "the Women's Way," (Pat Mulligan, tel. 838 3444), leads visitors through a female Dublin. The tour discusses the impact that women had on the city's art, literature, and politics (tours Mon.-Fri.; 1½ hr.; £5, students £3.50).

Dublin Footsteps (tel. 496 0641 or 845 0772) runs an "early morning" tour of Dublin's main attractions (meets at the O'Connell St. tourist office, 10am Mon.-Sat.), as well as tours along literary and medieval lines. (Literary tour Mon., Wed., Fri., Sun.; medieval tour Tues., Thurs., Sat. at 11am; 2½ hrs.; £4. Tours meet at Bewley's Café on Grafton St.; free coffee to finish the tour.) Those yearning for guidance in the matters of *céilí* and Guinness should try the **Traditional Music Pub Crawl,** which meets at Oliver St. John Gogarty's, on the corner of Fleet St. and Anglesea St. (May-Oct. Sat.-Thurs. 7:30pm; £5). **The Literary and Historical Performance Tour** puts its suffering guides into period costume as they make the sight-seeing circuit (pre-booked groups only; call Mark. tel. 478 0191; £5, students and seniors £4.50).

Bus Tours

Dublin Bus offers several bus tours. The **Dublin City Sightseeing Tour** covers the larger Dublin area and stops at the excellent Irish Museum of Modern Art (daily 10:15am and 2:15pm; £8). The **Dublin Heritage Trail bus** (tel. 872 0000), runs all day and allows you to get on and off at various sights. (April-Sept. daily 10, 11am, noon, 1:30pm, then every half-hour until 4, 6, and 7pm; £5.) Both tours depart from 59 O'Connell St.

SIGHTS

South Side

Trinity College & Nearby

Trinity College (tel. 677 2941) sprawls within its ancient walls in the very center of Dublin, between Westmoreland St. and Grafton St., fronting on the block-long traffic circle now called College Green. Pearse St. runs along the north edge of the college, Nassau St. to its south. Inside, stone buildings, a cobblestone walk, and spacious green grounds give the campus an illusory seclusion and allow for the occasional white-suited game of cricket. The British originally built Trinity in 1592 as a Protestant religious seminary "to civilize the Irish and cure them of Popery." The college became part of the accepted path which members of the Irish Anglican upper class trod on their way to high government and social position. TCD, as it is now known, became a stronghold and symbol of the Protestant Ascendancy. The Catholic Jacobites who briefly held Dublin in 1689 used it as a barracks and prison, but for the next hundred or so years it became a focus of Anglo-Irish society. Jonathan Swift, George Berkeley, Robert Emmett, Thomas Moore, Edmund Burke, Oscar Wilde, Samuel Beckett, and Robin Garvey are just a few of the famous Irish Protestants who spent years studying here. Until the 1960s, the Catholic church deemed it a cardinal sin to attend Trinity. Once the church lifted the ban, the size of the student body more than tripled.

The 1712 **Old Library** holds Ireland's finest collection of Egyptian, Greek, Latin, and Irish manuscripts, including the ***Book of Kells.*** Around 800 AD, Irish monks squeezed multicolored ink from insects to make the famous *Book,* a four-volume edition of the Gospels. Each page holds a dizzyingly intricate lattice of Celtic knotwork and scrollwork into which animals and Latin characters are interwoven. In 1007 the books were unearthed in Kells, where thieves had apparently buried them. In order to enhance preservation, only two volumes are on display. One page is turned each month. For your own amusement, you could ask the Trinity librarians why they won't return the *Book of Kells* to the town of Kells. Trinity owns other illuminated books, like the *Book of Durrow,* Ireland's oldest. Some of these are periodically put on display. Tourists viewing the *Book* should also check out the ever-changing science and history exhibits. Upstairs, in the Library's Long Room, are "Ireland's oldest harp"—the Brian Ború harp (which looks just like the one on Irish coins), and one of the few remaining 1916 proclamations of the Republic of Ireland. (Library open Mon.-Sat. 9:30am-5:30pm, Sun. noon-5pm. £3, students £2.25.) The line to see the *Book of Kells* is often lengthy, and visitors are herded onward by fastidious librarians. Ignore the pressure and pause to ponder away.

In Trinity's Davis Theatre, the **Dublin Experience** movie takes visitors in a 45-minute historical tour of Dublin, reminiscent of grade-school educational films. (Daily 10am-5pm, on the hour. £2.75, students £2.25. Combination ticket to Library and Dublin Experience £5.50, students £4.25.) **The Douglas Hyde Gallery** (no tel., but they do have paintings of fire and skulls), on the south side of campus, exhibits the works of modern Irish artists (open Mon.-Sat. 10am-5pm; free). During the academic year, TCD bulges with events and activities, which are listed on bulletin boards around campus (see Longer Term Stays, p. 87). Concerts and plays are posted at these points and elsewhere around campus.

Staring down Trinity from across College Green is a menacingly monolithic, Roman-looking building, the **Bank of Ireland** (tel. 677 6801). It was built in 1729 originally to house the 18th-century Irish Parliament. This Parliament represented the Anglo-Irish landowning class (the ones who attended TCD across the road). Its members envisioned a semi-independent Irish "nation" under the British crown and made up of the privileged Protestants of the Pale. After the Act of Union, the British sold the building to the bank on the condition that the bank blot out any material evidence of the legislature. The enormous curved walls and pillars were erected *around* the original structure to make the whole look more impressive. The bank inside is actually much smaller. Tourists can still visit the former chamber of the House of Lords. There, beneath a huge antique chandelier, is the gold mace of the old House of Commons. The last Speaker of the House refused to hand the mace over, saying he would keep it until an Irish assembly returned. Also on display is Maundy Money: special coins once given to the poor on the Thursday before Easter, and legal tender only for that day. (Open during regular banking hours Mon.-Wed. and Fri. 10am-4pm, Thurs. 10am-5pm. Guided tours Tues. 10:30am, 11:30am, 1:45pm. Free.)

South of College Green (away from the Liffey) run the three or so blocks of **Grafton Street,** off-limits to cars and ground zero for shopping tourists and residents alike. This crowded pedestrian street provides some entertaining observations, but nothing much to do or even to buy (most things are too expensive). Upstairs at the Bewley's Grafton St. branch is the **Bewley's Museum,** located in the coffee chain's former chocolate factory. Tea-tasting machines, corporate history, and a display on Bewley's Quaker heritage are among the curiosities that are quite fun for browsing. (Open daily 10am-7pm; free.)

Merrion Square & St. Stephen's Green

South of Trinity College at Leinster St., with Kildare St. at its back and Merrion Square in front of it, **Leinster House** provides chambers for the present-day Irish parliament. It holds both the *Dáil* ("doil") which does most of the government work and also the less powerful upper house, the *Seanad* ("SHAN-ad"). Together these two houses make up the parliament, called (in its entirety, in Irish) *An tOireachtas* ("on tir-OCH-tas"). When the *Dáil* is in session, visitors can view the proceedings by contacting the Captain of the Guard (tel. 678 9911; passport is necessary for identification). The *Dáil* meets, very roughly, Wednesday through Friday from January to July (10:30am-5pm). The Captain's office also conducts some tours of the *Dáil's* galleries (Sat. 10:30am-12:45pm and 1:30-4:50pm). Leinster House was once the house of the Duke of Leinster. When he built it, most of the urban upper-crust lived north of the Liffey. By erecting his house so far south, he was able to front it with an enormous lawn. The first Irishman to ride in a balloon ascended in 1785 from this same lawn. The airman had neglected to bring enough ballast, however, and drifted out over the Irish Sea, where well-aimed gunfire from the Dún Laoghaire barge brought him down.

Near Leinster House, a passel of museums pop up. The **National Museum,** Kildare St. (tel. 661 8811), focuses on legendary ancient Ireland and the equally heroic Easter Rising. One room gleams with the Tara Brooch, Ardagh Chalice, and other Celtic goldwork. Another, devoted to the Republic's founding years, offers plenty of historical information for the curious and shows off the bloody vest of James Connolly to pique the interest of the morbid. Connolly made a name for himself as a leading exponent of socialism in Ireland before he took part in the Easter Rising. After the rebellion, Connolly was unable to walk due to battle wounds and was also condemned to death by the British. Other chambers collect musical instruments and, oddly, Japanese ceramics. (Open Tues.-Sat. 10am-5pm, Sun. 2-5pm. Free.)

Connected to the National Museum, the **Natural History Museum** (tel. 661 8811) specializes in stuffed Irish wildlife. They even have an example of the extinct Great Irish Elk. They've got leeches and tapeworms, too (safely mounted). The collection is a good-sized one and contains tons of info, but everything is in need of organization and preservation (open Tues.-Sat. 10am-5pm, Sun. 2-5pm; free).

Down the street on Merrion Sq., the **National Gallery's** 2400 canvases (tel. 461 5133) include works by Brueghel, Vermeer, Hals, Goya, Rembrandt, and El Greco. The products of Irish artists comprise a major part of the collection, naturally. Portraits of Lady Gregory, Eliza O'Neill, James Joyce, George Bernard Shaw (who willed a third of his estate to the Gallery), and William Butler Yeats (by his father, John Butler Yeats) stare at one another in the four-story staircase. (Open Mon.-Sat. 10am-6pm, Thurs. 10am-9pm, Sun. 2-5pm. Free.) Nearby, the **National Library** chronicles Irish history and exhibits literary objects in its entrance room. (Library open Mon. 10am-9pm, Tues.-Wed. 2-9pm, Thurs.-Fri. 10am-5pm, Sat. 10am-1pm; free; academic reasons needed to obtain a library card and entrance to the reading room.)

Dublin may remember its Viking conquerors more fondly than its British ones, but the British had much more influence on the appearance of the capital today. **Merrion Square** and **Fitzwilliam Street** (near the National Museum) are plum full of Georgian buildings and their elaborate rows of colored doorways. W.B. Yeats moved from 18 Fitzwilliam St. to 82 Merrion Sq. Farther south on Harcourt St., playwright George Bernard Shaw and Dracula's creator, Bram Stoker, were once neighbors at #61 and #16, respectively. **#29 Lower Fitzwilliam Street** (tel. 702 6165) tries to give tourists an impression of late-18th-century Dublin domestic life. The National Museum has stuffed the Georgian house with period furniture, elegant drapes, and Irish crafts. Though the house hardly depicts the realistic 18th-century life of any social class, some of the objects make for interesting viewing (open Tues.-Sat. 10am-5pm, Sun. 2-5pm; free).

The prim Georgian townhouses continue up **Dawson Street,** which connects St. Stephen's Green to Trinity College, one block west of Leinster House. A few small and endearing churches line this street, as does **Mansion House,** home to Lord Mayors of Dublin since 1715. The house's various facades and additions give it an interesting but eclectic appearance. The Irish state declared independence here in 1919. The Anglo-Irish truce (not the Treaty) was signed here in 1921.

Kildare St., Dawson St., and Grafton St. all lead south from Trinity to **St. Stephen's Green.** The 22-acre park was a private estate until the Guinness clan bequeathed it to the city. The park today is constantly in use and has become a real center for activity. It's crowded with arched bridges, an artificial lake, flowerbeds, fountains, gazebos, pensioners, punks, couples, strollers, swans, ducks, trees, even more trees, and a waterfall. On sunny days, half of Dublin seems to fill the lawns. During the summer, even the ducks enjoy the outdoor theatrical productions near the old bandstand. (Gates open Mon.-Sat. 8am-dusk, Sun. 10am-dusk.)

Edging the green, **Newman House,** 85-86 St. Stephen's Green South (tel. 706 7422 or 706 7419), was once the seat of University College Dublin, the Catholic answer to Trinity. Influential Victorian intellectual and former Anglican John Henry Cardinal Newman was its first rector. The poet Gerard Manley Hopkins spent the last years of his life teaching classics to eager young faces at the new college. Joyce's years here are chronicled in *Portrait of the Artist as a Young Man.* Inside Newman House, the range of restored rooms has less kitsch than those at #29 Fitzwilliam. (Open June-Sept. Tues.-Fri. 10am-4pm, Sat. 2-4:30pm, Sun. 11am-2pm; £1, students 75p.)

The **George Bernard Shaw House,** 33 Synge St. (tel. 872 2077), lies between Grantham St. and Harrington St., off Camden Rd. and near the Grand Canal Bridge. It is of interest both as a period piece and as a glimpse into Shaw's childhood. Mrs. Shaw held recitals, sparking little George's interest in music, and kept a lovely Victorian garden, sparking George's interest in landscape painting. So how did he get into socialism in London? (Open May-Sept. Mon.-Sat. 10am-1pm and 2-5pm, Sun. 10am-1pm and 2-6pm. £1.75, children 90p. If it's too wet to walk, take bus #15, 16, 19, or 22 from O'Connell St.)

The **Irish Jewish Museum,** 3-4 Walworth Rd., off Victoria St. (tel. 453 1797) lies even farther from the city center. South Circular Rd. runs to Victoria St., and from there the museum is signposted. A restored, but unused, synagogue hulks above the exhibits, which cover the existence of Jews in Ireland from 1079—five arrived and were duly sent away—through the massive waves of European migrations. The most famous Dublin Jew is probably Leopold Bloom, hero of *Ulysses.* He's covered here, too. (Open May-Sept. Tues., Thurs., and Sun. 11am-3:30pm, Oct.-Apr. Sun. 11am-3:30pm. Donation requested.)

Temple Bar, Dame Street, & Cathedrals

West of Trinity College between Dame St. and the Liffey, the **Temple Bar** neighborhood wriggles with activity. Narrow cobblestone streets link up cheap cafés, hole-in-the-wall theaters, rock venues, and used clothing and record stores. The Irish transport authority intended to demolish the neighborhood and replace it with a seven-acre transportation center. As the transport authority acquired Temple Bar properties, they decided to lease the land (and make a profit) for the short term, until they had acquired all the necessary property. However, the artists and other transient types who moved into Temple Bar started a brouhaha about being forced into homelessness. In 1985 they circulated petitions and saved their homes and businesses from the rapacious transit project.

Government-sponsored Temple Bar Properties has changed its mind and now plans to spend over thirty million pounds to build eight arts-related tourist attractions in the Temple Bar. Though deadlines have been postponed until 1996, work continues on an expansion of the existing Temple Bar Art Gallery, a Children's Cultural Centre, a Photography Centre with school and gallery, and a Multi-Media Centre for video and high-tech arts.

South of the Temple Bar across Dame St. awaits another inviting, unpretentious shopping district. The **Dublin Civic Museum,** South William St. (tel. 679 4260) seems a bit out of place in the middle of all those shops. The pint-size, two-story townhouse holds photos, antiquities, and knick-knacks relating to the whole range of Dublin life, from the comparatively small-toed Vikings to the shoes of Patrick Cotter, the 8'6" "giant of Ireland." Another of the original 1916 proclamations of the Republic is held here. Photos of the 1907 Dublin Exhibition show a reconstructed Somalian village, complete with real Somalians, that was shipped in to Dublin. Disturbing. (Open Tues.-Sat. 10am-6pm, Sun. 11am-2pm. Free.)

At the west end of Dame St., where it meets Parliament St. and Castle St., sits **Dublin Castle** (tel. 677 7129). King John built the castle in 1204 on top of an old Viking fort. For the next 700 years Dublin Castle was the seat of British rule in Ireland and the office of the British Governor General. The present Dublin Castle structure actually dates mostly from the 18th and 19th centuries. The Birmingham Tower was once a prison. 50 insurgents died at the castle's walls on Easter Monday, 1916. Since 1938 the presidents of Ireland have been inaugurated here. The State Apartments, once home to English viceroys, now entertain EU representatives and foreign heads of state. If they're not entertaining state visitors when you get there, you can entertain the notion of a tour. (State Apartments open Mon.-Fri. 10am-12:15pm and 2-5pm, Sat.-Sun. and holidays 2-5pm, except during official functions. £1.75, students and children £1. Rest of castle is free.) The Visitors Centre exhibits photos of many of Dublin's architectural showpieces and of the Castle itself. Next door, the **Dublin City Hall** boasts an intricate inner dome and statues of national heroes like Daniel O'Connell. Designed as the Royal Exchange in 1779, it is open to the public.

Dublin's ecclesiastical beauties line up west of the Castle. All are owned by the Church of Ireland, none by the Catholic Church. As Ireland is overwhelmingly Catholic and even the Anglo-Irish aristocracy (which once had the funds to support lots of ornate churches) is a dead concept, the cathedrals and churches are now considered works of art more than than centers of worship.

Christ Church Cathedral (tel. 677 8099) looms at the end of Dame St., uphill and across from the Castle. Sigtyggr Silkenbeard, King of the Dublin Norsemen, built a wooden church on this site in 1038. Strongbow rebuilt it in stone in 1169. Further additions were made in the following century and again in the 1870s. Stained glass sparkles above the raised crypts (one of them supposedly Strongbow's own). The cathedral's cavernous crypt once held shops and drinking houses. Now, cobwebs hang down from the ceiling, fragments of ancient pillars lie about like bleached bones, and a mummified cat is frozen in the act of chasing a mummified mouse. (Open daily 10am-5pm except during services. Choral evensong Sept.-May Thurs. 6pm. £1 donation.) Christ Church also hosts **Dublinia** (tel. 679 4611), a charming re-creation of medieval Dublin with life-size reconstructions of a merchant's house and of Wood Quay c. 1200. Less charming is the buboe-covered mannequin in the Black Death display. (Open daily April-Sept. 10am-5pm; Feb.-March Mon-Sat. 11am-4pm, Sun. 10am-4:30pm. £4, students and children £3; includes admission to Christ Church.) Bus #50 and 50A from Aston Quay, or your feet, will carry you here.

From Christ Church, Nicholas St. runs south and downhill, becoming Patrick St. and encountering **St. Patrick's Cathedral** (tel. 475 4817). The body of the church dates to the 12th century, though many parts also date from Sir Benjamin Guinness's 1864 remodeling job. Three hundred feet long from stem to stern, it's Ireland's longest church. St. Patrick, who brought Christianity to Ireland and drove out all the snakes, allegedly baptized converts in the park next to the cathedral. Artifacts and relics from the Order of St. Patrick show up inside. Jonathan Swift, who wrote *Gulliver's Travels,* spent his last years as Dean of St. Patrick's. Sir Walter Scott said of his visit to St. Patrick's that "one thinks of nothing but Swift there....The whole cathedral is practically his tomb." His crypt rises above the south nave. (Open Mon.-Fri. 9am-6pm, Sat. 9am-5pm, Sun. 10am-4:30pm. £1, students 40p.)

Marsh's Library, St. Patrick's Close (tel. 454 3511), beside St. Patrick's Cathedral, is Ireland's oldest public library. A peek inside reveals its elegant wire alcoves, or "cages." The library has an extensive collection of early maps. Swift said of the library's founder, Archbishop Marsh, that "no man will be either glad or sorry at his death." (Open Mon. and Wed.-Fri. 10am-12:45pm and 2-5pm, Sat. 10:30am-12:45pm. £1 donation expected.)

Farther west, along High St., stands **St. Audoen's Church** (Church of Ireland), the oldest of Dublin's parish churches, founded by the Normans. Papal Bulls were read aloud here during the Middle Ages (open Sat.-Sun. 2:30-5pm). There is also a totally separate, Catholic St. Audoen's Church. **St. Audoen's Arch,** built in 1215 next to the church and now obscured by a narrow alley, is the only gate that survives from Dublin's medieval city walls. During the 16th century, walls ran from Parliament St. to the Dublin Castle, along the castle walls to Little Ship St. and along Francis St. to Bridge St., then along the Liffey.

Guinness Brewery & Kilmainham

From Christ Church Cathedral, follow High St. west (away from downtown) through its name changes to Thomas and then James to reach the giant **Guinness Brewery,** St. James Gate (tel. 453 6700; fax 454 6519). **The Hop Store,** on Crane St. off James St., is Guinness' sneaky way of perpetuating the legend of the world's best stout. Housed in a large warehouse which still smells of the hops that were stowed there for 200 years, it is near the site of Arthur Guinness' original 1759 brewery for which he signed a 9000-year lease. There are exhibits on the historical and modern processes of brewing stout, a short promotional film, and art exhibits on the top floor that showcase local artists. Best of all is the bar, where visitors get a complimentary glass of the dark and creamy goodness incarnate. This stuff is rumored to be the best Guinness in Dublin and hence, according to Dublin logic, the world's best beer. But is it really "good for you?" (Open Mon.-Fri. 10am-4:30pm, last tour 3:50pm. £2, students £1.50.) Bus #21A, 7, and 78A head here along the quays.

The Royal Hospital and Kilmainham Gaol lie farther to the west, a 20-min. walk from the city center. The **Royal Hospital Kilmainham** began in 1679; it wasn't a "hospital" in the modern sense, but an old-age home for retired or disabled soldiers. The facade and courtyard copy those of Les Invalides in Paris; the baroque chapel looks cool too (tours Sun. noon-4:30pm and by request; £1). Since 1991 the hospital has held the **Irish Museum of Modern Art** (tel. 671 8666), whose capacious, brightly-colored galleries might just as well be showing art in New York, Oakland, or Auckland; the museum project took some heat over its avant-garde use of this historic space. Modern Irish artists are intermixed with others as the gallery builds up a permanent collection (call for changing exhibits, artist talks, or concerts). (Museum and building open Tues.-Sat. 10am-5:30pm, Sun. noon-5:30pm; free. Guided tours Wed. and Fri. 2:30pm, Sat. 11:30am.)

From its completion in 1792 to Irish independence in 1921, **Kilmainham Gaol** (tel. 453 5984) managed to hold almost all the heroes of Ireland's struggle for independence. Parnell was confined here (with many other political criminals) in 1881 for fomenting Land League action. The leaders of the Easter Rising were confined here; many of them were executed in the same place. The jail's last occupant was Éamon de Valera. The tour ends in the prison chapel, where Easter Rebel Joseph Plunkett was married to his betrothed hours before his execution. The reception was a subdued affair. (Open May-Sept. daily 10am-6pm; April Mon.-Fri. 1-4pm, Sun. 1-6pm. £2, seniors £1.50, students and children 60p.) Take bus #51, 63, 69, 78A, or 79 from the city center to both the Museum and the Gaol.

Distant Sights

For an awesome view of Dublin and the action of Dublin Port, take bus #1 from the O'Connell St. stop outside the tourist office to its terminus at the Powerstation. Go around the station, past the dump, past the rocks, and onto the South Wall. The road extends two miles into Dublin Bay with the darling Poolbeg Lighthouse at the end, built in 1761. On a windy day, the long walk can feel like a boat ride.

Windmill Lane Studios, Windmill Lane. Not really worth the walk: from City Quay, turn right on Creighton St. and left on Hanover St. East. Where U2 ("that's the letter U and the numeral 2") record their stuff. Outside, graffiti artists pledge their undying love to Bono and his pop idol friends on the **U2 Wall,** and a plaque explains the "historical significance" of the place.

Chester Beatty Library and Gallery of Oriental Art, 20 Shrewsbury Rd. (tel. 269 2386 or 269 5187), take DART to Sandymount, bus #5, 6, 6A, 7A, or 8 from Eden Quay, or #10 from O'Connell St. If you're into Arabic calligraphy in illuminated copies of the Koran, you'll go nuts here. Strong Turkish collection of manuscripts and paintings. Also Biblical papyri from 200 AD, Japanese snuff bottles, and Chinese rhinoceros horn cups. Free admission; free guided tours Wed. and Sat. 2:30pm. Open Tues.-Fri. 10am-5pm, Sat. 2-5pm.

Museum of Childhood, 20 Palmerstown Park (tel. 973 223), take bus #13 or 14 from College Green. A private collection of dolls and toys from the 1700s to the present. Utterly charming. Dollhouse kitchens have tiny mice and rats. Tanya's Crystal Palace is a big dollhouse of 20 rooms, filled with tiny brass beds, porcelain sinks, and typewriters. Open Sun. 2-5:30pm, July-Aug. also Wed. 2-5:30pm; last admission 4:45pm. £1, children 75p.

Pearse Museum, St. Edna's Park, Grange Rd. (tel. 934 208). Bus #16 from O'Connell St. See Patrick Pearse's study and learn about his work as educator, writer, and revolutionary. Free; open daily May-Aug. 10am-5:30pm, Sept.-Oct. and Feb.-April 10am-5pm, Nov.-Jan 10am-4pm; closed daily 1-2pm.

North Side

O'Connell St. & Parnell Square

Rising from the river to Parnell Square, **O'Connell Street** is the commercial center of Dublin, at least for those who can't afford to shop on Grafton St. It's also said to be the widest street in Europe, though it's hard to imagine anyone traveling to Madrid with a yardstick to compare. In its Joycean heyday, it was known as Sackville Street. The name was changed in honor of "The Liberator" after independence. Smaller avenues leading off of O'Connell St. retain the old name. The center traffic islands are monuments to Irish leaders: Parnell, O'Connell, and James Larkin, who organized the heroic Dublin general strike of 1913. O'Connell's statue faces the Liffey and O'Connell Bridge; the winged women aren't angels but Winged Victories, though one has a bullet hole in a rather inglorious place.

Farther up the street, the newer statue of a woman lounging in water is officially the Spirit of the Liffey or "Anna Livia," unoffically and scathingly called "the floozy in the jacuzzi," "the whore in the sewer," (in Dublin, that rhymes too), or Anna Rexia. The even newer statue of Molly Malone, of ballad fame, on Grafton St. gets called "the tart in the cart." Decide for yourself whether Dubliners are mocking the city, the monument-making mentality, or simply women in general with this series of popular nicknames. One monument you won't see is Nelson's Pillar, a tall freestanding column which remembered Trafalgar outside the GPO for 150 years. The IRA blew it up in 1966 in commemoration of the 50th anniversary of the Easter Rising; Nelson's English head now rests in the Dublin Civic Museum.

The **General Post Office** presides over O'Connell St. Not just a fine place to send a letter, the Post Office was the nerve center of the 1916 Rising. Patrick Pearse read the Proclamation of Irish independence from its steps. When British troops closed in, mailbags became barricades. Outside, some bullet nicks can still be seen; inside, a glass case exhibits pennies fused together by the British army's incendiary bombing. A few blocks up O'Connell St., turn right on Cathedral St. to find the inconspicuous **Dublin Pro-Cathedral,** the city's center of Catholic worship, where tens of thousands once gathered for Daniel O'Connell's memorial service. "Pro" means "provisional"—Dublin Catholics want Christ Church Cathedral returned.

Overlooking the park, the **Hugh Lane Municipal Gallery,** Parnell Sq. North (tel. 874 1903 or 874 1904), confines modern art within the Georgian walls of Charlemont House. When Lane offered to donate his collection to the city, he did so on the condition that the people of Dublin contribute to the gallery's construction; the stinginess of the gift was viciously mocked by Yeats in a poem in the *Irish Times.* Lane's death aboard the Lusitania in 1915 raised decades of disputes over his will, which were resolved with a plan to share the collection between the gallery in Dublin and the Tate Gallery in London. (Open Tues.-Fri. 9:30am-6pm, Sat. 9:30am-5pm, Sun. 11am-5pm; free.)

Next door, the **Dublin Writers' Museum,** 18 Parnell Sq. North (tel. 872 2077; fax 872 2231), presents visitors with an interesting introduction to the city's rich literary heritage. Rare editions, manuscripts, and memorabilia of Beckett, Brendan Behan, Patrick Kavanagh, Sean O'Casey, Frank O'Connor, Swift, Shaw, Wilde, and Yeats blend with caricatures, paintings, and an incongruous Zen Garden. (Open Mon.-Sat. 10am-5pm, Sun. 11:30am-6pm, June.-Aug. Mon.-Fri. 10am-7pm; adults £2.60, students £2; combined ticket with either Shaw Birthplace or James Joyce Tower £3.95, students £3.20; ticket for all three £5.50, students £4.50). Adjacent to

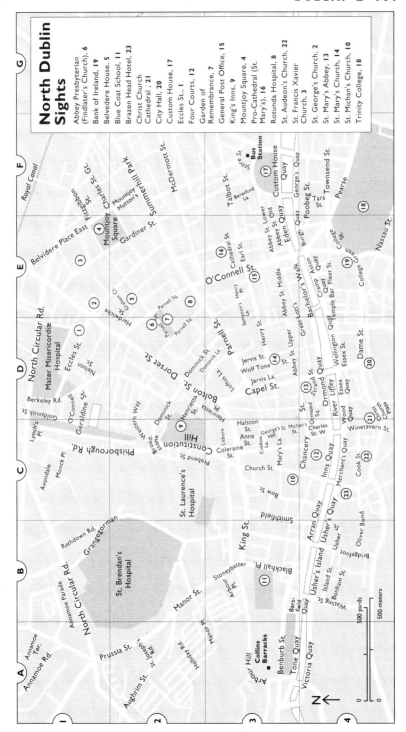

North Dublin Sights

Abbey Presbyterian (Findlater's Church), 6
Bank of Ireland, 19
Belvedere House, 5
Blue Coat School, 11
Brazen Head Hotel, 23
Christ Church Cathedral, 21
City Hall, 20
Custom House, 17
Eccles St., 1
Four Courts, 12
Garden of Remembrance, 7
General Post Office, 15
King's Inns, 9
Mountjoy Square, 4
Pro-Cathedral (St. Mary's), 16
Rotunda Hospital, 8
St. Audeon's Church, 22
St. Francis Xavier Church, 3
St. George's Church, 2
St. Mary's Abbey, 13
St. Mary's Church, 14
St. Michan's Church, 10
Trinity College, 18

the museum, the **Irish Writer's Centre,** 19 Parnell Sq. North (tel. 872 1302), is the administrative nerve center of Ireland's writing community, providing working and meeting space for the aspiring Swifts of today. Frequent poetry and fiction readings present current writings to the public. The center is not a museum, but if you ring the doorbell you can go in for information about Dublin's literary happenings.

Just past Parnell Sq., the **Garden of Remembrance** eulogizes the martyrs who took the GPO. A cross-shaped pool is plugged at one end by a statue representing the mythical Children of Lir, who turned from humans into swans. They cry, in Irish, "O generations of freedom remember us, the generations of the vision."

One block east of Parnell Sq. East, the new **James Joyce Centre,** 35 North Great Georges St. (tel. 873 1984), up Marlborough St. across Parnell St., raises the number of Dublin's Joycean institutions to a zillion and one. A well-stocked bookshop teems with Joyce criticism; inside, the museum features documents and photos from his life and times. Call for info on lectures, walking tours, and Bloomsday events. (Open Tues.-Sat. 10am-4:30pm, Sun. noon-4:30pm. £2, students £1.50, children 70p.)

Along the Quays

East of O'Connell St. at Custom House Quay, where Gardiner St. meets the river, is one of Dublin's architectural triumphs, the **Custom House.** It was designed and built in the 1780s by James Gandon, who gave up the chance to be St. Petersburg's state architect to settle in Dublin. The building's expanse of columns and domes suggests the mix of Rome and Venice that the 18th-century Anglo-Irish wanted their city to become. Carved heads along the frieze represent the rivers of Ireland; the Liffey is the only woman of the bunch. Several quays to the west, on Inn's Quay, stands another of Gandon's works, the **Four Courts;** from the quay or across the river, the building is monumentally impressive, but back and sides reveal 20th-century ballast. On April 14, 1922, General Rory O'Connor seized the Four Courts on behalf of the anti-Treaty IRA; two months later, after provocations, the Free State government of Griffith and Collins attacked the Four Courts garrison, starting the Irish Civil War. The building now houses the highest court in Ireland.

Mummies! Just up Church St., the dry atmosphere has effectively preserved the corpses in the vaults of **St. Michan's Church,** which inspired Bram Stoker's *Dracula.* Of particular interest in this creepy place of death is a 6'6" crusader (dead) and the hanged, drawn, and quartered bodies of two of the 1759 rebels (very dead). (Open Mon.-Fri. 10am-12:45pm and 2-4:45pm, Sat. 10am-12:45pm. £1.20, students and seniors £1, under 16 50p. Church of Ireland services on Sundays at 10am.) Farther north, uphill at the top of Capel St., the **King's Inns** on Henrietta St. were Gandon's last major building; from a cobblestone yard, two wings with pediments enfold a dome. Lawyers bark inside.

The **Irish Whiskey Corner,** Bow St. (tel. 872 5566), is located in a whiskey warehouse off Mary St. Learn how science, grain, and tradition come together to create the golden fluid with "the coveted appellation, whiskey." The film recounts the rise, fall, and spiritual renaissance of Ireland's favorite spirit (with the same narrator as the Waterford Crystal film!) The experience ends with a glass of the Irish whiskey of your choice. Feel the burn. (Tours Mon.-Fri. 3:30pm, May-Oct. additional tours 11am and 2:30pm, and 3:30pm on Sat.; £3 including whiskey tasting.) From O'Connell St., turn onto Henry St. and continue straight as the street becomes Mary St. then Mary Lane, then May Lane; the warehouse is on a cobblestone street on the left.

Distant Sights

Take bus #10 from O'Connell St. or #25 or 26 from Middle Abbey St. west along the river to **Phoenix Park,** Europe's largest enclosed public park. The "Phoenix Park murders" mentioned in *Ulysses* happened in 1882; the Invincibles, a tiny nationalist splinter group, stabbed the Chief Secretary of Ireland, Lord Cavendish, and his Under-Secretary, 200m from the Phoenix Column. A British Unionist journalist forged a series of letters purporting to link Parnell to the murderers; when the fakes were exposed, Parnell's stock rose even further. The Phoenix Column, a Corinthian column capped with a phoenix rising from flames, is something of a pun; the park's name actually comes from the Irish *Fionn Uísce*, meaning "clean water." The 1760-acre park incorporates the President's residence *(Áras an Uachtaráin)*, the U.S. Ambassador's residence, one of the world's oldest zoos, cricket pitches, polo grounds, and grazing red deer and cattle. The deer are quite tame and not to be missed; they usually graze in the thickets near Castleknock Gate.

Marino Casino, Malahide Rd. (tel. 833 1618), is a cute architectural gem and house of tricks. Funeral urns on the roof are chimneys, the columns are hollow and serve as drains, the casino has secret tunnels and trick doors, and the lions standing guard are actually made of stone. You can certainly gambol here, but you can't gamble; it's a casino only in the sense of "small house," built for the Earl of Charlemont by Sir William Chambers in 1758 as a seaside villa. Speaking of tricks: since then, the house's ocean view has vanished! (Open daily 9:30am-6:30pm, mid-June to Sept., Oct. daily 10am-5pm daily, Nov.-May Sat. 10am-4pm, Sun. 2-4pm; £1.50, students 60p. Take bus #20A or B from Eden Quay, or #27 or 27A from Lower Gardiner St.)

ENTERTAINMENT

Be it Seamus Heaney or the Pogues you fancy, Dublin is equipped to entertain you. *In Dublin* (£1.50) comes out every two weeks with feature articles and listings for music, theater, art exhibitions, comedy shows, movie theaters, and gay and lesbian info (listings include place, date, time, and price). The *Dublin Event Guide* (free; available at tourist info offices and Temple Bar restaurants) comes out every other Friday with ads in the back, slightly fawning reviews in the front, and reasonably complete listings in between. Hostel staff are often good, if biased, sources of info.

Music

Dublin's music world attracts performers from all over the country. Pubs are the scene of much of the musical action, since they provide musicians with free beer and a chance to play. (There is often a cover charge of £2-3 on better-known acts.) *Hot Press* (£1.50) has the most up-to-date music listings, particularly for rock. Its commentaries on the musical scene are usually insightful, and its left-leaning editorials give a clear impression of what the Dublin artistic community is thinking. *In Dublin* comes out less often and thus isn't quite so up-to-the-minute, but its listings are more comprehensive and it has a wider range of information. Record store clerks and habitués are one of the most valuable sources of info on the current Irish rock scene. Tower Records on Wicklow St. has reams of leaflets. Bills posted all over the city also inform of coming attractions. Scheduled concerts tend to start at 9pm, impromptu ones even later.

Traditional music is not a tourist gimmick, but a vibrant and important element of the Irish culture and the Dublin music scene. Both natives and foreigners can clap hands and stomp to the beat. Some pubs in the city center have traditional sessions nightly, others nearly so: **Hughes', The Brazen Head, Slattery's, Oliver St. John Gogarty, McDaid's, The International Bar, Mother Redcaps Tavern,** and **O'Dono-ghue's** are all good choices for trad (see Pubbin' in Dublin, p. 90). Traditional dancing or music are nightly events at **Comhaltas Ceoltóirí Éireann** ("co-UL-tus"), 32 Belgrave Sq., Monkstown (tel. 280 0295). From the Seapoint DART stop, Alma Rd. runs to Monkstown Rd. Belgrave Sq. is three blocks down on the left.

Big deal bands frequent the **Baggot Inn,** 143 Baggot St. (tel. 676 1430). U2 played here in the early '80s (some people are still talking about it). **Whelan's,** 25 Wexford St., the continuation of South St. George's St. (tel. 478 0766), is one of the hottest spots. Their posters cover the entire town. An **Béal Bocht** often hosts rock acts (see Theater, below). Big, big acts play to huge crowds at **Tivoli Theatre** (Francis St., tel. 454 4472), and will not only be well-publicized but also quite often sold out. **The Waterfront Rock Bar,** Sir John Rogerson's Quay (tel. 677 8466), was the big pub featured at the end of *The Commitments*. ("Tour of Irish Rock" nightly 8pm. Open Sun.-Thurs. until 11:30pm, Thurs.-Sat. until late.)

Country and western twang at **Brazen Head,** at **Barry's Hotel,** 1 Great Denmark St. (tel. 874 6943), or at the American-style **Bad Bob's,** 32 East Essex St. (tel. 677 5482). Customers mellow at **Rudyard's Wine Bar,** 15 Crown Alley (tel. 671 0846), to the sound of live jazz sessions Friday and Saturday night at 9pm. **McDaid's,** 3 Henry St. (tel. 679 4395), hosts acts on Mondays and Tuesdays at 8:30pm. On the North Side, **The Grattan,** 165 Capel St. (tel. 873 3049), hosts jazz on Wednesdays.

The **National Concert Hall,** Earl's Fort Terrace (tel. 671 1533), provides a venue for classical concerts and performances. July and August bring nightly shows (8pm; tickets £7-10, students ½ price). A summer lunchtime series makes a nice break from work on occasional Tuesdays and Fridays (tickets £2.50-3). Programs for the National Symphony and smaller local groups are available at classical music stores. Sunday afternoon jazz is a common phenomenon. *In Dublin* will have listings.

Dance Clubs

In recent years, clubs have displaced rock venues as the home of Dublin's nightlife. As a rule, these spots open at 10:30 or 11pm, but the action gets moving only after 11:30pm when the pubs close. Clubbing is not the least expensive evening entertainment, since the cover runs £4-8 and pints are a steep £2-2.50. Most clubs close at 3 or 4am, but a few have been known to last until daybreak at 6am. **Club Paradiso** (tel. 677 8788), at the Irish Film Centre, has an appropriately cinematic decor (IFC members only; see Cinema (p. 105) for membership info and directions; 11:30pm-late; £4). **UFO,** a mind-bogglingly intense club, is upstairs at Columbia Mills, Sir John Rogerson's Quay. **Temple of Sound,** in the Ormond Hotel on Ormond Quay, pumps out serious dance grooves on Thursday-Sunday nights (open 8:10pm-late; cover £3-8). **Rí-Rá,** 1 Exchequer St. (tel. 668 0995), in the Central Hotel, is a social epicenter for cool modern people but is open to anyone. To get home after Dublin Bus shuts down at 11:30pm, dancing fiends can take the **NiteLink bus** (Thurs.-Sat. midnight-3am hourly; £2), which runs designated routes to Dublin's outer city and its suburbs from the corner of Westmoreland and College St.

Gay & Lesbian Dublin

Dublin's progressive (for Ireland) thinking translates into an acceptance that was exemplified by the peaceful success of PRIDE, a week-long festival celebrating gay identity in July, 1995. This generally progressive attitude has encouraged the development of a small but vibrant gay scene, punctuated by organized events. *Gay Community News* offers the most comprehensive and up-to-date information on gay life and nightlife in Dublin (available at Books Upstairs Bookstore, Temple Bar Information Centre, the Well-Fed Café, among others). *In Dublin*'s gay page lists pubs, dance clubs, saunas, gay-friendly restaurants, bookshops, hotlines, and organizations. The listings are comprehensive but sometimes outdated. Copies of *Out* and *Advocate* magazines, when they exist, can found at Eason's bookstore (see Bisexual, Gay, & Lesbian Travelers, p. 22).

Gay Switchboard Dublin is a good resource for finding out about events and updates. It also sponsors a hotline (tel. 872 1055; Sun.-Fri. 8-10pm, Sat. 3:30-6pm). **Lesbian Line** offers similar services (tel. 661 3777; open Thurs. 7-9pm). **The National Gay and Lesbian Federation,** Hirschfield Centre, 10 Fownes St. (tel. 671 0939), in Temple Bar, publishes *Gay Community News* and offers counseling on legal concerns. It is not an info service but can provide advice. The lesbian community meets at **LOT** (Lesbians Organizing Together), 5 Capel St. (tel. 872 7770).

At the moment, **The George** is Dublin's only gay pub. **The Trinity,** Nassau St., across from Trinity College, becomes a women-only space on Saturday nights. **The Block,** upstairs from the George, is both bar and dance club (Fri.-Sat.). **Shaft,** 22 Ely Pl. (continue down Upper Merrion St. West) is where die-hard clubbers go when all else has closed. It has traditionally been gay-friendly, although in recent times that friendliness seems to have waned. Ask around for its present status. The basement-level dance floor gets kicking nightly around 11:30pm (Fri.-Sat. cover £3). **Pull** is a gay club at the Kitchen, on Essex St. (cover £4; open Sun. 11pm-2:30am). **Salon at** the **Cellary,** Fownes St. (see Food o' Dublin, p. 87), on Sundays becomes a night-club for women only (9:30pm-3am; £4, students £2.50). **Temple of Sound,** Ormond Hotel, Upper Ormond Quay (tel. 872 1811), hosts a dance club called **The Play-ground** on Sun. nights (starts 10:30pm; cover £5).

Theater

Dublin's curtains rise on the full range of mainstream productions, classic shows, and experimental theater. Showtime is generally 8pm. Dame St. and its Temple Bar alleyways are home to a few companies. The rest are scattered within a 10-minute radius of O'Connell Bridge.

Abbey Theatre, 26 Lower Abbey St. (tel. 878 7222), was founded by Yeats and his collaborator Lady Gregory in 1904 to promote Irish cultural revival and modernist theater, which turned out to be a bit like promoting corned beef and soy burg-ers—most audiences wanted one or the other. J.M. Synge's *Playboy of the Western World* was first performed here in 1907. The production occasioned storms of protest and yet another of Yeats' political poems. Today, the Abbey, like Synge, has become respectable. As part of the National Theatre, it receives government funding. Box office open Mon.-Sat. 10:30am-7pm. Tickets £8-13; student standby 1 hr. before show Mon. and Thurs., £5.

Peacock Theatre, 26 Lower Abbey St. (tel. 878 7222), downstairs, is more exper-imental. The usual evening shows plus occasional lunchtime plays, concerts, and poetry (£8, students £5). Box office open Mon.-Sat. at 7:30pm for that night's per-formance only; advance booking at the Abbey Theatre box office.

Gate Theatre, 1 Cavendish Row (tel. 874 4045), produces everything from Resto-ration comedies to Irish classics. Box office open Mon.-Sat. 10am-7pm. Tickets £10-12; student standby £6 Mon.-Thurs. at curtain time.

Project Arts Centre, 39 East Essex St. (tel. 671 2321), presents, not just theater, but all the performing arts, including avant-garde theater, dramatic readings, com-edy, and dance. Box office open daily 10am-6pm; tickets £8, concessions £6. The free gallery hosts rotating visual arts exhibitions (open same time as box office).

Gaiety, South King St. (tel. 677 1717), provides space for modern drama, ballet, pantomime, and the Dublin Grand Opera Society. Box office open Mon.-Sat. 11am-7pm; tickets £7.50-12.50.

Olympia Theatre, 72 Dame St. (tel. 677 7744). Old standbys like *The Sound of Music.* Box office open Mon.-Sat. 10am-6:30pm; tickets £8-15; ½-price student standby after 7pm.

Andrews Lane Theatre, Andrews Lane (tel. 679 5720), off Dame St. Dramatic classics, old and new—Shakespeare, Molière, Brecht.

An Béal Bocht, 58 Charlemont St. (tel. 475 5614), hosts traditional Irish-language theater Wed. at 9pm (£5).

City Arts Centre, 23-25 Moss St. (tel. 677 0643), parallel to Tara St. off George's Quay. Dublin's avant-garde theater explores sexual and political issues (£6, stu-dents £4).

Samuel Beckett Theatre, Trinity College (tel. 478 3397). Inside the campus. Hosts anything that happens to pass, from drama to dance, done by students or professionals.

Cinema

Ireland's well-supported film industry got a kick in the pants with the arrival of the **Irish Film Centre,** Eustace St., in Temple Bar (tel. 679 3477 or 679 5744). The IFC mounts tributes and festivals, including a gay and lesbian film festival in August and a French film festival in October. A variety of classic and European arthouse films appear throughout the year. You must be a "member" to buy tickets. (Weekly mem-bership £1; yearly membership £10, students £7.50; membership must be pur-chased at least 20 min. before start of show; each member can buy only 4 tickets per screening.) (Matinees £2; 5pm showing £2.50; after 7pm £4, students £3.) Other arty cinemas are the **Lighthouse Cinema,** 107 Fleet St. (tel. 873 0438; shows every night; £2 before 5pm, £3.50 after), and **The Screen,** D'Olier St. (tel. 671 4988 or 872

3922). First-run movie houses cluster on O'Connell St., the quays, and Middle Abbey St. The **Savoy,** O'Connell St., and the **Adelphi,** Abbey St., offer the widest selection of primarily American films.

Events

The tourist office's *Calendar of Events* and *Dublin Events Guide* describe Dublin's many festivals, provincial parades, mayor's balls, concerts, dances, and art shows. Ask about *fleadhs,* traditional day-long musical festivals. The **World Irish Dancing Championships** are held in late March or early April. For info, contact Cultúrann (see *Music,* above). The **Festival of Music in Irish Houses,** held during the second and third weeks of June, organizes concerts of period music in local 18th-century homes. The **Dublin Film Festival** (tel. 679 2937) in March features Irish and international movies and a panoply of seminars. The **Temple Bar Blues Festival** is a three-day blues extravaganza in mid-July. Bluesmen come from all over and have included Robert Cray and B.B. King. The Commitments would play here if they hadn't tragically disbanded. (Contact Temple Bar Information Centre for information, tel. 671 5717; most acts free; program guides available in July.)

St. Patrick's Day (March 17) occasions enormous parades, drunken carousing, and closed banks. TV coverage of March 17, 1993 showed the Irish gay and lesbian float cruising happily along with the rest of the Dublin parade. (Eating corned beef and cabbage on this day is an Irish-American, not an Irish, tradition.)

Dublin returns to 1904 each year on **Bloomsday,** June 16, the day on which the action of Joyce's Ulysses takes place. Festivities are held all week long. The **Joyce Centre** (tel. 873 1984) sponsors a mock funeral and wake, a lunch at Davy Byrne's, and a breakfast with Guinness, all as part of its Bloomstime program. On the day itself, a Messenger Bike Rally culminates in St. Stephen's Green with drink and food. Many bookstores have readings from Ulysses. Some of the better ones are Books Upstairs and Fred Hanna's (see Dublin's Literary Shopping, p. 107). Check out the June issue of *In Dublin* and the *Dublin Event Guide* for year-to-year details.

The **Dublin Theatre Festival** in late September and early October is a premier cultural event. Tickets may be purchased all year at participating theaters and at branches of the Irish Life Building Society (main office on Lower Abbey St., tel. 704 2000). As the festival draws near, tickets are also available at the Festival Booking Office, 47 Nassau St., Dublin 2 (tel. 677 8439; 50% discount with ISIC; student standby tickets £2-3).

Sports & Recreation

Dubliners, probably because they have more to distract them, aren't as sports-centered as their country cousins tend to be. Sports are still a serious business, though, as attested to by the frequency of matches and events. The seasons for **Gaelic football** and **hurling** (the national sports of Ireland) run from mid-February to November. Both are games of skill, stamina, and strength that have evolved from deep historical roots. Provincial finals take place in July, national semifinals in August (hurling on the 1st Sunday, football on the 2nd and 3rd Sundays), and All-Ireland Finals in September. Games are played in Croke Park and Phibsborough Rd. (tickets available at the turnstiles; All-Ireland Finals tickets sell out quickly). Home games of the Irish **rugby** team are played in Lansdowne Road Stadium (Oct.-March). **Camogie** (women's hurling) finals also take place in September. For sports information, check the Friday papers or contact the Gaelic Athletic Association (tel. 836 3232). **Greyhound racing** continues all year. Meets start at 8pm and end around 10pm (Mon. and Sat. at Shelbourne Park, tel. 668 3502; Tues., Thurs., and Fri. at Harold's Cross, tel. 497 1081). **Horses** race at Leopardstown Racetrack, Foxrock, Dublin 18 (tel. 289 2888).

SHOPPING

Dublin is not really a center for international trade, and consumer goods are generally expensive. Your time may be better spent in pubs and castles. That said, if something is made anywhere in Ireland, you can probably find it in Dublin. Tiny shops pop up everywhere along the streets both north and south of the Liffey, but Dublin's major shopping is on **Grafton St.** and **Henry St.** On pedestrianized Grafton St., well-dressed consumers crowd into boutiques and restaurants, and buskers aplenty lay out their caps for money. Nearby, Lord Powerscourt's 200-year-old townhouse on Clarendon St., now the **Powerscourt Townhouse Centre,** has been converted into a string of chic boutiques carrying Irish crafts. **Georges St. Market Arcade** on South Great Georges St. near Dame St. will suit the more casual shopper. The arcade includes a number of vintage clothing, jewelry, and used record stalls as well as a fortune teller. (Nose-piercing with stud, £1.25. Open Mon.-Sat. 8am-6pm.)

Teens and barely-twenties buy their used clothes and punk discs in the **Temple Bar. St. Stephen's Green Shopping Centre** is, well, a mall. On the North Side, **Henry St.,** off O'Connell, has cheaper goods, in price and quality, to suit a less finicky clientele. **ILAC,** another mall, lurks just around the corner on Moore St. (behind a rainbowed facade) and houses the main branch of the Dublin public library. **Clery's** (tel. 878 6000) on Upper O'Connell St. is Dublin's principal department store. They pride themselves on quality goods to meet every need. (Open Mon.-Wed. and Fri.-Sat. 9am-5:30pm, Thurs. 9am-8pm.)

Young couples have long planned to "meet under the Clery's clock." Perhaps they should also plan a trip to **Condom Power,** 57 Dame St. (tel. 677 8963), where a wide selection of prophylactics awaits (open Mon.-Sat. 9:30am-6pm). If you insist on carrying home a woolen souvenir, **Dublin Woolen Co.** Ha'penny Bridge, 41 Lower Ormond Quay (tel. 677 0301), has the best values in its huge selection of sweaters and tweeds (open Mon.-Sat. 9am-6pm).

Dublin's Literary Shopping

Waterstone's, 7 Dawson St. (tel. 679 1415), off Nassau St. Five floors of well-stacked books and informed reference staff. Open Mon.-Fri. 9am-8:30pm, Sat. 9am-7pm, Sun. noon-7pm.

Fred Hanna's, 27-29 Nassau St. (tel. 677 1255), across from Trinity College at Dawson St. Dublin's best-known, and with reason. Second-hand books mingle with new ones under the watchful eye of an intelligent staff. Any questions about contemporary Irish writing are best answered here. Open Mon.-Sat. 9am-5:30pm.

Hodges Figgis, 56-58 Dawson St. (tel. 677 4754). Part of an English bookstore chain, this large bookstore has a good selection for those with eclectic tastes. Open Mon.-Fri. 9am-7pm, Sat. 9am-6:30pm, Sun. noon-6pm.

Winding Stair Bookstore, 40 Ormond Quay (tel. 873 3292), on the North Side. Three atmospheric floors of good tunes, great Liffey views, and cheap café food. Used books, contemporary Irish literature, and literary periodicals. Open Mon.-Sat. 10:30am-6pm.

Eason's, 40-42 Lower O'Connell St. (tel. 873 3811). Lots of serious tomes and an extensive "Irish interest" section (*Let's Go: Ireland* £13.65). Wide selection of local and foreign magazines and newspapers. Special bargain section in the basement. Open Mon.-Sat. 8:30am-6:15pm.

Books Upstairs, 36 College Green, near Trinity Gate (tel. 679 6687). Dublin's alternative bookshop. Extensive sections on gay literature and women's studies. The principal distributor for *Gay Community News.*

Sinn Féin Bookshop, Parnell Sq. West (tel. 872 6100 or 871 6932). IRA paraphernalia, T-shirts, and rebel songs on tape. Open Mon.-Sat. 11am-5pm.

Records, Tapes & CDs

Besides Tower (tel. 671 3250), the musical megastores in Dublin are **HMV,** 65 Grattan St. (tel. 679 7817) and **Virgin,** 14 Aston Quay (tel. 677 7361). Most stores have roughly an equal selection of cassettes and CDs. Cassettes run from £6-12, CDs from £10-16.

Claddagh Records, 2 Cecilia St., Temple Bar (tel. 677 0262), between Temple Lane and Crow St. Best selection of traditional Irish music and a good variety of music from other countries and cultures. Open June-Sept. daily 10:30am-5:30pm, Oct.-May daily 12:30-5:30pm.

Freebird Records, 1 Eden Quay (tel. 873 1250), on the North Side facing the river. Slick, crowded basement shop below a newsstand proves its name with a good selection of indie rock, probably Dublin's best. Proprietors are refreshingly honest about which local bands they actually like. Open Mon.-Sat. 10:30-6pm.

Comet Records, 5 Cope St., Temple Bar (tel. 671 8592). Much like Freebird, but smaller and open later. More info on current groups and gigs, used LPs, and new indie CDs. Open Mon.-Sat. 10am-6pm.

Smile, 59 South Great Georges St. (tel. 478 2005). Good selection of American soul and jazz. Also has a wall of used books some of which expound on rock. "Shoplifters will be reincarnated as snails," they warn. Don't let it happen to you, sluggo.

NORTH OF DUBLIN

The suburbs north of Dublin are randomly scattered around the rocky coast and inland regions. Tract houses and factories crowd ancient castles and beach resorts. DART and suburban rail are by far the best way to travel (single tickets are never more than £1.50). Buses, however, can be confusing and unreliable. The best beach in Dublin is said to be the one at Dollymount, nicknamed the **Velvet Strand.** It's within walking distance of Malahide: to reach it, get off the train at Portmarnock, one stop before Malahide. If time allows for only one suburban jaunt, heather-crammed, peninsular Howth is the incontestable choice. Any of these towns can be seen in an afternoon, and all share Dublin's undiscriminating **phone code,** 01.

■■■ HOWTH

Only nine miles from Dublin, and quite DARTable, hilly Howth gives a quick look at Ireland's highlights—scenery, pubs, history, literature, a castle, an abbey, and fresh fish, all in one town. Howth, dangling off the mainland, looks out to sea from the north shore of Dublin Bay. Fish rather than people are central to Howth life. The food chain here proceeds from fishing boat to open-air vendor to hungry traveler.

The easiest way to reach Howth is by **DART.** Take a northbound train to the end of the line (6/hr.; 30 min.; £1). **Buses** bound for Howth leave from Dublin's Lower Abbey Street. #31 goes to the center of Howth (near the DART station; 1-2/hr.) and #31B climbs Howth Summit. Orient yourself with the *Guide to Howth Peninsula,* a hand-drawn map of Howth with sights and walking trails clearly labeled. It's posted at the harbor entrance, across from the St. Lawrence Hotel.

Financial matters are taken care of at the **Bank of Ireland,** 1 Main St. (tel. 839 0271; **ATM**). The **Post Office,** 27 Abbey St. (tel 831 8210), also exchanges currencies. C.S. **McDermott's Pharmacy,** 5 Main St. (tel. 832 2069) does the obvious (open Mon.-Sat. 9am-6pm, Sun. 10:30am-1pm).

ACCOMMODATIONS

Howth's B&Bs and the convenience of the DART (which doesn't service all of Dublin's suburbs) make it a fine base for hopping to Dublin. Prices don't vary much from one accommodating establishment to the next.

Glenn Na Smol (tel. 832 2936), on the left at the end of Nashville Rd. This is a full-service B&B. Mrs. Rickard's satellite dish pulls in MTV and CNN for the benefit of the post-literate. A generous supply of books suits wormier guests. Lip smackin' homemade bread and huge bathrooms. £17/person, w/bath.

Highfield (tel. 832 3936), 20 min. up Thormanby Rd. Highfield's sign is obscured by its hedges, but it's on the left as you go up the hill. Honeysuckle tumbles onto the lawn during the spring and summer. Inside, beautiful floral prints spill onto the bedspreads and wallpaper. There's no lounge, but there is a pay phone in the hall. £16/person, £17 w/bath.

Hazelwood (tel. 839 1391), in the Thormanby Woods estate off Thormanby Rd. Hazelwood offers peace and quiet in an already demure town. Ask for the room with the lavish bathtub. £17/person, single w/bath £19.

FOOD & PUBS

Quash your monstrous traveler's appetite with fabulous pizza and sundaes at **The Pizza Place,** 12 West Pier Rd. (tel. 832 2255). The lunchtime special, available until 2pm, includes small pizza, dessert, and coffee (£4.25; open daily noon-midnight). **Caffé Caira,** Harbour Rd., is a better-than-average chippy, and its tables soothe the Howth youth (burgers or fish £2-3, chips 75p). Hungry shoppers run to **Spar Supermarket,** on St. Laurence Rd. off of Abbey St. (open Mon.-Sat., 8am-10pm) After a day on your feet, stop for a pint in town at the classy **Cock Tavern,** 18 Church St. (tel. 832 3237), opposite St. Mary's Abbey. Rock bands entertain Wednesday-Friday nights at 9pm. The week winds down on Sunday afternoons with ballads. Book a seat in advance (or stand and regret it) to hear traditional music at **Ye Olde Abbey Tavern,** Abbey St. (tel. 832 2006 or 839 0282; music starts nightly 9pm; cover £4).

SIGHTS

Maud Gonne, Yeats' unyielding beloved, described her childhood in Howth in *A Servant of the Queen:* "After I was grown up I have often slept all night in that friendly heather…From deep down in it one looks up at the stars in a wonderful security and falls asleep to wake up only with the call of the sea birds looking for their breakfasts." A one-hour **cliff walk** rings the peninsula and trails through just such heather and past the nests of thousands of seabirds. A cairn reputed to be the grave of Griffan (the last pre-Christian King) will be of interest to pagan enthusiasts. The cleft in Puck's Rock, which marks the spot where the devil fell when St. Nessan waved a Bible at him, has Christian significance. To get to the trail head from Howth, turn left at the DART and bus station and follow Harbour Rd. around the corner and up the hill (about 15 minutes). The footpath begins where the cul-de-sac ends, at the top of this long, long hill. The trail is not only unmarked but also uncleared in places. Regardless, the views, and especially the springtime blooms of the slopes, are inspiring. For the less hearty, bus #31B cruises from Lower Abbey St. in Dublin to the cliffs' summit (see above).

The town of Howth itself occupies this long hill. The ruins of **St. Mary's Abbey** stand peacefully surrounded by a cemetery at the bend in Church St. The walls and arches of this 13th-century abbey are still quite sound. The courtyard, cordoned off, is nevertheless visible. You can get the key from the caretaker, Mrs. O'Rourke, at 13 Church St. The more modern **Howth Harbour** bustles with working fishermen. A strip of fresh fish shops lines West Pier. Thursday nights, when fishing boats come in, are the best time to buy.

Just offshore, **Ireland's Eye** once provided both religious sanctuary and strategic advantage for monks, as attested to by the ruins of **St. Nessan's Church** and one of the coast's many **Martello towers,** both located on the island. The monks eventually abandoned their refuge when pirate raids became too frequent. The island's long beach is now primarily a bird haven. **Frank Doyle & Sons** (tel. 831 4200) will jet you across the water. Their office is on the East Pier, the farthest from the DART of Howth's three piers. (Round trip £3, children £1.50; call ahead to schedule departure and return times.)

Aside from spectacular views, Howth can offer its own castle on the outskirts of town. To reach **Howth Castle,** take a right on Harbour Rd. as you leave the DART station. The castle turn-off, ¼ mile down the road, is marked by signs for the Deer Park Hotel and the National Transport Museum. The castle itself is a patchwork of different architectural styles, which gives its exterior an awkward charm. No massive gates protect the castle from invading hordes, but it is a private residence (not open to the public) belonging to the St. Lawrence family, which has occupied it for four centuries. You might try knocking if your surname is O'Malley. In 1575, the pirate queen Grace O'Malley paid a social call but was refused entrance on the grounds that the family was eating. Not one to take an insult lightly, Grace abducted the St. Lawrence heir and refused to hand him back until she had word that the gate would always be open to all O'Malleys at mealtimes.

At the end of the road on which the castle perches is the **National Transport Museum** (tel. (01) 848 0831), an amiable collection of old buses, tanks, cars, and trucks. (Open June-Aug. Mon.-Fri. 10am-6pm, Sat.-Sun. 11am-6pm; Sept.-May Sat.-Sun. noon-5pm; £1.50, children 50p.) Farther up the hill, the path leads around the Deer Park Hotel to the fabulous **Rhododendron Gardens**. The ending of Joyce's Ulysses is set "among the rhododendrons at Howth Head." The flowers blooms in June and July (always open; free).

Dyslexia and Defense

Martello towers, named after Cape Mortella in Corsica, are short, thick, and almost impenetrable towers. The English, upon encountering them in Corsica, decided to copy these brilliantly defensive towers (they were dyslexic, and spelled the name wrong). The paranoid British constructed these squat edifices all along the coasts, wherever they expected Napoleon to attack.

■■■ MALAHIDE

Eight miles north of Dublin, rows of prim and proper shops smugly line the main street in Malahide, a perennial "coastal" contender in Ireland's cutthroat "Tidy Town" competition. The gorgeous parkland and castle at Malahide Demesne partially justify the town's pride. Bus #42, which leaves from behind the Custom House (Beresford Place) in Dublin, drives right up to the park entrance. Suburban rail to Malahide leaves Connolly, Tara, and Pearse stations infrequently (£1.10). You can even take the DART to Sutton Station (one stop before Howth) and then take bus #102 to Malahide (Mon.-Sat. 3/hr.). Turn left from the rail station onto Coast Rd. to reach Malahide's center and all its facilities, at a four-way intersection between Church Rd. and New St. called "The Diamond." From the Diamond, the **tourist office** (tel. 845 0490) is down New St. towards the marina (open Mon.-Fri.10am-1pm and 2-6pm). Ask for the *Malahide Tourist Guide*, which has a town map.

Accommodations & Food Malahide hosts a number of inexpensive B&Bs along Coast Rd. and its tributaries, particularly along Biscayne St. (20 minutes from the Diamond). Since Malahide is only a ten-minute drive from the airport (bus #230 runs back and forth throughout the day, £1.10), it's convenient for travelers without the energy to drag themselves to Dublin. **Aishling,** Mrs. Noreen Handley, 59 Biscayne (tel. 845 2292), one block off Coast Rd., has pink carpets, curtains, and bedspreads covering firm, comfortable beds. Big breakfast includes fruit, yogurt, and homemade bread (£14/person, w/bath £15; open March-Oct.). **Pegasus,** Mrs. Betty O'Brien, 56 Biscayne (tel. 845 1506), impresses with welcoming, well-appointed rooms that boast elegant channel views. The full Irish breakfast includes smoked kippers for the daring (£14/person; open March-Nov.).

Most of the restaurants around the Diamond are greatly overpriced. Meat lovers will feel at home at **Oscar Taylor's,** (tel. 845 0099), ¼ mile down the Coast Rd. towards Port Marnoch. The steakhouse is a bit expensive, but the pub grub is affordable, and they have trad sessions on Wednesday nights at 9:30.

Sights Left off Main St. (heading north, past the railroad tracks), Malahide Demense envelops **Malahide Castle** (tel. (01) 846 2184; fax (01) 846 2537), the town's main attraction. The castle luxuriates in sweeping lawns and densely foliated paths. Oliver Cromwell, always one for soothing angry emotions, commented that here, and nowhere else, would he tolerate living on Irish soil. Now publicly owned, the well-preserved mansion houses a collection of Irish period furniture and part of the National Portrait Collection inside its regal walls. The Malahide Demesne also surrounds a church, playground, and stunning botanical gardens. (Castle open April-Oct. Mon.-Fri. 10am-5pm, Sat. 11am-6pm, Sun. 11:30am-6pm; Nov.-March Mon.-Fri. 10am-5pm, Sat.-Sun. 2-6pm. Demesne/Park open daily, June 10am-9pm, July-Aug. 10am-8pm, Oct. 10am-7pm, Nov.-Jan. 10am-5pm, Feb.-March 10am-6pm. £2.75, students £2.15.)

Between Malahide and **Portmarnock** (two miles down the coastal road toward Dublin) lies the **Velvet Strand**. This stretch of soft, luxurious beach makes a fantastic stop on a sunny day, and can hold its own with any Caribbean beaches.

■ NEAR MALAHIDE: DONABATE

In Donabate, four miles north of Malahide, the 18th-century **Newbridge House** (tel. 843 6534 or 843 6535) is surrounded by a 300-acre park. The ½-hour walk from the rail station, clearly marked, is as worthwhile as the house itself, as it takes you past the gardens of Donabate and through a lush tree-lined field. The rolling grass in the park is a favorite spot for family and school outings and a great spot for your picnic. The Archbishop of Dublin erected the mansion around 1740. It lacked electricity until the makers of the movie *The Spy Who Came in from the Cold* wired it up in the 1960s. Three rooms, in particular, should not be missed: the **kitchen** will blow your microwave-and-toaster preconceptions clear out of the water, the **private museum** is an attic full of very English, very eccentric collections (moth and ostrich eggs), and **Tara's Palace** is a luxurious 14-room, pre-Barbie dollhouse. (Open April-Sept. Tues.-Fri. 10am-1pm and 2-5pm, Sat. 11am-1pm and 2-6pm, Sun. 2-6pm; open Oct.-March Sat-Sun. 2-5pm; £2.50, students £2.15, children £1.35. Newbridge House and Malahide Castle combination ticket £4.50, students £3.50.) **Smyth Pub** (tel. 843 6053), across from the station, serves pub grub to weary travelers (sandwiches £1, salad plate £2.50). Take the infrequent bus #33B from Eden Quay to Donabate. Better yet, take the suburban rail from Connolly, Tara St., or Pearse Station in downtown Dublin to Donabate (£1.20).

SOUTH OF DUBLIN

The suburb/beach/port hybrids from Dún Laoghaire to Killiney form a nearly unbroken chain of snazzy houses and bright surf. The whole area is technically the "Borough of Dún Laoghaire." The individual cities are best thought of as neighborhoods within this larger town. A set of paths called the "Dún Laoghaire Way," "Dalkey Way," and so on connect the towns by what, someone has decided, is the best walking route. The separate parts combine into a whole trail that is three miles long. But getting from one town to the other is easy enough as long as you stay within ten blocks of the sea, on the path or not. For those who don't want to invest the shoe leather, the DART also makes for great (and less exhausting) coastal views between Dalkey and Bray. An entertaining ramble would begin with a ride on bus #59 from the Dún Laoghaire DART station to the top of Killiney Hill and proceed along the path through the park and down into Dalkey. The **phone code** is 01.

■■■ DÚN LAOGHAIRE

As Dublin's major out-of-city ferry port, Dún Laoghaire ("dun-LEER-ee"), for many tourists, is their first peek at Ireland. Fortunately it is a pleasant, well-developed town and a good spot to begin a ramble along the coast south of Dublin. The **tourist office** (tel. 280 6984) in the ferry terminal is accustomed to dealing with delirious travelers. They have a copious stock of maps and pamphlets on all of Dublin and the Borough of Dún Laoghaire. (Open June-Sept. Mon.-Sun. 10am-9pm; Oct.-Dec. Mon.-

Sat. 10am-9pm; Jan.-March Mon.-Sat. noon-9pm; April-May Mon.-Sat. 9am–9pm.) Ferry travelers can change money at the bureau de change in the ferry terminal, or they can wait for the **Bank of Ireland** on Upper George's St. (open Mon.-Wed. and Fri.10am-4pm, Thurs. 10am-5pm, and ferry arrival times; **ATM**). From the tourist office, Royal Marine Rd. climbs up to the center of town. George's St., at the top of Marine Rd., accommodates most of Dún Laoghaire's shops, many in the **Dún Laoghaire Shopping Centre** at the intersection (open Mon.-Wed. and Sat. 9am-6pm, Thurs.-Fri. 9am-9pm). Patrick St., which continues Marine Rd.'s path uphill on the other side of George's St., offers cheap eateries, open early and late, according to the ferry schedules. Reach Dún Laoghaire on the DART south from Dublin (£1.10) or on bus #7, 7A or 8 from Eden Quay.

ACCOMMODATIONS

Dún Laoghaire is so close to Dublin via DART that it is a convenient town from which to visit the city while avoiding the rigors of staying in the capital itself. As the port for the Stena-Sealink ferries, Dún Laoghaire is prime breeding ground for B&Bs, some more predatory than others.

Old School House Hostel, Elbana Ave. (tel. 280 8777), signposted on Elbana Ave., right off Royal Marine Rd. Full-service hostel sports a TV lounge, an eager 24-hr. staff, and a friendly atmosphere. Café enhances hostel life. Safety deposit boxes at reception and innovative lockers built into the beds. Sheets free; laundry (£2/wash, £1/dry). 6-bed dorm £8/person, quad £9/person, double £11/person; w/bath add 50p. Wheelchair access.

Marleen, 9 Marine Rd. (tel. 280 2456). Fall off the DART or ferry, and you'll be here—great location on the first block of Marine Rd., just west of the harbor. Friendly owners, TV in every room, and full Irish breakfast. £16/person.

Avondale, 3 Northumberland Ave. (tel. 280 9628). Next to Dunnes Stores. A crimson carpet leads honored guests to pampering rooms. Single £18, double £30.

Ariemond, 47 Mulgrave St. (tel. 280 1664). The rooms are a bit dark, but the beds are firm and comfy. £15/person, w/bath £17.

FOOD & PUBS

Stock up on provisions at **Quinnsworth Supermarket** (tel. 280 8441) in the Dún Laoghaire shopping center (open Mon.-Wed. and Sat. 9am-6pm, Thurs.-Fri. 9am-9pm) or at fruit stands and delis. Fast-food restaurants and inexpensive coffee shops line George's St. **The Coffee Bean,** 88b Upper George's St. (tel. 280 9522), virtually rolls customers out, filled to the brim with quiche (£3.75), soup and brown bread (£1.20), and scrumptious desserts (£1-1.50). A full Irish breakfast is served until noon (£2.45; open Mon.-Sat. 8am-5pm). **Bits and Pizzas,** Patrick St., gives a good return for your money (lunch special: pizza, cole slaw and tea £3.75; open Mon.-Sat. noon-6pm). Normally pricey **de Selby's,** 17/18 Patrick St. (tel. 284 1761 or 284 1762), will give you a free dessert if you prove that it's your birthday. The restaurant (also an art gallery) is named for the mad scientist in Flann O'Brien's novels (open Mon.-Sat. 5:30-11pm, Sun. noon-10pm).

The Purty Kitchen, Dunleary Rd. (tel. 284 3576), is a lively pub. Upstairs, the **Purty Loft** livens Dún Laoghaire weekends with groovy disco action (cover £3-5). From the harbor, turn right down Crofton Rd. (the pub is actually closer to the Monkstown DART station than Dún Laoghaire's). **Smyth's Pub,** Callaghan's Lane (tel. 280 1139), at the corner of George's St., is a pleasant old pub with tasty pub entrees and some cozy snugs as well.

SIGHTS

The **harbor** itself is a sight, filled with yachts, boat tours, car ferries chugging to Wales, and fishermen on the west pier. On a clear day, grab a picnic and head down to the piers to soak up the ambiance, the sun, or the fishy smells. Samuel Beckett's *Krapp's Last Tape* is set on one of the piers.

Otherwise, try the **National Maritime Museum,** Haigh Terrace (tel. 280 0969). From the tourist office, turn left on Queen's Rd. to the stone steps which lead up to Haigh Terrace. The museum is in the Mariners' Church. A giant lens has been moved here from its home in the Bailey Lighthouse, in Howth. Not only is the lens beautiful, but its mirrors reflected two million candelas. In the center of the museum stretches a longboat (akin to a rowboat) sent by revolutionary France to support the United Irishmen in 1796. (Open Tues.-Sun. 2:30-5:30pm; April and Oct.-Nov. Sat.-Sun. 2:30-5:30pm; £1, children 50p.)

■ ■ ■ MORE DARTABLE FUN

SANDYCOVE

Upper George's St. continues from Dún Laoghaire into dandy Sandycove. Restaurants and grocers gather on the street here, as they do farther north. Sandycove is pretty enough in a Victorian way, but its real allure is the **James Joyce Museum,** Sandycove Ave. West (tel. 280 9265). From the Sandycove DART station, walk down Islington Ave., then right along the coast to Sandycove Point; or take bus #8 from Nassau St. in Dublin to Sandycove Ave. West. The museum is a Martello tower (see Dyslexia and Defense, p. 110), one of many such along the coast. James Joyce stayed in the tower for six days in August 1904 as a guest of Oliver St. John Gogarty, a Dublin surgeon, poetic wit, man-about-town, and the tower's first civilian tenant. Unfortunately, Gogarty's other guest was an excitable Englishman with a severe sleepwalking problem. One night, as the foreigner paced, Gogarty shouted "leave him to me" and fired his shotgun into a row of saucepans. Joyce took the hint and left in the morning. A month later he escaped to the continent with Nora Barnacle. Part I of *Ulysses* is set in and near the tower, with Gogarty portrayed by Buck Mulligan, the Englishman played by "an Englishman," and Joyce, alias Stephen Daedalus, meditating on the wine-dark sea from the gun platform at the top of the tower. Another scene takes place at the Forty Foot Men's Bathing Place, below.

Sylvia Beach, Joyce's publisher, opened the tower as a museum in 1962. The two-room museum contains Joyce's death mask, his bookshelves, some of his correspondence, clippings of Ezra Pound's rave reviews, and lots of editions of *Ulysses,* including one illustrated by Henri Matisse. One letter to Italo Svevo mentions a briefcase "the color of a nun's belly." Genius! Upstairs, the Round Room reconstructs Joyce's bedroom; from the gun platform, you can stand in his shoes to see "many crests, every ninth, breaking, plashing, from far, from farther out, waves and waves." (Open May-Sept. Mon.-Sat. 10am-1pm and 2-5pm, Sun. 2-6pm; April and Oct. Mon.-Fri. 10am-1pm and 2-5pm; £1.90, seniors and ages 12-17 £1.40, ages 3-11 £1.)

At the foot of the tower lies the infamous **Forty Foot Men's Bathing Place.** A wholesome crowd with plenty of toddlers splashes in the shallow pool facing the road. But behind a wall, on the rocks below the battery and adjacent to the Martello Tower, men traditionally skinny-dip year-round—they don't even seem to mind that they're tourist attractions. The pool rarely contains 40 men, or even 20. Instead, the name derives from the *Fortieth* regiment of British *foot* soldiers, who made it their own semi-private swimming hole. Joyce's host, Oliver St. John Gogarty, once took the plunge here with a reluctant George Bernard Shaw in tow.

KILLINEY

"Europe was exhausting. Everything's at the top of a hill," joke the Kids in the Hall. You won't be laughing if you take the DART to Killiney ("kill-EYE-nee"), a posh suburb that's really just a DART stop on the beach, not an actual town (it does make a great start for a walk along the coast). Do yourself a favor and take bus #59 from the Dún Laoghaire DART station to its terminus on Killiney Hill. On foot from the Killiney DART station, you'll have to turn right on Station Rd. and climb up the countless flights of a pedestrian stairpath.

The cream of this crop is **Killiney Hill Park.** From the obelisk at the top, the views are breathtaking—that dark smudge on the horizon is called Wales. A path runs from the obelisk to Dalkey Hill. The **wishing stone** is on the way. If you walk around each level from base to top and then stand facing Dalkey Island and make a wish, it's bound to come true. The path slips off Dalkey Hill onto Torca Rd. Up the road on the left, **Shaw's Cottage** was the home of George Bernard Shaw during a fraction of his childhood. Steps descend from Torca Rd. to coastal Vico Rd., which runs to Dalkey. Killiney itself has a bonny beach. **Groceries,** for refreshment after the hard climb, are sold across from the Killiney Hill Park entrance next to atmospheric **Druid's Chair Pub** (tel. 285 7297), where you can down a pint in calm surroundings before making the final commitment to trek to the obelisk.

BRAY

Bray is a beach town where Dubliners find refuge. If you're looking for rural Irish charm, you won't find it here. But Bray is the southernmost point on the DART and therefore a jumping off point to Co. Wicklow's mountainous treats. The **tourist office** (tel. 286 7128) is the first stop south of Dublin which can give you info on Co. Wicklow. The office is adjacent to the Heritage Centre, downhill on Main St. next to the Royal Hotel (open June-Aug. Mon.-Fri. 10am-7pm, Sat. 10am-4pm, Sun. 2-4pm; Sept.-May Mon.-Fri. 10am-4pm). **Scotman's Hut,** 5 Albert Walk (tel. 286 9178), is the ideal Army-Navy store for hikers, providing equipment for those Wicklow hikes (open Mon.-Sat. 9:30am-6pm). David's Market in the DART station rents **bikes** for those who snub their noses at the bus to Enniskerry (tel. 287 6989; £4/4 hours, £10/day; deposit £20). Bray is a 45-minute DART ride from Connolly Station. Bus #45 also leaves Dublin's Burgh Quay for Bray, and bus #84 leaves from Eden Quay. Bray has good connections to Enniskerry, Co. Wicklow. Bus #85, from the DART station in Bray to Enniskerry (£1), runs more frequently than the Enniskerry-Dublin bus.

Bray's history since the Neolithic Age is on display in a small but well-designed **Heritage Centre,** on Main St. near the Royal Hotel (in the same building as the tourist office). Joe Loughman, local historian and phone repairman, gathered the center's artifacts by extorting them from the local populace in a good-natured exchange for working phones. The floor is a giant map of Bray (tel. 286 7128; open same hours as tourist office). Along the **Esplanade,** grim amusement palaces and B&Bs cater to a dwindling crowd of Dublin beachgoers. Low-confidence gamblers can try 2p slot machines in the **Fun Palace,** on the seafront (tel. 286 4450; open daily 10am-7pm). The **National Aquarium** (tel. 286 4688) is right on the beach and captivates a range of sealife. Unfortunately, it's all displayed in murky tanks (open April-Sept. Mon.-Sun. 10am-6pm; Oct.-March daily 10am-5pm; £2.50, students and seniors £2).

If you've had enough of silly amusements, climb free **Bray Head.** The trailhead is clearly marked at the end of the promenade. **Brandy Hole,** a cave at the foot of Bray Head, was once a smugglers' warehouse. Inland, the ruins of **Raheen A Cluig,** a 13th-century Augustinian church, look very small and very old. The climb to Bray Head takes a good 45 minutes.

B&Bs line the Strand, along the seafront. The cheaper ones are on Convent Ave. and Sidmonton Ave., both off the Strand. **St. Judes,** Convent Ave. (tel. 286 2534), entices customers with a comfortable atmosphere and colorful comforters (£13.50/person; open June-Sept.). **Sans Souci,** Meath Rd. (tel. 282 8629), next to Convent Ave., helps travelers forget their worries in well-decorated rooms. Only the luckiest guests get to sleep in the bed that once cushioned Sting's bones (low season £13.50/person, w/bath £16; July-Aug. £15/person, w/bath £18).

The shelves overflow with groceries at **SuperQuinn** market on Main St., north of the tourist center (open daily 8am-6pm). The surrounding shopping center also houses fruit stands and sandwich shops. In town, **Kincaid's,** Quinsborough Rd., serves pub grub (soup, roast chicken, and chips £5; open daily 8am-9pm). On the Strand, **Porter House** (tel. 786 0668) serves food until 8pm and has an impressive selection of imported beers—Chimay, Grolsch, and (if you honestly crave American beer) Rolling Rock. Trad on Wednesday, Friday, and Sunday nights.

EASTERN IRELAND

Appearances can be deceiving. Most tourists see Eastern Ireland from a bus window as they groove in that tourist track from Dublin direct to Cork or Galway. Without any inquisitive strangers to slow them down, the locals in these parts have dreamed up some pretty wacky ways to keep busy. Take Kildare: the town is picturesque and has some lovely pubs—now what's all this with horses and metaphysics, not to mention a theme park based on bogs? The tiny lakeland towns of Co. Monaghan, really a part of the Fermanagh Lake District, hold surprises like Hare Krishna Island. Standard tourist attractions in this region are the monastic city at Clonmacnoise and the ruins in Co. Meath. Counties Meath, Louth, Wicklow, and Kildare all hold goodies fit for daytrips from Dublin.

 # County Wicklow

Mountainous Co. Wicklow allows wilderness fans to lose themselves on deserted back roads, zoom down seesaw ridges by bicycle, and still be back in Dublin by nightfall. Wild as parts of it are, the whole county is in the capital's backyard. All its major sights are accessible by one bus or another from downtown Dublin, but traveling within the county is often best done by bike or car. The Wicklow Way hiking trail is an excellent reason for your feet to come to the county, and the remains of the monastic city of Glendalough are certainly worth a visit.

Ninth-century Vikings settled at present-day Wicklow and Arklow and used them as bases while raiding Glendalough and other monasteries. Norman invaders in the 1100s followed the same pattern, building defences on the coast while leaving the mountains to the Gaelic O'Toole and O'Byrne clans. English control was not fully established until the 1798 rebellion, when military roads and barracks were built through the interior so that the British Army could hunt down the remaining guerrillas. The mountains later produced a mining industry in the southern part of the county. Bray *is* in Co. Wicklow, but since it's on the DART, *Let's Go* covers it under South of Dublin (see Bray, p. 114).

WICKLOW MOUNTAINS

Over 2000 feet high, covered by gorse and heather and pleated by rivers rushing down wooded glens, the Wicklow summits are home only to grazing sheep and a few villagers. The main tourist attraction, Glendalough, is in the midst of the mountains and draws a steady summertime stream of coach tours from Dublin. The towns of Enniskerry, Ashford, Rathdrum, Avoca, and Blessington, all in the Wicklow Mountains, are on the tourist trail and are covered separately below. You'll need a map of the county, which is a bit difficult to navigate. Bray, Wicklow Town, Arklow, and Rathdrum all have free maps in the tourist offices.

■ ■ ■ GLENDALOUGH

In the 6th century, St. Kevin had a vision telling him to give up his life of ascetic isolation and found a monastery. Evidently reasoning that if you've got to be a monk, you'd might as well be a monk in one of the most spectacularly beautiful valleys in

Ireland, he founded Glendalough ("GLEN-da-lock," meaning "glen of the two lakes"). During the great age of the Irish monasteries—563 to 1152 AD—monastic schools were Ireland's religious and cultural centers, attracting pilgrims from all over Europe to the "land of saints and scholars." Supported by lesser monks who farmed and traded, the privileged brothers inscribed and illuminated religious texts and collected precious jewels and relics for the glory of God.

Practical Information The many tour buses, Dubliners, and backpackers who come to savor the scenery pass through **Laragh** ("LAR-a"), a village 1 mile up the road from the sites. Most pilgrims to Glendalough come by car; a few hike the Wicklow Way into town. The rest catch the private **St. Kevin's Bus Service** (tel. (01) 281 8119). The buses run from Dublin, St. Stephen's Green West (Mon.-Sat. at 11:30am and 6pm, Sun. 11:30am and 7pm; £5, £8 return). They also leave from Bray, just past the Town Hall (daily 12:10 and 6:40pm; £6 return). Buses return from the glen in the evening (Mon.-Fri. 7:15am and 4:15pm, Sat. 9:45am and 4:15pm, Sun. 9:45am and 5:30pm). In Laragh, the bus leaves from the phone booth across from the post office. **Hitching** is unpleasant, since almost all the cars going to Laragh and Glendalough are filled with nervous tourists. Hitchers do make it as far as the juncture of N11 with Glendalough's R755 by starting at the beginning of N11 in southwest Dublin (see To & From the Transportation Hublin, p. 75). **Wicklow Tours** (tel. (0404) 67718) runs a van to Avondale and Wicklow daily (9:40am-6:40pm every 1½hr.; to Wicklow £3, £5 return). **Bus Éireann** also runs tours to Glendalough daily from April to September (except on Mon., Tues., and Thurs. in March, and not on Tues. or Thurs. in Oct.). Buses leave Busaras Station in Dublin at 10:30am, travel along the coast, pass through Avoca, stop in Glendalough, and return to Dublin by 5:45pm. The driver is the tour guide, and admission fees are included in the cost (tel. (01) 836 6111 for booking; £15, children £8). In Laragh, **bike rental** is available from the **post office/video rental store,** on the road from Laragh (tel. (0404) 45236; £6/day, £21/week; deposit £20; open daily 9am-10pm).

Accommodation, Food, & Pubs The **Glendalough Hostel (HI/An Óige)** (tel. (0404) 45342) lies five minutes up the road past the Glendalough visitors' center. The dorms are cramped and the beds squeak, but the view is scintillating. A shop sells basic groceries. Rooms range from 24-bed dorm to private rooms with a bunkbed. (Lockout noon-5pm, unguarded luggage storage all day, bike storage. Kitchen open 7:30-10am and 5-10pm. Sheets 85p. Max. 3-day stay. Dorm £6, Oct.-May £5.) Also in Glendalough is the **Valeview B&B** (tel. (0404) 45292), where you can look at the mountains from under plush comforters (£15/person, £16/person w/bath). **Laragh** boasts another hostel and a clutch of B&Bs. The **Wicklow Way Hostel** (tel. (0404) 45398) is relatively new and has sturdy beds and warm comforters (sheets 50p). The attached coffeehouse serves inexpensive breakfasts. Kitchen with microwave open 7am-10pm; lounge with TV. (Co-ed dorm £6, no doubles.)

In Glendalough, **Mrs. Holden** pours tea and butters hot scones (£1.40) in her house, across from the entrance arch. Coffee and sandwiches are served as well (follow the "TEAS" signs; open April-Oct. daily 10am-5:30pm). In the town's hotel, the **Glendalough Tavern** serves a limited menu, but is much cheaper than the hotel restaurant (tel. (0404) 45135 or 45391; sandwiches £1.50, entrees £5). In Laragh, the **Laragh Inn** (tel. (0404) 45345) piles plates high with hot edibles (open noon-9pm; entrees £5-7; salads £4-7). The **Brudge Bar** has pub grub every night and sessions Saturday nights at 9pm, which pull all the local hostelers.

Sights Today only the **visitors center** (tel. (0404) 45352) and a handful of tourist trappings mark the ancient monastic spot. The center shows a film on the history of monasteries and conducts guided tours of the local ruins. (Open daily June-Aug. 9am-6:30pm, Sept. to mid-Oct. 9:30am-6pm, mid-Oct. to mid-March 9:30am-5pm, mid-March to May 9:30am-6pm. £2, students and children £1. Wheelchair access.)

The present ruins were only a small part of the monastery in its heyday, when wooden huts for low-status laborer monks were plentiful. Monks once hid in the

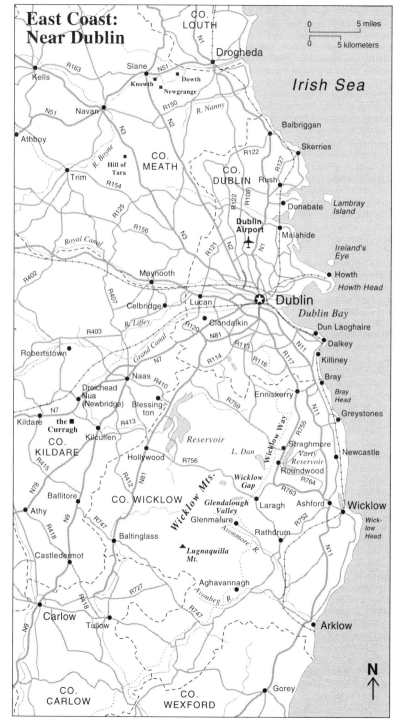

East Coast: Near Dublin

WICKLOW MOUNTAINS

CO. LOUTH

Irish Sea

0   5 miles
0   5 kilometers

Kells

R163

Slane N51

Drogheda

Knowth Dowth
Newgrange

N51

Navan

R150

R. Nanny

Balbriggan

N3

Skerries

Athboy

R. Boyne

CO. MEATH

R122

CO. DUBLIN

R127

Hill of
Tara

Rush

Trim

R154

R125

R122

R108

Donabate

Lambray
Island

R156

Dublin
Airport

Malahide

Royal Canal

N3

R121

N2

N1

Ireland's
Eye

R402

Maynooth

Howth

Howth Head

Celbridge

Lucan

Dublin

R407

R. Liffey

R120

N81

Clondalkin

Dublin Bay

R403

Grand Canal

R114

R115

R116

R117

Dun Laoghaire

Dalkey

Robertstown

N7

Killiney

Naas

R410

Enniskerry

Bray

Droichead
Nua
(Newbridge)

Blessing-
ton

R759

Bray
Head

Greystones

Kildare

the
Curragh

R413

Wicklow Way

R755

CO. KILDARE

Kilcullen

Reservoir

L. Dan

Straghmore
Varty
Reservoir

Newcastle

R415

Hollywood

R756

Wicklow
Gap

Roundwood

R764

Ballitore

R412

N81

CO. WICKLOW

Wicklow Mts.

Glendalough
Valley

Laragh

R763

Ashford

Wicklow

Athy

R418

R747

Glenmalure

Avonmore R.

Rathdrum

R752

N11

Wicklow
Head

Baltinglass

▲ Lugnaquilla
Mt.

N9

Castledermot

Aghavannagh

Avonbeg R.

R418

R727

R747

Carlow

Tullow

Arklow

Ng

N
↑

CO. CARLOW

CO. WEXFORD

Gorey

100-foot **Round Tower,** built in the 10th century as a watchtower and belltower. The entrance is 12 feet from the ground. When Vikings approached, the monks would climb the inside of the tower floor by floor, drawing up the ladders behind them. **St. Kevin's Cross** is an unadorned high cross: a crucifix (representing Christianity) merged with a ring signifying the sun (a pagan symbol). Early proselytizers hoped that combining the two would make Christianity more palatable to the Irish. The **Cathedral,** constructed in a combination of Greek and Roman architectural styles, was at one time the largest in the country. **St. Kevin's Church,** also jokingly known as St. Kevin's Kitchen, with its stone roof and round tower looks like it has a chimney for cooking. Built in the 11th century, it was used as a church until the 16th century. It lay derelict until the 19th century, when locals once again used it as a church until newer St. Kevin's Church was built a mile away.

The **Upper and Lower Lakes** are a short walk from the monastic site, across the bridge and to the right. A five-minute walk, the Lower Lake is serene. Near the spectacular Upper Lake, a half hour walk from the site, **St. Kevin's Bed** is the cave where he prayed. Local chieftains are buried in a church nearby. Legend says that when St. Kevin prayed, his words ascended in a vortex of flame and light which burned over the Upper Lake's dark waters with such intensity that none but the most righteous monks could witness it without going blind.

Sinners and Saints

Another legend linked to St. Kevin's Bed is the tale of Kathleen. Kevin was apparently an angelically beautiful man who wasn't interested in women. He was forced to move his hermitage to Glendalough to escape the lustful advances of the voluptuous Kathleen. Still she pursued him, so he withdrew to his cave near the Upper Lake. The princess scoured the area until Kevin's dog gave him away. Kathleen followed the dog to Kevin's cave, where she found him asleep and began to take advantage of the situation. Kevin awoke and angrily flung Kathleen into the lake, off the rocky ledge now called "Lady's Leap." She drowned. Kevin felt guilty, lived a life of atonement, and prayed that none might ever drown in the lake again.

■■■ THE WICKLOW WAY

The lonely mountain heights reach westward and upward, negotiable by foot, bike, or horse along many established trails. The 70-mile Wicklow Way, Ireland's first and best-known long-distance path, starts near Dublin and progresses south along the crests all the way to Clonegal in Co. Carlow. Parts of it are well-graded and even paved. Though the path is well-marked with yellow arrows, hikers should get the Ordnance Survey's *Discovery Series #56* for hiking in the northern part of the county and *Discovery Series #62* for hiking in south Wicklow. The latter covers the trail to Aghavannagh and has descriptive text on the reverse. Both are available in bookstores and tourist offices. Since the path is mostly out of sight and hearing range of the lowlands, traveling alone can be risky. It's a bad idea to drink water from the streams en route, and it is *illegal* to light fires within one mile of the forest.

The northern 45 miles of the path (from Dublin to Aghavannagh) are the most popular, have the best scenery, and offer better access to hostels. To reach the northern end of the path, take bus #47B from Hawkins St. in Dublin's city center to its terminus at Marlay Park in Rathfarnham, a Dublin suburb. Bus #47 also stops nearby. It takes three days to hike the northern section (assuming 7-8 hours/day of hiking). The entire trail takes six days.

From its start in Marlay Park the Wicklow Way piggybacks on **Kilmashogue Forest Trail,** which gives great views of Dublin and the distant Mourne Mountains. Farther on, the trail passes **Powerscourt Waterfall** in Enniskerry. The Knockree hostel is between the trail and Enniskerry, while the Glencree hostel is off the trail in the opposite direction from Knockree and Enniskerry. A "Greatest Hits" excerpt of the Wicklow Way would start in Enniskerry and end in Glendalough. Between the two, the trail climbs to the summit of **White Hill** (2073 feet), from which you can see the mountains of North Wales on a clear day. Soon after White Hill, the trail passes Annamoe, where a road and trail lead to Ashford, Devil's Glen, and the Tiglin Hostel (see Ashford, p. 121).

The trail then descends to Roundwood, a stop for **St. Kevin's Bus** (see Glendalough, p. 115), and runs alongside the Glenmacnass Rd. to Glendalough's impressive monastic ruins. The trail rises to visit **Poulanass Waterfall** and climbs a forest track towards **Mullacor** (at about 2300 feet, it's the highest point of the Way), then drops into **Glenmalure,** with another hostel and Mt. Lugnaquilla nearby. The trail crosses another mountain ridge and tiptoes across the **Dun River** over an iron bridge, 1½ miles southeast of the hostel at Aghavannagh. A detour east off the way between Glendalough and Aghavannagh leads to bus and rail stations in Rathdrum.

Past Aghavannagh, the trail makes smaller climbs amid mellower scenery, ending in Co. Carlow with views of antenna-topped Mt. Leinster. Long-distance hikers can connect here to the **South Leinster Way**. Bus Éireann serves the southern section of the Wicklow Way at Aughrim, Tinahely, Shillelagh, and Hackettstown.

An Óige prints the excellent white brochure *A Walking Guide for Hostelers #4,* which meticulously details hiking routes between An Óige/HI hostels in Co. Wicklow. These routes are not necessarily along the Wicklow Way, or indeed along any marked trail at all; the brochure is now hard to find, but may soon be reprinted. Get it from any of An Óige's Wicklow hostels or from their main office, 61 Mountjoy St., Dublin. Walking distances between An Óige hostels are: Tiglin to Glendalough, 5 hours; Rathdrum to Aghavannagh, 4 hours; Aghavannagh to Glenmalure, 5 hours; Aghavannagh to Glendalough, 7 hours. Other trails meander every which way through the Wicklovian wilderness.

ACCOMMODATIONS

Several hostels lie within five miles of the Wicklow Way; these fill up in July and August. For An Óige hostels, book ahead through the An Óige Head Office, 61 Mountjoy St., Dublin (tel. (01) 830 4555); call other hostels directly. The hostels are listed north to south, with distance from the Wicklow Way in parentheses. **Wicklow Way, Old Mill,** and **Glendalough hostels** are reviewed under Glendalough (see p. 116).

Knockree (An Óige/HI), Lacklan House, Enniskerry (tel. (01) 286 4036; on the Way), is a reconstructed farmhouse close to the village and to Powerscourt Gardens/Waterfall. From Enniskerry, take the left fork road leading from the village green, take a left at Buttercups Newsagent, and begin a steep walk, following signs for Glencree Drive. £5.50; Oct.-May £4.50.

Glencree (An Óige/HI), Stone House, Enniskerry (tel. (01) 286 4037; 3 mi. from the Way up a steep hill), is farther along Glencree Dr. from Enniskerry. The building was originally a barracks used by British army to stamp out leftover rebels from 1798. £5.50; Oct.-May £4.50.

Tiglin (An Óige/HI), a.k.a. **Devil's Glen,** Ashford (tel. (0404) 40259; 5 mi. from the Way), near the Tiglin Adventure Centre. 50 beds in a very basic accommodation. From Ashford, follow the Roundwood Road for 3 mi., then follow the signs for the Tiglin turnoff on the right-hand side (see Ashford, p. 121). £5.50/person; Oct.-May £4.50.

Wicklow Way Hostel (tel. (0404) 45398; on the Way), £6/person.

Glendalough (An Óige/HI; tel. (0404) 45342; 1½ mi.) £6/person; Oct.-May £5.

Glenmalure (HI/An Óige), Grennane (no phone; 2 mi.). Intimate country-cottage feel, maybe because it's the only habitation in sight. The Avonbeg River provides excellent fishing for brown trout and water for washing and cooking, which is handy since the hostel doesn't have running water. West of Glenmalure is an army range in the Glen of Imaal where military exercises are conducted. Stay out. £5.50; Oct.-May £4.50. Open July-Aug. daily; Sept.-June open weekends only.

■■■ WEST WICKLOW

Other Wicklow Mountain hostels are west of the tallest peaks in less spectacular but even less populated territory. Don't plan to hike here from the Wicklow Way, since you would have to pass through the Irish Army's target practice in the Glen of Imaal.

Baltyboys (An Óige/HI), a.k.a **Blessington Lake Hostel**, Blessington (tel. (045) 67266). A reconstructed old schoolhouse with excellent fishing and Russborough House nearby (see Blessington, below). £5.50; Oct.-May £4.50. Open March-Nov. daily; Dec.-Feb. Fri. and Sat. nights.

Ballinclea (An Óige/HI), Donard (tel. (045) 54657), near forest and Blessington Lake, but cut off from Glenmalure Hostel by the Army range in Glen of Imaal. From Dublin's Crampton Quay, try taking bus #65 to Donard (Sat.-Sun. 1/day; £1.10). £5.50; Oct.-May £4.50. Open March-Nov. daily; Dec.-Feb. Fri. and Sat. nights.

Rathcoran House (IHH), Baltinglass (tel. (0508) 81073; fax (01) 453 2183). A safer hiking destination from the western Wicklow hostels (since you won't have to make a huge detour around the Army). Easy access via Tullow to N81 road between Dublin and Wexford makes this a good starting or ending point for West Wicklow hikers. Bus Éireann runs to Dublin or Waterford twice daily via Baltinglass. £6.50, double £8/person; **camping** available. Open May to mid-Sept.

Two buses every day run from Busarus in Dublin to Baltinglass. The Baltinglass **tourist office** in Weavers Sq. (tel. 0508) 81634 or 81688) dispenses West Wicklow hiking info (open July-Sept. Mon.-Sat. 9am-1pm and 2-7pm).

BLESSINGTON

Since the Liffey was dammed to make a reservoir for Dublin's teeming, thirsty millions, Blessington in West Wicklow has become a popular recreation center. A pretty lakefront embellishes art-filled **Russborough House** (tel. (045) 65239; fax (045) 65054) built in 1741 for Joseph Leeson, a member of the old (Anglo-) Irish parliament. The architect was Richard Cassells, who is also responsible for Dublin's Leinster House and many of Trinity College's Georgian marvels. As at Powerscourt and Castletown, the design is Palladian, its central block flanked by colonnades and wings. Lavish trim is spread throughout the inside of the house like icing across a too-sweet cake. The house also holds paintings by Goya, Velasquez, and Rubens. These works of art were acquired by Alfred Beit (co-founder of DeBeers Diamonds) and tucked away in West Wicklow by his nephew, who now owns Russborough. The National Gallery of Ireland sometimes mounts exhibits here. The house is 2½ miles down the main road toward Ballymore. (Open June-Aug. daily 10:30am-5:30pm; April-May and Sept.-Oct. Sun. 10:30am-5:30pm. 45-min. tour of main rooms and paintings £3, students £2, ages 12-18 £1. Half-hour tours of the bedrooms £1.)

Turn to the Blessington **tourist office,** in the town square (tel. (045) 65850) for ideas on outdoor pursuits (open June-Aug. Mon.-Sat. 10am-1pm, 1:30-6pm, Sun. 2-6pm). The **Baltyboys Hostel (An Óige/HI)** a.k.a. **Blessington Lake Hostel,** Blessington (tel. (045) 67266), provides cozy accommodation in a reconstructed school house across Blessington Lake from Russborough House. Brown trout and perch await in the nearby lakes and in the upper Liffey River; rent rods in town (£5.50; Oct.-May £4.50. Open daily March-Nov.; Dec.-Feb. Fri-Sat.). Book through the An Óige head office, 61 Mountjoy St., Dublin (tel. (01) 830 4555).

From Dublin's Crampton Quay, Blessington is served by **bus** #65 (1/hr.; £1.10). On Saturday and Sunday, one bus continues on to Donard and the Ballinclea Hostel there. **Bus Éireann** passes through Blessington on its Dublin/Waterford route (2/day), connecting it with Baltinglass and its hostel. Blessington is on N81, which passes undulatingly from Dublin to Enniscorthy via Tullow. R410 road connects Blessington to Naas, from which N7 leads to nicer Kildare.

WICKLOW COAST

The natural sights and uncrowded towns of Wicklow coast seem a world away from urban Dublin. As a route to the southeast, it lacks the heavy-hitting historical sites of the inland route through Glendalough and Kilkenny, but its natural offerings are more intriguing.

ASHFORD

Ashford, six miles northeast of Wicklow on N11, provides access to both mountains and ocean. On Friday mornings the town trades goods and cattle at its **market-place.** The **Mount Usher Gardens** (tel. (0404) 40116 or 40205), on N11, encompass 20 acres of well-pruned rare trees, shrubs, flowers, and bees along the River Vartry. (Open mid-March to Oct. daily 10:30am-5:20pm; £3, students and seniors £2.) Gardeners will recognize Mount Usher as a prime example of a Robinsonian garden. This style stresses informality and natural design. Paths weave through the flora along a stream that is ornamented with cute miniature suspension bridges, splashing weirs, waterfalls, and subsidiary brooks. Two miles beyond Ashford on the road to Roundwood, imps may be hiding in the thickly wooded **Devil's Glen.** The glen is a chasm dug by the River Vartry's 100-foot waterfall, which tumbles into the **Devil's Punchbowl.**

Tiglin National Adventure Centre (tel. (0404) 40169; fax 40701), just 3½ miles from Ashford off the same road, challenges any takers. Experts teach mountaineering, rock climbing, canoeing, and kayaking. The center also arranges "Wild Wicklow" weekends, which explore particular aspects of the natural environment—it's called "eco-tourism." All courses include mountain biking, snorkeling, and full board in two-to-four-person dorm rooms. Weekend courses run Friday night to Sunday afternoon and cost £75 (including room and board). The course is also offered at a daily rate of £25; cost-cutting eco-tourists could combine days at Tiglin with nights at the Tiglin Hostel and meals at the grocers in Ashford.

The **Tiglin Hostel (An Óige/HI),** a.k.a. the **Devil's Glen Hostel** (tel. (0404) 40259), is simple, not pampering, accommodation (June-Sept. £5.50, Oct.-May £4.50). Book through An Óige's head office in Dublin (tel. (01) 830 4555). From the hostel, a scenic five-hour hike over Bookey's Bridge ultimately ends up in Laragh, next to Glenalough (maps available at hostel). **Bus Éireann** passes through Ashford on its route from Dublin to Wicklow (to Dublin or Wicklow 8/day, Sun. 6/day; £4.30, student £2.60).

■■■ WICKLOW TOWN

Wicklow Town is touted both for its coastal locale and for its usefulness as a departure point into the Wicklow Mountains. Older Wicklovians are chatty and friendly; the town's black-clad youth strive for urbanity. Wicklow also boasts an unusual level of ethnic diversity (for Ireland). While the town itself doesn't have any extraordinary charms, a few hours spent biking along the nearby coastal road can pleasantly occupy an afternoon. Long, skinny Main St. snakes past the Grand Hotel and the grassy triangular plot by the tourist office to its terminus in Market Square.

Practical Information Trains run to Dublin's Connolly Station and to Rosslare (Mon.-Sat. 4/day, Sun. 2/day; to Dublin £4). The station is a 15-minute walk east of town via Church St. **Bus Éireann** leaves for Dublin from both the street uphill from the Billy Byrne monument and from the Grand Hotel, at the other end of Main St. (Mon.-Sat. 9/day, Sun. 7/day; £3.50 return). **Wicklow Tours Ltd.** (tel. 67718) runs a van from the Bridge Tavern, Bridge St., to Avondale and Glendalough (July-Aug. daily departures 10am, noon, 2, and 4pm; to Glendalough £4, £6 return). **Dolan's Bus Service** (tel. (0404) 67420) runs buses daily (8:30am-11:30pm) from

Newcastle, 12 miles north of Wicklow Town, down the coast to Silver Strand and then Brittas Bay.

The **tourist office**, Fitzwilliam Sq. (tel. 69117; fax 69118), on Main St., can fill you in on the Wicklow Way and other county attractions. Their book and map selection, which includes *Let's Go: Ireland*, is excellent (open June-Aug. Mon.-Sat. 9am-6pm; Sept.-May Mon.-Fri. 9:30am-1pm and 2-5:30pm). **Bikes** may be rented from **Wicklow Hire** on Abbey St., the continuation of Main St. (tel. 68149; open Mon.-Sat. 8:30am-5:30pm; £6/day, £25/week; deposit £30; pump and lock included). An **AIB** bank conducts business on Main St.; **ATM**. Wicklow's **phone code** is 0404.

Accommodations Travelers will be content in almost any of the many B&Bs on Patrick Rd., uphill from Main St. and past the church. Wicklow Town can now accommodate hostelers in the **Wicklow Bay Hostel,** the Murrough (tel. 69213). From Fitzwilliam Sq., head toward the river, cross the bridge, and walk left until you see the big building called "Marine House." The friendly owners turned this abandoned beer-bottling factory into a cheery, spacious hostel with firm beds and spectacular sea views from the roof. (Dorm or double £8/person w/sheets; Irish breakfast £3, continental breakfast £1. Open March-Oct.) It takes a bit of energy to hike up Patrick Rd. to friendly Mrs. H. Gorman and son's **Thomond House,** Upper Patrick Rd. (tel. 67940). A veranda, panoramic views, and rooms as comfortable as your own are certainly worth the 15-minute walk. (£14/person, w/bath £16. If you call from Wicklow Town, Mrs. Gorman will pick you up. Open March-Oct.) The **Bridge Tavern,** Bridge St. (tel. 67718), has lots of hairy cats, snooker tables downstairs, and good value for its standard rooms (£10/person, w/bath £15).

Two **campgrounds** are both seven miles south of Wicklow off the Wexford Rd. (N11). **Johnson's** (tel. 48133; high season £5, low season £4; plus £1/person) and **River Valley** (tel. 41647; high season £6, low season £4; plus £1/person) are similar. Both are open March-Sept; both charge 40p for showers. From Wicklow, turn right off N11 at Doyle's pub. Johnson's is one mile down the road, River Valley 2½ miles.

Food & Pubs Main St., like Main Streets everywhere, is lined with greasy takeaways and fruit stands. **Fresh Today,** Main St. (tel. 68322), stocks stacks of fruits and vegetables that are, of course, fresh (open Mon.-Sat. 8:30am-6:30pm). **Quinnsworth,** Church St. offers an even wider selection of nutriments. The **Coffee Shop,** Fitzwilliam Sq. (tel. 68194), will provide a quick shot of caffeine before your hike and furnish you with salads (85p), sandwiches (£1.50), and baked goods. Plant yourself in the **Green Vase,** Main St. (tel. 66006), for fresh pizzas, friendly service, and more Italian fare (9-inch pizza £4; free delivery; open Mon.-Sat. 10am-11pm).

A number of pubs offer musical evenings for the delectation of Wicklow's residents. Every Thursday night, the **Bridge Tavern** on Bridge St. (tel. 67718) resounds with traditional music. It's also known to have informal squeezebox sessions on Wednesday and Saturday nights in the summer to calm the nerves of the snooker players in the back. Those not satisfied with listening should visit **Mulvihill's,** Market Sq. near the monument (tel. 68823). The comfortable little bar welcomes guest players, has plenty of seats for listeners, and throws its own sessions Thursday through Monday. Check the fence opposite the tourist office in Fitzwilliam Sq. for lists of concerts and events in town.

Sights True to its name, **Market Square,** at that end of Main St. farthest from the train station, holds open-air markets and displays a pike-less monument to local hero Billy Byrne, a pikeman in the 1798 rebellion. At the other end of Main St., an **abbey** keeps company with the remnants of a 13th-century **Franciscan Friary.** The abbey was founded at the same time as Black Castle and destroyed along with it. It was subsequently rebuilt and became a place of retirement for both Normans and native Irish, who considered it neutral ground. The first left past Market Sq. leads to **Black Castle.** Though only a few wind-worn stones remain, the promontory on which it was built elevates you to a great vantage point above the sea and meadows. The

Normans built the castle in 1169; the local O'Byrne and O'Toole clans immediately attacked and finally destroyed it in 1301. The staircase cut into the seaward side of the remains is reputed to access a tunnel to the nearby convent.

A cliff trail leads to **St. Bride's Head,** where St. Patrick landed on Travilahawk Strand in 432 AD. The local population greeted him by knocking the teeth out of one of his companions, later assigned to convert the locals in Wicklow. The trail itself is only slightly less threatening: it leads past cannons before arriving at St. Bride's Head. It takes about one hour to walk there (and another hour back). The heights of the cliff walk provide smashing views.

Beaches stretch south of Wicklow to Arklow. The closest ones to Wicklow are **Silver Strand** and **Jack's Hole.** The most popular is crowded **Brittas Bay,** midway between Wicklow and Arklow, where you can buy ultra-cheap crabs in summer. At the Billy Byrne monument, Wicklow Town's Main St. becomes Summer Hill (the coastal road), which will lead you to sun and sand.

■ NEAR WICKLOW TOWN

RATHDRUM

For the first weekend in June, cartooning is the life of Rathdrum. International and local cartoonists come to this town, where the streets are full of dogs, for the **International Cartoon Festival** (tel. (0404) 46183 or 46811) to exhibit and draw for the public and to hold workshops for budding artists (exhibition £1, related events free). The festival never stops at the **Cartoon Inn** (tel. (0404) 46774), on Main St., a pub with zany cartooned walls and a lip-smackin', belly-ticklin' lunch. The **tourist office** (tel. (0404) 46262) in the center of town will encourage you to stay and also to spend the money it will exchange for you. (Open Mon.–Fri. 9am-5:30pm, Sat.-Sun. 9am-6pm in summer.) There are a number of B&Bs around Rathdrum, but the cheapest option is **The Old Presbytery Hostel** (tel. (0404) 46173), a very clean and new hostel built from an old Presbyterian monastery (£8/person in 6-bed room, wheelchair accessible).

AVONDALE HOUSE

Rathdrum's position, perched over the steep wooded valley of the Avonmore river, makes the town picture-postcard pretty, but the best reason to visit is the **Avondale House** (tel. (0404) 46111). Avondale House was political leader Charles Stewart Parnell's birthplace and main residence until his death in 1891; the former home is now a Parnell museum where restorers have turned the clocks back to circa-1850 decor. The walls are decked with political cartoons and transcriptions of Parnell's love letters to Kitty O'Shea. The biographical video, although overripe with dramatic flourish, is a well-produced and genuinely interesting glimpse into Parnell's life and the history of Irish independence, two stories that are closely connected to each other.

Flora fanatics will faun over the five hundred acres of forest and parkland which surround the house and spread along the west bank of the Avonmore River. In 1904, the then-government of Ireland purchased Avondale and began its first silvicultural (forest-growing) experiment there: they wanted to figure out how best to reverse Ireland's severe deforestation. The plots of trees stretch out around the **Great Ride,** a grassy expanse that winds its way among the diverse tree species of Avondale's grounds. Otters play hide-and-go-seek on the river's muddy banks.

Prehistoric Celts operated a productive gold field somewhere in the Avonmore Valley, though no one knows quite where. Subsequent attempts to mine Wicklow Gold were made by one company which unfortunately set up shop in 1797 (a year later, all the miners decided they'd rather be rebels); another unsuccessful attempt was headed by Parnell himself. Avondale House is on the road from Wicklow Town to Avoca, one mile after Rathdrum, and before the Meeting of the Waters. Take Main Street heading towards Avoca and then follow the signs. (House and forest open daily 11am-5pm, 11am-4pm in winter; admission £2.50, seniors, students, and children £1.50.)

■■■ ARKLOW

Arklow has a long and fishy history—for the past two millennia it has made its living by fishing and shipping. When St. Kevin visited the town in the 5th century, he blessed the town's fishermen, guaranteeing prosperity. A more tangible blessing was bestowed by the Anglo-Irish government which built a modern harbor in the 18th century. Arklow blossomed into a strapping and well-known port and ship-building center. The town flops along a Main St. that runs parallel to the Avoca River. The harbor, beaches, and potteries are farther east of town center.

The Arklow **tourist office** (tel. 32484), really a trailer, parks in the town center, at the end of St. Mary's Rd. and Main St. (open all year, Mon.-Sat. 9:30am-1pm, 2pm-5:30pm). **Bank of Ireland** (tel. 32004) and **AIB** branches, with **ATMs**, are on Main St. **Trains** run to Arklow from Dublin on their way to Rosslare (Mon.-Sat. 4/day, Sun 2/day). **Bus Éireann** passes through Arklow on its way to Rosslare and Wexford (Mon.-Sat. 5/day, Sun. 3/day). Arklow is 40 miles south of Dublin on the N11 (Dublin/Wexford road). **Cycledom,** Upper Main St. (tel. 39989), sells camping equipment, repairs and rents bikes (£7/day, £20/week, deposit £40), and sells fishing bait and tackle (open Mon.-Sat. 9am-6pm). The **phone code** survives as 0402.

Accommodations & Food Those who can't resist Arklow's siren call head to Coolgreany Rd., which houses a passel of B&Bs. Turning right off of Station Rd. Main St. first becomes Upper Main St. and then Coolgreany. **Vale View** (tel. 32622) boasts huge bedrooms and good, firm beds; kudos to the glass-roofed "honeymoon suites;" (single £16; double £13, w/bath £15). **Dunguaire** (tel. 32774) is another comfortable B&B, with a good view of the green countryside from the spacious dining room (single £16, double £13.50, w/bath £15).

Cheap eats, but no Indian food, may be had at the **New Delhi,** Upper Main St. (tel. 39889), which is a take-out place with a few small tables (salads £2.40, sandwiches £1.30; open Mon.-Sat. 9am-6pm). Next door, **The Green Pepper** (tel. 39889) vends all kinds of produce (open 9am-6pm). **The River Walk Restaurant** (tel. 31657), next door to the paddleboats, has more sedentary river views (full breakfast all day for £3.75, chicken curry and rice £3.60; open daily 9am-10pm).

Sights Located about one mile from town, the north and south beaches are both safe for swimming, but grey and rocky; Florida it's not. A walk along the Avoca River is lovely, but a boat trip on the river is really splendid; paddleboats, rowboats, and canoes can be hired next door to the River Walk Restaurant for £2/person per half-hour, plus a bit of muscular exertion.

Next door to the town library, the seafoam-green **Arklow Maritime Museum** froths on St. Mary's Rd. between the train station and the Catholic Church. If you like ships, set sail for this one-room museum, which is nearly all that remains of Arklow's maritime past, when schooners from Arklow traversed the seven seas while voyaging to Europe and the Americas. Inform your curiosity about John Tyrrell and Sons, still a big source of local pride, who have been building ships in Arklow for 130 years. More recently, the family has constructed the racing yacht *Asgard II*. A piece of the first transatlantic cable, laid by an Arklow captain, is proudly displayed; also gawk at the newspaper headlines from the sinking of the *Titanic* (open daily 10am-1pm and 2-5pm; £1.50, students 50p).

St. Savior's Church, Rector-Rev. David Moynan (tel. 32439), on Upper Main St. at the roundabout, is a beautiful building with an international reputation for campanology (bell-ringing). The ringers strut their stuff on Sunday mornings. The church itself was built in 1899 out of Bath stone. When cut, this stone is so soft that it can be shaped by hand (it later develops a hardened surface). Morning prayers and Sunday services are held in the church. This area of Ireland produces the raw materials for ceramics, and Arklow is known for its finished products of all types, from bathroom ceramics (the warehouse is next to the beach for those combination sunbathing and redecorating days) to vases. **Arklow Pottery,** on the South Quay, was established in 1934; it mostly makes dinnerware. (Factory tours Mon.-Fri. Booking tel. 32401; individuals can join pre-booked groups; free. Factory open daily 9:30am-4:45pm.) The Arklow and Wicklow Vale **pottery outlets,** along the quays, sell glassware and ceramics straight from the kiln.

 # County Kildare

The towns immediately west of Dublin, in Co. Kildare, are still well within the city's orbit: the best sights—Kildare's horses and Lullymore's Peatland World—are easily seen as daytrips from Dublin. Only a bit farther from Dublin, though, the towns become shockingly tiny communities. Kildare's links to Dublin are more than just highways. The Pale—the border of official English rule—cut Co. Kildare in half. From the 13th to the 16th century, the FitzGerald Earls of Kildare had effective control over all of eastern Ireland. Today, mansions and the big-money Irish Derby evoke Kildare's former prominence.

■■■ MAYNOOTH

Maynooth ("ma-NOOTH") is sandwiched between two claims to fame: Carton House dominates one end of Main St., Maynooth Castle and St. Patrick's College the other. During the nineteenth century, Maynooth was home to Ireland's only seminary. A good number of today's priests both in Ireland and abroad are ordained here, at the National Seminary.

The **Citizens Information Centre,** Main St. (tel. 328 5477), is not a tourist office but will answer questions about the area (open Mon.-Fri. 10am-4pm). **Buses: #66** runs directly to Maynooth from Middle Abbey St., Dublin (2/hr.; 50 min.; £1.50); #67A, also from Middle Abbey St., takes the long way through Celbridge (2/hr.; £1.50). Suburban **trains** run from Connolly Station in Dublin (Mon.-Sat. 14/day, Sun. 4/day; 30 min.; £1.60). Maynooth is 12 miles west of Dublin on N4. Hitchers from Dublin stick out a thumb on Chapelizod Rd., between Phoenix Park and the Liffey, or even farther west where the same street becomes Lucan Rd. The copycat **phone code** is Dublin's 01.

Accommodations, Food, & Pubs The **Leinster Arms,** Main St. (tel. 628 6323), is primarily a pub, but it's also a great B&B value for groups. Guests pay a flat £22/room, with or without bath. Reserve ahead in summer, especially for the room with an attached kitchen. The pub downstairs serves both snacks and entrees for the kitchenless (sandwiches £1.10, vegetables £2.50, entrees about £5; open daily 10:30am-10pm). **St. Patrick's College** rents out singles and doubles in student apartments from mid-June to Sept. (£15/person for B&B; contact Bill Tinley at the conference center, tel. 708 3726). Enjoy light lunch fare at **Elite Confectionery,** Main St. (tel. 628 5521; soup of the day 85p, salad 80p, cheesecake £1; open Mon.-Sat. 8:30am-6:30pm).

Sights Maynooth Castle was built in 1176 by Maurice FitzGerald and dismantled in 1647. The powerful family controlled their vast domains from here. The edifice now lies in ruins in a sun-dappled field right off Main St. Pick up the key from Mrs. Saults at 9 Parson St., the road across from the castle, to become the sole, if temporary, resident of this castle. Hundreds of noisy birds take off in a huff when you climb the circular staircase into the roofless Great Hall (open whenever Mrs. Saults is home; free).

Next to the castle, **St. Patrick's College** draws in the tourists with interesting architecture and alluring, lush gardens. The **Visitors Centre,** on the left after passing through the arch, displays Christian artifacts and offers tours of the college (tel. (01) 708 3576; open Mon.-Sat. 11am-5pm, Sun. 2-6pm; tours £1.50, students £1). The arch leads into a world all its own that consists of the oldest swimming pool in Ireland (built in 1903), a cypress-shaded garden, and the **Ecclesiastical Museum** (tel. 628 5222). The museum contains a spectrum of priestly paraphernalia and an impressive collection of 19th century scientific instruments, including the induction coils of Dr. Nicholas Callan, their inventor. The unifying theme remains unclear (open Tues. and Thurs. 2-4pm, Sun. 2-5pm; free). Farther inside the arch grow the gorgeous gardens created in 1995 for the seminary's bicentennial. Maynooth was originally founded on fear: King George III granted permission for this first Catholic seminary in Ireland to open in 1795 out of fear that priests educated in Revolutionary France (the only other option) would acquire dangerous notions of independence. He later said that opening St. Patrick's "cost me more pain than the loss of the colonies." The Maynooth Seminary remained the only means of training Irish Catholic priests for much of the 19th century; it is now one of many centres of training and scholarship. At the other end of Maynooth's main drag, the Georgian **Carton House,** set at the end of a long, beautifully landscaped drive, impresses visitors with its imposing facade. Still privately owned, the house isn't open to the public.

■ NEAR MAYNOOTH: CELBRIDGE

The *raison d'être* of this town (pronounced "SELL-bridge") is **Castletown House** (tel. (01) 628 8252; fax 627 1811). The estate's driveway extends for a full half mile, spilling past its entrance gates to become the town's Main St. The grounds overlook the Liffey and are ideal for picnics; the shaded, bubbling creek is popular with young lovers. William Conolly, once Speaker of the Irish House of Commons, built himself this magnificent home, thus touching off a nationwide fad for Palladian architecture. Edward Lovett Pearce, who also designed the Parliament House/Bank of Ireland in Dublin (see Trinity College, Grafton Street, Christ Church, p. 88), finished the house after Conolly's death. From a central block, two wings and rows of colonnades stretch out in graceful arcs to hide the stables behind. Inside, sumptuous furnishings and baroque wallpaper (to match the grand colonnades) show off the luxurious life-styles of the rich and obscure Anglo-Irish gentry. Of particular note are the print room (the only one of its kind surviving in Ireland) and some garish chandeliers in the den. The **devil** allegedly visited the dining room one afternoon for tea, but no evidence of hoof-prints remains. Outside, the Obelisk, also known as Conolly's Folly, is merely an unruly stack of arches and towers conceived as a makework project during the severe winter of 1739. Americans may be surprised that the original plans for the Washington Monument looked like this, only bigger. (Open April-Sept. Mon.-Fri. 10am-6pm, Sat. 11am-6pm, Sun. 2-6pm; Oct. Mon.-Fri. 10am-5pm, Sun. 2-5pm; Nov.-March Sun. 2-5pm. Tours £2.50, students £1.)

Down Main St. from the House's entrance, **Celbridge Abbey** provides another opportunity for picnicking. The abbey and its gardens are maintained by mentally-challenged people, whom the Abbey houses and employs. The elegantly manicured gardens spread out behind the house, laced with two trails which tell stories about Jonathan Swift. He visited the abbey when courting a local lady, Vanessa. There's also a neat model railway (abbey open March-Oct. Tues.-Sun. noon-6pm; £1.50, students £1). Purchase picnic supplies for both dinner and lunch on the two lovely lawns at **Damien's Londis Supermarket,** Main St. (tel. (01) 628 8506; open Mon.-Sat. 8:30am-8pm, Sun. 9am-6pm). **Quinn's Salad Bar,** also on Main St., serves light and vegetarian fare (sandwiches £1, salads £2.50). **Buses** #67 and 67A run to Celbridge from Middle Abbey St., Dublin. #67A stops in Maynooth along the way. The suburban rail also has an infrequent service to Celbridge from Dublin.

■■■ KILDARE TOWN

Kildare Town is like many a twelve-year-old lass—it's still in its horse phase, and is likely to remain so for a long time. Purebreds are the lifeblood of the town. Racehorses are beautiful, elegant creatures, as anyone who's attended the Irish Derby well knows. Kildare seems imbued with some of their nervous energy and natural grace, especially in contrast with the town's mule-like neighbors. While Kildare's present religion centers around horses, its past was more influenced by Christianity. It grew around a church founded here in 480 AD by St. Brigid. The town's original name—*Cill Dara,* meaning "Church of the Oak"—derives from a story that Brigid founded the Church next to an oak tree that she saw in a vision.

Practical Information The Kildare **tourist office,** in the Square (tel. 22696), has a ferocious enthusiasm for local pubs (open June-Aug. Mon.-Sat. 10am-1pm and 2-6pm, Sept.-May Fri.only 10am-1pm and 2-6pm). Kildare is well connected by **trains** to Dublin's Heuston Station (Mon.-Sat. 30/day, Sun. 12/day; 30min.) and also by **Bus Éireann** to Dublin (1/hour; 1½hr.). Dublin-bound buses from Cork and Limerick also stop in Kildare. Kildare lies on the N7 (the Dublin-Limerick Rd.). Bikers will hate the N7—it's fast, has huge, scary, monster trucks, and one lane in each direction, so that cars must pass each other using the road shoulder/bicycle lane. The **phone code** is a galloping 045.

Accommodation, Food & Pubs Accommodation in Kildare isn't very forthcoming. Toward the Stud on the outskirts of town, **Fremont,** Tully Rd. (tel. 521604), has firm beds, well-decorated rooms, and a quasi-rural setting that allow visitors to dream of racehorses (£14/person, single £15). In town, the **Lord Edward Guest House B&B,** Dublin St. (tel. 522389), is more hotel than B&B, with professional staff and a TV in every room. Organists are welcome to jam on the organ in the lobby (single £18, double £30). **The Shell House** (tel. 521293), on the Dublin Rd. is worth a stop just to gawk. Once a thatched cottage with a bizarre form of weatherproofing, one of the conditions of sale was that the shells that cover all the outside walls of the house must be maintained. They are arranged to form pictures of local attractions, like the round tower and cathedral steeple. Inside, the beds are firm, the showers are hot, and the breakfast is light (single £14, double £28).

Good pubs are plentiful. **The Silken Thomas,** the Square (tel. 522232), has renowned food, ranging from bar snacks (basket of drumsticks and chips £3) to serious entrees (fisherman's platter £8). Lunch, lounge, and dinner menus variously served between 11am and 10pm. The pub's name isn't a euphemism, but a reference to "Silken Thomas" FitzGerald, who raised a revolt against the British in Dublin in 1534. **Li'l Flanagan,** in the back of the Silken Thomas (tel. 522232), is a small, delightfully scruffy, old-time pub. (Trad sessions at 9:30pm on Monday, Wednesday, Thursday, and Sunday nights, rock and easy listening on Friday and Saturday nights; no cover.) **Nolan's,** the Square (tel. 521528), is a low-key pub that served as a hardware store for several years. Sadly, the saws are gone, but they make up for it with trad sessions on Tuesday through Thursday nights (no cover).

Sights Kildare Town has a lovely little square lined with terrific pubs and old ladies on benches. In one corner of the square stands Kildare's **Round Tower,** originally built in the 10th century and capped with an incongruous 18th-century top. This is one of the few round towers in Ireland that visitors can actually enter and climb—most of the others have no floors inside. (Open Mon.-Sat. 9am-1pm and 2-5pm, Sun. 2-5pm; £1, children 50p.) **St. Brigid's Cathedral** lies in the shadow of the tower. The cathedral, an imposing building with old stonework, rests on the site where St. Brigid founded one of Ireland's first churches in 480 AD. She was one of the first powerful women in the Christian church: she even held power over bishops. Next to the church is **St. Brigid's Fire Temple,** a site of pagan rituals that Brigid possessed for Christianity. Only women were allowed to tend the fire which burned continually for 1000 years. There is an unadorned high cross on the site. Its uncarved surface indicates dates to the days before crosses were carved. (Cathedral open May-Oct. Mon.-Sat. 10am-1pm, 2-5pm, Sun. 2-5pm; tours of Cathedral are available upon request; free.)

The Irish National Stud, "where strength and beauty live as one," about one mile from Kildare in Tully (tel. 521617), does its best to make the town's horse fever contagious. (Don't use the gold and wrought-iron gates on the Dublin Rd.; instead, follow the plentiful signs for the turnoff from the main road.) Colonel William Hall-Walker, the mystical son of a Scottish brewer, started to breed thoroughbreds at Tully in 1900. Every time a foal was born, the Colonel would cast its horoscope; if it was unfavorable, the foal would be sold, regardless of how well it was bred. The "system" has proved remarkably successful.

Astrology aside, the whole place is still eccentric. The horses quaff naturally sparkling mineral water from the Tully River; its water is carbonated and has 260 parts per million of calcium, which is said to promote good bone formation. Hall-Walker stressed that the moon and stars should exercise their maximum influence on the horses, so skylights were incorporated into the roofs of all stables. Lantern roofs in the stallion boxes, built after Hall-Walker's death, continue his policy.

As the sights lose any practical purpose, things grow steadily weirder. The small **Irish Horse Museum** is housed in a converted groom's house and stallion boxes. It tells the history of the horse from its evolution to modern times, most vividly with the skeleton of Arkle, Ireland's greatest steeple chaser. **The Japanese Gardens,** also part of the Stud, are beautiful and truly bizarre, like a walk-through boardgame. Devised by Hall-Walker and built by two Japanese gardeners between 1906 and 1910, the gardens purport to tell "the story of the life of man" on a guided-by-numbers trail. From the entrance at the Gate of Oblivion (#1) visitors pass through the Cave of Birth (#2). Soon tough choices present themselves at the Parting of the Ways (#6): the smooth Path of Carefree Life, the narrow Path of Bachelorhood, or the Stepping Stones of Exploration that lead to Engagement Bridge (#8). Husband and wife go through some tough times (an uphill climb at #13, a temporary separation at #11) but before long the two are coasting down the Hill of Ambition to deposit the wife on the Chair of Old Age (#18), while the man's soul passes through the Gateway of Eternity (#20). (Irish National Stud, Irish Horse Museum, and Japanese Gardens open Feb. 12 to Nov. 12 daily 9:30am-6pm. Joint admission £4, students and seniors £3.)

■ NEAR KILDARE TOWN

THE CURRAGH

Entertainment in Kildare is understandably equinocentric. **The Curragh** racecourse (tel. (045) 541205), between Droichead Nua/Newbridge and Kildare on N7, hosts the **Irish Derby** ("DAR-bee") on the first Sunday in July. The race, sponsored by horse-crazy Budweiser, is Ireland's premier sporting and social event and one of the most prestigious races in the world. The atmosphere on race day is grand—everyone dresses like royalty. The Derby race itself is at 4pm. Other races are held from late March to early November (Irish Rail timetable lists dates; trains stop at The Curragh on racedays). (Admission £9 to Derby, £7.50 to other events; students and seniors get 50% off by purchasing tickets at the Enquiries booth, opposite the racecourse's VIP entrance.) The Curragh was once a headquarters for the British military presence in pre-1916 Ireland. In the important but hushed-up "Curragh mutiny" of 1914, British army officers (who wrongly thought they were about to be ordered north) stated that they would rather be fired than act against the Unionists.

PEATLAND WORLD & LULLYMORE

Near Kildare in Lullymore lurks campy **Peatland World** (tel. (045) 60133 or 60193). Located in the immense Bog of Allen, Peatland World comprises a museum and a natural history gallery. The natural history gallery expounds on the ecological diversity of the bogs and some of its eco-friendly post-peat-production uses. The museum explains the evolution of turf production from community activity to big business, with some attention to the "social impact of turf" over the centuries. On display are bog-preserved prehistoric artifacts, a model of an Irish cottage with a turf fire, and trophies from turf cutting competitions. With the 20th century came new economic pressures, and boglanders turned to their friend peat for relief. The museum displays their achievements: a model of a peat briquette factory and a peat-fueled power station, as well as a range of peat-based products, including a cosmetics line and clothing. (Open Mon.-Fri. 9:30am-5pm; £2, students £1.50, children £1.) Those bitten by the bog bug should certainly take a bog tour on the West Offaly Railway (see Near Athlone: Clonmacnoise, p. 148).

Tiny Lullymore is trying to capitalize on its monastic past with the **Lullymore Heritage Park** (tel. (045) 560353). The park shows relics and ruins from the town's 5th-century heyday, when the tiny community of Lullymore began as an early Christian settlement (open Mon.-Fri. 10am-6pm, Sat.-Sun. 2-6pm; £1, children 50p). To reach Lullymore from Kildare, take Allenwood Rd. to Rathangan Rd. It's a tricky hitch. Buses drive to nearby Allenwood from Dublin (6/day, Sun. 3/day; 1¼hr.).

Meath & Louth

Meath is a quiet, peaceful county, which makes it an appropriate home for the crypts of ancient, creeping terror that lurk among its hills. In pre-Norman times, after the builders of these crypts had faded into stony memory, Meath was considered Ireland's fifth province. In pre-Christian times, since it contained Tara, it was the political and spiritual center of Ireland. Vikings sailing up the Boyne built Drogheda, which today serves as a base for exploring the county's pleasantly morose charms. Farther north in Co. Louth, the Cooley Peninsula, almost an island, contains hills and water for bikers and sailors to enjoy. The land routes to Cooley are unpleasant. The boat trip is much more enjoyable and interesting.

BOYNE VALLEY

Among the towns, highways, back lanes, and furrows of the Boyne Valley are the richest sets of archaeological remains anywhere in Ireland. Slane and Trim have some of the best-preserved medieval castles (and a rock festival or two). The Celtic Hill of Tara and the neolithic tomb-mounds of Newgrange, Knowth, and Dowth puzzle professional archaeologists and amaze more casual visitors. Every so often the valley's farmers plow up weapons or artifacts from the 1690 Battle of the Boyne.

Buses from Dublin and Drogheda hit the major Boyne towns, but many famous sights are miles off the main roads, and service between towns is spotty. The several N-roads that criss-cross the valley make it easy to hitch, but the grand tour requires a fair degree of hiking. Bus fares from Dublin range from £3-6 return. Several tours herd visitors through the circuit of sites. **Celtic Twilight** (tel. (088) 54787) offers a full sight-seeing "Tour of the Royal Meath" (June-Aug.; £12). The coach leaves the Nassau St. entrance to Trinity College, Dublin at 10am and returns to Dublin at 5:30pm. **Sightseeing Tours** (tel. (01) 283 9973) visits Newgrange and Knowth on its Boyne Valley tour. The bus leaves the Dublin Tourist Office on O'Connell St. (June-Sept. daily at 1:20pm, return at 6pm; £14).

■■■ DROGHEDA

Founded by Vikings in 911, Drogheda ("DRA-hed-a") once rivaled Dublin as a center of trade and Armagh as a center of worship. It's still a busy port. Despite suburban development, old walls linger at unexpected points throughout the town. Most of the city is north of the River Boyne and is connected to the south side by St. Mary's Bridge. Most of the sights in Meath are within biking distance of Drogheda.

BOYNE VALLEY

PRACTICAL INFORMATION

Tourist Office: Donore Rd. (tel. 37070), in the bus station off Dublin Rd. Offers the *Traveler's Guide to Drogheda* (60p), which covers practical information, and *Drogheda* (£1), a historical summary with a better map and a walking tour. Open June-Sept. Mon.-Sat. 10am-1pm and 2-6pm.

Banks: AIB bank, West St. (tel. 36523). Open Mon.-Wed. and Fri. 9:30am-5pm, Thurs. 9:30am-7pm. **ATM. TSB** bank, West St. (tel. 38703). Same hours.

Post Office: West St. (tel. 38157). Open Mon.-Sat. 9am-5:30pm.

Phone Code: 041.

Trains: Station is east out of town on the Dublin Rd.: follow John St. south of the river, all the way. Station inquiries (tel. 38749). To Dublin (Mon.-Sat. 8/day, Sun. 3/day; ½hr.; £5 return) and Belfast (Mon.-Sat. 5/day, Sun. 3/day; 1½hr.).

Buses: leave from the bus station on John St. (tel. 35023). Inquiries desk open Mon.-Fri. 8:45am-7pm, Sat. 8:30am-1:30pm. Buses go to Athlone (Mon.-Sat. 2/day, Sun. 1/day; 2½hr.; £9); Belfast (Mon.-Sat. 4/day, Sun. 3/day; 2hr.; £8); Dublin (Mon.-Sat. 16/day, Sun. 7/day; 50min.; £4.80); Dundalk (Mon.-Sat. 11/day, Sun. 6/day; 40min.; £4.40); Galway (Mon.-Sat. 2/day, Sun. 1/day; 4½hr.; £12); Mullingar (Mon.-Sat. 2/day, Sun. 1/day; 2hr.£7.50).

Taxi Rank: Lawrence St. (tel. 38439).

Bike Rental: Irish Cycle Hire, Mayoralty St. (tel. 41067, 42338; fax 35369), off North Quay. This is the head office for Irish Cycle Hire, so they can produce many, many bikes. £6/day, £30/week; deposit £30. Helmet rental £5. Open Mon.-Sat. 9am-6pm. 10% discount with ISIC card, another 10% discount if you mention you got their name out of *Let's Go*. Also deals through **Bridge Cycles,** North Quay (tel. 34526); same hours and rates.

Hospital: Our Lady of Lourdes, Cross Lanes (tel. 37601).

Emergency: Dial 999; no coins required. **Garda:** West Gate (tel. 38777).

ACCOMMODATIONS

Drogheda's accommodations, like most everything in the town, are north of the River Boyne. **Harpur House,** William St. (tel. 32736), runs a small hostel in a big townhouse. Follow Shop St. up the hill, continue up Peter St. and take a right onto William St.; the hostel is on the right. The house is old and it shows, but the hostel rooms are airy, the beds are not bunks, and the house has a home-like feel absent in Dublin's industrial strength hostels. Simple B&B rooms provide additional privacy. (9-bed dorm £6, £9 w/breakfast; B&B £12). Buses from Harpur House do half-day sightseeing tours of the Boyne Valley (£10). A well-kept and backpacker-friendly B&B, **Abbey View House,** Mill Lane (tel. 31470) defines courtesy. Head west on West St. and take the first left after it crosses over to Trinity St. Sitting pretty right next to the River Boyne, the house has parking, bikes, canoes, a tunnel to Monasterboice, and big rooms with patchwork quilts (£12/person). **St. Laurence's Lodge,** King St. (tel. 35410) is a big B&B in a beautiful old Christian Brothers school. The rooms are pleasant, with firm beds, tea-makers and TVs (£15/person).

FOOD & PUBS

Groceries can be found on West St. at Dunnes Stores and Quinnsworth. (Both open Mon.-Tues. and Sat. 9am-6:30pm, Wed. 9am-8pm, Thurs.-Fri. 9am-9pm.)

Moorland Café, West St. (tel. 33951). If you laid all the kinds of pastries they serve here end to end, you'd get a line of baked goods from here to deepest, darkest Peru. Cafeteria-style grill, too (chicken-burger and fries £2.35). Open Mon.-Sat. 9am-6pm.

Hollywood West, West St. (tel. 38326). "American-style" diner with movie posters on the walls and hearty burgers and omelettes on the table (mushroom omelette with chips £3.40). Open Mon.-Wed. 9am-6pm, Thurs.-Fri. 9am-9pm, Sat. 9am-6:30pm.

The Pizzeria, Peter St. (tel. 34208). All kinds of Italian specialities. Very popular, so arrive before 9pm if you want to get a seat for dinner (pizza around £5). Open Mon.-Tues. 6-11pm, Thurs.-Sun. 6-11pm.

Eastern
Ireland

The Copper Kettle, 1 Peter St. (tel. (041) 37397), just up from the junction with West St., this seems like a hole-in-the-wall café. The offerings are simple but scrumptious (white coffee 60p, scones 25p). Open Mon.-Sat. 9:30am-5:30pm.

As the largest town in the area, Drogheda has a pretty active nightlife. Start at **Peter Matthews,** Laurence St. (tel. 37371), also known as McPhail's; dark wood engulfs you at this very old, very likable pub (live rock and blues Thurs.-Sun. nights). **The Weavers,** West St. (tel. 32816), is renowned for its lunchtime and dinner grub—more wood and darkness here (DJs spin top 40 tunes Fri.-Sun. nights; no cover). **Carberry's,** Back Strand, is the only place in town with trad music (Thurs. and Sun. nights), in a friendly, smoky environment.

Drogheda has a happening disco that draws dancers from miles around; The Earth, Stockwell Lane (tel. 30969) is a Flintstones-meet-techno sort of place, with fossils embedded in the walls and bar, rock-oriented bathrooms, and not a single straight wall in the place. (Open Thurs.-Sun. 11pm-2:30am; cover £5, usually £2 concession before midnight and on Sundays; Fri. and Sat. night are techno-dance music, Thurs. and Sun. more oriented towards '70s disco style.)

SIGHTS

Encounter a blackened shriveled head in the imposing, neo-Gothic St. Peter's Church on West St. (open 8:30am-8:30pm). Built in the 1880s, the church safeguards the head of the martyred saint Oliver Plunkett. Pious visitors light candles and pay homage. Look for Plunkett at the end of the left-hand aisle. The door of his London prison cell is also on display. Archbishops of Armagh sometimes lived in Drogheda until the 18th century. Most of the town's medieval churches (at one time there were as many as seven) were sacked or burned by Cromwell.

At the end of West St. stand the twin towers of **St. Lawrence Gate,** a 13th-century fortification outside the walls of the town, which is no less impressive for the fact that it never really faced a serious attack. At the top of the hill on St. Peter's St., the mossy **Magdalen Steeple,** dating from 1224, is all that remains of the Dominican Friary that once stood on the spot. The **Droichead Arts Centre,** Stockwell St. (tel. 33946; fax 42055), displays artwork and runs a theater which shows locally produced and traveling shows (open Mon.-Sat 10am-5pm; gallery free). In early August, Drogheda holds the **Drogheda Folk Festival,** a three-day festival of traditional music and drinking. On Old Abbey Ln., south of West St., are the few remains of the 5th-century **Priory of St. Mary,** perched among the urban refuse of the modern town.

■ NEAR DROGHEDA

The Battle of the Boyne raged at **Oldgrange,** five miles west of Drogheda. On July 1, 1690, Protestant forces under William of Orange (William III of England) defeated the Irish Catholic armies supporting the ousted Stuart king of England, James II, who fled the country weeks later. Though the Catholic armies fought for a year, the battle gave William control of Dublin, and James' flight made it clear that English Protestants would continue to control at least the eastern half of Ireland. Catholics, and English Jacobites, remembered the Battle of the Boyne as a momentous tragedy for centuries; the Ulster Protestants made it an occasion for celebration. Calendar reform has moved the battle's "anniversary" to July 12, Orange Day, when Protestant militants march all over Northern Ireland.

■■ BRÚ NA BÓINNE

The area southeast of the town Slane—*Brú na Bóinne* ("brew na BO-in-yeh," the Palace of the Boyne)—is saturated not with palaces, but with prehistoric tombs: Newgrange, Knowth, Dowth, and 37 more. All the tombs were made by an indigenous pre-Celtic neolithic culture with mind-boggling engineering talents. The tombs are older than the pyramids and older than Stonehenge; in July or August, you may grow old yourself waiting in the long lines to see them, especially at Newgrange. But the prehistoric architectural weirdness will prove worth the wait. All of Brú na Bóinne is very well signposted: all three of the passage-tombs are reached from the turnoff on N51, three miles from Slane and seven miles from Drogheda. Follow the turnoff road for about ½ mile, then take a right at the intersection for Knowth, a left for Newgrange and Dowth. The road is very well-travelled, and hitchers report an easy trip to and from the tombs. The **phone code** here, as in Celtic times, is 041.

NEWGRANGE

Newgrange, the most spectacular, most restored, and most visited of the sites, is the prime example of the passage-tomb. Built by a highly organized, religious society over 5000 years ago, using stones carted from Wicklow 40 miles away, Newgrange is covered with elaborate patterns and symbols mystifying to archaeologists. The inner chamber's roof was cobbled together without the use of mortar, and has stood since around 3200 BC. The tour is one part information and ten parts wild speculation (do the drawings represent "the triumph of life over death" or are they "art for art's sake?"), but it's the only way to see the inside of the tomb. The most dramatic moment of the tour is the recreation of the moment which actually occurs five days each year around the winter solstice, when the sun's rays enter at just the right angle to illuminate the inner chamber. Though this function was only recently discovered, the natives have told stories for thousands of years of how the people of the mound could "stop the sun." Watch for antique graffiti, left by visitors to Newgrange since the rediscovery of its passage in 1699. Bring a windbreaker or a warm sweater; it gets chilly inside even in summer. (Tours begin every 20 min. daily, June-Sept. 9:30am-7pm, Oct. 10am-5pm, Nov.-Feb. 10am-4:30pm, Mar.-Apr. 10am-5pm, May 9:30am-6pm; last tour 45 min. before closing; £3, students £1.25; tel. 24488; fax 24798). The **tourist office** is in Newgrange (just before the entry to the site, near the parking lot; tel. 24274; open April-Oct. daily 10am-7pm).

KNOWTH & DOWTH

West of Newgrange is the less frantic, and less restored, site of **Knowth** (rhymes with "mouth"). Knowth was inhabited continuously from 3000 BC until the Battle of the Boyne, so that the site today is a mishmash of Stone Age tombs, early Christian subterranean refuge tunnels, and Norman grain ovens. Among those who made use of the mounds were the mysterious "beaker people," not Muppets, but pre-Celtic tribes known only for their drinking flasks, who may have worshipped mead. The tour here is actually useful, and the guides are wonderfully knowledgeable. Though there is no tourist office, the admission office sells booklets about Knowth's history (tel. 24824; tours May to mid-June daily 10am-5pm, mid-June to mid-Sept. 9:30am-6:30pm, mid-Sept. to Oct. 10am-5pm; £2, students £1). East of Newgrange is **Dowth** (rhymes with "Knowth"), the third of the great passage tombs. Dowth is not open to the public, but you can still ramble about the mound's outside, badly damaged by the work of pillagers (there's a gaping hole at the top of the mound).

■■■ SAILING UP THE BOYNE

MELLIFONT ABBEY & MONASTERBOICE

Two of what were once the most important monasteries in Ireland crumble five miles north of Drogheda. Turn off of Drogheda-Collon Rd. at Monleek Cross and follow signs for either one. The more interesting of the two, **Mellifont Abbey** (tel. (041) 26459), has served as a grand setting for many of Ireland's tragedies. Founded by St. Malachy, a friend of Bernard of Clairvaux, Mellifont was the first Cistercian abbey in Ireland. The 1152 Senate of Mellifont saw the end of the independent Irish monastic system, as a papal legate divided Ireland into four bishoprics with Armagh as primate and confiscated the monasteries' tithes. Consequently, the monastic centers declined, along with the traditions of scholarship within their walls. Three years later, Cistercian pope Adrian IV issued a bull giving the English King authorization to "correct" Ireland, which served as approval for the Norman invasion of the 1170s.

The last of the O'Neills who once ruled Ulster surrendered to the English here in 1603, then evacuated Ireland for the Continent. Most of the grandeur of the place has disappeared as well, though a glimpse remains at the **old lavabo,** where monks once cleansed themselves of sins and grime. This bath of past ages will give you an idea of the original structure's impressiveness. (Open May to mid-June daily 10am-5pm, mid-June to mid-Sept. daily 9:30am-6:30pm, mid-Sept. to Oct. daily 10am-5pm; £1.50, students 60p.)

Just off N1, the monastic settlement of **Monasterboice** ("MON-ster-boyce"; always open; free), is well-known for its high crosses and round tower. Founded in 520, the monastery was one of Ireland's most wealthy until it was sacked and burned by Vikings in 1097. **Muiredach's Cross,** the first one you'll see upon entering, is one of Ireland's best examples of a high cross. A frenzy of sculpted Bible scenes, from Eve tempting Adam to the Judgement Day, cover the cross, the top of which is carved in the shape of a reliquary. The nearby West and North Crosses are similar but more timeworn. The 40-yard **round tower** does better service to the tourist as a viewing point than it did in protecting the monks from Norse invaders; if the tower is locked, try asking for the key at the house by the entrance gate.

HILL OF TARA

From prehistoric times until at least the 10th century, Tara was the political and sometime religious center of Ireland. The hill is home to a Stone Age tomb, an Iron Age fort, and the principal late Celtic royal seat—the combination has guaranteed Tara's popularity with tourists and archaeologists alike. As the seat of the powerful Uí Néill family, control of Tara theoretically entitled their warlord to be High King. Ownership of the hill was understandably disputed until the 10th century, but the arrival of St. Patrick (traditionally in 432, more likely closer to 400) deposed Tara from its position as the Jerusalem of Ireland. Tara's symbolic importance remains even in modern times; in 1843, Daniel O'Connell gathered a million people here for a Home Rule rally. The overlapping of bronze age, high king, and early Christian civilizations at Tara has confused historians and archaeologists for centuries, and today the historical function of many of the hill's structures remains unknown.

The enormous site is about halfway between Dublin and Navan on the N3. Take any Navan-bound **bus** from Dublin (13/day, Sun. 5/day; 1hr.) and ask the driver to let you off at the turnoff; it's about a mile straight up the hill to the site. The actual buildings—largely wattle, wood, and earthwork—have long been buried or destroyed; what you'll see is mostly a set of concentric and overlapping earthen rings and walls, whose traditional names correspond to the buildings the mounds were thought to cover. The whole history of Tara decamps at the **visitors center** (tel. (046) 25903), in an old church at the site. Aerial photos of Tara, essential for making sense of the place, are displayed here. The center shows a good 20-minute flick about Tara's history, complete with warrior-kings, pagan priestesses, and stormy, scary sound effects. After the film, an excellent guided tour circles the site. The full site encompasses 100 acres of many smaller mounds and ring forts, though you'll likely see only the sites at the top of the hill. (Visitors center open May to mid-June daily 9:30am-5pm, mid-June to mid-Sept. 9:30am-6:30pm, mid-Sept. to Oct. 10am-5pm. Mounds always open; free.)

Closest to the visitors center is the **Rath of the Synods,** a structure made of four concentric banks and ditches, lived in and/or used for ritual burials between the 2nd and 4th centuries AD. The name refers to its later use as a meeting place for gatherings of Irish bishops in the 5th-7th centuries. According to a rather propagandistic legend, St. Patrick himself preached at the first of these synods, unsuccessfully trying to convert the pagan king Laoghaire. **The Royal Enclosure,** a concentric hill fort from the Iron Age, contains a much older tomb, the **Mound of the Hostages.** Medieval scholars mistakenly thought that the King of Tara ritually took hostages and buried them here. Actually, those buried in the mound lived in the Stone and Bronze ages, 1500-2800 years before the first high kings.

Next, there's the **Royal Seat,** an ancient ring fort where the throne might have been located. **Cormac's House,** named for the first non-tribal king of Tara, Cormac Mac Airt, is right next door. This mound gives you the best view of the countryside; the Wicklow Hills and the Mourne Mountains can supposedly both be seen from here. Aspiring Indiana Joneses will be glad to know that neither mound has yet been excavated. The neighboring **Stone of Destiny,** a giant rock phallus of unknown origin, was said to give a scream when the authentic king drove past, a kind of Sword-in-the-Stone for Celts and the supposed place of inauguration for Uí Néill kings.

Outside of the Royal Enclosure is the **Rath Grainne,** named for Cormac's daughter, who is the heroine of an early Irish legend. Grainne was promised in marriage to the elderly Finn McCool, whom she didn't love. At the wedding feast, Grainne got everyone so drunk that she and her lover, Diarmuid, were able to sneak away. The Rath was the first stop on their flight, which ended with their tragic capture. Nearby, two long parallel banks of earth form what is still called, but no longer considered, the **Banquet Hall.** Excavations here haven't unearthed anything suggesting an ancient feast in this long passageway; it's more likely to have been a short road or plaza used in royal processions, at one end of which began the five provincial roads which radiated out from Tara. Archaeologists think they have actually found one of the roads—you can see its outline on the aerial map.

■ ■ ■ TRIM

A series of enormous, well-preserved Norman castles and abbeys that thrill even the most jaded tourist overlook this charming town on the River Boyne. Trim's **tourist office** on Mill St. (tel. 37111; open all year daily 9am-6pm) has a meaty amount of information on Meath, and the useful self-guided walking tour of Trim (60p). Next door to the office is the spanking-new **Meath Visitors Centre** (tel. 37227), which introduces the history of Trim with a multi-media presentation, an exhibit, and an excellent, dramatic slideshow (decapitations, the villainous Hugh de Lacy, and hideous plague rats—maybe Trim isn't so charming after all). (Open Mon.-Sat. 9am-6pm; £2, seniors £1.25, children 70p.) The **Bank of Ireland** surveys Market St. (tel. 31230; open Mon. 10am-4pm, Tues.-Fri. 10am-5pm). **Bus Éireann** stops on Castle St., in front of the castle, en route to Dublin (6/day; £5 return) and Athlone (1/day). Trim's **phone code** is a slim 046.

Accommodations, Food, & Pubs A handful of B&Bs makes a night in Trim an enticing possibility. The **White Lodge,** Lackanash New Rd. (tel. 36549; follow High St. to Navan Rd. and take the first right), has spacious, well-decorated rooms with TVs. (Single £18, double £27, w/bath £31). In the heart of town pumps **Brogan's,** High St. (tel. 31237), a pub that does hotel-like B&B (£13/person). Floral comfort blooms in **O'Briens,** Friars Park (tel. 31745), off Dublin Rd. The rooms are both spacious and neat (single £14, double £14/person, w/bath £15/person).

The **Pastry Kitchen,** Market St. (tel. 36166) puts sturdy breakfasts and luscious pastries and breads on the table (£2; breakfast served all day; open Mon.-Sat. 7:30am-6pm, Sun. 10am-6pm). The **Abbey Lodge,** Market St. (tel. 31549), presents a tremendous plate of roast stuffed chicken with fries and veggies (£3.50) with your pint. **McCormack's,** across from the Castle on Castle St. (tel. 31963), may show a lot of cricket on TV, but it's all Irish on Sun. nights when the *bodhrán,* tin whistle, and a fiddle or two liven things up (cover £1). The **Bounty** across the Bridge St. bridge (tel. 31640) is bedecked with spinning wheels, old umbrellas, and bulls' horns. On Emmet St., the bustling **Emmet Tavern** (tel. 31378) appeals to stomach and ears with its carvery and traditional Sat. and Sun. nights (cover £4).

Sights When Norman invader Hugh de Lacy first built **Trim Castle** in 1172, he couldn't know that 822 years later Mel Gibson would sack the place in the making of *Braveheart.* He was, however, aware that the unruly O'Connors of Connacht trashed the place a year later. A new castle, the one which Mel would actually attack, was constructed in the 1190s. King John of England dropped by long enough to rename it **King John's Castle.** For a few hundred years, the castle was an important fortification for all of Meath, and defended a walled town with separate gates and battlements. Richard II housed the young Prince Hal here in 1399, perhaps as a hostage to use against his then-rebellious father, Henry IV. The castle, which says it's the largest in Ireland, stands above the center of town and can be easily reached through the gate on Castle St. (closed for restoration in 1995, scheduled to reopen in 1996; free). **Walking tours** navigate the castle, starting from in front of the castle (tours July-Aug. daily 11:30am, 2pm, and 3:30pm; £2).

Across the picturesque river stand the 12th-century remains of **St. Mary's Abbey,** destroyed by Cromwell's armies. You can still see the **Yellow Steeple** (so called because of the yellowish gleam it gives off at twilight), the only remains of the holy sisters' old place (no steeplechase racers, but it was once home to "Our Lady of Trim," a miracle-performing statue). In front of the Yellow Steeple is what's left of **Talbot's Castle,** a 15th-century manor built by John Talbot, Viceroy of Ireland. The manor (built on the site of an old Augustinian abbey) has a very British air: Queen Elizabeth wanted it to be the country's first university, but it ended up as just a school. Outside the two ruins lies the **Sheep Gate,** the only surviving medieval gate of the once walled town. You can rid yourself of unwelcome warts at the **Newtown Cemetery,** far behind the Castle, by putting a pin between two tomb figures wrongly known as the **Jealous Man and Woman:** the name comes from the sword between them, which conventionally signified not resentment, but chastity. When the pin rusts (which shouldn't take long in this country) your warts will disappear.

Butterstream Gardens, ½ mile out of town on Kildalkey Rd., is one of Ireland's most frequently honored private gardens; in the summer of 1995, it was graced by the helicopter of Prince Charles as one of the few spots in Ireland that the gardener-prince demanded to see (Open May-Sept. daily 11am-6pm; £3). For one week each June (usually the last), the **Scurlogstown Olympiad Town Festival** fills Trim with horse fairs, carnival rides and traditional music concerts.

BEYOND THE VALLEY OF THE BOYNE

■■■ KELLS (CEANANNAS MÓR)

The name of Kells is known far and wide, thanks to a book which wasn't even written there. The monastery at Kells was founded by St. Columcille (also known as St. Columba) in 559, before the saint went on to found the more important settlement of Iona on an island west of Scotland. It was at Iona that the famous *Book of Kells,* an elaborately decorated Latin gospels, was started. It came to Kells in some form of development in 804 when the Columbans fled Iona. In 1007, the book was stolen, its gold cover ripped off, and the pages buried under sod and recovered two months later. It remained in Kells until 1661, when Cromwell carted it off to Trinity College, where it is now recovering. Kells is trying to get the book back, but Trinity won't agree. Even without the book, Kells can boast of some of the best preserved monastic ruins in Ireland, including an oratory, a round tower, and five high crosses.

Most maps refer to Kells only in Irish, as Ceanannas Mór. Bus Éireann stops outside of O'Rorke's Bar on Castle St. on its way to Dublin (Mon.-Sat. 17/day, Sun. 8/day; 1 hr.; £6 return). **AIB** bank is on John St. (tel. 40610; fax 41222; open Mon. 10am-5pm, Tues.-Fri. 10am-4pm), while the **post office** (tel. 40127) is on Farrel St. (open Mon.-Sat. 9am-5:30pm). Kells's **phone code** is decreed to be 046.

Accommodations, Food, & Pubs Kells can boast the area's only real hostel: **Kells Hostel,** on the Dublin-Donegal Rd. (tel. 40100; fax 40680), has a real jacuzzi and squash courts! The gym downstairs offers a special £2/session rate for hostelers. The dorms are clean and spacious, and beds are almost always available except on Slane Castle Concert weekend. Check in at Monaghan's Bar next door to the hostel. (Dorm £5.50, Sept.-May £5; 6-bed dorm £6.50; sheets 50p. Self-service laundry £2; snooker table available in the common room for 50p.) **Camping** is available behind the hostel, with full use of the indoor hostel facilities (£3/person). **Latimor House** (tel. 40133), ½ mile down the Oldcastle Rd. does B&B in a pretty, rustic setting. The house is full of antiques and the beds are firm with thick comforters. Relax to the lowing of the cows on the distant hills (single £14, double £28; from Market Sq., go down Cross St. and take the first right onto Canon St.).

After the cemeteries, stop in for a drink and some great grub at **O'Shaughnessey's**, Market St. (tel. 41110), everyone's favorite eating and drinking center (pizza £3, sandwiches £1.20). Trad session come to the pub on Wednesday nights, and balladeers do their thing on Friday, Saturday, and Sunday nights (music around 10pm; no cover). **Penny's Place** (tel. 41630) is a pink paradise on Market St., serving sensuous scones (35p; open Mon.-Sat. 9am-6pm).

Sights Despite its centuries-long tradition as a center of Christian learning, the monastery at Kells kept getting burned down by rival monasteries: the current church dates only to the 1700s, with the exception of the 12th-century belltower. Inside **St. Columba's Church** (tel. 40151) there's a replica of the Book; upstairs, copies of selected pages are enlarged for your viewing pleasure. The door should be open during daylight hours; if not, ask at the gate outside. Wander around and you'll find four large **high crosses,** some better preserved than others, scattered on the south and west side of the church and covered with Bible scenes. The 100-ft.-high **round tower** sheltered the monks, the relics of St. Columcille, and (less successfully) would-be High King Murchadh Mac Flainn, who was murdered there in 1076.

The most satisfying of the sights, however, is **St. Columcille's House,** on Church Lane, where the *Book of Kells* may have been finished. When facing the gates of the Church yard from Market St., walk up the lane on the right of the yard; you can't miss the only 8th-century house on the block. The key is available from Mrs. Carpenter, 100 yds. down the hill from Columcille's house on Church Lane. The place looks almost exactly as it would have in St. Columcille's day, except that the above-ground door you enter through now was originally part of a secret underground passageway from the churchyard—the original entrance began eight feet above the present ground level. Climb the ladder to the three tiny attic rooms for a glimpse of the sleeping quarters: they're alright for a monk, but not so fit for the entire families which lived here in the centuries before this one.

A town **Heritage Centre,** unfinished in 1995, should be open in 1996 on John St. The center will include an audio-visual presentation of the town's history, as well as the Market Cross, a high cross that served as a whipping and hanging post for the Fenian rebels of 1798. The Market Cross was originally in the town square, but trucks have been having this nasty tendency to run into it. The center will also contain a replica of the *Book of Kells,* which will be a relief to the tourists who invariable come here looking for it. If the center isn't open, don't despair; Monaghan's Pub, off the Dublin Donegal Rd. (tel. 40100), also has a copy displayed in their entryway. The best time to see it is early July, when the town holds a nine-day **Kells Heritage Festival** of traditional music, dancing, and rock.

Two miles down Oldcastle Rd., within the People's Park, is the **Spire of Lloyd,** a 150-ft.-high viewing tower erected by the old Headfert landlords. (Open Tues.-Fri. 2:30-5pm, Sat. 3:30-6pm, Sun. 2-6pm; £1, children 50p). From the top, behold spectacular Irish countryside as well as Northern Ireland itself. Next to the Spire is the **Graveyard of the Poor,** where the area's huge pauper population buried their dead in mass graves. The plot was a chaotic cow pasture until a few years ago, when the town scraped together the money to restore it. Now the grass is cut regularly, and there's a high sign which reads: "1838-1921, Erected to the poor interred here during the operation of the English Poor Law System. R.I.P."

Several historical sites are within the near vicinity of Kells, but bus service through most of the area is nonexistent. The best way to see the area is **Shamrock**

Experience, a backpacker-oriented tour that covers the Spire of Lloyd, the town of Oldcastle, and the neolithic tomb of Lough Crew, an excavated tomb of comparable size and age to Newgrange. (Contact Shane at Kells Hostel tel. 40100; tours leave Kells hostel at 10am, return at 4pm; £11, £9 for hostelers. The tour involves walking, so bring good shoes.) **The Dublin Bar** in Oldcastle is a pleasant little place.

■■■ DUNDALK

If you want to see the Cooley Peninsula, it's better to stay *on* it, rather than looking *at* it from Dundalk. Located at the mouth of Dundalk Bay, the very republican town of Dundalk may be a necessary stop for gathering information on the rest of Co. Louth and Cooley Peninsula, but it has little to attract tourists. Attacked by the Danes, the Normans, and the English, the town is all too familiar with its frontier role. Warfare and attrition have eradicated every trace of the city walls that protected modern Dundalk's 16th-century predecessor. With the evaporation of modern-day tensions here, the town's youthful atmosphere, enriched by the presence of a regional college, engenders a hopping pub and nightclub scene.

Practical Information Buses stop at the Bus Éireann station, Long Walk (tel. 34075). From the tourist office, walk east on Crowe St. and turn right after the parking lot. The station is at the end of the street. Buses run to: Belfast (Mon.-Sat. 4/day, Sun. 3/day; 90 min.; £6), Dublin (Mon.-Sat. 12/day, Sun. 6/day; 90 min.; £6), and Newry (Mon.-Sat. 12/day; 30 min.; £2.50, students £2). **Trains** (tel. 35521) pass through the Dundalk station, Carrickmacross Rd., en route to: Belfast (Mon.-Sat. 7/day, Sun. 4/day; 1hr.; £7), Newry (Mon.-Sat. 6/day, Sun. 3/day; 20 min.; £3.50), and Dublin (Mon.-Sat. 4/day, Sun. 3/day; 1hr.; £9.50). Take a **taxi** home from the nightclub—they run until 5am on weekends (tel. 33296 or 33333; 24-hr. service tel. 74777; £2 minimum; about £1/mile). N1 highway zips south to Dublin and north to Belfast, becoming A1 at the border. **Hitching** is less safe and much more difficult in and around Dundalk than elsewhere in the Republic.

The **tourist office,** Jocelyn St. (tel. 35484), hands out free maps marked with the city's few sights. They have the helpful, wide-ranging, and free "100% Proof," a guide to the pubs of Cos. Laois, Louth, Meath, and Westmeath and heaps of information on Carlingford Lough (open Mon.-Fri. 9:30am-1pm and 2-5:30pm). From the bus stop on Clanbrassil St., walk past the square and turn left onto Crowe St.; the tourist office is on the right after the library. The **National Irish Bank** (tel. 32156) is located on Earl St. (open Mon. 10am-5pm, Tues.-Fri. 10am-4pm). The **Bike Shop,** 11 Earl St. (tel. 33399), sells used bikes and rents new ones for £7 per day with a £30 deposit (open Mon.-Fri. 9am-1pm and 2-6pm, Sat. 9am-6pm). The **post office** (tel. 34444; open Mon.-Tues. and Thurs.-Sat. 9am-5:30pm, Wed. 9:30am-5:30pm) is on Clanbrassil St.; the **phone code** is a sight at 042.

Accommodations, Food, & Pubs If you must stay in town, **Oriel House,** 63 Dublin St. (tel. 31347), is inexpensive and serviceable with dark but comfortable rooms for £10/person. **Fáilte House,** a bit farther on the Dublin Rd. (tel. 35152), is larger and more motel-like, but has no showers (£14/person, £16 w/bath & TV).

Most restaurants cluster on Clanbrassil St. None will amaze you with heavenly delicacies, but there are plenty of cheap options. The **Imperial Hotel Coffee Shop,** Park St. (tel. 32241), stays open late to serve sandwiches (£1.60), quiche, and lasagne to hungry night owls (open daily 8am-10pm). The hotel also has a more elegant restaurant (salmon steak in champagne sauce £8). **Seanachaí,** 12 Park St. (tel. 35050; pronounced "SHAWN-na-kee"), has lots of traditional music and character, and a chummy bartender who is likely to slag (tease) you. The locals' pub, **Windsor Bar,** on Dublin St. (tel. 38146), is convenient to Oriel House. **Mr. Ridley's Nightclub,** 91 Park St. (tel. 33329), plays lots of old music (open Mon. and Thurs.-Sun. until 2:15am). The less rowdy hotel crowd congregates at **Tivoli,** at the Imperial Hotel, Park St. (tel. 32241; open Thurs.-Sun. 10pm-2:30am; cover £6).

Sights **St. Patrick's Cathedral,** Francis St. (tel. 34648), hides a beautiful, ornate Gothic interior behind a dark facade of gray stone (open daily 7:30am-5pm). **Louth County Library** (tel. 35457) and **Museum** (tel. 26578) are located next to the Cathedral in a refurbished old distillery and tobacco warehouse, respectively. (Museum hours are Tues.-Sat. 10:30am-5:30pm, Sun. 2-6pm; library hours are Tues.-Sat. 10am-5pm, Tues. and Thurs. also 6-8pm.) Behind **Green Church,** Church St., a stone marks the grave of Agnes Galt, Robert Burns's sister. **Seatown Castle,** which was originally the tower of a 13th-century Franciscan monastery, is situated at the corner of Mill Rd. and Castle Rd. Like Seatown Windmill, a block farther down Mill St., the monastery is in ruins and hardly worth the walk. Standing seven stories high, the **Seatown Windmill** used to be one of the largest in Ireland, but the wind has definitely been taken out of its "sails": they were removed in 1885.

COOLEY PENINSULA

There are numerous trails in the surrounding mountains and, in Carlingford Lough, the warmest waters in the northern half of the island for bathing. The area is also steeped in intriguing historical myths. It was the setting for, among others, part of the most famous Irish epic, the *Táin bo Cuailnge,* or "The Cattle Raid of Cooley" (see Legends & Folktales, p. 61). Although little material evidence remains of these legendary feats, the medieval settlements, built about 1300 years after the epics supposedly took place, are remarkably well-preserved. According to proud locals, Little Cooley Peninsula is the "best bit of Ireland," unjustifiably overlooked by tourists and the Bord Fáilte. Come during one of Carlingford's festival days and see for yourself what everyone else is missing. Cooley's **phone code** celebrates 042.

■■■ CARLINGFORD

Situated at the foot of Slieve Foy (the highest of the Cooley Mountains), the coastal village of Carlingford has changed remarkably little since its heyday in the 14th, 15th, and 16th centuries. The town's past is still visible in historic stone cottages and crumbling medieval fortifications. **The Holy Trinity Heritage Centre,** Church Yard Rd. (tel. 73454), housed in a former Church of Ireland, shows a short video and sells an informative map of "Medieval Carlingford" for £1. If they're giving a tour of the town, you can join in for £2.50. (Call for bookings; open Mon.-Fri. 10am-1pm and 2-4:30pm, Sat.-Sun. 1-6pm; admission to center £1.) **AIB** bank (tel. 73105) opens its doors on Newry St. (open Tues. and Thurs. 10:30am-12:30pm and 1:30-2:30pm). **Buses** (tel. 34075) stop along the waterfront on their way to Dundalk (4/day; 50 min.; £4.30, students £3.60) and Newry (1/day; 30min.; £3.50).

Accommodations, Food, & Pubs At the **Adventure Centre and Hostel,** Tholsel St. (tel. 73100), the friendly staff shows adventurers along long twisty corridors to rather dark rooms with wooden bunks and locker-room-style bathrooms; hot, hot showers. (8-bed dorm £6, 4-bed dorm £7, double £8/person; Feb.-June and Sept.-Nov. £1 less; sheets £1; open Feb.-Nov.) If there's a group staying at the Centre, meals are available (breakfast of cereal and juice £2.50, lunch £3.50, dinner £5). **B&Bs** in Carlingford tend to be posh and expensive. If the Adventure Centre is full, dance the hora all the way to the non-denominational **Shalom,** Ghan Rd. (tel. 73151), signposted from town center. All rooms have TV, hotpot, and bathroom (single £18, double £28). Otherwise, head to the Omeath Youth Hostel (see Around the Peninsula, below). **Carlingford House** (tel. 73118), well-posted from town center, has stately rooms (£15-18/person).

McKevitt's, down the street from the hostel, sells expensive groceries (tel. 73109; open Mon.-Thurs. 9am-6pm, Fri. 9am-8pm, Sat. 9am-6pm). Pub grub and good *craic* pile up at **Carlingford Arms,** Newry St. (tel. 73418). Look for daily dinner specials.

Traditional music plays here on the last Saturday of every month. **PJ's Anchor Bar,** across the street from the hostel (tel. 73106), is barely larger than a breadbox, but tight quarters induce close friendships. In good weather, the backyard provides a refreshing and less crowded alternative. Inside, publicans proudly display the clothes of the leprechaun caught in the hills several years ago.

Sights & Events **King John's Castle,** by the waterfront, is the largest and most foreboding of Carlingford's five medieval remains. Built in the 1190s and named for King John, who visited in 1210, the castle is usually locked. If renovations are complete, you might be able to finagle the key out of the Heritage Centre staff. **Taaffe's Castle,** towards town along the quay, was built in the 16th century as a merchant house on what was then the waterfront. You can't go in—now, as then, the castle is privately owned. In a tiny alley off Market Square, the turret-laden 16th-century **Mint** is fenestrated with five ornate limestone windows. At the end of the street, one of the old 15th-century town gates—**the Tholsel**—survives, leaving only a narrow path underneath for cars. Most impressive (and most accessible) of all is the mammoth **Dominican Friary** at the south end of town; the ruins are open for unrestricted exploration. Canoes, windsurfers, kayaks (all £12 for 2hr.), and sailboats (£14/2hr.) are all for hire at the **Adventure Centre,** Tholsel St. (tel. 73100)—be prepared to jostle with large groups of boisterous youngsters. Peadar Elmore's *MV Slieve Foy* (tel. 73239) goes **deep-sea fishing** (£15/person).

The village seems to have about as many annual festivals as it does houses. The **Leprechaun Hunt** in late May is a race through the hills to find 50 hidden "leprechauns," statuettes with tags marked £25, £50 or £100. The hunt actually was created by the legendary P.J. (see PJ's Anchor Bar, above) who is still remembered fondly as the man who almost convinced people that leprechauns existed. The winners get to keep the money. A mid-June **fleadh** manipulates traditional music and dancers; a **medieval banqueting weekend** in early July brings on parades, costumes, and indigestion; and **Cooley Vintage Day,** August 1, is a country fair with horses. The late-August **oyster fest** supposedly increases everyone's virility for a week; it definitely makes for a great lunch. The season ends in late September with a weekend **folk festival** that draws musicians from all over the Republic.

 # Cavan & Monaghan

The teeny towns of Co. Cavan and Co. Monaghan make fine stopovers on the way to the Northwest or to Northern Ireland's Fermanagh Lake District, especially since crossing the border has now become so easy and painless. Tourists are a rare breed in these counties—Hare Krishna Island, in particular, is a great place to avoid them.

BELTURBET

The little town of **Belturbet** overlooks the River Erne from a hill and has its own little citizen-run **Tourist Information Office,** along the main street (tel. (049) 22044; open summer daily 8:15am-9pm; call for winter hours) on the main street. Stop in at **The Seven Horses,** Main St. (tel. (049) 22166), for a pint of the blonde in the black among wagon wheel chandeliers, furry hides, and stuffed pheasants. Undoubtedly, you'll hear all about the long-awaited opening of the £30 million Shannon-Erne waterway. For the first time in 125 years you can travel from Belturbet to Carrick-on-Shannon by boat. **Turbet Tours** (tel. (049) 22360) sail the *Erne Dawn* from Belturbet to Ballyconnell. The 2½-hour trip either bores or inspires, depending on how you feel about water. Take the first right after Mrs. McGreevy's B&B—the marina is right down the road. (To Ballyconnell: April to mid-Sept. Tues. and Thurs. 11am, 1:30pm, Sat. 3pm. To Crom: Mon., Wed. and Fri. 3pm; £5 for either trip.) If you plan on spending the night in the area, stay at the hostel in Ballyconnell. If it's full, try Mrs. McGreevy's **Erne View House,** Bridge St. (tel. (049) 22289; single £15, double £25, both w/bath). Belturbet comes alive, believe it or not, the week of August 1st during the **Festival of the Erne,** when 20 women seek the title "Lady of the Erne."

Near Belturbet

Take the Killashandra and Crossdoney Rd. south of Belturbet and follow the signs to the hamlet of **Garthrotten,** where nature trails lace **Killykeen Forest Park** (tel. (049) 32541) and anglers cast their lines into lakes (park always open). The ruin of the **O'Reilly Clan Castle** stoically resists crumbling into Lough Oughter. Farther west, in Cornafean, is the **Pighouse Collection Folk Museum,** (tel. (049) 37248). Instead of pigs, what you'll find are over 3000 unusual items from daily Irish life wallowing in a converted pighouse. (Call ahead for hours; £2. Take the Crossdoney Rd. out of Killeshandra, turn right at the Arva signpost, then take the first right.) **On Yer Bike Tours** visits sites and scenery on wheels and by boat, June through September. They arrange bikes, admission fees, and refreshments (6-person minimum; 8-hr. tour £19.80/person). They also hire bikes out (£5/day, £25/week; deposit £30; for either service contact Michael, (tel. (049) 22219).

HARE KRISHNA ISLAND & BALLYCONNELL

Sandville House Hostel (tel. (049) 26297) is the best reason to halt your tracks around Ballyconnell. Its remote location, three miles south of town, and tremendous views ensure a quiet stay. Vent excess energy on the makeshift soccer field or volleyball court before settling by the fireplace in the converted barn. Call from Belturbet or Ballyconnell for pick-up by one of the friendly staff (£5; open March-Nov.).

Folks at the hostel can tell you all about the Hare Krishnas. Better yet, why not visit the Krishnas yourself at the extraordinarily un-Irish **Hare Krishna Island** (Inis Rath). Their presence here isn't aribtrary. Since the 6th century, the islands of Lough Erne have played host to various groups of Christian and pagan devotees. A 10-minute rowboat adventure takes you to an island gloriously stocked with deer, swans, peacocks, and rabbits. The only requirement for guests is an open mind to experience the Krishna way of life: waking up at 4am for prayers, dancing, readings, meditation, and recitation of the Hare Krishna mantra. The rest of the day is filled with services, chores, and indulging in *prasadam,* food specially prepared and offered to Krishna. But don't take more than you can eat, since Krishna etiquette requires leaving no food on your plate. Says one Krishna, "you'll never forget us." Boat pickup from Ballyconnell or Maguiresbridge—phone from either town and they'll pick you up if possible. If not, **Cabra Cars** (tel. (049) 23323) charges £10 from Sandville Hostel to the jetty and about £6 from Maguiresbridge. Reserve one day in advance; overnight guests preferred. Lodging and food are free. From Northern Ireland, call (013657) 21512. From the Republic, call (08 01365) 721512.

■■■ MONAGHAN TOWN

Monaghan ("MOH-nah-han") is indifferently pleasant—a busy market town in the center of the country, encircled by loads of tiny, egg-shaped hills called **drumlins.** Like many inland towns, there is nothing in Monaghan worth going out of your way to see. From Church Sq., walk up the Market St. hill to find the **tourist office** (tel. 81122, open June-Sept. Mon.-Sat. 9am-6pm; Oct.-May Mon.-Sat. 9am-5pm). You might be able to rent bicycles at **Clerkin's Cycles Shop,** Park St. (tel. 81113; call for rates; open Mon.-Wed. and Fri.-Sat. 8:30am-1pm and 2-6pm). Just north of Church Sq. lies the **post office,** Mill St. (tel. 82131; open Mon.-Tues. and Thurs.-Fri. 9am-5:30pm, Wed. 9:30am-5:30pm, Sat. 9am-1pm and 2-5:30pm). The **bus station** (tel. 82377; open daily 9am-9pm), north of Market Sq., runs buses to Dublin (7/day; 2hr.; £6, students £5) and Belfast (Mon.-Sat. 5/day; 1½hr.; £4.75, students £3.50). For **banks** try **AIB,** the Diamond, where the **ATM** accepts Visa. **Tommy's Taxis,** (tel. 84205), can scoot you farther afield. The **phone code** meditates on 047.

Accommodations, Food, & Pubs The best accommodation and only hostel/camping in the area is in Castleblayney (see p. 142). If you want to stay in town, **Ashleigh House**, 37 Dublin St. (tel. 81227), is a pleasant option. The rosy rooms are decorated with floral prints, and breakfast is "whatever you want" (single £14, double £26, both w/washbasin). Two doors down, **Argus Court**, 32 Dublin St. (tel. 81794), provides basic, no frills B&B (single £13, double £24; economy double £22).

Pizza D'Or, 23 Market St., behind the tourist office (tel. 84777) is a town institution; it stays open until after the discos close. Small veggie pizza £4.55 (open Mon.-Thurs. 5pm-1am, Fri.-Sun. 5pm-3:30am). **Genoa Restaurant**, 61 Dublin St. (tel. 82205), combines a coffee shop with fast food offerings. You can have an ice cream soda and small chips, all at one time, for 85p each (pizza margherita £2.95; coffee shop open Mon.-Sat. 10am-7pm, Sun. noon-7pm; fast food open Mon.-Sat. noon-12:30am, Sun. noon-1:30am). As expected, Monaghan has its SuperValu **supermarket**, on Church Sq. (tel. 81344; open Mon.-Wed. 9am-6pm, Thurs. 9am-8pm, Fri. 9am-9pm, Sat. 9am-6pm). For your health food needs (at health food prices), **Nature's World** (tel. 82882) lies across the street, providing everything from pumice to porridge (open Mon.-Sat. 9am-1pm, 2-6pm). **The Squealing Pig**, The Diamond (tel. 84562), with its barn-like wooden floor, green walls, large-screen TV, and crowd of twentysomethings gets the vote for the most popular pub in town.

Sights In the center of town, the **Monaghan County Museum**, Hill St. (tel. 82928), across from the tourist office, painstakingly chronicles Co. Monaghan exhibits of interest include a 14th-century Cross of Clogher (open Tues.-Sat. 11am-1pm and 2-5pm; free). Extremely thorough and specific, the **St. Louis Heritage Centre**, Market Rd. (tel. 83529), occupies the red-brick building in the convent school grounds. The center traces the Saint Louis Order of nuns. Dead sisters' hairshirts and cutlery are on display. A wax replica of the founder of the order presides over the whole scene. Barbie dolls model the evolution of nun fashion. (Open Mon.-Tues. and Thurs.-Fri. 10am-noon and 2:30-4:30pm., Sat.-Sun. 2:30-4:30pm; £1, children 50p; wheelchair access.)

■ NEAR MONAGHAN: CASTLEBLAYNEY

Twenty miles southeast of Monaghan, Castleblayney challenges sports enthusiasts and hikers at the **Lough Muckno Leisure Park,** at the end of the town's main street. The park consists of 900 acres of forests and trails around Lough Muckno, as well as a hostel, an adventure center, camping facilities, and Hope Castle Bar and Restaurant. Situated in a stoic stone building, the **Lough Muckno Leisure Park Adventure Centre (IHH)** (tel. (042) 46356), welcomes grungy backpackers to clean, airy, efficiently run accommodations (dorm £7; w/continental breakfast £9, w/full Irish breakfast £11; no self-catering). Camping space is also available (open St. Patrick's Day weekend to mid-Oct.; £4/tent plus £1/person).

The **Adventure Centre** offers both land and water activities for the energy-prone (open June-Sept. Tues.-Fri. 2-7pm, Sat.-Sun. noon-7pm; windsurfing £20/4 hr., tennis £2/hr.). After a day of activity, satisfy your appetite at **Barney's**, Main St. (tel. (042) 40120; chicken breast at £1.80; open Mon.-Sat. noon-1am, Sun. 3pm-1am). Or pack a picnic at **Spar Supermarket** on Main St. **Gunner Brady's**, Main St. (tel. (042) 40053), is a hoppin' place for pints. (Food is available Mon.-Sat. noon-7pm, daily specials £3.50; traditional music on Thurs. nights, live bands Fri.-Sun.).

If you don't care for windsurfing, you might want to look at some lovely lace in **Clones**, a petite town 20 minutes southwest of Monaghan on the N54 (serviced by the Monaghan-Cavan bus route). The Clones Lace Guilde, 10 Fermanagh Terrace (tel. (047) 51729 or 51051) has recently opened the **Canal Stores**, on the Cavan Rd. You can admire old lace, buy new lace, and even see the stuff being made.

Westmeath, Offaly, Laois, & Longford

With the exception of spectacular Clonmacnoise and its intriguing bog, these central counties are passages rather than destinations. Co. Westmeath, with nineteen lakes, is sometimes called the Land of Lakes and Legends—it's something like Minnesota, but smaller. Farming and fishing are the only occupations in Co. Westmeath. Farther south in famously soggy Co. Offaly, small towns civilize the peatland with rabid consumer culture. Co. Laois ("leesh") gets a lot out of its central location. Its county capital, Portlaoise, boasts a central mail sorting facility, shopping centers, a peat-powered generator with cooling towers, and a prison. The Slieve Bloom Mountains, between Mountrath, Kinnitty, and Roscrea, are unfairly neglected, but info is available in Birr. And no, we didn't forget forlorn **Co. Longford:** it's mostly harmless.

■ ■ ■ MULLINGAR

Plum in the center of Co. Westmeath, Mullingar is an ideal base for exploring the county's few attractions by day and discoing at night. The fishing and boating on Lough Ennell and Lough Owel are just minutes away, while Sligo and Galway, for which destinations passage through Mullingar is also necessary, are farther away.

Practical Information From the **train station** (tel. 48274), follow the road to the green bridge and turn right onto Dominick St. to reach town center (station open 6:30am-8:30pm; luggage storage £1/item). **Trains** chug to Dublin (Mon.-Sat. 5/day, Sun. 3/day; 1½hr.; £7) and Sligo (Mon.-Thurs. and Sat.-Sun. 4/day, Fri. 5/day; 2hr.; £8.50). **Bus Éireann** carries customers to: Athlone (3/day; 1hr.), Dublin (5/day; 1½hr.), Galway (3/day; 3hr.), and Sligo (3/day; 2½hr.). **O'Brien's Bus Co.** (tel. 48977) sends buses to Dublin (Mon.-Sat. 5/day, Sun. 3/day; £9.50 return). Bus Éireann stops at Miss Fitz's Hair Salon on Castle St.; O'Brien's buses stop in front of the post office on Dominick St.

The **tourist office** (tel. 48650; fax 40413) is far from town, ½ mile down the Dublin Rd. but clearly signposted (open June-Aug. Mon.-Fri. 9am-6pm, Sept.-May Mon.-Fri. 9:30am-5:30pm). The **Chamber of Commerce Tourist Information Centre** (tel. 44044 or 44285), in Market Sq., corner of Pearse and Mount St., is more convenient than the tourist office and almost as well-stocked with info, including the monthly *Calendar of Events* (open Mon.-Fri. 9:30am-5:30pm; also May-Sept. Sat.-Sun. 10am-4pm). The **post office,** Dominick St. (tel. 48393), is open Mon.-Sat. 9am-5:30pm. **TSB** bank, Oliver Plunkett St., has the longest hours of area banks (open Mon.-Wed. and Fri. 9:30am-5pm, Thurs. 9:30am-7pm). The **phone code** purrs 044.

Accommodations Palm trees shade the fish pond at **Grove House,** Grove Ave. (tel. 41974). From Oliver Plunkett St., turn right onto Dominick Pl., which leads directly to the front door. Fluffy pillows, warm comforters, and cherry rooms are only improved by the owners' genuine warmth (£12/person, w/bath £13; single £14; open Feb.-Nov.). Reservations are advised for rooms and access to the private sauna at **Auburn B&B,** Auburn Rd. (tel. 40507). Head down Mount St. and turn left onto Sunday's Well Rd. The B&B is opposite the park (£12.50/person, w/bath £15). The **Midland Hotel,** Mount St. (tel. 48381), hides its generic, impersonal rooms above the ground-floor pub (£10/person, £15 w/full Irish breakfast).

Food & Pubs The **Kitchen Fare Deli,** Mount St. (tel. 41294), is a great place to munch on delicious, lunch-sized, meat-filled salads (55p) and fruit scones (40p;

MULLINGAR

open Mon.-Thurs. 7:30am-6pm, Fri.-Sat. 7am-11pm, Sun. 11am-4pm). **The Greville Arms Hotel,** Pearse St. (tel. 48563), feeds restaurant meals at coffee-shop prices to Mullingar residents in a luxuriously red pub (smoked salmon, potatoes, salad, and peas £3.50; open daily 7am-9pm). The most youthful and popular pub in town is **Hughes'** (tel. 48237), on the corner of Pearse and Castle St. Candlelit trad sessions draw big crowds on Wednesday nights (variety of music Fri.-Sat.; no cover). **The Final Fence,** Oliver Plunkett St. (tel. 48688), hosts "Kamikaze Drinking Night" as well as a nightclub on Thursday to Sunday nights (starts at 11pm; cover £5).

Sights The modest **Market House Museum** (tel. 48152) on the corner of Pearse St. and Mount St., above the Chamber of Commerce Tourist Information Office, displays a peculiar array of weaponry and Iron Age implements. (Open by appointment, mid-July to mid-Sept. Mon.-Fri. 2:30-5:30pm.) Crowned with not one, but two spires, the **Cathedral of Christ the King** dominates the end of Mary St. The names of the 52 bishops who have presided over the diocese of Meath since 1117 AD are listed inside. An **ecclesiastical museum** (tel. 48338), also inside, displays wooden penal crosses and the vestments of St. Oliver Plunkett, Ireland's most recently canonized saint (cathedral and museum open Thurs. and Sat.-Sun. 3-4pm or by appointment; £1). South across the canal bridge, an immediate right and then a left will lead to the **Military Museum** at Colomb Barracks (tel. 48391). It's chilling to learn that some Irishmen privately fought for the Nazis in WWII out of pure hatred for England (open by appointment, call for scheduling; free). If you've been wondering, "How did Mullingar get its name?" or "What was James Joyce doing here?" then you should join a **Forgotten Heritage Guided Walking Tour,** which departs from the information center in Market Sq. (tel. (044) 44044; tours leave Mon.-Sat. 11:30am and 2:30pm; 90 min.; £2.50, students £1).

Anglers and aquaphiles can **rent boats** at **Lough Owel** (call Mrs. Doolan at tel. 42085) or **Lough Ennell** (call Eileen Hope at tel. 40807). Prices for both are the same: £10/day; £20/day for boat w/engine. **Sam's Tackle,** Castle St. (tel. 40431) sells fishing gear and maggots (£1.60/pint; open Mon.-Sat. 9:30am-6pm).

■ NEAR MULLINGAR

THE FORE TRAIL

Heading north of Mullingar, the Fore Trail first follows N4 to Coole, then turns east onto R395 and finally swoops back down to Mullingar on R394. The first stop on the trail is six miles north of Mullingar. Here, in the little village of **Multyfarnham**, monks still preserve their vows of chastity at a 15th-century **Franciscan friary.** Life-size wooden figures depict the stations of the cross. **Boats** are for hire from Tommy Newman (tel. (044) 71111; £9/day), and hiking trails also lace the area. Four miles north along N4 brings travelers on the trail to **Coole,** home of the 200-year-old Georgian mansion, **Turbotstown House.** Privately owned, the house is open to the public May-Sept. Some of the Midlands' famous **bogs** border Coole on the west. To the east is romantic, turreted **Tullynally Castle** (tel. (044) 61159; fax (044) 61856), one mile before Castlepollard. The largest castle in Ireland that is still used as a family home, its Gothic Revival towers are surrounded by 30 acres of gardens. (Castle open mid-June to mid-Aug. daily 2:30-6pm. Gardens open May-Sept. daily 2-6pm. Castle and gardens £3.50, students £2; gardens only £2, students 50p.)

The lakeshore town of **Fore** could be Glendalough with a little marketing. Fore was known for its seven wonders: water that flows uphill, water that won't boil, a tree that won't burn, a tree with only three branches (the Holy Trinity), a monastery that should have sunk into the bogs, a mill without a source of water to turn it, and a saint encased in stone (he vowed never to leave his cell). Fore was founded as a monastery in 630 AD by St. Fechin and rebuilt during the 11th, 13th, and 15th centuries. Today, it is the most extensive set of Benedictine ruins in Ireland. St. Fechin's Church, in the graveyard, is the oldest standing building. Though legends claims that St. Fechin himself built the church, realistically the remains date from the 11th

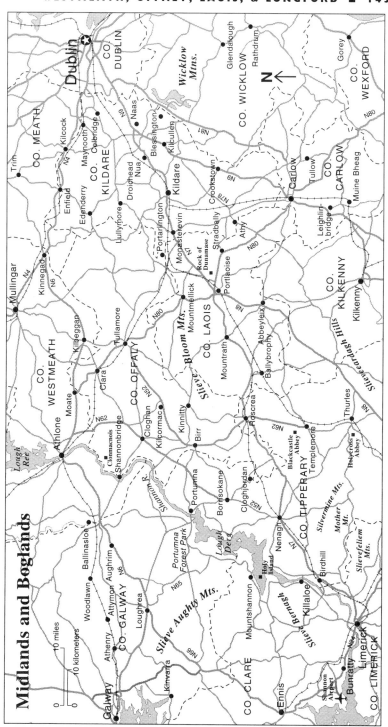

Midlands and Boglands

and 13th centuries. Parts of the cloister were even rebuilt around World War I (all always open; free). Fore Abbey can be reached from Kells with **Shamrock Experience** tours (tel. (046) 40127); (see Kells (Ceanannas Mór), p. 136). The Fore Trail continues along R395 to R394, then turns south to reach Collinstown Village. From the village, the trail turns east onto the Kells Rd. toward **Delvin,** where a golf course abuts the ruins of the 12th-century castle which once marked the western boundary of the British-controlled Pale (site always open; free). Returning to R394 along the Kells Rd., the trail carries on to **Crookedwood,** where a well-preserved 14th-century church with a stone roof sits in front of a ring fort (always open; free). The trail continues south until it returns to Mullingar.

THE BELVEDERE TRAIL

The **Belvedere Trail,** which covers the area south of Mullingar, follows N52 to N6 and then takes the Kilbeggan Rd. back to Mullingar. Four miles south of Mullingar, the 18th-century **Belvedere House and Gardens** (tel. (044) 40861) pompously promenade along the shore of Lough Ennel. The house seems to strive for imperial grandeur, with Roman gods frescoed along the ceiling. Robert Rochford, Lord Belvedere, for whom the house was built, also commissioned an Italian architect to create the fake and expensive "ruins" of a nonexistent abbey. His purpose was to obstruct his own of his brother's superior rose garden, of which the extravagant lord had grown jealous. The purpose-built ruin is now called, in his dishonor, "the Jealous Wall" (open April-June and Sept. daily noon-4:30pm; July-Aug. daily noon-6pm; £1, students 50p).

As the trail turns off N52 and onto N6, it passes by **Tyrellspass Castle** (tel. (044) 23105), an Irish stronghold that Cromwell tried to eradicate. The castle itself was built in 1411 and lay in disrepair until its restoration in 1979 (open daily 10am-6pm). Following N6 (the Dublin-Galway Rd.) east, Kilbeggan appears at the next major intersection. This small town is home to **Locke's Distillery** (tel. (0506) 32134), a former firewater factory converted into a museum (open May-Oct. daily 9am-6pm, Nov.-March daily 10am-4pm; £2, children £1). From Kilbeggan, the trail turns right, heading northeast to **Lough Ennell,** a major bird sanctuary also much favored by trout fishermen (for permits, call the Wildlife Service, tel. (044) 42771). On the shore of the lough await **Lilliput House** and **Jonathan Swift Park.** The park offers walking trails and fishing piers, but, sadly, no miniature mansion. According to local legend, Swift conceived *Gulliver's Travels* during a visit to Lough Ennell in the 1720s. Shortly after its publication in 1726, the area around the park was renamed Lilliput in his honor (grounds always open; free). The Belvedere Trail continues northeast and returns to Mullingar along N52.

■■■ ATHLONE

The geographical center of Ireland, Athlone warms a seat at the crossroads of the Galway-Dublin Rd. and the River Shannon. Its location makes it a travel hub, its rich history makes it a travel destination; if you have a car, Athlone serves as a great place to locate yourself to tour the rest of Ireland. The river rushes through town and flares into Lough Ree north of it. On one steep bank lie Church Street's shopping centers and greasy chip shops, while the historical left bank is home to the three typical components of an Irish town—the market square, the cathedral, and the castle. The river divides Athlone between two counties and two of the ancient provinces of Ireland—Co. Roscommon and Connacht on the left bank of the Shannon, Co. Westmeath and Leinster on the right.

Practical Information The **tourist office** in the castle (tel. 94630) has free copies of the *Athlone and District Visitors Guide* and the *Athlone Tourist Trail* (open June-Aug. Mon.-Sat. 9am-6pm; May and Sept.-Oct. Mon.-Sat. 10am-1pm and 2-5:30pm). **Bank of Ireland** (tel. 75111), and **AIB** bank (tel. 72089) adorn Church St.; both have **ATMs.** The **post office** is on Barrack St. (tel. 83544; open Mon.-Tues. and

Thurs.-Sat. 9am-5:30pm, Wed. 9:30am-5:30pm). The **laundromat,** Pearse St. (tel. 92930), washes and dries for £4/load. The **Athlone Youth Resource Centre,** Northgate St. (tel./fax 78747) offers info as well as secretarial services (Mon.-Fri., 10am-5:30pm). Athlone's **train and bus depot** (tel. 72651) is on Southern Station Rd., which loops off Church St. **Trains** leave for Dublin (8/day; 2hr.) and Galway (4/day; 1hr.). **Buses** shuttle off in all directions to: Dublin (8/weekday, 8/Sun.; 2hr.); Galway (9/day, 8/Sun.; 1½hr.); Tullamore and Rosslare (1/day); Cahir (1/day; 3hr.); and Dundalk (1/day; 3hr.). Athlone's **phone code** is a nurturing 0902.

Accommodations B&Bs inhabit Irishtown Rd. and its continuation towards Dublin. Closer to town is Mrs. Devaney's **Shannon View,** Sean Costello St. (a section of Church St.; tel. 78411), which offers crisp rooms with big beds and TVs (£13/person). Two doors down on Sean Costello St., a narrow hallway leads into respectable rooms with TVs and coffee-makers at **Mrs. Kennedy's** (tel. 75878; single £18, double £30). Across the river on Pearse St., **Higgins** (tel. 92519) has motel-like rooms over the pub, each with bath and TV (single £16, double £28). Three miles northeast on N55 (Longford Rd.), **Lough Ree Caravan and Camping Park** (tel. 78561) awaits. Follow turnoff signs for Lough Ree (open May-Sept.; £2.50/person).

Food & Pubs The shelves overflow at the **Quinnsworth Supermarket,** Athlone Shopping Centre, Dublin Rd. (tel. 72465; open Mon.-Wed. and Sat. 9am-6pm, Thurs.-Fri. 9am-9pm). **Bradbury's,** on Church St. (tel. 72058), can pass you a quick and decent cafeteria-style meal (baked potato £1.50, burger £1.10; open Mon.-Sat. 9am-6pm). **Beez Rock Diner,** in The Court off Church St. (tel. 75536), serves surprisingly good American diner food in a 50s hep cat den (veggie burger 80p, sirloin steak dinner £4.95; open Mon.-Wed. 11:30am-1am, Thurs.-Sun. 11:30am-4am). The **Hooker Tackle Shop,** Custume Place (tel. 74848), provides fishing equipment for catching your own dinner; and if you're unlucky, a pint of maggots is only £2.

The Westmeath Independent has entertainment listings. **Sean's Bar,** Main St. (tel. 92358), behind the castle, goes traditional on weeknights and Sunday afternoons. It traces an ancestry back to 1654; ask for the history lesson. The ruling elite drink at the classy **Prince of Wales Hotel,** Church St. (tel. 72626). Dim and wood-paneled, the **Keg,** Barrack St. (tel. 93031), hosts musicians (Fri.-Sat. nights) and Irish dancing (Thurs.). **Biddy Mulligan's,** Irishtown Rd. (tel. 73476), presents Blues on Mondays, Country on Tuesday, and a mix of other music the rest of the week to a lively, young crowd. **BoZo's Club,** at Conlon's on Dublingate St., honks its nose with delight (Thurs.-Sun.). **Dún na Sí,** on Mt. Temple Rd. (10 mi. east of Athlone; tel. 81183), has *céilí* around an open fireplace (first Fri. of the month; weekly July-Aug.).

Sights The course of English history took a pivotal turn at the 1691 **Siege of Athlone,** when William's army captured the Leinster half of town and laid the smaller Connacht town under siege. The Jacobites broke down the bridge and prevented its repair to stop the English advance. The jig was up after the Williamites fired 12,000 cannonballs into the Connacht half of town, forded the river, and stormed the castle. **The Athlone Castle Visitor Centre** (tel. 72107 or 92912) tells the story with stiff models and a noisy 45-minute audio-visual show. The local museum, also inside the castle, has a 1000-year-old chunk of butter, bronze age instruments, and other oddities. (Open May-Sept. daily 10am-6pm, multimedia show 1-4:30pm; £2.50, students and seniors £1.75; museum only, half-price.) Poking around Athlone Castle, with its grand Shannon views, is free (castle open May-Sept. daily 9:30am-6pm).

Take a free tour of the **Athlone Crystal Factory,** 28 Pearse St. (tel. 92867), which is what Waterford Crystal would be if it only had one glass-cutter; covet goods in the small factory shop (open Tues.-Fri. 10am-6pm). Two **ferry** companies cruise up the Shannon to Lough Ree; both Rossana Cruises and Shannon Holidays sail three times every day for 1½ hr. **Shannon Holidays** (tel. 72892; fax 74386) sails from the Jolly Mariner Marina (from the castle, cross the bridge and turn left, following the river—a 10-minute walk; open March-Oct.; £4, student, seniors, and under 16 £3.50). **Rossana Cruises** (tel. 92513) leave from the strand, across the river from the castle (£4.50, seniors and students £4, under 16 £3.50). For a faster trip, try **Hovercraft Tours,** Monksland (tel. 92658 or 74593), which will show you Lough Ree at 40 mph (from £5; departs every half hour from Hudson Bay Hotel).

Athlone celebrated its tercentenary of the siege with a festival and reenactment in 1991, and the last week in June still brings the **Athlone Festival** each year. The tourist office and many local businesses have the schedule of events, which include parades, exhibits, and free concerts. If you're an aspiring singer, go to Athlone in late autumn for the **John McCormack Golden Voice** opera competition, named for Athlone's most famous tenor. Contact Athlone Chamber of Commerce (tel. 73173; fax 73326) for details. You can get the inside scoop on town history from **Athlone Town Walks** (tel. 75814 or 74239), which meet at the castle and take one hour. (Tues.-Fri. at 11am, Sat.-Sun. at 3:30pm, adults £2.50, students £2).

O Johnny Boy, the pipes, the pipes are calling...

Athlone's native son, John McCormack is considered one of the finest tenors of the early 20th century. From his choir boy days in Athlone, McCormack went on to Dublin where he won first prize at *Feis Ceiol*, the National Irish Music Festival. The honor springboarded McCormack to Italy where he trained extensively for the opera. At the young age of 22, McCormack made his operatic debut in London as Luriddu in Pietro Masiagni's *Cavallina Rusticana*. Although a marquee name in opera, McCormack endeared audiences around the world with the Irish folk songs he invariably included in his recitals. McCormack often compared himself to old Irish minstrels. His variety of tone and enunciation while conveying meaning was a natural gift but nurtured by growing up around traditional Irish singing. After 1914, McCormack sang principally in concert and for those new-fangled phonograph records. In 1919, he became a U.S. citizen, but soon returned to his native Ireland and was made a papal count by Pope Pius XI. Although he retired in 1938, McCormack made charity appearances during the Second World War until his death in 1945.

■ NEAR ATHLONE: CLONMACNOISE

If Clonmacnoise were anywhere near the beaten path, it would be Glendalough with river views and without the weird tearooms. Instead, Clonmacnoise is a huge detour; but St. Ciaran's monastic city, and the perfect accommodation there, are worth the trip. To locals it is a graveyard, to historians a fantastically preserved ancient monastery, and to tourists the hot-spot of the bogs—but it's out of the way for everyone. St. Ciaran founded Clonmacnoise in 545 on the eastern (Leinster) shore of the Shannon. While studying on Aran, Ciaran had a vision in which he saw a huge tree growing in the center of Ireland, its fruit-laden branches stretched out to cover the whole land. St. Enda interpreted the dream: Ciaran was the tree, and he had to found a church in the center of Ireland to shelter the island with its grace. His settlement grew into a city and an important scholastic center. The precious *Book of the Dun Cow* was written by monks here around 1100. Its title refers to a legend that the book was written on vellum from St. Ciaran's cow; this Dun Cow traveled everywhere with Ciaran and produced milk for the whole monastery. Clonmacnoise also attracted a slew of religious artisans, as the carvings on the high crosses attest. The monks' *Annals* record a vision of manned ships passing through the air above the city in 748 AD; Seamus Heaney's squaring in *Seeing Things* retells the sighting.

The **visitors center** (tel. (0905) 74195) craves attention for its wheelchair-accessible displays. A number of high crosses (once located in the ruins themselves) and an audio-visual show are among the attractions. Groups should call ahead for guided tour bookings (included in entrance fee). Entrance to the ruins is through the visitors center. (Open daily, except Christmas; June-Sept. 9am-7pm, mid-Mar.-May and Sept.-Oct. 10am-6pm, Nov.-mid-March 10am-5pm; £2.50, students £1)

The **high crosses** that have been moved into the center from the ruins will reward lingering attention. The **South Cross,** a full nine feet high, shows the crucifixion within the circle on its west face; interlacing patterns and animals cover the rest. This cross, the oldest in the ruins, dates from the 700s. Only the shaft of the **North Cross** remains; it has abstract human and animal figures on three sides (the fourth is blank). The famous **Cross of the Scriptures** is gorgeous and easy to read (a replica stands in the churchyard). Ten feet high, it was built in memory of the High King Flann, who protected and funded Clonmacnoise until his death in 914. The west face shows the crucifixion within its circle; two small figures offer chalices on either side. Along the shaft are, in descending order, depictions of Christ's descent into hell, his betrayal, his arrest, and the guarding of his tomb. The better-preserved east face also shows a number of scenes: Moses praying for military victory, **God** on Judgment Day, St. Michael blowing a trumpet, and **Satan** pushing back the damned. The bottom panel shows Ciaran preparing to build his first church. The north face has more pagan designs—beneath the arm, a cat eats a fish; the second panel shows two cats dancing to a piper's tune.

The site itself is impressive for its lonely grandeur. The **cathedral** was destroyed by Vikings and rebuilt by monks several times; the structure now standing dates from about 1100, though the Romanesque west doorway and Gothic north door are from 1460. Over the north doorway arch, St. Dominic, St. Patrick, and St. Francis stand guard. The last High King of Ireland, Rory O'Connor, was buried inside in 1198. Other high kings are scattered around Clonmacnoise. **Temple Doulin** and **Temple Hurpain,** abutting each other behind the cathedral, are more crude.

Temple Ciaran, in the center of the churchyard, was probably constructed on the site of the original church. St. Ciaran is said to be buried close to the south wall. **O'Connor's Church,** built in 1000, still has Church of Ireland services on the fourth Sunday of the month at 10am. **O'Rourke's Tower,** the free-standing tower, had its top blown off by lightning in 1135. A ¼-mile walk from Clonmacnoise is the peaceful **Nun's Church.** Follow the path through the main site and bear left. The chancel, arc, and doorways are finely detailed—the best Romanesque architecture in Ireland.

The **tourist office,** at the entrance to the Clonmacnoise car park (tel. (0905) 74134), sells Kenneth MacGowan's excellent *Clonmacnoise,* a brown-covered guide to the monastic city (£2.50; open June-Aug. daily 9am-6pm, Apr.-May and Sept.-Oct. 10am-6pm). The best accommodation awaits at **Mr. and Mrs. Augustin Claffey** (tel. (0905) 74149), on the Shannonbridge Rd. near town. The couple restored the cottage across the road—it's white, with red trim windows and a peat roof, dating from 1843. On the windward side, the grass cozily slopes up to the windows to protect the house from storm damage. Charm is added by two double beds and a lambskin rug in the bedroom, peat fire and rocking chair in the sitting room, and a large modern bathroom, plus cooker and refrigerator. One lucky couple spent their honeymoon here. The price? £10/person. Have a great stay, but reserve well in advance. Another good spot is **Kajon House** (tel. (0905) 74191), past Perfection House and also on the Shannonbridge Rd. (single w/bath £14, double w/bath £29). Pitch a tent in the field next to the house for £1.50/person (local farmers also often permit camping). Along with a great view of the bog, Kajon House offers fresh scones to all guests. In its spare time it acts as a restaurant, dishing up Kajon cooking for breakfast and dinner (omelette and chips £4.75).

If you have a car, the easiest way to reach Clonmacnoise from either Athlone or Birr is on N62 to Ballynahoun and then follow the signs. Lacking a car, you can get there from Athlone by **Minibus Service** (tel. (0902) 74839), which departs from the front of the Athlone Castle at 11am (Mon.-Fri.), runs to both Clonmacnoise and the Clonmacnoise and West Offaly Railway, and returns around 4pm (adults £15, students £10, includes price of admission to both sights). Clonmacnoise is reachable by bike, but it's 14 miles of very hilly terrain, so you might want to think twice. Hitchers bound for Clonmacnoise first get a lift to Ballynahoun on the heavily trafficked

N62, and get a ride from there to Clonmacnoise. It might also be possible to hitch a ride there on a boat traveling down the River Shannon.

■■■ BIRR

William Petty labelled Birr *"Umbilious Hiberniae"*—loosely translated, Birr is Ireland's bellybutton. Its central location in Ireland gives it navel, not naval, qualities. The town is cute in a puckered-up sort of a way; many residents think it deserves more visitors than it gets. The tired Georgian houses along Birr's tree-lined malls contrast with the dramatic scale of the castle and its gorgeous gardens.

Birr makes a decent starting point for an expedition into the Slieve Bloom mountains to its east, and the tourist office staff are well-informed. The **tourist office** is on Rosse Row, across from the entrance to Birr Castle (tel. (0509) 20110; open May-Sept. daily 9:30am-1pm and 2-5:30pm). Ask for *Info Sheet #26F: The Slieve Blooms.* **AIB** bank (tel. (0509) 20069) offers an **ATM** in Emmet Sq. **P.L. Polan,** Main St. (tel. (0509) 20006), rents bikes at the corner of Wilmer Rd. (£7/day, £30/week, deposit £40). To Limerick take the Riverstown Rd., to Cashel the Roscrea Rd., to Cloghan Castle (see below) the Banagher Rd., to Athlone the Tullamore Rd. **Bus Éireann** runs to: Dublin (Mon.-Sat. 3/day, Sun. 1/day; 2hr.; £9); Cahir (1/day; 2hr., or to Cork 4hr.; £12); and Athlone (1/day; 50min.; £5).

Accommodations, Food, & Pubs Birr has a new and very comfortable hostel at the **Spinners Town House,** Castle St. (tel./fax (0509) 21673). It offers firm beds, friendly owners, and a bistro downstairs (7-bed dorm w/continental breakfast £10; double w/sheets and Irish breakfast £12.50/person, £15 w/bath). Right over the toy store on Main St. is **Kay Kelly's B&B** (tel. (0509) 21128), boasting a central location, fluffy beds and 24-hr. access to a plethora of toys. Mrs. Kelly offers the best advice in town on Birr's pubs and restaurants (single £15, double £28). For food, try the highly-recommended but cheap **Kong Lam,** which cooks up Chinese take-away at the end of O'Connell St. (chicken fried rice £3.50). A crowd of mixed ages gathers to watch sports and listen to music at **Craughwell's** on Castle St. (tel. (0509) 21839).

Sights You're welcome to tread on the Earl of Rosse's front lawn at **Birr Castle** (tel. (0509) 20056), which remains his private home. A babbling brook, a tranquil pond, the tallest box hedges in the world, and acres of lush woods and gardens make Birr Castle a stand-out even among Ireland's legions of showy *châteaux*. Don't miss the immense telescope, whose 72-inch mirror made it the world's largest from 1845-1917. The third Earl of Rosse used this very instrument to discover that nebulae could be resolved into separate star systems beyond our galaxy; the fourth Earl of Rosse used it to measure the heat of the moon. The castle's summer exhibitions have themes like "Sugar'n'Spice: Castle Cooking Down the Ages" and "Dressing for the Occasion." (Open daily 9am-1pm and 2-6pm, exhibitions open May-Sept. 2:30-5:30pm; £3.20, students £1.60; Nov.-Mar. £2.60, students £1.30.)

In town the **Slieve Bloom Environmental Display Centre,** Railway Rd. (tel. (0509) 20029), is in the Outdoor Pursuits Centre (from Emmet Sq., follow signs for Roscrea to reach Railway Rd.). The center explains the flora and fauna of the Slieve Blooms and also functions as a museum for the tiny town of **Kinitty.** (See *Slieve Bloom Mountains* pamphlet for more; open July-Sept. Mon.-Fri. 10am-6pm, Sat.-Sun. 2:30pm-6pm; free.) The blasted 19th-century factory by Elmsgrove Whiskey was once the R. and J. Wallace Distillery; in 1889 the distillery caught fire and coated the Camcor River with floating, flaming whiskey!!! **Birr Vintage Week,** which takes place in mid-August, involves a parade, a car rally, an antique and art fair, and much dressing-up, especially in Georgian costume.

■ **NEAR BIRR**

Seven miles north of Birr and 3½ miles from Banagher, the owners of **Cloghan Castle** (tel. (0509) 51650) welcome visitors. Built in 1249, the castle has been lived in for most of the time between then and now. Visitors can now see an intact defensive fortress, complete with spike holes and archery holes for 100 warriors. The castle shares 60 acres of park and lawns with Georgia O'Keeffe's favorite animal subjects, Jacob sheep (the kind with extremely curly horns). The tours take about 40 minutes. (Tours June-Sept. Wed.-Sun. 2-6pm; £3.50, seniors and students £2.50). From Birr, take the Banagher Rd. (also off N62—the Athlone Rd.—at Cloghan) to the center of Banagher; turn left at the small road opposite the chemist. At the Lusmagh Church continue straight and take the second right, opposite a stone windmill. The tower is one mile down.

SLIEVE BLOOM MOUNTAINS

Though only 2000 feet at their highest, the Slieve Bloom Mountains ("shleeve bloom") give the illusion of great height. None of this mucking around with foothills—the mountains burst up from plains within a parallelogram formed by Birr, Roscrea, Portlaoise, and Tullamore. Ard Erin (Irish for "highest in Ireland"), was once mistakenly thought to be the tallest peak in Ireland. **The Slieve Bloom Way** is a circular walking trail that passes mountain bogs, Ard Erin, waterfalls, and heaps of scenery. From these peaks all of Ireland is at your feet. The tourist office in Birr makes the best pre-mountain stop: hikers will need directions in *The Slieve Bloom Way (Info Sheet # 26F)*, theoretically available in any Bord Fáilte office, but definitely waiting for you in Birr. The office sells the Ordnance Survey's map *Slieve Blooms Sheet #54*. *New Irish Walk Guides*, found in bookstores, has more info on Bloom walks. The **Slieve Bloom Environmental Display Centre** discusses the flora and fauna you may encounter, as well as the history of the area. Remember, bogs are highly flammable: it is illegal to light fires anywhere on the Way. Mountrath, south of the Slieve Blooms in Co. Laois, and Kinitty northeast in Co. Offaly make good springboards; clever mountaineers can hike from one to the other.

ROSCREA

Ten miles south of Birr poses picturesque Roscrea. Among the shops and pubs on its narrow, winding streets are the remains of several medieval wonders. **St. Cronan's Monastery,** now divided in two by Church St., sports a finely worked Romanesque gable, a well-preserved high cross, and a round tower, which had 20 feet lopped off its height in 1798. On Castle St., a 13th-century **castle** surrounds the **Damer House,** the best preserved example of Queen Anne architecture in Ireland and the home of the Bog Butter, a thousand-year-old chunk of butter rescued from the bog. The **Roscrea Heritage Centre,** located in the castle (tel. (0505) 21850), is the closest thing in town to a tourist office; in addition to tours of the castle, it has the useful Roscrea Heritage Walk map (free). (Open June-Sept. daily 9:30am-6pm; castle tours: £2.50, seniors £1.75, students £1.) Fragments of the 15th-century **Franciscan friary** surround the parish church on Abbey St.

A branch of **Bank of Ireland** (tel. (0505) 21877) on Castle St. sports an **ATM.** Groceries abound at **Quinnsworth** in the Roscrea Shopping Centre, Castle St. (Open Mon.-Wed. and Sat. 9am-7pm, Thurs.-Fri. 9am-9pm). **Bus Éireann** stops in front of Christy Maker's pub on Castle St. (to Dublin, 3/day, 2 hr.; to Limerick, 3/day, 1 hr.). The clear winner among restaurants is the soothingly beautiful **Waterfront Gallery,** the Mall (tel. (0505) 22431; open Mon.-Wed. 9am-7pm, Thurs.-Sat. 9am-10pm, Sun. 12:30pm-7pm). Next door, the aptly named **Yellow House B&B** (tel. (0505) 21772) offers a warm reception and decent beds (£12/person, £15 w/bath). **The Roscrea Discount Centre,** Rosemary St., has plain rooms with TVs (£12.50).

PORTLAOISE

Portlaoise ("port-LEESH") is a decent-sized town with multi-stop shopping for people on their way to the Slieve Bloom Mountains and points west. Nearby, set in the middle of all that farmland, the **Rock of Dunamase** is worth a look. Take Stradbally Rd. east four miles; the Rock is on the left (follow the sign to "Athy/Carlow" at the big, red Catholic church). The Rock is a truly ancient fortress (it was recorded by Ptolemy), and passed between Irish and Viking hands many times over the years. The mound still bristles with fortifications. The Rock is a fantastic vantage point for viewing the Slieve Bloom Mountains (always open; free).

Back in town, the **tourist office** (tel. (0502) 21178) can provide you with *Info Sheet #26F: The Slieve Blooms* (free) to help you plan your hike (open Mon.-Sat. 9am-6pm). The regional **post office** (tel. (0502) 22339) enthusiastically sorts mail inside the shopping center on Lawlor Avenue (open Mon.-Fri. 9am-5:30pm, Sat. 10am-1pm and 2-5pm). **AIB** bank (tel. (0502) 21349) graces Lawlor Ave. with an **ATM.** There's a **laundromat** in the mini-mall across from the public library (wash and dry £4; open Mon.-Sat. 9am-6pm). **Jim's Country Kitchen** relaxes off Church St. (tel. (0502) 32616); turn off Main St. at Lombard and Vister. Low beams, a happy tea-time crowd, and a super *al fresco* experience are all in the cobblestoned courtyard. (Quiche and salad £3.60, tart and cream £1, cakes £1.20; open Mon.-Sat. 10:30am-5:30pm.) **O'Donoghue's B&B,** Kellyville Park (tel. (0502) 21353), just around the corner from Main St., is a large, hotel-like B&B with flower gardens and new beds (single £14, double £26, w/bath £30). The **train station** (tel. (0502) 21303) hides in a tall gray building at the curve in Railway St. (open daily 7:30am-9pm). **Trains** run to Dublin and to points south (Dublin 8/day; 1hr.; £10.50). **Bus Éireann** stops at Egan's Hostelry between Dublin and Cork (to Dublin 10/day; 1½hr.; £9). Be early: Bus Éireann buses feel free to leave 10 minutes early.

ATHY

Athy (pronounced "A-tie") is the modern name for the town that was marked on Ptolemy's map as *Ath-Ae*, Irish for the "Land of Ae." Ae was a popular King of Munster who died in a battle here. Later inhabitants grew tired of fording the River Barrow and so built a bridge, making Athy a natural commercial center for the area. Today, Athy is the largest town of South Co. Kildare, and a convenient stop on the Waterford-Dublin rail line. The **tourist office,** in the town hall building off Market St. (tel. (0507) 31859), is a good source of info on what to do in the Kildare area and will not try to con you into staying in Athy (open Mon.-Fri. 10 am-1pm, 2pm-4:30pm). Across the hall is the **Athy town museum,** which is just a room full of photographs and artifacts of local interest (open Tues. and Thurs. 2-4pm, Sat. 2-5pm). On Market St. is a **Bank of Ireland** (tel. (0507) 31616), with an **ATM.** Cross over the bridge and you can meet your grocery and postal needs at **SuperValu** and the **post office,** facing each other on Leinster St. Any other needs will be met down the road at **The Smuggler's,** Duke St. (tel. (0507) 31181), where pints are served amongst Athy antiques. You can also get a soup and sandwich for £2, or you can have bedroom with bath and breakfast for £14 per person. The **train station** (tel. (0507) 31966) is a 10-minute walk from the bridge, east on Market St. (Waterford-Dublin; 5/day Mon.-Sat., 3/day Sun.). **Bus Éirann** (tel. (010) 366111) stops near Tully's Pub, off Duke St. on the road to Portlaoise.

SOUTHEAST IRELAND

Southeast Ireland is the country's sunniest segment; it also belies the most English influence, since the Vikings, and then the Normans, made it their power base. Irish people take holidays on the beaches along the south coast, from cozy Kilmore Quay to tidy Ardmore. Waterford has the resources, and the grit, of a real city. Wexford is a charismatic town, packed with historical sites and convenient to many of the Southeast's finest attractions. Cashel has a superbly preserved cathedral complex; Ring is the region's sole *gaeltacht*. The happiest route to the south coast from Dublin is through Glendalough, Carlow and Kilkenny rather than along the coast. Plan to stop in Kilkenny and admire the medieval streets before you head south or west.

▨ Carlow & Kilkenny

■■■ CARLOW TOWN

The only town of any size in the county named for it, Carlow has hosted several of the most gruesome historical battles between Gael and foreigner due to its position on the southern edge of the Pale. During the 1798 rising, 417 Irish insurgents were ambushed in the streets of Carlow; they are buried in the gravel pits of Graiguecullen, across the River Barrow from Carlow. Part of the gallows from which they were hanged is now displayed in the county museum.

Contemporary Carlow is a small, busy town with surprisingly good nightlife. The town sits on the eastern side of the River Barrow, on the N9 (the Dublin-Waterford road). The Carlow **tourist office,** College St. off Tullow St. (tel. 31554), is worth a shot; it's in the Chamber of Commerce office, in front of the cathedral. Request the over-sized *Visitor's Guide to Country Carlow* for its decent map of the town (free) and be on your way (open Mon.-Fri. 9:30am-1pm and 2-5:30pm; June-Aug. also Sat. 10am-1pm and 2-6pm). Rent **bikes** from **Coleman Cycle,** 19 Dublin St. (tel. 31273; £7/day, £30/week; deposit £40; open Mon.-Sat. 8am-8pm). **Trains** run from Dublin's Heuston Station on their way to Waterford (Mon.-Thurs. and Sat. 4/day, Sun.3/day; 1¼hr.). **Bus Éireann** bounces from Carlow to: Athlone (daily 1/day; 2¼hr.); Dublin (Mon.-Sat. 6/day, Sun. 4/day; 1¾hr.); and Waterford via Kilkenny (daily 6/day; 1¼hr.). **Rapid Express Coaches,** Barrack St. (tel. 43081) runs a bus from Tramore-Waterford-Carlow-Dublin and back. (Mon.-Fri. 7/day, Sun. 5/day). From the **train station,** it's a 15-minute walk to the center of town; head straight out of the station down Railway Rd., turn left onto the Dublin Rd., and make a left at the Court House onto College St. The **phone code** here is undeniably 0503.

Accommodations A sweet little hostel on the banks of the River Barrow, the **Otterholt Riverside Hostel** (tel. 30404; fax 41318) is a half-mile from the center of town on the Kilkenny Rd. The hostel acts as a dorm for the local college during the school year, so pre-book from Sept.-May (6-bed dorm £6, sheets £1, laundry £3). A hostel slightly closer to town is **Verona,** Pembroke Rd. (tel. 31700 or 31846). Walking over the Dublin St. Bridge, Pembroke Rd. is the first right off Burrin St. Mrs. English makes room for everyone and supplies more info than the tourist office. Only two to three beds per co-ed room and only £5.50 per gentleman or lady make Verona ideal (private room, £6; bike shed; hot, hot showers. Open June-Sept.). Several **B&Bs** sprout up from the Kilkenny Rd. (N9), about two miles from the center of town; expect to pay about £13 per person.

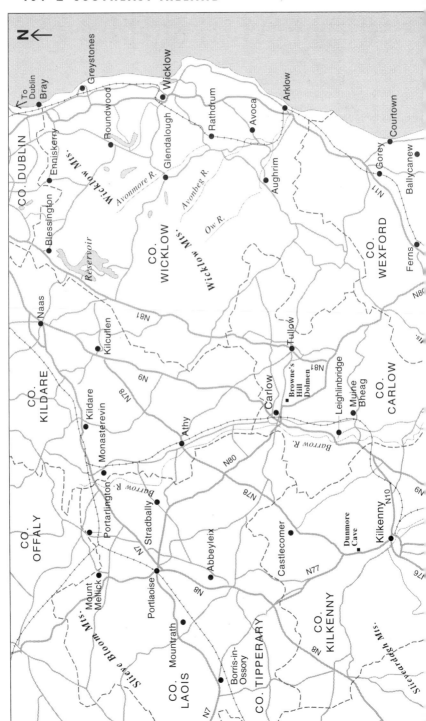

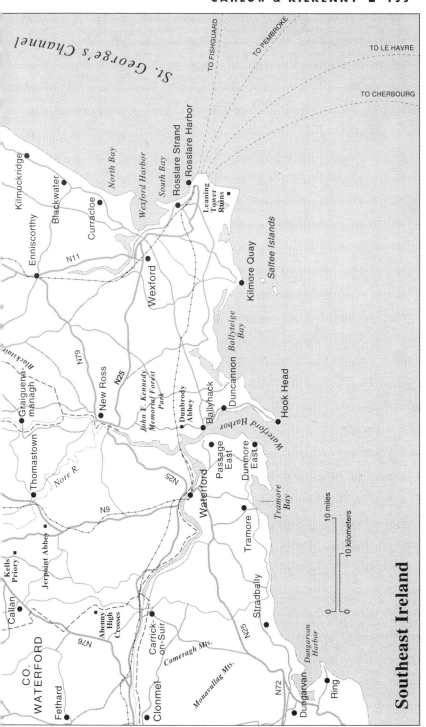

St. George's Channel

TO FISHGUARD

TO PEMBROKE

TO LE HAVRE

TO CHERBOURG

Kilmuckridge

Blackwater

Enniscorthy

North Bay

Curracloe

Rosslare Strand

Rosslare Harbor

Wexford Harbor

South Bay

Leaning Tower Ruins

N11

Wexford

Kilmore Quay

Saltee Islands

Blackstairs

Graiguena-managh

N79

New Ross

N25

John F. Kennedy Memorial Forest Park

Thomastown

Dunbrody Abbey

Ballyhack

Duncannon

Ballyteige Bay

Hook Head

Nore R.

N25

Waterford Harbor

N9

Passage East

Dunmore East

Jerpoint Abbey

Kells Priory

Callan

Waterford

Tramore

Tramore Bay

10 miles

10 kilometers

Ahenny High Crosses

Stradbally

CO. WATERFORD

N76

Carrick-on-Suir

Comeragh Mts.

N25

Fethard

Clonmel

Monavullag Mts.

N72

Dungarvan

Dungarvan Harbor

Ring

Southeast Ireland

Food & Pubs **Bradbury's,** on Tullow St. (tel. 32253), serves meals, tea and scones in a mild-mannered setting (quiche £1.60, full breakfast £3; open Mon.-Sat. 8:30am-6pm). **Scragg's Alley,** 12 Tullow St. (tel. 42233 or 40407), has hearty food (soup and roll £1, BBQ ribs £2.50; lunch served daily noon-2:30pm). Alternatively, **L&N Superstore,** Tullow St., has a huge range of groceries (open Mon.-Sat. 9am-6pm). Turn to the **Health Store,** Tullow St. (tel. 40118), for your goat's milk needs (open Mon.-Sat. 9:30am-1:15pm, 1:45-5:30pm).

Carlow grooves at **Scragg's Alley,** where pub-goers can hear live rock and traditional sessions Thursday and Saturday nights, and where partiers will find a nightclub with plenty of attitude Fridays through Sundays starting at 11pm. When An Emotional Fish played here the cover was £7.50, but it's usually free. **Tully's,** 149 Tullow St. (tel. 31862), is friendly and offbeat, with occasional live bands—squirm in the seats made out of church pews for a religious drinking experience. **The Owl,** 56 Dublin St. (tel. 43156), sings ballads on Saturdays to a crowd reclining on the red crushed velvet. **Alcock's,** 24 Groverney Sq. (tel. 41200), attracts an older crowd who enjoy the dartboard and the ballads upstairs. (Traditional ballads at 10pm on Fri. nights, Sept.-June. Bring your own ballads, please.) **O'Loughlin's,** 53 Dublin St. (tel. 32205), is dark and velvety, with typewriters strewn about; no music, but a lively, young crowd.

Sights The main attraction is outside of town. The **Brownshill Dolmen** is large and very heavy. Its capstone is the largest in Europe, weighs over 100 tons, and looks like a grounded UFO. Follow Tullow St. through the traffic light and straight through the roundabout; the dolmen is two miles away in a field on the right.

Turn right at the end of College St. onto Tullow St. and continue on to Castle St.; a left onto Mill Lane will take you around to **Carlow Castle,** behind the storefronts on Castle St. The castle is closed to the public, though you can get up very close without going through the locked gates. As an English stronghold, the castle was frequently attacked; during the 14th century, Carlow was considered so unsafe that English officers had to be paid danger money to live in town. The castle's ruined condition (two towers remaining from an original four) can be blamed on one Dr. Middleton, who intended to convert the castle into an asylum but wanted to enlarge the windows and thin the walls. He used dynamite to make his modifications. Oops.

The Carlow Museum, Haymarket (through the carpark behind Town Hall), looks like somebody's attic placed behind glass. An old bar and blacksmith shop are tritely reconstructed; on the plus side, there's an informative exhibit on the 1798 massacre (open Tues.-Sun. 10am-5:30pm, Sat-Sun. 2-5pm; £1, students 50p).

The best time to visit Carlow is during mid-June, when the town hosts **Eigse** ("egg-sha," meaning gathering), a ten-day festival of the arts. Artists from all over Ireland come to present visual, musical, and theatrical works; some events require tickets. Call the Eigse Festival office (tel. 40491) for more info.

■■■ KILKENNY TOWN

> There once were two cats from Kilkenny,
> Each thought there was one cat too many.
> So they fought and they hit,
> They scratched and they bit,
> 'Til instead of two cats there weren't any.

Touted as the best-preserved medieval town in Ireland, Kilkenny Town (pop. 19,000) is the modern incarnation of a Norman commercial center established in 1169. Following the British occupation of Ireland, it was said that the town's separate English and Irish communities scratched and hissed like "Kilkenny cats," a fable that their enmity inspired; even today Kilkennians call the Parliament St. area "Irish Town." But during the English Civil War, the Old English and the native feudal lords found common cause in Catholicism; they created the short-lived independent gov-

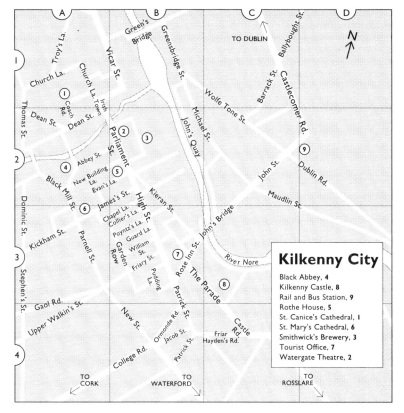

Kilkenny City

Black Abbey, **4**
Kilkenny Castle, **8**
Rail and Bus Station, **9**
Rothe House, **5**
St. Canice's Cathedral, **1**
St. Mary's Cathedral, **6**
Smithwick's Brewery, **3**
Tourist Office, **7**
Watergate Theatre, **2**

ernment called the Confederation of Kilkenny, between 1642 and Cromwell's invasion in 1649. Disagreements soon followed this attempt at cooperation; the two factions only joined administratively in 1844. Today, the town luxuriates in its affluence, evident in the boutiques and stately homes that line its pristine streets. Kilkenny's ancient architecture and rocking nightlife draw hordes of tourists—it's a not-to-be missed stop on everyone's southeast circuit.

ORIENTATION & PRACTICAL INFORMATION

The Castle dominates Kilkenny from the Parade. If you arrive at McDonagh Station, turn left on John St. and continue straight to reach The Parade. Otherwise, the town's main activity takes place in the triangle formed by Rose Inn St., High St., and Kieran St.

Tourist Office: Rose Inn St. (tel. 51500; fax 63955). Free maps. Demand the free *Kilkenny City and County Guide.* Open June-Sept. Mon.-Sat. 9am-6pm, Sun. 11am-5pm; Oct. Mon.-Sat. 9am-1pm and 2-5:30pm; Nov.-Feb. Tues.-Sat. 9am-1pm and 2-5:15pm; March-April Mon.-Sat. 9am-1pm and 2-5:15pm.

Financial Services: AIB Bank, The Parade (tel. 22089), at the intersection with High St. Open Mon. 10am-5pm, Tues.-Fri. 10am-4pm; **ATM. TSB,** High St. (tel. 22969). Open Mon.-Wed. and Fri. 9am-5:30pm, Thurs. 9am-7pm.

Post Office: High St. (tel. 21879). Open Mon.-Sat. 9am-5:30pm.

Phone Code: 056.

Trains: Everything stops at **McDonagh Station,** Dublin Rd. (for info call 22024). (Open Mon.-Sat. 8am-8pm, Sun. 10am-noon, 3-5pm, and 6:30-8:30pm; always staffed though ticket window opens only around departure times.) Kilkenny is on the main Dublin-Waterford rail route (Mon.-Sat. 4/day, Sun. 3/day; to Dublin, 2hr.; £9; to Waterford, 45 min.; £5; to Thomastown (south), 15 min.; £3).

Buses: McDonagh Station, Dublin Rd. (tel. 64933). Buses leave for: Clonmel (Mon.-Sat. 5/day, Sun. 3/day); Cork (3/day; 3hr.); Dublin (Mon.-Sat. 5/day, Sun. 4/day; £9); Galway (mid-June to mid-Sept. daily); Rosslare Harbour (mid-June to mid-Sept. daily); Thomastown (1/day); and Waterford (daily 5/day). **Buggy's Buses** (tel. 41264) run from Kilkenny to Castlecomer, with stops at Dunmore Cave and the An Óige hostel.

Hitching: Hitchhikers take N10 to Waterford, the Freshford Rd. to the N8 to get to Cashel, and N16 to go towards Dublin.

Taxi: K&M Cab (tel. 61333). £3 max. within the city.

Bike Rental: J.J. Wall Cycle, Maudlin St. (tel. 21236). £5/day; deposit £30.

Laundry: Brett's Launderette, Michael St. (tel. 63200). Wash and dry £4. Open Mon.-Sat. 8:30am-8pm. Last wash 7pm. Womb-like.

Pharmacy: Several on High St. Different one open Sun. according to a rotation system; check any pharmacy's door for the current one. Open Mon.-Sat. 9am-6pm.

Hospital: St. Luke's, Freshford Rd. (tel. 21133). Continue down Parliament St. to St. Canice's Cathedral, then turn right and take the first left to Vicar St.

Emergency: Dial 999; no coins required. **Garda:** Dominic St. (tel. 22222).

ACCOMMODATIONS

B&Bs average £12-14. Call ahead. Waterford Rd. and more remote Castlecomer Rd. have the highest concentration of beds.

Ormonde Tourist Hostel, Johns Green (tel. 52733), opposite the train station. This hostel boasts firm beds with floral duvets and a helpful staff. 24-hr. kitchen w/microwave. Laundry £4. Dorm £7, single £9, double £20; sheets free.

Kilkenny Town Hostel (IHH), 35 Parliament St. (tel. 63541). Clean, light, and bare rooms. Friendly, non-smoking environment; right next to the Smithwick's Brewery. Kitchen (7am-11pm) with microwave. Cyclist maps available. Checkout 10:30am. Laundry (wash and dry) £3. 4- to 8-bed room £5.50-6. Sept.-June: 50p discount to *Let's Go* readers, users, and abusers.

Foulksrath Castle (An Óige/HI), Jenkinstown (tel. 67674). Awesome 16th-century castle 8 mi. north of town. From Kilkenny, take the N77 (Durrow Rd.) and turn right at signs for Connahy. Buggy's Buses (tel. 41264) run from The Parade, Kilkenny to the hostel Mon.-Sat. at 11:30am and 5:30pm, leaving the hostel for Kilkenny Mon.-Sat. 8:25am and 3pm (20 min.; £1.50). Bike rental available. Dorm £5. Open all year.

Fennelly's B&B, 13 Parliament St. (tel. 61796), above the pub. Large, clean, floral rooms. Bathtub! Single £15, July-Aug. £20; double £27, £35 w/bath.

Church View B&B, 6 Dean St. (tel. 61734); it's over Siobhan's Café. Big beds in small rooms make sleeping comfortable, walking tough. TV in most rooms. £12.50/person, £15 w/bath; single £15.

Bregagh House B&B, Dean St. Handsome wood furniture and floral comforters; three stuffed quails. £13.50, £15.50 w/bath; in July-Aug., add £2. **Camping** in their giant backyard, with access to showers and toilets (£3).

Mrs. K. Dempsey, 26 James St. (tel. 21954). Geraniums, fluffy comforters, floral scent; soft carpets in cramped bedrooms. Two stuffed quails. £14, w/bath £16.

St. Mary's B&B, 25 James St. (tel. 22091). Renovations have brought bright rooms and a neat green carpet. £14/person, £16 w/bath.

Nore Valley Park, (tel. 27229), 6 mi. south of Kilkenny between Bennetsbridge and Stonyford, signposted from Kilkenny. A class act, with hot showers, laundry, and TV room. Hikers £2/person. Open March-Oct.

FOOD

The biggest grocery selection is in the **Super Quinn** (tel. 52444), in the new Market Cross shopping center off High St. (open Mon.-Wed. and Sat. 9am-6pm, Thurs.-Fri. 9am-9pm). Alternatively, stock up on supplies at the immense **Dunnes Supermarket,** several steps away from the tourist office (open Mon.-Wed. and Sat. 9am-6pm,

Thurs.-Fri. 9am-9pm). **Shortis Wong Delicatessen,** John St. (tel. 61305), sells noodles, spices, and canned, exotic, and baked foods (open Mon.-Sat. 9am-7pm, Sun. 10am-2:30pm).

Edward Lankton's, 69 John St. (tel. 65133). Voted the country's best pub food many, many times. Lunch menu (daily noon-3pm): steak sandwich £6.50, roast chicken £5.50. Dinner menu (daily 4:30-11pm) reaches double digits.

Italian Connection, 38 Parliament St. (tel. 64225). Gourmet Italian food in a mahogany setting colored with carnations. What more could you ask for? Lunch specials daily (noon-3pm). All pastas £5, pizzas £4-6. Open daily noon-11pm.

Kilkenny Kitchen, (tel. 22118), upstairs in the Kilkenny Design Centre across from the castle. A real swell cafeteria. Stuffed steak in red wine sauce, vegetables and potatoes £4.25, vegetarian quiche and salad £3.75, Irish whisky cake £1.35. Open Mon.-Sat. 9am-5pm, Sun. 10am-5pm.

M.l. Dore, High St. (tel. 63374), near Parliament St. A combo deli, restaurant, and bureau de change. Customers buried under copious ham or numerous knick-knacks. Soup and roll £1.15, roast chicken dinner £3.65. Open Mon.-Sat. 8am-11pm, Sun. 9am-11pm; evening meals served 5:30-10pm.

P.J. Crotty, 92 High St. (tel. 21099). Cafeteria-style restaurant with stunning sandwiches, breakfast, and pastries. Irish breakfast £3, cottage pie £3, banana milkshake 60p. Open Mon.-Sat. 8:30am-6pm.

PUBS

Pump House Bar, 26 Parliament St. (tel. 63924). Crammed with hostelers from across the street, this is a pub for the enthusiastic reveler. Throbbing rock music spills into the street; live rock bands play Thurs. nights.

Cleere's Pub, 28 Parliament St. (tel. 62573). Thespians converge for nightly poetry readings, improv comedy, and traditional and folk sessions. Tickets for some acts cost £3-5, discounts for students.

Kyteler's Inn, St. Kieran St. (tel 21064). This historical pub has a witch in the basement and butcher-blocks for tables. Mixed ages gather for food and *craic* in a relaxed atmosphere.

Fennelly's, 13 Parliament St. (tel. 64337), hosts an older crowd in its homey confines. Trad sessions Fri. nights during July and Aug. During the day, watch the House of Commons on their TV.

Lautrec's Wine Bar, St. Kieran St. (tel. 62720). From 5:30pm until the wee hours, serves wine in a dark, cavernous, French setting. Pub crawlers crawl here after pub closing time.

Maggie's, St. Kieran St. (tel. 62273), hosts trad music on Tuesday nights and live contemporary on Wed. Usually a younger crowd.

Caisleán Uí Cuain, 2 High St. (tel. 65406), at the intersection with the Parade. High-grade pub grub in a classy lounge (Greek salad £4.50, club sandwich £5; lunch served 12:30-3pm). Traditional music Mon. nights.

SIGHTS

All of central Kilkenny is a sight; most of the buildings have preserved their medieval appearance. **Tynan Walking Tours** (tel. 65929) is an excellent introduction to the juicy stories of the town's past. Tours depart from the tourist office on Rose Inn St. (mid-March-Oct. Mon.-Sat. 6/day, Sun. 4/day; £2.50, students £2). **The City Scope Exhibition** (tel. 51500), upstairs at the tourist office, shows city life in miniature. A detailed model of the city is used to show the changes in life and housing through the years. But the *real* city is right outside. (30-min. show Mon.-Fri. 9am-12:45pm, 2-6pm; Sat. 9am-12:45pm, 2-5:30pm; Sun. 11am-1pm, 2-5pm; £1, students 80p.)

Thirteenth-century **Kilkenny Castle,** The Parade (tel. 21450; fax 63488), housed the Earls of Ormonde until 1932. The Spencers—remote ancestors of Princess Di—sold it to them in the 1300s. A walk inside evokes images of swishing velvet robes and clashing swords. Many rooms have been restored to their former opulence: ogle the Long Room with its highly ornamented ceiling, designed like a Viking ship, and with portraits of English bigwigs, including that frumpy duo, William and Mary. In the basement, the **Butler Gallery** mounts modern art exhibitions. This level also houses a **café** in the castle's kitchen and shelters the castle's ghost, the spirit of a girl burned at the stake by the enlightened townsfolk. The formal flower garden and park adjoining the castle are beautifully maintained. (Castle and gallery open June-Sept. daily 10am-7pm; Oct.-March Tues.-Sat. 10:30am-5pm, Sun. 11am-5pm; Apr.-May daily 10:30am-5pm; access by guided tour only; £3, students £1. Gardens open daily 10am-8:30pm; free.) **The Kilkenny Design Centre** (tel. 22118) fills the castle's old stables with expensive and fine Irish crafts. (Open April-Dec. Mon.-Sat. 9am-6pm, Sun. 10am-6pm; Jan.-March Mon.-Sat. 9am-6pm.)

A Tudor merchant house built in 1594, **Rothe House,** Parliament St. (tel. 22893), is now a small museum of local archaeological finds and Kilkennian curiosities. The tour takes you through the three connected buildings, introducing the lifestyles of the 16th-century rich and famous. The Rothes were Kilkennian bigwigs, serving as sheriffs and mayors, and their banquet hall remains impressive. Exhibits show frightening dinner sporks. (Open April-Oct. Mon.-Sat. 10:30am-5pm, Sun. 3-5pm; Nov.-March Sat.-Sun. 3-5pm; £1.50, students £1.)

Kilkenny is blessed with legions of religious architecture. The finest is 13th-century **St. Canice's Cathedral;** the stone-step approach from Irishtown is lined with fragments of old sculpture from the cathedral itself, which was sacked by Cromwell's merry men. The name "Kilkenny" itself is derived from the Irish *Cill Chainnigh,* meaning "Church of St. Canice." Inside the church, medieval tombstones are embedded in the floor and walls. (Open daily 10am-6pm, except during services; cathedral free, donation requested.) The 100-foot-high tower, near the south transept, is a relic of the earlier 6th-century Church of St. Canice. For an additional 50p (students 20p), you can climb the series of steep ladders inside for a fine view of the town and its surroundings. **The Black Abbey,** off Abbey St., was founded in 1225 and got its name from the black habits of its Dominican friars. Within the heavy stone structure a fiery modern stained-glass window contrasts with older, subtler ones. Nearby **St. Mary's** is a lofty, narrow cathedral built in 1849 and hung with paintings of the Passion framed in gold leaf.

Crafty 14th-century monks are said to have brewed a light ale in St. Francis' Abbey; appropriately, the abbey's yard now contains the **Smithwicks Brewery** on Parliament St. The abbey is in ruins, but its industry survives: Smithwicks Brewery offers an audio-visual show and ale tasting. Smithwicks itself is a tasty brew (naturally best in Kilkenny), but the company also profanes the abbey by brewing Budweiser there. (Tours July-Aug. Mon.-Fri. 3pm; tourist office distributes free tickets.)

ENTERTAINMENT

The Kilkenny People is a good source for arts and music listings. **The Watergate Theatre,** Parliament St. (tel. 61674), puts on traditional Irish plays. (Tickets usually £5, students £3. Booking office open daily 10am-8pm). The anachronistic may wish to contact **The Order of Druids:** their Chief Scribe is at 18 Kickham St.

The last week of August is **Kilkenny Arts Week,** which has a daily program of concerts, recitals, poetry readings, and exhibitions by some of Ireland's top artists. Admission varies for individual events (free-£7; student tickets available); a week-long ticket costs £75, £65 before July 31 (student discounts available). Buy tickets from Kilkenny Arts Week at Rothe House, Parliament St. (tel. 63663), or the tourist office. For your comedy needs, visit Kilkenny in early June for the **Cat Laughs** (tel. 51254), a week-long festival that hosts Irish, English, and American comedians.

■ NEAR KILKENNY TOWN: DUNMORE CAVE

North of Kilkenny, on the road to Castlecomer, lurks the massive **Dunmore Cave** (office tel. (056) 67726), known as "the darkest place in Ireland." It contains fascinating, varied limestone formations. Recently unearthed human bones show that 40 people died underground here in 928 AD, hiding from marauding Vikings. (Open mid-June to mid-Sept. daily 10am-7pm; mid-Sept.-Oct. daily 10am-6pm; Nov.-Feb.

Sat.-Sun. 10am-5pm; mid-March to mid-June Tues.-Sat. 10am-5pm, Sun. 2-5pm. Last admission 45 min. before closing. £2, students £1.) There is no direct public transport to the cave, but **Buggy's Buses** (tel. (056) 41264) runs a bus between Kilkenny and Castle Comer that passes nearby (4/day; ask ahead of time to stop here). Or take N78 (Dublin Rd.) from Kilkenny; the turn-off for the cave, on the right, is after the split with N77 (Durrow Rd.).

County Tipperary

Trek south from Kilkenny Town or west from Waterford City to reach the medieval remains in south Tipperary, where Clonmel, Cahir, and Cashel bolster a plethora of castles and cathedrals. North Tipperary is a long way from the beaten tourist track, and for good reason—its acres are fertile, but not fascinating unless you're a farmer. From Cashel, keep going west until you reach Co. Kerry, or drop down south for a walk in the underrated Comeragh, Galtee, or Knockmealdown Mountains on your way to Co. Cork. Although Lismore is actually located in Co. Waterford, it is in this chapter along with the nearby Knockmealdown Mountains.

■■■ TIPPERARY TOWN

Good-bye to Piccadilly,/Farewell to Leicester Square.
It's a long way to Tipperary/And my heart lies there.

If the song is right, then you've come a long way for nothing. Tourists who don't know better go out of their way to see Tipperary, assuming that the famously-named town is as exciting as the World War I marching song. But "Tipp Town," as it's affectionately known, is primarily a market town for the region's fertile Golden Vale farming region. Compared with the surrounding area which can insinuate itself into your heart on a sunny day, Tipp Town itself is depressing.

Skip Tipp and head for the nearby **Glen of Aherlow** (above). The **tourist office** on James St., just off Main St. (tel. 51457), is a useful resource for trips into the nearby mountains. (Open Mon.-Fri. 9:30am-6pm.) **AIB** bank is on Main St. (open Mon.-Fri. 10am-12:30pm and 1:30-4pm; **ATM).** The **post office** hides on Davis St. (open Mon.-Fri. 9am-5:30pm, Sat. 9am-noon and 1-5:30pm). Tipp's **phone code** marches into war whistling "062."

The best B&B in Tipp is the aptly-named **Central B&B**, 45 Main St. (tel. 51117), which has a welcoming owner and spacious rooms—one boasts a four-poster brass and wrought-iron bed frame (£14/person, w/bath £15). Other B&B possibilities are on the Emly Rd. about ½ mile from town. Walk west down Main St. and continue straight. **The Brown Trout,** Abbey St. (tel. 51912), on the corner of the road to the Glen of Aherlow, has surprisingly reasonable prices (grilled trout £3.50) considering its chandelier, spanky red tablecloths, and multiple sets of flatware (open daily 12:30-3pm and 6-9:30pm).

You'll find hearty Irish food at the **Butler's Pantry** (tel. 51788), down Main St. just before the turnoff for Clonmel Rd. Meals come served in a diner-like atmosphere complete with vinyl booths. (Roast lamb, potato, and veggies £4. Open Mon.-Fri. 9:30am-8pm, Sat. noon-3pm, Sun. noon-6pm.) Fortunately, there is a full-scale **SuperValu** on Main St. (open Mon.-Wed. and Sat. 9am-6pm, Thurs. and Fri. 9am-9pm). Youth congregate in the **Underground Tavern,** James St., which looks a bit like a bankrupt winery with wine barrels that now function as tables (rock and pop Thurs., Sat., and Sun.). **Corny's Pub,** Davitt St. (later it becomes Limerick Rd., and even later Church St.) plays nightly trad that attracts an older crowd.

■■■ CASHEL

Truly magical when seen from a distance, the commanding **Rock of Cashel** rises above the town of Cashel. Three hundred feet above the plain, the dark limestone hill bristles with an elaborate complex of medieval buildings. The efficient **tourist office** shares space with the Heritage Centre in the recently renovated Cashel City Hall, Main St. (tel. 62511; open July-Aug. daily 9:30am-8pm; March-June daily 9:30am-5:30pm; Sept.-Feb. Mon.-Sat. 9:30am-5:30pm, Sun. noon-5:30pm). The **Cashel Holiday Hostel,** 6 John St. (tel. 62330), is also a **Rent-A-Bike depot,** which means that bikes can be rented here and returned elsewhere (£6/day, £30/week; deposit £30). **AIB** bank, Main St., does currency exchange and has an **ATM.** (Open Mon.-Wed. and Fri. 10am-12:30pm and 1:30-4pm, Thurs. 10am-12:30pm and 1:30-5pm.) The **post office** is also on Main St. (open Mon.-Fri. 9am-1pm and 2-5:30pm, Sat. 9am-1pm). Cashel's commanding **phone code** is 062.

Cashel lies inland between Waterford and Cork, tucked behind a series of mountain ranges on N8 from Cork to Dublin. **Bus Éireann** (tel. 62121) leaves from O'Reilly's on Main St., serving Dublin (3/day; 3hr.; £9, students £6.50), Cork (3/day; 1½hr.; £8, students £5.30), Limerick (4/day; £8.90, students £5), and Cahir (4/day; 15 min.; £2.40, students £2). Bus transport to Waterford is available via Cahir. Hitching to Cork or Dublin along N8 is a breeze; thumbing west to Tipp and Limerick on N74 is also feasible.

Accommodations Contributing greatly to the town's appeal as a backpackers' base, Cashel is graced with two excellent hostels. The **Cashel Holiday Hostel,** 6 John St. (tel. 62330), just off Main St., is extremely comfortable, with spacious bedrooms, a light-bathed kitchen, and an informative, gregarious staff. Their hints on the area's natural and archaeological sights have been known to keep backpackers in Cashel for an extended stay. (Laundry £3. Rent-A-Bike depot. 4- to 8-bed dorm £6; 4-bed dorm w/bath £7; private room £8/person. Key deposit £3.) **O'Brien's Farmhouse Hostel,** off Dundrum Rd. (tel. 61003; from town, make the first left after the Rock), is set in the shadow of the Rock with views of Hore Abbey. A large stone-walled kitchen and substantial beds fertilize its appeal. (Wash and dry £5. 6-bed dorm £6, private room £9; **camping** £3.50/person w/out use of hostel facilities.) The Rock attracts a fair number of tourists to Cashel, a fact reflected in the high quality (and high price) of local B&Bs. Just steps from the Rock on Moor Lance, you *can* go back to **Rockville House** (tel. 61760), which does credit to its outstanding location with crisp bedrooms.

Food & Pubs You can get anything you want at **Alice's Bistro,** 105 Main St. (tel. 62170), where an omelette and chips cost £3.75 (open daily 9am-10pm). **The Bake House,** across from the Heritage Centre on Main St. and upstairs from a bakery, is the town's best spot for scones, coffee, and light meals (open Mon.-Sat. 9am-9pm, Sun. 11am-7pm). **The Spearman Restaurant,** 97 Main St. (tel. 61143), offers a delicious but costly break from the brown-bread diet. (Open daily noon-2:30pm and 5-9:30pm. Sandwiches £1.50; dinner prices higher.) **SuperValu Supermarket,** Main St., offers the biggest selection of groceries (Mon.-Sat. 8am-9pm, Sun. 9am-6pm), while **Centra Supermarket** on Friar St. is open latest (daily 7am-10:30pm).

Good *craic* and nightly music entice locals to the best pub in Cashel, **Feehan's,** Main St. (tel. 61929; trad bands Tues. and Wed., trad session Thurs., Take a Chance on Fri.-Mon.). **O'Sullivan's,** across the street at 9 Main St. (tel. 61858), serves popular pints. Staid and well-appointed, **Dowling's,** 46 Main St. (tel. 62130), attracts a mixed crowd with trad music on Wednesdays.

Sights The elevated **Rock of Cashel** is a huge limestone outcrop dominated by a complex of secular and ecclesiastical buildings on top. The Rock itself has a number of legends, some historically substantiated and others of dubious origin, attached to it (see The Legendary Rock, below). On the Rock, **Cormac's Chapel,** a majestic, dual-towered structure, was consecrated in 1134. The interior displays ornate Romanesque carvings and a richly decorated sarcophagus, once thought to be in the tomb of King Cormac. A highlight of Cashel's illustrious history was the reported burning of the chapel by the Earl of Kildare in 1495. When Henry VII demanded an explanation, the Earl replied, "I thought the Archbishop was in it." Henry made him Lord Deputy. The 13th-century **Cashel Cathedral** survived the Earl, and though its vaulted Gothic arches no longer buttress a roof, the cathedral is unequalled in its grandeur. Beside the Rock, the 90-foot-high **round tower** is the oldest part of the Rock, probably dating from just after 1101.

The museum at the entrance to the castle complex preserves the 13th-century **St. Patrick's Cross.** Kings of Munster were crowned on the site marked by the *croix faux.* Access to much of the Rock is limited. (Rock open mid-June to mid-Sept. daily 9am-7:30pm; mid-March to mid-June 9:30am-5:30pm; mid-Sept. to mid-March 9:30am-4:30pm. Last admission 40 min. before closing. £2.50, students £1.) Far from the madding crowd and down the cowpath from the Rock, **Hore Abbey** looms silently. The last Cistercian monastery to be established in Ireland, its ruins are open, free, and afford a striking view of the Rock.

Heritage Centre, on Main St. (tel. 35362), will re-open in 1996. Exhibitions (both permanent and temporary) will include "Rock: From 4th to 11th century" and "Rock: 12th-18th century" with temporary exhibitions on such themes as Hore Abbey, Cashel Palace, and "Life in Cashel." (Open July-Aug. daily 9:30am-8pm; March-June daily 9:30am-5:30pm; Sept.-Feb. Mon.-Sat. 9:30am-5:30pm, Sun. noon-5:30pm; prices have not been set.) In Cashel proper, the **GPA-Bolton Library** (tel. 61944), on John St. past the hostel, displays a musty collection of books and silver formerly belonging to an Anglican archbishop of Cashel, Theophilus Bolton. The collection harbors ecclesiastical texts and rare fictional manuscripts, including a 1550 edition of Machiavelli's *Il Principe* and the first English translation of *Don Quixote.* (For a tour, call tel. (062) 61232; £2.50, students £1.50.) The **Brú Ború Heritage Centre** (tel. 61122), at the base of the Rock, performs Irish traditional music, song, and dance to international acclaim. (Performances June 15-Sept. 15 Tues.-Sat. at 9pm; £5.) Five miles west of Cashel on Tipperary Rd. stand the ruins of golden **Althassel Abbey,** a 12th-century Augustinian priory founded by the Red Earl of Dunster.

The Legendary Rock

The seat of Munster's Kingship since the days of the ancient Érainn (about 1-700 AD), the Rock was held for centuries by the Eóganacht (later MacCarthy) clan. They challenged the "High Kings" at Tara until subordinated to the Dál Cais king (Brian Ború's brother) in 859. Although Brian retained the title "King of Cashel," his real power was consolidated along the Shannon. (In legend, St. Patrick visited Cashel to baptize a fictional Eóganacht king, and accidentally pierced the king's foot with his pointy pastoral staff. The king didn't complain, thinking the injury part of the ceremony.) Cashel didn't become an ecclesiastical center until after 1101, when King Muirchertach O'Brien donated the site to the Church, thus ensuring the loyalty of the Irish church and rendering the Eóganacht powerless at the same time. Over the next few centuries, local political and ecclesiastical powers subsequently added to the construction on the Rock, creating a Gothic cathedral crammed between a round tower and a Romanesque chapel which, incredibly enough, fails to look incongruous.

■■■ CAHIR

"Cahir" (pronounced "care") means "city" in Irish, but the settlement is more a busy square (and one busy castle) than it is a city. The town's two prominent sights, Cahir Castle and the Swiss Cottage, can be explored in a few hours. Those planning on spending some time in the area should consider basing themselves in more scenic and hostel-blessed (and more pronounceable) Cashel.

C A H I R

Practical Information The well-signposted **tourist office,** Castle St. (tel. (052) 41453), knows surprisingly little about the mountains surrounding the town, but they do sell invaluable, if expensive, maps. (Open June-Sept. Mon.-Sat. 9:30am-6pm, Sun. 11am-5pm.) **Bus Éireann** runs from the tourist office to Limerick via Tipperary and to Waterford via Clonmel (both daily 7/day; Limerick 1hr., £7.30, students £4.20; Waterford 1¼hr., £7.70, students £4.30), also to Cork (4/day; 1½ hr.; £7, students £5), to Dublin (Mon.-Sat. 5/day, Sun. 4/day; 3 hr.; £10, students £7.50), and to Cashel (15 min.; £2.50, students £2). **Trains** leave from the station off Cashel Rd., just past the church, for Limerick and Rosslare (Mon.-Sat 1/day). **Hitchers** to Dublin or Cork station themselves on N8, which involves a 20-minute hike from the center of town. Those hoping to hitch to Limerick and Waterford wait just outside of town on N24 (Limerick/Waterford Rd.) which passes through the town square.

There are two hostels in the countryside, relatively close to Cahir. **Lisakyle Hostel (IHH)** (tel. (052) 41963), one mile south of Cahir on Ardfinnan Rd., is the more accessible of the two. The accommodations are truly rustic; even Wonderbras have more padding than the beds at this hostel (£6; **camping** £3.50). Reserve yourself a bed here at **Condon's Shop** on Church St., across from the post office. Condon's will also arrange lifts to the hostel. The **Kilcoran Farm Hostel (IHH)** (tel. (052) 41906) promises to be an education in rural living, with vocal sheep out back and an impressive collection of rusting farm tools. All rooms, singles or doubles, go for £6/person. From Cahir, take Cork Rd. for four miles, turn left at the Top Petrol Station, go ¼ mile, then veer right at the T-shaped junction. **Spring Hill,** along Cashel Rd. (tel. (052) 41754), is one of the better B&Bs (single or double £14.50).

For groceries, the best bet is **SuperValu Supermarket,** Bridge St., across the bridge from the castle (tel. (052) 41515; open Mon.-Wed. 9am-6pm, Thurs. 9am-8pm, Fri. 9am-9pm, Sat. 9am-7pm). The **Italian Connection,** Castle St. (tel. (052) 42152), serves bountiful plates of pasta (£5) on red tablecloths. (Open daily noon-11pm.) The **Roma Café,** Church St. (tel. (052) 41504), has late-night take-away and sit-down carbohydrates (cheese pizza £2.30; open daily noon-1am).

For an innocuous-looking town that panders to tourists, Cahir has a bizarre biker following. Consequently, it fosters a number of biker bars. Compare tattoos at **Black Tom's,** on the Limerick Rd. past SuperValu, a favorite among Tipperary's leather set that features live rock on weekends. **J. Morrissey,** on Castle St. across from the tourist office, holds traditional sessions every Tuesday night. **Galtee Inn,** Church St., and the **Castle Arms,** across from the tourist office on Castle St., attract fewer Harleys and more well-dressed ex-yuppies and older locals. They probably drive mopeds.

Cahir defines itself, physically and metaphysically, by **Cahir Castle** (tel. (052) 41011), one of the larger and better preserved castles in Ireland. It is exactly what every tourist envisions a castle to be—heavy, wet, and gray—which must be why so many tourists come to reinforce their preconceptions. Climb the towers for an unparalleled view of the tourist office and parking lot. (Open mid-June to mid-Sept. daily 9am-7:30pm; April to mid-June and mid-Sept. to mid-Oct. 10am-6pm; Nov.-March daily 10am-1pm and 2-4:30pm. £2, seniors and students £1. Last admission 30 min. before closing.)

The broad River Suir that flows into Waterford Harbour is still a mere stream in Cahir. The wildly green **river walk** follows it from the tourist office to the 19th-century **Swiss Cottage** (tel. (052) 41144) and beyond. Consisting of a charming jumble of architectural styles, the luxurious house approximates an aristocratic conception of the simple life. (Open May-Sept. Tues.-Sun. 10am-6pm; April 10am-1pm and 2-5pm; March and Oct.-Nov. 10am-1pm and 2-4:30pm. £2, students £1. Last admission 40 min. before closing. Wheelchair access.)

Fishing opportunities abound along the river walk past the Swiss Cottage: locals feed their families out of this river. Fishing licenses are required. For information, and for a free fly-tying demonstration, contact celebrated fly-tyer **Alice Conba,** Old Church St. (tel. 42348). Ms. Conba exhibits her framed, individually signed flies and is eager to enlighten individuals about her craft. Her collection includes dry flies, hair-winged salmon flies, and a unique gift idea: "beautifully crafted Fly Brooches."

■ NEAR CAHIR

The **Mitchelstown Caves** (tel. (052) 67246) drip two miles off the Cahir-Cork road in the town of Burncourt, about halfway between Cahir and Mitchelstown. The perfunctory tour lasts only 30 minutes, but the subterranean formations are so impressive that you leave in awe anyway. The stalactites and stalagmites formed over millions of years from rainwater filtering through the porous limestone. The dripping water deposited bits of rock in rippled, gooey structures. (Open daily 10am-6pm; £2.50.) Located about three miles from the caves, the tiny village of **Ballyporeen** has the dubious distinction of being home to Ronald Reagan's ancestors, now buried at Templetenny Cemetery in the village. (It's a pleasant enough village, despite its rather unfortunate associations.)

The **Galtee Mountains** rise abruptly from the flatlands due west of Cahir. The purplish range boasts Galtymore among its peaks, at 3654 feet Ireland's third-highest mountain. The north climb is most difficult. Serious hikers should invest in one of the excellent Ordnance Survey maps at the tourist office or local bookstore (£4.10). The *New Irish Walk Guides* have maps and routes for the Galtees, along with all the other mountains in the region (available in bookstores). Glenbarra is a popular base camp, accessible by driving west from Cahir towards Mitchelstown.

The **Glen of Aherlow (Ballydavid Wood) Youth Hostel (An Óige/HI)** (tel. (062) 54148), six miles northwest of Cahir off Limerick Rd. (signposted) is a renovated old hunting lodge. It makes a good home for trouncing around the Galtees. Bike hire available. (June-Sept. £6, March-May and Oct.-Nov. £5.50.) On occasion, dedicated hikers make the 10-mile trek across the mountains to the **Mountain Lodge (An Óige/HI),** Burncourt (tel. (052) 67277), a gas-lit Georgian hunting lodge in the middle of the woods. From Cahir, follow the Mitchelstown Rd. eight miles, turn right at the sign for another two miles on an unpaved path. (No showers. £5.50/person.) The **Kilcoran Farm Hostel** (tel. (052) 41906) also makes a convenient hiking home (see Cahir, p. 163). The campsite in the Glen of Aherlow, **Ballinacourty House** (tel. (062) 56230), is excellent. The staff provides detailed information on the Glen. (£6.25/tent, plus £1/person. Meals and cooking facilities available. Open April to mid-Sept.) They also operate a pleasant B&B and restaurant (double £16/person).

■ ■ ■ CLONMEL

Clonmel (pop. 16,000) derives its name from the Irish *Cluian Meala,* "the honey meadow." This medieval town on the banks of the River Suir ("sure"), bordered by the Comeragh Mountains, does have something sweet about it. Locally produced Bulmer's cider fills the air with sweet apple scents in the fall, and the *New York Times* recently declared the town the "optimism capital of Ireland." Clonmel now keeps itself plugging along as the county town of Co. Tipperary as well as the commercial center of its southern half.

ORIENTATION & PRACTICAL INFORMATION

The town's central street runs parallel to the Suir. From the station, follow Prior Park Rd. straight to Parnell St. and turn right. It becomes Mitchell St., O'Connell St., and eventually Irishtown. Businesslike Gladstone St. intersects O'Connell St.

Tourist Office: Nelson St. (tel. 22960), between the river and Parnell St. Open Mon.-Fri. 9:30am-5:30pm, Sat. 10am-4pm. Pick up the excellent *Clonmel and South Tipperary Guide* (free). "Self-guided walking tours" of Clonmel and the Nire Valley are printed on green-and-orange waterproof sheets (50p).

Bank: AIB bank, O'Connell St. (tel. 22500). Full services, including **ATM** that accepts all major cash systems.

Post Office: Emmet St. (tel. 21164), parallel to Gladstone St. Open Mon.-Fri. 9am-5pm, Sat. 9am-1pm.

CLONMEL

Phone Code: 052.

Trains: Prior Park Rd., a continuation of Gladstone St. farther north of the river. Train information (tel. 21982). Trains chug here twice a day between Limerick and Rosslare Harbour via Waterford. You'll change in Waterford (£6.50) or Limerick Junction (£11) before going anywhere else.

Buses: Bus information available at **Rafferty Travel** on Gladstone St. (tel. 22622). Open Mon.-Sat. 9am-6pm. Buses head to Clonmel from Cork (daily 3/day; £8, students £4.90), Dublin (daily 3/day; £8, students £6), Galway (Mon.-Fri. 5/day, Sun. 3/day; £12, students £7.50), Kilkenny via Carrick-on-Suir (Mon.-Sat. 4/day, Sun. 3/day; £3.50), Limerick via Tipperary (daily 5/day; £8.80, students £5), Rosslare (£10, students £6), and Waterford via Carrick-on-Suir (Mon.-Sat. 8/day, Sun. 5/day; £5.90, students £3.50).

Pharmacy: Joy's, 68 O'Connell St. (tel. 21204). Open Mon.-Sat. 9am-6pm.

Hospitals: St. Joseph's/St. Michael's, Western Rd. (tel. 21900).

Emergency: Dial 999 (no coins required). **Garda:** Emmet St. (tel. 22222).

ACCOMMODATIONS

Those intending to explore the Comeragh Mountains stay at **Powers-the-Pot Hostel,** Harney's Cross (tel. 23085), five miles uphill from Clonmel in the gorgeous Nire Valley. Following Parnell St. east out of town, turn right onto Waterford Rd. (not N24), crossing the Suir and continuing straight for four miles of arduous mountain road, to the signposted turnoff. Coming from Waterford on N24, Waterford Rd. is left at the first traffic light in Clonmel. Or call the hostel to arrange an evening pick-up. (Laundry; maps and walking guides for the Munster Way; freezing and smoking facilities for anglers. Dorm £5; **camping** £3/person. Open May to mid-Oct.)

The area past Irishtown, along the Cahir Rd. and Abbey Rd., is graced with numerous **B&Bs.** The options are relatively extensive in Clonmel, provided that you're willing to walk a mile or two to town. In Clonmel proper, gracious **Riverside House,** on New Quay overlooking the Suir (tel. 25781), entertains its guests with access to the river, and if all else fails, in-room BBC (£12.50/person).

FOOD & PUBS

Grocery shopping is a surreal experience at **Crazy Prices** on Gladstone St. (open Mon.-Tues. 9am-7pm, Wed.-Fri. 9am-9pm, Sat. 9am-6pm). **The Honey Pot,** Abbey St. (tel. 21457), sells health foods and bulk grains. Organic vegetable sellers parade their wares here on Fridays. (Open Mon.-Sat. 9:30am-6pm.)

Feathered Lane Café, Gladstone St. (tel. 26555), top floor of the Post House Bookshop. A cozy clone of the literary Winding Stair bookshop/café in Dublin. Tandoori chicken and two side salads £2.75, shepherd's pie £2.75. Open Mon.-Sat. 9am-6pm.

Busy Bees Bistro, Abbey St. (tel. 26899), on a side street between Parnell St. and New Quay. Well-prepared, healthy wholefood served on country pine tables make this Clonmel's "alternative" oasis. Less cerebral, but appreciably hipper than the Feathered Lane (French bread pizza £2.45; open Mon.-Sat. 9am-6pm).

Tom Skinny's Pizza Parlor, 4 Gladstone St. (tel. 26006). Bears a suspiciously close resemblance to fast food, but the pizza and ice cream are tasty. Mud pie £2, banana milkshake £1. Open daily noon-midnight.

Niamh's, Mitchel St. (tel. 25698). Locals love this comfortable and efficient deli/restaurant. Serves hot lunches, sandwiches, and Irish breakfast all day.

Tierney's, O'Connell St. (tel. 24467), is resplendent with wood panelling and polished brass. This may be the clubbiest, most luxurious pub in Ireland. With a restaurant upstairs and meals served all day, it feels less like a pub and more like a cushy club. For less genteel *craic*, the **Market Tavern,** Kickham St. (tel. 22838), off Gladstone St., is the favorite youth hangout. A disco club throbs here Friday to Sunday nights 9:30-11:30pm. Check *The Nationalist* for entertainment listings.

SIGHTS

A battery of **walking tours** are described in the tourist office's glossy leaflets *Clonmel Walk #1 and #2* (50p apiece), in the fat *Clonmel and South Tipperary* (free), and in the orange *Clonmel and the Nire* (£2.50). See Comeragh Mountains, p. 167, for day hike info. **West Gate**, straddling the west end of O'Connell St., was built in 1831 on the site of the old west gate by a rich, nostalgic citizen. **Old St. Mary's Church**, Irishtown, built in 1204, has an 84-foot-high octagonal bell tower and stained-glass windows. In the 1800s, **Hearn's Hotel** on Parnell St., was the nexus of Clonmel Mayor Bianconi's huge horsecart business, which competed successfully with the train in the 1850s. The **Franciscan Friary**, on Abbey St. between Parnell St. and the Quay, has housed the tomb of the Lords of Cahir since the 13th century though most of the current structure dates from the 1880s.

    Tipperary S. R. County Museum, Parnell St. (tel. 25399), has an art gallery featuring work of local artists as well as traveling exhibitions with no real relevance to Clonmel. More intriguing is the gallery upstairs, which concentrates on somewhat esoteric facets of local history—including relics of Carrick-on-Suir's prodigal cyclist Sean Kelly. (Open Tues.-Sat. 10am-1pm and 2-5pm; free.)

∎∎∎ THE MUNSTER WAY

The Munster Way footpath starts in Carrick-on-Suir, hits Clonmel, bypasses the Comeragh Mountains, and instead hits the Knockmealdowns full-force. It currently ends at the Vee Gap, eight miles north of Lismore. The best **map** to use for the Munster Way is sheet 22 of the 1:126,720 Ordnance Survey series.

COMERAGH MOUNTAINS

Nire Valley Walk #1 and 2, 50p apiece at the Clonmel tourist office, are excellent waterproof maps explaining Comeragh day hikes from Clonmel. For more extensive hikes, begin from **Powers-the-Pot Hostel**, ½ mile off the Munster Way (see Clonmel, p. 165). Other trails begin nearby and pass through the village of **Ballymacarby**, on the Clonmel/Dungarvan Rd. (R671), where B&B is available at the **Nire Valley Farmhouse** (tel. (052) 36149; £13/person, w/bath £14/person; open June-Aug.).

    The technical term for the mountain hollows so common in the mild Comeraghs is "cwms" (pronounced "kooms"). It's the only word in the English language without a vowel. From Powers-the-Pot, several trails wind through the mountains. Tony O'Brien's *Clonmel and The Nire* is the best guide to the area available (£2.50). The best **map** is the *Walking Guide to the Comeragh Mountains and the Nire Valley*, available in the Lismore and Clonmel tourist offices for a steep £8. If you're willing to wing it, head east from the hostel and follow the ridges south. The land is mostly open, and in good weather it's relatively hard to get lost.

KNOCKMEALDOWN MOUNTAINS

Straddling the Tipperary/Waterford border 12 miles south of Cahir, the Knockmealdown Mountains rise in a rippling wave. The spectacular **Vee Road** from Clogheen to Lismore encounters a series of switchbacks on its way to **Knockmealdown Gap**. About two-thirds of the way to the top, the pines give way to heather and bracken, and the remainder of the climb is scenic but treacherous for hikers. At the pass, a parking lot marks the path up to the top of **Sugarloaf Hill**. The walk takes about an hour and affords a panorama of patchwork fields on a clear day. From there, you can continue on to the Knockmealdown Peak, the highest in the range at 2,609 feet. Beautiful (and supposedly bottomless) **Bay Loch**, on the road down to Lismore, is the stuff of legend. The affable and decidedly unofficious **tourist office** in Clogheen (tel. (052) 65258; across from the Vee Rd. turnoff) is generous with local maps and lore (open Mon.-Sat. 10am-6pm). Descending from the gap to Lismore, the left fork to Cappoquin (R669) will bring you to **Mount Melleray Youth Hostel** (An Óige/HI;

tel. (058) 59390; £5.50/person; open June-Sept.). The idyllic **Kilmorna Farm Hostel** in Lismore (tel. (058) 54315) makes a far more luxurious if somewhat less convenient base for hiking in the range (see Lismore, below). Five minutes from the village on Cahir Rd., **camping** is available in **Clogheen** at **Parsons Green** (tel. (052) 65290), which is part gardens and part campsite. (Kitchen; laundry £2; £6/2-person tent.)

LISMORE

The disproportionate grandeur of Lismore's castle and cathedral reminds visitors that in the 8th century, the endearingly small town was a thriving center of monastic learning. Lismore, Co. Waterford still straddles the aptly named Blackwater River at the end of Vee Rd., across the Knockmealdowns from Cahir. **Bus Éireann** stops at O'Dowd's Bar on West St. and runs to Dungarvan (Mon.-Sat. 1/day; ½hr.), Waterford (Mon.-Sat. 1/day; 1¼ hr.), and Cork (Mon.-Sun. 1/day; 1¼hr.). The best way to get to Lismore is by foot or by bike, over the Vee or along the Blackwater River. **Hitching** to Dungarvan is also relatively easy. To get to Cork, hitchers first ride east to Fermoy, then south on N8. Lismore's **tourist office** (tel. (058) 54975) is in the Interpretive Centre (open June-Aug. Mon.-Sat. 9:30am-5:30pm, Sun. noon-5:30pm; April-May, and Sept. Mon.-Fri. 10am-5pm, Sun. 2-5:30pm; Oct. Sun. 2-5:30pm).

Swathed in foliage and standing over the Blackwater River, **Lismore Castle** is stunning. Once a medieval fort and bishop's residence, the castle was extensively rebuilt and remodeled in the 19th century into a romantic's ideal of a castle. In 1814, the Lismore Crozier and the *Book of Lismore*, two priceless artifacts thought to have been lost forever, were found hidden in the castle walls. Once home to Sir Walter Raleigh, the castle was also the birthplace of 17th-century scientist Robert Boyle (of chemistry-textbook, PV=nRT, fame). The castle is privately owned (occasionally accommodating guests at about £10,000/week). Admire the castle from the bridge over the Blackwater River, because its gardens are not worth their admission fee. (Lismore Castle Gardens tel. (058) 54424; open daily 1:45-4:45pm; £2.50, under 16 £1.50.) The bridge is also the starting point for the shady **Lady Louisa's Walk** along the tree-lined Blackwater.

Locals whisper that a secret passage connects the castle to the Protestant **Lismore Cathedral,** Deanery Hill. Although built in 1633 (by Boyle's father Richard) the west wall incorporates grave slabs from Lismore's 9th-century imminence. Lismore's **Interpretive Centre** (tel. (058) 54975), in the town square, includes a video presentation and a cursory exhibit stressing the 1000-year old *Book of Lismore*, with its vellum (calfskin) paper. (Open same hours as tourist office; £2, students £1.50). Oenophiles can taste the unsung virtues of the **West Waterford Vineyards** (tel. (058) 54283), five miles from Lismore off Dungarvan Rd. The Vineyard produces a sweet white wine in addition to seasonal fruit wines (pear and strawberry, for example; open daily 10:30am-8pm).

One mile from Lismore, the **Kilmorna Farm Hostel** (tel. (058) 54315) competes with the castle in luxury. The 18th-century coach house and stables were converted brilliantly (solid wood beds built by a local craftsman, gingham curtains, and fluffy duvets). They offer a common room with TV and a perfectly appointed kitchen (that even has matching plates!). The working farm provides fresh groceries and supports cows, chickens, and no fewer than six dogs. (Laundry £2.50. Breakfast £3. 3- to 6-bed dorm £7.50/person, double £9/person.) From town, walk up Chapel St. (to the left of the Interpretive Centre), take the first left, and follow the signs (or call for a lift). If the hostel is unexpectedly full, cheerful rooms open up behind unpromising doorways in the **Red House Inn** (tel. (058) 54248), across from the Interpretive Centre on Main St. (£12.50/person). Stock up on supplies at **Londis,** Main St. (open Mon.-Wed. and Sat. 9am-6:30pm, Thurs. 9am-7:30pm, Fri. 9am-9pm). **Eamonn's Place,** Main St. (tel. (058) 54025), is the best spot for a standard, substantial meal. (Open for lunch Mon.-Fri. 12:30-2pm, dinner Mon.-Tues. and Thurs.-Sat. 6-9pm). The **Red House Inn** (tel. (058) 54248) has traditional sessions on Fridays, much anticipated by Lismore's younger crowd. **Madden's Bar,** East Main St. (tel. (058) 54148), pleasantly serves pints in a history-rich pub.

Wexford & Waterford

Geography makes Co. Wexford the front door to Ireland for anyone coming from France, Wales, or England. Geography being destiny, Ireland's invaders—from the Vikings to the Normans to modern backpackers—have disembarked in Co. Wexford and moved on to conquer the natives elsewhere. Naturally, with so many people passing through, Wexford has been particularly prone to foreign influences. Christianity arrived here with St. Iba—after St. Declan but before St. Patrick. Co. Wexford and Co. Waterford were also the setting of one of the most pivotal of Ireland's historic tales: Dermot MacMurrough's invitation to Strongbow to take his daughter and the land. Still, regardless of all the strangers passing through her ports, some of Co. Wexford's residents retain the old Gaelic dialect, and some even continue to speak the Yola dialect, introduced by continental traders. Co. Wexford has mellow beaches, a splendid variety of pubs in Wexford Town, and more sun than any other part of the country. The beaches spread out just a few miles from businesslike Rosslare Harbour and pop up again at the county's southwest edge, along Waterford Harbour. Sights of antiquities are not as densely packed in industrial Co. Waterford as they are in other parts of Ireland; the inland parts of the county are dedicated to rural pastimes, especially agriculture. The commercial and cultural core of the Southeast is Waterford City, where crystal and sootier industries thrive, creating an urban environment totally different from the farmlands in the inner county. Now that Waterford has newly opened accommodations, it makes an ideal base for exploring the Southeast.

Slí Charman, (pronounced "SHLEE KAR-man") a.k.a. "An tSlí", is a pathway that runs 135 miles along Wexford's coast from the Co. Wicklow border through Rosslare and Wexford to Waterford Harbour. The path is sometimes a cliffwalk, but sometimes coincides with paved roads. While trekking the whole way is not as rewarding as hiking the Wicklow Way, short stretches of the path offer a good dose of stormy seascapes. Maps hang out at Bord Fáilte offices in Waterford, Tramore, Wexford, Rosslare, New Ross, Enniscorthy, and Arklow. Major roads in the region are the east-west N25 (Rosslare-Wexford-New Ross-Waterford), the north-south N11 (Wexford-Enniscorthy-Arklow-Dublin), and the N79 from Enniscorthy to New Ross.

■■■ ROSSLARE HARBOUR

Most people enter and leave Ireland through Rosslare Harbour: the town exists solely for this purpose. Rosslare Harbour normally denotes not a body of water, but the over-equipped village from which the ferries to France, England, and Wales depart: Rosslare Town is the less important town between Rosslare Harbour and Wexford on N25, while Rosslare Strand is the beach near Rosslare Town. Ferries run daily to Britain and almost as frequently to France. The town caters to this trade. Shops open and close with the arrivals and departures of the ferries, and B&Bs swamp N25 between Wexford and Rosslare Harbour. While the town of Rosslare Harbour itself is best seen from the porthole of a departing ferry, many Irish know the value of sunny beach towns like Rosslare Strand and Kilmore Quay. If you have to spend time in Rosslare Harbour, spend it at the beach south of the harbor. Hitchhiking anywhere around the ferry port can be very difficult. Neither locals surfeited with tourists nor a foreign family of four in an overstuffed car are likely to pick you up. Some hitchers try to convince a driver whose car has fewer than the allowed four passengers to take them on the ferry as part of their allotment—possible, but unlikely.

PRACTICAL INFORMATION

Tourist Office: The Rosslare area has two tourist offices: one manic-panic office in the ferry terminal and another overstaffed office 1 mi. from the harbor on the

Wexford Rd., in Kilrane. The **ferry office** (tel. 33623) runs on ferry time. Open daily 6:30-9:30am and 11am-8:30pm or 1-8:30pm, depending on ferry arrival times. The **Kilrane office** is more sedate (tel. 33232). Open May to mid-Sept. daily 11am-8pm. TravelSave stamps, but no ISIC cards.

Bank: Currency exchange at the **Bank of Ireland** (tel. 33304). Open Mon.-Fri. 10am-12:30pm and 1:30-4pm.

Post Office: In the **SuperValu,** between produce and checkout (tel. 33207). Open Mon.-Fri. 9am-1pm and 2-5:30pm, Sat. 9am-1pm.

Phone code: 053

Ferries: Trains and buses often connect with the ferries. Bus Éireann and Irish Rail have desks in the terminal (tel. 33592). There is also a bureau de change in the ferry port. **Stena Sealink** (tel. 33115, recorded info 33330; fax 33534; office open daily 9am-5pm), **Irish Ferries/Britain and Ireland line** (tel. 33158; fax 33544), and **Sea Lynx** (office open daily 7am-10pm) all operate from the ferry port. For info on ferries from Rosslare Harbour to England and France see (see Getting There, p. 27).

Trains: Trains run from the ferry port to: Dublin (Mon.-Sat. 3/day, Sun. 2/day; 2hr.; £10); Limerick (Mon.-Sat. 2/day; 2¾hr.; £18); Waterford (Mon.-Sat. 3/day; 1¼hr.; £8.50); and Wexford (Mon.-Sat. 3/day, Sun. 2/day; 20 min.; £3.50).

Buses: Buses run to: Galway, Killarney, and Tralee via Waterford (Mon.-Sat. 4/day, Sun. 3/day; £14); Cork (Mon.-Sat. 4/day, Sun. 3/day; £12); Limerick (3/day; £12, £16 return); Waterford (Mon.-Sat. 4/day, Sun. 3/day; £5, £7 return); Dublin (Mon.-Sat. 6/day, Sun. 5/day; 3hr.; £9); and Wexford (Mon.-Sat. 10/day, Sun. 8/day; 20 min.; £2.40). Buses stop outside the ferry port at J. Pitt's Convenience Store in Kilrane, and sometimes at the new Catholic church in Rosslare Harbour.

Taxis: It'll cost you, but you can call **Paddy's Taxis** (tel. 33533).

Emergency: dial 999; no coins required.

ACCOMMODATIONS

The nature and function of Rosslare Harbour makes accommodations here inevitably predatory (though admittedly convenient). Exhausted ferry passengers fill up both good and mediocre beds, while the better places to stay (down the Strand, in Kilmore Quay, and in Wexford) go untenanted. In Rosslare, more than anywhere in Ireland, take the Bord Fáilte shamrock as a measure of quality—there is a noticeable difference between approved and non-approved B&Bs on N25.

Mrs. David Power (tel. 31243). Its only drawback is the 1½ mi. separating it from the harbor. It's on the left-hand side of N25, marked only by a sign reading "Self-catering accommodations £5" and by belligerent cows across the road. A hostel in a converted farmhouse that would do most B&Bs proud, with comfy bunks, tea-makers, and a radiator to keep you toasty warm. July-Aug. £7.50/person (£5/person after the first 2 people); Sept.-June £5/person; sheets £1.

Rosslare Harbour Youth Hostel (An Óige/HI), Goulding St. (tel. 33399; fax 33624), signposted on the hill opposite the ferry terminal. It's off Rosslare Harbour's one street. Offers weak showers, cramped bunks, and a collection of continental youth. Not the nicest hostel in Ireland, but you only have to stay one night. Officially check-in is at 5:30pm, lockout from 9:30am-5:30pm, curfew at 11:30pm, and lights out at midnight. £6.50, Sept.-May £5.50; sheets 50p. MC, Visa accepted.

Clifford House, Christine Delaney (tel. 33226), on the main road. Climb the steps from the harbor and turn left. Bright, comfortable rooms with a nice view of the beaches that are just down the hill. Single £13, £15 w/bath.

Marianella B&B (tel. 33139), off N25 across the road from Anchors Restaurant. Run by Rosemarie Sinner, the large rooms are airy and bright, among the best on the highway. Cookies and tea thoughtfully laid out in every room. £13.50/person, £15 w/bath, single £17.50; family room available.

Mrs. O'Leary's Farmhouse, Killilane, in Kilrane (tel. 33134). Signposted from the N25, it's ½ mi. up N25, then 2 mi. west. Set on a 100-acre farm, Mrs. O'Leary's place is a holiday unto itself: gloriously rural, with a grassy lane leading to a secluded private beach. Mrs. O'Leary will pick you up if you call her from the ferry or the train station. Single £15, double £26, £28 w/bath.

Mrs. J. Foley, 3 Coastguard Station (tel. 33522). Down a gravel walkway next to the Great Southern Hotel, it's signposted off the main, the one, the only street. Offers, simply enough, a bed and (continental) breakfast. You get what you pay for. Noon check-out. £7/person, 2 or 4 persons/room. **Camping** £2/person.

Rosslare Holiday Caravan and Camping Park, Rosslare Strand (tel. 32427 or 45720), is opposite the Bay Bar, 5 mi. from the ferry. Take N25 (Wexford Rd.) for 1½ mi., turn right at Chusher's Bar in Tagoat, then turn right at the third junction (another 2 mi.). The park has a pretty setting near the beach and is a notch above closer campsites. Wheelchair access. Hairdryers, laundry, irons, and kitchen. £2.50/hiker or cyclist; caravan £6.50 (car & 2 people).

FOOD

The restaurants in Rosslare Harbour are expensive. The deluxe **SuperValu supermarket** is more popular with the hostel crowd. A tastefully laid out grocery store with a nice selection, the SuperValu is opposite the Rosslare Harbour Youth Hostel on the only road in town (open Mon.-Wed. 8am-6pm, Thurs.-Fri. 8am-7pm). Good things come to those who wait (and to those who trek a mile down the road toward Kilrane). There, on the left approaching from Rosslare Harbour, **Anchors Restaurant** (tel. 33366) serves family-style fare on wooden tables and dishes up inexpensive take-out. Their special supper (soup, entree, vegetables, tea or coffee, and dessert) is a bargain at £6. (Open daily 7am-11pm.)

■ NEAR ROSSLARE HARBOUR

OUR LADY'S ISLAND

Five miles south of Rosslare Harbour and seven miles east of Kilmore Quay in Broadway, Our Lady's Island is actually connected to the mainland. The peninsula contains the ruins of an Augustinian priory and a 15-foot **Leaning Tower** (tilted at a sharper angle than that overrated thing in Italy). The most remote site on the peninsula, **St. Vauk's at Carnsore Point,** is worth the penance. Each year (Aug. 15-Sept. 9) a group of pilgrims flocks around the holy island, where three girls once saw the Virgin Mary appear. The pilgrims are joined by birds of a religious bent, many of whom inhabit one of the world's largest **tern nesting sites,** where more than 2000 pairs of terns breed. The best time to see them is in summer, when they constantly catch fish for their chicks; most breeds head for Africa in the winter. From Rosslare Harbour, bikers and walkers should head north on N25, turn left in Tagoat, and follow the signs for Broadway. Camp at **St. Margaret's Caravan and Camping Park** (tel. (053) 31169), by the beach (£2/cyclist or hiker; open June-Aug.).

KILMORE QUAY

Coastal Ireland shines at its brightest thirteen miles southwest of Rosslare on Forlorn Point. The small fishing village of Kilmore Quay charms with its thatched, white-washed seaside cottages and its beautiful beaches. **Information** about Kilmore Quay can be had at the **Stella Maris Community Centre** (tel. (053) 29922), open throughout the year. The village berths its **Maritime Museum** (tel. (053) 29655 or 29832) in the lightship *Guillemot* (a lightship is a lighthouse that floats). The tour, offered hospitably in French, English, and German, encompasses both Irish naval history and the history of the town. One of the highlights is the set of dramatic photos of a 1989 storm, whose 50-foot waves devastated the community. (Open June-Sept. daily noon-6pm; £1, students and children 50p.) **Kilmore Seafood Festival** (tel. (053) 26959) runs in mid-July, with loads of cheap seafood, music, and dancing.

Kilmore Quay also sends boat trips out to the two **Saltee Islands,** formerly a pagan pilgrimage site and now Ireland's largest bird sanctuary with a winged population nearing 50,000. These puffin palaces and razorbill refuges are owned by Prince Michael Salteens, who bears no likeness to the cracker. A narrow ridge of rock connects the smaller island to the mainland. This land bridge, called **St. Patrick's Bridge,** was once used for driving cattle to the island for pasture. (Judging by the width of the road, they must have been thin cows.) Although ferry service was disrupted in 1995 by the dredging of the harbor, it should resume by spring, 1996. When running, boats leave the mainland each morning, stranding you for picnics, ornithology, bonding with gray seals, and discovery until 4:30pm. Contact Dick Hayes (tel. (053) 29704) for ferry times and rates.

Kilmore imbibes at **The Wooden House** (tel. (053) 29804), a friendly local pub with a (predictably) nautical decor. Pub grub, highlighting fresh fish, is also marine-themed (fried scampi £4.25). On Saturday, the Wooden House has music, and if you're really (really) lucky, disco! The overachieving pub also offers **B&B.** Small, low-ceilinged rooms with whitewashed walls almost resemble ship cabins. A sea breeze blasts right in the rooms (£12/person, June-Aug. £15). For large portions of very fresh seafood, take yourself across from the Maritime Museum to the **Silver Fox** (tel. (053) 29888).

One mile from town up the Wexford Rd., between Kilmore Quay and Kilmore Town, the **Kilturk Independent Hostel** (tel. (053) 29883) shelters weary souls. An old schoolhouse enlivened by a coat of new paint, the hostel has an impressive kitchen, funky TV lounge, and a new café, but no secure luggage storage. Fishing trips and tours of the islands are arranged daily (£8). Wheelchair access. (9-bed dorm £5.50; single, double, and family room £7/person.) Bus Éireann stops at the hostel on its way from Wexford to Kilmore Quay.

Bike rental is available at the aptly-named **Kilmore Quay Bike Hire** (tel. (053) 29781), at Island View House (£7/day, £30/week). **Bus Éireann** runs between Wexford Town and Kilmore Quay (Wed. and Sat. only, 2/day; 30 min.; £3.60 return). From Rosslare Harbour, take the Wexford Rd. to Tagoat and turn left, From Wexford, take the Rosslare Rd. and turn right four miles from town, at Piercetown.

■■■ WEXFORD TOWN

Thin, winding streets leading to fishing boats tied along the quay give Wexford Town a sleepy, small-town, southern European appearance that belies its prominence on the map and in the history books. In 1169, the Normans conquered the Viking settlement of *Wæsfjord* ("harbor of the mud flats") and built their characteristic fortifications. Narrow passages, cutting from Main St. down to the quays, survive as a testament to their efforts. Henry II spent Lent of 1172 in Selskar Abbey, doing penance for the murder of Thomas à Becket. Oliver Cromwell, trying to make sure that Wexford would be afraid and hence unable to aid more English kings or royalist forces, ravaged the town in 1649, slaughtering over 300 people in the centrally located Bull Ring. And in 1798, the rebellion which was sparked by revolutionary activities around the world found its bloodiest expression in Wexford. In contrast to its violent past, Wexford declared itself a nuclear-free zone in the 1980s. Spared many of the ravages of industrial development, Wexford retains the charm of an Irish town but offers the lifestyle and facilities of a city.

ORIENTATION & PRACTICAL INFORMATION

Wexford presents a sleepy face to anybody on the quays. Walk down lively and kinky Main St. instead. It runs one block inland, parallel to the quays. School St. and John St. (different sections of the same street) run parallel to Main St. one block farther inland. Redmond Square, with the train station, anchors the south end of Main St. The Bull Ring, at the city center, connects North and South Main St. The Twin Churches punctuate the skyline of an otherwise huddled harbor city. Aptly named Crescent Quay is where you'll find the tourist office and supermarkets. The Franciscan Friary, tall and inviolate, stands at the top of the hill, surveying the older city and train station to its right.

Hitching around Wexford Town can be quite rewarding. Hitchhikers to Dublin (N11) stand at the Wexford Bridge off the quays; those bound for Rosslare head south along the quays to Trinity St.; hitchers heading to Cork, New Ross, or Waterford continue down Westgate and turn left onto St. Ita's Terrace (N25). Take note: the N11 and the N25 are merged near the city, so be sure to specify either the Dublin Rd. (N11) or the Waterford Rd. (N25). You will achieve the most success if you get out thumbing before noon; the early bird gets the ride.

Tourist Office: Crescent Quay (tel. 23111). Centuries of sailors have sharpened their knives on the windowsills of the building, as the scars and blemishes attest. Grab the free *Junior Chamber Guide to Wexford.* Open mid-June to Sept. Mon.-Sat. 9am-6pm, Sun 10am-5pm; Oct.-June Mon.-Sat. 9am-1pm and 2-6pm.

Post Office: Anne St. (tel. 22587). Open Mon.-Tues. and Thurs.-Sat. 9am-5:30pm, Wed. 9:30am-5:30pm.

Phone Code: 053.

Travel Office: O'Donohoe Travel, Commercial Quay (tel. 22788). Sells ferry, rail, and airplane tickets. Not a specialist in budget or discounted travel, just the biggest travel agent in town. Open Mon.-Fri. 9:30am-5:30pm, Sat. 9:30am-1pm and 2-5pm. The nearest **USIT** office is in Waterford.

Banks: Bank of Ireland, Custom House Quay (tel. 23022). Open Mon. 10am-5pm, Tues.-Fri. 10am-4pm; **ATM. TSB** bank, 73/75 Main St. (tel. 41922). Open Mon.-Wed. and Fri. 9:30am-5pm, Thurs. 9:30am-7pm.

Trains: North Station, Redmond Sq. (tel. 22522), a 5-min. walk along the quays from Crescent Quay. Booking offices open around departure times. When the office is closed, buy tickets on the train. Someone is on duty to answer questions from 7am until last departure. Trains hustle to Dublin (Mon.-Sat. 3/day, Sun. 2/day; 3hr.; £10) and Rosslare Harbour (Mon.-Sat. 4/day, Sun. 3/day; 30 min.; £3).

Buses: Arrive in and depart from the train station. Buses run to Dublin (daily 5/day; 2½hr.) and to Rosslare Harbour (Mon.-Sat. 7/day, Sun. 5/day; 20 min.). Buses to and from Limerick connect with Irish Ferries and Stena-Sealink sailings (daily 2/day). From mid-July to Aug., buses run directly to Galway and other points west.

Taxi: Black Cab Co., South Main St. (tel. 47788 or 22245). 24-hr. service. £2.50 max. fare within the city.

Bike Rental: Wexford enjoys a glut of bicycle shops. **Hayes Cycle Shop,** 108 South Main St. (tel. 22462). Raleigh touring bikes £7/day, £30/week; deposit £40. Fishing tackle also available. Open Mon.-Sat. 9am-6pm. **The Bike Shop,** North Main St. (tel. 22514), £6.50/day, £30/week; deposit £20. Open Mon.-Sat. 9am-6pm. **Dave Allen Cycles,** 84 South Main St. (tel. 22516) £6/day, £30/week; deposit £20. Open Mon.-Sat. 8:30am-6pm.

Laundry: My Beautiful Launderette, St. Peter's Sq. (tel 24317), up Peters St. from South Main St. Get kissy with Daniel Day Lewis, or enjoy TV, videos, and complimentary tea or coffee while you wait. Wash £1.60; 2-min. dryer 50p; soap 30p. Showers, too (£1). Open Mon.-Sat. 10am-9pm. Sundays and holidays, access via video store next door, 3-8pm.

Youth Information and Resource Centre: South Main St. (tel. 23262). Tries to leave no question unanswered. Open Tues.-Fri. 10am-5:30pm, Sat. noon-4pm.

Pharmacy: Seven pharmacies along Main St. rotate Sunday and late hours; all open Mon.-Sat. 9am-1pm and 2-6pm.

Hospital: Wexford General Hospital, New Town Rd. (tel. 42233), on the N25.

Emergency: Dial 999; no coins required. **Garda:** Roches Rd. (tel. 22333).

ACCOMMODATIONS

The nearest hostels are about 10 miles away in Rosslare and Kilmore; staying in a B&B in Wexford Town proper is a more convenient way to see the city. Many B&Bs compete for customers along N25 (Rosslare Rd.), Bayview Drive off the Dublin Rd., or St. John's Rd. off Georges St.

The Abbey, Mrs. Donnelly, 3 Lower Georges St. (tel. 22787). Follow signs for White's Hotel. If Mary Poppins ran a B&B, this would be it. Potpourri and a delicately persistent floral theme inside and out. Great place, but closing after summer, 1996. £14/person.

Nancy Edwards, 51 St. Ita's Terrace (tel. 24597), on the New Town (a.k.a. Waterford) Rd. She has been running a B&B for 23 years, and remains chatty. Bright rooms with large beds. Single £13; double £24.

Carraig Donn, Mrs. Daly, New Town Court (tel. 42046), off the New Town (a.k.a. Waterford) Rd. Call from the center of town and Mrs. Daly will pick you up. The ideal grandmother presents large rooms and Brady Bunch decor. You'll smell fabulous thanks to cologne bottles in every room. £14/person. Wheelchair access.

Shanagolden, Marie Murphy, St. John's Rd. (tel 22156), continue up George's St. Photos and paintings of Marilyn Monroe and James Dean deck the walls, and thick comforters cover the beds. Single £13.50, double £25.

Ferrybank Caravan and Camping Park (tel. 44378 or 43274). On the eastern edge of town, across from the Dublin Rd. Take the bridge and continue straight to the camping site. Beautiful ocean-view, clean area. Swimming pool! £3/1-person tent, £5/2-person tent; showers 75p; laundry £1.50. Open Easter-Oct.

FOOD

Groceries abound. **L&N Superstore,** on Custom House Quay, and **Crazy Prices,** on Crescent Quay, are typical, large supermarkets with lots of cheap food. **Dunnes Store** has a wide selection of meats and sells clothes, too (fondly recall WalMart). (All open Mon.-Wed. 9am-6pm, Thurs.-Fri. 9am-9pm.) **Greenacres,** 56 North Main St., contains deli meats, exotic fruit, and a baby-changing facility; it's a step above the average local grocery stores.

Tim's Tavern, 51 South Main St. (tel. 23861). Pub grub elevated to *haute cuisine.* Tim's has won national awards for dishes like avocado, pear, and crab (£5.50), crab in garlic butter (£7), and lamb cutlets (£5). The same menu is cheaper at lunch, pricey at dinner. Lunch served daily noon-5pm, dinner 6:30-9:30pm. Traditional music Wed. and Sat. nights at 9:30pm.

La Cuisine, North Main St. (tel. 24986). Bakery and restaurant with a Parisian feel due to racks of delicious baguettes and a chatty, café atmosphere. Makes a mean chicken sandwich (£1.20) and tart apple tarts (£1). Open Mon.-Sat. 9am-6pm.

The Cellar, Cornmarket (tel. 24544), in the Wexford Arts Centre. As bohemian as it gets here: men sport goatees. Lunch special always includes a choice of at least two vegetarian entrees (£3). Chili bean pancakes with sour cream dressing and Navarin of lamb with vegetables are tasty treats. Open Mon.-Sat. 10am-6pm.

PUBS

The Centenary Stores, Charlotte St. (tel. 24424). Younger folk congregate in the pitch-dark back room of this former warehouse with high ceilings and brick walls. Excellent trad on Sun. morning as well as Tues. and Wed. nights. Blues and folk on Mon. night.

O'Faolain's, 11 Monk St. (tel. 23877). The friendliest and liveliest of Wexford's pubs; a crowd of all ages mingles here without generational strife. The place croons trad music on Sun. morning and Mon. night, mixed music on Sun. and Tues. nights, and ballads on Thurs. night.

The Goal Bar, 72 South Main St. (tel. 23727). Country, rock, or trad most nights, but something of a Russian roulette: pop in once too often, and bang! Karaoke! Occasional cover £1.

Archers, Redmond Sq.(tel. 22316). Full stomachs and friendly faces. Food served Mon.-Sat. noon-2:30pm, Sun. noon-2pm. Upstairs, **The Junctions** is Wexford's nightclub of choice. It thumps into the early hours of the morning (Thurs.-Sun. 10:30pm-2am; cover £6; teen disco on Fri.).

SIGHTS

The historical society runs free **walking tours** on random nights, departing from White's Hotel at 8:15pm; call the hotel (tel. 22311) for scheduled tours, and sacrifice to the *Let's Go* god in order to catch one. *Welcome to Wexford* (free from the tourist office) details a 45-minute self-guided walking tour. **Westgate Heritage Tower** (tel. 46506) also offers walking tours of Wexford (no regular schedule—call ahead to book a tour, or join a booked group. Price depends on size of group; 1½-2hr.)

The remains of the Norman **city wall** run the length of High St. to its north. At the intersection of High St. and Westgate St., **Westgate Tower** is the only one of six of the wall's towers that still stands. You can even see the barred and blackened cell that served as a lock-up for renegades. The tower gate now holds the **Westgate Heritage Centre** (tel. 46506). The audio-visual show dramatically recounts the history of Wexford. The fire and cannon special effects will blow your mind. (Open April-Sept. Mon.-Sat. 9am-5pm, also June-Sept. Sun. 2-6pm; £1.50, students £1.) The Heritage Centre has a design shop (tel. 46506) that sells pricey crafts (open same hours as center). Next door, the **Selskar Abbey,** site of King Henry II's extended penance, now acts as a windowbox for lush wildflowers. Alexander Roche built the abbey for his true love, after she, thinking him dead in the Crusades, entered a convent in her depression. The dark and frightening tower stairwell leads up to a precarious view of the town and the bay. (Enter through the tall, narrow wicket gate next to the center; open same hours as the center.)

The northern half of the city is studded with ancient buildings and monuments; southern Wexford Town, built on recent landfill, will have to wait a few years to be deemed historic. Separating North and South Main Streets, an open area marks the **Bull Ring.** Bullfights were inaugurated in 1621 by the town's butcher guild as a promotional device. The mayor got the hide while the poor got the meat. "The Pikeman," a statue of a stalwart peasant fearlessly brandishing a sharp instrument, commemorates the 1798 uprising (see History: The Protestant Ascendancy, p. 52), not famous Irish bullfighters. **Crescent Quay** held ship repair yards until the early 1900s. The statue facing the sea is Commodore John Barry, Wexford-born founder of the U.S. Navy. The bottom of the quay is reputed to be cobblestoned, though nobody has gone down to check.

The Friary Church in the Franciscan Friary, School St., houses the "Little Saint." This creepy effigy of young St. Adjutor shows the wounds inflicted by the martyr's Roman father. Franciscan monks have lived in town since 1240—their plain brown robes can still be seen bopping along Wexford's streets.

ENTERTAINMENT

The Wexford People (85p) lists events for all of Co. Wexford; the events section comes after "Farm Scene." The very active **Wexford Arts Centre,** in the Cornmarket (tel. 23764 or 24544), presents free visual arts and crafts exhibitions; evening performances of music, dance, and drama also take place in the center throughout the year. "Open mike" night, June through August on Wednesdays at 9pm, features poetry readings and songs. (Free for performers, £2 for audience; all events free with membership; yearly membership £15, students £5, includes free wine at exhibition openings; box office open Mon.-Sat. 10am-6pm.) Crouched backstage in an inconspicuous building on High St., the **Theatre Royal** produces performances throughout the year, specializing in the acclaimed **Wexford Festival Opera** during the last two weeks in October. For these festivities, three deserving operas are rescued from the artistic attic and performed in an intimate setting. For info on the opera festival and on regular performances, contact the Theatre Royal, High St. (tel. 22400; box office tel. 22144; open Mon.-Fri. 11am-5pm; opera tickets £34-48, available from early June; afternoon, late-night, and lunchtime concerts and operatic scenes £5-7).

■ NEAR WEXFORD TOWN

If you don't have a car, the best way to see the surrounding area is with a guided tour (rented bikes and cab rides are more expensive). **Westgate Minitours** (tel. 24655) runs buses from the tourist office to: the Irish National Heritage Park (departs Mon.-Sat. 10am and 1:30pm, Sun. noon and 2pm; £6 return); Johnstown

Castle Gardens (departs Mon.-Sat. 11am, Sun. 2:30pm; £6 return); and both (departs Mon.-Sat. 11am, Sun. noon; £10 return). All prices include admission.

The **Irish National Heritage Park** (tel. (053) 41733), in **Ferrycarrig**, is 2½ miles north of Wexford off N11. In the interests of education, this park—like Celtworld—regales visitors with 9000 years of replicated Irish culture, from the Stone Age to the arrival of the Normans. The park-like site features full-scale replicas of a dolmen (Stone-Age tomb), stone circles (Copper-Age planetariums), a cist burial, an *ogham* stone, a Viking ship, typical Irish homesteads, places of worship, and a Norman round tower. With everything so nicely packaged, who needs Ireland? The exhibits are even outside, so that you'll get soaked if it rains. No need to go anywhere else at all (open March-Nov. daily 10am-7pm, last admission 5pm; £3.50, students £3).

The **North and South Slobs** are messy, but in a delightful way: "slob" is the term for the cultivated mudflats to the north and south of Wexford Harbour that are protected from flooding rivers by dykes. The Slobs are internationally famous for the rare geese who winter there at the **Wexford Wildfowl Reserve** (tel. 23129). Ten-thousand of Greenland's white-fronted geese (one-third of the world population) descend on the Slobs from October to April, cohabiting with other rare geese, some from as far as Siberia and Iceland. The bathing rarities include Icelandic whooper swans, ducks, and 36 species of wading birds. Summer is a more mellow time for the Slobs, as most of its residents then are ordinary Irish birds. Excitement derives from the herons and grebes nesting and mating along the channels and streams. The **Reserve Centre** will help visitors spot whatever species wander through (open mid-April to Sept. daily 9am-6pm, Oct.-April 10am-5pm; free). The Reserve is on the North Slob, two miles north of Wexford town. Take the Castlebridge/Gorey Rd. to well-signposted Ardcavan Lane.

■■■ ENNISCORTHY

Fourteen miles north of Wexford Town, the hilltop town of Enniscorthy perches above the River Slaney. The town is exceptionally conscious of its Republican history: in 1798, rebels led by a local priest held the British at bay for 12 days before a defeat at nearby Vinegar Hill. And in 1916 Enniscorthy was one of the only towns to join Dublin's Easter Rising. Today, Enniscorthy sprawls across the river; its comelier west side incorporates a cluster of historic buildings, including a 13th-century Norman castle with an eclectic museum inside. If you have a few spare hours, spend them in welcoming Enniscorthy.

Practical Information The town **tourist office** (tel. 34699) is in the castle off Castle Hill Rd (the directions to get there? look for the big gray castle! open mid-June to mid-Sept. Mon.-Sat. 10am-6pm, Sun. 2-5:30pm). **AIB** Bank (tel. 33184) dispenses cash (ATM; open Mon.-Wed. and Fri. 9:30am-4pm, Thurs. 9:30am-5pm). The **post office,** Abbey Quay (tel. 33545), is off Mill Pack Rd. **Trains** running between Dublin and Rosslare stop in Enniscorthy (Mon.-Sat. 3/day, Sun. 2/day; to Dublin 2hr., £7.50; to Rosslare Harbour 50 min., £4.50). The railway station is on the first left after the new bridge. **Buses** leave from the Bus Stop Shop on Templeshannon Quay, opposite the castle, running south through Wexford and north through Ferns (10 min. from Enniscorthy). N11 motorway passes straight through Enniscorthy, heading north to Arklow, Wicklow, and Dublin, and south to Wexford. The **phone code** is indubitably 054.

Accommodations, Food, & Pubs Ivella, Rectory Rd. (tel. 33475), the right fork after the bridge past the railway station, is a shrine to the Kennedy brothers: a portrait of JFK and RFK greets guests in the lobby, and a bust of JFK has the place of honor on the mantle over the fireplace. Her American guests actually mail her Kennedy memorabilia. "I'm fond of the family," Mrs. Heffernan explains. Small rooms with low ceilings—watch your head (£13/person, singles £16). On the other side of the river lies Mrs. Ann Carroll's **Don Carr House,** Bohreen Hill (tel. 33458).

From Market Sq. take the first right on Main St., then left onto Bohreen Hill. Don Carr House comes equipped with two sumptuous sunrooms, high ceilings, and bouncy beds (£13/person, with bath £15). **Aldemar**, Summerhill (tel. 33668), is a little way up Bohreen Hill and to the right. The delightful Mrs. Agnes Barry provides tender lovin' care. The nearest hostels are in New Ross and Courtown; the latter makes a good stopover for the Dublin-bound. The **Anchorage Hostel,** Poulshone, Courtown Harbour (tel. (055) 25335), is a former B&B with great beaches nearby (£5/person, double £12; open May-Oct.).

Food eagerly awaits you on the shelves at the **L&N Supermarket** in the shopping center on Mill Park Rd., off Abbey Sq. (open Mon.-Wed. and Sat. 9am-6pm; Thurs.-Fri. 9am-9pm), or at the various pubs. **Killeen's,** Slaney St. (tel. 35935), dishes up roast chicken, potatoes, and vegetables for £4. They also have trad sessions on Saturday nights. Vegetarians or those seeking home-baked goodies should try **The Baked Potato,** 18 Ratter (tel. 34085), where food is hot and inexpensive (vegetarian lasagne, £3; open Mon-Sun. 9am-6pm). **The Antique Tavern** (tel. 33428) is a small but lively pub—great *craic* goes on amidst the antiques and curios, including a California license plate reading WEXFORD.

Sights Don't miss the **Walking Tour of Enniscorthy** (tel. 36800), which reveals the town's dirty little secrets with a provocative blend of drama and civic pride. Contact Maura Flannery at the **Castle Craft Shop**, across from the castle on Castle Hill Rd. (tel. 36800; fax 36130). Tours, in English, French, or Spanish, leave from the craft shop at noon or 2pm, or call to schedule a tour (£2, students £1.50, under 18 £1). The castle itself houses the tourist office, but the **Wexford County Museum** (tel. 35926) constitutes the bulk of the building. The museum chronicles Co. Wexford's collective stream of consciousness rather than any historical narrative. Starting with 13 items in 1960, curators scrounged for bequests, stuffing the castle from eaves to dungeon with such odd bits as ship figureheads and a collection of the world's police patches. A carving on the wall of the dungeon shows a young 16th-century man with his prominent scabbard. Receive your very own multi-media crash course in Co. Wexford history here. (£2, ages 13-18 £1, children 50p. Open June-Sept. Mon.-Sat. 10am-1pm and 2-6pm, Sun. 2-5:30pm; Oct.-Nov. and Feb.-May daily 2-5:30pm; Dec.-Jan. Sun. 2-5pm).

St. Aiden's Cathedral, Cathedral St. (continue down Main St.), was built in 1860 under the close personal supervision of architect Augustus Pugin, who littered Ireland's towns with his neo-Gothic creations. During renovations in 1994, Catholic masses were celebrated at the Protestant church down the road, an agreeably ecumenical gesture in a town whose history is punctuated by sectarian violence. In Market Square, a statue commemorates Father Murphy who, in 1798, led the town in rebellion. The Priest had been something of a Loyalist before an angry mob threatened to burn down his church. He was instantly affected with revolutionary zeal and promptly put himself at the head of the rowdy crowd.

Starting on the last weekend in June, eight days of festival and fructose redden Enniscorthy's streets during its annual **Strawberry Fair.** Sports events and a Strawberry Queen are featured—all for free. Pub theater performances draw the literati and "Lego Competitions" attract the child in each fair-goer. After all, strawberries, like pints of Guinness, are good for you.

■ NEAR ENNISCORTHY: FERNS

The view from the top of **Ferns Castle** is just what people expect of Ireland. **Ferns,** a tiny village eight miles north of Enniscorthy on the N11, was once capital of Ireland. The castle, whose profile smiles at you as you enter town, was once a large rectangle with cylindrical towers at the corners; only 1½ towers now remain. The stronghold was built in the 13th century by William Marshall, Strongbow's son-in-law, who locked up his daughter in the cellar to prevent her elopement. (Site always open; free; to climb around in the tower, get the key from the cool cat of a caretaker, Jim Gettings, 36 Castle View, 100 meters to the right of the castle.) **Bus Éire-ann** runs from Enniscorthy, stopping at the bend in Main St. (4/day; 10 min.; £2.90).

Down Main St., two sets of ruins skulk in the backyard of the Cathedral of St. Aiden (not to be confused with St. Aiden's Monastery of Adoration, a depressingly modern structure built in 1989). In the graveyard are three **high crosses,** as well as a granite stump which is said to mark the grave of Dermot MacMurrough, King of Leinster. The Romanesque archways of **Ferns Cathedral,** also in the cemetery, actu-ally date from the 10th century. After burning down the original 13th-century build-ing in a fit of pique in 1575, the O'Byrne clan was ordered to rebuild the Cathedral, and this crude reconstruction is what remains today. In a grassy field behind the churchyard are the ruins of **St. Mary's Abbey,** founded by Dermot MacMurrough in 1158 in order to save his much-blemished soul. The abbey helped save his skin, as well, when he took refuge here in 1167 while awaiting the arrival of his Norman ally, Strongbow. The Abbey's original charter entitled it to a portion of all the beer brewed in Ferns—ballast for both the body and the soul all at once—but the good times ground to a halt when Henry VIII shut down the monasteries in 1539. Farther up the Gorey Rd. lie more remains: the 16th-century **St. Peter's Church** and also **St. Mogue's Well,** founded in 607 by St. Moling as a real wishing well. (All sites always open and free.)

■■■ NEW ROSS

The old center of the city, rising steeply from the shores of the River Barrow, still preserves a faint medieval flavor. For a time in the 19th century, the town of New Ross joined forces with Waterford to handle over half of Ireland's shipping. The city's more recent past—its days in the 19th century as one of two major shipping centers—are only slightly more in evidence. Quay St./Mary St. continues from the bridge; North St., the main drag, becomes South St. as it crosses Mary St.

The prettiest way to reach New Ross is by cruising from Waterford on **The Gal-ley** (tel. 21723), which runs daily restaurant cruises from New Ross to Waterford. Eat lunch (April-Oct. at 12:30pm; 2hr.; £11, £5 for cruise only), tea (June-Aug. at 3pm; 2hr.; £5, £4 for cruise only), or dinner (April-Sept. at 7pm; 2-3hr.; £20, £9 for cruise only). **Bikes** travel free. It's easy to visit by land: **Bus Éireann** runs from Ryan's on the Quay to: Dublin (Mon.-Sat. 3/day, Sun. 2/day; 3hr.; £8); Rosslare Har-bour (Mon.-Sat. 3/day, Sun. 3/day; 1hr.; £7); and Waterford (Mon.-Sat. 7/day, Sun. 5/day; 34 min.; £3). New Ross is on the N25 (Wexford/Cork Rd.) and the N79 (Ennis-corthy/Waterford Rd.). If you're heading from Wexford to Waterford, you can skip the town altogether by taking the **ferry** across Waterford Harbour (see p. 183). Hitchers can find plenty of rides on either the N25 or N79, most in the morning or late afternoon.

The New Ross **tourist office,** in the JFK Centre (tel. 21857), overlooks the river traffic from North Quay St. (open Oct.-May Mon.-Sat. 9am-5pm; July-Sept. Mon.-Sat. 8am-8pm). The **post office** delivers on Charles St., off the Quay (tel. 21261; open Mon.-Fri. 9am-5:30pm). **TSB** bank (tel. 22060) is at 17 South St. (open Mon.-Wed. and Fri. 9:30am-5pm, Thurs. 9:30am-7pm). Wexford and Waterford are the closest places to rent bikes. New Ross's **phone code** takes long lunches at 051.

Accommodations Mac Murrough Farm Hostel (tel. 21383) is an awesome reason to be in New Ross. Follow Mary St. uphill to the Abbey and turn left, then take the first right, continuing through the square with a cross in the middle. Take a left at the supermarket, then a right at the Statoil Station; from there, follow the signs for two miles to the hostel. The sheep give a rowdy greeting (£5.50/night; sheets 50p). **Riversdale House,** William St. (tel. 22515), provides comfort and convenience for those who choose to stay in town. Follow South St. all the way to William St., then turn left up the hill. Friendly owners take pride in their commanding view of town (£16/person, single £20, all w/bath).

Food & Pubs The Sweeney, Mary St. (tel. 21963), is a cozy deli with a room full of palm trees and a menu full of sandwiches (90p), soup and bread (£1.25), and omelettes (£2.95; open Mon.-Tues. and Thurs.-Sat. 9am-6pm, Wed. 9am-2pm). **M&J Restaurant,** South St. (tel. 21833), serves coffee-shop fare (cheese sandwich 80p, full breakfast £3; open Mon.-Fri. 8:30am-9pm). **Hanrahan's,** North St. (tel. 21545), is a dark, sports-oriented pub with memorabilia from GAA hurling matches on the wall. The pub is one of the several local businesses bearing this name; in 1690, King James II stayed a night in Hanrahan's Inn while fleeing William of Orange.

Sights New Ross isn't much of a city for museums: most of its historical sights are still being used for practical purposes. The site of the **Tholsel,** South St., originally held a Norse tollbooth (*thol-sel,* "toll stall"). The timber proved structurally unsound in the mid-1700s; the current Tholsel, now the town hall, was built in 1749. Strongbow's grandson founded **St. Mary's Church,** off Mary St., in the 13th century. Even if you don't go in, at least hang out with the crows in the eerily beautiful graveyard. Get the key from Mrs. Culletan, 6 Church St., several houses down from the church. JFK memorabilia philanders in the tourist office lobby in the **John F. Kennedy Centre,** North Quay. See pictures of Jack being adored by throngs of Wexfordians during his 1963 visit, old parish registers containing the magic name, and a copy of the young JFK's **Harvard** yearbook entry. (Office open Mon.-Fri. 9am-5pm.) Outside New Ross, sights get more unusual. Four miles from New Ross on the N79 (Enniscorthy Rd.), the **Berkeley Costume and Toy Museum,** Berkeley Forest, houses a private collection of English rocking horses, Irish dresses, and 18th-century French and German dolls. (Open May-Sept.; tours 11:30am, 3, and 5pm; £3, children £1.)

Irish-Americans and Irish locals wanted to further honor the memory of JFK and decided to say it with flowers. They found 4500 different ways, which are displayed in a thesaurus of flora, **The John F. Kennedy Arboretum,** seven miles south of New Ross on the Ballyhack Rd. (tel. 388171; fax 388172). The park stunningly displays over 4500 species of trees and shrubs (all labeled) and 500 different rhododendrons, all dedicated to the memory of Ireland's favorite U.S. president. (Open May-Aug. daily 10am-8pm, April and Sept. 10am-6:30pm, Oct.-March 10am-5pm. Last admission 45min. before closing; £2, students £1.)

■ ■ ■ WATERFORD CITY

In 1003 AD, Vikings built Reginald's Tower to defend their longships in *Vadrafjord;* today, the tower overlooks the massive freighters which ply their trades in Waterford's busy harbor. The tower is a perfect symbol for the town, whose ideal position next to one of Ireland's natural ports has made it a military and commercial center for a millennium. Over the years, Waterford, so important to the nation militarily and economically, has endured sieges by Strongbow, the first Norman to invade Ireland, and by Cromwell; Strongbow's marriage to Dermot MacMurrough's daughter, Aoife, even took place at Reginald's Tower. These days, bikers lay siege to the town, making Waterford the "bikers' capital of Ireland." The city's street plan shows its split: narrow Viking-made streets battle wide commercial thoroughfares such as Broad St. and the Quay.

ORIENTATION & PRACTICAL INFORMATION

Most of Waterford, except the bus and train station, is on the south bank of the River Suir (pronounced "sure"). Merchants' Quay, Meagher's Quay, Custom House Parade ("The Parade"), and Adelphi Quay name each block of the street along the river, going west-to-east; the Quay is the strip of land between the river and this schizophrenic street. The main commercial street intersects the Quay at the Clock Tower; its blocks are named Barronstrand St., Broad St., Michael St., and John St.— from north to south. O'Connell St. becomes George St. and runs parallel to the river one block south of the Quay. **City buses** leave from the Clock Tower on the Quay and cost a flat fare of 70p for trips within the city. City bus timetables await at the Bus Éireann office (in the tourist office) or at Plunkett Station.

Tourist Office: 41 Merchant's Quay (tel. 75788), two blocks west of the Clock Tower. The office is behind a green facade between Hanover St. and Gladstone St. Ask for a map of Waterford and the free, ad-packed *Ireland's South East* guide; *The Waterford Guide* (£1.50) has good county-wide info. **Currency exchange,** Bus Éireann desk, Budget Rent-A-Car desk. Open July-Aug. Mon-Sat. 9am-6pm, Sun. 10am-1pm and 2-5pm; June and Sept. Mon.-Sat. 8am-6pm; Oct.-Feb. Mon-Fri. 9am-1pm and 2-5:15pm; March-April Mon.-Sat. 9am-1pm and 2-6pm.

Budget Travel: USIT, 36-37 Georges St. (tel. 72601; fax 71723). Near the corner with Gladstone St., one block east of Barronstrand St. As knowledgeable as the Dublin USIT office, without Dublin's lines. ISIC cards, Travelsave stamps, student fares to London. Deals in daily flights from Waterford to London and in a bus/ferry package to London (see Getting There, p. 27). Open Mon.-Fri. 9:30am-5:30pm, Sat. 11am-4pm.

Banks: Bank of Ireland, Merchants Quay (tel. 72074); **ATM.** Open Mon. 10am-5pm, Tues.-Fri. 10am-4pm. **TSB** bank, O'Connell St. (tel. 72988). Open Mon.-Wed. and Fri. 9:30am-5:30pm, Thurs. 9:30am-7pm.

Post Office: The Quay (tel. 74444), the largest of several. Open Mon.-Tues. and Thurs.-Fri. 9am-5:30pm, Wed. 9:30am-5:30pm, Sat. 9am-1pm.

Phone Code: 051.

Airport: tel. 75589. Served by British Airways and Suckling Airlines. Follow The Quay, turn right at Reginald's Tower, then left at the airport sign—it's 20 min. from town.

Trains: JFK's ancestors grew up in Waterford, and the city is still well-connected. Buses and trains leave from **Plunkett Station,** on the other side of the bridge from The Quay. For train info call: Mon.-Fri. 9am-5pm tel. 73401; after hours Mon.-Fri. tel. 73402; Sat. 9am-6pm tel. 73403; 24-hr. recorded timetable tel. 76243. Train station staffed Mon.-Sat. 9am-6pm, Sun. at departure times. Trains chug to: Limerick (Mon.-Sat. 2/day; 2¼hr.; £11); Kilkenny (Mon.-Sat. 4/day; 40 min.; £11); Dublin (Mon.-Sat. 4/day, Sun. 3/day; 2½hr.; £11); and Rosslare Harbour (Mon.-Sat. 3/day; 1hr.; £11).

Buses: Bus info tel. 79000. Office open Mon.-Sat. 9am-5:30pm, Sun. 2-5:30pm. Buses from Plunkett Station drive to: Dublin (Mon.-Sat. 8/day, Sun. 6/day; 3½hr.; £7); Kilkenny (daily 1/day; 1hr.; £5.90); Limerick (4/day; 2½hr.; £9.70); Cork (Mon.- Sat. 7/day, Sun. 5/day; 2½hr.; £9.70); Galway (Mon.-Sat. 4/day, Sun. 3/day; 4¾hr.; £13); and Rosslare Harbour (3/day; 1¼hr.; £8.80).

Hitching: Hitchers place themselves on the main routes, away from the tangled city center. To reach the N24 (Cahir, Limerick), N10 (Kilkenny, Dublin), or N25 (New Ross, Wexford, Rosslare), they head over the bridge toward the train station. For the N25 (Cork), they continue down Parnell St.; others take a city bus out to the Waterford Crystal Factory before they stick out a thumb (see Waterford, p. 183).

Bike Rental: Wright's Cycle Depot, Henrietta St. (tel. 74411; fax 73440). £7/day, £30/week; deposit £40. Open Mon.-Thurs. 9:30am-1pm and 2-6pm, Fri. 9:30am-1pm and 2-9pm, Sat. 9:30am-1pm and 2-5:30pm.

Luggage Storage: in Plunkett Station. £1/item. Open Mon.-Sat. 7:15am-9pm.

Laundry: Washed Ashore Launderette, The Quay (tel. 78925). Self-service wash and dry £5.60; serviced wash and dry £5.80. Open Mon.-Fri. 8:45am-5:45pm, Sat. 9am-6pm.

Crisis Lines: Samaritans, 13 Beau St. (tel. 72114). 24-hr. hotline. **Rape Crisis Centre** (tel. 73362). Mon. 10am-noon, Tues.-Wed. and Fri. 10am-noon and 2-4pm, Thurs. 10am-noon, 2-4pm, and 8:30-10pm.

Youth Information Centre: 130 The Quay (tel. 77328). Has information on work, travel, health, and a variety of support groups; they also provide information on gay and lesbian support groups. Open to all. Open Mon.-Fri. 9:30am-5:30pm.

Hospital: Ardkeen Hospital (tel. 73321). Follow The Quay to the Tower Hotel; turn left, then follow signs straight ahead to the hospital.

Emergency: Dial 999; no coins required. **Garda:** Patrick St. (tel. 74888).

ACCOMMODATIONS

In summer 1995, the Viking House Hostel was the only hostel we would recommend in Waterford. If it's full, stay in a B&B or in the An Óige hostel in Arthurstown. Most B&Bs in the city are unimpressive; those on the Cork Rd. are a better option.

Viking House Hostel (IHH), Coffee House Ln. (tel. 53827; fax 71730). In summer 1995, Viking House Hostel was the only hostel Let's Go would recommend in Waterford City. Follow The Quay east past the Clock Tower and the post office. A sign marks the turnoff; the hostel is on the right, behind another building. A luxurious and spanking-new hostel in the heart of Waterford. Slightly mushy beds are the only flaw. Staff is friendly and well-informed. Excellent facilities, good showers, and a large, beautiful lounge. The fireplace dates from the 15th century and was found on the site during construction. Free luggage storage, lockers £5 deposit. Kitchen 10am-10pm. Free sheets. 16-bed dormitory £7.50, 4- to 6-bed room w/bath £8.50, double £10; all w/continental breakfast.

Mrs. J. Ryder, Mayor's Walk House, 12 Mayor's Walk (tel. 55427). With a smile that defines "winsome," Mrs. Ryder (and her perennial guests) welcome *Let's Go* readers with advice, biscuits, and a seemingly endless pot of tea. Generous, flowery rooms. Single £13, double £25. Open March-Nov.

Derrynane House, 19 The Mall (tel. 75179). This B&B is the former home of the first governor of the state of Montana. Winding halls lead to plain, comfortable rooms with good, firm beds. Drown your sorrows in the bathtub! £13/person.

Beechwood, Mrs. M. Ryan, 7 Cathedral Sq. (tel. 76677). Elegant, silky rooms look out on pedestrian street and cathedral. Single £15, double £25.

Corlea House, New St. (tel. 75764), off Michael St. Small, cozy rooms, each with TV, are topped off by the owner's friendly manner. Single £13, double £25.

FOOD

Be sure to sample Waterford's contribution to classy cuisine, the *blaa*. Pronounced "blah," this is a floury white roll of Huguenot origins. Besides the *blaa*, Waterford gave the world the modern process of bacon curing. Thank you, Waterford! For cheap groceries, visit **Roches Stores** in the City Square Mall (open Mon.-Wed. and Sat. 9am-6pm, Thurs.-Fri. 9am-9pm). **Treacy's,** The Quay (tel. 73059), has a very large selection for a late-night grocery (even a small deli; open daily 9:30am-11pm). **The Late, Late Shop** (tel. 55376; fax 53223), farther up The Quay, gives you an extra hour to shop but a smaller selection (open daily 7:30am-midnight).

Chapman's Pantry, 61 the Quay (tel. 73833). A combination of a gourmet foodstore, bakery, and delicatessen-style restaurant. *Blaas* 12p, meals £3-4. Open Mon.-Sat. 9am-6pm.

Haricot's Wholefood Restaurant, 11 O'Connell St. The vegetarian and the meateater live in harmony with Haricot's tasty, innovative dishes as peacemakers. Seafood pancakes £4.70, raspberry and yogurt flan £1.65. Open Mon.-Fri. 10am-8pm, Sat. 10am-5:45pm.

Sizzlers Restaurant, the Quay. Cramped but atmospheric diner serves through the wee hours. Full Irish breakfast £3, burger and chips £3.50. Open Sun.-Wed. 7am-2am, Thurs.-Sat. 24 hrs.

Gino's, John St. (tel. 79513), at the Apple Market. Busy family restaurant serves pizza made right before your eyes. Make reservations for dinnertime, especially on Fri. and Sat. nights. Small pizza (for 1) £2.10 plus 45p/topping. Lunch special: small pizza with 2 toppings, ice cream, and tea or coffee £4. Open Mon.-Sat. 11am-8pm.

The Reginald, The Mall (tel. 55087). Right behind Reginald's Tower, this bar/restaurant serves rich, delicious food in a classy environment. Dinner is expensive, but lunch is reasonable. Lunch special £4.95, vegetarian specials £6.45. Lunch daily noon-2:30pm, dinner 3-10:30pm.

Crumbs, Michael St. Good food served quickly in a coffee-shop atmosphere. 9" pizza £3; soup with brown bread £1.10. Open Mon.-Sat. 9am-7pm.

PUBS

Waterford has 56 pubs and a city population of around 45,000. You do the math: we think they take their pubs rather seriously. You can find multiple pubs along the Quay, even more as you travel up Broad St. into town.

Geoff's Pub, 9 John St. (tel. 74787). Favored by Waterford's budding artists and the slick theater crowd. Wonder at a dark, smoky setting where cappuccino and Camus almost edge out Guinness and *craic.*

The Pulpit, John St. (tel 79184). A hip, young, and charismatic crowd is drawn by the upstairs nightclub, **Preachers.** Open Wed.-Sun. 10:30pm; cover £3-5.

Mullane's, 15 Newgate St. (tel. 73854), off New St., is famous for its hard-core trad sessions. A sprinkling of the young and a dash of tourists added to the older regular crowd results in the perfect mix. Sessions Tues., Thurs., Sat., and Sun. nights at 10pm—no cover.

The Wine Vault, High St. (tel. 53444; fax 53494). Drink wine in a classy bistro even after the pubs close. Jazz and blues sessions on Sat. nights; a glass of house red starts at £1.90. Open Mon.-Wed. until midnight, Thurs.-Sun. until 12:30am.

SIGHTS

You can cover all of Waterford's sights in a day, but only if you move quickly. The **Waterford Crystal Factory** (tel. 73311), one mile out on N25 (Cork Rd.), is the city's highlight. Forty-minute tours allow you to witness the transformation of molten glass into polished crystal. Many of the people taking the tour intend to buy something sparkly and expensive at its end; don't feel bad if you don't. Admire the finished products—and their outrageous prices—in the gallery. The least expensive item is a crystal snowman (£14). (Tours and audio-visual shows every 20 min.; April-Oct. daily 8:30am-4pm, showroom open 8:30am-6pm; Nov.-March daily 9am-3:15pm, showroom open 9am-5pm; £1.50.) Tours are wheelchair accessible. Book ahead via telephone or through the tourist office. The self-guided tour now in preparation should be ready by 1996. City bus route #1 (Kilbarry/Ballybeg) leaves the Clock Tower every 30 min. and passes the factory (70p).

Much of Waterford's history has unfortunately been converted into retail space. Because the city hasn't expanded outward since 1790, Viking, Victorian, and very modern structures are piled on top of each other. **Walking Tours of Historic Waterford** (tel. 73711; fax 50645) commence from the Granville Hotel on the Quay (March-Oct. daily at noon and 2pm; £3). The tours are a worthwhile way to get an understanding of Waterford's complex, tortuous history. They also give 25% off admission to Reginald's Tower and the Heritage Centre.

Reginald's Tower, at the end of The Quay (tel. 73501), has guarded the entrance to the city for 993 years. Its 12-foot thick Viking walls were almost impossible for invaders to penetrate. Climb the stone spiral staircase for bits of local history and old maps of Waterford, as well as a view of the city. Strongbow had his wedding reception here. Nearby, a wealth of Viking artifacts snatched from the jaws of bulldozers is now on display at the tiny **Waterford Heritage Centre,** Greyfriars St., off The Quay (tel. 71227). Highlights of the collection are the elaborate 13th-century gold brooches and Viking-era pencils. A cross-section of an archaeological dig on a Waterford street visually reveals the course of the town's history, from the floor of a Viking house to Norman-era rubbish to Michael Jackson-era Pepsi cans. (Open March-June and Sept.-Oct. Mon.-Fri. 10am-5pm, Sat. 10am-1pm; July-Aug. Mon.-Fri. 10am-8pm, Sat. 10am-1pm; £1, students 75p, 25% off with walking tour ticket.)

At the corner of Bailey's New St. and Greyfriars St. lie the ruins of the **French Church,** a Dominican monastery built in 1240 AD. The monastery was given to Huguenot refugees in the 17th century; today's visitors might be interested in its wide-open tombs. (Get the key from Mrs. White, 5 Greyfriars St., opposite the ruins.) Much of Waterford's more recent monumental architecture was the brainchild of John Roberts; the **Theatre Royal** and **City Hall,** both on The Mall, are his secular masterpieces. Both the Roman Catholic **Holy Trinity Cathedral** on Barronstrand St. and the Church of Ireland **Christ Church Cathedral** in Cathedral Square (up Henrietta St. from the Quay) were designed by Roberts in the 18th century. Through his work, Waterford became the only Irish town to have both faiths united by a common architect. Christ Church Cathedral has the rather unique tomb of Bishop Tunes Rice, which shows vermin chewing on his decaying corpse: a gruesome posthumous sermon on the ephemeral nature of human life. Scattered throughout town are remnants of the town's medieval **city walls;** the biggest blocks are behind the Theatre Royal on Spring Garden St. and on Patrick St., extending to Bachelor's Walk.

It's a Delicate Matter

The glass-making process at the Waterford Crystal Factory begins when raw ingredients are fed into pots kept at 1400°F. **Blowers** then huff and puff into a long tube with a globule of molten glass at its end, rotating the tube to create the shape of a vase or a fruit dish from the former globule. **Cutters** have the design patterns memorized, and cut two-thirds deep into the emerging crystal—not an easy feat. Both blowers and cutters apprentice for five years before qualifying for work. **Engravers** have it even tougher—it takes ten years to hone the special skills used in the factory. Video game junkies will be excited to learn that good eye-hand coordination is a crucial qualification for potential apprentices.

ENTERTAINMENT

The Munster Express (80p), a local newspaper, has some entertainment listings. **The Roxy,** O'Connell St. (tel. 55145), is Waterford's hottest nightclub; it also hosts live, occasionally major, acts. The pub downstairs is unremarkable, since the real action begins after pubs close. (Club open Wed.-Sun. midnight-2am; 70s and 80s rock Thurs. and Sun., acid/house Sat., live bands Fri.; cover £2-5). **Metroland,** the nightclub at **The Metropole,** Mary St. (tel. 78185), is a giant dance hall. Important gigs are well advertised around town. Speaking of important, **Boyzone** (an Irish N.K.O.T.B.) played here to kick off their debut single. Yay, Boyzone! Check the pub listings (above) for more music and club options.

The **Garter Lane Arts Centre,** Garter Lane 2, 22a O'Connell St. (tel. 77153), stages dance, music, and theater, and shows free exhibitions in an old Georgian building. In July and August, the Summer Arts and Crafts Fair fills the exhibition space, displaying handmade objects for sale. Down the street at Garter Lane 1, 5 O'Connell St., **screen/space** (tel. 57198) strikes a lowercase balance between art and capitalism. The result is a mix of smart second-run movies and cheap tickets. Information about Waterford's theater scene is available here. (Double features Wed.-Thurs. at 8pm. You must buy a membership in order to buy a ticket: yearly memberships are £2, tickets £1.50.)

■■■ WATERFORD HARBOUR

East of Waterford City, Waterford Harbour straddles the Waterford/Wexford county line. It is here that Oliver Cromwell coined the phrase "by hook or by crook," referring to his plan to take Waterford City by landing either at Hook Head or on the opposite side of the harbor, at Crooke. (Neither plan worked very well—Waterford held out for a very long time and escaped the Cromwellian destruction visited on places like Cork and Limerick.) Both sides of the harbor are host to historic ruins, friendly fishing villages, and gorgeous ocean views. Think of the scenic harbor as A-shaped: on the left slope of the A is popular beach destination Dunmore East while on the right slope is thin Hook Head. The crossbar represents the **Passage East Car Ferry** (tel. (051) 382488 or 382480), which carries coastal explorers between Passage East (six miles from Waterford City on the west side of the harbor) and Ballyhack on the east side, circumventing a 37-mile land route between them. From the Quay in Waterford, it's a swell bike ride to Passage East: turn left at the Tower Hotel and follow signs for Passage East and Dunmore East. From Wexford, follow signs for Ballyhack to reach the ferry. (Continuous sailings April-Sept. Mon.-Sat. 7:20am-10pm, Sun. 9:30am-10pm; Oct.-March Mon.-Sat. 7:20am-8pm, Sun. 9:30am-8pm. Pedestrians 80p, £1 return; cyclists £1, £1.50 return.)

DUNMORE EAST

Across Waterford Harbour from the Hook is **Dunmore East,** a tiny town in which fishing and tourism coexist uneasily. No ferry runs here; you'll have to travel the five miles south from Waterford City by foot, bike, car, or **Suirway** bus, which runs from the Quay in Waterford to Dunmore East (2/day; £1.50). The sandy strand attracts bathers and tanning frogs on the rare days when the sun is shining. At several points, trails descend to the isolated coves below, which are more secluded places to swim. At **Badger's Cove,** facing the docks, dozens of seagulls perch on the rocky cliff face and set up a frightening cacophony of echoing cries. These seagull nesting sites are the closest to human habitation, as far as we know. For an even more dramatic view, follow the gravel road past Dock Rd. to see the ocean crashing onto rocky coves. At the end of Dock Rd., behind the pink Harbour House, Irish surfer dudes at the **Dunmore East Adventure Centre** (tel. (051) 383783) will teach you to snorkel, sail, surf, kayak, or ride a horse. Bring a towel and swimsuit; they provide the equipment (£10/½-day, £22/full day, prices £2 higher July-Aug.).

As you follow Dock Rd., the hotels and B&Bs become more expensive. One of the more reasonable is **Creaden View,** Dock Rd. (tel. (051) 383339), with rooms overlooking the harbor (£15/person). Down the road, the **Dunmore Caravan and Camping Park** (tel. (051) 383200) has offices in the Park Shop. Most of the park is filled with trailers on blocks, but you can pitch a tent (hikers/cyclists £3, showers 50p). **Lucy's Kitchen** on the Strand (tel. (051) 383350) dishes up take-away food (chickenburger £1.40; open daily 8am-1am). Farther up the road, the **Ocean Hotel Restaurant** (tel. (051) 383136) creatively plays with its food (cream cheese and spinach pancakes with tomato and garlic sauce £5; open Mon.-Sat. 10am-10pm, Sun. 12:30-3pm and 4-9pm). Groceries are for sale at **Londis Supermarket** (open Mon.-Fri. 8:30am-8:30pm, Sat.-Sun. 9am-8pm). Dunmore's temporary residents gather at the pub in the **Strand Inn,** which they like for the pool table and the occasional live music.

PASSAGE EAST

Passage East is exactly that and nothing more: from here, people hop on the ferry that crosses the River Suir to the Wexford side. Passage is a small, friendly fishing village oriented around two open squares. **The Farleigh** (tel. (051) 382240) offers drinks to a tightly-knit but extraordinarily friendly crowd among red leather seats and nautical items. Several B&Bs in the village survive due to late-night ferry traffic. **Harbour Lights B&B** (tel. (051) 382646), facing the ferry, is lovely, with bare wood floors and wicker chairs in each room (£10/person). In September, Passage East kicks up its heels at the annual **Mussel Festival,** which features exhibitions, cooking demonstrations, fishing tips, and mussel-tasting (get your mouth muscles ready for all those mussels). The **Suirway** bus service (tel. (051) 382209) goes to Passage from Waterford (2/day; £1.50); buses depart opposite the tourist office in Waterford.

BALLYHACK

The profile that Ballyhack offers to its cross-channel neighbor is dominated by the 15th-century **Ballyhack Castle** (tel. (051) 389468 or 389164; fax 389284). Built by the Crusading Order of the Knights Hospitalers in the 1450s (a.k.a. the Knights of Malta), the castle now houses an unimpressive heritage center. A tour of the tower, empty except for cheesy Crusader mannequins, will take no longer than the 10 minutes that you have to wait for the ferry. (Open July-Aug. daily 10am-7pm; March-June and Sept. Wed.-Sun. noon-6pm; £1, students 50p). Next door to the castle in a building marked "The Half Door," a diminutive **tourist office** (tel. (051) 389468) is open in July and August. This is virtually the only place to find info on the Waterford

Harbour area. The pricey *Historic Hook Head* (£2) is nonetheless an invaluable guide to the area; get it if you plan to spend any time on the Hook.

Dunbrody Abbey (tel. (051) 388603), two miles from Ballyhack on the New Ross Rd., is a magnificent Cistercian ruin dating from 1190. Almost wholly intact, this abbey lets you wander through staircases and little rooms that are ideal for a game of medieval hide-and-go-seek. (Open daily 10am-6pm; go through the turnstile on the left side of the road, cross the field, and climb on in. Free.) Across the road, the **visitors center** (tel. (051) 389468) sits among the ruins of a castle once associated with the Abbey. The center has no info on the Abbey, but there is mini-golf and a hugely disappointing hedge-row maze—the hedges are two feet tall! Bring your hobbit friends. (Open June-Aug. daily 10:30am-6pm; £1.)

ARTHURSTOWN

Head south from Ballyhack past the ferry to the beginning of *Slí Charman* ("SHLEE KAR-man"), a coastal walking path that leads almost all the way to Dublin. Follow the path for just a few minutes until you round the bend to reach **Arthurstown,** which offers accommodations, a grocery, and little else. The **Village Store** corners the grocery store market (it's the only one around; open Mon.-Sat. 9am-6pm). The only competition is the prepared grub at the **King's Inn,** the local pub (tel. (051) 389173; salmon sandwich £1.70), which also sports a bureau de change. The first left coming from Ballyhack, across from Mardh Mere House, is the entrance to the **Arthurstown Youth Hostel (An Óige/HI)** (tel. (051) 389441). Once a coast guard barracks, it still has many of the original pine walls and moldings. Extensive renovations have turned a ramshackle building into a comfortable and respectable hostel; enjoy the antique fireplaces. (Curfew 10:30pm; lockout 10:30am-5pm. Kitchen open 7:30-10am; £6, under 18 £4.50; open June-Sept.) **Clogheen** (tel. (051) 389110) has plush green velvet and B&B. Blossoms pour out of the window to greet you at the front door, as do cats. (£12.50/person w/full breakfast, £10.50/person w/ continental breakfast). **Clendine House,** on the Ballyhack Rd. towards Duncannon (tel. (051) 389 258), is a huge house on a huge lawn. The rooms are suitably spacious and beautifully decorated with plush chairs and puffy duvets. You'll recognize it by the horses prancing in the front yard. (July-Aug. £13.50/person, £15 w/bath; Sept.-May £12, £13 w/bath. **Camping** on the lawn £5/tent, shower £1.)

DUNCANNON & HOOK HEAD

South of Arthurstown, the sunny and scenic **Hook Head Peninsula** begins. A circuit of the towns, ruins, and sea views of the peninsula is easily accomplished on a bike and eminently enjoyable and enlightening. From Arthurstown, head east on Duncannon Rd. and keep an eye out for the sharp right labeled "Duncannon."

One mile will bring you to Duncannon. **Duncannon Fort** perches on the cliffs at the edge of the village. The fort was attacked by the Spanish Armada in 1588, Cromwell in 1649, William of Orange in 1690, and the United Irishmen rebels in 1798. The Irish army took it over and refitted it during World War II, and it served as a summer camp until 1986. The original Elizabethan structures were used right up to the abandonment of the fort in 1945. Today, the tired site is being restored and turned into a museum. The tour is fascinating and brilliant; don't leave Duncannon without taking it. (Open daily mid-June to Aug. 10am-6pm; tours every hour on the hour; £1, students and children 50p. For info, call Roche's pub (tel. (051) 389188).)

Horse rides on the Hook can be arranged through the **Hook Trekking Centre,** one mile from Duncannon on the New Ross Rd. (call (051) 389166 to schedule). The Duncannon Festival runs the first week in July, offering fish, cheap tarts, and other inexpensive delectables (call Eileen Roche for details (tel. (051) 389188)). **Duncannon Campground** (tel. (051) 389193) is one half-mile from town on the Churchtown Rd. (open March-Oct.; £4-5/tent). **The Strand Stores,** also in Duncannon, sells groceries (daily 9am-10pm). Next door is the **Strand Tavern** (tel. (051) 389109) where you can appreciate the mugs above the bar as you eat a sandwich.

From Duncannon, the **Ring of Hook** road goes down to **Hook Head,** the tip of the peninsula. Welsh missionary St. Dubhan founded the first **Hook Lighthouse** in the 5th century, making it one of Europe's four oldest. The structure has beaconed continuously since then. On the eastern side of the peninsula is **Tintern Abbey** (tel. (051) 62321), founded in the 13th century as a daughter abbey of the Tintern in Wales, about which Wordsworth wrote. The Abbey is minutes from the Ballycullane stop on the Waterford-Rosslare train line (open all year; £1, students 50p).

■■■ TRAMORE

Tramore has beaches (*Trá Mór* means "big beach"), beautiful coastal views, and great places to stay, so it's too bad that the rest of the country only knows Tramore as the home of Celtworld, the made-for-tourists side-show of Celtic legend. Lots of amusements line up along the promenade in classic seaside-resort style; the **beach** itself is beautiful, wide, and shallow. The very professional **tourist office,** Strand Rd. (tel. 381572), can help you see past Celtworld (tourist office open June-mid-Sept. Mon.-Sat. 10am-12:45pm and 2-6pm). **Flanagan's,** Market St. (tel. 381252), rents **bikes,** but Tramore is so darn hilly that cycling won't be much fun (£7/day, £30/week, deposit £40). **Bus Éireann** stops on Strand St. en route from Waterford (1/hr., more during rush hour; 20 min.; £1.50, £2.25 return). Tramore's **phone code** is fixed as 051 in Celtic legend.

Tramore's is burdened with a staggering number of great places to stay. **The Cliff,** Church St. (tel. 381363), looks out on the ocean from a prime cliffside location. Technically a YWCA Hostel, its single and double rooms, each with wash basin, come closer to B&B status. The TV lounge seems entirely surrounded by the sea—who needs cartoons? (Co-ed. Resident pooch. No kitchen. £5.50/night. Sheet rental £2.50, continental breakfast £1, full Irish breakfast £2.50. Book well ahead July-Aug.) **Monkey Puzzle Hostel,** Upper Branch Rd. (tel. 386754), has a great dog that runs down the street to greet hostelers with a friendly wag; the kind owners await at the door. The hostel is named after an unusual, recently deceased tree. (£6.50, Sept.-May £5.50; laundry £2.)

Tramore is bursting with B&Bs, especially on Church Rd. **Venezia,** Church Road Grove (tel. 381412), signposted off Church Rd., is immaculate and glossy, with top-notch, firm beds (£13/person, £15 w/bath). For a killer view try **Turret House,** Church Rd. (tel. 386342), whose plain rooms are enlivened by the ocean. (Single £16, double £28, w/bath £32; Sept.-May prices £1 lower.) **Church Villa,** Church Rd. (tel. 381547), is, appropriately, across the road from Christchurch. TVs in every room add that special something (£13/person, £15 w/bath). By far the best of several nearby campsites is the family-style **Newtown Caravan and Camping Park** (tel. 381979 or 386189), 1½ miles from town off the Dungarvan Coast Rd. between the golf course and the **Metal Man,** a monument to shipwreck victims. (Hikers/cyclists £2.50, July-Aug. £3; showers 50p; open Easter-Sept.)

Tourist traps line up next to Celtworld and Splashworld; walk into town instead for regionally famous **Cunningham's Fish and Chips,** Main St. Fish and chips (£2.10), chicken and chips (£1.70; open daily 5pm-midnight). **The Sea Horse,** Main St. (tel. 386091), has great pub grub (4-course meals £7; food served noon-9pm). **Londis Supermarket** provides groceries right off Main St. (tel.383471; open Mon.-Sat. 8:30am-7:00pm.) Locals love to be hip and abbreviate their fave watering holes. **The Victorian House ("The Vic"),** Queens St. (tel. 390338), is blue and atmospheric. **The Hibernian ("Hi B"),** Main St. at the crossroads (tel. 386396), does disco on Friday through Sunday nights (cover £4).

Celtworld, The Promenade (tel. 386166), sometimes says it's educational, teaching foreigners about Irish folktales by dramatizing them. It may be a good attraction for kids, but not exactly an edifying experience for adults. The 40-minute show consists of five Irish legends told with pop-up-book-style special effects, followed by a sideshow of Celtic-themed parlor tricks. The giant killer eyeball that swoops at the audience is a nasty bit. Note the lack of books in the gift shop. (Shows start every 4 min.; July-Aug. daily 10am-10pm; Sept. 10am-6pm; April-May Mon.-Fri. 10am-5pm, Sat.-Sun. 10am-6pm; June daily 10am-8pm. Last ticket 1hr. before closing. £4, students £3.25, under 16 £3.) **Splashworld** next door (tel. 390176) has bubble pools, water slides, and wave machines. Yes, it's heated. (March-Oct. Mon.-Sun. 10am-10pm; Nov.-Feb. Mon.-Fri. noon-8pm, Sat.-Sun. 11am-6pm; £3.95 for a 2hr. session, students £3.25, children £2.95.) Adjoining **Laserworld,** (tel. 386565, fax 390146), lets you zap your friends in a glow-in-the-dark fantasy war-world. (June-Aug. Sun.-Sat. 10am-10pm, Apr.-May, and Sept.-Oct. 10am-6pm; £3.)

■■■ DUNGARVAN

The administrative headquarters for Co. Waterford, this busy market town concentrates on business and fishing. Main St. (also O'Connell St.) runs through the central square; Emmet St. (also Mitchel St.) runs parallel to Main St., one block uphill, and is home to the hostel and a number of B&Bs. The road to Cork veers off Emmet St. at the Garda station. contains B&Bs and the hostel. Turn off Emmet St. at the Garda station for the Cork Rd. The unreservedly helpful **tourist office,** on the Square (tel. 41741), is a good resource for information about the nearby Ring *gaeltacht.* (open June-Aug. Mon.-Sat. 10am-6pm). The best villages in West Waterford are inaccessible by bus—bikes can be rented at **Murphy's Cycles,** 68 Main St. (tel. 41376; open Mon.-Fri. 8:30am-7pm, Sat. 9am-6pm, Sun. 10am-6pm). It's a **Raleigh Rent-A-Bike** depot: £7/day, £30/week; deposit £30, £6 remote dropoff. **Bank of Ireland,** on the Square, has a 24-hr. **ATM** that accepts all major cash networks, as doe **AIB,** just steps away on Meagher St. (Both banks open Mon. 10am-5pm, Tues.-Fri. 10am-4pm). **Buses** run east to Waterford (Mon.-Fri. 11/day, Sat. 8/day, Sun. 5/day; 1hr.; £5.50, students £3.20), west to Cork (Mon.-Sat. 7/day, Sun. 5/day; £8, students £4.70), and north to Lismore daily, from Davitt's Quay. (Bus info. tel. (051) 79000.) The **phone code** in Dungarvan prefers to say 058 in Irish, thank you.

The **Dungarvan Holiday Hostel (IHH),** on the Youghal Rd. (tel. 44340), just off Emmet St. opposite the garda station, used to be a chapel for the Christian Brothers. Dark rooms and tightly packed beds perpetuate the ascetic life. (Four- to 6-bed dorm £6.50; July-Aug. double £7.50, Sept.-June £6; wheelchair accessible.) **Santa Antoni,** Mitchel St. (tel. 42923), is appreciably more welcoming with a gregarious owner. (Single or double £11/person.)

Ormond's Café, The Square (tel. 41153), a few doors down from the tourist office, serves outstanding desserts and even the meals to precede them in its stonewalled back rooms (quiche £2.50; open daily 8:30am-5:30pm). **An Bialann,** 31 Grattan Sq. (tel. 42825), is a little café with overstuffed vinyl booths and 40p scones and butter (open daily 9am-8:30pm). There's an **L&N Superstore** on Main St. (open Mon.-Wed. and Sat. 9am-6pm, Thurs.-Fri. 9am-9pm).

The **Govs,** 13 Main St. (tel. 41149), is probably the best pub in town, at least when they hold their rousing trad sessions (Tues.-Wed.; ballads Thurs.). Other good bars are **Paddy Foley's** on The Square, **Downey's,** Main St., and **Davitt's Quay,** by the Quay of the same name. If you have transportation try **The Seanachie** ("The Storyteller;" tel. 46285) on N25 to Cork, about 10 miles from Dungarvan. The food is terrific and terrifically expensive (dinner £12). They pump out marathon trad sessions nightly and all-day *craic.*

The **Dungarvan Museum** (tel. 41231), at the end of Lower Main St. above the library, spares nothing in its breathless and well-mounted story of Dungarvan. From the Ice Age to Vikings, Cromwell, and maritime trade, it's in there. (Open Mon.-Fri. 2-5pm; free.) One-hour **Walking tours** of medieval and Georgian Dungarvan leave the tourist office three times a day during July and August (£2). **King John's Castle,** presiding over Davitt's Quay, was built by none other than King John around 1200. The castle has 7-feet-thick walls but has nevertheless been in various states of disrepair at least since 1299. Now it's between a warehouse and industrial complex, certainly not a tourist thing.

There's not much else to see in Dungarvan itself, but deep-sea and in-shore **fishing** is excellent just off the coast—fishermen claim to have caught 16 varieties in a day, including blueshark, conger, and ling. Book a boat at **Gone Fishin'** (tel. 43514), 42 Lower Main St., a professional outfit with plenty of experience guiding less professional anglers to a catch. A deep-sea expedition leaves daily at 9:30am, returning at 6:30pm (£20; rod and tackle hire £7; open Mon.-Sat. 9am-6pm). **Baumann's,** 6 St. Mary St. (tel. 41395) dispenses fishing tackle, licenses, and a wealth of inside info.

■■■ ARDMORE

Pastel houses and thatched cottages line Main St., which eventually disappears into the sea. Besides having a great **beach,** Ardmore says it's the oldest Christian settlement in Ireland, and has the ruins to back up its claim. St. Declan christianized the area between 350-450 AD. St. Declan's feast day, "Pattern Day," is July 24—a big deal in Ardmore. Ardmore set another record on August 27, 1989, when 704 people wriggled their way into the *Guinness Book of World Records,* making the world's longest human centipede!

The **tourist office** (tel. 94444) on the Dungarvan Rd., is two doors down from the visually offensive, youth-thronged arcade. The staff gives out an excellent leaflet outlining a one-hour **walking tour** of town (open Easter-Sept. daily 10am-8pm). Ardmore is a three-mile detour off Cork-Waterford Rd. (N25). Hitching from the junction to the town can be slow. Buses run to: Cork (Mon.-Sat. 3-5/day, Sun. 1/day; 1½hr.; £7.30, students £4.20), Dungarvan (July-Aug. Mon.-Thurs. 2/day; all year Fri.-Sat. 2/day; 40min.; £3.10, students £2), and Waterford (July and Aug. Mon.-Fri. 2/day; all year Sat. 1/day; 2hr.; £7.70, student £4.30). Their **phone code** is 024.

Ardmore's tranquil, seaside location is conducive to B&Bs with brilliant sea views. **Byron Lodge,** Middle Rd. (tel. 94157), has literary aspirations, a large flower garden, and rooms with sunny alcoves. From Main St., take the street that runs uphill between the two thatched cottages (£13.50/person, w/bath £15.50; single £14; open Easter-Sept.). The **Cush B&B** (tel. 94474) is another wise choice (single £15.50, double £13.50). **Camping** in Ardmore is available along the beach at **Healy's** (tel. 94181; just look for the caravans; about £3.50/tent), but some travelers just pitch their tents on the beach.

Ardmore's limited food offerings reflects its size and popularity as a daytrip rather than a traveling destination. The local favorite is **Cup and Saucer,** Main St. (tel. 94501), which has a delightful flower garden out back for sunny days (garlic potatoes £1.40, cottage pie £4; open daily 10am-9pm). **Paddy Mac's,** Main St. (tel 94166), prepares good pub fare (open smoked salmon on brown bread £3.50) and holds rousing trad sessions on Thursday nights and Sunday afternoons in the presence of an encouragingly mixed crowd. **Quinn's Foodstore,** in the town center, has the best selection of groceries (open daily 8am-10pm). **Riley's** pub is small but attracts the homespun "Fiddling Farmers," as well as a gaggle of older locals Tuesday nights. **Keever's Bar,** Main St., should be "Keever's Bars"—there are two of them, quite separate, but both offer good *craic.*

The free walking tour guide to Ardmore serves as a useful introduction to the town's historic monuments. The **cliff walk** winds along the coast with views of the beach. The **cathedral,** built piecemeal between 800 and 1400, covers the site of St. Declan's monastery. Its west gable is carved ornately with long rows of human figures. The tiny **Beannachán** (oratory) is the oldest building in the graveyard. St. Declan is said to be buried inside, and the faithful avow that soil from the saint's grave cures diseases. The cathedral and its graveyard are marked unmistakably by the 97-foot-high **round tower,** where strange head-shaped projections suggest ancient head-hunting rites. Farther along the St. Declan pilgrimages, the **St. Declan's Stone** is perched at water's edge (just right from Main St. along the shore).

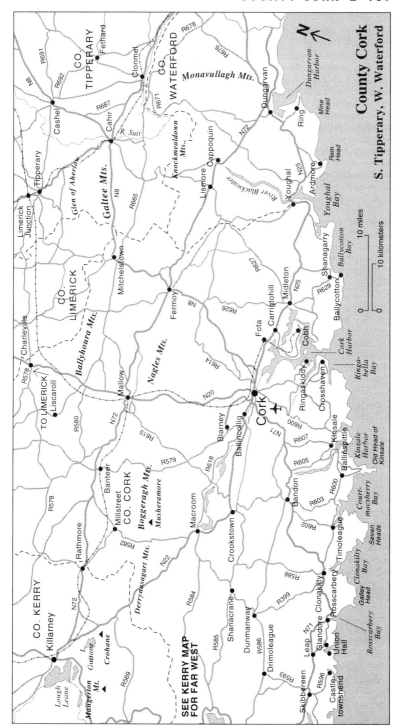

County Cork
S. Tipperary, W. Waterford

SOUTHWEST IRELAND

Traveling west from Cork City means moving from an English-influenced, 20th-century landscape into one that often looks untouched: the scenery is lush, the fishermen enthusiastic, and the roads lousy. This is the most fertile of the West's scenic coasts; its history stretches back millennia, and the derelict monuments that once had spiritual significance to ancient civilizations now bestow a sense of timelessness on the open landscape. Life in the Southwest is leisurely and localized: the newly-settled foreign expatriates, the remote pubs that stay open until 3am, and the stretches of wild, open, undeveloped land are all tributes to the region's informal and decidedly anti-urban atmosphere. If you're short on time, spend a day or two in Cork City, try to visit an island or coastal town in West Cork, then zip up to the mountains on one of the three peninsulas. Get to know a few places well rather than doing the typical tourist's whirlwind tour through Cork, Killarney, the Ring of Kerry, and Dingle.

County Cork

County Cork incorporates both the Republic's second-largest city and some of its most deserted seashores. Eastern Cork's superb harbors made it a prosperous trading center, while its distance from Dublin and the Pale gave the English less leverage over it. Perhaps as a result, Cork was a center of patriotic activity during the 19th and early-20th centuries. Headquarters of the "Munster Republic" that the anti-Treaty forces controlled during the Civil War, the county produced both military planner, spymaster, and administrative genius Michael Collins, as well as the man who assassinated him in 1922. Cork City replaces the old patriotic energies with mercantile and cultural ones, while the sea towns of Kinsale and Cobh gaily entertain tall ships along with stooped backpackers. "West Cork" means the southwestern third of the county, once the "badlands" of Ireland whose ruggedness and isolation rendered it lawless and largely uninhabitable. Ex-hippies and antiquated fishermen have replaced the outlaws, and they do their best to render the villages laid-back and ultra-hospitable. The salt-sprayed, wind-tossed Roaringwater Bay and Mizen Head mark Ireland's land's end and provide the closest thing to solitude that the country can offer. Ireland's rich archaeological history is particularly visible in Cork. Ring forts of Celtic warrior-tribes and stone circles of their more peaceful predecessors dot the Cork countryside alongside the more recent ruins of medieval castles and abbeys.

■■■ CORK CITY

Cork shows its true colors on weekends (and especially on days of hurling matches, when the entire city seems inebriated): families stroll the shops along Patrick St. and Oliver Plunkett St., shoppers haggle for goods at the English Market, and young and old alike fill the city's cafés and pubs. Though it's 400 years older than Dublin (St. Finbarr founded a monastery here around 600 AD), there's almost no history left to be seen: the old city burned down in 1622, Cromwell expelled half its citizens in the 1640s, the English Duke of Marlborough laid siege to it in 1690, slum clearances and an 1853 flood required more new building, and the British torched the city again in 1920 during the Irish War of Independence. In between all these depredations, Cork became fairly prosperous—shipping, butter, and Henry Ford's first European factory kept the town expanding faster than anyone could tear it down. Cork is still growing, as new bistros and cafés open everyday, and the city rocks on weekends.

ORIENTATION & PRACTICAL INFORMATION

Downtown Cork is the tip of an arrow-shaped island in the River Lee; most streets downtown were Venice-style canals until the 1700s, when Cork discovered pavement. Plentiful bridges link the island to Cork's residential south side, and to its north side, including the poorer Shandon district. Downtown action concentrates on Oliver Plunkett St., Patrick St., and Paul St. (all parallel to the Lee) as well as the north-south streets that connect them, including the Grand Parade and a number of pedestrian walkways. Heading west from the Grand Parade, Washington St. becomes Western Rd. and then N22 to Killarney; to the north of the Lee, MacCurtain St. flows east into Lower Glanmire Rd., which then becomes N8 and N25. Cork is compact and pedestrian-friendly; it's hard to get lost. City buses crisscross Cork and its suburbs; from downtown, catch the buses (and their schedules) at the bus station on Merchant's Quay or on Patrick St., across from the Father Matthew statue. Downtown buses run every 20 to 40 minutes (reduced service on Sunday) from about 7:30am to 11:30pm and cost 65p.

Tourist Office: Tourist House, Grand Parade (tel. 273251), near the corner of South Mall and Grand Parade downtown. The £1 *Tourist Trail* leaflet gives you a rundown on all the sights. The office also runs free guided walking tours of the city in July and August. Call for schedules. Open May-June Mon.-Sat. 9:15am-6pm; July-Aug. Mon.-Sat. 9am-7pm, Sun. 2-5pm; Sept.-April Mon.-Sat. 9:15am-5:30pm.

Budget Travel Office: USIT, 10 Market Parade (tel. 270900), in the Arcade off Patrick St. Large, helpful travel office sells TravelSave stamps (which are essential for student discounts on bus and rail travel), Rambler, and Eurotrain tickets. Open Mon.-Fri. 9:30am-5:30pm, Sat. 10am-2pm. USIT has a second office at University College, across from Boole Library (tel. 273901; open Mon.-Fri. 9:30am-5:30pm).

An Óige/HI (Irish Youth Hostel Association): 1-2 Redclyffe, Western Rd. (tel. 543289); open nightly after 5pm.

Banks: TSB bank, 4/5 Princes St. (tel. 275221). Open Mon.-Wed. and Fri. 9:30am-5pm, Thurs. 9:30am-7pm. **Bank of Ireland,** 70 Patrick St. (tel. 277177), open Mon. 9:30am-5pm, Tues.-Fri. 9:30am-4pm. **American Express: Heffernan's Travel,** Pembroke St. (tel. 275625). AmEx desk is open Mon.-Fri. 9:30am-1pm and 2:30-5pm.

Post Office: Oliver Plunkett St. (tel. 272000). Open Mon.-Sat. 9am-1pm and 2-5:30pm.

Phone Code: 021. **Directory Assistance:** dial 1190.

Airport: Aer Lingus and **Manx Airlines** (tel. 311000) and **Ryanair** (tel. 313000) connect posh Cork Airport to Dublin, the Isle of Man, various English cities, and Paris. A taxi (£6) or bus (19/day; £2.50) will deliver you to Cork City. The airport is 5 mi. south of Cork on Kinsale Rd.

Trains: Kent Station: Lower Glanmire Rd. (tel. 504777), across the river from the city center in the northeast part of town. Open daily 7am-8pm. Lockers £1. Cork has good train connections to Dublin (Mon.-Sat. 7/day, Sun. 5/day; 3hr.; £31.50, students £12); Limerick (Mon.-Sat. 5/day, Sun. 3/day; 1½hr.; £12.50, students £6); Killarney (Mon.-Sat. 4/day, Sun. 3/day; 2hr.; £12.50, students £6); and Tralee (Mon.-Sat. 4/day, Sun. 3/day; 2½hr.; £16, students £7).

Buses: Parnell Pl. (tel. 508188), 2 blocks from Patrick's Bridge on Merchants' Quay. Inquiries desk open Mon.-Fri. 9am-6pm; April-Sept. Mon.-Fri. 9am-6pm, Sun. 9am-5pm. **Luggage storage** £1.30/item, 80p/each additional day (open Mon.-Fri. 8:35am-6:15pm, Sat. 9:30am-6:15pm). Bus Éireann goes to all major cities: Bantry (Mon.-Sat. 3/day, Sun. 2/day; £8.80, students £5); Galway (Mon.-Sat. 5/day, Sun. 4/day; £12, students £7.50); Killarney (Mon.-Sat. 7/day, Sun. 5/day; £8.80, students £5); Limerick (Mon.-Sat. 6/day, Sun. 5/day; £9, students £5.30); Rosslare Harbour (Mon.-Sat. 3/day, Sun. 2/day; £13, students £8); Skibbereen (Mon.-Fri. 6/day, Sat. 4/day, Sun. 3/day; £8.80, students £5); Tralee (Mon.-Sat. 7/day, Sun. 5/day; £9.70, students £6); Waterford (Mon.-Sat. 6/day, Sun. 5/day; £9.70, students £6); Dublin

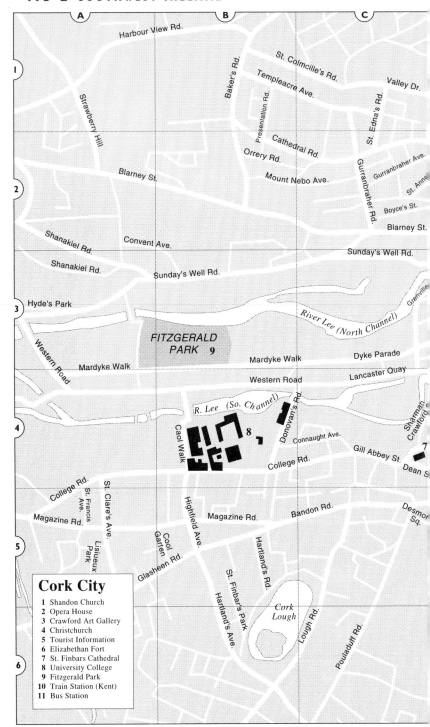

Cork City

1 Shandon Church
2 Opera House
3 Crawford Art Gallery
4 Christchurch
5 Tourist Information
6 Elizabethan Fort
7 St. Finbars Cathedral
8 University College
9 Fitzgerald Park
10 Train Station (Kent)
11 Bus Station

Fair Hill

Assumption Rd.

Glen Rd.

Redemption Rd.

Gerald Griffin St.

Watercourse Rd.

Pope's Rd.

Wolfe Tone St.

N

0   yards   220

0   meters   200

Cathedral Rd.

Cathedral Walk

Youghal Old Rd.

Mary Aikenhead

Old Market Pl.

Rathmore Park

Glen Ryan Rd.

Shandon St.

Eason's Hill

Roman Hill

John's St.

Leitrim St.

John St.

Richmond Hill

St. Patrick's Hill

Audley Pl.

Blarney St.

1

John Redmond St.

Dominick St.

Park

Sidney

Belgrave Pl.

North Mall

Pope's Quay

Camden Pl.

Wellington Rd.

Military Rd.

Bachelor's Quay

Kyrl's Quay

Lavitt's Quay

MacCurtain St.

Summer Hill

Henry St.

Grattan St.

North Main St.

St. Paul's St.

2

St. Patrick's Quay

Lower Glanmire Rd.

Sheares St.

Liberty St.

Castle St.

Paul St.

3

Drawbridge St.

Merchant St.

Merchant's Quay

Anderson's Quay

Penrose's Quay

Railway St.

10

Washington St.

St. Patrick's St.

Maylor St.

Parnell Place

Hanover St.

Grand Parade

Oliver

Prince's St.

Marlborough St.

Plunkett St.

11

Wandesford Quay

South Main St.

4

South

Cook St.

Mall

Morrison's Quay

Lapp's Quay

Albert Quay

Victoria Quay

Bishop St.

Proby's Quay

6

Sullivan's Quay

Cove St.

Drinan St.

Mary St.

George's Quay

Union Quay

Angelsea St.

South City Link Rd.

Albert St.

Albert Rd.

Victoria Rd.

Barrack St.

Abbey St.

Evergreen St.

Douglas St.

Sawmill St.

South Terr.

Copley St.

Gas Works Rd.

Mount Carmel

Industry St.

Presentation Pl.

Townshend Pl.

Tower St.

Quaker Rd.

Rutland St.

Infirmary Rd.

Friars Walk

St. Patrick's Rd.

Summerhill South

High St.

South Douglas Rd.

South City Link Rd.

Old Blackrock Rd.

(Mon.-Sat. 4/day, Sun. 3/day; £12, students £8.50); Belfast (Mon.-Sat. 2/day, Sun. 1/day; £17, students £12.80); Sligo (3/day; £16, students £9.50).

Ferryport: Ferries to France and England dock at **Ringaskiddy Terminal,** 9 mi. south of the city. The 40-min. bus from the terminal to the bus station in Cork costs £3. See Getting There (p. 27) for air and ferry details.

Hitching: Hitchhikers headed for West Cork and County Kerry walk down the Western Rd. past both the HI hostel and the dog track to the Crow's Nest Pub. Those hoping to hitch a ride to Dublin, Waterford, or the east stand along Lower Glanmire Rd., on the hill to the train station.

Car Rental: Great Island Car Rentals, MacCurtain St. (tel. 503536), £25/day, £160/week for subcompact standard; min. age 25. **Budget Rent-a-Car,** Tourist Office, Grand Parade (tel. 274755), £44/day, £190/week; min. age 21.

Bike Rental: The Bike Store, 48 MacCurtain St., next to Isaac's (tel. 505339) and at the An Oige Hostel on Western Rd. (tel. 543289). Rents mountain bikes and trekking bikes at £7/day, £30/week; deposit £30 (or you can leave your passport). Return at any Rent-A-Bike depot for an extra £5. Open Mon.-Sat. 9am-6pm. **Bike Repair: Hardings,** 15/17 South Terrace (tel. 273930). Open Mon.-Thurs. 9am-6pm, Fri.-Sat. 9am-5:30pm.

Bookstores: Collins Bookshop, Carey's Ln. (tel. 271346), between Patrick St. and Paul St. Small bookshop with extensive Irish history section, local travel guides, and good vibes. Open Mon.-Sat. 9am-6pm.

Camping Supplies: Outside World and the **Tent Shop,** Parnell Pl. (tel. 278833), next to the bus station. 2-person nylon tent £14/wk.; deposit £8. Extensive stock of camping supplies, including boots and clothing.

Laundry: College Launderette, Western Rd. by the University. Large load, full service £4.45. Open Mon.-Sat. 6am-6pm. **Cork Launderette Service,** 14 MacCurtain St. (tel. 501421). £1/small load, £2/large load, 10p/min. drying time. Open Mon.-Sat. 9am-8:30pm.

Pharmacies: Hayes, Conygham, & Robinson, 71-2 Patrick St. (tel. 270977). Open Mon.-Fri. 9am-5:30pm. **Regional Late Night Pharmacy,** Wilton Rd. (tel. 344575), opposite the Regional Hospital. Take bus #8. Open Mon.-Fri. 9am-10pm, Sat.-Sun. 10am-10pm. **Phelan's Late Night,** 9 Patrick St. (tel. 272511). Open Mon.-Sat. 9am-10pm, Sun. 11am-6pm).

Bisexual, Gay, and Lesbian Information: The Other Place, 8 South Main St. (tel. 278470 or 278471), is a resource center for gay and lesbian concerns in Cork and hosts a gay mixed disco every Fri. and Sat., 11:30pm-2am. **The Other Side Bookshop,** downstairs, sells new and second-hand gay and lesbian publications. **Gay Information Cork** (tel. 271087) offers a telephone helpline Wed. 7-9pm.

Hotlines: Rape Crisis Centre, 26 MacCurtain St. (tel. 968086). 24-hr. counseling. **AIDS Hotline,** Cork AIDS Alliance, 16 Peter St. (tel. 276676). **Samaritans** (tel. 271323) offers a 24-hr. support line for depressed or suicidal individuals.

Hospital: Mercy Hospital, Glenville Pl. (tel. 271971). £10 fee for access to emergency room. Or take bus #8 to **Cork Regional Hospital** (tel. 546400).

Emergency: Dial 999; no coins required. **Garda:** Barrack St., inside the Elizabeth Fort (tel. 271220).

ACCOMMODATIONS

With six hostels ranging from the adequate to the sublime, there is little reason to seek out budget B&Bs in Cork. Most of the city's hostels and B&Bs are concentrated in two areas: on Western Rd. near University College and across the Lee on Lower Glanmire Rd., near the bus and train station.

Campus House (IHH), 3 Woodland View, Western Rd. (tel. 343531), a 15-min. walk, or take bus #8. An extremely helpful and ebullient staff greets you with Cork info at this intimate and luxurious hostel with comfortable beds and superb showers. £5.50, sheets 50p.

Isaac's (IHH), 48 MacCurtain St. (tel. 500011). Follow Patrick St. across the river and take the second right. This bright and clean industrial-sized hostel has high ceilings, polished wood floors, and exposed brick arches. It is an attractive option in a renovated-loft sort of way, and it is conveniently close to the bus and train stations. Organized trips, bike rental, and café (continental breakfast £1.25, Irish £1.95). 24-hr. reception. Disabled access. Dorm £5.75, 4-6 person room w/bath £7.50, single £17.25, double £15.50.

The Cork City Hostel, 100 Lower Glanmire Rd. (tel. 509089). From the train station, turn right and walk 100 yds. The hostel is on the left. Small and a little creaky (especially the lumpy beds), but splendidly offbeat. Walls painted funky colors combine with the lingering scent of patchouli oil to give this hostel a kick-back, alternative feel. Videos at night; fire in winter. 2-6 person dorm £5.50.

Garnish House, Western Rd. (tel. 275111). Large, airy rooms, fluffy comforters, fruit and flowers in every room, free laundry service, fresh scones when you arrive: let yourself be spoiled. Single £16, w/bath £18.

An Óige (HI), 1-2 Redclyffe, Western Rd. (tel. 543289), a 15-min. walk from the Grand Parade, or take bus #8. Comfortable, if somewhat dreary, bunkrooms in a lovely Victorian townhouse with a welcoming front lawn. Currency exchange, bike rental, laundry, hostel vans to Blarney Castle (£2 return), and pool table. Continental breakfast £1.75, 4-course dinner £4.75. Check-in 5pm-midnight. Lockout 10am-5pm. Midnight curfew. £6/person; Sept.-May £5. Sheet rental 50p.

Sheila's Budget Accommodation Centre (IHH), 3 Belgrave Pl. (tel. 505562), by the intersection of Wellington Rd. and York St. Red and gray decorating scheme in a quiet building near the train station; why venture to the store when they sell ramen at the front desk? Reception open 8am-3am, no lockout. Non-smoking rooms. Checkout 10:30am. Breakfast £1.50. 6-person dorm £5.50, 4-person dorm £7.50, single £11, double £9/person. Linen 50p. Key deposit £1.

Fairylawn House, Western Rd. (tel. 543444). Spacious, bare rooms can't compare with the lovely gardens out front. Continental breakfast included. Single £11.50, double £10.50/person (w/continental breakfast).

Kinlay House (IHH), Bob and Joan Walk (the street), (tel. 508966), down the alley to the right of Shandon Church. Located in seedy Shandon, Kinlay House is stark but functional. 24-hr. reception. Lockers in rooms. Free continental breakfast, kitchen with microwave. Laundry £3.60. Dorm £7, single £15, double £10.50/person. 10% discount with ISIC.

Kelly's Independent Hostel, 25 Summerhill South. From downtown Cork follow Parnell Pl. south (it becomes Anglesea St. once you cross the Lee), then turn right on Lanford Row. A small, struggling hostel. Bike rental; laundry £2.50; continental breakfast £1.50. 4-8 person dorm £5.50; Nov.-March £5. Double £7/person.

Camping: Cork City Caravan and Camping Park (tel. 961866), southwest of the city center on Togher Rd., ½ mi. beyond Lough Rd. Bus #14 runs every 20 min. Tent £3.50, 2-person tent £6.50. £1/extra person. Open Easter-Oct.

FOOD

Don't attempt to explore the center of Cork on an empty stomach—intriguing restaurants and cafés are abundant and live in close proximity to each other. Particularly appealing are the lanes connecting Patrick St. to Paul St., Carey Lane and French Church St. The **English Market** hops with a mesmerizing display of fresh fruit, meat, fish, and cheese. One stand is even exclusively devoted to olives and olive oils (accessible from Grand Parade, Patrick St., and Princes St.; Wed. and Sat. are the best days to visit). **Quinnsworth Supermarket** on Paul St. is the biggest grocery story in town (open Mon.-Wed. and Sat. 9am-6pm, Thurs.-Fri.9am-9pm) and the **Quay Co-op** stocks health foods (see listing below). Cork's historic role as a meat-shipping center meant that Corkonians often got stuck eating the leftovers: feet, snouts, and other parts we'd rather not mention since it might ruin your lunch. Hence Cork's local specialties include *cruheen* (pig's feet), *drisheen* (blood sausage; its texture is a cross between liver and Jell-O), and Clonakilty black pudding (a curious mixture of blood and grain). For the less carnivorous, a quasi-religious mission can be made of discovering the city's tastiest scone: scones of both varieties, brown and fruit, can be had at every café, restaurant, and newsstand.

CORK CITY

Quay Co-op, 24 Sullivan's Quay (tel. 317660). Funky music, fresh flowers, and an alternative crowd at this combination restaurant/grocery store. Vegetarian and vegan entrees (dinner £6). Open Mon.-Sat. 10am-10:30pm, Sun. 6:30-10:30pm.

The Gingerbread House, Paul St. (tel. 276411). Enormous windows, vaulted ceilings, cool jazz, and heavenly breads and pastries—an essential fixture in Cork's café culture. Open Mon.-Sat. 10am-10:30pm, Sun. 6:30-10:30pm.

The Harlequin, 21 Paul St. (tel. 272270). Big sandwiches (£1.50-2), 22 different flavors of herbal tea, and plenty of angst. Music and poetry "celebration" on Mon. 7:30-10:30pm; cover £3. Open Mon.-Sat. 9am-7pm.

Kelly's, 64 Oliver Plunkett St. (tel. 273375). Big portions of Irish favorites—this food will stick to your ribs. Corned beef and cabbage £4, roast lamb £4.95. This Cork institution is open daily noon-9pm.

Bully's, 40 Paul St. (tel. 273555). Tasty Italian dishes in an intimate setting (cheese pizza £3). Extensive wine list. Open Mon.-Sat. noon-11:30pm, Sun. 5-11pm.

The Delhi Palace, 6 Washington St. (tel. 276227). Consume like a maharajah without paying the price. Vegetarian dishes £3.25-3.95, meat dishes £4.50-6.25. Lunch Thurs.-Sat. 12:30-2:30pm; dinner daily 5:30pm-12:30am.

Lennox's, 137 Bandon Rd. (tel. 275618). From Western Rd. turn onto Donovan's Rd. and go uphill until you hit Bandon Rd., then make a left. You haven't had chips until you've been to Lennox's. Fish £1.50, chips 70p. Open Mon.-Thurs. noon-2pm and 5pm-1am, Fri.-Sat. noon-1:30am, Sun. 5pm-1am.

Scoozi, Winthrop Ave. (tel. 275077). You're forgiven for loving burgers, pizza, and pasta served in a pleasant wood-and-brick room. Lunch £4-5, dinner £5-7. Open Mon.-Sat. noon-11pm, Sun. 5-11pm.

Café Paradiso, Western Rd. (tel. 277934). Creative vegetarian entrees and blissful desserts are worth the splurge. Don't miss the superb foccaccia served with olive oil for dipping. Fresh tagliatelle £6, soup and bread £1.90. Open Tues.-Sat. 10:30am-10:30pm.

Gino's, 7 Winthrop St. (tel. 274485), between Patrick and Oliver Plunkett St. Inarguably the best ice cream in Munster: try zabaglione (Italian eggnog) or the healthier "Fruit of the Forest." 65p/scoop. Open Mon.-Sat. noon-midnight, Sun. 1pm-midnight.

Tribes, Tuckeys St. (tel. 276070), by Christ Church. Aggressively hip coffeehouse that serves exotic teas and cappuccino after the pubs close down. The schizophrenically painted walls (red, green, and purple complemented by racy paintings) will give you an extra kick. Open daily 9am-4am.

PUBS

Cork's pubs have all the variety of music and atmosphere you'd expect to find in Ireland's second largest city. Pubs compete for Irishmen along Oliver Plunkett St., Union Quay, and South Main St. Cork is the justly proud home of **Murphy's,** a thick, sweet stout that sometimes, and especially in Cork, tastes even better than Guinness. Beamish, a cheaper stout, is also brewed here.

An Spailpín Fánach, 28 South Main St. (tel. 277949). One of Cork's most popular pubs, and probably the oldest (it opened in 1779). The name (pronounced "AHN Spal-PEEN FAH-nak") means "the potato picker." Brick walls, stone floors, wooden trim, great traditional music, open fire, and a mature crowd. Live music Sun.-Fri. Pub grub (Irish stew £3.50) served Mon.-Fri. noon-3pm.

Isaac Bells, Patrick's Quay (tel. 506521). Spirited Monday night jam sessions with traditional instruments draw a decidedly diverse and untraditional bunch; the music, some of the best you'll hear, is raw and authentic.

The Donkey's Ears, Union Quay (tel. 964846). The most "alternative" of the Quay pubs; loud and vibrant, with an edge. Live rock, hip-hop, funk, and reggae.

The Lobby, 1 Union Quay (tel. 311113). The most famous venue in Cork, the Lobby has given some of Ireland biggest folk acts their start. Live music nightly, of varying magnitude and cover charge.

An Phoenix, 3 Union Quay (tel. 964275). Blues and bluegrass Tues. in this dark, mysterious pub with old wine casks embedded in the walls. Upstairs attracts a younger crowd with loud indie rock.

Loafer's, 26 Douglas St. (tel. 311612). Cork's sole gay and lesbian pub shines with a colorful interior and relaxed atmosphere.

The Thirsty Scholar, Western Rd. across the street from Jury's Hotel. Steps from campus, this congenial pub is proof that students will walk no farther for a pint than they absolutely have to.

Sir Henry's, South Main St. (tel. 274391). The music is loud and the smoke is thick in this surreal, cave-like pub, which doubles as a club. It's no hallucination—the walls *are* dripping. Live rock Sunday nights.

Charlie's, Union Quay (tel. 965272). Smallest of the pubs on Union Quay. A mixed and fun crowd is attracted to good music—folk, trad, rock, or blues nightly.

SIGHTS

Cork's character derives not only from its history but also from its modernity; the city has a smattering of captivating sights that can be reached easily by foot. For guidance, pick up *The Tourist Trail* at the tourist office (£1), or take advantage of one of the free walking tours (ask the tourist office for details).

The Old City

You might start seeing Cork from the center of the old city—Christ Church Lane off the Grand Parade, just north of Bishop Lucey Park. Walk down the lane (keeping the park on your left) and you'll emerge on South Main St., once the city's main drag. To your right will be steepleless **Christ Church,** now the Cork Archives (closed to tourists). The church is an emblem of the persistence of Catholicism in Cork; it has been burned to the ground three times since its consecration in 1270, but rebuilt promptly each time, most recently in 1729. Edmund Spenser married Elizabeth Boyle here in 1594, in tribute to which he wrote his *Prothalamium* and *Epithalamium* ("before- and after-marriage poem").

Nestled against the church is the small but dynamic **Triskel Arts Centre,** Tobin St. (tel. 272022), the locus of Cork's cultural libido. The Centre maintains a small gallery with rotating contemporary exhibits. The Centre also runs a brilliant café, and organizes a wide variety of cultural events (music, film, literature, theatre, and the visual arts; open Mon.-Sat. 10:30am-5:30pm; free). Continuing south along Main St., you will pass (and no doubt recognize the odor of) the **Beamish Brewery,** which produces Cork's own stout for budget drinkers. Crossing the **South Gate Bridge,** turn right onto Proby's Quay, in the shadow of St. Finbarr's Cathedral, and then left onto obscure Keyser Lane. When you reach the top of the stairs, you'll see the **Elizabethan Fort,** a star-shaped, ivy-covered remnant of English rule in Cork (always open; free). Built in 1601 after the Elizabethan English clobbered Hugh O'Neill's forces at the Battle of Kinsale, the fort's ruins now sequester the Garda station. Climb the stairs just inside the main gate to get to the top and enjoy the fort's most valuable asset—its view.

Down the street, **St. Finbarr's Cathedral** (tel. 963387) stands as a testament to the Victorian aesthetic ideal of Gothic bombast. St. Finbarr allegedly founded his "School of Cork" here in 606; no trace of the early foundation remains. Built between 1735 and 1870, the present church appears centuries older; designer William Burgess, who oversaw the mosaics, furniture, and metalwork as well as the overall plans, took his love of the Gothic era so far as to dress up in 13th-century robes. (Cathedral open daily 10am-1pm and 2-5:30pm, Oct.-April daily 10am-1pm and 2-5pm; free.)

Shandon

On the other side of the Lee, North Main St. becomes Shandon St., heart of the unimaginatively named Shandon neighborhood, which is less affluent than the rest of Cork but has more neighborhood pride and a cooler accent: "Cork" becomes "caulk." Walk up Shandon St. until you see Donnelly's Diner on the left; then take a right down the unmarked Church St. and walk straight to **St. Anne's Church** (tel. 501672), Cork's most famous landmark. (Most people call it **Shandon Church,** since the steeple is "Shandon Tower" and it's in the Shandon neighborhood.) The red and white (sandstone and limestone) sides of the steeple inspired Cork's ubiquitous "Rebel" flag; the salmon on top of the church spire represents the River Lee. Like most of Cork, the original church was ravaged by 17th-century pyromaniacal English armies; construction of the current church began in 1722. Four clocks grace the four sides of Shandon's tower. Notoriously out of sync with each other, the clocks have been held responsible for many an Irishman's tardy arrival at work. This trend has earned the Church its endearing nickname, "the four-faced liar." For £1.50, visitors can subject the city to their experiments in bell-ringing (sheet music provided; open Mon.-Sat. 9:30am-5pm). Just opposite the church is the **Shandon Craft Centre,** Church St., where artisans practice weaving, crystal-cutting, and pottery; the circular **Firkin Crane Centre,** a performance hall, is next door.

Emmet Place & Western Road

Walk down the other side of the hill, re-cross the north fork of the Lee, and you'll arrive at the monstrous, cement **Opera House,** erected 20 years ago after the older and elegant opera house went down in flames. The adjacent **Crawford Municipal Art Gallery,** Emmet Pl. (tel. 273377), boasts one of the most important collections of Irish art and features contemporary and avant-garde traveling exhibitions (open Mon.-Sat. 10am-5pm; free).

Cork's other major sights are on the western edge of the city; coming from the Grand Parade, walk down Washington St., which soon becomes Western Rd. **University College Cork (UCC),** built in 1845, has its main entrance on the Western Rd. Gothic windows; long, echoing, stony corridors; a smattering of ivy; and grassy expanses make for a fine, secluded afternoon walk or picnic along the Lee. Tours of the campus tell the story of George Boole, the Cork professor of mathematics (and the mastermind of Boolean logic) upon whom Sir Arthur Conan Doyle based the character of Prof. James Moriarty, Sherlock Holmes' nemesis. (Tours depart Western Rd. gate June 19-Aug. 30 Mon.-Fri. at 2:30pm; £2, students £1.50.) Across the street from the College entrance, signs point to the **Cork Public Museum,** Fitzgerald Park (tel. 270679), set in long public gardens studded with statues and flowers. The museum's exhibits are intriguing and astoundingly esoteric. The splendid gardens of **Fitzgerald Park** are worth the walk. (Open June-Aug. Mon.-Fri. 11am-1pm and 2:15-6pm, Sun. 3-5pm; Sept.-May Mon.-Fri. 11am-1pm and 2:15-5pm, Sun. 3-5pm; free.)

The **Cork City Gaol** is an easy walk from Fitzgerald Park; cross the footbridge at the western end of the park, turn right on Sunday's Well Rd., then follow the abundant signs. A tour of the jail tells the story of individual Cork prisoners and the often miserable treatment they endured (for punishment, prisoners were forced to run for hours on a "human treadmill" which was used to grind grain). Be sure to catch the captivating film at the end of your tour: it explains "why some people turned to crime." (Our theory: repressed libido and not enough lunch.) (Open daily 9:30am-6pm; winter Sat.-Sun., 10am-4pm; £3, students and seniors £2, children £1.50.)

ENTERTAINMENT

You'll find it easy to enjoy Cork. If you tire of drinking, take advantage of Cork's music, dance clubs, theaters, and sports—or just explore the innumerable cafés and bookshops. Pick up a copy of *In Cork,* Cork's biweekly guide for staying down with it (available at **Triskel Arts Centre** and at various locations around the city, including the **In Cork** office, 14 Tobin St. (tel. 278544)). The nightlife is bustling, but a fly-by-night affair: fashions and hip bands change nightly.

Music & Clubs

Cork bands are big these days: the Sultans of Ping F.C. (who sound like the love child of the Wedding Present and They Might be Giants) and the gentler Frank and Walters are two. But you're not likely to hear them in Cork (the Sultans just toured Japan). Popular local bands include Tree House, The Orange Fettishes, Mr. NSF (Not-So-Famous), Mickey Rourke's Fridge, and L.I.P. However, what is hip one week can be passé the next. The **Lobby** (see Pubs, p. 196) is a consistently sound choice for live music. **Nancy Spain's,** 48 Barrack St. (tel. 314452), is one of the city's most popular venues, often featuring live rock and blues (cover £5). **Charlie's Bar,** Union Quay (tel. 965272), has live folk, rock, blues, trad, and poetry nightly. Check the pub listings above for other venues.

Nightclubs fill up when the pubs close, but be aware before you plunk down your £2-5 cover charge that most close at 2am. **Norma Jeans,** Oliver Plunkett St. (tel. 271217), grooves to dance and top-40 (open nightly 10:30pm-2am; cover £5). **Gorby's,** Oliver Plunkett St., revels nightly in hip-hop, hard-core, and retro (cover £1-3), while **The Keg,** Gravel Ln. (tel. 271120), jams in students to hear the disks spin (nightly 10:30pm-2am; cover £4). Head to **City Limits,** Coburg St. (tel. 501206), for Comedy Nite (Fri. 9:30-11pm; £4) or to the **Grand Parade Hotel** for Irish "set" dancing on what looks like a movie set (Fri. 9:30-11:30pm). **Sir Henry's,** South Main St. (tel. 274391), is a funky pub and nightclub with live rock Sunday nights. **The Half Moon Club** (tel. 274308), tucked behind the Opera House on Half Moon St. delights with jazz, blues, and traditional music (Thurs.-Sat.; check Opera House box office for listing; bars open at 11:30pm).

Theater & Film

Cork's theater scene has been revitalized by the opening of the **New Granary,** Mardyke Quay (tel. 904275), with performances of new scripts by local and visiting theater companies. **Triskel Arts Centre** (tel. 277300), simmers with avant garde theater and performance art and hosts regular concert and film series. **Everyman's Theatre** (a.k.a. "the Palace"), MacCurtain St. (tel. 501673), stages big-name concerts, musicals, plays, and even opera (open Mon.-Sat. noon-11pm; tickets £6-15). The **Opera House** (tel. 270022) presents an extensive program of dance and performance art (open Mon.-Sat. 10:15am-7pm); catch one of the free lunchtime concerts at the **Firkin Crane Centre,** Dominick St. (tel. 507487), near Shandon Church, every Friday in July and August (concerts begin at 1:15pm). For a fix of mainstream American celluloid (and the occasional Irish or art-house flick), head to the **Capitol Cineplex** (tel. 272216), at Grand Parade and Washington St. (£3.50, matinees £2).

Sports

Cork is sporting-mad: its soccer, hurling, and Gaelic football teams are perennial contenders for national titles. Be cautious in venturing into the streets on game days (especially during championships): screaming, jubilant fans will either bowl you down or, worse yet, force you to partake in the revelry. Tickets to big games are £13-15 and often scarce, but Sunday after-work matches are inexpensive (£1-4) or free. **Hurling** and **Gaelic football** take place every Sunday afternoon (3pm) from June to September in the Gaelic Athletic Association Stadium in Blackrock (take bus #2); call the GAA (tel. 385876), or consult *The Cork Examiner*. After saving on brown scones and hostel beds, blow your money at the **Cork Greyhound Race Co.,** Western Rd., ¼ mi. beyond the An Óige hostel. Races cost £3 (free after 9pm) and run year-round, Monday, Wednesday, and Saturday 8-10pm. On a rainy afternoon, **The Mardyke Club** (tel. 270276) goes bonkers with billiards, bowling, and quasar (laser tag £2.50/person; open daily 10am-11pm).

Festivals

The **Cork Choral Festival** (tel. 308308; last weekend in April) fills city churches with international singing groups while the **Cork Folk Festival** (tel. 317271), held in various pubs and hotels, jams in September. Also popular is the **International Film Festival** during the first week of October at the Opera House and the Triskel Arts Centre; documentaries and shorts elbow the features for attention (contact the Triskel Arts Centre, tel. 271711). See the big names for free in local pubs during the three-week-long **Guinness Jazz Festival** in October (call 273946 for information).

■ NEAR CORK CITY

BLARNEY

While sucking down tour bus fumes and standing in line with tourists from around the globe, you may forget why you're in Blarney. The main attraction is, certainly, **Blarney Castle** (tel. 385252), and its terrifically overrated **Blarney Stone.** Not only are the stone's origins obscure (some say it was brought from Jerusalem during the Crusades, others claim it's a chip off the Scottish Stone of Scone), the stone itself is obscure, too; it's just a slab of limestone among others in a castle wall. Tourists don't doubt its magic, though; they lean over backwards to kiss the stone in hopes of acquiring the legendary eloquence bestowed on those who smooch it. The term "blarney" itself, meaning "smooth-talking b.s.," was supposedly coined by Queen Elizabeth I after a series of particularly frustrating negotiations with the devious Irish Lord Dermot MacCarthy, who resided at Blarney Castle. The Irish themselves consider the whole thing a bunch of blarney; they're mostly interested in the sanitary implications of hundreds of people kissing the same rock. More impressive than the stone is the castle itself, built in 1446 as a stronghold for the final generations of independent, Irish-speaking feudal aristocrats. A trip to the top of the castle is rewarding even for those who are sufficiently confident with the gift of gab—the view, if you're lucky enough to get one, is enough to make up for the tour group from Topeka. (Open May-Sept. Mon.-Sat. 9am-6pm, Sun. 9:30am-5:30pm; Oct.-April Mon.-Sat. 9am-sundown, Sun. 9:30am-sundown; £3, seniors and students £2, children £1.)

Two hundred yards from the castle lies the **Rock Close,** a beautifully manicured rock-and-plant garden supposedly built on sacred Druid grounds. After you receive the ancient, mystical vibes, walk around the fields and explore the limestone cave near the castle (bring a flashlight, unless you actually enjoy groping your way in total darkness). The crowds tend to confine themselves to the castle, making the Rock Close and adjacent fields a perfect place for a picnic. The nearby **Blarney House** (tel. 385252), obscures its historical past with modern renovations; a trip to the Laura Ashley shop in Cork would achieve the same degree of authenticity. (Open mid-June-mid-Sept. Mon.-Sat. noon-5:30pm, but call ahead; £2.50, students £2.)

Across from the castle is the other main attraction of Blarney Village, the **Blarney Woolen Mills** (tel. 385280; open April-Oct. daily 9am-7pm, Nov.-March 9:30am-5:30pm). The outlet store (tel. 381624) dispenses tourist info and sells Aran sweaters (£25 and up), woolens, and the standard tourist fare; you can also tour the mill (Mon-Sat. 9:30am-5pm; free). On the town square, **St. Helen's Restaurant,** located above **SuperValu,** serves cheap sandwiches (open daily 9am-6pm) while **The Blarney Stone** cooks up Irish specialties (soup and bread £1.30, stew with vegetables £4; open daily 12:30-10pm). Trad music and pub fare can be had at the **Muskerry Arms** (tel. 385505), as can line dancing for the truly brave on Sunday afternoons (music nightly 9:30-11:30pm).

If you must find a place to stay, the new **Blarney Tourist Hostel** (tel. 385580 or 381430), two miles from town on the Killarney Rd., rents basic and functional beds in a converted farmhouse (£5). **Bus Éireann** runs buses from Cork to Blarney (Mon.-Sat. 16/day, Sun. 10/day; £2.60 return). From July 5 to August 25, they also offer the **Cork Tourist Trail bus,** which trundles from the Cork bus station to the City Gaol, the Ballincollig Powder Mills, Blarney Castle, and back to Cork (Tues.-Thurs. 4/day; £2, children £1). But if you're weary of buses, Blarney is a short and pleasant bike ride from Cork. The **phone code** in Blarney is steadfastly 021.

COBH

Until the 1950s, Cobh (pronounced "KOVE") was Ireland's main transatlantic port; for many of the 2.5 million emigrants who left from Cobh harbor between 1848 and 1950, Cobh was the last they saw of their country. Cobh was also the *Titanic's* last port of call before the "unsinkable" ship struck an iceberg on her maiden voyage, killing 1683 people. Later, when the Germans torpedoed the *Lusitania* during

World War I, most survivors and some of the dead were taken back to Cobh in life-boats, accounting for the town's mass grave of 150 victims. Pick up the "Cobh Tour-ist Trail" map at the **tourist office** (tel. 813301; up the hill from the train station, on the right; open Mon.-Sat. 11am-1pm and 2-6pm, Sun. 3-6pm). Cobh is best reached by **rail** from Cork (Mon.-Sat. 12/day, Sun. 5/day; 25 min.; £2.50 return). Cobh's **phone code** rocks at 021.

In remembrance of its eminent, if tragic, history, Cobh recently established a museum called **The Queenstown Story** (tel. 813591), adjacent to the Cobh railway station. The museum's flashy, if somewhat contrived, multi-media exhibits trace the port's eventful history, with sections devoted to emigration, the *Lusitania*, the *Titanic*, and the peak and decline of transatlantic travel (open daily 10am-6pm; £3.50, students £2). In June 1995, the Cork-Cobh train ran into the museum, caus-ing minor damage—not an auspicious start for a museum in this crash-prone town. **St. Colman's Cathedral** towers over Cobh; its ornate French Gothic spire domi-nates the town's architectural landscape and gives a great view of the harbor. Com-pleted in 1915, the cathedral boasts the largest carillon in Ireland, consisting of 47 bells weighing over 7700 pounds! (Cathedral open daily 8am-8pm; free.) The small **Cobh Museum,** housed inside the Scots Church on High Rd., deals almost exclu-sively with Cobh's maritime history (open daily 2-6pm; free).

Despite its sometimes tragic past, Cobh revels in its maritime heritage. The tourist office, in fact, occupies the recently restored site of the Royal Cork Yacht Club, reputed to be the world's first yacht club. Today's visitors take advantage of the har-bor for all types of water sports. **International Sailing** (tel. 811237) on East Beach rents canoes (£8/3hr.), sailing dinghies (from £22/3hrs.) and windsurfers (£18/3 hrs.; open daily 10am-6pm).The **fishing** shop (tel. 813839), across the street rents fishing poles and tackle (£5/day; deposit £20; open daily 9am-6pm). The third week in July brings **Coi's Cuan Festival,** a celebration of traditional Irish music and story-telling. The **Cobh People's Regatta** during the second week of August and the **Deep-Sea Angling Festival** in early September draw crowds to Cobh harbor.

Pubs, restaurants, and B&Bs face Cobh's harbor from Beach St. **Rumble's Bistro,** 2 Casement Sq. (tel. 812397), across from the *Lusitania* Memorial, cooks quiche (£1.75), pastries, and ethnically diverse entrees (chicken curry, rice, and garlic bread £3.90). Enjoy delicious scones or a full Irish breakfast (£2.50) while admiring the oil paintings of local Cobh artists at **Kate's Coffee Pot,** 8 Pearse Sq. (tel. 814191; open Mon.-Sat. 7:30am-6pm, Sun. 9:30am-6pm). Alternately, buy a picnic at **Super-Valu supermarket** on West Beach and eat it at John F. Kennedy Park, near the waterfront (supermarket open Mon.-Sat. 9am-6pm, Thurs.-Fri. 9am-9pm). Cobh's pubs are young and rowdy, reflecting the town's renewed vitality. The **Rob Roy,** Pearse Sq. (tel. 814001), attracts a young and aloof crowd with a smoky atmo-sphere, pool table, and loud American rock. The **Rotunda,** 14 Casement Sq. (tel. 811631), across from the *Lusitania* monument, is more sedate, with plush ban-quettes of crimson velvet. Heading east on Beach St., stop in at **Connie Dulan Pub** (tel. 813788), or head straight for the relentlessly cheery (and totally unmistakable) **Well House** (tel. 811739), which beckons with a Miami Vice-inspired windsurfing mural. This bar is Cobh's answer to the American phenomenon of the sports grille; big-screen TVs captivate local fans.

South of Midleton on R629, visionary Stephen Pearce throws ceramics at the **Shanagarry Pottery Shop** (tel. (021) 646087; open Sun.-Mon. noon-5:30pm, Tues.-Sat. 10am-5:30pm). Three miles south of Shanagarry, the picturesque village of **Bal-lycotton** juts into the Atlantic. On the way back to Cork, the best place to stop for refreshment is the **Barryscourt Castle Craft & Tea** (tel. (021) 883864) in Carrigto-hill, on N25 between Cork and Midleton. The restored **Castle,** built in 1206, was the seat of the Earls of Barrymore until the 18th century (open daily 11am-6:30pm).

■ ■ ■ YOUGHAL

Thirty miles east of Cork on N25, beach-blessed Youghal (pronounced "YAWL" or "Y'all" for cute Texans) can make an excellent daytrip or a stopover on the way to

Waterford and points east. If you made it through the movie *Moby Dick* with Gregory Peck, you've made it through Youghal—it was filmed here in the 1950s. Recently the town of 7500 became home to the more mundane production of carpets and computers.

The helpful **tourist office**, Market Sq. (tel. 92390), on the waterfront behind the clocktower, distributes a free "tourist trail" booklet, and can steer you to traditional sessions in the town's pubs. (Open June-Sept. Mon.-Fri. 9:30am-7pm, Sat.-Sun. 10am-6pm; Oct.-May Mon.-Fri. 9:30am-5:30pm.) **Buses** stop in front of the public toilets on Waterford Rd. (just before it becomes one-way), and travel to Cork (Mon.-Sat. 12/day, Sun. 9/day; 50 min.; £5.50, student £3.20), and Waterford (Mon.-Fri. 6/day, Sat. 8/day, Sun. 5/day; 1½-2hr.; £8.80, students £5). **Hitching** to Cork or Waterford along N25 is viable. Ahoy, matey—the white whale of a **phone code** is 024.

Hillside, 6 Strand St. (tel. 92468), is a puzzling cross between a hostel and a B&B, but it is by far the cheapest place to stay in town. The owner sold off all the antiques that once graced the house, so now you'll have to make do with knit afghans covering spongy beds (2- to 4-bed room £7.50/person). **Devon View,** Pearse Sq. (tel. 92298) is considerably nicer, if slightly garish: antique furniture and silver in the dining and sitting rooms, all rooms with bath, TV and phone (£13/person, £15 single). The only **camping** park is no longer open, but locals report that some travelers set up their tents on the beach for a night.

Thankfully, y'all are not in Youghal for the food. For a town with its action, Youghal is lacking in its restaurant options. The **Coffee Pot,** 77 North Main St. (tel. 92523), is extremely popular among locals, serving pastries, soup, and light meals (soup and brown bread £1.35; open daily 9:30am-7:30pm). Desperate carnivores are appeased at the **Old Well Restaurant** next door (open daily 9:30am-9pm). In times of crisis, you can always rely on the **SuperValu** in the town center near the tourist office (open Mon.-Thurs. 9am-6pm, Fri. 9am-9pm, Sat. 9am-8pm).

In contrast to the slim restaurant pickings, good pubs abound. Beer lovers fill their tums with liquefied starch instead of solid food. **The Nook,** North Main St., is the most "universal" watering hole, with *craic* and live music Wednesdays and Fridays through Sundays (trad on Wed.). **Moby Dick's,** Market Sq. (tel. 92756), on the waterfront, is popular with red-haired local youth. The **Grattan Bar** (tel. 93161), near the tourist office, is best in the early evenings and at lunchtime. Locals gather to play darts in the **Central Star,** North Main St. (tel. 92419), where elderly patrons make weekend singalongs a rather memorable experience.

Historical **walking tours** of the town (1½ hr.) leave from the tourist office (tel. 92390; June-Aug. Mon.-Sat. at 11am and 3pm; £2.50). The huge **Clockgate** (1777) straddles the narrow, crowded Main St. From here you can see the old city walls, built on the hill sometime between the 13th and 17th centuries. The tower served as a prison and a low-budget gallows (prisoners were hanged by the windows). Off North Main St. on Church St., two remarkable buildings stand side-by-side: **St. Mary's Church** and **Myrtle Grove.** Myrtle Grove was the residence of Sir Walter Raleigh when he served as Mayor here from 1588-89. Pay due respect to the corner of the garden where he is said to have planted the first Irish potatoes. (Only open for guided tours in Aug. on Mon., Wed., and Fri. 2:30pm and 4pm. £3, students £2.)

WESTWARD HO!

From Cork City, there are two routes to Skibbereen and West Cork: an inland route and a coastal route beginning in Kinsale. Two major **bus routes** depart from Cork City and serve West Cork: a coastal bus runs from Cork to Skibbereen, stopping in Bandon, Clonakilty, and Rosscarbery. An inland bus travels from Cork to Bantry, stopping in Bandon and Dunmanway (both 3/day, Sun. 2/day). Charming hitchers are reported to have no problems in these parts.

■■■ THE INLAND ROUTE

Cyclists and hitchers wishing to save time or avoid crowds should consider one of the inland routes from Cork to Skibbereen, Bantry, the Beara, or Killarney, instead of the coastal N71 through Clonakilty. Popular routes are Cork-Macroom-Killarney, Cork-Macroom-Ballingeary-Bantry/Glengarriff, and Cork-Dunmanway-Bantry/Skibbereen. The view of sunsets through the Shehy Mountains around Dunmanway and Ballingeary wins glowing praise.

South of Macroom on R587, **Dunmanway** is less a town than a single busy main square. **Bus Éireann** voyages from Cork to Dunmanway (4/day, Sun. 3/day; £6.30, students £4.10) and from Dunmanway to Glengarriff via Bantry (3/day, Sun. 2/day). Buses leave in front of The News Basket on the square. The best place to stay (or eat) is the **Shiplake Mountain Hostel (IHH)** (tel. (023) 45750), in the hills three miles from town. Call for a ride from Dunmanway; or follow Castle St. (next to the Market Diner) out of town until you see the hostel sign, then turn right. Shiplake commands a view of the lakes and mountains, does pub runs, offers horseback riding (£3/½-hr.), rents bicycles (£3.50/day), and cooks Ireland's best vegetarian pizza. A cute but extremely popular gypsy caravan (trailers painted in bright colors) behind the hostel accommodates couples or families. (Groceries available; dorms £5; caravan £6.50; **camping** £3/person, £4/person w/tent rental; meals £2-4.) Back in town, **An Toísín** pub, Main St., 200 yards from the square, rings with live music on the weekends. Good pub stops are made at the dark-green **Southern Bar,** Clonakilty Rd., on the left side of the road as you leave town, or the **Arch Bar.**

Northwest of Dunmanway on R584, **Ballingeary** and the quiet **Tig Barra Hostel (IHH)** make a good base for exploring **Gougane Barra Forest** or the **Shehy Mountains** (tel. (026) 47016; hostel £5; **camping** £3/person; laundry £3; open mid-March-Sept.). The mountains around Dunmanway and Ballingeary erupt with hiking and biking possibilities. Either hostel will give details.

■■■ KINSALE

Big-boated anglers, swimming parties, and gourmets salivating before Kinsale's famed Good Food Circle (of 12 expensive restaurants) fill the town with money as its population temporarily quintuples every summer. Luckily, Kinsale's best attractions—its pubs, its forts, and its seaside location—don't discriminate by class.

Kinsale has held a grimmer role in history than its pleasant present suggests. Elizabethan English armies destroyed the native Irish followers of Ulster chieftain Hugh O'Neill in the 1601 Battle of Kinsale while O'Neill's supposed Spanish allies watched the action from ships stationed nearby. Some historians blame Spanish duplicity; others, poor military communications. In any case, the Brits won, leading to decisive British control over Munster and Leinster and to the Flight of the Earls. (See History: Feudalism, page 52.) Kinsale was legally closed to the Gaelic Irish for almost two centuries after the English victory. In 1688, the freshly deposed King James II of England, trying to gather Catholic Irish support for a Jacobite invasion of Scotland, entered Ireland at this very spot; for his efforts, James had a fort named after him. Kinsale historically had a reputation as a smuggling port of some magnitude. The attention of the outside world turned to Kinsale again in 1915, when the *Lusitania* sank just off Old Head of Kinsale.

Orientation & Practical Information Kinsale is a half-hour drive southwest of Cork City on R600—an easy daytrip. The city parks itself at the base of a U-shaped inlet; facing the tourist office, Charles Fort and the Scilly Walk are to the left, the piers, Compass Hill, and James Fort are to the right, and the town center is behind you. The **tourist office,** Emmet Pl. (tel. 772234, Oct.-May 774026), in the brown-and-red building, gives out free maps and sells postcards and guidebooks (open March-Nov. Mon.-Sat. 9:30am-6pm; June-Aug. Mon.-Sun. 9:30am-7pm). **Bank of Ireland,** Pearse St. (tel. 772521), provides VISA-friendly **ATM** services (open

Mon.-Fri. 10am-4pm). Rent **bikes** at **Deco's Cycles,** 8 Main St. (tel. 774355), for £6 per day (open June-Aug. daily 9am-8pm, Sept.-May daily 9:30am-6pm). **Buses** between Cork and Kinsale stop at the Esso station on the Pier (Mon.-Sat. 6/day, Sun. 4/day; £3.60, students £2.20). The **telephone code** just can't help being 021.

Accommodations Although Kinsale caters to an affluent tourist crowd with hotels and plush B&Bs in profusion, there are two excellent hostels just outside of town. The **Castlepark Manua Centre** (tel. 774959), which opened in June 1995, dazzles with colorful comforters, polished wood floors, and expansive views over the marina, but no kitchen yet. This stone-faced "centre" doesn't call itself a hostel and doesn't quite feel like one. The centre, which shares a rugged peninsula with James Fort, is a half-hour walk from the town center (dorm £8, w/sheets and breakfast). Ferries run regularly from the Trident Marina (south of the tourist office, at the end of the pier); call the hostel for ferry schedules. Closer to town, **Dempsey's Hostel (IHH),** Cork Road (tel. 772124), offers clean rooms in a small, prim house (dorm £5; sheets 50p; shower 50p). In town, the **Yello Gallery,** 43 Main St. (tel. 772393), provides B&B (single £13.50, shared bath). The **campground** nearest to Kinsale is **Garrettstown House Holiday Park** (tel. 778156), six miles west of Kinsale on R600, in Ballinspittle. (Buses run Thurs. 3/day, Fri. 1/day and Sun. 1/day; Sun. bus runs June 26-Aug. 21 only.) (Open May 14-Sept. 30; £2.75/tent.)

Food & Pubs Kinsale is Ireland's gourmet food capital: locals claim it's the only town in Ireland that has more restaurants than pubs. The Good Food Circle has 12 restaurants which uphold both Kinsale's well-deserved culinary reputation as well as its reputation for tourist-scalping expense. The budget-conscious fill their baskets at the **SuperValu supermarket,** Pearse St. (tel. 772843; open daily 9am-9pm).

Café Palerma, on Pearse St. (tel. 774143), serves delicious Italian food and sinful desserts, like Death By Chocolate (fresh pasta £4-5, chicken cacciatore £6.50; open daily 10am-11pm). **The Yello Gallery,** 43 Main St. (tel. 772393), is a small café with artistic aspirations—its walls display a different exhibit of contemporary Irish art each month (sandwiches, salads, pasta £3-5.50; open Sept.-May daily 8am-6pm; June-Aug. daily 8am-10pm). **La Scala,** (tel. 772529) just off Market Sq., satisfies pizza cravings, while **1601,** Pearse St. (tel. 772529), helps the pub grub-deprived.

The stucco-colored **Spaniard** (tel. 772436) rules over the Kinsale pub scene from the hill on Scilly Peninsula (follow the signs ¼ mile to Charles Fort). Stone walls, dark wood paneling, low-beamed ceilings, and a bar the length of the Shannon— how can the stout *not* taste good? (Lively trad sessions Wed., other nights vary.) **The Greyhound,** Market Sq. (tel. 772889), attracts a young crowd, while **1601** (see above) serves traditional music along with *de riguer* chips. Downhill from The Spaniard, and farther on the Scilly Walk, **The Spinnaker** (tel. 772098), presides over the harbor and plays loud American rock. Those who make the walk to Charles Fort are rewarded with the inviting **Bulman Bar** (tel. 772131), a picturesque spot for liquid iron therapy—Ireland's own black gold, Guinness.

Sights The half-hour trek up **Compass Hill** south from Main St. rewards with a view of the town and its watery surroundings. More impressive is the view from Charles Fort (tel. 772263), a classic 17th-century star-shaped fort that remained a British naval base until 1921. (Sack the fort mid-June-mid-Sept. daily 9am-6pm; mid-April to mid-June and mid-Sept. to mid-Oct. Mon.-Sat. 9am-5pm, Sun. 9:30am-5:30pm; £2, students and children £1; guided tours on request.) Reach Charles Fort by following Scilly Walk (pronounced "SILL-ee," silly), a sylvan path along the coast.

In 1915, the *Lusitania* sank off the Old Head of Kinsale, a promontory south of the town of Kinsale; over 1000 civilians died. As it turned out, a German torpedo was to blame, and the resulting furor helped propel the United States into World War I. Hearings on the *Lusitania* case took place in the Kinsale Courthouse, now a low-key **Regional Museum,** Market Sq. (tel. 772044), which is home to the "Holy Stone" of Kinsale. (Sporadic hours; call for admission; 50p.) Just beyond Market Sq., the west tower of the 12th-century **Church of St. Multose** (patron saint of Kinsale) bewitches visitors; the old town stocks still stand inside (tel. 772220; open daylight hours; free). **Desmond Castle,** Cork St., a 15th-century custom house, served as an arsenal during the 100-day Spanish occupation in 1601. It was put to use in the 18th century as a prison for salty French and American soldiers (open June-Sept. daily 9am-5pm; £1, students 40p.).

Across the harbor from Charles Fort, the ruins of star-shaped **James Fort** delight with secret passageways and panoramic views of Kinsale (always open; free). To reach the fort, follow the pier away from town, cross the bridge, then turn left. After exploring the ruins and the rolling heath, descend to Castlepark's hidden arc of beach, nestled behind the hostel. Rent windsurfing equipment, kayaks, and dinghies from the **Kinsale Outdoor Education Centre** (tel. 772896). Full-day deep-sea fishing trips can also be arranged at **Castlepark Marina** (tel. 774959; £20/person, £5 rod rental).

■■■ COASTAL ROUTE

From Kinsale, southerly R600 sits watch over farming valleys before hugging the coast and wide, deserted beaches on the way to Timoleague and Clonakilty; from Cork, N71 carries buses and cars to Bandon and then on to Clonakilty.

Six miles east of Clonakilty along watery R600, **Timoleague** slumbers on the Ardigheen Estuary. **Buses** from Cork rarely stop here (Mon.-Fri. 2/day) and traffic from Kinsale is light. Timoleague's main attraction is the shell of a **Franciscan Abbey** founded in 1240 (always open; free). Ravaged by English armies throughout the 1600s, the abbey was abandoned by frustrated monks in 1696. Now it hosts an overgrown and desolate graveyard. Down the road past the town church are the unimpressive remains of **Timoleague Castle,** built in 1215. Smell flowers or pick your own raspberries at the well-maintained **Castle Gardens,** more fun than the castle itself (open June-Aug. daily 11am-5:30pm; £1.50).

The most compelling reason to visit Timoleague is the brilliant hostel and restaurant, **Lettercollum House** (tel. (023) 46251), perched on a hill above the village. The hostel's owners took an imposing Victorian mansion and transformed it into a spectacularly funky hostel. Cornflower-blue walls are enlivened with the owner's ebullient oil canvas, and stained-glass windows illuminate spacious rooms. To top it off, the huge kitchen and blissfully firm pine beds are the icing on this cake (8-bed dorm £5.50, double £8; open mid-March-Oct.). Lettercollum House's **restaurant,** specializing in organically grown vegetarian meals, has racked up various gourmet awards and itself justifies the detour through Timoleague. (Open Wed.-Sun. for dinner beginning at 7:30pm; Sun. brunch is served at 1:30pm; *Table d'hote* menu for hostelers £13.50.) **Dillon's** (tel. (023) 46390) beckons the after-dinner Lettercollum crowd with delicious desserts (créme caramel), good tunes (folk and jazz), and the sacred nectars of Éire on tap (open Mon.-Sat. noon-11:30pm, Sun. 12:30-2pm and 4-9pm). For those resolute souls who resist the hostel's lures, camping is available at **Sexton's Caravan and Camping Park** (tel. (023) 46347), two miles from town on Clonakilty Rd. (£4.50/tent).

■■■ CLONAKILTY

Once a linen-making town with a workforce of over 10,000 people, Clonakilty (pop. 3000; the slick crowd says "Clon") lies between Bandon and Skibbereen on N71. Military leader, spy, and organizational genius Michael Collins was born near Clonakilty in 1890; a bit earlier, so was Henry Ford. Like Kinsale, tidy Clon is a vacation spot whose animated streets and vibrant pub scene rival its natural attraction, Inchydoney Beach. However, Clon appeals more to the "looking-for-our-roots" set than to the budget traveler. The **tourist office** (tel. 33226) vacations at 9 Rossa St. (open June-Sept. Mon.-Fri. 9am-6pm, Sat. 9am-1pm). **Buses** from Skibbereen (3/day;

£4.30, students £2.60) and Cork (Mon.-Fri. 6/day, Sat.-Sun. 3/day; £5.90, students £3.70) stop across from the newsagent on Pearse St. Clon's **phone code** is a great lunch special at 023.

Accommodations, Food, & Pubs There is no hostel in the town of Clonakilty, but stately and totally organic **Lettercollum House**, six miles away in Timoleague, is worth a special trip (see *Timoleague*, above). Book early for Mrs. McMahon's **Nordav**, just east of town at 70 Western Rd. (tel. 33655). Set back from the road behind a well-groomed lawn and splendid rose gardens, her B&B features enormous, airy rooms (£15/person w/full Irish breakfast). **Ashville**, on Clark St. (tel. 33125), overwhelms the senses with brown, flowery carpeting and velvety crimson wallpaper (open March-Sept.; £12/person). **Desert House Camping Park** (tel. 33331) is one mile southeast of town on a dairy farm: follow the signs (open May-Sept.; £4/tent).

Famous (or notorious) for its black pudding, a sausage-like concoction made from blood and grains, Clonakilty is visibly lacking in the way of cheap, non-pub food. **Fionnuala's Little Italian Restaurant,** 30 Ashe St. (tel. 33125), attempts to please with candles in wine bottles that illuminate your antipasto (£1.50-3) or pizza (£3-5). (Open daily 10am-3:30pm and 6-10pm). **Karen's Café**, Pearse St. (tel. 33456), serves pastries and simple sandwiches (£1-3, open summer daily 9am-6pm, winter Mon.-Sat. 9am-6pm), while **Jade Garden,** 20 Pearse St. (tel. 34576), will treat you to surprisingly excellent take-away Chinese (chicken chow mein £3.20). Brown bag it at **Lehane's Supermarket,** Pearse St. (open Mon.-Thurs. 9am-1:15pm, Fri.-Sat. 9am-9pm, Sun. 9am-1:15pm).

There's music aplenty in Clonakilty. The most popular pub is **De Barra's,** Pearse St. (tel. 33381), with folk and traditional music nightly all year. Though the pub is huge (3 rooms, 2 bars, and a beer garden), come early if you want to sit down—in this town of pubs, De Barra's is the center of action. Around the corner, **Shanley's,** 11 Connolly St. (tel. 33790), juggles folk and rock nightly in summer, five nights a week in winter; national-level stars have played here. **Blackbird's,** 3 Connolly St. (tel. 33654), is known for occasional live blues, while **An Teach Beag** (tel. 33250), nestled behind O'Donovan's Hotel on Recorder's Alley, features traditional music and storytelling sessions.

Sights To fill the hours before the pubs pick up, join the locals at **Inchydoney Beach,** billed as one of the nicest beaches east of Malibu. Arrive in the morning, before everyone else does. (Camping here is permitted, but uncommon.) You can walk the three miles to Inchydoney or rent a bike. **Healy's Bikes,** Rossa St. (open daily 9am-6pm) rents for £5 per day or £25 per week. **MTM Cycles,** 33 Ashe St. (tel. 33584) charges £7 per day or £30 per week but allows drop-off at other Raleigh Rent-a-Bike depots for £6. On Inchydoney Rd. you'll pass the **West Cork Model Village** (tel. 33224), where 1940s-era West Cork has been replicated in miniature, complete with model railways and smokestacks. Back in town, the **Clonakilty Museum,** Western Rd., displays the first minute book of the Cloghnikilty Corporation (dated 1675) and other historical Clon minutiae. (Open May-Oct. Mon-Sat. 10:30am-5:30pm and Sun. 3-5pm; Nov.-April Sun. 3-5pm; £1, students 50p.) Then explore the ancient **Templebryan Stone Circle** or the **Lios na gCon Ring Fort,** two miles east; the ring fort has been "fully restored" based on clues its excavators dug up.

■■■ CLONAKILTY TO SKIBBEREEN

If you head due west on a bus from Clonakilty to Skibbereen, you would miss the rugged and pretty countryside in between. Pastures give way to forests and to heaths too rocky or too hilly to be farmed. Sleepy towns dot the hills, each with a few rows of pastel houses, a couple of pubs, and a B&B or two. This combination of rugged vitality with quiet beauty is quintessentially Corkian. As long as you're in the area, stop by **Connolly's Bar** (tel. 33215), in Leap, reputed to host the best music in West Cork.

ROSSCARBERY

Eight miles west of Clonakilty, Rosscarbery sits by the sea along N71. From town, head east along the coast road to reach **beaches** and the **Galley Head Lighthouse.** Built in 1641, **Castlefreke Castle,** 1½ miles east of town off the coast road, housed generations of Carberys until the 1950s, when Lord Carbery renounced his family and moved to Kenya. Today it's the centerpiece of a public park.

West of Rosscarbery, off the Glandore Rd. (R597) in the Rowry River valley, lie the ruins of a 17th-century mansion called **Coppinger's Court.** The place looks as if it had just recently been bombed, though in fact it burned down in 1641 (always open; free). A mile farther along the Glandore Rd., the famous **Drombeg Stone Circle** (150 BC) is a well-preserved example of West Cork's recumbent stone circles. Archaeologists speculate that the horizontal ("recumbent") stone was used for human sacrifice; one victim was unearthed here in the 1950s.

UNION HALL & CASTLETOWNSHEND

Just across the water from the overrated hamlet of Glandore, the fishing village of **Union Hall** was once a hangout for Jonathan Swift and family. Now it's home for **Maria's Schoolhouse** (tel. (028) 33002), formerly the Union Hall National School, now a legendary hostel gloriously redecorated with Sante Fe furniture. High ceiling and peat fire in the huge common room, spanking-new bunkbeds down the hall— this hostel is reason enough for a detour en route to Skibbereen. (Dorm £7, double £9; laundry £3; breakfast £4.50; wheelchair accessible; open March-Sept.) To get to Maria's, turn right in the center of Union Hall, left at the church, and proceed one-half mile (or call Maria for a lift). Back in town, **Dinty's Bar** (tel. (028) 33373) plays music on weekends, while all-talk **Nolan's Bar** (tel. (028) 33589) supplies civilized gossip. Prehistoric artifacts reside in the **Ceim Hill Museum** (tel. (028) 36280; open daily 10am-7pm).

From Union Hall, the most scenic route to Skibbereen is via **Castletownshend,** an Anglo-Irish hamlet that makes its way down to the sea. On the way to the sea, you'll pass **Rineen Forest and Castle,** built around 1580 using the latest grouting technique (sand and lime mixed with horsehair and blood to strengthen the walls). The castle is almost intact, except for cannonballs which Cromwell's army embedded in its walls. **Knockdrum Fort,** just west of town, is a typical ring fort. The tribal center was built by the Celts between 1300 BC and 400 AD and then fortified with walls and ditches. In Castletownshend itself, you can defend the **Townshend Castle** (tel. (028) 36100; open Sun.-Fri. 2:30-6:30pm; £2). **Mary Ann's Bar and Restaurant** (tel. (028) 36146) serves yummy, cream-laden bar food and seafood dishes.

SKIBBEREEN & THEM ISLANDS

From Clonakilty on, the population starts to thin out. Mountains rise up inland, rocky ridges replace smooth hills, and sunset-laden shoals proliferate as Ireland's south coast starts to look like its west. Crossroads along N71 link mellow tourist towns and hardworking fishing villages. "Blow-ins," refugees from urban America and Northern Europe, have settled in the area by the hundreds. They are usually kick-back expats who appreciate the quiet pace and extraordinary scenery of the southwest but have shaped its culture to their own tastes. Trad music thrives in these small towns, attracting long-time locals and artsy expats alike.

The islands in the stretch of ocean between Baltimore and Schull may be the wildest, remotest human habitations in all of southern Ireland. High cliffs stagger into the sea in which many a ship has found a watery grave. The O'Driscoll clan of pirates informally ruled the bay for centuries, sallying into the Atlantic for raids, offloading brandy (gold too, but the brandy mattered more) from Spanish galleons, then speeding home through secret channels among the islands. Though all nine O'Driscoll castles stand in ruins, the clan still dominates much of the area. During the last weekend in June, the O'Driscolls assemble in Baltimore to elect a clan chieftain and to revel for three days. Those in Baltimore who are not named O'Driscoll regard the gathering as something of a joke, but a good party nonetheless.

■■■ SKIBBEREEN

The biggest town in West Cork unites blue-collars and blow-ins within its varied landscape: you'll find as many hardware stores here as bohemian galleries and cafés. When Algerian pirates attacked Baltimore in 1631, the scared survivors moved north, establishing Skibbereen as a sizable settlement. The town is now the gateway for land-lovers to Roaringwater Bay and the Beara Peninsula, and consequently something of a tourist haunt. The best day to visit is Friday, when farmers tote in plants, fresh produce, cakes, and pies for the weekly **market** (1:30pm in summer, 2:30pm in winter).

Practical Information & Orientation Comely Skibbereen is L-shaped, with Main and Bridge Streets comprising the height and North St. the base, while the clock tower, Tourist Office, and stately "Maid of Erin" statue compose the junction. **Buses** stop in front of Calahane's Bar, Bridge St. (the continuation of Main St.), connecting to Baltimore (June-Sept. Mon.-Sat. 4/day; £2.10), Cork (Mon.-Fri. 5/day, Sat. 3/day, Sun. 2/day; £8.80, students £5) and Clonakilty (Mon.-Fri. 3/day, Sat. 2/day; £4.30, students £2.60). **Hitchers** stay on N71 to go east or west, but switch to R595 (Market St. becomes R595 past the roundabout) to go south to Roaringwater Bay.

> **Tourist Office,** North St. (tel. 21766). Open July-Aug. Mon.-Sat. 9am-6pm; June and Sept. Mon.-Sat. 9:15am-5:30pm; Oct.-May Mon.-Fri. 9:15am-1pm and 2:15-5:30pm.
>
> **Banks: AIB,** 9 Bridge St. (tel. 21388; **ATM** accepts VISA). **Bank of Ireland,** Market St. (tel. 21700). Both offer currency exchange and are open Mon.-Fri. 10am-4pm, Wed. until 5pm.
>
> **Post Office:** The Square. Open Mon.-Sat. 9am-5:30pm.
>
> **Phone Code:** 028.
>
> **Bike Rental: Roycroft Stores,** Ilen St. off Bridge St. (tel. 21235). Open Mon.-Wed., Fri.-Sat. 9am-1:10pm, 2:15-6pm, Thurs. 9am-1pm; £7/day, £35/week. Return bike to Schull or Rolf's Hostel in Baltimore for free.
>
> **Laundry: Bubble and Suds Laundry,** 18 North St. (tel. 22621). Open Mon.-Sat. 10am-6pm. Small wash and dry £3.10.
>
> **Hospital:** tel. 21677.
>
> **Emergency:** Dial 999; no coins required. **Garda:** tel. 21088.

Accommodations Gloriously-situated **Mont Bretia,** four miles from town (tel. 33663), is just a step from heaven in a light and airy old farmhouse adorned with Indian rugs and paintings. Call for a lift (from Leap or Skibbereen) to this unassuming B&B. The food is deliciously and almost absurdly plentiful; and the cozy bedrooms are enticing, complete with fluffy terry bathrobes. (B&B £15/person; £6.50/main course, £8/2-course dinner.) To reach Mont Bretia from Skibbereen, take the road east towards Leap for one mile and turn left onto Drinagh Rd. Follow this road for three miles, passing the Adrigole creamery. Take the second left (marked by a sign for "Sprucedale"); Mount Bretia is the second house on the left. If Mont Bretia is full, try a B&B in town. **Ivanhoe,** North St. (tel. 21749), offers big beds and bathrooms for £13/person. **Mrs. Dwyer's Millview,** Market St. (tel. 21016), past the Maid of Erin statue, greets guests with red roses, a bathtub, and friendly mustiness (£11.50/person; open May-Sept.).

Food & Pubs Cafés cluster on Main St. and North St., making a handful of inviting options. **O'Donovan's,** 12 Bridge St. (tel. 21163), has a window full of yummy baked goods—try one of their colossal brown scones on the terrace out back (hot lunch £4). Ever-versatile, the **Stove,** Main St. (tel. 22500), serves copious breakfasts and Irish specialties for lunch (full Irish breakfast £3; open Mon.-Sat. 8am-6pm). The **Wine Vaults,** Main St. (tel. 22743), provides an excuse for a mid-day pub stop—they serve delicious sandwiches, pizzas, crêpes, and a good vegetarian selection (vegetable and bean chile £3.50; food served noon-12:30pm and 5-8pm). The **Backroom Bistro,** 48 North St. (tel. 22556), serves Burmese (!) specialties (lunch £5, dinner £7; open Mon.-Sat. noon-3pm and 7-10pm). Skib's **SuperValu market** (tel. 21400) dispenses bargains (open Mon.-Sat. 9am-6:30pm).

Kearney's Well, 52-53 North St. (tel. 21350), attracts a young, lively crowd with music nightly in summer, five nights a week in winter. Traditional music is generally featured on Friday and Sunday nights. In the aura of good beer, tourists and residents meld comfortably into an almost alternative crowd in the **Wine Vaults** on Main St. (tel. 22743) and in the cavernous but cheery **Bernard's** on Main St., behind O'Brien's Off License. Locals gather in **Baby Hannah's,** Main St., which seems to have converted most of its furniture to sawdust. **Sean Og's,** Market St. (tel. 21573), hosts contemporary folk and rock on Friday and Saturday nights.

Sights The **West Cork Arts Centre,** North St. (tel. 22090), across from the town library, hosts about twelve exhibits a year by Irish artists and craftsfolk. It also draws poetry readings, concerts, dance performances, and other cultural events to West Cork. Stop by the Centre (and its small but impressive craft shop) to get wired into the local arts scene. (Gallery open Mon.-Sat. 11am-6pm; free.) The **gardens** at nearby **Liss Art** (tel. 22368) promise to "induce new perceptions of light and sky" through experiences of nature, as conceived by new-age landscape architects. They remain something of a source of mystery for most locals. Among the 50 acres of gardens are a waterfall garden and the surreal "Irish sky garden," designed by American artist James Turrell (entrance to gardens by appointment; £5). The **Creagh Gardens** (tel. 22121), 3½ miles west of town on the Baltimore Rd., are less mysterious. Here, a woodland setting constrasts with well-maintained gardens (open daily 10am-6pm; £2, children £1). At the end of July, Skibbereen celebrates **Welcome Home Week** and **Maid of the Isles Festival,** featuring free street entertainment and culminating in the crowning of a local girl as "Maid of the Isles."

Once equipped with bicycles or lifts, explorers head south to circle **Lough Ine** ("lock EYE-na"), Northern Europe's only salt-water lake, where clear rapids change direction with the tide. Originally a fresh-water lake, the lough was inundated when sea levels rose after the last ice age. It is now a stomping ground for marine biologists, since it shelters dozens of sub-tropical species. A 30-minute ascent through the moss-strewn **Knockomagh Wood** (adjacent to the Lough; trails leave from the carpark) affords a view of nine towns and the Mizen Head. One-half mile up the hill from Lough Ine, **The Old School** (tel. 20172) is an outcrop of hospitality amid the barren heath (£12-14/person, open March-Nov.).

■■■ BALTIMORE

The tiny fishing village of Baltimore (pop. 200) and its harbor serve as the point of departure for Sherkin Island and Cape Clear Island. In the center of the village stand the stone remains of *Dún na Sead* ("The Fort of the Jewels"), a 16th-century O'Driscoll castle. The O'Driscoll family congregates here to elect a chieftain and to stage a family gathering, complete with live music, jammed pubs, and inebriated Irishmen. Artists, like seagulls, congregate in Baltimore in spring and fall for bright, dramatic seascapes. Follow Baltimore's main road through town (with the pier on your right) for about a mile to the **Beacon,** a bulbous white lighthouse perched on a magnificent cliff with views over the ocean and across to Sherkin Island. Ferry rides to the island (particularly to Cape Clear) offer similarly superb views.

The **tourist office** (tel. 20441), 50 steps up from the ferry depot, is non-Bord Fáilte and keeps sporadic hours. The craft shop next door, **Islands Craft,** dispenses helpful information on Sherkin and Cape Clear, including historical accounts of the islands and the more basic ferry schedules (open April-Oct. Mon.-Sat. 11am-4:30pm, Sun. 12:30-5:30pm). Inquire at **Algiers Inn** (tel. 20352) for information about deepsea angling. Scuba divers willing to brave Baltimore's icy waters are rewarded with a number of wrecks, including **Kowloon Bridge,** the largest shipwreck in the world. To arrange dives or rentals, contact the **Baltimore Diving & Watersports Centre** (tel. 20300), across from Brendan McCarthy's pub (full set of equipment w/wetsuit £20/day, £70/week). **Buses** run to and from Skibbereen (June-Aug. Mon.-Sat. 5/day, Sun. 4/day; Sept. daily 4/day; £2, £2.75 return; the post office has a full schedule in its window). The **phone code** for Baltimore and the islands is steadfastly 028.

Accommodations, Food, & Pubs A visit to Baltimore requires a stay at **Rolf's Hostel (IHH)** (tel. 20289), run by a charming German family in a 300-year-old stone farmhouse, five minutes from town off the Skibbereen road. Comfortable pine beds with llama-hair blankets and a dining room with stunning views (and delicious food) are hard to resist. (Dorms £6, double £10/person; camping £3.50/person; bike rental £6/day; laundry £3.15.) **Rolf's Hostel** not only provides heavenly beds but also serves delicious pasta, vegetarian dishes, and Malaysian specialties (main courses £4-6). **Café Opus,** next door, offers a more extensive menu and an elegant ambiance for those who want to splurge a bit. The **Lifeboat Restaurant** (in the post office building; tel. 20101) serves cheap soup, sandwiches, and pizza in a glassed-in room on the harbor's edge (entrees £1-3; open 10am-5:30pm). Stock up on food for the islands at **Cotter's** (tel. 20106; open daily 10am-8pm). All of Baltimore's pubs offer food and drink. **Declan McCarthy's** (tel. 20159) is the liveliest pub, with live trad and folk nightly in summer (no cover). The surprisingly comfortable stools and tables outside **Bushe's Bar** (tel. 20125) are prime spots for scoping out the harbor (and the locals), while cozy **Algiers Inn** (tel. 20352) attracts a younger crowd.

■ NEAR BALTIMORE

SHERKIN ISLAND

Just a hop on the ferry from Baltimore, Sherkin Island offers stunning, cliff-enclosed beaches, wind-swept heath, and a sense of unhurried ease. **Ferries** depart from Baltimore June-Sept. at 10:30am, noon, 2, 4, 5:30, 7, and 8:30pm, and leave the island at 10:45am, 12:15, 2:15, 4:15, 5:45, 7:15, and 8:45pm (in winter, 1-3/day; £3 return). Call Vincent O'Driscoll (tel. 20125) for information, or check the listings in Baltimore (above) at Island Craft or at Cotter's.

If you're looking for isolation, **Island House,** on the main road, ten minutes from the ferry landing (tel. 20314), is attractive. An old farmhouse with Indian bedspreads, paintings, and strains of cool jazz, it offers mesmerizing views from rustic (charming, if not exactly modern) rooms (£14/person; open April-Sept.). **Murphy's Bar,** close to the ferry landing, next to Dún-na-Long ruins (tel. 20116), opened in June, 1995. It serves a mean pint with expansive views of the bay. By summer, 1996, the bar should be joined by a full restaurant and accommodations (call for room info). The amiable **Jolly Rodger,** across the street (tel. 20379), also has live music most weekends in summer. The **Abbey,** on the main road (tel. 20181), is the only food store on the island, and it stocks only the basics (open summer daily 9am-6pm, winter Mon.-Fri. 9am-6pm).

When you get off the ferry, you'll encounter the ruins of a 15th-century **Franciscan abbey** founded by Fineen O'Driscoll (not Fineen "the Rover"—who comes later). Vengeful troops from Waterford sacked the abbey in 1537 to get back at the O'Driscolls for stealing Waterford's wine. The ruins are currently undergoing renovation and are closed to the public. North of the abbey (behind Murphy's Bar) lie the ruins of **Dún-na-Long Castle** ("fort of the ships"), built around the same time as the friary by our favorite buccaneer clan and sacked by Waterford in 1537 (always open; free). Stay straight on the main road from the ferry dock and you'll pass the blue-green **Kinnish Harbour** and Sherkin's yellow one-room schoolhouse, where the island (pop. 90) educates its children. The beaches on Sherkin are sandy, gradually sloped, and great for swimming: **Trabawn Strand, Cow Strand,** and the bigger **Silver Strand** are all on the west side of the island (follow the main road and bear right after Island House B&B). The defunct **lighthouse** on Horseshoe Harbour stares across the channel toward the unsightly Beacon. This spot affords some of the best views on the island. The island's allure lies not in its "sights," of course, but in its scenery and seclusion: nature is the main attraction on this island.

CAPE CLEAR ISLAND (OILEÁN CHLÉIRE)

Before the Famine, Cape Clear Island supported a completely self-sufficient population of 1200. Today, its main industry still is farming; and the landscape of patchwork fields separated by low stone walls hasn't changed much since the Spanish galleons stopped calling here hundreds of years ago.

Ferries to and from Baltimore: May Mon.-Fri. 2/day, Sat.-Sun. 1/day; June and Sept. daily 2/day; July-Aug. daily 3/day; Oct.-April. Mon.-Thurs. and Sat.-Sun. 1/day, Fri. 2/day; £5; £8 return. Call Capt. O'Driscoll (tel. 39135) for more information. Ferries to the island **from Schull** leave daily, in June at 2:30pm, in July-Aug. at 10am, 2:30pm, and 4:30pm. Another ferry service from Baltimore cruises via Heir Island to Schull (Sun.-Mon. and Wed.-Fri. at 11:15am, 1:30, and 4pm; £6/any 2-stage journey).

Once you get to the Cape, life is leisurely and hours are approximate: the island's stores and pubs keep flexible hours and B&Bs arise and decline according to individual resident's inclination to host guests. For an updated version of opening hours, as well as general island information, check the bulletin board at the end of the pier. The island's grocery store, **An Siopa Beag** (tel. 39119), stocks the essentials in a white building a few hundred yards to the right as you walk down the pier (open Mon.-Sat. 10am-1pm and 2-5pm, Sun. 11am-5pm). The island **co-op** (tel. 39119) doubles as an information office (open Mon.-Fri. 9:30am-1pm and 2-5pm). **Cistin Chiarain** (tel. 39184) serves sandwiches, soup, and pastries next to the harbor (open daily 10am-8pm). **Cotter's** serves bar food until 8pm.

What the Cape Clear pub scene lacks in variety it makes up for in stamina. Cape Clear Island has no resident authorities to regulate after-hours drinking, and if any have the impudence to sail over from the mainland, their lights give revellers plenty of time to close up shop. The island's 130 people support three pubs. You can enjoy an afternoon pint with a young (but not unseemly) crowd at **Paddy Burke's** (tel. 39115), 100 yards up the hill on the right (open noon-6pm). **Cotter's** opens at noon and is liveliest in the afternoon and early evening, while **Club Chléire** (tel. 39184), behind the café, has live sessions most nights, which often last until 4am or later.

The **An Óige Hostel (HI)** (tel. 39144) is about ten minutes from the pier, keeping left on the main road. The strict curfew of this institutional hostel may shackle some, but at least you can light a peat fire and fall asleep to the sound of the waves just a few feet outside. This spare and rather sullen hostel evokes the real estate mantra— "location, location, location." Lockout 10:30am-5pm; midnight curfew. (June-Sept. £5.50/person; April-May and Oct. £4.50/person; sheets 50p.) Inarguably more hospitable is **Cluain Mara** (tel. 39153), a short stumble up the hill from Paddy Burke's. (£14/person (singles more), w/bath £15). The gracious innkeeper also rents out a spacious self-catering apartment across the road for £20, posing an attractive alternative to the hostel for groups. The island's **campsite** (tel. 39149) is a five-minute walk from the harbor: go up the main road, turn right at the yellow general store, then continue, bearing left (open June-Sept.; £5).

About a 25-minute walk up a bone-shatteringly steep hill is the island's **Heritage Centre,** which is half a room containing everything from a butterfly collection to items recovered from shipwrecks. Maps of the island (20p) decipher the code of numbered posts marking the archaeological and historical sites. (Open June-Aug. Mon.-Sat. 2-5:30pm; £1, students 50p, children 30p.) The museum's summer staff consists of teenage students converging on the island to perfect their Irish. It's comforting to walk into the pubs or post office and hear islanders keeping alive Ireland's native language. On the road to the center, **Cleire Goats** sells **goat's milk ice cream** for a mere 85p and even raises the animals responsible (goatsicles also for sale in the craft shop across from Cotter's). Past the center, a right turn leads to the **windmills** which generate ¾ of the island's electricity. On a misty day you'll hear the eerie noise of their motion long before you see them. Cape Clear also shelters gulls, stormy petrels, cormorants, and ornithologists. The **bird observatory,** the white farmhouse on North Harbour, is one of the most important in Europe. Cape Clear hosts an annual **International Storytelling Festival** (tel. 39157) during the first week of September, featuring puppet workshops, music sessions, and a week's worth of memorable tales.

THE MIZEN HEAD PENINSULA

If you've made the mistake of skipping Cape Clear Island, you'll have to pass through Ballydehob on the land route to Schull, Crookhaven, and Mizen Head. Bally-dehob is only worth a stop for a pint of Guinness. Otherwise spend your time exploring craggy tips and secluded beaches along the peninsula. Schull is a more ideal destination. With a great hostel and an excellent B&B/bakery, Schull is the place to hang your hat. The **phone code** for the Mizen Head Peninsula is 028.

SCHULL

A jovial seaside hamlet 45 minutes from Cape Clear by ferry, or four miles west of Ballydehob by road (R592), Schull makes the best base from which to explore the Mizen Head Peninsula. Intermittent ferries connect Schull to Cape Clear and to Baltimore. A **bulletin board** on Main St. *is* the tourist office, as it currently exists. The **bus** to Cork and Goleen (2/day) stops in front of Griffin's Bar on Main St. Either sing half-clothed on a Schull street corner or get cash at **AIB** bank, 3 Upper Main St. (tel. 28132), which has an **ATM** that accepts VISA (open Mon.-Fri. 10am-12:30pm and 1:30-4pm). Schull's appeal for budget travelers is immeasurably enhanced by the opening of the **Schull Backpackers' Lodge,** Colla Rd. (tel. 28681). A brand-new wooden lodge, the hostel is bright and immaculate, with fluffy, cheerful comforters on pine beds; a sparkling kitchen; and incredible showers (4- to 6-bed dorms £6, double £8/person; sheets 50p). **Adele's B&B, Coffee Shop and Bakery,** Main St. (tel. 28459), will warm you up with dark wooden floors and small fireplaces (£12.50/person w/continental breakfast). Three miles from town on the way to Goleen, **Jenny's Farmhouse** (tel. 28205) offers friendly, quiet B&B (£10/person; call for possible pick-up in Schull).

Schull is a prime destination for scone and brown bread connoisseurs, as the town's bakeries compete for top honors. **Adele's** bakes decadent cakes and pastries and dishes up tasty soups, salads, and sandwiches (£1-3) in a proper tea room (open May-Oct. for lunch and tea daily 9:30am-7pm, dinner Wed.-Sun. 7-10pm). Not to be outdone, the multi-talented **Courtyard,** across the street (tel. 28390), bakes eight types of bread (70p-£1.10/loaf). The Courtyard also sells a variety of gourmet foods, wholefoods, soups, and sandwiches. This place also serves plentiful dinners, with such specialties as warm goat's cheese salad with sun-dried tomatoes and basil (£5.85; dinner menu served daily 6-9pm). On weekends, the adjacent **pub** features traditional music, jazz, and blues (open Mon.-Sat. 9am-6pm). **The Bunratty Pub** (tel. 28341), up the hill on Main St., concocts some of West Cork's best pub fare (lunch served Mon.-Sat. noon-7pm, Sun. 12:30-2pm). **Cotter's Yard,** Main St., distinguishes itself with Mizen Mud Pie (£1.85; open Mon.-Sat. 11am-8pm, Sun. 11am-5:30pm). The **Bunratty Inn** (tel. 28341) and **Al Tigin's** (tel. 28337) host live folk and rock during the summer. Finally, before leaving, stock up for Mizen forays at one of Schull's **grocery stores** on Main St.—**Spar Market** (open daily 7am-9pm) or smaller **Hegarty's,** across the street (open Mon.-Sat. 8am-10pm, Sun. 9am-9pm).

Schull's location on a calm harbor near numerous shipwrecks makes it a boater's or diver's paradise. The **Watersports Centre** (tel. 28554) rents dinghies, windsurfers, snorkeling apparel, wetsuits, and diving gear (open Mon.-Fri. 9:30am-1pm and 2-6pm, Sat. 10am-1pm and 2-6pm). They offer some of the cheaper rates on the bay, so take advantage of them if you're set on taking to the sea. Terrestrial types can rent bikes at **Freewheelin'**, Cotter's Yard, Main St. (tel. 28165), for £8/day or £45/week (open Mon.-Sat. 11am-5pm; bikes can be returned to Schull Backpacker's Lodge).

FARTHER ON: MIZEN HEAD

The Mizen becomes more scenic and less populated the farther west one goes from Schull. Depending on when you go, Mizen can be mobbed on sunny Sunday afternoons, as beach-goers and sun-worshippers pack sandy beaches. **Bus Éireann** only goes as far as Goleen (2/day; inquire in Schull or Ballydehob for schedule). Hitching can also be rewarding if it is high-traffic season for camping—but a perfect daytrip to Mizen Head is made by bike.

Goleen itself seems to move at half-pace: dogs roam the streets in this block-long town. You can spend a night in **Heron's Cove B&B** (tel. 35225), where £16.50 rents a modern room with a view of the cove (and a balcony and a TV). The **restaurant** downstairs lovingly serves seafood (mussels with wine and cream £5; May-Sept. daily noon-9:45pm).

From Goleen, the slightly longer but worthwhile coast road roams to Barley Cove and Mizen Head. **Crookhaven,** a one-mile detour, is perched at the end of a peninsula. It's a haven for Euroyachts which swarm to the village every summer. Nevertheless, at the end of Crookhaven Pier, **O'Sullivans** (tel. 35319) serves sandwiches, desserts, and cold pints on the water's edge (salmon sandwich £2.40). **Barley Cove Caravan Park,** 1½ miles from Crookhaven (tel. 35302), offers camping to a sea of cooler-sporting, satellite-disked campers. (£4.50/tent, July to mid-Aug. £5.50/tent; £1/extra person; showers 50p; mini-market and laundry available; bike rental £5/½-day, £8/day; deposit £20 for campers or £40 for non-campers; open May 7-Sept. 11.) A cheaper (it's free) and infinitely more romantic (there are no caravans) option is to camp on or near the **Barley Cove Beach,** a gorgeous ¼-mile of sand whose warm, shallow coves satisfy bathers who won't brave the frigid sea itself. Rest easy—camping is legal here and you have no fear of a 4am citation by local beach rangers.

Three miles past Barley Cove, Ireland ends at spectacular **Mizen Head,** whose cliffs rise to 700 feet. **The Mizen Head Lighthouse,** built in 1909, was recently automated and electrified; and the buildings nearby were turned into a museum, the **Mizen Vision** (tel. 35115). To get to the museum (it's on a small island), you'll have to cross a suspension bridge. The museum assembles lighthouse paraphernalia and sheds light on the solitary lives of lighthouse-keepers, all set to the sound of seagulls and sea-surf amplified by loudspeakers. (Open June-Sept. daily 10:30am-5:30pm; Oct.-May call 32553; £2, students £1.50.)

BEARA PENINSULA

Untold numbers of visitors traveling up and down Ireland's southwest coast skip the Beara altogether. This region has much of the majesty of the Ring of Kerry but also a more profound sense of tranquility. The spectacular **Caha** and **Slieve Miskish Mountains** march down the spine of the peninsula, separating the Beara's rocky southern coast from its lush northern coast. West Beara remains remote—stark Atlantic coastline is traversed by a few single-track roads upon which travelers precariously dodge mountains, rocky outcrops, and an occasional herd of sheep. For unspoiled scenery and solitude, the Beara is superb; if you're looking for pubs, people, and other signs of civilization, you might be happier on the Iveragh or Dingle Peninsulas. The dearth of cars west of Glengarriff makes cycling the Beara a joy (weather permitting), but means that hitchhikers may find themselves admiring the same views for longer than their sanity can bear.

Existence Chanting

The Beara Peninsula is bleak and unspoilt, but it was here that the first humans supposedly set foot on Ireland. When the first invaders of the island landed in about 2000 BC, the Milesians actually had to bring the land into existence. According to *The Book of Invasions*, the Milesians were pressured into composing (quite literally) the land. It was necessary for their bard, Amergin, to chant the land into existence, before they could set foot on shore:

> *I am wind on sea*
> *I am wave in storm*
> *I am sea sound*
> *I am hawk on cliff*
> *A word of art*
> *A piercing point that pours out rage*
> *The god who fashions fire in the head*
> *Who if not I?*

■■■ BANTRY

According to the *Book of Invasions*, the first human beings landed in Ireland just a mile from Bantry. Bantry's second "invasion" is more generally agreed upon by historians: English settlers seized Bantry and drove out the 17th-century Irish. Irishman Theobald Wolfe Tone tried to return the favor by attacking the town in 1796. A day or two in civilized Bantry may pay off with a cruise round the bay, a visit to Wolfe Tone Square on Saturday afternoon, or an expedition to the Armada exhibit.

PRACTICAL INFORMATION

Bantry is settled at the east end of Bantry Bay. Sheep's Head stretches due west, while journeying north then west will bring you to the Beara Peninsula. Hitchers, cars and bicyclists stay on N71 to get in or out of town.

Tourist Office: Wolfe Tone Sq. (tel. 50229). Open June-Sept. Mon.-Sat. 10am-6pm.

Banks: AIB, Wolfe Tone Sq. (tel. 50008). **Bank of Ireland,** Wolfe Tone Sq. (tel. 51377); both open Mon.-Wed. and Fri. 10am-4pm, Thurs. 10am-5pm; both have **ATMs** that accept VISA.

Post Office: 2 William St. (tel. 50050). Open Mon.-Tues. and Thurs.-Sat. 9am-5:30pm, Wed. 9:30am-5:30 pm.

Phone Code: 027.

Buses: Buses stop outside of Lynch's Pub in Wolfe Tone Sq., several doors from the tourist office toward the pier. **Bus Éireann** heads to: Cork via Dunmanway and Bandon (Mon.-Sat. 3/day, Sun. 2/day; £8.80, students £5); Glengarriff (Mon.-Sat. 3/day, Sun. 2/day; £2.70, students £2). June-Sept. only, buses go to: Skibbereen (Mon.-Sat. 2/day, Sun. 1/day; £4.30, students £2.60); Clonakilty (Mon.-Sat. 1/day); Killarney via Kenmare (Mon.-Sat. 2/day); and Schull (Mon.-Sat. 1/day). **Berehaven Bus Service** (tel. 75009) stops in Bantry on the way to and from Cork (see Castletownbere, p. 218).

Bike Rental: Kramer's, Glengarriff Rd., Newtown (tel. 50278). Open daily 9am-6pm; £6/day; deposit £20.

Laundry: The Wash Tub, Wolfe Tone Sq. Wash and dry £3.50; open Mon.-Sat. 10am-6pm.

Pharmacy: Coen's Pharmacy, Wolfe Tone Sq. (tel. 50531). Open Mon.-Tues. and Thurs.-Sat. 9:30am-1pm and 2-6pm, Wed. 9:30am-1pm.

Hospital: Bantry Hospital, Bridge St. (tel. 50133), ¼ mi. past the library.

Emergency: Dial 999; no coins required. **Garda:** Wolfe Tone Sq. (tel. 50045).

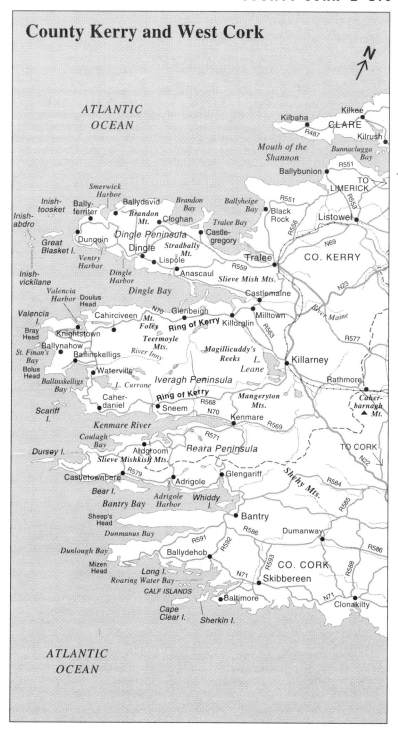

County Kerry and West Cork

N

ATLANTIC
OCEAN

Kilbaha
Kilkee
CLARE
R487
Kilrush

Mouth of the
Shannon
Bunnaclugga
Bay
R551

Ballybunion
TO
LIMERICK
R551

Smerwick
Harbor
R553
Inish-
toosket
Bally-
ferriter
Ballydavid
Brandon
Bay
Ballyheige
Bay
Black
Rock
Listowel
Inish-
abdro
Brandon
Mt.
Cloghan
Tralee Bay
R556
N69
Great
Blasket I.
Dunquin
Dingle Peninsula
Castle-
gregory
CO. KERRY
Dingle
Stradbally
Mt.
Ventry
Harbor
Lispole
Tralee
Inish-
vickilane
Dingle
Harbor
Anascaul
R559
Slieve Mish Mts.
N23
Dingle Bay
Castlemaine
Valencia
Harbor
Doulus
Head
N70
Glenbeigh
Milltown
River Maine
Valencia
I.
Cahirciveen
Mt.
Foley
Ring of Kerry
Killorglin
R577
Bray
Head
Knightstown
Teermoyle
Mts.
R563
St. Finan's
Bay
Ballynahow
Ballinskelligs
River Inny
Magillicuddy's
Reeks
Killarney
Bolus
Head
Waterville
Iveragh Peninsula
L.
Leane
Ballinskelligs
Bay
L. Currane
Rathmore
Scariff
I.
Caher-
daniel
Ring of Kerry
Sneem
R568
N70
Mangeryton
Mts.
Caher-
barnagh
Mt.
Kenmare River
Kenmare
R569
Coulagh
Bay
R571
TO CORK
Dursey I.
Ardgroom
Beara Peninsula
N22
Slieve Mishkish Mts.
Shehy Mts.
Castletownbere
R579
Adrigole
Glengariff
R584
Bear I.
Adrigole
Harbor
Whiddy
I.
R585
Bantry Bay
Bantry
Sheep's
Head
Dunmanus Bay
R591
R586
Dumanway
Dunlough Bay
Ballydehob
R592
R586
Mizen
Head
Long I.
R593
CO. CORK
R588
Roaring Water Bay
N71
Skibbereen
CALF ISLANDS
Cape
Clear I.
Baltimore
N71
Clonakilty
Sherkin I.

ATLANTIC
OCEAN

BEARA PENINSULA

ACCOMMODATIONS

Bantry Independent Hostel (IHH), Bishop Lucey Place (tel. 51050). Walk up the Glengarriff Rd. (Marino St.), turn left at the fork and walk ¼ mi. to this small, friendly hostel above town, nestled among the trees. Pleasant kitchen w/microwave and music. 6- to 8-bed dorm £5.50, private room £7.50/person; sheets 50p. Open mid-March to Oct.

Harbour View Hostel, Harbour View (tel. 51313), just to the left of the fire station along the water. Brand-new bunkbeds and thick comforters grace this seaside hostel. Dorm £5.50, quad £7.50/person; sheets 50p; breakfast £3.50.

Eagle Point Camping and Caravan Park, Glengarriff Rd. (tel. 50630), 4 mi. from town in Ballylickey. This spacious campground occupies its own private peninsula and offers such frills as its own private beach and tennis courts. Laundry, TV room, free showers. Plenty of privacy for tents; £3.50/person. Open May-Sept.

FOOD & PUBS

Bantry has numerous inexpensive lunch restaurants. For an evening meal, pub fare at the **Snug** or the **Wolfe Tone** may be the best value. **SuperValu** is on New St. (open Mon.-Thurs. 9am-6pm, Fri. 9am-9pm, Sat. 9am-5pm), while **Essential Foods** on Main St. stocks health food (open Mon.-Sat. 10am-1pm and 2-5:30pm).

The 5A Café, Barrack St. (tel. 51581). Serves savory vegetarian food at laughably low prices to a kick-back café crowd (soup and brown bread £1). Open Mon.-Sat. 10am-4:30pm, also Thurs.-Sat. 6-9pm.

The Bakehouse, New St. (tel. 51233). Eat irresistible pastries in a trellised café downstairs or dinner in the inviting **Garden Café** upstairs. Bakehouse open Mon.-Sat. 9am-5:30pm; upstairs open Wed.-Sun. 6:30-11pm.

O'Siochain, Bridge St. (tel. 51329). Solid, well-prepared food in a coffee house atmosphere. Sandwiches £1.50, pizza and entrees £3.50-5. Open Mon.-Sat. 9am-9pm, Sun. 10am-10pm.

O'Connor's, Wolfe Tone Sq. (tel. 50221). Renowned for their seafood. You can eat mussels 8 different ways. Satisfy your shellfish cravings at lunch (mussels and pasta £5; dinner prices much higher). Open daily noon-9:30pm, bar/lunch menu available until 5pm.

Bantry nightlife has kicked into overdrive thanks to **Caill an Ceann** (a.k.a. the Bantry Folk Club), Wolfe Tone Sq. They play live music most nights, hosting both nationally known musicians and impromptu sessions. **The Wolfe Tone,** Wolfe Tone Sq. (tel. 50900), has music every Thurs. and Sun. during the summer and cooks excellent Indonesian food (£3.50-6). **J.J. Crowley's** offers country and ballads every summer weekend. As any good seaside town should, Bantry sports its token **Anchor Bar,** New St. (tel. 50012): this one is garnished with a working miniature lighthouse.

SIGHTS

The town's highlight is undoubtedly **Bantry House** (tel. 50047), a Georgian manor with an imposing garden overlooking Bantry Bay. The tired mansion, currently being renovated, houses art and furnishings collected by the Second Earl of Bantry. The former seat of the four Earls of Bantry (and the current residence of the same, though now less wealthy, family), the House was transformed into a hospital during Ireland's Civil War and again during the "Emergency" (neutral Éire's term for World War II). More impressive than the house are the manicured gardens and the view of the bay from the grand lawn, which is littered with plaster statues and poised cannons pointed to sea. The long and shaded driveway to the house is a two-minute walk from town on Cork Rd. (Open daily 9am-8pm. House £3, students £1.75; gardens free.)

Next door to Bantry House is the **1796 Bantry French Armada Exhibition Centre** (tel. 51796). In 1796 Theodore Wolfe Tone, whose last two names now grace streets from Kells to Sligo, arranged for 50 French ships to sail to Ireland and aid his anti-British insurrection. A storm fatefully intervened: thirty ships turned back and ten sank, of which one, recovered in 1985, is modeled at the Armada Centre. The centre focuses on Wolfe Tone's general revolutionary activities and the revolutionary trend at the time. The museum's proximity to Bantry House is historically ironic, given the fact that Richard White, owner of Bantry House at the time of the Armada's sailing, was instrumental in rallying British resistance to the threatened invasion. (Open daily 10am-6pm; £2.50, students £1.50.)

Sea trips circumnavigate the harbor or drop you at **Whiddy Island,** a prime spot for repressed ornithologists. Trips leave from the pier hourly (tel. 50310; run June-Sept. daily 10am-6pm; £4 return). For two weeks in August (usually beginning on the second weekend), the **Bantry Bay Regatta** employs the best sailors in Ireland. Bantry is gearing up for an epic **bicentennial** celebration of Wolfe Tone's aborted revolution. Festivities are scheduled for the entire year, so ask around for details.

Sheep's Head is the empty space on your map west of Bantry. Largely ignored by the heavy-footed herd of tourists stampeding through Skibbereen, Bantry, and Glengarriff, this narrow finger of land is best explored on a daytrip by bike or on foot. Bantry makes a good homespot. Cyclists head west along the cove-filled southern shore, and return by the barren and windswept northern road, while hikers explore the spine of hills down the middle. Inquire in Bantry for directions.

Sheep's Head itself is marked by the requisite lighthouse and its spectacular (and untouristed) cliff-top vistas. If you're lucky, you might see the tide change in Bantry Bay, where incoming breakers meet the outgoing tide and create a mini-maelstrom. For a snack on the way out, try the highly recommended **Tin Pub** in Ahakista, on the southern road—the corrugated iron "shack" serves yummy sandwiches. You can also try the nearby celebrated Japanese restaurant.

■ ■ ■ GLENGARRIFF & GARINISH

Glengarriff identifies itself as a "gateway" to the Beara peninsula. If you're wise (or already well-stocked with Guinness paraphernalia), proceed quickly through this touristy gateway. To aid the throngs passing through, Glengarriff is graced with two separate **tourist offices.** The staffs of both are helpful and friendly. The large, privately-run office is located "in the village" next to the public bathrooms (open daily 9am-6pm). The smaller Bord Fáilte office is on Bantry Rd. (tel. 63084), next to the Eccles Hotel (office open July-Aug. Mon.-Sat. 10am-1pm and 2:15-6pm). **Bus Éireann** runs to Glengarriff from Bantry (Mon.-Sat. 5/day, Sun. 2/day; winter Mon.-Sat. 3/day, Sun. 2/day; 25 min.; £2.70, students £2). Another route runs between Killarney and Glengarriff via Kenmare (June to mid-Sept. Mon.-Sat. 3/day; Kenmare 45 min.; £3.70, students £2.20; Killarney 1¾ hr.). Buses stop in front of Casey's Hotel on Main St. **Berehaven Bus Service** (tel. 70007) also runs buses to Cork (Mon.-Sat. 3/day, Sun. 2/day; 2¾ hr.) and Bantry (Mon. 2/day, Tues. and Thurs.-Sat. 1/day). The **phone code** plays automatic for the people at 027.

Accommodations, Food, & Pubs There has been a recent proliferation of "hostels" (often private houses stocked with beds and billed as cheaper, if less private, alternatives to the town's B&Bs) in Glengarriff. Thus, if you must stay in Glengarriff, you have a number of budget alternatives. **St. Anthony's Hostel,** Bantry Rd. (tel. 63109), is small and comfortable among its rhododendrons, but a 10-minute walk from town. (2- to 6-bed dorms £5, sheets 50p, laundry £4.) Still farther from town on the Kenmare Rd., the **Glengarriff Independent Hostel** compensates for its remote location with a sparkly kitchen and huge windows looking out over the sylvan scene (dorms £6). As for B&Bs, **Island View House** (tel. 63081), next to the Eccles Hotel off the Bantry Rd., offers pleasant, sunny rooms set above the harbor (£13.50/person, £15.50 w/bath). In town, **Maureen's,** Main St. (tel. 63201), offers comfortable rooms for £12.50, £13.50 w/bath. Two **campsites, Dowling's** (tel. 63154) and **O'Shea's** (tel. 63140), flank the Castletownbere Rd. 1½ mi. from town (both open mid-March to Oct.; £5/tent). Sandwiches and excellent pastries can be found at **The Coffee Shop,** Main St. (tel. 63073; cake slice £1.50), while **Johnny Barry's** and **The Blue Loo,** both on Main St., serve standard pub grub.

Sights Glengarriff's proximity to the lush **National Forest** is its kindest attraction, where hiking trails allow you to meander among giant rhododendrons and moss-strewn evergreens. Walking trails in the area range from pebbled walks for the most sedentary, scone-eating tourists to rugged climbs for serious hikers. *Let's Walk Around Glengarriff,* available at hostels in town and at the tourist office, outlines several walks in the park; but more intense hikers should pick up maps at the tourist office in town. For the truly committed, Glengarriff is a good starting point for the 130-mile **Beara Way** walking path.

The town's popularity, however, really results from **Garinish Island,** formerly a rocky outcrop inhabited only by gorse bushes; now, a million hours of labor and countless boatloads of topsoil later, it's now an exotic flower garden! Three ferry companies along the main Bantry Rd. overcharge—a return trip will put you out a steep £5 (students £4); prices are somewhat negotiable, especially from September to June. Garinish's **Latinate Garden,** also known as Illnacullin, blooms and flour-ishes with the seasons and offers an expensive view of the peninsula's mountains. (Open daily July-Aug. Mon.-Sat. 10am-5:30pm, Sun. 11am-6pm; April, June, and Sept. Mon.-Sat. 10am-5:30pm, Sun. 1-6pm; March and Oct. Mon.-Sat. 10am-4:30pm, Sun. 1-5pm; £2.50, students £1.50.) Boats usually leave every 10-20 minutes, depending on the weather and the crowd. Nearby, **Lake Eskenohoolikeaghaun** ("Lake of Twelve Cows") wins Ireland's longest-name contest, but pales miserably beside Wales' offering: the town of Llanfairpwllgwyngyllgogerychw-yrndrobwllllantysiliogogogoch. Glengarriff's water gets more attention for its fishing than its aesthetic value: Upper and Lower Lough Avaul are stocked with brown and rainbow trout (fishing permit required) while Barley Lake, nearby rivers, and the ocean, do not require permits. For more details, pick up the free *Fishing in Glen-garriff* and ask around by the piers.

The breathtaking **Healy Pass** branches north off east-west R572 near Adrigole; it's a narrow, winding road which takes you through the green and rocky Caha Moun-tains to Lauragh. The **Glanmore Lake Youth Hostel (An Óige/HI)** makes a good base for hiking or fishing in the little-explored mountains near Lauragh. The hostel itself is housed in a stately former schoolhouse with great mountain views; and, due perhaps to the lack of traffic, it is prim and immaculate. (Dorm £5.50, £4.50 in low season; open Easter-Sept.) Follow signs from town, it is located three miles from Lauragh on a dead end road.

■■■ CASTLETOWNBERE

In contrast to Glengarriff, the fishing town of Castletownbere is an unpretentious relief: this largest town on the Beara Peninsula reverberates daily with the sounds of ferry engines, cars, loud children, and wind over the world's second-largest natural harbor, Berehaven Bay. During the summer, the town supports street musicians, fes-tivals, and long-distance cyclists who stop here for a pint. Winters show the town's true calling: working hard for the fruit of the sea, not catering to outsiders.

The bathroom-sized **tourist office,** behind O'Donoghue's by the harbor, gives away heaps of maps (open June-Sept. Mon.-Sat. 11am-5pm). The **AIB** bank on Main St. accepts VISA (open Mon. 10am-12:30pm and 1:30-5pm, Tues.-Fri. 10am-12:30pm, and 1:30-4pm). There is also an **ATM** on Main St. **Bus Éireann** operates a summer service between Castletownbere and Killarney, via Kenmare (June 26-Sept. 2 Mon.-Sat. 2/day; £8.80, students £5). **Berehaven Bus Service** (tel. 70007), heads to Bantry via Glengarriff (Mon. 2/day, Tues.-Sat. 1/day; Glengarriff 45 min., £2.70; Bantry 1½hr., £4) and to Cork (Thurs. only; 3hr.; £8) from the parking lot next to O'Donoghue's. Two **minibus** services leave Cork for Castletownbere Mon.-Fri. (and Sat. in summer) 6pm and Sun. 8pm: phone **Harrington's** (tel. 74003) or **O'Sullivan's** (tel. 74168) for mandatory reservations (both buses £8). **Bike hire** is available at

SuperValu on Main St. (tel. 70020; open Mon.-Sat. 9am-7pm, Sun. 9am-1pm; £7/day; deposit £20). The **phone code** for Castletownbere and Bere Island is 027.

Two miles west of town on Allihies Rd., just past the fork to Dunboy Castle, the **Beara Hostel** (tel. 70184) offers comfortable beds in a pleasantly rural setting. The high-spirited Ella Baetz can cure any ailment with her homemade chicken soup. (Dorm £5, private room £7/person; camping £3.50; laundry £2.) **Castletown House,** Main St. (tel. 70252), above the Old Bank Seafood Restaurant, offers spacious rooms and lots of info (£13.50; w/bath £15.50).

Four miles farther, and a good deal more isolated, is the euphoria-inducing **Garranes Farmhouse Hostel** (tel. 73147). This luxurious and intimate cottage perched above the sea has a view to inspire meditation (dorm £5.50, single or double £7/person). Stay on the Allihies Rd.; if you hit a fork in the road, you've gone too far. Phone ahead to confirm that all the space hasn't been gobbled up by the Buddhist center next door and to arrange a possible lift from town. Next door to the Garranes Farmhouse Hostel is the **Dzogchen Buddhist Centre,** where dabblers and devotees alike practice meditation. There are no drugs or altered states involved. The aim is to become more "natural"—to free yourself from passing feelings of anger, passion, or guilt by distancing your actions from your thought. If you don't believe it, attend a **meditation session,** every Saturday at 8pm and most other evenings in summer.

Seafood spawns in almost all of Castletownbere's restaurants. **Jack Patrick's,** Main St. (tel. 70319), serves enormous platters (open Mon.-Fri. 10:30am-9pm, Sat. 10:30am-7pm). Across the street, **Niki's** (tel. 70625) expands the seafood options with creativity (open daily 10am-3pm and 7-9:30pm). **Murphy's,** Main St. (tel. 70244), offers seafood for £3-6 or a 4-course lunch for £4 (open Mon.-Sat. 9am-8pm). **SuperValu,** Main St. (tel. 70020), sells the largest selection of foodstuffs (open Mon.-Sat. 9am-7pm, Sun. 9am-1pm). **O'Donoghue's** pub, Main St. on the square, lures a younger catch with its pool table and sunny (or starry) tables outside. **O'Shea's,** across the square, is the fishing crowd's pick.

Two miles southwest of Castletownbere on the Allihies Rd., **Dunboy Castle** shelters two separate ruins. Cows roam the crumbling Gothic-style halls of its 18th- and 19th-century mansion, and ¾ mile past the gate stand the ruins of the 14th-century O'Sullivan Bere fortress (pedestrians and cyclists 50p). The road that runs past the castle soon becomes a shady trail that passes a number of sheltered coves perfect for swimming, as long as you don't mind jellyfish.

■ NEAR CASTLETOWNBERE: BERE ISLAND

Cape Clear Island it isn't. While Bere Island's proximity to the mainland and its dedication to shipping rupture its tranquility, the island still offers fantastic views of the Beara peninsula. Two **ferries** chug to Bere Island: **Murphy's Ferry Service** (tel. 75004) leaves from the pontoon three miles east of Castletownbere off the Glengarriff Rd. but lands you much closer to the island's "center," Rerrin Village (daily 4/day; £4 return, students £3). The other company, **Bere Island Ferry** (tel. 75009), leaves from the center of Castletownbere but drops you inconveniently on the western end of the island (June 21-Sept. 2, 5/day, Sun. 4/day; £3 return). A *Let's Go* researcher was stranded here for hours when her ferry from the island left half an hour early, so don't plan to catch the last one just as it leaves. Bere Island used to be a British naval base—forts and other military remnants are still scattered around the island. These days, **Glenan's Sailing School** (tel. 75012) has taken over the island; and at night the pubs stay open long after the land-lubbers are asleep. **Hotel Bere Island** (tel. 75018), actually a pub and a store, is situated at the top of a long hill (from the Bere Island Ferry take a left after the pier and keep walkin'… and walkin') and has a commanding view of Berehaven Harbour. (Open Mon.-Sat. 10am-midnight, Sun. 10am-3pm and 7pm-midnight.) If you plan to stay, you've no choice but to drop your bags at **Mrs. Sullivan's Harbour View** (tel. 75011), a half-hour walk from the Bere Island Ferry on the way to Hotel Bere Island. Fairly large rooms go for £13/person, w/bath £15. In Rerrin Village, four miles from Hotel Bere Island, **Kitty**

Murphy's Café is your best bet for food while **Desmond Sullivan's** will pamper you in the Guinness department.

■ ■ ■ THE REST OF THE RING

Past Castletownbere, the Beara Peninsula stretches out with rugged knolls, cliff-lined coasts, and desolate villages. The utter isolation of this part of the Ring is at once part of its appeal and pain to hitchers, who may get lucky or, more likely, frustrated by a lack of cars rather than a lack of friendliness. If you are hitching, timing is everything; if not, rent a cycle.

Tiny **Allihies** dangles west of Castletownbere, along R575; the town consists of one street set above the Atlantic and at the foot of the Slieve Mountains. There's a superb hostel here. **Bonnie Brae's,** Main St. (tel. (027) 73107), next to the very red O'Neill's pub, is an excellent base for exploring the nearby coastline. They premiere brightly painted bunkrooms, a sun-drenched kitchen, and excellent karma. (Dorm £6, double £7.50/person; **camping** £3/person; bike hire £6/day; laundry £3; Open May-Sept.) One mile south of the village (and well-marked by signs) lies the spare **Allihies Youth Hostel (An Óige/HI)** (tel. (027) 73014), which threatens to compound the sense of bare isolation in Allihies (dorm £5.50; sheets 60p; open June-Sept.). **The Atlantic,** Main St. (tel. (027) 73072), prepares succulent seafood right off the boat and offers B&B (open daily 9am-10pm). **O'Neill's Bar** (tel. (027) 73008), next to Bonnie Brae's, serves pub grub all day (lasagna £4). **O'Sullivan's,** a few minutes downhill, sells everything necessary for a first-class picnic on Dursey and even rents bikes to get you there (open daily 9am-9pm; mountain bikes £7/day). Allihies' four pubs cater mostly to locals. Usually one pub—seemingly chosen by tacit consensus among the villagers—is quite lively each night. **O'Neill's** is a safe bet, and the **Oak Bar** hosts trad music every Thursday night.

This blunt northern head of the peninsula is choked with architectural fossils. Children's gravestones crumble outside the **Celtic Church,** two miles from Allihies, and marked on some maps and signs as Point Nadistiert. The collapsing entrance to a series of caves stands nearby. **Mass Rocks** dot the fields surrounding the village, and the shafts of abandoned **copper mines** dot Allihies' upper slopes. Paltry evidence of a booming mid-19th century mining industry, the shafts themselves are fenced off. **Ballydonegan Strand** is just short of town on the Castletownbere Rd. More pristine and secluded are the white sands of **Garnish Strand,** across from the post office on the Dursey Rd. The **Windy Point House,** at the cable car a few minutes away, sustains scone-deprived beachgoers.

The best scenery on the Beara is on **Dursey Island,** reached by Ireland's only cable car (tel. (027) 73017). The car makes the 10-minute aerial trip continuously Mon.-Sat. 9-11am, 2:30-5pm, and 7-8pm; Sunday hours vary (£2 return). The English Army laid waste to Dursey Fort in 1602 after raiding the unarmed garrison and callously tossing many soldiers over the cliffs to their doom. The whole of Dursey Island is best seen by bike; a trip to the western tip provides a stunning view of the sea and a chance to observe the island's much-vaunted migrant bird flocks. There is no accommodation on the island, but camping is legal.

Ten miles to the northeast of Dursey Island via some of the most barren land and some of the most exciting road in Ireland lies the colorful hamlet of **Eyeries,** even sleepier than its neighbor to the west. Head to the **beach** here; or ask for directions to **Ballycrovane,** where the tallest *ogham* stone in Ireland (17½ ft.) stands (it's on private property and not well signposted). Five minutes east of the village, the **Ard Na Mara Hostel** (tel. (027) 74271) makes you feel like a friend of the family.

The only other thing to see on the northern side of the Beara—except for mountains, forests, and sea—are the **Derreen Gardens** (tel. (064) 83103), where you can lose yourself in the mossy tunnels that run through evergreens. (½ mi. north of Lauragh on the coast road. Open daily April-Sept. 11am-6pm; £2.) Heading east past Eyeries, you pass through Ardgroom, a small village with…drum roll please…a good pub. **The Holly Inn** takes its name from the flora sprouting on its walls.

County Kerry

Various places in County Kerry claim to be Europe's westernmost inhabited land. They're all wrong (the honor goes to Hellisandur, Iceland) but the ubiquitous mistake reveals something about Co. Kerry. Consisting of a string of towns, forests, mountains, and peninsulas so far from the Continent, Co. Kerry can believe its own fictional version of European commerce and geography. The county is so removed from Dublin's metropolitan orbit that when its residents think about the big, bad city, they think of Cork. Famous for its natural beauty, the county can subsist economically from the tourism trade along the Ring of Kerry. If you spend enough time here, you may come to agree that the world worth seeing is bounded by the River Shannon and the Beara Peninsula.

The Iveragh Peninsula (colloquially equated with the Ring of Kerry road) has the lake-filled Killarney National Park at its base, Bray Head near its tip, and noxious tour buses traveling between the two. Even so, the views are incomparable. The Dingle Peninsula is slightly less visited: narrow roads protect Slea Head, the West Dingle *gaeltacht,* and the Blasket Islands from tour bus madness. Summer bus transport throughout Kerry is all too available; in the low season, public transportation grows sparse along coastal routes.

■■■ KILLARNEY

Package-tour guests love Killarney unreservedly; but if you can peek behind the polyester, dodge the shamrock-emblazoned buses, and find your way into the mountains and parks, you will be amply rewarded with some of the most spectacular inland scenery in Ireland. Use Killarney as a base to get to the mountains and the natural attractions, and don't plan on finding "authentic" Irish culture in a town so tailored to tourism. Few of the folks with big cameras and belt buckles will be hiking up Macgillycuddy's Reeks, or rowing out to Innisfallen Island in the National Park.

ORIENTATION & PRACTICAL INFORMATION

Killarney packs itself into three very crowded major streets. **Main St.,** in the center of town, begins at the Town Hall and the tourist office, then becomes High St. **New St.** and **Plunkett St.** both intersect Main St. New St. heads west to the Knockreer Estate and toward Killorglin. Plunkett St. becomes College St. and then Park Rd., heading east to the bus and train stations. East Avenue Rd. begins by the bus and train stations, bends, then becomes the Muckross Rd. en route to the Muckross Estate and Kenmare.

Tourist Office: Main St., in the Town Hall (tel. 31633). Exceptionally helpful and deservedly popular. Open July-Aug. Mon.-Sat. 9am-8pm, Sun. 9am-1pm and 2:15-6pm; June and Sept. Mon.-Sat. 9am-6pm; Oct.-May Mon.-Fri. 9:15am-5:30pm, Sat. 9:15am-1pm.

Banks: TSB bank; 23/24 New St. (tel 33666). Open Mon.-Fri. 9:30am-5pm, Thurs. until 7pm. **AIB** bank; Main St., next to the tourist office (tel. 31922). Open Mon.-Fri. 10am-4pm, Wed. until 5pm. **ATM;** Main St. at New St.; accepts Mastercard/Access and Visa.

American Express: International Hotel (tel. 35722), around the corner from the tourist office. Moneygrams, travelers cheques, but no client mail service. Open Mon.-Fri. 9am-8pm, Sat.-Sun. 9am-7pm.

Post Office: New St. (tel. 31288). Open Mon.-Sat. 9am-5:30pm.

Phone Code: 064.

Trains: Killarney Station off East Avenue Rd. (tel. 31067), near the intersection with Park Rd., past the Great Southern Hotel. Open Mon.-Sat. 7:30am-12:45pm and 1:45pm-6:10pm, Sun. ½ hr. before train departures. Trains flee to Cork (daily

3/day; 1½hr.; £12.50, students £5.50), Dublin (Mon.-Sat. 5/day, Sun. 4/day; 3½ hr.; £33.50, students £11.50), Galway (Mon.-Sat. 4/day, Sun. 2/day; 6hr.; £28.50, students £10.50); Limerick (Mon.-Sat. 6/day, Sun. 3/day; 2hr.; £14, students £6.50), and Sligo (Mon.-Sat. 3/day, Sun. 1/day; £33.50, student £11.50). No trains leave after 6:30pm.

Buses: off East Avenue Rd. (tel. 34777), across from the Great Southern Hotel. Open daily 8:30am-5:50pm. Buses travel to: Cork (Mon.-Sat. 7/day, Sun. 4/day; 2hr.; £8.80, students £5); Dingle (Mon.-Sat. 6/day, Sun. 4/day; 2hr.; £7.30, students £4.20); Dublin (daily 3/day; 6hr.; £14, students £9); Galway (Mon.-Sat. 7/ day, Sun. 6/day; 7hr.; £13, students £8), Limerick (daily 4/day; 2hr.; £9.30, students £5.60); and Sligo (Mon.-Sat. 2/day, Sun. 3/day; 7½hr.; £17, students £10). From June-Sept., buses leave Killarney for the **Ring of Kerry tour** (daily 2/day), which stops in Killorglin, Glenbeigh, Kells, Cahirsiveen, Waterville, Caherdaniel, Sneem, and Moll's Gap (£12, students £7.50; a return, which allows you to get on and off as often as you wish, is £9.70 for students). A bus to Cahirsiveen does the northern half of Ring of Kerry (summer Mon.-Sat. 4/day, Sun. 2/day, off-season Mon.-Sat. daily; 1½hr.; £7.30, students £4.20). The **Dingle/Slea Head tour** (Mon.-Fri. 2/day) stops in Inch, Annascaul, Dingle, Ventry, Slea Head, Dunquin, and Ballyferriter (£9.70, students £6). Bikers should remember that a charge of about £5 is levied for carrying bikes.

Bike Rental: Killarney Rent-a-Bike, Market Cross (tel 32578), Main St. at New St. £5/day, £25/week, free panniers; 10% discount with ISIC. Open daily 9am-6pm.

Laundry: J. Gleason's Launderette (tel. 33877), down the lane next to Spar Market on College St. £4.50/load. Open Mon.-Sat. 9:15am-6pm, Thurs.-Fri. 9:15am-8pm.

Pharmacy: Sewell's Pharmacy, corner of Main and New St. (tel. 31027). Open Mon.-Sat. 9am-6:30pm.

Hospital: District Hospital, St. Margaret's Rd. (tel. 31076). Follow High St. 1 mi. out from town center.

Emergency: Dial 999; no coins required. **Garda:** New St. (tel. 31222).

ACCOMMODATIONS & CAMPING

Finding a cushy B&B is easily accomplished. Killarney is also home to a handful of excellent hostels—six lie within easy walking distance of town center, while three are in rural settings near the National Park. However, there is no camping allowed in the National Park.

Bunrower House (IHH), Ross Rd. (tel. 33914). Follow Muckross Rd. out of town and take a right onto Ross Rd. at the Esso station. The hostel is about ¾ mi. down the road, on the left. Like its sister hostel, the Sugán, the "Bun" has a common room with peat fire and good vibes. There's always music in the air. Upstaging its sibling, though it offers spacious bunkrooms, sky-lit toilets, outstanding showers, and a resident golden retriever. 6-bed dorm £6, double £8.50/person; sheets 50p. Camping in the quiet yard is the closest you can legally get to the experience of sleeping in Killarney's big National Park (£3).

The Sugán (IHH), Lewis Rd. (tel. 33104), 2 min. from the bus or train station: turn right, then left onto College St. Lewis Rd. is the first right. Late nights spent in the stone common room with a glowing turf fire, candlelight, and groovy music give the hostel an incomparable ambiance. Small, ship-like bunk rooms blur the distinction between intimacy and claustrophobia. Hostelers can enjoy a superb 3-course dinner for £4.50. 4- to 8-bed dorm £6.

Neptune's (IHH), Bishop's Lane (tel. 35255), the first walkway off New St. on the right. Large and clean with good showers and solid mattresses. 10% discount to USIT cardholders. Laundry £3.50, bikes £5/day. Free tour booking (save £1). Lockers £1. 4- to 8-bed dorm £6, double £8; sheets 50p.

The Four Winds Hostel (IHH), 43 New St. (tel. 33094). Situated in town but very close to the entrance to the National Park, the Four Winds is comfortable and handy. Bikes £5/day; laundry 50p. 4- to 14-bed dorm £6, double £8/person.

The Railway Hostel, Park Rd. (tel. 35299), across the street from the bus and train stations. Big and bright hostel with skylights, excellent beds, and a pool table. The

Railway Hostel is surprisingly friendly for its large size. Bikes £5/day. 4- to 12-bed dorm £6.50, double £8/person.

Atlas House, Park Rd. (tel. 36144). Take College St. past the bus station, then turn left onto Park Rd. With carpeted lobby and satellite TV, Killarney's newest budget accommodation comforts those who miss the Holiday Inn. Atlas House tries to be more hotel than hostel: prices include linens and a continental breakfast. Dorm £7, double w/bath £11/person.

Peacock Farms Hostel (IHH) (tel. 33557). Take Muckross Rd. out of town and turn left at Muckross Village, just after the hotel. Take that road 2 mi. and follow the signposts—if you think you are nearly there, you haven't gone far enough. As a less taxing alternative, call for a ride from the bus station. Overlooking Lough Guitane and surrounded by Killarney's rocky slopes, this fairly isolated hostel makes a good base for hiking, biking, or fishing. It's designed for quiet, serious hostelers—no pub runs. Dorms £5. Open May-Sept.

Aghadoe Hostel (An Óige/HI) (tel. 31240). In Aghadoe, 3 mi. west of town on the Killorglin Rd., this hostel occupies a stone mansion with magnificent views of the surrounding mountains. They organize National Park and Ring of Kerry trips; nightly pub runs, and maybe even a shuffleboard game. Midnight curfew. Free van from the bus and train stations. Breakfast £2, packed lunch £2.50, cafe for dinner (lasagna w/salad £3.50). June-Sept. £6.50, Oct.-May £5. Bike rental £6/day.

Black Valley Hostel (An Óige/HI) (tel. 34712), 12 mi. from town on the Gap of Dunloe Rd., Black Valley was one of the last places in Ireland to receive electricity. Buy food in town or eat at the hostel. Pickup is available from the bus/train station. Lockout 10:30am-5pm. Midnight curfew. £5.50; Oct.-May £4.50.

Fossa Caravan and Camping Park (tel. 31497), 3½ mi. west of town on the Killorglin Rd. Kitchen, laundromat, and tennis courts—how quaint. £3.50/cyclist or hiker. Open mid-March to Oct.

Flesk Caravan and Camping (tel. 31704), 3 mi. from town on Muckross Rd. July-Aug. £3.25/cyclist or hiker, Sept.-June £3.

FOOD

Food in Killarney is affordable at lunchtime, but prices skyrocket as the sun sinks. **Quinnsworth,** on New St., is the town's well-stocked grocer (open Mon. 9am-8pm, Tues.-Wed. 9am-7:30pm, Thurs.-Fri. 9am-9pm, Sat. 9am-7pm). A disturbing number of fast-food joints and take-aways stay open until 2 or 3am nightly.

The Sugán, Lewis Rd. (tel. 33104). Delicious and generous vegetarian-friendly dinners are a bargain (3-course dinner £4.50; dinner served daily 6-9pm).

An Taelann, Bridewell Lane (tel. 33083), on the left off New St. Incredible vegetarian food accompanies inedible but nourishing philosophy books. Soup and bread (£1.20), veggie pancakes, and baked goat cheese. Lunch £1-5, dinner entrees £6-7. Open Tues.-Sat.12:30-4pm and 6:30-10:30pm.

Bricin, 26 High St. (tel. 34902). Reasonably priced Irish lunches in a dignified quasi-art gallery setting (Irish stew £3.50). Open daily 10am-10pm.

Robertino's, 9 High St. (tel. 34966). Eat bruschetta and antipasti in the company of plaster Greco-Roman goddesses. Pasta dishes £5-7. Open daily 12:30-4pm and 5-10:30pm. **Allegro's,** next door, is run by the same owners and specializes in more democratically priced pizzas (£3.95).

Busy B's Bistro, 15 New St. (tel. 31972). Open late, and it's not Burgerland. Burgers, sandwiches, salads (£1.20-3), and mugs of decent coffee. Open Mon.-Sat. 8am-3am, Sun. 9am-3am.

PUBS

The battalions of jig-seeking tourists make it hard to find a decent pub in Killarney; a few have retained some character in spite of it all. During the summer, traditional music can be heard nightly around town.

Yer Mans, Plunkett St. (tel. 32688). Uncontestedly the best pub in town, it is frequented by a young, almost alternative crowd who actually live in Killarney. The pub consoles guests with turf fires, sawdust on the floor, and Guinness served in jam jars on request (£1.25). Trad nightly in summer, 5 nights per week in winter. If you arrive before 10:30pm, you can stay in their alter-ego "club" **Rudy's** without paying their cover charge.

Fáilte Bar, College St. (tel. 33404). A relaxed, mixed (and large) crowd converges at this well-regarded dark and woody pub. Traditional music Mon.-Tues., folk and rock nightly.

Buckley's Bar, College St. (tel. 31037). Tourist-tolerant drinkers warm themselves by the peat fire. Lively traditional sessions nightly, from 9:30pm.

Mustang Sally's, Main St. (tel. 35790). Loud rock music, some of it live, scares away the tourists.

Kiely's Bar, College St. (tel. 31656). Local bands play folk and rock nightly. Open until 1am Mon., Wed., and Fri. (cover £2.50 after 11pm), this pub attracts thirsty exiles from the town's more atmospheric pubs which close earlier.

SIGHTS & ENTERTAINMENT

Congested with pubs, souvenir shops, and disoriented foreigners, Killarney's charm is elusive. The glories of Killarney are to be discovered in the National Park just beyond city limits. The neo-Gothic **St. Mary's Cathedral** on New St. seats 1400 and boasts three altars, one the size of a tennis court, inside its rough limestone exterior (always open; free). Killarney's festivals are worth anthropological exploration: locals take them quite seriously and come out *en masse*. In mid-May and mid-July, horses gallop around the race course on Ross Rd., competing in the **Killarney Races** (tickets available at gate; £3-5). The **Killarney Regatta** in July draws rowers and spectators to Lough Leane. **Gaelic football matches** are held in Fitzgerald Stadium on Lewis Rd. most Sunday afternoons and some weekday evenings (Kerry's fanatical rivalry with Cork comes to a head when Cork's team comes to town).

Several **nightclubs** around Killarney simmer from 10:30pm until 1:30 or 2am. Most charge £4-5 cover but often offer discounts before 11pm. **Rudy's Nightclub,** above Yer Mans on Plunkett St. (tel. 32688), plays alternative music nightly for Killarney's ruthlessly hip element. **Revelles,** East Avenue Rd. (tel. 32522), in the East Avenue Hotel, clogs with disco bums on Friday through Sunday nights, while **Scoundrels** in the Eviston House Hotel on New St. (tel. 31640) attracts an even younger crowd (Wed.-Sun.; free Fri. before 11pm). Check the *Killarney Advertiser* (free) for happenings around town and the *Kingdom* (70p) for county events.

■ KILLARNEY NATIONAL PARK

Scooping a series of glens and strewing about ice-smoothed rocks and precarious boulders, the Ice Age had a dramatic impact around Killarney. The resulting 10,000-hectare park, stretching west and south from Killarney towards Kenmare, incorporates a string of forested mountains and the famous **Lakes of Killarney:** huge **Lough Leane (Lower Lake),** medium **Middle (Muckross) Lake,** and smallest **Upper Lake,** two miles southwest and connected by a canal. Ireland's last indigenous herd of red deer, numbering about 850, roams the glens that surround the lakes.

Although the Kenmare Rd. curves along the southeastern shores of the lakes, hitchhiking is both difficult and unnecessary. The park's major scenic attractions are only a few miles apart and connected by hundreds of paths ideal for walking or mountain biking. But don't attempt to explore the park without a decent map. Maps from the Killarney tourist office or the **Information Centre** behind Muckross House (tel. 31440; open daily June-Sept. 9am-6pm) may suffice for outings along most trails, but serious hikers should buy the 1:25,000 Ordnance Survey map.

The three most frequented destinations are the **Ross Castle/Lough Leane** area, **Muckross House** on Middle Lake, and the **Gap of Dunloe,** which is bordered on the southwest by Ireland's highest mountain range, **Macgillycuddy's Reeks** (most of the peaks are under 3000 feet). The Gap of Dunloe is a full-day excursion, but the others are close to town and can be managed in several hours or stretched over a full day, depending on your mode of transport. Hikers and bikers should take the necessary precautions whether traveling alone or in groups; see Camping (p. 41).

The best way to explore the park is to find the most remote, least visited spots. There are plenty that are just as magical as the main attractions. If you have the time, consider walking the 129-mile **Kerry Way.** The first (or last) leg, the **Old Kenmare Road,** passes through the spectacular Torc and Mangerton Mountains and can be managed in one day (from Killarney, follow the Kenmare Rd. four miles and turn left just beyond the main entrance to Muckross House—the path leaves from the car-park on this side road). If you plan on hiking the rest of the Kerry Way, take a good map, pack lightly, and do not attempt the trail from October to March, when rains make the uneven and mountainous terrain dangerous. The Killarney bookstore sells a "Kerry Way" guide, with topographic maps of each stretch of the Way. Also available are excellent 1:50,000 Ordnance Survey maps of the Iveragh that include minor roads, trails, and archaeological points of interest. Unfortunately, the maps are expensive (£4.60) and are far from being waterproof.

ROSS CASTLE & LOUGH LEANE

From town, **Knockreer Estate** is a short walk down New St. The original mansion housed the Grosvenor family (of National Geographic fame) and, before that, the steadfastly Catholic Earls of Kenmare. The current building, dating only from the 1950s, is unimpressive but still gives great views of the hills. You can drive to **Ross Castle** (turn right on Ross Rd. off Muckross Rd.; tel. 35851), but the numerous footpaths from Knockreer are more scenic (a one-mile walk). The castle, built in the 14th century by the O'Donoghue chieftains, was the last one in Munster to hold out against Cromwell's army. General Ludlow captured it in 1652 by sailing across the lake, fulfilling the prophecy that only by water would the castle be taken. In the last two decades the castle has been completely renovated, and it shows: the limestone is clean, the wood beams fresh. The castle tours are preoccupied with the O'Donoghue clan's vaguely paranoic, and ultimately futile, measures to repel intruders (open daily June-Aug. 9am-6:30pm, May 9:30am-5pm, Sept. 9am-6pm, Oct. 9am-5pm; £2.50, students £1). Past the castle, paths lead to the wooded and relatively secluded **Ross Island**—not an island at all, but a peninsula shaped like a lobster claw stretched out into Lough Leane.

The view of Lough Leane and its mountains from Ross Island is great, but the best way to see the area is from the water. Two **waterbus services,** Pride of the Lakes (tel. 32638) and Lily of Killarney (tel. 31068), leave from behind the castle for lake cruises every 30 to 60 minutes daily in summer (£5/person). You can hire your own rowboats by the castle for £3/hour, or take one of the **motorboat trips** (tel. 32252; £4/person) to **Innisfallen Island.** Since the motorboat trips take an hour in the water but only leave you 20 min. on the island, rowing is a wiser choice.

On the island are the stoic remains of **Innisfallen Abbey.** St. Finian the Leper founded the abbey around 600 AD. The abbey was eventually transformed into a university during the Middle Ages (High King Brian Ború was educated here). The *Annals of Innisfallen,* now entombed at Oxford, recount world and Irish history. Written in Irish and Latin by 39 monastic scribes, the annals were supposedly finished when the last scribe put pen to parchment in 1326. At the abbey's center is a yew tree: yew and oak groves were sacred to the Druids, so abbeys were often built in and around them. Now the abbey walls are crumbling. The separate Augustinian abbey is so ruined it's barely recognizable. (Both ruins always open; free.)

MUCKROSS HOUSE & ABBEY

Three miles south of Killarney on Kenmare Rd. lie the remains of **Muckross Abbey,** whose construction has been dated to 1448. Cromwell tried to burn it down, but enough still stands to imitate the grace of the part-Norman, part-Gothic cloisters and passageways.

From the abbey, signs direct you to **Muckross House** (tel. 31440), a massive 19th-century manor which has a garden that blooms brilliantly in early summer. The grand and proper house (completed in 1843) reeks of aristocracy, commanding a regal view of the lakes and mountains. Upon first visiting Muckross House, the philosopher Bishop George Berkeley proclaimed: "Another Louis Quatorze may make another Versailles, but only the hand of the Deity can make another Muckross." (Open July-Aug. daily 9am-7pm, mid-March to June and Sept.-Oct. daily 9am-6pm, Nov. to mid-March Tues.-Sun. 11am-5pm; £3, students £1.25.) **Muckross Traditional Farms** lie outside the House. Traditional cottages recreate rural life in early 20th-century Co. Kerry. The view from here is spectacular, and the expansive lawns are perfect for a mid-afternoon nap or picnic. The trees seem to be from another world, or at least another continent: the flora is typical of sub-tropical climes. (Same hours and prices as the house. Joint ticket £4, students £2.)

From Muckross House, it's a two-mile stroll to the **Meeting of the Waters**—walk straight down the front lawn and then follow the signs. The paved path is nice, but the dirt trail through the **Yew Woods** is more secluded. The Meeting of the Waters is the natural sight that is intended to justify a trip, but the real focus of tourists is **Dinis Cottage,** serving pizza, drinks, and pastries (open June-Sept. daily 10am-5pm). If you're coming from the cottage, the roaring influx of water straight ahead is Upper Lake, while the forks to the left and right lead to Middle Lake and Lough Leane. The path returns you to the main (Kenmare/Killarney) road, from which it's about a mile to **Torc Waterfall** (turn left, toward Killarney). A short walk through the mossy woods brings you to the cascading 60-foot drop. Following the trail past the waterfall, you can make your way up Ford Mountain which afford dramatic views of the lakes.

GAP OF DUNLOE

The easiest way to reach the deservedly hallowed Gap of Dunloe is to follow the Killorglin Rd. for five miles, then turn left on the road to Beaufort. You will pass the entirely ruined Dunloe Castle, an Anglo-Norman stronghold which Cromwell's armies effectively demolished. There is also a set of *ogham* stones (c. 300 AD) inscribed with a form of writing unique to the early Christian period in Ireland (see Archaeology, p. 59). Before the Gap, you'll pass **Kate Kearney's Cottage** (tel. 44116). "Kate Kearney" was an independent mountain-dwelling woman famous for brewing the near-poisonous *poitín* (moonshine). Now her former home is a pub attracting droves of tourists (open daily 9am-midnight; traditional music Wednesday, Friday, and Sunday nights).

Past the cottage, walking or cycling are the only options because cars are banned along the seven-mile stretch of road near the Gap. The Gap itself divides **Macgillycuddy's Reeks** (Ireland's tallest range) from the lake-studded **Purple Mountains.** Locals say the best time to "run" the Gap is during the late afternoon, after the masses have cleared the road and returned to their hotel rooms. After running the Gap, you can either retrace your trail or head back to the Kenmare/Killarney Rd. South of the Gap, **Lord Brandon's Cottage** (tel. 34730) serves soup and sandwiches (£1-3) to bellowing German visitors (open June-Sept. daily 9am-4pm).

RING OF KERRY

The Southwest's most gorgeous peninsula once embodied the tough, romantic spirit of Ireland but has more or less sold out to attract the masses. Legions of visitors, drawn by national and international publicity, board buses and pay exorbitant fees for brief real-life glimpses of what they've already seen on travel brochures. Find a good hostel in a small town on a windy day by the sea, however, and you may be able to duplicate the exhilaration of life on the Ring of Kerry in the days before package tourism.

The term "Ring of Kerry" is often used to describe the entire Iveragh Peninsula, but it more correctly refers not to a region, but to a set of roads: N71 from Kenmare to Killarney, R562 from Killarney to Killorglin, and the long loop of N70 west and back to Kenmare. Stay away from the prepackaged Ring of Kerry private bus tours based out of Killarney. **Bus Éireann** does a somewhat better summer circuit through all the major towns on the Ring (daily 2/day), since you can get off anywhere and anytime you like. (Unfortunately, you will have to pay in increments for the trip, since they don't offer one single Ring package that allows you to get on and off.) Generally, towns on the Ring fill up between noon and 6pm as the buses move through, but become relaxed and authentic by evening as the crowds return to Killarney: don't let the mobs deter you from spending a night or two on the Ring. Buses travel around the Ring counterclockwise, from Killarney to Killorglin, west along Dingle Bay, east along Kenmare River and north from Kenmare to Killarney. Some people advise bikers to travel against tour bus traffic, which may not be necessary if traveling in the afternoon or during other "non-prime" tour bus times.

■■■ KENMARE

Kenmare's location subjects it to a fast-moving flow of sightseers: most people traveling through the Beara, the Ring of Kerry, and Cork pass through the town, but few stay more than a night. Despite Kenmare's tourist orientation, it manages to retain an appealing pace and attraction. The town is relentlessly cheery, dotted with tasteful craft shops and tempting restaurants alongside all the less appealing tourist fare. If its charm feels somewhat artificial, Kenmare seems more palatable than larger and more densely-touristed Killarney to the north.

ORIENTATION & PRACTICAL INFORMATION

Kenmare's streets form a triangle: Henry St. is the lively base while Main St. and Shelbourne St. form the other two sides. Main St. flows into the Square, which contains a lovely park, and then becomes N71 to Moll's Gap and Killarney; N70 to Sneem and the Ring of Kerry also branches off this road. From Kenmare, cunning travelers take N70 west, not N71 north, to do the Ring clockwise and avoid tour bus traffic.

Tourist Office: The Square (tel. 41233). Open May-Sept. Mon.-Sat. 9am-6pm; July-Aug. Mon.-Sat. 9:30am-7pm, Sun. 11am-5pm.

Bank: AIB, 9 Main St. (tel. 41010). Open Mon.-Fri. 10am-12:30pm and 1-4pm, Wed. 10am-12:30pm and 1-5pm; **ATM** accepts VISA.

Post Office: Henry St. (tel. 41490), at the corner of Shelbourne St. Open Mon.-Fri. 9am-1pm and 2-5:30pm, Sat. 9am-1pm.

Phone Code: 064.

Buses: Leave from Roughty's Bar on Main St. to: Killarney (Mon.-Sat. 3/day, Sun. 1/day; 1hr. 20 min.; £4.80, students £2.80); Tralee (Mon.-Sat. 3/day, Sun. 1/day; 2hr.; £7.70, students £4.30); Sneem (June-Sept. Mon.-Fri. 2/day; 35 min.); and Cork via Bantry (June-Sept. Mon.-Sat. 2/day, Sun. 1/day; 4hr.; £9.70, student £7).

Bike Rental: Finnegan's, (tel. 41083), on the corner of Henry and Shelbourne St. £6/day. Open Mon.-Sat. 9:30am-6:30pm.

Laundry: The Laundry Basket, Market St., just off the Square. Wash and dry £4.50. Open Mon.-Fri. 10am-1pm and 2-6pm, Sat. 10am-1pm and 2-3pm.

Pharmacy: Sheahan's, Main St. (tel. 41354). Open Mon.-Sat. 9am-6pm.

Hospital: off the Old Killarney Rd. (tel. 41088). Follow Henry St. past the Square.

Emergency: Dial 999; no coins required. **Garda:** Shelbourne St. (tel. 41177).

ACCOMMODATIONS

Fáilte Hostel (IHH), corner of Henry and Shelbourne St. (tel. 41083). Not the white building that says "private hostel" but the one across the street. Comfortable couches and a VCR are useful for rainy days. Great kitchen equipped with the mysterious but ever-stoked Ada cooker. Dorm £6, double £8/person.

La Brasserie, Henry St. (tel. 41379). Newly-opened as a B&B, La Brasserie offers cheery, spacious rooms and a satisfying, lunch-skipping breakfast; £12/person.

Keal Na Gower House B&B, the Square (tel. 41202). Sleep comfortably within earshot of a brook in this small B&B; one room with bathtub, the other two with brook views. Single £15, double £28.

Sunville B&B (tel. 41169). 1 mi. out of town on the Kilgarvan Rd.; £12.50/person.
Ring of Kerry Caravan and Camping Park, Sneem Rd. (tel. 41366), 2½ mi. west
of Kenmare. Overlooks mountains and bay; £3.50/person. Open May-Sept.

FOOD & PUBS

Good food is plentiful, if pricey, in Kenmare. Stick to the smaller cafés for the lowest
prices. **SuperValu** on Main St. opens Mon.-Thurs. 8am-8pm, Fri. 8am-9pm, Sat. 8am-
6:30pm, and Sun. 8:30am-5pm. **The Pantry** on Henry St. (tel. 41296) sells wholefoods (open Mon.-Fri. 9am-8pm, Sat. 10am-6pm).

Mickey Ned's, Henry St. (tel. 41591). A young crowd wolfs down decadent cakes
and open-faced sandwiches in this bustling café. Try the carrot cake! Open Mon.-
Sat. 9am-5:30pm.
La Brasserie Bistro, Henry St. (tel. 41379). Reasonably priced meals all day long in
a spacious dining area; ice cream (50p/scoop) for dessert. Open daily 9am-9pm.
Án Leáth Phigin, 35 Main St. (tel. 41559). Succulent Italian cuisine in what feels
and looks like a 100-year old Irish cottage. Homemade pasta £6-9; smaller portions
£3-4. Open daily 6-10pm.
The Purple Heather, Henry St. (tel. 41508). Excellent bistro fare; save room for
one of the sinful desserts (omelettes £4; open daily 10:45am-11pm).

Kenmare's pubs attract a hefty contingent of tourists. Native revelers, however, are
afforded too much good music to quibble over polyester. **Crowley's,** Henry St. (tel.
41472), asks "When you've got frequent spontaneous traditional sessions, who's got
time to think about interior decorating?" **Moeran's Bar,** on the corner of Main St.
and Shelbourne St., pays homage with live trad most nights in the Lansdowne Arms
Hotel (tel. 41368) to English composer E.J. Moeran (who spent his final months in
the hotel). **Murty's,** New Rd., just off Henry St., has live bands Wednesday, Friday,
and Saturday nights. A warning to stout drinkers with Cork allegiances: you'll *have*
to settle for Guinness here.

SIGHTS

There are plenty of good hikes in the country around Kenmare, but few sights in the
town itself. The ancient **stone circle,** a five-minute walk from The Square down
Market St., is the largest of its kind in Southwest Ireland (55 feet in diameter) and
worth a visit simply for its proximity to town (£1). The new **Kenmare Heritage
Centre** shares a building with the tourist office and focuses on the town's prowess
for lace-making as well as the general history of Kerry and Kenmare (same hours as
the tourist office; £2, students £1.50). Invented in 1862 by the lacemaking nuns at
the Kenmare convent as a source of revenue to alleviate poverty in the town, the
Kenmare techniques were once the envy of anyone who understood lacemaking.
Local artisans are working to resurrect the craft. **Demonstrations** take place in the
lace center above the tourist office (open Mon.-Sat. 10am-1pm and 2-6pm; free).
    Seafari Cruises (tel. 83171) explores Kenmare Bay and its colonies of otters,
seals, and whales, daily, departing from the pier (follow the Glengarriff Rd. and turn
right just before the bridge). Cruises last 1½-2hr. and cost £7.50, students £6. You
can fish at the **Ardtully Castle Salmon Fishery** on Roughty Rd. (£10/day, £30/
week. For permits contact Mr. John O'Hare, 21 Main St.; open daily 9am-7pm.)

■ ■ ■ SNEEM

Tourists make Sneem their first or last stop along the Ring, and the town has
adapted to please them. Sneem won Ireland's "Tidy Town" competition in 1987,
and nine years later it still defines itself by the dubious honor. Ever been to Lego-
land? More grass, fewer plastic bricks.
    The Ring of Kerry **bus** leaves for Killarney via Kenmare from the Square (June-
Sept. daily 2/day; 1hr.; £5.50, students £2.80). If Sneem's **phone code** took out an

ad in the personals, it would read "Slim, attractive **064;** likes long walks on the beach and leather."

Sneem's only hostel, the **Harbour View Hostel** (tel. 45276), ¼ mile from town on the Kenmare Rd., used to be a motel and still looks like one—comfortable ranch-style units (with hairdryers!) scattered in a gravel lot. (**Camping** £3; private rooms £7.50/person, dorm £6.) Occupying a former stone convent, **Woodvale House,** Pier Rd. (tel. 45181), just off the Square, has charming rooms with mountain views and a large Victorian sitting room (£11/person, w/bath £15). They also offer pictur-esque **camping** in the backyard (£3) and laundry (wash £2.50, dry 50p/15 min.). Three doors up from the Texaco station, the unmistakably blue **Homestead** (tel. 45179) is very friendly and all dolled up with Irish lace (£12).

Charlie Chaplin once frequented the **Green House Tea Room** (tel. 45208), next to the bridge in the town center (Irish stew £4; open Easter-Oct. daily 8:30am-9pm). On the other side of town, the simply-titled **Coffee Shop** (tel. 45331) is cosier, with mismatched furniture, sandwiches, and pastries (open Easter-Oct. daily 10am-9pm). The **Blue Bull** (tel. 45382), next to the wool shops on the Square, is a pub noted for its seafood (pub grub £3-5, served noon-8:30pm) and hosts traditional and country music (July-Aug. Mon., Wed., and Fri.). The **Green Linnet** pub, across the bridge on the Caherdaniel Rd. (tel. 45224) reverberates to eclectic beats three nights a week.

■■■ CAHERDANIEL

Tiny Caherdaniel has little to attract the Ring's drove of travel coaches—just a village with several pubs and restaurants and gorgeous stretches of white beaches. The **bus** stops in Caherdaniel at the junction of the Ring of Kerry Rd. and the town's own Main St. Buses go to Sneem and Killarney (June-Sept. daily 2/day; Sneem 30 min., £2.90, students £1.70; Killarney 1½hr., £7.30, students £3.80). Caherdaniel's **phone code,** 066, is looking for a committed partner who enjoys Thai and tennis.

The **Village Hostel** (tel. 75277), across the street from Skellig Aquatics, resides in the first English police building to be deserted in the 1916 Revolution. (Midnight curfew. Climbing trips arranged. £6. Open Feb.-Nov.) One-quarter mile west of town on the Ring of Kerry Rd. is the intimate seven-bed **Carrigbeg Hostel** (tel. 75229), which feels more like a B&B with its extremely warm owner and cozy kitchen with a stone fireplace. (Laundry £2.75. £5. Free lift from Caherdaniel.) Campers get their beauty sleep one mile east of town on the Ring of Kerry Rd. at **Wave Crest Camping Park** (tel. 75188), overlooking the beach. (£3/cyclist or hiker. Showers 50p. Open April-Sept.)

The **Courthouse Café** serves the most affordable food in town (sandwiches £1.50; open daily 9:30am-12:30am, only take-away after 9pm). **Freddy's Bar** sells groceries (open daily 9am-9pm) and serves pints to locals. In summer, the bright yel-low **Blind Piper** (tel. 75126) attracts a lively crowd with planned or spontaneous trad sessions most nights.

To reach **Derrynane Strand,** the soul of Caherdaniel, follow the signs from the center of town to Derrynane House. The strand here is one of Ireland's finest, with two miles of white sand. **Derrynane House** (tel. 75113), just up from the beach, was the cherished residence of Irish patriot Daniel "the Liberator" O'Connell, who won Catholic Emancipation in 1829. Inside the house, look for the dueling pistol that O'Connell used to kill challenger d'Esterre, and the black glove he wore to church for years afterwards to mourn his victim. The half-hour film on O'Connell presents an engrossing and refreshingly multi-faceted image of the acerbic barrister. It's easy to understand how O'Connell, who believed strictly in non-violence and adherence to the law, captured the support and imagination of the country. (Open May-Sept. Mon.-Sat. 9am-6pm, Sun. 11am-7pm; March, April, and Oct. Tues.-Sun. 1-5pm; £1.50, seniors £1, students and children 60p.)

Offshore lies a shipwreck, rumored to be a smuggling ship financed by Maurice "Hunting Cap" O'Connell, Daniel's uncle. If you can dive, it's worth a look. Contact **Derrynane Sea Sports** (tel. 75266) or **Skellig Aquatics** (tel. 75277) for rental information. If you can motivate yourself for several miles of uphill hiking or pedaling to get there, the pre-Christian **Staigue Fort,** west of town, will make you feel tall and powerful. The largest and one of the best preserved forts on Ireland, Staigue Fort stands high on a hill overlooking the sea below. Skip the "heritage center" devoted to the fort, which runs the danger of being a rip-off tourist attraction.

■■■ WATERVILLE

It's Coney Island without the hot dogs, roller coaster, and New Yorkers. Okay, that makes Waterville just a town along a clean pebbly beach on Ballinskelligs Bay, but it's a damn fine beach. The town is a universal stopping point for tour buses, which accounts for its dearth of quaintness. Nearby, tiny towns like Ballinskelligs and Portmagee provide departure points for the ultra-remote monastic remains of Skellig Michael.

The **tourist office** soaks up sea spray across from Butler Arms Hotel on the beach (open Mon.-Fri. 9am-7pm, Sat. 9:30am-3:30pm, mid-Sept. to late June Mon.-Fri. 9am-5pm). The Ring of Kerry **bus** (June-Sept. daily 3/day) stops in Waterville in front of the Bay View Hotel on Main St., with service to Caherdaniel (20 min.; £2.20, students £1.70), Sneem (50 min.; £4.30, students £2.30) and Killarney (2hr.; £8.60, students £4.40). In the off-season, **Dero's** (tel. 31251) fills in with a Ring of Kerry bus all its own (1/day; reservations required). **Bus Éireann** travels to Cahersiveen Mon.-Fri. at 8:20am (also Sat. from June-Sept.). The Bay Area's **phone code** rings 066.

The grand stone edifice that is now the **Waterville Leisure Hostel (IHH)** (tel. 74644) has all the hostel amenities you could ask for (VCR, pool table, laundry). Bear right at the fork at the Butler Arms Hotel and walk five minutes up the hill. (£2 wash, 30p/3-min. dry. Dorms £6, double £7/person. Wheelchair accessible.) Back in the town center, the **Stella Maris B&B** (tel. 74249) has a plethora of rooms with views for £12.50/person w/bath. If, for some bizarre reason, you're planning a night in Ballinskelligs, you could stay at the quiet **Prior House Youth Hostel (An Óige/HI)** (tel. 79229) near the beach overlooking Ballinskelligs Bay (midnight curfew; June-Sept. £5.50; Easter-May and Sept. £4.50).

Fifty yards from the tourist office, **The Huntsman** (tel. 74124) vends an unusual variety of take-away dishes, but don't be put off by high prices on the sit-down menu (fish and chips £2.25, poached salmon *au vin blanc* £6.60; open Mon.-Sat. 10:30am-4pm and 6-9:30pm). The **Silver Sands,** on the main street (tel. 74161), caters to bourgeois vegetarians and their carnivorous dates (entrees £3-6; 3-course vegetarian dinner £9.90). The **Lobster Bar and Restaurant,** Main St. (tel. 74255), is worth a visit just for the icon outside—a giant lobster clutching a Guinness—though their pub food isn't bad, either (fisherman's soup and bread £2.50, lunch specials £4; open pub hours). The Lobster is also the liveliest pub in town, with a pool table and live music on weekends. **Mick O'Dwyer's** (tel. 74248) does the disco thing (Wed. and Sat. 11pm-1:30am; cover £3). Charlie Chaplin's old haunt is the **Fishermen's Bar** (tel. 74205), which is linked to the Butler Arms Hotel (open July-Sept.; trad Thurs. and Sat.).

Two miles from town, **Lough Currane** lures anglers, boaters, and divers with its numerous picnic-friendly islands and its submerged castle ruins. **Waterville Boats** (tel. 74255) rents rowboats (£10/day) and fishing poles (£5/day).

Ballinskelligs village isn't worth a special trip, but if you're there to catch a boat, check out the ruins, near the pier, of the **Ballinskelligs Monastery,** the crumbling twin of the Skelligs Rocks monastery. It was here that the monks moved from their lofty heights to start Europe's first "university." Two miles south of Ballinskelligs, **Bolus Head** affords great views of the Skelligs and the bay on clear days.

■ SKELLIG MICHAEL

Eight miles offshore the Iveragh Peninsula, the **Skellig Rocks** (and their 2306 steps) break the ocean's surface: Little Skellig is a bird sanctuary and not accessible to the public, but the larger Skellig Michael makes an exciting (if expensive) voyage. Early Christian monks founded an austere settlement in the 6th century along the cragged faces of the 714-foot high rock which George Bernard Shaw once called "not after the fashion of this world." The old walls now service 40,000 pious gannets, petrels, guillemars, kittiwakes, and puffins.

The fantastic and stomach-churning **ferry voyage** takes up to 1½ hr., depending on where you begin. From Ballinskelligs, it's only 45 minutes. Mrs. Walsh (tel. 76155) sails from Reenard Pier, near Cahersiveen (£15); Joe Roddy (tel. 74268) and Sean Feehan (tel. 79182) depart from Ballinskelligs (£20), and Michael O'Sullivan (tel. 74255) leaves from Portmagee (£20). Roddy and O'Sullivan will also give you a lift from Waterville. The boats run mid-March to October, depending on the weather—phone ahead for reservations and to confirm that the boats are operating. They usually leave between 9:30am and noon and land for at least two hours on the island. The grass-roofed **Skellig Experience** visitor center (tel. 76306) is just across the Portmagee Bridge on Valentia Island. Videos and models engulf visitors in Virtual Skellig. The video is a good diversion on a rainy day, provided you ignore the theatrically intoned rhetorical questions posed by the center's video presentation. (Open daily April-Sept. 10am-6pm; £3, students £2.70.)

■ ■ ■ CAHERSIVEEN

Perhaps because it's the Iveragh Peninsula's biggest town, Cahersiveen ("care-si-VEEN") hasn't allowed foreigners to drag it down or gloss it up. It's a businesslike place serving the prosaic needs of its full-time residents. After Waterville and Sneem, Cahersiveen's hustle may come as a relief.

Practical Information Cahersiveen enjoys (or tolerates) two **tourist offices:** one in the old Protestant church on Main St. (tel. 72996; open June-Sept. daily 9:30am-7pm) and one in the former barracks on the road to Ballybarbery castle (tel. 72589; open Mon.-Sat. 10:30am-6pm, Sun. 11am-4pm). Main St. is home to **AIB** bank (tel. 72022; open Mon. 10am-12:30pm and 1:30-5pm, Tues.-Fri. 10am-12:30pm and 1:30-3pm; **ATM),** as well as the eyesore of a **post office** (tel. 72010; open Mon.-Fri. 9:30am-1pm and 2-5:30pm, Sat. 9:30am-1pm). The Ring of Kerry **bus** stops in front of Banks Store on Main St. (June-Sept. daily 2/day) and continues on to: Waterville (25 min.; £2.70, students £1.70); Caherdaniel (1½hr.; £3.10, students £1.70); Sneem (2hr.; £6.30, students £3.40); and Killarney (2½hr.; £9, students £5). One bus route heads directly east to Killarney (Sept.-June Mon.-Sat. 1/day; July-Aug. Mon.-Sat. 2/day). Cahersiveen's **phone code** masquerades as 066.

Accommodations Stay at the **Sive Hostel (IHH),** (pronounced like "hive") 15 East End, Main St. (tel. 72717), for mighty *craic*. Comfortable and remarkably friendly, with free live music by the resident songwriter/warden and great sunsets from the third-floor balcony. (Dorm £6, double £7/person.) Behind its charming bay window and flowerpot facade, newly opened **Mortimer's Hostel,** Main St., competes with Sive for the town's friendliest hostel honors (dorms £6/person). At the west end of town, the **Mannix Point Caravan and Camping Park** (tel. 72806) adjoins a waterfront nature reserve, facing across the water toward the romantic ruins of Ballybarbery Castle. Mannix Point's common area (complete with turf fire) feels like a relaxed hostel. It's one of the best camping parks in the country. Camping fee includes hot showers and use of a cooker-less kitchen—bring your own stove (£2.75/person; open mid-March to mid-Oct.).

Food & Pubs Generous **Grudle's,** Main St. (tel. 72386), serves huge slices of cakes and pies, if you still have room for dessert (vegetarian quiche £3.25, cake slice £1.50; open daily 9am-10pm). **Brennan's,** 13 Main St. (tel. 72021), serves inspired soups of the day and Irish stew (£4). Their cake-like brown bread could pass for dessert. Dinner is expensive, but lunch and early bird specials make Brennan's affordable (open Mon.-Sat. noon-12:30pm and 6-9:30pm, Sun. 6-9pm). Try **The Shebeen,** (tel. 72361), near the Sive Hostel on Main St. (open daily 9:30am-10:30pm) or **Teac Culann** (tel. 72400) in the center of town (Irish stew £4). The **Point Bar,** Reenard Point (tel. 72165), located basically on a pier, prepares unbelievably fresh fish. And after a few pints at this most endearing pub, people don't seem to mind the interruptions of the Valentia ferry (fresh fish £5-9; open daily 10:30am-11:30pm).

Cahersiveen still has several **original pubs** on Main St.—once common in rural Ireland during the first half of this century, these establishments were a combination of watering hole, general store, blacksmith, leather shop, and farm goods store. The **Anchor Bar** (tel. 72049), towards the west end of Main St., is one of the best. Don't come before 10pm, and be sure to take your drink into the kitchen for an unforgettable night. **Mike Murt's** (tel. 72396) seethes with pure Irish character. Come here to chat with the locals during the afternoon, but be prepared to tell your life story to the entire pint-clutching ensemble. **The Skellig Rock** (tel. 72305) and the decidedly un-Irish **Teac Culann** (tel. 72400) are the best pubs for music. **The Shebeen,** Main St., plays trad several nights a week.

Sights Every schoolchild in Ireland knows that Cahersiveen is the birthplace of Daniel O'Connell. The Catholic Church in town that bears his name is the only one in Ireland named for a layperson. O'Connell, the "Liberator," is celebrated at a new **Heritage Centre** (tel. 72589) housed in the town's former guard barracks (see tourist office, above). Aside from its promotional promise of being "a most arresting experience," the center is an engrossing introduction to the life of O'Connell, complete with sections devoted to the Famine and Irish rebellions under British rule (open Mon.-Sat. 10am-6pm, Sun. 1-6pm; £2.50, students £1.50). Two miles northwest of the town (signposted from downtown), the ruins of the 15th-century **Ballybarbery Castle**, once held by O'Connell's ancestors, commands great views of mountains and sea. Two hundred yards past the castle turnoff lie two well-preserved stone forts: **Leacanabuaile Fort** lets you walk atop its 10-foot-thick walls while **Cahergal Fort** encloses a 10th-century beehive hut.

■ VALENTIA ISLAND

Valentia Island makes an appealing respite from the Ring of Kerry pilgrimage. Valentia lacks much of the Atlantic starkness of Cape Clear or Sherkin Island, but it offers accessibility (connected to the mainland by a land bridge) and a feeling of relaxation. Valentia Island is archaeologically and historically rich. The first transatlantic telegraph cable infused Valentia with cable operators and allowed some of the island's families to work at cable stations around the globe. Valentia Island hosts two restaurants on the island that are deserving of a special, if rather expensive, trip.

Ferries depart from Reenard Point, three miles west of Cahersiveen off the Ring of Kerry road. Ferries run often, but there's no set schedule: ask at the Point Bar in Reenard or the Royal Pier Bar on the island (going rates are £3-4 return). A bridge ties Valentia to the mainland at Portmagee, ten miles west of Cahersiveen, but hitching there is difficult. To get to Portmagee, go south (from Cahersiveen) or north (a longer trip from Waterville), then west on R565. Hard-core bikers can also make a worthwhile trip following the "loop" (Waterville to Ballinskelligs, Portmagee to Knightstown to Cahersiveen). The island's **phone code** wires 066.

The ferry drops you off at **Knightstown,** the island's population center, where the monstrous **Royal and Pier Hostel (IHH)** (tel. 76144) looms before you. The once-luxurious hotel, built on the occasion of Queen Victoria's one-night stand on the island retains only some of its aged grandeur and even less of its mattresses' firmness (dorm £6). The **Valentia Island Hostel (An Óige/HI)** (tel. 76154) in the old coast guard station signposted off the main road, provides only the bare necessities. (Midnight curfew; £5.50/person; open June-Sept.) Knightstown's smattering of B&Bs are more inviting and reasonably priced. A few blocks up the hill from the pier, **Altazamuth House** (tel. 76300) may lack complexity, but with crisp taste and rich pine undertones, it is worthwhile at £12/person. **Spring Acre,** across from the pier (tel. 76141), has bedrooms with enormous waterfront windows. If you've been very good, you may get one for £13.

Ogling is encouraged at the **Gallery Kitchen** (tel. 76105), on the main road in town. Creative meals are served amid sculptures and drawings of half-clothed people (fresh pasta £6; open daily 1-4pm and 6:30-9:30pm). Two miles from Knightstown (on the road to the Quarry), the **Lighthouse Café** (tel. 76355) serves comforting meals and sublime desserts in a candlelit cottage overlooking Valentia lighthouse. It's quite possibly the best reason to visit the island (open Mon.-Thurs. 10am-8pm, Fri.-Sun. 10am-midnight).

The road from town to the **old slate quarry** offers some of Valentia's best views across Dingle Bay. The quarry itself supplied the slate that roofed the Paris Opera House and the British Parliament, and is now the site of an astoundingly tacky "sacred grotto." Bring a flashlight to explore the quarry's dark recesses. At the opposite end of the island, you can hike up to the ruins of a Napoleonic lookout tower at **Bray Head,** with views to the Skelligs. On the way there, you'll pass the turnoff for **Glanleam Subtropical Gardens** (tel. 76176), a smaller and less-manicured version of Garinish Island (open daily 11am-5pm; £2.50, students £1.50).

■■■ KILLORGLIN

The Ring of Kerry traditionally commences in Killorglin, though this should be your last stop if driving behind gigantic tour buses isn't your cup of tea. 13 miles west of Killarney, Killorglin lives in the shadow of Iveragh's mountain spine and the tourism generated by them. But if you are traveling clockwise around the Ring on N70, stop at the **Quarry in Kells** (tel. 77601). This restaurant/craft shop/convenience store comes complete with magnificent views and dark green benches. The shop is particularly inviting to haggard bikers cycling against hurricane-like winds. Killorglin's hibernation is interrupted every year from August 10-12, when it holds the riotous **Puck Fair,** a livestock festival culminating in the crowning of a particularly virile he-goat as King Puck. The pubs stay open for 72 straight hours to refresh the exuberant musicians, dancers, and singers. During the rest of the year, residents plan the next fair, show off their mountains, and entertain the Ring crowd.

The spiffy **tourist office** (tel. 61451) is on the corner of Iveragh Rd. and Upper Bridge St., beside the library (open May-Sept. Mon.-Sat. 9:30am-6pm, Sun. 10am-3pm). **AIB** bank (tel. 61134) is on the corner of Main St. and New Line Rd. (open Mon. and Wed.-Fri. 10am-4pm, Tues. 10am-5pm), while the **post office** (tel. 61101) is on Main St. (open Mon.-Fri. 9am-5:30pm, Sat. 9am-1pm). Rent a bike at **O'Shea's** on Main St. (tel. 61919; open Mon.-Sat. 9am-6pm; £6/day, £30/week). The omnipresent Ring of Kerry **bus** stops in Killorglin next to the tourist office. (June-Sept. 2/day; Cahersiveen 50 min.; £5, students £2.60; Waterville 1¼ hr.; £5.90, students £3.10; Sneem 3hr; £8.80, students £5.) The eastbound bus from Cahersiveen goes more directly to Killarney (Sept.-June Mon.-Sat. 1/day, July-Aug. Mon.-Sat. 2/day). The **phone code** sings chim-chimminy at 066.

Laune Valley Farm Hostel (IHH), 1½ mi. from town off the Tralee Rd. (tel. 61488), shares its land with a yardful of cats, dogs, chickens, and ducks (save your table scraps for the ducks). Milk and eggs from farm for sale. (Dorm £6, double £8/person, all w/bath; **camping** £3.50/person. Wheelchair accessible.) **Orglan House** (tel. 61540), atop a small hill on the Killarney Rd., proffers grand views from immaculate rooms and relieves you from brown bread-induced delirium with its delicious breakfasts (single £18, double £30). **Laune Bridge House** (tel. 61161), a few doors down from Orglan, opens its florid and comfortable rooms to travelers (£14/person w/bath). Commune with RV people at **West's Caravan and Camping Park** (tel. 61240), one mile east of town on the Killarney Rd. Pool table, tennis, and fishing (rackets and rods for hire) are available. (July 9-Aug. 20 £3.50, low season £3; open Easter to mid-Nov.)

The Fishery, corner of Lower Bridge St. and Tralee Rd. (tel. 61670), is the town's most popular restaurant and a haven for senior citizens. The Fishery features seafood and Irish music and dancing galore. The lounge/bar downstairs serves simpler standards (smoked salmon and brown bread £3.95), while the restaurant upstairs serves more complete dinners (open 10am-11:30pm). Across from the tourist office hunkers **Bunker's** (tel. 61381), a pink-faced restaurant offering fish and chips takeaway. Their regal purple pub lies next door. The live music wraps up at 11:30pm, but you can get food until 1am. The **Bianconi Restaurant** on Lower Main St. (tel. 61146) is touristy, but the salads are bountiful (open Mon.-Sat. 11am-9pm, Sun. 12:30-2pm and 5:30-9pm). Drinkers at the **Old Forge,** Main St. (tel. 61231), are immersed in stone and darkness (music Tuesdays, and Thursdays and Sundays in summer).

The **Cappanalea Outdoor Education Centre** (tel. 69244), seven miles southwest of Killorglin on the Ring of Kerry Rd., offers canoeing, rock-climbing, windsurfing, hillwalking, fishing, and orienteering (open daily 10am-5pm; any activity £9/½ day, £17/day; book a few days in advance). **Cromane Beach** is only four miles west of town (take New Line Rd.—it branches off Main St. south of the Square). Five miles off the Killarney Rd., the 16th-century **Ballymalis Castle** lies on the banks of the River Laune in view of Macgillycuddy's Reeks. Frustrated golfers can play a round at the **Killorglin Golf Club** (tel. 61979, 1½ miles from town on the Tralee Rd.), whose green fees are much more affordable than those in nearby Killarney (18-hole-green fees £12, £5 to rent a half-set of clubs).

DINGLE PENINSULA

The Dingle Peninsula really has some of the best beaches Co. Kerry can offer, and droves of tourists are realizing this: Dingle Peninsula is getting more crowded by the day. Shoot past Slieve Mish (where the ancient goddess Ériu presides over both Irish sovereignty and the yearly cycle) and the flat farming country of East Dingle. Base yourself in Dingle Town, an upscale fishing village whose cafés and bookstores are beginning to feel more touristy and less authentic. The coast to the west of Dingle Town combines striking scenery with *gaeltacht* communities. Dingle Town, while good for nightlife, is not the most amenable of towns for spontaneous backpackers who hope to find a room without reservations. In contrast, the Blasket Islands offshore are a symbol of vanishing coastal culture: a ghost settlement is all that remains on Great Blasket, while traditional hand-built *curraghs* ply the waters around Brandon Bay and Blasket Sound. Explore Dingle's *bohareens* (side roads) by bike: the entire western circuit, from Dingle out to Slea Head, up to Ballydavid, and back, can easily be covered in a day. The Cloghane/Brandon area in the north remains most free of foreigners; Slea Head, Dunquin, and the Blasket Islands are the most inspiring spots. Maps available in area tourist offices describe "The Dingle Way," a walking trail which circles the peninsula. While Dingle Town is well-connected to Killarney and Tralee, public transport within the peninsula is scarce. **Buses** to towns on the peninsula run daily in July and August, but only two or three times per week the rest of the year. For detailed bus information, call the Tralee station (tel. (066) 23566).

■■■ DINGLE TOWN

For now, *craic* in Dingle is still authentic, but the word is out about the fabulous pubs, the breathtaking views, the smart cafés, and the too-cute dolphin, Fungi, who charms the whole town from his permanent residence in Dingle Bay. And, as everyone here moans, it's starting: hostels, restaurants, and expensive souvenir shops multiply, and the town just keeps getting more popular with travelers. If Dingle manages its growth successfully, it could follow the lead of Galway. If not...Killarney looms. Scour the deserted parts of the peninsula for vistas and *ogham* stones, then come here in the evening for the *craic* and the high-quality nightlife.

ORIENTATION & PRACTICAL INFORMATION

Dingle lies in the middle of the south coast of Dingle Peninsula. R559 heads east to Killarney and Tralee and west to Ventry, Dunquin, and Slea Head. A narrow road north through the Connor Pass branches to Stradbally and Castlegregory.

Downtown Dingle approximates a grid pattern, though it's just a bit more confusing than you'd expect. The lack of street signs in English complicates matters. Strand St. and Main St. parallel Dingle Harbour, while the Mall, Dykegate St., and Green St. run perpendicular to the shore, uphill from Strand St. to Main St. On the eastern edge of town, Strand St., the Mall, and Tralee Rd. converge in a roundabout.

Tourist Office: Corner of Main St. and Dykegate St. (tel. 51188). Great if you like standing in line. Open April-Oct. Mon.-Sat. 9:30am-6:30pm, Sun. 11am-5pm.

Banks: AIB bank, Main St. (tel. 51400). Open Mon. 10am-12:30pm and 1:30-5pm, Tues.-Fri. 10am-12:30pm and 1:30-4pm. The **ATM** accepts most major cards. **Bank of Ireland,** Main St. (tel. 51100). Same hours, similar **ATM** services.

Post Office: Upper Main St. (tel. 51661). Open Mon.-Fri. 9am-1pm and 2-5:30pm, Sat. 9am-1pm.

Phone Code: 066.

Buses: Bus stop on Ring Rd. is behind Garvey's SuperValu. Bus information is available from the Tralee bus station (tel. (066) 23566). **Bus Éireann** rushes out of Dingle to Ballydavid (Tues. and Fri. only, 3/day; £3.15 return); Dunquin and Ballyferriter (summer Mon.-Sat. 4/day, Sun. 1/day, winter Mon. and Thurs. 2/day; £2.30, students £2); Killarney (June-Sept. Mon.-Sat. 10/day, Sun. 2/day, Oct.-May Mon.-Sat. 3/day, Sun. 2/day; 1½hr.; £7.30, students £4.20); and Tralee (June-Sept. Mon.-Sat. 7/day, Sun.4/day, Oct.-May Mon.-Sat. 3/day, Sun. 2/day; 1hr. 10 min.; £5.90, students £3.50). From June-Sept. two additional buses a day (Mon.-Sat.) tour the entire peninsula from Dingle.

Bike Rental: Paddy's Bike Shop, Dykegate St. (no phone). £5/day, £25/week. Open daily 9am-7pm. **Raleigh Rent-A-Bike: Foxy John Moriarty's,** Main St. (tel. 51316). £5-6/day, £25-30/week. Open daily 9:30am-8pm.

Camping Equipment: The Mountain Man, Strand St. (tel. 51868). Open July-Aug. daily 9am-9pm, Sept.-June daily 9am-6pm.

Laundry: Níolann an Daingin, Green St. (tel. 51837), behind El Toro. Open Mon.-Sat. 9am-5:45pm. Medium wash and dry £5, large £6.

Emergency: Dial 999; no coins required. **Garda:** the Holy Ground (tel. 51522), across from Tig Lise.

ACCOMMODATIONS

There are several good hostels in Dingle, though some are a fairly long walk from town. You'll need your own transport to reach the rustic accommodations east of Dingle. B&Bs along Dykegate St. and Strand St. tend to fill up fast in July and August. Ballintaggart and Rainbow Hostels are reasonably close to town center, Marina Inn and Grapevine Hostel are in town, while the others are way out there.

Grapevine Hostel (tel. 51434), Dykegate St., off Main St. Just a short stagger from Dingle's finest pubs, the Grapevine rewards hostelers with comfortable bunk rooms, each with toilet and superb shower, and a common room with a fireplace, CD player, and dangerously cushy chairs. Book ahead before *craic*-seeking hordes arrive. Laundry £4. 8-bed dorm £6, 4-bed dorm £6.50.

Rainbow Hostel (tel. 51044), 15 min. west of town on Strand Rd. (at the corner of Dunquin Rd., go straight and inland). Irish folk legend Christy Moore knows the owner and bunks at this small, hip hostel when in Dingle. Cooking is a joy in the huge wood-paneled kitchen. Laundry £2, bikes £5/day, free lifts to and from town, angling trips £10/3 hr., dolphin trips £5/person. July-Aug. £6/person, Sept.-June £5/person, double £7.50/person; **camping** £2.50.

Ballintaggart Hostel (IHH) (tel. 51241), about a 25-min. walk east of town on the Tralee Rd. With crystal chandelier and enormous bunk rooms, Ballintaggart is set on the grand estate where the Earl of Cork poisoned his wife in an upstairs room (which her ghost supposedly haunts to this day). The hostel consequently attracts a loud bunch of budget mystics. Horse treks £10/1½ hr., longer trips available. Wetsuits £6. Free shuttle to town. Groceries. Kitchen locked after 10pm. Laundry £1.50. Bike hire £5/day. 10- to 12-bed dorms £5, July-Aug. £6; double £6.50/person, July-Aug. £8/person; **camping** £3.

Marina Hostel, Strand St. (tel. 51660), across from the pier. Great location, intimate quarters, and extremely friendly staff. Dorm £6, double £8/person; **camping** £3

Lovett's Hostel, Cooleen Rd. (tel. 51903), opposite Moran's Garage on the east side of town. A 5-min. walk from the town center, close to the bay. Not much to it, but good if the other hostels are full. Laundry £1 (no dryer). Free sheets. Sept.-June dorm £5, double £6.50/person; July-Aug. dorm £6, double £7/person.

Avondale House, Dykegate St. (tel. 51120). Mrs. Houlihan's jovial rapport (not to mention homemade brown bread and jam) draws guests back to her centrally located home (and its even nicer annex) year after year. From £13.50/person.

Kirrary House, (tel. 51606), across from Avondale House. With good cheer and pride, Mrs. Collins puts guests up in her delightful rooms. £14/person w/bath.

The Marina Inn, Strand St. Simple, airy rooms are a bargain. Double with breakfast £10/person.

East of Dingle

Seacrest Hostel (IHH), Lispole (tel. 51390), 3 mi. east of Dingle. With extremely kind and interesting owners, this hostel also boasts great views. It is, however, a bit out of the way if you are afoot.

Phoenix Hostel (tel. 66284), on the Dingle-Killarney Rd. (R561), 5 mi. west of Castlemaine. Attached wholefood café serves interesting vegetarian and Asian food (3-course meal £5.50 for hostelers; open daily 9am-midnight). Funky, relaxed country house with Indian-print tapestries and spiritually-elevating books (not to mention a bathtub). Bikes £5/day, laundry £3, breakfast £2. Pub runs. 6-bed dorm £7, double £9.50/person; sheets £1; **camping** £3.50.

Mountain Road B&B, Lispole (tel. 51149), 5 mi. east of Dingle, just off the Tralee Rd. Eat a wholefood breakfast in this remote B&B with a beautiful sign out front. £12; open May-Sept.

FOOD

Dingle is blessed with a handful of congenial cafés that attract a fairly intellectual crowd. **SuperValu supermarket,** Strand St. (tel. 51397), stocks a SuperSelection of groceries and juicy tabloids (open Mon.-Sat. 9am-9pm, Sun. 9am-6pm). **An Grianán** on Dykegate St., next to the Grapevine Hostel, offers a selection of crunchy wholefoods (open Mon.-Sat. 9am-1:30pm and 2-6pm).

An Café Litearta, Dykegate St. (tel. 51388), near Main St. Coffee, fresh scones, brown-bread sandwiches, and an intellectual atmosphere in this excellent bookstore/cafe. Open Mon.-Fri. 10am-5:30pm, Sat.-Sun. 11am-5:30pm.

Café Ceol, Green St., opposite the church and behind Dick Mack's pub. Outside seating, exotic wholefoods, and great live traditional music (which usually starts at 7:30pm) will keep you here for hours and hours. Dinner entrees £6-9. Open daily 1-3pm and 6-9pm, later when there's music. During the day, try one of the sweet crepes at **Cul an Tí** downstairs. (Open daily 10am-6pm.)

Deirdre's Wholefood Cafe, Craft Village, just off the Strand west of town. Delicious vegetarian lunches prepared with fresh ingredients. Vegetarian pizza £3.50. Open Mon.-Sat. 10am-7pm.

Tig Lise, Bridge St. (tel. 51001). Simple bistro food served at bright, cheery tables with checkered tablecloths. Quiche and salad £2.50. Open Mon. 9am-6pm, Tues.-Sun. 9am-10pm.

Greany's, Bridge St. (tel. 51694), next to Tig Lise. Hearty, heavy seafood in tight quarters. Big sandwiches (big!) and excellent chips. Open daily 12:30-9pm.

COUNTY KERRY ■ 237

DINGLE PENINSULA

PUBS

Though only 1500 people live in Dingle permanently, the town has 52 pubs: in theory, every single inhabitant could hoist a Guinness simultaneously without anyone having to scramble for a seat. Many pubs are beginning to cater to tourists, but the town still produces more *craic* than it knows what to do with.

O'Flaherty's Pub, Holy Ground (tel. 51461), a few doors up from the traffic circle. Memorable jam sessions most nights in this well-decorated pub. Too many people have discovered the great atmosphere. Get here by 9pm if you want a seat. All types of music.

An Droichead Beag, Lower Main St. (tel. 51723), also referred to by its English name, "The Small Bridge." This pub can be crowded, but it still unleashes the best traditional music in town, playing nightly in summer.

Dick Mack's, Green St. (tel. 51070), opposite the church. A leather bar—"Dick Mack's Bar, Boot Store, and Leather Shop," that is. The proprietor leaps between the bar and his leathertooling bench. Shoeboxes and whiskey bottles hang from the walls. The lack of music and harsh lighting encourages conversation.

Star, Strand St. (tel. 51855). Older clientele and a sophisticated atmosphere. Hushed music ideal for intellectualizing (or scamming).

Murphy's, Strand St. (tel. 51450). The Lost Generation sidles up to the super-long bar in this American-infected pub. Rock, blues, and trad.

McCarthy's, Upper Main St. (tel. 51205), across the street and a few doors up from the post office. Quiet, intimate, undiscovered pub. Good *craic* when there's music (trad Mon. and Wed.).

Jack Neddy's, on the corner of Green St. and Strand St. Defines "unpretentiousness"—the sign outside the green-trimmed building says simply "Bar." Frequented by locals who, if you're lucky, will break into a spontaneous singing chorus.

SIGHTS

Fungi the Dolphin swam into Dingle Bay one day in 1983 with his mother, and the pair immediately became local celebrities. Dolphins were not uncommon in the bay, but Fungi actually liked it around Dingle, cavorting with sailors and swimmers, flirting with TV cameras, and jumping in and out of the water for applause. Mom has died, but Fungi remains rather fond of humans in wetsuits and boats. Humans, however, have become far too fond of Fungi, and wetsuited tourists incessantly swarm around him. **Boat trips** to see the dolphin leave from the pier constantly in summer. Most cost around £5 and guarantee that you'll see the dolphin. In the morning (before 9am) and evening (after 6pm) when Fungi isn't following boats, he often hangs out in a little cove east of town. To get there, walk two minutes down the Tralee Rd., turn right at the Skellig Hotel, and then follow the beach away from town. On the other side of a stone tower, the small beach will probably be packed with Fungi-seekers. You can rent a **wetsuit** from Flannery's (tel. 51967), just east of town off the Tralee Rd. (£14/3 hr., £20 overnight) or from Seventh Wave (tel. 51548), ½ mile west of town on the Dunquin Rd. (£9-11/3 hr., £14 overnight; deposit £40), or just jump in as you are. Ballintaggart Hostel rents suits cheap to its guests (see Accommodations, above).

Deep-sea angling trips (tel. 51337) leave daily in summer at 10am and 6pm from the pier. Land-bound **Sciúird Archaeology tours** (tel. 51937) take you from the pier on a three-hour whirlwind bus tour of the area's ancient spots (3/day; £6.50/person; book ahead). The same company also coordinates historic walking tours of Dingle Town (2/day; £2.50/person).

Summer festivals periodically turn the town into a carnival: the **St. Brendan Festival** (three days in mid–July) involves *curragh* races, duck races, and street entertainment. The **Dingle Races** (second weekend in August) are geared more for children than for horses, while the **Dingle Regatta** (usually the third Sunday in August) attracts mariners from around the country.

■■■ WEST DINGLE

DUNQUIN (DÚN CHAOIN) & SLEA HEAD

No matter how tight you think your schedule is, you will inevitably be waylaid by glorious **Slea Head.** Slea Head is inspiring—people stay for hours and don't feel guilty. The unmistakable **Enchanted Forest Cafe,** adorned with cute bears and flowers, serves sandwiches and sweets with great views of Slea Head from the side (4 large cookies £1; open daily 11am-6pm). There's plenty of space on the head to **camp,** though in high season you'll have some neighbors. *Ryan's Daughter* and parts of *Far and Away* were filmed around Slea Head, and it's not difficult to understand why Hollywood cigar-chompers chose this place to represent what millions of moviegoers would idealize as Ireland. Green hills, interrupted by rough stone walls and sheep, lead down to jagged cliffs chiseled away by the sea.

The road from broad horseshoe-shaped **Ventry Beach** out to Slea Head passes hundreds of Iron Age and early Christian stones and ruins. **Dunbeg Fort** and the **Fahan Group** of beehive-shaped stone huts (known as oratories) built by early monks cluster on hillsides over the cliffs. (Landowners who display signs charge 50p-£1 to visit the ruins.)

North of Slea Head, the scattered settlement of **Dunquin** consists of stone houses, a pub, and plenty of spoken Irish, but no grocery store. Stock up in Dingle or in Ballyferriter if you're going to stay here or on Great Blasket. Familial **Kruger's** features pub grub and frequent spontaneous music sessions. Its adjacent **B&B** charges £13.50/person. Along the road to Ballyferriter, **An Óige Hostel (HI)** (tel. (066) 56121) provides adequate and clean bunkrooms and a spacious, window-walled sitting and dining room which looks out onto the sea. (Lockout 10:15am-5pm; curfew midnight. £6.50/person, Oct.-May £5.50/person. Sheets 60p. Breakfast £1.75.) Two miles past Dunquin, about halfway to Ballyferriter, **Tig Aine** (tel. 56214), a gallery and café, charms visitors to this stone cottage with views of the cliffs. Stop in for a fluffy scone and pot of coffee, or call ahead for dinner, a full Irish meal with vegetables grown in their private garden (£5.50).

The stunning architecture of the **Blasket Centre** (tel. (066) 56371), across the road from the youth hostel, enhances the museum's outstanding exhibits. Writings by renowned Great Blasket authors and photographs create an incredibly authentic (and moving) vision of life on the island. The museum concentrates on the writers, who rediscovered the richness of the Irish language and its oral tradition. (Open July-Aug. daily 10am-7pm, Easter-June and Sept. to mid-Oct. daily 10am-6pm; £2.50, students £1.)

BLASKET ISLANDS (NA BLASCAODAÍ)

The Blaskets comprise six islands: Beginish, Tearaght, Inishnabro, Inishvickillane, Inishtooskert and Great Blasket. Ferries sail to Great Blasket, which is now occupied by a handful of isolation-seeking summer residents. Evacuated in 1953, the Blasket Islands have famously come to stand for the elegiac vision of an antiquated *gaeltacht* culture, once inhabited by poet-fishermen, proud but impoverished and aging villagers, and memoirists reluctantly warning that "after us, there will be no more." Blasket writers themselves, in English and Irish, helped produce and publicize that vision. The well-known memoirs *Twenty Years a-Growing* (Maurice O'Sullivan), *The Islander* (Thomas O'Crohan), and *Peig* (Peig Sayers, recently published in English) are obscure in America but required (and often dreaded) reading for Irish students. The buildings from the well-chronicled village still stand. Mists, seals, and occasional fishing boats may continue to pass the Great Blasket forever, but the vision of desolation may leave visitors mournful at the disappearance of the primitive ways of life exemplified by the Blaskets.

Days on somnolent Great Blasket are long and meditative: wander through the mist down to the white strand, follow the grass paths of the island's ten-mile circumference, explore the stone skeletons of former houses in the village, and observe the puffins and seals that populate the island. Those spending the night can enjoy fresh fish and wholefood dinners in the **café** near the old village for £5—the portions are massive (try the seaweed!). (Open daily 10am-6pm when there are customers.) **Campers** can pitch their tents anywhere for free. There's no hot water, food (other than in the café), or electricity, so if you plan to stay, stock up on supplies in Dingle or Ballyferriter. Keep in mind that if the weather is bad, the boats don't run—people have been stuck here for two weeks during gales. **Boats** for the Blaskets depart from Dunquin May to September daily, every hour from 10am to 6pm, weather and ferry operator's mood permitting (tel. (066) 56455; £10 return).

The Last Islander

The famous autobiographers of the Blasket Islands described 19th- and early-20th century Irish life on the island and were concerned with the possible eradication of Irish culture. By 1953, most of Great Blasket's residents were old, with the exception of a 19-year-old who represented "the future" to everyone else on the island. The youngster came down with meningitis during weather so severe that no boats could leave for the mainland's hospital. The sea calmed down only two days after his death. By the end of that year, everyone had moved to the mainland.

BALLYFERRITER (BAILE AN FHEIRTÉARAIGH)

Ballyferriter is West Dingle's closest approximation to a town center. After visiting the Blasket Centre, which is something of a shrine to the almost extinct Irish oral tradition, Ballyferriter (an authentic *gaeltacht*) stands as a testament to the language's continued existence—even the Guinness signs are in Irish. The views aren't as spectacular as at Slea Head, but the town is a lively center of Irish culture and language.

Many people are lured to Ballyferriter by the musical strains and prosaic voices inside **Peig's Pub,** Main St. (tel. (066) 56388), where there are frequent trad sessions in the evenings and occasionally during lunch in the summer. Peig's makes a welcoming spot for an appetizing meal (including vegetarian options; daily specials £4.95). Across the street, **Murphy's** (tel. (066) 56224) serves pub food, and **Ocatain** specializes in seafood and occasionally lures in local musicians.

The largest grocery in town is **Ollmhargadh Market,** in the town center (open in summer daily 9am-9pm, winter daily 9am-7:30pm). Five minutes outside town on the Dunquin Rd., the simple **Black Cat Hostel** (tel. (066) 56286) crosses your path in a tacky but friendly sort of way. (Kitchen closed 10:30am-4pm. Check-in 2:15pm, checkout 10.30am. £6/person.) The B&B next door, **An Speice** (tel. (066) 56254), charges £12, w/bath £13.

Back in town, the **Heritage Centre** (tel. (066) 56333) brims with photos and text relating to the area's wildlife, archaeology, and folklore (open June-Sept. daily 10am-5:30pm; £1). The Heritage Centre is a noble attempt at making the area's history accessible, but to get a true feel for the past, you should visit the ancient sites themselves. From Ballyferriter, follow the signs to **Dún An Óir** (the Fort of Gold), an Iron Age fort where, in 1580, the English massacred over 600 Spanish, Italian, and Irish soldiers who openly supported the Irish Catholics' rebellion against Queen Elizabeth's Protestantism. From the main road, signposted roads branch to **Riasc,** a puzzling monastic site with an engraved standing slab, to the **Dillon Stone** (a monument erected by early British settlers to which Protestants flock every year on January 7), and to Ballydavid.

■ ■ ■ NORTH DINGLE

A winding cliffside road runs north from Dingle via the 1500-foot **Connor Pass** and affords tremendous views of the valleys and the bays beyond. Buses won't fit on the road, but private automobiles can and do squeeze through the pass. A slight detour west on the north side of the Connor Pass (watch for the signs) leads to the quiet hamlet of **Cloghane.** From here you can hike north along the scenery-splashed main road to **Ballyquin Strand** and **Brandon Point** or west (and up) to 3127-foot **Mt. Brandon** and its surrounding lakes. (Follow the signs west from Cloghane.) **The Saint's Road** to the summit was cleared by St. Brendan. It might have been easy for someone who could cross the Atlantic in a leather boat, but for most people, it's quite a hike. Climb on the west side from Ballybrack, or try the more impressive ascent from the Cloghane side, which begins between Brandon Point and Cloghane (watch for signs).

Back toward Tralee in **Stradbally,** narrow beds and triple-decker bunks make for perilous nights in the friendly **Connor Pass Hostel (IHH)** (tel. (066) 39179; £6/person; open mid-March to Sept.). The hostel makes a good base for hikes in the **Slieve Mish Mountains** to the east. The 2713-foot ascent to **Cáherconree** culminates with views of the peninsula, the ocean, and the Shannon Estuary. In summer, swimmers escape on daytrips to the huge, empty strands west of the hostel.

If you're intent on exploring north Dingle, **Castlegregory** may make a better base—there's actually a grocery store here. The quiet **Lynch's Hostel** (tel. (066) 39128) is the better of the two hostels in town, with only 2-4 beds per room (£6/person; bikes £5/day, £30/week). A **supermarket** across from the visitor information office opens daily 8:30am-10pm. **Ferriter's Pub** plays trad and ballads on Wednesdays and weekends. **Ned Natterjack's** (named for the rare and quite vocal Natterjack toad, not to be confused with a frog, that resides in this area), plays trad on weekends. **O'Riordan's,** south of the village on the Dingle-Tralee Rd. (tel. (066) 39379), prepares outstanding soups, salads, pizzas, and baked goods.

From Castlegregory, head north up the sandy **Maharees Peninsula** where you can play a round of golf at the **Castlegregory Golf Club** (tel. (066) 39444; £10), rent windsurfers from **Focus Windsurfing** (tel. (066) 39411; from £7/hr., with wetsuit), or swim at numerous strands. A **bus** to Tralee runs erratically (July-Aug. Mon., Wed., Sat. 3/day; Tues. and Thurs. 2/day; all year Fri. 3/day; £3.80, students £2.20).

NORTH KERRY

■■■ TRALEE

While tourists tend to identify Killarney as the core of Kerry, residents correctly see Tralee (pop. 20,000) as the county's economic center. The commerce and industry frequently makes visitors, fresh from Dingle or the Ring, perceive Tralee as an unwelcome return to urban reality. But there's plenty for tourists to do here these days: local effort and buckets of EU development funds have gone towards building new, splashy attractions. Precious minutes are most wisely spent at Kerry the Kingdom museum, the folk theater next door, and the radiant rose gardens. In contrast to the painfully tourist-oriented feel of Tralee's sights, the rest of the town is quite authentic: locals dilute the smattering of visitors in pubs, restaurants, and shops.

ORIENTATION & PRACTICAL INFORMATION

Tralee's streets are hopelessly knotted—find the tourist office immediately and arm yourself with a free map. The main street in town—variously called the Mall, Castle St., and Boherboy—is a good reference point. Ashe St. and Edward St. branch north off the Mall while the stately Denny St. shoots south. To the west, the Mall encounters the Square and a haphazard system of one-way streets, before dead-ending at Russell St. (also called Prince's Quay, Slaughton's Row, and Rock St.). To get to Dingle Rd. (N86), follow Prince's Quay away from the town center to the traffic circle; to Tarbert, Listowel, and N69, follow Edward St.; to Ardfert, go up Rock St. and take your first left onto Pembroke St.; to Killarney or Limerick, head away from the town on Boherboy and take N21 at the roundabout; and to Killorglin and the Ring of Kerry, turn right off Castle St. onto Moyderwell and follow N70.

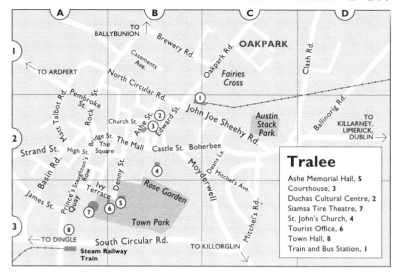

Tourist Office: Ashe Memorial Hall, at the end of Denny St. (tel. 21288). From the station, go into town on Edward St., right on Castle St. and left onto Denny St. The staff is extremely kind and helpful. Open Mon.-Sat. 9am-7pm, Sun. 9am-6pm.

Banks: Bank of Ireland, Castle St. Open Mon. 10am-5pm, Tues.-Fri. 10am-4pm. **AIB** bank, corner of Denny and Castle St. Open Mon.-Fri. 10am-5pm. Both have **ATMs** that accept most major credit cards.

Post Office: Edward St., off Castle St. (tel. 21013). Open Mon. and Wed.-Sat. 9am-5:30pm, Tues. 9:30am-5:30pm.

Phone Code: 066.

Trains: on the corner of Edward St. and John Joe Sheehy Rd. (tel. 23522). Ticket office open Mon.-Sat. 7-7:30am, 9:30-9:55am, 1:30-2:20pm, and 5-5:35pm; Sun. 7:20-7:50am, 1-1:40pm and 4:30-5:30pm. Phone inquiries taken Mon.-Fri. 10am-1pm and 2:25-5:15pm. Trains tie Tralee to: Cork (Mon.-Sat. 8/day, Sun. 7/day; 2½hr.; £17, student £7); Killarney (Mon.-Sat. 8/day, Sun. 7/day; 40 min.; £5.50, students £3.50); Galway (£33.50, students £12); Dublin (Mon.-Sat. 6/day, Sun. 3/day; 3-4hr.; £33.50, students £12); Waterford (Mon.-Sat. 3/day; 4hr.; £33.50, students £12); and Rosslare Harbour (Mon.-Sat. 2/day; 5hr.; £33.50, students £12).

Buses: on the corner of Edward St. and John Joe Sheehy Rd. (tel. 23566). Station open Mon.-Sat. 8:30am-6pm, Sun. 11am-6pm. Buses run to: Cork (Mon.-Sat. 6/day, Sun. 4/day; 2½hr.; £9.70, students £6); Dingle (July-Aug. Mon.-Sat. 9/day, Sun. 5/day; Sept.-June Mon.-Sat. 4/day, Sun. 2/day; 1¼hr.; £5.90, students £3.50); Killarney (June-Sept. Mon.-Sat. 14/day, Sun. 8/day; Oct.-May Mon.-Sat. 5/day, Sun. 2/day; 40 min.; £4.40, students £2.60); Limerick (Mon.-Sat. 5/day, Sun. 4/day; 2hr.; £9, students £5.30); and Galway (Mon.-Sat. 5/day, Sun. 4/day; £13, students £8).

Airport: Kerry Airport (tel. 64644), off N22 halfway between Tralee and Killarney. Manx Airlines (tel. (01) 260 1588) flies to London for at least £99 return (7-day advance purchase required).

Taxi: Kingdom Cabs, 48 Boherboy (tel. 27828). Cabs park on Denny St. at the intersection with the Mall and charge £1/mile, less for longer distances.

Bike Rental: O'Halloran, 83 Boherboy (tel. 22820). £5/day, £25/week. Open Mon.-Sat. 10am-6pm.

Camping Equipment: Landers, Courthouse Lane (tel. 26644), has an extensive selection. Open Mon.-Sat. 9am-6pm.

Laundry: The Laundry, Pembroke St. (tel. 23214). Open Mon.-Sat. 9am-6pm.

Hotlines: Samaritans, 44 Moyderwell (tel. 22566), 24-hrs. **Cura** (tel. 27355), unplanned pregnancy hotline.

Pharmacy: Kelly's Chemist, the Mall (tel. 21302). Open Mon.-Thurs. 9am-6pm, Fri. 9am-8pm, Sat. 9am-6pm.

Hospital: Tralee County General Hospital, off Killarney Rd. (tel. 26222).
Emergency: Dial 999; no coins required. **Garda:** High St. (tel. 22022).

ACCOMMODATIONS

While Tralee is neither especially charming nor picturesque, it boasts five good hostels. A number of pleasant B&Bs line Oakpark Rd., while a smattering of others sit on Boherboy, by the traffic circle.

Finnegan's Hostel (IHH), 17 Denny St. (tel. 27610). At the end of the city's most dignified street, this majestic 19th-century townhouse contains part of the old town castle. The hostel's central location is enhanced by grand doorways, moldings, and a common room furnished with oriental rugs, garish lamps, and velvet furniture. Spacious, wood-floored bunk rooms are named after Ireland's literary heroes and reinforce the hostel's musty aura. £6/person, double £7.50/person.

Collis-Sandes House (tel. 28658). Follow Edward St./Oakpark Rd. 1 mi. away from town, taking the first left after Halloran's Foodstore and turning right at the sign. This grand stone mansion is fit to be a 4-star hotel, with its arched entryways, high ceilings, and coats of arms. The pitch-and-put on the front lawn detracts from its grandness. Free lifts to town. Dorm £6-7, double £8. Wheelchair accessible.

Sean Og's Hostel, Church St. (tel. 27199). Walk up Barrack Ln., the pedestrian walkway off the Mall opposite Denny St., and make the first right. Small, downtown hangout with a cozy, warm sitting room. Dorm £6, double £7.50/person.

Lisnagree Hostel (IHH), Ballinorig Rd. (tel. 27133), on the left fork just after the traffic circle (follow Boherboy away from town), ½ mi. from town and close to the bus/train station. Small, relaxed hostel perfect for families or couples (lots of doubles and quads). Dorm £6, private room £7-8/person; laundry £4.50.

Droumtacker Hostel, (tel. 25922), 2 mi. out of town off Listowel Rd. Smaller and less imposing than Collis-Sandes House, Droumtacker is a quiet rural haven. Hostelers can choose among multiple common rooms. Free pickup from the bus station. £5.50/person; **camping** £3.50.

Dowling's Leeside, Oakpark Rd. (tel. 26475). About ½ mi. from town center on Edward St./Oakpark Rd. Pamper yourself at this cheerful B&B, decorated with country pine antiques and cushy chintz chairs. Flowers outside, but no lace in sight. Single £16, double £30.

Bayview Caravan and Camping Park, (tel. 26140 or 23319), 1 mi. from town on Ballybunion Rd.; follow Rock St. north. Tents July-Aug. £3/person, April-June and Sept.-Oct. £2.50/person. Open April-Oct.

FOOD

Tralee may be slightly disappointing for those seeking fine cuisine, but it does have two vegetarian restaurants and a slew of fast-food joints for those lacking time or creativity. If all else fails, there's a **Quinnsworth Supermarket** in the Square (open Mon.-Tues. 9am-7pm, Wed.-Fri. 9am-9pm, Sat. 9am-6pm) and a health food store, **Sean Cara** (tel. 22644) across the street (open Mon.-Wed. and Sat. 9am-6pm, Thurs. 9am-8pm, Fri. 9am-9pm). **Counihans Newsagent** on the corner of Prince's St. and Ivy Terrace sells groceries until 11pm.

Finnegan's, below the hostel on Denny St. (tel. 27610). Incomparable *craic* in the company of thick stone and mortar walls, rough wooden benches draped in rugs, and candlelight. Dinners are fairly expensive (entrees £6-10), but the food, wine, and atmosphere are sublime.

The Old Forge, Church St. (tel. 28095), next to Sean Og's Hostel. Something of a Tralee institution, with authentic Irish specialties. Lamb £4.25, Irish breakfasts £3, and lighter fare, too. Open July-Aug. Mon.-Sat. 9am-10pm; Sept.-June. Mon.-Sat. 9am-6pm.

Brat's Place, Milk Market Ln. (pedestrian walkway off the Mall). Substantial, conscientiously prepared vegetarian food uses mostly local and organic ingredients. Potatoes, spinach, and goat cheese £4. Delicious desserts £1-1.50. Open Mon.-Sat. 12:30-3pm.

The Skillet, Barrack Ln. (tel. 24561), off the Mall. If the pizza doesn't exhilarate you, the photos of Mt. Everest will (the owner was the first Irishman to climb it). Pizzas £3 (lunch only). Chicken curry and chips £6.95. Open daily 9am-10pm.

Roots, 76 Boherboy (tel. 22665). An ever-changing menu of vegetarian food, in gargantuan portions (£3-4). Open Mon.-Fri. 11am-3pm, also Wed.-Fri. 7-9pm.

Pizza Time, next to Quinnsworth on the Square. Pizza £3.50-6. Open every day of the week, even when the rest of Tralee is closed.

PUBS

Baily's Corner Pub, (tel. 23230), corner of Ashe and Castle St. This relaxing pub reigns supreme, with outstanding trad sessions Tues.-Thurs. nights. Kerry's Gaelic-football legacy hangs on the walls while real-life players drink at the bar.

Paddy Mac's, the Mall. Another Tralee favorite with many a trad session, compensating for its lack of physical charm.

Val O'Shea's, Bridge St. (tel. 21559). Trad music plays nightly all summer (less frequently in winter) in this unpretentious pub. Dark, intimate back room encourages making friends.

Betty's, Strand St., right off Slaughton's Row past the garda station. This pub gets loud Fri.-Sun. when there's music; at other times, regulars chat freely.

Abbey Inn, the Square (tel. 22084). Tough, hip biker crowd comes to hear live rock and reggae. When U2 played here in the early '80s, the manager made them sweep the floors to pay for their drinks because he thought they were so bad. Open until 1am Mon., Thurs., and Fri. (cover £2 those nights).

SIGHTS

Ireland's second-largest museum is **Kerry the Kingdom,** Ashe Memorial Hall, Denny St. (tel. 27777), where all the resources of display technology are marshaled to tell the story of Co. Kerry from 8000 BC to the present. The museum devotes barely a display case to the Famine, but an entire room of videos and dioramas chronicles the rise and fall of the Kerry Gaelic-football team. "Geraldine Tralee" downstairs is a reconstruction of medieval Tralee seen from a small moving cart. You even get the old city's stench for part of the ride! (Open March-July and Sept.-Oct. Mon.-Sat. 10am-6pm, Sun. 2-6pm; Aug. Mon.-Sat. 10am-7pm, Sun. 2-6pm; Nov.-Dec. Mon.-Sat. 2-5pm. £3.90, students £3.50.)

Across the street from the brilliant museum, the **Roses of Tralee** bloom each summer in Ireland's second-largest town park. The rose gardens, designed in 1987, could convert even the most reluctant into rose smellers. On Denny St., the **Wellspring Gallery** (tel. 21218) displays contemporary Irish painting, sculpture, and ceramics (open Mon.-Sat. 10am-6pm). The gray carpeting in **St. John's Church,** Castle St., dampens the echo and the Gothic mood, but the stained glass is worth a look (always open).

The building on the Prince's Quay traffic circle that looks like a cross between a Gothic castle and a space-age solarium is actually Tralee's new £4.5-million **Aquadome** (tel. 28899). Inside, a wave pool, river rapids, and speedy waterslide are all substantially warmer than the Atlantic. Whirlpools, steam room, sauna, and enough lifeguards to fend off any lawsuit (£5; open daily 10am-10pm).

Just down Dingle Rd. (N86/R559) is the **Blenneville Windmill and Visitor Centre** (tel. 21064). Blenneville's is the largest operating windmill in Britain or Ireland, and you can even climb to the top. Before it generated electricity, the windmill was used to grind wheat. Recalling Blenneville's status as Kerry's main port of emigration during the Famine, a small **museum** focuses its attention on the "coffin ships" that sailed from Ireland during and after the Famine (open April-Oct. daily 10am-6pm; £2.75, students £2.25).

ENTERTAINMENT

The **Siamsa Tíre Theatre** (tel. 23055), at the end of Denny St. next to the museum, is Ireland's national folk theater. It mounts brilliant summer programs depicting traditional Irish life through mime, music, and dance. (Productions in July-Aug. Mon.-Sat.; May-June and Sept. Mon.-Tues., Thurs., and Sat. Shows start at 8:30pm. Box office open Mon.-Sat. 9am-10:30pm. Tickets £8.) The **Duchas Cultural Centre,** Edward St., puts on dance and music (July-Aug. Thurs. 8:30pm; £3).

Less culturally-elite entertainment is available in Tralee's two nightclubs. The **Brandon Hotel,** Prince's St. (tel. 23333) plays disco on Wednesdays and Fridays through Sundays. **Horan's,** Boherboy (tel. 21933), blasts country-western and disco on Thursday through Sunday nights. Both stay open until 1:45am and charge a £4-5 cover. **Greyhound races** run every Tuesday and Friday at the track on Brewery Rd., off Oakpark Rd. (£2.50 plus whatever you squander on bets). The **Tralee Races** occupy the whole town during the week of the Rose festival (admission £5).

Budding sociologists should save the last week of August for the **Rose of Tralee International Festival.** A maelstrom of entertainment surrounds the event, a competition between young women of Irish ancestry from around the world for the "Rose of Tralee" title. Rose-hopefuls or spectators can call the Rose office, in Ashe Memorial Hall (tel. 21322). For local goings-on, check *The Kerryman* (85p).

■ NEAR TRALEE

Take Fenit Rd. (R558) out of town for views of the Tralee Bay and the Dingle Peninsula and for the new **Fenit Sea World** aquarium (tel. 36544). Eels and prawns frolic in huge tanks containing native sea life, much of it captured just off the pier (open daily 10am-8pm; £3, students £2.50). Beyond the pier, deserted beaches stretch for miles. From the aquarium, a tangle of backroads (or take R551 from Tralee) lead to **Ardfert,** where St. Brendan the Navigator founded his **monastery** in the 6th century. The Office of Public Works has taken over the crumbling structures, but you can still gambol in most of them for free. If you're curious, go inside for a guided tour, but the "museum" itself isn't worth the price (center open daily 9:30am-6:30pm; £1.50, students 60p). Ardfert's real gem, though, is the neverending **Banna Strand** (watch for the signs from town center or anywhere along Tralee-Ardfert Rd.). Roger Casement was put ashore here by a German U-boat in mid-April 1916, returning from his mission to secure German arms for an Irish rebellion. He showed up a day after the arms had—the British captured and hanged him. A monument on the beach remembers his unfortunate landing.

Twelve miles from Tralee in **Castleisland** on Limerick Rd. (N21), visitors can amuse themselves with stalagmites in the **Crag Cave** (tel. 41244). Divers discovered the cave in 1983 (there was no terrestrial entrance until humans blasted one). Now a good portion of its six miles is open to guided tours. (Open mid-March to Oct. 10am-6pm, July-Aug. 10am-7pm; £3, students £2.50.)

TARBERT

Anyone traveling between Co. Kerry and Co. Clare should take the 20-min. **Tarbert-Killimer car ferry** (tel. (065) 53124), thus avoiding the 85-mile land detour via Limerick. (Sailings April-Sept. Mon.-Sat.7am-9:30pm, Sun. 9am-9:30pm; Oct.-March Mon.-Sat. 7am-7:30pm, Sun. 10am-7:30pm.) Boats sail every hour on the half hour and return on the hour from Clare. £2/passenger or cyclist, £3 return, £7/car including passengers.) There's also a hostel in Tarbert, the **Nest** (tel. (068) 36165). A simple place with a garden in the backyard, the Nest is a stone's throw off the Foynes Rd. (Dorm £6. **Camping** £3.50. Open June-Aug.)

From mid-June through September, **Bus Éireann** travels from Galway and Doolin to Tralee, Killarney and Cork via the Tarbert-Killimer ferry (Mon.-Sat. 3/day, Sun. 2/day; Galway to Tralee £13, students £8). During the rest of the year, the nearest bus stop to Killimer is in Kilrush, eight miles north, with connections to Milltown Malbay and Ennis (late June to late Aug.). Those arriving in Killimer in mid-afternoon will have an easy time finding rides to Kilrush from the power station employees of nearby Moneypoint, who get off work at 4:30pm sharp. A bus runs to Tarbert from Limerick (late June to late Aug.), but no buses arrive in Tarbert from Tralee.

WESTERN IRELAND

Dubliners will tell you to get out of their dirty old town, and that the west is the "most Irish" part of Ireland. Yeats would agree: "For me," he said, "Ireland is Connacht." For less privileged Irish, Connacht has sometimes meant poor soil, starvation, and emigration. When Cromwell uprooted the native Irish landowners in Leinster and Munster and resettled them west of the Shannon, he was giving them a raw deal. The West was also hardest-hit by the potato famine: entire villages emigrated or died, and the population of every Western county is still less than half what it was in 1841. But from Connemara north to Ballina, hikers, cyclists, and hitchhikers enjoy the isolation of boggy, rocky, or brilliantly mountainous landscapes.

Galway City is a different story, a successful port that's now a boomtown for the young. The rest of Co. Galway now draws summer tourists to its rugged scenery and Irish-speaking villages. To the south, the barren moonscape of the Burren, the Cliffs of Moher, and a reputation for being the center of the trad music scene attracts travelers to Co. Clare. Western Ireland's gorgeous desolation, tragic history, and enclaves of traditional culture are now its biggest attractions.

Limerick & Clare

The Dál Cais (later O'Brien) clan invaded Clare around 744 AD, ruthlessly exterminated the natives, who were called the Corcu Modruad, and prepared themselves for a 300-year rise to power and high-kingship. Counties Limerick and Clare are substantially less violent today. The poverty of Western Ireland is most visible in Limerick City but is alleviated a bit by Shannon Airport. Geology defines Co. Clare: fine sands glisten on the beaches of Kilkee, limestone slabs higher than some skyscrapers mark the Cliffs of Moher, and 100 square miles of exposed limestone form Ireland's weirdest landscape, the Burren.

■ ■ ■ LIMERICK CITY

Limerick City is in the middle of a facelift—it has been for years—but a number of factors keep it sagging: high unemployment, grimy industry, and an unimaginative grid of streets littered with neon, plastic, and abandoned buildings. The situation is exacerbated by the recent elimination of the Shannon stopover rule, which had required all planes from North America to touch down in Shannon. That said, Limerick won't be a major tourist center, but it can be a pleasant city where people actually want to spend a couple of nights. Delightful red-brick 18th-century Georgian architecture lines the classier streets, while Limerick's two rivers and numerous quays hold great potential for development.

The Vikings settled around Limerick in 922, presaging a millennium of turbulent history. The area was also prime O'Brien country until the Norman invasion in the late 12th century. Later, during the English Civil War, Limerick was the last stronghold of Royalist support against Cromwell's army. When the city finally did break, it took Cromwell's commander, Henry Ireton, with it (he died at 3 Nicholas St. of plague he caught in Limerick). Forty years later, the Jacobites made their last stand here against Williamites. The battle resulted in the infamous Treaty of Limerick, a promise of limited civil rights for Catholics which the English had no intention of keeping (see The Protestant Ascendancy (1688-1801), p. 52). The treaty became a sore point in British-Irish relations for the next 150 years or so. Later, this unpromising terrain became a center of manufacturing: the world's first mass-produced clothing rolled off a Limerick assembly line. The city gained more renown in April 1919 when a workers' soviet chose the eve of the War of Independence to lead a general strike.

ORIENTATION & PRACTICAL INFORMATION

Limerick's streets conform to a grid pattern, bounded by the River Shannon on the west and by the Abbey River on the north. **O'Connell St.** fosters most of the city's activity in its few blocks. Following O'Connell St. north, cross the Abbey River to reach King's Island, which is dominated architecturally by St. Mary's Cathedral and King John's Castle. The city itself is easily navigable by foot, but to reach the suburbs, catch a **city bus** (65p) from Boyd's or Penney's on O'Connell St. (buses run Mon.-Sat. 8am-11pm; 2/hr., Sun. 1/hr.). Buses #2, 5, and 8 access the University, while bus #6 follows Ennis Rd.

Tourist Office: Arthurs Quay (tel. 317522), in the space-age glass building. From the station, walk straight down Davis St., turn right on O'Connell St., then left just before Arthurs Quay Mall. Excellent, free city maps. Open July-Aug. Mon.-Fri. 9am-7pm, Sat.-Sun. 9am-6pm; March-June and Sept.-Oct. Mon.-Sat. 9:30am-5:30pm; Nov.-Feb. Mon.-Fri. 9:30am-5:30pm, Sat. 9:30am-1pm.

Budget Travel Office: USIT, O'Connell St. (tel. 415064), kitty-corner to Bank of Ireland. Issues ISICs and Travelsave stamps. Open Mon.-Fri. 9:30am-5:30pm, Sat. 10am-1pm. Also located at University of Limerick (tel. 332073).

American Express: Riordan's Travel, 2 Sarsfield St. (tel. 414666). American Express Travelers Cheques redeemable, commission-free. Client mail service. Open Mon.-Fri. 9:30am-5:30pm, Sat. 10am-1pm and 2:30-5pm.

Post Office: Main office on Lower Cecil St. (tel. 315777), just off O'Connell St. Open Mon. and Wed.-Sat. 9am-5:30pm, Tues. 9:30am-5:30pm.

Phone code: 061.

Trains: Colbert Station, just off Parnell St. (tel. 418666). Enquiries desk open Mon.-Fri. 9am-6pm, Sat. 9am-5:30pm. Trains from Limerick go to: Dublin (Mon.-Sat. 11/day, Sun. 8/day; 2hr.; £25, students £10.50); Waterford (Mon.-Sat. 2/day; 2hr.; £17, students £8); Rosslare (Mon.-Sat. 2/day; 3½hr.; £23, students £10.50); Ennis (1/day); Cork (7/day, Sun. 6/day; 2½hr.; £13.50, students £7); Killarney (Mon.-Sat. 4/day, Sun. 3/day; 3½hr.; £15, student £7.50); and Tralee (4/day, Sun. 3/day; 2¼hr.; £15, student £7.50).

Buses: Colbert Station, just off Parnell St. (tel. 313333 or 418855; 24-hr. talking timetable tel. 319911). Open June-Sept. daily 8:45am-6pm; Oct.-May Mon.-Sat. 8am-6pm, Sun. 3-7pm. Most buses leave from the station, but some depart from Penney's or Todd's downtown on O'Connell St. Limerick sends buses to: Cork (6/day; 2hr.; £9, students £5.30); Dublin (Mon.-Fri. 7/day, Sun. 4/day; 3hr.; £10, students £7.50); Galway via Ennis (Mon.-Sat. 7/day Sun. 6/day; Ennis 1hr., £9, students £5.30; Galway 2hr., £9.30, student £5.30); Killarney (Mon.-Sat. 6/day, Sun. 3/day; 2½hr.); Sligo (Mon.-Sun. 3/day; 6hr.); Tralee (Mon.-Sun. 5/day, 2hr.; £9, students £5.30); Waterford (Mon.-Thurs. and Sat. 5/day, Fri. 6/day, Sun. 4-5/day; 2½hr.; £9.70, students £6); and Wexford and Rosslare Harbour, with some timed to meet the ferries (Mon.-Sun. 2-3/day; 4hr.; £12, students £7.50).

Luggage storage: in Colbert Station. Lockers £1/day, 24-hr. limit.

Bike Rental: Emerald Cycles, 1 Patrick St. (tel. 416983). £7/day, £30/week; deposit £40. £12 charge for return at other locations. **Rent-A-Bike,** An Óige Youth Hostel, 1 Percy Sq. (tel. 411090). Mountain bike £7/day, £30/week. £5 charge for return at other Rent-A-Bike depots.

Laundry: Speediwash Laundrette & Dry Cleaners, 11 St. Gerard St. (tel. 319380). Wash and dry £4.40. Open Mon.-Sat. 9am-6pm.

Camping Equipment: River Deep, Mountain High, 7 Rutland St., corner of O'Connell (tel. 400944). Open Mon.-Sat. 9:30am-6pm.

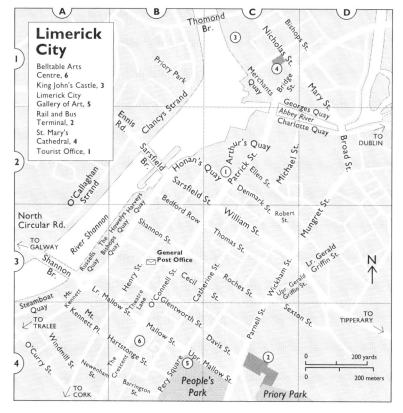

Limerick City

Belltable Arts Centre, 6
King John's Castle, 3
Limerick City Gallery of Art, 5
Rail and Bus Terminal, 2
St. Mary's Cathedral, 4
Tourist Office, 1

Pharmacy: Arthurs Quay Pharmacy, Arthurs Quay Mall (tel. 416662). Open Mon.-Wed. 9am-7pm, Thurs.-Fri. 9am-9pm, Sat. 9am-6pm.
Emergency: Dial 999. **Garda:** Henry St. (tel. 414222), at Lower Glentworth St.

ACCOMMODATIONS

For a city of its size, Limerick has a dearth of budget accommodation. If Limerick itself is somewhat lacking in charm, the hostels do little to compensate. The existing hostels are adequate, however, by summer 1996, a promising new hostel may be open (inquire at the tourist office). For those seeking some quiet, Ennis St. houses B&B after B&B, most priced around £15.

An Óige Hostel (HI), 1 Pery Sq. (tel. 314672). From Colbert Station, walk straight down Davis St. to the monument and turn left onto Percy Sq. A pleasant, old Georgian house conceals the usual An Óige restrictions. Metal bunks. Bring your own utensils! Midnight curfew; sheets 85p. 12- to 14-bed dorm June-Sept. £6.50, Oct.-May £5.50.
Barrington Hostel, George's Quay (tel. 415222), near St. Mary's Cathedral. From the station, walk straight out and 3 blocks down Davis St. Turn right on O'Connell St., walk about 10 min., and make the first right after the bridge. Fairly comfortable beds occupy a large former nurses' dormitory. Its central location only partially compensates for loud traffic outside. £6.50/person.
Parklodge Holiday Hostel, Dublin Rd. (tel. 400404). Follow signs to Dublin from O'Connell St.; at N24, N7 roundabout, stay on Dublin Rd. Hostel is about 200 yards farther on your left. Or take Bus #2, 5, or 8 from Penney's downtown. This

"hostel" feels more like a roadside motel, complete with faux cherry closets and traffic outside. Double £7.50/person.

Plassey Village, University College Limerick, off Dublin Rd. 2 mi. from Limerick (tel. 333644). Take Bus #2, 5, or 8 from Penney's downtown. Single bedrooms in luxurious, condo-like dorms on the University campus. Free Internet hookup! Good for longer stays. Reception open Mon.-Fri. 8am-9pm, Sat.-Sun. 8-noon and 5-9pm. Laundry £3.80. Lunch and dinner available. Students £10/night, £40/week.

St. Anthony's, 8 Coolraine Terrace, Ennis Rd. (tel. 452607), 1 mi. from city center. Pleasant rooms look out onto a flourishing garden. Homemade brown bread and jam await in the morning. *Let's Go* special: £11.50/person, w/bath £13/person.

FOOD

Limerick must have more fast-food joints than do all the truck stops in Ohio combined. Stock up at Quinnsworth **Supermarket** in Arthurs Quay Mall (open Mon.-Wed. 9am-7pm, Thurs.-Fri. 9am-9pm, Sat. 9am-6pm) or at **Eats of Eden,** Henry St. (tel. 419400), a well-stocked health food store (don't miss the apples; open Mon.-Fri. 9am-6pm, Sat. 9am-5:30pm).

The Green Onion Café, Evlen St. (tel. 400710), just off O'Connell St. Crimson-sponged walls etched with musings surround diners. Excellent bistro fare at prices more reasonable than might be expected. Open daily noon-10pm.

Dolmen Gallery and Restaurant, Honan's Quay (tel. 417929), across from the tourist office. Enjoy vegetarian goulash (£4) or other daily specials while critiquing the current exhibit. Decadent afternoon tea (£3.50, daily 3-5:30pm) includes enough sweets to last a week. Open Mon.-Sat. 10am-5:30pm.

The Grove, 11 Upper Cecil St. (tel. 410084). Hearty, appealing wholefood. They now offer sit-down in their small café in addition to take-away. Cheese and lentil pie with two salads £3. Open Mon.-Sat. 9:30am-6pm.

Java's, 5 Catherine St. (tel. 418077). Flavored coffees, herbal teas, and desserts placate the late-night crowd. Open daily 8am-4am.

Moll Darby's, 8 Georges Quay, (tel. 417270), just across the Abbey River. Appealing and quintessentially Italian, down to the red-checkered tablecloths, candles, and flowing red wine. Open daily 5:30-11pm.

PUBS

Traditional music is played nightly around town. You can pick up the tourist office's Guinness guide to Irish music for schedules or you can opt for one of the local gig "Guides" for more detailed information and local gossip. A large student population ensures plenty of more raucous options.

Nancy Blake's, Denmark St. (tel. 416443). One of the best pubs in town. A young crowd filters in and out of three large stone rooms (each with its own bar) and a romantic outdoor patio. Trad inside every Sun.-Wed., rock and blues outside nightly, live bands Fri., Sun., and sometimes Sat.

Locke Bar, George's Quay (tel. 413733). Hip, but without the grunge baggage of Doc's or the Henry Cecil pub. Pleasant, Quay-side seating with festive Christmas lights! Owner Richard Costello, who used to play rugby for Ireland's national team, now plays trad music Sun.-Tues. nights.

Doc's, Michael St. at the corner of Charlotte's Quay in the Granary (tel. 417266). Spacious, interesting pub in a former warehouse. Large outdoor beer garden, complete with palm trees and waterfalls, is invariably packed with tumescent youth. Music on Wed., Thurs., and Sun. nights.

The Henry Cecil, Lower Cecil St., between O'Connell St. and Henry St. (tel. 416988). Huge, multi-level pub similar in atmosphere to Doc's. Upstairs, a DJ spins nightly. His selections include techno-infused trad that would make any self-respecting fiddler cringe. Downstairs, traditional sessions on Mon.-Wed.

SIGHTS

Shannonside Walking Tours (tel. 311935) leave the tourist office Mon.-Fri. June-Aug. at 11am and 2:30pm. Tours focus primarily on the old English city on King's Island, including St. Mary's Cathedral and King John's Castle (£3.50, students £2.50). The tours skip the area around the Daniel O'Connell monument on **O'Connell St.,** which is dominated by red-brick Georgian townhouses with brightly-painted, stately doorways. The consistently gracious, if slightly decrepit, buildings are indicative of careful town planning during the late-18th and early-19th centuries. The buildings sharply contrast with the discordant architecture on Lower O'Connell St. The proliferation of modern, plastic stores and restaurants farther down O'Connell St. obviously were built with no such sensitivity.

A few decades after the Normans invaded Ireland and displaced the O'Brien dynasty from the Limerick area, King John ordered a castle built for protection. **King John's Castle,** on Nicholas St. (tel. 411201), still defends Limerick, although the ranks of prospective invaders have dwindled significantly. Walk across the Abbey River and take the first left after St. Mary's Cathedral. Today, the castle's presence is more educational than physically impressive, with well-prepared exhibits supplying a survey of history from the Vikings to the present. The importance of military strength becomes obvious outside, where the mangonal is displayed. Easily recognizable from its use in *Monty Python and the Holy Grail*, the mangonel used to catapult pestilent animal corpses into enemy cities and castles. (Open daily 9am-6pm. £3.50, students £1.90.)

Close by is **St. Mary's Cathedral** (tel. 416238), built by the O'Briens in 1172, whose delicate glass windows belie a rough interior. On the side of the altar, fold-down seats are built into the wall (called "misericords"). Their elaborate carvings depict the struggle between **good** and **evil.** Nightly sound and light shows here provide a surreal, and somewhat irreverent, introduction to Limerick's history. (Church open Mon.-Sat. 9am-1pm and 2-5pm. Light shows Mon.-Fri. at 9:15pm; £2.50, students £1.50.) Across the river, in the city proper, Irish paintings can be critiqued for free at the **Limerick City Gallery of Art,** Percy Sq. (tel. 310633; open Mon.-Wed. and Fri. 10am-1pm, Thurs. 2-6pm; free). More modern and abstract art decks the walls at the **Belltable Arts Centre,** O'Connell St. (tel. 319866; gallery open Mon.-Sat. 9am-6pm; free).

The small but fascinating **Hunt Museum** (tel. 333644), in the Foundation Building on the university campus, is worth a special trip. The museum's collection, ranging from bronze age tools to the most "perfect" of Leonardo da Vinci's four "Rearing Horses," is impressive and enhanced appreciably by an excellent guided tour (tours daily at 11am and 3pm; open Mon.-Sat. 10am-5pm. £2, students £1). As long as you're at the University, stop by the **National Self-Portrait Collection** (tel. 333644) which displays itself in Plassey House (open Mon.-Fri. 10am-5pm; free).

ENTERTAINMENT

Limerick has a nightclub scene worthy of the Republic's third-largest city. Most social events seem to congregate according to word of mouth, but a few nightclubs are safe bets. **Doc's** (see Pubs, above) revels with a rave-like disco Thursday through Sunday nights (cover £3-6). **Baker's Place,** Dominick St., a few doors down from the Clock Tower on Davis St. (tel. 418414), has live music nightly, with a club pumping music Tuesday through Sunday nights. **The Works,** on Bedford Row next to the Cinema, has a club operating nightly.

The **Belltable Arts Centre,** 69 O'Connell St. (tel. 319866), stages excellent, if somewhat bizarre, productions year round. (Box office open Mon.-Sat. 9am-6pm and prior to performances; tickets £5-7). The **Theatre Royal,** Upper Cecil St. (tel. 414224), hosts any large concerts that come to town. Phone or ask at the tourist office for current offerings. The **University Concert Hall** on the university campus (tel. 331549) attracts opera, dance, and classical and traditional music (tickets £8-14). Greyhounds race every Monday, Thursday, and Saturday night at the Market's

Field on Mulgrave St. (several blocks up William St.). Races start at 8pm and cost £3. The free **Limerick Events Guide,** at the tourist office, has details on all events.

■■■ LOUGH DERG

Lough Derg plays host to affluent middle-aged tourists, or "cruisers," who navigate their private boats upriver from Limerick to the small towns of Killaloe, Mountshannon, and Portumna. Younger, land-based travelers are much rarer here than they are farther west. Archaeological attractions are not the draw; visitors come to the lake for swimming, windsurfing, and other recreational activities. The **Lough Derg Way** walking path starts in Limerick, follows the western bank of the Shannon up to Killaloe, then crosses over to Ballina. The trail traces along the eastern shore of the lough beneath Arra Mountain, where Fintan the White, consort of Cesair, survived the flood (see Legends & Folktales, p. 61). His refuge is marked by the Neolithic tombs known as the "Graves of the Leinstermen."

Killaloe and Mountshannon lie along the Lough Derg Drive northeast of Limerick. Public transport virtually ignores Mountshannon and Killaloe, though buses sometimes do venture forth from Limerick (3/week; £3.50, students). Hitchhikers report an easy time getting to Killaloe from Limerick or from Dublin Rd. (from Dublin Rd., hitchers station themselves on R494 and hitch to Ballina, just across the river). Thumbing farther north to Mountshannon may require a bit more patience.

Fifteen miles out of Limerick along the Lough Derg Drive and just south of the lake itself, **Killaloe** ("KILL a loo") feels distant from the industry of the big city with its rolling hills and nautical orientation. Old churches and oratories remember Killaloe's 7th-century function as a religious center, when St. Lua (*Molua* in Irish) and St. Flannan made it their home. High King of Ireland Brian Ború lived here too (from 1002-1014 AD), though no one is sure quite where.

At the base of the town on Royal Parade lies **St. Flannan's Cathedral,** built between 1195 and 1225 and still in use. Inside the Cathedral, the Thorgrim Stone is written in Scandinavian Runic characters and again in the Irish monks' *ogham* script as a prayer for the conversion of Thogrim, a Viking, to Christianity. This rare occasion to observe Runic writing in Ireland, is made particularly significant given the *ogham* "translation." Market Sq. may have once held Brian Ború's palace of Kincora. The other candidate for the coveted site-of-Ború's-palace award is the abandoned fort known as **Beal Ború,** 1½ miles out of town toward Mountshannon, and unfortunately not much to see. Behind the tourist office, a **heritage center** occupies itself with the legendary Ború. (Open Mon.-Sat. 10am-6pm. £1.50, students 70p.)

Lough-related activities abound in Killaloe. The **Derg Princess** leaves from just across the river in **Ballina,** Co. Tipperary, for relaxing, if not informative, 1½-hr. cruises (tel. (061) 376364; £6). Two **boat rental** companies, **Whelan's** (tel. 376159) and **Haskett** (a.k.a. Killaloe; tel. (061) 376693), station themselves across from the tourist office and rent out motorboats for fishing or cruising (£7/hr., £30/day). A boat (and a bit of navigational prowess) will allow you access to **Holy Island** (see below). In mid-July, Killaloe recognizes its most famous ex-resident with **Féile Brian Ború,** four days of music, watersports, and various Ború-revering activities.

The **tourist office** (tel. (061) 376866), in Lock House on the Killaloe side of the bridge, can provide information on several rural walks around Killaloe. (Open June-Sept. daily 10am-6pm.) Main St. is home to **AIB** bank (tel. (061) 376115; open Mon. and Wed.-Fri. 10am-4pm, Tues. 10am-5pm) and, farther uphill, the **post office** (tel. (061) 376111; open Mon.-Fri. 9:30am-12:30pm and 1:30-5:30pm, Sat. 9:30am-12:30pm). A couple of miles north of Killaloe, indulge in an afternoon of watersports at the **Shannonside Activity and Sailing Centre** (tel. (061) 376622; windsurfing £8/hr.; canoeing or kayaking £3/hr; sailboats from £10/hr.).

Though you can make Killaloe a daytrip from Limerick, several nice B&Bs near town also compete for your attention. **Kincora House,** across from Crotty's Pub (tel. (061) 376149), is very hospitable and will serve you a healthy breakfast on request (£16/person). Super-fresh seafood makes the **Dalcassian,** Main St. (tel. (061)

376762), near the cathedral, a local favorite (open daily 11am-5pm and 6-9:30pm; dinner entrees £7-9; bar menu until 5pm). Next to the bridge in Ballin, **Molly's** serves elevated pub grub (Irish stew £4) and pleasant river views (and *al fresco* pints if the weather allows; food served from 12:30-9pm). The best place to stock up for a picnic is **McKeogh's,** on Main St. in Ballina (open Mon.-Wed. 9am-7:30pm, Thurs.-Fri. 9am-9pm, Sat. 9am-8:30pm, Sun. 9:30am-1pm).

■■■ LIMERICK TO ENNIS

Fifteen miles west of Limerick off Ennis Rd. (N18) along the north shore of the river, **Shannon Airport** sends jets to North America and Europe (tel. (061) 471444; Aer Lingus info tel. (061) 471666). The airport has spawned unsightly industrial development (and some much-needed employment) in the coastal areas west of Limerick. Until a couple years ago, all transatlantic flights to Ireland were obliged by Irish law to stop first at Shannon. Bus Éireann hits the airport from Limerick (Mon.-Sat. 20/day, Sun. 11/day; 45 min.; £3.50, students £2) and from Dublin (Mon.-Sat. 6/day, Sun. 4/day; 4½hr.; £10, students £8). The airport provides direct ground transport to Ennis, Galway, Westport, Tralee, and Killarney. **Car rental** opportunities abound. The cheapest is **Thrifty** (tel. (061) 472649; from £25/day, £160/week; min. age 23).

BUNRATTY

Eight miles northwest of Limerick along the Ennis Rd., **Bunratty Castle and Bunratty Folk Park** (tel. (061) 361511) amalgamates a collection of historical attractions found, separately, all over Ireland. Bunratty Castle says it's Ireland's most complete medieval castle, with superbly restored furniture, tapestry, stained-glass windows, and a historically significant virginal. The castle derives much of its popularity from the medieval feasts that it hosts nightly for deep-pocketed tourists. Local lasses, dressed in period costume, serve much wine and meat to would-be chieftains.

The folk park took root in the Bord Fáilte-approved 60s, when builders at Shannon Airport couldn't bear to destroy a quaint cottage in order to build a new runway. Instead, they moved the cottage to Bunratty. Since then, reconstructions of turn-of-the-century houses from all over Ireland and a small village of old-fashioned stores (now catering to modern tourist tastes) have been added. (Open July-Aug. daily 9:30am-7pm; Sept.-June daily 9:30am-5:30pm; last admission 1 hr. before closing. Castle closes at 4:15pm. £4.50, students £2.20.) Try not to visit in mid-afternoon during the high season: the thick queue of tourists on the narrow castle stairways will make for an annoying and treacherous experience. The Bunratty complex also claims one decent but still tourist-friendly pub. The first proprietress at **Durty Nelly's** (founded 1620) earned her name by serving Bunratty soldiers more than just beer. All buses between Limerick and Shannon Airport pass Bunratty (Mon.-Sat. 20/day, Sun. 11/day; £3.10 return, students £2.75). The Limerick bus station also sells combination bus and admission tickets to the castle for £6.

NEWMARKET-ON-FERGUS

Between Bunratty and Ennis on N18, this little village contains a bonanza of castles, ruins, and archaeological projects. Unfortunately, few are within walking distance. Ask for directions at the **tourist office** on Main St. (tel. (061) 368744; open Mon.-Sat. 10am-5:30pm). Buses run from Limerick to Newmarket (Mon.-Sat. 7/day, Sun. 4/day; 45 min.; £3.50, students £2).

One-half mile towards Ennis from Newmarket, anyone can explore the grounds of **Drumoland Castle** (tel. (061) 368144), former home of Lord Inchiquin and the O'Brien Clan and now a pricey hotel. Pheasant shooting, clay pigeon shooting, horse riding, dear stalking, tennis, and golf take place on the premises; try not to get shot at as you roam past the peacocks. Make a right off the Ennis Rd. at the sign for Mooghaun B&B to reach the **Mooghaun Ring Forts** and the beautiful **woods** surrounding them. Archaeologists at the site are looking for burial remains to clue them in to the forts' purpose, and will gladly chat about their work.

Save your time and money for the lesser-known **Craggaunowen Project** (tel. (061) 367178), two miles from Knappogue Castle and near the village of Quin. You can tour a *crannog* (Bronze Age lake dwellings) and see the leather boat in which Tim Severin crossed the Atlantic in 1976. Akin to the Hunt Museum, this well-done re-enactment claims "free admission for visitors who show their commitment to 'Our Living Past Experience' on Bank Holidays by coming in Celtic costume." (Open mid-March to mid-April Fri.-Sun. 10am-5pm; mid-April to mid-May daily 10am-6pm; mid-May to mid-Sept. daily 9am-6pm; mid-Sept. to mid-Oct. daily 10am-6pm; mid-Oct. to mid-Dec. Fri.-Sun. 10am-4pm; last admission 45 min. before closing; £3.10, students £2.)

There's no hostel in Newmarket, and most B&Bs involve a considerable hike into the countryside: consider basing yourself in Limerick or Ennis. After dark, the **Weaver's Inn,** Main St. (tel. (061) 368144), a cross between an Irish pub and an Asian restaurant, is the most popular joint (open 12:30-3pm and dinner 6-10pm). **The Hunter's Tavern,** Main St. (tel. (061) 368577) and the **Tradaree Arms,** Main St. (tel. (061) 368193; trad sessions Fri.) are also worth a look.

■■■ ENNIS

Twenty miles northwest of Limerick, the narrow, high-walled streets and bustling crowds of Ennis (pop. 16,000) make it an attractive place. Makeshift stands vend fruit along the river, and pubs shake with trad music on weekends. Sure, the standard historical stuff is there, but no one comes to Ennis for the scenery. Instead, they head through Ennis, southwest to Kilkee and the sea or northwest to the Cliffs of Moher, Doolin, and the Burren.

PRACTICAL INFORMATION

Ennis Tourist Office: O'Connell Sq. (tel. 41670), in the Upstairs Downstairs shop, will copiously answer your queries. (Open June-Sept. daily 9am-9pm; Oct.-May Mon.-Sat. 9am-6pm, Sun. 10am-6pm.)

Shannon Region Tourist Office: (tel. 28366), ½ mi. from the bus station on Clare Rd., books accommodations, looks like a rest stop on a highway, and seems designed to serve the car-equipped. From the station, follow Clon Rd. and take a left onto Clare Rd. (Open May-Oct. daily 9am-5:45pm; Nov.-April Tues.-Sat. 9am-1pm and 2-6pm.)

Banks: Bank of Ireland, O'Connell Sq. (tel. 28615). Open Mon.-Tues. and Thurs.-Fri. 10am-4pm, Wed. 10am-5pm. **ATM. AIB,** Bank Pl. (tel. 28089). Open same hours. **ATM.**

Post office: Bank Pl. (tel. 21054). Open Mon.-Tues. and Thurs.-Fri. 9am-5:30pm, Wed. 9:30am-5:30pm, Sat. 9:30am-2:30pm.

Phone code: 065.

Trains: next to the bus station. **Station** (tel. 40444) open Mon.-Sat. 7am-5:30pm, Sun. 15 min. before departures. Trains leave for Dublin via Limerick (Mon.-Sat. 2/day, Sun. 1/day; £16, students £9.50). You're better off catching the train from Limerick, where 9-11/day leave for Dublin.

Buses: The **station** (tel. 24177) is a 10-min. walk from the town center on Station Rd. Open Mon.-Fri. 7:15am-5:30pm, Sat. 7:15am-4:45pm. To: Limerick (12/day, Sun. 7/day; 50 min.; £5, students £3); Galway (6/day; 1¼hr., £7.30, students £4.30); Dublin via Limerick (5/day; 4hr.; £10, students £8); Cork (7/day, Sun. 5/day; 3hr.; £10, students £6); Kilkee (2-3/day, Sun. 1/day; 1hr.; £6.90, students £4.10); Doolin (3/day, Sun. 1/day; 1½hr.; £6.50, students £3.20); Shannon Airport (Mon.-Fri. 13/day, Sat. 9/day, Sun. 10/day; 40 min.; £3.50, students £2). Also a West Clare line (Mon., Sun. 2/day): Lisdoonvarna, Ennistymon, Lahinch, Miltown Malbay, Doolin, Kilkee, and Kilrush. The crowded **post bus** runs from the post office to Liscannor and Doolin on the coast. (Mon.-Sat. 2/day; Ennis to Doolin £2.50, students £1.) Arrive early to get a seat.

Bike Rental: Michael Tierney Cycles and Fishing, 17 Abbey St. (tel. 29433). Rentals and repair. Tierney helpfully suggests routes through the hilly country-

side. £3.50/afternoon, £7/day, £30/week; deposit £20. Open Mon.-Sat. 9:30am-6pm. **Irish Cycle Hire/Railbike,** Ennis Train Station (tel. (041) 41067). £6/day, £30/week; deposit £30. Open daily 9am-8pm.
Luggage Storage: in the bus station on Station Rd., off O'Connell St. Lockers for 50p. Coaches for £80,000. Open Mon.-Sat. 7:30am-6:30pm, Sun. 10am-7:15pm.
Pharmacy: O'Connell Chemist, Abbey St. (tel. 20373). Open Mon.-Sat. 9am-6pm, Sun. 11am-1pm.
Samaritans: tel. (1850) 609090. 24 hrs.
Emergency: Dial 999; no coins required. **Garda:** tel. 28205.

ACCOMMODATIONS, FOOD, & PUBS

Right on the river, across Club Bridge from Abbey St., the **Abbey Tourist Hostel (IHH),** Harmony Row (tel. 22620), is a 300-year-old labyrinth. The hostel itself is clean and comfortable, but the showers can be erratic. (Reception open 9:30am-10:30pm. July-Aug. dorm £5.50, private room £7/person; Sept.-June dorm £5, private room £6.50; semi-private room £6; sheets 50p, laundry £2.50.) **Derrynane House** (tel. 28464), in the Square, will put a roof over your head right in the middle of town (£15/person, all w/bath). Dinner and pubs go hand in hand, but there are a few alternatives. Dunnes **supermarket** lurks on O'Connell St. (tel. 40700; open Mon.-Tues. 9am-7pm, Wed.-Sat. 9am-9pm, Sun. noon-6pm). The **Food Emporium,** Abbey St. (tel. 20554), does deli favorites (sandwiches £1.10, rolls £1.25). **Derrynane House** (see above) cooks up satisfying, belt-loosening breakfasts between 9am and noon (Irish breakfast £2.50). But pubs are where it's really at. **Brandon's Bar,** O'Connell St. (tel. 28133), serves huge plates of spuds, meat, and veggies (entrees £3.50) alongside its pints. **O'Connell Bar** (tel. 28464), near the square, will fry up scampi (£3.75). **Brogan's,** Abbey St. (tel. 29480), is your supplier of Irish stew (£5.50) in the afternoon or early evening. It becomes even more popular and smoky in the evening as young people flock here for the *craic.* **Cruises Pub,** next to the Friary on Abbey St. (tel. 41800), stuffs its customers with griddle scones and muffins with cream and jam (70p) or the special club sandwich (£3.95; music nightly in summer). Ennis has its fair share of dark and woody pubs serving dark and frothy pints, the darkest and woodiest being **The Usual Place,** O'Connell St., *Let's Go's* pick for the coziest pub in Ireland.

SIGHTS

Ennis's four main streets—O'Connell St., Abbey St., Bank Place, and Parnell St.—meet in **O'Connell Square,** where a high statue of Daniel O'Connell watches over his hometown. The original O'Connells were Catholic landowners dispossessed by Cromwell. Almost two hundred years later in 1828, Ennis residents elected Catholic barrister Daniel O'Connell to represent them at Westminster. As a Catholic, he was refused his seat. The resulting political uproar led to Catholic Emancipation in the U.K. (1829). "The Liberator" was thrust into being the leader of Catholic Ireland for the next twenty years. A 10-minute walk from the town center on the Mill Rd. stands the **Maid of Erin,** a life-size statue remembering the "Manchester Martyrs," three nationalists hanged in Manchester in 1867.

Abbey St. leads northeast to the ruined and roofless 13th-century **Ennis Friary** (tel. 29100), famous for the slender panes and peaked points of its east window. In 1375 the seminary housed and taught 350 Franciscan monks and 600 students. It was the last theological school in Ireland to survive the Reformation. Inside, depictions of the Passion adorn 15th-century **McMahon tomb.** The tombstones within the friary often announce the name and profession of the man who paid for the stone in larger letters than the name of the deceased. (Open mid-May to Sept. daily 9:30am-6:30pm; £1, students 40p.) Across the street from Ennis Friary, a block of sandstone inscribed with part of Yeats's "Easter 1916" remembers the Easter Rising.

A few doors from the Abbey House Hostel on Harmond Row, **de Valera Library and Museum** (tel. 21616) adds a door from the Spanish Armada to its collection of the ex-Taoiseach's stuff, which includes his private car. IRA weapons and Land

League banners recall Ennis's political life. (Museum and library open Mon. and Thurs. 11am-5:30pm, Tues.-Wed. and Fri. 11am-8pm; free.) Saturday is **Market Day** in Market Sq. All conceivable wares are sold below a statue of crafty Daedalus.

CLARE COAST

Those traveling north to Co. Clare from Tralee and the southwest should take note of the **Tarbert-Killimer car ferry** (tel. (065) 53124), which makes a 20-minute trip across the Shannon estuary, preempting an 85-mile drive via Limerick City (see Tarbert, p. 244).

■■■ KILKEE

In Kilkee, on the southwest tip of Clare, three rows of Victorian houses arranged along a beautiful sheltered beach look out to sea. Gorgeous cliffs rise high on eroded islands where farms lay hundreds of years ago. Irish, not foreign, holiday makers come here. The deafening arcades and fine white beaches fill with crowds in the summer. A healthy pub scene makes up for the abounding plastic storefronts. During the rest of the year the deserted town offers solitary cliff walks.

The **tourist office** pops up in the central square across from the Stella Maris Hotel (tel. 56112; open June-Sept. daily 10am-6pm). The **ATM** at the **Bank of Ireland,** O'Curry St. (tel. 56053) puts cash in your pocket. (Open Mon. 10am-12:30pm and 1:30-5pm, Tues.-Fri. 10am-12:30 and 1:30-4pm.) The **post office** (tel. 56001) is on Circular Rd. (open Mon.-Fri. 9am-3pm, Sat. 10am-1pm). **Bus Éireann** (tel. 24177, in Ennis) scrapes by twice a day for Ennis and Limerick and three times a day for Galway and Cork. All buses stop outside Kett's Bar. Rent **bikes** and get your greens from **Rosarie's** on O'Curry St. (tel. 56622; £6/day, £32/week; deposit £20; open May-Sept. daily 9:30am-8pm). **Williams,** opposite the post office on Circular Rd, also rents bikes (£6/day, £30/week; a Raleigh dealer). Kilkee's **phone code** is 065.

The welcoming **Kilkee Hostel (IHH)**, O'Curry St. (tel. 56209), is so clean that you won't even mind if your toothbrush falls on the floor. The family-run place creates an atmosphere of bonhomie between travelers. (Dorm £6; sheets 50p; laundry £3; **bikes** £6/day.) Rooms live up to the billing of **Bay View B&B** (tel. 56058), a large pink building smack in the town center on the corner of O'Connell and O'Curry St. (single £15, double £26, both w/bath).

If you wouldn't mind being fat and lazy, you could live your whole life between the beach and O'Curry St. A **Centra Stores supermarket** sells victuals on the corner of O'Curry St. and Circular Rd. (open summer Mon.-Thurs. 9am-8:30pm, Fri.-Sun. 9am-9pm; winter daily 9am-8pm). **Country Cooking Shop** specializes in desserts for the decadent traveler. Adjoined **Pantry** is a café/restaurant run by the same folks (tel. 56576; Irish breakfast £3; chicken, leek and vegetable pie £4; open Easter-Sept. daily 8:30am-9:30pm). **Eats & Treats,** O'Curry St. (tel. 56866) serves snacks to hungry beach bums (nachos £2.90, bagel with cream cheese £1; open April-Oct. daily 9am-7pm). **Purtills,** O'Curry St. (tel. 56900) is a full restaurant—a rare breed in these parts. (Chicken kebabs £6.50. Open Easter-Sept. daily 6-10pm; Oct.-March Sat.-Sun. 6-10pm.) Kilkee's pub crawl is famously fun. Begin at **Strand Hotel** and continue to the **Stella Maris Hotel Bar,** then **Michael Martin's Pub** (opposite the tourist office). If you're still standing, move on to **Central Bar** (tel. 56103), **Richie's,** and the **Myles Creek Pub** (tel. 56670), all on O'Curry St. After last call, head to **Waterfront** (tel. 56838), a nightclub above the amusement center at the end of O'Curry St. Music sounds out between 11pm and 2am (Mon.-Thurs.; cover £3).

The **Westend Cliff Walk** begins to the left of the seafront, where **Diamond Rocks** sit on the side of the harbor. The collection of quartz rocks called Diamond Rocks today are farther up the coast than the originals. The first rocks are now a slippery kelp-coated mussel bed—locals come out at low tide with nets. A gravel path leads

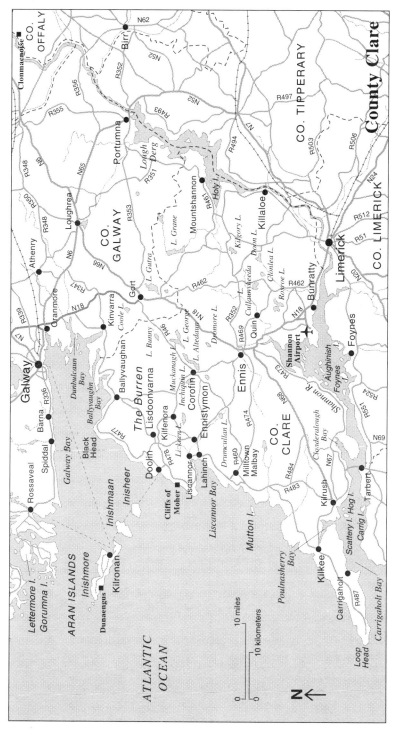

out from the car park. Four **"Pollock Holes"** provide natural rock pools for swimming (the fourth is a men's nudist bathing spot).

The path out to the (new) Diamond Rocks leads into **Loop Head Drive,** which passes through small villages, ruined farmhouses, and plenty of pasture to **Loop Head** itself, at the very tip of Co. Clare. Only a lighthouse and four electrical fences stand between the road and the crashing water at the foot of the cliffs. The Loop Head Drive passes through Carrigaholt village, seven miles south of Kilkee on the Shannon Estuary. Boat trips geared for **dolphin watching** set out from here into the waters where approximately 60 bottlenosed dolphins have made their home (tel. (088) 584711; £8).

■■■ KILKEE TO DOOLIN

MILTOWN MALBAY

Once you've enjoyed Kilkee and the sea, only small towns stand between you and the awesome Cliffs of Moher. Most of the people who stop and stay in these towns are looking for golf courses, in large supply here. Miltown Malbay, 20 miles north of Kilkee on coastal N67, wakes up only during the first week of July, when the **Willie Clancy School of Traditional Music** lets fly one of Ireland's larger musical celebrations. People from all corners of the globe flock here in the thousands to their pre-booked accommodations.

Miltown pubs are, not surprisingly, praised for their trad sessions. The very best ones are usually on Monday nights. **Cleary's** (tel. (065) 84201) has trad music nightly, while **Wilson's** (tel. (065) 84189) goes one step farther and hosts both trad and folk nightly. **Clancy's** (tel. (065) 84077) and **The Lark's Inn** (tel. (065) 84308) also join the action (trad Fri.-Sun. nights). **O'Friel's Bar,** Main St. (tel. (065) 84275), has an adorable yellow and jade interior (Irish stew £4). **Mary's Place Restaurant & Pizzeria** (tel. (065) 84551) on Ennis Rd. is a little bit of heaven in Miltown. (Fresh salmon bisque with bread £1.75; 9" 5-topping pizza £3.50. Open July-Aug. Mon.-Sat. 10am-8pm, Sun. noon-8pm; Sept.-June Mon.-Sat. 10am-8pm, Sun. 5-7:30pm.) **Spar Supermarket & Bakery,** Main St. (tel. (065) 84093; open Mon.-Sat. 9am-9pm, Sun. 9am-1:30pm) has just what you'd expect. Halfway between Miltown and the beaches at Spanish Point, **Three Corner View** (tel. (065) 84362) has rooms with TVs (£11.50/person). The affordable **Station House** (tel. (065) 84008) at the old railway station doesn't skimp on its pillows (£12.50/person). The **tourist office,** Main St. (tel. (065) 84730), is happy to see you (open June-Sept. Mon.-Fri. 10am-8pm, Sat.-Sun. 10am-7pm). The **Bank of Ireland** (tel. (065) 84018) stares back stonily from across the street (open Mon.-Wed., Fri. 10am-12:30pm and 1:30-4pm, Thurs. 10am-12:30pm and 1:30-5pm). **Byrne's** on Ennis Rd. (tel. (065) 84079) rents and repairs **bikes** and has a limited supply of camping equipment. (Bikes £7/day, £30/week; deposit £40; open Mon.-Sat. 9:30am-6:30pm.)

LAHINCH & LISCANNOR

Golfers cluster in a triad of towns north of Miltown Malbay on N67, near Liscannor Bay. Tiny **Lahinch,** a seaside resort, calls itself "the St. Andrews of Ireland." The wide beach below the town also attracts a large summertime beach population. A **tourist office,** Church St. (tel. (065) 81730) can help you out (open June-Sept. daily 10am-7pm). A **post office** (tel. (065) 81001) on Main. St. can exchange currency (open Mon.-Fri. 9am-1pm and 2-5:30pm, Sat. 9am-1pm). The nearest bank and **ATM** are in **Ennistymon,** about two miles east.

Clean bunkrooms and a waterfront location are the main attractions at **Lahinch Hostel (IHH;** tel. (065) 81040) on Church St. in the town center. (Dorm £6, 4-bed room £7, double £8; sheets free, laundry £2.) The **Lahinch Caravan & Camping Park** on N67 (tel. (065) 81424) rents **bikes** (£1/day; open daily 9am-9pm) and has plenty of space for **camping** (£3/tent; open Easter-Sept.). **Mrs. O'Brien's Kitchen,** Main St. (tel. (065) 81020) cooks breakfast all day (open March-Sept. daily 8am-

10:30pm). **Kenny's Bar,** Main St. (tel. (065) 81433), resounds with ballads, trad, and rock (music 5 nights/wk. in summer, 3 nights/wk. in winter).

The 26-mile **Burren Way** crosses the village of **Liscannor.** Not a lifestyle choice but rather a hiking trail, the Burren Way is marked with yellow arrows that eventually point to the Cliffs of Moher and Doolin. The lengthy slice of trail from Liscannor to Doolin runs along cliffs sprinkled with wildflowers. John P. Holland, inventor of the submarine, grew up in these parts. Depopulated bunkrooms and a huge, echoing kitchen take up space at the **Village Hostel (IHH;** tel. (065) 81385) on the main road in Liscannor. The hostel is functional. (Dorm £5.50, private room £6.50/person; sheets 50p; **bikes** £6/day; **camping** £3.50/person). The Cliff Top Centre (tel. (065) 81031) on the main road houses a **Spar supermarket** and a **restaurant** (rainbow stir-fry teriyaki £3; open noon-10pm). **Egan's** has lots of fresh food (large crab sandwich with salad £4.75) and even more pints. Locals love the little bar that is **Joe McHugh's** (tel. (065) 81163; steak and kidney pie with salad £3.50). Trad music harmonizes nightly in summer, Tuesdays and Fridays in winter.

CLIFFS OF MOHER

From the edge of the Cliffs of Moher, you can look 700 feet straight down into the open ocean. These cliffs are so high that humans actually see gulls whirling below them. Visiting the Cliffs of Moher is like seeing a world being created out of Chaos. Tourists, often filing behind tour guides, cluster where the road ends at the cliffs, though the better views are a bit farther off the road. Occasionally marked paths wander along the cliffs; tourists drop away after the first curve. Wallace Stevens based his wonderful poem "The Irish Cliffs of Moher" on photographs—he'd never been here. You shouldn't miss the chance.

The **tourist office** (tel. (065) 81171; open July-Aug. daily 9am-6:30pm; mid-March to June and Sept.-Oct. 10am-6pm) and unnecessary **O'Brien's Tower** compete for tourists' attention near the parking lot, where cars must pay £1. (Tower open, weather permitting, June-Aug. daily 9:30am-6:30pm; mid-March to May and Sept.-Oct. 10am-6pm; 70p, students 50p.) The Tower marks the highest point of the cliffs, but what's a few more feet on top of 700? A teashop refreshes feet and souls exhausted by the experience (soup £1.20; open same hours as tourist office). The Cliffs brush against R478 three miles south of Doolin. Road to the cliffs are, naturally, well marked. **Bus Éireann** clangs by on the summer-only Galway-Cork route (Mon.-Sat. 3/day). The **Burren Way** and several non-linear bike trails lead more elusively through raised limestone to the Cliffs. It's quite easy to find a ride to the cliffs from Lisdoonvarna or closer Doolin, since practically everybody is going your way.

■■■ DOOLIN

Ireland sees Doolin ("Fisherstreet" on some maps) much as Europe views Ireland: windy, beautiful, musical, oriented around pubs, and overtouristed. Twenty years ago, Doolin was a blip on the map. Today Dubs and foreigners outnumber residents 10 to 1, a fact which makes most Clare folk scowl at any mention of the town. Many excellent musicians have begun to shy away from Doolin on account of the crowds, instead preferring quieter towns like Miltown Malbay and Ballyvaughan. Still, Doolin's near-legendary status as the trad capital is slow to die. All three pubs—O'Connor's, McGann's, and McDermott's—are still justly famous for world-class music. Great *craic* is generally a guarantee.

Doolin is shaped like a barbell, made up of two smaller villages about one mile apart from each other (Martin Breen's *The Doolin Guide and Map* has good info; £3). The **Lower Village** (Fisherstreet) is closer to the shore and the **Upper Village** (Roadford) is farther up the road. A **traveling bank** comes to Doolin's shores every Thursday from 10:30-11:15am, but bureaux de change abound. The **post office** (tel. 74209) operates from the Upper Village (open Mon.-Fri. 9am-5:30pm, Sat. 9am-1pm). The **Doolin Café** (tel. 74429) rents **bikes** (£6/day; deposit £40), runs one- and two-day tours of the Burren (£18/day, including rental; 4 person min.), and even repairs bicycles (open April-Oct. daily 9:30am-9:30pm; call Nov.-March). Doolin's **phone code** answers to 065.

A three-mile-long, paved, and bicycle-friendly segment of the **Burren Way** links Doolin to the Cliffs of Moher. The steep climb along the road from Doolin to the Cliffs is more than offset by the thrilling glide back down and by the anticipation of another night of carousing at the pubs. **Boats** leave the pier on the other end of town for the Aran Islands, but boats from Galway and Rossaveal are cheaper under almost any circumstances (see Galway City, p. 264).

ACCOMMODATIONS

The immense popularity of Doolin's pubs has necessarily flooded the area with places to stay. Book ahead at all times.

> **Aille River Hostel (IHH)** (tel. 74260), ¼ mi. downhill from the Upper Village, by the river. Small, relaxed hostel with groovy ambiance. Live music almost every night. Warms its stone common-room floor with a stove. Free laundry! Dorm £6, private room £7; **camping** £3.50. Open mid-March to Oct.
>
> **Doolin Hostel (IHH)** (tel. 74006), Lower Village. Quiet, modern hostel includes everything you could ever need: shop, bureau de change, bus ticket sales. Very clean, comfortable, safe, and pink. Free tennis court and rackets. Reception 8am-9pm. Sheets 50p, laundry £2.50. **Bikes** £6/day. Dorm July-Aug. £6.75, Sept.-June £6.50; £5 key deposit. MC, Visa.
>
> **Fisher Street Hostel** (tel. 74006), in Lower Village, across the road from Doolin Hostel and also run by Paddy. The rates are the same as those at the Doolin Hostel, but this one has more 2- and 4-bed rooms w/bath (£8/person).
>
> **Rainbow Hostel (IHH)** (tel. 74415), Upper Village. Small, with rainbow-colored rooms. Cheerful appearance, casual atmosphere. Free 30-min. guided walking tours of the Burren for hostelers. July-Aug. £6.50; Sept.-June £6; laundry £3.
>
> **Westwind B&B** (tel. 74227), Upper Village, in the same driveway as the Lazy Lobster. Pleasing to the eye and comforting to the legs. Run by a friendly young couple. Vegetarian or meaty breakfasts are available. So is advice for spelunkers or other Burren explorers. Dorm June-Aug. £11; Sept.-May £10.
>
> **Campsite** (tel. 74127), near the harbor, has a kitchen and laundry. £4/tent plus £1/person; showers 50p; laundry £3.

FOOD & PUBS

Doolin has many excellent but costly seafood restaurants. Luckily, all three pubs serve excellent grub. **The Doolin Deli** (tel. 74633), near O'Connor's in the lower village, packs overstuffed sandwiches (£1.30) and stocks groceries (open June-Sept. Mon.-Sat. 8:30am-9pm, Sun. 9:30am-9pm). Positive karma fills the **Doolin Café** (tel. 74429), Upper Village, where meat lovers, vegetarians, and vegans are all fed and cared for. Feast on the Doolin Café Special of local cheeses, cured ham, mixed salad, brown bread, and fruit (£4.50) or snack on a homemade cinnamon fruit scone (55p; open daily 9:30am-2pm and 6-9:30pm).

People definitely come to Doolin for the pubs. Both O'Connor's and McGann's have won awards in the past for the best trad music in Ireland. **O'Connor's,** Lower Village (tel. 74168), never stops (music nightly and Sun. afternoons all year). It provides drink, food, and song (garlic mussels and brown bread £3.95; B&B, tel. 74242, £14/person w/bath). **McGann's,** Upper Village (tel. 74133), has music nightly at 9pm in the summer, weekends in winter, and Irish stew in both seasons (£4.50). **McDermott's,** Upper Village (tel. 74328) ranks right up there (chicken curry and rice £4; music nightly in summer, weekends in winter). Most sessions start at 9:30pm to standing room only in summer. O'Connor's tends to be the most crowded despite its being the largest.

■■■ LISDOONVARNA

Lisdoonvarna's relative fame comes from its **Matchmaking Festival,** by far the best known of the several once held all over Ireland. On these occasions, farm boys—their crops safely harvested—gathered together to pick their mates (and, one hopes, vice versa). The five-week-long festival still fills the town each September, but today's Irish women tend to stay home and make jokes about the randy bachelors and foreign women who go. The town's other claim to fame is as the title of a Christy Moore song that was written about a massive music festival held here in 1983. During the rest of the year, the pubs range from lively to pathetic. Half-empty posh hotels and innumerable pub names (The Matchmaker, the Lonely Hearts, etc.) testify to thousands of men who thought the town would do for them what they couldn't do for themselves.

The **Lisdoonvarna Tourist Information Centre** (tel. 74630; open June-Sept. daily 10am-6pm; Oct.-May 10am-6pm Mon.-Fri.) is buried in the Spa Wells Shop (signposted from town center). **Bus Éireann** stops at the corner just up from Burke's on either side of the road. Rent **bikes** at **Burke's Garage,** the Square (tel. 74022; £5/day, £30/week; deposit £40; open daily 9:30am-7pm). A few miles inland amid scrubby hills, Lisdoonvarna weds the R476, R477, and R478 to N67. R478 leads southwest to Doolin and the Cliffs of Moher; N67 heads northeast through the Burren to Ballyvaughan. Plenty of unmarked bike paths and trails circumvent the roads. Lisdoonvarna's **phone code** is a perky, red-haired, and available 065.

The **Burren Holiday Tourist Hostel (IHH),** Doolin Rd. (tel. 74300), disguises itself in Kincora House with a red and gold carpeted staircase reminiscent of a palatial hotel. A turf fire flickers in the cheery pub downstairs, and in the summer traditional set dancing rocks the bar. Delicious meals £3-6. Excellent rental **bikes** £5; laundry £3; bureau de change with rates as good as those in town. (Mid-Sept. to June dorm £6, double £7; July to mid-Sept. dorm £6.50, double £8.) Dream of genie under the foot-high, comfy comforters at Mrs. O'Connor's **Roncalli House** (tel. 74115; single £18, double £24, all w/bath). In town, Mrs. Barrett's hospitable **Marchmont House** (tel. 74066) is within stumbling distance of the pubs (single £19, double £28).

Imperial Hotel offers a soup and main course special (£4.90) until 9pm (open March-Oct.). The **Family Value supermarket** in the Square can also provide your dinner (open daily 8:30am-10pm). Possibilities for a pint and an earful of music abound. The **Roadside Tavern,** Doolin Rd. (tel. 74084), looks more like an antique shop than a bar. The nightly trad music (March-Sept. at 9:30pm) gives it away, though (Oct.-Feb. weekends only). The tavern also serves yummies (soup £1.20, Burren smoked salmon sandwich £2; noon-8:30pm). The **Kincora Bar** (tel. 74007), by the Burren Tourist Hostel, has a less cultured interior (high season music daily; set dancing every Thurs. night; off-season music weekends only). Beef stew in Guinness (£4.50) is the best seller on the menu. The large, bright red **Matchmaker Bar** (tel. 74042) could symbolize hell or love, depending on your mood. Far more men than women line the bar here (live music after 9pm; open March-Oct.).

Festival-goers and others take advantage of Lisdoonvarna's mineral springs at the **Spa Wells Health Centre,** Sulfur Hill Rd. (tel. 74023), ¼ mile from the center of town. The springs were discovered in the early 1700s, and Lisdoonvarna began to boom. If you can't stay for a bath, at least savor their aromatic sulfur water (30p/glass; electric sulphur bath £10, full massage £18, sauna £4). The **Lisdoonvarna Smoke House** (tel. 74432), between the Burren Holiday Hostel and the center of town, can tell you more than you ever needed to know about smoked salmon in a single, seven-minute video (open March-Oct. daily 10am-7pm).

■■■ COROFIN

The small village of Corofin, "the crossing place of Finn," nestles among seven lakes and the River Fergus but is only a few miles from the barren Burren. Corofin is usually overlooked by tourists eager to reach Ennis or Doolin. Buses from Ennis to Lahinch, and vice versa, pass through Corofin only once a day (Mon.-Sat.).

The approved **tourist office** in town resides in the multi-functional **Corofin Village Hostel and Camping Park,** Main St. (tel. (065) 37683). Clean, modern facilities plus bend-over-backwards hosts equal joyous hostelers. The common room has a piano and a TV. Campers have separate facilities. Laundry £5; **bikes** £5/day, £25/week; bureau de change. (Dorm £6, private room £7.50; **camping** £3/hiker or cyclist, £4.50/family.) The **post office** is on Main St. (open Mon.-Fri. 9am-1pm and 2-5:30pm, Sat. 9am-1pm). **MacNamara's Convenience Store,** Main St. (tel. (065) 37602) is just that (open daily 8am-9pm). **Cahir's Bar** (tel. (065) 37238) and **McNamara's,** are similar only in that both are along Main St. Modern Cahir's is younger and livelier (music 3 nights/week in summer, Sun. nights in winter). Pool, darts, games, and a TV provide endless entertainment. McNamara's is mellower.

The **Clare Heritage and Genealogical Research Centre,** Church St. (tel. (065) 37955), explores the region's past. The interpretive museum, located in an 18th-century church proclaims itself "a microcosm of 19th-century Ireland." The Genealogical Centre, across the street, may be able to help you find yourself (varying prices). The **Teác Celide,** on Main St. near the post office, puts Clare heritage into action on Thursday evenings with organized music, song, set dancing, and of course brown bread and tea.

One and one-half miles south of Corofin, the **Dysert O'Dea Castle and Archaeology Centre** (tel. (065) 37722) discovers the more distant past. The museum, inside a restored 15th-century tower, displays and explains archaeological features of the surrounding lands (open May-Sept. daily 10am-6pm; £1.80). A **history trail,** which stays within two miles of the center, leads you to the sights themselves (about 25 of them). Well preserved, 12th-century **St. Tola's Cross** is visited by the trail, as is a **battlefield** from 1318, where Conor O'Dea and a few of his friends defeated the intruding Normans and put off English domination for another two centuries. The **Dromore National Nature Reserve** and its cool lakes are just a few miles west of Corofin. **Guided tours** are available, but the nature trails allow you to amble at your own pace. Fishing is rampant in the many lakes and rivers around. **Burke's** shop (tel. (065) 37677) can help you out with hiring gillies and boats.

THE BURREN

The Burren begins around Lisdoonvarna when bare limestone pops up amid the grasses and sheep. Limestone plains, spines, and outcroppings dominate this 100-square-mile region, called the Burren. The elaborate moonscape includes rare wildflowers, flat stone pedestals, and jagged hills resembling gray skyscrapers bombed to rubble.

Oliver Cromwell famously complained that the Burren had "no wood to hang a man, no water to drown him, and no earth to bury him." He was two-thirds wrong. There's not much wood—nothing grows above knee-level. Instead, orchids, gentians, and other rare wildflowers proliferate. But the water in the Burren's underground rivers has hollowed out 25 miles of caves under the earth. The area's crazy geology has spawned its own lingo: *furloughs* (temporary lakes that disappear into the limestone), *clints* (a type of rock outcropping), and *grikes* (cracks in clints) make up much of the landscape. It also has its own species of colored snails, orchids, ferns, and a green butterfly. Wild goats and Irish hares patrol and fertilize the area. Geologists have decided that the Burren's layers formed undersea before the last Ice Age, as decaying shells turned to powder and mixed with sediment. Earthquakes brought the rock to the surface; advancing glaciers cracked it open.

Ancient tribes roamed the Burren, building settlements out of the ever-present stone. Since no one would bother to invade the area, these encampments were never attacked or disassembled. The fieldless region is now a field day for paleoarchaeologists. Along with the distinctly Burren-esque vocabulary, certain archeological terms are frequently thrown around, noticeably "dolmen" (a prehistoric burial sites marked by a huge upright stone) and "souterrain" (an underground passage used as a pantry or an escape tunnel). The R480 road south from Ballyvaughan through Caherconnell is particularly rich in archaic refuse: the Gleninsheen wedge tomb, the Poulnabrone dolmen, and the Caherconnell stone fort all date from the third millennium BC. At last count, the Burren National Park contained about 120 massive dolmens and wedgetombs and some 500 stone forts.

The way to see the Burren is to walk or cycle in it. George Cunningham's *Burren Journey: West* is worth a look (£3), as is Tim Robinson's meticulous map (£3.60). The Burren Rambler maps (£2) are extremely detailed. Any of the Burren's tourist offices is bound to stock these. Cheapskates can grab lesser-quality maps of the region for free at any tourist attraction, hostel, or eatery: the *North Clare Wonderland Cycling Guide* isn't bad. The **Burren Way** and its subsidiary walking trails traverse terrain as sterile as steel and patches of pulverized stone teeming with blue-headed grasses and red-winged butterflies. The 26-mile trail passes through Ballyvaughan, Ballynalackan, Doolin, and Liscannor. Yellow arrows and the occasional symbolic "walking man" point the way throughout northwest Co. Clare.

Bus service in the Burren is poor. **Bus Éireann** connects Galway, Kinvara, Ballyvaughan, Lisdoonvarna, and Doolin infrequently. During the summer (June-Oct.), some of those buses every weekday continue over the Shannon car **ferry** at Killimer to Killarney and Cork. Bus stops are at the Doolin Hostel in Doolin, Burke's Garage in Lisdoonvarna, Linnane's in Ballyvaughan, and Winkles in Kinvara. Other infrequent but year-round buses run from some individual Burren towns to Ennis (Bus Éireann info: tel. (065) 24177). **Brian's West Clare Shuttle** supplies a door-to-door Galway to Doolin service every morning, with stops at hostels in Fanore and Lisdoonvarna if prearranged. At about noon, Brian arrives in Doolin and then turns right around (£5; book ahead at tel. (091) 767801 or (088) 517963). Hitchhiking requires persistence; bikes are the best bet.

KILFENORA

A small town five miles southeast of Lisdoonvarna along R478, Kilfenora calls itself "the heart of the Burren." It's certainly a useful stopover. Tourists, most of them on bicycles, stop here for a pint, some grub, and a walk through the **Burren Centre** (tel. (065) 88030), which explains the formation of the Burren and shows an excellent film on the biology of the Burren. The adjacent tea room serves cheap lunches. (Open March-May and Oct. daily 10am-5pm; June-Sept. daily 9:30am-6pm. Centre and film £2, students £1.50.) A **tourist office** sits next to the Centre (tel. (065) 88198) and sells the helpful Burren Rambler map series (£2; open June-Oct. daily 9:30am-6pm).

Next to the Burren Centre, Catholic masses still take place in the nave of the **Kilfenora Cathedral** where the Pope is bishop (Sunday 9:45am). The rest of the Cathedral and its graveyard stand open to the sky. The structure itself dates from 1190, but the site has held churches as early as 1055. (Tours of the cathedral July-Aug. £1, ask at the tourist office.) West of the church is the elaborate **Doorty Cross,** identifiable by carved scenes of three bishops and Christ's entry into Jerusalem. Odd birds and menacing heads cover its sides. Another of the "seven crosses of Kilfenora" is railed off in the field just beyond the church.

Remarkably, Kilfenora has only three pubs. **Linnane's** (tel. (065) 88157) may be filled with tourists during the afternoon, but at night things pick up with trad sessions four nights a week all year. Red vinyl covers just about everything at **Nagle's** (tel. (065) 88011; music Fri.-Sun. in summer). **Vaughan's** (tel. (065) 88004) entertains locals with music most nights and set dancing two nights a week in summer.

Ms. Mary Murphy, Main St. (tel. (065) 88040), runs a comfortably central B&B with snug comforters and bathrooms attached to the rooms (single £14, double £24; open June-Sept.). Bicycles stack up at **Howrt Bicycles** (tel. (065) 88127; hourly or daily rental up to £6). The **post office** (tel. (065) 88001) is on Main St. across from the grocery store (open Mon.-Fri. 9am-5:30pm, Sat. 10am-1pm).

KINVARA & DOORUS

Galway Bay's shore makes a sharp turn at **Kinvara**, Co. Galway, where the rocky pastures of the pre-Burren landscape sprout pretty, rugged foliage. The view across the bay can't be beat. The guides at **Dunguaire Castle** (tel. (091) 37108), just a short distance along the shore, will show you around the fortified tower house and tell a number of stories. They both explain why clockwise staircases are easier for right-handed knights to defend and swear to a bizarre tale about St. Colman and some flying plates. (Open May to Sept. daily 9:30am-5pm. £2.25, students £1.25.) East of Kinvara, the landscape quickly dies off into the dull farmland of southern Co. Galway. Yeats's summer homes, Coole Park and Thoor Ballylee, stand a bit off N18 between Ardrahan and Gort, tantalizingly close to Kinvara. But it's difficult to hitch from Kinvara to Gort, no official bus connects them, and it's just too far to walk (see Near Galway, p. 272). **Bus Éireann** hits Kinvara on its Galway-Doolin route (June-Sept. Mon.-Sat. 4/day, Sun. 2/day; Oct.-May Mon.-Sat. 1/day).

Across the street from the hostel is **Tully's**, where a grocery and bar keep company in smoky surroundings. The acoustics make it a favorite of musicians; its close proximity to the hostel means they sometimes end up there when pubs close. **Flatley's** (tel. (091) 37112), also on Main St., is locally renowned for the quality of its weekend trad sessions. The **Café on the Quay** is perfectly named (tel. (091) 78134; mussel platter £5; open April-Oct. daily 9am-9:30pm; Nov.-March daily 9am-5pm). Back on Main St., **Partners** (tel. (091) 37503) makes hunger disappear (vegetarian quiche and salad £3.50; open March-Oct. Mon. and Wed.-Sat. 10am-10pm, Sun. 12:30-10pm).

Johnston's Hostel (IHH), Main St. (tel. (091) 37164), uphill from the Quay, is a relaxing place to end the day. The gargantuan common room was converted from an old dance hall. Upstairs, the spacious 4-bed rooms are blessed with fireplaces and colorful walls. Reputedly the first independent hostel in Ireland, a shocking number of people have met here and subsequently married. Sheets £1, showers 40p donation; laundry expected in 1996. (Dorm £6; **camping** £3.50. Open June-Sept.) Mary Walsh's **Cois Cuain B&B** (tel. (091) 37119) reposes in manicured gardens on the Quay (no singles, double £28; open May-Aug.). The **Londis supermarket** (tel. (091) 37508) does its thing on the main road (open daily 9am-9pm) **Kinvara Pharmacy**, Main St. (tel. (091) 37397) can soothe your blisters (open Mon.-Sat. 9:30am-6pm).

For those with an urge to sail, **Michael Linane** (at the Kinvara inlet) will take groups of four people on a tour of the bay and across to the village of **Doorus**, Co. Galway. Yeats and Lady Gregory stayed here while planning the Abbey Theatre and collaborating on plays. The house they inhabited is now the isolated **Doorus House Hostel (An Óige/HI)** (tel. (091) 37512). The large, well-appointed hostel has an inviting common room with a turf fire. (Dorm June-Sept. £6; Oct.-May £5.) Toni the warden, happily helps hostelers plan their routes. A 10-mile roundtrip to the **Aughinish Peninsula** is particularly rewarding. Part of the road is surrounded on both sides by the sea. If you make the trip, down a pint at the blessedly secluded **Linnane's Pub** (tel. (065) 78120). Depending on your frame of mind, Doorus can be a haven or an inconvenience. Walking or cycling will bring out the best in Doorus. Traught Stround is just a five-minute walk from the hostel. Campers can pitch a tent in the field nearby and wake to the slosh of waves. If none of this interests you, you'll do much better to stay in Kinvara. Fortunately, Michael Linane will sail you right back (round-trip sailing £6/person). The Galway-Doolin **bus** will stop on request at the turnoff on the Ballyvaughan Rd. (June-Sept. Mon.-Sat. 4/day, Sun. 2/day; Oct.-May Mon.-Sat. 1/day); from there it's a two-mile walk.

BALLYVAUGHAN

Eight miles west of Kinvara on N67 along the jagged edge of Galway Bay, Ballyvaughan ("BAH-lee VUH-han") is actually in the Burren, which you can't say about

Kinvara. Ballyvaughan is, however, lined with unpleasant rows of identical "holiday cottages." Needless to day, Ballyvaughan's pubs have a reputation for excellent trad sessions, especially since Doolin's crowds have scared trad musicians farther afield.

Prehistoric bears once inhabited the two-million-year-old **Aillwee Cave** (tel. (091) 77036 or 77067), two miles south of Ballyvaughan and over ¾ mile deep. You'll hear all about bears on the 30-minute tour, but you'll be gaping at spectacular rocks and waterfalls. The engineering required to open the cave to the public is almost as impressive as the geology itself. Be sure to look up when you get outside. (Open July-Aug. daily 10am-6:30pm; mid-March to early Nov. Mon.-Fri. 10am-5:30pm. £3.85, students £3.)

In town, the **Dállan Gallery** (tel. (065) 77156), located in the same building as the tourist office, is a more civilized attraction. An eclectic range of contemporary work from fabric paintings and metal work to witch dolls are on display (open May-Sept. daily 9am-6pm). One mile out of Ballyvaughan on N67 is the turnoff for **Newtown Castle and Trail** (tel. (065) 77200). The 16th-century home of the O'Loghlens, Princes of the Burren, has been restored. Ancient Clare manuscripts and Bardic Poetry recitals are seen on the hour-long **tour.** Another hour-long guided tour covers about ¾ mile and discusses the geology and archeology of the Burren. A Victorian folly "gazebo" (a children's miniature castle) and an 18th-century military waterworks system are both a part of the latter tour. (Open Easter to early Oct. daily 10am-6pm; castle or trail tour £2, both tours £3.50.)

The Burren Way leads down to the pier and **Monk's Pub** (tel. (065) 77059), which churns out seafood specialities (fishcakes with salad £4.50). Music abounds most nights in summer, Friday through Sunday in winter. Back in town, **Greene's** is a small card-playing locals' pub with an older crowd. The menu consists entirely of one daily special (about £5), but it's huge and available from noon to midnight. **O'Brien's** (tel. (065) 77003) has a younger, louder, and livelier crowd and music four nights a week in the summer (weekends in winter). The food is good, cheap, and plentiful (smoked salmon platter £3; food served noon-8:30pm). **The Tea Junction Café** (tel. (065) 77174) tempts you to ruin your appetite with Marianne's famous chocolate cake (£1.25). Marianne will also provide breakfast and take-away. She even remembers the vegetarians among us (vegetable and bean chili pita pocket £3; open mid-March to Oct. Tues.-Sun. 10am-6pm). **Spar Supermarket** (tel. (065) 77077) can sell you fresh bread from their bakery (open June-Aug. daily 8:30am-9pm; Sept.-May daily 9:30am-8pm). There's no hostel in Ballyvaughan, but B&B is available at **Gentian Villa** (tel. (065) 77042), on the main road on the Kinvara side of town, where all rooms have a bath (£14/person; open Easter-Oct.). Monk's Pub provides Raleigh **bike hire** (£7/day, £30/week). A **tourist office** (tel. (065) 77105) sits just off the main road on the Lisdoonvarna side of town (open June to mid-Oct. daily 9am-8:30pm).

If you insist on a hostel, take the scenic journey to **Fanore,** eight miles west of Ballyvaughan on R477 after Black Head. The small **Bridge Hostel** (tel. (065) 76134), on the banks of the river just up from the bridge on the main road, has panache, an open fire, and lovely showers. Graham and Frances can help you plot your path around the area so as not to miss the good stuff. (Dorm £5.50, private room £7; **camping** £3/person.) Homemade brown bread (£1.20) and evening meals sometimes (about £3.50). Open March-Oct.

County Galway

Lots of people visit both Galway City and the terrain to its west, but they do so for disparate reasons. The city is the world headquarters of *craic,* especially during its many festivals. Land west of Galway, on the other hand, offers peaceful, rugged scenery at its best. Clifden has thriving nightlife; Inishbofin has that as well as a rugged life. Cong, a popular hamlet just over the Mayo border (we cover it under Co. Galway), has grassy natural attractions and stony ruined ones. Avoid east Co. Galway: Ballinasloe may excite farmers, but even the cows wouldn't recommend it.

■■■ GALWAY CITY

Galway City is fit to burst (with crowds) during the spring and summer. The crowds of *craic*-seekers, along with students and hard-working residents, congest the cobblestone lanes at midday. But by late afternoon, most people have already chosen a pub to patronize for the evening. An oligarchy of 14 families of Welsh descent (the "Tribes of Galway") ruled the region until the late 18th century and grew rich from trade with Spain. Under their direction, Galway became the three-way intersection connecting the fertile inland districts to the ships of the European maritime trade and to Connemara. Galway's popular university, its relative wealth, and its proximity to the Connemara *gaeltacht* make it a likely place to find literary and theater culture in both of Ireland's languages. But by no means does "high" culture dominate the town. People here speak of poems over a pint or see plays in a pub. Above all else, Galway is a social city full of energy found in pubs as well as theaters.

ORIENTATION & PRACTICAL INFORMATION

Any transport to Galway will deposit you in **Eyre Square,** a central block of lawn and monuments with the train and bus station on its east side. A string of lonely B&Bs beg for business northeast of the square along Prospect Hill. The real town, or the part you'll want to visit, spreads out south and west of the square. Williams St. descends southwest into the cobblestone area around High St., Shop St., and Quay St.: Galway's "Left Bank," where most of the food and the pubs are concentrated. A bridge leads over the River Corrib and past Nuns' Island to Dominick St., where hostels and pubs compete. From there, both a path and a road stretch past the quays for a mile or two to Salthill's bayfront arcades. After passing the cathedral, Abbeygate St. becomes University Rd., so called because it passes University College Galway. Suburban Renmare, one mile east of the center, slumbers peacefully by its bird sanctuary. To reach it from the station, follow the path next to the railway tracks.

City buses costing 60p leave from Eyre Sq. at 20-minute intervals. Buses roll to each area of the city: #1 to Salthill, #2 to Knocknacarra (west) or Renmare (east), #3 to Castlepark, and #4 to Newcastle and Rahoon. (Service runs Mon.-Sat. 8am-9pm, Sun. 11am-9pm.) Or walk—it's good for you (just like Guinness). Hitchhikers abound in Galway. Dozens at a time wait on Dublin Rd. (N6), scouting rides to Dublin, Limerick, or Kinvara. Most catch bus #2, 5, or 6 from Eyre Sq. to this prime thumb-stop. University Rd. leads drivers to Oughterard and Clifden via N59.

> **Tourist Office:** Victoria Pl. (tel. 563081), just over one block southeast of Eyre Sq. Information on ferries and planes to the Arans make the usual pamphlet mania more exciting than ever. Open July-Aug. daily 8:30am-7:30pm; Easter-July and Sept.-Oct. Mon.-Sat. 9am-5:45pm, Sun. 9am-12:45pm; Nov.-March Mon.-Fri. 9am-5:45pm, Sat. 9am-12:45pm. **Salthill office** (same phone), visible from the main beach. Open June to mid-Sept. daily 9am-5:45pm; July-Aug. 9am-8:30pm.
>
> **USIT (Student Travel):** Kinlay House, Victoria Place, Eyre Sq. (tel. 565177), across the street from the tourist office. Offers the usual student discounts and sells *Let's Go.* Open June-Aug. Mon.-Fri. 9:30am-5:30pm, Sat. 11am-1pm and 1:30-4pm; Sept.-May Mon.-Fri 9:30am-5:30pm, Sat. 11am-2pm.
>
> **Banks: Bank of Ireland,** 19 Eyre Sq. (tel. 63181). Open Mon.-Wed. and Fri. 10am-3pm, Thurs. 10am-5pm; **ATM. AIB,** Lynch's Castle, Shop St. (tel. 67041). Exactly the same hours; **ATM.** Salthill: **Bank of Ireland** (tel. 22455). Open Mon.-Wed. and Fri. 10am-4pm, Thurs. 10am-5pm; **ATM.**
>
> **American Express:** John Ryan's Travel, 1 Williamsgate (tel. 67375). Client mail held. Open Mon.-Fri. 9:15am-5:30pm, Sat. 10am-1pm and 2:15-4pm.
>
> **Post Office:** Eglinton St. (tel. 62051). Open Mon.-Sat. 9am-6pm. Expect long lines.

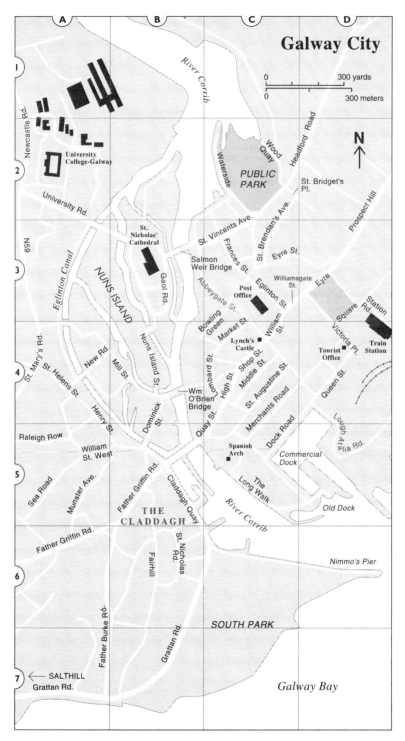

Galway City

Phone Code: 091.

Galway Airport: tel. 75569, in Carnmore.

Trains: Eyre Sq. (tel. 61444). Open Mon.-Sat. 7:40am-6pm. Trains to: Athlone (6/day, Sun. 3/day; 1hr.; £7, students £6) continue to Dublin (3hr.; £13, students £9); transfer at Athlone for all other lines. **Irish Rail/Iarnród Éireann office:** (tel. 64244 or 61444). Open Mon.-Fri. 9am-5:30pm.

Buses: (tel. 62000). Open daily 8am-8:30pm; Sept.-June Mon.-Sat. 8am-6pm. **Bus Éireann** runs regularly Mon.-Sat., less frequently on Sun. Buses depart Eyre Sq. for: Athlone (11/day, Sun. 9/day; £7, students £5.30), Ballina (6/day, Sun. 2/day; £9.70, students £6), Belfast (2-3/day, Sun. 1/day; £16.90, students £12.10), Clifden (June-Sept. Mon.-Sat. 6/day, Sun. 2/day; Oct.-May Mon.-Sat. 2/day, Sun. 1/day; £7, students £5), Cork (daily 5/day; £12, students £7.60), Doolin (June-Sept. 3/day; Sun. 1/day; Oct.-May 1/day; £8.20, students £4.60), Dublin (8-9/day, Sun. 7-8/day; £8, students £6.50), Ennis (8/day, Sun. 6/day; £7.30, students £4.30), Limerick (7/day, Sun. 6/day; £9, students £5.30), Rosslare (3/day; £16, students £9.50), Shannon Airport (5/day, Sun. 3/day; £9, students £5.30), Sligo (5/day, Sun. 3/day; £10.50, students £6.50), and Westport (5-7/day, Sun. 1/day; £8.80, students £5). Private bus companies specialize in the Dublin-Galway run. **P. Nestor Coaches** (tel. 97144; Mon.-Thurs. and Sun. 2/day, Fri. 4/day, Sat. 5/day; £5 single or day return, £8 open return; leaves from Imperial Hotel, Eyre Sq.) and **Citylink** (tel. 64163; Mon.-Thurs. and Sat.-Sun. 2/day. Fri. 3/day; same prices as Nestor's; leaves from Supermac's in Eyre Sq.) both trip back and forth between Galway and Dublin. A **West Clare Shuttle** to Doolin, Lisdoonvarna, and Fanore leaves various Galway hostels on request (June-Sept. daily 1/day; £5). Bus tours of Connemara also available (see Connemara, p. 282).

Luggage Storage: in the train station. Backpacks and large bags £2/day, other bags £1/day. Open Mon.-Sat. 7:30am-10pm, Sun. 11am-7pm.

Taxis: Big O Taxis, 21 Upper Dominick St. (tel. 586166). **Rice Edward,** 12 Oaklands, Salthill (tel. 22860). **Galway Taxis,** (tel. 61111), 7 Mainguard St., around the corner from McSwiggan's Pub; 24-hr. service. **Hackneys: MGM** (tel. 757888), **Claddagh** (tel. 589000), **Moycullen** (tel. 85818; 24 hrs.). Call to book; flat rate within city, by the mile outside.

Car Rental: Budget Rent-a-Car, Eyre Sq. (tel. 66376).

Bike Rental: Europa Cycles, Hunter Buildings, Earls Island (tel. 563355), opposite the cathedral. £3/day, £5/24hrs., £25/week; deposit £30. Open Mon.-Sat. 9am-6pm, Sun. 10am-2pm and 4-6pm. **Celtic Cycles,** Queen St., Victoria Place (tel. 566606), next to the Celtic Hostel. £7/day, £30/week; deposit £40 or ID; remote dropoff charge £12. Open daily 9am-6pm.

Camping Equipment: River Deep Mountain High, Middle St. (tel. 563938). Open Mon.-Sat. 9:30am-6pm.

Bookstores: Eason & Son, Ltd., 33 Shop St. (tel. 562284). Huge selection and specials on Irish literature. Open Mon.-Thurs. 9am-6:15pm, Fri.-Sat. 9am-8:45pm.

Laundry: The Bubbles Inn, 18 Mary St. (tel. 63434). Wash and dry £4; last wash 4:30pm; open Mon.-Sat. 8:45am-6:15pm. **Prospect Hill Launderette,** Prospect Hill (tel. 568343). Wash and dry £4; open Mon.-Sat. 7:30am-7pm.

Youth Information Centre: Ozanam House, St. Augustine St. (tel. 562434). Open Mon.-Fri. 9am-5pm. Also an AIDS resource center.

Bisexual, Gay, and Lesbian Information: P.O. Box 45 (tel. 566134). Lesbian line open Wed. 8-10pm; gay line open Tues. and Thurs. 8-10pm. "Call for information on basketball, videos, discussion groups."

Rape Crisis Centre: 3 St. Augustine St. (tel. (1 800) 355355).

Hotline: Samaritans, 14 Nun's Island (tel. 561222). 24-hr. phones.

Pharmacies: Commins, Shop St. (tel. 562924). Open Mon.-Sat. 9am-6pm. **Really's,** 17 William St. (tel. 62332). Open Mon.-Fri. 9am-9pm.

Hospital: University College Hospital, Newcastle Rd. (tel. 524222).

Emergency: Dial 999; no coins required. **Garda:** Mill St. (tel. 563161).

ACCOMMODATIONS

Over the last two years the number of hostels in Galway has almost tripled. Nevertheless, during weekends and big festivals, finding a pleasant bed can be extremely difficult. Reserve hostel beds or pay the steep price during Galway Arts Week (mid-July) and the Galway Races (late July to early Aug.). Try to arrive in town before 5pm if you can't make reservations in advance. Despite all the competition, Galway's truly excellent hostels are few and far between. It's always a good idea to see the rooms before you decide to stay. **Woodquay** hostels cluster about five minutes from Eyre Sq. around the Salmon Weir. **Dominick St.** hosts its own fleet on the west side of the River Corrib, and **Eyre Sq.** hostels are closest to the bus and train stations. B&Bs should set you back from £12-15 a night per person. Most of them, along with a few hostels, are in **Salthill**, a mile away. If you're a club-goer, give some thought to staying in Salthill, as the majority of post-midnight nightlife is there. (If you get into town late, you may be forced to stay in Salthill anyway.) **Renmare** is a sedate Galway suburb with a few B&Bs of its own.

Hostels & Camping

Galway

Salmon Weir Hostel, St. Vincent's Ave., Woodquay (tel. 61133). Turn right onto St. Vincent's Ave. off Francis St. (formerly Eglinton St. in Eyre Sq.). Galway's best hostel. One-night visitors beset with "Weir Syndrome" become week-long guests. Videos, pubcrawls, BBQs, and friendly folk turn any trip into a treat. Clean and truly comfortable townhouse. Free tea, coffee, washing powder, and peace of mind. Curfew 3am. Laundry £4. June-Aug. 4- or 6-bed dorm £6.90, double £9/person; May £6.50 and £8.50 respectively; Sept.-April £5.90 and £7.50.

The Westend (formerly Owen's Hostel), Upper Dominick St. (tel. 583636), across from the Arch View Hostel. Artsy, creative travelers in flannel shirts or flowery skirts enjoy storytelling, jugglers, and musicians in an unbelievably mellow atmosphere (bordering on unconsciousness). Fall into bed just seconds away from Monroe's and Roisín Dubh pubs. Old house with creaking floorboards (best when barefoot) and free tea and coffee. Curfew 3am; laundry £3-5. July-Aug. dorm £7, private room £10/person; Sept.-June dorm £5.50, private room £8/person.

Quay Street Hostel (IHH), Quay St. (tel. 568644 or 561094). Shop St. becomes Quay St. Uncrowded bunkrooms, some with skylights, and an unbeatable location in the city center. Open fire in common room. Laundry £3.50. July-Aug. dorm £7, 6-bed room £8, 4-bed room £8.50, w/bath £10, double w/bath £11.50. June-Sept. dorm £6.90, 6-bed room £7.50, 4-bed room £8, w/bath £9, double w/bath £11.50. Visa, MC accepted.

Kinlay House, Merchants Rd. (tel. 65244), across from the tourist office. Brand new, spotless, and friendly. Washcloths, bars of soap, blue duvets, and closet space in airy, uncrowded rooms resemble real luxury. Awesome medieval mural in dining room. 24-hr. computerized reception. Free continental breakfast. Bureau de change. Laundry £4. 6-bed room £7; 4-bed room £10.50, w/bath £11.50; double £12.50, w/bath £13; single £17. Oct.-June £7, £9.50, £10.50, £12, £12.50, £16.50, respectively. 10% discount with ISIC.

Great Western House, Eyre Sq. (tel. 61150), across from bus and train station. Massive, 250-bed complex. Clean and hotel-like with friendly staff. Pool table and sauna are big draws. Towel warmers in smaller rooms make you feel like (toasty) royalty after a shower. 24-hr. reception; laundry £5; bikes £6/day; bureau de change; free continental breakfast. July-Sept. 8- or 10-bed dorm £7.50, 4-bed room w/bath £11.50, double w/bath £14. March-June and Oct. £7, £10.50, £13 respectively. Nov.-Feb. £6.50, £9.50, £12 respectively.

The Galway Hostel, Eyre Sq. (tel. 566959), next door. Soft yellow walls and attractive, airy rooms (some with balconies) which look out onto Eyre Sq. Chinese floor tiles, super-clean bathrooms, heaters in rooms. For 80 beds the kitchen is way too small. Discounted laundry nearby, £3 per load. 8- to 14-bed dorm £6.90; 4-bed dorm £7.50, w/bath £9.50/person; double w/bath £10.50/person.

Celtic Tourist Hostel, Queen St., Victoria Pl. (tel. 586606 or 521559 at night), around the corner from the tourist office. Sit back, relax, and look out the big windows in the sitting room. Big kitchen. Large yet cramped dorms. Microwave and VCR. Laundry expected for 1996. Raleigh bike depot. Sheets £1. July-Aug. dorm £6.90, private room £9.90; Sept.-June dorm £5, private room £7.60.

Corrib Villa (IHH), 4 Waterside (tel. 62892). Just past the courthouse, about 4 blocks from Eyre Sq. down Eglinton St. Spacious, old Georgian house is rumored to get a little chilly when the weather turns poor. Curfew 3am. July to mid-Sept. £6; mid-Sept. to June £5.

Woodquay Hostel, Woodquay (tel. 62618). Yellow and red paint brightens bunks. Tunnel-like hallways. The rooms are satisfactory, if unexciting. Laundry £4, sheets £1. Breakfast available July-Aug. (scrambled eggs on toast £1.50). July-Aug. dorm £6.50, w/bath £6.90, private room £7.50. Sept.-June dorm £5.90, w/bath £6.50, private room £6.50.

Salthill

The Grand Holiday Hostel (IHH), Promenade (tel. 21150). Bus #1 from Eyre Sq. runs here. Once a hotel, always well-vacuumed. Fresh and tidy rooms overlooking the sea substitute for rose-colored glasses. Currency exchange. Bikes £6/day. Laundry £3; sheets 50p. July-Aug. dorm £6.50, double £9; Sept.-June dorm £5.50, double £8. **Strawberry Fields Café** (tel. 26919), on the ground floor, serves American food (breakfast £2.50; open 7am-10:30pm).

Stella Maris (IHH), 151 Upper Salthill (tel. 21950). Bus #1 from Eyre Sq. Mega-blue hallway, reminiscent of the sea, leads to 3- or 6-bed rooms. Large common room looks out onto the real sea. Staff on duty 24 hrs. Sheets 50p. June-Aug. dorm £6.50, twin £7.50, double £8.50; Sept.-May £5.50, £6.50, £7.50 respectively.

Camping: Salthill Caravan and Camping Park (tel. 22479). On the bay, ½ mi. west of Salthill. Crowded in summer. £2.50-3/hiker or cyclist. Open April-Sept.

Bed & Breakfasts

St. Martin's, 2 Nuns Island (tel. 68286), on the west bank of the river at the end of Dominick St. (visible from the Bridge St. bridge). Gorgeous riverside location with a grassy lawn, right in the city center. A mere £12.50/person.

Brasstacks, Diana Walsh, 3 St. Helen's Street (tel. 24728). Off Newcastle Rd., a 10-min. walk. Henry St. (right from the end of Dominick St.) becomes St. Helen's St. In a word, amicable. £12.50/person.

Mary Ryan's, 4 Beechmount Rd. (tel. 23303), in Highfield Park, 20 min. from Galway. Bus #2 from Eyre Sq. to Taylor's Hill Convent will take you there. A respectable B&B at hostel prices that fills up fast. £6/person; open June-Sept.

Grianan, Mrs. S. O'Kelly, 12 Glenard Ave., Salthill (tel. 22151), off Dr. Mannix Rd. Bus #1 from Eyre Sq. is fastest. Kind Mrs. O'Kelly treats you to all the comfort of a soft and cushy B&B for almost half the normal price. Single £8 w/continental breakfast. Double £13 w/Irish breakfast.

FOOD

Because Galway is full of students in winter, there are plenty of excellent cheap eats. Because Galway is full of tourists in summer, there are also a fair number of second-rate rip-offs. Stick east of the river and near the short blocks around Quay St., High St., Shop St., and Abbeygate St. for good values. **Roches Stores,** Eyre St. (tel. 61211), is a department store and cheap supermarket economically rolled into one (open Mon.-Thurs. and Sat. 9am-5:30pm, Fri. 9am-9pm). **Evergreen Health Food,** 1 Mainguard St. (tel. 64215), offers food from its shelves as well as from a menu (open Mon.-Thurs. and Sat. 9am-6:30pm, Fri. 9am-8pm). Two other stores, **Healthwise** (tel. 68761) and **Honeycomb Health** (tel. 68995), are both on Abbeygate St. On Saturdays, a **market** (8am-1pm) sets up in front of St. Nicholas Church on Market St. Fishers may wander through the pubs all evening, selling cups of fresh mussels (around £1) and other shellfish from the bay. Buy. Eat. Go completely nuts.

The Home Plate, Mary St. (tel. 61475). Expect a wait between noon and 3pm, when the whole city lines up to bat. Colossal servings even include a beverage for washing down big mouthfuls. Some take-away available. Vegetarian fajita £2.90, BIG sandwiches £2. Open Mon.-Sat. 10am-8pm.

McDonagh's, 22 Quay St. (tel. 65001). Quite possibly the best chippy in the world. Certificates, newspaper clippings, and magazine articles line the wall to prove it.

The pride and joy of the collection is an official recognition from the former Soviet fleet naming this the best chipper at any port of call. Especially crowded after the pubs close. Cod fillet and chips £3.10. Open Mon.-Sat. noon-midnight, Sun. noon-11pm. Restaurant (open daily noon-11pm) is pricier than take-away.

The Couch Potatas, Upper Abbeygate St. (tel. 61664). A good potato can't be beat (or mashed in this joint). "Hawaii 5-0" is a baked potato with ham, cheese, pineapple, and onion (£3.50). The "Pavoratti" adds meatballs and cheese to the basic potato (£3.50). Spuds & butter £1. Crowded at lunchtime with all types. Open Mon.-Sat. noon-10pm, Sun. 1-10pm.

Java's, Upper Abbeygate St. (tel. 67400). A carbon copy of the great Seattle coffee-house, even to the stamped cards that give every 10th drink free. The lack of orig-inality doesn't bother Galway's disaffected, somber-eyed youth. They sit here for hours in the afternoon, reading and smoking, smoking and talking. After mid-night, loud, drunken intellectuals drive the sober ones to seek solitude elsewhere. 34 varieties of coffee (90p), 27 of tea (70p). Salad and sandwiches of fewer variet-ies. Open Mon.-Sat. 9am-4am, Sun. noon-4am.

Scotty's Casual Gourmet, 1 Middle St. (tel. 66400). The upstairs deli prepares foot-long subs and fresh salads. Tuna sub £2.25. Open Mon.-Sat. 7:30am-5:30pm.

Le Café de Paris, Cross St. Two-level café and creperie attempts a *français* atmo-sphere. Croissants 45p, omelette with salad and brown bread £1.20. An adjoining bakery also offers sandwiches. Open Mon.-Sat. 8am-9pm, Sun. 10am-9pm.

Food for Thought, Lower Abbeygate St. (tel. 65854). Coffeeshop and wholefood restaurant serves perplexing vegetarian dishes (£2.25) and mind-bogglingly big sandwiches from £1.10. Scones 45p. Open Mon.-Fri. 8am-7pm, Sat. 8am-6pm.

The Runner Bean, Mary St. (tel. 569292). Surrounds every meal of the day with a lemon-colored casual setting. House special breakfast £1.95, seafood chowder with baguette £1.95. Open daily 9am-11pm (breakfast served 9am-noon).

Fat Freddy's, Quay St. (tel. 67279). Everyone under 25 goes here. And since every-one in Galway is under 25, it's always ridiculously crowded. Eccentric mix of Ital-ian dishes and chowder. Large cheese pizza £4.60. Open daily noon-10:30pm.

Nimmo's Restaurant and Winebar, (tel. 563565), above the antique shop by the Spanish Arch. Intimate room with Persian carpets for tablecloths. Arrive early to be seated for dinner. Ritzy, but moderately priced, daily specials like salmon in herb sauce (£5.50). Open Tues.-Sun. 12:30-3pm and 7-11pm.

PUBS

Half the businesses in downtown Galway seem to be pubs. There is an average of five on every block, so there's no excuse for stopping and staying in one that doesn't suit you. Fabulous, fast-paced traditional music usually blazes from several pubs each night. Unfortunately, second-rate musicians exist alongside the good ones. Good and bad versions of rock, guitar-folk, country, blues, and metal also rear their heads. The most talked-about pubs congregate on Dominick St. and Quay St.

The Quays, Quay St. (tel. 68347). Popular with everyone under 25, including large numbers of scamming yuppies and Americans. The massive, multi-floored interior was built with carved wood taken from the balconies and stained glass windows of an old church. Fabulous atmosphere is a bit forced, but good *craic* is generally guaranteed. It's worth a visit simply to see the curious interior.

McSwiggan's, 3 Eyre St., Woodquay (tel. 68917), around the corner from Eddie Rockett's. Just as popular with twentysomethings as The Quays. Dark, worn-wood interior with paneled glass. The back of the bar is forever hidden behind unnumbered corners and crannies. The bog-preserved tree need only be men-tioned for tourists to flock. Good restaurant upstairs. Trad Sat.-Sun. nights.

The King's Head, High St. (tel. 566630), continue down Shop St. Crazy student hangout. Most people who drink here are under 21. All kinds of music nightly. Lunchtime theater Mon.-Sat. 1-2pm, £2. Popular Sun. brunch jazz 12:45-2:15pm.

Roisín Dubh, Dominick St., (tel. 66540), "The Black Rose." Old bicycles and dead branches on the walls. Set dancing Tues. nights, trad Mon.-Tues., rock Wed.-Thurs., folk Fri.-Sat.

Seaghan Ua Neachtain (a.k.a. Knockton's), Quay St. (tel. 68820). A dark maze of secret nooks and fireplaces. Mixed crowd interested primarily in the good trad which blares out every Mon., Wed., and Fri.-Sat.

Busker Browne's, Cross St. (tel. 563377), next to Knockton's. Huge. 3 bars and 4 floors. The top one is a medieval banquet hall lined with long tables. Be careful not to get so spirited that you throw your bones on the rushes.

Monroe's, Dominick St. (tel. 63397). Home to the alternative nation. Dark and scary cave-like interior serves as a refuge for bandannas, long hair, pierced body parts, and dreadlocks. Wear black. Live, loud bands nightly.

Taaffe's, Shop St. (tel. 64066). Everyone from tweed-capped men to platform-shoed mods comes here to hear quality trad nightly (except Good Friday). Barman claims that there is "no useless bric-a-brac to distract from the job of drinking here," but the unabashedly green walls aren't necessarily aids to concentration.

The Cellar Bar, Eglinton St. (tel. 563966). Your source for music. Nightly trad and ballads upstairs, live bands downstairs (9pm).

Waterfront, Ravens Terrace, off Dominick St. Gay friendly.

The Lisheen, 5 Bridge St. (tel. 563804). Outstanding and ceaseless trad nightly and Sunday morning. You'll easily forget your hangover. Musicians welcome.

SIGHTS

The commercial and cultural Galway overshadows its historic aspects. The tourist office sells the *Medieval Galway Map,* which isn't worth £3.50, and simply gives away the *Junior Chamber Galway Tourist Guide,* whose price reflects its value.

Galway's **Catholic Cathedral,** officially known as the "Cathedral of Our Lady Assumed into Heaven and St. Nicholas," looms above the Salmon Weir Bridge. It's located across the river from most of the city, where Gaol Rd. and University Rd. meet. The 25-year-old domed structure was severely criticized for its eclectic design. The boring outside reveals no hints about the controversy. The impressive inside, where circles of Connemara marble intersect with elaborate mosaics, was the main subject of debate. The inside walls of the dome depict the stations of the cross. (Excellent tours and mood-setting organ practice, Mon.-Fri. 3:30-5:30pm; also open Sun. for masses.) Closer to the center of town near the Church of St. Nicholas, the tiny **Nora Barnacle House,** 8 Bowling Green (tel. 64743), exposes a few letters and photos relating to James Joyce and his wife. Joyce visited the house in 1909 and 1912. Nora reputedly inspired much of his writing, including a short story, *The Dead,* which was based on a love affair she once had. The table where Joyce composed a few lines to Nora draws the admiration of Joyce addicts. (Open mid-May to mid-Sept. Mon-Sat. 10am-1pm and 2-5pm; £1.)

Shop St. runs past **Lynch's Castle,** an elegant stone mansion with incongruous gargoyles that dates from the early 16th century. The Lynch family ruled Galway from the 13th to the 18th centuries. Exhibits inside the edifice analyze the castle's architecture and heraldry and relate a family legend. In the late 1400s, Lynch junior killed a Spaniard whom he suspected of liking his girlfriend. The son, sentenced to hang, was so beloved by the populace that not one man would agree to be the hangman. Lynch senior, the lord of the castle, was so determined to administer justice that he had to hang his own son. The window from which junior supposedly was hanged is that behind St. Nicholas Church. A skull and crossbones designed into the glass remembers the just deed. The castle now houses the Allied Irish Bank (bank and exhibits open Mon.-Wed. and Fri. 10am-3pm, Thurs. 10am-5pm; free).

Many Lynches lie together in their family tomb in the **Church of St. Nicholas,** Market St., behind the castle. The church, strangely full of oddities from a wide range of sources, devotes some of its attention to a heritage project. Columbus stopped to pray here before going off to meet the American Indians; a stone marks the spot. Glorious stained glass and relics from the Connacht Rangers provide more distractions for short attention spans. Unnecessary tours cost £1.50, students £1. (Open May-Sept. daily 9am-5:45pm; free.)

By the river, the Long Walk makes a pleasant stroll which will bring you to the **Spanish Arch,** the only surviving gateway to the old trading town. Built in 1584 as a defensive bastion for the port, the Arch is more famous than it is impressive. Yet this worn, one-story stone curve is revered by townspeople. The **Galway City Museum** (tel. 67641), in Tower House next to the arch, can show you up the stairs to the top of the arch. A knife-sharpener by a peat fire and some fishy statistics next to the big one that didn't get away in 1918 are the highlights of this small museum. Intriguing old photographs of the Claddagh line the walls and could occupy you for hours. (Open May-Oct. daily 10am-1pm and 2:15-5:15pm; for opening times Nov.-April, check at the tourist office; 60p.)

Across the river, the neighborhood called the **Claddagh** centers itself around Dominick St. Until the 1930s, this area was an independent, Irish-speaking, thatched-cottage fishing village. The cottages have long ago been replaced by stone bungalows, but a bit of the small-town appeal and atmosphere still persist. The famous Claddagh rings, traditionally used as wedding bands, are mass-marketed but still remarkable examples of Celtic metalworking. The rings depict the thumb and forefingers of two hands holding up a heart. The ring should be turned around upon marriage: once the crown faces inward, the wearer's heart is attached and no longer available for viewing.

From the Claddagh, the waterfront road leads west to Salthill. The coast here alternates between pebbles and sand, curious to see and fun to play in, and an ocean sunset should not be passed up. The **Corrib Princess** sails from Galway's Woodquay on a guided tour of Lough Corrib to the north (tel. 592447; June-Aug. daily 2:30pm and 4:30pm; 90 min.; £5). Energetic types can hire a rowboat to visit the ruins of **Menlo Castle,** the burned-down seat of the Blake family. Anyone lucky enough to see the sun in Galway can't resist **Salthill** where sandy beaches flirt with discos.

ENTERTAINMENT

Culture crowds into Galway itself; music of all varieties barrages Salthill's clubs. *The Advertiser* and *Galway Guide* are free and provide listings of events. The **Galway Arts Centre,** 47 Dominick St. (tel. 65886), may be able to inform you (open Mon.-Sat. 10am-5:30pm). The center also hosts rotating art or photography exhibits and frequent workshops on dance, writing, and painting.

The **Druid Theatre Company,** Chapel Lane (tel. 68617), off Quay St., produces four Irish-themed plays each year (box office open Mon.-Sat. noon-6pm, until 8pm on show nights; tickets £7, students £5; buy tickets at least a week in advance). **The Punchbag Theatre,** Quay Lane. (tel. 565422), tops the Druids by staging five shows a year, both contemporary and traditional—but always Irish (box office open Mon.-Fri. noon-6pm; £8, students £6). For a pint with your play, try **Taylor's Pub,** Upper Dominick St. (£3.50, including lunch) or the **King's Head,** High St. (tel. 66630, 1-2pm, £2). The mostly Irish-language theater **an Taibhdhearc** ("TIVE-yark"), Middle St. (tel. 62024), has launched quite a few Irish actors into the limelight. Poetry readings and other artsy events share the space with full-blown plays. Some shows are bilingual, giving non-speakers a lyrical earful of Irish language and drama (box office open Mon.-Fri. 10am-6pm, Sat. 2-6pm; £7, student £5). Along different lines, the Omniplex 7-screen **cinema** (tel. 67800) is five minutes from town on the Headford Rd. and shows the usual mainstream flicks.

Between 11pm and midnight, the pubs empty out in Galway proper. The tireless then decide to go dancing. The **nightclub** population is denser in Salthill, but Galway can satisfy the immobile. In the center of town, **Central Park,** 32 Upper Abbeygate St. (cover £4), and **GPO,** Eglinton St. (tel. 563073), both throw crowds into a tizzy. GPO reserves Friday nights for comedy and Sunday for Funky Jazz.

Groups will find a hackney service the best way to get to Salthill. The walk along the waterfront takes about 20-35 minutes, but is not recommended after dark. Salthill's biggest nights are Wednesday, Friday, and Saturday. Those who go on other nights will find the clubs more or less empty. All the clubs charge a £3-6 cover for a sweaty night inside dripping walls; those listed here all lie on Upper Salthill, the main road. A major hot spot, **C.J.'s,** 143 Upper Salthill (tel. 22563), rocks to pop. **The Castle** (tel. 255083) is famous (or infamous) for its raves (cover £4). **The War-**

wick plays alternative or blues. The crowd and the music selection are both mixed at **The Oasis Club,** Kings Hill (tel. 22715; cover weekdays £2, weekends £3). Only for the adventurous, **Vagabonds** branches out with theme nights, including Irish-only bands, techno, and rave (cover £3.50). **Feet First** bounces to hip-hop on Wednesday nights at Vagabonds. Sundays bring a gay disco to **Liberation.** Night-clubs all open between 10 and 11pm, but don't expect them to get going until 11:30pm. Either way, clubbers lose: they can enjoy the pubs and stand in line, or skip the pub only to find the discos empty. The action stops early, at 2am in summer, 1:30am in winter.

Festivals knock at Galway's door at the rate of about one major event every month. At the **Galway Poetry and Literature Festival,** or the **Cúirt** (tel. 65886), the very highest of the nation's brows gather together in the last week of April. Past guests have included Nobel prize-winner and Caribbean poet Derek Walcott and reggae star Linton Johnston. For twelve crazed days in mid-July the **Galway Arts Festival** (tel. 583800)—the largest of its kind in Ireland—reels in famous trad musicians, rock groups, theater troupes, filmmakers and comedians. Last year, Michelle Shocked and a 10-piece Japanese drum orchestra turned heads (in different directions). The highlight of the Festival is a colorful and joyous **Macnas Parade.** The town is packed to overflowing for the festival, so be sure to reserve a bed. The same is true of the famous **Galway Races,** which commence at the end of July or beginning of August and last for one week. Those attending the races celebrate horses, money, and stout, not necessarily in that order (tel. 753870; tickets £2 at the gate).

■ NEAR GALWAY

COOLE PARK

W. B. Yeats's two best-known residences are about twenty miles south of Galway near Gort, where N18 meets N66: one is now a ruin and national park, the other restored as it was when he lived there. One mile north of Gort on N18 (the Galway Rd.) and well before Ardrahan, **Coole Park** was Lady Augusta Gregory's estate. This friend and theatrical collaborator of Yeats welcomed him to her home many times. The estate was purchased by the Gregorys in 1768 and finally sold to the state in 1928. Lady Augusta Gregory, its last inhabitant, supposedly planted another tree on the grounds every time she was paid a fee or royalty for her writing. In the picnic area, the famous great copper beech "autograph tree" bears the initials of some of Ireland's most important literary figures: George Bernard Shaw, W.B. Yeats, Sean O'Casey, John Masefield, and Douglas Hyde, Gaelic League founder and first president of Ireland. Along with Yeats, Gregory, Synge, Douglas Hyde, Hugh Lane, and others gathered at Coole Park to rejuvenate Irish literature (see Much of Edgeworth's extensive body of mostly historical fiction was typical of its age. She began her career with ideas about the connection between moral worth and social position. Some of her stories reveal a subtle romantic preoccupation with the achievement of personal integrity through solitude. But her innovations and the anomalies in her writing add a twist to the writings of an author otherwise representative of her era. Edgeworth was a woman in the midst of men. She, with her family, moved to Ireland when most people went the other way (even her literature posits a westward flight). She also realized, as few at this time did, that there existed a British social reality, not entirely separable into England and Ireland. Finally, Maria Edgeworth paved the way for future literary journals by raising the question of a compromise between the modern and the antiquarian. This legacy, more than any other, substantially determined the concerns of later writers, including those of the Revival., p. 65). In Yeats's own work the estate stood for the beautiful aristocratic order to which the wars of the Twenties and the crass, materialistic industrialists were laying waste: "ancestral trees/Or gardens rich in memory glorified/Marriages, alliances and families/And every bride's ambition satisfied." The house itself was ruined by the 1922 Civil War; only the foundations are visible now. The yew walk and garden, however, are preserved as part of a national forest and wildlife park.

Coole Park's **Visitors Centre** (tel. (091) 31804) is in the right place, but it eschews Yeats in favor of local rocks, trees, and furry wildlife. (Open mid-April to mid-June Tues.-Sun. 10am-5pm; mid-June to Aug. daily 9:30am-6:30pm; Sept. daily 10am-5pm. Last admission 45 min. before closing. £2, students £1.) A mile from the garden, **Coole Lake** spreads out (always open; free). Yeats watched nine-and-fifty swans here "all suddenly mount/And scatter wheeling in great broken rings/Upon their clamorous wings." You can see them, too.

THOOR BALLYLEE

In 1916, Yeats bought and renovated a 13th- and 14th-century tower, **Thoor Ballylee.** Three miles north of Coole Park a road turns off Galway Rd. and runs ¾ mile down an unfrequented road to Thoor Ballylee. Yeats bought his poetic retreat from the government for £35. Major repair work still left the tower habitable only during the summer. The poet lived there with his family off and on from 1922, but abandoned the tower permanently after his health failed in 1928. While the poet was cloistered here writing "Meditations in Time of Civil War," Republican forces blew up the bridge by the tower. In Yeats's account, they "forbade us to leave the house, but were otherwise polite, even saying at last 'Good-night, thank you.'"

Yeats always assumed that after his descendants moved out, Thoor Ballylee would "become a roofless ruin that the owl/May build in the cracked masonry and cry/Her desolation to the desolate sky." The **Visitors Centre** (tel. (091) 31436) that now exists there was never in the plans. A film on Yeats's life and presentations in seven languages inform all visitors. The tower's current 1961 interior restores its look c.1926, the year Yeats wrote "The Tower." (Open Easter-Sept. 10am-6pm; £2.50, students £2.)

ARAN ISLANDS (OILEÁIN ÁRANN)

The three Aran Islands—Inishmore, Inishmaan and Inisheer—poke up out of Galway Bay 15 miles southwest of Galway City. Visitors are bewildered by the stark limestone landscapes that drop straight into the sea, prehistoric and historic ruins, and people whose traditions have attracted tremendous attention. Dublin-born writer John Millington Synge met with Yeats in 1894 looking for some creative criticism. Yeats told him to go to the Arans, learn Irish, and write plays about the islanders. Synge did, and became instantly famous (see Literature: 1880-1939, p. 65). Robert Flaherty's groundbreaking film *Man of Aran* (1934) added to the islands' fame. All this fame and the islands' reputation for harboring traditional ways of life have stimulated a somewhat mercenary tourist industry.

The flocks of high-season visitors to the Arans give residents of really isolated islands (like Inishbofin and Cape Clear) the willies. During July and August, throngs of curious foreigners surround every monument and pub on Inishmore. Luckily, the empty spaces between the sites (those not accessible by mini-bus) are still deserted. Tourists are rarer on the other two smaller islands than on Inishmore. The scenery remains awe-inspiring, regardless of the number of people who see it. The lifestyle also remains traditional: locals still make *curraghs* (small boats made from curved wicker rods tied with string and covered with cowskin and black tar). Some of them retain local styles of dress, footwear, and fishing, and many speak Irish.

If ferries in Galway gave you a headache, here they're twice the trouble. Double-check with fishermen to find out where and when the boats are coming. Luxurious tourist amenities don't exist, but on the plus side, you may be able to camp in a field for a small fee; be sure to ask the relevant farmer. (Don't be surprised if some irregularity in the planting or harvesting schedule renders all fields temporarily off-limits.) The **phone code** for all three islands is 099.

GETTING THERE

Three ferry companies—Aran Ferries, Island Ferries, and O'Brien Shipping/Doolin Ferries—operate boats to the Aran Islands. They use three points of departure—Galway, Rossaveal (several miles west of Galway), and Doolin—to get to the three islands. The majority of ferries float to Inishmore, the largest Aran Island. Fewer boats dock at Inisheer, the smallest island, and Inishmaan, the middle island, is hardest of all to reach. Boats from Galway City to Inishmore take 1½ hr.; boats from Rossaveal to Inishmore or from Doolin to Inisheer take only ½ hour. None of the ferry companies charges to bring **bicycles** on board.

If the ferry leaves from Rossaveal, the company making the trip will provide a shuttle bus from Galway City to Rossaveal, usually for £3. The hitch is difficult and chancy. On the other hand, a boat departing from Rossaveal will always wait at the Rossaveal pier, if necessary, for its own company's bus from Galway to arrive. The closest hostels to Rossaveal are in Inverin and Spiddal (see Galway City to Clifden, p. 283), but unless you have transport it's easiest to stay in Galway.

Ferries serving Inishmore are reliable (always leaving daily) and generally on time. Even in the summer, ferries to the smaller islands are less certain. And if they are running, they're liable to leave either port early or late. Don't get stuck the day before your flight for Idaho leaves. The best idea is to formulate firm travel plans and take them to the three ferry companies in Galway on a comparison-shopping spree.

Island Ferries (tel. (091) 61767, after hours (091) 72273), is based in the Galway Tourist Office. The *Aran Sea Bird* serves all three islands year-round from Rossaveal. A bus connects Galway with the ferry port (£3 return; departs 1½hr. before sailing time). Ferries leave from Rossaveal for: Inishmore (35min.; £12 return, students £10) and to Inishmaan or Inisheer (£18 return, students £16). The *Sea Sprinter* connects Inishmore with Inisheer via Inishmaan (£8 return per island). They also offer a package for students, which includes the bus from Galway, return ferry to Inishmore, one night's accommodation at the Mainistir House Hostel, and continental breakfast (£19).

Aran Ferries (tel. (091) 568903, after hours (091) 565352), is also based in the Galway Tourist Office. Sends ferries to Inishmore from Rossaveal (April-Oct.; 30 min.; £12 return, students £10). A connecting bus from Galway departs 1¼hr. before sailing time (£3 return). The *Aran Flyer* also journeys from Galway to Inishmore (June to mid-Sept.; 90 min.; £15 return, students £13).

O'Brien Shipping (tel. (091) 67283 or 61854), shares space in the Galway Tourist Office. Year-round service departs from Galway, goes to all three islands (for the same price), and returns to Galway (90min.; £15 return, students £12). Another service follows the same path but returns to Doolin (90 min. from Galway, 20 min. to Doolin; £20, students £18).

The Doolin Ferry Co. (tel. (065) 74455 after hours (065) 71710), has an office at The Pier in Doolin and a representative in the Galway Tourist office. Year round from Doolin to: Inisheer (£15 return, students £13), Inishmaan (£18 return, students £15), and Inishmore (£20 return, students £18). Inter-island trips £8 return.

Fly to the Arans, if you must, on **Aer Árann** (tel. (091) 93034), located 19 miles west of Galway at Inverin. Reservations are accepted over the phone or in person at the Galway Tourist Office. (All year 4/day; 6 min. to Inishmore, serves all three islands; £18, students £15; £35 return, students £29.)

■■■ INISHMORE (INIS MÓR)

Inishmore (pop. 900) is the largest and northernmost of the Aran Islands. Crowds disembark at Kilronan, spread out to lose themselves amid the stone walls and stark cliffs, and then coalesce again around any major sight. Minivans and "pony traps" traverse the island incessantly, begging anyone on foot to climb aboard and pay up. The landscape resembles that of the Burren in Co. Clare. Dozens of ruins, forts,

Aran Islands

Brannock Islands

Inishmore (Inis Mór)

Onaght (Eoghanacht)
The Seven Churches (Na Seacht d'Teampaill)
Clochán na Carraige
Dún Eoghanachta
Kilmurvy (Cill Mhuirbhigh)
Dún Aengus (Dún Aonghasa)
Blind Sound

Oatquarter

Teampall I Chiarain
Heritage Center (Ionad Arann)
Kilronan (Cill Rónáin)
Killeany Port
Killeany Bay
Killeany (Cill Éinne)
Temple Benan (Teampall Bheanáin)
Dún Dúchathair

Lighthouse
Straw Island
Dog's Head

Puffing Holes
Clinewalee Point

Museum (Múseam)
Port
Loch Mhuirbhigh
Loch Ceann Gainimh

Leaba Dhairmada 'is Ghráinne (Bed of Diarmuid and Brainne)
Baile an Mhothair
Trá Leitreach
An Córa
Cill Port Cheannannach

Gregory's Sound (Sunda Ghráin)
Synge's Chair (Cathaoir Synge)
Dún Chonchúir
Dún Fearbhai

Inishmaan (Inis Meáin)

An Sunda Salach

Cnoc Raithni
Baile an Chaisleáin
St. Kevin's Church (Teampall Chaomháin)
Formna
Plassy Wreck
Dún Formna
Cill na Seacht ninion

An Baile Thios
Baile an Lurgáin
Baile an tSéipéil
Tobar Éinne
Lighthouse

Inisheer (Inis Oirr)

South Sound (An Sunda ó Dheas)

Walking Trails

3 miles
3 kilometers
0

N ←

churches, and "minor sites" (holy wells and kelp kilns) inhabit the island. Exactly 437 kinds of wildflowers rise from the stony terrain.

Practical Information Ferries land in Kilronan (Cill Rónáin), where you couldn't possibly get lost. The **tourist office** (tel. 61263) changes money, holds bags during the day (75p), and sells Tim Robinson's meticulous and invaluable map (£3; open May to mid-Sept. daily 10am-7pm). Bikes are great for exploring island paths and can be rented at **Mullen's Aran Bicycle Hire** (tel. 61132; £5/day, £21/week; deposit £5; open March-Nov. daily 9am-8pm). **B&N Bicycle Hire** (tel. 61402) at the base of the Ti Joe Mac Bar/Hostel also rents bikes (£5/day, £20/week; deposit £5; open Feb.-Sept. daily 9am-7pm; Oct.-Jan. daily 9am-5pm). Strangely enough, bike theft here is a problem: lock it up, hide it, or don't ever leave it. **Minibuses** roam the island: flag them down for a ride (£5 return to Dún Aengus). The buses also offer organized two-hour tours of the island for about £5. The **post office** (tel. 61101; bureau de change; open Tues.-Sat. 9am-5pm, Mon. 9am-1pm) is up the hill from the pier, past the Spar Market. The **phone code** for all of the Arans is 099.

Accommodations It's not a bad idea to spend the day on Inishmore and the night in one of the less crowded hostels on the other islands. **Mainistir House (IHH)** (tel. 61169) offers decent hostel accommodations just ½ mile from Kilronan (from the pier, go uphill and turn right after the supermarket). Mainistir deserves its excellent reputation for huge "vaguely vegetarian" dinners (£7), and the common room is a comfortable space to settle after dinner. But the rooms are packed, especially during summer. (Dorm £7.50 w/morning porridge, scones, tea/coffee; double £20. Laundry £4; bikes £5.) By the harbor, the **Aran Islands Hostel** (tel. 61255) has a stone common room and large blue dorms which suffer slightly from the noisy pub next door and from infrequent staffing. The kitchen and common room are in a separate building across the street. (July-Aug. £6/person; April-June and Sept.-Oct. £5; open April-Oct.; laundry £3.) **Dún Aengus Hostel** (tel. 61255), is more personable, but hides 4 miles west in Kilmurvey, a 10-minute walk from Dún Aengus. (July-Aug. £6/person, at other times £5; shuttle service included; laundry £3.)

Bed down in style across the street from the ocean at Mrs. G. Tierney's ivy-covered **St. Brendan's House** (tel. 61149). (£12/person, £10 w/continental breakfast; Nov.-March £9.50 and £7.50; tea/coffee facilities in rooms). Across from the pier, **Bay View House** (tel. 61260) has everything you need under one roof (Feb. to mid-May £15/person; mid-May to mid-Nov. £16/person; restaurant and coffee shop downstairs). Three miles west of Kilronan, **Mrs. B. Conneely's Beach View House** (tel. 61141) lives up to its name and more. It also offers views of Dún Aengus and framed versions of the Alps (single £18, double £26; open May-Sept.). **Johnston Hernon's Kilmurvey House** (tel. 61218) offers ready access to Kilmurvey Beach, near Dún Aengus (single £16, double £26; open April-Sept.).

Food, Pubs, & Entertainment **Spar Market** (tel. 61203), past the hostel in Kilronan, seems to be the island's social center, too (open Mon.-Sat. 9am-8pm, Sun. 10am-7pm). Restaurants tend to be expensive and aren't open in winter. You may want to stick to tea houses, which serve homemade soups and snacks. **Bay View House** (tel. 61260) caters to every budget (open Feb.-Nov.: coffee shop daily 9am-6pm, restaurant daily 6-9pm). **An Seán Chéibh** (tel. 61228), an embellished chippy with outdoor seating, is a short walk left from the harbor (fresh Aran fish £2.50). (Open June-Sept. Mon.-Thurs. 9am-11pm, Fri.-Sun. 9am-1am; March-April and Oct. daily 9am-5pm; May daily 9am-9pm.) Pubs are a way of life here. **Joe Watt's Bar,** east of the harbor on the main road, offers food, music, and conversation to accompany thick pints. The **American Bar** (tel. 61303) attracts younger islanders and droves of tourists (music most nights in summer). Traditional musicians occasionally strum on the terrace at **Tí Joe Mac** (tel. 61248). On Friday, Saturday, and Sunday nights in summer, the first steps of a *ceilí* begin at midnight at the

dance hall (cover £3). If you haven't seen it already, **Man of Aran** is also shown here (summer 3/day; £3).

Sights The sights are crowded but the paths between them desolate and unmarked (most people travel by minibus). The tourist office's £3 maps correspond to yellow arrows that mark the trails, but markings are frustratingly infrequent and can vanish in fog. The trails themselves seem to disappear at times. Anyone exploring the island on foot should bring a compass. The £1.50 brochure called *Inis Mór* is helpful.

The island's most impressive (and best known) monument, dating from the first century BC, is magnificent **Dún Aengus** *(Dún Aonghasa)*, four miles west of the pier at Kilronan. The fort's walls are 18 feet thick and form a semi-circle around the sheer drop at Inishmore's northwest corner. One of the better-preserved prehistoric forts in Europe, Dún Aengus commands a thought-provoking view of miles of ocean from its hill. Many have been fooled by an imaginary island that appears on the horizon. The vision was so realistic that it appeared on maps until the 20th century. Down the side of the cliff, **Worm Hole** is a saltwater lake filled from the limestone aquifer below the ground. The bases of the surrounding cliffs have been hollowed by mighty waves to look like pirate caves. Two roads lead to the fort from Kilronan, one inland and the more quiet one along the coast. On the way to the fort past **Kilmurvey** (Cill Mhuirbhigh), **The Seven Churches** lie three miles west of Kilronan. These scattered groupings of religious remains stimulate speculation about the island's former inhabitants. The island's best **beach** lies flat at Kilmurvey.

In Kilronan, the new **Aran Islands Heritage Centre** *(Ionad Árann)* (tel. 61355) caters to inquisitive tourists who walk uphill from the pier. *Curraghs,* soil and wildlife exhibits, old Aran clothes, and a cliff rescue cart constitute this local effort. (Open April-Oct. daily 10am-7pm; £2, students £1.50.) The **Black Fort** (Dún Dúchathair), a mile south of Kilronan over eerie terrain, is even larger than Dún Aengus and about 1000 years older.

■■■ INISHMAAN (INIS MEÁIN)

Inishmaan (pop. 300) is where Synge set *Riders to the Sea*. The island's gloomy remoteness is its main attraction. From the ferry, Inishmaan resembles a stepped mesa on which sheep and houses have been dropped. Its cliffs are less spectacular than those on the other islands. Inishmaan's famous emptiness and silence hit hardest when you enter the interior. Only a hermit or an anthropology major would want to spend the night here: on a gray day, the desolation can be unnerving.

At the pier, a small coffeeshop inside an old Irish cottage dispenses food and **tourist information** all on one plate (tel. 73010; open Easter-Sept. daily 9am-6pm). The island's tiny village spreads out along the road west of the pier to divide the island in half. B&B and victuals can be had at **Dún Fearbhai** (tel. 73085), the first house on the right walking uphill from the pier (£12/person). The restaurant concentrates on perfecting seafood (lunch under £5, dinner from £6, soup £1.20; open June-Sept. daily 9am-9pm). A self-catering cottage is available for £150/week. **Mrs. Faherty** (signs from the pier show the way) also runs a cheerful B&B (tel. 73012; single £13, double £22; open mid-March to Nov.). A **post office** (tel. 73001), public phone, and **shop** (tel. 73002, open Mon.-Sat. 9am-8pm) constitute the majority of the village. The center of life on the island, Padraig O'Conghaile's thatched **pub,** serves pub grub all day.

The **Inishmaan Way** brochure (£1.50 in Galway or Inishmore tourist office) describes a five-mile walking route covering all the island's sights. One mile north of the pier is Inishmaan's safest and most inviting beach, **Trá Leitreach. Synge's Chair** is a not-so-cozy nook between cliffs overlooking George's Sound. **Dún Chonchúir,** a 7th-century fort, looks over the entire island. Near the village of **Baile an Mhothair,** 8th-century **Cill Cheannannach** left its remains on the shore. Islanders were buried here for ages under simple stone slabs, until the mid-20th century. Halfway across the island on the main road hunches Synge's cottage, where the Anglo-Irish author wrote much of his Aran-inspired work, from 1898-1902. A small **museum** in the Knitwear factory (tel. 63009) records island history (in Irish) near Dún Chonchúir. Ferries to the mainland visit the middle island sporadically, which makes getting on and, more importantly, off the island a questionable affair.

■■■ INISHEER (INIS OÍRR)

Someone has described the Arans as "quietness without loneliness," but Inishmore isn't always quiet and Inishmaan can get lonely. Only Inisheer (pop. 300) fulfills the promise of the famous phrase. This smallest island is fewer than two miles across in either direction. Islanders and stray donkeys seem to be present in approximately even proportions on this island which leaves a predominant impression of labyrinthine stone walls.

Tourist information is cheerfully offered up in English or Irish at the red-gated office near the main pier (tel. 75008; open June-Sept. daily 10am-6pm). A **post office** resides farther up the island in a white house with green trim (tel. 75001; open Mon. 9am-1pm, Tues.-Sat. 9am-5:30pm). Rothair Inis Oírr (tel. 75033) rents bikes of all colors (£5/day, £25/week). See the island from a different perspective with a pony cart **island tour** (tel. 75092).

The best of the Aran Island hostels is found on Inisheer. The **Brú Hostel (IHH)** (tel. 75024), visible from the pier, is clean and spacious. Upper-level rooms have skylights for stargazing. The hostel organizes *curragh* trips. Call ahead in July and August. (4- to 6-bed dorm £6, private room £8, w/bath £9.50. Sheets 75p, laundry £2. Irish breakfast £3, continental breakfast £1.50.) **Rory's Hostel** (tel. 75077) is a tiny 8-bed stone cottage behind the post office (£5). The **Ionad Campála Campground** (tel. 75008) stretches its tarps near the beach for camping aficionados who don't mind chill winds off the ocean (£2/tent, £10/week; showers 50p; open May-Sept.). A list of Inisheer's 17 B&Bs (a lot of B&Bs for one small island) hangs on the window of the small **tourist office** next to the pier. Both **Máive Searraigh** (tel. 75024) and **Bríd Póil** (tel. 75019) run B&Bs to satisfy Bord Fáilte standards.

Marb Gan é (tel. 75049), serves coffee and treats by the pier (homemade soup with brown bread £1.30; open June-Sept. daily 10am-6pm) and even offers B&B (£12/person). **Sharry's Restaurant** (tel. 75024), next door to the Brú Hostel, cooks food (full Irish breakfast £3.50, prawn cocktails £2; open June-Sept. daily 8:30am-9pm). **Tigh Ned's** pub lies next to the Brú Hostel and caters to a younger crowd, while the pub at the **Ostan Hotel** (tel. 75020), just up from the pier, is exceptionally crowded, dark, and mellow (grub served 11am-9:30pm). **Tigh Ruairí** (tel. 75002) is another pub/shop just up the road (shop open daily 9:30am-8:30pm, Sept.-June Mon.-Sat. 10am-6pm, 11am-1pm Sun.).

The Inis Oírr Way covers the island's major attractions in 6½ miles. The first stop is in town at **Cnoc Raithní**, a bronze-age tumulus (stone burial mound) 2000 years older than Christianity. Walking along the An Trá shore leads to the romantic overgrown graveyard of St. Kevin's Church *(Teampall Chaomhain)*. This St. Kevin, patron saint of the island, was believed to be a brother of St. Kevin of Glendalough. Each year on June 14, islanders hold Mass in the church's ruins to commemorate St. Kevin. His grave nearby is said to have great healing powers. Below the church, a pristine sandy beach stretches back to the edge of town. Farther east along the beach, a grassy track leads to **An Loch Mór**, a 16-acre inland lake where wildfowl prevail. Above the lake is the stone ring-fort **Dún Formna**. Continuing past the lake and back onto the seashore is the **Plassy wreck**, a ship which sank offshore in 1960 and washed up on Inisheer. From the wreck, look for the Inisheer lighthouse, then head north. The walk back to the center leads through **Formna Village** with its typical Aran old thatched houses, and on out to **Cill na Seacht nInion**, a small monastery with a stone fort. The remains of the 14th-century **O'Brien castle**, which Cromwell razed in 1652, sit atop a nearby knoll. On the west side of the island **Tobar Einne**, the Holy Well of patron St.Enda, supposedly has healing powers.

LOUGH CORRIB

Three hundred and sixty-five islands dot Lough Corrib, one for each day of the year. The eastern shores of Lough Corrib and Lough Mask stretch quietly into fertile farmland. The western shores slip into bog, quartzite scree, and the famously rough country in Connemara. The island of Inchagoill, right in the middle of the lough, is the location of the oldest Christian monument other than the Roman Catacombs (see *Let's Go: Rome, 1996*).

■ ■ ■ OUGHTERARD

Tourists seldom stop here, which adds to the town's appeal. While everyone else hurries to Clifden and the sea, you can stop to sample the lake and islands as an appetizer. Oughterard is attached to Lough Corrib's western flank at the base of the northwesterly Maam Turk Mountains, on N59 between Galway and Clifden.

An independent **tourist office** (tel. (091) 82808) helps out on Main St. (open May-Aug. Mon.-Sat. 9am-7pm, Sun. 10am-2pm, Sept. April Mon.-Fri. 9am-5pm). The **post office** (tel. (091) 82201) sends letters from Main St. (open Mon.-Fri. 9am-1pm and 2-5:30pm, Sat. 9am-1pm). The **Bank of Ireland,** Main St. (tel. (091) 82123), jealously guards the only **ATM** between Clifden and Galway (open Mon.-Wed. and Fri. 10am-12:30pm and 1:30-4pm, Thurs. 10am-12:30pm and 1:30-5pm). **Bus Éireann** coaches from Galway to Clifden stop in Oughterard (4-6/day, Sun. 2/day; Sept.-June 1/day; ¾ hr. to Galway, 2hr. to Clifden). **Hitchhikers** report easy going, at least in summer, between Galway and anything west or northwest. **Keogh's Launderette** (tel. (091) 82542), just a few steps from the bank, can help you clean up your act (open Mon.-Sat. 9am-1pm and 2-6pm). **Frances Geoghegan's Pharmacy,** Main St. (tel. (091) 82348) is open Mon.-Tues. and Thurs.-Sat. 9:30am-1:45pm and 2:15-6pm, Wed. 9:30am-1pm.

Accommodations Oughterard's **Lough Corrib Hostel (IHH)** (tel. (091) 82866), is blessed with a stereo and the best showers in Ireland. Hostelers enjoy conversations with the funny owner about anything from the sticky fur of koalas to frogs to long-neck lamps. Bike rental £6, £5 for hostelers; boat trips to Inchagoill £5; canoe rental £5.50; fishing rods £3; sheets £1. (Dorm £6, private room £8; **camping** £3. Open April-Nov.) Oughterard's other hostel, **Canrower House,** Station Rd. (tel. (091) 82388), brings new and modern facilities to the middle of nowhere (about a mile out of town). Laundry £3.50, key deposit £5, continental breakfast £2; rowboats £14/day. (May-Sept. dorm £7.50, private room w/bath £9; Oct.-April dorm £6.50, private room w/bath £8.50; **camping** £5/person.) The **Western Way,** Camp St. (tel. (091) 82475), has rooms (single £14, double £25). Mrs. Walsh's **Carrbury Arms,** Camp St. (tel. (091) 82367), has decidedly pink rooms (£13/person).

Food & Pubs Considering the size of Oughterard, the selection of eateries covers all tastes. Follow the yellow brick road to **Corrib County,** Main St. (tel. (091) 82678). All three meals are served here, though lunch is most affordable (tuna sandwich £2.50; open April-Oct. daily 8:30am-10pm). **O'Fatharta,** Main St. (tel. (091) 82692), has stones and a fire (and water and air). (Smoked salmon quiche with chips £4.75. Open Easter-Sept. daily 11am-10pm.) Good pub grub, nightly traditional music, and brilliant *craic* hover around the boat hull bar at **The Boat Inn,** the Square (tel. (091) 82196; music nightly in summer, weekends in winter; Irish stew £4.95; food served 10:30am-9pm). **Power's Bar** (tel. (091) 82712), a few doors down, is a local favorite (live Irish rock every Sat. night). **The Angler's Rest,** Main St. (tel. (091) 82203), exudes the grimy, groovy atmosphere of pubbing past. **Keogh's Grocery,** the Square (tel. (091) 82583), sells food, fishing tackle, and hardware. (Open winter Mon.-Sat. 8am-10pm; summer Mon.-Sat. 8am-8pm, Sun. 9am-

9pm.) Adjoining **Keogh's Bar** (tel. (091) 82222) encourages people to eat, drink, and be merry (pizza w/chips £2.50; music Fri.-Sun. nights).

Sights One mile south of town, a turnoff from N59 heads for the 16th-century **Aughnanure Castle** (tel. (091) 82214), where a river red with peat curves around a three-room fortified tower. The secret chamber, feasting hall, and murder hole are highlights of the high-quality tour, which mixes interesting local history with odd facts about the O'Flaherty clan. The key to the castle roof, from which the view is tremendous, can be borrowed from the ticket booth. (Open mid-June to mid-Sept. daily 9:30am-6:30pm. £2, students £1.) Glann Rd. covers the nine miles from Oughterard to the infamous **Hill of Doon,** where the pre-Celtic Glann people annually sacrificed a virgin. The practice supposedly continued in secret until the Middle Ages. The **Western Way Walk** (16 miles) begins where Glann Rd. ends and passes along the lake shore to Maam, at the base of the Maamturk Mt. range.

Great Irish contemporary art is on display in town at Peter Conneely's avant-garde **West Shore Gallery** (tel. (091) 82562), in Oughterard of all places. (Open Mon.-Sat. 10am-6pm, 6 exhibits/year.) In June, Oughterard hosts the **Currach Racing Championships.** Competitors assemble from all over Ireland.

Anglers worldwide know of Lough Corrib and the Mayfly bait that miraculously arises from it. The EU designated the lake a "salmonid," meaning that it should be preserved as a special trout and salmon lake. If you're interested, ask Greg Forde (tel. (091) 82678) about renting a **fishing boat** (about £25/day). Enquire at the **Fuschia Craft Shop** (tel. (091) 82644) about Lough Corrib cruises to Cong (2/day; £8 return, including 1½hr. stop on Inchagoill Island) and Inchagoill Island (July-Aug. 2/day; £5 return). Bikes are £3 on either trip. See Inchagoill madness (p. 282).

■■■ CONG

Cong, Co. Mayo (pop. 300) was designated by legend as the site of the First Battle of Moytura between the pre-human Fir Bolg and the god-like Túatha de Danann, and so began its career with a few big hits. Cong is a romantic and beautiful town with immediate access to islands in the loughs on either side of it. Opulent Ashford Castle, where the Guinness clan once lived, stands firmly in Cong. Oscar Wilde made fun of it and Ronald Reagan and Jason Priestley slept in it; regardless, it's an impressive castle. John Wayne and Maureen O'Hara shot *The Quiet Man* here in 1951, an event which will never be forgotten in town. Obsessed moviegoers come here and quote the whole film. The *craic* and the ruins top off the list. Not only do caves, graves, and an abbey litter the area, but so does the Dry Canal, a failed make-work project.

PRACTICAL INFORMATION

The town's privately established **tourist office,** Abbey St. (tel. 46542), will point you toward Cong's many wonders, all listed in the free *Get to Know Cong* (open May-Oct. daily 10am-6pm). *Cong: Walks, Sights, Stories* (£2.50), available from the town's hostels, describes good hiking and biking routes. The **post office** (tel. 46001) is on Main St. (open Mon.-Sat. 9am-5:30pm). **O'Connor's Garage,** next door (tel. 46008), rents Raleigh bikes. (£7/day, £30/week; students £5/day, £30/week; deposit ID. Open daily 9am-9pm.) **Buses** leave for Westport, Ballina (Mon.-Sat. 2/day), Clifden (Mon.-Sat. 1/day), and Galway (Mon.-Sat. 1-2/day) from outside Ryan's Hotel. Cong's **phone code** starred opposite John Wayne in *092.*

ACCOMMODATIONS, FOOD, & PUBS

Both the **Quiet Man Hostel** and the **Cong Hostel,** owned by the same helpful family, are perfect if you've got no place to go and you're feeling down. Both hostels offer a laundry service that miraculously picks up, washes, dries, and folds for £4. Other bonuses include free fishing rods (deposit £20), returnable guidebooks (deposit £2.50), guided tours of *The Quiet Man* locations (£2.50), and free screenings of the film *Un Taxi Mauve,* also made near Cong. No one will stop you from **camping** on Inchagoill Island.

> **Quiet Man Hostel (IHH),** Abbey St. (tel. 46511), across the street from Cong Abbey. Spacious and central. Shows *The Quiet Man* nightly and names its rooms after the movie's characters. Bike rental £6. Dorm £6. Open April-Sept.
> **Cong Hostel (IHH)** (tel. 46089), a mile down the Galway Rd. Clean and comfortable. All rooms have skylights. Screening room for nightly *The Quiet Man* showings. Playground, picnic area, and games room. Bikes £6; rowboats £6/2hr., £15/day. Dorm £6, double £8/person; continental breakfast £2.50, full Irish breakfast £4; **camping** £3 (separate facilities).
> **Courtyard Hostel (IHH)** (tel. 46203), several miles east of Cong, in Cross. Clean and fresh hostel will renew your *chi.* Bikes £5/day; one round of 18-hole golf £3. Dorm £5.50, private room £6.50; **camping** £3.
> **White House B&B,** Abbey St. (tel. 46358), across the street from Danagher's Hotel. Smothered in geraniums and ivy. £13.50/person.

Just across the street from the White House B&B, locals down mammoth meals and countless pints at **Danagher's Hotel and Restaurant** (tel. 46494). Gimme, gimme, gimme (roast lamb, vegetables, and potatoes £5.95; pub hours). The most brilliant *craic* in the region occurs here, and youth from all over the county come in for the weekend discos. **The Quiet Man Coffee Shop,** Main St. (tel. 46034), is obsessed with Hollywood. (Soup and sandwich £2.60, milkshake £1.50; open Easter-Sept. daily 10am-6pm.) Cooks can go crazy at **O'Connor's Supermarket** on Main St. (Open daily 9am-9pm.)

SIGHTS

From 1852 to 1939, the heirs to the Guinness fortune (later Lord and Lady Ardilaun) lived in **Ashford Castle.** Big-deal diplomatic visitors stay in the Castle, now a hotel. *The Quiet Man* was shot on the castle grounds. John Wayne and Maureen O'Hara took over an entire tower when they stayed here. Oscar Wilde informed Lady Ardilaun that she could improve her gardens by planting petunias in the shape of a pig. Though lacking such clever designs, the grounds do hold exotic plants. A pleasant walk from the castle along Lough Corrib leads to a stone monument, which recalls Lord Ardilaun: "Nothing remains for me/What does remain, is nothing," written by the grieving Lady Ardilaun. The castle-hotel is expressly closed to visitors (signs read "Residents Only!"), and to see the gardens you'll have to pay £2.

A sculpted head of its last abbot keeps watch over the ruins of the 12th-century **Royal Abbey of Cong,** located near Danagher's Hotel in the village (always open; free). The last High King of a united Ireland, Ruairi ("Rory") O'Connor, retired to the abbey for his final 15 years after repeatedly leading Gaelic armies against Norman troops and failing. Ironically, centuries later, it was General Rory O'Connor who disunited the twenty-six counties and sparked the Irish Civil War by seizing the Four Courts in Dublin in 1922. Across the abbey grounds, a footbridge spans the River Cong. Abbey monks used to sit and fish in a small stone house to the left. Continu-

---

Ceremonious Failure

Clonbur, where **Mount Gable** rises up above the flatness, was the site of a 19th-century engineering disaster. The famous four-mile **Dry Canal** is a deep, empty groove in the earth just east of Cong off the Galway Rd., near the Cong Hostel and clearly signposted. The useless canal is punctuated by locks just as if water were flowing through it. In the 1840s, engineers remembered too late that the ground around Cong was composed of porous limestone. The canal-opening ceremony was a surprising failure, as water that was let into the canal from Lough Mask promptly vanished into the absorbent walls. The canal could have been sealed and made useful, but by the mid-1850s, trains had already replaced canals as the most efficient means of commercial transport.

ing past the **Monk's Fishing House,** the footpath takes you to **caves,** called Pigeon Hole, Teach Aille, and Ballymaglancy Cave, and to a 4000-year-old burial chamber, **Giant's Grave.** (Both hostels have detailed cave maps for you to borrow.) Spelunkers have free access to caves, but Kelly's Cave must be unlocked (the key is held at the Quiet Man Coffee Shop). Spelunking safety requires a friend who knows when to expect you back, two torches (flashlights), and waterproof gear.

■ NEAR CONG: INCHAGOILL

Inchagoill ("INCH-a-gill"), a forested island in the middle of Lough Corrib, has been uninhabited since the 1950s. A deserted monastery and two churches, about which very little is known, are the prime targets. The only other building of note on the island is the **Coffee House** built in 1860 by the Guinness family.

The two churches hide down the right-hand path from the pier. **St. Patrick's Church,** built in the 5th century, is now only a pile of crumbling stone. The name Inchagoill means "Island of the Foreigners," which suggests that Christians in Ireland were still "foreigners" when the monastery was built. The famous **Stone of Lugna,** supposedly the tombstone of St. Patrick's nephew and navigator, stands three feet high among the stones surrounding the church. The inscription on the stone reads *'LIE LUGUAEDON MACCI MENUEH,'* or "stone of Luguaedon the son of Menueh," which may be an interpretation of an earlier inscription in *ogham* characters. The stone is almost certainly the second-oldest inscribed Christian monument in the world (the oldest are the catacombs of Rome). The **Church of the Saint** dates back to the 12th century. Its archway is lined with carved heads. Inchagoill's only current full-time residents are a colony of **wild rats.** During the day they do their own thing, but at night they come out to play. Would-be campers should take these furry fellows into consideration. **Ed Hickey** at Lough Corrib Hostel in Oughterard can take you out to Inchagoill or bring you back "anytime" (£5 return). The **Corrib Queen** (tel. (092) 46029) sails daily from Lisloughrea Quay, on the Quay Rd. in Cong. (June-Aug. 4/day; 1½hr.; £7 return including tour of island.)

CONNEMARA

A lacy net of inlets and islands along the coast and a rough gang of inland mountains (with some bogs in between) make up the famously rugged Connemara, the thinly populated western arm of Co. Galway. The land has little agricultural value and was therefore of little interest to Ireland's English occupiers. The Famine hit hardest here, where subsistence farming was the norm. But Connemara is ideal for camping, since the coast is dotted with small beaches and almost all of the offshore islands are accessible by land bridge or by local fishing boat. Ireland's largest *gaeltacht* stretches along the south Connemara coast, west from Galway City to Carna. The Irish government has taken various steps to preserve and encourage the use of the language. Corporate development incentives, designed to pump money in and prevent poverty-stricken Irish speakers from leaving the *gaeltacht,* have tended only to fill target towns with immigrating English-speaking technicians. Connemara-based Irish-language radio, *Radio na Gaeltachta*, has been more successful in spreading knowledge of Irish.

As with much of the western coast, the most rewarding way to absorb Connemara is on bike. Consider renting in Galway, then cycling northwest to Clifden via Lough Corrib and Cong, though the roads get a bit difficult toward the end of the ride. If you have neither the time for a long ride nor the docility for a guided tour, a public bus runs from Galway to Clifden via Cong. The three-hour ride passes through the most miraculous parts of Connemara. Hitchhikers may receive a personal guided tour from drivers. N59 from Galway to Clifden is the main thoroughfare; R336, R340, and R341 are more elaborate coastal loop roads.

Buses serve southern Connemara from Galway many times a day (summer up to 8/day) and less often serve northern Connemara (Mon.-Sat. 1/day). **Lally's Coaches** (tel. 62905) gives tours of Connemara that leave from the tourist office in Galway at 10am (return 5:30pm; £10, students £9). **Western Heritage** (tel. 21699) offers a number of different sightseeing tours to Connemara, the Burren, the Cliffs of Moher, and Lough Corrib. Tours take a full or a half day (£8-10, students £7-9). **Michael Nee** (tel. 51082) runs a private bus service to Clifden and Cleggan, connecting with the 2pm ferry to Inishbofin (operates June-Sept.; £5, £7 return). **Bus Éireann** (tel. 562000) conducts a day tour of Connemara that departs Galway Railway Station at 9:45am (late June-Sept.; £6). **O'Neachtain's** does full- or half- day guided tours of Connemara (tel. 83188). As always, tourist offices have more info on specific tours.

GALWAY CITY TO CLIFDEN

There are two ways to get to Clifden from Galway. The inland route, which passes through Oughterard, Maam Cross, and Recess, is faster but less scenic. The coastal route weaves in and out of numerous peninsulas and along stretches of beach. Hitchers take the inland route. The **Brú Hostel** (tel. (091) 83678) is a friendly place in **Spiddal** (Dorm £6.50, Sept.-June £6; double £8/person; **camping** £3. Laundry £3.) Up the street from the hostel is the mansion where The Waterboys recorded *Fisherman's Blues* (the house appears on the cover). The hostel can arrange a tour of the home for fans. The bus stops outside the very yellow An Cruiscin Lan pub and goes to Galway (6-8/day, 1/Sun.; 40 min.).

The landscape becomes progressively more stark west of Spiddal. **Connemara Tourist Hostel,** Aille, Inverin (tel. (091) 93104), lies two miles west of Spiddal. It shocks with tango-colored bathrooms but comforts with a relaxed atmosphere (£5.50; midnight curfew). The **Indreabhán Youth Hostel (An Óige/HI)** (tel. (091) 93154) is five miles farther from Spiddal. Only a ten-minute walk from the sea, this hostel is spartan and rarely full (June-Sept. £6.50; Oct.-May £5.50; sheets 85p; 11:30pm curfew). The coastal bus from Galway stops at both hostels.

Those continuing along the coast to **Gortmore** and the northern peninsula should make the detour to **Rosmuck,** a small peninsula that juts into Kilkieran Bay. The **cottage of Padraig Pearse** (tel. (091) 74292) squats in a small hillock overlooking the northern mountains. Pearse and his brother spent their summers here learning Irish and dreaming of an Irish Republic. The Republic-come-true named the cottage a national monument. (Open late-May to early-Oct. daily 9:30am-1:30pm and 2:30-6:30pm; £1, students 40p.)

The roads and beaches south of Clifden offer opportunity for hours of wandering. Seven miles south along R341, **Ballyconneely** sits on an isthmus near the wonderfully sandy **Coral Strand. Roundstone,** a quiet holiday resort eight miles southeast of Ballyconneely, is home to **Roundstone Musical Instruments** (tel. (095) 35808). They are the only full-time *bodhrán* ("BOW-rawn") makers in the world (see Traditional Music, p. 70). (Open daily 8am-7pm; Sept.-Feb. Mon.-Fri. 8am-7pm.)

■■■ CLIFDEN (AN CLOCHÁN)

As the region's only community big enough to be called a town, Clifden has become a miniature Killarney: five hostels, tons of tourbuses, and countless bureaux de change are bound to take their toll on even the most staunchly Irish of communities. In summer you're almost certain to hear more German than English or Irish. The past half decade has seen Clifden's nightlife rocket from nonexistent to famous. People who would never have left Galway years ago now come here at night for *craic.* Waterfront buildings provide a scenic backdrop to Clifden Bay. And where the buildings end, the beach begins. On account of its size, geography, and general cheerfulness, Clifden remains the best base from which to explore Connemara. N59 makes a U-turn at Clifden. Most traffic is from Galway, two hours southeast, but the road does continue northeast to Letterfrack and Connemara National Park. Hitchers usually wait at the Esso station on N59.

CONNEMARA

PRACTICAL INFORMATION

Tourist Office: Market St. (tel. 21163). Open May and Sept. Mon.-Sat. 10am-5pm; June-Aug. Mon.-Sat. 9am-6pm.

Banks: AIB bank, The Square (tel. 21129). Open Mon.-Fri. 10am-12:30pm and 1:30-4pm, Wed. open until 5pm. **ATM** accepts Visa, MC, Plus. **Bank of Ireland,** Sea View (tel. 21111). Open Mon.-Fri. 10am-12:30pm and 1:30-5pm.

Post Office: Main St. (tel. 21156). Open Mon.-Fri. 9am-5:30pm, Sat. 9am-1pm.

Phone Code: 095.

Buses: Buses from Galway run through Oughteraard and then to Clifden (June-Aug. Mon.-Sat. 6/day, Sun. 2/day; Sept.-May 1/day; 2 hr.). A summer service runs between Westport and Clifden (mid-June to August 1-2/day; 1½ hr.). **Bus Éireann** leaves from Cullen's Coffeeshop on Market St. **Michael Nee** (tel. 51082) runs a private bus to Galway and Cleggan, leaving from The Square (June-Sept.; to Galway £5, £7 return; to Cleggan £2, £3 return). Inquire at the tourist office.

Taxi: Desmond Morris, Ben View House, Bridge St. (tel. 21256).

Bike Rental: Mannion's, Bridge St. (tel. 21160, after hours 21155). £7/day, £30/week; deposit £10. Open Mon.-Sat. 9am-6:30pm, Sun. 10am-1pm and 5-7pm.

Boat Rental: John Ryan, Sky Rd. (tel. 21069). Prices negotiable.

Laundry: Hillview Laundrette, Church Hill (tel. 21836). Open Mon.-Sat. 9am-6pm; wash and dry £3.75.

Pharmacy: Clifden Pharmacy (tel. 21821). Open Mon.-Fri. 10am-12:45pm and 1:30-6:30pm, Sat. 10am-2pm.

District Hospital: tel. 21301 or 21302.

Emergency: Dial 999; no coins required. **Garda:** tel. 21021.

ACCOMMODATIONS

The Clifden Town Hostel, Market St. (tel. 21076). The certainty of a clean, uncrowded room and a friendly staff, plus a location in the middle of it all, make up for unrelenting modernity. Sheets £1 when busy, otherwise free; bikes £5/day. 4- or 5-bed dorm £6; private room £7.50/person high season, £7 low season.

Leo's Hostel (IHH), Sea View (tel. 21429). The reputation of its "loo with a view" has spread far and wide. This big old house is feeling its age, but a turf fire and good location outweigh other considerations. Sleeping huts—essentially wooden tents—and cabins for all-out budget travelers. Bikes £5/day, £4 low season; laundry £3; sheets free. Double cabin £6/person, quad hut £5/person; **camping** £3/person. Sept.-June dorm £5, private room £6/person; July-Aug. £1 more for each.

Brookside Hostel, Hulk St. (tel. 21812). Owner will painstakingly plot a hiking route for you. Parking available. Tickets on *M.V. Queen* to Inishbofin £8 return; from Rossaveal to Aran Islands £10 return; laundry £5. Sept.-June dorm £5; July-Aug. £6. Availability and rates of private rooms vary.

Bayview Hostel, Market St. (tel. 21866), behind King's Garage. Small, cute hostel from the pages of a decorating magazine. A bit tight, but humans are social creatures. Bikes £5/day; curfew 2am (key available); laundry; microwave. Dorm £5 (Nov.-Feb. £4.50); private room £6/person.

Blue Hostel, Sea View (no tel.). Converted townhouse is cramped but has all the necessities plus some: 2 kitchens, tea and coffee, microwaves, TV, VCR, and *free* laundry. £5/person; open summer only.

Crannmer, Churchill (tel. 21174). Family restaurant has 2 impeccable rooms (w/bath) for post-feast slumber. Coffee/tea facilities. Double £25, single negotiable.

White Heather House, The Square (tel. 21085). Centrally located, tastefully decorated rooms. Part of the sea is even visible. £12/person.

Kingston House, Mrs. King, Bridge St. (tel. 21470). Spiffy rooms with a partial view of the church. £13.50/person, w/bath £15; no singles July-Aug.

FOOD & PUBS

Finding a good restaurant or café in Clifden requires little effort; fitting the prices into a tight budget is more difficult. **O'Connor's SuperValu,** Market St., may be the best place to score some vittles (open Mon.-Sat. 9am-7pm, Sun. 11am-1pm).

Connemara Kitchen, Market St. (tel. 21054). This hybrid of deli and wholefood take-away sells frozen, but delectable, full meals. Bombay chicken with lentils £3; cauliflower and potato curry £2. Open daily 10am-6pm.

My Tea Shop, Main St. (tel. 21077). Sit on honey-colored wooden picnic benches to have lunch. The breakfast of vegetarian pizza, muesli, and coffee (£3.75) will keep you full all day. Dinner entrees all under £6. Open Sept.-June Mon.-Sat. 9am-6pm; July-Aug. daily 9am-9pm.

E.J. King's, The Square (tel. 21330). Crowded bar serves incomparable fare on exceptionally old wood furniture. Irish stew £4.95. Pub hours.

Doris', Market St. (tel. 21427). All walks of culinary life meet here—the Asian specialties, pasta, pizza, homemade ice cream, and waffles all get thumbs-up from locals. As expected, lunch is cheaper than dinner. Sweet and sour pork £4.90. Open daily noon-10pm.

Derryclare Restaurant, The Square (tel. 21440). Dark wood adds class. Lunch specials are a particularly good value (½ dozen oysters £3). Dinner, of course, is priced a bit higher (veggie pizza £5.85). Open daily 8am-10:30pm.

Crannmer, Churchill (tel. 21174). The breakfasts are widely acclaimed (£3.75) and dinner is no let-down. The filling 4-course Tourist Menu (£10.50) is a bargain compared to individual prices. Soup and Greek salad less than £5. Breakfast 7:30am-noon; closed for lunch; dinner 6-10:30pm.

Drinks by the huge open fire agree with everyone at **The Central,** Main St. (tel. 21430). Bring your own instruments to frequented favorite **Mannion's,** Market St. (tel. 21780), which has music nightly in summer (Fri.-Sat. in winter). Residents of Clifden congregate at **Lowry's,** Market St. (tel. 21347), more often than elsewhere (nightly music in summer, Sat. only in winter). **E.J. King's,** The Square (tel. 21330), is a talking, laughing, shouting pub that rocks the casbah, while **Humpty's** (tel. 21511), across the street, rolls with a rowdier bunch.

SIGHTS AND ENTERTAINMENT

There are no cliffs in Clifden itself. But ten-mile **Sky Road,** which loops around the head of land west of town, paves the way to some dizzying cliffs and makes an ideal cycling route. One mile along Sky Rd. stands the gate to the ruins of **Clifden Castle,** the former mansion of Clifden's founder, John D'Arcy. Farther out, a peek back at the opposite side of the bay reveals the spot where U.S. pilots Alcock and Brown landed after crossing the ocean in a biplane. One of the nicer ways to acquaint yourself with Connemara is by hiking south to the Alcock and Brown monument, three miles past Salt Lake and Lough Fadda.

Connemara Heritage Tours, Market St. (tel. 21379), led by an inspiring archaeologist, explore the history, folklore, and archaeology of the region (Easter-Oct. daily at 9:30am and 2pm; 4hr.; £10, students £8). The same friendly fellow organizes a **tour of Inishbofin** that delves into the island's natural history, archaeology, geology, and place names (leaves from Clifden daily at 11am, return 6:15pm; bus, ferry, and tour £20, students £18). The entrepreneurial archaeologist has also developed a **tour of the Aran Islands** along the same lines (Easter-Oct. leaves Clifden Wed. at 9am, return at 6:30pm; ferry, bus, and tour £26).

Clifden is closely associated with artists, and one school of painters in particular. Two galleries in town, the **Lavelle Art Gallery** (tel. 21882) and **Clifden Art Gallery** (tel. 21788; open May-Oct.), both on Main St., display local artists' works (and sell them to the non-budget traveler). The Lavelle brothers can also relate an interesting story about shoe-gazing. **Irish night** hits Clifden Town Hall every Tuesday at 9pm (July-Aug.), reviving an ancient culture of traditional music, dance, and song. The **Clifden Regatta** floats in during the first weekend in July. The rather alarming **Clifden Country and Blues Festival** takes place in September.

■ NEAR CLIFDEN: CLEGGAN

Ten miles northwest of Clifden, tiny Cleggan, the center of Connemara's fishing industry, offers more visual charms than Clifden but without any tourist population. Like most towns that rely on the sea, Cleggan is a no-nonsense place: people here talk fish and football and little else. **Omey Island,** just offshore of Claddaghduff a few miles due south of Cleggan, has rolling sandhills and minor ruins for exploration. But this island's accessibility is its truly unique attraction: it can be reached on foot at low tide. Bareback riding along the Cleggan Strand makes for more good stories (£10/hour; contact the **Cleggan Trekking Centre** at Master House Hostel).

People come to the airy **Master House Hostel (IHH)** (tel. (095) 44746) and find it difficult to part from the turf fire. Formerly a courthouse, shop, and headmaster's residence (hence the name), the hostel is now full of plants and bright wood. Sheets £1; laundry £3; book in advance for bikes at £5/day; Irish breakfast £2.50, continental £1.25. (Dorm £6, private room £8/person; **camping** £3.) Cleggan lacks a dirt cheap restaurant. **Oliver's Seafood Bar** (tel. (095) 44640) fills the gastronomical gap with seafood, sandwiches, and a currency exchange (seafood chowder £2). Upscale **Pier Bar** (tel. (095) 44690) is by the quay. **Kings Convenience Store,** farther down the road (tel. (095) 44642), will sell you provisions and ferry tickets to Inishbofin on the *M.V. Queen.* (£10 return, students £8, bikes free; open May-Sept. daily 9am-9pm, Oct.-April daily 9am-7pm). Transport to Cleggan is limited to an irregular **Bus Eireann** service (1-3/wk. from Clifden and Galway) or **Michael Nee's** more frequent private bus from Clifden (June-Sept. 3/day, Oct.-May 2/wk.; £2, £3 return).

■■■ INISHBOFIN

On the island of Inishbofin (pop. 200), seven miles from Cleggan at the western tip of the Connemara, travelers can choose between complete solitude on white beaches or drinking and dancing until dawn with seasoned locals. Inishbofin keeps time according to the ferry, the tides, and the sun; visitors to the island easily slip into a similar habit. A fishing boat which ran aground years ago still lies tilted on its side in the harbor. Weathered, black-capped men stroll along the shore, grasping tight their pipes and their memories. Inishbofin is infinitely less spoiled than the Aran Islands. Package tours are still an unrecognized concept here, on an island which seems to be out of this world, or at least past known boundaries.

Ferry tickets are sold at the Brookside Hostel in Clifden, the Master House Hostel in Cleggan, and at the Cleggan pier. Two **ferries,** the *M.V. Queen* (Malachy King, tel. (095) 44642) and the *M.V. Dun Aengus* (Paddy O'Halloran, tel. (095) 45806), leave Cleggan Pier three times every day (Easter-Sept.) for Inishbofin. During the winter months (Oct.-Easter), when the 45-minute crossing is even rougher, only the *Dun Aengus* operates (it's also the island's mail boat). Both charge £10 (students/hostelers £8) and carry bikes free.

Accommodations, Food, & Pubs The best hostel in all Connemara is quite possibly the **Inishbofin Island Hostel (IHH)** (tel. (095) 45855), up the hill past the church. The hostel will bless you with pine bunks, a large conservatory, and views that are constantly entertaining. People come for a night and stay months. (Dorm £6, private rooms from £8/person; sheets £1; laundry £2.) **The King's House** (tel. (095) 45833), just before the hostel, furnishes B&B in light and airy rooms with views (£13.50/person) and furnishes bikes for £7/day. Remote **Horseshoe B&B** sets itself apart on the east end of the island (tel. (095) 45812; £12/person). You'll also find **The Lobster Pot** here (tel. (095) 45807), a little restaurant with the best view in Connemara—the long, silent beach leaves customers speechless. Butter comes in a seashell (milkshakes £1.25, seafood chowder £1.80; open June-Aug. daily 11:30am-6pm). Closer to the pier on the west end, **Day's Pub and Hotel** (tel. (095)

45829) serves food all day and drink all night. The nightlife is unusually vibrant and the music surprisingly frequent during summer (4 nights/week). The small disco at the hotel often bulges with a young, well-traveled crowd. **Murray's Pub,** a 15-minute walk west of the pier, is smaller and more sedate, the perfect place for conversation, slurred or otherwise. **Shop** (tel. (095) 45819), near the pier provides groceries and island maps (£1; open late May to mid-Sept. daily 10am-8pm).

Sights A folk tale recalls the instance when two fishermen lit a fire on the island. The flames broke a spell which had been cast to imprison a witch. The witch struck a white cow upon her release, and the cow instantly became a rock. Consequently, the island is now called Inis Bó Finne (Island of the White Cow). It takes roughly three days to thoroughly walk around the island's periphery. The **east end** of the island is more quiet than the harbor and equals its natural splendor. A large, deserted beach lies at the end of the road which leads past the hotel to the eastern side. A trek to the **west end** of the island takes longer but affords more dramatic views of massive coves and blow-holes. Inishbofin is a favorite breeding ground for grey seals (most visible during mating season, late Aug.-early Oct.). The island also provides a perfect climate for those trees hospitable to the corncrake, a bird hard to find on the mainland except in Seamus Heaney's poems. The **Connemara Summer School** (tel. (095) 41034), held on Inishbofin during the first week of July, teaches about the island's ecology.

The expected rocks and ruins begin at a menacing **Cromwellian fort** (across Inishbofin Harbour from the pier), constructed to hold prisoners before transportation to the West Indies. At low tide, the **Bishop's Rock,** a short distance off the mainland, becomes visible. Cromwell once tied a recalcitrant priest to the rock and forced his comrades to watch as the tide rose over their colleague. From the northwest tip of the island, a collection of offshore rocks, **The Stags,** are visible. Past the hotel, at the eastern end of the island lie the ruins of a 15th-century Augustinian Abbey. The abbey was built on the site of a monastery built in 667 AD by St. Colman. A few gravestones and a well from the 7th-century structure remain extant.

■ ■ ■ CLIFDEN TO WESTPORT

CONNEMARA NATIONAL PARK

East and northeast of Clifden, the country hunches up into high hills and collapses into squishy, grass-curtained bogs interrupted only by the rare bare rock. The landscape of the Connemara National Park conceals a number of curiosities, including hare runs, orchids, bogs, and roseroot. The park is actually pretty tame as far as national parks go.

Letterfrack hasn't quite achieved town status: it's actually three pubs at the crossroads on the edge of the national park. The local **bus** from Galway to Clifden via Cong and Leenane stops in Letterfrack as well (late June-Aug. Mon.-Sat. 11/week; Sept. to mid-June Tues., Thurs., and Sat.-Sun. 1/day). A summer-only route goes from Clifden to Westport via Letterfrack (Mon. and Thurs. 2/day; Tues.-Wed. and Fri.-Sat. 1/day). **Hitchers** report average waits on the main road (N59), but a lack of cars frustrates thumbers on the byways. Uphill, on the way from town to the park, the **Old Monastery Hostel** (tel. (095) 41132) provides high-ceilinged rooms in the stately 300-year-old house. Downstairs, a cozy café cooks quality vegetarian buffet dinners (£5) and free organic breakfasts: tea, coffee, and homemade scones. (Roomy showers; laundry £3; bikes £5/day. Dorm £6; private room £7.50/person.) Good pub grub, seafood, groceries, and plentiful pints are available at **Veldon's** (tel. (095) 41046), which also sporadically sponsors music (steak sandwich £3.95; open June-Aug. daily 9:30am-1:30pm and 2:15-9:30pm; Sept.-May daily 9:30am-1:30pm and 2:15-7pm). **The Bard's Den,** across the intersection (tel. (095) 41042) is lit by a large open fire and skylight. The walls are hung with original Connemara baskets (disco

Counties Galway, Mayo, and Sligo

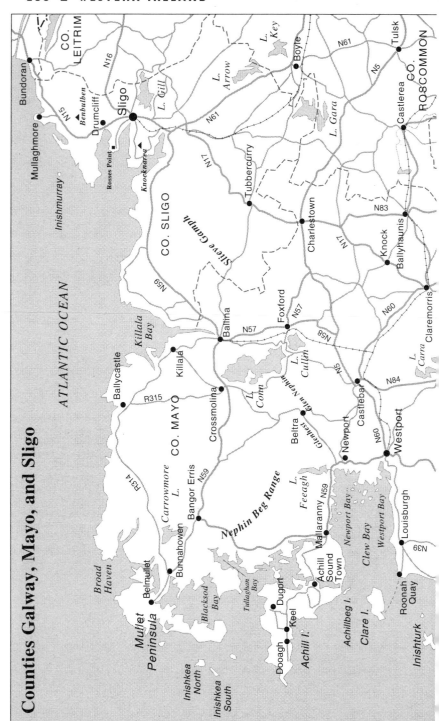

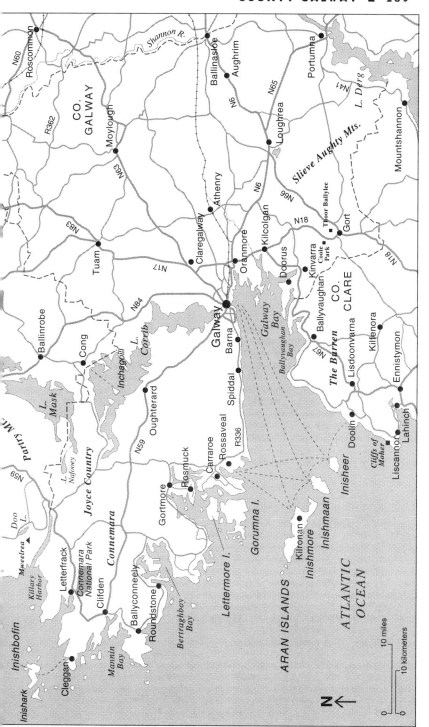

Fri. and Sun. in summer). The **Bank of Ireland Traveling Bank** stops in Letterfrack (daily 2:40-3pm).

Outside Letterfrack, **Connemara National Park** (tel. (095) 41054) occupies 2000 hectares of mountainous countryside, while unnumbered birds occupy the park. The far-from-solid terrain of the park is composed of bogs with a screen of grass and flowers over it. It's wisest to wear shoes and pants that you won't mind getting dirty, or perhaps even throwing away. Guides lead walks over the hills and through the bogs (July-Aug. Mon., Wed., and Fri. 10:30am; free) and speak on ecological and archaeological subjects (July-Aug. Wed. 8:30pm; free). The **visitors center** excels at explaining bogs, turf, and other ground cover in the park. (Park open May and Sept. daily 10am-5:30pm; June daily 10am-6:30pm; July-Aug. daily 9:30am-6:30pm. £2, students £1.)

Two short, signposted trails which begin at the visitors center afford satisfying views of Ballinkill Harbour, Inishbofin, and Inishark. Experienced hikers often head for the **Twelve Bens** *(Na Benna Beola*, a.k.a. the Twelve Pins), a rugged range that reaches 2400-foot heights and is not recommended for single or beginning hikers. The Bens are accessed through the park. Trailheads are located behind Diamond Hill. Diamond Hill itself has been climbed so many times (by so many feet that dislodge so much soil and stone) that soil erosion endangers the hill and everything around it. Visitors today are asked not to ascend the hill at all. Hikers base themselves at the **Ben Lettery Youth Hostel (An Óige/HI)** (tel. (095) 34636) in Ballinafad, far away from anything else. (Easter-June and Sept. £4.50, July-Aug. £5.50.) The hostel is eight miles east of Clifden; the turnoff N59 is west of Roundstone road.

KILLARY HARBOUR

Farther east along N59, Killary Harbour, Ireland's only fjord, breaks through the mountains to the town of **Leenane,** which wraps itself in the skirts of the **Devilsmother Mountain.** *The Field* was filmed here in 1989, and no one in town will ever forget it. The murder scene was shot at Aasleagh Falls. At **Leenane Cultural Centre** (tel. (095) 42323), on the Clifden-Westport Rd., spinning and weaving demonstrations clarify what happens to the wool of the sheep that graze right outside (open April-Oct. daily 10am-7pm; £2, students £1). Gemstone and silver jewelry at **Killary Crafts,** across the road from Hamilton's, are the products of a different, but also local, craftsmanship (open April-Sept. daily 10am-8pm). Stop for a pint at **Gaynor's Lounge** (tel. (095) 42261) or at next-door neighbor, **Hamilton's** (tel. (095) 42262); or perhaps, stop at both. Hamilton's hides behind a tiny shop that is open daily 8:30am-12:30am. It's hard to fight the temptation for an eggburger and chips (£2.80) from the **Village Grill** (tel. (095) 42253; open daily 10am-10pm). **Bay View House** (tel. (095) 42240), on the northern side of town along N59, boasts a bizarre dining room that was once a chapel (single £20-24, double £29). **Killary Harbour Hostel (An Óige/HI)** (tel. (095) 43417) perches on the very edge of the harbor shore seven miles west of Leenane. The hostel has an unsettlingly gorgeous waterfront location. Wittgenstein wrote *Philosophical Investigations* here. A hostel shop sells baked beans and other necessaries. At £5.50 a night from June-August (March-May and Sept. £4.50), it's a wonderful bargain. At a spot five miles off N59, it's also inconveniently remote.

County Mayo

Co. Mayo's appeal is largely a result of its distance from well-traveled paths. Bogs, beaches, and big fish fill the county and attract travelers of all veins. The best scenery is found along the inlets around the Belmullet Peninsula; the best fish swim in Lough Conn and Lough Cullin. Mayo's one big moment in history occurred in 1798,

"The Year of the French," when General Humbert landed at Kilcummin. Combining French soldiers, Irish revolutionaries and Irish rural secret societies into an army, Humbert briefly controlled half the county, from Killala to Castlebar. The English retaliated and won at Ballina and Ballinamuck. The village of Cong, Co. Mayo is covered under Co. Galway (see Cong, p. 280).

■ ■ ■ WESTPORT

Mayo's population centers are seldom its most interesting places, but Westport is becoming an exception to this disheartening rule. Westport has an exciting, thriving pub life and plenty of good cafes. Its many conveniences make it an entirely agreeable stop between Connemara and Mayo's islands, to the northwest. The town's layout, with a central Octagon and Georgian architecture, is the result of similar Anglophile town planning as famous Westport House. Hopes of making the town a major port on the order of Galway or Cork more or less died with the Act of Union, and the House has lost whatever stateliness it once had. N60 passes through Clifden, Galway, Sligo, and Castlebar on its way to Westport. Hitchers report that it's an easy route.

ORIENTATION & PRACTICAL INFORMATION

Westport's North Mall and South Mall run parallel to each other, one on each side of the river. Most of the town extends off South Mall. Perpendicular to it, Bridge St. favors pubs, eateries, and Sunday strolls. Most activity centers on The Octagon (the junction of James St., Peter St., and Shop St.), or at the clock tower at the other end of Shop St., where it meets High, Mill, and Bridge St.

Tourist Office: North Mall (tel. 25711). Open Mon.-Sat. 9am-6pm.
Banks: Bank of Ireland, North Mall (tel. 25522). Open Mon., Wed., and Fri. 10am-4pm, Thurs. 10am-5pm; **ATM. AIB,** Shop St. (tel. 25466). Open Mon.-Wed. and Fri. 10am-4pm, Thurs. 10am-5pm; **ATM.**
Post Office: North Mall (tel. 25475). Open Mon.-Sat. 9am-5:30pm.
Phone Code: 098.
Trains: Trains arrive at the **Altamont St. Station** (tel. 25253 or 25329 for inquiries, Mon.-Sat. 9:30am-6pm), a 5-min. walk east of town on the continuation of the North and South Malls. The train goes to Dublin via Athlone and Castlebar (daily 3/day; Dublin £14, students £10, Fri. and Sun. £20).
Buses: For Westport bus info, call the tourist office (tel. 25711). Almost no buses leave Westport on weekends. Buses leave from the Octagon and travel to: Ballina (Mon.-Sat. 1-3/day, Sun. 1/day); Castlebar (Mon.-Sat. 6/day); Louisburgh (Mon.-Sat. 2/day; £4.30); Galway (Mon.-Fri. 2/day; £9.70); Knock (Mon.-Sat 3/day, Sun. 1/day; £6.70); and Belfast via Sligo (Mon.-Sat. 1/day).
Taxis: Brendan McGing, Lower Peter St. (tel. 26319).
Bike Rental: Breheny & Sons, Castlebar St. (tel. 25020).
Bookstore: The Bookshop, Bridge St. (tel. 26816). Open July-Aug. daily 9am-9pm, Sept.-June daily 10am-6:30pm.
Laundry: Westport Washeteria, Mill St. (tel. 25261), near the clock tower. £3.50, self-service £2.50, soap 40p. Open Mon.-Tues., Thurs. and Sat., 9:30am-6pm, Wed. 9:30am-1pm.
Travel Agency: Westport Travel, 4 Shop St. (tel. 25511). USIT prices for students; Western Union Money Transfer point. Open Mon.-Sat. 9:30am-6pm.
Pharmacy: O'Donnell's, Bridge St. (tel. 25163). Open Mon.-Sat. 9am-6:30pm. Rotating Sunday openings are posted in pharmacy doors.
Emergency: Dial 999; no coins required. **Garda:** Fair Green (tel. 25555).

Impractical Information and Disorientation: Clay Pigeon Shooting (tel. 21926), Liscarney, Leenane Rd. Open daily 11am-dark.

ACCOMMODATIONS

Westport's B&Bs, with their faux-wood headboards, are easily spotted on the Castlebar and Altamont Roads. Most charge £13-15 for the pleasure of waking up beside one of these stylish objects.

Old Mill Holiday Hostel (IHH), James St. (tel. 27045), between The Octagon and the tourist office. Firm pine beds line up in a renovated mill and brewery. The showers are often compared to a second date—hot and full of pressure. Book ahead during festival weeks. Bedroom lockout 11am-1pm; kitchen and common room lockout 11pm-8am. Sheets 50p; laundry £2. £5, July-Aug. £6.

Club Atlantic (IHH), Altamont St. (tel. 26644 or 26717), a 5-min. walk from North or South Mall. This massive, 140-bed complex across from the train station "has it all": pool table, ping-pong, video games, Irish videos, a shop, an elephantine kitchen, and even an educational exhibition on Croagh Patrick. Bikes £6/day, £30/week. Sheets £1; laundry £2. June and Sept. £5.90; July-Aug. £6.50; mid-March to May and Oct. £5.50. Double June-Sept. £6.90/person; mid-March to May £5.90. Single £9. **Camping** £4.

The Granary Hostel (tel. 25903), 1 mi. from town on the Louisburgh Rd., near the main entrance to Westport House. A garden and conservatory flank the 150-year-old converted granary. In general, the outside is nicer than the inside—showers and most bathrooms are detached from the house. Dorms are crowded and the kitchen is small. Dorm £5. Open Jan.-Nov.

Altamont House, Altamont St. (tel. 25226). In business for 29 years and still going. Roses peep in the windows of spacious rooms. £13.50/person; all rooms w/shower; open March-Dec.

FOOD

Gorge on Spam and Hobnobs from the **SuperValu supermarket** (tel. 27000) on Shop St. (open Mon.-Wed. 9am-7pm, Thurs.-Fri. 9am-9pm, Sat. 9am-6:45pm). **Country Fresh** (tel. 25377) sells juicy fruits and vegetables (open Mon.-Fri. 8am-6:30pm, Sat. 8am-6pm; closes early on Wednesdays during winter). The **country market** by the Town Hall at The Octagon vends farm-fresh vegetables, eggs, milk, and butter (Thurs. 10:30am-1:30pm).

Circe Café and Wine Bar, Bridge St. (tel. 27096). Patrons smoke languidly to the beat of jungle music as they watch the pig mobile spin. Creative lunches are affordable before 5:30pm (spinach pancake £2.75), then double in price. Open June-Sept. daily 10am-10pm, Oct.-May daily 10am-6pm.

The Continental Health Food Shop and Café, High St. (tel. 26679). It's difficult to decide whether the fireplace or the menu of sandwiches (under £3) is the greater attraction in this cozy cottage. Open Tues.-Sat. 10am-6pm.

Bernie's High Street Café, High St. (tel. 27797). Soft light, ecru-colored walls, and healthy plants are comforting. Caesar salad £3.10, crab with avocado and lemon £6. Open Mon.-Sat. noon-9pm, Sun. 1-9pm.

McCormack's, Bridge St. (tel. 25619). Pastries, teas, and simple meals on floral tablecloths. Praised by locals as an exemplary teahouse. Daily special, potato, and salad £4. Open June-Sept. Mon.-Sat. 10am-6pm; Oct.-May Tues.-Sat. 10am-6pm.

Cafolla, Bridge St. (tel. 25168). Eat in or take away, the food is still incredibly cheap. Plain pizza £1.75, omelettes from £2.60. Open June-Sept. Mon.-Sat. 11am-1am, Sun. noon-11pm; Oct.-May Mon.-Sat. 11am-11pm, Sun. 5-11pm.

The Urchin, Bridge St. (tel. 27532). A menu full of old favorites. Fish chowder and bread £1.50, quiche and salad £3.20. Lunch is affordable, dinner isn't. Open daily 10am-10pm.

PUBS

Westport is blessed with *craic* as good as the food. Search Bridge St. to find a scene or session that suits. In case of a musical or social emergency, call the southwest Mayo **pub hotline** (tel. 27371) for a rundown of music in Westport and Newport.

Matt Molloy's, Bridge St. (tel. 26655). Owned by the flutist of the Chieftains. All the cool people, including his friends, go here. Trad sessions nightly in summer.

The West, corner of Bridge St. and South Mall (tel. 25886), on the river. Choose between the light and creamy outside and the dark and woody inside. Friendly Westport youth come attached to both settings. Live rock most nights in summer.

Pete McCarthy's, Quay St. (tel. 27050), uphill from the Octagon. Old, dark, and smoky pub attracts regulars—you know the score. Trad on weekends in summer.

The Towers (tel. 26534), down by The Quay, 1 mi. from town center. Fishing nets and excellent grub hook lots of customers. Beef in Guinness, a uniquely Irish specialty, is worth £4.90. Music thrice a week in summer, twice in winter.

O'Malley's Pub, Bridge St., across from Matt Molloy's. The pool tables and neon beer signs on the walls don't exactly harmonize with all the dark wood.

SIGHTS

The current commercial uses of **Westport House** (tel. 25430) would horrify its former elite inhabitants, the Marquesses of Sligo. A carnival and the bog-preserved butter in the museum are hardly worth the entrance fee. The zoo and train ride betray an emphasis on entertaining families with children. (Open May and early Sept. daily 2-5pm; June and late Aug. daily 2-6pm; July to mid-Aug. Mon.-Sat. 10:30am-6pm, Sun. 2-6pm. Admission May-June and Sept. £5, July-Aug. £6; students £3.50.) More interesting and much cheaper is the **Clew Bay Heritage Centre,** at the end of The Quay. The narrow interior (a bit like the stock room of a shop) crams together a pair of James Connolly's gloves, a sash belonging to John MacBride, and the stunning original photograph of Maud Gonne that graces her biographies. A full genealogical service is available (open July-Aug. Mon.-Fri. 9am-5pm, Sat.-Sun. 3-6pm; Sept.-June Mon.-Fri. 9am-4pm; £1).

Perfectly conical **Croagh Patrick** rises 2510 feet over Clew Bay. The summit has been revered as a holy site for thousands of years. Perhaps because of its height, it was sacred to **Lug,** sun god, god of arts and crafts, and temporary ruler of the Túatha de Danann (see Legends & Folktales, p. 61). St. Patrick, reenacting a Biblical parable, prayed and fasted here for 40 days and nights in 441 AD before he banished snakes from Ireland. The deeply religious climb Croagh Patrick barefoot on the last Sunday in July. Not coincidentally, this date also Lug's holy night, Lughnasa. Others climb the mountain just for the exhilaration and the view from the top. It takes about four hours total to climb and then descend the mountain. Shod climbers start their excursion anytime from the village of Murrisk, several miles west of Westport on R395 to Louisburgh. Buses drive along this road to Murrisk (July-Aug. Mon.-Fri. 3/day, Sept.-June Mon.-Sat. 2/day). Pilgrims and hikers also set out for Croagh Patrick along a path from **Ballintubber Abbey** (tel. (094) 30709), several miles south of Castlebar and 19 miles from Murrisk. Founded in 1216 by then King of Connacht Cathal O'Connor, the abbey still functions as a religious center today.

■ NEAR WESTPORT

LOUISBURGH

The wild, mountainous landscapes south of Westport, clearly more exhilarating than the farmlands of inner Mayo, are rocky and barren. **Louisburgh,** a dull town 13 miles west of Westport on R395, is the best base for exploring the area or for trips to Clare Island. In the Square, the **Granuaile Heritage Centre** (tel. (098) 66195) honors Grace O'Malley, 16th-century Pirate Queen of Clew Bay. Wax figures depict Gaelic chieftains, Queen Elizabeth, and Grace herself in pirate gear while a documentary tells the whole story. (Open March-May Mon.-Fri. 2-5:30pm, June Mon.-Sat. 10am-6pm, July-Sept. daily 10am-7:30pm, Oct.-Nov. Mon.-Fri 11am-5:30pm; £2.25, students £1.50.) The many O'Malleys in town willingly relate a spiced-up version of Grace's life to those who miss the Heritage Centre.

Old Head Strand, two miles northeast of town, is one of the finer beaches in the **Clew Bay** area and along the coast, though **Carramore Strand** is closer to town (one mile away). Mountain-type people will have to travel a bit farther. Fifteen miles south of town, calm **Doolough** ("Black Lake") offers a choice of several heart-pounding climbs up the Sheffrey Hills, the Mweelrea Mountains, or Ben Gorm. The south end of the lake leads into an enchanted wooded dell which runs into the River Bundarragh. Cars and bikes can head back to Westport on the scenic route, which bends left at the south end of the lough. The loop from Westport to Louisburgh to Killary Harbour and back to Westport covers 40 miles. Cars are few and far between.

The **tourist information** point (tel. (098) 66400) is ensconced on Bridge St. (Open June-Aug. 10am-1pm and 2-5:30pm.) The **post office** also exchanges currency on Main St. (open Mon.-Fri. 9am-1pm and 2-5:30pm, Sat. 9am-1pm). **Staunton's Pharmacy,** the Square (tel. (098) 66139), is open Mon.-Sat. 10:30am-7:30pm, Sun. 12:30-1:30pm. **Durkan's Foodstore,** Bridge St. (tel. (098) 66394), will satisfy your appetite (open June-Aug. daily 9am-9pm; Sept.-May Mon.-Sat. 9am-9pm). **Village Tea Shop** (tel. (098) 66577) serves light luncheons to bridge groups (open Mon.-Sat. 11:30am-5pm, Sun. 2-5pm). Its own **Aimhirgin Gallery** displays sculpture and ceramics. Bread and beer sustain customers at **Durkan's Weir House,** Chapel St. (tel. (098) 66140; lasagne, salad, and brown bread £4.95; food served daily noon-10pm). The attached restaurant has fancier food (seafood pancake w/lobster sauce £3.95; open daily from 6:30pm). Mary O'Malley's **Rivervilla** (tel. (098) 66246) is in Shraugh, ¾ mile from Louisburgh (signs mark the way). Her riverside farmhouse is open to guests mid-April to October (£13/person). **Old Head Forest Caravan and Camping Park** (tel. (098) 66021 or 66455) helps guests enjoy tennis and clean laundry. (50p/person in a small tent. Caravans and large tents: Mid-May to June and mid-Aug. to mid-Sept. £4.50, July to mid-Aug. £5.50. Open mid-May to mid-Sept.)

CLARE ISLAND

Four miles west of Louisburgh, boats leave Roonah Point for **Clare Island** (pop. 150), a scenic dot in the Atlantic that is less popular than Inishmore and Achill but not quite as isolated as Inisheer and Inishbofin. The most exotic things about this island is its history of pirates. Grace O'Malley ruled the 16th-century seas west of Ireland from her base on the eastern end of this island, which later became a coast guard station. Throughout the 16th century, her notorious (but wealthy) galley fleet exacted tolls from all ships entering and leaving Galway Bay. The ferocious pirate also abducted the grandson of Dublin aristocrats when they refused her entrance into their castle (see Howth, p. 108). Grace was supposedly laid to rest here, on the island that was close to her heart and purse, under the ruins of Clare Island Abbey halfway down the beach. Ascending Knockaveen Hill requires little energy; climbing Croaghmore takes more effort, but the reward is greater. Many visitors make a search for buried treasure on the west coast of the island, where the cliffs of **Knockmore Mountain** (1550 feet) rise vertically out of the sea. (Maps and printed directions are available at the tourist office in Louisburgh.) **Clare Island Historical Safaris** (tel. (098) 25048) will organize a one-day exploration of a megalithic tomb, Bronze Age cooking sites, a 12th-century abbey, and Grace O'Malley's 15th-century castle. (£25/person, including transport and meals; reduced rates for groups; minimum of 6 people for a tour.)

The **Bay View Hostel** (tel. (098) 26307), just up the beach road on the right side of the harbor, offers two deals. A bed (of the four in every dorm) costs £7, while a combined hostel and ferry package (*The Very Likely* leaves Roonagh Quay for Clare Island 6/day in summer) costs £15. The hostel also serves lunch between noon and 3pm sharp; show up at 3:01 and you lose (evening meal is also an option). Mrs. O'Malley's **Cois Abhain** (tel. (098) 26216), down by the harbor, will even pick you up along with providing a bed and a breakfast (single £15, double £24).

Charlie O'Malley's **Ocean Star Ferry** (tel. (098) 25045) crosses the bay from Roonah Quay in 15 minutes (£10 return, bikes free). Since the ferry delivers cargo to the island's permanent residents, it only stops running in the worst storms and gales. (July-Aug. 3/day; May-June and Sept. 2/day; call Oct.-April.) Chris O'Grady (tel.

(098) 26307) operates a **bus-ferry scheme**. A coach leaves The Octagon in Westport at 10am to meet the 11am ferry to Clare Island. The ferry returns from Clare at 5pm; buses carry passengers back to Westport by 6:15pm (July-Aug. daily 1/day; £15). O'Grady's advertised "student" prices apply only to Irish prepubescents.

DELPHI

Three kinds of people go to Delphi: the artistic, the rich, and the athletic. Delphi isn't really a town since it doesn't even have a pub. But this tiny hamlet has rivers and lakes that are perfect for photos, picnics, and fishing (contact the Delphi fishery, tel. (095) 42213 for permits). The Lodge sells seclusion to the rich and famous. The Prince Charles visit in 1995 was, and still is, a huge deal for locals. And the **Delphi Adventure Centre** (tel. (095) 42307) provides activities for energetic travelers (and hostel accommodation during the summer season). Adventurous types can try surf-skiing, rock climbing, and abseiling, among other activities, for £18/day. Times of kitchen access are limited. The coffeeshop has a pool table for those with sore muscles (soup and brown bread £1.30). You can hire a bike for £7/day, or you can relax in the sauna for £3. Laundry £5; sheets, pillow, and duvet £2. (Dorm £5.50, double £8/person; **camping** £5/2-person tent. Open July-Aug.)

■■■ ACHILL ISLAND

Achill Island is Co. Mayo's most popular holiday refuge and, measuring 15 by 12 miles, Ireland's largest island. Ringed by glorious beaches and cliffs, Achill's interior consists of bog, bog, mountain, bog, and bog. Hardly an acre of land is cultivable. The island's several towns divide its large tourist trade among them. Keel is most central and convenient to the island's sights, but the best hostel is in Achill Sound Town and the best scenery is in the far west of the island. Recent Nobel-winning novelist Heinrich Böll once lived in Dugort.

Buses run infrequently from Achill Sound Town, Dugort, Keel, and Dooagh to Westport (summer Mon.-Sat. 4/day, winter Mon.-Sat. 2/day; £5.50 return, students £4.30), and to Sligo, Enniskillen, and Belfast (summer Mon.-Sat. 3/day; winter 2/day). **Atlantic Drive** lines the south shore. **Hitchers** report relative success during July and August, but cycling is more reliable and just as easy. There's no bank on the island, so change money on the mainland or suffer rates that resemble piracy. The **phone code** for all Achill Island agrees on 098.

ACHILL SOUND TOWN

About six miles south of Achill Sound Town (from the road onto the island take a left at the crossroads), two sets of ruins crumble near each other. The ancient **Church of Kildavnet** was founded by Dympna when she fled to Achill Island to escape her father's incestuous desires. The remains of **Kildownet Castle,** really a fortified tower house dating from the late 1400s, proudly stand nearby. Grace O'Malley, the swaggering, seafaring pirate of medieval Ireland, once owned the castle (ask at the house next door for the key). The **Atlantic Drive** roams along the south coast from the ruins past beautiful beaches and up to Dooega, Keel, and Dooagh.

The buildings that cluster on the island, just past the bridge, constitute Achill Island Town. The bevy of buildings incorporates a wee **tourist office** (tel. 45384; open mid-June to Aug. Mon.-Sat. 10am-1pm and 2-5:30pm), a **post office** and Bureau de Change (tel. 45141; open Mon.-Fri. 9am-12:30pm and 1:30-5:30pm), a SuperValu **supermarket** (open Mon.-Sat. 9am-6pm), and a pharmacy (tel. 45248; open July-Aug. Mon.-Sat. 9:30am-6pm; Sept.-June Tues.-Sat. 9:30am-6pm). **Achill Sound Hotel** (tel. 45245) rents bikes (£6/day, £30/week; deposit £30; open daily 9am-9pm).

Achill Sound Town accommodates flocks of tourists at two hostels. The **Wild Haven Hostel** (tel. 45392) is just like home. Painted signs point the way from the main road. This establishment imitates more expensive inns with its polished floors, antique furniture, and an open turf fire in a cozy sitting room. Lockout 11am-3:30pm, except on rainy days. Breakfast £3.50, bikes £6/day, £30/week; sheets £1.

ACHILL ISLAND

(Dorm £6; private room £8; **camping** £3.50.) Just before the bridge to Achill Sound Town, the **Railway Hostel** (tel. 45187) is a simple, multi-kitchened, casual family affair at a prime location—a pub is just across the street. (Continental breakfast £2.50, full Irish £3.50; bikes £5/day; laundry £2; sheets £1. Dorm £5, private room £6/person, all w/bath.) The proprietors can be found at Mace Supermarket, in town. Opposite the Railway Hostel, **Alice's Harbour Inn** (tel. 45138) does more than its share for the tourist industry. The owners allow **camping** and will provide tourist info if the office is closed. The inn also feeds hungry souls (Achill cod w/vegetables and chips £4.95; food served 10am-10pm). In the summer of 1994, **Eric Clapton,** in the words of locals, was caught "slobbering over a guitar" here during an impromptu jam session.

KEEL & DOOAGH

Keel fades gracefully into its spectacular three-mile strand, Trawmore, flanked by cliffs and rocks. Two miles north of Keel on the road looping back to Dugort, the **Deserted Village** is populated only by stone houses closely related to early Christian *clocháns*. They were used until the late 1930s in summer as pasture and shelter for fattening cattle. Some of these "booleying" houses are scheduled for restoration. The site is used in the summer months for an **Archaeological Summer School** (call Theresa McDonald, tel. (0506) 21627) which sponsors evening lectures at the Warecrest Hotel (tel. 43153) in Dooagh (8:30pm; £4).

Pedal out with groceries in your pack from **O'Malley's Island Sports** (tel. (098) 43125; bikes £7/day, £30/week; open Mon.-Sat. 9am-9pm, Sun. 9am-7pm) in the **Spar Supermarket.** The bike can carry you to **Keel Sandybanks Caravan and Camping Park** (tel. 43211), where you can get sand in your tent (July-Aug. £5.50/tent, late May-June and Sept. £4). An infinitely more comfortable, though more expensive option, is Mrs. Joyce's **Marian Villa** (tel. 43134), a 20-room hotel/B&B with a veranda that looks onto the sea (£18/person and up, all w/bath and TV). A few pints can aid sleep on the less-than-large bunks at the **Wayfarer Hostel (IHH)** (tel. 43266). Central location and a short walk to Trawmore Strand. (Microwave and laundry; sheets 50p. £5.50, private room £6.50; open mid-March to mid-October.)

Drunken inspiration is encouraged at the vinyl **Annexe Inn** (tel. 43268). The pub has pictures of dead sharks and trad sessions nightly July-Aug., but only on Saturdays in winter. The large **Mináun View Bar,** across the street from the caravan park, is legendary for its Republican fervor. Although there are numerous decadent chippies, more nutritious food is available at the **Beehive Handcrafts and Coffee Shop** (tel. 43134) where sweaters alternate with wooden tables (soup and brown bread £1.30; open daily 10am-6:30pm). At **Calvery's** (tel. 43158), next to the Spar Supermarket, pink and green tablecloths only improve the already flavorful fresh cod (£3.75) and Gammon steak (£3.20; open daily 9am-10pm).

Two miles up the road from Keel in **Dooagh** ("DOO-ah"), **Corrymore House** (tel. 43333) was one of several Co. Mayo estates owned by the infamous Captain Boycott. His mid-19th-century tenants went on an extended rent strike that turned his surname into the eponymous verb. The **Folklife Centre** displays household utensils, furniture, and farm implements from the turn of the century (open daily 10:30am-5pm). Dooagh hosts a music, dance, art, and writing **festival week** (call Dr. Paddy Loneen, tel. 45284) during August. The activities culminate in a free, open-air show of arts.

The **Abha Teangai Restaurant and Guest House** (tel. 43414) has a number of guises. It is both a vegetarian restaurant (veggie stirfry £5.50) and gallery displaying local artists' work (open daily 9am-10:30pm). In August, the art gallery turns into a heritage center, displaying the usual crafty assortment of baskets, *curraghs,* and woven goods. **B&B** is also available here for £12. **The Pub,** just a bit farther down the main street, is managed by the well-loved mistress of the house. Don Allum, the first man to row both ways across the Atlantic, made his first stop upon landing in Ireland at The Pub. Pictures document him savoring his Guinness instead of depicting his landing. Four miles into Achill's wild west past Keem Bay, the **Croaghaun**

Mountain are the source of the stream on **Achill Head.** The mountains provide bone-chilling views of **Croaghaun Cliffs,** Europe's highest sea-cliffs. The climb to the top of the cliffs from Keem Bay is less strenuous but provides similar views.

DUGORT

A right turn in Achill Sound Town leads to the northern part of the island, where Dugort has slept through the 20th century and may sleep through the 21st as well. The tiny hamlet is picturesquely perched atop a sea-cliff. Mist-shrouded Slievemore Mountain looms to its east. Germans flock here to see the former cottage of Heinrich Böll, now a retreat for artists-in-residence. His favorite pub, the **Valley,** still serves pints to literary pilgrims. Modern-looking cemeteries and abandoned buildings west of Dugort are the result of a futile mid-1800s effort to convert the islanders to Protestantism by sending in Irish-speaking missionaries. On the other side of **Slievemore Mountain** gapes the chambered tomb known as **Giant's Grave** (easily accessible from Dugort). Other megalithic tombs lurk nearby. The main signposted tomb after McDowell's Hotel towards Keel is easiest to find, one mile straight up from the road. It has been eroded away to a sinuous beauty reminiscent of a Henry Moore sculpture. **McDowell's Hotel** (tel. (098) 43148) hires out sports and activity equipment. **Boats** leave for the **seal caves** from the pier at Dugort (up the road from the Strand Hotel) daily at 11am and 6pm.

Seal Caves Caravan and Camping Park (tel. (098) 43262) lies between Dugort Beach and Slievemore Mountain (July-Aug. £2.50/hiker or biker; April-June, and Sept. £2/hiker or biker; open April-Sept.). A softer pillow for your head awaits at **Valley House Hostel** (tel. 47204). The 100-year-old house is furnished, in a paroxysm of fading splendor, with antique furniture, massive windows, and an open turf fire. An in-house pub is the most luxurious of amenities (£5; open Easter-Oct.). The woman who once owned the house was brutally murdered. Her murderer's story became the basis for Synge's *Playboy of the Western World.* The road to the hostel turns left off the main road two miles east of Dugort at the valley crossroads. Nearby, self-proclaimed seafood specialist **Atoka Restaurant** (tel. 47229) feeds hearty portions to applauding locals (entrees £5-6; open May-late Sept. daily 8:30am-11pm). Those who stay for B&B get a big breakfast, too (£12/person).

■ ■ ■ MULLET PENINSULA

Unlike its popular neighbor to the south, the Mullet Peninsula is not part of the cool crowd. The peninsula itself remains desolate and untouristed. Remote **Belmullet** occupies the slender strip of land between Broad Haven and Blacksod Bay, which connects the soggy mainland to an equally soggy (but more unusual) peninsula. Equestrian trails, guided tours and walking paths unroll from Belmullet to the sea, where amateur anglers crowd the waters. The farther you get from Belmullet, the wilder the landscape becomes. Small white cottages dot the rugged bogland, while the sea rages on either side of the peninsula (the end of which is a small *gaeltacht*). An infrequent bus service runs to the Mullet Peninsula from Ballina. A summer service connects the towns to Dublin (July-Aug. Mon.-Sat. 2/day; Sept.-June Mon.-Sat. 1/day).

The **Erris Tourist Information Centre** (tel. 81500) serves the area well (open June-Sept. daily 9:30am-7:30pm; Oct.-May 9am-5:30pm). The **Bank of Ireland** (tel. 81311) monopolizes peninsula finances (open Mon.-Wed. and Fri. 10am-12:30pm and 1:30-5pm). The **Centra Supermarket** (open Mon.-Fri. 9am-7pm, Sat. 9am-9pm) is across Main St. from **Lavelle's Pharmacy** (tel. 81053; open Tues.-Fri. 9:30am-6:30pm, Mon. 9am-11pm, Sat. 10am-8pm). The **post office,** at the end of Main St. (tel. 81032), is open Mon.-Sat. 9am-2pm and 3-5:30pm. **Belmullet Cycle Centre,** American St. (tel. 81424) does a good trade in rentals (£6/day; deposit £10; reduction for group rentals; open Mon.-Sat. 9am-6pm). The **Garda** can be reached at tel. 81038. The area's **phone code** recedes to 097.

Eight miles south of Belmullet, the **Ten Degrees West Hostel and Watersports Centre** (tel. 82111) is a patch of L.A. grafted onto remote, windy Elly Bay. Bright murals, a young Irish-speaking staff, and a waterfront location combine to ensure a relaxing holiday. Call ahead during summer months. (Dorm £5, **camping** £2; Irish breakfast £1.50, dinner £3.50.) To reach Ten Degrees West, cross the bridge and stay on the main road, keeping the sea to your left. **Pollatomish,** between Belmullet and Ballycastle, invites you to its **An Óige Youth Hostel** (tel. (091) 84511; lockout, midnight curfew; July-Aug. £5/person, April-June and Sept. £4; open April-Sept.). B&Bs are a bit closer to Belmullet; many provide tackle rooms for fishing. **Mrs. Anne Reilly,** on the Ballina Rd., overlooks Broadhaven Bay (tel. 81260; single £13), while **Mill House B&B,** American St. (tel. 81181), near the bridge, offers cute rooms for £12.

The **Curragh Café** serves good chips and better Guinness. A jukebox, video games (10p), and disco keep the Irish-American connection alive. **The Appetizer** (tel. 81056) serves coffee shop fare on Main St. (chicken sandwich £1.10; open Mon.-Sat. 10am-5pm). **Clan Lir,** also popular with the young folk, gets rowdy during the football games. Suave international males smoke across the street at **Lavelle's,** reputedly Mayo's only gay pub. Birdwatchers and a youthful crowd flock to the **Anchor Bar,** Barrack St. (tel. 81007), which keeps a log of ornithological sightings.

Bogseeing package tours assemble at **Turasoireacht Lorrais** (tel. 82292), known in English as the **Erris Tourist Organization.** Pony trekking at the **Duvullaun Riding Centre** is £5/hour. **Boat trips** can be taken to the islands off the Mullet Peninsula by contacting Josephine and Matt Geraghty (tel. 85741). Most trips visit Inishkea and can go to the Achill Islands (daily; off-season 3/week; £10 return or single when busy, £12 otherwise; minimum of six persons). **The Belmullet Sea Angling Competition** in mid-July (tel. 81076) awards £2/lb. for the heaviest halibut, as well as money prizes for variety, and a life jacket for the best specimen caught. **Watersports** go for reasonable rates at the Ten Degrees West hostel (surfing, windsurfing, sea kayaking, etc. cost £8 per ½-day, £5/hr.; see above).

■■■ BALLINA

What Knock is to the Marian cult, Ballina ("bah-lin-AH") is to the religion of bait and tackle: hordes of pilgrims in olive green waders invade the town each year during the fishing season, from February to September. Some anglers fish without pause for three days and three nights when the salmon are biting. But the town also has attractions for the non-ichthyologist traveler, not the least of which are the many walks along the river with lovely vistas and a hip hostel. Forward-looking Irish President Mary Robinson grew up in Ballina, too (see Current Events, p. 58).

PRACTICAL INFORMATION

Tourist Office: Cathedral Rd. (tel. 70848), along the river next to St. Muredach's Cathedral. Open Easter-Sept. Mon.-Sat. 10am-5:30pm.

Banks: Bank of Ireland, Pearse St. (tel. 21144). Open Mon.-Wed. and Fri. 10am-4pm, Thurs. 10am-5pm; **ATM** accepts Visa, MC; **Irish Permanent Building Society,** Pearse St. (tel. 22777). Open Mon.-Fri. 9:30am-5pm; **ATM** accepts AmEx, Visa, Plus.

Post Office: Casement St. (tel. 21498). Open Mon.-Sat. 9am-5:30pm.

Phone Code: 096.

Trains: Train Station: Station Rd. (tel. 71818), near the bus station. Open Mon.-Fri. 7:30am-6pm, Sat. 9am-1pm and 3:15-6pm. Service to Dublin via Athlone (Mon.-Sat. 3/day, Sun. 2/day; £14, students £10).

Buses: Bus Station: Station Rd. (tel. 71800 or 71825), a 5-min. walk from the town center (turn left out of the station and walk straight). Open Mon.-Sat. 9am-6pm. Buses to: Athlone (Mon.-Sat. 1/day; £11, students £6.50), Dublin via Mullingar (3/day; 4hr.; £8, students £4.40), Galway (Mon.-Sat. 7/day, Sun. 5/day; 3hr.; £9.70, students £6), Donegal (£10, students £6), Sligo (Mon.-Sat. 6/day; 2hr.; £7.30, students £4.20), and Westport (1-3/day; 1½hr.; £6.30, students £3.70).

Taxis: **Mulherin Taxi Service,** the Brook (tel. 21783).
Bike Rental: Gerry's Cycle Centre, 6 Lord Edward St. (tel.70455). £7/day, £30/
week; collection service available. Open Mon.-Sat. 9am-7pm.
Luggage Storage: At bus station, £1.30/piece.
Pharmacy: McKane's, O'Rahilly St. (tel. 21698).
Emergency: Dial 999; no coins required. **Garda:** Walsh St. (tel. 21422).

ACCOMMODATIONS

The Salmon Weir Hostel, Berret St. (tel. 71903), is reason enough to come to Ballina. Glorious, luxurious, harmonious—all the good adjectives seem to apply. This
dream hostel has an outdoor patio, fantastic kitchen, and heavenly beds that even
smell clean. Most rooms have river views. (Bike rental £7/day, laundry £4.50. Bed
with sleeping bag £6.50 dorm £7.50, private room £9/person. Full Irish breakfast
£3.50, continental £1.80.) From the bus station, turn right, take your first left (after
the small shop), then the first right, and again the first left onto Barrett St. The hostel
is on the right. If by chance the hostel is full, the river, the lake, and seafishing are
just a cast away from the **Evergreen B&B,** near town on the Dublin Rd. (tel. 71343;
single £15, double £28, both w/bath). In town, try Ms. Galvin's **Greenhill,** on Cathedral Close behind the tourist office (tel. 27674; single £15, double £26). **Belleek
Camping and Caravan Park** (tel. 71533) is two miles from Ballina toward Killala
on R314, behind the Belleek Woods (£3/hiker with tent; laundry and kitchen; open
March-Oct.).

FOOD & PUBS

Aspiring gourmets can prepare for a feast at Quinnsworth **supermarket** (tel. 21056)
on Market Rd. Gourmands have it good, too.
Cafolla's, Bridge St. (tel. 21029). Cheap, fast, and almost Italian. Small cheese and
tomato pizza £2, veggie kebab £2.65. Open Mon.-Sat. 10am-10pm.
Jordy's, Pearse St. (tel. 21916). Get caught up in the intimacy of fishing nets and
flowers. Jordy specializes in grilling but can placate vegetarians, too. Vegetarian
stirfry £3.40, cake £1.25. Open Mon.-Sat. 9:30am-midnight, Sun. 11am-midnight.
Tullio's, Pearse St. (tel. 21890). Exudes elegance but foregoes high prices. Crab
claws in garlic butter £3. Open daily noon-3pm and 6-10pm.
Brogan's Bar and Restaurant, Garden St. (tel. 21961). Some of the best meat in
town. Grilled Moy salmon steak with side salad £6.95.

Down by the river, on Clare St., **Murphy's** (tel. 22702) serves pints to twenty-some-
things settled into the dark wood furnishings. **Longneck's,** a popular disco spruced
up with adobe walls and sombreros, is in the same building. **Hogan's,** O'Rahilly St.
(tel. 22527), has a hint of the Victorian in its old pictures and stained glass windows.
A mixed crowd and plenty of *craic,* however, ensure that the traditional elements
dominates. **Gaughan's,** across the street, emphasizes its addictive and traditional
atmosphere by selling pipe tobacco and snuff. **An Bolg Bui,** just before the bridge
on Bridge St. (tel. 22561), is Irish for "the yellow belly." The pub calls itself a "young
fisherperson's pub." Along with pouring pints, it displays its talents and fearlessness
by organizing fishing trips, tackle, and licenses. **Doherty's** next door (tel. 21150)
revels more exclusively in the angling lifestyle. **The Loft,** Pearse St. (tel. 21881),
rocks with all kinds of music nightly in summer, less frequently in winter. Or sink
into the **Armada Bar** (see Sights, below).

SIGHTS

Christmas comes twice a year here, once in December and once in the second
week of July during the **Ballina Salmon Festival** (tel. 71877), which has been
swinging since 1964. All of Mayo is hooked for Wednesday's **Heritage Day,** when
the streets are closed off and life reverts to the year 1910. All aspects of traditional
Irish life are staged. Greasy pig contests, a traditional Irish wake, donkey-driven butter churns, steam-driven vehicles, bands, and pageants center on Wednesday but
overflow into the rest of the week, which culminates in a dance and fireworks.

Trace out walks along the river in the bird-rich **Belleek Woods** ("bah-LEEK") around **Belleek Castle,** a fairytale forest without the big, bad wolf. To reach the Beleek Woods entrance, cross the lower bridge near the cathedral on Pearse St. and keep Ballina House on your right. Beleek Castle is an expensive hotel, but its **Armada Bar,** furbished entirely with wood from a sunken Spanish Armada galleon, is accessible, affordable, and appealing. Downstairs, another hotel bar carouses in a medieval banquet hall. Owner Marshall Doran gives tours of the castle and even allows a look at his own extensive fossil collection and an **armory museum** with exhibits dating as far back as the 16th-century (tel. 22400; by appointment only; £2).

A nearby dolmen, called "Table of the Giants," dates back to 2000 BC. It supposedly marks the burial site of four Maols who murdered Ceallach, a 7th-century bishop of Connacht. They were caught, hanged at Ardaree (the "Hill of Executions") and commemorated with the huge rock.

Fifteen minutes northeast of Ballina on the scenic Quay Rd. (R297), the gorgeous Enniscrone (or Inishcrone) Strand stretches along the east shore of Killala Bay. Opposite the long beach, the dreamy, family-run **Kilcullen's Bath House** (tel. 36238) simmers and steams, leaving you weak all over. Steam baths in cedarwood cabinets which leave only the head exposed and cool seaweed baths can relax even the most excitable traveler (no time limits, towels supplied; £6/seaweed bath, £7/steam bath and hot & cold seaweed baths). Post-soak, a tea room with views of the Strand awaits. (Both open June and Sept.-Oct. daily noon-9pm; July-Aug. daily 11am-10pm; Nov.-May Sat.-Sun. noon-8pm.) Fishing enthusiasts should contact John McDonagh (tel. 45332) for guidance and equipment. Equestrian land-lubbers can ride horses seven miles north of Ballina along the road to Sligo, at **Ox Mountain Slopes Ltd.,** Cloonkeeland, Corballa (tel. (096) 36451; pony trekking £8/hour).

■ NEAR BALLINA

BALLYCASTLE

Tidy Ballycastle is bordered by rich farmland on one side, by bogs on the other. The town closely resembles the set of a romance movie set in a pre-Famine village: stunning beaches for the love scenes, two tantalizing, remorse-inducing churches, and the Ceide ("KAY-ja") cliffs in case love sours. R314 crosses Ballycastle on its way west from Ballina to Belmullet; R315 leads due south to Crossmolina. **Tourist info** (tel. (096) 43256) is available from Moy Valley Resources Ltd., Lower Main St. (open Mon.-Sat 10:30am-5pm, Sun. 1-4pm). **Ulster Bank** opens its mini-office Tuesday 10am-noon. The **post office** (tel. (096) 43036) on Main St. will send your letters. **Bus Éireann** has a service to Killala and Ballina (Mon.-Sat. 3/day). The **phone code** is 096.

Accommodations, Food & Pubs Opulent—nay, *palatial*—digs, huge meals, and potpourri under the pillow grace Mrs. Chambers' B&B, **Suantai,** on the edge of town toward Killala (no phone). **Ceide House B&B** and restaurant, Main St. (tel. 43105), offers a double feature that starts with distinctly Mayo cuisine (open daily 9am-9pm) and ends the show in comfortable lodgings (£13). A tearoom and bar march side by side to the beat of different drums at **Barrett's** (tel. 43006; open 10:30am-12:30am). **McNamee's Supermarket,** Main St. (tel. 43057), sells peanut butter, jelly, and more. Forget rebellions and revolutions: at the **Castle Lounge** (tel. 43031), an olive green interior captures the spirit of 1976 (salmon sandwich £1.60).

Sights Apart from the **Catholic Church** in town, any structures of real significance are outside Ballycastle. To see the sights, walk across town toward **Ceide Fields,** turning right at the sign for the fisheries. From there, the road follows a bucolic route to the ocean, passing Dun Briste and stoic **Downpatrick Head.** The multi-layered rock formation supposedly broke off from the mainland as a demonstration of the power of God. The occurrence reinforced St. Patrick's authority, which had been challenged by a pagan king. In modern times, a car manufacturer used a helicopter to place one of its vehicles upon Dun Briste and made a spectacular TV commercial.

Five miles toward the Mullet Peninsula, the **Ceide Fields** are open to visitors through an **interpretive center** (tel. 43325), which offers exhibits, films, guided tours, murals, and an excavated Stone Age wall. One thousand hectares of bog around the center have buried Stone Age farming settlements. The center is of some architectural interest as well, as it was built around a re-erected 5000-year-old Scotch pine that had been dug out of the bog. And if all the muck gets you down, the Ceide Cliffs rise high nearby. (Open mid-March to May and Oct. Mon.-Sat. 10am-5:30pm; June-Sept. Mon.-Sat. 9:30am-6:30pm; tours every hour, film every ½-hour; £2.50, students £1; wheelchair accessible.)

LOWER MOY VALLEY

Ten miles south of Ballina on N26, the massively over-hyped **Foxford Woolen Mills,** Main St. (tel. (094) 56756), are the one and only attraction in the town of Foxford. The mill was founded by an entrepreneurial nun a century ago and today is open for tours. The mill itself is full of religious icons. A showroom displays a series of life-like tableaux chronicling the run-of-the-Mill history. (Open May-Oct. Mon.-Sat. 10am-6pm, Sun. noon-6pm; Nov.-April Mon.-Sat. 10am-6pm, Sun 2-6pm; 1-hour tours, 3/ hour; £2.75, students £1.75.) Between Foxford and Swinford on N57 is the **Carraig Abhainn Farm** (tel. (094) 56444). Barn dances, trad music, and farm animals drag in the locals (open Easter-Sept. Mon.-Sat. 10am-6pm, Sun. 1-6pm; £2.50).

The general frenzy of fins and hooks continues west of Foxford, across the lakes in the minuscule town of **Pontoon.** The **Tiernan Brothers' North Mayo Angling Centre,** Upper Main St. (tel. (094) 56731, ask for Thomas; open daily 7am-late) may become your spiritual guide. Gillies (guides) for one full day cost £30, but advice is free. **Cooltra Lodge** (tel. (094) 56640), a 14-bed hostel, monopolizes a great location 100 yards away from the Pontoon Bridge at the intersection of Lough Conn and Lough Cullin (dorm £5, private room £6/person; bikes £4/day; open June-Sept.).

The **Bellacorick Bog Train** (tel. (096) 53002) departs from its station on N59 between Ballina and Bangor, west of Crossmalina. The guided rail tour chugs through blanket bog, Ireland's first windfarm, and the flora and fauna of the Nephin Mountains (open May-Sept.; £3, students £1.50).

■ ■ ■ KNOCK

At 8pm on August 21, 1879, St. Joseph, St. John, and the Virgin Mary appeared at Knock with a cross, a lamb, an altar, and a host of angels. The visions materialized before at least fifteen witnesses, who stood in the rain for two hours watching the apparitions and chanting the Rosary. The Catholic hierarchy endorsed the reports, and Knock quickly developed into a major pilgrimage site. The streets overflow with entrepreneurs hawking anything (keychains and ashtrays included) emblazoned with the Knock label, implying a few comparisons to an overcrowded beach resort. While the objects that zealots buy may strike atheists as amusing, the town itself—holy and intent—never could. To anyone interested in the sociology of Catholicism or the psychology of religion, Knock will prove fascinating.

Knock lies midway between Galway and Sligo on N17 and makes a convenient and holy roadside stop for folks hopping directly from one to the other. Knock's **tourist office** (tel. (094) 88193) is suitably central (open May-Sept. daily 10am-6pm). Two doors down, the **shrine office** (tel. (094) 88100) hides to the left of the Presbytery and sells such literature as *The Vision in Marble, Hymns of Knock,* and official Knock calendars. The *Knock Pilgrim's Guide* (70p) contains a useful map (open June-Oct. daily 8:30am-10pm, Nov. 10am-6pm). **Bus Éireann** stops at Coleman's or at Lennon's, depending on the route. Buses depart for Westport or Roscommon and Athlone (Sun. 1/day) and Sligo (Sun. 3/day) and arrive from Athlone, Ballina, Castlebar, Galway, Roscommon, Sligo, and Westport (all Mon.-Sat. 2-3/ day). The **post office** is in Henegan's by the traffic circle (tel. (094) 88210; open

Tues.-Sat. 9am-5:30pm). A **Bank of Ireland** is located in the tourist office building. Testifying to the drawing power of Knock, **Horan Cutríl Airport** (tel. (094) 67222), closest to Charlestown 11 miles from the city, attracts pilgrim cash with direct flights to the U.K.

There's little opportunity and no reason to stay the night. "Hostels" in town are for the sick or elderly. Campers stay at **Knock Caravan and Camping** (tel. (094) 88223), about ¼ mile from the roundabout on the Claremore Rd (N17). (Laundry; July-Aug. £5.50/caravan and 25p/person, £4/cyclist or hiker; March-June and Sept.-Oct. £5/caravan and 25p/person, £3.50/cyclist or hiker.) Mrs. Carney's **Burren,** on Kiltimagh Rd. (tel. (094) 88362), induces restful slumber (£13.50/person). Food prices are aimed toward the masses. When bread and water lose their appeal, head for **Beirne's Restaurant** (tel. (094) 88161), on the main road (£6/3-course lunch; open daily noon-6pm). **Ard Mhuire's** (tel. (094) 88459) is an attractive split-level restaurant on Main St. (soup and roll £1.20; roast beef, veggies, and potatoes £4.25; open April-Oct. 9:30am-7:30pm). **Wally's,** Main St. (tel. (094) 88408), sends you on your way burdened with food (burger and chips £1.50; open June-Sept. daily noon-1:30am; Oct.-May daily 6pm-1:30am).

Despite all the pilgrims it attracts (a 1979 Papal visit drew a half-million faithfuls), Knock is a tiny, one-street town, and all of the religious sights are clustered along its one street. The Apparition supposedly appeared in the **Courtyard of Statues,** next to the Church of the Apparition. Due to its holy associations, numerous healings are said to have occurred in the courtyard. The enormous **Church of Our Lady** holds 20,000 people and resembles a basketball arena. Mass times are posted in the processional square and are held in various buildings (services at 8, 9:30, 11am, noon, 3, and 7pm). Signs everywhere command visitors to keep quiet and off the grass, but the devout can collect holy water at one of 18 automatic dispensers near the statues. The **Knock Folk Museum,** to the right of the basilica (tel. (094) 88100), portrays rural 19th-century life. The eyewitness accounts of the apparition and charming old photographs of Irish life are the best reasons to visit. (Open July-Aug. daily 10am-7pm; May-June and Sept.-Oct. daily 10am-6pm; £1.50.)

▓ Roscommon & Leitrim

■■■ CARRICK-ON-SHANNON

Water, water everywhere—and, probably, Guinness to drink. Lough Allen and Lough Key empty into the River Shannon in and around Carrick-on-Shannon. Anglers catch pike; yachtsmen drop in. Natural beauty attracts tourists to the Lough Key Forest Park. Two major streets, Bridge and Main, meet at the town's clock tower. The Famine Museum in nearby Strokestown is a useful, moving reminder of the catastrophe endured by western Ireland during the mid-19th century.

PRACTICAL INFORMATION

Tourist Office: (tel. 20170), on the Marina. Open Sept.-June Mon.-Sat. 9am-1pm and 2-5pm; July-Aug. Mon.-Sat. 9am-1pm and 2-8pm.

Bank: AIB, Main St. (tel. 20055). Open Mon. 10am-5pm, Tues.-Fri. 10am-4pm; **ATM.**

Post Office: St. George's Terrace (tel. 20020). Open Mon.-Fri. 9am-5:30pm, Sat. 9am-1:30pm and 2:30-5:30pm.

Phone Code: 078.

Trains: The train station (tel. 20036), a 10-min. walk southwest of town, sends carriages to: Sligo (3/day, Sun. 2/day; 1hr.; £4, students £2) and Dublin (2½hr.; £10, students £7).

Buses: Buses leave from Coffey's Pastry Case for Athlone (1/day; 1½hr.), Boyle (3/day; 15 min.), Sligo (3/day; 1hr.; students £4.10), and Dublin (3/day; 3hr.).
Taxis: P. Burke, Bridge St. (tel. 21343).
Bike Rental: Geraghty's, Main St. (tel. 21316). £6/day, £20-25/week; deposit £20. Fishing tackle £15/week. Open daily 9am-10pm.
Boat Rental: Michael Lynch, Villa Maria, (tel. 20034).
Laundromat: McGuire's Washeteria, Main St. (tel. 20339). Open daily 10am-6pm. Wash & dry £4.50.
Pharmacy: Cox's, Bridge St. (tel. 20158). Open Mon.-Sat. 9am-1pm and 2-5pm.
St. Patrick's Hospital: Summerhill Rd. (tel. 20011 or 20287; nights 20091).
Emergency: Dial 999; no coins required. **Garda:** Shannon Lodge (tel. 20021).

ACCOMMODATIONS, FOOD, & PUBS

Clean, comfortable bunk rooms, a smiling dog, and a microwave are found at the **Town Clock Hostel (IHH)** (tel. 20068), at the junction of Main and Bridge St. (£5, sheets 50p; open June-Sept.). B&Bs border Station Rd. and the manicured lawns of St. Mary's Close. Mrs. Clarke's **Sunnybank,** Station Rd. (tel. 20988), has several luxurious rooms reminiscent of Robin Leach's nasal commentary (£13.50/person; open April-Oct.). **Aisling,** St. Mary's Close, (tel. 20131), behind the Church of Ireland on Main St., corners the market on cozy abodes. It also pampers guests with a TV and coffee/tea facilities in each room (double w/bath £28; open April-Nov.).

To eat at **Coffey's Pastry Case,** Bridge St. (tel. 20929), without sampling the cake selection is a sin (pizza slice w/three salads £2.85; open Mon.-Sat. 8:30am-9pm, Sun. 10:30am-7:30pm). Chinese lanterns illuminate chicken and chips (£2.50) at the **Soda Fountain,** Main St. (tel. 21675; sandwiches from £1, chocolate sundae £1.25; open Mon.-Sat. 10am-7pm; Sun. noon-3pm; no soda fountain). **Chung's Chinese Restaurant,** Main St. (tel. 21888), cooks up a storm. Order take-away and save big. (Sweet 'n' sour chicken take-away £4.50, £5.80 eat-in; open Sept.-June Mon., Wed., and Thurs. 6-11pm, Fri.-Sat. 6pm-midnight; July-Aug. Mon.-Thurs. 6-11pm, Fri.-Sat. 6pm-midnight, Sun. 12:30pm-midnight.)

Wash down great meals to the tune of traditional sessions (every Wednesday, Friday, and Saturday in summer, impromptu sessions in winter) at **Cryan's Pub,** in The Riverside Inn on Bridge St. (tel. 20409). Move in with the Lost Generation and locals in the splendidly furnished **Flynn's Corner Pub,** Main St. (tel. 20003), near the tiny town clock. Find down-market drinks just across the town bridge at **Ging's** (tel. 21054), which boasts a beer garden on the River Shannon. They don't serve food, "just drink—and plenty of it."

SIGHTS

The **Angling Information Centre,** two miles from Carrick-on-Shannon in Drumsna (tel. 20694), supplies boats (£15/day), tackle, bait, and even info. For still more detailed information, the Angling and Tourism Association (tel. 20489) is the place. Fishing tackle is sold at **Holt's,** Bridge St. (tel. 20184; open daily 7:30am-10pm).

Cyril Cullen and his wife sell fuzzy Irish knits and handmade porcelain for reasonable prices in their shop on Main St. (tel. 20100). Some sweaters are made from the wool of their own Jacob sheep. At the intersection of Main and Bridge St., teeny, tiny **Costello Memorial Chapel,** reputedly the second smallest in the world, provides a permanent, safe haven under glass for the coffins of Mr. and Mrs. George.

■ NEAR CARRICK-ON-SHANNON

STROKESTOWN

15 miles south of Carrick on R368, where it meets N5 from Longford, poses the 18th-century **Strokestown Park House,** on Main St. (tel. (078) 33013). The former family estate of the Mahons has been expansively restored. The family's dark history of Irish blunders includes fighting as mercenaries for Oliver Cromwell, evicting 3006 tenants during the Famine, and subsidizing a number of coffin-ships (the infa-

mous emigration ships). By 1847, the worst year of the Famine, the tenants had had enough oppression and killed Denis Mahon. The house was occupied until 1979. A casual, unforced grandeur remains. Stags' heads, Chippendale bookcases, and velvet curtains seem to naturally belong here, but meager servants' quarters, kitchen, and underground service tunnel reveal the other side of the coin.

The **Famine Museum,** located in the old stables next to the house, moves and angers visitors more than anything in the house itself. Photographs and drawings of sallow, wide-eyed, starving tenants are from a world totally different from the one depicted in the renovated house. They also display accounts of dead Irish peasants on the roadsides, their mouths green from eating grass. One million people died in the Famine—more were forced to leave their country, never to return (see Famine (1841-1870), p. 54). (Open May-Sept. Tues.-Sun. 11am-5pm; museum £3; house £2.50; guided tours are available.)

LOUGH RYNN & LOUGH KEY

The Earls of Leitrim once roamed the 100-acre **Lough Rynn Estate** (tel. (078) 31427), just outside Mohill, 15 miles east of Carrick on N4 to Dublin. A walled Victorian garden and the turret house overlooking 600 acres of lake are remnants from the past century. A pleasant walking tour will guide you into the beautiful parklands, which include angling spots and the country's oldest monkey-puzzle tree. (Open late April-Aug. daily 10am-7pm; £1.50, cars £3.50; tours £1/person, last tour at 4pm.) The **Lough Rynn Caravan Park** (tel. (078) 31054) services campers on the shores of Lough Rynn (£2/tent, £5/caravan; open March-Oct.).

Four miles west of Carrick-on-Shannon on the road to Boyle, the **Lough Key Forest Park** (tel. (079) 62363) bursts with rhododendrons in the springtime. Its 850 acres and 33 forested islands are worth exploring any time of the year. Underground chambers, "bog gardens" displaying peat-loving plants, and boat tours strew themselves across the shores. Numerous signposts won't let you miss the round tower, fairy bridge, and wishing chair (always open). North of the Lough lies the site of Ireland's most important pre-human battle, in which the Túatha De Danann defeated Ireland's indigenous demons, the Formorians (see Legends & Folktales, p. 61). For camping details, see Accommodations, listed above.

■■■ BOYLE

The last major city on the Dublin-Sligo route, Boyle makes a convenient stop before launching into the Curlieu Mountains. Its geographic position has brought much trade to the town historically. Presently, Boyle is overlooked by tourists as a destination in its own right, but recent developments promise an interesting, if short, stay.

PRACTICAL INFORMATION

Tourist Office: Main St. (tel. 62145), inside the main gates of King House. Open May to mid-Sept. 9am-5pm.

Banks: National Irish Bank, at Bridge and Main St. (tel. 62058). Open Mon. 10am-5pm, Tues.-Fri. 10am-3pm; **ATM. Bank of Ireland,** Main St. (tel. 62015). Open Mon. 10am-12:30pm and 1:30-5pm, Tues.-Fri. 10am-12:30pm and 1:30-4pm.

Post Office: Carrick Rd. (tel. 62029 or 62028). Open Mon.-Tues. and Thurs.-Fri. 9am-5:30pm; Wed. 9:30am-5:30pm, Sat. 9am-1pm and 2-5:30pm.

Phone Code: 079.

Trains: The **station** (tel. 62027), past the Town Clock on the road to Roscommon, lies on the Dublin-Sligo route. Trains go to Dublin (3/day; 2½; £10, students £7) and Sligo (3/day; 40 min.; £4, students £2).

Buses: The stop is outside the Royal Hotel on Bridge St. Services to: Dublin (daily 3/day; 3¼ hr.); Sligo (daily 3/day; 45 min.); and Athlone (daily 1/day; 1¼hr).

Bike Rental: Sheerin Cycles, Main St. (tel. 62010). Raleigh rent-a-bike agent; £7 day, £30/week; deposit £40. Open Mon.-Tues. and Thurs.-Sat. 9:30am-1pm and 2-6pm.

Taxi: McHughs (tel. 63344).
Pharmacy: Patrick J. Ryan, Patrick and Main St. (tel. 62003). Open June-Sept. Mon.-Thurs. and Sat. 9am-6pm, Fri. 9am-6:30pm; Oct.-May Mon.-Tues., Thurs., and Sat. 9am-6pm, Wed. 9:30am-1:15pm, Fri. 9am-6:30pm.
Emergency: Dial 999; no coins required. **Garda:** Military Rd. (tel. 62030).

ACCOMMODATIONS, FOOD, & PUBS

The best and only hostel in the area is the **Town Clock Hostel (IHH)** (tel. (078) 20068) in nearby Carrick-on-Shannon (see Accommodations, food, & Pubs, p. 303). Every visitor to Boyle's **Abbey House,** Abbeytown Rd. (tel. 62385), gets an individually decorated room (£15/person). **Avonlea** (tel. 62538), on the Carrick Rd. just before you enter Boyle, puts up Annes by the dozen (single £15, double £28). The **Lough Key Forest Caravan & Camping Park** (tel. (079) 62212), and its laundry facilities are just a five minute drive from Boyle on the Carrick Rd. (£7.25/tent, £2.50/hiker or cyclist; open Easter-Aug.).

D. H. Burke, Main St. (tel. 62208) fulfills the duties of a supermarket (open Mon.-Thurs. 9:30am-6pm, Fri. 9:30am-8pm, Sat. 9:30am-7pm). **Una Bhán Restaurant** (tel. 63033), located within the gates of the King House, nourishes cross-country travelers (breast of chicken and salad £2.50; open daily 9:30am-6:30pm). **Chung's Chinese Restaurant,** Bridge St. (tel. 63123), has bunches of bean sprouts (open Mon.-Tues. and Thurs.-Sun. 5:30-11pm). **The Royal Hotel,** Bridge St. (tel. 62016), more than the average tourists' watering hole, pours pints of coffee and cups of beer. The coffee shop part will feed you (lasagne £2.50; open 10:30am-6pm; lunch served 12:30-3pm) and the bar will comfort you (shepherd's pie £2.10; dinner 6-9pm).

SIGHTS & ENTERTAINMENT

Gothic arches curve over the green lawns of magnificent **Boyle Abbey** (tel. (079) 62604; on A4), built in 1161 by Cistercian monks. The central arched walls are perfectly preserved, though they lack a roof. The walls seem to have been gently placed from outer space. (Open mid-June to mid-Sept. daily 9:30am-6:30pm; £1, students 40p; key available from the caretaker in off-season.)

King House, Main St. (tel. 63242), recently re-opened its doors and its four Georgian floors. Compare its present condition to the photos of a tree growing through the formerly derelict house. Built by Sir Henry King around 1730 for entertaining VIPs, it remained the family home for 50 years. The house is now decked out in 3-D displays and interactive exhibits chronicling the history of the "Kings of Connaught" and their elite dwelling, including its years as a military barracks. King House is also home to the **Boyle Civic Art Collection** of paintings and sculptures (open April and Oct. Sat.-Sun. 10am-6pm; May-Sept. daily 10am-6pm; £3, students £2.50; last admission at 5pm).

New in town, **Frybrook House,** Bridge St. (tel. 62170), lies on the banks of the Boyle River. Built in 1752, this Georgian house has been restored and refurbished to resemble its glory days. Henry Fry, for whom the house was built and named, was invited by Lord Kingston of King House to move to Boyle. Though not as grand as King House, Frybrook is noble in its own right. Of particular interest is the intricate plasterwork, of which 80 percent is original, and the array of smooth, dark Irish Georgian furniture. The house is still used as a residence, so only the bottom floors are open for viewing. An exception, however, is made in the case of the original ocular windows on the upper floors (open June-Aug. daily 2-6pm; £2.50, students £2; tour included).

NORTHWEST IRELAND

The farmland of the upper Shannon gradually gives way to Sligo. Sligo Town, itself alive and kicking, is surrounded by landscapes and monuments close to the heart of William Butler Yeats. A mere sliver of land connects Co. Sligo to Co. Donegal, the most remote and most foreign of the Republic's counties. Donegal's windy mountains and winding coasts are a dreamlike landscape. Don't leave the country before seeing the inspiring Inishowen Peninsula (Derry, in Northern Ireland, is readily accessible from here). Hitchhikers report that the upper Shannon region is difficult to thumb through and that they often end up relying on trucks. Drivers in Donegal are said to be much friendlier.

▓ County Sligo

If W.B. Yeats had never existed, County Sligo would be merely a pretty coastal stretch of hills, low cliffs, and choppy waves between boggy north Mayo and mountainous Donegal. As it is, the county is something of a literary pilgrimage site. The preadolescent Yeats divided his time between London and his mother's family in Sligo Town. The windswept landmarks near Sligo Bay became symbols and settings for many of his poems, and it has now become impossible to disassociate the landscape from the lyrics. It's easiest (and most exciting) to spend the nights in Sligo Town; everything else can be seen either on daytrips or on the way to Enniskillen or Donegal.

■ ■ ■ SLIGO TOWN

The gray River Garavogue gurgles along, swans and all, through the commercial, industrial, and market center that is Sligo Town (pop. 18,000). As you approach the town by rail, two imposing hills, Knocknarea and Benbulben, loom in the mist beyond train windows like possessive guardians competing for prominence in Sligo's stormy seaside landscape. W.B. Yeats was raised here by his mother's family, the Pollexfens, who owned a mill over the Garavogue. Most of Sligo can (and does) boast of some connection to the poet. Though quiet during the day, Sligo evenings bop to the beat of some 70 pubs and discos. Musical offerings range from Gaelic lays to Gaelic rock to Garth Brooks. Sligo rang in 1995, its 750th year of townhood, with a boisterous bonfire and celebrations.

ORIENTATION & PRACTICAL INFORMATION

Both trains and buses pull into the same station on Lord Edward St. From the station, take a left and follow Lord Edward St. straight onto Wine St., then turn right at the post office onto O'Connell St., which is the main street. More shops, pubs, and eateries beckon from Grattan, left off O'Connell.

Tourist Office: Temple St. on the corner of Charles St. (tel. 61201). From the station, turn left along Lord Edward St. Then turn right onto Adelaid St. Follow this up the hill past the cathedral and around the corner onto Temple St. to find the Northwest regional office with information on Donegal, Monaghan, Cavan, Leitrim, and Sligo counties. They offer a few freebies, but the bulk of the literature will cost you. Open May-June Mon.-Fri. 9am-6pm, Sat. 10am-2pm; July-Aug. Mon-

Sligo Town

Cathedral of the Immaculate
Conceptionl, **7**
Dominican Abbey, **5**
Rail and Bus Station, **1**
Sligo Art Gallery, **4**
St. John's Church, **6**
Tourist Information and Hawks
Well Theatre, **2**
Yeats Gallery and County
Museum, **3**

Sat. 9am-8pm, Sun. 10am-2pm; Sept.-April Mon.-Fri. 9am-5pm. There's also an info booth on O'Connell St. in Quinnsworth arcade (open Mon.-Sat. 10am-5:30pm).

Travel Agencies: Broderick's Travel, O'Connell St. Arcade (tel. 45221). USIT rates for students. Open Mon.-Sat. 9am-6pm.

Banks: AIB, 49 O'Connell St. (tel. 41085). Open Mon.-Wed. and Fri. 10am-4pm, Thurs. 10am-5pm; **ATM** accepts Visa, MC. **TSB,** 31 O'Connell St. (tel. 45360). Open Mon.-Wed. and Fri. 9:30am-5pm, Thurs. 9:30am-7pm.

Post Office: Wine St. (tel. 42593), on the corner of O'Connell St. Open Mon.-Tues. and Thurs. 9am-5:30pm, Wed. 9:30am-5:30pm.

Phone Code: 071.

Airport: Sligo Airport, Strandhill (tel. 68280). Open daily 9am-8pm.

Trains: McDiarmada Station, Lord Edward St.(tel. 69888; open Mon.-Sat. 7am-6pm, Sun. 20 min. before departure) sends trains to Dublin, via Carrick-on-Shannon and Mullingar (Mon. 4/day, Tues.-Sat. 3/day, Sun. 3/day;£12, students£8.50).

Buses: Station (tel. 60066) open Mon.-Thurs. 9:30am-6pm, Fri. 9:30am-7pm, Sat. 9:30am-4:30pm, Sun. 2-5pm. Buses fan out to: Belfast (Mon.-Sat. 1/day; 4hr.; £11.50, students £7.90); Derry (Mon.-Sat. 4/day, Sun. 2/day; 3hr.; £10, students £6); Dublin (3/day; 4hr.; £8, students £7); Galway (Mon.-Sat. 4/day, Sun. 2/day; 2½hr.; £10.50, students £6.50); Drumcliff (10 min.; £1.60); and Westport (Mon.-Sat. 1/day; 2¾hr.; £9.70, students £6).

Luggage Storage: In the train station; £1.30/piece.

Taxi: Cab 55, tel. 42333; **Finnegan's,** tel. 77777, 44444, or 41111 (for easy dialing if you're drunk); at least £3 in town, 50p per mile outside.

Bike Rental: Gary's Cycles, Quay St. (tel. 45418), £6/day, £25/week; deposit £30. Open Mon.-Sat. 9am-6pm. **Flanagan's Cycles,** Connelly and High St. (tel. 44477;

after hours tel. 62633). £7/day, £30/week; deposit £35. They offer other deposit destinations and do repairs. Open Mon.-Sat. 9am-6pm.

Bike Repair: P.J. Coleman, Stephen St. (tel. 43345).

Boat Rental: Peter Henry (tel. 42530), Blue Lagoon; rowboat £12/day; w/motor £25/day plus fuel.

Bookstore: Keohane's, Castle St. (tel. 42597). Big and smart. Sells Kirby's *The Yeats Country* and *Sligo, Land of Yeats's Desire.* Open Mon.-Sat. 8am-6:30pm, Sun. 8am-1:30pm.

Camping: Out & About, 20 Market St. (tel. 44550). All your outdoor needs met indoors. Open Mon.-Sat. 9:30am-6pm.

Laundry: Gurries, High St. (tel. 69268). Small wash and dry £3-4, large (like 30 pairs of jeans) £10-14. Open Mon.-Sat. 9am-7pm; last wash 4:45pm.

Early Closing Day: Monday; afflicts mostly grocery shops.

Hotline: Samaritans: tel. 42011. 24 hrs.

Pharmacy: E. Horan, Castle St. (tel. 42560), at Market St. Open Mon.-Sat. 9:30am-6pm. Local pharmacies post schedules of rotating Sun. openings.

Hospital: General Hospital, the Mall (tel. 42161).

Emergency: Dial 999; no coins required. **Garda:** Pearse Rd. (tel. 42031).

IMPRACTICAL INFORMATION

Wind Surfing: Sligo Yacht Park, Rosses Point (tel. 77168).

Woodcarver/Storyteller: Michael Quirke, Wine St. (tel. 42724). Open Mon.-Sat. 9am-6pm.

Fork Lift Rental: Meadowbank Industrial Estate (tel. 69890).

Falconry Courses: Michael Devlin (tel. 83211).

Tennis: Ballincar House Hotel (tel. 45361). Private hard court £2/hr.

ACCOMMODATIONS

There simply are not enough hostels in Sligo to handle the hordes of invading tourists, especially during the Yeats International Summer School weeks in mid-August. The cheaper options are often overcrowded and chaotic. B&Bs abound five minutes (on foot) out of town on Pearse Rd.

Eden Hill Holiday Hostel (IHH), Pearse Rd. (tel. 43204), entrance via Marymount or Ashbrook. 10 min. from town, but worth it. Cozy rooms and a Victorian sitting parlor. An open fire fosters new friendships. Kitchen with 2 microwaves. TV and VCR in common room. Esso station nearby is open 24 hrs. for munchies. Wash and dry £2; bikes £7/day. **Camping** £3/day. Dorm £6, private room £7/person.

White House Hostel (IHH), Markievicz Rd. (tel. 45160 or 42398), the first left off Wine St. after it crosses the bridge. Just 5 min. from the train station, it fills fast. The epitome of a hip hostel, White House has bunks named after the likes of Jimi Hendrix, James Connolly, and Socrates. Call to reserve a woolly blanket and avoid disappointment. Dorm £6; sheets £1; key deposit £2.

Yeats County Hostel, 12 Lord Edward St., across from bus station. Acceptable hostel beds if all the others are full. £5, sheets £1.

Glenview B&B, 1 mi. out of town on the Strandhill Rd. (tel. 62457). Friendly Mrs. Kane keeps four fine private rooms. Single £18, double £28.

Renati House, Upper Johns St. (tel. 62014). Businesslike and spotless and the cheapest B&B near the tourist office. Single £18.50, double £27.

Camping: Greenlands Campground (tel. 77113 or 45618), on Rosses Point, 5 mi. west of town (see below; buses run Mon.-Sat. 4-6/day; £1.65). At the end of Rosses Point Rd., Greenlands flanks the spectacularly situated green land of a golf club. Laundry free. Hikers and bikers £5/tent, July-Aug. add 50p/person. Open late May-Sept. On the other side of the bay near Strandhill, **Buenos Ayres,** Seahill Rd. (tel. 68120), is within earshot of the surf and just off the airport road (buses run Mon.-Sat. 4-6/day; £1.60). Laundry facilities. £5/hiker or biker, July-Aug. £5/tent plus 50p/person. Open Easter to mid-Sept.

FOOD

"Faery vats/Full of berries/And reddest stolen cherries" are not to be found in Sligo today. The demands of international visitors have, however, induced culinary development in Sligo. **Quinnsworth Supermarket,** O'Connell St., might even sell berries (open Mon.-Tues. 9am-7pm, Wed.-Fri. 9am-9pm, Sat. 9am-6pm). **Tír na nÓg,** Grattan St. (tel. 62752), stocks health foods and, for those sophisticated dinners, wine and soft cheese balls (open Mon.-Sat. 9am-6pm).

Kate's Kitchen, Market St. (tel. 43022). Not quite a restaurant, this combination deli-wholefood shop varies its take-away menu each day. French bread with gourmet toppings, vegetarian delights, homemade soups (£1), and fresh sandwiches from £1.15. Open Mon.-Sat. 9am-6:30pm.

Hargadon Bros., O'Connell St. (tel. 70933). It's reputation precedes it. Be prepared to scramble for a seat. (See Pubs, below, for more.) Veggie lasagne and two salads £3; restaurant open 10:30am-7pm; Sept.-June 10:30am-4pm.

The Cottage, Castle St. (tel. 45319). Irish-Asian flair (the Irish part is the pine furnishing). Kebabs of sundry varieties for £3.85. Open Mon.-Sat. 9am-6pm.

Lyon's Café, Quay St. (tel. 42969). Tucked away upstairs, this cute café brews Bewley's tea and bakes a selection of cakes. Chicken hotpot with potatoes and veggies £3.50. Open Mon.-Sat. 9am-6pm; lunch served 12:30-2pm.

Robert's Restaurant, Stephen St. (tel. 43320). Has all four food groups: it's inexpensive, sells pastries, makes ice cream, and serves hot meals. Daily lunch specials (salmon, potatoes, and veggies £4.25). Open Mon.-Sat. 9am-6pm; July-Aug. also open Sun. 11am-6pm; lunch served 12:30-3pm.

PUBS

Sligo loves its pubs. Many pubs have live music during the summer. The weekly *Sligo Champion* (50p) lists events and venues.

Hargadon Bros., O'Connell St. (tel. 70933). Open fires, old Guinness bottles, poitín jugs, and dark, intimate nooks—nothing's changed here since 1868. The traditional pub of all traditional pubs, but no music.

The Bear and Cat, Thomas Bridge St. (tel. 41310), don't really get along, but the pinball machines entertain kids. Cynical not-quite-young people hang out here. Live bands once or twice a week.

Shoot the Crows, Castle St., but clean up after yourself. Naked men carouse with snakes on the mural outside: an apt introduction to the epicenter for social gatherings of cool modern people. Music on Tues. and Thurs.

Connolly's, Markievicz Rd. (tel. 67377), a few steps from White House Hostel. Oldest pub in Sligo.

McGarrigle's, O'Connell St. (tel. 71193). 18th-century lanterns light the wooden barrel-tables. Live music draws crowds Tues. and Thurs.; impromptu sessions other nights.

McLynn's, Old Market St. (tel. 60743). The *International Pub Guide* ranks McLynn's as the best pub for music in Sligo. Music on Fri. nights.

The Clarence, Wine St. (tel. 42211). Crowds stumble to this nightclub after the pubs close Tues.-Sat. nights. Live band Sat. (cover £3.50). The lounge bar has lounge music on lounging weekends.

SIGHTS

Yeats praised peasants and aristocrats (at least in principle) and disdained modern middle-class merchants and industrialists. Appropriately, most of the Yeatsian sights are at least a mile from mercantile Sligo town (see Near Sligo Town, p. 310). The 13th-century **Dominican Abbey,** Abbey St., is one of the best preserved abbeys of its type. It boasts cloisters and ornate coupled pillars that, though old and disused, can hardly be described as ruins. A new staircase now allows visitors to view the equally intriguing upper floors. A defaced monument stone, which until quite recently bore the names of a mother and her child, graces the sacristy. Tradition claims that the mother's descendants, not wanting a public reminder of their forebears' illegitimacy, hired a stonemason to chisel the names away in secret. (Open summer daily 9:30am-6:30pm; £1.50, students 60p; last admission 45 min. before closing; otherwise, ask for the key from Mrs. McGuinn, 6 Charlotte St.) The oldest of Sligo's churches is the 17th-century **St. John's Church,** on John St. (open Mon.-Sat. 10am-5:30pm; free). Next door, the hulking **Cathedral of the Immaculate Conception** is best visited at dawn or dusk, when the sun's rays stream through dozens of truly magnificent stained glass windows.

The Yeats Art Gallery, Stephen St., houses one of the country's finest collections of modern Irish art, including a number of works by Jack Butler Yeats (William Butler's brother) and contemporaries such as Nora McGuinness and Michael Healy. Among the museum's other treasures are some first editions of Yeats and original publications by the Dún Emer Press and Cuala Press. The gems among these are a few illustrated broadside collaborations by Jack and W.B. Yeats. The **Sligo County Museum** preserves small reminders of Yeats: pictures of his funeral and Countess Markievicz's prison apron. (Museum open June-Sept. Mon.-Sat. 10:30am-12:30pm and 2:30-4:30pm, April-May and Oct. Mon.-Sat. 10:30am-12:30pm. Gallery same hours as museum but closed Mon. Both free.) The **Sligo Art Gallery** in the Yeats Memorial Building, Hyde Bridge (tel. 45847), hosts traveling exhibitions of Irish art (open daily 10am-5:30pm when there's a traveling exhibit).

ENTERTAINMENT

The Hawk's Well Theatre, Temple St. (tel. 61526 or 62167), beneath the tourist office, presents modern and traditional dramas, ballets, and musicals. The theater also sponsors lectures and conferences (partially linked to the Yeats Summer School). The theater box office is at 6 Union St. (open daily 10am-6pm; £6, students £4). **The Blue Raincoat Theatre Company,** Quay St. (tel. 70431), produces one-act plays, some quite naturally by Yeats (June-Aug. Mon.-Fri. at 1pm).

A monthly *Calendar of Events,* available and free at the tourist office, will clue you in. Late August brings the **Sligo Arts Festival** and its variety of attractions to town: traditional music, jazz, blues, rock, classical music, short story readings, comedy, and dance (contact the Sligo Arts Festival Office, Wine St.; tel. 69802). For two weeks in August, the internationally renowned **Yeats International Summer School** opens some of its poetry readings, lectures, and concerts to the public. International luminaries such as Seamus Heaney are regular guests. (For an application, contact the secretary of the Yeats Society, Yeats Memorial Building, Douglas Hyde Bridge, Sligo; tel. 42693, call Mon.-Fri. 10am-1pm and 3-5pm.) In July, the **Summer Festival** climaxes with a national fiddling competition.

■ NEAR SLIGO TOWN

LOUGH GILL

Lough Gill is just a short distance southeast of Sligo. From town, take the Enniskillen Rd. and turn off at the Lough Gill signs. Signs from the main road point to **Holywell,** a rather unusual shrine, with a well and waterfall. During the Penal Law years, secret masses were held at this site. If by chance the British Military approached, the congregation would disband and pretend to be enjoying a football game. The main road itself reaches **Dooney Rock,** on the south shore of Lough Gill near Cottage Island. Here, Yeats's "Fiddler of Dooney" made "folk dance like a wave of the sea." An even younger Yeats wrote **"The Lake Isle of Innisfree,"** about an actual island in Lough Gill where "peace comes dropping slow." To see it yourself, descend to the edge of the Lough.

Along the same route lies **Dromahair,** which still shelters Creevelea Abbey. Founded in 1508 as the Friary of Killanummery, its active days ended in 1650 when Oliver Cromwell expelled monks from the confiscated monastery. Since 1721 it has been used as a burial site. Dromahair is the farther point of the Lough Gill route. From here, turn left onto R286 to head back to Sligo Town.

On the route back stands **Parke's Castle** (tel. (071) 64149), a 17th-century planta-tion castle. Originally built for protection from the British, its waterfront location enables a quick getaway across the Lough. (Open mid-April to May Tues.-Sun. 10am-5pm; June-Sept. daily 9:30am-6:30pm; Oct. daily 10am-5pm; £2, students £1.) Two miles before town, a left turn leads to Hazelwood. Yeats walked in this park "among long dappled grass" in "The Song of Wandering Aengus." The sculpture trail makes a particularly interesting walk.

Lough Gill is accessible by boat and by bus. **The Wild Rose Water-Bus** (tel. (071) 64266) offers a number of tours: a Sligo-Parke's Castle-Garavogue-Lough Gill-Sligo trip (daily; 3 hr.; £4.50); a Parke's Castle-Innisfree trip (3/day; 1hr.; £3.50); a Doorly Park (Sligo)-Parke's Castle trip (daily; 1 hr.); and a night cruise of the Lough that departs from Parke's Castle (Mon., Wed., and Fri. 9pm). **Lough Gill Tours,** 57 Moun-tain Close (tel. 642 66), does a tour of the Garavogue and Lough Gill (stopping at Parke's Castle, 3½hr., £4.50), and Innisfree Island (1hr., £3.50). In July and August, **John Howe's bus company** (tel. 42747) departs from the Sligo tourist office to guide visitors through Yeats country (3hr.; £7). Information on self-guided **walking tours** is available from the tourist office.

YEATS, YEATS, YEATS

Yeats is laid to rest in **Drumcliff churchyard,** four miles northwest of Sligo on N15 (Bundoran Rd.) under bare Benbulben's head. The epitaph was chosen by the poet himself: "Cast a cold eye/On life, on death./Horseman, pass by!" Yeats died in France in 1939. World War II prevented his wife, Georgie, from shipping his body back to Ireland for several years. An engraving marks her tomb, at his feet. Some of Yeats's roots are in the churchyard: one of his ancestors was rector here many years ago. A high cross dating from 1000 AD guards the entrance to the graveyard (always open; free). Just outside, the **Old Stables** (tel. 44946) caters to literary pilgrims' needs with bulging pots of tea and a convenient bureau de change (open June-Sept. Mon.-Fri. 9am-6pm, Sun. 1-6pm). **Buses** run from Sligo to Drumcliff (Mon.-Sat. 3/ day; Sun. 1/day summer only; 10 min.; £2.60 return, students £1.65). **Hitching** is reportedly painless along the four-mile stretch of N15. A few miles northeast of Drumcliff, **Glencar Lake** is the subject of more literary excursions. It was men-tioned in Yeats's "The Stolen Child." Stunning views of Knocknarea and Benbulben and the smashing Glencar Falls add thoughts of natural beauty to those of literary genius. The lake is marked by a sign about one mile north of Drumcliff on N15.

North of Drumcliff, eerie **Benbulben**—the subject of Yeats's eponymous poem—protrudes from the landscape like the keel of a foundered boat. The climb up the 1729-foot peak is rather windy, and the summit can be downright gusty. Marks of old turf cuttings on the way up remember one of the mountainside's essential uses. Clear signs guide travelers to Benbulben from the Drumcliff Rd. Ask for detailed directions to trailheads at the gas station in Drumcliff (the only one).

Four miles west of Drumcliff is **Lissadell House** (tel. 63150), where poet Eva Gore-Booth and her sister Constance Markiewicz (second in command in the Easter Rising and later the first woman elected to the Dáil) entertained Yeats and his circle. The gaunt house has lost some of its luster, and the carpets are wearing thin, but the Gore-Booth family still lives here and allows tours. Henry Gore-Booth was an Arctic explorer and avid hunter—his harpoons, stag heads, and stuffed birds create a macho atmosphere that must have given mild-mannered Yeats the willies. Yeats wrote that the sitting room was "as high as a church and all things in good taste." Admire the double staircase made of Kilkenny marble and find where Constance Markiewicz scratched her initials on a window pane in the ante-room with her dia-mond ring. (Open June to mid-Sept. Mon.-Sat. 10:30am-12:15pm and 2-4:15pm; £2.15. Grounds open year-round; free.) Take your first left after Yeats Tavern Hostel on the Drumcliff Rd. and follow the signs. Near Lissadell and the village of Carney, the excellent food at **Laura's Pub,** just past Orchard Inn, justifies the prices (chicken Kiev £3.50).

INISHMURRAY & MULLAGHMORE

Mullaghmore, 15 miles north of Drumcliff, is one of the departure points for faraway **Inishmurray**, a tiny monastic island which looks like a hill fort with no hill. Founded around 600 AD, pounded by Vikings around 800, and finally abandoned in the 1940s, the windswept island is now a deserted maze of stone walls and altars. The power of the *Clocha Breaca* (cursing stones), found on the islands, can be unleashed on your worst enemies. Be careful of your wish, however, as it will rebound on you if it is unjustified. No regular scheduled ferries go to Inishmurray: to get there you should be rich or find a group of 8-12 others who want to see the island. Then try boatman **Brendan Merrifield** (tel. (071) 41874; £95), who organizes driving or angling trips and parties. **Mullaghmore** itself is a beautiful fishing village with two long miles of sheltered beach, a headland, and **Classiebawn Castle,** the residence and murder scene of Lord Mountbatten. You can feasibly visit Mullaghmore on a daytrip from Sligo but you'll be more comfortable doing so from Bundoran, just five miles away. B&Bs are expensive here, but dinner at **Eithne's Restaurant** (tel. (071) 66407) is worth the splurge. The meal will keep you fed for an entire day or more (open summer daily, lunch 12:30-3pm, *à la carte* dinner 6:30-10pm).

CARROWMORE & KNOCKNAREA

A fantastic assortment of passage graves spooks visitors south of Sligo. Just three miles from town, **Carrowmore** remains Ireland's largest group of megalithic tombs. More than 60 passage tombs and stone circles mark the fields, some pre-dating Newgrange (see Newgrange, p. 133) by seven centuries. The excellent **interpretive center** (tel. 61534) explains their meaning (open May-Sept. daily 9:30am-6:30pm; £1, students 60p).

The mountain **Knocknarea** faces Benbulben, on the opposite shore of Sligo Bay. Queen Mebdh, or Maeve, the villain of the *Táin bo Cuailnge* (see Legends & Folktales, p. 61) is reputedly interred in the cairn on the summit. She is buried standing up to face her enemies in Ulster. Her notoriety is evident from the size of the cairn, which is about three times that of Creevykeel. Decades ago, tourists started taking stones from the cairn as souvenirs; to preserve the legendary monument, local authorities created a "tradition" that any unmarried man or woman who brought a stone *up* the mountain to place *on* the cairn would be married within the year. The plot succeeded, the cairn survives. The stunning mountain also makes a cameo appearance in Yeats's "Red Hanrahan's Song about Ireland"—"The wind has bundled up the clouds high over Knocknarea/And thrown the thunder on the stones for all that Maeve can say."

Knocknarea is a long walk from Carrowmore: walk in the direction away from Sligo from the **Visitors Centre.** Take a right at the church, then the first left to the sign *Mebdh Meirach*. The hour-long walk up the path gets boggy and slippery: walk softly and carry a big stick (or bring a friend to lean on). From Sligo, turn right at the bottom of O'Connell St., and walk straight—for an hour. The reward is a stunning view of the misty bay and heathered hills.

 # County Donegal

Though its name means "fort of the foreigner," tourists are still likely to feel a bit out of place in this most remote, least Anglicized, of Ireland's "scenic" provinces. Donegal takes second to Cork in size, second to none in glorious wilderness. There's more forest (that is, less deforestation) than in Connacht, and the coastline alternates glorious beaches with majestic cliffs. The biggest cliffs are around Slieve League, and Inishowen makes the best cycling or driving route. In between the

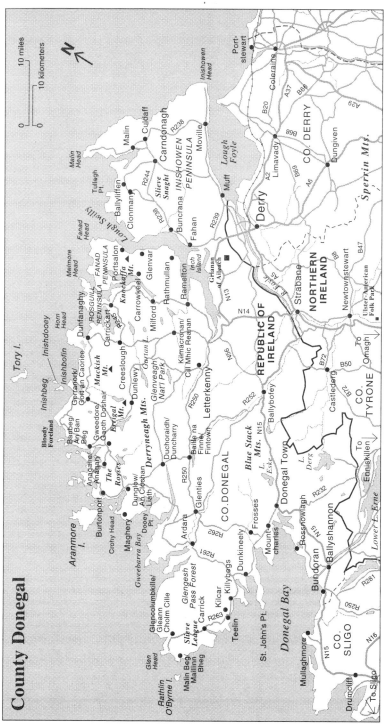

County Donegal

larger pockets of civilization, distance from all things English has preserved the biggest *gaeltacht* in the country.

Donegal's decent harbors and their remoteness from London made it a stronghold for Gaels (especially the Northern Uí Néill, Ó Domhnaill (O'Donnell), and McSwain (McSweeney) clans) until the Flight of the Earls. After years of English occupation (though few English actually lived in this barren "wasteland"), Donegal was given to the Irish state in 1920. Its largely Catholic population would have put at risk the Protestant majority that was Northern Ireland's reason for being. Today, cottage industries, fishing boats, and the underwear factory help the county keep body and soul together. Since the ceasefire, the tourist industry has started to pick up as well, but be assured that you'll encounter fewer camera-toting tourists here than anywhere else in the country. One of the best books on any Irish region is J. J. Tohill's *Donegal: An Exploration*, a historical work to complement your travel guide.

GETTING THERE & GETTING AROUND

Donegal has the public transportation to get you where you want to go, but only if you're willing to wait. There are no trains past Sligo and Derry into Donegal, and buses tend to hit smaller towns only once per day, sometimes in the early morning. **Cycling** is always fun, though the distances are large and the terrain is hilly; most towns, including major towns like Letterkenny, Donegal town, Sligo, and Dungloe, rent bikes. **Hitchers** report very short waits and friendly drivers on the main roads, especially those north of Donegal town; byways are largely devoid of drivers, but any that pass will usually pick up hitchers who look friendly or desperately hungry.

Bus Éireann (tel. (01) 366111) connects Dublin with Letterkenny (tel. (074) 21309; Mon.-Sat. 4/day, Sun. 3/day; 4 hr.; £10, £13 return), Donegal town (Mon.-Sat. 4/day, Sun. 3/day; 4 hr.; £10, £13 return), and these two towns with some of the smaller villages in the southern half of the region. **Lough Swilly Buses** (Derry tel. (0504) 262017; Letterkenny tel. (074) 22400) fan out over the northern area, connecting Derry, Letterkenny, the Inishowen Peninsula, the Fanad Peninsula, and western coastal towns as far south as Dungloe. Swilly also offers a Runabout ticket: eight days of unlimited travel (£18, students and children £9). **McGeehan's Bus Co.** (tel. (075) 46101 or 46150) runs to and from Dublin each day, passing through almost every town on the way (Donegal to Dublin £11, £15 return). **John McGinley** (tel. (074) 35201; Dublin tel. (01) 4513804) runs a similar service, based in Falcarragh (Mon.-Thurs. 1/day; Fri.-Sun. 3-4/day; £9, £12 return). **Feda O'Donnell** (tel. (075) 48114; in Galway tel. (091) 761656) runs up and down the Donegal coast, connecting northwest Ireland with Galway (from Letterkenny, 1/day; £8, £12 return), and carries bikes for free. Bus prices on the main routes like Letterkenny-Dublin fluctuate due to competition. McGeehan's offers **day tours** of Co. Donegal from Donegal Town, Ardara, and Glenties, mid-July to Sept. On Tuesdays the tours cover the Killybegs peninsula and Ardara; on Wednesdays, Glenties and the Rosses; on Thursdays, Carrickart, Rosguill, and the Fanad Peninsula. All tours leave from the Donegal tourist office, Ballybofey, or Letterkenny (with connections from Ardara and Glenties) and cost £10/person or £25 for all three days. One last hint: private bus companies tend to be more extensive than Bus Éireann, and their drivers more open to persuasion if you want to be let off on the doorstep of a remote hostel.

■ ■ ■ BUNDORAN

Bundoran, at the mouth of Dobhran River, is the first stop in Donegal when arriving from Sligo or Leitrim. A thriving seaside resort, its hopping nightlife, water sports, and horseback riding attract an overwhelming crowd of partiers. The population of the town swells from 2000 to 20,000 during the summer. The masses of vacationers disappear once you travel even a bit farther into the remoter regions of the county.

Information is available from the **tourist office,** over the bridge on Main St. (open May-Sept. Mon.-Sat. 10am-1pm and 2-6pm). Farther down the street roosts Bundoran's own **post office** (tel. 41224; open Mon.-Fri. 9am-5:30pm and Sat. 9am-1pm).

AIB bank is on Main St. (open Mon.-Wed. and Fri. 10am-4pm, Thurs. 10am-5pm; **ATM**). **Bus Éireann** and **Feda O'Donnell** coaches leave regularly from the bus station on Main St. for Donegal Town and Sligo. The **phone code** whistles 072.

Every other house in Bundoran seems to be a B&B; the cheaper and more quiet ones are farther down main street, away from the bridge. The most affordable option is the **Homefield Hostel (IHH)**, Bayview Avenue (tel. 41288), just around the corner from the old church on Main St. (dorm £7, double £8-10/person w/bath; all w/continental breakfast; dinner £5; laundry £4). Homefield also organizes horseback riding, bicycle rentals (£6/day, £30/week; deposit £30), hill walking, fishing, and local tours. The hostel is a two-minute walk from the Bundoran bus stop: take a left at McGrath's guest house. **Coel na Mara** (tel. 41287) has splendid views of Donegal Bay from its bedrooms (£15/person). **Dartry View Caravan and Camping Park** (tel. (072) 41794) hangs out at the east end of Bundoran (£6/tent, April-May £5.50; open Easter-Sept.).

For the fish enthusiast, **Conroy's** at the west end of Main St. (tel. 41280) is fishlicious. Fresh fish and smoked salmon at low prices are always available (fish 'n chips £3). The **Ould Bridge Bar,** on the corner of Main St. and Church St. (tel. 42050), cooks budget lunches. The "Bridge" is also a haven for trad music at night (sessions Tues. and Thurs. nights). **Brennans,** on Main St., is a real, old pub experience; it's been in the same family for over 100 years and hasn't changed much. People from all around flock to Bundoran's nightclubs and discos.

Aughross Cliffs (meaning "headlands of the steeds") was once the grazing ground for war horses. A leisurely stroll here past the Northern hotel is contrasted by the impressive view of mighty Atlantic waves on your left. Curious natural sights include the **Fairy Bridges,** the **Wishing Chair** (so called because the natural stone formation looks like one), and the **Puffing Hole,** where water spouts up in an impressive display through a hole in a bed of rock. Farther along are the golden beaches of Tullan Strand. Bundoran is a mecca for Donegal's surfers. **Fitzgeralds,** Main St. (tel. (072) 41223), reports on conditions and provides equipment.

■■■ BALLYSHANNON

St. Patrick once offered to make Ballyshannon "a second Rome." Though still popeless, the town does host the raucous annual **Ballyshannon Folk & Traditional Music Festival** (tel. 51049; tickets on sale after July 29), which attracts about as many people as a papal visit might. The festival itself is on the August bank holiday weekend, but informal sessions begin during the last week of July. Tickets for the entire weekend cost £25 and admit purchasers to performances, afternoon music workshops, and a jammed campsite. During the rest of the year, Ballyshannon twiddles its musical thumbs by the River Erne, which splashes over the Falls of Assaroe (or *Ess Ruaid*) just west of the bridge. Though the falls are one of Ireland's most ancient pagan holy sites (representing the domineering male river flowing into the joyous female sea), there's little to see other than water. Ballyshannon, only 30 miles from both Sligo and Donegal Town, is a convenient stop between the two.

Ballyshannon's **tourist office** consists of a desk in the Abbey Centre Cinema complex at the end of Tirconaill St. (tel. 51375; open July-Aug. Mon.-Sat. 9am-7pm). Ask here about guided walking tours. The **post office** (tel. 51111; open Mon.-Fri. 9am-1pm and 2-5:30pm, Sat. 9am-1pm) settles halfway up Castle St., as does the **AIB** bank (tel. 51169; open Mon.-Wed. and Fri. 10am-4pm, Thurs. 10am-5pm; **ATM**). Call the **police** at tel. 51155. **Buses** leave the depot just beside the bridge (tel. (074) 31008) on their way to Sligo (Mon.-Sat. 11/day, Sun. 5/day; 1hr.;£5.50) and Donegal Town (Mon.-Sat. 10/day, Sun. 3/day; 25 min.;£3.50). The **phone code** screams 072.

Accommodations, Food, & Pubs **Duffy's Hostel (IHH),** Donegal Rd. (tel. 51535) just outside town, offers a warm Irish welcome. Duffy's is fairly small and doesn't accept reservations, so an alternate plan is a good idea (dorm £5, double £6/person; **camping** £3; open March-Oct.). **Hillcrest B&B,** Tirconaill St. (tel. 52203), offers rooms for £13 per person. At **Mullac naSi,** (tel. 52702), Mrs. Nolan-Coyle hospitably houses guests in big, comfortable rooms overlooking Erne Estuary (£15/person); she can also arrange pony trekking. If all else fails, look in Bundoran (see above) for a bed.

Cúchulainn's, Castle St. (tel. 51814), serves the same food—anything and chips—upstairs and down. Upstairs is infinitely more pleasant. (Small cheese pizza £1.50; upstairs restaurant open daily 12:30-10pm; downstairs self-service open Mon.-Fri. 12:30pm-1:30am, Sat. 12:30pm-4am, Sun. 1pm-1:30am.) **Ember's Restaurant** (tel. 52297), upstairs from Paddy Donagher's Pub, Main St., offers typical pub grub alongside more interesting dishes in a pleasant setting. Lunch served noon-3pm: baked brie £2.75, fruit salad £1.85. Dinner (6-10pm) is more expensive, but the vegetarian stir-fry and pasta dishes are priced within the stratosphere (£5-7). **Spar Supermarket** sells groceries at the end of Tirconaill St. (Open Mon.-Thurs. 9am-8pm, Fri.-Sat. 9am-8:30pm, Sun. 11:30am-8pm.) Locals flock to **Sean Óg's,** Castle St. (tel. 51585), for music every Wednesday and *craic* all week long. The newest and most happening bar is the **Cellar,** at the White Horse Bar just down the road toward Bundoran (tel. 51452). Acoustic music beats on Wednesday and Saturday nights, and traditional music shows a good time on Fridays. **The Thatched Pub,** Bishop St. (tel. 51147), looks like an old-time kitchen and has music (usually traditional) every night in July and August and weekends all year. **Herman's Nite Club,** Main St., rocks Friday to Monday (cover Fri.-Sun. £2; Mon. no cover), but most locals head to Bundoran for night life (see Bundoran, above).

Sights **Allingham's Bridge** connects the town's two halves and honors Ballyshannon's most famous native, the poet William Allingham: he inspired Yeats to study the folklore, mythic beliefs, and ancient traditions of Sligo. Most of the town lies north of the river, where Main St. divides halfway up a hill. This hill, named Mullach na Sídh (Hill of the Faires) has a panoramic view and is believed to be the burial site of the legendary High King Hugh, supposedly drowned by the Assaroe Falls. From the left fork of Main St., a left turn just past the Imperial Hotel will bring you to **St. Anne's Church,** where poet Allingham is buried. His grave lies on the south side of the church, marked by a white slab. Back by the river, a fish pass at the power station allows tourists to watch the ancient biological cycle of salmon and trout struggling upstream during spawning season, around June. Trying to distinguish the sun-god in salmon form—believed to swim past every night after dipping into the western ocean—is a challenge.

Just outside Ballyshannon, the river meanders past the barely visible 12th-century **Cistercian Abbey of Assaroe.** It was built on an ancient pagan holy site. The Cistercians were brilliant water engineers: they canalized the river to harness its hydraulic power for running a water mill. The **water mill** still operates; restorers have added a neat tea shop (open June-Aug. daily 10:30am-6:30pm; Sept.-May Sun. 1:30-6pm). Outside the mill, a tiny path leads to the **Abbey Well,** blessed by St. Patrick (what hasn't been?). Pilgrims bless themselves with its water each year on August 15 (though they avoid the river, which Patrick cursed). Nearby, a tiny **cave,** cut into stone and marked with the Catsby Cross above the door, harbors a rough stone altar (in use long before Christianity confiscated it). The cave also contains a Mass rock which was used during Penal Days and two hollow stones that were used for holy water. To reach the cave, take a right after you cross Allingham's bridge and follow the river bank for about 100 yards. Trails to the caves and the well get quite muddy and slippery. To get to the mill hill from town, continue up the left fork of the main road, past the Thatched Pub. From there, take the second left down a tiny lane.

■■■ DONEGAL TOWN

Most international travelers regrettably begin their tour of Co. Donegal with a stay in Donegal Town. An inevitable stopover between Sligo or Fermanagh and the splendor of the north and west, Donegal Town itself has few natural and historical wonders to offer tourists. However, as far as night life, amenities, bustling social activity, and souvenirs are concerned, this is the place to be. The **International Arts Festival,** held on the last weekend of June, brings such diverse activities as parachuting, theater, storytelling, and traditional music that render the town a summertime center of entertainment. The town is too far south to make a good base for traveling around the rest of Donegal, but its tourist office—by far the county's best—can tell you about more remote, more scenic destinations along the northern coast.

PRACTICAL INFORMATION

Tourist Office: Quay St. (tel. 21148), south of the Diamond on the Sligo Rd. Loads of brochures on the entire county, as well as a basic, free map of the city; be sure to stop here before heading north. Open July-Aug. Mon.-Sat. 9am-8pm, Sun. 10am-1pm and 2-6pm; Sept.-Oct. and Easter-June Mon.-Sat. 9am-6pm.

Banks: AIB bank, the Diamond (tel. 21016). Open Mon.-Wed. and Fri. 10am-4pm, Thurs. 10am-5pm; **ATM. Bank of Ireland,** the Diamond (tel. 21079). Open Mon.-Wed. and Fri. 10am-4pm, Thurs. 10am-5pm; **ATM.**

Post Office: Tirconaill St. (tel. 21030), north of the Diamond. Open Mon.-Sat. 9am-5:30pm.

Phone Code: 073.

Buses: Bus Éireann (tel. 21101) runs to: Dublin (Mon.-Sat. 5/day, Sun 3/day; 4hr.; £10) via Ballyshannon (25 min.; £3) and Galway (Mon.-Sat. 3/day, Sun. 2/day; 4hr.; £13) via Sligo (1hr.; £7.30). Buses stop outside the Abbey Hotel, where timetables are also posted. **McGeehan Coaches** (tel. (075) 46150) ride to Dublin at least once a day. **Feda O'Donnell** (tel. (075) 48114) leaves for Galway every day.

Airport: tel. (075) 48232. Flights to Glasgow.

Taxis: tel. 35162.

Bike Rental: C.J. O'Doherty's, Main St. (tel. 21119). £6/day, £25/week; deposit £30. Open Mon.-Sat. 9am-1pm and 2-6pm. **The Bike Shop,** Waterloo Pl. (tel. 22515). £7/day, £30/week; deposit £40. Open Mon.-Sat. 9am-6pm.

Laundry: Eleanor's Launderette, Upper Main St. Wash £1.75, dry 25p/5 min.; £1 charge for dry without wash. Open Mon.-Sat. 9am-6pm. Last wash 5:30pm.

Pharmacy: Begley's Chemist, the Diamond (tel. 21232). Open Mon.-Fri. 9am-6pm, Sat. 9am-7pm.

Hospital: tel. 21029.

Emergency: Dial 999; no coins required. **Garda:** tel. 21021.

ACCOMMODATIONS

Donegal Town Hostel (IHH), 1 mi. out on the Killybegs Rd. (tel. 22805). High on a hill, overlooking the main road, this adequate but not-so-friendly hostel has a large kitchen and not-so-large bedrooms. The overflow building that is sometimes used isn't nearly as nice. £5.75/person; £2.50 surcharge for leaving after 11am; sheets 50p; laundry (wash and powder) £4.50.

Bosco House (tel. 35382), 4 mi. west of Donegal Town, in Mountcharles. An easy cycle out the Killybegs Rd. from Donegal (hitchers report it's not difficult to get a ride). The wardens might pick you up. While convenient to the services of Donegal, small, musical Mountcharles is also less noisy and less crazy. The owner of this old house painted with bright colors is a traditional musician who often brings hostelers to his gigs. 2- to 6-bed dorms; sheets 50p; open March-Oct.

Ball Hill Youth Hostel (An Óige/HI), (tel. 21174), 3 mi. from town; proceed 1½ miles out of Donegal on the Killybegs Rd., turn left at the sign, and keep moving for another 1½ mi. towards the sea; taxi ride runs about £3-4. An old coastguard station sitting on a high cliff, this hostel has been under new management since Easter, 1995; manager Kevin welcomes hostelers with open arms. 3-course dinner available at nearby Mountcharles Hotel for £5. Curfew 12:30am, no lockout. 8-bed dorms. May-Sept. £6/person, Oct.-April £4.50/person.

Atlantic Guest House, Main St. (tel. 21187). A 17-room guest house with long corridors and an unbeatable location. Each clean room has a TV, coffee/teapot, and sink. £12.50/person, w/bath £17.50; prices negotiable in off-season (around £16).

Aranmore House, Killybegs Rd. (tel. 21242). Seven clean, white rooms line up like peas in a pod in Mrs. Keeny's large home, a 3-min. walk from the library.

Open fire in the lounge. Free coffee and tea. Single £13.50, w/bath £15; double £27, w/bath £30. Open Easter-Oct.

FOOD & PUBS

Cafés and take-aways compete for tourists' attention in Donegal as adolescent boys in T-Birds cruise the strip scoping for cute chicks. Most inhabit the Diamond and the streets near it. **Foodland Supermarket** (tel. 21016) has an accurate name (open Mon.-Thurs. 9am-8pm, Fri. 9am-9pm, Sat. 9am-7:30pm). Nature store **Simple Simon's** (tel. 22687) sells fresh baked goods, local cheeses, and (inedible) crafts from around the world (open Mon.-Sat. 9:30am-6pm).

The Blueberry Tea Room, Castle St. (tel.22933). Justifiably popular. Sandwiches, daily specials and all-day breakfast (veggie and cheese croissant w/salad £2.50). Also carries that all-important selection of fine wines. Open daily 8am-9pm.

Errigal Restaurant, Main St. (tel. 21428). Local hangout with the cheapest dinner in town—their potatoes are freshly chipped every day. (Fresh fish and chips £2-4, chicken dinner £3.50.) Open Mon.-Sat. 9am-10:20pm, Sun. 3-10:20pm.

Stella's Seafood Bar, at McGroarty's Pub, the Diamond. Serves creative, healthy food using organic vegetables. Dinner is expensive but delicious (shellfish pancakes £10.95). Lunch is more reasonable (pita filled w/garlic mussels, baked potato, and veggies £4.50). Live trad on Thurs. Open Mon.-Sat. noon-9pm.

Harbour Restaurant, Quay St. (tel. 21702). Fish and chips (£3-4), sandwiches and chips (£2). Hearty steaks and baked potatoes, too! Open daily 11am-9pm.

Donegal puts on a good show at night, especially in the summertime. Pubs have tons of events during the International Arts Festival; keep a sharp lookout for the happening places. During the winter, the trad dries up, but rock and blues still happen on the weekends. **Schooner's,** Upper Main St. (tel. 21671), has traditional and contemporary sessions, particularly during the summer. **Olde Castle Restaurant Bar,** Castle St., is more restaurant than bar, with no music but a good mix of people. *Á la carte* menu served until 10:30pm. **Charlie's Star Bar,** Main St., spouts live rock, country, and blues. **The Abbey Hotel,** the Diamond (tel. 21014), draws tourists to its folk cabaret and to its lively summer disco (July-Aug. Tues. and Wed.). **The Stables,** Castle St. (tel. 21056), confines its trad action to Monday. **The Cellar Bar,** Upper Main St. under the Coach House (tel. 22855), features trad nightly. Confident musicians and singers are welcome to perform as well. **Nero's,** Main St. (tel. 21111), plays the fiddle while Donegal burns (dancing Thurs.-Sat., live bands Sun.).

SIGHTS

Donegal's historic locations don't really explain the masses of visitors crowding its streets, but once you elbow your way around the Eurotourists, the few old buildings can be interesting. **Guided tours** (tel. 22312), of the town leave from the chamber of commerce (Mon.-Fri. at 11am and 2pm; £2). **Donegal Castle** takes up prime real estate space just north of the Diamond, smack in the center of town. Most residents consider the 15th-century castle an inexplicable oddity, but its spiral staircase is worth climbing, if only to see the finely carved stone fireplace. (Castle closed for renovations; will re-open when the U.S. budget is balanced.)

Just a short walk from the tourist office along the river south of town awaits a ruined **Franciscan Friary.** Thirteen delicate arches and their supporting pillars are all that remain of the original 15th-century cloister. Founded in 1474 by Red Hugh O'Donnell's wife, the friary was abandoned quite unceremoniously in 1608. Four of the monks who fled—Brother Michael O'Cleery, Fearfeasa O'Maolconry, Peregrine O'Duignean, and Padraig O'Cleary—wrote the *Annals of the Four Masters,* an important narrative history of Ireland. The narrative dates back to the time of Noah's grandmother, 40 years before the **Great Flood,** and continues until 1618 AD. The monks may have actually written the masterpiece in another, more-ruined monastery near Bundoran, but it has become tradition to claim that they completed the classic of Irish literature here, in Donegal Town. An obelisk in the center of the Diamond recalls the four holy men, as does **St. Patrick's Church of the Four Masters,** about ½ mile up Main St.: a fine example of stolid, Irish Romanesque architecture (open Mon.-Fri. 9am-5pm; free).

Just south of Donegal Town, one mile out on the Ballyshannon Rd. at the **Donegal Craft Village** (tel 22225), six craftspeople open their workshops to the public. The work of Invereske potters (tel. 22053), a batik artist (tel. 22015), a jewelry designer (tel. 21742), a handweaver (tel. 22228), a jewelry metalworker (tel. 22225), and a porcelain crafter (tel. 22200) make fantastic gift alternatives to the mass-produced leprechauns sold in the Donegal Town stores (workshops open July-Aug. daily 9am-6pm, Sept.-June Mon.-Sat. 9am-6pm, Sun. 11am-6pm). The **Donegal Drama Circle** presents summer theater at the Bosco Centre, Tirconnaill St., in July and August (tickets £4, students £2). Posters all over town give details.

■ NEAR DONEGAL TOWN: STATION ISLAND

Several miles due east of Donegal Town, Co. Donegal's **Lough Derg** (there's another Lough Derg along the Shannon) encircles **Station Island.** Ireland's most important place of pilgrimage, Station Island witnesses a three-day barefoot religious ordeal every summer, the subject of Seamus Heaney's long poem *Station Island.* Though St. Patrick never visited Lough Derg, legend has it that he visited nearby Saints Island, where he temporarily descended into Purgatory. The pilgrimage involves three days of similarly hellish fasting and circling the island barefoot. "Lough Derg soup" has become an island delicacy; the pilgrims, who aren't allowed to eat, snack on this concoction of boiled water flavored with salt and pepper. Hardcore Catholics scowl at a recent addition to the pilgrim's calendar: a special one-day retreat to the island that some think is too easy. For budget-traveler pilgrims, **Bus Éireann** visits Lough Derg daily from Whit Sunday to the Feast of the Assumption on its Dublin-Cavan-Enniskillen route. The Galway-Sligo-Lough Derg route runs both ways on Sundays, but only *to* Lough Derg *from* Galway Mon.-Sat. (so don't go on Monday, or you'll have to stay the entire week). Regular ferry service picks up pilgrims at the lakeshore. The "Lough Derg Journey" at the new **Pettigo Visitor Centre** (tel. (072) 61546) lets you visit the area in virtual reality. Real boat trips can be arranged through the Centre. (Centre open March-April Sat. 10am-5pm, Sun. 2-5pm; May-Oct. Mon.-Sat. 10am-5pm, Sun. noon-5pm. Boat trips March-April Sat. 12:05pm and 3pm, Sun. 4pm; May-Oct. Mon.-Sat. 12:05pm and 3pm, Sun. 3pm and 5:30pm; center £2, students £1.50; center and boat £4, students £3.) Bring nothing but warm clothing and a repentant heart. Contact the Monsignor of Lough Derg, Fr. Mohan, Pettigo, Co. Donegal for more info (tel. (072) 61550).

KILLYBEGS PENINSULA

The road west (N56) along Donegal's southern edge winds within yards of the Atlantic coast and then swerves inland around huge cliffs and tiny villages. High passes through heather link the scarce houses on the northern half of this most southerly of Donegal's peninsular protrusions. Although it is not particularly appealing (especially to the nose), the prosperous fishing harbor of **Killybegs** has some of the only services in the area. **AIB** bank, on Main St., is open Mon.-Wed. and Fri. 10am-12:30pm and 1:30-5pm. **McGee's Chemist** on Main St. (tel. (073) 31009) sells aspirin and toothpaste (open Mon.-Sat. 9:30am-6pm). The **post office** is located on Main St. (tel. (073) 31060; open Mon.-Fri. 9am-1pm and 2-5:30pm, Sat. 9am-1pm). **Buses** run from Donegal town to Killybegs (Mon.-Sat. 3/day; early July-Aug. 5/day). The early-morning bus on Saturday continues on to Glencolmcille at Rossan Point. Otherwise, a bus skips directly to Glencolmcille from Donegal Town (Mon.-Fri. 1/day). **McGeehan Coaches** (tel. (075) 46150) also has a service (at least 1/day) to Donegal and Dublin from most towns on the peninsula. Hitching can be unrewarding; N56 (from Killybegs) is quicker to Glencolmcille, but not as pretty as the northern road. **Cycling** is ideal, except for the hilly terrain.

MOUNTCHARLES & ST. JOHN'S POINT

The coastline becomes more rugged and more dramatic farther west, but there's nothing shabby about the eastern towns. In **Mountcharles,** (the first town after Donegal Town) the **Bosco House Hostel** (see Accommodations, p. 317) puts up traditional music fans and story-tellers during the mid-July **Seamus MacManus Festival** (tel. (073) 35125). **The Cellar Bar,** in the Seamount Hotel (tel. (073) 35490), has trad sessions (summer Sat. and Sun. evenings). You can go **deep-sea fishing** in Donegal Bay from the Mountcharles Pier (daily 11am-5pm; £20/person; contact Michael O'Boyle at tel. (073) 35257).

Ten miles past Mountcharles, a turnoff leads to **St. John's Point,** which has fantastic views across to the Sligo coastline. Another mile past the St. John's turnoff, in **Bruckless,** the **Gallagher's Farm Hostel** (tel. (073) 37057) sits about ¼ mile off the main road. Mr. Gallagher built the wonderfully clean, well-outfitted hostel himself; he also provides trail info for walks around the gently undulating countryside. Two kitchens (and a third one for campers), a huge fireplace, and a ping-pong table may make you want to stay forever. Separate bathrooms are outside. (Dorm £6; **camping** £3.50/person; continental breakfast (with fresh baked scones) £3; laundry (wash and powder) £2.50.)

KILCAR

A stunning eight miles along N56 takes shoppers to tiny Kilcar, a base for many of the area's weavers. **Studio Donegal** (tel. (073) 38194) sells handwoven tweeds fresh off the loom (open Mon.-Fri. 9am-5pm; also open July-Aug. Sat. 10am-6pm). Downstairs, **Mary's Tea House** cooks up homemade soups and sandwiches (£1 each; open Mon.-Fri. 9am-7pm, Sat. 10am-6pm, Sun. 2-4pm). The Tweed Factory Craft Shop & Tea Rooms doubles as the **Northwest Tourism Information Centre** (tel. (073) 38002; open Mon.-Fri. 9am-7pm, Sat. 10am-6pm, Sun. 2-4pm).

Traditional music fans should visit Kilcar during the **Francie "Dearg" Byrne Memorial Fleadh,** on the third weekend in July. The first week of August sees a street Theatre Festival featuring music, dance, tomfoolery, and surprises. **Johnny Joe's** pub has traditional music every Tuesday and Friday all year. At the **Piper's Rest,** Main St. (tel. (073) 38205), the music sessions are often unplanned—trad music on Wednesday and Saturday nights, but aspiring musicians can volunteer to perform anytime. **Teelin Harbour Cruises** (tel. (073) 39079 by day, 39117 in the evening) ships out along the Slieve League coast. (Boat trips July-Aug.; 1½-2hr.; £6/person.) Closer to home, **Jim Maloney** of Kilcar (tel. (073) 38316) provides cruises or fishing trips at £6/person; rods and tackle also available.

Several miles farther along the coast road from Kilcar to Carrick, **Dun Ulun House** (tel. (073) 38137) is a luxurious alternative to hostel life. Sleep in large, flowery beds at night and wake up to continental breakfast in the morning. You may even hear live music played by Mrs. Lyons's talented daughters. (Sept.-June £12.50/person, July-Aug. £13.50/person, all w/bath; dorm beds may be available for £7.50, £6 in low season; laundry £5; bike rental £6/day, £30/week; deposit £20.) Farther down the road and five minutes from the beach, the **Derrylahan Hostel (IHH)** (tel. (073) 38079) welcomes guests like long-lost cousins; don't even *think* about refusing the initial cup of tea. The showers stay hot, the laughter and wit never run dry, and the on-premise grocery shop stays well-stocked. Campers have separate showers and kitchen facilities. (Dorm £5; private room £7/person; **camping** £3.) Phone the hostel for a pick-up from Kilcar or Carrick. Buses pass the hostel daily on the way to Killybegs and Glencolmcille.

CARRICK

Smaller than Kilcar, Carrick has good pubs, trad and folk music every night, and the hiker's dream: ready access to **Slieve League,** whose stunning cliffs drop straight into Donegal Bay. In late October and early November, Carrick hosts the annual **Carrick Fleadh,** one of the better music festivals around. The Carrick **tourist office,** at the junction of Killybegs and Kilcar Rd. (tel. (073) 39377), will shower you with kindness and information (open Easter-Sept., daily 10am-8pm). Just south of Carrick, Mrs. Maloney, at **Teelin Bay House** (the third B&B on the road to Teeling; tel. (073) 39043), is deservedly famous for the care she bestows upon her guests. It's a bit of a hike but the view just keeps getting better. You'll have to book well ahead (£12/person).

Fishing is fabulous and rewarding around Carrick. River angling requires both a license and a permit—get one upstairs from **McGinley's Supermarket** on Main St. (tel. 39120). Rods and tackle are also sold there (license £3, 1-day permit £10; open Mon.-Sat. 9am-9m, Sun. 9am-2pm). Head for **Salmon Leap,** just south of Carrick (follow signs for Teelin), for the best salmon; the **Glen River** is best for trout.

In clear weather it'd be unconscionable *not* to visit **Slieve League,** a well-known, 2000-foot mountain arranged in the midst of a precipitous, beautiful coastline which is itself composed of (mere) 1000-foot cliffs. To reach the mountain, halfway down Carrick's main street, turn left and follow signs for Teelin. In Teelin, turn right to follow signs for Bunglass; at the end of the road sits a car park with fantastic views. From here, a cliff path heads west along the coast. After about 10 minutes on the path, you'll approach **Eagle's Nest,** where 70 years ago a child was supposedly lifted from the cliff by a golden eagle. Farther along (about ½ hour from Bunglass), the clifftop narrows to two feet. On one side of this pass—called **One Man's Pass**— the cliffs drop 1800 feet to the sea. On the other side, the cliffs drop a measly 1000 feet to a rocky floor. There are no railings, and most people go across on their butts or hands and knees (the less courageous and more sane can take a route slightly inland). After bringing hikers perilously close to death at One Man's Pass, the path continues all the way along the cliffs to **Rossarrel Point,** near Glencolmcille. The entire Slieve League way usually takes four hours. It's always a good idea to ask a local expert for advice. *But never go to Slieve League in poor weather.* Use extreme caution if you plan to cross the pass. People have died attempting this under poor conditions.

■ ■ ■ GLENCOLMCILLE (GLEANN CHOLM CILLE)

N56, less dramatic then the mountain paths, is a more convenient route to Glencolmcille ("glen-kaul-um-KEEL") at the westernmost point of the peninsula. Named after St. Colmcille, who founded a monastery here, this Irish-speaking town and pilgrimage site sits between two huge cliffs in a starkly beautiful valley of barren rolling hills and sandy coves. Travelers with cars stop in the tiny town center. A walk along the desolate, wind-swept cliffs to the west of the village will rid you of their presence. Glencolmcille's **tourist office** is on Cashel St. (tel. (073) 30116; open April to mid-Nov. daily 9am-9pm). The town's own craft village has an **exchange bureau** with a better rate than that at the **post office** east of the village center (post office open Mon.-Fri. 9am-1pm and 2-5:30pm, Sat. 9am-1pm). **McGeehan's buses** leave from Biddy's Bar to go to Killybegs and Ardara daily. **Bus Éireann** has services to Donegal Town. Ask at the hostel or tourist office for details.

Accommodations, Food, & Pubs The Dooey Hostel (An Óige/HI) (tel. (073) 30130), incredibly, is located in a cave in the side of the hill. Solid bedrock forms one wall of the hostel's entrance hall. To reach the hostel, turn left just past the village and follow the signs about ¾ mile uphill. Several kitchens grace the hostel (you can have a private lunch here), which houses guests in 2- to 8-bed dorms, most with stunning views of the sea (dorm £6, private room £6.50/person; sheets £1). To stay past 11am, you must pay a £2.50 fee or book for the next night. **Camping** is £3.50/person. Mrs. Ann Ward's **Atlantic Scene** (tel. (073) 30186), near the hostel, lives up to its name. You'll stay up just to admire the view longer (£12; open May-Oct.). There are also B&Bs in the village itself.

The **Lace House Restaurant and Café,** above the tourist office on Cashel St., serves typical Irish food (roast beef, potatoes, and veggies £5, sandwiches £1.30; open Easter-Sept. daily 11am-10pm). **An Bradan Feasa** (tel. (073) 30213), at the Cultural Centre, is affordable only at lunchtime (fried trout £6; open Mon.-Sat. 10am-9:30pm). The **teashop** in the Folk Village tempts with sandwiches and Guinness cake (80p). The **grocery shop** on Cashel St. supplies the basics. (Open Mon.-Sat. 9:30am-10pm, Sun. 9:30am-1pm and 7-8pm.) The village has three pubs and lots of trad and folk music in the summer—look for the signs to find out which pub has music on a given night. **Biddy's** (a.k.a. Cross Roads Bar) is at the mouth of the Carrick Rd. It's small and cozy, but **Roarty's,** farther down Cashel St., has more trad music and a bigger crowd during the summer (open Wed., Thurs., and Sat.). **Glen Head Tavern** pours a refreshing afternoon pint.

Sights Glencolmcille's craft movement was begun in the 1960s as a cure for unemployment; all remaining energy is used to run a small **folk village.** The village is comprised of wooden replicas of old buildings with immaculately thatched roofs. Houses dating from 1700, 1850, and 1900 are joined by a schoolhouse from the 1850s. The school is open to the general public, but only those taking guided tours get to see the insides of the houses while hearing descriptions and explanations of furniture and tools from each period of Irish history. A short path through the village leads past various reconstructed remains found around this area, including a Mass Rock (where undercover services were held during the time of Catholic persecution), a sweat house (an early sauna), and a lime kiln. The shop (tel. (073) 30017) stocks homemade heather, fuschia, and seaweed wines (free samples w/tour) along with whiskey and Guinness marmalade, good for those hung-over breakfasts. (Village open Easter-Sept. Mon.-Sat. 10am-6:30pm, Sun. noon-6pm; tours April-June and Sept. every hour, July-Aug. every half hour; £2.50.) Just down the road, **Foras Cultúir Uladh** ("The Ulster Cultural Institute"; tel. (073) 30248) displays local crafts, a facsimile of the *Book of Kells* and archaeological exhibits. Its shop offers a good selection of Irish books and tapes (open daily 9am-6pm; free).

Fine beaches and cliffs make for excellent hiking in all directions. A five-mile walk southwest from the village terminates at **Malinbeg,** a winsome hamlet on the edge of a sandy cove. Formerly notorious for its smuggling tunnels (some of which may still be in use), **Silver Strand** is now ideal for those seeking tranquility (and low population density) on a spacious beach. From here, you can laboriously walk up and

---

Read This Gray Box About Devilish Imps

While St. Patrick was the savior for much of Ireland, his act of banishing demons to the North put that part of the country in danger. The demons, angry and resentful, set up a fiery river around their territory, which no one could enter upon pain of death. The demons also surrounded their land with a dense mist so that no one could see their evil works. Colmcille, a religious man who was always at war with the devil, approached the burning stream in the company of his trusted servant, tu Cerc. The Devil thereupon hurled a holly rod through the mist that struck and fatally wounded tu Cerc. Colmcille was so incensed that he threw the javelin back through the mist to clear a line of sight for further vengeance and punishment. The holly javelin stuck in the ground and grew into a holly tree which stands at the spot to this day. An angel appeared to guide Colmcille, bidding him to use his Dub Duaibsech bell to destroy the evil imps. Colmcille, with the help of this bell, turned all the demons into fish and sent them to the sea where they could no longer endanger people. These demon fish were distinguishable from others by being red in color and blind in one eye; fishermen were, of course, advised to avoid these evil fish. Colmcille, whose valor is celebrated to this day, triumphed over the evil forces of the Devil.

along the Slieve League coastline (see Carrick, p. 320). North of Glencolmcille, **Glen Head** is easily identifiable by the martello tower at its peak. A sandy beach links the cliffs here to each other. The head is an hour's walk from town through land rich in prehistoric ruins, including dolmens and court cairns (pre-Celtic burial sites). The tourist office and hostel in town each have a wall-map showing the locations of the major sites. A third walk from town begins at the Protestant church and ascends a hill to the ghostly "famine village" of Port. Haunted by crying babies, this surreal village has been empty since all of its inhabitants emigrated during the Famine. The only current resident, according to local rumor, is an eccentric artist who lives in the isolated bay without electricity or water. The "beach" nearby is covered with pretty egg-shaped stones. The visible phallic rock sticking out of the sea is just what it appears to be: the only part of the Devil's anatomy still visible after St. Colmcille banished him to the ocean.

The road east from Glencolmcille to Ardara passes through the spectacular **Glengesh Pass.** Nine hundred feet above sea level itself, the road tackles the surrounding mountains with hairpin turns. Though a more difficult hitch or bike ride than the route through Killybegs, the views make this route worth your while.

■■■ ARDARA

Originally the center of the Donegal tweed industry, Ardara ("ar-DRAH") is now a major attraction for tourists with high credit card limits and the need for tweed. Prices don't differ much from store to store, but discount vouchers may be available at the Heritage Centre. Souvenirs spill out of the shops and into the L-shaped pair of streets. The brand-new **Ardara Heritage Centre** (tel. (075) 41704), in the middle of town, tells the story of tweed with live demonstrations and shows a film about local attractions. For those who are curious: Donegal tweeds incorporate dyes made from Ireland's four elements: lichen, blackberries, heather, and soot. (Centre open March-Oct. daily 9:30am-6pm; £2, students £1.) The tearoom at the center serves snacks and refreshments daily from 9:30am-6pm (fresh salmon and mayonnaise sandwich £3.50). Ardara has its moment in the sun on the first weekend of June during **Weaver's Fair,** which brings musicians and weavers to town.

The **Drumbarron Hostel,** the Diamond (tel. (075) 41200), is clean and charismatic, if a little rough. The kitchen has flagstone floors, dorms have 4-8 beds/room, and the hostel has a 1am curfew (£6/person; continental breakfast £2, full breakfast £3-3.50). Next door, **Laburnum House,** the Diamond (tel. (075) 41146), has grand rooms and windows that stretch to the floor (£11.50/person). **The Lobster Pot,** Dungloe Rd. (tel. (075) 41463), sells cheap burgers (£1-1.50) and pricey but tasty fresh seafood dinners (salmon steak £9; open daily noon-1am). Check out the colorful selection of mugs at **Nancy's,** Front St., while diving into smoked mackerel (£3.25) or oysters (£3; trad music Sat.). The Central Bar, known as **Peter Oliver's,** Main St. (tel. (075) 41311), has traditional music every single night during July and August. **Bikes** can be rented at **Donald Byrne's,** West End, beyond town on the Killybegs Rd. (tel. (075) 41156; £7/day, £30/week; deposit £40). **Ulster Bank** (tel (075) 41121 or 41201), is located on the Diamond (open Mon.-Wed. and Fri. 10am-12:30pm, 1:30-4pm; Thurs. 10am-12:30pm and 1:30-5pm). You can call a cab from **Hillhead Cabs** (tel. (075) 41463). The **post office** is opposite the Heritage Centre (tel. (075) 41101, open Mon.-Fri. 9am-1pm and 2-5:30pm, Sat. 9am-1pm). **Chemist,** Front St., is the local pharmacy (open Mon.-Sat. 10am-1pm and 2-6pm). The bus stop and bus information are at the Spar **supermarket,** Main St. (tel. (075) 41107; open Mon.-Sat. 8:30am-8pm, Sun. 8:30am-1pm). Pony treks start from Castle View Ranch, 2½ miles from Ardara town center (tel. (075) 41212; £8/hr., £40/day).

To enjoy beautiful walks along the peninsula located east of Ardara, head south through town and turn right at the horse-riding sign towards Loughros Point ("LOW-crus"). At the next horse-riding sign, either turn right for a beautiful view of Ardara Bay or continue straight to Loughros Point to sight the sea. The **Maghera Caves,** located five miles from the town center, make another pleasant excursion from Ardara. The six caves vary in size and depth; all require a flashlight. At low tide you can enter the Dark Cave, once the refuge of *poteen* makers. A rising tide, however, could trap you inside. To reach the caves, follow the main road south past the Loughros turnoff, then follow the signs several miles west on small roads. The road that passes the caves continues through a mountain pass until it reaches Dungloe.

MIDWEST COAST

Coastal N56 from Glenties to Dungloe, on the midwest coast, bumps and bounces along. The beautiful, sandy beaches of the midwest are isolated by the grand Derryeagh Mountains. Expect a leisurely pace in this, the largest *gaeltacht* in Ireland. Buses run infrequently, so be sure to plan your schedule—or not, because you may decide to stay.

DUNGLOE (AN CLOCHAN LIATH) & CROHY HEAD

Dungloe ("dun-LO"), known locally as the Capital of the Rosses, is a busy market town where travelers stock up before hurrying on to Crohy Head or the mountains. Hundreds of party-lovers flock to Dungloe in the last week of July for the **Mary from Dungloe Festival** (tel. 48519), named after a popular old song about the tragic love affair between Mary and a local lad. The population swells to 80,000 during this 10-day celebration, which attracts famous musicians to both trad and modern parties. The highlight of the festival, of course, is the selection of the annual Donegal ambassador, Mary from Dungloe. For festival information and ticket bookings, call the Festival Booking Office (tel. (075) 21254; open Mon.-Sat. 10am-6pm).

Crohy Head, the peninsula to the southwest of Dungloe, collects strangely-shaped rock formations around a jagged coast. **Crohy Head Youth Hostel (An Óige/HI)** (tel. 21950), in an old coast guard station, offers stupendous views over the Atlantic (April-May £4.50, under 18 £3.50; June-Sept. £5.50, under 18 £4). To reach the peninsula and the hostel from Dungloe, turn onto Quay Rd. halfway down Main St. and follow the less than smooth road out.

The Dungloe **tourist office** (tel. 21297), close to the shore, finds rooms and sells all sorts of maps (open June-Oct. Mon.-Fri. 10am-1pm and 2-5pm, Sat. 9-11:45am). The Main St. sports a **Bank of Ireland** (tel. 21077), an **AIB** bank (tel. 21179; both open Mon.-Wed. and Fri. 10am-12:30pm and 1:30-4pm, Thurs. 10am-12:30pm and 1:30-5pm), and the **post office** (tel. 21179; open Mon.-Fri. 9am-1pm and 2-5:30pm, Sat. 9am-1pm). The hostel rents **bikes** (tel. 21021; £6/day; deposit £10). Just across from the caravan park (see below), **Green's Launderette** (tel. 21021) cleans up (large wash and dry £4.50, small wash and dry £3.50; open Mon.-Fri. 9am-6pm). The pharmacy works out of **O'Donnell's Chemist**, Main St. (tel. (075) 21386; open Mon.-Sat. 9am-6pm). The **phone code** hollers 075.

Greene's Independent Holiday Hostel is attached to the **Dungloe Caravan and Camping Park** (tel. 21021), on Carnemore Rd. near the Esso filling station. Two 8-bunk dorms, a family room and a large kitchen constitute this basic, clean hostel. Dorm £6.50, low season £6; sheets 50p; laundry £3.50. Camping £5/tent plus £2/car and 30p/person (people are packed like sardines during the festival). Farther down Main St., across the bridge and up a hill, the **Hillcrest B&B**, Barrack Brae (tel. 21484), sits atop a steep slope. The rooms are gorgeous and the proprietors are kind to boot. Great views and solitary tranquility add to the attractions (£12/person, w/ bath £14).

At the **Riverside Bistro,** Main St. (tel. 21062), snacks (BLT £2) and vegetarian meals (vegetable lasagne £5) are affordable (open daily 12:30-3pm and 6-10pm). **Sweeney's Hotel,** Main St. (tel. 21033), supplies tasty treats (ham and cheese sandwich £1.85; lunch served 11:30am-3pm). Dinners are much dearer, my dear; you may have to settle for the large starters (mussels in garlic butter £3.25). Cheap Chinese food is the specialty at **Evergreen** on Main St. (tel. 21880), across the bridge and up the hill. (Most entrees are less than £4.50; open Mon.-Wed. noon-1:30pm, 5:30pm-midnight, Thurs. 5:30pm-midnight, Fri.-Sat. 5:30pm-1am, Sun. 6pm-midnight.) The Cope **supermarket,** Main St., opens its doors daily 9am-6pm and Fridays until 7pm. **Beady's,** Main St. (tel. 21219), entertains with trad and a bartender whose infectious laughter will set off long-suppressed giggles. **The Midway,** Main St. (tel. 21251), has music most summer nights, but don't expect the fiddle here.

BURTONPORT & ARRANMORE ISLAND

About five miles north of Dungloe, **Burtonport** is sea-obsessed, used mostly for the Arranmore ferry that docks there. The fishing village is also a good base for fishing and boat trips to the many uninhabited islands in the area. The **tourist office** is just past the Ferry Booking Office to the left of the ferryport (tel. 20101; open Mon.-Sat. noon-6pm, Sun. 2-6pm). **Sea anglers** leave from the cabin on Burtonport Pier (tel. (075) 42077) most summer mornings (10am) and some evenings (4pm; £10). Book in advance. **Campbell's Pier House** (tel. (075) 42017) presents a happy face, spacious rooms, wonderful carved wooden doors, and a tiny kitchen where you can make tea and coffee (£14/person; w/bath £18). The **Lobster Pot,** Main St. (tel. 42012), prices its lunches and entrees reasonably (chicken chasseur £5; open daily 1-10pm). **Skippers Tavern** (tel. (075) 42234), sings and rings with trad most nights; **O'Donnell's Bar** (tel. (075) 42255) pours a more quiet pint. Both serve pub grub. **The Cope,** at the top of the town (tel. 42004), is the largest **grocery** on either side of the water; make sure you stock up before boarding the ferry. (Open Mon.-Sat. 9am-6pm.) The **post office** (tel. (075) 42001) is pat in the middle of town (open Mon.-Fri. 9am-1pm, 2-5pm, and Sat. 9am-1pm).

Just off the coast lies **Arranmore Island** (it appears on some old maps as "Aran" or "Arran Island"). The **ferry** from Burtonport (tel. (075) 20532) takes a brief 20 minutes (July-Aug. Mon.-Sat. 8/day, Sun. 7/day; Sept.-June 2-3/day). Dock office opens daily 8:30am-7:30pm; £5 return, hostelers £4, students £3. About 700 people (most with some connection to Chicago, IL—honestly) live in the sheltered southeast corner of the island.

A well-marked footpath—**the Arranmore Way**—encircles the island and will lead you to the lighthouse, high above impressive cliffs and rushing water, at the far tip of the island. When you walk right out to the point, the inlet to the right is splashy and loud. The tourist office sells a map of trails on the island (50p). A full perambulation of Arranmore Way takes a good five hours, longer if you're searching for Arranmore's pearls. Four priceless O'Donnell pearls were a gift to Red Hugh O'Donnell from Philip II for Red Hugh's help in saving Spanish sailors when Armada ships went down off the coast. The pearls were last seen on Arranmore Island in 1905—you might be the one to unearth them.

Along the shore to the left of the ferry port stretches a string of pubs, houses, and the **Arranmore Island Youth Hostel (An Óige/HI)** (tel. 20574), just 100 yards from the ferry and *right* on the water. Very basic, the hostel is fine in good weather, but there's little common space to squeeze into when it rains (dorm £5.50, under 18 £4; pillow £1; open June-Sept.). There are plenty of B&Bs; **Ward's B&B,** (tel. 20511) promises clean, spacious rooms and great ocean views (£12/person).

O'Donnell's (a.k.a. Atlantic View Bar), Reilly's, Philly's Bar, Phillbhnán, Andrew's Bar, and **Glen Hotel** comprise the list of Arranmore's pubs (a long list for a small population). Each Wednesday during the summer, the entire island will flock to one of these for traditional music (the location rotates). With 24-hour licenses to service fishermen returning from sea, some pubs provide "refreshments" into the wee hours of the morning. The only **grocery store** on the island is attached to Phillbhnán pub—it closes at 6pm, but the bartender might be convinced to help someone in dire need of supplies. **Bonners Ferryboat Restaurant** (also the Booking Office) sells some snacks.

THE ROSSES AND CROLLY

To the north and west of Burtonport stretch the haunting, untouched, Irish-speaking **Rosses,** an environmentalist's dream. Locals will tell you that this is the "real" Donegal, where peat cutting and salmon fishing keep the economy alive. In fact, the area produces all of its own energy (as well as much employment) with a hydroelectric plant and a small peat-fired generator. Massive peat farming is in evidence on the main N56 from Dungloe to Crolly. Cutting approaches cast mining proportions here, as whole families frantically make use of every dry moment. A wind farm, to supplement energy sources, is in the planning stages.

North of Burtonport on the Coast Road dwells the little village of **Kincasslagh.** Its main attraction is the **Viking House** hotel, owned by country singer Daniel O'Donnell, an effective ambassador for Donegal. His elderly fans flock from all over the world whenever Daniel invites them to his place for tea. A minor road heads west to **Cruit Island,** not really an island at all but rather a peninsula with nice beaches and a host of thatched cottages. **Aran Trail Bikes** (tel. (075) 43213) rents cycles, which are an ideal way to see the Rosses (ask for Smith's House; £10/day, £25/4 days, £35/week; deposit £40; open Mon.-Sat. 11am-6pm). Farther north, the magnificent stretch of sand known as **Carrickfinn Strand** is marred only by the presence of tiny **Donegal Airport.**

Heading into the heart of the Donegal *gaeltacht,* the village of **Annagry** marks the area of **Rannafast,** famous for its Gaelic story-telling tradition. *Seanachies* like the MacGrianna brothers and Mici Shean Neill actively perpetuate the Irish language and the narrative tradition through their stories and tales. Working to keep alive a language that is still in some danger of extinction, an Irish school in Annagry recruits dozens of teenagers every summer for Gaelic camps (see The Irish Language, p. 60). Not much farther, **Leo's Tavern,** where Clannad and Enya raged, has become a kitschy tourist attraction, its walls lined with silver, gold, and platinum discs.

At the intersection of the coast road and N56, **Crolly** is the gateway to northwest Donegal. Crolly Bridge is the only infrastructural link in the area. There was once another bridge some distance downstream, but local tradition maintains that a rival pub owner blew it up so that all traffic would pass his own door. **Paddy Oig's** pub (he's not the arsonist) has everything a body could need: camping, good pub grub, great traditional music, and Irish dancing in summer. **Coillín Darach Caravan & Camping Park** is just behind the pub and sports a craftshop, tennis court, and modern facilities (July-Aug. £5; Sept.-April £3.50; May-June £4).

The postmistress at the Crolly Post Office is a good source of information on the area and its accommodations. She can point you toward the youth hostel. A scenic four-mile walk through the hills, which include every version of natural beauty available, descends into Tor, site of the **Screag an Iolair Hill Hostel** ("SCRAG an UH-ler"; tel. (075) 48593). The hostel gives visitors a warm welcome and a warmer cup of tea. The building itself is full of hidden nooks and crannies. The land comes complete with its own neolithic stone circle and semi-wild "arboretum" planted by hostelers of yore. This peaceful and mystically soothing hostel is witness to frequent trad sessions, poetry readings, and art exhibits (£6/person; laundry £2; open all year, but call ahead in winter). The sore of foot or weary of spirit may call the warden to pick them up in Crolly. Those who accept the challenge of walking or biking should take the Tor Road out of Crolly. The road first passes a deserted village on the shores of still Lough Keel and then, at the old Tor school, it swings right. Hostel-seekers, however, should continue straight ahead at the school, past the hostel sign. The road descends past Ashardan Waterfall and Lake and finally into Glen Tor. Crolly and the hostel nearby make a good base for exploring the unspoiled heath lands of the **Derryveagh Mountains** and the red deer that are virtually its sole inhabitants. Trails for hikers of varying abilities, most clearly shown on the *Ordnance Survey Discovery Series I,* begin at the hostel in Tor. As the trails are often hard to follow, hikers should inform the hostel warden of their plans in case of emergency.

One mile north of Crolly, N56 and the coastal road diverge. N56 turns inland and, after about five miles, reaches R251. This road leads east through Dunlewey, past the foot of conical **Errigal Mountain,** and eventually to Glenveagh National Park. The whole length of the drive is studded with stunning views. At the foot of Errigal Mountain in Denlewey village, the **An Óige Errigal Youth Hostel** (tel. (075) 31180) is a traveler's haven. (June-Sept. members £6, under 18 £4.50; low season members £5, under 18 £4.) The marked trail that begins at the east end of Dunlewey leads up the side of the mountain to the 2466-foot summit. Lovely Dunlewey Lake and the Poison Glen guard the trailhead at the foot of the mountain. In a mythical battle, Lugh slew Balor of the Evil Eye. Poison from the Eye supposedly permeated the ground in the Glen, but most practical people attribute the name to an abundance of spurge in the Glen. Three strenuous hours to the summit reveals another frightening **One Man's Pass,** similar to that at Slieve League. The less foot-sure or foolhardy will find a number of shortcuts that bypass the pass. The **Lakeside Centre Dunlewey** offers boat tours, loads of info, trad sessions with dancing on Tuesdays, and a café with heavenly scones. (Centre open Mon.-Sat. 11:30am-6pm, Sun. 12:30-7pm; café open Mon.-Sat. 10:30am-6pm, Sun. 11am-7pm; boat trip £2.50, students £2.)

BUNBEG & BLOODY FORELAND

Where N56 moves inland, R257 continues along the coast to Bunbeg. The coastal route is one continuous strip of attractive scenery—perfect for cyclers, since there's little traffic. But hitchers tend to stay on N56, where cars pass more often. **Bunbeg Harbour,** the smallest enclosed harbor in Ireland, was a main port of exit and entry in the height of Britain's imperialism. Relics from that period line the harbor: military barracks, grain stones, and a Martello tower. The amiable **Hudi Beag's** pub (tel. (075) 31016) hosts intense, almost professional, trad sessions on Monday nights. Lunches for little money are available at **Errigal View Hotel** (tel. (075) 31355), which also caters to vegetarians (open Mon.-Sun., lunch noon-2:15pm, dinner 6-9:15pm). A ferry to **Tory Island** leaves from the harbor daily at 9am (tel. (075) 31991 or 31340; £12). Halfway from town to the harbor, a pair of stone pillars marks a rough path that leads to the gorge through which the Clady River rushes. The coastal strip north of Bunbeg is crowded with commercialism: this Gweedore area is actually the most densely populated rural region in Western Europe.

About seven miles north of Bunbeg, the **Bloody Foreland,** named for the deep-red of the sea on sunny days, juts into the ocean. Legend attributes the color of the sea to the blood of sailors who perished in the wrecks of old Spanish galleons. The sandy headland at **Magheraroarty,** farther west, offers miles of both unspoiled beaches and clear views. A mythical holy well here remains full of fresh water despite the tide's passing over it twice a day. **Ferries** to **Tory Island** leave from both Bunbeg (see above) and also from Magheraroarty at 11:30am and sometimes 1:30pm (tel. (074) 35661; £12). Bloody Foreland is best circled counter-clockwise from Bunbeg through Gortahork and then to Magheraroarty.

TORY ISLAND

Barren Tory Island, visible from the Bloody Foreland, sits far off the coast. The island is named for its "tors" (hills). Its age-old reputation as a harbor for pirates prompted people to equate the word "Tory" with "pirate" or "rascal." The use of "Tory" to mean "Conservative" derives from this Irish slang. ("Whig" originally meant a Scottish horse thief.) The original Tory Island pirates were the Fomorians, sour-tempered bad-guy demons of myth who inhabited Ireland since the beginning of the world. They attacked each mythical settlement one after the other until the Túatha de Danann supplanted them on the mainland. The Fomorians then retreated to Tory Island and the northwest ocean, from where they periodically raided the mainland. Their leader in these invasions was Balor of the Evil Eye, who lived in a certain cave on Tory Island. Human pirates used the island in the glory days of smuggling. Today, if an islander appears particularly difficult to deal with, mainlanders attribute it to a pirate ancestry. A recent tradition claims that a stone on one of the island's hills has power to fulfill wishes. Islanders have been known to use the stone to wish shipwrecks on invaders, most recently in 1884, when a gunboat coming to collect taxes was wished to the bottom of the Atlantic. The islanders still pay no taxes (though they do pay to maintain a school).

This small, Irish-speaking community has thus far managed to maintain a strong sense of independence and separateness, though a recent spurt in the tourist industry opened a hotel and a hostel and threatens the island's uniqueness and isolation. Islanders themselves refer to the mainland as "the country." Ferry service to the island is more regular and reliable than it used to be, but the king of the island—Rí an Oileáin, or Patsy Dan Rodgeres—still greets all visitors who disembark from the boat. Many of the island's unusual traditions remain intact, including the superstition which deters people from rescuing those drowning after having fallen off of a boat (make sure to spot the life-jackets on any ferry). **Donegal Coastline Cruises** (tel. (075) 31320) runs boats from one of three ports on the mainland: Bunbeg, Portnablagh, or Magheraroarty. (June-Sept.; from Bunbeg 1/day at 9am, 1¼hr.; from Magheraroarty 1/day at 11:30am and sometimes 1:30 and 5pm, 1½ hr.; from Portnablagh 1/wk. on Wed.; £14 return, students £12; bicycles free.) Times depend on tides and weather and are subject to change: travelers have been stuck here for a few days (in summer) or even a few weeks (in winter) because of storms.

The island's 130 people manage to support a surprising number of businesses, including a shop, a new hotel and restaurant, a tea and craft shop, and **Gailearai Dixon** (the Dixon Gallery). The gallery showcases the work of local artists well-known for their unique, child-like painting style. The youth hostel, **Brú Thorái, Radharc Na Mara** (tel. (074) 65145) costs £5 and is the best place to stay while exploring the islands' bleak, wind-swept scenes. Historical sights are few, but the monastery that St. Colmcille founded in the 6th century is still present in the Round Tower and Tau Cross close to the town center.

NORTHERN DONEGAL

FALCARRAGH & DUNFANAGHY

Northeast of the Bloody Foreland, white beaches stretch along the coast from Falcarragh to Dunfanaghy. The area's only **tourist information** spouts from the Bord Fáilte office in Falcarragh, located at the school (tel. (074) 65070; open Mon.-Sat. 10am-5pm, Sun. noon-5pm). The town's **post office,** Main St. (tel. (074) 35110), is open Mon.-Fri. 9am-1pm and 2-5:30pm, Sat. 9am-1pm. Financial services to satisfy anyone are available at the **Bank of Ireland** and its friendly **ATM** (tel. (074) 35484; open Mon.-Wed. and Fri. 10am-12:30pm and 1:30-4pm, Thurs. 10am-12:30pm and 1:30-5pm). Irish-speaking **Falcarragh** lives pub life to the fullest. The **Shamrock Lodge,** in the center of town, is especially buzzing with human activity that continues well into the night (rhythm and blues Friday nights, trad Saturday nights). Upstairs at the small but intimate **Shamrock Lodge Hostel (IHH),** Main St. (tel. (074) 35859), guests peek down the stairs at the revelry. The rooms are cozy and comfortable, as are the wee kitchen and living room (£6, double £7/person). Next to the post office, **Patricia McGraddy** offers B&B in a modern abode. Guests are welcome to jam on her piano (£12/person). Eat to the twang of country & western's top hits at **John's Restaurant,** Main St. (fish fingers and "fries" £1.90; open Mon.-Sat. 10am-10pm, Sun. 2-10pm). The **Gweedore Bar,** Main St. (tel. (075) 35293), earns the town's favor with a pleasant atmosphere and a reasonable lunch menu (roast chicken, veggies, potatoes £2.90; lunch served 12:30-2:30pm).

Along the coast, 5½ miles north of Falcarragh and 1½ miles south of Dunfanaghy, the **Corcreggan Mill Cottage Hostel (IHH)** (tel. (074) 36507) has a definite hip character. It consists of two amazingly comfortable cottages, each with exposed wood beams, handy-dandy sleeping lofts, well-stocked kitchens, and tastefully adorned walls. If you're lucky and in season, you can buy vegetables from the organic garden (dorm £6; camping £3; laundry £2; sheets 50p). Most hostelers get groups together to hire the services of **John McGinley's Buslines** (to Falcarragh and nearby areas £1 return; to Bunbeg and Dunlewey £2 return). Hitchers usually find it easy to get a ride to the pubs in Falcarragh. Farther on towards Dunfanaghy, Francis Stewart provides comfortable, snuggly **B&B** (tel. (074) 36281; £12/person).

In Dunfanaghy, **Danann's Restaurant,** Main St. (tel. (074) 36150), specializes in slightly expensive but praiseworthy seafood. (Entrees from £7 and up; early 3-course dinner £10, 6-7pm only; open June daily 6-9:30pm; July-Sept. daily 6-10pm.) **Arnold's Hotel,** Main St. (tel. (074) 36208), has a number of traveling aids, including the reasonably-priced **Garden Bistro** (open 10am-9:30pm; á la carte 7-9pm). The **Whisky Fly** (tel. (074) 36208), also in the Arnold Hotel, has traditional music Monday and Friday, folk music Wednesday, and sing-alongs Saturday nights during the summer. Otherwise, the town is quiet, though the **village shop** is open daily from 9am to 11pm for groceries.

GLENVEAGH NATIONAL PARK

Fourteen miles northwest of Letterkenny on the eastern side of the Derryveagh Mountains, **Glenveagh National Park** (tel. (074) 37088) is justly one of the more popular national parks in Ireland, as it excels in quality and quantity. The founder of the Glenveagh estate, John Adair, had a nasty reputation that doesn't suit the beauty of the park. In the cold April of 1861, he evicted 244 tenants on trumped-up charges. Many of them decided to emigrate to Australia while others were forced into a subsistence lifestyle in the workhouse. The park itself features 10,000 hectares of forest glens and mountains. Glenveagh is so large that hundreds of people can easily lose themselves in isolation (or simply lose themselves—take a good map just in case).

Many visitors climb Mt. Errigal and Slieve Snacht to boast that they have climbed the two highest mountains in Ireland. Large crowds, especially in summer, take the free minibus from the entrance to the castle, 2½ miles away (last trip 1½ hrs. before park closes). **Glenveagh Castle** is less than 200 years old but looks like a medieval keep with its thick walls, battle-ready rampart, turrets, and round tower. The gardens and greenhouse are clearly more modern, though. Marked trails head off from the castle, uphill and down. The ½-mile walk uphill to a viewpoint behind the castle is definitely worth the sweat. Some travelers even go to Glenveagh specifically to deer-watch (best done at dusk): one of the largest herds of red deer in Europe roams the park. (Park and castle open April-May daily 10am-6:30pm; June-Sept. Mon.-Sat. 10am-6:30pm, Sun. 10am-7:30pm; Oct. Sat.-Thurs. 10am-6:30pm. Park £2, students £1; same prices for castle. Garden tours July-Aug. Tues. and Thurs. at 2pm leave from the Castle Courtyard.) For those who can't make up their minds about what to see, guided nature walks leave from the **visitors center** (July-Aug. Wed. 2pm). Park rangers (tel. (074) 37088) lead hill walks on some Saturdays and can always dole out Glenveagh hiking info.

On the other side of the park, quite close to Letterkenny, **Glebe House and Gallery,** in Churchill (tel. (074) 37071), displays a large collection of Donegal folk art and a rare collection of international Victorian folk art. The gallery also houses an impressive collection of fine arts: paintings (Louis de Brocquy), ceramics (Picasso) and other works by leading 20th-century artists. (Open around Easter and late May-late Sept. Sat.-Thurs. 11am-6:30pm; last tour 5:30pm. £2, students £1.) Hostels in Crolly and Errigal are most convenient to Glenveagh National Park.

ROSGUILL PENINSULA

The Irish-speaking village of **Carrigart** sits at the base of one of the more beautiful drives in Donegal—the **Atlantic Drive** around the Rosguill Peninsula—and provides the shops and services necessary before setting out on the road. The **post office,** Main St. (tel. (074) 55101), performs all the necessary functions (open Mon.-Fri. 9am-1pm and 2-5:30pm, Sat. 9am-1pm). Money matters are of concern to the **National Irish Bank** (open July-Aug. Mon.-Fri. 10am-noon, Sept.-June Mon.-Tues. and Thurs.-Fri. 10am-noon). Soap and aspirin are available at **Joy's Pharmacy,** Main

St. (tel. (074) 55124; open summer Mon.-Sat. 10am-7pm, winter Mon.-Tues. and Thurs.-Sat. 9am-6pm, Wed. 10am-1pm).

In Carrigart, stay with Mary Gallagher at **Cuan-na-long,** or "Ship-haven" (tel. (074) 55597). The rose garden has been known to bewitch guests (dorm £13.50, double £15/person). A friendly staff at **Greim-Blasta,** Main St., serves toasted sandwiches (£1.50) and decadent, luscious desserts (open daily 8am-8pm). Down the road, the upscale **Weaver's Restaurant** (tel. (074) 55204) specializes in fresh-from-the-ocean seafood (trout £7.95; open July-Aug. daily 10am-10pm; Sept.-June Fri. 6:30-10:30pm, Sat.-Sun. 10am-10pm). The **Carrigart Indoor Market** (tel. (074) 55795), just around the corner, sells more knick-knacks than edibles (open Mon.-Sun. 11am-6pm). The **North Star** (tel. (074) 55110), across the way, is Carrigart's favorite pub by far, but nightlife is more lively in Downings. Rent your wheels at **C.C. Cycles** (tel. (074) 55427; £1/hr., £5/day; open Mon.-Sat. 10am-6pm).

The Atlantic Drive leads from Carrigart to the very tip of the peninsula, where **Trá na Rosann Youth Hostel (An Óige/HI)** (tel. (074) 55374) watches from the top of a hill four miles from the tiny town of **Downings.** The setting is unbeatable (you're almost on top of the whole world); the design is rustic but surprisingly comfortable (flag stone kitchen and warm lounge). (£5.50, under 18 £4.50.) A convenient shop is 50 yards from the hostel. Drink down a draught where the locals mill around, at nearby **Singing Pub,** a thatched bar with low ceilings, great grub, and trad music nearly every night. Downings itself is a prosperous and prim village known for its fishing and tweed industries.

■■■ FANAD PENINSULA

The Fanad Peninsula juts into the Atlantic between Lough Swilly and Mulroy Bay. Diminished in size but not in attractiveness by its larger neighbor, Inishowen, the Fanad Peninsula's small area comforts cyclists. During the summer, the peninsula's lush greenery makes a striking complement to the sandy beaches. Winter brings even better views. The eastern edge, outlined by the villages of **Ramelton, Rathmullan,** and **Portsalon,** is by far the more attractive of the two, with colorful old houses and sweeping views across Lough Swilly. The Knockalla Mountains are attractive but not terribly challenging to climb. The route from Kreevykeel to the breathtaking viewpoint at Saldan Ha Head, near Portsalon, provides a thorough impression of the peninsula.

RAMELTON

A river runs through the pretty little town of Ramelton, the eastern gateway to the peninsula. Famous in bygone days for its salmon, Ramelton refuses to demolish the last fish house in all of Ireland. The building, formerly used for smoking salmon, is now a restaurant and the **Fish House Craft Gallery** (tel. (074) 51316; open May-Sept. daily 10am-7pm). The building maintains some of its original character with an interior of bare stone and rough-hewn logs and the requisite view of the water (chicken and mushroom crepe £2.50). For feasts at surprisingly affordable prices in a more refined setting, cross the street to **Mirabeau Steak House,** the Mall (tel. (074) 51138; salmon steak £5).

To discover the area's heritage, follow Main St. uphill from the fish house. Past Crammond House, a right at Mary's Bar will bring you to Back Lane, the old Presbyterian Meetinghouse. Francis Makemie preached here before founding the first American Presbytery in 1706. The building now houses the town library and the humble **Ramelton Heritage Centre** (tel. (074) 51266). As part of Irish Genealogical Project Centres, the center in Ramelton will help you trace your Donegal ancestors for a fee (registration £10; open Mon.-Thurs. 9am-4:30pm, Fri. 9am-4pm). It has info on other national heritage centers as well. For some bonus *craic* join the crowds that flock to this mouth of the Lennon Estuary during the beginning of July for the **Lennon Festival.** Carnival, parade, pageant and much more fun and games are all yours.

One mile out of town on the Milford Rd., Mrs. Kathleen Curran provides a mattress and a meal in beautiful, quiet **Clooney House** (tel. (074) 51125; single w/bath £14, double w/bath £28). In the town center, **Crammond House,** Market Sq. (tel. (074) 51055), has enormous, pretty rooms intended mostly for families (single £18.50, double £27; open Easter-Oct.). Friday night trad sessions, a good pint, and a funky bathroom recommend **Sweeney's. Bridge Bar** (tel. (074) 51119) has music almost every night (trad on Sundays). **Conway's** (tel. (074) 51297) pours proper pints in an old thatched cottage to the beat of trad and ballads every Saturday.

National Irish Bank, the Mall (tel. (074) 51028), has money, money, money. It's a rich man's world. The mail arrives at the **post office,** Main St. (tel. (074) 51001; open Mon.-Fri. 9am-5:30am, Sat. 9am-1pm). **Bridge Launderette,** the Mall (tel. (074) 51333), can clean your filthiest socks (open Mon.-Sat. 9:30am-6pm; wash and dry £3.90). A **pharmacy** (tel. (074) 51080) also graces Main St. (open Mon.-Tues. and Thurs.-Sat. 9am-1pm and 2-6pm, Wed. 9am-1pm). Whoriskey's/Spar **Supermarket** (tel. (074) 51006) sells groceries (open Mon.-Sat. 8:30am-9pm, Sun. 9am-9pm).

RATHMULLAN

Five miles north along the main coastal road is Rathmullan, an ancient town of historical significance and sandy beaches. In 1607, the last powerful Gaelic overlords, Hugh O'Neill and "Red Hugh" O'Donnell, set sail from Rathmullan for the Continent along with 99 of their retinue. They had decided to abandon Ireland after a series of military defeats. The event is known, and lamented, as the Flight of the Earls. The tales of O'Neill and O'Donnell (see Feudalism (1200-1607), p. 51) are very much alive and present at the **"Flight of the Earls" Heritage Centre** (tel. (074) 58178), on the coast. Helpful staff use a variety of media—artwork, literature, and wax models—to explain the entire area's history in detail. The center, housed in a renovated Martello tower built to defend Ireland from Napoleon, is historic in itself. (Open June-Sept. Mon.-Sat. 10am-6pm, Sun. noon-6:30pm; £1, students 50p, families £3.) **Tourist info** is also gladly dispensed at the Heritage Centre (tel. (074) 58229). Around the corner, the remains of romantic 16th-century **Rathmullan Priory** loom. Overgrown with weeds, the crumbling priory affords good views across the lough. Also important in more recent republican history, Rathmullan was the place where the famous champion of Irish independence, Wolfe Tone, was arrested in 1798.

Mrs. McFadden's **Martello B&B,** Kerrs Bay Rd. (tel. (074) 58207), is an old, low-ceilinged house in the middle of town. Guests can experience an unique old-world feeling in this 1806 house (TV and sink in each room; single £12, double £22). **Deeney's Supermarket,** Kerrs Bay Rd. (tel. (074) 58148), supplies basic gastronomic needs (open Mon.-Sat. 9am-1pm and 2-8pm, Sun. 9am-1pm and 3-6pm). **An Bonnán Bui** (tel. (074) 58453) concocts a remarkably creative menu (tuna and spring onion sandwich w/salad for lunch £2.50, poached trout for dinner £5.50; open Easter-Sept. Wed.-Mon. 11am-11pm). Quiet **Pier Hotel** (tel. (074) 58178) serves cheap pub grub (sandwiches £1, breaded haddock £4.50; open for lunch mid-June to mid-Aug. Mon.-Sat. 12:30-5:30pm, Sun. 1-2:30pm, dinner Mon.-Sun. 5:30-8:30pm; reservations required; line dancing every Thursday). A romantic wooded lane runs parallel to the beach from behind the hotel. The **Water's Edge Pub and Restaurant** (tel. (074) 58182) is set on the very spot where the Earls set sail. The **Beachcomber Bar** (tel. (074) 58125) across the street from the hotel, offers a similar panoramic view (occasional trad and disco, no cover).

GLENVAR & PORTSALON

North of Rathmullan, a dozen slow brooks cross the road as the land rises over the **Knockalla Mountains** and **Glenvar.** Beyond this stretch of road, the coast at its most arresting arcs dramatically between mountain and shore. About halfway to Portsalon, a signposted lane leads from the main road to **Bunnaton Hostel,** Glenvar (tel. (074) 50122), high on a hill above the lough. Once an HI hostel, glorious Bunnaton has now declared independence. Sidle up to the cozy fireplace or amble along the beaches (£5; private room £7.50/person; sheets £1). Continuing north, the main road becomes both mind-bogglingly steep and breathtakingly beautiful. Just before Portsalon, the road crests a hill: an indescribable view of beaches and the northern peninsula suddenly materializes. **Mike's Bikes,** Doaghbeg (tel. (074) 59207), rents bikes for this perfect cycle (£6/day, £30/week; deposit £35).

Descend into **Portsalon,** the source of these beautiful views. It was once a resort town, but the resort hotel burned down three years ago, leaving just 100-year-old **Rita's** (tel. (074) 59135), a triptych of a restaurant, general store, and pub. It's the perfect place to eat a filling four-course lunch for £6, sip a pint by the picture windows, and stock up on provisions (restaurant and store open daily 10:30am-8:30pm). To reach Rita's, take the first right toward the pier after the golf club. The **Portsalon B&B** (tel. (074) 59101), next to the post office on the main road, attempts to replace the former resort hotel with big, new rooms perfumed by the rosebushes outside (£12/person). **Camping** is available next to the huge Warden Beaches (rated second best in the world by a British expert) at the **Knockalla Holiday Centre** (tel. (074) 59108), five miles south of Portsalon (kitchen and laundry facilities, shop, TV and game room; £6/2-person tent; open Easter to Oct.).

About one hour north of Portsalon by bike, the **Great Arch of Doaghbeg,** a mass of rock detached from seaside cliffs, keeps the lonely **Fanad Lighthouse** company. Over 80 feet wide, the arch is visible from the cliffs, though not from the main road itself. From Fanad Head, the route down the western side of the peninsula winds in and out of the inlets of **Mulroy Bay.** For westward-facing accommodation, stay with Mrs. Borland at the **Avalon Farmhouse** (tel. (074) 59031), on Main St. in tiny Tamney (homemade jam, attractive decor; £13.50/person, w/bath £15; open March-Sept.). Farther south at the foot of the Knockalla Hills, **camping** right on Mulroy Bay in **Rockhill Park,** Kerrykeel (tel. (074) 50012), is another option (tents £5; open mid-April to Oct.).

■■■ LETTERKENNY (LEITIR CEANA INN)

Letterkenny is Donegal's commercial and ecclesiastical center. The "white-streaked hill face" on the shores of River Swilly captured its place in history in 1992 by becoming the fastest growing town in Europe. The only traffic light in Co. Donegal can be found here, at the intersection of Main St. and Port Rd., although a pedestrian light that most people hope is temporary has also been added. Letterkenny is a functioning city rather than a tourist destination. It serves tourists as a practical hub for exploring the surrounding attractions, but the town itself is probably of greater importance for college students and residents. **Letterkenny Bus Service (Handy Bus)** extensively services city routes (70p).

PRACTICAL INFORMATION

Tourist Offices: Bord Fáilte (tel. 21160), 1 mi. past the bus station on the Derry Rd. Open Sept.-June Mon.-Sat. 9am-5pm, July-Aug. Mon.-Sat. 9am-5pm, Sun. 10am-2pm. Has info on all Donegal. **Chamber of Commerce Visitors Information Centre,** 40 Port Rd. (tel. 24866 or 25505), fills in the gaps with tons of Letterkenny-specific info. From outside, this Chamber of Commerce office may look like a china shop, but the pamphlets and friendly advice inside are no bull. Open June-Sept. Mon.-Sat. 9am-5pm; Oct.-May Mon.-Fri. 9am-5pm.
Banks: AIB, 61 Upper Main St. (tel. 22877 or 22807). Open Mon.-Wed. and Fri. 10am-4pm, Thurs. 10am-5pm; **ATM.**
Post office: halfway down Main St. (tel. 22454). Open Mon-Tues. and Thurs.-Sat. 9am-5:30pm, Wed. 9:30am-5:30pm.
Phone code: 074.
Buses: at the junction of Port Rd. and the Derry Rd., in front of the Quinnsworth Supermarket. **Bus Éireann** (tel. 21309) makes tours of Inishowen Peninsula and Giant's Causeway (from Letterkenny £7; call to book). They also run regular service to: Derry (Mon.-Sat. 3/day, Sun. 2/day; 40 min.; £3), Dublin (Mon.-Sat. 4/day,

Sun. 3/day; 5hr.; £10 return), Galway (Mon.-Sat. 3/day, Sun. 2/day; 4hr.), and Sligo via Donegal Town (Mon.-Sat. 3/day, Sun 2/day; 2½hr. to Sligo, 1½hr. to Donegal). **Feda O'Donnell Coaches** (tel. (075) 48114) drives to Galway via Donegal Town (1/day; Galway 4¼hr., Donegal ¾hr.) and to Crolly via Dunfanaghy (1/day; Crolly 1½hr., Dunfanaghy ¾hr.). They run more extensive services on Fri. and Sat. **Lough Swilly Buses** (tel. 22400) head north towards the Fanad Peninsula (Mon.-Sat. 2/day), to Derry (Mon.-Sat. 7/day), and south to Dungloe (Mon.-Sat. 2/day; fares £3-7). **John McGinley Coaches** (tel. 35201) sends one bus every day to Gweedore (1¼hr.) via Dunfanaghy (¾hr.) and another to Dublin (4hr.; £8). **McGeehan's Bus** (tel. (075) 46101) goes to Killybegs (1/day; £7) and Glencolmcille (1/day; £6). **Northwest Busways** (tel. (077) 82619) sends buses around Inishowen (Mon.-Sat. 2/day), making stops in Buncrana (50 min.; £2.60), Carndonagh (1½hr.; £3.70) and Moville (2hr.). **Doherty's Travel** (tel. (075) 21105) has buses that leave for Dungloe and Burtonport from Dunnes Supermaket (1/day; £4, £6 return).
Taxi: Letterkenney Cabs, tel. 21373.
Bike Rental: Church St. Cycles (tel. 26204) near the cathedral. £7/day, £30/week; deposit £40. Open Tues.-Sat. 10am-6pm.
Laundry: Peerless Clean-up, High Rd. (tel. 24538). Wash and dry: small load £3.90, large load £4.90-5.90. Open Mon.-Sat. 9am-8pm.
Hotlines: Samaritans: 20 Port Rd. (tel. 27200). **Letterkenny Women's Aid:** Port Rd. (tel. 24985). Open Mon.-Fri. 9am-5pm.
Pharmacy: Kelly's Pharmacy, Main St. (tel. 22354). Open Mon.-Sat. 9:30am-6pm, Sun. noon-2pm.

ACCOMMODATIONS

The Manse Hostel (IHH), High Rd. (tel. 25238). From the bus station, head up Port Rd. towards town and turn right up the lane marked "Cove House B&B." Continue past the playground, through the parking lot, and 50 yards up the road. The hostel is across the street. The longer way around goes farther down Port Rd. and then makes a sharp right onto High Rd. Diane, the warden, is also the IHH regional representative. Well-equipped kitchen with microwave and free coffee. Saggy beds in 3- or 4-bed dorms, some with sinks. Clean and tidy. £5.
Rosemount Hostel, 3 Rosemount Terrace (tel. 21181). Unceasingly friendly. Rather dark 6- to 8-bed dorms are upstairs; bathrooms are downstairs. Outside the hostel, elaborate floral arrangements in every window and on every porch along Rosemount Terrace are a feast for the eyes. Dorm £5. Open mid-June to Sept.
Port Hostel, 24 Port Rd. (tel. 25315). Upstairs from a funky craft shop and café. Small, bare kitchen, free sheets, and no bunk beds. The common room isn't terribly inviting, but the park outside is. Dorm £5 in summer, £4 in winter. Single £7.50. Double £6/person.
McClafferty's, 54 Main St. (tel. 21581). Clean, hotel-like rooms hover above a pub, but remain surprisingly quiet even in the evening. £13/person, £16 w/bath.
White Gables, Mrs. McConnelogue, Dromore (tel. 22583), just off the Derry Rd. 1½ mi. out of town. Clean rooms, no fuss. The upstairs balcony has spectacular views over Letterkenny and the surrounding countryside. Call ahead for pickup from town. £13.50/person, w/bath £14.50.

FOOD

As every college town does, Letterkenny, too, offers a fair share of cheap meals. **Quinnsworth,** behind the bus station (tel. 22555), is all you could want in a grocery store (open Mon.-Wed. and Sat. 9am-6pm and Thurs.-Fri. 9am-9pm). **The Natural Way,** 55 Port Rd. (tel. 25738), hawks health food (even chocolate bars), soya milk, and eggs from free-range chickens (open Mon.-Sat. 9am-6:30pm).

Pat's Too, Main St. (tel. 21761). Hearty, take-away meals for the budget student or traveler. Delivery available. 9-inch pizza £3-4.50, lasagna £3-3.50. Open Mon.-Fri. noon-2:30pm and 5pm-midnight, Sat.-Sun. 5pm-midnight. **Pat's Pizza,** Market Square, is the restaurant version of Pat's Too, with the welcome addition of seafood dishes and daily specials. Open Mon.-Sun. 5pm-midnight.

Bakersville, Church St. (sandwich bar tel. 21887, bakery tel. 25926). At lunchtime, locals pay tribute to its cheap, delicious coffee, laudable sandwiches (£1.30), and delectable pastries. Open Mon.-Sat. 8am-6pm.

Galfees, in the basement of the Courtyard Shopping Centre, Main St. (tel. 27173), has a dual personality. It features both a fresh sandwich bar (sandwiches £1-1.50; open 9am-6pm), and a full restaurant with a broad selection of seafood, Italian, and Mexican food—something for the whole family. The evening menu (stuffed taco shells £4; served 5-8pm) is cheaper than the later dinner menu (vegetarian pasta special £6.50; served 6:30-10pm).

PUBS

McGinley's, 25 Main St. (tel. 21106). Clearly a happening pub. Live sessions ring out on Thurs.-Sat. nights

McClafferty's, 54 Main St. (tel. 21581). Another popular spot where stained glass windows lend special lighting effects and set the mood.

Cottage Bar, Main St. (tel. 21338) wins for music. Trad music on Thurs. nights.

The Pub, 50 Main St. (tel. 26032). Need we say more?

Downtown, 19 Main St. (tel. 25291), rocks with trad sessions on Mon.

Hotel Clanree, 1 mi. out on Derry Rd. (tel. 24369), transforms itself into a night-club for disco lovers on Sat. and Sun. nights (cover £5-6).

SIGHTS

Neo-Gothic **St. Eunan's Cathedral,** perched high above town on Church Ln., looks most spectacular when floodlit at night (like a castle in the sky). Moving away from the traffic light, Church Ln. emerges right off Main St. Proposed as a "resurrection of the fallen shrines of Donegal," construction on the cathedral lasted 11 years, all of which were years of economic hardship and depression. A detailed guidebook (£2.50) describes the brief history and relevance of each part of the cathedral. (Open daily 8am-5pm, except during the five Sunday masses at 8, 9, 10, 11:15am, and 12:30pm. Free.) Although St. Eunan's is not even one hundred years old, its burgeoning congregation has already outgrown it. Out of necessity, a second, modern cathedral has recently been built on the edge of town. Opposite the cathedral, the

---

Heads or Tails

Before turning to more spiritual affairs, Saint Colmcille was a ferocious swordsman. During these early years, a great monster lurked in the pool up on Meenaroy where the river that runs through Letterkenny rises. Locals called the monster Swileach because it had 200 eyes on each side of its head (that's 400 total). The local chief, Feardorocha, begged Colmcille to help him kill the monster in defense of the community.

Early one morning, both warriors set out for the pool. Upon their arrival there, Swileach reared out of the water and attacked them. Cowardly Feardorocha suddenly panicked and fled, leaving Colmcille to fight the monster single-handedly. This brave young man drew his sword and, with a mighty blow, halved the monster. Still not defeated, the monster's tail wrapped itself around Colmcille, trying to squeeze the life out of him. Miraculously, Colmcille managed to free himself from the iron grip and proceeded to make *ciolar coit* of the monster, carving it into many pieces (an ancient version of sushi).

Colmcille then set out after the cowardly chief. He caught up with Feardorocha as the latter was trying to ford the river near Conwal. As Colmcille was about to strike the deserter in reprisal, Feardorocha begged for mercy. He requested that the saint at least wash the monster's blood off his blade before exacting revenge. Colmcille did so and found that his anger abated. The kindly saint pardoned Feardorocha and remarked that this water would wash away the anger of any future person who washed his hand in it. He decided to name the river Swilly after the monster he had slain.

smaller but more historical **Parish Church of Conwal** (Church of Ireland) shelters a number of tombstones with intriguing inscriptions, some of which date from the 17th century (Sunday services at 8 and 10:30am).

Donegal County Museum, High Rd. (tel. 24613), exhibits anything and everything having to do with Co. Donegal. Artifacts date from all periods, including the Iron Age, Medieval Ireland, and the post-modern era (open Tues.-Fri. 11am-12:30pm and 1-4:30pm, Sat. 1-4:30pm; free).

■ NEAR LETTERKENNY: BALLYBOFEY

Ballybofey ("BAL-lee-BA-fay"), halfway between Letterkenny and Donegal Town, remains unblemished by tourism. As the road from Donegal Town passes through Barnesmore Gap, previously notorious as an 18th-century haven for highway robbers, mountains rise dramatically on either side of it. The **Finn Farm Hostel (IHH)** (tel. (074) 32261) is 2½ miles from Ballybofey. A sign marks the left turnoff 1½ miles out on the Glenties road; the hostel is another ¾ mile up the dirt road. While the facilities are average, the structure itself, an abundance of traditional musicians, and horses distinguish this hostel from many others. (£9; sheets free; **camping** £2/person, £3 w/kitchen; open March-Oct.) Wednesdays bring organized sessions (BYOB), but musicians often burst into spontaneous song. The hostel's setting is perfect for pony treks (hostelers £5/hr., £7/hr. for non-hostelers). Several pubs in town also try their hand at trad. Strains of songs are heard at **Bonners Corner Bar** on Glentin St. on Thursday nights (tel. (074) 31361); **Gallens Lounge,** Navenney St. on Sunday nights (tel. (074) 31053), and **Jacksons Hotel** (tel. (074) 31021) on Friday nights.

INISHOWEN PENINSULA

It would be a shame to leave Ireland before seeing the Inishowen Peninsula, an untouristed mosaic of mountains, forests, meadows, and beaches. The white sands are deserted, the pubs are filled with traditional music almost nightly, and residents are happy to share their land and laughter. The peninsula is dotted with many villages and two towns (Buncrana and Cardonagh), but it should really be thought of as a whole, since the sights never cease. It takes three or four days to see the whole shebang properly without a car.

The nearest commercial center to Inishowen is Derry, whose residents are well aware of Inishowen's allure and often vacation there. **Lough Swilly** (tel. (08 01504) 262017) runs buses from Derry to points on the Inishowen: Buncrana (Mon.-Fri. 10/day, Sat. 12/day, Sun. 4/day; 35 min.); Moville (Mon.-Sun. 5/day; 50 min.); Carndonagh (Mon., Wed., Fri. 4/day, Tues. and Thurs. 3/day, Sat. 4/day; 1 hr.); and Malin Head (Mon., Wed., Fri. 2/day, Sat. 3/day; 1½ hr.). Lough Swilly also connects Buncrana directly to Carndonagh (Mon.-Sat. 3/day; 50 min.). **Northwest Buses** (tel. (077) 82619) runs from Shrove through Moville, Culdaff, Carndonagh, Ballyliffen, Clonmany, Fahan, Buncrana, and on to Letterkenny (Mon.-Fri. 2/day; Sat. 1/day), and from Shrove to Derry via Moville (Mon.-Sun. 2/day; 1 hr.).

Inishowen's inland landscape is unusual (especially compared to Ireland's Midlands), but the northern and western shores are by far the more striking. The clearly posted **Inishowen 100** road takes exactly 100 miles to navigate the peninsula's perimeter. Drivers will find this the best route for seeing Inishowen. Even hitchers will have an easy and pleasant time on this road, since any traffic tends to stop for people in isolated areas. Cycling can be arduous around Malin Head due to ferocious winds. In fact, cyclists may want to use the roads that crisscross the peninsula to shorten long distances between sights. Most of the inland roads look exactly alike, so good directions and a good map are an absolute necessity. (Available at tourist offices in Buncrana and Cardonagh, the map published by the Inishowen Tourism Society is most comprehensive for £3.)

■■■ GRIANAN OF AILEACH

Ten miles south of Buncrana at the bottom of the peninsula, the hilltop fort Grianan of Aileach ("GREEN-ya of ALL-ya") is a logical place to start or finish a tour of Inishowen. This site has been a cultural center for at least 4000 years: first as a temple for sun-worship, then as a seat of power for the northern branch of the Uí Néill clan, and finally as a "mass rock" where Catholics worshipped in secret during the time of the Penal Laws. The fort's name translates approximately into "the sun-house of Aileach." This denomination derives from three sources: the fort's pre-Celtic role as a place of sun-worship, the Celtic belief that the sun-goddess Gráine hibernated here in winter, and the legend of a divine Scottish maiden-princess named Aileach who supposedly lived here. Much of the present stone structure is a 19th-century reconstruction, but the tri-level earthworks are original. Away from the carpark beyond the fort, a cross marks the site of a healing well supposedly blessed by Saint Patrick.

In light of its long history, the fort not surprisingly figures in a number of legends and tales. Inishowen (Owen's Island) even gets its name from events that took place here. Owen was the son of **Niall of the Nine Hostages**, the semi-legendary ancestor of the Uí Néill/O'Neill clan. One story claims that Niall slept with an old hag to gain sovereignty over Ireland. As ruler, he captured young St. Patrick and brought him to Ireland as a slave. Having escaped captivity and begun his missionary work, St. Patrick baptized Niall's son Owen at this very same hillfort. This act consecrated the Uí Néill fortress as a Christian holy site and ensured its continued significance. The fate of Grianan Aileach was finally sealed in the 11th century when Donal McLaughlin, the reigning Prince of Inishowen, was defeated by Brian Ború's grandson, Murtagh O'Brien. Each of O'Brien's men was ordered to carry away one stone from the royal palace of Aileach so that it could never be a challenger's set of power.

For the fort, turn left two miles along the Letterkenny Road from Bridgend. The turnoff is at the Burt Circular Chapel, a modern-day replica of the ancient fort. The fort itself is on top of the two-mile hill. No public transport comes near here, so the car-less will have to cycle, walk, or choose to hitch (drivers are particularly nice on the two-mile incline). A more pleasant shortcut returns to Buncrana: take the first left at Burt Circular Chapel. The **Grianan of Aileach Interpretive Centre** hunches at the foot of the hill in an old stone church of Ireland, just past St. Aengus Church (the circular chapel). (Centre open all year daily 10am-6pm; £2, students £1. Restaurant open all year daily 10am-10pm.)

■■■ BUNCRANA

North of Fahan, Buncrana curls up catlike in the long shadows of the mighty 2019-foot **Slieve Snacht.** Summer tourism and the Fruit of the Loom's sweatshirt and T-shirt factory (underwear is produced in Malin Town) fortify Buncrana. Bord Fáilte operates a summertime **tourist office** (tel. 62600) on the shorefront (open late May to mid-Sept. Tues.-Sun. 10am-1pm and 2-6pm). **AIB** bank (tel. 61087) counts money at 8 Market Sq. (open Mon.-Wed. and Fri. 10am-12:30pm, 1:30-4pm, Thurs. 10am-12:30pm and 1:30-5pm; **ATM). Bank of Ireland,** Main St. (tel. 61399), imitates its competition with an **ATM** (open Mon.-Wed. and Fri. 10am-4pm, Thurs. 10am-5pm). The **post office** (tel. 61010) crowds onto Main St., too (open Mon.-Fri. 9am-5:30pm, Sat. 9am-1pm). **E. Tierney Chemist's,** Lower Main St. (tel. 62412), is the friendly local pharmacy (open Mon.-Sat. 9:30am-6pm, Sun. noon-4pm). **Valu-Clean,** Main St. (tel. 62570), is particularly valuable for its washing machines (wash and dry £4.30; open Mon.-Sat. 9am-6pm). Buncrana's **phone code** is actively 077.

Accommodations, Food, & Pubs

The bedrooms at **Rattan House,** Swilly Rd. (tel. 61222), give a choice of TV or stunning ocean view. A kitchen is occasionally available; coffee and tea are constantly accessible (£14/person). **Ross-na-Rí House,** Ballymacarry (tel. 61271), is unfortunately divided from the sea by a hill and a factory, but Mrs. A. McCallion makes her own breads and jams to compensate.

From Main St., take a right at Mill Brae and cross the bridge onto Old Lane. The second left will carry you to Ross-na-Rí (single £15, double £26). **Mill View B&B,** Mill Brae, Lower Main St. (tel. 62043), is well-conceived and closer to the center of town. A chatty proprietor shows guests to clean, spacious, and well stocked rooms and bathrooms (single £15, double £24). **Swilly Villa,** Shore Front (tel. 61307), is convenient to tennis courts and bike hire at the leisure center next door. The lounge is beautiful, but the rooms aren't quite (TVs and hot pots in some rooms; single £13.50-17.50, double from £27).

Kitchens jostle with banks on Main St. The **Ubiquitous Chip,** 47 Upper Main St. (tel. 62530), scours the world for creative recipes. Happily, chips are not a main theme of the excellent menu. "Chicken Bang! Bang! Curry Dip" (£6.75) is one of the spicier dishes on the menu. (Marinated lamb steak in mint sauce £5.95; open July-Aug. daily noon-11pm, Sept.-June Mon.-Fri. noon-11pm.) **Dorothy's Kitchen,** 3 Church St. (tel. 62639), combines cultures in a French-bread pizza (£1.80; open daily 11am-1am). **O'Donnell's supermarket,** at the bus depot (tel. 61719), can also help (open Mon.-Sat. 7:30am-9pm, Sun. 7:30am-8pm). **Rodden's Pub,** Main St. (tel. 62395), has occasional impromptu trad sessions. The **West End Bar,** Main St. (tel. 61067), hosts live music every weekend and offers pool for entertainment at other times. **O'Flaherty's Lounge Bar** (tel. 61305), on Main St., also has characteristically Inishowen trad sessions.

Sights Two castles overlook Swan Park: the stately Queen Anne-era **Buncrana Castle,** in which Wolfe Tone was imprisoned after the French "invasion" of 1798 failed, and the 1430 **O'Doherty Keep,** near Castle Bridge. To get to the park, walk up Main St. towards the shorefront. At the cinema crossroads, walk straight down Castle Avenue. The park is beyond the Castle Bridge, which arcs 100 yards to the right. Not quite Arthurian, the castle is more like a derelict mansion and is closed to the public anyway. But the park itself is peaceful and pleasing. A **coastal walk** begins at Castle Bridge, goes past the keep, turns left at the Castle, and then ascends the hill. Ned Point's Fort, also along the coast, was built in 1812 but is surprisingly (and not very pleasantly) modern looking. The path finally reaches Porthaw Bay and culminates in beautiful Dragill Strand. Friar Rogerty's Rock, beyond the beach, witnessed the martyring of a local clergyman in 1632.

Just north of Buncrana, the multifarious **Tullyarvan Mill** (tel. 61613) surveys the history of Irish textiles from early modern linen and wool through Fruit of the Loom. The main attraction of a smaller wildlife exhibit is a colony of Ireland's rarest mammal, the Pine Marten. Disabled people produce and sell crafts inside the restored early, 19th-century corn mill. (Mill open Easter-Sept. Mon.-Sat. 10am-6pm, Sun. 2-6pm.) Once a week in summer the mill hosts a night of story-telling, trad, and Irish dancing (8:30-11:30pm, call to find out which night; £1-2).

■■■ WEST INISHOWEN

DUNREE HEAD & THE GAP OF MAMORE

Six miles northwest of Buncrana, Dunree Head pokes out into Lough Swilly. The **Guns of Dunree** (tel. (077) 61817) stay polished and inactive inside an old fort here, one of six that were built to defend Lough Swilly against hypothetical Napoleonic invaders. The forts were used through both World Wars. Some of the guns from those wars are also on display in **Fort Dunree** ("the fort of the heathen"), the first and only professionally-designed military museum in Ireland, complete with historical video. The fort's most impressive feature is its location overlooking Lough Swilly, where it is surrounded by nesting gulls and puffins. The mammoth searchlights used in WWII are still lit at times to search for people lost at sea. (Open June-Sept. Mon.-Sat. 10:30am-6pm, Sun. noon-6pm; £1.50, students/children 75p.)

Farther north along the Inis Eoghain 100 toward Clonimarry, a sign points left to the edge of the **Gap of Mamore.** This breathtaking pass teeters 800 feet above sea level between Mamore Hill and Urris. The rocky pass itself is exhilarating; the views are much more than magnificent. The views over the mountains to the Atlantic can be seen only if you head through the pass from east to west (from inland to coast). The road through the pass rises steeply and proves difficult for cyclists. It's easier to drive, though the hairpin turns over the sea are daunting. Yet the struggle of climbing the pass on bike or foot may add to the elation and satisfaction of travelers. Queen Mebdh of Connacht, Cú Chulainn's archenemy in the Táin (see Legends & Folktales, p. 61), is supposedly buried near the Gap of Mamore (and at Knocknarea, Co. Sligo, and in a few other places).

The road descends from the gap onto chilly northern beaches. The Inis Eoghain 100 proceeds to Lenan Head and inviting Lenan Strand. Heading north again, the road passes over Dunaff Head, through Rockstown Harbour, and past Tullagh Bay. Two miles from Clonmany, the road arrives at the **Tullagh Bay Caravan and Camping Park** (tel. (077) 76289), sprawling between mountains and sea. One of the choicest beaches on the peninsula is just steps from the front flap of your tent. (Laundry; kitchen; shop and café; £4/tent and 50p/person; showers 20p; open May 15-Sept. 15.)

CLONMANY & BALLYLIFFIN

North of the gap, two tiny towns, **Clonmany** and **Ballyliffin,** are separated by one mile. Clonmany hosts a local trad festival the first week of August. **Keg O' Poteen** (tel. (077) 76415) serves "keg" burgers (£1) and pints of legal alcoholic beverages on Main St. The pub's misleading name probably comes from Inishowen's pride in its old reputation for distilling the best poitín (moonshine) in Éire. Live music ranges from country to Irish ballads (Fri.-Sun.). Traditional singing fills the weekend air in and around **McFeeley's** (tel. 76122), across the street at Corner House.

Apart from its neighbor's festivities, Ballyliffin's own highlights are three long miles of golden sands on Pollan Strand. From the northern end of the beach, ruined **Carrickbrahey Castle** is visible. It has been the seat of both the MacFaul and O'Doherty clans. The **Doagh Farm,** on the Isle of Doagh (tel. (077) 76493), organizes pony treks along the beach, which gives views of curious Five Finger Strand. The farm includes a zoo where domestic and wild animals rub noses. (Entry to farm £1. Shop and tearoom open daily 10am-5pm. **Camping** available. Farm scheduled to reopen in May, 1996.) In the meantime, wanderers can stay at **Castlelawn House** just behind the Strand Hotel in Ballyliffin (tel. (077) 76600; £16/person, all w/bath).

■■■ NORTH INISHOWEN

CARNDONAGH

Carndonagh, or "Carn," is Inishowen's main market town. Two miles from the head of Trawbreaga Bay, it's an ideal, if noisy, hub for exploring north Inishowen. **Inishowen Tourism,** Chapel St. (tel. (077) 74933), just off the Diamond, is independently funded (open July-Aug. Mon.-Fri. 9:30am-7pm, Sat. 10am-6pm, Sun. noon-6pm; Sept.-June Mon.-Fri. 9:30am-5pm; free accommodation service). In the middle of it all sits an **AIB** bank, the Diamond (tel. (077) 74388; open Mon. 10am-12:30pm and 1:30-5pm, Tues.-Fri. 10am-12:30pm and 1:30-4pm). The **post office,** Bridge St. (tel. (077) 74101), handles mail with care (open Mon.-Fri. 9:30am-1:30pm and 2:30-5:30pm, Sat. 9:30am-1pm). **Rent-a-bike,** Pound St. (tel. (077) 74840), rents bikes for further exploration (£6/day; passport/driver's license as deposit; open Mon.-Sat. 9am-6pm). For late night jaunts, Carn Cabs provides **taxis** (tel. (077) 74580). **Valu-Clean,** Bridge St. (tel. (077) 74150), washes and dries (£4.60; open Mon.-Sat. 9am-6pm). **McLaughlin's,** the Diamond (tel. (077) 74120), is the town's pharmacy (open Mon.-Tues. and Thurs.-Sat. 10am-7pm, Wed. 10am-6pm).

Mrs. Mary Kearney, at **Roadside,** Glentogher (tel. (077) 74506), welcomes guests to her quiet home three miles from town on the Derry Rd. (£12/person). The rooms sparkle and shine at Mrs. Kathleen Brett's **Dunshenny House,** Millbrae (tel. (077)

74292), ½ mile down Chapel St. (£13/person w/full breakfast; £11.50 w/continental breakfast; no singles in high season). One mile out of town on the Malin Rd., **Ashdale House B&B** (tel. (077) 74017) takes advantage of its peaceful rural setting (spacious double £26, w/bath £30). **Trasbreaga Bay House,** the Diamond (tel. (077) 74352), contents cheap budget travelers (chicken nuggets and chips £2.05, sandwiches £1; open Mon.-Sat. noon-9pm, Sun. 12:30-2:30pm and 4-10pm). The **Corncrake Restaurant,** Malin St. (tel. (077) 74534), is at the forefront of grunge (lunch £4 and up; open April-May Mon.-Sat. 11am-7pm, June onward daily 10am-9pm). Tiny, modest **Bradley's Bar,** Bridge St. (tel. (077) 74526), has royal bathrooms (Queen Victoria supposedly used the toilet in the men's room). **The Sportsman Inn,** the Diamon (tel. (077) 74817), hosts trad on weekends.

Commercial Carn has but one lone sight to offer. The old Church of Ireland hulks ½ mile down Bridge St. Outside its walls, the 7th-century **Celtic cross** known as Carin Carndonagh is all that remains of the monastery that St. Patrick founded when he brought Christianity to the peninsula. Two ornamented shorter pillars flank the cross. One of them depicts David playing his harp. Another ancient pillar, this one displaying Christ's crucifixion, stands erect in the graveyard of the church.

MALIN

North of Carndonagh, Malin is yet another former winner of the Tidy Town contest. All starch and pleasantries, the town even has a perfectly manicured central green. R242 coincides with the Inis 100 five miles northwest of town as it winds toward Lagg. The sand dunes here are reputedly the highest in Europe, towering 100 feet high in some places. A little farther on, **Five Fingers Strand,** named for five standing rocks that jut into the bay, looks picture postcard-perfect with rugged slopes contrasting golden sand and blue water. The water looks tempting but is dangerous for swimming. High above the beach, **Knockamany Bens** provide views of the whole peninsula. Turn left at the little white church to get to the top of this worthwhile detour. Nearby **Malin Ostriches,** Ballylannon (tel. (077) 70661), farms ostriches for their feathers, meat, and leather (open Sat.-Sun. 1-6pm or by appointment; £1.)

The northernmost point in Ireland, **Malin Head** is a barren tooth of dark rock jutting up from the ocean spray. Until the 19th century, Malin Head was the site of an annual pilgrimage: young men and women "frisked and played in the water all stark naked" in celebration of the sea god's affair with the goddess of the land. Though the Irish youth no longer play this spectator sport, the Head instead gives today's travelers views of the Paps of Jura in Scotland (on a clear day, of course). Old water towers still stand like sentries over the point. The "EIRE" marked on the cliffs below identified Ireland as neutral territory to would-be Nazi bombers, but less patriotic names spelled out by more recent visitors make this peace signal hard to see. One mile from the head, **Hell's Hole,** a 250-foot chasm, roars devilishly with the incoming tide. A path to the left of the car park leads here. The path continues to naturally formed **Devil's Bridge,** which arcs over a chasm. The bridge is no longer safe to walk on, so the Devil is stuck where he is. The beaches around Malin Head have a reputation for semi-precious stones: casual walkers sifting through the sands may find jasper, agate, small opals, or amethysts—the **Malin Pebbles.** The five-mile **Atlantic Circle** road, which tours the perimeter of Inishowen's tip, also yields arresting views.

Two miles from Malin Head, Mrs. Doyle at **Barraicín** (tel. (077) 70184) keeps a friendly, comfortable B&B and tends a beautiful garden. A bulletin board with maps and photos of local sights helps plan the day's agenda (single £16, w/bath £20; double £26, w/bath £28). If you're traveling there by bus, get off at the phone booth that stands a bit past the Malin Head Post office. A broader view recommends Mrs. Anne Hawes' **Highview B&B** (tel. (077) 70283), ½ mile farther down the Malin Rd. The beds are so comfortable that you won't want to get up, but the spacious sitting room has such a great view that you won't want to go to sleep, either (single £18, double £30, all w/bath). Four miles southeast of Banba's Crown (the Signal Tower), **Mrs. Bridge McEleney's B&B** (tel. (077 70223) shrinks back just a bit from the cliffs

(£12/person). Sore feet will also find rest and revitalizing brew at **Farren's,** Ireland's northernmost pub. Back towards Malin Town, **Bree Inn** (tel. (077) 70161) delivers heaping plates of food (fish and chips £2.30; open daily 12:30-11:30pm). In Malin Town itself, all are welcome to eat at the **Malin Hotel** bar (tel. (077) 70645) or a lift a pint at **McLeans'** (tel. (077) 70607).

■■■ EAST INISHOWEN

Opposite Malin Head, **Inishowen Head** looks over to the carnival lights of Portrush and gathers sunbathers and swimmers at **Shroove Strand. The Drunken Duck** (tel. (077) 81362) is a friendly, shroving pub. It was named after a local woman whose beer leaked into her ducks' feeding trough—ask the bartender to pour a good pint of Guinness into yours. Mrs. McCann's warm welcome complements the cozy atmosphere at **Rockall B&B** (tel. (077) 81024), on Culdaff Rd. in Shroove. The smoked salmon she serves for breakfast is a rarity; badger-watching at night is an oddity. Tea facilities; TVs on request (£13/person, w/bath £15). Charlie McCann will also expertly direct you to Port a Doris, a delightful little cove with its share of semi-precious Shroove pebbles. The nimble of limb can hurdle the gate to the cliff walk and find a route to the shore.

GREENCASTLE

The road south from Inishowen Head leads to **Greencastle,** a small fishing village near the misty ruins of a seaside castle and fort. Greencastle's castle, built in 1305, warrants exploration. The Irish government maintains a center for training professional fishing boats in Greencastle. The most celebrated of Greencastle's skippers is Seamus McCormick, honored in 1970 by a small town in Tyrone for "the first Irish naval victory over the British." The British Navy, suspecting illegal fishing, had boarded his boat, but instead of sailing to the British pier at Portrush as ordered, McCormick hurried back to Greencastle with the British stuck on board. Relics of life on the seas are the center of attention at the newly-opened **Greencastle Maritime Museum,** on the shorefront. Occupying an old coastguard station, the well-organized museum displays an impressive collection of seacraft, including a 19th-century rocket cart, a traditional but brand new Fanad *curragh,* a wildfowling punt complete with swivel gun, and plenty of ship models and photographs (open July-Aug. daily 10am-6pm; £1, students 50p).

Fish of all kinds are available at **Kealey's Seafood Bar** (tel. (077) 81010), which has an affordable lunch menu (salmon with anchovy butter £4.50; open Tues.-Sun. 12:30-5pm and 7-9:30pm). **Old Fort Inn** (tel. (077) 81044) was originally a Martello Tower; today it fights off thirst. From its walls, Rathlin Island and Giant's Causeway are visible. An adjoining restaurant specializes in home baking (open daily noon-9:30pm). In a quietly secluded mansion overlooking Lough Foyle, Mrs. Anna Wright warmly welcomes guests to the **Manor House** (tel. (077) 81011). Walk along the beach or on the road to Culdaff to find it (£15/person). On the other side of town, **Brooklyn Cottage** (tel. (077) 81087) equips all rooms with a TV. The view is wonderful, but the cottage isn't quite as comfortable as home (£18/single, double £30, all w/bath; open Feb.-Nov.).

MOVILLE

A few paces farther south along a coastal path is the grassy seaside promenade of **Moville. Peter Bush** at the Coast Guard Station (tel. (077) 82402; open Mon.-Fri. 9am-5pm) rents boats to any takers. You can rent jet-skis at **Rent-a-Jet,** Quayside (tel. (077) 82052), at the water's edge beside the Hair O' the Dog Saloon (jet-skiing £11-12.50/hr., skiing £7.50/10 min.; open Sat.-Sun. 2pm-dusk, Wed. 6pm-dusk).

After an active day on the water, search for fossils in the floor o' the **Hair O' the Dog Saloon** (tel. (077) 82600; live music weekends). **Rosato's,** 7 Malin Rd. (tel. (077) 82247), prepares tasty dishes (big sandwiches £2.50, prawns in garlic butter £2.25; open daily noon-9pm). On Main St., **Barron's Cafe** (tel. (077) 82472) has cheap snacks and more filling meals of every variety (lamb cutlets w/peas £3.70, fresh salmon salad £5; open Mon.-Sun. 9:30am-9:30pm). The **Moville Holiday Hostel,** Malin Rd. (tel. (077) 82378), on the edge of town, was converted from old farm buildings. Large four and eight bed dorms and a health food shop occupy an attractive wooden interior (dorm £6, w/bath £9; sheets £1). Mrs. B. McGroarty offers B&B in a cute white house at **Naomh Mhuire,** Bath Terrace (tel. (077) 82091; single £14, double £26; open Easter-Sept.). For a view of Lough Folye, stay with Mrs. McGuinness at **Dunroman B&B** (tel. (077) 82234), off the Derry Rd. Guests can look at the lake or plop down in front of TVs in comfy rooms (single £12.50, w/bath £14). The **Mace Supermarket** deals in edibles on the main street (open daily 7:45am-9pm). **Hannon's Pharmacy**, Main St. (tel. (077) 82649) cures ills (open Mon.-Sat. 9:30am-1pm and 1:30-6pm, also July and Aug. Sun. noon-2pm). The **post office** functions on Malin Rd. (tel. (077) 82016; open Mon.-Fri. 9am-1pm, 2-5:30pm, Sat. 9am-1pm).

MUFF

On the southeast coast of the Inishowen Peninsula, just five miles from Derry, the tiny village of Muff boasts just one good chippie and one brilliant hostel. Martin Cooke's warm welcome makes the **Muff Hostel (IHH)** (tel. (077) 84188) a *Let's Go* home-away-from-home and the hosteler's best friend. Between Inishowen and Derry, it makes a perfect base for exploring both. (Kitchen and hot showers; dorm £5; open March-Oct.) The benefits are unending: **Lough Swilly Buses** offers a £3.50 same-day return ticket to Malin Head for guests of the Muff Hostel. Hostelers also get a 15% discount (Mon.-Fri.) at **Ture Inn** down Moville Rd. (tel. (077) 84262; food served after 6pm), where special Sunday brunches cost only £6.95. Trad jams enliven the atmosphere on Wednesday and Friday nights. (Hostelers can charter a minibus for the return trip, £1/person; otherwise, it's a 25-minute walk.) Down the road in Bridgend, **Harry's** (tel. (077) 68444) provides the perfect end-of-Ireland celebratory meal: mouth-watering surf, turf, and veggie meals (£6-8; open daily 5:30-10:30pm; bar open 4-11:30pm).

■ NORTHERN IRELAND

The strife that makes the North infamous hides the land's beauty and appeal from international travelers. What they're missing includes the string of seaside villages on the Ards Peninsula; the pockets of womb-like green collectively called the Glens of Antrim; one of the world's strangest geological sights, the Giant's Causeway; the beautiful Fermanagh Lake District; and a thrilling folk park in Omagh. Pub culture and urban neighborhoods show everyday life in a divided (and, most of the time, for most people, peaceful) society.

AN INTRODUCTION

HISTORY & POLITICS

There's a place called "Northern Ireland," but there are no "Northern Irish." The political entity's citizens still identify themselves along secular rather than geographic lines—namely as Catholics or as Protestants. The 900,000 Protestants are generally **Unionists** (who want the six counties of Northern Ireland to remain in the U.K.); the 600,000 Catholics tend to identify with the Republic of Ireland, not Britain, and many are **Nationalists** (who want the six counties to be part of the Republic). The conflict between them has proven to be one of the world's most intractable.

The 17th-century's **Ulster Plantation** systematically set up English and Scottish settlers on what had been Gaelic-Irish land, and gave Derry to parts of the City of London (hence the name "Londonderry"). Over the following two centuries, merchants and working-class emigrants from nearby Scotland settled in northeast Ulster. Their ties to Scotland, proximity to England, and bourgeois leanings meant that Counties Antrim and Down developed an Industrial Revolution economy, based on linen and shipbuilding, while the rest of the island remained agricultural. Protestant Unionists in the South were a thin layer of economic interests; but Ulster Plantation and Scottish settlement, over the course of 300 years, had created a working-class and middle-class population in northeast Ulster who identified with England and the Empire and didn't want Home Rule. The **Orange Order,** widespread by 1830, organized the Protestants and held parades which celebrated their supremacy.

Edward Carson and his ally **James Craig** translated Ulster Unionism into terms the British elite understood. When Home Rule looked likely in 1911, Carson held a mass meeting, and Unionists signed a Covenant promising to resist. When Home Rule appeared imminent in 1914, the Unionist **Ulster Volunteer Force (UVF)** armed itself by smuggling guns in through Larne—an act which inspired Nationalists to smuggle their own guns in through Howth. World War I gave Unionists more time to organize, and gave British leaders time to see that the imposition of Home Rule on all of Ulster would mean havoc as the UVF fought the IRA who fought the police. The 1920 Government of Ireland Act created two parliaments for North and South. The Act went nowhere in the South and was quickly superseded by Treaty and war, but the measure—intended as a temporary one—became the basis of Northern Ireland's government until 1973. The new Parliament met at **Stormont,** near Belfast.

The new statelet included only six of the nine counties in the province of Ulster. Carson and Craig had approved these odd borders. Their intent was to create the largest possible area which would have a permanent Protestant majority. Craig became the North's first Prime Minister. He, his successor **Sir Basil Brooke,** and most of their Cabinet ministers, thought in terms (as Brooke put it) of "a Protestant

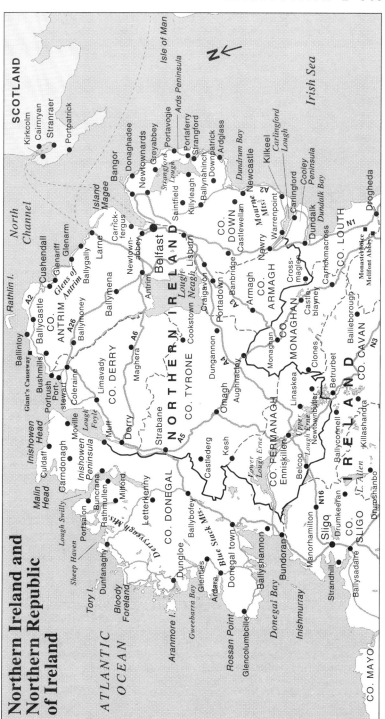

Northern Ireland and Northern Republic of Ireland

state for a Protestant people." Orange lodges and other militant groups continued to control politics, while the Catholic minority boycotted elections. Anti-Catholic discrimination was widespread. The **Royal Ulster Constabulary (RUC),** the new police force in the North, supplemented its ranks with part-time policemen called Bs and **B-Specials,** whose presence became notorious excuses for Orange militants to bear arms. The IRA continued sporadic campaigns against the North through the '20s and '30s with little result. After the 1920s, the movement was gradually suppressed inside the Irish state.

The depressing '30s sent the Northern economy into the dumps, requiring more and more British subsidies, while the Stormont Cabinet aged and dithered. **World War II** gave Unionists a chance to show their loyalty; the Republic of Ireland stayed neutral and stayed out, but the North welcomed Allied troops, ships, and air force bases. The need to build and repair warships raised employment in Belfast. The Luftwaffe firebombed it towards the end of the war, making Belfast one of the U.K.'s most-damaged cities. In a famous speech of May 1945, Churchill thanked the North and attacked Éire's neutrality.

Over the following two decades a grateful British Parliament poured money into Northern Ireland. The North's standard of living stayed higher than the Republic's, but discrimination and joblessness persisted—during the '50s, Ulster unemployment was twice that of Wales. Stormont failed to match social reforms across the water, parliamentary districts were painfully and unequally drawn to favor Protestants, and the working classes' sectarian obsessions frustrated labor activists. Large towns were segregated by religion, perpetuating the cultural separation. After a brief, unsuccessful try at school desegregation, Stormont ended up granting subsidies to Catholic schools. Violence had receded. Barring the occasional border skirmish, the IRA was seen as finished by 1962, and received a formal eulogy-like farewell in the *New York Times.* **Capt. Terence O'Neill** became the third Stormont Prime Minister in 1963. He tried to enlarge the economy and to soften discrimination, meeting in 1965 with the Republic's Prime Minister, **Sean Lemass.** O'Neill may have epitomized the liberal Unionist attitude when he said, "If you treat Roman Catholics with due kindness and consideration, they will live like Protestants."

The economy grew, but the bigotry stayed, as did the Nationalist community's bitterness. The American civil rights movement inspired the 1967 founding of **NICRA** (the **Northern Ireland Civil Rights Association**), which tried to end discrimination in public housing. NICRA tried to distance itself from constitutional concerns, though many Catholics didn't get the message: the Nationalist song "A Nation Once Again" often drowned out "We Shall Overcome" in demonstrations. Protestant extremists who didn't get the message included the forceful **Dr. Ian Paisley,** whose **Ulster Protestant Volunteers (UPV)** overlapped in membership with the illegal, paramilitary, resurrected UVF. The first NICRA march was raucous, but nonviolent. The second, in Derry in May 1968, was a bloody mess, disrupted by Unionists, then by the RUC's water cannons. This incident is usually thought of as the culmination of the Troubles.

Catholic **John Hume** and Protestant **Ivan Cooper** formed a new civil rights committee in Derry, but were overshadowed by Bernadette Devlin's student-led, radical **People's Democracy (PD).** The PD encouraged, and NICRA opposed, a four-day march from Belfast to Derry starting on **New Year's Day 1969.** Paisleyite harassment was nothing compared to the RUC's assault on Derry's Catholic Bogside once the marchers arrived. After that, Derry authorities agreed to keep the RUC out of the Bogside—it became **"Free Derry."** O'Neill, granting more civil rights concessions in hopes of calming everyone down, was deserted by more of his hardline Unionist allies. On August 12, 1969, Catholics based in Free Derry threw rocks at the annual Orange parade through the city. The RUC attacked the Catholics, and a two-day siege ensued. Free Derry "won," but the violence showed everyone that the RUC couldn't maintain order. The British Army arrived—it's still there.

O'Neill quit in 1969. Between '70 and '72, Stormont leaders alternated concessions and crackdowns, to little effect. The rejuvenated IRA split in two, with the

Marxist "Official" faction fading into insignificance as the new **Provisional IRA** (the **Provos,** or PIRA) took aim at the Protestants. More hopefully, the **Social Democratic and Labor Party (SDLP)** was founded in 1970. By '73, it had become the moderate political voice of Northern Catholics. The British troops became the IRA's main target. British policies of internment without trial outraged Catholics, and led the SDLP to withdraw from government. The pattern was clear: any concessions to the Catholic community might provoke Protestant violence, while anything that seemed to favor the Union risked explosive IRA response.

On January 30, 1972, British troops fired into a crowd of protesters in Derry; the famous event, called **Bloody Sunday,** and the ensuing reluctant British investigation increased Catholic outrage. The Stormont government was finally dissolved in 1973. The **Sunningdale executive,** which split power between Catholics and Protestants, was immediately crippled by a massive Unionist work stoppage, and its lasting replacement was **direct British rule** from Westminster. A 1973 referendum asking "Do you want Northern Ireland to remain part of the United Kingdom?" showed that a majority still supported the Union. The verdict didn't stop the violence.

In 1978, 300 Nationalist prisoners in the Maze Prison in Northern Ireland began a campaign to have their "special category" as political prisoners restored. The campaign's climax of sorts was the H-Block **hunger strike** of '81—ten prisoners fasted themselves to death. Their leader, **Bobby Sands,** was the first to go on hunger strike. He was elected to Parliament from a Catholic district in Tyrone and Fermanagh even as he starved to death. Sands died after 66 days and became a prominent martyr—his face is still seen on murals in the Falls Rd. section of Belfast.

Sands's election to Parliament was no anomaly. The hunger strikes galvanized the Nationalists, and support for **Sinn Féin,** the political arm of the IRA, surged in the early '80s. British Prime Minister Margaret Thatcher and Taoiseach Garret FitzGerald signed the **Anglo-Irish Agreement** at Hillsborough Castle in November 1985. The Agreement grants the Republic of Ireland a "consultative role" but no legal authority in how Northern Ireland is governed. It improved relations between London and Dublin, but infuriated extremists on both sides. Protestant paramilitaries began to attack the British Army, while the IRA continued its bombing campaigns in England. In 1991-2, the Brooke Initiative led to the first multi-party talks in the North in over a decade—Sinn Féin was not included. In December 1994, the **Downing Street Declaration,** issued by John Major and Taoiseach Albert Reynolds, invited the IRA to participate in talks if they refrained from violence for three months.

On August 31, 1994, the IRA announced a "complete" cessation of violence. Wanting a permanent end to terrorism, Unionist leaders bickered over the meaning of this statement. Nonetheless, Sinn Féin leader **Gerry Adams** defended the statement and called for direct talks with the British government. His efforts came to fruition; and for the first time in 75 years, the Sinn Féin and British ministers met head-on. The talks have proceeded sluggishly and precariously. The breakdown of Reynolds' coalition in the South and Major's problems in the Conservative party have threatened the progress of the negotiations. The discussion centers around the decommissioning of IRA arms and a return to some level of Home Rule for the province. In February 1995, Major issued his **joint framework** proposal. The document suggested the possibility of a new Northern Ireland Assembly, the "harmonizing powers" of the Irish and British governments playing a role in that Assembly, and the right of the people of Northern Ireland to choose their own destiny. Although the past year has shown amazing promise and initiative, the quantifiable results are minimal. In the words of one reporter, "the British government appears snail-like, the Unionist politicians obstructive, and Irish Republicans belligerent."

In some sense the Sinn Féin is planning its own end by pursuing these talks. The party has no agenda if the IRA disbands and its electoral clout has never risen above 13% in Northern elections. The SDLP, still led by John Hume, continues to work on behalf of Catholics within a constitutional framework. Paisley still heads the extremist **Democratic Unionist Party,** but the moderate **Official Unionist Party (OUP),** led by **James Molyneaux,** gets more votes. The Irish Constitution retains its paper claim to the six counties, though many young Southerners are sick of Republican platitudes and fear bombs in Dublin if the North ever changes hands. Some speculate that the North's drain on Britain's budget, army, and image might someday make a British withdrawal likely even against the majority's wishes. The Loyalists fear this, too, and have killed more people in the past few years than the IRA.

Overseas attention to the politics and bombs obscures the weird but often calm tenor of life in the North. Northern Ireland has one of the lowest crime rates in the world—people in England are more likely to be the victims of crime. Fringe groups on both sides aren't nearly as visible as the huge division in civil society which sends Protestants and Catholics to separate neighborhoods, separate stores, separate pubs, and often separate schools, with separate (though similar) traditional songs and separate slang. The split can be hard to see in Belfast (where everyone frequents downtown) or on the north Antrim coast (where everyone's on holiday). But the separation is unavoidable in Derry. Unemployment and poor housing are seen as the most pressing problems. Some writers describe the North's conflicts in terms of class: according to these essayists, the moderate middle class wants peace, but the working classes have less to lose and support the extremists.

SECURITY

Terrorists and paramilitaries on both sides want nothing less than to injure a tourist. As long as you stay out of Derry's Bogside and Belfast's Falls, Shankill, and Sandy Row after dark (and South Armagh altogether), you're unlikely to see trouble. Use common sense in conversation, and try not to take a political side or religious bent. Be aware of word choice: "Ireland" can mean the whole island or the Republic of Ireland, depending on who's listening. It's best to refer to "Northern Ireland" or "the North" and "the Republic" or "the South." "Southern Ireland" is never acceptable.

Since the ceasefire, **border check-points** have been removed and one rarely sees armed soldiers and vehicles in Belfast or Derry. It may still be unsafe to hitch in South Armagh. Do not ever take **photographs** of soldiers or of military installations or vehicles: if you do, your film will be confiscated and you may be detained for questioning. Taking pictures of political murals is not considered to be a crime, though it will mark you as a tourist. Some urban areas have **"control zones,"** where there's no parking due to fear of car bombs. Since **unattended luggage** can also conceal a bomb, it will be viewed with suspicion. Large sectarian parades are sometimes occasions for conflicts, though the first Orange day after the ceasefire was quite uneventful. Except for a showdown in Portadown, Co. Armagh, parades went quite smoothly. Still it may be wise to avoid large cities on July 12 (Orange Day) and on any other day in July or August (the "marching season") when there's a big Orange or Catholic march scheduled. Avoiding towns on these days is recommended as much for avoiding traffic congestion and closed stores as for safety reasons. Rural and holiday areas like the Glens and the Causeway Coast are untouched by the parades. As in the Republic, nonpolitical crime is much rarer than it is in America, although the crime rate seems to be going up.

MONEY

Money in Northern Ireland is in British pounds (£), called "pounds sterling" to distinguish them from the Irish pound or "punt." Notes printed in Northern Ireland have the same value as the notes printed in England, Scotland, and the Isle of Man, but look different and are *not* accepted in the rest of the U.K. If you're going from the North to England, Scotland, Wales, or to the Isle of Man, remember to swap your Northern Ireland pounds for Bank of England notes before you leave. English, Scottish, and Manx notes *are* accepted in Northern Ireland and on the borders around Northern Ireland; most towns will have shops that take "punt for pound" or the other way around. (The punt currently has a higher value than the pound, but the difference is fractional.)

■■■ BELFAST

The second-largest city on the island, Belfast is in some ways more cosmopolitan than Dublin. Over 400,000 people (one-fourth of the North's population) live in Belfast, making the city the center for Northern Ireland's commercial, artistic, and para-military worlds, entirely separate from those of the Republic. The student scene fosters the development of pubs, hole-in-the-wall cafés, and urban bustle. There's also some long-term unemployment, which make the poorer parts of the city recruiting grounds for extremist groups. The Troubles were unforgettable here. Armed British soldiers patrolled the streets during the Troubles, frequent military checkpoints slowed traffic and pedestrians, and stores advertised "Bomb Damage Sales." Although some may think that Belfast would be indelibly marked by its part in the 25-year conflict, travelers can be surprisingly oblivious to its dramatic recent history. Except for the numerous murals in the Falls, Shankill, Sandy Row, and East Belfast areas, the heavily protected police stations, the stark Peace line and uninhabited nearby houses, and the occasional bombed building, little physical evidence of violent division remains. The Troubles may have had unintended positive results, from the brilliantly grim irony of Belfast's literati, to the black taxi services (started in response to a bus strike), to the ban on cars downtown, which produced a prosperous shopping zone—a lesson for urban planners everywhere. Dockyards, smoke, and architecture look across the ocean to England and Scotland, while the pristine hills behind the small city remind it of its Irish component; it's hard to know in which direction, if any, the people and culture may someday tilt.

Belfast began as a base for "Scotch-Irish" Presbyterian settlement and then became a 19th-century industrial center, resembling Liverpool and Birmingham, with world-famous shipyards, factories, and exports. Gathering slums, smoke, flax mills, and social theorists as it went, Belfast by 1900 looked much more British than Irish. The Protestant majority that controlled the city felt British, too. Irish fear of Protestant violence (as skillfully managed by Unionist leaders like Carson) was instrumental in creating the present divided island. Some combination of Irish tradition with bicultural social angst has made Belfast in the last few decades arguably more important to the arts than Dublin. Actor/director Kenneth Branagh, singer Van Morrison, and a handful of contemporary poets have been influenced by Belfast's mix of excitement and unease.

SECURITY

The working class neighborhoods of West Belfast are sharply divided by the **peace line**—a physical wall that runs halfway between the Catholic Falls Rd. and the Protestant Shankill Rd. The wall was inspired by the fact that most violence occurs at the interfaces between Catholic and Protestant areas. Since the ceasefire, parts of the wall have been removed, but the neighborhoods are still distinct and separate. Even when sectarian conflict was at its worst, Belfast was actually safer for tourists than most American cities (both military and paramilitary groups strongly discourage non-political crime). The city center, the "Golden Mile," and the university area to its south rarely saw any trouble. West Belfast, however, full of joblessness and amazing political art, is best seen by day. Those planning to visit the docks for the nightlife should go to and from their chosen destinations in a taxi. Remember that it is against the law to take pictures of soldiers, or of any military item or installation—and this law is enforced. Many downtown curbs are control zones, where there's no parking permitted due to a well-founded fear of car bombs. Although peace has been restored for over a year now, some of these traffic regulations are still being enforced, possibly because they are the best way to maintain the bustling activities of the pedestrian shopping zones. For a few days around July 12, when the Protestant Orangemen hold their proud, angry parades, many Catholics leave the city and cultural events dry up not so much to avoid violence, as to get away from street blocks and congestion. July 12 and 13 are official holidays and the last two weeks of July are traditionally the quietest time of the summer. The parades in 1995 saw no

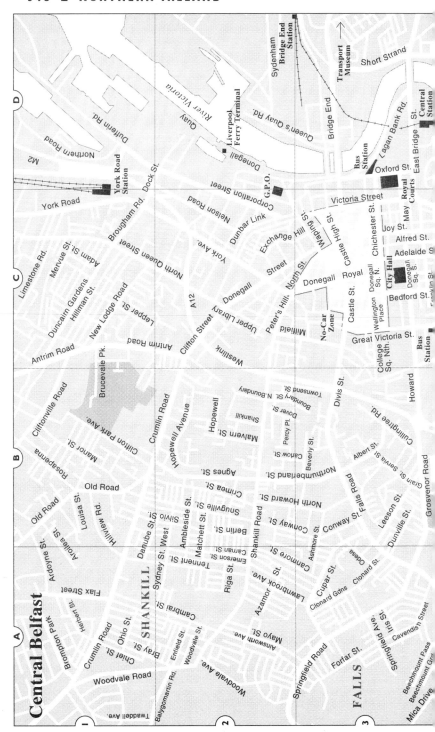

Central Belfast

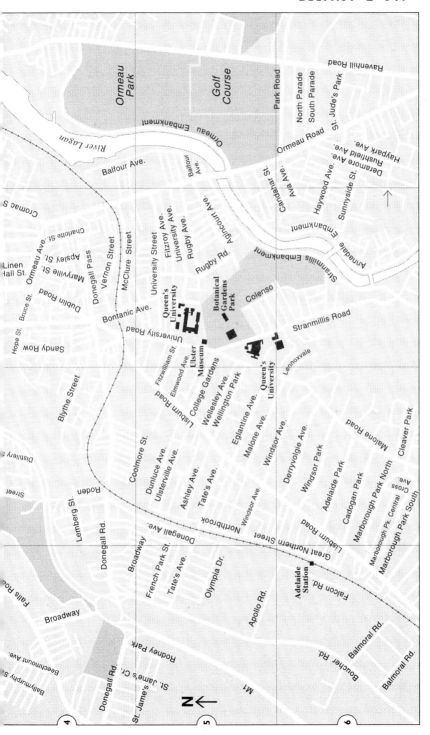

violence, but as always, large cities like Belfast have higher risks of conflicts during such a tense time.

GETTING THERE

For information on **ferries** and **hovercraft** to Belfast and Larne from England and Scotland, or on flights to Belfast from anywhere, refer to the Essentials section (see To Belfast & Larne, p. 34).

From **Belfast International Airport** in Aldee Grove, a **shuttle bus** runs to Belfast's Europa/Glengall St. bus station in the city center and to the central train station (Mon.-Sat. 2/hr.; Sun. 1/hr.; 70 min.; £3.50, £5.50 return). An audio-visual stand and an information desk, both on the ground floor of the airport, will fortify you with preliminary orientation. **Avis, Hertz, Europcar,** or **McCausland** all rent cars. The three companies have desks on the ground floor and have similar rates (about £39/day, £185/week). Rows of **taxis** offer to transport you to the city for about £20.

From **Belfast City Airport** (tel. (01232) 457745), **trains** run to Belfast Central Station (Mon.-Sun. 15/day; 6 min.; 60p). A **taxi** downtown costs about £5. **Manx Airlines** (tel. (01345) 256256) flies into Belfast City Airport four times a day. Jersey European also lands here. The airport has no currency exchange, but has **ATMs.**

From the **ferry terminals at Larne,** take either a bus or a train into Belfast city center. (Buses run Mon.-Fri. 17/day, Sat. 15/day, Sun. 3/day; 1 hr.; £2.30, £4.80 return. Trains roll Mon.-Fri. 20/day, Sat. 16/day, Sun. 6/day; 45 min.; £2.80, £4.70 return.) **Flexibus** (tel. 233933) connects the Sea Cat hovercraft terminal with Central Station, Oxford St. Station, Donegall Sq. Station, and the Europa Bus Centre (8/day; 50p, children 25p).

To reach the city center on foot from the **Sea Cat terminal** on Donegall Quay, turn left for one block. Turn right just before the Customs House on Albert Sq. and after two blocks turn left onto Victoria St. (not Great Victoria St.). At the Clock Tower, turn right again onto High St., which runs into Donegall Place, where a left will lead to Donegall Sq. at the end of the street.

Trains roll in from: Larne (Mon.-Fri. 20/day, Sat. 16/day, Sun. 6/day; 45 min.; £2.80, £4.70 return); Derry (Mon.-Fri. 7/day, Sat. 6/day, Sun. 3/day; 2¼ hr.; £7, £9.70 return); and Dublin's Connolly Station (Mon.-Sat. 7/day, Sun. 3/day; 2½ hr.; £13, £19.50 return). All trains arrive at **Belfast Central Station,** East Bridge St. (tel. 899411). To reach Donegall Square from Central Station, turn left and walk up East Bridge St. to Victoria St. Turn right here, then left onto May St. after two blocks. A free **Rail-Link bus** runs from Central Station to Donegall Square for those encumbered with luggage (Mon.-Sat.). For British rail enquiries, call tel. 230671.

Buses come to Belfast's **Europa/Glengall St. Station** (tel. 320574 or 333000) from Dublin's Busáras Station (Mon.-Sat. 4/day, Sun. 3/day; £9.50, £12 return) and from Derry's Foyle St. Station (Mon.-Sat. 6/day, Sun. 4/day; £5.30, £9.30 return). Buses from Northern Ireland's east coast arrive at the **Oxford St. Station** (tel. 333000 or 232356). All others arrive at Europa/Glengall St. Across the street from the Oxford St. bus station, Chichester St. leads straight to Donegall Square North. From the Europa/Glengall St. Station, a left at the Great Victoria St. exit leads to Howard St. Donegall Square appears soon after taking a right onto Howard St.

M1 and M2 motorways join to form a backwards "C" through Belfast. A1 branches off from M1 around Lisburn and heads south to Newry, where it changes to N1 before continuing through Dundalk and Drogheda to Dublin. M2 merges into A6, then heads northwest to Derry. Larne is connected to Belfast by the A8. **Hitching** is notoriously hard in and out of Belfast—most people take the bus out as far as Bangor or Larne before they stick out a thumb.

ORIENTATION

Belfast spreads out from City Hall in Donegall Sq., six blocks west of the River Lagan and the harbor. A bustling, pedestrianized shopping district extends for four blocks between City Hall and the enormous Castlecourt Shopping Centre to the north. Donegall Place, which becomes Royal Ave., bisects the pedestrian area as it leaves

Donegall Sq. Two blocks west of the center, Great Victoria St. runs south until it meets Dublin Rd. at Shaftesbury Sq. The stretch of Great Victoria between Shaftesbury and the Opera House is known as the "Golden Mile." South of the square, Dublin Rd. becomes University Rd. and leads to the red bricks of Queen's University and a neighborhood of B&Bs, pubs and cafés.

Divided from the rest of Belfast by the Westlink Motorway, West Belfast is both poorer and more politically volatile than the city center. There remains a sharp division between sectarian neighborhoods. A Catholic in a Protestant neighborhood would draw looks of suspicion. The Protestant neighborhood stretches along Shankill Rd., just north of the Catholic neighborhood which is centered on Falls Rd. The two are literally separated by a wall. The River Lagan divides industrial East Belfast from the rest of the city. The shipyards and docks that brought Belfast fame and fortune extend north on both sides of the river as it grows into Belfast Lough.

GETTING AROUND

Public transportation within the city is provided by the red **Citybus Network** (tel. 246485), supplemented by the Ulsterbus "blue buses" to the suburbs. Citybuses going south and west leave from Donegall Sq. East; those going north and east leave from Donegall Sq. West (73p). Travel within the city center costs 42p. Money-saving four-journey tickets cost £2.30. Seven-day gold cards allow unlimited travel in the city (£10). Seven-day silver cards permit unlimited travel in either North Belfast, West/South Belfast, or East Belfast (£6). All these transport cards and tickets can be bought from the kiosks in Donegall Sq. and around the city (open Mon.-Sat. 7am-6pm). A free **Rail-Link** bus connects the rail station and the city center, but you must have a train ticket to ride. Citybus services run from 5am to 11pm, though some routes have shorter hours. Late **Nightline** buses cover routes from Shaftesbury Sq. to various parts of the city (maps are posted in Donegall Square; depart Fri.-Sat. midnight, 1, and 2am; £1.50).

PRACTICAL INFORMATION

Tourist Office: St. Anne's Court, 59 North St. (tel. 246609). The usual, as well as an excellent map of the city with bus schedules (free). Helpful staff will get you where you need to go and find you a place to stay (in summer, call until 10pm for accommodations). A 24-hr. computerized info point in the outside wall helps travelers arriving at all times. Open Sept.-June Mon.-Sat. 9am-5:15pm; July-Aug. Mon.-Fri. 9am-7pm, Sat. 9am-7pm, Sun. 10am-4pm. The **Northern Ireland Tourist Board,** in the same building, doesn't provide walk-in tourist info.

Irish Tourist Board (Bord Fáilte), 53 Castle St. (tel. 327888). Limited info on the Republic of Ireland. The focus is clearly on Dublin. Open Oct.-Feb. Mon.-Fri. 9am-5pm, March-Sept. Mon.-Fri. 9am-5pm, Sat. 9am-12:30pm.

Budget Travel Office: USIT, 13b The Fountain Centre, College St. (tel. 324073), near Royal Ave. Sells ISICs and Travelsave stamps (£5.50) for 50% discount on trains. Books ferries and planes. Open Mon.-Fri. 10am-5:30pm, Sat. 10am-1pm. **Additional offices:** Queen's University Student Union (tel. 241830), open Mon.-Fri. 10am-5pm. **STA agent:** Arrow Travel, 48 Bradbury Pl. (tel. 232492). Student rates for ferries and planes. Open Mon.-Fri. 9am-5:30pm, Sat. 9:30am-2pm.

Youth Hostel Association of Northern Ireland (YHANI): 22 Donegall Rd. (tel. 324733). Books YHANI hostels free, international hostels for £2. Sells HI membership cards (senior £7, under 18 £3). Open Mon.-Fri. 9am-5pm.

U.S. Consulate General: Queens House, Queen St. (tel. 228239). Open Mon.-Fri. 1-5pm. **Canada, Australia,** and the **Republic of Ireland** are not represented.

Financial Services: Thomas Cook, 22/24 Lombard St. (tel. 236044). Cashes Thomas Cook travelers checks with no commission, others with 2% commission. Open Mon.-Fri. 9am-5:30pm. Belfast International Airport office: (tel. (01849) 422536). Open Mon.-Fri. 7am-8pm, Sat.-Sun. 7am-10pm. **American Express:** Hamilton Travel, 10 College St. (tel. 322455). Client mail held. AmEx Travelers Cheques cashed without fee, others £3 commission. Open Mon.-Fri. 9am-5pm, Sat. 10am-1pm.

Banks: First Trust, 14-16 Donegall Sq. East (tel. 326118). **Bank of Ireland,** 7 Donegall Sq. North (tel. 246241). **Ulster Bank,** 47 Donegall Pl. (tel. 320222). **Halifax Bank** 10-11 Shaftesbury Sq. (tel. 247777), also at 41 Arthur St., off Chichester St. near Donegall Sq., and at the Castlecourt Shopping Centre. All have **ATMs;** most close at 3:30pm.

Post Office: Central Post Office, 25 Castle Pl. (tel. 323740). Open Mon.-Fri. 9am-5:30pm, Sat. 9am-1pm. *Poste Restante* mail comes here. **Postal code:** BT1 1NB. **Branch offices:** dozens, two of which are: **Botanic Garden Post Office,** 95 University Rd. (tel. 381309), across from Queen's University; **Shaftesbury Sq. Post Office,** 7-9 Shaftesbury Sq. (tel. 326177; postal code: BT2 7DA). Open Mon.-Fri. 9am-5:30pm, Sat. 10am-12:30pm.

Telephones: Even in Belfast, fewer than half of public phones accept phonecards (available at most grocery stores). Coins are a necessity when exploring the city. **Phone code:** 01232.

Taxi: Huge **black cabs** run set routes to West Belfast, collecting and discharging passengers along the way (standard 55p charge). Two sets of signs identify the cabs. Those heading to Catholic neighborhoods are marked with a Falls Rd., Andersontown, or Irish-language sign; those going to Protestant neighborhoods are painted with a "Shankill" sign or a red poppy. The cabs are heavily partisan (see West Belfast, p. 359). Ordinary 24-hr. metered cabs abound: **City Cab** (tel. 242000; wheelchair accessible); **Diamond Taxi Service** (tel. 646666); **Fona Cab** (tel. 233333).

Car Rental: McCausland's, 21-31 Grosvenor Rd. (tel. 333777). £39/day, £185/week. Ages 21-70 only. Open Mon.-Thurs. 8:30am-6:30pm, Fri. 8:30am-7:30pm, Sat. 8:30am-5pm, Sun. 8:30am-12:30pm. 24-hr. car return at Belfast International Airport Office (tel. (01849) 422022). Belfast City Airport office (tel. 454141). £10 surcharge to drive in the Republic. **Budget,** Great Victoria St. (tel. 230700). £39-59/day, £195-395/week. Ages 23 and over. Open Mon.-Fri. 9am-5:30pm, Sat. 9am-1:30pm. Offices at both airports open 24 hrs. **Avis,** 69/71 Great Victoria St. (tel. 240404). £41/day, £155/week. Fri. afternoon to Mon. morning special £67.50; deposit £35. Ages 23 and over. Open Mon.-Fri. 8am-6pm, Sat. 9am-1pm. Most car rental companies require returns to be made to Northern Ireland offices.

Bike Rental: None in city center. **E. Coates,** 108 Grand Parade (tel. 471912). £4/day; deposit £30. Open Mon.-Fri. 9am-5:30pm. **McConvey Cycles,** 476 Ormeau Rd. (tel. 491163). £7/day, £40/week; deposit £30. Open Mon.-Sat. 9am-5:30pm.

Luggage Storage: Arnie's Hostel will hold bags during the day for those staying there, as will the **YHANI,** 22 Donegall Rd. (tel. 324733).

Camping Equipment: The Scout Shop and Camp Centre, 12/14 College Sq. East (tel. 320580). Huge selection of anything you need. Ring the bell to get in. Open Mon.-Sat. 9:15am-5pm.

Bookstore: Eason's, Castlecourt Shopping Centre, Royal Ave. (tel. 235070). Large Irish section, lots of travel guides. Open Mon.-Wed. and Fri.-Sat. 9am-5:30pm, Thurs. 9am-9pm. **Familia,** Belfast Family History and Cultural Heritage Centre, 64 Wellington Place (tel. 2353952). Big Irish section. Open Mon.-Fri. 9:30am-5:30pm, Sat. 10am-5pm.

Library: Linen Hall Library, 17 Donegall Sq. North (tel. 321707). (See Sights, p. 356.) Open Mon.-Wed. and Fri. 9:30am-5:30pm, Thurs. 9:30am-8:30pm, Sat. 9:30am-4pm. Extensive collections of pre-19th-century newspapers and maps, info on the Troubles, genealogy. Free Irish language courses. Visitor's Pass to the library w/photo ID.

Laundry: Student's Union, Queen's University, University Rd. Wash £1, dry 20p. Open Mon.-Fri. 9am-9pm, Sat. 10am-9pm, Sun. 2-9pm. Students only. **Duds & Suds,** University Rd. (tel. 243956). Popcorn and TV while you wait! Wash £1.50, dry £1.50. 15% discount for students and seniors. Open Mon.-Fri. 8am-9pm, Sat. 8am-6pm, Sun. noon-6pm. Last load 1½ hr. before closing.

Bisexual, Gay, and Lesbian Information: Carinated Counseling: (tel. 238668). Open Thurs. 7:30-10pm. Odd name, cool people.

Crisis Lines: Samaritans: (tel. 664422). 24 hrs. **NI Council on Disability:** (tel. 491011). Open Mon.-Fri. 9am-5pm. **Rape Crisis Centre:** 41 Waring St. (tel. 321830). Open Mon.-Fri. 10am-6pm, Sat. 11am-5pm.

Pharmacy: **Boot's,** Donegall Place (tel. 242332). Open Mon.-Wed. 9am-5:30pm, Thurs. 9am-8:45 pm, Fri. 9am-8pm, Sat. 9am-6pm.
Hospitals: Belfast City Hospital, Lisburn Rd. (tel. 329241). From Shaftesbury Sq. follow Bradbury Pl. and take the right fork. **Royal Victoria Hospital,** Grosvenor Rd. (tel. 240503). From Donegall Sq., follow Howard St. west into Grosvenor Rd. **Ulster Hospital,** Dundonald St. (tel. 484511).
Emergency: Dial 999; no coins required. **Police:** 65 Knock Rd. (tel. 650222).

ACCOMMODATIONS

Nearly all of Belfast's accommodations are located near Queen's University, south of the city center. Relatively safe and convenient to pubs and restaurants, this area is by far the best place to stay in the city. Bus #59, 69, 70, 71, 84, and 85 run there from Donegall Sq. East. B&Bs multiply between Malone Rd. and Lisburn Rd. south of Queen's, and the YWCA and the independent hostel are in this area. B&Bs are surprisingly busy during the summer; reservations are recommended.

Hostels & University Housing

Arnie's Backpackers (IHH), 63 Fitzwilliam St. (tel. 242867). Relaxed, friendly atmosphere provides a real respite from tiring travels. Small 6-bunk rooms. Kitchen always open. Luggage storage during the day. Dorm £7.
YHANI Belfast Hostel, 22 Donegall Rd. (tel. 324733). Clean, airy, ultra-modern rooms with 2-6 beds, some with private bath. No kitchen. They'll return your cycle to Dublin's Rent-a-bike but keep the deposit. Wash and dry £2.50, powder 40p. Coffee shop open daily 7:30am-8pm. Dorm £9, w/bath £10.50; charge for check-in after 11pm. Book 2 weeks ahead for weekends. Wheelchair access.
YWCA, Queen Mary's Hall, 70 Fitzwilliam St. (tel. 240439). Co-ed. Bright, spic'n'span rooms with sinks. Limited self-service kitchen open 7am-11pm. Always full during school year; in summer, book 1-2 weeks in advance. £1 wash (no dry); dinner £5. B&B £13/person, 3-bed dorm w/out sheets £8/person.
Queen's University Accommodations, 78 Malone Rd. (tel. 381608). Bus #70 or 71 from Donegall Sq. East runs here. On foot, Great Victoria Rd. runs into Malone Rd. An undecorated but furnished dorm: spacious single or twin rooms with sinks and desks. Strong, reliable showers; little ventilation. 24-hr. kitchen with toaster and little else; common rooms with TV; free laundry. Single £7 for U.K. students only, £8.70 for international students, £11-16 for non-students; double £17.40. Open mid-June to mid-Sept., and Christmas and Easter vacations.

Bed & Breakfasts

The university-area B&Bs are all similar in price and quality. Though individual houses are often full, you can usually find a bed somewhere in the neighborhood.

Mrs. Davidson's East-Sheen Guest House, 81 Eglantine Ave. (tel. 667149). The best deal in Belfast, if you can get a room. Sweet Mrs. D. serves enormous breakfasts, and every room has a teapot, sugar cubes, and biscuits. Rooms are bright and clean. £15/person (£16.50 as of Jan. 1, 1996).
The George, 9 Eglantine Ave. (tel. 683212). Reassuringly spotless but cramped rooms, all with shower and TV. Cushy leather couches by the big picture window in the common room. Single £17, twin double £34, double w/shower £36, double w/bath £40. Family room available for £46.
Marine House, 30 Eglantine Ave. (tel. 381922). High ceilings in the huge common room. Rooms vary in size. Single £18, double £34, double w/bath £40, triple £15.
Eglantine Guest House, 21 Eglantine Ave. (tel. 667585). Vinyl headboards shine in tiny singles. Tea, coffee, and fresh bread. Single £16-18, double £34, triple £48.
Liserin Guest House, 17 Eglantine Ave. (tel. 660769). Comfy beds invite you to flop down in pastel rooms. One single has a skylight. Coffee, tea, and biscuits available all day in the dining room. Single £18, double £34.
Camera House, 44 Wellington Park (tel. 660026 or 667856). Nondescript rooms with TVs and phones. Single £18, twin w/shower £38, double w/bath £45.

Drumragh House, 647 Antrim Rd. (tel. 773063), several mi. north of city center. Citybus #123 and 45 stop in front of this house with large rooms in a more residential neighborhood. Pretty gardens at the foot of Cave Hill. £15/person.

Pearl Court Lodge, 67 Malone Rd. (tel. 662985). Comfortable rooms give ready access to the University. £18/person.

FOOD

Belfast offers alternatives to the bland and greasy frying tradition. Dublin Rd. and the Golden Mile (of Great Victoria St.) have the highest concentration of restaurants. Bakeries and cafés dot the shopping areas, but most close with the shops at 5:30pm.

The **Mace Supermarket** on the corner of Castle St. and Queen St. sells cheap groceries (open Mon.-Wed. and Fri.-Sat. 9am-6pm, Thurs. 9am-9pm). For fruits and vegetables, plunder the lively **St. George's Market,** East Bridge St., in the enormous warehouse between May St. and Oxford St. (open Tues. and Fri. 7am-3pm). **The Nutmeg,** 9A Lombard St. (tel. 249984), supplies healthy foods, baked goods, and raw ingredients (open Mon.-Sat. 9:30am-5:30pm).

Queen's University Area

Bluebells, 50 Botanic Ave. (tel. 322622). A hangout for the young intellectuals who spend hours here. Great food, homemade ice cream (small cone 35p), and newspapers. Big bowl of soup and homemade bread £1.25. Open Mon.-Sat. 8am-10:30pm, Sun. 9am-8pm.

Bookfinders, 47 University Rd. (tel. 328269). Smoky, atmospheric bookstore/café has the lived-in look. Moussaka and salad (£3.20) or soup and bread (£1.40) amid stacks of old books. Occasional poetry readings. Open Mon.-Sat. 10am-5:30pm.

Cloisters Bistro, in the Queen's University Student Union, University Ave. (tel. 324803). Mediocre but cheap cafeteria food. Open Mon.-Fri. 8:30am-6:30pm, but closes at 3pm during school vacations.

The Attic Restaurant, 54 Stranmillis Rd. (tel. 661074). A tiny second-floor restaurant that practically spills out the windows to the Victorian balcony. Light fare for lunch (homemade soup, chicken sandwich, and tea £2.50). Heartier food at dinner (huge roast and potatoes £7). Open Mon.-Sat. 11:30am-3pm and 5-10:30pm, Sun.11am-3pm and 5-9pm.

The Greek Shop, 43 University Rd. (tel. 331135). Bring your own wine for a Bacchanalian feast, complete with stuffed grape leaves (£2.75). Feast at lunch but fast at the more expensive dinner (souvlaki £6). Open Mon. noon-3:30pm, Tues.-Fri. noon-3:30pm and 6-10pm, Sat. 1-2:30pm and 6-10pm.

The Tea House, 245 Lisburn Rd. (tel. 611292). This centaur-like establishment is a secondhand bookstore upstairs and a dark café with good vegetarian dishes downstairs. Open Mon.-Sat. 10am-4:15pm.

The Golden Mile & the Dublin Rd.

Larry's Piano Bar/Restaurant, 36 Bedford St. (tel. 325061), next to Ulster Hall. Cozy booths and intimate tables crowned by high ceilings. Guests are entertained by jazz and blues while they dine in style at the only piano bar in town (high tea £5.95, chocolate truffle rum roll £2.75). All the waitstaff sing and dance and will gladly see you do the same. Waltz away on starched cloth but watch out for the glasses. Open 5pm-1:30am for dinner.

Café Equinox, 32 Howard St. (tel. 230089), behind the gift store. Sleek black café serves chic double espressos and clearly the best sandwiches in Belfast. Open Mon.-Wed. and Fri.-Sat. 9:30am-5pm, Thurs. 9:30am-9pm.

Banana's, 4 Clarence St. (tel. 339999). Ceiling fans, palm trees, and Caribbean food with an Irish twist (bacon and banana sandwich with salad, £3.25). Cheaper food during happy hour (5-7pm). Open Mon-Sat. noon-3pm and 5-11pm.

Harvey's, 95 Great Victoria St. (tel. 233433). A yuppie pizza joint with big wooden booths and seafood pizza (£5.75). Open daily 5pm-midnight.

Spuds, 23 Bradbury Pl. For the hungry insomniac and the post-club crowd. Huge baked potatoes laden with curry, chili, and other indigestible delights (£1.10-1.80). Open Mon.-Thurs. and Sat. 11am-3am, Fri. 11am-4am, Sun. 11am-1am.

North of Donegall Square

Spice of Life, 62 Lower Donegall St. (tel. 332744), across from St. Anne's Cathedral, behind the tourist office. Earthy atmosphere and cheap, wholesome veggie food. Student special: large soup and sandwich £1.50. Vegan ice cream 55p/scoop. Nothing over £3. Open Mon.-Sat. 10am-5pm.

Bambrick's, corner of Wellington Pl. and College Sq. (tel. 423203). Many notice the intricate mosaic exterior before seeing the café itself. Unlimited cup of coffee (75p) washes down a full Irish breakfast (£1). Eggplant parmesan w/potato £3. Open Mon.-Fri. 9:30am-4:30pm, Sat. 11am-4pm.

Delaney's, 19-27 Lombard St. (tel. 231572). Tall wooden booths seat cowboys at this "American-style," bison-bedecked hangout. Hearty portions of soup and quiche and an enticing salad bar. Moussaka and potato £3.15. Open Mon.-Wed. and Fri.-Sat. 9am-5pm, Thurs. 9am-8pm.

Nick's Warehouse, 35-39 Hill St. (tel. 439690), 3 blocks east of Royal Ave. Known for a fun crowd and veggie food. Lunch £3-6 at wine bar. Open daily noon-3pm.

PUBS

Pubs were prime targets for sectarian violence at the height of the Troubles, in the 60s and 70s. As a result, most of the popular pubs in Belfast are relatively new, though some have recreated a traditional flavor. Ask the student staff at the Queen's University Student Centre about current hip night spots. The *Bushmills Irish Pub Guide*, by Sybil Taylor, relates the history of Belfast's pubs (£7 at tourist office).

Queen's University Area

The Queens University Student Centre, (tel. 324803), hops and bops during termtime: 2 popular bars, discos 6 days a week (cover £2), and occasional live bands. In summer, the bars are quiet, but discos continue on Thurs. and Sat.

The Elms, 36 University Rd. (tel. 322106). A rough-around-the-edges student bar for those who don't want frills. Live bands most nights, trad on Thurs.

The Botanic Inn (the "Bot"), 23 Malone Rd. (tel. 660460). Students.

The Eglantine Inn (the "Egg"), 32 Malone Rd. (tel. 381994). More students. Some young professionals pop in for a drink at lunch.

The Empire, 42 Botanic Ave. (tel. 328110). Cheap pizza to go with all that beer. Big-screen TV. Stand-up comedy on Tuesdays from Sept.-June (cover £3.50).

The Golden Mile and the Dublin Road

Lavery's, 12 Bradbury Pl. (tel. 327159). The popular, if rather unattractive, place to be for all (cool) kinds of people—bikers to students to road-hog intellectuals.

Morrisons, 21 Bedford St. (tel. 248458). A new pub with a painstakingly reconstructed "traditional" atmosphere. Always packed.

Crown Liquor Saloon, 46 Great Victoria St. Famous, convivial place for an afternoon pint, but in the evenings it fills with an older, tourist crowd. The National Trust was quick to claim this property—with its gilt ceilings, gas lamps, and Victorian booths—as its own.

Robinson's, 38-40 Great Victoria St. (tel. 247447). Recently bombed but none the worse for the wear. Incredibly lively, it offers four floors of bars, including a motorcycle-themed "Rock Bottom" sporting a real Harley in the basement and "The Spot" on the top floor, which hosts live rock bands Thurs.-Sat. "Fibber Magee's," at the back of the ground floor, serves traditional Irish lunches. Trad sessions on Mon. nights.

North of Donegall Square

Queens Bar, 4 Queen's Arcade (tel. 321347). Friendly, low-pressure atmosphere in a tiny alley off Donegall Pl. attracts a broad mixture of people, gay and straight. Upscale lunchtime pub grub (tuna and red bean salad w/crusty bread £3).

The Crow's Nest, 26 Skipper St. (tel. 325491), off High St., across from the Albert Memorial Clock. A jovial gay and lesbian crowd. Popular disco Thurs.-Sat. nights at 9:30pm (cover £1). Ask the helpful staff for other frequented gay hangouts.

Kelly's Cellars, 30 Bank St. (tel. 324835), off Royal Ave. near the Primark building. Favored, smoke-stained, working-class bar. The oldest pub in Belfast that hasn't been renovated. Trad on Thurs., folk or rock Fri.-Sat. cover £1.

The Parliament Bar, Dunbar St., around the corner from the Duke. Gay and lesbian crowd parties at discos on Tues., Fri. and Sat. nights, sways to classical music on Mon. nights, and even swings to golden oldies.

Near the Docks

The pubs by the docks are full of unique character and are also among the few in Belfast that have survived the violence of the past 25 years intact. A cab should be used for transport to and from the dock area, as it can be dangerous at night.

The Rotterdam (the "Rott"), 54 Pilot St. (tel. 746021). Crammed to the rafters with an odd assortment of flotsam and jetsam, from wooden shoes to spiked flails. The odds and ends were contributed mostly by foreign sailors. Live music 6 days/week, ranging from folk to jazz to blues.

Pat's Bar, 19 Prince's Dock St. (tel. 458603). The Rotterdam's twin.

The Front Page, 9 Ballymoney St. (tel. 324924). Packs the locals in nightly. Plays live music on weekends.

SIGHTS

The **tourist office** on North St. will arm you with a valuable free map listing bus routes and most major sites and limitless brochures in an attempt to make the city navigable. A more detailed Greater Belfast area map is also available for £3. The *Belfast Civic Festival Trail* pamphlets, basically self-guided walking tours of various neighborhoods, are detailed and interesting. **Citybus** (tel. 458484) offers a 3½-hour "Belfast City Tour" of the city's major architectural landmarks. (July-Aug. Wed. 1:30pm, leaving from Castle Place; £6.50, students £4.50; advance booking required.) Recent peaceful developments have also made possible the Citybus "Belfast: A Living History" tour. The coach guides gawking tourists through the Falls, Shankill, and Sandy Row areas, pointing out murals and places of recent significance. (Tues., Thurs., and Sat. 9:30am and 2pm; £6.50, students £4.50; free, illustrated souvenir booklet included.) One-hour **walking tours** focus intensely on Belfast's history; they leave the tourist office daily at 2pm (£2.50, students £2).

Donegall Square

Belfast City Hall, Donegall Sq. (tel. 320202 ext. 2618), is the administrative and geographical center of Belfast, distanced from the crowded streets by a grassy square. Its green copper dome, 173 feet high, is visible from any point in the city. Neoclassical marble columns and arches figure prominently in A. Brunwell Thomas's 1906 design. Inside, a grand marble staircase ascends under the watchful dome to the second floor. Portraits of the city's Lord Mayors somberly line the halls. The City Council's oak-paneled chambers, used only once a month, are deceptively austere considering the Council's reputation for rowdy meetings (they sometimes devolve into fist fights). If you want to see the council in action, befriend a councillor—they can sign you in with 48-hr. notice. Otherwise, there is no public access to debates. Glass and marble shimmer in three elaborate reception rooms. In the City Hall gardens, marble statues of Queen Victoria and Sir Edward Harland (of Harland and Wolff shipyard fame) stand over the crowds on the grass. An inconspicuous pale gray stone column commemorates the 1942 arrival of the U.S. Expeditionary Force, whose soldiers were stationed here to defend the North from Germany. The interior of City Hall is accessible by guided tour (Sept.-June Wed. 10:30am; July-Aug. Mon.-Fri. 10:30am and 2:30pm; 1hr.; free, but due to security, reservations must be made a day in advance).

Across the street from City Hall, the **Scottish Provident Institution,** built in 1902, is recognizable by its asymmetrical roofline and 16 sculpted lions' heads. Other decorations depicting the loom, ships, and spinning wheel represent the industries which made Belfast prosperous. The northwest corner of Donegall Sq.

shelters the wood-paneled **Linen Hall Library,** 17 Donegall Sq. (tel. 321707). The library contains a famous collection of political materials. Devoted librarians scramble for every Christmas card, poster, hand bill, and newspaper article related to the Troubles that they can get their hands on. "A History of Linen Hall Library 1788-1988" is assigned the call number LIB.04 KIL (open Mon.-Wed. and Fri. 9:30am-5:30pm, Thurs. 9:30am-8:30pm, Sat. 9:30am-4pm).

Cornmarket

Just north of the city center, a shopping district envelops eight blocks around Castle St. and Royal Ave. This area, known as Cornmarket after one of the commodities originally sold here, has been a marketplace since Belfast's early days. The barricades which prevent private automobiles from entering happen to fall roughly where the old city walls stood in the 17th century. Just across College Sq., **The Old Museum Arts Centre** (tel. 235053) mounts rotating art exhibits and hosts frequent concerts (open Mon.-Fri. 9am-5:30pm, Sat. 10am-5pm; free). Tucked into the chaos of Rosemary St., the **First Presbyterian Church of Belfast** achieves fame by being the oldest church in the city (open Wed. 10:30am-12:30pm).

Although the Cornmarket area is dominated by modern buildings, snapshots of old Belfast remain in the tiny alleys, known as the **Entries,** which connect some of the major streets. A drink at any of the pubs along these alleys excites feelings of nostalgia. On Ann St., a hand and an umbrella stick out of the wall over an umbrella store. The entrance to Pottinger's Entry, which contains the old **Morning Star Pub** in all its traditional splendor, is right across the street. Farther down Ann St., **Joy's Entry** was the alley where the *Belfast News Letter* was printed for over 100 years. The only establishment in the entry—**Globe Tavern**—is disappointingly modern on the inside. Off Lombard St., **Winecellar Entry** is the site of Belfast's oldest pub, **White's Tavern,** which has been serving drinks since 1630. It's still an ideal place for an afternoon pint. This part of town also holds the city's oldest public building, **The Old Stock Exchange,** on the corner of North and Waring Streets. The tireless Charles Lanyon designed a new facade for the building in 1845 when the original was deemed not grand enough.

St. Anne's Cathedral Area

Belfast's newspapers all set up shop north of the Cornmarket shopping district, around the still active Church of Ireland cathedral (on Donegall St.), which is called the **Belfast Cathedral** or **St. Anne's.** To keep from disturbing regular worship, this cathedral, begun in 1899, was built around the smaller, earlier church already on the site. Upon completion of the cathedral's exterior, the earlier, now enclosed, church was removed brick by brick from inside. The mosaic above the Chapel of the Holy Spirit depicts St. Patrick arriving in southeast Co. Down and bringing Christianity to Ireland. The tops of each of the cathedral's 10 interior pillars depict somebody's idea of the 10 basic professions of Belfast: Science, Industry, Healing, Agriculture, Music, Theology, Shipbuilding, Freemasonry, Art, and Womanhood (a nice enough profession, but the pay stinks). (Open daily 9am-6pm.)

North Belfast

At the bottom of the hills that rise outside the city sits **Belfast Castle,** presented to the city by the Earl of Shaftesbury in 1934. Though in perfect condition, the castle is closed to the general public. However, anyone can walk through the grounds. At the top of **Cave Hill,** on which the castle was built, **McArt's Fort** is the Fort of Matudan, the ancient Ulster King, where the more modern United Irishmen plotted rebellion in 1795. The summit is nicknamed "Napoleon's Nose." Its breath-taking view over the city and Belfast Lough is certainly nothing to sneeze at. Marked trails lead north of the fort to five caves in the area. Historians believe that the caves are actually ancient mines, of which only the lowest is accessible.

The Docks & East Belfast

Belfast has its own combined version of a leaning tower and Big Ben: the precarious **Albert Memorial Clock Tower.** Designed in 1865 by W. J. Barre, the tower leans at the entryway to the docks area, where Oxford St. briefly parallels the Lagan. The Albert of mention is Prince Albert, Queen Victoria's consort.

Although the docks area was the activity hub of old Belfast, continued commercial development and Belfast's urban revisionism have obliterated anything old enough to remember the city's founding. The stately **Custom House,** built by Charles Lanyon in 1857, stands between Queen Sq. and Albert Sq. on the approach to the river from the clock tower. Designed in an imaginative E-shape, it rests on an elaborate pediment of Britannia, Neptune, and Mercury, the god of trade. This is Belfast's answer to Dublin's famous Custom House (Belfast's is closed to the public).

An organ with port and starboard lights carries the tune at **Sinclair Seamen's Church,** Corporation St. (next to Donegall Quay), the church with a theme. The minister delivers his sermons from a pulpit carved in the shape of a ship's prow; collections are taken in miniature lifeboats. (Sun. services 11:30am and 7pm; open July-Aug. Wed. 2-4pm, or call tel. 757730.) The exterior was designed by prolific **Charles Lanyon,** the same architect who designed The Custom House and virtually every other notable mid-19th-century Belfast building (except the Albert Memorial Clock Tower, and he was mad about that). Lanyon later became mayor of Belfast.

Farther south along Donegall Quay, **Lagan Lookout** provides a walkway across newly built **Lagan Weir** and offers an interpretive center (tel. 315444) with displays on the history of Belfast and the harbor. The £14-million weir was built to eliminate the Lagan's drastic tides, which used to expose stinking mud flats during ebb. The weir is part of a huge development project for Belfast which includes the **Laganside Trail** along the far side of the river, a road/rail bridge (currently under construction), and a huge hotel and concert hall (also under construction, but scheduled to open in 1996 to seat over 2000). The walkway across the weir provides an unusual perspective on the city. The interpretive center, on the other hand, is of benefit only for those intensely interested in the history of the Lagan and its curbmasters. But the center does mention the thrilling story of Houdini's near brush with death in Donegall Bay (open Mon.-Fri. 11am-5pm, Sat. noon-5pm, Sun. 2-5pm; £1.50).

The twin cranes, nicknamed **"Samson and Goliath,"** of the Harland and Wolff shipyard in East Belfast are clearly visible from anywhere across the river. During the 19th and early 20th centuries, Harland and Wolff fashioned Belfast into one of the world's premier shipbuilding centers. The builder's most famous single creation was, unfortunately, the *Titanic.* The shipyards figure in numerous poems and novels set in Belfast, notably at the end of Paul Muldoon's "7, Middagh St." Back on the western side of the Lagan, the **One Gallery,** 1 Oxford St. (tel. 310400), exposes the city to the work of contemporary Belfast artists (open Mon.-Fri. 10am-4pm; free).

Queen's University Area

South of city center, the main building of **Queen's University** sits back from the road in its revival Tudor red brick. Designed by the overworked Charles Lanyon in 1849, it was modeled after Magdalen College, Oxford. Only the facade was finished properly; the sides are disappointing. The **Visitors Centre** (tel. 335252), which has the usual exhibits and memorabilia, is in the Lanyon Room to the left of the main entrance to the building (open Mon.-Sat. 10am-4pm). The University has its own art collection, **Fenderesky Gallery,** 5 Upper Crescent (tel. 235245), which puts up contemporary shows all year (open Tues.-Fri. 11:30am-5:30pm, Sat. noon-5pm).

On warm days, a majority of the student population suns itself at the **Botanic Gardens** (tel. 324902), down the street. Meticulously groomed, the gardens offer a welcome green respite from the gray Belfast streets. The **Tropical Ravine House** provides a break from the cold Irish weather—it's about 95°F inside. The ornate **Palm House** overflows with greenery at a much more comfortable temperature. (Gardens open daily 8am-dusk; Tropical House and Palm House open Mon.-Fri. 10am-noon and 2-5pm, Sat.-Sun. 2-5pm; free.) Amid the Botanic Gardens, the **Ulster**

Museum (tel. 381251), off Stranmillis Rd., has developed a variety of exhibits for its huge display halls. Irish art, local history, and antiquities are all subjects for investigation. The treasure salvaged from the *Girone*, a Spanish Armada ship that sank off the Causeway Coast in 1588, is on show here. The Mummy of Takabuti and a Maori War canoe add an exotic note. It takes at least 1½ hours to see the museum properly (open Mon.-Fri. 10am-5pm, Sat. 1-5pm, Sun. 2-5pm; free).

South Belfast

No perfumery could compete with the 100,000 rose bushes at **Sir Thomas and Lady Dixon Park,** Upper Malone Rd. The gardens were founded in 1836 and include the stud China roses that were imported between 1792 and 1824 and provided the foundation for current British roses. New strains of roses are tested at the City of Belfast International Rose Trials from late June to early August, which is held here. The Belfast Parks Department (tel. 320202) excites guests with promises of the red squirrel and the elusive bluebell glade. Buses #70 and 71 from Donegall Sq. East run to the roses. The public search room at the **Public Record Office,** 66 Balmoral Ave. (tel. 661621), allows you to trace your ancestors (but won't do it for you; open Mon.-Fri. 9:15am-4:45pm). Out the Ballynahatty Rd., a strange earthen ring with a dolmen in the middle goes by the name of **Giant's Ring.** Little is known about the 200-yard-wide circle.

The Golden Mile

Belfast's pride and joy, the **Grand Opera House** on Great Victoria St., has been cyclically bombed by the Provos, restored to its original splendor at enormous cost, and then bombed again. The **Grand Opera House Ticket Shop,** 17 Wellington Place (tel. 241919; 24-hr. information line tel. 249129), sells tickets for performances (open Mon.-Wed. 8:30am-8pm, Thurs. 8:30am-9pm, Fri. 8:30am-6:30pm, Sat. 8:30am-5:30pm). The Opera House is at its best during performances (musicals, operas, ballets, and concerts), but it is possible to arrange a visit during the day. Call the booking office (tel. 241919; open Mon.-Sat. 9:45am-5:30pm) to make an appointment, or ask at the stage door on Glengall St. If there's no rehearsal at the moment, they'll give you a tour. Farther down Great Victoria St., the plush **Europa Hotel** has the dubious distinction of being "Europe's most bombed hotel." Across the street from the Europa Hotel, the **Crown Liquor Saloon,** Great Victoria St., is a showcase of carved wood, gilded ceilings, and stained glass, all fully restored by the National Trust. The box-like snugs fit groups of two or ten comfortably. Just ring the buzzer when you want another round (see Pubs, p. 355).

Great Victoria St. proceeds south to **Shaftesbury Square,** where the one neon sign allows tourism officials to compare it to Piccadilly Circus. Nearby, the **Arts Council Gallery,** 56-60 Dublin Rd. (tel. 321402), shows the work of contemporary artists from Belfast to Oslo (open Tues.-Sat. 10am-6pm; free). Two blocks farther down the Golden Mile, the **Crescent Arts Centre,** 2 University Rd. (tel. 242338), dedicates lots of gallery space to Belfast artists (open Mon.-Sat. 10am-5pm; currently closed for renovations but scheduled to open in spring 1996). The center also teaches 8-week courses on innovative subjects like yoga, trapeze, tai chi chuan, trad music, ballet, and drawing (1 class/week; £24 total).

WEST BELFAST

Separated from the rest of the city by the Westlink motorway, the working-class neighborhoods of West Belfast lie at the heart of political tensions in the North. The Catholic area (centered on Falls Rd.) and the Protestant neighborhood (centered on the Shankill) are grimly separated by the **peace line,** a literal gray wall separating the two warring parts of town. Following the ceasefire, parts of the peace line were perforated to allow free passage from one region into the other. But along the wall, abandoned houses with blocked-up windows still point to a troubled past and an uncertain future. These two neighborhoods embody both the raw sentiment that drives the Northern Irish conflict and the casual calm with which those closest to the Troubles approach daily life. These epicenters of political violence in Belfast are unique to the city and may intrigue the curious. Not a "sight" in the traditional sense, West Belfast is presented here for anthropological exploration, not consumer tourism. It is polite (and wise) to remember that residents usually object to being scrutinized as social anomalies. The murals in the Falls and Shankill are constantly changing. The sections below describe only a handful of murals. We provide a glossary to decode the symbols and terms of others.

Practical Information

With care and common sense, the Falls and Shankill can be visited in **safety.** Stay far away after dark. By day, visit in a car, on foot, or in a black cab. The Protestant Orangemen's marching season, around Orange Day on July 12, is an exciting but risky time to visit the area, since the proud, angry parades can inspire political violence (though this consequence is less likely to occur since the ceasefire). Other ceremonial occasions, such as the Catholic West Belfast Festival (August 7-15), may also be dangerous times to visit. *Never* take pictures of soldiers, police, or military installations; if you do, your film will be confiscated and you may be detained for questioning. You can freely take pictures of murals and buildings, but if you want snapshots of people, be sure to ask their permission for the sake of both courtesy and safety. To see both the Falls and Shankill, the best plan is to visit one, then return to the city center before heading out to the other. The area around the peace line is still desolate and the least safe of these areas.

Black cabs are the community shuttles that whisk West Belfast residents to the city center along set routes, picking up and dropping off passengers on the way. For the standard fare (55p), you can ask to be let off anywhere along the route. Black cabs can also reasonably be hired by groups for **tours** of the Falls or Shankill (£10/hr.). **Catholic black cabs,** identified by signs which read "Falls Rd.," "Andersontown," or which are written in Irish, leave the city center from Donegall Sq. and the taxi park on Castle St. **Protestant black cabs,** identified by red poppies or "Shankill" signs, head up and down the Shankill Rd. from their base at the top of North St.

The Falls

The Falls is larger than Shankill and still growing. Moving west on Divis St., away from the city center, a high-rise apartment building marks the site of the **Divis Flats,** an ill-fated housing development built by optimistic social planners in the 1960s. This project experienced some of the worst of Belfast's Troubles in the '70s. The political affinities of its residents are evident from the many tri-colored flags flying from the windows. The lower, six-story apartments, like much of the ugly and shabby public housing in this neighborhood, are being torn down and replaced with more attractive low-rise houses.

Continue west as Divis St. turns into the Falls Rd. The **Sinn Féin office** on the right is marked by the wire cage enclosing the building and surveillance camera outside. To get in, ask next door at the Republican bookstore, marked *"Sioppa na hEalaine."* (You have to ring a bell to be admitted to the bookstore.) Tell the shopkeeper that you're a tourist interested in seeing the Republican sights of West Belfast, and you will be probably escorted to the office next door. Sinn Féin sometimes gives tours of the neighborhood if they can get a group together. If not, they will give you a map which shows the largest groups of murals and other sites of Republican significance. On the side of the bookstore is a large mural with a portrait of the "martyred" hunger striker, Bobby Sands, and an advertisement for the Sinn Féin newspaper, *An Phoblacht.*

The Falls Rd. soon splits into Andersontown Rd. and Glen Rd. Here, on the left, are the Celtic crosses of **Milltown Cemetery,** which contains the bones of many who died for the Republican cause. Inside the entrance, a memorial to Republican casualties is bordered by a low green fence on the right. Bobby Sands's grave stands here. Another mile along the Andersontown Rd. lies the road's namesake—a housing project (formerly a wealthy Catholic neighborhood)—and several good murals.

Shankill & Sandy Row

North St., to the left of the tourist office, quickly turns into Shankill Rd. as it crosses the Westlink and then arrives in Protestant Shankill. The **peace line** looms at the end of any of the side roads to the left. Many of the neighborhood's murals have been painted on the sides of the buildings that front the Shankill Rd. At Canmore St., a significant mural on the left depicts the Apprentice Boys "Shutting the Gates of Derry—1688" as the Catholic invaders try to get through. A little farther, also on the left and across a small park, a big, faded mural labeled "UVF—then and now" depicts a modern, black-garbed "soldier" and a historical soldier side-by-side. The densely decorated **Orange Hall** sits on the left at Brookmount St. The side streets to the right guide you to the **Shankill Estate**, home of more murals. Through the estate, the **Crumlin Road** heads back to the city center past an army base and the courthouse and jail, which are on opposite sides of the road but linked by a tunnel.

The Shankill area is shrinking as middle-class Protestants abandon it, but **Sandy Row,** another Protestant area, has more to show. It begins at Donegall Rd. next to the youth hostel at Shaftesbury Sq. An Orange Arch, with King Billy on top, marks the entrance to the Protestant area. Nearby murals show the Red Hand of Ulster, a British bulldog, and King Billy crossing the Boyne. While murals in the more volatile Falls and Shankill areas are often defaced or damaged, better-preserved and more elaborate murals adorn the secure Protestant enclave of East Belfast, across the Lagan. Several line Newtownards Rd. One truly awe-inspiring mural likens the UVF to the ancient hero, Cuchulainn—Ulster's defender. It eerily resembles a mural in Derry which represents the Irish army in these same mythical terms, seeing the army also as Cuchulainn. Ulster's legendary warrior is apparently the only symbolic figure admired by both sides of the struggle.

A Primer of Symbols in the Murals of West Belfast

The Red Hand: the symbol of Ulster (found on Ulster's crest), usually used by Unionists to emphasize the separateness of Ulster from the rest of Ireland.

Blue, White & Red: the colors of the British flag; often painted on curbs, signposts, etc., to demarcate Unionist murals and neighborhoods.

Bulldog: represents Britain.

King Billy/William of Orange: sometimes depicted on a white horse, crossing the Boyne to beat the Catholic King James II at the Battle of the Boyne in 1690. The Orange Order was later founded in his honor. He is a major Protestant icon.

The Apprentice Boys: a group of young men who shut the gates of Derry to keep the besieging troops of James II out of Protestant Derry, beginning the great siege of 1689. They have become Protestant folk heroes, inspiring an honorary association in their name. The slogan **"No Surrender,"** also from the siege, has been appropriated by radical Unionists, especially Rev. Ian Paisley.

Lundy: the name of a Derry leader who advocated surrender during the siege; now a term for anyone who wants to give in to Catholic demands.

Taig: phonetic spelling of an Irish given name, Teague; slang for a Catholic.

Star of David: allies the North with Israel, equating the IRA with the PLO.

Orange & Green: colors of the Irish Republic's flag; often painted on curbs and signposts in Republican neighborhoods.

Landscapes: sometimes imply Republican territorial claims to the North.

The Irish Volunteers: Republican link to the earlier (nonsectarian) Nationalists.

Éireann go bráth: "Ireland forever;" a popular IRA slogan.

Tiocfaidh ár lá: "Our day will come;" Irish is a sure sign of a Nationalist mural.

Phoenix: symbolizes united Ireland rising from the ashes of British persecution.

Lug: Celtic god, seen as the protector of the "native Irish" (Catholics).

Nelson Mandela and **Native Americans:** attempts to align the IRA with oppressed groups throughout the world and throughout history.

ARTS AND ENTERTAINMENT

ARTS & ENTERTAINMENT

Belfast's many cultural events and performances are best covered in the free, monthly *Arts Council Artslink* (at the tourist office and all art galleries). Daily listings appear in the daily *Belfast Telegraph* (also a Fri. arts supplement) as well as in Thursday's *Irish News*. The **Crescent Arts Centre,** 2 University Rd. (tel. 242338), supplies general arts info and more specific news about their own exhibits and concerts. Queen's University and the University of Ulster host many arts events during the school year. July is a slow month for the arts in Belfast; around July 12, the whole city shuts down. For more extensive information on pub entertainment (including special guests), pick up the free, bi-weekly, two-page news bulletin *That's Entertainment*, available at most pubs and the YHANI hostel.

Theater

Belfast's theater season runs from September to June. Some plays are produced in the summer, but most playhouses "go dark" for the tourist season. The truly **Grand Opera House,** Great Victoria St. (tel. 241919; 24-hr. information 249129), boasts an impressive mix of large productions of opera, ballet, musicals, and drama. During the opera season in September, tickets can be purchased by phone (tel. 381241; £8-30; student standbys available 45 min. before performance, £5). Tickets for other events are available at the box office, 17 Wellington Pl. (open Mon.-Sat. 9:45am-5:30pm). **The Arts Theatre,** 41 Botanic Ave. (tel. 324936), houses its own company but hosts touring troupes as well. (Open Aug.-June; box office open Mon.-Sat. 10am-7pm; tickets £3-7.) **The Lyric Theatre,** 30 Ridgeway St. (tel. 381081), mixes Irish plays with international theater. **The Group Theatre,** Bedford St. (tel. 329685), specializes in comedies to make you laugh. (Open Sept.-May; box office open Mon.-Fri. noon-3pm; tickets £2.50-3.) **The Old Museum** (tel. 235053) also puts on a few plays (see Sights, p. 356), as does **The Ulster Hall** (see Music, below).

Music

Ulster Hall, Linenhall St. (tel. 229685), brings music for a wide range of tastes to town (box office open Mon.-Sat. 9am-5pm). **The Grand Opera House** (see Theater, above) also resounds with less shrill notes. The only other music in Belfast is that found in pubs. For traditional music, try **Madden's Bar,** 74 Smithfield (tel. 244114), on Wednesday through Saturday nights; **Kelly's Cellars,** 30 Bank St. (tel. 324835) on Thursday; **The Parador Hotel,** 473 Ormeau Rd. (tel. 491883), on Thursday; **The Duke of York,** Lower Donegall St. (tel. 241062), on Monday and Thursday; and **Morrisons,** 21 Bedford St. (tel. 248458), on Sunday.

Anything and everything blasts from **The Rotterdam** almost every night of the week. **The Elms** has folk/rock bands most nights and trad on Thursday. **The Front Page** plays a wide range of music mostly on weekends. **Robinson's** spends a long weekend (Thurs.-Sat.) with rock and dance bands upstairs (see Pubs, p. 355). **The Limelight,** Ormeau Rd. (tel. 325968), rocks on Thursday and Sunday. **The Manhattan,** Bradbury Pl., will help you chill to jazz, and the **Drumkeen Hotel,** Upper Gallwally (tel. 491321), can put you in a loose, jazzy mood on Wednesday. More of the same can be found at the **Terrace Restaurant,** 255 Lisburn Rd. (tel. 381655), on Thursday and **The Cutter's Wharf,** Lockview Rd. (tel. 662501), on Sunday.

The **Ulster Orchestra** plays a series of free summer-time concerts on Friday nights at Ulster Hall, sponsored by the BBC. (For info and free tickets, send a stamped, self-addressed envelope to BBC Ticket Unit, Broadcasting House, Ormeau Ave., Belfast BT2 8HQ.)

Dance Clubs

Nightclubs provide another opportunity for release. The **Dome and Limelight** complex, Ormeau Ave. (tel. 325968), is basically a dance club with a pub attached. Monday is gay and lesbian night (straights also welcome); Friday and Saturday are student-only discos; Tuesday is for everyone; Thursday and sometimes Sunday bring a live band (9pm; cover £1-7). Crowds flock to **Lavery's,** 12 Bradbury Place (see

Pubs, p. 355), for discos every night except Sundays (cover £1 Mon.-Wed., Thurs. £2, Fri.-Sat. £2.50). **Queen's University Student Centre** (tel. 324803) has student-only discos 6 nights a week during term time and Thursday and Saturday during the summer (cover £2). **The Crow's Nest** (see Pubs, p. 355) has dancing for gays and lesbians (Wed.-Sat. cover £1); straights are welcome. **Parliament Bar** (see Pubs, p. 355) has a disco for gays and lesbians Thursday (cover £2) and Sunday (free); straights are unwelcome.

Events: The Belfast Festival at Queen's

Belfast reigns supreme in the art world for three weeks each November when Queen's University hits the town with its annual festival. Over 300 separate performances of opera, ballet, film, and comedy invade venues across the city, drawing groups like the Royal Shakespeare Theatre. Tickets for the most popular events sell out months ahead of time, although there's almost always something to see if you haven't planned ahead. For advance tickets and schedules, write to: Mailing List, Festival House, 25 College Gardens, Belfast BT9 6BS by August. Ticket sales by mail begin Sept. 15. From Oct. 15 through the festival's end, tickets are available by phone (tel. 667687).

■ NEAR BELFAST

ULSTER FOLK AND TRANSPORT MUSEUM

Five miles east of Belfast on the way to the Ards Peninsula on the Bangor Rd., the **Ulster Folk and Transport Museum** (tel. (01232) 428428) stretches over 60 acres in Cultra. The Folk Museum is the better half of this marriage. More than 25 buildings dating from the past three centuries have been moved from their original locations around Ulster and reconstructed stone by stone on museum property. Each of the buildings has been restored inside and out, and visitors may wander freely. Since this is an *Ulster* museum, all nine of its counties contribute: Monaghan, Cavan, and Donegal plus the six that comprise Northern Ireland. The buildings collected here represent all different regions and social classes: along with the more pleasant side of life, visitors can enter into the one-room building which an 18th-century family once shared with their livestock. An entire village is slowly materializing near the entrance. The set of old cottages comes complete with an 18th-century church from Kildare, Co. Down, a public weighbridge from Donaghadee, Co. Down, a coal distributer's shop from Belfast, and an 18th-century one-room schoolhouse from Ballycastle, Co. Antrim. In the printer's shop on "Main Street," an original 1844 newspaper press prints posters for upcoming museum events. Little written commentary accompanies the reconstructions, but the buildings' attendants can answer any questions. Comprehensive displays in the exhibition hall near the entrance treat textiles, farming, and crafts, and are geared for visitors who already have some interest in the techniques. The museum also hosts many special events, including pipe ban tattoos, flute performances, and textile exhibitions.

The Transport Museum and the Railway Museum are across the road from the Folk Museum. Inside the **Transport Museum,** some horse-drawn coaches, cars, bicycles, and planes trace the history of moving vehicles. A *Titanic* exhibit, which includes original blueprints, details the Belfast-built ship and its fate. The hangar-like **Railway Museum** stuffs in 25 old railway engines. Half a day is just long enough to see the museums here, but spending fewer than two hours would be foolish. Ulster-buses #1 and 2 from Oxford St. Station run to Cultra. (Open July-Aug. Mon.-Sat. 10:30am-6pm, Sun. noon-6pm; April-June and Sept. Mon.-Fri. 9:30am-5pm, Sat. 10:30am-6pm, Sun. noon-6pm; Oct.-March Mon.-Fri. 9:30am-4pm, Sat.-Sun. 12:30-4:30pm; closed Dec. 24-26. £3.30, HI members £2.20.)

CARRICKFERGUS

Eight miles northeast of Belfast on the Antrim coast, Carrickfergus was thriving when Belfast was but a village. Carrickfergus is now past its heyday, but it can back up its claim to being Ireland's oldest town with massive **Carrickfergus Castle.** It's the oldest Norman castle in Ireland and the only attraction in this suburb-port, whose major artistic products are the poet Louis MacNeice and a rock fanzine called *Mos Eiseley.* The rectory on North Rd. was MacNeice's boyhood home. The poem he wrote about his hometown describes "The little boats beneath the Norman castle,/ The pier shining with lumps of crystal salt." The town itself is named after King Fergus, who drowned just offshore in 531 AD. He had come to the town to find a cure for his skin disease.

A well-stocked **tourist office** (tel. 366455) hangs out in the new mall on Antrim St., which also contains the Knight Ride attraction. (Open April-Sept. Mon.-Fri 9am-6pm, Sat. 10am-6pm, Sun. noon-6pm; Oct.-March Mon.-Sat. 10am-5pm, Sun. noon-5pm.) **Ulster Bank** is at 37 High St. (tel. 351309; open Mon. 9:30am-noon and 1:30-5pm, Tues.-Fri. 10am-noon and 1:30-3:30pm; **ATM).** The **post office,** 46 Antrim St. (tel. 351640), has a passport photo booth (open Mon.-Thurs. 9am-5:30pm, Fri. 9:30-5:30pm, Sat. 10am-12:30pm). The **postal code** is BT3 878. **Trains** chug into the station at the top of North St. (tel. 351286) from Belfast and continue to Larne. (Mon.-Fri. 20/day, Sat. 17/day, Sun. 6/day; 20 min. from Belfast, 30 min. from Larne.) **Buses** drop you off in the center of town but pick you up at the bus stop on Joymount. Buses to Belfast also stop on the main road, next to the Harbour Car Park. Buses head to Belfast (Mon.-Fri. 38/day, Sat. 15/day, Sun. 13/day; 1hr.; £1.60, £2.70 return) and rarely to Larne (June-Sept. Mon.-Sat. 1/day; 35 min.; £1.15). Pharmacy services are available at **McFarlands,** 10 High St. (tel. 362541). The **phone code** is 01960.

Jean Kernohan's **Marathon House,** 3 Upper Station Rd. (tel. (01232) 862475), in Greenisland, is a picture-perfect B&B set back from the road in a beautiful English garden. Trains from Belfast stop in Greenisland, which is not far at all from Carrickfergus. The B&B is a short five-minute walk up the hill from the station (£15/person). High St. is most likely place to find sustenance. The **Old Tech Griddle,** 20 High St. (tel. 351914), cuts huge slices of quiche (£1.35) and makes cheap sandwiches (£1; open Mon.-Sat. 9am-5:30pm). **Mauds,** Scotch Quarter (tel. 367428), sells Guinness ice cream alongside other, more palatable flavors (open daily 9am-9pm). Only for the adventurous, the **Dobbins Inn Hotel,** 6-8 High St. (tel. 351905), sells traditional Ulster food: champ (mashed potatoes mixed with scallions simmered in milk) and black pudding (a type of blood sausage made with oats). (Fried black pudding with onions and apples in soda bread £2.75; food served 5:30-8:30pm.)

The **castle** (tel. 351273), seat of English power in Ulster from the 12th through the 17th centuries, has weathered its tumultuous 800-odd years well. A brigade of Disneyesque fiberglass figures inhabits the castle. Cuthbert the Crossbowman & Co. notwithstanding, the castle is exciting to explore. Practically every room is open (including the latrines), and you can read (or ignore) as much history as you want from the ubiquitous signs. From the train station, Victoria St. leads to cobbled, pedestrianized North St. The castle rises where the road meets the water (bus drivers will let you call out right outside if you ask). (Open April-Sept. Mon.-Sat. 10am-6pm, Sun. 2-6pm; Oct.-March Mon.-Sat. 10am-4pm, Sun. 2-4pm; £2.70.)

Most of the old **town wall** survives. An entry behind town hall gives access to the remaining chunk of wall. The archway at North Gate is still intact (but does it prove or disprove the local tradition that the arch would stand until a wise man joined the Borough Council?). The Irish and Scotch parts of town lie outside the walls of this very English town. Excavations of the Irish, or West Gate, area revealed skulls that are believed to have been displayed on pikes following a gruesome execution. **Knight Ride,** Antrim Rd. (tel. 366455), is the town's newest attraction. For all its advertisements, it still doesn't compete with the castle. This theme ride re-enacts the town history which a fictitious older resident of Carrickfergus tells his annoyingly enthusiastic grandson. A life-size mural at the end of High St. depicts a day in 1536. After the ride, a walk-through exhibit fills in the gaps of the story. (Open Oct.-March Mon.-Sat. 10am-5pm, Sun. noon-5pm; April-Sept. Mon.-Sat. 10am-6pm, Sun. noon-6pm. £2.70. Joint ticket with castle £4.85.)

Down & Armagh

Those parts of the North that lie south of the Lagan aren't visited as often as the Causeway Coast because their attractions are more subtle. The Ards Peninsula, which points south from Belfast, is sandier than the northern coast of the island. And while everything along the Causeway is focused on one sight, the Ards Peninsula is pleasing and fun in its entirety. The Mourne Mountains, almost directly south of Belfast and near the Republic, slope scenically just inland from the beach party at Newcastle. Co. Armagh is situated inland from Belfast and is seldom visited, except by religious pilgrims. The southern half of Armagh is known as a flashpoint for Troubles (the area around Crossmaglen has been especially dangerous). Though the political situation is still volatile and the county is not free of violence, safety conditions are improving. Armagh Town, itself has a full plate of cultural attractions.

■ ■ ■ BANGOR

Close both to Belfast and to open sea, Bangor was once *the* seaside resort for Belfast residents. The town now caters especially to families and older vacationers. Parks accost visitors from the left and right. As a beach town built for urbanites, Bangor can offer its share of entertainment. Besides, its location makes it an inevitable stop on the way down the Ards Peninsula.

PRACTICAL INFORMATION

Tourist Office: Tower House, 34 Quay St. (tel. 270069). From the bus and train stations, a left down Main St. leads to the Marina. Turning right along the water, the road runs past the Royal Hotel to Tower House. Open July-Aug. Mon.-Fri. 9am-7pm, Sat. 10am-7pm, Sun. 2-6pm; Sept.-June Mon.-Fri. 9am-5pm, Sat. 10am-4pm.

Banks: Halifax Bank, 20 Main St. (tel. 270013). Open Mon.-Fri. 9am-5pm, Sat. 9am-noon. **ATM** accepts Plus and Visa. **First Trust,** Main St. (tel. 270628). Open Mon.-Fri. 9:30am-4:30pm. **ATM** takes Visa and Mastercard.

Post Office: Main St. Open Mon.-Fri. 9am-5:30pm, Sat. 9am-12:30pm. **Postal Code:** BT20 5ED.

Phone Code: 01247.

Buses: Abbey St. (tel. 271143). To: Belfast (26/day; ¾ hr.; £1.75, £2.50 return) and all towns on the Ards Peninsula, including Donaghadee (34/day; ½ hr.; £1.10) and Newtownards (34/day; 25 min.; £1.10).

Train Station: Abbey St. (tel. 270141), next to the bus station. To Belfast (40/day; 20 min.; £2.20, £3.50 return) and Carrickfergus (£3.80).

Bike Rental: Sampson's Cycles, 109 High St. (tel. 462929). £5/day, £30/week; deposit £60. Open Mon.-Sat. 9am-5:30pm.

Pharmacy: Boot's Pharmacy, Main St. (tel. 271134). Open Mon.-Fri. 9am-5:30pm, Sat. 9am-6pm.

Hotline: Samaritans, 92 Dufferin Ave. (tel. 464646). Open daily 9:15am-10pm.

Emergency: Dial 999; no coins required. **Police:** Castle Park Ave. (tel. 454444).

ACCOMMODATIONS, FOOD, & PUBS

Without hostel or campground, this city that hosts families and senior citizens also teems with B&Bs in the £12-15 range. They're listed in the tourist office window. Coastal Seacliff Rd. and inland Princetown Rd., near the train and bus stations, are full of choices. **Tara Guesthouse,** 51 Princetown Rd. (tel. 468925), pampers guests with spacious rooms, all with bath and TV (£16/person). **Pierview House,** 28 Seacliff Rd. (tel. 463381), alters its flexible rates, depending on the size of the room, length of stay, and time of year (£13-15/person). **St. Ives,** 58 Seacliff Rd. (tel. 469444), has rooms replete with video equipment (£14/person).

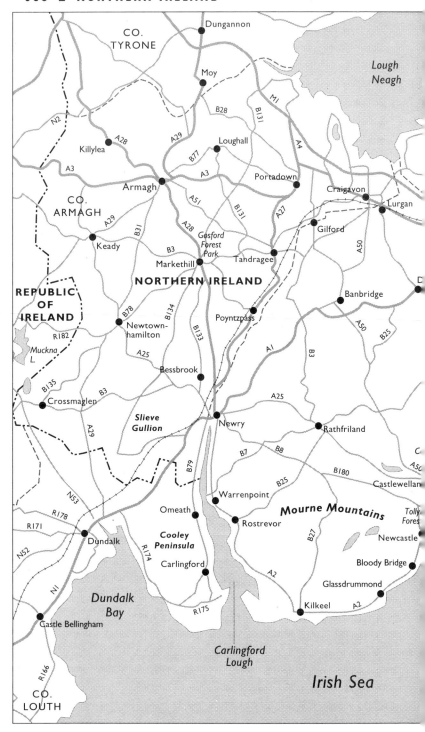

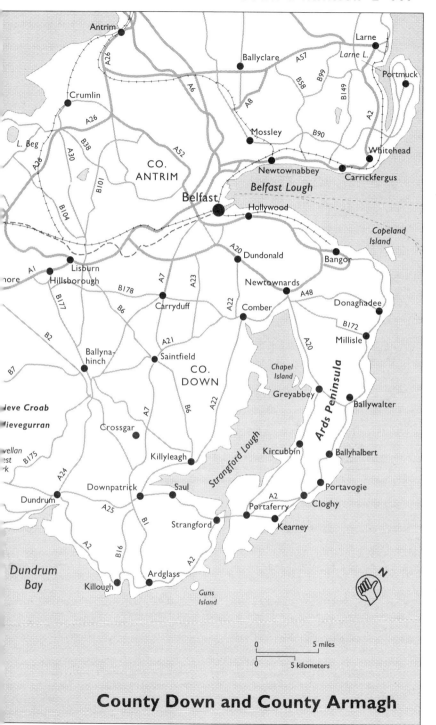

County Down and County Armagh

Sandwich Express, 48 Bingham St. (tel 462131), just off High St., seats its customers at a counter and serves them grilled cheese sandwiches (85p; open Mon.-Sat. 8:30am-4pm). Hearty meals await hearty folk at the **Bungy Jump Café Restaurant,** 99/101 Main St. (tel. 461529). Rubber cords hold up the framed photographs of jumpers in action (prawn and garlic pita £3.95, 12" pizza £4.95-5.95; open Mon.-Sat. noon-7pm, weekend brunch noon-4pm). **Wosley's,** 24 High St. (tel. 460495), envelops patrons in red velvet. Dinner special for two includes two 9" pizzas and two bottles of beer (£7; open Mon.-Thurs. noon-6pm, Fri.-Sat. noon-7pm, Sun. 12:30-2pm). Pubs congregate in the triangle on High St. and along the waterfront. **Jenny Watts,** High St. (tel. 270401), has a Sunday lunch jazz session, a Tuesday ribs and folk night, and a nightclub upstairs on Friday and Saturday nights. Across the street, **Wosley's** regulars sing along to disco four nights a week (Wed.-Sat.). **The Windsor** (tel. 473943) watches over the Marina from 24 Quay St., and the **Steamer Bar,** 30-32 Quay St. (tel. 467699), plunges you deep into a nautical mood.

SIGHTS

North Down Visitors and Heritage Centre, Town Hall, Castle Park (tel. 271200), has a model of obliterated Bangor Abbey and much faded paraphernalia from Bangor's heyday as a seaside resort. The Jordan room displays an unrelated collection of Far Eastern art. Around the Heritage Centre are 129 acres of sometimes wooded, sometimes grassy **Castle Park.** Trail guides will steer you through the grounds and the arboretum. Nearby, 37-acre **Ward Park** (up Castle St. or Hamilton Rd. from Main St.) entices with tennis courts, bowling greens, and a cricket pitch. A string of lakes down the middle also harbors a wildlife sanctuary. The **North Down Coastal Path** forays for 15 miles from Holywood through Bangor and Groomsport to Orlock Point. Along the way are abandoned WWII lookouts, Helen's Bay (a popular bathing spot), Crawfordsbum Country Park, an old fort with a massive gun, and a giant redwood. Bicycles are banned from the path. The region it covers is recognized for its colonies of Black Guillemots, which look like penguins. The Bangor-Holywood portion, more striking than the rest, should take 3½ hours to walk.

The path also passes through the picturesque village of Crawfordsbum, which boasts Ireland's oldest hotel. **The Old Inn** on Main St. dates bates to 1614. (Open July-Aug. Tues.-Sat. 10:30am-5:30pm, Sun. 2-5:30pm; Sept.-June Tues.-Sat. 10:30am-4:30pm, Sun. 2-4:30pm; free; wheelchair access.) The **Crawfordsbum Country Park** is one of the more popular forest parks in Northern Ireland, as it offers both coastal paths and green forests. The **Visitors Centre** spouts about the park's natural history (tel. 8533621; park open daily 8:30am-dark; center open daily 9am-5pm).

In mid-June, the week-long **Bangor and North Down Festival** brings in gymnasts and bands for events such as a masquerade barbecue. Deep-sea **fishing boats** (B.J. Meharg, Bangor Harbour Boats, tel. 455321) leave the marina for some good sport (June-Aug. Mon.-Sun. 3/day; Sept.-Oct. Sat.-Sun. 1/day; £5). The same boats make trips to Black Head (£7), Carrickfergus (£4), Orlock (£8), Copeland Islands (£4), and Rockport Reef (£4).

ARDS PENINSULA

Bounded on the west by tranquil Strangford Lough, the Ards Peninsula guards the rest of Co. Down from the agitated Irish Sea to its east. The Strangford Lough shore from Newtownards to Portaferry is crowded with wildlife preserves, historic houses, crumbling ruins, and spectacular lake views. On the eastern shore of the Ards, each wee fishing village seems tinier, and twice as nice as the one before.

Ulsterbus leaves Oxford St. Station in Belfast to traverse the peninsula, stopping in almost every town. **Trains** roll no farther than Bangor. From the south, a **ferry** crosses frequently between Strangford and Portaferry (see Portaferry, p. 370). The Ards Peninsula can be seen efficiently and attractively by bike.

DONAGHADEE

The fishing villages which line the coast south of Bangor each consist of little more than one harbor and a few pubs each. The largest is **Donaghadee,** famous for its life-boat and lighthouse. Donaghadee was Ulster's most important passenger port from the 17th century until 1849, when the mail boat began to patronize Larne. The composer Franz Liszt spent several days here waiting for a ship to bring him and his piano back to England. **Ulsterbus** drives to Donaghadee from Bangor (34/day; ½ hr.; £1.20) and from Belfast (24/day; 55 min.; £2).

A well-spent morning would include walks along the waterfront or a stroll to the still-operational first electrical lighthouse in Ireland. Past the lighthouse, the formerly communal potato fields called the **town commons** spread along the shore. An old ruined *motte* (pronounced "moat") towers above the village. It held all the ammunition used to blast stone from the hill for building the harbor. In July and August, Quinton Nelson (tel. (01247) 883403) skips boats out to the **Copeland Islands,** a wildlife sanctuary just offshore. Everyone in town knows about the **RNLB Sir Samuel Kelly.** In 1953, the *Samuel Kelly* rescued scores of passengers when the ferryboat *Princess Victoria,* on its way from Scotland to Belfast, sank just offshore. The spruced-up boat is now displayed on Lemons Wharf. Donaghadee's summer festival arrives at the end of July and the beginning of August. The week-long party includes dancing, kite-flying, absailing, and lots of music.

A restful night in Donaghadee can be spent at **The Deans,** 52 Northfield Rd. (tel. (01247) 882204; £17/person) or at **Waterside B&B,** 11 New Rd. (tel. (01247) 888305), which isn't on the waterside (£14.50/person). Locals will entertain you at **The Moat Inn,** 102 Moat St. (tel. (01247) 883297), where a huge burger and a pint of Guinness are a mouth-watering bargain at £3. **Grace Neill's Pub,** 35 High St., has been in business since 1611. This lucky pub has catered to Peter the Great, Oliver Cromwell, and, more benignly, Judith Macartney.

South of Donaghadee, gnat-sized fishing villages buzz along the eastern shoreline. **Millisle, Ballywalter, Ballyhalbert, Portavogie, Cloughey,** and **Kearney** make good stops on an afternoon's drive, but none require a special visit. **Portavogie** is charming, and **Millisle** is home to the **Ballycopeland Windmill.** A2 runs the length of the shore, where hitching is reportedly easy.

MOUNTSTEWART & GREYABBEY

Five miles south of Newtownards on A20 stands **Mountstewart House and Gardens** (tel. (012477) 88387 or 88487). Held by a string of Marquesses of Londonderry, both house and garden are now National Trust property and are worth a long detour to see. The house looks much as Lady Edith Stewart left it in the 1930s. The 22 chairs in the formal dining room, purchased by the 3rd Marquess of Londonderry, once held the butts of Europe's greatest diplomats at the 1814 Congress of Vienna, which divvied up the post-Napoleonic continent. The Mountstewart grounds boast 18 gardens that cover 98 acres. They range from a wild rhododendron wood to the Red Hand of Ulster in the Shamrock Garden to a wooded walk around a five-acre mini-lake. In summer, watch for the Italian gardens' magnificent roses and symmetrical beds of herbaceous plants. The much acclaimed Dodo Terrace is also evidence of Lady Londonderry's participation in the First World War. Lacking a proper banqueting spot, Lady Edith had a two-story pavilion built ¼ mi. into the woods. Her ornate **Temple of the Winds** tops a hill with a super view of Strangford Lough. To reach the temple, go out towards the main road, turn left, and walk about ¼ mile. (House open May-Sept. daily, including bank holidays, except Tuesdays, 1-6pm. Last Tour starts at 5pm; April and Oct. Sat.-Sun. 1-6pm. Gardens open April-Sept. daily 10:30am-6pm; Oct. Sat.-Sun. 10:30am-6pm. Temple closed in 1995 season, scheduled to reopen in April, 1996; open same days as house, 2-5pm. Admission £3.30 for house and garden, £2.70 for gardens only.)

Two miles farther south on A20 lies miniscule **Greyabbey,** whose Main Street consists of four pubs, several antique stores, two art galleries, and a few other general shops, including the **post office**/news agent/gift shop. For those with precious antiques to sell, Greyabbey is also home to **Sotheby's** Northern Ireland office in Grey Abbey House (tel. (012477) 88668), which provides free valuations of antiques for sale, by appointment only (open Mon.-Sat.). The ruins of the eponymous grey **Cistercian abbey** provide views of neighboring Grey Abbey House and the medieval "physick" (emphasis on "sick") herb garden. Only some foundations of the abbey and the walls of the main buildings, including the entire chapel, are left intact. The abbey is known as the first church in Ireland to have been built in the Gothic rather than the typical Romanesque style. The abbey was built in 1193 with the support of Affreca, wife of John de Couny and daughter of the King of Man, who vowed during a storm at sea to found a monastery if she survived. Turn left on the A20 to reach the abbey—it's at the end of the road. (Open April -Sept. Tues.-Sat. 10am-7pm, Sun. 2-7pm; £1, seniors and children 50p; wheelchair accessible.) **Buses** from Newtownards run to Mountstewart (18/day; 15 min.; £1.35) and Greyabbey (20 min.; £1.40). Buses from Newtownards come infrequently; though not recommended, some find it faster to hitch. Wait for the bus outside the **police station,** Main St. (tel. (012477) 88222).

PORTAFERRY

A relatively untouristed but expanding fishing village at the tip of the Ards Peninsula, Portaferry grabs its moment in the sun each year during the **Galway Hookers Festival.** Fish nets, not fishnets, characterize these boating beauties, which hail from western Ireland. Hookers are traditional boats with thick black bottoms and billowing sails. The Galway Yacht Club sails a bunch of them to Portaferry for a big party every year on the fourth weekend in June. For general info, call the **Ards Borough Council Community Relations/Tourism** (tel. (012477) 812215); sailing info can be obtained from John McAlea (tel. (012477) 29532). Book B&Bs far, far in advance.

The main non-hooker attraction in town is **Exploris,** The Ropewalk (tel. (012477) 28062). Located near the dock, next to small, ruined Portaferry Castle, Exploris houses snazzy exhibits on local ocean and seashore ecology. Pet the rays and pick up small ocean creatures, but watch out for the 5-ft. long Conger Eels and the Exploris mascot with BIG teeth, the wolf fish. The Exploris complex also includes a café, gift shop, park with duck pond, picnic area, children's playground, caravan site, woodlands, tennis courts, and bowling green. (Aquarium open Mon.-Fri 10am-6pm, Sat. 11am-6pm, Sun. 1-6pm. £3; students, seniors, and children £2.15.)

The posh Portaferry Hotel greets visitors off the ferry, but *Let's Go* readers may want to skip next door to the **Portaferry Barnholm Youth Hostel (YHANI),** 11 The Strand (tel. (012477) 29598). This self-catering, ferry-ready hostel has clean, large rooms, no bunks, semi-private bathrooms, and magnificent views. Reservations are recommended, since the hostel is often full (£8.95/person). Otherwise, trek to the B&Bs in the center of town. **Mrs. Adair,** 22 The Square (tel. (012477) 28231) will accommodate you for £13/single, £25/double. Just off The Square, **White's B&B,** 25 High St. (tel. (012477) 28580), also poses as a tea house and café during the day (£14/person; w/4 course dinner £20). The **Tara Caravan Park,** 4 Ballyquentin Rd. (tel. (012477) 28459), has space (£2.50/tent; open April-Oct.); campers can also settle across the Lough in Strangford (see Strangford, below).

For cheap food during the day, try the pint-sized **Coffee Pot,** The Square (tel. (012477) 28971). Toasted sandwiches (£1.30) and banana milkshakes (55p) will arrive with lightning speed (open Mon.-Sat. 10am-5pm). Other cafés abound on Castle Street. **Joe's Hot Spot,** 18 The Square, is the place to be for late-night take-away. (Open Tues.-Sat. 12:30-1:30pm and 5-11pm, Sun. 4:30-7:30pm, Mon. 12:30-1:30pm.) Everyone sails into the **Fiddler's Green,** Church St., where pub-owner Frank leads rowdy traditional sing-alongs amid nautical paraphernalia and welcomes live folk bands on some evenings. **M.E. Dunnigan's,** Ferry St., has the simple charm of every "smallest pub in Ireland," where everybody knows your name. Just across the street is the more spacious and youthful **The Quiet Man.**

The Portaferry tourist office trailer parks by the ferry dock (mid-June to Aug.; open Mon.-Fri. 10am-5pm, Sat. 11am-5pm, Sun. 1-5pm). **Northern Bank,** 1 The

Square (tel. (012477) 28028; open Mon. 10am-12:30pm and 1:30-5pm, Tues.-Fri. 10am-12:30pm and 1:30-3:30pm; **ATM** accepts only VISA), and the **post office,** 2 The Square (tel. (012477) 28201; open Mon.-Tues., Thurs.-Fri. 9am-1pm, 2-5:30pm, Wed. 9am-1pm, Sat. 9am-12:30pm) are both within spitting distance of the bus stop. The **postal code** is BT22 1LN. **Ferries** (tel. (01396) 86637) leave from the waterfront at 15 and 45 minutes past the hour for a 10-minute chug to Strangford. (Boats run Mon.-Fri. 7:45am-10:45pm, Sat. 8:15am-11:15pm, Sun. 9:45am-10:45pm; admission 60p, seniors and ages 5-12, 30p.) **Buses** stop at The Square, in the center of town, from Newtownards via Greyabbey (18/day; 50 min.; £2.60).

ST. PATRICK'S VALE

When St. Patrick's boat was swept into Strangford Lough in 432 AD, he probably didn't expect the surrounding area to be revered in remembrance of him. All over this verdant yet dramatic region lie reminders of the famous patron saint's footsteps. The towns in St. Patrick's Vale are also famous for sea activities, varieties of wildlife, lively festivals, and the breathtaking Mourne Mountains.

STRANGFORD

This tiny Viking village huddles across the Lough from Portaferry, northeast of Downpatrick on A25 and north of Ardglass on A2. Apart from its friendly residents, the main attraction of the village is its proximity to the Castle Ward National Trust property. Two miles from Strangford, **Castle Ward House and Estate** (tel. (01396) 881204), resides atop a hill. One wing of the house, built in 1768, is classical, which satisfied Lord Bangor; the other is Gothic, to please Lady Anne. (They split up soon after the house was built.) The 700-acre estate includes a temple, a tower house, a restored corn mill, and the **Strangford Lough Wildlife Centre.** From Strangford, head up A25 towards Downpatrick. Where the Lough curves to the right, head off the road onto a driveway between two white houses which will take you to a path along the water's edge. To reach Castle Ward House, you can either follow the path (dappled with sunlight on a nice day) or return to the road (only another ¼ mile), from which you approach the estate through its main gates and get a splendid view of the Lough. (House open May-Aug., Sun.-Wed. and Fri.-Sat., 1-6pm, April and Sept.-Oct. Sat.-Sun. 1-6pm; Estate and Grounds open all year, dawn to dusk; Wildlife Centre open July-Aug., Sun.-Wed. and Fri.-Sat., 2-6pm; April-June and Sept. Sat.-Sun. 2-6pm; admission to House £2.60, to Estate £3.50/car (Nov.-March £1.75/car), free if you walk; Wildlife Centre free with estate admission.)

In Strangford, the inviting **Cuan Bar and Restaurant,** 6 The Square (tel. (01396) 881222), serves creative pub food during the day (fresh battered cod w/tartar sauce £4.85; food served Mon-Sun. 11:30am-11pm). Locals nurse their pints on the curved velvet seats at **The Lobster Pot,** 11 The Square (tel. (01396) 881288). Another popular spot is **The Hole in the Wall Bar & Lounge** (tel. (01396) 881301), on the road to Downpatrick (open 11:30am-11:30pm). The **Castle Ward Caravan Park** (tel. (01396) 881680), on the Castle Ward National Trust property, charges £6 per tent (open mid-March-Oct.; free showers). Showers and bathrooms are inadequate for such a large crowd, but clean. **Ferries** leave Strangford for Portaferry on the hour and half-hour (Mon.-Fri. 7:30am-10:30pm, Sat. 8am-11pm, Sun. 9:30am-10:30pm).

■■■ DOWNPATRICK

Down's county seat, Downpatrick, tries to entertain as much as it governs. The country around it shelters religious and archaeological sights related to St. Patrick and links the rolling hills of Ards Peninsula to the more dramatic Mourne Mountains.

PRACTICAL INFORMATION

Tourist office: 74 Market St. (tel. 612233). Posh. Grab literature on all of Co. Down, useful maps, or souvenirs from the gift shop. Open Mon.-Sat. 9am-5pm, Sun. 10am-5pm (July-Aug. open til 6pm daily).

Banks: Northern Banks, 58 Market St. (tel. 614011). Open Mon. 9:30am-5pm, Tues.-Fri. 10am-3:30pm; **ATM. Bank of Ireland,** 80-82 Market St. (tel. 612911). Open Mon.-Fri. 9:30am-4:30pm; **ATM.**

Post office: 65 Market St. (tel. 612061). Open Mon.-Fri. 9am-5:30pm, Sat. 9am-12:30pm. **Postal code:** BT30 6LZ.

Phone code: 01396.

Buses: 83 Market St. (tel. 612384). Frequent buses to Belfast (Mon.-Fri. 29/day, Sat. 11/day, Sun. 6/day, 45 min.; £2.80); Newcastle (Mon.-Fri. 14/day, Sat. 9/day, Sun. 3/day, 20 min.; £1.85); Strangford (Mon.-Fri. 7/day, Sat. 4/day; 25 min.; £1.55).

Taxis: 96 Market St. (tel. 614515); run 10am-3:30am.

Hospital: Downe Hospital (tel. 613311).

Emergency: Dial 999; no coins required. **Police:** Irish St. (tel. 613434 or 615011).

ACCOMMODATIONS, FOOD, & PUBS

The town itself simply lacks them. Three miles out on the Strangford Rd., **Hillcrest,** (tel. 612583), offers stellar views of hills rolling down to the Lough. Warm welcome, but no pickup from town (£14/person). Take the Strangford bus and ask to be let off at Buckshill. **Mrs. Coburn,** 47 Roughal Park (tel. 612656), is more accessible (open March-Sept.; single £14, double £25). To reach her B&B, follow Church St. out of town to the roundabout; cross the park and the road on the other side and take the first left up the steep hill that is Roughal Park (a 10-min. walk). The closest campground is Castle Ward, near Strangford; the nearest hostel is in Newcastle.

Downpatrick does a better job feeding visitors than housing them. Drink Bewley's coffee and nibble on sandwiches while discussing the latest art exhibit at the **Down Arts Café,** Irish St. (tel. 615283). The staff provides info about activities in town (open Mon.-Sat. 10am-4:30pm). If you'd like to sit, don't be put off by the take-away look of **Oakley Fayre's** bakery, 52 Market St. (tel. 612500)—hiding behind it, a large coffee shop serves pastries, sandwiches, and filled baked potatoes (chicken salad sandwich £1.60, steakburger £2.35; open Mon.-Sat. 9am-5:15pm). Chinese food simmers on Scotch St. and English St.

Dick's Cabin, 40 Church St. (tel. 612800), stays open until 1am (live bands Tues.-Sat.). **Turley's** and **Phil's,** side by side on Scotch St., are smaller and less glossy but popular with locals. **De Courcy Arms,** 14 Church St. (tel. 612522), is filled with students. **Hootenanny,** 21 Irish St. (tel. 612222), has bands on Saturday and trad music on Sunday during meals; stays open on Sunday until the last person drops.

SIGHTS

Just up the hill from the tourist office, **Down County Museum and Heritage Centre.** The Mall (tel. 615218), does regional history with unusual flair. Housed in the old jail, the museum introduces you to people from St. Patrick to a gang of 19th-century prisoners and their look-alike dummies. (Open July to mid-Sept. Mon.-Fri. 11am-5pm, Sat.-Sun. 2-5pm; mid-Sept. to June Tues.-Fri. 11am-5pm, Sat. 2-5pm. Free.)

Next door to the museum, **Down Cathedral** (tel. 614922; Church of Ireland) sits atop the **Hill of Down,** originally a Bronze Age hill fort. The medieval illuminated *Book of Armagh,* now cohabiting with its cousins in Trinity College library, claims that St. Patrick is buried in the hill. Rebuilt in 1818, the present cathedral incorporates stone carvings from its medieval predecessor into its own walls and houses the only private pew boxes still in use in Ireland. (Open Mon.-Fri. 10am-5pm, Sat.-Sun. 2-5pm, except during services; free.) In the graveyard, a stone commemorates the so-called **grave of St. Patrick**—although Patrick is believed to be buried under the actual church, the stone has become legend. The **Down Arts Centre,** 2-6 Irish St. (tel. 615283), converted from the old Town Hall, hosts traveling exhibitions (free) and stages dramatic performances (mostly in autumn). (Open Mon., Fri., Sat. 10am-4:30pm, Tues., Thurs. 10am-10pm; tickets are £5, £2.50 for students.)

■ NEAR DOWNPATRICK

St. Patrick dominates the landscape and mentality here, but the area has a variety of remains from 8000 years of continuous occupation. Most masterful and famous of all is **Saul** (two miles northeast of Downpatrick on the Strangford Rd.) where St. Patrick is believed to have landed in the 5th century. After being converted to Christianity, the local chief gave Paddy a barn *(sabbal)* which later became the first parish church in Ireland (open daily until 6pm). A 1932 replica of an early Christian church commemorates the landing. Nearby, **St. Patrick's shrine** consists of a huge granite statue of the saint, bronze panels depicting his life, and an open-air temple. Even nonbelievers will appreciate the 360° view of the lough, the mountains, and, on a clear day, the Isle of Man. Located off Ardglass Rd. from Downpatrick, the **Struell Wells** have water running through underground channels from one well to the next. Their curative powers are believed to have originated long before St. Patrick arrived on the scene with Christianity.

One mile from Downpatrick on the Belfast road are the last ruins of the **Cistercian Inch Abbey.** Founded by John de Courcy in 1180, little of the monastery remains. The site itself, on an island in the Quoile River, is spectacular. (Open April-Sept. Tues.-Sat. 10am-7pm, Sun. 2-7pm; admission 75p.) The **Quoile Pondage Nature Reserve,** off the Strangford Rd. (tel. (01396) 615520), offers hiking trails and picnic sites around a lake which was converted from salt to fresh water by human activity. The flood-control barrage also resulted in an unusual collection of vegetation, fish, and insect life. The Quoile Countryside Centre provides a plethora of information (open April-Sept. daily, 11am-5pm; Oct.-March Sat.-Sun. 1-4:30pm).

■ ■ ■ NEWCASTLE & THE MOURNES

On a sunny day with an ocean breeze, Newcastle is an attractive preliminary to Slieve Donard. When the weekend arrives, however, Newcastle becomes as idyllic as the Jersey Shore as children crowd the streets and vacationers squabble over a place in the lines for waterslides. No one competes for places on the beach any more, since it is quite polluted and far from ideal for swimming. Anyone looking for natural beauty heads up into the mountains or north along the untrammeled dunes. Situated at the foot of Slieve Donard, the highest peak in Northern Ireland, Newcastle is by far the best base from which to explore the hypnotic Mourne Mountains, which deserve a few days.

The 15 rounded peaks of the Mourne Mountains sprawl across the southeastern corner of Northern Ireland. Volcanic activity spewed five different kinds of granite onto the mountains 75 million years ago, resulting today in a rainbow of rocky color. No road penetrates the center of the mountains, leaving solitude welcome to walkers. The fifteen peaks form a skewed figure eight with two large valleys in the middle. The larger of these holds **Ben Crom** and **Silent Valley,** reservoirs built in the early 1900s to supply water to Belfast, and still in use.

ORIENTATION & PRACTICAL INFORMATION

The main road in town stretches along the waterfront, changing names from Main St. to Central Promenade to South Promenade. Those who thumb a ride stand at either end of the main road: south for Kilkeel or north for Downpatrick.

Tourist Office: 10-14 Central Promenade (tel. 22222), about halfway down the street. Free map and visitor's guide of Newcastle's complex street plan. Open Mon.-Sat. 10am-5pm, Sun. 2-8pm (2-6pm Sept.-May).

Banks: AIB/First Trust Bank, 28/32 Main St. (tel. 23476). Open Mon. 9:30am-5pm, Tues.-Fri. 10am-3:30pm; **ATM. Northern Bank,** 60 Main St. Open Mon. 9:30am-5pm, Tues.-Fri. 10am-3:30pm. **Ulster Bank** is also on Main St.

Post Office: 35 Central Promenade (tel. 22418). Open Mon.-Wed. and Fri. 9am-12:30pm and 1:30-5:30pm, Thurs. and Sat. 9am-12:30pm. **Postal Code:** BT33 0DJ.

Phone code: 013967.

Buses: 5-7 Railway St. (tel. 22296), at the end of Main St., away from the mountains. Buses run to: Belfast (Mon.-Fri. 23/day, Sat. 16/day, Sun. 10/day; 70 min.; £3.60), Downpatrick (Mon.-Fri. 17/day, Sat. 12/day, Sun. 4/day; 40 min.; £1.85), Kilkeel (Mon.-Fri. 16/day, Sat. 12/day, Sun. 8/day; 40 min.; £1.90), Newry (Mon.-Fri. 11/day, Sat. 12/day, Sun. 1/day; 40 min.; £3.90).

Taxi: Donard Cabs: tel. 24100 or 22823.

Bike Rental: Wiki Wiki Wheels, 10B Donard St. (tel. 23973). £6.50/day, £30/wk. They also have panniers. Driver's license or credit card deposit. Open Mon.-Sat. 9am-6pm, Sun. 2:15-6pm.

Pharmacy: G. Maginn, 9 Main St. (tel. 22923). Open Mon.-Sat. 9am-6pm. **Chemist,** 49 Central Promenade (tel. 23248). Open Mon.-Sat. 9am-6pm.

Camping Equipment: Hilltrekker, 115 Central Promenade (tel. 23842). Trail maps, tips for hiking in the Mournes, info about guided tours, and hiking boots (£2.50/day, deposit £10). Open daily 10am-5:30pm.

Emergency: Dial 999 (including mountain rescue); no coins required.

Police: South Promenade (tel. 23583).

ACCOMMODATIONS

B&Bs in this summer-resort town are relatively expensive. Of the area's numerous **campsites,** the Tollymore Forest Park is probably the most scenic, but the mountains themselves are a free and legal alternative, especially if you like sleeping under the stars without electricity or water.

Newcastle Youth Hostel (YHANI/HI), 30 Downs Rd. (tel. 22133). Clean, spacious, central, and on the waterfront. The helpful, amiable proprietor will show you the way to the well-furnished kitchen. The only drawback is a scarcity of showers. Free laundry! Lockout 11am-5pm, in theory. Curfew 11:30pm, not always enforced. £6.30/person, under-18 £5.30. Open all year. MC/Access, Visa.

Glenada YWCA, 29 South Promenade (tel. 22402). 8-bunk rooms in a posh building with lots of common space and balconies overlooking the sea. No kitchen. Often filled with groups, so call in advance. Ask for the backpackers' rate (£8/person w/breakfast). Family suite w/kitchen also available for 6 people (£25). (With student ID, £12.50/person, otherwise £14 or £16.) Wheelchair access.

Glenside Farm House, 136 Tullybrannigan Rd. (tel. 22628), a long, if lovely, 1½-mi. walk from the town (take Bryansford Rd. and look for signs). Clean, simple rooms. Small single £11. Double £20.

Castlebridge House, 2 Central Promenade (tel. 23209). Understandably popular, with cozy rooms, an ideal location overlooking the bay, and a fabulous sitting room. Mrs. Lynch will even give you the run of her kitchen at night. £14/person.

Arundel, 23 Bryansford Rd. (tel. 22232). Just off the southern end of Central Promenade, with a huge lounge, comfy beds, loads of flowers, and a mountain instead of an ocean view. £15/person.

Ashmount B&B, 19 Bryansford Rd. (tel. 25074). Clean, comfortable, well-lit rooms. Not much of a view, but cheap for Newcastle (£12/person).

Camping: Tollymore Forest Park, 176 Tullybrannigan Rd. (tel. 22428), a 2-mi. walk along A2 (hitchers report it's not hard to get a ride). Excellent facilities include a café with delicious doughnuts, showers, a wildfowl exhibit and arboretum, and 584 hectares of well-marked walks and gardens. Oh, and a well-lit camping area with electricity. May-Sept. £8.50/tent; Oct-April £5.

FOOD & PUBS

The nougat-like density of take-aways, candy stores, and ice cream shops on the waterfront could keep you on a permanent sugar high. **Maud's,** at Castlebridge

Court, 139 Main St., flaunts Orgasmic Pooh Bear (honeycomb and vanilla) ice cream. It also serves up soup and sandwiches (open Mon.-Fri. 11am-10:30pm, Sat.-Sun. 11am-11:30pm). Several other bakeries have similarly light fare.

> **Brambles,** 4 Central Promenade (tel. 26888). Tasty Canadian recipes (what *are* Canadian recipes?) stand out in the culinary sameness of the North. Homemade quiche, pizza and pancakes (soup with organic wheat bread £1.50). Tempting desserts are all homemade and reasonably priced. Open Easter-Sept. Mon.-Fri. 10am-7pm, Sat.-Sun. 10am-11pm; Oct.-Easter Mon.-Fri. 10am-7pm.
>
> **The Mariner Hotel,** 59 Central Promenade (tel. 23473). Full meals are available from the bar menu during pub hours (lasagne, garlic bread, and veggies, £3.95).
>
> **Central Park Restaurant/Nite Club,** (tel. 22487) on the south end of Central Promenade. Prepares filling meals at reasonable prices. Live bands perform on weekends, and the night club is open until 1am.
>
> **Cygnet Coffee Shop,** Savoy Lane (tel. 24758), just off Main St. behind the modern Catholic Church. Coffee shop fare (sandwiches, quiche, pastries) with particularly good taste. Open Mon.-Sat. 10am-5:30pm, Sun. 11:30am-5:30pm.

Newcastle is not the place for a quiet drink. Popular (and packed) spots include the **Anchor Bar,** 9 Bryansford Rd. (tel. 23344), which draws a sociable crowd of mixed ages though proper dress is required and **The Oaks,** 62 Main St. (tel. 26400), where younger people smoke and play pool. Nearly everyone listens to country-western music and sings along with Neil Diamond. For a classier and dearer drink, head to **Percy French,** in the Slieve Donard Hotel, at the northern end of the beach (tel. 23175). Before he became a bar, Mr. French wrote a popular ballad about the Mourne Mountains. He also wrote the lines, "Remember me is all I ask, and yet, if remembrance prove a task, forget;" hopefully remembering won't be too difficult.

SIGHTS: THE MOURNE MOUNTAINS

Before heading for the hills, stop at the **Mourne Countryside Centre,** 91 Central Promenade (tel. 24059), where the friendly and knowledgeable staff will help you plan your hike. *Mourne Mountain Walks* (£5), which maps 10 good one-day hikes, is sold here. Those planning to stay in the Mournes overnight ought to buy the *Mourne County Outdoor Pursuits Map* (£3.50), a detailed topographical map. The Mourne Countryside Centre offers guided walks on Mondays in the summer. (Transportation costs £1-2; meet at 10am sharp at the Centre, but it's best to call ahead of time.) The center will photocopy parts of maps for day hikes (open Mon.-Fri. 9am-5pm, Sat.-Sun. noon-6pm; winter hours may vary). If the center's closed, ask for maps at the tourist office and advice at **Hilltrekker** (see *Practical Information,* page 374). Seasoned hikers looking for company might want to join the **Mourne Rambling Group** (tel. 24315), which sends groups into the Mournes each Sunday. Shuttlebuses—open-top, when weather permits, for a great view—run between Silent Valley and Ben Crom (July-Aug. Mon.-Sat. 11:15am-6pm). **Ulsterbus'** *Mourne Rambler* makes three trips through the mountains to drop off hikers (July-Aug. Mon.-Sat., drop-off at 9:30, 10:45, pick-up at 3:30; £3 return). This bus is the best way to get to the trailheads even if you have a car, because it allows you to begin and end your hike in different places. Ulsterbus also gives one-hour tours of the mountains that leave from Belfast (tel. (01232) 333000).

The **Mourne Wall,** built in the early 1900s, encircles the interior of the mountains just short of the peaks. Originally built to mark the catchment area for the reservoirs below, the wall is a favored hike. Following the length of the 22-mile wall takes a strenuous eight hours; many people break it up with a night under the stars. Wilderness **camping** is legal and popular; common spots include the north end of Ben Crom reservoir and the shores of Lough Shannagh and the Trassy River. Hare's Gap and the shore of Blue Lough at Annalong are also good places to pitch. Remember to bring warm clothing as the mountains get cold and windy at night.

The **Brandy Pad,** an old path running from Bloody Bridge (2 miles south of Newcastle) right across the mountains, is also frequented; it was used in the 1800s to smuggle brandy and tobacco from the Isle of Man. Hiking along the Glen River is an attractive option. When water levels are high, the numerous little waterfalls are breathtaking. Locals swim in the crystal-clear (and cold) tiny pools. The Mourne's highest peak, **Slieve Donard** (850m) towers above Newcastle, challenging those below to a tough but manageable day hike to its summit (5-hr. return). The record for running up and down is fabled to be a hard-to-believe 45 minutes. The peak next door, **Slieve Commedagh,** ("the mountain of watching") is 2500 feet high. It, too, is best reached from Newcastle. To reach either peak, head to the **Donard Park,** on the corner of Central Promenade and Bryansford Rd. Follow the dirt path at the back of the car park carefully (it crosses 2 bridges) and you will hit the Mourne Wall. At the wall, turn left for Slieve Donard, right for Slieve Commedagh. Two Mountain Rescue teams stand by for emergencies.

■ NEARBY FOREST PARKS

Two forest parks, managed by the Dept. of Agriculture for both timber production and recreation, are just a hop, skip, and a jump away from Newcastle. **Tollymore Forest Park** lies just two miles west of town, at 176 Tullybrannigan Rd. (tel. (013967) 22428). A network of marked trails and Ireland's unique Strawberry Tree, in the arboretum, are highlights. The Strawberry Tree, also found in Spain, grows wild in Ireland and produces berries, edible but very sour, which turn from white to red. Trails range from one to nine miles in length; the walks will afford glimpses of diverse wildlife, including deer, foxes, badgers, and if you're particularly quiet, otters; be sure to hike down to Salmon Leap Falls. The park is well-equipped with a campground (see Newcastle: camping), visitors center, café, and arboretum (open year-round daily 10am-sunset; £2.50/car). Take the Bryansford bus and ask to be let off at Tollymore (buses run Mon.-Fri. 6/day, Sat. 6/day, Sun. 2/day). **Murlough National Nature Reserve,** on the Dundrum Rd. (tel. (013967) 51467), has sand dunes, heath and woodlands (£1.50/car; beach and walks always open). Since Newcastle Bay is now so polluted, Murlough is the closest beach still safe for swimming. Take the Downpatrick or Belfast bus and get off at Murlough. (Visitor center open June-mid-Sept. daily 10am-5pm; guided walks for observation of seabirds and seals.)

Farther north, **Castlewellan Forest Park,** The Grange, Castlewellan (tel. 78664), spreads itself out in the hills just north and east of the Mournes. (From Newcastle, take A50 past its junction with A25.) Inside the park, a Scottish baronial castle overlooks a small lake surrounded by Castlewellan Gold, the park's unique species of cypress. The castle itself is now a Christian Conference Centre and off limits to the public, but the Park is impressive in itself. There's an arboretum, a tropical birdhouse, and a photographer on hand for wedding photos (just in case). The Sculpture Trail creatively displays sculptures made of natural materials. The lake overflows with trout; fishing permits are available April to mid-October (call the park for info). For £8.50 you can pitch a tent here too—but only if you've booked far in advance. (Oct.-Easter £4; call Mon.-Fri. 8:30am-4:30pm for info and site booking. Park open daily 10am-sunset; £2.20/car; no charge on foot.) **Buses** run from Newcastle to Castlewellan (Mon.-Fri. 26/day, Sat. 20/day, Sun. 6/day; 10 min.; 80p).

■■■ CARLINGFORD LOUGH

KILKEEL

South of Newcastle, the largest fishing fleet in Northern Ireland contributes to Kilkeel's fascinating, if a little fishy, harbor; every evening it buzzes with action as boats come in with their day's catch. For a view of the harbor, avoid the obvious but drab Harbour Drive; instead, walk down Kockchree Ave. (off Greencastle St.), and turn left onto the Cliff Walk. The town itself has little to offer other than fish, but inland, miles of stone "ditches" (walls) and hedges carve the countryside into neat parcels.

The **tourist office**, 6 Newcastle St. (tel. 62525), is open Mon.-Sat. 10am-5pm. The **post office**, 4 The Square (tel. 62225), delivers (open Mon.-Wed. and Fri. 9am-1pm and 2-5:30pm, Thurs. 9am-1pm, Sat. 9am-12:30pm). The **postal code** is BT34 4AA. **First Trust Bank**, 30 Greencastle St. (tel. 62237), has an **ATM** (open Mon.-Fri. 9:30am-4:30pm). **Buses** stop at 54 Greencastle St. and travel to Newry and Warrenpoint (Mon.-Fri. 12/day, Sat. 11/day, Sun. 4/day; Newry £2.60, Warrenpoint £1.80) and Belfast (Mon.-Fri. 13/day, Sat. 9/day, Sun. 6/day). The **phone code** is 016937.

Accommodations, Food, & Pubs The best reasons to visit Kilkeel are the McGlues and their alluring farmhouse B&B, **Heath Hall**, 160 Moyadd Rd. (tel. 62612). Tea, sandwiches, advice on seeing Co. Down, and limitless kindness are some of Heath Hall's wondrous features (single £13.50, double £26). Closer to town, just off the main road, Mrs. Haugh's B&B, **Homesyde**, 7 Shandon Dr. (tel. 62676), welcomes visitors with televisions and sinks in each room (£12.50/person). Both Mrs. Haugh and Mrs. McGlue will pick up lost or tired travelers from town, but please call ahead for a lift.

The Old Mill, 10-14 Knockchree Ave., serves up hot meals, pizza and salads (shepherd's pie £1.50; open Mon.-Sat. 10am-10pm; Oct.-May Mon.-Thurs. 10am-6:30pm, Fri.-Sat. 10am-10pm). **Jacob Hall's Bar**, 8 Greencastle St. (tel. 64751) offers "good music and the best of *craic*"; trad music on Wed. and Thurs., disco on Fri. and Sat.

Sights Head towards Newcastle on A2 to get to both Slieve Binnian and Silent Valley; about one mile from Kilkeel, take a left at the Aircraft Furnishings Co. (you'll see British and American flags in front; for tours of the factory, call 62471). From here, hike three miles uphill to the park. Hitchers report a good amount of success, and much less exhaustion than walkers, on that road. **Slieve Binnian** (2400 ft.), a good day-hike, is renowned for the scenic views from the top. **Silent Valley**, a well-managed park with an information center, rather expensive café, and craft shop, is the site of Belfast's reservoir (center open all year, daily 10am-6:30pm). From Kilkeel, head straight out the Moyadd road to the park. From there, a three-mile path runs up the side of Silent Valley to Ben Crom reservoir. In July and August, you can travel this route by shuttle bus (May-June and Sept. weekends only; £1). (Reservoir grounds open June-Sept. daily 10am-6:30pm; Oct.-April 10am-4pm. £2/car.)

WARRENPOINT

Farther along the coast on the A2, the pretty harbor town of **Warrenpoint** sports both an idyllic, isolated inlet and an animated waterfront. Pick up tourist info and free maps at the **Town Hall**, (tel. 52256) opposite The Square on Church St. The helpful and well-informed staff will be glad to assist you (open Mon.-Fri. 9am-5pm). The **post office**, 9 Church St. (tel. 52225; open Mon.-Tues. and Thurs. 8:30am-5:30pm, Wed. 8:30am-1pm, Fri. 9am-5:30pm, Sat. 9am-12:30pm), will hold mail if you mark it with the **postal code**, BT34 3HN. Get money at **Ulster Bank**, 2 Charlotte St. (tel. 52323; open Mon.-Fri. 9:30am-4:30pm). **Stewarts Cycles**, 7 Osbourne Mews (tel. (016937) 73565), off Marine Parade, has bikes (£5/day, £20/week; open Mon.-Tues. and Thurs.-Fri. 10am-noon and 2-6pm, Sat. 10am-1pm and 2-6pm). Warrenpoint has a sporadic summertime ferry service to Omeath on the Cooley Peninsula (in the Republic). **Red Star Passenger Ferry** (tel. (016937) 72682) is a great tradition (operates June-Sept. 1-6pm from Marine Parade, weather permitting; £1.50 return). Carlingford Lough cruises are also available on the **Maiden of Mourne**, (tel. 72950) an enclosed water coach, from Easter-mid-Sept. (weather permitting, £3).

Glen Rosa B&B, 4 St. George's St. South (tel. 72589), is central but dark (£13.50; open Feb.-Oct.). Rooms for the night can also be had next door from **Mrs. Joan O'Hare**, 6 St. George's St. (tel. 73265), which is also slightly dark, but with clean and comfortable rooms (£13/person). A mile out of town, **Firóne**, 74 Upper Dromore Rd. (tel. (016937) 74293; Duke St. turns into Upper Dromore Rd.), offers homemade jam in the kitchen and potted plants in the bathroom (£14.50/person).

The Cobbler, 29 Church St. (tel. (016937) 72714), cooks up creative food (fruit and vegetable fritters with salad £3; open Mon.-Thurs. 9:30am-6pm, Fri.-Sat. 9:30am-10pm, Sun. 12:30-10pm). **Diamonds Restaurant,** The Square (tel. 52053), offers pasta, burgers (£2.50), seafood, and desserts. Upstairs seats have a good view of the Lough. Try the chicken Kiev for £5.95 (open Mon.-Thurs. 10am-7pm, Fri.-Sat. 10am-10pm, Sun. 12:30-10pm). Warrenpoint has a lively nightlife which satisfies all ages. On weekend nights, **Mac's Bars,** 1-2 Marine Parade (tel. (016937) 52082), caters to the young and the restless. Check out the Ode to Mac's, which promotes the joys of various liquors, inscribed on the outside wall. If you prefer nursing pints with the locals, **Bennett's,** 21 Church St. (tel. 52314), is the place to be. Try the Guinness' Meals for dinner (Wed.-Sat. 7-9:30pm).

Warrenpoint and the surrounding area host several lively festivals during the summer months. Thousands of people gather here to witness the **Maiden of the Mournes Festival** in August; maidens from Ireland and some parts of the U.S. gather to display their personality and talent. This event is preceded by the **Fiddler's Green Festival** in **Rostrevor** (three miles from Warrenpoint along A2). Musicians from Ireland and abroad present original compositions. Rostrevor is also known for Kilbroney Park (more wildlife) and Rostrevor Forest, which rises rapidly to the altitude of 1600 feet.

NEWRY

Located on the main route between the North and South of Ireland, Newry has been pillaged by waves of invaders traveling between the two over the centuries. Quite a few have wrought some destruction in the town, including Medbh's army and those running from or to the Troubles. Despite this, Newry's residents claim with studied nonchalance that their lives have not been affected by the ceasefire (except for the removal of barricades). Newry is neither particularly dangerous nor visually dramatic—there's not much to make it a tourist attraction by itself, but there's no real reason to avoid it. Newry is actually well-known as an over-sized shopping center, which may be a good reason for avoiding it. Given the town's position at the tip of Carlingford Lough, between Belfast and Dublin, it's quite a convenient stop.

Newry's **tourist office** (tel. (01693) 68877), located in the Town Hall, has free maps and more free advice. To reach it from the bus stop, walk up the Mall, with the canal on your left, past a bridge. The street will curve to your right as you approach Town Hall (open Mon.-Fri. 9am-5pm, Sat. 10am-4pm). The **post office** is located at 50-52 Hill St. (tel. (01693) 62156; open Mon.-Fri. 9am-5:30pm, Sat. 9:30am-12:30pm). The **postal code** will cook you a lunch of BT34 1JD.

Buses to and from the Republic stop either on Mary St., a block south of the pedestrianized city center and behind the Newry Market, or opposite the Ulsterbus depot on Monaghan St. (to Dundalk: 7/day; 30 min.; £2.50). Call **Bus Éireann** in Dundalk for scheduling info (tel. (042) 34075, in Ireland). **Ulsterbus** stops along the Mall, the road just west of the two canals. Each route has its own stopping point; look for the posted schedules. Get driven to: Belfast (Mon.-Fri. 25/day, Sun. 13/day; 70 min.; £4.10) and Armagh (Mon.-Fri. 8/day, Sat. 7/day; 60 min.; £2.60). Newry's **train station** (tel. (01693) 69271) is 1½ miles out of town on Camlough Rd. Trains go in both directions to: Belfast (7/day; 40 min.; £4.45) and Dublin (5/day; 80 min.; £10.90). Hitching is reportedly quite slow around Newry—stick to public transportation.

Most B&Bs are quite far out of Newry. **Marymount B&B,** Windsor Ave. (tel. (01693) 61099), wins the award for convenience. Walk down Trevor Hill, past the roundabout, and straight down Belfast Rd. Take the second right and walk uphill to Mr. And Mrs. O'Hare's open arms (£15/person). **The Ambassador Restaurant,** 81 Hill St. (tel. (01693) 65307), doles out hearty daily specials (prawn roll or breast of chicken £2; open Mon.-Wed. 8am-7pm, Thurs.-Fri. 8am-8pm, Sat. 8am-7pm). The **Brass Monkey** on Trevor Hill (close to the roundabout on Belfast Rd.; tel. (01693) 63176) entices with affordable lunches daily between noon-6pm but more expensive *à la carte* and steaks between 6-10pm. Live bands and a lively crowd, but more like the States than Ireland—age 21 and up only. If you find yourself with a bit of time on your hands, stop at **Timoney's,** 6 Canal St., for delicious homemade ice cream (open daily 9am-9pm) or visit the first Protestant church (St. Patrick's, built in 1578 and still operating). If you have energy as well as time, walk up and up and up the **Flagstaff Hill** for an exquisite view of Carlingford Lough and Slieve Gullion. (It's easier to take the Dundalk bus to Flagstaff and then walk.)

ARMAGH & AROUND

The best time to visit Armagh is during apple blossom season in May, when the surrounding countryside, known as the "orchard of Ireland," is covered in pink. The Apple Blossom Festival brings a number of events to the city and culminates in a lavish May Ball. County Armagh's other population centers, Craigavon and Portadown near Lough Neagh, are industrial centers of little interest to tourists. South Armagh, considered unsafe for tourism until the last months of 1994, boasts several attractive recreational forest areas, the largest being **Slieve Gullion Forest Park.** Call the Forest Officer (tel. (01693) 38284) for more information.

■■■ ARMAGH

Armagh (pop. 52,000) has been revered as the ecclesiastical capital of Ireland since St. Patrick legendarily chose the town as his base. Its name is of pagan origin. Deriving from *Ard Macha* ("Macha's Height"), it was named after the legendary pagan Queen Macha. But the city, with its magnificent cathedrals, has been and remains the administrative center for both the Catholic Church in Ireland and the Protestant Church of Ireland. Armagh's vibrant history, which stretches from pre-historic activity at nearby Navan Fort to associations with Jonathan Swift, has been partially dimmed by sectarian violence in the past decade. Its new-found glory flashes brightly every March 17 when people journey from far and near to celebrate St. Patrick's patronage of the city.

ORIENTATION & PRACTICAL INFORMATION

Armagh's street plan is quite confusing. Head to the clearly signposted **tourist office** on English St. for a free map. A long grassy park, called **The Mall,** occupies prime real estate just east of the city center, which is defined by English St., Thomas St., and Scotch St. (The Mall, which used to be a race course, was converted into an innocent park when betting and racing were deemed activities inappropriate to the sanctity of an ecclesiastical city.) Just west of the city center, the two cathedrals sit on neighboring hills—the Catholic Cathedral lifts two neo-Gothic spires, the Church of Ireland a medieval-looking tower. While **buses** stop along both sides of The Mall, most of them leave from the bus station on Mall West.

Tourist Office: Old Bank Building, 40 English St. (tel. 527808). From the bus station, turn left, and walk past The Mall to the roundabout. Turn left up the hill onto College St. and then take the first left. The tourist office is 15 yds. ahead on the right, in the large building with the sign for St. Patrick's Trian. Be sure to pick up the "Essential Guide for Visitors to Armagh" and a wealth of other info. Open April-Sept. Mon.-Sat. 9am-5:30pm, Oct.-March Mon.-Sat. 9am-5pm.

Bank: Northern Bank, 78 Scotch St. (tel. 522004). Open Mon. 9:30am-5pm, Tues.-Fri. 10am-3:30pm.

Post Office: 31 Upper English St. (tel. 510313). Mail is held at 46 Upper English St., just across the street (tel. 522856). Open Mon.-Fri. 9am-5:30pm, Sat. 9am-7pm.

Postal Code: BT61 7BA.

Phone Code: 01861.

Buses: Mallview Terrace, Mall West (tel. 522266). To: Belfast (Mon.-Fri. 20/day, Sat. 15/day, Sun. 9/day; 70 min; £4); Enniskillen (Mon.-Sat. 2/day; 2hr.; £5.30, students £4.40); Newry (Mon.-Sat. 5/day; 50 min.; £2.60).

Bike Rental: None in Armagh town; you might try **Brown's Bikes,** 32 Cormeen Rd. (tel. 522782), in Killylea, 3½ mi. away, on the Killylea bus route. (£4/day, £20/week; deposit required.)

Pharmacy: J. W. Gray, corner of Russell and English St. Open Mon.-Sat. 9am-6pm.

Hospital: Tower Hill, off College Hill, tel. 522341.

Emergency: dial 999, no coins required. **Police:** Newry Rd., tel. 523311.

ACCOMMODATIONS

Armagh has few B&Bs, but they are seldom full. **Padua Guest House,** 63 Cathedral Rd. (tel. 522039 or 523584) is just past the Cathedral (#63 is next door to #10). Kind Mrs. O'Hagen and her large doll collection greet guests with a cup of tea. Watch color TV in some rooms; hear the loud cathedral bells in all of them (£12/person). Mrs. McRoberts will kindly welcome you to **Desart Guest House,** 99 Cathedral Rd. (tel. 522387; £14-16/person). **Clonhugh Guest House,** College Hill (tel. 522693), north of the tip of The Mall, makes a mighty effort. Mrs. McKenna's house is so full of bric-a-brac that you may not be able to sit, but her bedrooms are very comfortable (single £15, double £30). **Gosford Forest Park,** off A28, (tel. 551277; ranger tel. 552169), has room for tents seven miles southeast of Armagh. The park includes a castle, old walled garden, poultry sheds, and miles of nature trails. (Park open daily 10am-sunset; £2/car, £1/person.) The Market Hill bus will drop you within walking distance of the park (**camping** £8/2-person tent, Oct.-Easter £5).

FOOD & PUBS

The lack of restaurants that are open late may be a result of formerly soldier-strewn streets. What little Armagh has for restaurants is scattered across English St. and Scotch St. The best bet may be to pick up supplies at **Emerson's,** 57 Scotch St., or at **Dunne's,** English St., for a picnic on the Mall or near the old Friary (see Sights, below). Get fresh fruit, vegetables, and almost anything else at **Shambles Market** (tel. 528192), across from the Catholic Cathedral (Tues. and Fri. 9:30am-5pm). **Rainbow Restaurant,** 13 Upper English St. (tel. 525391), serves colorful chicken curry and rice for £2.95 (open Mon.-Sat. 8:30am-5:30pm). Sleek **Fat Sam's,** the Shambles (tel. 525555), offers a dazzling variety of sandwiches (curried chicken with pineapple and sweet corn, £1.50; open Mon.-Fri. 8:45am-6pm, Sat. 9:15am-5pm). At **Hester's Place,** 12a English St. (tel. 522374), the unpretentious enjoy cheap, juicy burgers (£1.50; open Mon.-Sat. 9am-5pm). For non-drinkers, the **Pub with No Beer** on Thomas St. offers cheap pies and stews (£2.50-3), tea and coffee, and less noisy entertainment from 9-10:30pm. **The Station Bar,** 3 Lower English St. (tel. 523731), a more traditional pub, has trad on Tuesdays and folk on Thursdays. **Harry Hoots',** on Railway St. (tel. 522103), another popular hangout, calls out to passers-by. The **Northern Bar,** across the street (tel. 527315 or 527316), provides live entertainment and dancing, and hoots right back.

SIGHTS

Armagh's twin cathedrals are the city's pride and joy, not to mention its main attractions. **The Church of Ireland Cathedral of St. Patrick** (tel. 523142) is a 19th-century restoration of a 17th-century structure that was based on a 13th-century plan. Graves of famous dead people include that of the great Irish King, Brian Ború. (Open April-Sept. daily 10:30am-5pm; Nov.-March daily 10:30am-4pm; services Sun. at 10, 11am, and 3:15pm; tours June-Aug. Mon.-Sat. 11:30am and 2:30pm; free.) Across town the **Catholic Church of St. Patrick** raises its heady spires from Cathedral Rd. Opened in 1873 to a crowd of 20,000 spectators, the cathedral's imposing exterior and exquisite mosaic interior are marred only by ultra-modern, granite furnishings in the sanctuary. (Open daily 9am-5pm; services Sun. at 9, 10:30am, and noon; free.)

In the center of town, **St. Patrick's Trian** (tel. 527808) shares a building with the tourist office. Most of the exhibits emphasize St. Patrick's role in Armagh. *The Armagh Story* is a walk-through display and audio-visual presentation in which pictures and characters from the past relate the lengthy history of the town. A smaller, but nonetheless well-done, display recreates Swift's *Land of Lilliput.* (Open April-Sept. Mon.-Sat. 10am-7pm, Sun. 1-7pm; Oct.-March Mon.-Sat. 10am-5pm, Sun. 2-5pm; £3.25, students £2.40.) Up College Hill north of The Mall has the **Armagh Observatory,** founded in 1790 by Archbishop Robinson (of Demesne Palace fame). Would-be astronomers can observe the modern weather station and a refractory telescope dating from 1885. The Robinson Dome provides self-guided tours (grounds open Mon.-Fri. 9:30am-4:30pm). Those without a physics degree can stargaze in the **Planetarium,** College Hill (tel. 523689). Booking ahead is strongly recommended as seating is limited to 100 people. (Open Sept.-March Mon.-Fri. 10am-5pm, show at 3pm, Sat. 1:30-5pm, shows at 2 and 3pm; April-June Mon.-Fri. 10am-5pm, show at 3pm, Sat.-Sun. 1:30-5pm, shows at 2 and 3pm; July-Aug. Mon.-Fri. 10am-5pm; shows hourly 11am-4pm, Sat.-Sun. 1:30-5pm, shows at 2 and 3pm; free.)

At the **Armagh County Museum** (tel. 523070), on the east side of The Mall, undiscriminating historians have stuffed a panoply of 18th-century objects—old wedding dresses, pictures, stuffed birds, jewelry, and militia uniforms—into huge wooden cabinets. (Open Mon.-Sat. 10am-1pm and 2-5pm; free.) On Friary Rd. south of town center, the ruins of the 13th-century **Franciscan Friary,** the longest-standing friary in Ireland, occupy a peaceful green corner of the **Palace Demesne.** The palace, its chapel, and its stables were built by the 18th-century Archbishop of Armagh, Richard Robinson. These and a number of other structures in town, including the observatory, were all a part of his plan to rebuild the entire city. Although the palace is closed to the public, its stables have been converted into a high-class tourist attraction. **The Palace Stables Heritage Centre** (tel. 529629) puts on a slick multi-media show about "A Day in the Life" of the closed palace—July 23, 1776. (Open April-Sept. Mon.-Sat. 10am-7pm, Sun. 1-7pm; Oct.-March Mon.-Sat. 10am-5pm, Sun. 2-5pm; £2.80, students £2.20.) Close your visit to Armagh with a peek at an open first edition of *Gulliver's Travels,* covered with Swift's own scrawled marginalia, at the **Armagh Public Library,** Abbey St. (tel. 523142; open Mon.-Fri. 10am-12:30pm and 2-4pm).

■ NEAR ARMAGH

Twelve miles east of Armagh, in Tandragee, the **Tayto Crisp Factory** (tel. (01762) 840249), housed in the old O'Hanlon castle near an even older Celtic holy site, gives free 1½-hour tours Mon.-Fri. at 10:30am and 1:30pm. Call ahead to make sure they have room. To get there by bus, you'll have to go to Portadown and change buses.

NAVAN FORT

On the outskirts of Armagh, **Navan Fort,** also called *Emain Macha* ("AHM-win maka"), was the capital of the Kings of Ulster for 800 years. The whole area is an archaeological site of primary importance to historians of Iron Age Ireland. The legendary founding of the fort is attributed to Queen Macha (see Queen Macha, p. 382). St. Patrick probably chose Ard Macha as a base from which to spread Christianity because of its relative proximity to this pagan stronghold. The **Navan Centre** (tel. (01861) 525550), built deep into the hill, presents a 70-minute program of films and interactive exhibits on the legends associated with the site and the factual archeological evidence of the hills. The powerful and often violent stories about this, the first capital of Ulster, will inspire you to explore the fort itself (¼ mile from the center). Few parts of the earthworks are still visible. The overgrown fort mount may seem disappointingly lacking in evidence of human civilization, but the view is excellent. The center and fort are located on the Killylea Rd. (A28), two miles west of town. (Centre open July-Aug. Mon.-Sat. 10am-7pm, Sun. 11am-7pm; April-June and Sept. Mon.-Sat. 10am-6pm, Sun. 11am-6pm; Oct.-Mar. Mon.-Fri. 10am-6pm, Sat.

11am-6pm, and Sun. noon-6pm; £3.75, students £2.50; the fort is free and always open.) Nearby, artificial ritual pools called the **King's Stables** and **Loughnashade** (Lake of the Treasures) are the receptacles where the ancient Celts dumped everything from gold jewelry to iron weapons to a human head, presumably as offerings to the gods. The grisly remains are no longer visible, however, and the pools themselves aren't spectacular.

Queen Macha

For 800 years, Navan Fort served the Kings of Ulster as their capital. Legend holds that the founding and the name of the fort, *Emain Macha*, are derived from a story concerning the pagan Queen Macha. The queen supposedly raced and defeated King Conchobar's horses. She subsequently collapsed and died while giving birth to twins (*emain*, in Irish). As retribution, Conchobar's warriors were cursed to suffer Macha's birth pangs in the future. In honor of the tragedy and in respect for the successful and powerful queen, the name of the Ulster king's capitol was attributed to the twins of Queen Macha. The queen's curse finally took effect when Queen Medbh of Connacht invaded Ulster in search of King Conchobar's bull (see Legends & Folktales, p. 61). The king's soldiers began to suffer Macha's birth pangs, rendering them unable to fight. Fortunately, King Conchobar had one particularly strong and immune warrior, Cú Chulainn, who fights and defeats each of Medbh's warriors one by one, thus saving Ulster from utter ruin.

LOUGH NEAGH & OXFORD ISLAND

The U.K.'s largest lake sits smack in the center of Northern Ireland's industrial heartland, touching five of the North's six counties. Legend has it that the Isle of Man was scooped out of Lough Neagh and flung into the sea by a giant. Birdwatching, water-skiing, and various aquatic activities are just about the only amusement in the towns around the Lough; its shores are best seen as daytrips from Belfast or Armagh.

On the southeast shore of the Lough, the **Lough Neagh Discovery Centre,** Oxford Island National Nature Reserve, Craigavon (tel. (01762) 322205), contains acres of wooded parkland for exploration, with or without a guided tour. Boat rides to the islands run several times daily. Audio-visual displays in the center itself successfully detail the lake's ecosystem and wildlife. (Open April-Sept. daily 10am-7pm; Oct.-March Wed.-Sun. 10am-5pm; last admission 1 hr. before closing; £2.) The lakeshore hosts hundreds of bird species every year. The **Kinnego Caravan Park,** Kinnego Marina, Lurgan (tel. (01762) 327573), receives campers (£5/2-person tent).

■ Antrim & Derry

North of lively Belfast, the smoke stacks of Larne cease to obstruct views of the sea as the wooded mountains of the nine Glens of Antrim take over. They were formerly the stomping grounds of the Ulaid dynasty for over a thousand years. Today, tiny, non-dynastic towns nestle into a coastline dotted with beaches. The towns are linked by a flat road that proclaims cyclists' paradise. Farther west, natural formations become even more staggering and inspire contemplation of the massive forces that caused the Causeway. The garish lights and lively atmospheres of Portrush and Portstewart, however, will cause light-headedness rather than sobriety. The northern coast culminates at Derry, the North's second largest city whose turbulent history matches the dramatic coastal landscape. The inland woods and country parks provide a welcome change from the stormy seas and massive forms. The Sperrin Mountains can last for days.

■■■ LARNE

The **ferries** that depart for Scotland from here are the only imaginable reason for a trip to Larne. But now that the Hoverspeed Seacat goes directly to Belfast, few pedestrians will want to use the Larne ferry (see Getting There, p. 27). Two ferry companies operate from Larne: **Sealink** (tel. (01574) 273616) and **P&O Ferries** (tel. (01574) 274321). Travelers should arrive 45 minutes early, as ferries often leave early and, when they don't, they're often full. **Larne Town** itself lies 15 minutes down the coast and inland from the harbor. From the harbor, the first right after the ferry port becomes Curran Rd. after the bridge and then turns into Main St. when it reaches town.

Practical Information The **tourist office**, Narrow Gauge Rd. (tel. (01574) 260088), makes life a little easier. The office has loads of info, a free town map, and a surprisingly good geological and historical exhibition (open Mon.-Sat. 9am-5pm; July-Sept. Mon.-Wed. 9am-5pm, Thurs.-Fri. 9am-7:30pm, Sat. 9am-6pm, Sun. 11am-6pm). **Halifax Bank** (tel. (01574) 270214), on the corner of Broadway and Main St., has an **ATM** that accepts Plus and Visa (open Mon.-Fri. 9am-5pm, Sat. 9am-noon). Larne's **post office**, 78 Main St. (tel. (01574) 272518), feels an affinity for the **postal code**, BT4 01AA. **Trains** run between Belfast's Central Station and Larne Harbour (Belfast office tel. (01232) 741700, Larne office tel. (01574) 270517; Mon.-Fri. 22/day, Sat. 17/day, Sun. 7/day; 50 min.; £2.90). **Buses** leave frequently from Larne (tel. (01574) 272345) for Belfast's Oxford St. Station (Mon.-Sat. 17/day, Sun. 3/day; 50-min. express or 1½-hr.; £2.40). Those departing on a ferry from Larne should ensure that their train or bus terminates in Larne Harbour, not a 15-minute walk away in Larne Town.

Accommodations, Food, & Pubs Most people wouldn't choose to stay in Larne, but if you're too weary to travel anywhere else, there is certainly no shortage of accommodation. The B&Bs most convenient to both the harbor and the bus and train stations lie along Curran Rd. A right turn from the bus station leads to a round-about. From here, Circular Rd. crosses Curran Rd., the first road on the right. From the harbor, the first right after the ferry port crosses a bridge and turns into Curran Rd. **Mrs. McKane,** 52 Bay Rd. (tel. (01574) 274943), just off Curran Rd., stocks her rooms with TVs and hotpots (single £13, double £24, w/bath £30). Guests can see the sea from their beds at **Moneydara,** 149 Curran Rd. (tel. (01574) 272912; single £15, double £26). **The Curran Caravan Park,** 131 Curran Rd. (tel. (01574) 273797 or 260088), midway between the harbor and town, has lawn bowling, putting greens, and grubby bathrooms (£4/person, hook-up £1.50; £6.50/caravan).

In the center of town, **Stewart's Supermarket,** on Broadway, has an ample selection of food (open Mon.-Tues. and Sat. 9am-5:30pm, Wed.-Fri. 9am-9pm). Main St. alternates coffee shop with bakery. The lunch menu is affordable at **Carriages,** 105 Main St. (tel. (01574) 275132), as opposed to its dinner menu. Cheap pizza persists all day, though. (Seafood flan with salad £3; open daily noon-11pm.) **Maud's,** Main St. (tel. 278065), will tide you over with ice cream, snacks, and tea (sandwiches £1-1.25; sundaes £1.95; open Mon.-Sat. 11am-9pm, Sun 11:30am-8pm). The cozy and unique atmosphere at lamp-lit **Bailie,** 111-113 Main St. (tel. (01574) 273947), is perfect for cuddling. Thursdays and Sundays feature live music while Fridays and Saturdays amplify less entertaining karaoke. The **Rising Tide,** 87 Main St. (tel. (01574) 272259), also entertains to live music on some nights.

GLENS OF ANTRIM

North of Larne, nine lush green valleys, or "glens," slither from the hills and high moors of Co. Antrim down to the seashore. Though there is absolutely nothing to

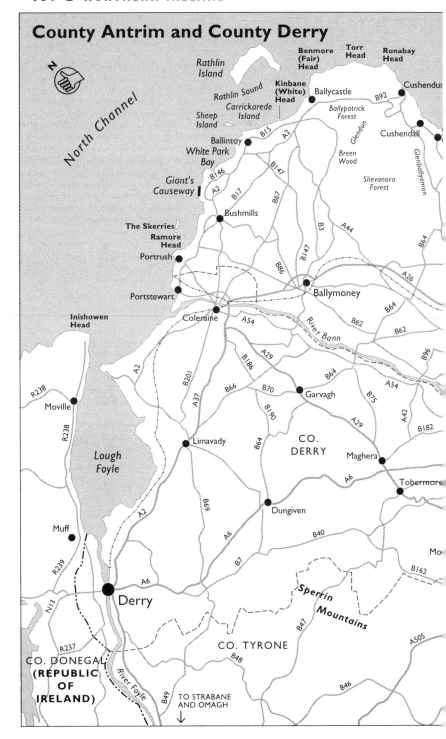

County Antrim and County Derry

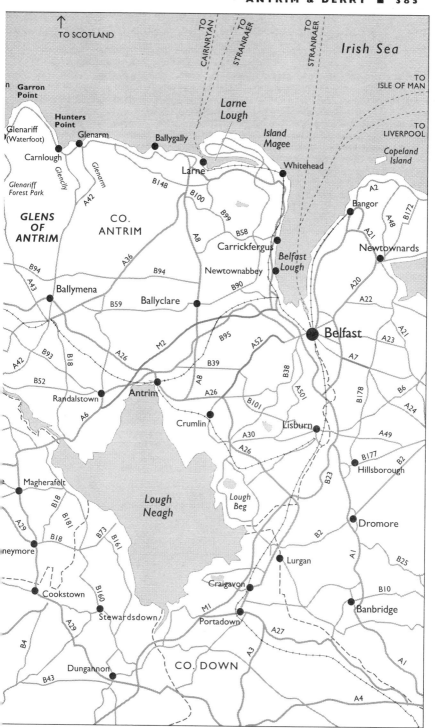

see in the glen towns, people inexplicably love visiting them. A2 connects the small towns at the foot of each glen to each other. For once, this road along the rocky shore is suitable for any mode of transport: driving, biking, or hitching. The glens themselves (and the mountains and waterfalls) can best be seen by heading inland from one of the base towns. The area's only hostel is in Cushendall.

Bus service through the glens is scant at best. Two Ulsterbus routes serve the area (in Belfast tel. (01232) 320011, in Larne tel. (01574) 272345). Bus #162 from Belfast stops in Larne, Ballygally, Glenarm, and Carnlough (Mon.-Fri. 10/day, Sat. 8/day, Sun. 2/day), and sometimes continues to Waterfoot, Cushendall, and Cushendun (Mon.-Fri. 4/day, Sat. 3/day). An infrequent summertime Antrim Coaster follows the coast road from Belfast through to Coleraine, stopping at every town and village (June-Sept. Mon.-Sat. 2/day). The Ulsterbus Express bus from Belfast to Portrush doesn't go anywhere near the Glens. Most rides in the glens average £2-4.

Hitching is decent, but the winding narrow road between cliffs and the sea wall doesn't allow for easy stopping. The photo opportunity points and crossroads are the best places to try your luck. **Cycling** is fabulous. The coast road from Ballygally to Cushendall is both scenic and flat, if tortuous. After the road divides north of Cushendall, the coastal route, which passes the spectacular views of Torr Head, runs through hills that make even motorists groan. The inland route, through Ballypatrick Forest, is more manageable but still far from flat. The Cushendall and Whitepark Bay YHANI/HI hostels each rent bikes and allow drop-off at the other (£6/day, £5/additional day, £30/week; deposit £30; £5 drop-off charge; pannier bags £5).

BALLYGALLY

The tiny village stretches along the water's edge, surrounded by a wide sandy beach and gentle hills. Well-preserved **Ballygally Castle,** built in 1625 by a Scotsman who needed a fortified home, dominates the strip. Also called the **Halfway House Hotel,** coach travelers in the past used to stop off here on their journeys between Larne and Glenam. The Castle's **ghost** room is inhabited by a female spectre whose physical body plummeted from the tower window hundreds of years ago. Now, an occasional fortune-teller will read your future there. The rocky outposts that appear in the sea, just before entering the village, are rumored to be the submerged ruins of another castle.

In its basement, the **Dungeon Bar** (tel. (01574) 583212) has live folk music on Fridays and trad on Saturdays. **Lough Restaurant,** 260 Coast Rd. (tel. (01574) 583294), serves sandwiches (£1) and a standard Irish snack menu (£2-2.75; open daily 11am-8:30pm). The adjoining **grocery store** (tel. (01574) 274117) has a large stock of food (open daily 9am-9pm). Fifty yards up the road from the point where the bus stops as it enters town, B&B with a view can be had at **Té an Téasa,** 4 Coastguard Cottages, Coast Rd. (tel. (01574) 583591). The bright, modern house distinguishes itself with a funky staircase (£12.50/person). Also along the coast road but nearer to Larne, the **Carnfunnock Country Park** (tel. (01574) 260088 or 270541) provides **campsites** (£5) and a walled garden, where sundials of all shapes and sizes tell the time and give timely advice, e.g. "Hasten slowly". One sundial even points a beam of light, rather than a shadow, at the correct hour. The hedge maze next to the garden is shaped like Northern Ireland; the entrances and exits to the maze are at the major ports. Inquire at the visitors center for entrance to the maze (open daily 8am-8pm). Ballygally's **post office,** Coast Rd. (tel. (01574) 583229; open Mon.-Tues. and Thurs.-Fri. 9am-1pm and 2-5:30pm, Wed. 9am-1pm, Sat. 9am-12:30pm), knows the difference between the **postal code,** BT40 2QX, and the **phone code,** 01574.

GLENARM

Six flat, winding, coastal miles along A2 lead up to Glenarm ("glen of the army"), the southernmost glen. At its foot lies Glenarm Village. The village itself is small, quiet, and unexciting, but the forest is a rare pleasure. You can kiss the road goodbye and hike the six miles along the **Ulster Way** trail (a good map is necessary, of course). Glenarm Village is graced with several pubs, a few stray artists, and the grand entrance to **Glenarm Forest,** where trails trace the river's path for miles (open daily 9am-sunset). The village has been the seat of the MacDonnells, the Earls of Antrim, since they first arrived from Scotland in the 13th century. Today, the 13th Earl of Antrim still resides here in **Glenarm Castle.** Just off the main street, the Castle hides behind the trees north of the river. Only the 17th century gate is visible from outside.

Margaret's B&B and Café, 10 Altmore St. (tel. (01574) 841307), provides the only alternative to pub grub in town. It doubles the pleasure with large, comfortable rooms and religious sayings on the walls. (B&B £14/person. Café open Mon.-Sat. 9am-midnight.) Either **Heatherdew Tavern,** 1 New Rd. (tel. (01574) 841221), or the **Bridgend Tavern** (tel. (01574) 841247; occasional trad in summer), on Toberwine St., will pour you a pint. A **festival** shocks this sleepy town during the first week of July. Just before entering Glenarm, the **madman's window** appears on the right. The elements have worn this huge hole through a gigantic block of chalk. Glenarm's **post office** (tel. (01574) 841218) is halfway down Toberwine St. (open Mon.-Tues. and Thurs.-Fri. 9am-1pm and 2-5:30pm, Wed. and Sat. 9am-1pm). The **postal code** is BT44 0AP.

WATERFOOT & GLENARIFF

Nine miles farther up the coast, the village of Waterfoot guards Antrim's broadest glen, Glenariff, often deemed the most beautiful of the nine. (Waterfoot itself is sometimes called Glenariff—don't get lost.) Thackeray labeled Glenariff "Switzerland in miniature," presumably because it was steep and pretty, since secretive banks and trilingual skiers are rare. Glenariff's **coastal caves** are worth exploring. They gape on the way to the Red Bay pier from town. Due to the Penal Laws, Catholics learned their Catechism in the School Cave under dripping stalactites.

Four miles down the road from the village at **Glenariff Forest Park,** waterfalls splash down shaded hills to feed the **River Glenariff.** If you're starting from south of the park, you can save yourself the three-mile uphill hike to the official entrance by taking the downhill road marked with red arrows. It branches left towards the Manor Lodge Restaurant. From the north Cushendall, A2 (Glenariff Rd.) goes past flat-topped **Lurigethan** (1153 feet) on the right. The ruined walls of **Red Bay Castle** are straight ahead just before you pass under Red Arches. The road then veers away from the sea (it doesn't follow signs to Glenariff). After about four miles, signs point left to the park. Once inside, paths marked by red arrows begin at the **Manor Lodge** and climb up the **Waterfalls Trail.** A 1¾-mile walk shadows the River Glenariff as it crashes over jagged rocks. Just inside the park entrance, a trail veers left to follow the river downstream (and downhill). Bridges cross streams and sweet-smelling flora up to the **Waterfall Restaurant,** still within the forest park. The café has tasty "quickies" for £3. (Park open March-Oct. Mon.-Sun. 10am-dusk. £2.50/car, £1/person.) The Cushendun-Ballymena **bus** (Mon.-Sat. 4/day, Sun. 1/day) passes the park entrance. Ask to be dropped off here and wave your arms for the driver's attention to get back on.

If you would rather not camp at **Glenariff Forest Park Camping,** 98 Glenariff Rd. (tel. (012667) 58232; tents £5-7.50), find one of the many farmers in the area who welcome campers (ask in town), stay in Waterfoot itself, or settle just up the road in Cushendall. At **Glen Vista,** 245 Garcon Rd. (tel. (012667) 71439), near the beach at the foot of the glen after the caravan park, bright, clean rooms overlook the sea (£12/person; open June-Sept.).

Waterfoot may be a one-street town, but it has two charismatic pubs. **The Mariners' Bar,** 7 Main St. (tel. (012667) 71330), has trad every Sunday and some summer weeknights, as well as varied live music on Friday and Saturday nights. **Harvey's,** across the street, has a beer garden. **The Glens of Antrim Feis,** one of Northern Ireland's major music and dance festivals, is held here in late June/early July.

■■■ CUSHENDALL

Considered the capital of the Glens region, **Cushendall,** two miles north of Water-foot, is an unpretentious town with no arcades and no neon. Instead, the town fosters happening pubs and takes advantage of its lucky location: moors, hills, and the rough seashore form a triangle with the town at its center. Three of the nine glens (Glenballyeamon, Glenaan, and Glencorp) are closer to Cushendall than to any other human habitation.

PRACTICAL INFORMATION

Tourist office, Mill St. (tel. (012667) 71180), near the bus stop and opposite the library. They'll surprise you with a wealth of information. Open Mon.-Fri. 10am-1pm and 3-7:30pm, Sat. 10am-1pm and 2-4:30pm; mid-June to Aug. also open Mon.-Sat. 6-8pm.

Banks: Northern Bank, Shore St. (tel. (012667) 71243). Open Mon 9:30am-5pm, Tues.-Fri. 10am-3:30pm.

Post office, Mill St. (tel. (012667) 71201). Open Mon. and Wed.-Fri. 9am-1pm and 2-5:30pm, Tues. and Sat. 9am-12:30pm. The **postal code** is BT44 0RR.

Buses: call the Ballymena bus station (tel. (01266) 652214) for information.

Bike Rental: Ardclinis Activity Centre, 11 High St. (tel. (01266) 71340). Mountain bikes £10/day; deposit credit card, passport, or £50; wetsuits £5/day.

Camping equipment: O'Neill's Country Sports, Mill St. (tel. (012667) 72009). They also sell fishing tackle. Open Mon.-Thurs. and Sat. 9:30am-5:30pm, Fri. 9:30am-8pm, Sun. noon-5:30pm.

Pharmacy: Gillan Pharmacy, 2 Mill St. (tel. (012667) 71523). Open Mon. and Wed.-Sat. 9:30am-5:30pm, Tues. 9:30am-1:30pm.

ACCOMMODATIONS

Cushendall Youth Hostel (YHANI/HI), Layde Rd. (tel. (01266) 71344), 1 mi. from town. A "YHA" sign appears on a wall along the (uphill) road that forks left from Shore St., but the warden will pick you up if you plan ahead. A recent architectural tune-up generated a phenomenal kitchen where future Julia Childs get color-coordinated cutting boards. Curfew 11:30pm, key available. Bike rental. Members £6.30, under 18 £5.30. Open March-Dec.

Glendale, Mrs. O'Neill's, 46 Coast Rd. (tel. (012667) 71495). It's hard to imagine a warmer welcome or a better bathtub. £13/person, w/bath £15.

Shramore, 27 Chapel Rd. (tel. (012667) 71610). Three quiet, restful rooms and a bathtub for £13/person. Open May-Sept.

Cushendall Caravan Park, 62 Coast Rd. (tel. (012667) 71699), adjacent to Red Bay Boatyard. Summer £7.25/tent, winter £4.40/tent.

Glenville Caravan Park, 22 Layde Rd. (tel. (012667) 71520). £3/tent.

FOOD & PUBS

After all those trees in the Glens, it's nice to be around lively people and pubs again. **Spar supermarket,** Bridge St., is open 365 days a year, 366 days every leap year (8am-10pm).

Gillian's Home Bakery and Coffee Shop, 6 Mill St. (tel. (012667) 71404). Simple food that you could cook yourself, but it's cheap. Hot dog 70p, beans on toast £1.50. Open Mon.-Sat. 9am-8pm, Sun. 11am-8pm.

The Moyle Inn, Bridge St. (tel. (012667) 71300). Everything and anything with chips. Open Mon.-Sat. 10:30am-5pm.

Harry's, Mill St. (tel. (012667) 72022). Bar snacks are quick and satisfying (turkey supreme and rice £3.20; served Mon.-Sat. noon-5pm, Sun. noon-3pm) but evening meals are more expensive and complex, and are served in a less pub-like atmosphere (roast half-chicken, bacon, and sweet corn £6.75; served daily 6-9:30pm).

Joe McCollam's, 23 Mill St. (tel. (01266) 71330), a.k.a. "Johnny Joe's." A tiny, ancient, and completely traditional barroom that will soothe feet and spirits.

Lively traditional nights feature impromptu singing, fiddling, tall tales, and drinking until 11pm (summer Thurs. and Sat.-Sun.).

Lurig Inn, 5 Bridge St. (tel. (01266) 71527), is right next door. Music plays most nights and much less common *ceili* dancing on the first Friday of every month.

SIGHTS

The sandstone **Curfew Tower** endures in the center of town on the corner of Mill St. The tower was built in 1825 to contain rowdy townspeople after a riot or a revel. Today it is privately owned and closed to the public. The remnants of a Franciscan Friary, **Layde Church,** lie just a short walk from the hostel along the coast road to Cushendun. The church was appropriated for use as a Protestant church until the 1800's. Inland from the church, **Tieveragh Hill,** known locally as Fairy Hill, embodies a gate to the Otherworld that is inhabited by ancient "little people." The tiny folk play haunting music on Halloween, which coincides with the Celtic new year's festival of Samhain. **Lurigethan Hill** would soar above town if it weren't for its remarkable flattened top.

Ossian's Grave molders on the lower slopes of Tievebulliagh Mountain. In fact a neolithic burial cairn dating from around 2000 BC, it is linked only by tradition with the Ulster warrior-bard Ossian who, according to legend, was buried here in about 300 AD (see Legends & Folktales, p. 61). This merry poet, while relating his family's adventures to St. Patrick, allegedly tried to convince the saint that Christianity was far too restrictive for the boisterous Gaels. This episode was later incorporated into young Yeats's first long poem. A2 leads north from Cushendall towards Ballymoney to the lower slopes of Tievebulliagh, where a sign points the way. The steep walk up the southern slope of Glenaan itself rewards with views of the lush valley. Powerboats for racing on the waves are available at **Red Bay Boats Ltd.,** 21 Dalnade Park (tel. (01266) 71331; £8/1 hr., £6/hr. for 2-5 hrs., and £32/6 hrs.). Every Friday of the summer, **McMullan's Sea Angling Service** (tel. (01266) 71282) sends a fishing boat from the pier at 6:30pm (£5; book ahead).

■ NEAR CUSHENDALL: CUSHENDUN

Five miles north of Cushendall on A2, the tiny, picturesque seaside village of Cushendun was bought in its entirety by the National Trust in 1954. Since then, Big Brother has been able to protect the town's "olde," quaint, squeaky-clean image from any danger. Cushendun has none of the hustle and little of the bustle which characterizes is larger neighbor to the south. This picture-perfect village's largest attraction is a set of **sea caves** that perforate its vast beach. The caves were carved out of the stone cliffs by a sea which was once much higher than it is now. The largest cave, located just past the Bay Hotel, provides the only entrance to **Cave House,** which was built in 1820. It is currently occupied by the Mercy religious order but closed to the public. From behind the hotel, an insupportably steep path leads to the cliff top.

The **National Trust** office, 1 Main St. (tel. (01266) 74506), plays up the town's two attractions with displays on Cushendun's history and the sea caves. They also sell a good map of walks in the area (50p; open daily 1-5pm; Easter-June and Sept. Sat.-Sun. 1-5pm). You can sip tea downstairs in a tourist-priced **tea room** (burgers 90p, big sandwiches £1.20; open daily 11:30am-6:30pm). **The Bay Hotel,** 20 Strandview Park (tel. (01266) 74267), provides simple rooms, breakfast, and nice views (£16/person). It also supplies bar snacks and pub grub (chicken royal £4.75; open daily 12:30-3pm). **The Villa,** 185 Torr Rd. (tel. (01266) 761252), one mile from town, is a 19th-century farmhouse converted into a B&B. It lies on a particularly scenic portion of the Ulster Way hiking trail (£20/person). Mrs. McKay's **Sleepy Hollow B&B,** 107 Knocknacarry Rd. (tel. (01266) 761513), is cheaper (£15/person). Camping at **Cushendun Caravan Site,** 14 Glendun Rd. (tel. (01266) 761254), is cheapest. TV/game room; wash and dry £1.50. (£7.25/tent; open March-Sept.) The multi-talented **Bay Hotel** has folk music in the bar on Saturdays. **Buses** pause at

Cushendun's one grocery shop (open daily 8:30am-10pm) on their way to Water-foot (Mon.-Sat. 9/day, Sun. 1/day) and Ballycastle (Mon.-Sat. 2/day).

CAUSEWAY COAST

Past Cushendun, the northern coast shifts from lyrical into dramatic mode: 600-foot cliffs dominate yielding white beaches. The Giant's Causeway, for which the whole region is named, is a honeycomb of black and red hexagonal columns. The rock for-mations, suited to a science fiction scene, extend off the coast in the direction of Scotland. The Giant's Causeway itself is seldom less crowded than the towns which lead up to it.

A2, which can be comfortably biked or driven, connects the main towns along the Causeway. Ulsterbus #172 runs between Ballycastle and Portrush along the coast (Mon.-Fri. 7/day, Sat. 6/day; 1hr.) and makes frequent connections to Ports-tewart. In good summer weather, the open-topped **Bushmills Bus** (Coleraine bus station, tel. (01265) 43332) outlines the coast between Coleraine (five miles south of Portrush) and the Giant's Causeway (July-Aug. Mon.-Sat. 4/day, Sun. 2/day). The summertime **Antrim Coaster** bus (tel. (01232) 333000) runs up the coast from Bel-fast to Portstewart (June and Sept. Mon.-Sat. 2/day, July and Aug. daily 2/day). Ulster-bus also runs package **tours** in the area that leave from Belfast or elsewhere. From points farther south along the coast, many rely on their thumbs or the express bus from Belfast (June-Sept. 9/day). Those **hitching** along A2 or the inland roads (margin-ally quicker) find that the lack of cars slows them down.

CUSHENDUN TO BALLYCASTLE

Seven miles north of Cushendun, just south of Ballycastle, **Fair Head** magnetically attracts international hikers. Challenging basalt cliffs plummet straight down to rocky scree. Bikes should be left at home: the hills are so horrific that cyclists will spend more time walking than wheeling. Those in cars should head straight for this stretch of road, though they seldom do. The lack of autos translates into poor hitch-ing conditions. High **Torr Head**, halfway to Fair Head from Cushendun, is the clos-est spot to Scotland in all Ireland. Just to the south, a steep road from Crockanore runs down to undiscovered **Murlough Bay**, protected by the National Trust.

A2 straight from Cushendun to Ballycastle is more manageable for cyclists, with one long climb but an even longer descent from a boggy plain. Part of the high plain has been drained and planted with evergreens. The result is secluded **Ballypatrick Forest,** which includes a forest drive and several pleasant, pine-scented walks. **Camping** is allowed with a permit from the ranger or the Forest Office (tel. (012657) 62301), two miles toward Ballycastle on A2 (basic facilities; £4/tent). Past the forest, the landscape is even more desolate. A few miles north, a high hollow contains a **vanishing lake** which can appear and disappear into the bog in less than a day. When the lake is full, it has fish in it. (Where do they go when it empties?)

An Unforgettable Affair

Legend maintains that a certain Princess Taisie, whose royal presence was often seen along this coast, was so beautiful that suitors came from far and wide to compete for her hand. Two of her most ardent admirers, trying to determine who had the right to wed the Princess (they didn't want to bother her with the question), engaged in a duel. One of the headstrong suitors was mortally wounded. As he lay dying, he called a liegeman to his side. The liegeman swore that he would exact revenge upon the winner of the duel. This dedicated ser-vant appeared as a happy guest at the wedding reception. But when the groom's attention was diverted, the liegeman seized his moment. He waltzed the bride to the edge of the cliffs and threw her over. Her body washed up at Fair Head.

■■■ BALLYCASTLE

The Glens of Antrim and the Causeway Coast converge upon L-shaped Ballycastle, a bubbly seaside town with a busy beach. Weekend discos induce revelers to travel miles to get to town. Weekdays are a little more navigable. Though Ballycastle (not the only town with this name) means "town of the castle," don't look for a castle here. The progenitor of the town's name was demolished in 1856. While Ballycastle is not unpleasant, those desiring to visit the famous sights to its west (Giant's Causeway) or the south (Glens of Antrim) may want to stay closer to those attractions.

ORIENTATION & PRACTICAL INFORMATION

Ballycastle's main street runs perpendicular to the waterfront. It starts at the ocean as Quay Rd., becomes Ann St., and then Castle St. Most restaurants and shops are found along Ann St. and its successor, Castle St. As Quay Rd. meets water, the road takes a sharp left onto North St., where more stores and food await. The amusement grounds and "park" here make it a popular meeting place for young people. Unfortunately, the groovy coastal walk beyond North St. has been closed for safety reasons. Most B&Bs perch on Quay Rd., as does the hostel.

Tourist Office: Sheskburn House, 7 Mary St. (tel. 62024). 24-hr. computerized information outside. Open July-Aug. Mon.-Fri. 9:30am-7pm, Sat. 10am-6pm, Sun. 2-6pm; Sept.-June Mon.-Fri. 9:30am-5pm, Sat. 10am-4pm.

Banks: First Trust Bank, 32-34 Ann St. (tel. 63326). Open Mon.-Fri. 9:30am-4:30pm; **ATM** accepts Mastercard and Visa.

Post Office: 3 Ann St. (tel. 62519). Open Mon.-Tues. and Thurs.-Fri. 9am-1pm and 2-5:30pm, Wed. 9am-1pm, Sat. 9am-12:30pm. **Postal code:** BT54 60H.

Phone Code: 012657.

Ferry: See Rathlin Island, page 392.

Buses: stop at the Diamond. Get rides to: Cushendall (Mon.-Sat., 3/day; 40 min.; £2.40); Portrush (Mon.-Sat. 7/day; 1hr.; £3.60); and Belfast (Mon.-Sat. 6/day, Sun. 4/day; 3hr.; £5.40).

Taxis: tel. 62822 or 62537.

Bike Rental: J. Spence, Castle St. (tel. 62487). £5/day; no deposit.

Pharmacy: McMichael's, 10 Ann St. (tel. 63342).

ACCOMMODATIONS

Watch out for the Ould Lammas Fair on the last Monday and Tuesday in August. B&Bs fill almost a year in advance, and even hostel beds fill weeks before the big event. **The Castle Hostel,** 62 Quay Rd. (tel. 62337), has a central location, crowded but comfortable co-ed bunk rooms, no lack of modern showers, and *two* kitchens (dorm £5; laundry £1). **Camping** in the backyard is an option for the strictest of budget travelers (£3). Just up the road towards town, you can eat or sleep at **Fragrens,** 34 Quay Rd. (tel. 62168). Mrs. Frayne will spoil you with TV, a navigable tub, and free tea and coffee. (Separate smoking and non-smoking rooms; £13/person, w/bath £15; £2 less for continental breakfast; dinner £7.) **Hilsea,** 28 North St. (tel. 62385), is a large, businesslike guest house offering bright, slightly sterile rooms overlooking Rathlin Island and the Sea of Moyle (£15/person).

FOOD & PUBS

Brady's Supermarket, 54 Castle St. (tel. 62349), is just ten minutes from the hostel (open Mon.-Sat. 9am-9pm, Sun. 10:45am-9pm). Closer still, the **Fruit Shop,** the Diamond (tel. 63348), sells greens (and reds and oranges; open Mon.-Sat. 8am-6pm). **Beach House Cafe,** Bayview Rd. (tel. 62262), is close to the pier. Romantic views of the bay and Fair Head are marred only by the loud amusement park. Serves sinful but cheap desserts and snacks, as well as full meals (sundaes £1.80-2, lasagne £2.30; open daily 9am-9pm). **The Strand Restaurant,** North St., plays Bryan Adams, but it redeems itself with a large menu that includes several vegetarian dishes (vegetable pie £4.95) and dandy desserts (crepes £1.95; open daily 11am-10pm). Savory pizzas that will feed at least three (£6-7) slip onto your tables at the subterranean grotto called **Cellar Pizzeria,** 11a The Diamond (tel. 63037). (Delivery for orders of £5 or more daily 6-11pm. Open Sept.-May Mon.-Sun. 5-11pm; June-Aug. Mon.-Sat. 12:30-3pm and 5-11pm, Sun. 5-11pm.)

Though renowned for its nuttiness during the Fair, Ballycastle is lively throughout the entire year. Tourists usually head for tiny **House of McDonnell,** Castle St. (tel. 62975), which has trad on Wednesdays and Fridays in summer. The **Anglers' Arms,** 12 North St. (tel. 62155), promises fun with nightly sing-alongs during the summer; occasional live music adds to the enjoyment. **The Central Bar,** 12 Ann St. (tel. 63877), has all kinds of live music (Wed., Sat., and sometimes Tues. nights). **McCarroll's Pub,** 5 Ann St. (tel. 62123), spins traditional reels and jigs every Thursday. Locals fill the **Boyd Arms,** 4 The Diamond (tel. 62364), in appreciation of folk music (Fri.). For the fast-paced, the weekend disco at the **Marine Hotel,** North St. (tel. 62222), provides entertainment (cover Sat. £4, Sun. £5). The hotel also organizes line dancing on Wednesday nights (£3/person).

SIGHTS

Just off the Diamond, **Boyd Church** raises its octagonal spire over a sandstone interior, most of which is covered by carpet. The Boyd family ruled Ballycastle through the 17th and 18th centuries. The town's development is largely attributed to Hugh Boyd (landlord 1727-1765). The **Ballycastle Museum** on Castle St. will take you by the hand to guide you through the town's history (open summer Mon.-Sat. noon-6pm; free). **Antiques and Galley,** 38 Quay Rd. (tel. 63078) shows and sells old things and paintings (open Mon.-Sat. 11:30am-6:30pm, Sun. 2:30-6pm). Outside town on the road from Cushendall, the **Bonamargy Friary** lies in ruins: the Mac-Donnell vault holds the remains of the first Earls of Antrim. Near the main entrance, a flat tombstone marks the **grave of the Black Nun.** As a sign of humility, Julia Mac-Quillan chose her grave here, where people would be forced to step on her.

Visitors to Ballycastle will be better off if they want to do things rather than just observe objects. **Christopher McCaughan,** 45 Ann St. (tel. 62074), goes fishing on summer nights in his boat, the *Lady Moyle,* and will be happy to have you on board. You could just **fish** off the pier, where pollock, mackerel, colefish, plaice, and cod abound (inquire at the tourist office about licenses). The old stone harbor, now filled with silt, has been covered with ten grass **tennis courts** and a **bowling green** near the beach (£1.40/hr., racket and ball rental 70p). **Celtic Journeys,** 111 Whitepark Rd. (tel. 69651), organizes afternoon rambles, day walks, and weekend trips around North Antrim, including Rathlin Island. Guides emphasize local wildlife and myths (prices vary).

On the last Monday and Tuesday of August, Ballycastle hosts Northern Ireland's oldest and most famous fair, the **Ould Lammas Fair.** The fair was originally a week-long fiesta but is now crammed into two, frenzied days. Continuing the traditions of the ancient Celtic harvest festival, the fair jams Ballycastle's streets with vendors selling cows, sheep, crafts, and baked goods. It packs pubs even more densely with traditional musicians. *Dulse* (nutritious seaweed dried on local roofs, reputedly good for the brain!) and *yellow-man* (sticky toffee made from a secret recipe) are two curiosities associated almost exclusively with the fair. Both are worth a try.

■ NEAR BALLYCASTLE

RATHLIN ISLAND (FORT OF THE SEA)

Just off the coast at Ballycastle, boomerang-shaped Rathlin Island is the ultimate in escapism for 20,000 puffins, the odd golden eagle, and about 100 human beings, including the famous Mary Black. Its windy surface can support few trees; its perimeter is lined with 200-foot cliffs. A leaflet, available at the Ballycastle tourist office, describes the island's walks and sights. A new **interpretive center** (no tel.) on Rathlin Island also has maps (10p) of walks to the extreme points of the island: East Lighthouse, West Lighthouse, and Rue (South) Lighthouse. The center gives an interesting display of the small island's interesting history (open daily 11am-5pm; free). While Rathlin makes a beautiful day-trip in nice weather, be warned that there is absolutely nothing to do in bad weather.

The island generates two-thirds of its own electricity with three wind turbines, visible from most parts of the island. Electricity was brought to the island as recently as September, 1992. The wind machines are named **Conn, Ardh,** and **Fiachra,** who were the three sons of mythical chieftain Lir. He was forced to spend 300 years in the Sea of Moyle after being cursed by the boys' wicked stepmother. Another legend claims that Robert the Bruce, a Scottish national hero, hid in one of the many caves underneath the east lighthouse after his defeat by the English in 1306. He was inspired by a spider who shared the cave. The arachnid tried enduringly to climb up its thread to the roof of the cave. The previously dispirited Robert returned to Scotland with renewed determination and won the Scottish throne.

A **minibus** (call Johnny Curry tel. (012657) 63905) sometimes runs from the pub to the **bird sanctuary** at the tip of the island (£2.50 return). The bus will wait while you take in the lighthouse area. The lighthouse itself is the best point from which to view birds, but it's usually locked. Call the warden (tel. (012657) 63935) in advance to gain entrance. The bus also makes occasional trips to Rue Point. Here, visitors can clamber over (and comb through) the remains of **Smuggler's House,** whose wall cavities supposedly hid contraband. Ironically, the official tax house is just yards away. Rathlin residents were known for their hatred of tax collectors who clogged their harbor (Ushet Port). Fair Head looms a few miles away and seals frolic here freely. No matter how good a swimmer you may be, don't try swimming to Fair Head. The currents are notoriously vile.

The island town has one pub and a few stores, all within 300 yards of the dock. **Mrs. McCurdy,** the Quay (tel. (012657) 63917), offers B&B from £13 (open March-Sept.). The **Richard Branson Dive/Holiday Centre,** the Harbour (tel. (012657) 63915), brings divers to the island. If there's extra space in their bunkroom, they may let you stay for £10 (B&B £12). The Holiday Centre is named after the hot-balloonist who crashed just short of Rathlin Island. Rumor has it that the island's lads battled strong currents to save him from drowning but refused to complete the rescue until he promised to donate money to Rathlin. **MacCraig's Bar** (tel. (012657) 63974) may also allow camping on its grounds. The bar—the single entertainment center for the entire island—takes care of the snacks (big sandwiches £1.10), pool (20p/game), video games, and on occasion discos and karaoke. The head of **Duncan,** Rathlin's last Highland bull who went loco and had to be shot, graces the wall of this otherwise normal looking pub. Spectacular views from the outdoor tables and opportunities for exchanging stories with locals and visitors alike are other notable features.

Two **ferries, Rathlin Venture** (tel. (012657) 63917) and **Iona Isle** (tel. (012657) 63901), run to the island daily from the pier at Ballycastle. (To Rathlin 10:30am, in summer also 12:15pm; from Rathlin 4pm, in summer also 6pm.) The ferries may leave early (or late), so passengers should arrive a few minutes early. (Single £3.30; £5.60 day return.)

BALLINTOY & CARRICK-A-REDE ISLAND

Five miles west of Ballycastle, the village of Ballintoy inspires smiles with a picturesque church and a tiny, equally attractive, harbor. Just off the coast, **Sheep Island** is home to puffins, razor bills, shag, and kittiwakes. It also has the largest cormorant colony in Ireland, none of which explains the island's name. Until recently, 11 sheep were taken to the island each year to graze—10 were thought to be too few (the sheep would get too fat) and 12 were thought too many (they would starve). Access to the island is now restricted to protect the nesting birds.

Smaller and better-known **Carrick-a-rede Island** lies offshore, to the east of Ballintoy. Carrick-a-rede means "rock in the road," a reminder of the fact that the island presents a barrier to migrating salmon returning to their home rivers. Fishermen have been setting up their nets for 350 years exactly at that point where the fish have to go around the island. To reach the nets, the fishermen string a rope bridge between the main road and the island. Crossing the flimsy bridge over the dizzying 80-foot drop to rocks and sea below is now a popular activity for tourists. Be extremely careful in windy weather, as the bridge has been known to flip over! A sign one mile east of Ballinatoy marks the turnoff for the bridge from the coast road.

The wildlife and walks on the island are just as interesting as the bridge is thrilling. Humans can get quite close to cliff-nesting black-and-white razor bills (which look like mini-penguins) as well as more mundane gulls. A fishing hut totters on the east side of the island, from which salmon nets stretch out into the sea. On a clear day, you can even see the Hebrides. The **National Trust Information Centre** (tel. (012657) 62178) on the mainland has info about the island. For 50p, they'll give you a certificate stating that you successfully crossed the bridge (open May-June daily 11am-6pm, July-Aug. daily 10am-6pm). The center has a convenient carpark (open April-Sept.; £1.50/car) and allows **camping** for one night only (tel. (012657) 62178 or 31159; £1.50/person; tent must be down by 10am; no facilities except toilets).

■■■ GIANT'S CAUSEWAY

Advertised as the eighth natural wonder of the world, the Giant's Causeway is deservedly Northern Ireland's most famous sight. In the absence of weekend crowds, it easily lives up to the reputation. 40,000 hexagonal columns of basalt form a honeycomb path from the foot of the cliffs far into the sea. Geologists have decided that the Causeway resulted from an unusually steady cooling of lava, which stimulated crystallization, but legend holds otherwise (see McCool Story, below).

The Causeway Visitors Centre (tel. (012657) 31855), near its head, caters to all needs. It sells an excellent leaflet of walks (45p) that will guide you the eight miles back to Whitepark Bay or along several shorter circular walks. Every 15 minutes, it also run minibuses the ½ mile to the columns (70p return). An audio-visual show informs the curious about the fact and fiction of the Causeway (£1, students 80p). (Centre open July-Aug. daily 10am-7pm, Sept.-June 10am-5pm. Causeway always open. £2/car to park in the lot, free just outside the center.) There are gift shops and tea rooms aplenty outside the center (tea room closes at 6:15pm). Many paths loop to and from the Causeway. Two leave the visitors center, one along the cliff and another along the coast. They merge after four miles. When making a circuit of the two, it's best to go out by the low road and return by the high one, as the lower one is by far more stunning. The well-tended track winds through naturally sculpted amphitheaters and inlets studded with bizarre, creatively named formations (such as the "organ"). Although not essential, the center's trail leaflet contains a helpful map and basic geological and human history. To see the Causeway itself in its full glory, it's necessary to at least go the 2½ miles to **Hamilton's Seat.**

McCool Story

Irish legend states that Finn McCool, the warrior giant, fell in love with a female giant on Staffa Island, off the Scottish coast. The devoted lover built the Causeway to bring her across to Ulster, a story which explains the existence of similar beehive-esque rock formations on Staffa. The legend continues to tell of McCool's desire to fight the Scottish giant Benandonner. But when he realized how big his Scottish rival was, McCool decided to use wit instead of brute force. The wily giant, with the help of his wife, disguised himself as an infant. When the Scottish giant saw the size of this Irish "baby", he was terrified by the anticipated proportions of the father. Benandonner quickly fled back to Scotland, destroying the Causeway on his return trip in order to ensure that the huge father McCool would never be able to cross the sea to challenge him.

WHITEPARK BAY

Two miles west of Ballintoy, just around the point from the harbor, lie the golden sands of Whitepark Bay, owned by the National Trust. A well-kept, cement-walled **YHANI Youth Hostel (HI)** (tel. (012657) 31745) overlooks this stunning beach. Two large dorms (each with about 20 beds) and two smaller 6-bed rooms constitute this easygoing hostel, so distant and different from those in the city. The lounge has a stunning ocean view in case you didn't get enough during the day. A major renovation will add 2-, 4-, and 6-bed rooms with baths to the existing dorms, but will also close the hostel from October 1995-April 1996. **Bike rental** is available here (£6/day; non-hostelers £8/day; deposit passport or credit card). And if you're biking or hiking between Whitepark Bay and Ma Cool's Hostel in Portrush, the angelic wardens will transport your pack. (Lockers 50p/day, deposit £2.50; wash and dry £2. Dorm £6.30, under 18 £5.30; non-members £7.50.) Buses from Portrush via the Giant's Causeway (daily 3/day) and from Ballycastle (daily 5/day) stop in front of the hostel on request. Every morning, hostelers set out for the Giant's Causeway, an easy four-mile hitch north along A2 or a rocky, sweaty eight miles along the windswept but rewarding **North Antrim Coastal Path.** Three miles from the hostel, you can proceed on four hooves (tel. (012657) 32764; **horses** £5/hr.; ask for directions at hostel).

BUSHMILLS

On its own merits, it's no slouch of a seacoast. Nevertheless, the shores west of Giant's Causeway and Whitepark Bay may seem comparatively tame and unpopular. Two miles west of the National Trust Visitors Centre, **Bushmills** remains the home of **Bushmills Irish Whiskey.** Distilling since 1609, the family-owned Bushmills is the oldest functioning whiskey producer in the world. The fact that Sir Thomas Phillips issued the distillery license to himself does not detract from the authenticity of the product. Indeed, in the 18th century, when roads were virtually non-existent, this was the only welcome respite gentlefolk could get on their travels. When the distillery is operating, you get to see actual whiskey being made. Production stops on occasion, but (less interesting) tours are still held. Around Christmas and the second week in October, both distilling and tours cease. For just £3000, you can buy a barrel of the Millennium Whisky scheduled to be opened in the year 2000. (Tel. (012657) 31521; tours, with free sample, every 15 min.; June-Aug. Mon.-Thurs. 9am-noon and 1:30-4pm, Fri. 9am-4pm, Sat. 10am-4pm; Sept.-May Mon.-Thurs. 9am-noon and 1:30-3:30pm, Fri. 9-noon; £2.)

■■■ PORTRUSH

By day, Portrush's merry-go-rounds, water slides, and arcades go full-throttle as throngs of Irish vacationers roam the streets and its two beaches. By night, however, the same roaring hordes produce some of the North's best nightlife, with live music nightly in at least one pub in town. Portstewart's beaches and the Giant's Causeway are within easy cycling distance.

PRACTICAL INFORMATION

Tourist Office: Dunluce Centre, (tel. 823333), on the way to town. Dead posh. They won't hold your pack but will answer your questions. 24-hr. computerized info outside. Open June-Sept. daily 9am-8pm, Oct.-May Mon.-Sat. 9am-5pm, Sun. noon-5pm.

Banks: First Trust, 25 Eglinton St. (tel. 822726). Open Mon.-Fri. 9:30am-4:30pm; **ATM. Ulster Bank,** 33 Eglinton St. (tel. 823730). Open Sept.-June Mon.-Fri. 9:30am-12:30pm and 1:30-4:30pm; July and Aug. Mon.-Fri. 9:30am-4:30pm; **ATM.**

Post Office: 23 Eglinton St. (tel. 823700). Open Mon.-Tues. and Thurs.-Fri. 9am-12:30pm and 1:30-5:30pm, Wed. 9am-1pm, Sat. 9am-12:30pm. **Postal code:** BT56 8DX.

Phone Code: 01265.

Trains: Station: Eglington St., (tel. 822395), in the center of town. Carriages from Belfast (Mon.-Sat. 8/day, Sun. 2/day; 2hr.; £5.90, £9 return) and Derry (Mon.-Sat. 7/day, Sun. 2/day).

Buses: Dunluce St. (tel. 824065). Regular buses to Portstewart (30/day; 13 min.; 90p). Ulsterbus #172 (4/day) runs along the coast to Bushmills (20 min.), the Giant's Causeway (25 min.), and Ballycastle (1hr.). The open-topped Bushmills bus (#177) goes to Portstewart, Bushmills, and the Giant's Causeway in good weather (daily 5/day). **Ulsterbus** also has day tours to Ards Peninsula (£8), Roe Valley (£4), and Silent Valley (£7.50); inquire at tourist office or bus station.

Taxis: tel. 822777 or 824901.

Bike Rental: Causeway Coast Cycles, 6 Bath St. (tel. 824334). £5/day, £30/week; deposit £30.

Surfing Equipment: Atlantic Drive & Surf, 102 Main St. (tel 823273). Rent or buy. Surfboard £8/day, wetsuit £8/day; deposit credit card.

Early closing day: Sept.-June on Wednesday; July-Aug. none.

Pharmacy: Heron Chemist, 5-9 Main St. (tel. 822324). Open daily 9am-11pm.

Emergency: Dial 999; no coins required. **Police:** tel. 822721.

ACCOMMODATIONS

Except for the YHANI hostel in Whitepark Bay, Portrush is the best place to stay before or after seeing the Giant's Causeway. If anything can, **Ma Cool's Hostel,** 5 Causeway View Terrace (tel. 824 845), can make staying in Portrush a pleasure. Friendly hostelers and wardens gather in the common room to exchange travel stories. (Free coffee; microwave; wash and dry £2; dorm £6.) From the bus stop, a left onto Dunluce St., then a right onto Eglinton St., then another quick left onto Mark St. (it runs into Causeway View Terrace) will bring you to your home away from home. From the train station, Mark St. is the second left after turning right out of the station. Though there are no signs on the way, the hostel *will* appear not long after Mark St. crosses Main St.

Portrush supports so many B&Bs that tourists seem a more common breed than residents. Nearly every other townhouse along Mark St., Kerr St., and Mount Royal is a B&B. Most are indistinguishable in size, character, and price. **Atlantis,** 10 Ramore Ave. (tel. 824583), offers an ocean view in a comparatively quiet neighborhood. Use of the kitchen and free tea and coffee are added bonuses (high season £13/person, low season £11/person). **Causeway House,** 26 Kerr St. (tel. 824847), is central to the hubbub (high season £13/person, low season £12.50/person).

FOOD

The proliferation of fast food in Portrush may seem all-encompassing, but a few good restaurants hide amid the neon. If you're not up to the search, stock up on groceries at **Cost-Cutter,** Main St. (tel. 823715; open Mon.-Fri. 9am-7pm, Sat. 9am-6pm, Sun. 10am-5pm).

Dionysus, 53 Eglinton St. (tel. 823855). Godlike Greek food. Lots of vegetarian and vegan dishes. All entrees £4.75. Open Mon.-Sat. 5:30-10pm, Sun. 5:30-9:30pm.

Ramore Restaurant and Wine Bar, the Harbour (tel. 823444). An elegant and expensive treat. Delicious, creative homemade breads are a specialty. Chicken cordon bleu £8. Open Tues.-Sat. 6:30-10:30pm.

The Singing Kettle, 315 Atlantic Ave. Comfortable coffee shop could become a favorite. Sells exotic burgers and sandwiches. Garlic mushrooms in homemade roll £1.75. Vegetarian version of Ulster fry £3. Banana milkshake 95p. Charmingly (or maybe frustratingly) vague opening hours, but typically open daily 10am-6pm.

Boogies' Diner, 47 Eglinton St., (tel. 822561). American-style 50s diner. Open Mon., Thurs., and Sat. 11am-2am, Tues.-Wed., Fri., and Sun. 11am-9pm.

PUBS & ENTERTAINMENT

The **Harbour Bar,** 5 Harbour Rd. (tel. 825047), is a spit-in-the-sawdust sailors' pub, popular with the locals. The adjacent Harbour Inn also serves good pub grub. At the other end of the social spectrum, **Ramore Wine Bar,** the Harbour (tel. 823444), offers harbor-side elegance. The **Alpha Bar,** 63 Eglinton St. (tel. 823889), the **Atlantic Bar,** and adjacent **McNally's,** Atlantic Ave. (tel. 822727), all have Irish charm and superior *craic.* The **Londonderry Hotel** (more commonly called the **Derry**), Main St. (tel. 823693), next to the Atlantic and McNally's, is the place to be on Saturdays, but **Shunter's,** in the railway station, draws crowds on Tuesdays.Partiers make tracks for **Traks Nightclub,** at the railway station (tel. 822112; cover charge). Popular **Station Bar** (tel. 823509), next door, pounds the drums.

Finish your evening (or begin your morning) at a Portrush institution, **Beetles Bar and Disco** (a.k.a. Kelly's; tel. 823539), just outside Portrush on the Bushmills Rd. Kelly's has not one, but *eleven* bars and *three* discos (from punk to house to '70s funk). Excessive and sometimes downright tacky, every sector of youth culture in Northern Ireland fits in somewhere here. (Regular rave nights.)

Northern Irish theater companies travel to Portrush to present their acts on the **Summer Theatre** stage (tel. 822500), in the old town hall. (Nightly shows at 8pm; tickets £4; box office open in summer Mon.-Sun. 10:30am-12:30pm and 6:30-8pm.)

SIGHTS

The biggest sight around—the Giant's Causeway—isn't even here. The most widely advertised attraction in Portrush itself is the over-hyped **Dunluce Centre,** Dunluce Arcade (tel. 824444), which tries to capitalize on every fact or story. Moving seats in the Turbo Tours theater make Dino Island that much more real. A multimedia presentation on local folklore will not knock your socks off. For 50p you can climb a squat tower to look at the view. (Open June-Aug. daily 10am-10pm; Sept. Mon.-Thurs. 11am-6pm, Fri.-Sun. 11am-10pm; Oct.-Dec. weekends 2-7pm. Turbo Tours £2, off-peak £1.75; whole center £4, off-peak £3.50.) In refreshing contrast, the understated **Countryside Centre,** 8 Bath Rd. (tel. 823600), on the waterfront, is small but lovingly cared for. The assortment of displays includes wildlife exhibits, a tide pool with sea urchins and starfish, and loads of old pictures. A (free) viewing platform outside can help identify the many land masses in the distance (open June-Sept. Wed.-Mon. noon-8pm, Tues. noon-5pm.; viewing platform always open).

■ NEAR PORTRUSH: PORTSTEWART

Thoughtful town planning has saved this smaller town from Portrush's garish fate, but by no means is Portstewart any less crowded than its larger neighbor. Carnival lights are the only thing resembling the merry-go-round mentality of Portrush vacationers. A fantastic beach, popular with surfers, and a popular pub bring more hip throngs to Portstewart. At high tide the sea comes right up to the wall of the main street. A path to the beach runs around the convent on the main street.

Portstewart's tiny **tourist office,** Town Hall (tel. 832 286), opens only for the summer tourists (open Mon.-Sat. 10am-1pm and 1:30-4pm). **First Trust,** 13 the Promenade (tel. 833723), offers financial services inside and out at the **ATM.** The **post office,** 90 the Promenade (tel. 832001) does the usual (open Mon.-Fri. 9:30am-4:30pm). A pharmacy distributes plasters at **Super Chem,** the Promenade (tel. 833844; open Mon.-Sat. 9am-9pm, Sun. noon-9pm). **Not Just Books,** 49 the Promenade (tel. 834600), sells old stamps and prints as well as the usual assortment of books (open Mon.-Sat. 11am-10pm). **Buses** coming into town stop on the Promenade. Portstewart's **phone code** is 01265.

Accommodations, Food & Pubs The Victoria Terrace area, on the left as you head out of town on the Portrush Rd., is laden with beds. From the bus stop, face the sea, turn right, and follow Main St. around the corner. Victoria Terrace juts out to the left. The **Causeway Coast Independent Hostel,** 4 Victoria Terrace (tel. 833789), is friendly and comfortable if not luxurious. Free laundry and immediate access to ice cream (dorm £5, double £6.50/person; sheets sometimes 50p). **Salem,** 5 Atlantic Circle (tel. 834584), provides B&B at £13/person.

Surprisingly good cooks live in Portstewart, which also cultivates a tradition of superb ice cream. **Mace Supermarket,** on the Promenade, has the usual groceries and tons of cheeses (open Mon.-Sat. 8:30am-11pm). **Good Food and Co.,** 44 the Promenade (tel. 836386), makes quiche (80p), sandwiches, breads, and pastries (open Mon.-Sat. 9am-10pm; Sept.-June Mon.-Sat. 9am-6pm). **Ashiana Tandoori Restaurant,** 12 the Diamond (tel. 834455), offers exotic evening meals. Curry-starved tourists indulge themselves in inexpensive Indian food (king prawn curry madras £4.95; open Mon.-Thurs. 12pm-midnight, Fri.-Sat. 5pm-2am, Sun. 5-11pm). Sixty-three steps above the Promenade, **Cassioni's** (tel. 834777) serves its beloved pizza, pasta, and more (open daily 5-11pm). **Morelli's Sundae Garden,** the Promenade (tel. 832150), is infamous for its superb high-calorie and sugar concoctions and their creative names, like the pink panther waffle (Irish beauty sundae £3.10, single scoops available; open daily 9:30am-11:30pm). **The Chocolate Strawberry,** the Promenade (tel. 833377), serves hot food only during mealtimes (lasagne £3; noon-2:30pm and 5-7:30pm), but "Bananarama" milkshakes are always available. Most of the town and all of its students head for the **Anchor Pub,** 87 the Promenade (tel. 832003), to put back some pints by the fire. Summer Wednesdays bring live rock and roll, while term-time Mondays see folk night. The upstairs **disco** pounds all year (Mon.-Sat. 10pm-1am; cover Fri. and Sat. £1.50).

Sights Portstewart has a high road and a low: one coastal walk to Portrush and one path along the **cliffs** to the convent (the big white building with the cross). **The Strand,** ½ mile west of town, is owned and preserved in all its long beauty by the National Trust. A small but dedicated group of surfers call the waters around here and Portrush home. For those who dare to try out the Irish waves, **Ocean Warriors** (tel. 836500), located at the intersection of the road to the beach and the Promenade, rents wetsuits (£4/5 hr.), surf boards (£10/½-day), and body boards (£3/½-day). According to locals, September brings the best surfing on 8- to 10-foot waves. Kowabunga, dude. The **Flowerfield Arts Centre,** 185 Coleraine Rd. (tel. 833959), shelters traveling art exhibitions, holds frequent lectures on subjects ranging from local history and folklore to the royal family, and hosts jazz concerts (£4). Sand sculptures are also displayed in appropriate weather.

■■■ DERRY CITY

Derry's long and troubled history has given rise to powerful popular symbols used by both sides of the sectarian conflict. The siege of Derry in 1689 created Protestant folk heroes out of the "Apprentice Boys," who closed the city gates on the advancing armies of the Catholic King James II. More recently, the violence of the early 70s reached a pinnacle in "Bloody Sunday," so-called by Republicans as a symbol of what they see as continuing British tyranny. Even the city's name has strong political associations. The Northern and British governments call it, officially, "Londonderry," as do many Northern Protestants. Catholics and the Catholic-majority City Council call the city "Derry." The shorter name, used colloquially by some Protestants, is less politically charged and is the preferred usage for visitors to the city.

For all this, modern Derry is in the middle of a determined and largely successful effort to cast off the legacy of the Troubles, or "Bothers" as they're known here. With the ceasefire and foreign investment rolling in, it seems that Derry residents can entertain a realistic hope of prosperity and consensus. Most parts of the city, and especially the downtown area, show evidence of Derry's rapid development. Construction and commerce are booming there. The recent success of "Impact '92," a huge festival celebrating cultural diversity, did much to improve the city's image and morale, as well as successfully revitalizing the tourist industry. Five sons of Derry called The Undertones were one of the world's best and catchiest rock and roll bands between 1977 and 1981. Derry's rock scene is still thriving; gig posters crowd any available wall. While its controversial history is one of Derry's more fasci-

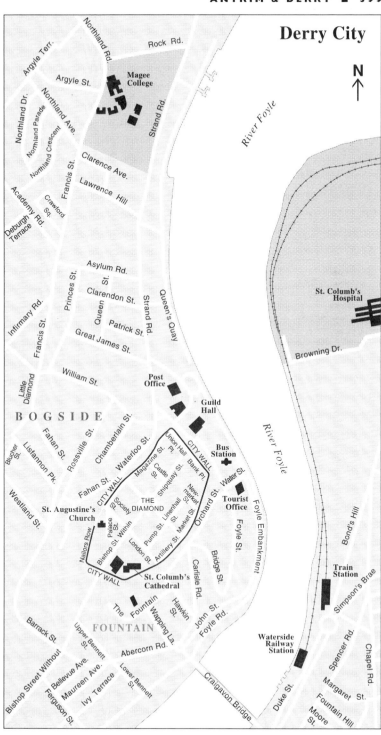

Derry City

N

nating characteristics, its brilliant rock scene and the improving cultural scene are attractions in their own right.

ORIENTATION & PRACTICAL INFORMATION

Downtown Derry denotes the old city within the walls plus the pedestrianized shopping district around Waterloo St., just northwest of the walls. The grid layout of inner Derry's streets resembles the geometrical construction of many modern cities, noticeably New York City. Inside the old city, four main streets connect the four main gates (Bishop's Gate, Ferryquay Gate, Shipquay Gate, and Butcher's Gate) to the central square—the **Diamond.** The university area can be reached by taking a left off Strand Rd. just past Strand Bar. The **Bogside** neighborhood is west of the walls. The Protestant **Waterside** neighborhood, with the train station, has settled across Craigavon Bridge, on the east shore of the River Foyle.

Tourist Office: 8 Bishop St. (tel. 267284). The nonetheless friendly staff doesn't give recommendations but does distribute the truly useful *Derry Tourist Guide* and free but illegible maps. **Bord Fáilte** keeps a desk here, too (tel. 369501). Open July-Aug. Mon.-Sat. 9am-8pm, Sun. 10am-6pm; Oct.-June Mon.-Thurs. 9am-5:15pm, Fri. 9am-5pm.

Budget Travel: USIT, Ferryquay St. (tel. 371888). ISICs, YHANI, and HI cards, and Travelsave stamps. Open Mon.-Fri. 9:30am-5:30pm, Sat. 10am-1pm.

Banks: First Trust, Shipquay St. (tel. 363921); open Mon.-Fri. 9:30am-4:30pm. **Bank of Ireland,** Shipquay (tel. 264141); open Mon.-Wed. and Fri. 10am-3:30pm, Thurs. 9:30am-5pm. **Northern Bank,** Guildhall Sq. (tel. 265333); open Mon.-Wed. and Fri. 10am-3:30pm, Thurs. 9:30am-5pm. All have **ATMs.** The **Richmond Centre,** a shopping center next to the Diamond (tel. 260636), has a bureau de change; open Mon.-Wed. 9am-5:30pm, Thurs.-Fri. 9am-9pm, Sat. 9am-6pm.

Post Office: 3 Custom House St. (tel. 362274). Open Mon. 8:30am-5:30pm, Tues.-Fri. 9am-5:30pm, Sat. 9am-12:30pm. Unless addressed to 3 Custom House St. *poste restante* letters will go to the Postal Sorting Office (tel. 362577) on the corner of Great James St. and Little James St. **Postal Code:** BT48 6AA.

Phone Code: 01504.

Eglinton/Derry Airport: Eglinton (tel. 810784). 7 mi. from Derry. Flights to Manchester, Glasgow, Jersey, London, Birmingham, Edinburgh, and Dublin.

Trains: Duke St., the Waterside (tel. 42228), on the east bank. Trains from Derry only go east, to Coleraine, Ballymena, Lisbum, and Belfast (Mon.-Fri. 7/day, Sat. 6/day, Sun. 3/day; to Belfast 2½hr.; £7). A sideline from Coleraine zips north to Portrush. No rail lines connect Derry to the Republic.

Buses: Foyle St., between the walled city and the river. **Ulsterbus** (tel. 262261) serves all destinations in Northern Ireland and some in the Republic. To: Belfast (Mon.-Fri. 12/day, Sat. 9/day, Sun. 6/day; 1½-3hr.; £5.50); Enniskillen (Mon.-Fri. 5/day, Sat. 3/day, Sun. 1/day; 2½hr.; £5); Dublin (Mon.-Sat. 3/day, Sun. 2/day); Galway (Mon.-Sat. 4/day, Sat.-Sun. 2/day; 5½hr.); Letterkenny (Mon.-Sat. 4/day, Sat.-Sun. 2/day; 40 min.); Donegal Town (Mon.-Sat. 4/day, Sat.-Sun. 2/day; 1½hr.); and Sligo (Mon.-Sat. 4/day, Sat.-Sun. 2/day; 2½hr.). **Lough Swilly** private bus service (tel. 262017) heads to Inishowen, Letterkenny, and the Fanad Peninsula. Buses to: Malin Head (Mon.-Sat. 3/day; 1½hr.; £6); Letterkenny (Mon.-Sat. 11/day, Sun. 8/day; 1hr.); Buncrana (Mon.-Fri. 10/day, Sat. 12/day, Sun. 4/day; 35 min.). **Northwest Busways** (tel. (0035377) 82619) has offices in the Republic. Buses depart Derry from Patrick St., opposite the Multiplex Cinema, for Inishowen.

Taxi: Quick Cabs, Custom House St. (tel. 260515). **Tower Taxis,** Bishop St. (tel. 371944). Derry also has a fleet of **black cabs** (tel. 260247) with set routes, though it's neither as extensive nor as famous as the Belfast black cab system.

Car Rental: Ford Rent-a-Car, Desmond Motors Ltd., 173 Strand Rd. (tel. 360420). £36.75/day, £183.75/week; deposit £180. Must be over 25. Open Mon.-Fri. 9am-1pm and 2-5:30pm. Weekend package: Fri. 4pm-Mon. 9am, £73.50.

Bike Rental: Rent-A-Bike, Magazine St. (tel. 372273), at the YHANI hostel. £6/first day, £5/additional day, £30/week; deposit passport or £50.

Laundry: Duds 'n' Suds, 141 Strand Rd. (tel. 266006). Pool table and big screen TV. Wash £1.50, dry £1.50. Open Mon.-Fri. 8am-9pm, Sat. 8am-8pm.

Women's Centre, 24 Pump St. (tel 267672). Open Mon.-Fri. 9:30am-5pm.

Bisexual, Gay, and Lesbian Information: Carafriend Counselling (tel. 263120). Open Thurs. 7:30-10pm.

Disabled Services: Disability Action, 58 Strand Rd. (tel. 360811), serves the physically or mentally disabled.

Hotline: Samaritans, 16 Clarendon St. (tel 265511). Open 10am-8pm. Phone service 24 hrs., all year.

Pharmacy: Connor's Pharmacy, 3a/b Strand Rd., (tel. 264502). Open Mon.-Wed. 9am-5:30pm, Thurs.-Fri. 9am-9pm, Sat. 9am-6pm.

Hospital: Altnagelvin Hospital, Glenshane Rd. (tel. 45171).

Emergency: Dial 999; no coins required. **Police:** Strand Rd. (tel 367337).

ACCOMMODATIONS

Oakgrove Manor is the only acceptable hostel in Derry City. The Muff Hostel, just across the River Foyle in the Republic, is also a good choice. If these are both full, university housing and the YMCA are farther but will satisfy your needs.

Oakgrove Manor (YHANI/HI), Magazine St. (tel. 372273). A colorful mural on the side of the building identifies this modern, spacious, and institutional hostel. Centrally located. Not always well supervised. Curfew 2am, checkout 10am strictly enforced. Scantily-equipped kitchen with harsh fluorescent lights. Laundry in basement: wash 60p, dry 60p, powder 50p. Sheets 50p; towels 50p; pool table 20p. Ulster fry £2.50, continental breakfast £1.50. Large dorm £8.70; single w/shower and breakfast £15; double w/shower and breakfast £28.

Muff Hostel, Muff, Co. Donegal, Republic of Ireland (from the North, tel. (00 353 77) 84188). Just 5 mi. outside Derry, this friendly hostel combines the best of two worlds: relaxed and solacing accommodation in the country for the evening and easy access to the busy city during the day. Martin Cooke's invigorating welcome will keep you here for days. Lough Swilly buses leave Foyle St. in Derry for Muff (Mon.-Fri. 8/day, Sat. 7/day, last bus 6:10pm; 60p, 75p return).

Magee College, Northland Rd. (tel. 265621, ext. 5233). Truly institutional dorms. Free showers, kitchens, and laundry available during Easter week and again mid-May to Sept. Mandatory reservations accepted Mon.-Fri. 9am-5pm (rooms are available for weekends, but you must arrive during office hours). Single £6, double £10. Take the Ballygoarty or Rosemont bus from Foyle St., or walk ½ mi. up Strand Rd. and turn left after the Strand Bar.

YMCA, 51 Glenshane Rd. (tel. 301662), 3 mi. from city center. Accepts both sexes into an old house with clean but starkly furnished bedrooms. £5/person. Open mid-July to mid-Sept. From Foyle St. take the Tullyalley bus down Glenshane Rd.

Florence House, 16 North Land Rd. (tel. 268093). Large, sunny bedrooms in a townhouse around the corner from the university. £14/person.

Joan Pyne, 36 Great James St. (tel. 269691). Small flowery rooms shelter tired souls back from popular Bogside pubs, just minutes away. £15/person, w/bath £17.

Grace McGoldrick, 10 Crawford Sq. (tel.265000). In the middle of it all and often full of contented guests. Single £15, double £28.

FOOD

Restaurants, mostly around the walled city, tend to be expensive. Take-aways and cafés are a better option. Wellsworth **supermarket,** Waterloo Pl., is in the pedestrianized shopping district around the corner from the post office (open Mon.-Tues. and Sat. 9am-5:30pm, Wed.-Fri. 9am-9pm). **Scoop-A-Market,** 19 Strand Rd. (tel. 262939), sells health foods and dispenses free recipe hints (open Mon.-Thurs. 9am-6pm, Fri. 9am-9pm, Sat. 9am-6pm).

Freddy's Bistro, Castle St. (tel. 373222), around the corner from the hostel. Creative food in a funky atmosphere includes lots of veggie options. Indonesian meatballs with spiced yogurt and rice £5, veggie stir-fry £3. Bring your own wine. Open Mon.-Sat. 11am-10pm, plus summer Sundays 1-8pm.

The Sandwich Co., the Diamond (tel. 372500), corner of Ferryquay St. and Bishop St. Freshly constructed sandwiches (£1-2.45, smoked salmon supreme £1.85). Live folk music in summer, Fri. at 4pm. Open Mon.-Sat. 8:3am-5pm.

Bewley's, Shipquay St. (tel. 372512). This café has velvety seats and much to remind you of Dublin (lunch specials £3.85 noon-3pm). Open Mon.-Wed. and Sat. 9am-6pm, Thurs.-Fri. 9am-8pm, Sun. 11am-5:30pm.

Rafters Restaurant, Northwest Rd. (tel. 372819). Kudos to that vegetarian food.

Boston Tea Party, 13 Craft Village (tel. 264568). Wrought-iron tables and flowered curtains are ever so quaint. Every July 4, diners throw the flowered curtains into the River Foyle with merriment and war-whoops. Open daily 9am-5:30pm.

Anne's Hot Bread Shop, William St. (tel 269236), in the Bogside. A Derry institution. Open late, late, late. Big portions, no frills. How long does bread have to be heated until it becomes toast? Open daily 8am-3am.

PUBS

Derry may not satisfy every craving at dinner, but it compensates with a superb drinking scene, in quality *and* quantity. Trad and rock music flare up most nights.

The Dungloe, 41-43 Waterloo St. (tel. 267716). Loved all around. Almost nightly trad music downstairs (10pm). Live blues or rock or even "alternative" discos upstairs (cover £1-2; 11pm).

Peadar O'Donnell's, 63 Waterloo St. (tel. 372318). An old-style pub named, in traditional style, for the famous Donegal man who organized the Irish Transport and General Workers Union and took an active role in the 1921 Irish Civil War. Bric-a-brac crowds the walls. Bric-a-brac crowd of all ages fills the benches.

The Gweedore Bar, 59-61 Waterloo St. (tel. 263513). Next door to Peadar's, this Victorian pub imitation offers trad, rock, and bluegrass most weekends. The tourist lure extends to an assortment of Guinness memorabilia, and some is for sale.

The Carraig Bar, 113-119 Strand Rd. (tel. 267529), or "Rock." Destroyed by a bomb in 1973, no signs of the violence remain in the splendid Victorian bar with stained glass. Lively, friendly students. Discos Wed.-Sat. Please look and be cool.

Bound for Boston, Waterloo St. Busy, full of young people. Tues. trad sessions and occasional rock and blues downstairs (no cover); disco Sat. and Sun. and alternative or reggae bands other nights upstairs (cover £2). Why the Derry obsession with Boston? As they advertise, "Bring a towel and your dancing slacks."

The River Inn and **Gluepot,** (tel. 267463). These two adjoining pubs on Shipquay together occupy the site of "the oldest bar in Ireland." The River Inn often has music, but the Gluepot is stickier.

The Townsman Bar, 33 Shipquay St. (tel. 260820). Hip folk squeeze together to fit into this popular pub. The original interior is from an old chemist shop, complete with ghastly 19th-century medical tools. A low front bar contrasts nicely with the French country house behind. A comfortable attic room tops the list.

SIGHTS

Harry Bryson's animation and his love for the city he claims never to have left make for an entertaining (though far from impartial) **walking tour.** Amusing and shocking anecdotes constitute a good part of the tour's substance. (Tour leaves from the tourist office June-Aug. Mon.-Fri. 10:30am and 2:30pm; 1½hr.; £1.50. Sept.-May call tel. 365151 ext. 307 or the tourist office to arrange a tour.) **Foyle Civic Bus Tours,** presented by Ulsterbus, run a circuit of six stops, including the University, Guild Hall, and St. Eugene's Cathedral (July-Aug. Tues. and Thurs. 2pm; £3).

Derry's earliest associations are religious. It was both a Celtic holy place (the name Derry comes from the Old Irish *daire,* meaning "sacred oak grove") and site of a monastery founded by St. Columcille (kol-um-KEEL) in the 6th century. The city itself was built as the crowning achievement of the Ulster Plantations at the beginning of the 17th century. After the "Flight of the Earls" in 1607, when the O'Neill and O'Donnell chieftains fled to Europe, much of Ulster was left without local leaders. The English seized the moment and asserted their mastery of the area by taking land from the native Catholic residents and granting it to Protestant settlers from England and Scotland. Derry itself was granted to the London guilds, which built the walled city of "London"-derry. After withstanding several rebellions by the displaced local Catholics, the city experienced the famous 105-day siege in 1689. In addition to the beloved Apprentice Boys, the siege created a villain for present-day Protestants to revile. **Robert Lundy,** the city's leader who advocated surrender during the siege, is labeled a traitor. His effigy is still burnt every year at an August 12th ceremony commemorating the closing of the gates. A reviled and grotesque caricature can be seen in the Tower Museum (see below).

In the 18th and 19th centuries, Derry became an industrial center for port and linen. As the River Foyle receded, working-class settlements developed outside the walls. Partition made Derry a border city, and a Catholic majority made it a headache for Unionist leaders and the locus of some of the most blatant discrimination. The civil rights marches that sparked off the Troubles originated here in 1968. "Free Derry" (the western, Catholic part of the city, controlled by the IRA and a "no-go area" for the army from 1969-72), "Bloody Sunday" (Jan. 30, 1972, when British troops fired on demonstrators and killed 14), and "Operation Motorman" (the July 1972 army effort to penetrate the "no-go" area and arrest IRA leaders) became powerful logos for Derry Catholics and Republicans everywhere. While the protestant and Catholic communities are still sharply divided, recent years have seen them coexisting peacefully. Moves to mix religions in the Derry school system may someday unify civil society—when today's 5-year-olds are all grown up.

The Walls

Eighteen feet high and 20 feet thick, Derry's city walls were erected between 1614 and 1619. They've never been breached or attacked, hence the nickname "the Maiden City." The walls are accessible in their entirety to the public. Wherever there are steps, visitors can freely climb to the top. Seven **cannons** along the northeast wall, between Magazine Gate and Shipquay Gate, were donated by Queen Elizabeth I and the London Guilds who "acquired" the city during the Ulster Plantation. A plaque on the outside of this section of wall marks the water level of the Foyle in the days when it ran right along the walls. (It's now 300 feet away.) The stone tower along the southeast wall, past New Gate, was built to protect **St. Columb's Church,** sheltered inside the wall.

Stuck in the center of the southwest wall, **Bishop's Gate** was remodeled in 1689 into an ornate triumphal gate in honor of King William III, the Protestant contestant in the battles of 1689. Bishop's Gate is accessible only on foot—its closeness to the courthouse means that cars (possibly carrying carbombs) are prohibited. The **northwest wall** supports a massive cannon, "Roaring Meg," which was donated by London fishmongers in 1642 and used in the 1689 siege. The sound of the cannon alone was rumored to be enough to strike fear into the hearts of enemies. The massive marble platform that stands here now was built to hold a marble statue of the Rev. George Walker, joint-governor of Derry (and one of the threatening individuals) during the siege. The first statue placed here of the joint-governor was blown up in 1973. Its replacement was ready in 1992, but hours before its unveiling an anonymous phone call threatened to blow the new one up if it were placed overlooking the Bogside. The authorities backed down, and the marble Rev. Walker II now stands securely within the city walls. His platform is currently being converted to add to the viewpoints already existing on the city walls. A bit farther, between Royal Bastion and Butcher's Gate, lurks **Memorial Hall** where the modern-day Apprentice Boys have their headquarters. They still maintain the traditions of the 13 Guild apprentices who shut the city gates thereby launching the Great Siege of Derry.

Within the Walls

The tall spire of **St. Columb's Cathedral,** Bishop St. (tel. 267313), is visible from almost any nook or cranny in Derry. The cathedral shouldn't be confused with less grand St. Columba's Church outside the walls, which commemorates the same saint in different orthography. Built between 1625 and 1633, St. Columb's Cathedral was the first Protestant Cathedral in Britain or Ireland (all the older ones were actually confiscated Catholic Cathedrals). The original spire is thought to have been made of wood coated with lead. But during the Great Siege, the lead was removed and smelted into bullets and cannonballs, resulting in the steeple's present stony appearance. The interior is fashioned of roughly-hewn stone and holds an exquisite Killybegs altar carpet, a bishop's chair dating from 1630, and hand-carved oak pew ends, of which no two are the same. A tiny, museum-like **chapterhouse** at the back of the church also displays some curiosities: the original locks and keys for the four main city gates, part of Macaulay's *History of England*, and relics from the 1689 siege. Outside in the graveyard, the tombstones lie flat on the ground. They were leveled in an attempt to protect the graves from defacement by Jacobite cannonballs during the siege. (Open Mon.-Sat. 10am-5pm. Cathedral free, chapterhouse 50p. Call ahead to arrange a free cathedral tour.)

Just outside Shipquay Gate stands the neo-Gothic **Guildhall** (tel. 365151), home to the City Council. First built in 1890, wrecked by fire in 1908, and destroyed by bombs in 1972, today's structure contains replicas of the original stained-glass windows. Those in the main hall depict one version of the history of Derry. Among the bountiful rarities is the Mayor's chain of office, which was officially presented to the city by William III. (Open Mon.-Fri. 9am-5pm; free tours July-Aug. 9:30am-4:30pm.) The Guildhall also sponsors various concerts, plays, and exhibitions throughout the year. A more detailed history of Derry is revealed at the award-winning **Tower Museum,** just inside Magazine Gate (tel. 372411). A series of short videos and written explanations teach you more than you ever wanted to know. The last video presents an engaging and unbiased summary of the city's recent turbulent past. The whole museum deserves at least 1½ hours of exploration. (Open Tues.-Sat. 10am-1pm and 2-5pm; last entrances 12:30 and 4:30pm. £2.75, students £1.)

The **Derry Craft Village** was designed in the medieval style. It was built by entrepreneurial youth from the Bogside in an abandoned lot from cast-away building materials. The village encompasses cafés, craft shops, and **Bridie's Cottage.** The cottage will give you "A Taste of Ireland," an evening of Irish song, dance, and storytelling (Tuesday, Thursday, and Saturday 8:30pm). **Teach Ceoil (Music House)** hosts informal *ceili* in the same building on Wednesdays and Fridays; the £5 fee includes supper and traditional bread and tea. (To book, call Mary McLaughlin tel. 269033.)

Outside the Walls

Down by the river near Craigavon Bridge, the **Foyle Valley Railway Centre** (tel. 265234) promises to be a fantastic sight—someday. The old steam railway station gives a small but colorful tribute to the Golden Age of Train Tracks, when four railway systems, instead of the current one, met in Derry. A steam train chugs 1½ uneventful miles down a track and right back again. (Open April-Sept. Tues.-Sat. 10am-5pm, Sun. 2-6pm; Oct.-March Tues.-Sat. 10am-5pm. Collection free; train ride £2 on weekends.) **Magee College,** 15 minutes east of city center, has been a part of the University of Ulster since October 1984. Magee changed allegiances several times. Originally, in 1879, a member of the Royal University of Ireland, by 1909 it had become part of Trinity College in Dublin. A grassy carpet is laid before the main building, on a high hill. Built in 1865, the neo-Gothic building shines among its clumsy neighbors.

Brilliant **murals** in both Protestant and Catholic neighborhoods remind anyone who cares to look that Derry's recent turbulent history is far from over. Especially since the ceasefire, the areas which contain this genre of pop art are safer than many big American cities, though there is something of a watchful, cautious feeling in the streets. Tourists must, however, remember not to photograph police, soldiers, or military installations. The famously Protestant sections of Derry are **Waterside,** to the east of the River Foyle, and the **Fountain Estate,** west of the river. The Fountain is reached from the walled city by exiting through the left side of Bishop's Gate.

Though Waterside is more populous, the Fountain holds the better Protestant murals and curb paintings. Some Loyalist murals grace the Waterside along Bond St. and Irish St. Most of the murals convey clear meanings (see The Falls, p. 360).

The best-known Catholic neighborhood, the **Bogside,** is easily recognizable. A huge mural, just west of the city walls at the junction of Fahan St. and Rossville Square, declares "Welcome to Free Derry." The politically loaded phrase is sometimes used by activists to describe the Bogside and Creggan areas. The mural has recently been expanded to mark various significant events, including Derry's victory in the 1993 All-Ireland Gaelic Football Competition. Nearby, a stone monument commemorates the 14 protesters shot on Bloody Sunday. Many of the other murals in this neighborhood are also memorials to Bloody Sunday, which became a symbol of the British Army's behavior during the Troubles. They can be found along the street that proceeds from the first right (at the Bogside Inn) past the "Free Derry" mural. The better murals are in the housing projects on either side of the street. On the back of the community center on the left, murals reflect on the role of the "Bothers" in the daily life of Derry. They depict children playing amid murals and memorials. In both Belfast and Derry, peace groups have lately organized children of all religions to paint big, glorious, and non-sectarian murals. "The Auld Days" (at the junction of William and Rossville St. in the Bogside, across from Pilot's Row Community Centre) is one of several renditions of a formerly peaceful city. One piece of popular art, at the end of Craigavon Bridge, also reflects hopes for future peace. Recently unveiled in July of 1992, the Carlisle Square sculpture shows two standing men reaching out to each other across a divide in the walls they stand upon.

ENTERTAINMENT

Derry has a limited but active arts scene. Both Irish and international artists get exposure at **Orchard Gallery,** Orchard St. (tel. 269675; open Tues.-Sat 10am-1pm and 2-6pm). The **Foyle Arts Centre,** (tel. 266657 or 363166), on Lawrence Hill off Strand Rd., promotes a broad range of arts, including music, drama, dance, and fine arts. The **Rialto Entertainment Centre,** Market St. (tel. 262567 or 260516), has all those favorites plus photography. **St. Columb's Hall,** Orchard St. (tel. 267789), welcomes traveling musicians and theater groups to the town's largest playhouse. The hall also houses **Orchard Cinema** in an intimate theater (tel. 262845; box office open Mon.-Fri. 10am-4pm; tickets £5-10). The **Guildhall** (tel. 365151) combines government and artistic functions. Shows include jazz concerts and dance championships. The **Gordon Gallery,** 7 London St. (tel. 374044), exhibits and sells Irish arts (open Tues.-Fri. 11am-5:30pm, Sat. 11am-1pm). The **Strand Multiplex Quayside Centre,** Strand Rd. (tel. 373900), brings Hollywood movies to town. *Let's Go's* pub listings of Derry include many trad and rock venues (see Pub listings, above). Rock gigs also haunt **The Waterloo, Caspers,** and **Legends.** Discos groove upstairs at the **Strand Tavern,** Strand Rd. (tel. 266446; Thurs. techno/house £2). The **Squires Night Club,** just behind the Townsman, is popular with all kinds of people (Mon. and Thurs.-Sat., cover £3.30).

▨ Tyrone & Fermanagh

■■■ OMAGH

The area surrounding Omagh ("OME-ah"), as opposed to the city itself, tends to attract tourists. Sights of spectacular beauty and museums with masterful and moving exhibitions dot the region: a mist-shrouded mountain range, a pine-scented forest park (in a country where trees are as rare as sunshine), the top-notch Ulster American Folk Park and Ulster History Park, not to mention a brilliant hostel. Omagh doesn't have the urban character of Galway or the solitude of Inishbofin, but there are plenty of other reasons to stay in Omagh. A5 links Omagh to Derry and Armagh; A32 lumbers toward Enniskillen.

Practical Information Omagh's **tourist office** (tel. 247831, after hours 240774) is in the center of Market St. (open Oct.-March Mon.-Fri. 9am-5pm; April-Sept. Mon.-Sat. 9am-5pm). The **post office** is at 7 High St. (tel. 242970; open Mon.-Fri. 9am-5:30pm, Sat. 10am-12:30pm); the **postal code** is BT78 1AB. **Halifax Building Society** (tel. 246931) provides pounds at 22 High St. (open Mon.-Fri. 9:30am-5pm, Sat. 9am-noon; **ATM**). **Abbey National Building Society,** 59 High St. (tel. 247121) is open Mon.-Tue. and Thurs.-Fri. 9am-5pm, Wed. 9:30am-5pm, Sat. 9am-noon. For those who didn't leave home without it the **ATM** accepts American Express, Visa, and Plus. **Conway Cycles,** 1 Old Market Pl. (tel. 246195), rents bikes in the alley across from the tourist office (£8/day, £40/week; deposit £30; open Mon.-Sat. 9am-5:30pm). **Ulsterbus** runs from the station on Mountjoy Rd. (tel. 242711) to: Belfast (Mon.-Fri. 9/day, Sat. 8/day, Sun. 4/day; 2 hr.; £5.40, student £4.60); Derry (Mon.-Sat. 11/day, Sun. 4/day; 1hr.; £3.90, student £3.30); Dublin (Mon.-Sat. 6/day, Sun. 4/day; 3hr.; £8.90, students £7.40); and Enniskillen (Mon.-Fri. 7/day, Sat. 5/day, Sun. 1/day; 1 hr.; £3.60, student £3.10). The station **stores luggage** for 50p/bag (open Mon.-Sat. 9am-5:45pm). The **phone code** reverberates at 01662.

Accommodations, Food, & Pubs You'll forget you're on a budget at the **Glenhordial Hostel,** 9a Waterworks Rd. (tel. 241973). This new hostel boasts sparkling cleanliness, a conservatory, a wok, hair dryer, and a plethora of other luxuries. Bill and Marella Fyffe will share a pint with hostelers and ensure a pleasant stay. From the bus station, walk up B48 towards Gortin. Veer right at the first fork (by the car showroom). Follow that road (and the hostel signs) for two miles. Call for pick-up; the Fyffes will get you at the bus station if they're home. (£6/person, sheets free. Bikes £7.50/day, laundry £1. Wheelchair access.)

Closer to town, the **4 Winds,** 63 Dromore Rd. (tel. 243554), defines cozy accommodation. Mr. Thomas, a retired chef, provides tea and coffee and a filling Irish breakfast. Call for pick-up or directions for the 10-minute walk (£13/person; optional evening *á la carte* from £6.50, July-Sept. only; packed lunches on request; discounts for stays over 4 days). Pitch a tent and eat baked beans eight miles north of Omagh at **Gortin Glen Caravan and Camping Park,** Gortin Rd. (tel. (016626) 48108), in a forest park (£4/2-person tent).

At **Expressway,** (tel. 243637), opposite the bus station, sit down to lunch with Marilyn Monroe (meat, chips, and veggies, £2.70; served until 5pm) or order from their take-out menu (open Mon.-Sat. 8:30am-6pm). The **Pink Elephant,** 19 High St. (tel. 249805; open daily 8am-5:30pm), offers a similar deal for £2.90, and serves breakfast from 8-11am (£2.50). **O'Doherty's at Sally O'Brien's,** 35 John St. (tel. 242521) has history. The legend of Sally who died of a broken heart will make you weep in your Guinness. Once you've recovered, head next door to **Sally O'Brien's,** a nightclub with live bands (Fri. 18 and over, Sat. 21 and over, Sun. 25 and over).

Sights Five miles north of Omagh on Strabane Rd., the **Ulster American Folk Park** (tel. 243292), attracts tourists, residents, and frogs. Over 2 million people emigrated from Ulster between 1700 and 1900, and the museum chronicles some of their history and experiences. The indoor exhibition includes life-sized clay figures of such Ulster-American heroes as Davy Crockett and frighteningly accurate, full-scale tableaus of a famine cottage, a New York City Irish tenement, and a big black bear. Outside, a 19th-century rural village, including schoolhouse, meetinghouse, and working forge, educates visitors about life in bygone Ireland. More awesome, however, is the **Ship and Dockside Gallery** in which a 100-feet brig sits in front of dockside brick buildings, transported from Belfast and Derry. On the ship, visitors can walk through the cramped living quarters of the emigrants, while the sounds of creaking timbers, wind, waves, and seagulls induce seasickness. After disembarking, visitors walk through an "American" town and a 19th-century Pennsylvania back-country village, complete with log cabin, fancy house, corn crib, and giant barn. Ask one of the guides how soap was made; you won't like what you hear. Watch out for loose, squealing pigs. To get to the park from Omagh, stay on Strabane Rd. for five miles, or take the Omagh-Strabane bus (Mon.-Fri. 14/day, Sat. 13/day, Sun. 5/day; 10 min.; £1.15, students £1). (Park open Easter-Sept. Mon.-Fri. 11am-6:30pm, Sun. 11:30am-7pm; Oct.-Easter Mon.-Fri. 10:30am-5pm; £3.50, students £1.70. Wheel-chair access. Last admission to park 1½ hrs. before closing.) Access to the Emigra-tion Database containing ships' passenger lists is available (Mon.-Fri. 9:30am-4:30pm; fees vary).

Less spectacular than the Folk Park but well worth seeing is the **Ulster History Park** (tel. (016626) 48188), seven miles out of town on Gortin Rd. You'll know you're there when you see three round buildings wearing large witch hats. (The Omagh/Gortin bus stops right outside: Mon.-Sat. 2/day; £1.30, student £1.10.) Designed to trace settlement in Ireland from the Stone Age, the park contains full-scale reconstructions of neolithic huts, passage tombs, a round tower, a *crannog* (see Archaeology, p. 59) and a castle. Be on the lookout for anachronisms such as a butter churn in a ring fort and a radio in a monk's stone hut. An exhibition explains the history of Ulster (pre-Christian to the Plantations) for those not in the know. (Open April-Sept. Mon.-Sat. 10:30am-6:30pm, Sun. 11:30am-7pm; Oct.-March Mon.-Fri. 10:30am-5pm.) Last admission to the park one hour before closing (£3, students £1.50). The deer-infested, "purely coniferous" **Gortin Glen Forest Park** is just a three-minute walk up from the History Park (exit left). Nature trails and breath-tak-ing views abound. Archaeology enthusiasts should check out Ireland's answer to Stonehenge. Situated between Omagh and Cookstown, Creggan overflows with 44 well-preserved monuments dating from the Neolithic Period.

■ NEAR OMAGH: SPERRIN MOUNTAINS

Less than a half hour northeast of Omagh by car, the truly underrated **Sperrin Mountains,** covered with hare and heather, sprout up. A few too many tour buses beep through, but the area is beautiful. Walkers and cyclists can pick up the **Ulster Way** 3½ miles east of Sperrin. This section of the trail is over 25 miles long: it weaves through the heart of the mountains and then meets A6 main road 4 miles south of Dungiven. Those with cars should cruise along the Plumbridge-Sperrin Rd. (B47, commonly known as the Glenelly Rd.) for vivacious vistas. Purchase a copy of *The Ulster Way: Accommodation for Walkers* (30p) from the tourist office in Omagh and book ahead. The **Sperrin Heritage Centre** (tel. (016626) 48142) is on Glenelly Rd. between Cranagh and Sperrin. Glaciation, bootlegging in the Poteen Mountains, and the discovery of gold are all hot topics. For 65p you get to try your own luck with a pan (open May-Oct. Mon.-Fri. 11am-6pm, Sat. 11:30am-6pm, Sun. 2-7pm; £1.80).

■ ■ ■ DUNGANNON

Fourteen miles northwest of Armagh, the busy but uninteresting town of **Dungan-non** sits at the beginning of M1 to Belfast. Buses scurry between Armagh and Dung-annon (Mon.-Fri. 6/day, Sat. 5/day, Sun. 1/day; 30 min.; £1.95, students £1.70). The **Killymaddy Tourist Information Centre** on Ballygawley Rd. (tel. (01868) 767259) can help you plan a visit to the area (open June-Aug. Mon.-Thurs., Sat.-Sun. 9am-5pm, Fri. 9am-6pm; April-May and Sept. Mon.-Fri. 9am-5pm, Sat.-Sun. 10am-4pm; Oct.-Mar. Mon.-Fri. 9am-5pm). Local bus #80 covers the three miles between the town center and the **Tyrone Crystal Factory** (tel. (01868) 725335), where tours show you each intricate step involved in the crystal-making process. (Tours run Mon.-Thurs. 9:30am-3:30pm, Fri. 9:30am-noon, Sat. 9:30am-3:30pm; £2.) A few miles away (also on bus route #80), the town of **Coalisland** has turned an old corn-mill in the center of town into its own **heritage center** (tel. (01868) 748532). Its exhibits teach visitors about the area's industrial history. (Open June-Sept. Mon.-Fri. 10am-8pm, Sat. 11am-6pm, Sun. 2-6pm; Jan.-May, Oct.-Dec. Mon.-Fri. 10am-6pm.

Just off M1, six miles east of Dungannon, **Peatlands Park** (tel. (01762) 851102) contains native reserves, an interpretive center with interactive displays on the natural and human history of peat bogs, and a small railroad which was originally used to carry turf out of the bogs. Turf-cutting demonstrations on busy days. (Park open daily June-Sept. 9am-9pm; Oct.-May 9am-dusk; visitor center open June-Sept. daily 2-6pm. Both free; railroad 70p.)

FERMANAGH LAKE DISTRICT

Upper and Lower Lough Erne extend on either side of Enniskillen like the two blades of a propeller. They lure vacationers to a lake district several times larger, and infinitely less trampled, than England's. Lower Lough Erne is north of Upper Lough Erne. The upper lough (which flows down into the other, and hence lower, lough) extends south into Co. Cavan, in the Republic. Hiking, biking, canoeing, windsurfing, and orienteering provide the action in the area. Everything cool is within 20 miles of Enniskillen, the county's only sizable town.

■■■ ENNISKILLEN

Busy Enniskillen (pop. 14,000) lies on an island between Upper and Lower Lough Erne. Its shops and services are an excellent source for information and equipment for touring Ireland's accessible Lake District. Enniskillen is also a city in its own right. The city will never forget the 1987 Remembrance Day bombing that killed 11 people, injured 61, and shocked hundreds. There is, however, less tension here than in the bigger towns of Northern Ireland.

ORIENTATION & PRACTICAL INFORMATION

Enniskillen's main street is actually comprised of five smaller ones. From west to east they run: Darling St., Church St., High St., Townhall St., and East Bridge St. Queen Elizabeth Rd. parallels the main street to the north; Wellington Rd. parallels it to the south. Sligo Rd. and Derrygonnelly Rd. lie across the bridges on the west side of the town center (cross the bridge by Enniskillen castle—Derrygonnelly Rd. is straight ahead, Sligo Rd. to your left). The Dublin/Belfast Rd. is at the other end of the city center.

Tourist Centre: Fermanagh Tourist Information Centre, Wellington Rd. (tel. 323110), is across the street from the bus station. With plenty of information and a well-informed staff, this office is actually a pleasure to visit. Ask about guided town walks in the summer. Open June and Sept. Mon.-Fri. 9am-5:30pm, Sat. 10am-6pm, Sun. 11am-5pm; July-Aug. Mon.-Fri. 9am-6:30pm, Sat. 10am-6pm, Sun. 11am-5pm; Oct.-May Mon.-Fri. 9am-5pm.

Banks: First Trust Savings Bank, 8 East Bridge St. (tel. 322464). Open Mon.-Fri. 9:30am-4:30pm; **ATM** accepts Visa and MasterCard. **Halifax Building Society,** 20 High St. (tel. 327072). Open Mon.-Fri. 9am-5pm, Sat. 9am-noon; **ATM** accepts Plus and Visa.

Post Office: East Bridge St. (tel. 324525). Open Mon.-Fri. 9am-5:30pm, Sat. 9am-12:30pm. **Postal code:** BT74 7BW.

Phone code: 01365.

Bus Station: Wellington Rd. (tel. 322633), across from the tourist office. Very clean, very swanky. Open Mon.-Sat. 9am-5:30pm. Bus service to Belfast (Mon.-Fri. 10/day, Sat. 8/day, Sun. 6/day; 2¼hr.; £5.70, students £4.90); Derry (Mon.-Fri. 7/day, Sat. 4/day, Sun. 3/day; 3hr.; £5.40, students £4.60); Dublin (Mon.-Fri. 4/day, Sat. 5/day, Sun. 3/day; 3hr.; £9.70, students £7.50); Sligo (Mon.-Sat. 1/day; 1hr.;

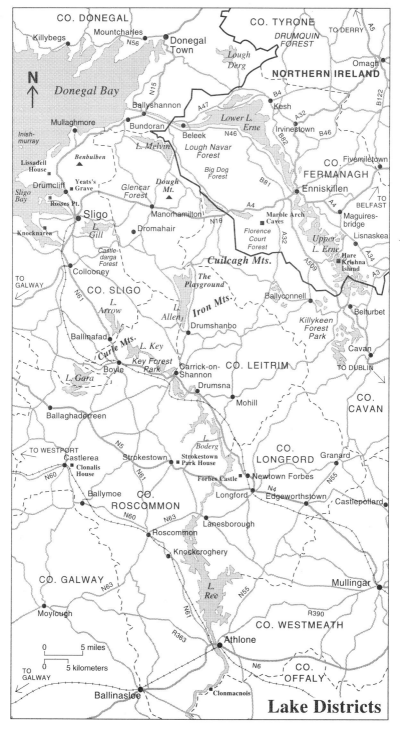

Lake Districts

£7.30, students £3.80); and Galway (Mon.-Sat. 2/day; 5hr.; £12.40, students £8.10).

Taxis: Call-a-Cab, tel. 324848; **Diamond Taxis,** tel. (0800) 123444 (free call).

Luggage Storage: Ulsterbus Parcel-link (tel. 322633), at the bus station. Open daily 9am-5:30pm; 50p/bag.

Bike Rental: Erne Tours, Round 'O' Quay, Derrygonnelly Rd. (tel. 322882). £7/day, £35/week. **Spokes and Sports,** Church St. (tel. 325251). £6/day, £25/week; deposit £35.

Laundry: Paragon Cleaners, 12 East St. (tel. 325230). £4-6/load, varies by weight. Open Mon.-Sun. 9am-5:30pm.

Hospital: Erne Hospital, Cornagrade (tel. 324711). "Good Samaritan" policy: those who fall ill while on vacation in Enniskillen receive free treatment.

Emergency: Dial 999; no coins required. **Police:** tel. 322823.

ACCOMMODATIONS

Backpackers are limited to a remote hostel, 11 miles from town, or B&Bs which are almost always full in high season. Call ahead for a room or you'll be sleeping in the bus station (although it *is* a swanky bus station...).

Castle Archdale Youth Hostel (YHANI/HI) (tel. 28118), 1 mi. off the Kesh-Enniskillen Rd. Take the Pettigo bus from the station and ask the driver to let you off at Lisarrick. Walk 1 mile left down Kesh-Enniskillen Rd., then turn right into the park, at a small church, and walk 1 mile. Hitchers report little luck. The hostel occupies one corner of a stately 19th-century home—the hostel is neither in, nor identical with, the castle. The mammoth bunk rooms are contrasted by a tiny kitchen. Large groups and small children can be noisy. On the plus side, hot showers and lovely surroundings provide stress-relief. £6.30/person; laundry £2.

Curraig Aonrai, 19 Sligo Rd. (tel. 324889). Look for the sign on Sligo Rd. Mrs. Mulhern doesn't think it's fair to charge her guests more than £12 a night for her aqua and pink rooms. Closest B&B to town center (5-min. walk). Aqua bathtub!

Abbeyville, 1 Willoughby Ct. (tel. 327033). Well marked 10-min. walk down the Derrygonnelly Rd. Mrs. McMahon's flowery rooms are stocked with TVs and piles of tourist info (from £14/person). Pink bathtub!

Rossole House, 85 Sligo Rd. (tel. 323462). The expensive but spiffy option—£15/person, double w/bath £32 (no singles). Located in a gorgeous stone Georgian house on the Lough shore. TVs in all rooms.

Lough Melvin Holiday Centre, Garrison (tel. 58142), 25 mi. out of Enniskillen on A4/B52 Rd. A convenient stopover on the way from Enniskillen to Sligo Town. Spelunking, sailing, and pony-trekking for your entertainment (£6/½-day, £11/full day). Caters mostly to groups, so the hostel will either be jam-packed or empty. £7.50; single £11; double £20; continental breakfast £1.8, fisherman's breakfast £4.50. Camping is available March-Sept.; £5/tent.

Lakeland Canoe Centre, Castle Island (tel. 324250, evenings 322411), is within walking distance of town with a free ferry service (8am-12pm) and sports equipment for hire. Dorm £9; camping £4/person.

FOOD & PUBS

Franco's, Queen Elizabeth Rd. (tel. 324424). Cozy nooks, wooden tables, candles in bottles, and red napkins inhabit this popular bistro. Pizza from £4.45, pasta from £5.95, and seafood. Opens at noon, closes late.

Barbizon Café, 5 East Bridge St. (tel. 324556). A totem pole, miniature palm tree, and surreal paintings keep company with Enniskillen's falafel-chomping crowd. Chicken kebab sandwich £2.50. Open Mon.-Sat. 8:30am-6pm.

The Crowe's Nest, High St. (tel. 325252). Gas masks, swords, and other aids to digestion are exhibited in glass cases around this pub/grill. Tourists are attracted by its central location. Live music Mon.-Thurs. nights. Lasagne and salad £3.90, all-day breakfast (2 eggs, 2 strips of bacon, 2 tomatoes, 2 sausages, 2 homemade potato pancakes, toast, chips) £3.90.

Geraldo's, Forthill St. (tel. 322228), opposite Dunnes Stores, does fresh pizzas and home-made ice cream. Seating is sparse; take-away is wisest. Veggie pizza £2.85, plain pizza £2.35, small cone 45p—try the Bailey's flavor. Open Mon.-Wed. 12:45pm-11pm, Thurs.-Fri. 12:45pm-midnight, Sat. noon-midnight, Sun. 2-11pm.

Aisling Centre, 37 Darling St. (tel. 325811), serves light lunches and snacks. Great afternoon tea special (3-5 pm): £1 buys you tea, a scone and pastry.

Bush Bar, 26 Townhall St. (tel. 325210). Narrow, woody, happy bar. "St. Anthony Fund" boxes line the bar to make you feel guilty as you pay for your pint. West coast cod pie, wrapped in shamrock crust £4. Trad Mon. and Tues. nights.

White Star Bar, 1 Church St. (tel. 325303). Barmaids scuttle between beseeching drinkers. Well-stocked bar (more than just beer), young crowd, and dark room. Music Fri.-Sun. nights. "Home-cooked" roast beef £3.25.

Blakes of the Hollow, 6 Church St. (tel. 322143). Reads "William Blake" on the front. So old and red that they put it on a postcard; try traditional Gaelic coffee.

SIGHTS

Inside Enniskillen's grand castle, the **Fermanagh County Museum** (tel. 325050 or 325000) presents a comprehensive look at rural Fermanagh, beginning with a wild-flower exhibition and culminating in a large-scale tableau of a 1930s country kitchen. The Museum of the Royal Inniskilling Fusiliers and Dragoons is a military historian's playground. (Open July-Aug. Sat.-Mon. 2-5pm, Tues.-Fri. 10am-5pm; May-June and Sept. Mon. and Sat. 2-5pm, Tues.-Fri. 10am-5pm; Oct.-April Mon. 2-5pm, Tues.-Fri. 10am-5pm; £1.50, students £1.)

One and a half miles south of Enniskillen on A4, **Castle Coole** (tel. 322690) rears up in neoclassical *hauteur*. The National Trust spent £7 million restoring it for tourists. The acres of landscaped grounds are covered by buttercups and wild daisies (and the occasional unicorn). The castle grounds are 10 minutes along on the Dublin Rd.; the castle itself appears at the end of a 20-minute hike up the driveway. (Open April-May and Sept. Sat.-Sun. 1-6pm; June-Aug. Fri.-Wed. 1-6pm. Last tour 15 min. before closing; £2.50.) Diagonally across the street from the castle entrance, the **Ardhowen Theatre** poses by the lake shore, satisfying dance, drama, music, and film enthusiasts (tel. 325440; tickets available from the box office Mon.-Sat. 9am-5pm, and until 9pm on the night of a performance; £5-8).

If you don't have time to explore the surrounding Lake District, Erne Tours Ltd. offer a quickie, 1¾-hr. **tour** of upper Lough Erne, including a half-hour stop at the very cool Devenish Island (see below). Tours on the **MV Kestrel** leave from the Round 'O' Jetty in Brook Park, two minutes down the Derrygonnelly Rd. (Tel. 322882; May-June Sun. 2:30pm.; July-Aug. daily 10:30am, 2:15, and 4:15pm, also Tues., Thurs., and Sun. 7:15pm.; Sept. Tues., Sat., and Sun. 2:30pm; £4; 50p discount on morning trips. "Humor" free.)

■■■ LOWER LOUGH ERNE

DEVENISH ISLAND

The ruins on tiny Devenish Island are an imperative destination for anyone, from the amateur to the professional, with an interest in Irish medieval history and archeology. St. Molaise founded a monastic center here in the 6th century. Viking raids and Plantation reforms finally put an end to the long monastic life by the 17th century, when the whole congregation moved to Monea, on the mainland. **St. Molaise's House,** an old oratory, an 81-feet round tower (dating from the 12th century), and an Augustinian priory (from the 15th century) are all that remain today. The **round tower** is completely intact—you can even climb to the top. From Enniskillen, sail on the **M.V. Kestrel's** tour of the lakes (see above), which includes an ample half-hour stop on the island. If you want to see only the island, the **Devenish Ferry** leaves from **Trory Point.** (April-Sept. Tues.-Sat. 10am-7pm, Sun. 2-7pm; £2.25, includes ticket to small museum on island.) Ask the driver of the Pettigo bus to let you off at Trory ferry stop, or drive four miles out of Enniskillen on the Irvinestown Rd. to the ferry terminal sign, at a gas station. However you travel the 10 minutes to the island, dress warmly, because strong winds howl. **Boa Island** and **White Island** are also of interest for their many brilliant examples of both pagan and Christian carvings. You can drive across Boa Island on the Kesh-Belleek Rd., while a ferry service based at the Castle Archdale Marina runs an hourly boat to White Island. (Tel. (01365) 631850; open June-early Sept. Tues.-Sat. 10am-7pm, Sun. 2-7pm; £2.25.)

BELLEEK

At the tip of Lower Lough Erne, on the national border, tiny Belleek is famous for its delicate, lace-like china. Tours of the **Belleek Pottery** factory feature the tradesmen in action. The **Visitors Centre** (tel. (013656) 58501) is both museum (with originals like "Crouching Venus" and "The Prisoner of Love") and shop—nothing at discount prices, though, since anything with a flaw is destroyed. (Tours available Mon.-Fri. 9:30am-12:15pm, 2:15-4:15pm, last tour on Fri. at 3:15pm; £1. Visitors center open March-June and Sept. Mon.-Fri. 9am-6pm, Sat. 10am-6pm, Sun. 2-6pm; July-Aug. Mon.-Fri. 9am-8pm, Sat. 10am-6pm, Sun. 11am-8pm; Oct. Mon.-Fri. 9am-5:30pm, Sat. 10am-5:30pm; Nov.-Feb. Mon.-Fri. 9am-5:30pm). Also in Belleek, **ExplorErne** (tel. (013656) 58866), chronicles the history and heritage of the Lough Erne region (open June and Sept. Mon.-Fri. 9am-5:30pm, Sat. 10am-6pm, Sun. 11am-5pm; July-Aug. Mon.-Fri. 9am-6:30pm, Sat. 10am-6pm, Sun. 11am-5pm; mid-March to Easter Mon.-Fri. 9am-5pm; Easter-May Mon.-Fri. 9am-5pm, Sat. 10am-6pm, Sun. 11am-5pm; £1). Belleek is 25 miles from Enniskillen on the Derrygonnelly Rd. (A46).

ULSTER WAY

Serious hikers should consider tackling the Fermanagh stretch of the Ulster Way. These 23 miles of forested paths are marked by wooden posts with yellow arrows and stenciled hikers. Leading from Belcoo to Lough Navar, the path is neither smooth nor level, so those on bikes or in wheelbarrows should think again. Take a detailed map and food—shops and transport are scarce. The tourist office's *Ulster Way* pamphlet and the Fermanagh section of *The Ulster Way* (both £1.50) contain detailed descriptions of the route, its sights, and its history.

■■■ FLORENCE COURT & THE MARBLE ARCH CAVES

Ten miles southwest of Enniskillen, both Florence Court and the Marble Arch Caves can be combined into one daytrip. **Florence Court** (tel. (01365) 348249), an 18th-century Georgian mansion, was completed twenty years before Castle Coole. The building is surrounded by the **Florence Court Forest Park,** which also includes an impressive walled garden. The Rococo Court once housed the Earls of Enniskillen; the third Earl left behind his fossil collection for visitors' delectation. To get there take Sligo Rd. out of Enniskillen, then turn left onto the A32 (Swanlinbar Rd.) and follow the signs. (Estate open all year 10am to 1hr. before dusk. Florence Court open April-May and Sept. Sat.-Sun. 1-6pm; June-Aug. Wed.-Mon. 1-6pm; £2.50.)

Four miles farther on the road from Florence Court to Belcoo (take the Sligo bus to Belcoo and walk three miles, following the signposts; the indirect route makes this a fairly difficult hitch) are the **Marble Arch Caves** (tel. (01365) 348855), a subterranean labyrinth of hidden rivers and weirdly sculpted limestone. Most of the eerie caves are accessible only by boat tour. When the water level is high, the tour is only half its length and much less interesting. Call before you show up, as the caves are "rained out" often and the half-tour isn't worth it. (Open late March-Sept. daily 11am-4:30pm; £5, students £4.50; the half-tour is only £4.50, students £3.)

■ ISLE OF MAN

The Isle of Man (or "Mann" to its friends) is a pint-sized anomaly floating in the middle of the Irish Sea, equidistant from Ireland and Britain. Why an anomaly? Well, the 70,000 Manx are British and swear allegiance to Queen Elizabeth, but they aren't part of the United Kingdom—the Isle of Man has its own legislature (the world's oldest), its own flag (a pinwheel with feet), its own currency, and its own post office, which complement its own fauna (weird cats and sheep and now extinct ponies, cows, and pigs), its own language (now nearly dead), and its previous unique approaches to human rights legislation (banned homosexuality and sanctioned corporal punishment—now no longer in practice).

The Manx clearly relish their eccentricities, though nowadays they do worry that they are becoming too mainstream: "thy throne of home rule," as the Manx national anthem sings, "makes us free as thy sweet mountain air." Manx home rule has also spawned the lax tax laws that created the island's huge offshore finance industry and gave it some (unwanted?) international attention. The low taxes lured hundreds of tycoons too rich to live in high-tax Britain; these "tax exiles" now zip around Douglas in their expensive cars, leaving the young Irish immigrants who work for them to suck down their cigar fumes. The *Manx Independent* has big debates over this perceived dilution of Manx culture; 50% of the population was born off-island, pulling the Isle of Man closer to Ireland, Britain, and the rest of the world. The EU has also had a big effect: it pressured the Manx government to de-criminalize homosexuality in 1992 and to abolish capital and corporal punishment in 1993.

It would take a lot more than legislation to rob Mann of its charms. The island is beautiful: ringed by cliffs, sliced by deep valleys, and criss-crossed by lovable antique trains. It is small enough to be thoroughly explored, and far enough off the beaten track to supply real discoveries. The Manx language, a close cousin to Irish and Scots Gaelic, is taught in schools and in newspaper columns, and is still heard when the Manx legislature's laws are proclaimed on July 5 on Tynwald Hill. Manx (tailless) cats are still bred on the island, as are the terrifying, four-horned Manx Loghtan sheep. The three-legs-of-Mann emblem appears on every available surface, asserting the Manx identity with the slogan "Quocunque Jeceris Stabit": whichever way you throw me, I stand (like a weeble-wobble). The Isle of Man has rolled through the political and cultural changes on either side of the Irish Sea without losing its independence or its moxie: visitors will come to cherish the fierce and indomitable Manx spirit the three legs represent.

> The Isle of Man shares an international phone code with Britain of 44. See Essentials (p. 44) for dialing instructions. All British pounds (from England, Scotland, or Northern Ireland) are accepted in the Isle of Man; however, Manx bills and coins are not accepted outside the Isle. Exchange before you leave, or save your interesting Manx currency for souvenirs. The Isle of Man issues its own stamps; British stamps are not valid.

■■■ GETTING THERE

The Isle of Man is a logical stopover between England or Scotland and the Republic or Northern Ireland. It's also possible (and about as expensive as a round trip) to travel from Belfast or Dublin to Douglas, then to return to the Irish city from which you did not depart.

BY FERRY

The **Isle of Man Steam Packet Company** has a monopoly on ferry service to the island, with sailings between Douglas and Heysham, Liverpool, and Fleetwood in

England; Ardrossan in Scotland; and Belfast and Dublin in Ireland. Heysham and Liverpool are the only routes covered all winter. In 1994, a high-speed SeaCat catamaran replaced the ferry for most sailings to and from Belfast, Dublin, Liverpool, and Fleetwood, cutting the sailing time almost in half. Sailings to and from: **Belfast** (May-Sept. 2-4/week, usually on Mon., Fri., and Sun.; 2½hr. by SeaCat, 4½hr. by ship); **Dublin** (May-Sept. 2-4/week, usually on Thurs. and Sun.; 2½hr. by SeaCat, 4½hr. by ship); **Heysham** (June-Sept. 1-2/day; Jan.-March Mon-Fri. 1/day; 3¾hr.); **Liverpool** (July-Aug. Mon., Wed., Fri., and Sat.; Oct.-May only Sat.; 2½hr. by SeaCat, 4½hr. by ship); **Fleetwood** (June-Sept. 1/week; 2 hr. by SeaCat, 3½ hr. by ship); and **Ardrossan,** Scotland (in cooperation with Caledonian MacBrayne; June-Aug. 1/week on Sat. or Sun.; 8hr.).

Fares vary with the popularity of the sailing time (highest on summer weekends, lowest in winter). 1995 one-way fares ranged from £20-28, students and seniors £15-28, bikes free. Return tickets are about 10% cheaper than two singles, but only if you return within five days. Thus, it's nearly as cheap to go from England to the Isle of Man to Ireland as to do a round trip. Some sailings fill up weeks in advance during the summer. For **reservations,** call the Douglas office of the Isle of Man Steam Packet Co. (tel. (01624) 661661; fax (01624) 661065; open Mon.-Sat. 7am-7pm, Sun. 6am-11:30am and 12:30-7:30pm) or the Belfast office: W.E. Williames, Northern Rd. (tel. (01232) 351009; open Mon.-Fri. 9am-5:15pm). Bookings can also be made through travel agents.

BY TRAIN/FERRY COMBINATION

Combination Sea/Rail tickets are available from any British Rail station to Douglas and will save you money if you're planning to return to the same city. The ferry crossing is by ship from Heysham. From **London,** the whole trip takes about 8hr. and costs £88-99 return; from **Edinburgh,** 9hr. and £69-84. Higher fares apply from Friday to Sunday and from June to September. Combination tickets are available from some travel agents, but many in Douglas don't sell them. It's best to reserve your space on the ferry directly with the Isle of Man Steam Packet Co., especially since advance reservations (on rail and ferry) save quite a bit of money. British Rail passes qualify for discounts on combined Sea/Rail tickets.

BY AIR

Manx Airlines flies from Ronaldsway Airport (tel. (01624) 823311), in the south of the island, to Belfast, Cork, Dublin, London, Manchester, Glasgow, and seven other British destinations. **Jersey European** flies between Ronaldsway, Blackpool, and Belfast daily. For info and reservations, call Manx Airlines: U.K. tel. (01345) 626629 or (01624) 824313, Dublin tel. (01) 260 1588; or call Jersey European (tel. (01345) 676676). Easier still, call a travel agent. USIT offers a student flight from Belfast to Ronaldsway (£78 return). **Knight Air** (tel. (01345) 626489) flies from Leeds. As always, booking two weeks in advance is a less expensive choice.

■■■ ONCE THERE

GETTING AROUND

The Isle of Man has an extensive and reliable system of public transportation, managed by **Isle of Man Transport,** Strathallan Crescent, Douglas (train info tel. 663 3666, bus info tel. 662525; open Mon.-Sat. 7:30am-10pm, Sun. 8am-4pm). The 7-day **Freedom Ticket** gives free passage on any public transport on the island (buses, railways, and horse trams) for £24. Similar multi-day tickets are less of a value. Discount tickets and a comprehensive bus/train timetable (50p) are available from the major bus and train stations, newsagents, some bed and breakfasts, and the tourist office in Douglas.

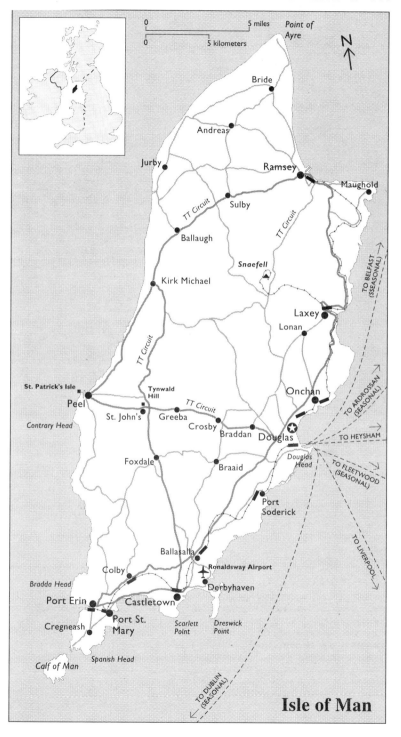

Isle of Man

Buses

Frequent buses connect the four major towns and reach every tiny hamlet on the island. While they lack the romance of the antique railroads, buses, particularly the double-decker ones, offer prime vantage points from which to view the island. Return tickets on buses are usually 15-20% cheaper than two singles. A **three-day Bus Rover** discount ticket allows unlimited bus travel on three days out of seven (£9.90), a good deal if riding trains (which are less extensive) doesn't interest you. It's more difficult to make the **one-day Bus Rover** ticket (£4.30) worth its price.

The **Tours (Isle of Man) Bus Tour Company** (tel. 676105) provides transportation from Douglas to events, such as concerts and parades, and makes daytrips to towns and sights around the island. The buses drop off passengers in the morning or before the event and pick up passengers in the afternoon or after the event (£1.50-3.70 for a return). Schedules are posted at the Douglas tourist office and the Crescent Leisure Centre, Central Promenade, Douglas. Tickets can also be bought at the Discovery Guides Centre on Harris Promenade and the Booking Office at Villa Marina, Loch Promenade. Full-day "Round the Island" tours leave at 10:15am and stop in Peel, Ramsey, and Port Erin. They arrive back in Douglas by 5pm. More localized daytrips, with fancy names like "Northern Nomad" or "Southern Experience," are also available. The schedule of other tours (including vintage coach tours in a '40s bus and mystery tours) changes weekly. (Full-day tours £7.40-8, half-day and evening tours £3.50-3.70.)

Trains

Thousands of "railway enthusiasts" come from Britain each year to experience the shaky, clackety rides in the original Victorian cars of both the electric and steam trains. Most of these dedicated people have been on all the steam trains in Britain and compare notes when they get together. A subset enjoy taking pictures of the trains, for whom the Manx bus company runs a special service known as the "chasing bus." Its sole purpose is to follow the route of a particular train and reach each stop before the train. At each stop, bus passengers pile out to take photos of the train as it passes. They they scramble back onto the bus, hoping that the coach will be able to beat the train to the next station, where they all pile out to take pictures again. In fact, the term **train spotting** has weaseled its way into British slang to mean something that is boring and pointless. Inquire at bus station for details.

The unique Isle of Man Railways, all at least 100 years old, run up and down the east coast, from Port Erin in the south to Ramsey in the north. A separate line of the electric railway branches off at Laxey, 6 miles north of Douglas, to head northwest to the top of Snaefell, the island's highest peak. The **Steam Railway,** dating from 1873, used to cover much of the island, but only the line south from Douglas to Port Erin is still running. The newer **Electric Railway** (dating from 1893) runs north from the other end of Douglas to Ramsey. The M.E.R. (Manx Electric Railway) boasts the two oldest trains in the world (the #1 and #2 trains). 1995 marks the centenary of the Snaefell Line, first opened to the public on August 21, 1895. The two miles of Douglas between the Steam and Electric Railway Stations is covered by bus or by **horse-drawn trams**.

The Electric Railway runs 10am to 6:15pm (April-June and Sept.-Oct. 5/day; July-Aug. 14/day). The Steam Railway runs 10am to 5:30pm (April-June and Sept. and the last week of October 4/day; July-Aug. Mon.-Thurs. 6/day, Fri.-Sun. 4/day). Less useful but more atmospheric than the 3-day bus ticket, the **3-day Rail Rover** ticket includes unlimited travel on the Steam, Electric, and Snaefell Mountain Railways (valid 3 days out of 7; £13). A similar one-day costs £8.80. Tickets for children are half price.

By Bike or Thumb

The island's small size makes it easy to get around by bike. The southern three-fourths of the island is covered in rolling hills which present a manageable challenge to cyclists. Bike rental is available but expensive in Douglas and Ramsey. Since the ferry carries bikes for free, it's wiser to import them. Some of the walking trails described below are open to bikes, but many are not. Back roads are fairly quiet.

For tired walkers, hitching provides a legal, socially acceptable alternative to public transport. The scarcity of hitchhikers on the island probably relates more to the lack of budget travelers and the ease of public transport than to any difficulty in getting lifts. Locals claim that the Isle of Man is one of the safer places for hitching. Nonetheless, *Let's Go* does not recommend hitching (see By Thumb, p. 38).

By Foot

The Isle of Man is a walker's paradise. The short distances between towns and sights make it feasible to walk from place to place. Three long-distance **hiking trails** are marked and maintained by the Manx government. **Raad ny Foillan,** or "The Road of the Gull," is a 90-mile path, marked with seagull signs, which traces the island's perimeter and passes through the major towns. **Bayr ny Skeddan,** or "The Herring Road," marked with herring signs, covers the less spectacular 14 miles between Peel in the west and Castletown in the east. (Walking east to west allows you to see the sunset at Peel.) The end of this trail overlaps with **Millennium Way,** which begins at Castle Rushen in Castletown and goes north to Ramsey. This trail follows the course of an ancient highway for 28 miles, described in a pamphlet available from tourist offices. Each town on the Isle also contains smaller trails marked with "Public Footpath" signs. The tourist office in Douglas and in some of the other towns have a free sheet which describes Raad ny Foillan and Bayr ny Skeddan and lists places to stay along Raad ny Foillan. Several books, available at tourist offices, bookstores, or the Manx Museum, give detailed descriptions of the walks around the island. The "Walks of Man Natural History" is the best pamphlet at tourist offices. Walking info can also be obtained from the **Venture Centre** (tel. 814240), the **Isle of Man Rambling Association** (tel. 624095), and the **Manx Discovery Guides** (tel. 673444).

ACCOMMODATIONS

Although the Isle of Man has no youth hostels, competition for the declining tourist trade has produced plenty of inexpensive guesthouses, most of them in Douglas. The *Isle of Man Holiday Guide,* available from the tourist office, lists all of the approved accommodations on the island, including some campgrounds. B&Bs or guesthouses which aren't on this list are operating illegally (which doesn't mean that they're bad). Though many B&Bs often fill up, it should still be possible to find a cheap place to stay, except during **T.T. races** (the first two weeks in June). B&Bs raise their rates but still fill up a year in advance for the races.

The other cheap option is **camping,** made more pleasant by the island-wide ban on trailer caravans (campers). Camping on the island must be done on a campsite, unless you find the "common land," where you can pitch your tent for free. It's located near the remote northern tip of the island. Ask in the Douglas tourist office.

EVENTS

These are as much reasons to avoid Mann as they are reasons to go to the Isle of Man. During the motorcycle races, crowds are huge and raucous. A calendar of events can be obtained from the tourist office and are also listed in detail in the *Official Guide to the Isle of Man: What's On.*

T.T. (Tourist Trophy) Race Weeks. First 2 weeks in June; all kinds of crazy events, and huge crowds. Jazz, music, and theater come with the races. The races have spawned a bit of geography. Islanders often give directions in relation to the "T.T. Circuit," which is marked on the Isle of Man map.

Manx Heritage Festival. Week of July 5. Music recitals and flower displays in the island's churches. Tynwald Fair sees the pronouncement of new laws on July 5, which is the Isle of Man Bank Holiday and Manx National Day.

Southern "100" Motorcycle Races. Mid-July. Call tel. 822546 for info.

International Football Festival. Last week in July. Gangs of large, noisy, beer-drinking men from across Britain (*very* international) play ball. Info tel. 661930.

Manx Grand Prix Motorcycle Races and Vintage Motorcycle Rally. Last weekend in August. Race info tel. 627979.

■■■ AN INTRODUCTION

HISTORY

The Isle of Man has been populated since at least 4000 BC; farming settlements on the island go back thousands of years. In legend, St. Patrick brought Christianity to Mann circa 450. The pattern of Christianization points to the Isle of Man's strong ties to Ireland: both share unique features like round towers and Celtic crosses. The Vikings landed on Mann in the 800s and established the **Tynwald**—the world's oldest legislature. In 1079, Godred **"King Orry"** Crovan took over the Isle of Man in the Battle of Skyhill (near Ramsey). He strengthened the Tynwald and the island's defenses. Scottish and English domination of the island began in 1265. Direct rule ended in 1405 when Henry IV gave Mann to the **Earls of Derby.** The Derbies died out and were succeeded by the **Atholls** (a popular street name on the Isle today); however, in 1765 the **Isle of Man Purchase Act** granted the island to the Crown, albeit for a fee. Then, as now, the island's unique tax status had enriched it and nearly ruined it: because Mann was outside the British customs union, smugglers would import goods to the Isle and then float them by night to England and Ireland, thereby avoiding the high British tariffs. The Atholls collected a modest customs duty, the Manx merchants prospered, and the Crown lost revenue. England responded by forcing the Isle of Man into its customs union; deprived of tax revenue, the island fell into poverty. The **Manx language** fell out of favor among the upper classes; by 1900, every islander would be able to speak English. **Henry Loch** was chosen by the Crown to be Governor of the Island in 1863. He raised tax revenue, began public works improvements such as breakwater construction, and strengthened the House of Keys. Today the Isle has total control over its internal affairs and finances. Its continuing customs union with the U.K. remains a bone of contention among the Manx—many want to lower Manx duties, thereby stimulating tourism and trade just as the low taxes have stimulated the financial industry. Fourteen percent of the population is currently involved in finance.

PUBS & FOOD

Like Manx accents, Manx food generally resembles that of England, with a few unique quirks. After cats and motorcycle racing, the island is most famous for its **kippers,** smoked herring which are usually eaten at breakfast. Manx kippers, caught and smoked locally (especially in Peel), are said to be tastier and more oily (that's a good thing) than the typical English variety. For those who can't stomach any breakfast food that looks back at them, an even greasier option is common: most hotels and guesthouses include a full, cooked English breakfast (eggs, bacon, sausage, bread, mushrooms, tomatoes—all fried—as well as cereal, toast, juice, and tea) in the price of a room. Such a breakfast makes it tempting to skip lunch and wait for dinner; unfortunately, cheap meals are difficult to find in the evenings. Lunch is a better time to eat cheaply, in the pubs or simple cafés common throughout the island. Pub lunches are of the same flavor as in Ireland: soup, sandwiches, or simple hot meals. The few pubs with more extensive menus are usually also more expensive. Cheap cafés tend to serve basic and boring salads, sandwiches, burgers, and meals based on the "meat, potato, and two veg" model. The more expensive dinner restaurants, like the supermarkets, tend to have a more cosmopolitan selection of food than can be found in Ireland (i.e., they've heard of tacos). A highlight of Manx cuisine is the fresh seafood; a lowlight is the proliferation of fast-food restaurants (takeaways) which inevitably spring up wherever tourists' arteries can be found.

Manx **pubs** are open Monday to Saturday 11am to 10:45pm, Sundays noon-1:30pm and 8-10pm. Legal drinking age is 18, but those between ages 15-18 are also allowed into bars as long as they don't drink. Closing times are enforced fairly strictly, although some bars have late licenses. Pubs are generally friendly, and women on their own are usually welcome. Because many people come to the island for week-long vacations, Douglas pubs are busy every night. Most of the rest of the island is quiet, although the smaller towns tend to boast one or two lively pubs. The island has two **breweries,** Bushy's at Mt. Murray and Okells in Douglas (there used to be over 100), and up until a few years ago it was difficult to find any imported beers in local pubs. The local ales and lagers are still very popular: try Old Bushy Tail or T.T. Pilsner. Both breweries proudly advertise their compliance with the Manx Pure Beer Act of 1874 which prohibits any chemicals, "opium or grams of paradise" in their brews. For information about obtaining hand-crafted beers, souvenirs, or brewery tours, call Ian Cains or Martin Brunnschweiler at tel. 661244.

■ ■ ■ DOUGLAS

The capital of a none-too-large country, Douglas really is a grape-sized metropolis. It's in there: there's culture (the famed Gaiety Theatre and the remarkable Manx Museum), diversity (rich old Brits, struggling young Irish, and a spattering of "others"), restaurants (some even serve banana milkshakes), and even commercialism.

Douglas bloomed in the Victorian era after it was named the capital of the island, replacing smaller Castletown Harbour. The Victorian tourist boom still dominates the landscape: Douglas wouldn't quite be itself without the railway and horse tram network, promenades, and the Gaiety Theatre. The turn of the 20th century was Douglas's high point, though the government is optimistic about the next century.

GETTING THERE

From the **airport,** the main coast road heads 8 miles northeast to Douglas. The Port St. Mary/Douglas bus drives this route (Mon.-Sat. 7:30am-11pm every ½ hr., every hr. on Sun.; 25 min.; £1.25). The steam train will stop at Ronaldsway Airport if you notify the guard first. The **ferry/SeaCat terminal,** designed to look like the three legs of Mann, lies at the southern end of Douglas, near the bus station and shopping area. The tourist information office is in the terminal itself. Stock up on pamphlets before walking north along the seaside to reach the promenades.

The **Electric Railway** runs from Ramsey via Laxey (July-Aug. 4/day, April-June and Sept.-Oct. 5/day; 1¼hr.; £3). **Steam trains** arrive from Port Erin via Castletown (4-6/day from April-Sept.; 65 min.; £3.55). **Buses** arrive from Port Erin (24/day; 50 min.; £1.70), Peel (24/day; 35 min.; £1.40), and Ramsey (30/day; 50 min.; £1.80). The central Douglas bus station is on Lord St. (open Mon.-Sat. 8am-5:40pm).

GETTING AROUND

During the summer, **horse-drawn trams** (streetcars; tel. 675522) run along tracks up and down the Promenade every few minutes between 9am and 8-10pm (April-Sept.). The service is slow but inexpensive and very quaint: elsewhere, people pay lots of money for this kind of thing. Stops are posted every 200 yards or so, so you can get on or off almost anywhere you want. **Buses** also run along the Promenade every few minutes, connecting the Bus and Steam Railway stations with the Electric Railway and Onchan (bus station to Electric Railway 55p). Local buses are covered by the Bus Rover **passes,** and both buses and horse trams are covered by the 7-day Freedom Ticket. A 7-day ticket covering local buses within Douglas and Onchan (£6) probably won't do most tourists much good. Another ticket costs £4.20 for 10 journeys, and may be a better value. The £1.20 "Ride-A-Day" ticket for horse trams is probably a safer buy. The 1-day or 3-day Rail Rovers also include the #30 bus service running between the Electric Railway Station and the Steam Railway Station, including stops on the Promenade and embarkation at Villa Marina, Loch Peninsula.

DOUGLAS

ORIENTATION & PRACTICAL INFORMATION

Douglas stretches for two miles along the seafront, from Douglas Head in the south to the Electric Railway terminal in the north. Douglas Head is separated from the rest of town by the River Douglas, which flows into the harbor. Just north of the river, the shopping district spreads around Victoria St., and turns into Duke St. and pedestrianized Strand St. The Promenade, which changes its name frequently, is a wide street that runs along between the long crescent of beach and a continuous row of grand but slightly tattered Victorian terrace houses. Summer Hill branches inland, just before the Electric Railway station. The neighborhood village of Onchan is north and east. At the point where Harris turns into Central Promenade, Broadway leads up a steep hill to Nobles Park, site of recreation facilities and the start of the T.T. course.

Tourist Office: Sea Terminal Building (tel. 686766). A dizzying array of helpful leaflets and lists of everything from nice views to ballroom dance venues. Bus and rail timetables and passes for sale here. The indispensable *Isle of Man: What's On* guide is most valuable. Open May-Aug. daily 9am-7:30pm; Sept.-April Mon.-Thurs. 9am-5:30pm, Fri. 9am-5pm, Sat. 9am-1pm.

Travel Agent: There are no budget travel agencies, but **Lunn Poly Holiday Shop,** 83 Strand St. (tel. 612848), offers cheap flights. Open Mon.-Sat. 9am-5:30pm.

Financial Services: Thomas Cook, Strand St. (tel. 626288). Open Mon.-Wed. and Fri.-Sat. 9am-5:30pm, Thurs. 10am-5:30pm. **American Express: Palace Travel,** Central Promenade (tel. 662662), in the Palace Hotel. **A.T. Mays Travel Agents,** 1 Regent St. (tel. 623330). Bureau de change is convenient to the ferry terminal for trading Manx money into English bills before you leave. Open Mon.-Fri. 9am-5:30pm, Sat. 9am-5pm.

Banks: Isle of Man Bank, (tel. 637100), corner of Regent and Strand St. Open Mon.-Fri. 9:30am-3:30pm; **ATM. TSB,** 78 Strand St. (tel. 673755). Open Mon.-Thurs. 9:30am-4pm, Fri. 9:30am-6pm; **ATM.**

Post Office: Regent St. (tel. 686114). Wide range of interesting Manx stamps, though nothing old since the island only started issuing stamps in 1973. For free info pack on Manx stamps, call tel. 686132 or write Philatelic Bureau, Circular Rd., Douglas, IOM, IM99 1PB. Open Mon.-Fri. 9am-5:30pm, Sat. 9am-12:30pm.

Phones: Strand St.; Villa Marina Arcade; Harris Promenade. Cardphones are common, cards are sold in any post office or newsagent.

Phone Code: 01624 for the whole island.

Transportation: Isle of Man Transport, Strathallan Crescent (trains tel. 663366, buses tel. 662525). Open Mon.-Sat. 7:30am-10pm, Sun. 8am-4pm. See Getting There (p. 413), Getting Around (p. 414), and Once There: Getting Around (p. 419) for more.

Taxis: A-1 Taxis (tel. 674488). 24-hr. service to the whole island.

Car Rental: Athol Car Hire, Hill St. (tel. 623232; fax 620782; Ronaldsway Airport tel. 822481). Europcar agent. Nissans. Cheapest cars £24/day, £105/week if reserved 10 days in advance. Cheaper rates on weekends and in winter. Free delivery of car. Ages 23-75 only. **E.B. Christian and Co.,** Bridge Garage (tel. 673211, fax 677250; airport 822126). Fords. £24/day; £124/week. Ages 21-75. Drivers ages 21-22 must leave a £100 deposit. Hotel collection service available. **Cleveland Self-Drive Car Hire,** 30a Esplanade Lane (tel. 621844; fax 628833). Nissan, Ford. £18/day, £100/week, including taxes and insurance. Ages 23-70.

Bike Rental: Eurocycles, 8a Victoria Rd. (tel. 624909), off Broadway. 18-speed mountain bikes £7/day, £35/week; deposit ID. **HSS Hire Shops,** 32 South Quay (tel. 622987). Mountain bikes £12.50/day, £6.25/additional day for 3 days, £25/week; deposit £100. Open Mon.-Fri. 8am-5:30pm, Sat. 8:30am-noon.

Bookstores: Manx Museum Shop (tel. 675522) The best selection of books on Manx history and culture (see Sights, p. 423). Open Mon.-Sat. 10am-5pm.

Libraries: Manx Museum Library. Every book relating to Manx studies, genealogical information, and history (see Sights, p. 423). Open Mon.-Sat. 10am-5pm.

Launderette: Broadway Launderette, 24 Broadway (tel. 621511). £2.50 wash, 20p dry. Open Mon.-Wed. and Fri.-Sat. 8:30am-5:30pm, Sun. 9am-2pm.

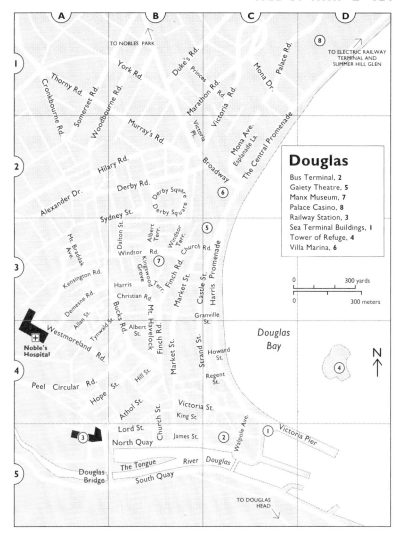

Douglas

Bus Terminal, **2**
Gaiety Theatre, **5**
Manx Museum, **7**
Palace Casino, **8**
Railway Station, **3**
Sea Terminal Buildings, **1**
Tower of Refuge, **4**
Villa Marina, **6**

Weather: tel. (01696) 888300. 24 hrs.

Bisexual, Gay, and Lesbian Info: Carrey-Friend (tel. 611600), Thurs. 7-10pm. **Ellan Vannin Gay Group,** P.O. Box 195, Douglas IM99 1QP (no phone).

Crisis Hotline: Samaritans, 5 Victoria Pl. (tel. 663399), near Broadway. Drop-ins 10am-10pm; hotline 24 hrs.

Pharmacy: Flynn's Pharmacy, 44 Duke St. (tel. 674014). Open Mon.-Sat. 9am-6pm.

Hospital: Nobles Hospital, Westmoreland Rd. (tel. 663322).

Emergency: Dial 999, no coins required. **Police:** tel. 631212.

ACCOMMODATIONS AND CAMPING

Inexpensive guesthouses (in the £10-13 range) can be found on the promenades, but the majority of them cluster on Church Rd., around Broadway, on Castle Mona

Ave. (off Central Promenade), and around Mona Drive (halfway up Central Promenade). The Mona Drive area is quietest but farthest from the center of town.

Merridale Guest House, 30 Castlemona Ave. (tel. 673040). Clean, comfortable bedrooms with sinks and coffee/tea facilities. Sells rover and freedom tickets. Fran and Ken are encyclopedia of info on IOM. No vacancies for T.T. '96. £14/person for one night; £12/person for more than 1 night. Open March-Sept.

Pat's B&B, 27 Derby Rd. (tel. 623689), off Broadway to the left. Small and cozy, with an orderly garden. Fresh flowers on the tables. Sinks in all rooms. The cheapest place in town at £10/person. Open March-Oct.

Glen View, 7 Stanley Terrace (tel. 674360), part of Broadway, about 200 yds. from the Promenade on the right. The house itself is quiet, but the neighborhood is not. Clean, basic rooms with sinks. £13/person; min. stay 2 nights.

Sea Nook, 10 Empire Terrace (tel. 676830). Turn off Central Promenade next to the Imperial Hotel, turn right after 50 yds. onto Empire Terrace. Small but pleasant rooms with views of Douglas Bay. All have sinks and teapots. Single £14, double £22. Open May-Sept.

Nobles Park Grandstand Campsite, on the site of the T.T. races' start and finish line. Only campground in Douglas. Showers £1, toilets free. £4.50/site. Open June-Sept. except during the races (first 2 weeks in June). For info and reservations, call the Douglas Corporation (tel. 621132) Mon.-Fri. 9am-5pm.

Glenlough Farm Campsite, (tel. 851326), Union Mills, 3 mi. out on the Peel Rd., lies on the Peel and Abbeylands bus routes. Unlimited space and fresh farm produce. Shop available during T.T. races. Open May-Sept. £3.20/person.

FOOD

Groceries can be found at the enormous **Safeway,** Chester St. (tel. 673039), near the Manx Museum (open Mon.-Thurs. and Sat. 8:30am-8pm, Fri. 8:30am-9pm). Fresh and cheap fruits and vegetables tempt the palate at **Robinson's,** Strand St. (no tel.; open daily 8am-6pm). **Holland and Barrett Health Food Store,** Strand St., sells things that crunch when you step on them (open Mon.-Tues., and Thurs.-Sat. 9am-5:30pm, Wed. 9:30am-5:30pm). **La Pâtissier Bakery,** Strand St., has organic wholewheat bread (70p) along with a whole range of other baked goods.

Crusoe's, North Quay (tel. 663337). Offers pizza, simple meals, and a salad bar amid tropical decor, complete with fake palm trees. Chicken dinner £5.50, pizzas £4. Open daily noon-10pm.

L'Experience, Summer Hill (tel. 623103), near the Electric Railway station. Surprisingly good French cooking at reasonable lunchtime prices (French ploughman's lunch w/Brie £2.75). Expensive dinners. Lunch Mon. and Wed.-Sat. noon-2pm, dinner Mon. and Wed.-Sat. 7-11pm.

Saagar Tandoori, 1 South View, Summerhill (tel. 674939). Good Indian food with a lovely bay view (vegetable rice £2.75, prawn bhuna £4.95). Open daily noon-2:30pm and 6pm-midnight.

Dynasty Peking and Szechuan Restaurant, Central Promenade (tel. 613061). Tempting platters for reasonable prices. Sweet and sour chicken £5.80. Open Tues.-Thurs. and Sun. 5:30-11pm, Fri.-Sat. 5:30-11:30pm.

Taylor's, Castle St. (tel. 624561). Victorian tea room specializing in veggie burgers (choice of 4 types; with salad and pasta £3.70) and pancakes with lots of toppings (£1.80). Banana milkshake £1.20. Open daily 10am-6pm.

Trams Bistro, Harris Promenade (tel. 626011), next door to the Sefton Hotel. Has comfortable indoor or outdoor seating with a great bay view. Casual café atmosphere. Manx kippers £2.40. Open daily 11am-10pm.

PUBS

Manx pubs are not known for the quality of their music. While pubs are busy and fun every night of the week, entertainment generally falls into either the disco or country-singer category. Irish music and jazz appear only for special events. In summer, hordes of young people roam the streets until the wee hours of the morning, while the hotel bars generally fill with older people. Women tend to dress up for nights out.

Bushy's Bar, (tel. 675139), at the intersection of Loch Promenade and Victoria St. One of the island's most popular pubs has live rock bands on weekends (cover £3), and tasty Bushy's beer to recommend it. A bubbly crowd spills out into the square in front of the bar on summer evenings. Open Mon.-Sat. until 11:45pm.

Cul-de-Sac Bar and Pizzeria, 3 Market Hill (tel. 623737). Claims to have the largest selection of beer on the island, including Hell Lager and Elephant Beer. Youthful crowds munch pizza and snacks in the dark interior to the accompaniment of piped-in dance music or occasional live rock. Cheap lunch specials (prawn salad and garlic bread £3) available Mon.-Fri. noon-2pm, Sat. noon-6pm. Other food available Mon.-Sat. 5:30pm-late. Closed Sun. in winter.

Brendann O'Donnell's, 16-18 Strand St. A self-proclaimed *seanachi* (storyteller), this popular pub displays its Irish origins with a lengthy story written outside its door. Look for the traditional cobbler's tools and few old shoes in the windows.

Quids Inn, 56 Loch Promenade (tel. 611769). A money-saver for serious drinkers: pay £1 to get in and £1 per drink. Closed during the day in winter.

Stakis Hotel and Casino, Central Promenade (tel. 662662). Enormous and rather garish complex with nightclub, bars, and casino. Bars open until 3:30am. All kinds of people, from local teens to elderly tourists.

SIGHTS

Sightseeing in Douglas has to begin with the Victorian transportation network. The Steam Railway, Electric Railway, and Horse Trams are a living transportation museum. The **Electric Railway and Horse Tram terminal** marks the northeastern boundary of Douglas (look for the enormous, Hollywood-style "Electric Railway" sign). See Laxey (page 425) and Ramsey (page 426) to find uses for the terminal.

Just 100 yards toward town, Summer Hill, on its way to neighboring Onchan, runs past the entrance to **Summer Hill Glen,** a moist green corridor of forest that follows a stream for half a mile up a narrow river valley. A network of paths allows for exploration of the glen, a peaceful place during the day. On summer evenings, however, the glen is transformed into Mother Goose's worst nightmare. Blinking colored lights depict familiar nursery rhymes and dinosaurs. A giant, billboard-like painting with moving parts presents the teddy bear's picnic. Meanwhile, '30s-style recordings of children's songs play in an endless loop. The top of Summer Hill Glen reaches Glencrutchery Road, the last leg of the T.T. motorcycle race course. A half-mile left down Glencrutchery Rd. lies huge **Nobles Park,** where the T.T. races begin and end. The park contains a campground, tennis courts, lawn bowling, and mini-golf. Yet another set of landscaped gardens, **Villa Marina** spreads out where Broadway and Harris Promenade meet. The gardens are often used as an open-air theater.

Just past the Villa Marina on Harris Promenade sits one of the more impressive reminders of the island's Victorian heyday, the **Gaiety Theatre** (tel. 625001). The remarkable, newly restored stained-glass awning of the theater is unmistakable. The gilded and cherubic interior is even better. Frequent performances offer a glimpse of the theater in action, but to see the fascinating antique machinery under the stage you'll have to take a guided tour. The theater was designed by Frank Matcham, who designed most of the Victorian theaters in England. After years of decay, the Gaiety is gradually being restored to its original splendor. An enormous drop painting and backstage machinery, including a "grave trap" and two "demon traps," impress visitors. A little old lady sitting in seat D-14 is one of the theater's three ghosts. (Tours every Sat. at 10:30am, also July-Aug. Thurs. 2:30pm; 1¼ hr. Tea and scones afterwards. Free, but donation encouraged.)

Just south of the Gaiety Theatre, the shopping district begins. From here, signs lead to a parking garage with an elevator to the **Manx Museum** (tel. 675522). The terrific museum, which takes about three hours to see properly, chronicles the natural and human history of the island from the Ice Age to the present. A 20-minute introductory film gives a useful background on the whole island. The impressive

DOUGLAS

map gallery contains a huge 3-D model of the island with an accompanying computer database of IOM info. A 12,000-year-old Irish Elk skeleton, a reconstruction of the "Pagan Lady's Grave" discovered at Peel Castle, and displays on the wartime internment of resident aliens on the island all vie for visitors' attention. The museum also contains the **National Art Gallery** and a library stocked with every book on Manx subjects. (Museum and library open Mon.-Sat. 10am-5pm; free.)

The thing that looks like a little castle sitting on a rock in Douglas Bay is the **Tower of Refuge.** It sits on treacherous Conister Rock, which has caused many shipwrecks. The tower was built in 1832 to provide a shelter for shipwreck survivors to wait out the storm in, until they were rescued. The southern end of Douglas is marked by **Douglas Head,** which has lovely views back onto Douglas town.

ENTERTAINMENT

Most visitors to the Isle of Man want to participate in, rather than watch, their entertainment. As a result, the arts and entertainment scene here tends to be heavy on hypnotists and country crooners, low on theater and concerts. Jazz and trad are usually available to those who keep their eyes open.

The splendid **Gaiety Theatre** (tel. 625001) is the only theater of note on the island, but it does its best to fill the hole in the Manx arts scene with a complete range of musical and theatrical productions. The theater's season runs from March through December, but its busiest period is from July to October, when there are plays most nights. (Box office open Mon.-Sat. 10am-4:30pm and performance nights; tickets £4-12; discounts for seniors and children.) The Royal Hall at the **Villa Marina,** Harris Promenade (tel. 628855), has a variety of tacky entertainment. They'll stoop to anything from Ron Ricco the Hypnotist to professional wrestling. Occasionally, however, a pearl like the Chinese State Circus and others appears among the seaweed of '70s tribute bands. The **Summerland Complex** (tel. 625511), next to the Electric Railway terminal, has a similarly cheesy spectrum of summer entertainment on top of their cinema. Films are also shown at **Palace Cinema,** Central Promenade (tel. 676814). Both have mostly popular first-run films.

The **Gaiety Theatre** (see above) has occasional classical music and rare popular groups. The self-explanatory Hour of Popular Classical Music at **St. Thomas' Church,** Church Rd., showcases local talent (mid-May to mid-Sept. Wed. 7:45pm; free). Douglas pubs like **Bushy's Bar** have live, average rock and folk often in summer. The nightly live music scene at **Champs Entertainment Bar** (tel. 621218) in the Rutland Hotel, Queens Promenade, tends toward country (May-Sept. from 7:30pm). **Smuggler's** (tel. 629551), in the Admiral Hotel, Loch Promenade, hosts folk bands (April-Sept. Thurs. 8:40pm; cover £1.50) and the **Ridgeway Hotel,** Ridgeway St. (tel. 675612), has live music on Thursdays, Fridays, and Saturdays. The Summerland Complex (see above) boasts the **Manx Youth Orchestra** every Sunday night (admission free) and a summer cabaret, too (Mon.-Sat. 8pm).

On summer nights, Douglas overflows with youthful activity of both a local and a tourist flavor. Perhaps "local" is the wrong word, since much of Douglas' under-30 population is made up of foreigners (especially Irish) who've come here in search of jobs. In any case, the party crowd is very dedicated.

The **Stakis Hotel Complex** has a popular nightclub and a casino, both open until 3:30am. **Paramount City,** Queens Promenade (tel. 622447), turns into a nightclub called **The Dark Room** on Wed., Fri., and Sat. (9pm-2am; Wednesdays free; Fri. and Sat. free before 10pm, £2.50 after 10pm; over 21 only). It also contains the **Director's Bar,** which serves until 2am. **Jimmy B's,** Central Promenade, in the Castle Mona Hotel, sings along with karaoke on Thurs. (Mon.-Sat. 8pm-2am; over 21 only). **The Tardis,** Barrack St. (tel. 661547), is a reminder of the frightening number of Doctor Who fans on this island (open Mon.-Sat. 10pm-1:45am; Mon.-Thurs. free, Fri.-Sat. cover £2). Or rub elbows with Tony Bennett fans while ballroom dancing at the **Villa Marina Garden Room,** Harris Promenade (tel. 628855; Feb.-June Fri. at 8pm).

■ NEAR DOUGLAS

On the western edge of Douglas, about two miles from the Douglas bus station on the Peel Rd., the village of **Braddan** offers two sights of interest to visitors. The old church, next to the old cemetery, houses a major collection of Viking-era **Manx crosses** along with a few Celtic-period crosses. The typical Viking-style animalistic designs on these burial stones include depictions of dragons and runic inscriptions. The old church (as distinct from the new church) is on the Peel Rd. Also in Braddan, **Bushy's Brewery,** Mount Murray, offers tours by appointment (tel. 661244).

Three miles south on the Castletown Rd. from Douglas, fields full of happy old horses draw visitors to the **Isle of Man Home of Rest for Old Horses** (tel. 674594), Bulhrenny. Most of the happy horsies (saved by the Home from slaughterhouse doom) used to pull the trams back and forth across Douglas. A museum shows exactly how this came about. A little band of retired beach-ride donkeys have joined their cousins. (Open late May to mid-Sept. Mon.-Wed. 10am-4:50pm.) For those who prefer younger horses, the **Manx Equestrian Centre** (tel. 621852 or 675901) offers pony trekking through the countryside. They will pick you up from town. On your own, follow Broadway to Ballaquayle Rd., which turns into Ballanard Rd.—a two-mile trip from Douglas. (£5/hr., £10/half-day, £20/day including lunch.)

Northeast of Douglas, the neighboring village of **Onchan** is indistinguishable from Douglas itself. Families flock to the Onchan Pleasure Park for mini-golf and go-carts. The town's real treasures, several well-preserved Celtic-era **cross slabs,** lie in the porch of the village church on Church Rd. Take any Onchan bus to Avondale Rd., continue in the bus's direction, and turn right onto Church Rd. If it's open, **Molly Carrooin's Cottage** makes an interesting stop. It's the preserved cottage of a 19th-century washerwoman. (Open June to mid-Sept. Tues. and Sun. 2:30-4:30pm; free.)

■■■ LAXEY

Laxey is a quiet, picturesque village which seems to have changed very little since its heyday as a mining and mill town in the late 19th century. The town's main attraction is the old mine itself, which has a giant, restored waterwheel (72 feet in diameter), said to be the largest in the world. It is named the **Great Laxey Wheel (a.k.a. Lady Isabella).** Visitors can wander freely along the network of paths around the remains of the old lead and zinc mine workings. Only the above-ground parts of the mine are open, but the intrepid can climb the spiral steps to the small platform at the top of the wheel for a view of the surrounding valley. (Call tel. 675522 for info; wheel open Easter-Sept. daily 10am-5pm; £1.80.) After 5pm, the wheel no longer turns, but you can walk into the mine without paying. The way to the Wheel from the railway station is well-signposted, leading past the tiny **tourist office** and craft shop (tel. 862007; open Easter-Oct.), then up imaginatively named Water Hill.

While the town's peace and quiet are a welcome change from Douglas, accommodation and inexpensive food are hard to find. **Brown's Café,** Ham and Egg Terrace (tel. 862072), near the train station, serves typical sandwiches and salads (open daily 9:30am-6pm). The public footpath along the river ends up on the beachfront. Burgers and ice cream are available along the beach. **La Mona Lisa,** Minorca Hill (tel. 862488) serves pizza (£4-5) and pasta (£4.20-4.50) amid fake plants on the well posted road to the **Quarry Road Campsite** (tel. 861241; kitchen and bathrooms; open May-Sept.). The **Shore Hotel** serves tall, frothy pints at picnic tables. Right next to the tavern are two traditional looking cottages labeled **Blacksmith** and **Woodcanier.** Old implements, including a turnip docker and an iron bender, sit outside for inspection. More convenient to the award-winning train station is **Mine's Tavern.** The interior is designed to resemble a train carriage and is filled with railway memorabilia. Tasty food and outdoor seating add to your enjoyment (summer pudding £2, lasagne verdi £4.50; tel. 861484; open Mon.-Sat. noon-2pm and 6-9pm, Sun noon-2:45pm).

Shoppers may be drawn to the old **Laxey Woolen Mills,** Glen Rd. (tel. 861395), downhill from the train station, where cloth is still woven on hand looms for the benefit of tourists and moth connoisseurs. (Open Mon.-Sat. 9am-5:30pm, Sun. 2-5pm.) Laxey is accessible by **train** from Douglas (11/day; 30 min.; £2.30, £3.80 return) or Ramsey (11/day; 45 min.; £2.40, £4 return), or by bus (£1.25).

■ NEAR LAXEY: SNAEFELL

Laxey is also known to tourists as the beginning of the Snaefell Mountain Railway, a separate Electric Railway line which climbs the rattly, creaky five miles to the 2036-foot summit of **Snaefell,** the highest point on the island. It's rumored that Ireland, England, Scotland, and Wales are visible from the summit on clear days. If you find anyone who has been up there on a clear day, let us know. Perhaps remnants of the "mists of Mannanan" are left here from the time when the ancient Celtic sea-god, Mannanan, is said to have lived on the island, protecting it from invaders by hiding it in the mist.

Even if the view from the top is less than perfect, the ride on the 100-year-old train along the precipitous hillside and the views of the neighboring valleys and Sulby Reservoir are worth the trip. The train stops at **Murray's Motorcycle Museum** (tel. 861719) just before the summit, allowing bikers and fans the chance to peek at the 120 vintage machines (open mid-May to Sept. daily 10am-5pm; £2). The summit boasts a café, bar, shop, and a video about the history of the Manx railways. If you thought that the creaks and rattles emanating from the train on the way up the mountain were disturbing, wait until you hear the squealing of the brakes on the way down. (Trains depart Laxey for the summit Easter-Sept. daily 10:30am-3:30pm; return from Laxey £5.25, from Douglas £6.40.)

■ ■ ■ RAMSEY

The second-largest town on the island, Ramsey lies on the northwest coast where the Electric Railway line ends and the low northern plain begins. The town retains its Victorian feel in the harbor area (though the harbor itself is quite unattractive) and offers few sights of interest to tourists. But it is convenient to points north and west, like Maughold, the Point of Ayre, and Jurby.

The small **tourist office** (tel. 812228) is in the library in the town hall. The Ramsey **post office** (tel. 812248) is on Court Row. Banks include the **Isle of Man Bank** (tel. 812829) and **Barclays** (tel. 813596), both on Parliament St. (both open Mon.-Wed. and Fri. 9:30am-3:30pm, Thurs. 9:30am-5:30pm, with **ATMs).** The **Electric Railway** runs to Ramsey from Douglas via Laxey (April-May 12/day, mid-Sept.-Oct. 5/day; 1¼hr.; £5 return). **Buses** arrive from Douglas at a blistering pace (30/day, 50 min. £1.75). Bikes, ideal for exploring the area, can be rented at **Ramsey Cycles,** Bowring Rd. (tel. 814076). Three-speed bikes go for £4/day, £20/week, mountain bikes for £6/day, £40/week; no deposit (open Mon.-Sat. 9am-5:30pm).

Most of the accommodations in town are rather upscale. It would be cheaper and more relaxing to stay at Maughold (see Maughold, p. 427). The only affordable B&Bs in town are **Whitestones,** the Vollan (tel. 813824), a smoke-free B&B on Mooragh Promenade (single w/bath £17, double w/bath £30) and **Stanleyville Guest House,** Stanley Mount West (tel. 814420; £16/person).

There are scarcely any restaurants open for dinner. Stock up at **Safeway's,** Christian St. (tel. 813228; open Mon. 8:30am-7pm, Tues.-Thurs. until 8pm, Fri. until 9pm, Sat. 8am-7pm). Popular **Francesco's** (tel. 814692) right next to the Viking Hotel is a real treat. Cheery Italian atmosphere accompanies good food (pasta £5.95, fish £5.95; open Tues.-Sat. noon-1:30pm, and 7-9:30pm). For coffee-shop food with an international flair, try **Gophers,** 2 West Quay (tel. 815562)—the proprietors speak eight languages and make baked potatoes with fillings like Melted Manx cheese (£3.50), plus ploughman's lunch with wine (£4.50). (Open daily 10am-about 6pm.) The **Mitre Hotel,** Parliament St. (tel. 813045), serves ocean views with the pints.

Nearby, **Grove Rural Life Museum** (tel. 675522), formerly the summer home of a wealthy English merchant, has been restored to its original condition as an upper-class Victorian country house. Designed to complement to the Cregneash Folk Museum (see page 430), which represents the poorer class of Victorian farmers, the Grove is less engaging than its counterpart. Besides, there are Manx cats in the garden. The Museum is one mile out of town, on A9 to Andreas. (Open Easter-Sept. daily 10am-5pm; £1.80.) The town itself contains the **shipyard** where one of the earliest iron ships, the famous *Star of India*, was built. On the edge of town lies 40-acre **Mooragh Park,** complete with lake, gardens, and bowling and putting greens all built on land reclaimed from a marsh. You can rent rowboats, canoes, or sailing dinghies here from 11am (tel. 813375). Sailing and windsurfing lessons also available (£14.50/2 people; open Eater to June weekends only, June-Sept. daily). Ramsey hosts **Yn Chruinnaght** (tel. 815705) in the last week in July. The inter-Celtic festival features music, dance, art, and literature from all the Celtic nations: Mann, Scotland, Ireland, Wales, Cornwall, and Brittany.

■ NEAR RAMSEY

MAUGHOLD

Three miles southeast of Ramsey, Maughold makes a terrific excursion from Ramsey by bike along the coast road (or by bus from Ramsey). The **Maughold Churchyard** contains the best collection of Celtic and Norse Manx crosses on the island, as well as the remains of three early Christian chapels, or *keeills,* dating from as early as 800. Manx crosses date from early Christian times. They are Celtic crosses, similar to those found in Ireland (a cross with a circle), but show a Norse influence. Some depict scenes from Norse mythology, though supposedly symbols of Christianity.

The church itself, parts of which date from the 11th century, was named after St. Maughold. Legend has it that he was an Irish sinner who was tied up and cast adrift in the Irish Sea by St. Patrick as punishment. When he washed up on Maughold Head, he was so grateful to have survived that he founded an abbey on the site of the present church, whence Christianity spread across Mann. A road leads from the churchyard to the lighthouse on **Maughold Head,** where a nice walk across the cliffs known as the **Maughold Brooghs** begins. **Cardle Vooar Farm** (tel. 812160) provides accommodation (£13/person; open April-Oct.). The **Venture Centre** at Maughold (tel. 814240) offers a number of unique outdoor activities, including grass-skiing, absailing, clay pigeon shooting and archery.

POINT OF AYRE

From Ramsey, the main coastal road leads north through **Bride** and eventually, after seven miles, to the **Point of Ayre,** the northern tip of the island. A walk along the coast here affords spectacular views of the mountains of Scotland, only 17 miles away. To the west lies The Ayres, a region of elevated sand dunes rich in plant and bird life. **Ayres Visitors Centre** (tel. 801985) has displays on wildlife inside and nature trails outside. (Centre open mid-May to Sept. Wed.-Sun. 2-5pm; free.) **Buses** run from Ramsey to Bride (Mon.-Sat. 4/day, Sun. 2/day; 15 min; 90p.). From there, the center is two miles down the road west from of Bride. The north road leads to the Point of Ayre. Buses also run from Ramsey directly to the Point of Ayre (Mon.-Sat. 2/day; 20 min.; 90p).

■ ■ ■ CASTLETOWN

Nine miles south of Douglas, Castletown retains much of its energy and all of its history from its stint as the old capital of the island. (The town was "de-throned" because its harbor was too small.) The **tourist office** is located at the Town commissioner's office at the Civic Centre (tel. 825005). The Square and the narrow streets to the north and west of it contain most of the town's history and businesses, including the **IOM Bank,** 3 Market Sq. (tel. 822503; open Mon.-Wed. and Fri. 9:30am-3:30pm, Thurs. 9:30am-5:30pm; ATM) and the **post office,** Arbory St. (tel. 822516; open Mon.-Fri. 9am-12:30pm and 1:30-5:30pm, Sat. 9am-12:30pm). **Buses** from Port Erin/Port St. Mary (20/day; 25 min.; £1.10) and Douglas (20/day; 35 min.; £1.40) stop next to the castle. The **Steam Railway** station is a five-minute walk out of town toward Ballasalla (4-6/day; to Douglas, 40 min.; to Port Erin, 20 min.).

Accommodations, Food, & Pubs The most inexpensive place to stay in town is **Sandymount,** Bowling Green Rd. (tel. 822521), a large, beloved house near the beach. From the Castle, go across the footbridge, walk right along the sea to Bowling Green Rd., and head to its other end. From the railway station, turn left (away from town center), go 200 yards to the rotary, and turn right. The house is on the left (£14.50/person; open April-Sept.). The only year-round option is **The Rowans,** Douglas St. (tel. 823210), facing the beach (£16.50/person).

Simple meals, omelettes (£2.85-3.40), baked potatoes (£2-3), and sandwiches (£1.30-2.30) are available at **Ye Olde Bakery Café,** 31 Malew St. (tel. 823092). More substantial fare is on the snack menu at **Bunter's Bistro,** Parliament Sq. (tel. 822400), next to the old House of Keys (parliament) building. (Lasagne £3.25; open Mon.-Fri. noon-2pm and 7-10pm, Sat. 7-10pm). **Chablis Cellar Restaurant,** 21 Bank St. (tel. 823527), overlooking the harbor, has beautiful new decor but is only affordable at lunch. Lunch hours are Mon.-Sat. noon-2pm; lite bite menu 2:30-5pm (sandwiches £2.25-3). The **George Hotel,** Market Sq. (tel. 822533), offers a historic atmosphere and a surprisingly complete bar menu (chili con carne with rice £3.50; food served Mon.-Sat. noon-2pm). The lively, friendly **Glue Pot,** at the Hotel, overlooking the harbor, sticks to drinkers from all over the island.

Sights In summer, guided **walking tours** of Castletown leave from the tourist office, Tuesdays at 11am (£1.50 for 1¼-hr. tour; for info, call 823209). Otherwise, call guide Hugh Jackson (tel. 824412). The former seat of the Lords of Man, **Castle Rushen** (tel. 825761) dominates the center of town. The castle, which had its origins with the last Viking king, Magnus, around 1250, is one of the best preserved castles in the British Isles. Practically every room in the castle is open for exploration, and plaques explain the uses of each room during each period of the castle's history. The banquet hall has been reconstructed to resemble its appearance in the 1400s: a 15th-century Lord of Man feasts on 15th-century food, surrounded by 15th-century furniture. Even the castle kitchens and the workmen's sheds in the courtyard have been reconstructed. A "high-ranking" officer sits on the garderobe (toilet), with appropriate sound effects. Several rooms are also given over to exhibits which chronicle the history of the island and the castle through its use as an 18th-century prison. You can purchase a pamphlet on the history of the castle at reception for 50p. (Open Easter-Sept. daily 10am-5pm; £3, students £2.50.)

In the middle of the square, on the site of the former market cross (where two accused witches were burned at the stake in 1617), stands a tall pedestal with nothing on top. Intended as a monument to a popular former governor of the island, the structure was left unfinished due to lack of funds. The odd-looking structure beside the castle is a **dial** erected to commemorate John Wesley's Methodist preaching here in 1771. It tells the time by both the sun and the moon.

From the castle, a short walk toward the pier, across the footbridge and around the corner leads to the small **Nautical Museum,** (tel. 675522) with its 18th-century yacht and replica ship's cabin. (Open Easter-Sept. daily 10am-5pm; £1.80.) ¼ mile down the road, across from King William College, rises a small hill with a ruin at the top. Probably originally a prehistoric burial mound, this site, know as **Hango Hill,** is where the Manx patriot Illiam Dhone (William Christian) was executed for treason after he supported greater Manx independence from Britain.

Two miles north on the main Douglas Rd., the village of **Ballasalla** houses the ruins of the medieval Cistercian **Rushen Abbey.** Ballasalla also holds a rare opportunity to pet or purchase a **Manx cat.** These tailless cats appeared on the island only

300 years ago; they are characterized by their absent tail, long hind legs, awkward walk, and intestinal problems. Some surmise that they represent a cat/rabbit cross-breed. Demand an answer from **Mr. F. J. Wadsworth,** The Sycamores, Airport Rd. (tel. 824 345): he breeds and sells Manx cats. Completely tailless "rumpies" cost £100, while tiny-tailed "stumpies" go for £50.

■■■ PORT ERIN

Near the southern tip of the island, Port Erin lost its competition with Douglas to replace Castletown as the island's major port when its breakwater fell into the sea in 1884. As a result, Port Erin has remained small and quiet, despite the preponderance of tourist accommodation. While the B&Bs here are slightly more expensive than those in Douglas, the town's saner atmosphere and beautiful setting make it a tempting place to stay.

PRACTICAL INFORMATION

Tourist Office: Commissioners Office, Station Rd. (tel. 832298). A few pamphlets and advice on accommodations (no bookings). Open Mon.-Fri. 9am-5pm, Sat. 9am-noon.

Banks: IOM Bank, Station Rd. (tel. 822503). Open Mon.-Wed. and Fri. 9:30am-3:30pm, Thurs. 9:30am-5:30pm.

Post Office: Church Rd. (tel. 833119). Open Mon.-Wed. and Fri. 9am-1pm and 2-5:30pm, Thurs. 9am-1pm, Sat. 9am-12:30pm.

Trains: To Douglas: 4-6/day; 65 min.; £3.75. Station's coffee shop open daily 10am-4:30pm.

Buses: To Douglas: 20/day, 55 min., £1.70. To Peel: 3/day, 50 min., £1.75. From the bus stop, turn right, then right again at the Haven Bar. This street goes past the train station and down to the Upper Promenade. Buses to Douglas and Port St. Mary leave from Bridson St.

Fishing: Sea Sports, Strand Rd. Rents rods for fishing from the Port Erin pier (£4.50/day). Open daily 10am-6pm.

Horses: Port Erin Stables, (tel. 621852 or 675901). Free pickup from town. Beginners welcome. Half-day pony trek £10.

Pharmacy: Woodworth's Chemist, Orchard Rd. (tel. 832139). Open daily 9am-6pm, except Sat. open 9am-5:30pm.

ACCOMMODATIONS

York House, The Promenade (tel. 832440). A friendly welcome; clean, simple rooms with teapots and sinks; huge breakfasts (vegetarian option). £12/person.

Epworth, Church Rd. (tel. 832431), off the Promenade near the center of town. Popular and comfortable with sinks in the room. £14.50/person. Open May-Sept.

Anchorage, Atholl Park (tel. 832355). Great, green views of a glen from many bedrooms. £16/person, w/bath £18.50/person. Open March-Oct.

Brobourne House, The Promenade (tel. 832369). Outstanding breakfasts and a view of the beach that can't be beat. Catch up on *Doctor Who*—TVs in all rooms. From £15/person, w/bath £18; winter £13/person, w/bath £16/person.

FOOD

Port Erin will keep you well-fed. If you tire of inexpensive restaurants, try the **Shop-rite Supermarket,** Orchard Rd., behind the bus stop (Open Mon.-Tues. 9am-5:30pm, Wed.-Fri. 9am-8pm, Sat. 8:30am-5pm).

Cozy Nook Café, Lower Promenade (tel. 835020), right on the beach. Incredible setting on the beach with views of the bay and Mourne Mountains on a clear day. Sandwiches (£1.30-1.50) and salads (£2.50-3.25). Summer evenings (6:30-9pm) are chef's night off: cook-your-own-barbecues from a choice of veggie burgers, steak, chicken, or other meat, with baked potato, salad, and bread for £3-5.50.

Open April-Sept. Mon.-Sat. 10:30am-5pm, 6:30-9pm, Sun. 10:30am-9pm (early closing in bad weather); Oct.-March Fri.-Sun. 10am-6pm.

DaVinci's Brobourne House, The Promenade (tel. 832369). Offers interesting pasta dishes, pizza, steaks, and seafood. 7" pizzas from £2.50, pasta £4-5. Open Mon. and Wed.-Sat. 7-10pm, Sun. noon-3pm and 7-10pm.

The Cherry Tree Grill, Bridson St. (tel. 833811), in the Cherry Orchard Hotel, has some affordable meals: vegetable moussaka £4.20, tortellini in cheese and mushroom sauce £4.10. Interesting and filling starters as well (assorted satay £3.40, dim sum £3.75). Open Mon.-Sat. 11am-9:45pm, Sun. 4-9:45pm.

SIGHTS

Port Erin's major attractions are natural ones. Cruises to the **Calf of Man,** the small island and bird sanctuary off the southern tip of Man, leave from the Port Erin pier during the summer daily in good weather. Visitors can choose between a 1¼-hr. cruise around the Calf, with good views of the cliffs, seals, the odd basking shark, and countless sea birds, or a ferry service. The ferry gives anywhere from an hour to a whole day to explore the island and its bird observatory and herds of native, four-horned Loghtan sheep. (Tel. 832339; April-Sept. Cruises leave 10:15am daily; ferries leave 10:15, 11:30am, and 1:30pm daily, last return at 3:30pm; £6 return.) To get to the Calf, you can also charter a boat from Port St. Mary. Bob Taylor at **Gemini Fishing Charter and Sightseeing** (tel. 832761) can arrange wildlife watching or sea angling trips.

The **Railway Museum,** in the railway station, is free but suitable for die-hard rail fans only. Its collection of old photographs is nothing to look down your nose at. (Open April-Oct. 9am-noon and 1-4pm.) The **Marine Interpretation Centre** (tel. 832027), in the University of Liverpool's Department of Marine Biology, will interpret nature for you. A small room is full of displays and a video on the ecology of the Calf and surrounding waters. (Open Mon.-Fri. 10am-5pm; free.) To reach the University from Port Erin, face the sea, turn left, and walk as far as you can. A pleasant path begins across from the Port Erin Royal Hotel, leading north along the cliffs past sandy coves to **Bradda Head,** which is capped by a key-shaped tower built to honor local philanthropist and safe-maker William Milner. This short walk, especially peaceful and beautiful at sunset, offers views across to the Mourne Mountains of Northern Ireland. On some days, the Mournes seem to "come right into the bay," a sure sign that the next day will be rainy, or that a disastrous earthquake has just struck Co. Down. Erosion makes it dangerous to leave the path.

The 1½-mile road to Cregneash, past the strange Neolithic **Meayll Circle** (a chambered burial mound) makes a nice walk. The **Cregneash Village Folk Museum** (tel. 675522) is a fascinating preservation of 19th-century life in a farming village. Farmers and craftspeople in traditional dress demonstrate their skills for the visitors. You can also read about how Manx ponies, cattle, and pigs (referred to as "purrs") became extinct, and gaze at the still existing Loghtan sheep and an occasional Manx cat. Be sure to watch the ten-minute video at the shop. (Open Easter-Sept. 10am-5pm; £2.) The 6-mi. portion of the coastal walking path *(Raad ny Foillan)* between Port Erin and the fishing village of **Port St. Mary** to the east is a manageable walk with stunning views of cliffs and sea. (Buses run back to Port Erin frequently.) The *Southern Walks* pamphlet, free from tourist offices, describes these walks.

The **Erin Arts Centre,** Victoria Sq. (tel. 832662) hosts several events. The **Mannanan International Festival of Music and the Arts** features all kinds of classical music, dance, drama, and lectures in late June and early July. **Sundays at Eight** is a monthly happening (first Sundays of the month) of classical recitals. Contact the Arts Centre for more info. At Port St. Mary, Wednesday is **Craft and Heritage Day** during the summer. The fair is held at Town Hall, the Promenade (open 10am-4pm).

■■■ PEEL

The "most Manx of all towns" or "the Sunset City," Peel is a beautiful fishing town on the west coast of the island. Narrow streets and small stone buildings have hardly changed since the days when its fishers sailed from Kildare to the Hebrides. The town is the headquarters of the big-time Manx kipper industry; except for connoisseurs of brine, visitors to Peel will more likely enjoy its cathedrals and coastal walks.

PRACTICAL INFORMATION

Tourist Office: Town Hall, Derby Rd. (tel. 842341). Has pamphlets with self-guided walking tours. Open Mon.-Thurs. 9am-5:15pm, Fri. 9am-4:30pm.

Financial services: IOM Bank, Atholl St. (tel. 842122). Open Mon.-Wed. and Fri. 9:30am-3:30pm, Thurs. 9:30am-5:30pm. **ATM.**

Post Office: Market Pl. (tel. 842282). Open Mon.-Wed. and Fri. 9am-12:30pm and 1:30-5:30pm, Thurs. and Sat. 9am-12:30pm.

Buses: Station is on Atholl St. To reach Market Pl., turn left, then right onto Douglas St., which runs into Market Pl. Buses go to Douglas (30/day, 40 min.), Ramsey (10/day, 40 min.), and Port Erin (3/day, 55 min.).

ACCOMMODATIONS

The Haven Guest House, 10 Peveril Ave. (tel. 842585). Non-smoking. All rooms have teapots, TVs, radios, and bathrooms, so there is no need ever to leave them. £17/person. Open all year.

Seabourne House, Mount Morrison (tel. 842571). Vegetarian breakfasts offered (an easy escape from kippers) and tea-making facilities. £14/person.

Kerrowgarrow Farm, Greeba (tel. 801871). Dairy farm in the countryside 4 mi. from Peel on the Douglas Rd. Sinks and TVs in all rooms. £15/person.

Peel Camping Park (tel. 842341). Laundry, game room, TV room, supermarket close by, disabled-accessible bathroom. £3.50/person. Open May-Sept.

FOOD & PUBS

There's not much decent food to be found in Peel—everyone's too focused on kippers. **Peel Wholefoods,** 5 Douglas St., sells health food to crafty eaters (open Fri.-Wed. 9:30am-5pm, Thurs. 9:30am-7pm). The best bet for food is the **Creek Inn Pub,** The Quay (tel. 842216), which serves meals all day (crab salad £5; food served Mon.-Sat. 11am-11pm, Sun. noon-1:30pm and 8-10pm), and the best place to drink is the **White House Hotel,** a former farmhouse on the Tynwald Rd. Other food options are the **Bay Tree Café,** corner of Derby Rd. and Christian St., which serves the expected sandwiches and snacks (Mon.-Sat. 9am-5pm), and **Hong Kong Delight,** Atholl Pl. (tel. 842944), which also serves the expected (£5-6; Mon.-Sat. 5-10:30pm, Sun. noon-2pm and 5-10pm).

SIGHTS

Peel Town Walks (tel. 842852) start from Point Odin's Raven, The Quay, with a special focus on the town's architecture and personalities (Wed. 2:30pm; tours last 1½hr.; £1.50). Alternatively, the free *Peel on Foot* self-guided walking tours (there are three in the series) are available at the tourist office.

Peel Castle is located on **St. Patrick's Isle,** now connected to the mainland by a causeway, where the first Christian missionaries (followers of St. Patrick) landed around 450. A second wave of missionaries from Iona (St. Columba's crew) came around 550; many Manx churches are still named for them. In the 800s, Viking raids forced the Christians to build stone churches instead of ones made out of timber and sod. In the 10th century, the clever monks added round towers, the better to see you with, my dear Viking. The path over the rocks around the castle offers views of nothing but the sea, as well as a good vantage point to see the **seals** which often feed in the surrounding waters and their complement of seagulls waiting to snatch the leftover fish. The castle's name is derived from an earlier fort made of timber, or "piles," built by the Viking King Magnus Barefoot. The castle has a ghost, in the form of a black dog, the **Moddey Dhoo,** which supposedly frightened one of the resident soldiers to death in the 17th century. A mark on the ground in front of the castle's entrance is evidence of a medieval system of timekeeping: when the shadow of the castle's corner hit the mark at noon, it was time to change the guard. Peel Castle was the site of a major archaeological excavation which uncovered the "Pagan Lady's Grave," now on display at the Manx Museum (see page 423). Inside the castle are a 10th-century Irish-style round tower, built as a place of refuge for the monks during Viking raids, and the 13th-century **Cathedral of St. German.** The damp, eerie **Bishop's Dungeon** under the cathedral was used for hundreds of years to punish sinners for terrible offenses such as missing church.

The two **kipper factories** on the island are in Peel. They don't give factory tours (just think of what you're missing!), but you can buy fresh kippers from the factory stores: try **Devereau,** Mill Rd., the largest curers of Manx kippers in the known universe. You can even write them for mail-order, vacuum-sealed kippers. While munching on your factory-fresh kippers, learn all about the history of the factory that produced it at **The Leece Museum,** Castle St. The very small museum tells all about the history of Peel, especially its fishing industry. (Open mid-May to mid-Oct. Mon.-Sat. 2-4pm.) Learn about more tastebud-pleasing foodstuffs at **Davisons' Chocolate Factory,** 1 Douglas St. (tel. 843524), which does have tours (every ½-hr. Mon.-Fri. 11am-4pm).

Peel hosts the **Theatre Set Up** (tel. 842104) every mid-July. This open-air Shakespeare festival is held at Peel Castle. **Viking Boat Races** (tel. 843640), held in August, pit teams of twenty rowers in Viking-style boats against the unforgiving bay and their own Nordic stamina.

Easy Law-making

Tynwald Hill is an ancient site of the original Tynwald (parliament) from Norse times, and is still the site of **Tynwald Fair,** where Manx laws are proclaimed on July 5. Acts which are passed by Tynwald and the Governor (a rubber-stamp representative of the Queen) are read in Manx and English at the open-air meeting. This reading turns acts into law. But the fact that they are Tynwald laws doesn't mean that they are enforceable. For example, capital punishment by hanging is still allowed by the Tynwald constitution but no longer enacted. Homosexuality, on the other hand, is still officially illegal yet never prosecuted. "Tynwald" comes from the Norse for "assembly field." The Norse have met at this assembly field since at least the 9th century. The island's long experience with parliamentary procedure has led to legal innovations like a nationwide transferable vote system for the lower house, the House of Keys. (Keys means "chosen"—the Vikings picked the most worthy to represent them.) Voters rank the candidates on their ballot, which means that a strong faction is less likely to win a divided election. The first women's suffrage was granted by Tynwald in 1881, though only to property owners.

■ LONDON

At first glance, London is kind to the expectations of visitors stuffing their mental baggage with bobbies and Beefeaters, nursery rhymes and "Masterpiece Theatre," Sherlock Holmes and history books. The relatively small area embraced by the Underground's Circle Line seems filled to bursting with the "big sights," and all the city's double-decker red buses seem to spin around the mad whirl of Piccadilly Circus. But central London is just a speck on the Greater London map. Beyond Tower Bridge looms the glossy, pyramid-tipped Canary Wharf skyscraper, centerpiece of the world's largest and most controversial redevelopment. The Victorian doorway inscribed with an Anglican piety may belong to a Sikh or a Muslim in a city internalizing its imperial past. What makes London not just "quite interesting," but rather, enthralling, can be found partly in this, a tension between the close quarters of central London and the expansive boroughs; between the cluttered, "familiar," and sometimes fictional past of the heritage industry and a riotously modern present.

Unless you're coming by ferry from the Continent, it's likely that you'll be arriving via London. Most flights to Ireland connect in London (see Getting There, p. 27). Remember that London travel agents offer some economical train-and-ferry or bus-and-ferry connections to Ireland, Northern Ireland, and the Isle of Man—see Getting There for details, or stop in at one of the budget travel offices listed below in Practical Information. For an absolutely dapper little book packed with first-rate info on this city, grab a copy of *Let's Go: London*.

ORIENTATION & PRACTICAL INFORMATION

London is divided into boroughs and postal code areas, and into informal districts. Both the borough name and postal code prefix appear at the bottom of most street signs. The city has grown by absorbing nearby towns, which is reflected in borough names such as "City of Westminster" and "City of London" (or simply "The City").

Central London, on the north side of the Thames and bounded roughly by the Underground's Circle Line, contains most of the major sights. Within central London the vaguely defined **West End** incorporates the understated elegance of Mayfair, the shopping streets around Oxford Circus, the theaters and tourist traps of Piccadilly Circus and Leicester Square, the exotic labyrinth of Soho, chic Covent Garden, and London's unofficial center, Trafalgar Square. East of the West End lies **Holborn,** center of legal activity, and **Fleet Street,** the traditional journalists' haunt.

Around the southeastern corner of the Circle Line is **The City:** London's financial district, with the Tower of London at its eastern edge and St. Paul's Cathedral nearby. Farther east is the **East End,** ethnically diverse and working-class, and the epic construction site of **Docklands.** Moving back west, along the river and the southern part of the Circle Line is the district of **Westminster,** the royal, political, and ecclesiastical center of England, where you'll find Buckingham Palace, the Houses of Parliament, and Westminster Abbey. In the southwest corner of the Circle Line, below the expanse of **Hyde Park,** are gracious **Chelsea,** embassy-laden **Belgravia,** and **Kensington,** adorned with London's posher shops and restaurants.

Around the northwest corner of the Circle Line, tidy terraces border **Regent's Park;** nearby are the faded squares of **Paddington** and **Notting Hill Gate,** home to large Indian and West Indian communities. Moving east towards the Circle Line's northeast corner leads to **Bloomsbury,** which harbors the British Museum, London University colleges, art galleries, and specialty bookshops. Trendy residential districts stretch to the north, including **Hampstead** and **Highgate,** with the enormous Hampstead Heath and fabulous views of the city.

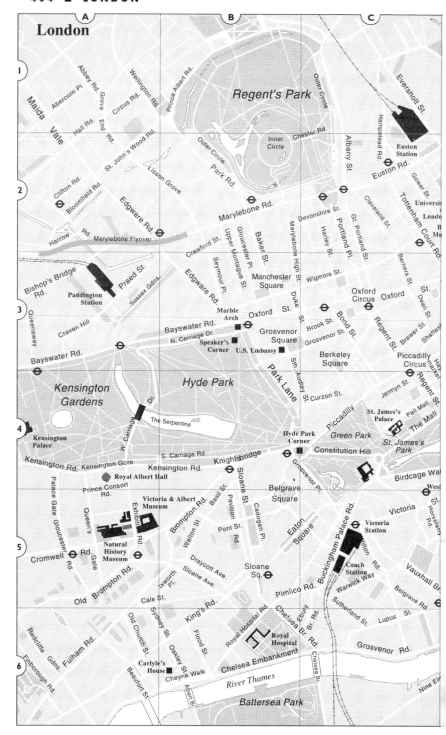

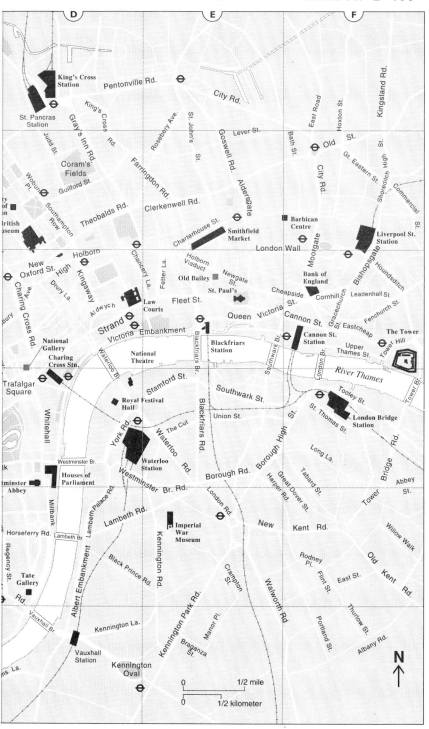

Trying to reach a **specific destination** in London can be frustrating. Numbers often go up one side of a street and down the other. One road may change names four times in fewer miles, and a single name may designate a street, lane, square, and row. A good map is key. For a day's walk, London Transport's free map will do, but those staying a week or longer ought to buy a London street index. *London A to Z* (that's "ay to zed," by the way), *Nicholson's Streetfinder*, and the *ABC London Street Atlas* (all £2 and up) are excellent.

For the most part, London is a tourist-friendly city. It's hard to unwittingly wander into unnerving neighborhoods; these areas, in parts of Hackney, Tottenham, and South London, lie well away from central London. The areas around King's Cross/St. Pancras and Notting Hill Gate tube stations are a bit seedy at night. Avoid parks, heaths, and the riverbanks in all areas after dark. Late trains on the tube out of central London are usually crowded and noisy. But waiting late at night at less central stations can be unsettling. In general, unattended packages will be taken either by thieves or by the police, who are paranoid (and rightly so) about terrorist bombs. Leave nothing unattended.

Tourist Offices: London Tourist Board Information Centre: Victoria Station Forecourt, SW1 (tel. (0839) 123432, recorded message only, 48p per min.). Tube: Victoria. Info on London and England, a well-stocked bookshop, theater and tour bookings, and an accommodations service (£5 booking fee, plus 15% refundable deposit). Open April-Nov. daily 8am-7pm; Dec.-March Mon.-Sat. 8am-7pm, Sun. 8am-5pm. **British Travel Centre:** 12 Regent St., SW1 (tel. (0171) 495 4466). Tube: Piccadilly Circus. Down Regent St. from Lower Regent St. tube exit. Run by the British Tourist Authority and ideal for travelers bound for destinations outside of London. Pleasantly relaxed compared to LTB, but similarly long queues. Open Mon.-Fri. 9am-6:30pm, Sat. 9am-5pm, Sun. 10am-4pm; Nov.-April Mon.-Fri. 9am-6:30pm, Sat.-Sun. 10am-4pm. **City of London Information Centre:** St. Paul's Churchyard, EC4 (tel. 606 3030). Tube: St. Paul's. Specializes in the City of London but answers questions on all of London. Helpful staff. Open 9:30am-5pm; Nov.-March Mon.-Fri. 9:30am-5pm, Sat. 9:30am-12:30pm.

Budget Travel: London is *the* place to shop for cheap bus, plane, and train tickets to North America, Africa, Asia, and Australia. Browse the ads in *Time Out* or the *Evening Standard*. Campus Travel is affiliated with USIT, the Irish student travel organization. **Trailfinders,** 42-50 Earl's Ct. Rd., W8 (tel. 937 5400). Tube: High St. Kensington. Busier branch at 194 Kensington High St., W8 (tel. 938 3232). Tube: High St. Kensington. Travel services. Both branches open Mon.-Wed. and Fri.-Sat. 9am-6pm, Thurs. 9am-7pm, Sun. (telephone only at Earl's Ct.) 10am-4pm.

Embassies and High Commissions: U.S., 24 Grosvenor Sq., W1 (tel. 499 9000). Tube: Bond St. **Canada,** MacDonald House, 1 Grosvenor Sq., W1 (tel. 629 9492). Tube: Bond St. or Oxford Circus. Visas Mon.-Fri. 8-11am. **Australia,** Australia House, The Strand, WC2 (tel. 379 4334; emergency tel. 438 8181). Tube: Aldwych or Temple. Visa and passport inquiries tel. 438 8818. Open Mon.-Fri. 9:30am-3:30pm. **Ireland,** 17 Grosvenor Pl., SW1 (tel. 235 2171). Tube: Hyde Park Corner. Open Mon.-Fri. 9:30am-1pm and 2:15-5pm. **New Zealand,** New Zealand House, 80 Haymarket, SW1 (tel. 930 8422). Tube: Charing Cross. Open Mon.-Fri. 10am-noon and 2-4pm. **South Africa,** South Africa House, Trafalgar Sq. WC2 (tel. 930 4488). Tube: Charing Cross.

Post Office: Save hassle and have mail sent to **Trafalgar Sq.,** 24-28 William IV St., London WC2N 4DL (tel. 930 9580). Tube: Charing Cross. Open Mon.-Sat. 8am-8pm. If you don't specify a post office, mail will be sent to either Trafalgar Sq. or London Chief Office, King Edward Bldg., EC1 (tel. 239 5047). Tube: St. Paul's. Open Mon.-Tues. and Thurs.-Fri. 8:30am-6:30pm, Wed. 9am-6:30pm.

Telephones: Most phones accept change or phonecards, but not both. The blue Mercurycard phones are cheaper than BT phones, but harder to find. London has 2 **city codes:** 0171 (central London) and 0181 (outer London). Use the code only if you are calling from one area to the other. All London numbers listed in *Let's Go* are (0171) unless otherwise indicated.

Flights: Heathrow Airport (tel. (0181) 759 4321) is the world's busiest airport. From Heathrow, take the **Underground** to central London (45 min.). London Transport's **Airbus** (tel. 222 1234) zips from Heathrow to central points, including hotels (1hr.; £5). Most charter flights land at **Gatwick Airport** (tel. (0293) 535353). From there, take the BR Gatwick Express train to Victoria Station (daily 5:30am-8pm every 15 min., 8pm-1am every 30 min.; £8.50 return). **National Express** (tel. (0990) 808080) buses run 5:30am-11pm from Victoria Station to Gatwick (every hr.; 1hr.; £6.50). Taxis take twice as long and cost 5 times as much. British Rail's Stansted Express runs to **Stansted Airport** (tel. (01279) 68 0500) from Liverpool St. station (£10).

Trains: 8 major stations: Charing Cross, Euston, King's Cross, Liverpool St., Paddington, St. Pancras, Victoria, and Waterloo. All stations linked by the Underground. **Travel Centres** at its mainline stations and at 12-16 Regent St. (tube: Piccadilly Circus); The Strand (tube: Charing Cross); Victoria St.; and King William St. All open Mon.-Fri. 9am-5pm. Talking timetables: To East Anglia, Essex, Southern England, Northeast, East, and South London: tel. 387 8775. To the South Midlands, West of England, South Wales, West London, and Republic of **Ireland via Fishguard:** tel. 387 5790. To the East and West Midlands, North Wales, Northwest England, Scotland via West Coast, Northwest London, **Northern Ireland,** Republic of **Ireland via Holyhead,** and the **Isle of Man:** tel. 387 7070. To East and Northeast England, Scotland via East Coast, and North London: tel. 278 2824. To continental Europe: tel. (0891) 8887131.

Buses: Victoria Coach Station (tube: Victoria), located on Buckingham Palace Rd., is the hub of Britain's denationalized coach network. **National Express coaches** (tel. (0990) 808080) service an expansive network. Outer London area served by **Green Line** (tel. (0181) 668 7261) coaches, which leave frequently from Eccleston Bridge behind Victoria Station. Purchase tickets from the driver. Discounts include the one-day **Rover** ticket (£6, valid on almost every Green Line coach and London Country bus Mon.-Fri. after 9am, Sat.-Sun. all day).

Luggage Storage: Very restricted, due to recent bomb threats. Storage companies in the London area charge £3-5 per item per week (check the Yellow Pages under "Storage Service").

Public Transportation: The **Underground** (or **Tube**) is fast, efficient and crowded. It opens about 6am; the last train runs around midnight. Buy your ticket before you board and pass it through automatic gates at both ends of your journey. On-the-spot £10 fine if you're caught without a valid ticket. The **Travelcard** is a must for budget travelers. One-day Travelcards cannot be used before 9:30am Mon.-Fri., and are not valid on night buses (adult one-day Travelcard, zones 1 & 2, £2.80). Travelcards can be used on the Underground, regular buses, British Rail (Network SouthEast), and the Docklands Light Railway. The one-week and one-month Travelcards can be used at any time, and are valid for Night Bus travel. (1-wk. Travelcard, zones 1&2, £13; 1-mo. Travelcard, zones 1&2, £50. Bring a passport-sized photo). **Night buses** (the "N" routes) run frequently throughout London 11pm- 6am. All pass through Trafalgar Sq., and many stop at Victoria as well. Pick up a free brochure about night buses, which includes times of the last British Rail and Underground trains. The **bus** network is divided into 4 zones. In and around central London, one-way fares range from 50p to £1.20, depending on the number of zones you cross. Pick up free maps and guides at **London Transport's Information Centres** (look for the lowercase "i" logo on signs) at the following major tube stops: King's Cross, Piccadilly Circus, Oxford Circus, St. James's Park, Liverpool St., Hammersmith, and Heathrow Terminals 1, 2, 3 station (most open Mon.-Fri. 8am-6pm; central London stations also have weekend hours).

Taxis: Hail your own or call a radio-dispatched taxi (tel. 272 0272 or 253 5000). London fares are steep, and 10% tip is standard. In addition to licensed black cabs, there are tons of unregulated "minicabs" in the Yellow Pages. **Ladycabs** (tel. 272 3019) has only women drivers.

Hitchhiking: Anyone who values safety will take a train or bus out of London. Hitchers check the University of London Union's **ride board,** on the ground floor of 1 Malet St., WC1 (tube: Russell Sq.), or ask at youth hostels. **Freewheelers** is a ride-share agency. £10 annual membership required. You must pay for five matchups (each £1) in advance. Single-sex matching available. Call (0191) 222 0090, or write to Freewheelers, Ltd., 25 Low Friar St., Newcastle upon Tyre, NE1 54E.

Disabled Travelers: Call **Disability Information and Advice Service** (tel. 275 8485), or the **Greater London Association for the Disabled** (tel. 274 0107). 24-hr. travel info hotline (tel. 222 1234).

Bisexual, Gay, and Lesbian Information: London Lesbian and Gay Switchboard (tel. 837 7324). 24-hr. advice and support service. **Bisexual Helpline:** tel. (0181) 569 7500. **Lesbian Line** (tel. 251 6911 or 253 0924).

Hotlines: Samaritans, 46 Marshall St., W1 (tel. 734 2800). Tube: Oxford Circus. 24-hr. crisis hotline. **London Rape Crisis Centre** (tel. 837 1600). 24 hrs.

Pharmacy: Every police station keeps a list of emergency doctors and pharmacies in its area. Listings under "Chemists" in the Yellow Pages. **Bliss Chemists,** 5 Marble Arch, W1 (tel. 723 6116), is open 9am-midnight. **Boots Chemists** has branches throughout London.

Medical Assistance: You can receive free treatment in the casualty ward (emergency room) of any hospital. Try **Westminster Hospital,** Dean Ryle St., Horseferry Rd., SW1 (tel. 746 8000; tube: Pimlico) or **Royal London Hospital,** Whitechapel Rd., E1 (tel. 377 7000; tube: Whitechapel).

Emergency: Dial 999; no coins required.

ACCOMMODATIONS

Write well in advance to reserve rooms for summer. From London's spectrum of accommodations, private hostels and university halls of residence are the best buys. Check for reduced weekly rates in hotels. Sleeping outdoors is unsafe and illegal.

YHA/HI Hostels

Cheap, cheery, and full of the young, London's YHA hostels can be a welcome relief from dreary urban B&Bs. Groups gobble space early, but some beds are kept free for individuals. Reserve ahead for July and August; if not, it's still worth calling (central tel. 248 6547). Bring a padlock to secure your personal locker.

Oxford Street, 14-18 Noel St., W1 (tel. 734 1618; fax 734 1657). Tube: Oxford Circus. Heart of London and Soho. Small, plush rooms for 2-4. 24-hr. security. Spacious TV lounge. Currency exchange. Baggage room. Reception open 7am-11pm. No curfew. £16.70/person, under 18 £13.60.

City of London, 36 Carter La., EC4 (tel. 236 4965). Tube: St. Paul's. From the City Information Centre on the opposite side of St. Paul's Cathedral, go left down Godliman St. Take the first right onto Carter Lane. Centrally located and newly refurbished. Reception open 7am-11pm. Single or double £22.20, under 18 £18.70. Triple or quad £19.70, under 18 £16. 5-8 bed dorm £19.10 (under 18 £16). 10-15 bed dorm £14.20 (under 18 £11.10).

Earl's Court, 38 Bolton Gns., SW5 0AQ (tel. 373 7083; fax 835 2034). Tube: Earl's Court. Townhouse in leafy area. 24-hr. security. Currency exchange. Reception open 7:30am-10:30pm. 4-16 per room. No curfew. £17.10/person, under 18 £15.

Highgate, 84 Highgate West Hill, N6 (tel. (0181) 340 1831). Tube: Archway. An unassuming Georgian house set along a residential street in the middle of historic Highgate village. One of the more "traditional" rough-it hostels, where 20 people sometimes share 1 shower and 1 toilet. Reception open 8:45-10am, 1-7pm, and 8-11:30pm. Strict midnight curfew. £11.85/person, under 18 £7.90.

Rotherhithe, Island Yard., Salter Rd., SE16 (tel. 232 2114). Tube: Rotherhithe. 15min. walk down Brunel Rd. to Salter. Welcome to *2001: A Space Odyssey.* Complete facilities (they're in the process of installing new showers) and tightly-packed but immaculate rooms, mostly with 2 or 6 beds. No curfew. 24-hr. security. £16.50/person, under 18 £13.50. Wheelchair access.

Epping Forest, Wellington Hall, High Beach, Loughton, Essex 1G10 (tel. (0181) 508 5161). Tube: Loughton (zone 6, 45 min. from central London), or BR: Chingford (zone 5), then a good 2 mi. walk through the forest. Taxi from the station is a few pounds. A retreat from London havoc and prices. Set in the heart of 6000 remote acres of ancient woodland. £4.45-6.55/person. Open Feb.-Dec.

Private Hostels

Private hostels, which do not require an HI card, generally have a youthful clientele. Some have kitchen facilities and there are rarely curfews.

Central University of Iowa Hostel, 7 Bedford Pl., WC1 (tel. 580 1121; fax 580 5638). Tube: Holborn or Russell Sq. Bright, spartan, clean rooms. Near the British Museum. 2-week max. stay. Reception open 8am-1pm and 3-8pm. Laundry. Single £17, double £15.50/person, triple/quad £14/person. Open mid-May to mid-Aug.

Astor's Museum Inn, 27 Montague St., WC1 (tel. 580 5360; fax 636 7948). Tube: Holborn, Tottenham Ct. Rd., or Russell Sq. Prime location across from British Museum. 24.-hr. reception. Continental breakfast. No curfew; co-ed. 10-bed dorm £13, 6- and 8-bed dorm £14, 4-bed dorm £15. MC, Visa.

Tonbridge School Clubs, Ltd., corner of Judd and Cromer St., WC1 (tel. 837 4406). Tube: King's Cross. Right price for desperadoes. Seedy area. Blanket and foam pads on gymnasium floor. Non-British students with passports only. Reception open 10-11:30pm. Check-out 10am. Hot showers, storage. £3/person.

Palace Court Hotel, 64-65 Prince's Sq., W2 (tel. 229 4747 or 4412; fax 727 5437). Tube: Bayswater or Notting Hill Gate. Keg parties every Wed. night, outdoor patio area, and airy, comfortable rooms. Much boisterous activity. Sheets and cozy duvets included. English breakfast. Call ahead. 6-bed dorm £11, 4-bed dorm £12, double £14/person.

Palace Hotel, 31 Palace Ct., W2 (tel. 221 5628 or 243 8157). Tube: Notting Hill Gate or Queensway. Bright rooms and an excellent social space. Continental breakfast. 8-bed dorm £10. Cash only.

Quest Hotel, 45 Queensborough Terrace, W2 (tel. 229 7782). Tube: Queensway. Communal, clean, and sociable; staff throws one theme party a month. Continental breakfast included. English breakfast £2. Pool room and kitchen open. Key deposit £3. Call ahead. 4-8 bed dorm £11.50-14. MC, Visa.

Albert Hotel, 191 Queens Gate, SW7 (tel. 584 3019). Tube: Gloucester Rd., or bus #2 from S. Kensington. A substantial walk from the tube; take a right on Cromwell then left on Queen's Gate. Hotel is about ¼mi. on your right. The bus is quicker. Stately lounges with plush couches. Pool table, color TV. 24-hr. reception. Reserve ahead. No lockout or curfew. Dorm £10-12.50, double £35, quad £52.

Curzon House Hotel, 58 Courtfield Gdns., SW5 (tel. 581 2116). Tube: Gloucester Rd. Tidy and cool. Most rooms have tall ceilings and mammoth windows that overlook a gracious park. Continental breakfast. Single-sex dorm £13, single £28, double £18/person, triple £17/person, quad £17/person. Visa, MC.

Elizabeth House (YWCA Hostel), 118 Warwick Way, SW1 (tel. 630 0741). Tube: Victoria. Anyone over 5 welcome. Friendly. Continental breakfast included. Reserve early with £10 deposit. Dorm £15, single £21, double £40-45.

Victoria Hotel, 71 Belgrave Rd. SW1 (tel. 834 3077; fax 932 0693). Tube: Pimlico. From the station, take the Bessborough St. (south side) exit and go left along Lupus St. Take a right at St. George's Sq.; Belgrave Rd. starts on the other side. Whimsical splashes of color brighten the standard rooms with bunk beds. Cozy kitchen, TV lounge, pool table. Dorm £11-14. MC, Visa.

University Halls of Residence

London's university residences often accommodate visitors for limited periods during the summer break and during Easter vacations. Many of these halls are characterized by box-like rooms and institutional furniture. Most charge around £20 and contain all singles, offering more privacy than a hostel. Call well in advance (by April for July reservations), as conference groups tend to snatch up rooms early. **King's Campus Vacation Bureau,** 552 King's Rd., London SW10 OUA (tel. 351 6011), controls bookings for a number of residence halls where students of **King's College** of the University of London live during the academic year. Rooms are available from early June to mid-September.

Carr Saunders Hall, 18-24 Fitzroy St., W1 (tel. 580 6338). Tube: Warren St. Turn right off Tottenham Ct. Rd. onto Grafton Way, then left onto Fitzroy St. A newer

London School of Economics building. English breakfast. Min. 4 nights. Single £21.50, double £42.

Connaught Hall, 36-45 Tavistock Sq., WC1 (tel. 387 6181; fax 383 4109). Tube: Russell Sq. Head left from the station and turn right onto Woburn Pl.; the first left is Tavistock Sq. Small, single, typical dorm bedrooms. Reception open Mon.-Sat. 8am-midnight, Sun. 9am-11pm. Singles £19.50. English breakfast. Reservations recommended. Open July-Aug.

John Adams Hall, 15-23 Endsleigh St., WC1 (tel. 387 4086; fax 383 0164). Tube: Euston. Heading right on Euston Rd., turn right onto Gordon St., and first left onto Endsleigh Gdns.; Endsleigh St. is the second right. Elegant London University building. Discount if stay exceeds 5 nights. Reception open 7:30am-10pm. Single £21.50, double £37. Open July-Aug.

Ingram Court, 552 King's Rd., SW10 (tel. 351 6513). Tube: Sloane Sq. or Fulham Broadway. From Sloane Sq., take the bus #11 or 22 to Lot's Rd.; or walk 10 min. from Fulham Broadway. One of the more beautiful college residence halls. Single £19.50, double £15.25/person.

Lightfoot Hall, Manresa Rd. at King's Rd., SW3 (tel. 333 48 98 or 351 6011; fax 333 4901). Tube: Sloane Sq. or South Kensington. From South Kensington, take bus #49; from Sloane Sq., bus #11 or 22. Rooms in a modern, institutional block. Single £20 (£13 for students), double £16/person.

Queen Alexandra's House, Kensington Gore, SW7 (tel. 589 3635 or 589 4053). Tube: South Kensington, or bus #52 to Royal Albert Hall. Women only. Write weeks in advance for a booking form. Cozy rooms. Single £23.

University of North London, Arcade Hall, Holloway Rd. Tube: Holloway Rd. Self-contained flats with kitchens for groups of 4-6 on a weekly basis. Reservations must be made at **Accommodations Advisory Office,** Stapleton House, 277-281 Holloway Rd., N7 (tel. 753 5041); all payments in advance. £40/person/week.

Bed & Breakfasts

The number of B&Bs boggles the mind. While some are about as indistinct as blades of grass, many feature distinctive furnishings and a warm, welcoming atmosphere.

Near Victoria Station

Although accommodations can be fairly expensive, guests at B&Bs around Victoria Station are within close proximity to London's attractions. In the summer, prudent visitors make reservations at least two weeks in advance.

Melbourne House, 79 Belgrave Rd., SW1 (tel. 828 3516). Past Warwick Sq.Tube: Pimlico. Rake Bessborough St. (south side) exit and go left along Lupus St. Turn right at St. George's Sq.; Belgrave Rd. is on the other side of the square. Modern showers have smashing water pressure. Very well-run and clean. Book ahead. Single £22-25, w/bath £35-40; double w/bath £48-58; triple w/bath £65-75. MC, Visa.

Luna and Simone Hotel, 47-49 Belgrave Rd., SW1 (tel. 834 5897 or 828 2474), past Warwick Sq. Bus #24 stops at the doorstep, or walk from Pimlico. Clean and well-maintained. TV, phones, hairdryers. Single £25; double £36, w/bath £48; triple £48, w/bath £60. Winter discounts. English breakfast. MC, Visa.

Marne Hotel, 34 Belgrave Rd., SW1 (tel. 834 5195). Tube: Victoria. Arranges home stays for students, with Homestay U.K. High-ceilinged rooms with TVs. Showers cramped but functional. English breakfast. Single from £26; double £38, w/bath £45; triple £55. Discounts if stay exceeds 5 nights. AmEx, MC, Visa.

Alexander Hotel, 13 Belgrave Rd., SW1 (tel. 834 9738). Upstairs rooms dark and cozy. Downstairs pretty, newly decorated. All with TV, radio, bath. English breakfast. New TV lounge with great couches. Single £35, double £45. MC, Visa.

Earl's Court

The area feeds on the tourist trade—beware the hustlers. Travel agencies, take-away eateries, currency exchanges, and souvenir shops dominate. The area also has a vibrant gay and lesbian population.

York House Hotel, 27-29 Philbeach Gdns., SW5 9EA (tel. 373 7519; fax 370 4641). Helpful, experienced manager. French, Spanish, and Arabic spoken. TV lounge, garden. English breakfast. Reception open 7am-11pm. Single £24.70, double £38.80-55, triple £49-65, quad £56. Reserve in advance.

Mowbray Court Hotel, 28-32 Penywern Rd., SW5 (tel. 373 8285 or 370 3690; fax 370 5693). Striped reception area leads to a lounge decorated in '70s style, with bar and cigarette machine. Expensive, but stupendous services proffered by Tony and Peter. Family rooms available. Superb continental breakfast. Single £35, w/bath £42; double £45, w/bath £52; triple £55, w/bath £62. Book ahead. MC, Visa.

Kensington & Chelsea

These hotels prove convenient for those who wish to visit the stunning array of museums that line the southwest side of Hyde Park. Prices are a bit higher but hotels here tend to be significantly more sober and comfortable than many at Earl's Court.

Abbey House Hotel, 11 Vicarage Gate, W8 (tel. 727 2594). Tube: Notting Hill Gate. After a series of renovations, it has achieved a level of comfort that can't be rivaled at these prices. Palatial rooms with color TVs, washbasin, fresh towels, and billowing curtains. English breakfast. Reserve ahead. Single £34, double £55, triple £66, quad £76. Winter discounts. No credit cards.

Vicarage Hotel, 10 Vicarage Gate, W8 4AG (tel. 229 4030). Tube: Notting Hill Gate. Posh! Red velvet and gold frame a sweeping staircase. Small immaculate bedrooms. Luxurious TV lounge. Full English breakfast included. Reserve in advance. Single £34, double £55, triple £66, quad £76. No credit cards.

Bloomsbury

Despite its proximity to the West End, Bloomsbury maintains a fairly residential demeanor. Gracious, tree-filled squares and a prime location (within Zone 1 on the tube) make hotel prices a pound or two higher here.

Arran House, 77-79 Gower St., WC1 (tel. 636 2186 or 637 1140; fax 436 5328). Relatively large rooms with hotpots, TVs, Japanese lanterns, and working fireplaces. Spotless bathrooms, and a lovely garden. English breakfast. Single £28-38, double £42-55, triple £55-70, quad £64-80, quint £70. MC, Visa.

Ridgemount Hotel, 65-67 Gower St., WC1 (tel. 636 1141 or 580 7060). Tube: Goodge St. Cheery pink bedspreads, firm beds. English breakfast; laundry. Single £27-39, double £39-49, triple £52.50-61.50, quad £57-72. No credit cards.

Thanet, 8 Bedford Pl., WC1 (tel. 636 2869 or 580 3377). Tube: Russell Sq. Dependable hotel on a pretty tree-lined street. Well-kept rooms are simply furnished and spacious. All come with shower, toilet, TV, radio, phone, and hotpot. English breakfast. Single £49, double £64, triple £75, quad £85. MC, Visa, AmEx.

Celtic Hotel, 62 Guilford St., WC1 (tel. 837 9258 or 837 6737). Go left when exiting the station. Take a left onto Herbrand St., and then left again onto Guilford. Basic, sparsely furnished rooms and clean facilities. Fresh pastel color scheme balances out darkly lit hallways. 24-hr. reception. TV lounge. Single £30.50, double £42.50 when paid in advance. English breakfast.

Hotel Apollo, 43 Argyle St., WC1 (tel. 837 5489). Tube: King's Cross. From the tube station take Euston Rd. and turn left onto Argyle St. Bright white with blue trim, this hotel stands out from others on the street. English breakfast. Rooms come with sinks, lace curtains, TVs. Single £22, double £32.

Paddington & Bayswater

These neighborhoods are located near many of London's finest attractions. Whiteley's, London's first large, indoor shopping mall, is within walking distance. Slightly decrepit B&Bs cluster around Norfolk Sq. and Sussex Gardens. As you travel west, the hotels increase in character. (Tube: Paddington, unless otherwise noted.)

Hyde Park Rooms Hotel, 137 Sussex Gdns., W2 (tel. 723 0225 or 723 0965). Recently renovated rooms bright and airy. Single £20-25, double £30-3, family £49. Discount for small children. Visa, MC, AmEx.

Compton House Hotel and Millard's Hotel, 148-152 Sussex Gardens, W2 (tel. 723 5096; fax 723 6225). Respectable and clean. Single £25, w/shower £30; double £32, w/shower £44; triple £48; w/shower £60. MC, Visa.

Barry House Hotel, 12 Sussex Pl., W2 (tel. 723 7340; fax 723 9775). Bright rooms with TVs and kettles. Single £30, w/bath £38; double w/bath £56; triple w/bath £72; quad w/bath £80. AmEx, Visa, MC.

Ravna Gora, 29 Holland Park Ave., W11 (tel. 727 7725; fax 221 4282). Tube: Holland Park. Sedate and family-run, with room for 50 guests. Convenient to, yet removed from, Holland Park and the crowds of Portobello. Breakfast. 24-hr. reception. Single £28, double £46-56, triple £54-66, quad £68-80. MC, Visa.

FOOD

London presents a tantalizing range of foreign and English specialties. With Indian, Lebanese, Greek, Chinese, Thai, Italian, West Indian, and African food inexpensive and readily available, the city has few rivals when it comes to diversity. If you eat but one meal in London, let it be Indian—British Indian food is rivaled only by India's. Meals are cheaper on Westbourne Grove (Tube: Bayswater), or near Euston Station (Tube: Euston) than in the West End.

Supermarkets are cheaper than corner shops and stock inexpensive food. **Safeway** stores punctuate King's Rd., Edgware Rd. (not far from Paddington), and the Brunswick Shopping Centre opposite the Russell Sq. Tube stop. **Sainsbury** has a branch on Victoria Rd. not far from Victoria Station, and another on Cromwell Rd. Ubiquitous **Europa Food** stores are expensive but stay open until 11pm.

The West End

Mandeer, 21 Hanway Place, W1 (tel. 323 0660 or 580 3470). Tube: Tottenham Ct. Rd. Hidden in the upper reaches of Soho, Mandeer offers some of the best Indian food around. Food is fresh, primarily organic, and all vegetarian. Try the *panir matter* (cheese cubes, peas, and onions in a spiced sauce, £4.50). Open Mon.-Sat. for lunch (self-service) noon-3pm, dinner 5:30-10pm.

The Stockpot, 18 Old Compton St., W1 (tel. 287 1066). Tube: Leicester Sq. or Piccadilly. Beloved by locals. The cheapest place in Soho to soak up some style. Divine apple crumble drowned in hot custard 85p. Open Mon.-Tues. 11:30am-11:30pm, Wed.-Sat. 11:30am-11:45pm. Sun. noon-11pm. Also at 40 Panton St.

Lorelei, 21 Bateman St., W1 (tel. 734 0954). Tube: Tottenham Ct. Rd., Leicester Sq., or Piccadilly Circus. Small wall lamps reveal a tidy Italian restaurant with a wistful mermaid mural. Perfect place for an inexpensive oven-baked pizza. Mushroom pizza £3.90. Open daily noon-midnight.

Lok Ho Fook, 4-5 Gerrard St. (tel. 437 2001). A busy place with extensive offerings with lots of seafood, noodles, and vegetarian dishes. Noodles, fried or in soup, £2.80. Dim sum is made fresh when you order. Open noon-11:45pm daily.

Neal's Yard Bakery and Tea Room, 6 Neal's Yard, WC2 (tel. 836 5199). Only organic flour and filtered water are used in the delicious breads here. A plethora of baked goods, sandwiches, and salads—all vegetarian. Large three-seed loaf £1.95. Bean burger £1.90, take-away £1.60. Open Mon.-Sat. 10:30am-5pm.

Sofra, 36 Tavistock St., WC2 (tel. 240 3773). This Turkish restaurant serves the freshest of foods in a cool Mediterranean atmosphere to match. Attentive and friendly waitstaff. Live music by a Turkish guitarist. Open daily noon-midnight.

Food for Thought, 31 Neal St., WC2 (tel. 836 0239).Foliage decorates this tiny basement restaurant offering excellent vegetarian food at moderate prices. Tasty daily specials from £2.80. Open Mon.-Sat. 9:30am-8pm, Sun. 10:30am-4:30pm.

City of London & East End

The Place Below, in St. Mary-le-Bow Church crypt, Cheapside, EC2 (tel. 329 0789). Tube: St. Paul's. Hip executives enjoy attractive and generous vegetarian dishes. Quiche and salad £5.55. Savory tomato, almond, and saffron soup £2.40. Cheaper take-away and 11:30am-noon. Open Mon.-Fri. 7:30am-2:30pm.

Jazz Bistro, 340 Farringdon St., EC1 (tel. 236 8112). Tube: Farringdon. Exit right on Cowcross, left on Farringdon. Exciting jazz bar/restaurant with a suave Latin

American feel. Meals are as excellent as the tunes. Happy hour (5:30-7:30pm) is an excellent time—all drinks £1.50. Open noon-1am. Cover £2.

Crown and Anchor, Hill House, Shoe La., EC4 (tel. 583 4180). Tube: Blackfriars. Younger executives ingest inexpensive food in this low-ceilinged but spacious pub. Barbecued chicken with rice £2.50. Open Mon.-Fri. 11am-11pm.

The Gallery Café Bar, Unit 1, 9 Leather La., EC1 (tel. 404 5432). Tube: Chancery La. A sleek café with floor-to-ceiling glass windows and marble tables. Identical twins behind the counter serve up unbelievable desserts to hip clientele. Sandwiches from £1, homemade pizza slices from £1.50. Open Mon.-Fri. 7am-4pm.

Kensington, Knightsbridge, Chelsea, & Victoria

City Harvest, 38 Buckingham Palace Rd., SW1 (tel. 630 9781). Tube: Victoria. A fresher sandwich bar than most in the area, with chalkboard specials and a busy take-away lunch scene. Conventional sandwiches £1-1.40, fancy sandwiches £2.30-3. Open Mon.-Fri. 7am-5pm, Sat.-Sun. 9am-3pm.

Ambrosiana Crêperie, 194 Fulham Rd., SW10. Tube: South Kensington. Airy storefront with cane chairs and small tables. Savory crêpes £4.60-6 (try the combination of salami, asparagus, onions, and cheese). Sweet crêpes slightly cheaper. Open Mon.-Fri. noon-3pm and 6pm-midnight, Sat.-Sun. noon-midnight.

Sticky Fingers, 1a Phillimore Gdns. (tel. 938 5338). Does the name sound familiar? Former Rolling Stone Bill Wyman makes sure that you don't forget for which group he played. Princess Di sometimes dines here with the kids. It's a tourist trap, but if you're into the Stones, you have to stop by, at least for a Stones drink. "Rocks Off" and "One Hit" cocktails £4.25.

Planet Poppadum, 366 King's Rd. (although they may be moving soon), SW2 (tel. 823 3368 or 3369). Tube: Sloane Sq., then bus #11 or 22. This *Balti* brasserie and bar manages to fuse elements of Euro-chic, Indian take-away, and futuristic modern styling into a spicy new-wave South Asian synthesis. Hipsters crowd in late at night. Tikka take-away served up from behind the sushi counter. Open Mon.-Fri. 5:30pm-midnight, Sat.-Sun. noon-midnight. MC, Visa, Eurocard.

Chelsea Kitchen, 98 King's Rd., SW3 (tel. 589 1330). Tube: Sloane Sq., then bus #11 or 22. 5-10min. walk from the tube. Locals rave about the eclectic menu of cheap, filling, tasty food: *spaghetti bolognese,* Spanish omelette £2.30. Breakfast served 8-11:25am. Open Mon.-Sat. 8am-11:30pm, Sun. 9-11:30pm.

Bloomsbury & North London

Wagamama, 4 Streatham St., WC1. Tube: Tottenham Ct. Rd. Go down New Oxford St., taking a left onto Bloomsbury St. "Positive Eating & Positive Living." Strangers sit elbow-to-elbow at long tables slurping happily from their massive bowls of ramen. Pan-fried noodles, rice dishes, and vegetarian soups also available. Noodles in various permutations £3.80-5.70. Open Mon.-Fri. noon-2:30pm and 6-11pm, Sat. 1-3pm and 6-11pm, Sun. 12:30-3pm and 6-11pm.

Mille Pini Restaurant, 33 Boswell St., WC1 (tel. 242 2434). Tube: Holborn. Take Southampton Row and turn right onto Theobald's Row. Boswell St. is the second left. Terrific brick-oven pizza £4-4.50, pasta £4.50-4.80, and homemade pastries. Divine *tiramisu* £2.40.

Crank's Restaurant/Take-Away, 9-11 Tottenham St., W1 (tel. 631 3912). Another branch of London's original health food restaurant. Crisp blond wood and white brick interior; frosted glass atrium ceiling in rear. Large portions of vegetarian and vegan dishes. Salad platter (quiche or vegetable tart with 2 salads) £4.50. Open Mon.-Fri. 8am-7:30pm, Sat. 9am-7:30pm.

Chutney's, 124 Drummond St., NW1. Tube: Warren St. A cheerful café serving vegetarian dishes from Western and Southern India. *Dosas* (filled pancakes) £2.45-3.50. Lunch buffet Mon.-Sat. noon-2:45pm and Sun. noon-10:30pm, £4.95. Take-away 6pm-11:30pm. Open noon-2:45pm and 6-11:30pm. Visa, MC.

Café Olé, 119 Upper St., N1 (tel. 226 6991). A hip pasta bar/café adorned with colorful ceramic plates and painted floral borders on the salmon walls. Bustling with Islington trendies of all ages, the atmosphere remains comfortable. Huge breakfast £3.80. Open Mon.-Sat. 8am-11pm.

Indian Veg Bhelpoori House, 92-93 Chapel Market, N1 (tel. 837 4607 or 833 1167). One of the best bargains in London. All-you-can-eat lunch buffet of 18 vegetarian dishes and chutneys for £3.25. Dinner buffet £3.50. Open noon-3pm and 6-11pm. MC, Visa.

Nontas, 16 Camden High St., NW1 (tel. 387 4579). Tube: Mornington Crescent or Camden Town. This wonderfully intimate restaurant is one of the best Greek venues in the city. The incomparable *meze* (£8.75) offers a seemingly interminable selection of dips, meats, and cheeses. Open Mon.-Sat. noon-3pm and 6-11:30pm. *Ouzerie* open Mon.-Sat. 8:30-11:30pm. AmEx, MC, Visa.

Coffee Cup, 74 Hampstead High St. NW3 (tel. 435 7565). The place to be seen if you're young, rich, and "with-it." Arguably the center of Hampstead's nightly social scene. Marble tables on the sidewalk are packed by noon and stay that way until midnight. Open Mon.-Sat. 8am-midnight, Sun. 9am-midnight.

Paddington & Bayswater

Café Grove, 253 Portobello Rd., W11 (tel. 243 1094). Tube: Ladbroke Grove. Atmospheric music pulses through this art gallery/coffeehouse. Sandwiches £1.90-3.10. Omelettes £3.25-5.25. BYOB. Open Mon.-Fri. 9am-11pm, Sat. 9am-7pm, Sun. 10:30am-6pm.

The Garden, 1 Hillgate St., W8. Tube: Notting Hill Gate. A small, tasteful establishment with the cheapest lunches around. Homemade pasta with chicken and mushrooms £2.50. Sandwiches £1.25-2.25. Open Mon.-Sat. 8am-3:30pm.

The Grain Shop, 269a Portobello Rd. (tel. 229 5571). Step inside and you'll be amazed by the surprisingly large array of tasty foods in this take-away joint. Organic whole grain breads are baked daily on the premises; 75p-£1.80 for a fresh loaf. Groceries also available, many organic. Open Mon.-Sat. 10am-6pm.

Gallery Café, 74 Tavistock Rd. (tel. 221 5844). Tube: Ladbroke Grove. An unpretentious vegetarian café just off Portobello Rd. south of the Westway. Lunch specials £2.50 with salad. Get a mix of hot foods, salads, or both £4, small £3. Many locals eat lunch here everyday. Open Mon.-Fri. 9am-5pm, Sat.-Sun. 9am-7pm.

The Belair Diner, 23 All Saints Road, W11 (tel. 229 7961). Tube: Westbourne Park or Ladbroke Grove. Behind a rust-red exterior, sample dishes from a variety of international cuisines while listening to a mix of funk and jazz music. Well-prepared West Indian, South American, and African dishes. Fried plantains £2. Open Mon.-Sat. 11am-11:30pm and often on Sun. but call to make sure.

Khan's, 13-15 Westbourne Grove, W2. Tube: Bayswater. Cavernous, noisy, and crowded and the best bargain around for delicious Indian cuisine. Chicken *saag* (chicken cooked with spinach) £3. *Nan* bread 95p, rice £1.40. Chicken *tikka masala* £3.40. Open noon-3pm and 6pm-midnight.

Penang, 41 Hereford Rd., W2 (tel. 229 2982). Tube: Bayswater. The standard interior hides magnificent Malaysian and Thai cuisine. Tangy lemon chicken £4. *Sayor lodeh* (mixed vegetables cooked in savory coconut milk gravy) has a well-deserved reputation (£3). Open Mon.-Sat. 6-11:30pm, Sun. 6-11pm.

PUBS

London's 7000 pubs are as colorful as their country counterparts, but in London the clientele varies widely from one neighborhood to the next. Avoid pubs near train stations; many prey on naïve tourists. For the best pub prices head to the East End. Stylish, lively pubs cluster around the fringes of the West End. Many historic alehouses lend an ancient air to areas recently swallowed up by the urban sprawl, such as Highgate and Hampstead.

The Dog and Duck, 8 Bateman St., W1 (tel. 437 4447). Tube: Tottenham Ct. Rd. One of Soho's best. Local TV and advertising professionals crowd in at lunch for the inexpensive pints. Evenings bring locals and a theater crowd.

Lamb and Flag, 33 Rose St., WC2, off Garrick St. Tube: Covent Garden or Leicester. A traditional English pub, with no music and still separated into 2 sections — the public bar for the working class, and the saloon bar for the businessmen, though today the distinction is not obvious.

World's End Distillery, 459 King's Rd. near World's End Pass before Edith Grove (tel. 376 8946). Tube: Sloane Sq. This pub isn't wedged into a street corner like most others; it stands alone and grandiose. If the universe collapsed and nothing but the World's End remained, we would not weep.

The King's Head, Hogarth Pl., SW5. Tube: Earl's Ct. From Earl's Ct. Rd., head east on Childs Walk or Hogarth Pl. The place to get loose. Billions of lusty tourists packed into a classic pub—smoky atmosphere and all.

The Old Crown, 33 New Oxford St., WC1 (tel. 836 9121). Tube: Tottenham Ct. Rd. A thoroughly untraditional pub. Cream-colored walls, faded pine-green bar, green plants, and funky brass crowns suspending the light fixtures from the ceiling. Also a restaurant/café serving salads, hummus, tea, and Mexican specialties.

Black Friar, 174 Queen Victoria St., EC4. Tube: Blackfriars. Probably the most exquisite and fascinating pub in all of London. The edifice's past purpose as a 12th-century Dominican friary is celebrated not only in the pub's name but also in its structure.

The Blind Beggar, 337 Whitechapel Rd., E1 (tel. 247 8329). Tube: Whitechapel. You may be sitting where George Cornell sat when he was gunned down by rival gangster Ronnie Kray in 1966. Spacious pub with a conservatory and a garden.

Slug and Lettuce, 1 Islington Green, N1. Tube: Angel. Upper St. changes its name to Islington Green as it passes by the Green. Good observation post for spotting Islington trendies (inside or outside). Try upstairs for a cozy setting.

King of Bohemia, 10 Hampstead High St. (tel. 435 6513). Most pubby of Hampstead High St. hangouts, but still has upscale clientele that swarm to outdoor seating in summer. Library-like, elegant seating in back.

The Dove, 19 Upper Mall, SW6 (tel. (0181) 748 5405). Tube: Hammersmith. Make the trip to the 300-year-old tavern for a delicious lunch overlooking the Thames.

The Brixtonian, 11 Dorrell Pl., SW9 (tel. 978 8870). Tube: Brixton. A cozy, artsy bar removed from the market area. Green picnic tables on the pedestrian walk outside can be an ideal base for a quiet, slow drink with a loved one.

Prospect of Whitby, 57 Wapping Wall, E1, London Docks (tel. 481 1095). Tube: Wapping. 600-year old pub with sweet riverside terrace. Open ceilings and a rustic flagstone bar with a serious view of the Thames.

SIGHTS

London is best explored on foot. When your soles begin to ache, the **London Transport Sightseeing Tour** (tel. 222 1234), provides a cursory, but convenient, overview of London's sights (9:30am-5:30pm every ¼hr. (Nov.-Feb. every ½hr.) from Baker St., Haymarket, Marble Arch, Oxford Circus, and Victoria St., near the station. £9, under 16 £5; discount if ticket purchased at Travel Info Station inside Piccadilly Circus and Oxford Circus tube stops; otherwise pay conductor).

Mayfair to Parliament

An auspicious beginning to a day's wander is **Piccadilly Circus** and its towering neon bluffs (Tube: Piccadilly Circus). At the center of the Nash's swirling hub stands a fountain topped by a statue everyone calls Eros but is actually supposed to be the Angel of Christian Charity. North are the tiny shops of Regent St. and the renovated seediness of **Soho,** a region which sports a vibrant sidewalk café culture where pornography once reigned supreme. Outdoor cafés, upscale shops and slick crowds huddle in **Covent Garden,** to the northeast. **Piccadilly,** running off the Circus, is lined with exclusive stores, including **Fortnum and Mason.** Paths across **Green Park** lead to **Buckingham Palace** (Tube: Victoria or Green Park), now open to tourists. (Tours Aug.-Sept., £8.50.) The Changing of the Guard occurs daily (April-July) or every other day (Aug.-March) at 11:30am unless it's raining. Arrive early or you won't see a thing.

The **Mall,** a wide processional, leads from the palace to **Admiralty Arch** and Trafalgar Square. **St. James' Park,** south of the Mall, shelters a duck preserve and a flock of lawn chairs. The center of a vicious traffic roundabout, **Trafalgar Square** (Tube: Charing Cross), centers on Nelson's Column, a 40-foot-high statue astride a 132-foot column. Political Britain branches off **Whitehall,** just south of Trafalgar. Draped in black velvet, Charles I was led out of the **Banqueting House** (corner of Horse Guards Ave. and Whitehall) and beheaded. The building now hosts less lethal state dinners. (Open Mon.-Sat. 10am-5pm but closed for government functions; £2.90, seniors and students £2.25.) The Prime Minister resides off Whitehall at **10 Downing Street,** now closed to tourists. In the middle of Whitehall is the **Cenotaph,** a monument to Britain's war dead. Whitehall ends by the sprawling **Houses of Parliament** (Tube: Westminster). Access to the House of Commons and the House of Lords is extremely restricted since a member was killed in a bomb blast in 1979. Your best bet is to send a written request to the Public Information Office, 1 Derby Gate, Westminster, SW1. Technically speaking, **Big Ben** is neither the tower nor the clock, but the 14-ton bell, cast when a similarly proportioned Sir Benjamin Hali served as Commissioner of Works. Church and state tie the knot in **Westminster Abbey,** coronation chamber to English monarchs for the past 684 years, as well as the site of **Poet's Corner,** the **Grave of the Unknown Warrior,** and the elegantly perpendicular **Chapel of Henry VII.** Britain bestows no greater honor than burial within these walls. The abbey plumber is buried here among such greats as Elizabeth I, Darwin, Dickens, and Ben Jonson (whose last name is misspelled with an *b* on his tomb). Ask about the story surrounding the Stone of Scone. (Abbey open Mon.-Sat. 7:30am-6pm, Wed. 6-7:45pm, Sun. in-between services; free. Chapels and transepts open Mon.-Fri. 9am-4:45pm, also Wed. 6-7:45pm, Sat. 9am-2:45pm and 3:45-5:45pm; £4, students £2; all parts of the abbey £3 Wed. 6-7:45pm. Photography permitted Wed. evenings only.)

Hyde Park & Kensington to Chelsea

Hyde Park shows its best face on Sundays from 11am to dusk, when soapbox orators take freedom of speech to the limit at **Speaker's Corner** (Tube: Marble Arch, *not* Hyde Park Corner). To the west, **Kensington Gardens,** an elegant relic of Edwardian England, celebrates the glories of model yacht racing in the squarish Round Pound. From the gardens you can catch a glimpse of Kensington Palace. The **Royal Albert Hall,** on the south edge of Hyde Park, hosts the Proms, a gloriously British festival of music. Up Brompton Rd. near Knightsbridge, **Harrods** (Tube: Knightsbridge) vends under their humble motto, *Omnia Omnibus Ubique* ("All things for all people, everywhere"). (Open Mon.-Tues., and Sat. 10am-6pm, Wed.-Fri. 10am-7pm.) Still-fashionable **King's Road** (Tube: Sloane Sq.), to the south in **Chelsea,** attempts to do justice to its bohemian past; the area has sheltered both Oscar Wilde and the Sex Pistols.

Regent's Park to Fleet Street

Take a picnic from Harrods to the expanse of **Regent's Park,** northeast from Hyde Park across Marylebone (Tube: Regent's Park). The **London Zoo,** in the north end, has mambos, Asian lions, and piranhas. (Open daily 10am-5:30pm; Oct.-March 10am-4pm. £7, students £6.) **Camden Town** (Tube: Camden Town), bordering the park to the northeast, sports rollicking street markets.

Bloomsbury—eccentric, erudite and disorganized—is known for its literary and scholarly connections, including the **British Museum. Fleet Street** is the traditional den of the British press, though nearly all the papers have moved to cheaper real estate. Close by are the **Inns of Court,** which have controlled access to the English Bar since the 13th century.

City of London & the East End

Once upon a time, "London" meant the square-mile enclave of the **City of London;** the rest of today's metropolis were far-flung towns and villages. The **Tower of London** was the grandest fortress in medieval Europe and the palace and prison of English monarchs for over 500 years. Its best-known edifice, the **White Tower,** is also the oldest, begun by William the Conqueror. In 1483, the "Princes in the Tower" (Edward V and his brother) were murdered in the **Bloody Tower** in one of the great unsolved mysteries of history. Two of the wives of jolly King Henry VIII were beheaded in the courtyard, and in 1941 Rudolf Hess was sent to the Tower after his parachute dumped him in Scotland. The **Crown Jewels** include the Stars of Africa, cut from the enormous Cullinan Diamond, which was mailed 3rd-class from the Transvaal in an unmarked brown paper package. (Tube: Tower Hill. Open Mon.-Sat. 9:30am-5pm, Sun. 2-5pm; Nov.-Feb. Mon.-Sat. 9:30am-4pm. £6.70, students and seniors £5.10.) Next to the Tower is **Tower Bridge,** one of London's best-known landmarks. The walkways provide one of London's best views and a new exhibition inside the bridge explains its history. (Tube: Tower Hill. Open 10am-6:30pm; Nov.-March 10am-5:15pm. £5.) Other shrapnel of history are scattered throughout the City, among them 24 Christopher Wren churches interspersed with the soaring steel of modern skyscrapers. Peruse smaller churches, such as the Strand's **St. Clement Danes** of "Oranges and Lemons" fame, or the superb **St. Stephen Walbrook** near the Bank of England (Tube: Bank). True-blue cockney Londoners are born within earshot of the famous bells of **St. Mary-le-Bow,** Cheapside. In the German Blitz in 1940, **St. Paul's Cathedral** stood firm in a sea of fire. Climb above the graves of Wren, Nelson, and Wellington in the crypt to the dizzying top of the dome; the view is unparalleled. (Tube: St. Paul's. Open Mon.-Sat. 8:30am-4pm; ambulatory and crypt open Mon.-Sat. 8:45am-4:15pm; galleries open Mon.-Sat. 10am-4:15pm. Cathedral, ambulatory, and crypt £3, students £2.50. Cathedral, ambulatory, crypt, and galleries £5, students £4.) The immense **Barbican Centre** (Tube: Barbican or Moorgate) is one of the most impressive and controversial post-Blitz rebuilding projects.

The **East End** is a relatively poor section of London with a history of racial conflict. A large working-class population moved into the district during the Industrial Revolution, soon followed by a wave of Jewish immigrants fleeing persecution in Eastern Europe who settled around **Whitechapel.** Notable remnants of the former East End community include the city's oldest standing synagogue, **Bevis Marks Synagogue** (Bevis Marks and Heneage La., EC3; tel. 626 1274; tube: Aldgate: from Aldgate High St. turn right onto Houndsditch; Creechurch Lane on the left leads to Bevis Marks). In 1978, the latest immigration wave brought a large Muslim Bangladeshi community to the East End. At the heart of this community is **Brick Lane** (tube: Aldgate East), a street lined with Indian and Bangladeshi restaurants, colorful textile shops, and grocers stocking ethnic foods. (To reach Brick Lane, head left up Whitechapel as you exit the tube station; turn left onto Osbourne St., which turns into Brick Lane.) On Sundays, vibrant market stalls selling books, bric-a-brac, leather jackets, and salt beef sandwiches flank this street and Middlesex St., better known as **Petticoat Lane.** The **East London Mosque,** 84-86 Whitechapel Rd. (tel. 247 1357; tube: Aldgate East), was London's first to have its own building.

The South & Outskirts

Lesser-known but equally rewarding treasures lie south of the river. **Southwark Cathedral,** a smallish, quiet church, boasts London's second-best Gothic structure and a chapel dedicated to **John Harvard** (Tube: London Bridge). West along the riverbank, a reconstruction of Shakespeare's Globe Theatre is underway; it should open in autumn in 1995. South London's entertainment history lives on in the externally brutal but internally festive **South Bank Arts Centre** (Tube: Waterloo).

The genteel Victorian shopping and residential district of Brixton (tube: Brixton) became the locus of a Caribbean and African community who followed large-scale Commonwealth immigration in the 1950s and 1960s. Most of the activity in Brixton centers around the **Brixton Market** at Electric Ave., Popes Rd., and Brixton Station Rd. Choose from among the stalls of fresh fish, vegetables, and West Indian cuisine, or browse through the stalls of African crafts and discount clothing. Nearby, on the corner of Coldharbor and Atlantic, the **Black Cultural Archives,** 378 Coldharbor Lane (tel. 738 4591), mounts small but informative exhibits on black history.

The transport system that encouraged London's urban sprawl blurs the distinction between the city and its surroundings. If Hyde Park seemed but a small bit of green, **Highgate** and **Hampstead Heath** will prove that there is an English countryside. To the east, Karl Marx and George Eliot repose in the gothic tangle of **Highgate Cemetery,** Swains Lane. (Tube: Archway. **Eastern Cemetery** open Mon.-Fri. 10am-4:45pm, Sat.-Sun. 11am-4:45pm. £1.50. **Western Cemetery** access by guided tour only Mon.-Fri. at noon, 2, and 4pm, Sat.-Sun. hourly 11am–4pm. £3. Camera permit £1, valid in both sections.)

London **Docklands,** the largest commercial development in Europe, has utterly changed the face of East London within the space of 10 years. As part of the Thatcher government's privatization program, redevelopment of the area was handed over to the private sector—in the form of the **London Docklands Development Corporation (LDDC)**—along with a generous helping of public funds. Since then, the LDDC has been at the helm of what it calls "the most significant urban regeration program in the world." The best way to see the region is via the **Docklands Light Railway (DLR)** (tel. 918 4000), a futuristic, totally automatic, driverless elevated rail system. All tickets, Travelcards, and passes issued by London Transport, London Underground, and British Rail are valid on the DLR provided they cover the correct zones. The wheelchair-accessible DLR is replaced by bus on weekends and weekdays after 9:30pm. The first stop for any Docklands tour should be the **Docklands Visitors Centre** (tel. 512 1111; DLR: Crossharbor, then left up the road).

Head by train or boat to red-brick **Hampton Court** (tel. (0181) 781 9500 or 781 9666 for recorded information and special events) for a quirky change of pace. Its grounds contain the famous hedgerow maze (British Rail: Hampton Court). From the first Monday before Easter until the end of September, a boat runs from Westminster Pier to Hampton Court, leaving in the morning at 10:30, 11:15am, and noon, and returning from Hampton Court at 3, 4, and 5pm. The trip takes 3-4 hours one way (adult one way £7, £9 return).

Windsor Castle (tel. (01753) 868286 or 831118 for 24-hr. information line) is the Queen's country retreat. British Rail serves Windsor and Eton Central station and Windsor and Eton Riverside station, both of which are near Windsor Castle (street signs point the way).

Just west of central London on the Thames lie the serene and exotic **Kew Gardens.** Lose yourself in the controlled wilderness of the grounds, or explore the Victorian and modern glasshouses containing thousands of plant species. (Tube or British Rail: Kew Gardens. Open Mon.-Fri. 9:30am-6:30pm, Sat.-Sun. 9:30am-7:30pm, last admission ½hr. before closing).

Museums

British Museum, Great Russell St. (tel. 636 1555 or 580 1788 for recorded info), Tube: Tottenham Ct. Rd. or Holborn. The closest thing this planet has to a complete record of the rise and ruin of world cultures. Among the plunder on display are the Rosetta Stone (whose inscriptions allowed French scholar Champollion to decipher hieroglyphics) and the Elgin Marbles. Also hoards an early manuscript of *Beowulf* and 2 of 4 surviving copies of the *Magna Carta.* Open Mon.-Sat. 10am-5pm, Sun. 2:30-6pm. Free. Special exhibits £3, students £2.

National Gallery, Trafalgar Sq. (tel. 839 3321 or 747 2885 for recorded info), Tube: Charing Cross. One of the world's finest collections of European painting; heavyweight works by da Vinci, Turner and Velázquez. The new Micro Gallery, a computerized, illustrated catalogue, will print out a free personalized tour. Open Mon.-Sat. 10am-6pm, Sun. 2-6pm. Free.

National Portrait Gallery, St. Martin's Pl. (tel. 306 0055), opposite St. Martin's in the Fields. Tube: Charing Cross. Doubles as *Who's Who in Britain.* Open Mon.-Fri. 10am-5pm, Sat. 10am-6pm, Sun. noon-6pm. Free.

Tate Gallery, Millbank (tel. 821 1313), up the Thames from Parliament Sq. Tube: Pimlico. The best of British artists such as Gainsborough, Reynolds, and Constable, along with works by Monet, Dalí, and Matisse. The vast J.M.W. Turner collection rests in the Clore Gallery, an extension of the main building. Both open Mon.-Sat. 10am-5:50pm, Sun. 2-5:50pm. Free.

Victoria and Albert Museum, Cromwell Rd. (tel. 938 8500 or 938 8441 24-hr. recorded info or 938 8349 current exhibits). Tube: South Kensington. A mind-boggling array of fine and applied arts from all periods and places. Open Mon.-Sat. 10am-5:50pm, Sun. 2:30-5:50pm. "Donation" £4.50, students £1.

Institute of Contemporary Arts, the Mall, SW1 (tel. 930 3647 for recorded info). Tube: Piccadilly Circus or Charing Cross. Outpost of the avant garde. Three galleries, a cinema featuring first-run independent films, and experimental space for film and video. Galleries open Sat.-Thurs. noon-7:30pm, Fri. noon-9pm. £1.50.

Madame Tussaud's, Marylebone Rd., NW1 (tel. 935 6861). Tube: Baker St. The classic waxwork museum. Open Mon.-Fri. 10am-5:30pm, Sat.-Sun. 9:30am-5:30pm. £4.20, seniors £3.25, children £2.60.

Museum of London, 150 London Wall, EC2 (tel. 600 3699 or 600 0807 for 24-hr. info). Tube: St. Paul's or Barbican. From Londinium to the Docklands. Free lectures Wed.-Fri. 1:10pm. Open Tues.-Sat. 10am-6pm, Sun. noon-6pm, bank holidays 10am-6pm, last entry 5:30pm. £3.50, students £1.75. Free after 4:30pm.

Museum of Mankind, 6 Burlington Gardens. (tel. 323 8043). Tube: Piccadilly Circus. Engrossing assemblage of artifacts from non-Western societies. Open Mon.-Sat. 10am-5pm, Sun. 2:30-6pm. Free.

Museum of the Moving Image (MOMI), South Bank Centre, SE1 (tel. 928 3232 or 401 2636 for 24-hr. information). Tube: Waterloo, or Embankment and cross the Hungerford footbridge. Charts the development of image-making with light, from Chinese shadow puppets to film and TV. Countless clips and famous props. Open daily 10am-6pm; last entry 5pm. £5.50, students with ID £4.70.

Natural History Museum, Cromwell Rd., SW7 (tel. 938 9123 or 938 9242 for group bookings). Tube: South Kensington. Permanent exhibits include "Discovering Mammals," "Creepy Crawlies," "Ecology: A Greenhouse Effect," "Primates," and the superb dinosaur exhibits, with tantalizing computer displays and realistic life-size models. Open Mon.-Sat. 10am-6pm, Sun. 11am-6pm. £5.50, concessions £3. Free Mon.-Fri. 4:30-6pm, Sat.-Sun. 5-6pm. Wheelchair accessible.

Sir John Soane's Museum, 13 Lincoln's Inn Fields, WC2 (tel. 405 2107). Tube: Holborn. The idiosyncratic home Soane designed for himself will intrigue all. Famous artifacts on display include Hogarth paintings, the massive sarcophagus of SETI I, and casts of famous sculptures. Open Tues.-Sat. 10am-5pm; lecture tour Sat. at 2:30pm (arrive by 2pm). Free.

ENTERTAINMENT

On any given day or night, Londoners and visitors can choose from the widest range of entertainment. For guidance consult the weekly *Time Out,* or *What's On.*

Theater, Music, & Film

London **theater** is unrivalled. Seats cost about £8-30 and up, and student/senior standby (with an "S" or "concessions" in listings) puts even the best seats within reach—around £7 shortly before curtain (come two hours early to get a seat). **Day seats** are sold cheaply (9-10am, the day of performance) to all; queue up earlier to snag one. The **Leicester Square Ticket Booth** sells half-price tickets on the day of major plays (open Mon.-Sat. noon-2pm and 2:30-6:30pm; long wait. £1.50 fee; cash only). Standby tickets for the **Royal National Theatre,** on the South Bank (tel. 928 2252; tube: Waterloo) sell two hours beforehand (£8-12, students £6.50, 45 min. before). The **Barbican Theatre** (tel. 628 2295; Tube: Barbican or Moorgate), the London home of the Royal Shakespeare Co., student and senior standbys for £6.50 from 9am on the day of performance. Often, more exciting performances for significantly less cash are to be found on the **Fringe,** smaller less commercial theaters.

Most major **classical music** is staged at the acoustically superb **Royal Festival Hall** (tel. 928 8800; Tube: Waterloo) and the **Barbican Hall** (see Sights, above). Hampstead Heath's **Kenwood House** and the **Marble Hill House** have low-priced outdoor concerts on summer weekends (tel. 973 3427 and 413 1443). Opera and ballet embellish the **Royal Opera House** (tel. 304 4000; tube: Covent Garden) and the **London Coliseum** (tel. 632 8300; tube: Charing Cross or Leicester Sq.). Londoners have been lining up for standing room in the **Royal Albert Hall's "Proms"** (BBC Henry Wood Promenade Concerts), the most popular and endearing feature of the London music scene, for nearly a century.

Every **pop music** phenomena that didn't take off in London gets there at some point. Ticket offices and record shops list concerts. **The Marquee,** 105 Charing

Cross Rd., WC2 (tel. 437 6603; Tube: Leicester Sq. or Tottenham Ct. Rd.), is a loud, band-churning machine (cover £5-7). **Brixton Academy,** 211 Stockwell Rd., SW9 (tel. 326 1022; tube: Brixton), is a larger, rowdy venue for a variety of music including rock and reggae (advance tickets £9-15). **Ronnie Scott's,** 47 Frith St., W1 (tel. 439 0747; Tube: Leicester Sq. or Piccadilly Circus), has London's greatest jazz (cover from £14). Find fine folk at **Bunjie's,** 27 Litchfield St., WC2 (tel. 240 1796; Tube: Covent Garden), where the crowd transcends all bounds (cover £3, students £2).

Electric Cinema, 191 Portobello Rd. (Tube: Ladbroke Grove or Notting Hill Gate) which is the first Black cinema in Britain. (£6, concessions £4). **Gate Cinema,** Notting Hill Gate (tube: Notting Hill Gate) screens recent foreign language and art films. (Tickets £6, concessions £3. Rotating Sunday matinees £4.) **Cinema Fumée,** 211 Stockwell Rd. (tel. 924 9999; tube: Brixton), is a cinematic celebration of the cancer stick, where 800 people watch cult flicks while smoking (call to check dates and movies; £6.50). **Notting Hill Coronet,** Notting Hill Gate Rd. (tel. 727 6705; tube: Notting Hill Gate), is London's last full-time smoking cinema (£5.75).

Dance Clubs

London pounds to 100% Groovy Liverpool tunes, ecstatic Manchester rave, hometown soul and house, imported U.S. hip-hop, and Jamaican reggae. Many clubs host a variety of provocative one-night stands (like "Get Up and Use Me") throughout the week. If you're looking for a truly underground dance experience, keep your ear to the ground. While news of serious raves travels exclusively by word of mouth, they can attract thousands of revelers "in the know," who congregate in abandoned warehouses or in open fields outside the city. As always, check listings in *Time Out* and *What's On* for the latest.

The Fridge, Town Hall Parade, Brixton Hill, SW2. Tube: Brixton. Night bus N2. A serious dance dive with a multi-ethnic crowd. Immensely popular weekly "Love Muscle" every Sat. night crowds with busy mixed-gay clientele. The Fridge cools down during the summer months. Open Fri.-Sat. 10pm-6 am.

The Garage, 22 Highbury Corner, N5. Tube: Highbury and Islington. Night bus N19, N73, N96. Local club specializing in indie rock. Women only on Sat. nights. Cover £3-6. Open daily 7:30pm-2am.

Gossips, 69 Dean St., W1. Tube: Piccadilly Circus or Tottenham Ct. Rd. A dark basement club renowned for a wide range of great one-nighters. Anything goes, from heavy metal to ska to psychedelia to reggae. Open Mon.-Sat. 10pm-3:30am.

Hippodrome, Charing Cross Rd., WC2 (tel. 437 4311). Tube: Leicester Sq. Infamously enormous, loud, and tourist-ridden; leave your blue jeans and trainers behind. Mon. night is "PSST!!"—the biggest U.K. students' night around. Cover £2 before 11pm, £3 before midnight with U.K. student ID. Pints go for £1.50 all night. Thurs. and Fri. party with "BUSH!" Dance it up to the house/party mix. Professional dancers and laser shows. Open Mon.-Sat. 9pm-3am.

Iceni, 11 White Horse St., W1 (tel. 437 4311). Tube: Green Park. Off Curzon Street. 3 beautiful floors of deep funk entertainment in this stylish Mayfair hotspot. Board games for those who can't keep the beat. Open Wed.-Sat. 10pm-3am.

Offbeat Entertainment

College of London Fashion, 20 John Povices St., W1 (tel 629 9401). Tube: Oxford Circus. Offer yourself to the students at the LCF's beauty-therapy department, where they learn how to give everything from cathiodermie to pedicures. Prices from £2.50. Open Mon.-Fri. 9am-8pm.

The Cooltan, in the Old Dolehouse, 372 Coldharbour Lane, SW9 (tel. 737 2745). Tube: Brixton. Offers meditation classes, usually on Friday nights 7:30-9:30pm; donations accepted. For information call the co-op, or contact Friends of the Western Buddhist Order (tel. 673 5570). A variety of other classes, like life-drawing, T'ai Chi Ch'uan, yoga, and drum workshops, are offered; call for details.

Porchester Baths, Queensway, W2 (tel. 792 3980 or 792 2919). Tube: Bayswater or Royal Oak. In the Porchester Centre. A Turkish bath with steam and dry heat rooms and a swimming pool. Rates are high (£15.40/3hr.), but devoted fans keep taking the plunge. Men bathe Mon., Wed., and Sat.; women bathe Tues., Thurs., and Fri. Open Mon.-Sat. 10am-10pm. Open Sun. 10am-4pm (women only), 4-10pm (mixed couples). Swimwear must be worn at all times.

Speakers' Corner, in the northeast corner of Hyde Park. Tube: Marble Arch. Crackpots, evangelists, and political activists speak their minds and compete for the largest audience every Sun. 11am-dusk.

BISEXUAL, GAY, & LESBIAN LONDON

Travelers coming to London will be delighted by the range of London's very visible gay scene, which covers everything from the flamboyant to the cruisy to the mainstream. For information contact the **Lesbian and Gay Switchboard** (tel. 837 7324; 24 hrs.), or the **Bisexual Helpline** (tel. (0181) 569 7500; Tues.-Wed. 7:30-9:30pm).

The Angel, 65 Graham St., N1 (tel. 608 2656). Tube: Angel. A buzzing café/bar with a consistently balanced male-female ratio. Eclectic menu of light meals, like Japanese noodles with stir-fry and tofu, all under £3. Free live music Sun. Open Mon.-Sat. noon-midnight, Sun. noon-11:30pm.

Balans, 60 Old Compton St., W1 (tel. 437 5212). Tube: Leicester Square. Flower arrangements and zebra-print lampshades create a glamorous ambience in this brasserie/bar. Full bar. Live blues, acoustic, and vocal performers Mon.-Sat. 11pm-1am. Open Mon.-Thurs. 9am-2am, Fri.-Sat 9am-2:30am, Sun 9am-1am.

Drill Hall Women-Only Bar, 16 Chenies St., WC1 (tel. 631 1353). Tube: Goodge St. A much anticipated one-nighter located in the lobby of one of London's biggest alternative theaters. Dim lighting and red walls. Crowded and laid back. Open Mon. 6-11pm.

Wilde About Oscar, 30-31 Philbeach Gdns., SW5 (tel. 835 1858 or 373 1244). Tube: Earl's Ct. In the garden of a gay B&B. A definite splurge, but worth it. Candles and flowers make an intimate dining encounter. Open daily 7pm-midnight.

Wow Bar, at Michael's 122-126 Wardour St. (tel. 373 9859). Tube: Earl's Court. Take a right out of the station, then another right at Old Brompton Rd. Saturday night fever disco lights splash around biker men in leather outfits. A bit more hard-core than other local gay bars.

G.A.Y., at London Astoria 2, 157 Charing Cross Rd., WC2 (tel. 734 6963). Tube: Tottenham Ct. Rd. A 3-nights-a-week pop extravaganza amidst chrome and mirrored disco balls. Unpretentious clientele (very mixed, in both gender and orientation). Open Mon., Thurs., Sat. 10:30pm-3, 4, and 5am. Cover Mon. £3, £1 w/w/flyer; Thurs. £3, free before midnight w/student ID; Sat. £6, w/flyer £5.

Heaven, Villiers St., WC2 (tel. 839 3852), underneath The Arches. Tube: Embankment or Charing Cross (Villiers is off of the Strand). Still the oldest and biggest gay disco in Europe. Three dance floors, high-tech lighting, pool tables, bars, and a capacity of nearly 4000 means you'll never get bored. Open 10:30pm-3:30am.

Up to the Elbow, fortnightly at the Laurel Tree, 113 Bayham St., NW1 (tel. 485 1383). Tube: Camden Town. Exit the station left, then cross to the right; Bayham is parallel to Camden High St. Housed in a small, black-painted, windowless room above the Laurel Tree pub. Every other Fri. 9pm-late. Cover £3, students £2.

SHOPPING

Books

Dillons, 82 Gower St., WC1 (tel. 636 1577), near University of London. Tube: Goodge St. Also on The Strand near Trafalgar Square. The most graceful bookstore in London. Open Mon. and Wed.-Fri. 9am-7pm, Tues. 9:30am-7pm, Sat. 9:30am-6pm, Sun. noon-6pm.

Hatchards, 187 Piccadilly, W1 (tel. 437 3924). Tube: Green Park. Oldest and most comprehensive of London's bookstores, recently expanded. Come in for 10 min. and stay for 2 hours. Open Mon. and Wed.-Fri. 9am-6pm, Tues. 9:30am-6pm, Sat. 9:30am-6pm, Sun. 11am-5pm.

Bell, Book and Radmall, 4 Cecil Ct., WC2 (tel. 240 2161). Tube: Leicester Sq. A small antiquarian bookstore with a zippy staff, an exceptional selection of American and British first editions, and an impressive supply of science-fiction and detective novels. Open Mon.-Fri. 10am-5:30pm, Sat. 11am-4pm.

Clothing & Shoes

Radio Days, 87 Lower Marsh, SE1 (tel. 928 0800). Tube: Waterloo. Fantastic selection of collectibles and memorabilia from the 1920s-1960s. Dresses, books, valises, and classic traveling trunks. Open Mon.-Fri. 10:30am-5pm, Sat. 11am-4pm.

Accupuncture, 3 Tisbury Ct., W1 (tel. 439 3703), off of Wardour St., next to Village Soho. Tube: Piccadilly Circus. A super-tiny and hard-to-find shop known for its vintage racks, '70s and '80s fashion gems, the occasional contemporary Westwood outfit, and, crucial to the contemporary fashion scene, Adidas. Open Mon.-Sat. 11am-7pm. No credit cards.

Flip, 125 Long Acre, WC2 (tel. 836 7044). Tube: Covent Garden. Dozens of 50s and 60s blouses and sweaters, plus the usual jeans and menswear. Open Mon.-Wed. and Fri.-Sat. 10am-7pm, Thurs. 10am-8pm, Sun. noon-6pm.

Paul Smith, 23 Avery Row, W1 (tel. 493 1287), off of Brook St. Tube: Bond St. The seconds and out-of-season outlet for the witty yet elegant menswear store. Savings of up to 50% off regular retail prices. Open Mon.-Wed. and Fri. 10:30am-6:30pm, Thurs. 10:30am-7pm, Sat. 10am-6pm.

Vivienne Westwood, 6 Davies St., W1 (tel. 629 3757). Tube: Bond St. Brilliantly radical, although more staid of late. Open Mon.-Wed. and Fri.-Sat. 10:30am-6pm, Thurs. 10:30am-7pm. Also an **outlet** at 40-41 Conduit St., W1 (tel 439 1109; tube: Oxford Circus). Save 30% on used samples, as much as 75% on items from last year's collection. Open Mon.-Sat. 10:30am-6pm.

Specialty Shops

Honour, 86 Lower Marsh, SE1 (tel. 401 8220). Tube: Waterloo. Fetish gear for the '90s: rubber, leather, and harnesses galore. A good resource for information on upcoming gothic, pagan, and fetish happenings. Open Mon.-Fri. 10:30am-7pm, Sat. 11:30am-5pm.

Into You, 144 St. John St., EC1 (tel. 253 5085). Tattooing, body-piercing, and related literature and items. Open Tues.-Fri. noon-7pm, Sat. noon-6pm.

The New Power Generation, 21 Chalk Farm Rd., NW1 (tel. 267 7951). Tube: Chalk Farm. A 3-floor store dedicated to (and owned by) the artist formerly known as Prince. Open Mon.-Thurs 10am-5:30pm, Fri-Sun. 10am-6pm.

GLOSSARY

Many Irish-English words and usages duplicate those in England; some don't. Words derived from Irish are listed separately below. "Traveler" can mean someone like you, but sometimes refers to several thousand poor families who roam the Republic in caravans, living at "halting sites;" these "travelers" face vicious discrimination.

aubergine	eggplant
bangers and mash	sausage and mashed potatoes
bap	a soft bun, like a hamburger bun
bedsit	one-room apartment, sometimes with kitchen
bill	check (in restaurants)
biro	ball point pen
busker	street musician
candy-floss	cotton candy
caravan	trailer, mobile home
cheap	inexpensive (not "shoddy")
chemist	pharmacist
chips	french fries
chipper	fish and chips vendor
coach	bus (long-distance)
concession	discount on admission (for students, OAPs, etc.)
crisps	potato chips
dear	expensive
dole, on the dole	welfare or unemployment benefits
dolmen	chamber formed by huge stones
drumlin	small hill
DUP	Democratic Unionist Party; led by Ian Paisley
dustbin	trash can
en suite	with bathroom (and usually shower)
fag	cigarette
first floor	first floor up (second floor)
flat	apartment
fook	emphasis
football	Gaelic football in South, soccer in North
fortnight	two weeks
gaol	pronounced (and means) "jail"
ground floor	first floor
hire	rental
hoover	vacuum cleaner
INLA	Irish National Liberation Army, an IRA splinter group
IRA	Irish Republican Army
lavatory, lav	bathroom
left luggage	luggage storage
to let	to rent
loo	bathroom
lorry	truck
Loyalist	pro-British
mate	pal
motorway	highway

IRISH-ENGLISH WORDS

nappies	diapers
Nationalists	those who want Northern Ireland to be a part of the Republic of Ireland
the North	relatively neutral term for Northern Ireland
OAP	old age pensioner; a senior citizen
off-license	retail liquor store
Orangemen	A widespread Protestant Unionist group
OUP	Official Unionist Party; the largest party in Northern Ireland
pants	underwear
petrol	gasoline
pissed	drunk
pub grub	quality bar food (see page 73)
publican	barkeeper
punt	Irish pound
quay	"key"; a waterside street
queue up, "Q"	line up
rashers	bacon
redundancies	job layoffs
Republican	see *Nationalist*
return ticket	round-trip ticket
roundabout	rotary road interchange
rubber	eraser
RUC	Royal Ulster Constabulary, the Northern Ireland police force
SDLP	Social Democratic and Labor Party; moderate Nationalist party in Northern Ireland
self-catering	accommodation with kitchen facilities
self-drive	car rental
to shift	to chat with the intention of hooking up
single ticket	one-way ticket
to slag	to tease and ridicule in the inimitable Irish fashion
to snog	to kiss
snooker	a game like pool
snug	enclosed booth within a pub
sterling	British pound
stone	14 pounds (in body weight)
strand	beach
subway	underground walkway
sultanas	similar to raisins or currants
take-away	take-out food
The Troubles	understatement of Northern Ireland's Protestant/Catholic conflict
toilet	bathroom
torch	flashlight
trad	traditional Irish music
trainers	sneakers
traveler	(sometimes) an ethnic group (see above)
UDA	Ulster Defence Association (Unionists)
UDR	Ulster Defence Regiment, the British Army unit in Northern Ireland
UFF	Ulster Freedom Fighters (Unionists)
Unionists	those who want Northern Ireland to remain part of the U.K.

UVF and UDF	Ulster Volunteer/Defence Force (Unionist paramilitary groups)
way out	exit
zed	letter "Z"

■ ■ ■ IRISH WORDS & PHRASES

The following bits of the Irish language are either used often in Irish English or are common in Irish place names. Spelling conventions do not always match English pronunciations: for example, "mh" sounds like "v," and "dh" sounds like "g."

aerphort	AYR-fort	airport
aisling	ASH-ling	vision or dream, or a poem or story thereof
An Lár	on lahr	city center
Ar aghaidh linn: Éire	uhr EYE linn: AIR-ah	*Let's Go: Ireland*
Baile Átha Cliath	BALL-yah AW-hah CLEE-ah	Dublin
bodhrán	BOUR-ohn	traditional drum
Bord Fáilte	bored FAHL-tshuh	Irish Tourist Board
Conas tá tú?	CUNN-us thaw too?	How are you?
céilí	KAY-lee	Irish dance
craic	krak	good cheer, good pub conversation, a good time
Dáil	DOY-il	House of Representatives
Dia dhuit	JEE-a dich	good day, hello
Dia's Muire dhuit	JEE-as MWUR-a dich	reply to "good day"
dún	doon	fort
Éire	AIR-uh	Ireland; official name of the Republic of Ireland
fáilte	FAWLT-cha	welcome
feis	fesh	an assembly, Irish festival
Fianna Fáil	FEE-in-ah foil	"Soldiers of Destiny;" political party
Fine Gael	FINN-eh gayl	"Family of Ireland;" political party
fir	fear	men
fleadh	flah	a musical festival
gaeltacht	GAYL-tokt	a district where Irish is the everyday language
garda, Garda Siochána	GAR-da SHE-och-ANA	police
go raibh maith agat	guh roh moh UG-ut	thank you
inch, innis, ennis	inch, innis, ennis	island; river meadow
kil	kill	church; cell
knock	nok	hill
lei thras	LEH-hrass	toilets
lough	lohk	lake
mná	min-AW	women
mór	more	big, great
ní hea	nee hah	no (sort of; it's tricky)
oíche mhaith dhuit	EE-ha woh ditch	good night
ogham	AG-um	early Irish, written on stones
Oifig an Phoist	UFF-ig un fwisht	Post Office

poitín	po-CHEEN	moonshine; sometimes-toxic homemade liquor
rath	rath *or* rah	earthen fort
sea	shah	yes (sort of; it's tricky)
seanachaí	SHAN-ukh-ee	storyteller
Seanad	SHAN-ud	Senate
Sinn Féin	shin fayn	"Ourselves Alone;" the political wing of the IRA
sláinte	SLAWN-che	cheers, to your health
slán agat	slawn UG-ut	goodbye
slieve *or* sliabh	shleev	mountain
sraid	shrawd	street
Taoiseach	TEE-shukh	Prime Minister
teachta dála (TD)	TAKH-ta DAH-lah	member of Irish parliament
telefón	TEL-eh-fone	telephone
Tír na nÓg	cheer na nohg	Land of Youth
trá	thraw	beach
uilleann	ILL-in	"elbow;" bagpipes played with the elbow

USEFUL PHRASES

It's said that Eskimos have 40 different words for snow.

How is the weather today?	*Conas atá an aimsir inniú?*	CUNN-us a thaw un AM-shir in-YOU?
It is…	*Tá sé…*	thaw shay
cloudy	*scamallach*	SCOM-ull-uckh
cold	*fuar*	FOO-ur
cool	*finuar*	fin-OOR
wet	*fliuch*	flukh
frosty	*ag cur sioc*	egg cur shuk
Tomorrow it will be…	*Amárach, beidh sé…*	um-AW-ruckh beg-shay
raining	*ag cur báistí* or *fearthaine*	egg cur BAWSH-tee *or* FAR-han-a
snowing	*ag cur sneachta*	egg cur SHNOKH-ta
windy	*gaofar*	GWEE-fur
showery	*ceathach*	KYAH-ukh
foggy	*ceomhar*	KYO-wur
damp	*tais*	tash
I am…	*táim…*	thaw im
tipsy	*súgach*	SOO-gakh
drunk	*ar meisce*	uhr MEH-shka
very drunk	*ar dearg mheisce*	uhr jar-eg-VEH-shka
quite drunk	*ólta*	OLE-ta
blind drunk	*caoch ólta*	KWEE-ukh OLE-ta

Index

Don't forget to call home!

While LET'S GO sets you on the road to adventure, AT&T connects you to your loved ones back home.

When traveling abroad you can rely on AT&T USADirect Service to make calling home easy and affordable. From over 130 countries, you'll get connected directly to an English-speaking AT&T Operator, so there are no language barriers to overcome. You'll know how to use the phone from practically anywhere you travel! And, it won't blow your budget either. You can access USADirect Service with your AT&T Calling Card, local phone company calling card, by calling collect or with an AT&T Global PrePaid Card™.

Now, AT&T and LET'S GO are offering you a $5 AT&T Global Prepaid Card which will connect you to AT&T USADirect Service, so you can see for yourself just how great it is. For FREE! Here's the deal:

To receive your $5 AT&T Global Prepaid Card™

1. Fill out the survey on the other side of this page.

2. Clip and include the "proof-of-purchase corner" from the upper left hand corner of the back of this book.

3. Enclose in a stamped envelope and mail it to us at the address indicated on the survey **ON OR BEFORE 5/31/96**.

4. Allow 4 weeks for delivery.

LET'S GO® AT&T

Name

Address

City   State

Zip   Telephone #

AT&T Calling card (exclude pin #)

<u>Please circle your answers - pick one response per question:</u>

1. Have you ever heard of AT&T USADirect Service?
   1. Yes   2. No

2. How do you plan on paying for your phone calls while you are abroad?
   1. Calling card   2. Call collect   3. Coins   4. Other

3. Where would you like to get information on how to call home from abroad?
   1. Newspaper/magazine   2. TV   3. Direct mail   4. Travel agent
   5. Hotel   6. Study abroad orientation program

4. How old are you?
   1. Under 17   2. 17-23   3. 24-30   4. 31-40   5. 41-55
   6. over 55

5. Where did you purchase the guide?
   1. Superstore   2. Chain store   3. University store
   4. Independent book store   5. Other

6. Why did you buy LET'S GO?
   1. I used it before   2. The AT&T offer
   3. Friend/Fellow traveler recommended it   4. Store clerk recommended it
   5. Saw it in bookstore display   6. Other

Fill out this survey, clip and include the "proof of purchase corner" from the upper left hand corner of
the back of this book. Enclose in a stamped envelope and mail it to us, at the address below **on or
before 5/31/96**. Limit one per customer. No photocopies will be accepted.

Address: LET'S GO / AT&T Promotion
                P.O. Box 15680
                Mascoutah, IL 62224

                Thank you.

Sponsor not responsible for lost, late, mutilated, postage due or misdirected mail.
Void where taxed, prohibited or restricted by law.

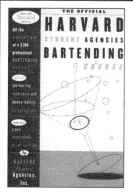